CORPORATE ACCOUNTING

A Simplified Approach

For B.Com. (Hons.) and other Professional Courses

Naseem Ahmed
M.Com. Ph.D. (Aligarh)
Reader, Department of Commerce
Zakir Husain College (University of Delhi)

PUBLISHERS & DISTRIBUTORS (P) LTD

Published by

ATLANTIC

PUBLISHERS & DISTRIBUTORS (P) LTD

B-2, Vishal Enclave, Opp. Rajouri Garden,
New Delhi-110027
Phones : 25413460, 25429987, 25466842

Sales Office
7/22, Ansari Road, Darya Ganj,
New Delhi-110002
Phones : 23273880, 23275880, 23280451
Fax : 91-11-23285873
web : www.atlanticbooks.com
e-mail : info@atlanticbooks.com

Printed in India
at Nice Printing Press, Delhi

Dedicated to

My Parents

Acknowledgements

The author gratefully acknowledges with thanks the kind favour of the Directors of Studies:

- The Institute of Chartered Accountants of India
- The Institute of Cost and Works Accountants of India
- The Institute of Company Secretaries of India

for having granted permission to use question papers of past examinations of their respective institute.

Preface

I feel great pleasure to place in the hands of esteemed readers its long awaited first edition of *Corporate Accounting*. Although there is no dearth of books on Corporate Accounting, yet there always remains a scope for improvement in the matter of style, presentation and amendments in subject matters.

This text provides a comprehensive coverage of each topic. As the field of accounting is expanding in scope and contents, the number of topics for corporate accounting course have increased and the traditional topics requiring update have been given extensive coverage. In recognition of time limit the materials included in the text have been structured to suit the requirements of students. Each chapter is a self-contained unit, making it possible to exercise substantial flexibility in sequencing the course material. The presentation of each chapter permits going into greater depth of the subject matter. The explanatory working notes provide an insight into solution process which develops understanding the most intricate problems in a simple way.

The basic philosophy of the book is to provide a conceptual foundation for the topics presented so that the students can understand the reasoning underlying the procedures.

A distinguishing feature of this book is the use of multidimensional illustrations for each chapter. In this way the reader can clearly see each step of the process. The material coverage has been properly focused so as to enhance the grasping power of the students on the advanced corporate accounting problem. The logic and theory underlying the procedures are stressed to provide an anchoring point for understanding each accounting treatment. The main aim throughout the book is to replace memorisation with understanding and doing.

Every effort has been made to make this book the most comprehensive, advanced and current corporate accounting text possible. The latest changes in the Accounting Standards of the appropriate topics such as Amalgamation (AS-14) Revised, Consolidated Financial Statements (AS-21), Cash Flow Statement (AS-3) Revised including Accounting for the Banking companies etc have been incorporated in the text. This will facilitate learning in consistent with current accounting practices.

At the end of each chapter materials have been designed to provide a wide range of assignments from focused exercises requiring understanding of basic concept to problems and cases requiring more integrated solution skill. Since for many students corporate accounting provides an important part of their preparation for professional examinations, selected questions from CA, ICWA and CS have been included. In areas where adequate questions were not available from past examinations, original questions have been developed.

In the end I extend my deepest appreciation for my colleagues, friends and family members who provided support and encouragement necessary to complete this book.

I am also thankful to Atlantic Publishers and Distributors (P) Ltd for bringing out this edition in a record time despite their hectic work schedule and other priorities.

I am sure my efforts and work will meet the warm response from students and teachers alike whose suggestions will always be welcomed to improve the overall quality of the present work.

C-12/516, Yamuna Vihar **NASEEM AHMED**
Delhi-110053
Phone : 65253363 (R), 9811072671 (M)

Contents

1

Accounting for Share Capital

Meaning of Company

The term "Company" may be defined as a group of persons associated together to achieve some common objectives. Section 3 (1) of the Companies Act defines company as a company formed and registered under this Act. However, section 566 of Companies Act, 1956 lays down that a joint stock company is one which is "having permanent paid up or nominal capital of fixed amount divided into shares, also of fixed amount, held and transferable as stock and formed on the principles of having for its' members only– the holders of those shares or stock and no other person".

According to justice Lindley, a company is "an association of many persons who contribute money or money's worth to a common stock, and employ it in some common trade or business (for a common purpose) and who share the profit or loss arising there from". Whereas Chief Justice Marshall defines company as "an artificial being, invisible and existing in the contemplation of law. Being a mere creation of law, it possesses only the property which the charter of it's creation confer upon it, either expressly or as incidental to it's very existence."

These above mentioned legal and juristic definitions of the term company fail to reveal it's attributes or characteristics fully. Hence considering it's characteristics a company may be defined as an artificial person created by law with a common purpose and capital divisible into transferable shares with limited liability having a separate legal entity with perpetual succession and a common seal."

Thus the salient features of the company can be explained as under :

Artificial Person

A company is an artificial person. That is the law regards it as a person. It can act as a natural person like entering into contracts, owning a property or making and receiving payments etc. but like natural person it has no body and mind. Thus a company is a creation of law and exists in the eyes of law only. It has a name and can sue and can be sued in that name. However, it does not enjoy the same fundamental rights as enshrined in the constitution for a natural person.

Separate Legal Entity

This attribute makes a company altogether different from it's members (Shareholders) who constitute it. And that is why the company can enter into contracts with it's members and vice versa. The company and it's members can be a debtor and a creditor of each other. However, a company cannot be regarded as the agent or trustee of members (Shareholders) and vice versa. A member cannot be sued for the debts or obligations of the company. Similarly a member cannot bind his company by his acts or dealings with the third party.

Perpetual Succession

Since a company has a separate legal entity, it's existence is not affected by the death, lunacy or insolvency of it's members. Shareholders may go, share holders (new) may come, the company's existence remains un-affected. The Company continues it's operation subject to the compliance of legal requirements of the Act under which it has been formed even if all of it's founder members die.

Limited Liability

The liability of the members of a limited company is limited to the face value of the shares held by each of them. Since a company has a separate entity it follows that it's members are not as such liable for it's debts. Even if the assets of the company are not sufficient to satisfy fully the claims of creditors of the company, members cannot be asked to pay more than the face value of the shares held by them. In no case private assets of the members can be attached to satisfy the claims of the creditors of the company.

However, if the number of members falls short of minimum limit (Seven in case of public company and two in case of private company) it shall be treated as an "unlimited company". Every member of such a company shall be liable to the debts of the company (as in case of partnership) to the extent of his interest in the company. If such a company carries on business even after six months, a member shall be liable severally for the whole debts of the company contracted during that time.

Transferability of the shares

The shares of companies are freely transferable except in case of private companies. Every shareholder of a public limited company is free to transfer his shares. A private company puts certain conditions/restrictions on the transfer of shares, thus right to transfer is not taken away absolutely.

Common Seal

Since a company is an artificial person, it takes the help from natural persons who act on it's behalf. All the acts of the company done through directors/officials are authenticated by the common seal of the company. The common seal is affixed on all documents of the company as a token of company's approval. Thus, common seal is the official signatures of the company. Any document which does not bear the company's common seal is not binding.

KINDS OF COMPANIES

The companies can be classified on the basis of their formation, public participation, and liability etc. These may be explained as under :

1. Statutory Company

A statutory company is formed and governed by Special Acts of Legislature or Parliament. These companies with extensive powers are monopoly, public welfare or utility organisations which work in the national interest to meet the needs of public in general. Such companies are not required to frame any Memorandum or Articles of Association. These include Reserve Bank of India, Life Insurance Corporation of India, State Bank of India, Unit Trust of India, Industrial Finance Corporation of India, Railways, Delhi Vidhut Board, Delhi Jal Board, Air India, State Trading Corporation etc.

2. (I) Registered Company

A company which is incorporated and registered under companies Act 1956 is known as Registered company. Companies are required to fulfill certain legal formalities & prepare certain legal documents to be submitted with the Registrar of Joint Stock Companies. The registered companies are governed by the provisions of Companies Act 1956. These Companies may be classified as:

(a) Companies limited by shares

(b) Companies limited by Guarantee

(c) Unlimited Companies

(a) A Company in which liability of a member is limited to the extent of face value of shares held by him is known as a **Company limited by shares.** The liability of a person who is holding fully paid shares of the company is nil, whereas if a person is holding partly paid shares, then the liability will be restricted or limited to the extent of unpaid/uncalled amount. A company limited by shares may be a private or a public company.

(b) Where Memorandum of Association of a company makes it mandatory for the members to contribute a specified sum towards the assets of the company in the event of liquidation, it is known as a **Company limited by guarantee.** Such a company may or may not have share capital. The guaranteed sum is over and above the share capital. Non-profit making organisations such as Clubs Trade Associations or Societies etc. for promoting art, science , or social welfare sports, culture are the examples. It should be remembered that guarantee sum is required to be paid by members on liquidation and that too in case of a short fall only.

(c) **Unlimited Companies.** In case of unlimited company, the liability of a member is unlimited (as in case of partner's liability in a partnership firm). Members are required to make good all debts and obligations of the company on winding up. The members have to contribute the necessary amount to pay off the creditors of the company fully. However, such types of companies do not exist in India.

(II) A registered company which is limited by shares may further be classified on the basis of public participation such as :

Private Company

Public Company.

A Private Company is one which by its's Articles of Association.

(i) Restricts the rights of the members to transfer shares

(ii) Limits the number of it's members to fifty (50) and

(iii) Prohibits any invitation to the public to subscribe for it's shares or debentures.

A Private Company is registered with minimum two members and is required to put "private Limited" after it's name except in case of unlimited companies. Private Companies are not required to hold statutory meeting, file prospectus or statement in lieu of prospectus.

A Public Company means a company which is not a Private Company. [Companies Act, 1956 Section 3 (I) (IV)] Thus, a public limited company is free from the restrictions imposed on a private company. There is no restriction on transfer of shares, maximum number of members or on public invitation to subscribe it's shares. However, the minimum number of members has to be seven.

3. Other kinds of Companies

(i) *Government Company*

According to Companies Act 1956, a Government company is a company in which not less than 51% of the paid up capital is held by Central Government or by State Government or by both.

(ii) *Foreign Company*

A company which is incorporated outside India and under the law of that country but has a place of business in India before or after commencement of the Companies Act 1956.

(iii) *Holding Company*

According to Companies Act 1956, a holding company may be defined as "any company which directly or indirectly, holds more than fifty percent of equity share capital of other company/companies or controls the composition of Board of Directors of other company/Companies. In other words, a holding is one which controls one or more companies either by means of holding shares or by having powers to appoint directly or indirectly the whole or majority of Board of Directors of that company/ companies.

(iv) *Subsidiary Company*

A Company whose majority of shares are held by other (Holding) company or composition of Board is controlled by other (Holding) company is known as subsidiary company.

"FORMATION OF A COMPANY"

Any seven (7) persons in case of public limited company and any two (2) persons in case of a private limited company, can form themselves into a joint stock company. There are certain legal formalities which are to be completed for bringing a company into existence. The formation of a company involves three important stages.

(I) Preparation of necessary documents

(II) Payment of necessary fees and filing of documents

(III) Registration and receipt of certificate of incorporation and commencement of business.

I The promoter/promoters (person or group of persons who conceives/conceive the idea of forming a company to run a business) get the following documents prepared for the purpose of filing with the registrar.

(1) **Memorandum of Association**, known as charter of the company must be signed by at least by seven persons in case of public company any two persons in case of private company. The purpose of Memorandum of Association is two-fold. Firstly, to point out to the outsiders dealings with the company wether their contractual relationship with the company shall be within it's objects or beyond it's jurisdiction (Ultra vires) which do not bind a company and secondly to convey the degree of risk exposed to the investment made by shareholders. The Memorandum of Association contains the following clauses.

(i) Name Clause

(ii) Situation or Registered Office Clause

(iii) Objects Clause

(iv) Liability Clause

(v) Capital Clause

(vi) Association or Subscription Clause

(2) The Articles of Association

The Articles of Association of a company contains rules and regulations in respect of internal administration of the company. The Memorandum of Association establishes and regulates the relationship of the company with the outsiders while the Articles of Association establishes a binding contract between the company and members and amongst the members interse. The A/A contains details of internal management regarding :

(i) Director's qualification, appointment, removal, rights, duties and remuneration.

(ii) Division of share capital in to different classes of shares & their voting rights etc.

(iii) Issue, transfer, forfeiture and reissue of shares.

(iv) Meetings of directors and shareholders.

(v) Audit etc.

(3) Preparation of prospectus or statement in lieu of prospectus for private companies.

(4) List of directors and their written consent to act as directors and written undertaking to take up and pay for the qualification shares.

(5) A Statement of Nominal/Authorised Capital.

(6) A Statutory declaration that all requirements of the Companies Act and the rules there under in respect of registration have been complied with. The declaration shall be signed by any of the following:

(a) An advocate of a Supreme Court or High Court

(b) An attorney entitled to appear before a High Court.

(c) A Company Secretary or a Chartered Accountant who is also engaged in the formation of the company

(d) A director or any other officer of the company such as manager or secretary.

II Payment of necessary fees and filing of documents

When all the legal requirements have been complied with and the above mentioned documents are filed with the Registrar of joint stock companies along with the necessary fees, the Registrar of companies will consider the application and if satisfied will enter the name of the company in the register and will issue a Certificate of Incorporation in the name of the company.

III Certificate of Incorporation and Commencement of Business.

Once the Certificate of Incorporation is granted, the company comes into existence as a legal person. A private company or a company having no share capital is entitled to commence business immediately on receipt of Certificate of Incorporation which is a conclusive proof that company has complied with all the requirements of the Companies Act 1956 in respect of registration and the company has been duly registered under the Companies Act 1956.

However, a public company has to obtain another certificate before starting business. This certificate is known as "Certificate of Commencement of Business" which can be obtained after fulfilling following conditions and filing necessary documents with the Registrar.

(i) A copy of the prospectus or a Statement in Lieu of Prospectus.

(ii) The minimum number of shares subscribed and paid for in cash.

(iii) The qualification shares taken up by the directors and paid for in cash.

(iv) There is no liability to repay the application money.

(v) The condition of "Minimum Subscription" has been fulfilled.

(vi) A declaration by an advocate or officer of the company that all conditions of the Act have been satisfied.

The Registrar, if satisfied, grants certificate to commence business. On receipt of such a certificate a public company can only then start a business.

MAINTENANCE OF BOOKS OF ACCOUNTS

Section 209 of the Companies Act requires that books of accounts shall be maintained at company's registered office unless the Board of Directors decide to keep at other place. If it is so, the Registrar of the companies should be informed with in seven days of such a decision to keep the "Books of Accounts" at any other place. Each company is required to keep the proper books of accounts in respect of:

(i) All money received and spent and the details thereof

(ii) All sales and purchases of goods by the company.

(iii) All assets and liabilities of the company.

(iv) In case of a company engaged in production, processing manufacturing or mining activities, the details relating to material, labour and other items of costs as required by Central Government.

Where a company has a branch office, the proper books of accounts relating to transactions effected at the branch are kept at branch office and a proper summarised returns are sent to the Head Office for each quarter.

However, proper books of accounts shall not be deemed to be kept if books of accounts fail to give a true and fair view of the state of affairs of the company.

In order to comply with the provisions of Companies Act a company usually maintains the following books of accounts.

(i) Three column Cash Book

(ii) Purchases Book

(iii) Sales Book

(iv) Bills Receivable Book

(v) Bills Payable Book

(vi) Debtors' Ledger

(vii) Creditors' Ledger

(viii) General Journal

(ix) General Ledger

(x) Returns Inward Book

(xi) Returns Outward Book and

(xii) Cost Accounting records

STATUTORY BOOKS

In addition to above mentioned books of accounts the following statutory books are required to be maintained by a company under different provisions of Companies Act. These are :

(1) Register of Investments not held in it's own name (U/s 49)

(2) Register of Mortgages and charges. (U/s 143)

(3) Register of Members (U/s 150)

(4) Register of Members Index (U/s 151)

(5) Register of Debenture holders (U/s 152)

(6) Foreign Register of Members and Debenture holders (U/s 157 & 158)

(7) Minute Books (U/s 193)

(8) Register of contracts, companies and firms in which the directors are interested. (U/s 301)

(9) Register of Director, Managing Director or Secretary (U/s 303)

(10) Register of Directors' Shareholding. (U/s 307)

(11) Register of loans made, guarantees given or securities provided to companies. (U/s 370)

(12) Register of investments in shares and debentures (U/s 372)

STATISTICAL BOOKS

A part from the statutory books and other books of accounts, each company maintains the following statistical books:

(1) Application and Allotment book (Shares & Debentures)

(2) Shares Call Book & Debenture Call Book.

(3) Register of Transfers (shares & Debentures)

(4) Register of Directors' & Managing Directors' attendance

(5) Register of power of attorney.

(6) Dividend Register

(7) Interest Register

(8) Register of transfer certificates (Shares & Debentures)

(9) Register of share warrants

(10) Register of sealed documents

(11) Register of probates.

SHARE CAPITAL

The Capital of a company is divided in to different units of certain denomination which are known as shares. According to section 2 (46) of the companies Act 1956, "a share means share in the capital of a company and includes stock except where a distinction between stock and share is expressed or implied." A unit may be of Rs. 10, 20, 50 or 100 each or for any other of (lower/higher) denomination with is known as face value. If a company has total Capital of Rs. 50,00,000 divided into 50,000 units, the value (face value) of each unit (Share) will be Rs. 100 (Rs. 50,00,000 ÷ 50,000 units). Thus the company will have share capital divided into shares of Rs. 100 each. No trading concern can run without capital However, the companies limited by guarantee or unlimited companies need not to have share capital. The various types of capital which are shown in the Balance Sheet of a company are as under :

Authorised or Nominal or Registered Capital.

This refers to the maximum amount a company can raise during it's life time by issuing various kinds of shares. The number and par value (face value) of each class of shares that a company can issue as per capital clause of Memorandum of Association.

Issued Share Capital

It refers to the portion of Authorised share capital which has been offered for public subscription, or shares issued to renders or promoters for a consideration or bonus or rights shares issued to existing shareholders.

Subscribed Share Capital

This refers to that amount of issued share capital which has actually been subscribed by and allotted to public including allotment made to vendors, promoters & existing shareholders.

Called up Capital

This represents that part of Subscribed Share Capital which the allottees are required to pay.

Paid up Capital

This represents that portion of subscribed Capital for which consideration in cash or kind has been received. The difference between called up amount and paid up amount shows the unpaid amount which represents calls-in-arrears.

Reserve Capital

When a company, as per the provisions of Companies Act 1956 (Sec. 99) , reserves any portion of subscribed capital, by a special resolution, to be called up only in the event of liquidation, it is known as Reserve Capital. This simply means capital (uncalled amount) reserved for winding up only. This uncalled amount will be demanded from shareholders only in case of winding up. It has no use during the life time of the company.

> It should be noted that Un-issued Capital, Uncalled Capital or Reserve Capital is not shown in the Balance Sheet or else where.

CLASSIFICATION OF SHARES

Companies usually issue two types of shares as authorised and permitted by Companies Act 1956. These are preference shares and equity shares which are also known as ordinary shares.

1. Preference Shares

As the term itself suggests that these are the shares which enjoy preferential rights as regards payment of dividend during the life time of the company and repayment of capital in the event of liquidation. However, preference shareholders cannot compel or force a company to pay dividend except in case where company has already paid equity dividend. This simply means that preference shares carry a right of dividend at a fixed rate before any dividend is paid on equity shares. These shares do not carry any voting right. The preference shares are classified into following categories.

(i) *Cumulative Preference Shares*

Preference Shares are always deemed to be cumulative unless otherwise stated in the Articles.

In case of cumulative preference shares dividends accumulate if not paid due to inadequacy of the profits or otherwise. The dividend payable on these shares go on accumulating till it is fully paid off. The arrears of dividend have to be paid before any divided is paid to equity shareholders. However, in case of winding up of a company the arrears of dividend are payable only if it is expressly stated in the Articles.

(ii) *Non-Cumulative Preference Shares*

Such shares do not enjoy right to claim arrears of dividend if not declared and paid in any of the year due to inadequacy of profit. The right to claim dividend lapses and shareholders cannot claim arrears of dividends of any year out of the profit of subsequent years.

(iii) *Participating Preference Shares*

Such type of preference shares are entitled to a dividend at a given rate and a share in the profits (residual) left after paying preference, and equity dividend at a specified rate. The right to participate may also extend to surplus assets if available after satisfying the claims of equity shareholders in the event of liquidation.

(iv) *Non-participating preference shares*

These preference shares carry a right to claim dividend at a given rate only. Holders of such shares are not entitled to share either the surplus profits or surplus assets. All preference shares are deemed to be non-participating unless otherwise expressly stated in the Articles.

(v) *Redeemable Preference Shares*

Redeemable Preference Shares are those shares which can be redeemed after a specified period of time in accordance with the terms of issue. That is, the preference share holders are entitled to get their money back during the life time of the company.

(vi) *Irredeemable Preference Shares*

Such shares are not redeemable during the lifetime of the company but on winding up. However, Companies Amendment Act 1988 expressly prohibits issue of irredeemable shares. Now, no company can issue such type of shares.

(vii) *Convertible Preference Shares*

Such shares can be converted into equity shares as per the terms of issue within the stipulated period of time.

(viii) *Non-Convertible Preference Shares*

The holder of such shares do not enjoy the right to get their preference shares converted into equity shares.

2. Equity Shares

According to section 85(2) of Companies Act, 1956, "an equity share is one which is not a preference share". Such shares do not enjoy any preferential rights as regards to payment of dividend or refund of capital. That's why these are known as ordinary shares. The equity shareholders are the last to claim in the assets of the company and entitled to residual surplus left after meeting the claims of Debenture holders, Creditors and Preference share holders. However, these shares carry voting rights.

Sweat Equity Shares

The Companies (Amendment) Act 1999 has authorised companies to issue equity shares to it's employees or directors at a discount or for a consideration other than cash for providing know-how or making available rights in the nature of intellectual property rights or value additions etc. Thus, when a company allots equity shares as per the above terms of issue, such equity shares are known as "sweat equity shares". However, such an issue should be authorised by a special resolution passed in general meeting. The resolution will specifically mention the number and value of equity shares to be issued to various class of employees or directors as per the SEBI's guide lines. It is to be noted that companies can issue sweat equity shares after one year from the date when the company was entitled to commence business. The unlisted companies can issue such shares as per the guide lines as may be prescribed.

Stock

Section 94(1) (C) of the Companies Act 1956 states that when all the shares of a company have been fully paid up these may be converted into stock, if authorised by Articles. Conversion is done because it is convenient method of denoting the capital of the company without affecting the rights of shareholders who continue to enjoy same rights and powers as before. However, stock is divisible into smaller factions and each may have different nominal value as desired. Stock cannot be issued directly and can be transferred in fraction.

DISTINCTION BETWEEN SHARES AND STOCK

Basis of distinction	Shares	Stock
1. Paid up amount	Shares may be fully or partly paid up.	Stock is always fully paid up.
2. Issue	Shares may be issued directly to the public after incorporation	Stock cannot be issued directly and just after incorporation.
3. Transfer	Shares cannot be transferred in fraction because a share is not divisible.	Stock may be transferred in fraction.
4. Nominal Value	Shares are of equal denomination (nominal value)	Stock may be dividend into unequal nominal value.
5. Number	Shares are always serially numbered.	Stock is not numbered.
6. Registration	Shares are always registered.	Stock may be registered or unregistered both.

DISTINCTION BETWEEN PREFERENCE SHARE & EQUITY SHARE

Basis	Preference Share	Equity Shares
1. Right to claim dividend	A preference share holder has the right to receive dividend before any dividend is paid to equity shareholders.	Equity shareholders don't have any preferential right with regards to dividend payment. In this case dividend is a residuary decision.
2. Rate of Dividend	Preference Shares carry pre-determined dividend rate which is fixed at the time of issue..	Rate of dividend may vary year after year. The rate depends upon availability of divisible profits and the management policy.

3. Arrears of dividend	Preference shareholders have the right to claim arrears of dividend except when it is provided otherwise in the Articles. *i.e.* preference shares are non-cumulative.	Question of arrears of dividend does not arise.
4. Right to vote & participation in management.	Usually, preference shares do not carry any voting right except in special circumstances and thus have no say in management.	Equity shares always enjoy voting rights and have their say in managerial affairs.
5. Capital Structure	A company can not have only preference shares in it's capital structure. Hence a company cannot be formed with preference shares only.	A company may have only equity shares in it's capital structure and it can be formed with equity shares alone.
6. Redemption	Preference shares are redeemable on or before the stipulated period of time as per terms of issue. The stipulated period cannot exceed ten years in any case.	Equity shares are always irredeemable. However, on liquidation they are entitled to surplus or residuary assets of the company.

ISSUE OF SHARES

A public company can issue it's shares either for "Cash" or for "consideration other than cash" to collect capital from the public. For this purpose the company, at first, issues a prospectus inviting the public to subscribe it's shares as per the terms of issue mentioned there in. The prospectus contains information relating to the number and class of shares offered and the manner & time at which share money is to be paid on application, allotment and calls, the minimum subscription, the date of opening and closing the subscription lists. It should comply SEBI's guide lines prescribed in this behalf.

SEBI'S GUIDELINES`

To provide a degree of protection to the investors and safeguard their rights and interest so that there is a steady flow of savings into the market, the SEBI has framed certain guidelines which have been made effective from 29th May 1992. The salient features of such regulations are as follows :

(1) As per the guidelines only listed companies and those who have applied for listing can make public issue. The pricing of issue is to be based on the track record as given under :

(A) The following companies are required to issue shares at par only.

(i) New companies promoted by persons without track record.

(ii) Existing private closely held companies without a three year track record of consistent profitability.

(iii) Existing private closely held companies with a three year track record of consistent profitability.

(iv) Dis-investment with a view to become public by existing private closely held companies without three year tack record of profitability.

(B) Following companies are allowed free pricing of it's shares, That is these companies can issue shares either at par or at premium.

(i) New companies promoted by existing companies with a five year track record of consistent profitability.

(ii) Companies which do not have year track record but had been promoted by existing companies with a five year track record of consistent profitability.

(iii) Dis-investment with a view to become public by existing private closely held companies with a three year tack record of profitability.

(iv) Existing public limited companies making further issue.

(2) Companies issuing shares at premium should disclose the net assets value (NAV), low and high prices of shares for the last two years to justify price of issue.

(3) In case of public issue at par, minimum number of shares for which application is to be made should be fixed at 200 shares of the face value of Rs. 10 each.

(4) Where issue is to be made at premium or comprises of debentures the total amount payable in respect of each instrument by each applicant shall not be less than Rs. 2,000 irrespective of the size of premium.

(5) All issues are made subject to promoter's contribution to the issue and to a lock in period of 5 years (in some cases 2 years only) for the shares so subscribed by them.

(6) The minimum application money shall not be less than 25% of issue price.

(7) The issue price is applicable to all investors uniformly. However, in case of composite issues which combine a public & rights issue the company may follow different pricing policy for the two issues.

(8) No bonus issue can be made within twelve months of any public/right issue.

(9) Shares are to be allotted in tradeable lots which is of Rs. 1,000 each. For example for a share of the face value of Rs. 10 each, the tradeable lot shall be 100 shares.

(10) Companies making issue of less than 50 crores will collect the full amount on application.

(11) In case of maga issue exceeding the size of Rs. 250 crores, the amount to be called upon application/allotment and on various calls should not exceed 25% of the total issue.

(12) The Capital issue should be made fully paid within 12 months from the date of issue. However, this will not apply to issues of Rs. 500 crores or more.

(13) Under-writing is now optional for the full issue. Minimum requirement of 90% subscription is mandatory only for public and rights issue and not in case of offer for sale of securities. In case of non-receipt of 90% of the issued amount from public subscription within 60 days from the date of closure or 120 days from the date of opening of the issue, the company must refund the amount of subscription.

(14) If the issue is oversubscribed, the allotment has to be made on pro-rata basis. No retention of over-subscription is permissible.

(15) The reservation for promoters, directors, friends, relatives and association has been made uniform at 20% of total issue. However, in case of employees of issuing and promoting companies the ceiling of 10% is applicable.

(16) Subscription list for public issues should be kept open at least for three working days and disclosed in the prospectus.

(17) Rights issues should not be kept open for more than 60 days.

(18) The gap between closure dates of public and rights issues should not exceed 30 days.

(19) SEBI has the right to modify and interpret the guidelines. Any violation of the guidelines is punishable offence.

PROCEDURE AND ACCOUNTING TREATMENT

As already stated shares may be issued for cash or for consideration other than cash. When shares are issued for cash it should satisfy the provisions of Companies Act 1956 and the guide lines framed by SEBI (Securities Exchange Board of India) in this regard. However, the following procedure may be noted.

Issue of prospectus

Every public issue must be accompanied by an issue of "prospectus" or "statement in lieu of prospectus". It is simply an invitation to public to subscribe shares. The prospectus contains the detailed information about the company, terms of issue, number and types of shares offered, the minimum subscription, the date of opening and closing the issue (subscription lists), details of projects for which issue is made, amount payable on application and allotment, details of underwriting, preliminary expenses, details about the preferential rights if any, Number of shares and debentures issued within two years for a consideration other than cash, particulars of premium received within two years, names and addresses of auditors, details of holding of directors, promoters and their interest in any other property, details of voting rights if shares are of more than one class, prospects, profitability, market price of the share etc. The application form attached there to provides the details of procedure to apply for shares.

Receipt of applications and application money

The prospective shareholders, having satisfied with the information given in the prospectus, apply for the shares in the prescribed form together with application money which should by at least 5% of the face value of shares. The application has to be deposited with the Banker of the company. The company may demand from investors the full value on application or is free to ask to pay in different instalments. According to section 69 of the Companies Act 1956, the amount paid by applicants (by cheque or drafts) has to be kept in a scheduled bank against the concerned applicants accounts till the "minimum subscription" stated in the prospectus has been received. In case company fails to raise minimum subscription, within 120 days from the date of issuing prospectus, the application money so received has to be refunded within next ten (10) days (or within 130 days from the date of issue of prospectus Otherwise, the directors will be liable to pay back application money along with the interest @ 6% per annum for a period falling after the expiry of 130 days from the date of issue of prospectus. However, some bankers have introduced the scheme of stock-invests for the convenience of the investors to avoid delay in the refund or non-receipt of share application money or allotment letter from the issuing company.

Allotment of Shares

On receipt of applications the Board of Directors proceed to allot shares as per SEBI's guidelines and in accordance with the provisions of Companies Act 1956 (Section 69 & 70). However, Companies Act does not impose any restriction on private company to allot it's shares. However, a public company has to comply with certain requirements which are already explained earlier.

Minimum Subscription

As per the provisions of Companies Act 1956 no allotment shall be made unless the amount stated in the prospectus as "minimum amount" has been subscribed for. This minimum amount is known as "Minimum subscription" which is fixed to meet the following :

(a) Preliminary expenses and underwriting commission.

(b) Cost or purchase price of any property to be purchased out of proceeds of

(c) Repayment of any money taken (borrowed) to meet the above mentioned expenses and cost of property.

(d) Working Capital requirements etc. (estimated)

As per SEBI's guide lines the amount of minimum subscription has been fixed at 90% of the amount of issue which is to be subscribed within 120 days from the date of issue. However, there may be two possibilities :

(i) Over-subscription

(ii) Under-subscription

Stock-invest scheme

Stock invest is an instrument under which investors, who want to purchase shares or debentures of certain companies, has to open account for a deposit with the bank, issuing stock-invests. The bank in turn issues the stock-invests of desired amount against the deposit made or credit balance of saving or current account of the applicant in favour of shares/debentures issuing companies. That is the issuing bank fills in the name of securities issuing company on the stock-invests before these are delivered to the investors. When an investor wishes to apply for any public issue, he will enclose the stock-invests before these are delivered to the investors. When an investor wishes to apply for any public issue, he will enclose the stock-invest with the share application and send it to the banker of the company. In case of non-allotment, the stock-invests are returned to the investors or to the banker of the applicant. If there is partial/prorata allotment the banker presents the stock-invests in respect of shares allotted only. If Shares are allotted to the investor, the banker of the company will collect the money from the payee bank. The salient features of stock-invests scheme are :

(i) Stock-invests are issued in favour of securities issuing company against the deposit or credit balance standing to the credit of investor's account.

(ii) Blank stock-invests are not issued.

(iii) Stock-invests scheme is meant for individual investors and mutual funds only.

(iv) Interest on stock-invests deposits is allowed upto the date of allotment.

(v) Only those stock-invests are encashed against which allotment has been made. However, excess application money need not to be refunded by the company.

(vi) Stock-invests instrument is neither negotiable nor transferable.

(vii) Stock-invests instrument is valid for a period of six months from the date of issue.

Over-Subscription & allotment

When number of shares applied for exceeds the number of shares meant for public subscription, the issue is said to be over-subscribed and the Board of Directors have to find a criterion for allotment. The directors have the power either to reject the certain applications and accept the rest or accept all the applications partially by adjusting excess application money. Thus there may be three possibilities:

(i) The directors may allot the shares to some of the shares to some of the applicants and reject the applications of the others. This situation is termed as full allotment.

(ii) All applicants may be allotted arbitrarily without following any specific criteria or basis. This is known as partial allotment. or

(iii) A prorata allotment may be made to the applicants. This prorata (proportionate) allotment may be applied in respect of some applicants or all applicants.

Applicants, whose applications have been turned down by the directors, are sent letter of regrets and their application money is refunded. For remaining applicants, share application money is adjusted on allotment or even on share calls. It is to be noted that only those applications may be rejected which are incomplete in any respect. As per SEBI's guidelines only those applications can be rejected which suffer from any infirmity.

Under-Subscription and allotment

When public response to a public issue is poor and number of shares applied for falls short of number of shares meant for public subscription, such a situation is termed as under subscription. However, the condition of minimum subscription" must be satisfied failing which the process of allotment cannot take place legally. As far as amount due on various instalments is concerned, the number of shares applied for is taken as basis and not the number of shares offered for public subscription.

Calls, Calls-in-Advance and Calls-in-Arrears

When the directors of the company make a demand from the allottees of shares to pay further a sum towards the value (cost) of shares already allotted to them, such a demand is known as call. There may be maximum three calls viz, First Call, Second Call and Final Call.

In case of over-subscription, when an applicant's application money exceeds far more than the amount due on allotment the balance is transferred to Calls-in-advance account. Sometimes, on allotment an allottee pays entire sum including due on call or all calls, it is also termed as calls-in-advance. However, it should be noted that a company may accept calls-in-advance only if it is provided in the Articles of Association. Interest @ 6% per annum is allowed on calls-in-advance or at the rate mentioned in the Articles. The amount so received is adjusted against the calls money as and when it becomes due.

Sometimes, shareholder fails to pay money due on any call, the amount remaining so unpaid, is treated as calls-in-arrears. The company may charge interest at the rate prescribed in the Articles of Association from due date to the date of payment. In the absence of Articles. Table A provides for interest @ 5% per annum. However, the Board of Directors have the power to waive payment of interest on calls-in-arrears.

ACCOUNTING TREATMENT

Journal Entries: (Issue at par for cash in instalments)

(1) On receipt of application money

Bank A/c	Dr.	— Amount actually received
To Share application A/c		— Amount actually received

(2) On transfer of application money:

Share application A/c*	Dr.	— Application money in respect of which allotment is made.
To Share Capital A/c		

*A combined entry may be recorded

(3) On refund of application money :

Share application A/c* Dr. — Refund in respect of rejected
To Bank A/c applications.

(4) On adjustment of application money on allotment.

Share application A/c* Dr. Excess application money
To Share allotment adjusted on allotment

(5) On adjustment of application money towards first call or & final call.

Share application A/c* Dr. With the excess application
To Calls-in-Advance money adjusted on calls.

(6) On allotment when money becomes due:

Share allotment A/c Dr. With the amount due on
To Share Capital A/c

(7) On receipt of allotment money:

Bank A/c Dr. — With the amount actually
To Share allotment A/c received on allotment.

(8) On making the call money due

Share Call A/c (First/second/or final) Dr. — With the amount due on call.
To Share Capital A/c

(9) On adjusting the Calls-in-Advance, if any.

Calls-in Advance A/c Dr. — With amount of calls-in-
To Share Call A/c advance

(10) On receipt of Call money.

Bank A/c Dr. — With the amount actually
To Share Call A/c received.

(11) On calls-in-Arrears No Entry

In case call money remains due on the date of closing of books of accounts, the following entry may be recorded.

Calls-in-Arrears A/c Dr. — With the amount remaining
To Share Call A/c outstanding.

(12) In case the Shareholder pays calls-in-arrears along with interest.

Bank A/c Dr.
To Calls-in-Arrears/Share Call A/c**
To Interest A/c

(13) On making the interest on Calls-in-Advance due, if any.

Interest on Calls-in-Advance A/c
To Share holder's A/c

(14) On making the payment of such interest

Share holder's A/c Dr.
To Bank A/c

**In case calls-in-Arrears are paid before the date of closing or opening of call-in-Arrears account.

Illustration (1) Calls-in-Advance, Calls-in-Arrears & Interest thereon).

On 1.1.2002 X Ltd. issued 50,000 equity shares of Rs. 10 each payable as under :

Rs. 3 on application

Rs. 3 on allotment

and the balance in two equal calls. The due date being :

Application	—	1st Feb. 2002
Allotment	—	1st March 2002
First Call	—	1st May 2002
Final Call	—	1st July 2002

Articles of Association authorises to charge interest @ 10% p.a. on calls-in-arrears and to pay @ 5% p.a. on calls-in-advance, if any.

Applications for 55,000 shares were received. The directors sent the letter of regrets to the applicants of 5,000 shares and allotments were made for the rest. All money due was received on due dates except the following.

P— holding 1,500 shares paid the entire amount due along with the allotment

Q— holding 3,000 shares paid the entire amount due on first call with the amount due on final all.

Record journal entries assuming that interest remains due and accrued on all calls-in-arrears and calls-in-advance.

Date	Particulars	L.F.	Debit Rs.	Credit Rs.
2002	Bank A/c Dr.		1,65,000	
Feb. 1	To Share Application A/c			1,65,000
	(Being application money on 55,000 shares @ Rs. 3 per share received)			
	Share Application A/c Dr.		1,65,000	
	To Share Capital A/c			1,50,000
	To Bank A/c			15,000
	(Being application money on 50,000 shares transferred to share Capital A/c and the rest returned as per Board's resolution no—dated—)			
March 1	Share Allotment A/c Dr.		1,50,000	
	To Share Capital A/c			1,50,000
	(Being share allotment money on 50,000 shares transferred to Share Capital A/c as per Board's resolution no—dated—)			
	Bank A/c Dr.		1,56,000	
	To Share Allotment A/c			1,50,000
	To Calls-in-Advance A/c			6,000
	(Being allotment on 50,000 shares @ Rs. 3 and Calls-in-Advance on 1,500 shares @ 4 each received)			

Contd.

2002			Rs.	Rs.
May 1	Share First Call A/c	Dr.	1,00,000	
	To Share Capital A/c			1,00,000
	(Being first call money transferred to Share Capital A/c as per Board's resolution no—dated—)			
	Bank A/c	Dr.	91,000	
	Calls-in-Advance A/c	Dr.	3,000	
	To Share First Call A/c			94,000
	(Being first call money on 45,500 @ Rs. 2 received and Calls-in-Advance of 1,500 shares adjusted)			
May 1	Interest on Calls-in-Advance A/c	Dr.	50	
	To Share holder's A/c			50
	(Being interest due on calls-in-advance on 1,500 shares @ Rs. 4 per share @ 5% p.a. for 2 months)			
July 1	Share Final A/c	Dr.	1,00,000	
	To Share Capital A/c			1,00,000
	(Being share final call on 50,000 shares @ Rs. 2 transferred to share Capital A/c)			
	Bank A/c	Dr.	1,03,000 (1)	
	Calls-in-Advance A/c	Dr.	3,000	
	To Share Final Call A/c			1,00,000
	To Share First Call A/c			6,000
	(Being final Call & arrears of first call received)			
	Interest on Calls-in-Advance A/c	Dr.	25	
	To Share holder's A/c			25
	(Being interest due on Calls-in-Advance on Rs. 3,000 for 2 months @ 5% p.a.)			
	Share holder's A/c	Dr.	100	
	To Interest on Calls-in-Arrear A/c			100
	(Being interest due on calls-in-arrear on 3,000 shares @ Rs. 2 per share for 2 months @ 10% per annum)			

Note: Normally, a Cash Book is maintained to record the cash & Bank transactions (receipts & payments) and hence such entries are not recorded in the journal proper but in the Cash Book. In the above illustration if a Cash Book is maintained the journal entries relating to non-receipts & non-payments (due) transactions only will be recorded as shown above and the Cash Book shall be prepared as under.

CASH BOOK

Date	Particulars	Rs.	Date	Particulars	Rs.
2002			2002		
Feb. 1	To Share Application A/c	1,65,000	Feb. 1	By Share Application A/c	15,000
Mar. 1	To Share Allotment A/c	1,50,000	July 1	By Balance c/d	5,00,000
Mar. 1	To Calls-in-Advance A/c	6,000			
May 1	To Share First Call A/c	91,000			
July 1	To Share Final Call A/c	97,000			
July 1	To Share First Call A/c	6,000			
		5,15,000			5,15,000

BALANCE SHEET OF X LTD. AS ON .....

Liabilities	Rs.	Assets	Rs.
Authorised Capital	--------	Cash at Bank	5,00,000
.....Shares of Rs. 10 each			
Issued and Subscribed Capital			
50,000 Shares of Rs. 10 each fully paid	5,00,000		
	5,00,000		5,00,000

Illustration (2)

(Over-subscription and different scales of allotment)

Z Ltd. made an offer of 10,000 shares of Rs. 10 each payable Rs. 3 on application; Rs. 4 on allotment and the balance on first & final call. 43,825 shares were applied for, including an application for 300 shares from a person who paid for the full face value of the shares. Owing to heavy over-subscription allotment were scalled down as follows :

Applicants for 11,825 shares (in respect of applications for 500 or less) received 5,750 shares (including the applicant of 300 shares who got 150 shares).

Applicants for 32,000 shares (in respect of applications for more than 500 shares) received 4,250 shares.

The amount received was first applied towards allotment and call money (after satisfying the money due on application) and the balance was returned.

You are required to show the cash book and ledger accounts to record the above transactions.

[B.Com. (D.U.) - Modified]

Solution (2)

TABLE SHOWING MONEY RECEIVED, ADJUSTED, DUE & REFUNDED.

Serial No.	No. of shares applied for	No. of shares allotted	Money received on Application	Money Adjusted		Calls-in-Advance	Money adjusted on call	Money to be received		Refund
				on Application	on allotment			on Allotment	on Call	
	1	2	3	4	5	6	7	8	9	10
	Rs.	Rs.	Rs.	Rs.	Rs.	Rs.	Rs.	Rs.	Rs.	Rs.
I	300	150	3,000	450	600	450	450	—	—	1,500
II	11,525[1]	5,600	34,575	16,800	17,775*[2]	—	—	4,625[3]	16,800	—
III	32,000	4,250	96,000	12,750	17,000	12,750	12,750	—	—	53,500
	43,825	10,000	1,33,575	30,000	35,375	13,200	13,200	4,625	16,800	55,000

*(1) 11,825 – 300 = 11,525

*(2) 34,575 – 16,800 = 17,775

*(3) Balancing figure = 4,625

CASH BOOK (BANK A/c)

	Rs.		Rs.
To Share Application A/c	1,33,575	By Share Application A/c	55,000
To Share Allotment A/c	4,625	By Balance c/d	1,00,000
To Share Call A/c	16,800		
	1,55,000		1,55,000

SHARE APPLICATION A/c

	Rs.		Rs.
To Share Capital A/c	30,000	By Bank A/c	1,33,575
To Share Allotment	35,375		
To Calls-in-Advance	13,200		
To Bank A/c (Refund)	55,000		
	1,33,575		1,33,575

SHARE ALLOTMENT A/c

	Rs.		Rs.
To Share Capital A/c	40,000	By Share Application A/c	35,375
		By Bank A/c	4,625
	40,000		40,000

CALL-IN-ADVANCE A/c

	Rs.		Rs.
To Share Call A/c	13,200	By Share Application A/c	13,200
	13,200		13,200

SHARE CALL A/c

	Rs.		Rs.
To Share Capital A/c	30,000	By Calls-in-Advance A/c	13,200
		By Bank A/c	16,800
	30,000		30,000

SHARE CAPITAL A/c

	Rs.		Rs.
To Balance c/d	1,00,000	By Share Application A/c	30,000
		By Share Allotment A/c	40,000
		By Share Call A/c	30,000
	1,00,000		1,00,000

ISSUE OF SHARES AT PREMIUM [SECTION 78]

The Companies (Amendment) Act 1999 has substituted the word "securities" for the word "Shares" wherever it occurs in section 78. Accordingly "Share premium" should be read as "securities premium".

When a company issues shares (securities) at a price higher than it's face value, it is said to be issue of shares at premium. *i.e.* Excess amount received by a company over and above the face value of shares is known as premium. For excmple, if a company issues shares of Rs. 20 each at Rs. 25 per share, then Rs. 5 will be treated as share premium (securities premium). According to section 78 of the companies Act." whre a comapny issues shares at a premium, whether for cash or otherwise, a sum equal to the aggregate amount of the premium collected on shares must be credited to "Share Premium" (Securities Premium) Account. The amount of the premium cannot be utilised except for the purposes stated U/s 78 sub-section (2). The company, accordingly, may use the premium for the following purposes:

(1) For paying up unissued shares of the company to be issued to members of the company as fully paid bonus shares.

(2) For writing off preliminary expenses of the company.

(3) For writing off the expenses or commission paid or discount allowed on any issue of shares, or debentures of the company.

(4) For providing for any premium payable on redemption of preference shares or debentures or for buy back purposes as per section 77.

In case a company uses securities premium for any other purpose it is treated as reduction of paid up capital and this will require the complaince of provisions laid down U/s 100 of the Act.

Hence, the premium so received on issue of shares should not be treated as revenue receipt/ profits but as capital receipt and it should be shown separately on the liabilities side of the Balance Sheet under the head "Reserve & Surplus". The premium may be collected either on application or on allotment. However, securities premium should be segregated and credited to "Securities Premium" Account.

I Accounting Treatement : (For premium only*) Due basis)

(a) If premium is to be collected on Application.

(1)	Bank A/c To Share Application	Dr.	...including premium
(2)	Share Application A/c	Dr.	...Amount received
	To Share Capital A/c		...transfer to share Capital
	To Securities Premium A/c		...transfer to Share premium

(b) If premium is to be collected on Allotment.

Share Allotment A/c	Dr.	...Amount due
To Share Capital A/c	Dr.	....to Share Capital
To Securities Premium A/c		...Tr. to Share premium

*Rest of the entires will be recorded as usual.

II Accounting treatment : For the share premium under Receipt Method.

(i) No entry is passed when share premium becomes due

(ii) On receipt, "Securities premium" account is credited with the amount of share premium received. However, under this method "Securities premium account" is not debited at the time of forfeiture of those shares on which premium is not received.

> To maintain uniformity in approach, only first method (due basis) of premium has been adopted throughout the book."

Issue of Shares at Discount [Section 79]

Where a company issues shares at a price lower or less that it's face value, the shares are said to be issued at discount. For example if a company issues shares of Rs. 10 each at Rs. 9 each, the shares are issued at a discount of Re. 1 per share This discount on issue of shares is treated as a loss of capital nature and is shown on the assets side of the Balance Sheet under the head "Miscellaneous Exenditure" until it is written off. However, the following conditions must be satified as laid down U/s 79 before shares are issued at discount.

(i) The shares must belong to a class already issued.

(ii) At least one year has elapsed since the date when the company was entitled to commence business.

(iii) The issue must be authorised by a resoluation passed in the general meeting and sanctioned by Company Law Board.

(iv) The resolution must specify the maximum rate of discount which cannot exceed 10%. However, in special circumstances a higher rate may be sanctioned by the Company Law Board.

(v) The issue must be made within two (2) months from the date of receiving the sanctions of the Company Law Board or within a period as sanctioned by the Company Law Board.

It should be noted that a newly incorporated company cannot issue shares at discount. Even an existing company cannnot issue shares at discount if it is a new class of shares. In case an old existing company has already issued shares at discount, then prospectus of subsequent issues should contain particulars of discount allowed on earlier issue. Annual financial statements must give details of discount till it is written off.

Accounting Treatment

Share discount is usually allowed on allotment, hence the following entry will be recorded on allotment which is different from the situation when shares are issued at par or premium. All other entires will be recorded as usual.

Share Allotment A/c	Dr.	—(with the amount due on allotment)
Discouint on Issue of Shares A/c	Dr.	—(with the amount of discount)
To Share Capital A/c		(with the total)

ISSUE OF SWEAT EQUITY SHARES

Sweat Equity Shares are issued by a company to it's employees, officers or whole time directors either at a discount or for consideration other than cash, for providing know-how or, making available rights in the nature of intellectual property rights or value addition, by whatever name called. It means when shares are issued in appreciation of their technical, managerial or other valuable services, at a concessional rate or free of cost known as sweat equity shares.

Conditions:

(i) The issue of Sweat equity shares is authorised by special resolution passed by the company in the general meeting.

(ii) The resolution specifies the number of shares, current market price and the consideration if any, being paid along with the class of employees, officers and directors to whom sweat equity shares are to be issued.

(iii) Not less than one year has elapsed since the date on which the company was entitled to commence business.

(iv) SEBI's guidelines shall be applicable in case of a listed company issuing sweat-equity shares. In case of unlisted copany- in accordance with guidelines as prescribed.

(v) Sweat-Equity shares must be of a class of shares already issued by the company.

> It should be noted that all restrictions, limitations, and provisions relating to equity shares shall be applicale to sweat-equity shares also.

LIEN ON SHARES

Lien means "right to retain possession of a certain property of other party unitl a certain claim is settled. The right of lien on shares is not conferred on a company by the statute. It must be clearly provided in the Articles of Association. A company has first and paramount lien on all shares (except fully paid up) for amount due from any shareholder. Lien also covers debts due by a shareholder to a company in his capacity as a customer. It also extends to all dividends payable thereon and the assets receivable by the shareholders upon winding up. It continues even after the death of a shareholder.

A lien gives the company such rights as it has under the general law if the shares were expressly charged. The lien can be enforced by a company even in case of a time-barred debt.

However, in the following cases a company loses lien if:

(i) It registers a transfer of shares subject to the lien of the transferee.

(ii) A member pledges his shares to a third party as security for a loan and the company has notice there of and then incurs a liability to the company. In such a case the pledgee has priority over the lien of the company. For examople if shares are given to a bank as security for an overdraft after giving notice to the company and subsequently the shareholder becomes indebted to the company giving rise to a lien in favour of the company. In that case, the Bank will have priority over company's claim.

FORFEITURE OF SHARES

When a shareholder fails to pay money due on allotment, first call or any other call i.e. on any due date, the company may sue the defaulting shareholder or forfeit the shares. Generally the company follows the second approach. The Articles of Association of the Company usually authorises the directors to forfeit the shares of a member on non-payment of any call or calls on or before the due date. However, a proper notice must be served to the holder. In short, the following conditions must be satisfied.

(i) The forfeiture must be authorised by Articles of the Company.

(ii) Defaulting shareholder must be served at least 14 days notice to pay the amount due.

If the shareholder fails to pay the amount even after notice, the directors may pass a resolution to forfeit such shares. The holder (Defaulting) ceases to become a member of the company with immediate effect and his name is removed from the register of the members without making any refund of the amount already paid by him.

In the absence of express provisions in the Articles regarding forfeiture, the provisions contamed in "Table A" will be applicable.

Accounting Treatment

The effect of forferture reduces the share capital & hence it is debited with the called up value and amount due but not paid (either on allotment or on calls) is credited to respective account and amount actually paid by holder is credited to "Share forfeited" Account. The forfeiture entry is passed on the following grounds:

1. When shares were issued at Par

Share Capital A/c	Dr. —	(No. of shares X Amount Called up per share)
To Share Allotment A/c	—	Amount due & not paid
To Share First Call A/c	—	Amount due & not paid
To Share Final Call A/c*	—	Amount due & not paid
To Share Forfeited A/c	—	Amount paid by holder

(Being ... shares forfeited for non-payment of allotment, first call & final call money as per the directors resolution no... dated...]

In case the amount due on call or calls has been trenaferred to "Calls-in-Arrears" A/c, the following entry will be recorded in forferture :

Share Capital A/c	Dr.	(No. of Shares X Amount Called up per share)
To Calls-in-Arrears A/c	—	[Amount due]
To Share Forfeited A/c	—	[Amount paid by holder]

*If final Call is not made then it will not be credited

Example (1)

X was holding 100 shares of Rs. 10 each on which he did not pay allotment money at the rate of Rs. 3 per share and first call Rs. 2 per share. He had paid only application money @ Rs. 2 per share. The directors forfeted all the shares held by X. Record journal entry.

Share Capital A/c	Dr.	700	
To Share Allotment A/c			300
To Share First Call A/c			200
To Share Forfeiture A/c			200
(Being forferture of 100 shares as per directors resolution no.— dated]			

2. When shares were issued at "discount".

In case of forfeiture of shares which were originally issued at discount, the discount on issue of shares has to be cancelled. For this purpose "Discount on Issue of shares A/c" is to be credited with the amount of discount allowed to defaulting shareholder whose shares are being forfeited. The following entry is recorded:

Share Capital A/c	Dr.	(No. of shares X called up value per share)
To Discount on Issue of Shares A/c	—	(with the amount of discount)
To Share Allotment A/c	—	(If due & not paid)
To Share Calls A/c	—	(Amount due)
To Share Forfeited A/c	—	(Amount paid by shareholder)
(Being ... Share forfeited for non-payment of Allotment, & Call money as per Board's resolution no... dated...]		

Example (2)

Y was allotted 200 shares of Rs. 10 each which were issued at 10% discount. He paid Rs. 2 per share on application but could not pay the allotment money of Rs. 3 per share and the first and final call. His shares were forfeited. Pass journal entry for the forfeiture of shares.

(200 × 10)	Share Capital A/c	Dr.	2,000	
(200 × 1)	To Discount on Issue of shares A/c			200
(200 × 3)	To Share Allotment A/c			600
(200 × 4)	To Share First & Final Call A/c			800
(200 × 2)	To Share Forfeited A/c			400
	(Being 200 shares forfeited for non-payment of allotment and call money as per Board's resolution no. dated....)			

(3) When shares were issued at "Premium".

According to section 78 of Companies Act 1956, share premium once received cannot be cancelled even if these shares are forfeited at any stage. Hence no cancellation of share premium is to be effected. The forfeiture entry will be recorded as if shares were originally issued at par.

But if the shares, on which premium has become due but has not been received, are forfeited then the share premium has to be cancelled by debiting the "Securities Premium Account".

Example (3)

Z Ltd. issued 50,000 shares of Rs. 10 each at 20% premium payable as under :

	Rs.
On Application	2
On Allotment	5 (including premium)
On First Call	3
On Final Call	2

P who was holding 200 shares did not pay his allotment and first call and his share were forfeited. S who was the holder of 300 failed to pay both the calls and his shares were forfeited. Pass forfeiture entries.

(i)	Share Capital A/c	Dr.	1,600	
	Securities Premium A/c	Dr.	400	
	To Share Allotment A/c			1,000
	To Share First Call A/c			600
	To Share Forfeited A/c			400
	(Being 200 shares of P forfeited)			
(ii)	(300 × 10) Share Capital A/c	Dr.	3,000	
	(300 × 3) To Share First Call A/c			900
	(300 × 2) To Share Final Call A/c			600
	(300 × 5*) To Share Forfeited A/c*			1,500
	(Being 300 shares of S forfeirted)			

*Excluding premium

Surrender of shares

When a shareholder is not able to pay further calls on shares held by him, returns the shares to the company for cancellation. This voluntary return of partly paid shares under such a situation is known as surrender of shares. Accounting treament on surrender of shares is the same as in case of forfeiture. No separate or distinct entry is required to be recorded. Same set of entries are recorded as discussed and illustrated above.

Note : Share Forfeited Account will continue to be shown on the liabilities side of the Balance Sheet until the forfeited shares are reissued.

REISSUE OF FORFEITED SHARES

A Company, subject to any contrary provisions in the Articles, may re-issue the shares at any time according to it's convenience either at par or at discount or at premium irrespective of terms of original issue. However, the amount of concession (discount on reissue) cannot exceed the proportionate amount forfeited on such shares. In other words the minimum reissue price cannot be less than the unpaid balance on such shares.

It should be noted that the amount of concession (discount on reissue) is adjusted against the Share Forfeited Account. However, if shares were originally isued at discouint, then the (original) discount account will always be debited along with the Bank A/c and Share Forfeited Account as shown in the following illustrations. The proportionate balance of Share Forfeited A/c after the discount on reissue will be transferred to Capital Reserve.

Accounting Treatment:

1. *When shares were issued at Par and Reissued at discount.*

a. Bank A/c Dr. (Amount actually received)
Share Forfieted A/c Dr. (Conscession or discount on Reissue)
To Share Capital A/c (Paid up value of shares)

b. Share Forfeited A/c Dr.
To Capital Reserve A/c*
(Being (proportionate) balance transferred to Capital Reserve)

*(No. of forfeited shares reissued X Rate of forfeiture (Amount per share) Less No. of shares reissued X Rate of discount (Concession on reissue)

2. *When shares were issued at discount and Reissued also at discount*

a. Bank A/c Dr. (Amount Received)
Discount on Shares A/c Dr. (Original discount on issue)
Share Forfeited A/c Dr. (discount/concession on reissue)
To Share Capital A/c (paid up value)

b. Share Forfeited A/c Dr.
To Capital Reserve A/c

Example (4) (Reissue of Forfeited shares originally issued at Par)

X Ltd. forfeited 50 shares of P who paid application money @ Rs. 2 per share, 150 shares of Q who paid Rs. 2 on application Rs. 3 on allotment and 300 shares of R who paid 2 on application, Rs. 3 on allotment and Rs. 3 on first call. They all failed to pay their arrears along with the final call. The directors forfeited all these Shares of Rs. 10 each which issued at par. All these share were reissued @ Rs. 9 per share credited as fully paid. Pass Journal entries.

Solution (4)

			Rs.	Rs.
	Share Capital A/c (500 × 10)	Dr.	5,000	
	To Share Allotment (50 × 3)			150
	To Share First Call A/c (200 × 3)			600
	To Share Final Call A/c (500 × 2)			1,000
	To Share Forfeited A/c*[1]			3,250
	(Being 500 shares were forfeited as per Board's resolution no.... dated....)			
	Bank A/c	Dr.	4,500	
	Share Forfeited A/c	Dr.	5,00	
	To Share Capital A/c			5,000
	(Being forfeited shares reissued)			
	Share Forfeited A/c	Dr.		2,750
	To Capital Reserve A/c			2,750
	(Being balance of Share Forfeited A/c transferred to Capital Reserve)			

*1 Share forfeited amount has been worked out as under :

	Rs.
P paid application money on 50 shares @ Rs. 2	100
Q paid application & allotment on 150 shares @ Rs. 5 (2 +3)	750
R paid application, allotment & first call @ Rs. 8 (2 + 3 + 3) on 300 shares	2,400
	3,250

Example (5) (Reissue of forfeited shares originally issued at premium)

N Ltd. forfeited 200 shares of Rs. 10 each issued at a premium of 20% D, the holder paid Rs. 2.50 per share on application but did not pay Rs. 4.50 per share (including premium) on allotment and first call of Rs. 3 per share. His shares were forfeited after the first call. K another holder of 300 shares failed to pay the two calls-the first second & final call. His shares were also forfeited after the final call.

Of these, directors reissued 400 shares @ Rs. 9 per share credited as fully paid up, the whole of the D's shares being included. Pass necessary journal entries to record above transactions.

(b) What difference will it make if shares are reissued @ Rs. 11 per share credited as fully paid.

Solution : 5

JORURNAL ENTRIES

			Rs.	Rs.
	Share Capital A/c	Dr.	1,600	
	Securities Premium A/c	Dr.	400	
	To Share Allotment A/c			900
	To Share First Call A/c			600
	To Share Forfeited A/c			500
	(Being 200 shares of D forfeited for non-payment of allotment allotment and first call.)			
	Share Capital A/c	Dr.	3,000	
	To Share First Call A/c			900
	To Share Final Call A/c			600
	To Share Forfeited A/c			1,500
	(Being 300 shares of K forfeited for non payment of two calls)			
	Bank A/c	Dr.	3,600	
	Share Forfeited A/c (B.F.)	Dr.	400	
	To Share Capital A/c			4,000
	(Being reissue of 400 shares @ Rs. 9)			
	Share Forfeited A/c	Dr.	1,100	
	To Capital Reserve (1)			1,100
	(Being proprotionate balance of share forfeiture transferred to Capital Reserve)			
(b)	Bank A/c	Dr.	4,400	
	To Share Capital A/c			4,000
	To Securities Premium A/c			400
	(Being 400 shares reissued @ Rs.11)			

	Share Forfeited A/c Dr.		1,500	
	To Capital Reserve (2) A/c			1,500
	(Being amount forfeited on 400 shares transferred to Capital reserve)			

Working Note :

(1) Capital Reserve = Amount forfeited on shares reissued Less discount (Concession) allowed on reissue.

			Amount forfeited
I	Shares forfeited 200 @ Rs. 2.5		Rs. 500
	(D) Application money		
II	Shares forfeited 300 @ Rs. 5		Rs. 1,500
	(K) Application & Allotment money		

No of shares reissued

		No.	Rs.	Amount forfeited Rs.
I	D's whole shares	200	@ 2.5	500
II	K's Shares	200	@ 5	1,000
		400	Total	1,500
	Less discount (Concession) allowed on reissue			400
	Capital Reserve			1,100

2. In the second situation since no discount has been allowed on reissue rather these shares have been issued at premium, hence entire amount forfeited on 400 shares reissued, has been transferred to Capital Reserve.

3 However, the amount forfeited on shares not reissued will be shown on the liabilities side of Balance Sheet as Shares Forfeited Account.

Illustration (3)

(Shares issued at discount, undersubscription, forfeiture & reissue)

X Ltd. invited applications for 80,000 shares of Rs. 10 each at a discount of 5% payable as follows :

	Rs.
On application	2
On allotment	2.50
On First & Final Call	balance

Applications were received for 75,000 shares and all of these were accepted. All money due was received except the first and final call on 800 shares which were forfeited. Of these 500 shares were reissued @ Rs. 9 credited as fully paid. Assuming that all requirements of the law were complied with, pass entries in the journal and Cash Book and prepare a Balance Sheet to reflect these transactions. Bank entries to be shown in Cash Book only.

Solution : 3

JOURNAL ENTRIES

		Rs.	Rs.
Share Application A/c	Dr.	1,50,000	
To Share Capital A/c			1,50,000
(Being application money on 75,000 shares transferred to share Capital A/c)			
Share Allotment A/c	Dr.	1,87,500	
Discount on Shares A/c	Dr.	37,500	
To Share Capital A/c			2,25,000
(Being 75,000 shares allotted and 5% discount allowed as per Board's resolution no. dated)			
Share First & Final A/c	Dr.	3,75,000	
To Share Capital A/c			3,75,000
(Being amount due on final Call @ Rs. 5 per share on 75,000 shares)			
Share Capital A/c	Dr.	8,000	
To Discount on shares A/c			400
To First and Final Call A/c			4,000
To Share Forfeited A/c			3,600
(Being forfeifure of 800 shares for non-payment of first and final call as per Board's resolution no... dated...)			
Discount on shares A/c (500 × .50)	Dr.	250	
Shares Forfeited A/c (Balancing figure)	Dr.	250	
To Share Capital A/c (500 × 1*)			500
(Being 500 forfeited shares reissued at discount of Re. 1 per share (10 – 9)			
Share Forfeited A/c	Dr.	2,000	
To Capital Reserve A/c			2,000
(Being profit on reissue (forfeited– discount on reissue) transferred to Capital reserve) $\left(\frac{3,600 \times 500}{800}\right) = 2,250 - 250)$			

* Bank entry (500 × 9) Rs. 4,500 has been recorded in the Cash Book

CASH BOOK

Dr.	Rs.		Cr. Rs.
To Share Application A/c (75,000 @ Rs. 2)	1,50,000	By Balance c/d	7,13,000
To Share Allotment A/c (75,000 @ Rs. 2.50)	1,87,500		
To Share First & Final Call A/c (74,200 @ Rs. 5)	3,71,000		
To Share Capital (500 @ Rs. 9)	4,500		
	7,13,000		7,13,000

BALANCE SHEET OF X LTD.

As on........

Liabilities	Rs.	Assets	Rs.
Authorised Share Capital .....Shares of Rs....each		Cash at Bank	7,13,000
		Discount on Shares (3)	37,350
Issued & Subscribed Capital 74,700 Shares of Rs. 10 each fully paid	7,47,000		
Share Forfeited Account (2)	1,350		
Capital Reserve	2,000		
	7,50,350		7,50,350

Working notes:

(1) Bank entries have been recorded in Cash Book only.

(2) Shares forfeited 800 @ Rs. 4.50 (app. & allot)

Forfeited Shares Reissued 500

Remaining unissued 300

Forfeited amount on 300 shares @ Rs. 4.50 = Rs. 1,350

(3) Discount on Shares = 5% of Share Capital

i.e. 5% of Rs. 7,47,000 = Rs. 37,350 or

Rs. .50 per share *i.e* 74,700 × .50 = 37,350

Illustration (4)

(Over- Subscription different scales of allotment, issue at premium & Share forfeiture)

Vyoma Ltd. issued 6,000 shares of Rs. 100 each at a premium of Rs. 25 per share payable as under :

	Rs.
On Application	45 (including premium)
On Allotment	40
On First & Final Call	balance remaining

Applications were received for 11,000 shares. The directors scaled down the allotment as under:

	Shares applied for	Shares allotted
Ist Category (0 - 25) Shares	7,000	4,200
IInd Category (25 - 50) Shares	3,500	1,400
IIIrd Category (>50) Shares	500	400

It was also resolved that excess application money to be adjusted against the money due on allotment and surplus if any would be refunded.

X an applicant of 10 shares defaulted on payment of allotment money. Y the holder of 80 shares failed to pay the call money. Their shares were forfeited after the respective calls were made and later on reissued @ Rs. 80 & Rs. 60 per share respectively credited as fully paid.

You are required to pass journal entries. All working should form part of your answer. Also prepare a Balance Sheet.

Solution (4)

Table showing money received on application, it's adjustment & refund.

Category	No. of Shares Applied for	No. of Shares Allotted	Application Money Received	Amount Adjusted @ Rs. 45 on Application	Amount Adjusted @ Rs. 40 On allotment	Balance to be received on allotment	Money to to Refunded
			Rs.	Rs.	Rs.	Rs.	Rs.
I (0 - 25)	7,000	4,200	3,15,000	1,89,000	1,26,000	42,000	—
II (25 - 50)	3,500	1,400	1,57,500	63,000	56,000	—	38,500
III (> 50)	500	400	22,500	18,000	4,500	11,500	—
	11,000	6,000	4,95,000	2,70,000	1,86,500	53,500	38,500

JOURNAL ENTRIES

			Rs.	Rs.
	Bank A/c	Dr.	4,95,000	
	To Share Application A/c			4,95,000
	(Being application money received on 11,000 shares @ Rs. 45 pershare)			

			Rs.	Rs.
	Share Application A/c	Dr.	4,95,000	
	To Share Capital A/c (6,000 × 20)			1,20,000
	To Securities Premium A/c (6,000 × 25)			1,50,000
	To Share Allotment A/c*			1,86,500
	To Bank A/c*			38,500
	(Being application money transferred to Share Capital A/c Securities Premium A/c and adjusted on Allotment & balance refunded)			
	Share Allotment A/c	Dr.	2,40,000	
	To Share Capital A/c			2,40,000
	(Being allotment money due on 6,000 shares @ Rs. 40)			
	Bank A/c*2	Dr.	53,440	
	To Share Allotment A/c			53,440
	(Being allotment money received)			
	Share First & Final Call A/c	Dr.	2,40,000	
	To Share Capital A/c			2,40,000
	(Being first & final call money due on 6,000 Shares @ Rs. 40 per share)			
	Bank A/c	Dr.	2,36,560	
	To Share First & Final Call A/c			2,36,560
	(Being call money received on 5,914 shares @ Rs. 40 per share)			
	Share Capital A/c	Dr.	8,600	
	To Share Allotment A/c (2)			60
	To Share First & Final Call A/c (3)			3,440
	To Share Forfeuted A/c			5,100
	(Being forfeiture of 86 shares for non payment of allotment money)			
	Bank A/c	Dr.	5,280	
	Share Forfeited A/c	Dr.	3,320	
	To Share Capital A/c			8,600
	(Being reissue of 6 shares @ Rs. 80 per share and 80 shares @ Rs. 60 per share)			
	Share forfeited A/c	Dr.	1,780	
	To Capital Reserve A/c			1,780
	(Being profit on reissue transferred to Capital reserve)			

* Please refer to table

BALANCE SHEET OF
As on....

Liabilities	Rs.	Assets	Rs.
Authorised Capital			
.....Shares of Rs.....		Cash at Bank	7,51,780
Issued & Subscribed Capital			
6,000 Shares of Rs. 100 each fully paid	6,00,000		
Securities Premium	1,50,000		
Capital Reserve	1,780		
	7,51,780		7,51,780

Working notes :

(1) Money adjusted on allotment & money refunded has been shown in the table.

(2) Money received on allotment has been worked out as under. X the applicant of 10 shares has been allotted 6 shares because he belongs to first category where rate of allotment is

7,000 : 4,200 or 60% of 10 shares $\frac{4,200}{7,000} \times 10 = 6$ shares

	Money paid by a X on application 10 × 45 =	450
Less	appliaction money adjusted for 6 shares 6 × 45	270
	Excess app. money to be Adjusted on allotment	180
	X was required to pay on alotment = 6 × 40 =	240
Less	Excess application money =	180
	Money not paid by X	60

Money due (after adjustment) Rs. 53,500 as shown in the table less Rs. 60 *i.e.* money received on allotment is Rs. 53,440

(3) Money not received on first & final Call

		Rs.
X - 6 shares @ Rs. 40	=	240
Y - 80 shares @ Rs. 40	=	3,200
		3,440

(4) **Share Forfeited Amount**

Money paid by X on 10 shares @ Rs. 45 = 450 but premium on 6 shares allotted to X cannot be forfeited. Hence money forfeited in case of X = Rs. 450 – 150 = 300

Money paid by Y on 80 Shares = 4,800

(@ Rs. 20 + 40)

5,100

(5) CASH BOOK

	Rs.		Rs.
To Share Application A/c	4,95,000	By Share Application A/c	38,500
To Share Allotment A/c	53,440	By Balance c/d	7,51,780
To Share First & Final Call A/c	2,36,560		
To Share Capital A/c	5,280		
	7,90,280		7,90,280

PRO-RATA ALLOTMENT AND IT'S ACCOUNTING TREATMENT

Pro-rata means proportionately - where shares are allotted in proportion of number of shares applied for. This situation arises in case of over subscription where all applicants are entertained and the directors please every applicant by alloting the shares in proportion of number of shares applied for. Alternatively, the directors may turn down the applications of a few applicants and accomodate the remaining applicants on pro-rata (proportionate) basis or it is quite possible the directors may accepts some of the applications in full, reject some and make allotment for the remaining on pro-rata basis. As far as it's accounting treatment is concerned, "Pro-rata" allotment does not require any additional calculations & working as long as there is no default on allotment. It should be remembered that in case of over subscription, the applicants pay application money more than what is required on application. In case of no default it becomes a simple case of adjustment of surplus money received on application.

However, if any allottee makes a default on allotment and subsequently his shares are forfeited, such a situation demands an additional careful working on the part of students to calculate amount due from the defaulter on allotment and amount forfeited there on For instance A company issues 50,000 shares for which applications are received for 80,000 shares and directors make allotment on pro-rata basis. If a person is holding 100 shares, he must have paid application money on $\left(\frac{100 \times 8}{5}\right)$ *i.e.* 160 shares. In case of forfeiture (suppose he does not pay any other call). The amount forfeited will be calculated on the basis of 160 shares i.e. shares applied for - being the basis of payment of application money. And similary, he will be required to pay on allotment on the basis of no. of shares allotted less excess application money. Therefore, students are required to note following points.

(1) In a question whether the word allottee or holder is given or applicant. In case it is allottee or holder given, calculations must be made to find out number of shares applied for by applying the following formula.

$$\frac{\text{Total number of shares applied for}}{\text{Total number of shares allotted}} \times \text{Shares allotted to defaulter}$$

However, if in the question applicant is given, then students are required to findout number of shares allotted.

i.e.
$$\frac{\text{Total number of shares allotted}}{\text{Total number of shares applied for}} \times \text{Shares applied for by defaulter}$$

(2) Calculate application money paid by applicant/allottee or holder on the basis of number of shares applied for:

In fact this is the amount which will be tranferred to shares forfeited account in case of default & forfeiture.

(3) Calculate total amount due on allotment on the basis of total number of shares allotted and deduct the excess application money in all.

(4) Findout defaultter's dues on allotment on the basis of number of shares allotted to him as reduced by the excess application money paid by him.. This amount is credited to share allotment account at the time of forfeiture.

Illustration (5)

(Pro-rata allotment & forfeiture of shares)

G.L. Ltd. invited applications for 25,000 shares of Rs. 10 each issued at 25% premium payable as under :

On application	Rs. 7.50 per share (including premium)
On allotment	Rs. 3.00 per share
On First & final Call	Rs. 2.00 per share

Applications were received for 30,000 shares and the Board decided as under :

(i) To refuse allotment to an applicant for 1,000 shares

(ii) To give full allotment to the applicants for 5,000 shares

(iii) To allot the remaining shares on pro-rata basis.

(iv) To utilise the surplus received on application against the sum due on allotment.

An applicant to whom 250 shares were allotted on pro-rata basis failed to pay the amount due on the allotment and his subsequent failure to pay first and final call, his shares were forfeited. Of these 150 shares were reissued @ Rs. 8 per share credited as fully paid.

Give journal entries, prepare Bank A/c and a Balance Sheet to give effect to above mentioned transactions.

C.A. (Inter) Adapted.

Solution (5)

JOURNAL ENTRIES

		Rs.	Rs.
	Bank A/c Dr.	2,25,000	
	To Share Application A/c		2,25,000
	(Being application money received on 30,000 shares @ Rs. 7.50 per share)		
	Share Application A/c Dr.	2,25,000	
	To Share Capital A/c (25,000 × 5)		1,25,000
	To Share Allotment A/c (4,000 × 7.50)		30,000
	To Securities Premium A/c (25,000 × 2.50)		62,500
	To Bank A/c (1,000 × 7.50)		7,500
	(Being application money transferred to Share Capital A/c, Securities Premium A/c, and adjusted on allotment on 4,000 shares & balance refunded)		

Contd.

		Rs.	Rs.
Share Allotment A/c	Dr.	75,000	
To Share Capital A/c			75,000
(Being allotment money due on 25,000 shares @ Rs. 3 per share)			
Bank A/c[1]	Dr.	44,625	
To Share Allotment A/c			44,625
(Being allotment money received)			
Share First & Final Call A/c	Dr.	50,000	
To Share Capital A/c			50,000
(Being amount due first & final call due)			
Bank A/c	Dr.	49,500	
To Share First & Final Call A/c			49,500
(Being call money received)			
Share Capital A/c	Dr.	2,500	
To Share Allotment A/c (2)			375
To Share First & Final A/c			500
To Share Forfeited A/c (3)			1,625
(Being 250 Share forfeited for non payment of allotment and call money)			
Bank A/c	Dr.	1,200	
Share Forfeited A/c		300	
To Share Capital A/c			1,500
(Being 150 shares reissued @ Rs. 8 per share			
Share Forfeited A/c	Dr.	675	
To Capital Reserve A/c[4]			675
(Being profit on reissue transferred to Capital Reserve)			

BANK ACCOUNT

	Rs.		Rs.
To Share Application A/c	2,25,000	By Share Application A/c	7,500
To Share Allotment A/c	44,625	By Balance c/d	3,12,825
To Share First & Final Call A/c	49,500		
To Share Capital A/c	1,200		
	3,20,325		3,20,325

BALANCE SHEET OF --------
As on ------

Laibilities	Rs.	Assets	Rs.
Authorised Capital ----- shares of Rs. -----each		Cash at Bank	3,12,825
Subscribed & paid up Capital 24,900 shares of Rs. 10 each fully paid	2,49,000		
Securities Premium	62,500		
Capital Reserve	675		
Share Forfeited Account	650		
	3,12,825		3,12,825

3. Calculation of Amount Forfeited on 250 shares

Total Money paid by, @ Rs. 7.50 per share, defaulter allottee on 300 shares	2,250
Since application money includes premium which cannot be forfeited but transferred to " Securities Premium only (250 × 2.50) hence deduct	625
	1,625

It should be noted that the amount to be transferred to securities premium account is calculated on the basis of 'shares allotted" and not on shares applied for"

4. Calculation of Capital Reserve

	Amount forfeited on 250 shares	1,625
Less	Amount pertaining to shares forfeited but not re issued $\left(\frac{1,625}{250} \times 100\right)$	650
	Maximum amount that can be allowed on shares re issued	975
Less	discount (Concession on re issue) 150 @ 2	300
	Capital Reserve	675

It should be remembered that the Capital reserve is the difference between the "amount forfeited on shares re issued" & the actual discount (Concession) on such shares.

Working notes :

	No. of Shares Applied for		No. of Shares Issued
	30,000		25,000
Shares rejected	1,000		—
	29,000		25,000
Full Allotment made to	5,000		5,000
	24,000		20,000
	24		20
Ratio	6	:	5

i.e. for every 6 six shares applied for number of shares alloted is 5

		Rs.
(1)	**Money received on allotment**	
	Amount due on 25,000 shares @ Rs. 3 per share	75,000
Less	Excess Application money on 4,000 shares due to pro-rata allotment	30,000
		45,000
Less	Amount not paid by defaulter allottee	375*
	Amount Received	44,625
(2)	***Amount due but not paid by defaulter (allottee) on allotment**	Rs.
	Amount due on 250 Shares @ Rs. 3 per share	750
Less	Excess application money	375
	Money due and not paid by defaulter allottee	375
	He paid on application on $\left(\frac{250 \times 6}{5}\right)$ = 300 Shares	
	@ Rs. = 7.50 per shares	= 2,250
Less	Money Adjusted on application on 250 shares	= 1,875
	Excess application money to be adjusted on allotment	375

Illustration (6) (Over-subcription, pro-rata & forfeiture)

X Ltd. issued a prospectus inviting applications for 20,000 shares of Rs. 10 each at a premium of Rs.2 per share payable as follows :

	Rs.
On Application	2
On Allotment	5 (including premium)
On First Call	3
On Final Call	2

Applications were received for 30,000 shares and pro-rata allotment was made on the application for 24,000 shares Money over-paid on applications was employed on account of sum due on allotment.

Ramesh, to whom 400 shares were allotted failed to pay the allotment money and on his subsequent failuare to pay the first call his shares were forfeited. Mohan, the holder of 600 shares, failed to pay the two calls and his shares were forfeited after the second call.

Of the shares forfeited, 800 shares were sold to Krishna credited as fully paid for Rs. 9 per share, the whole of Ramesh's share being included.

Show journal and Cash Book entires and the Balance Sheet.

C.S. (Inter) - Modified

Solution (6)

JOURNAL ENTRIES

		Rs.	Rs.
	Share Application A/c Dr.	48,000	
	To Share Capital A/c		40,000
	To Share Allotment A/c		8,000
	(Being application money tranferred to Share Capital A/c and to Share Allotment A/c due to pro-rata allotment)		

Contd.

		Rs.	Rs.
Share Allotment A/c	Dr.	1,00,000	
To Share Capital A/c			60,000
To Securities Premium A/c			40,000
(Being amount due on allotment on 20,000 shares)			
Share First Call A/c	Dr.	60,000	
To Share Capital A/c			60,000
(Being first call money due on 20,000 shares)			
Share Capital A/c	Dr.	3,200	
Securities Premium A/c	Dr.	800	
To Share Allotment A/c (3)			1,840
To Share First Call A/c			1,200
To Share Forfeited A/c			960
(Being forfeiture of 400 shares for non-payment of allotment and first call money)			
Share Final Call A/c	Dr.	39,200	
To Share Capital A/c			39,200
(Being money due on 19,600 shares on final call)			
Share Capital A/c	Dr.	6,000	
To Share First Call A/c			1,800
To Share Final Call A/c			1,200
To Share Forfeited A/c			3,000
(Being forfeiture of 600 shares for non-payment of both calls)			
Share Forfeited A/c	Dr.	800	
To Share Capital A/c			800
(Being discount allowed on reissue of 800 shares @ Re.1 difference between paid up value and reissue price *i.e.* 10 – 9 per share)			
Share Forfeited A/c	Dr.	2,160	
To Capital Reserve A/c (4)			2,160
(Being profit on reissue of 800 shares transferred to Capital reserve)			

CASH BOOK (BANK COLUMN)

	Rs.		Rs.
To Share Applicaiton A/c	60,000	By Share Application A/c	12,000
To Share Allotment A/c(2)	90,160	By Balance c/d	2,40,360
To Share First Call A/c	57,000		
To Share Final Call A/c	38,000		
To Share Capital A/c (Reissue)	7,200		
	2,52,360		2,52,360

BALANCE SHEET OF....
As on ....

Liabilities	Rs.	Assets	Rs.
Authorised Capital		Cash at Bank	2,40,360
... Shares ... of Rs.			
Issued Capital			
.... Shares of Rs.			
Subscribed and Paid up Capital			
19,800 Shares of Rs. 10 each fully paid	1,98,000		
Securities Premium (5)	39,200		
Share Forfeited Account	1,000		
Capital Reserve	2,160		
	2,40,360		2,40,360

Working notes:

		Shares Applied for	Shares Issued
(1)		30,000	20,000
	Pro-rata allotment made on	24,000	20,000
	Shares rejected and money refunded there on	6,000	—

Thus rate of prorata = 24 : 20 or 6 : 5

For every 6 shares applied for 5 shares have been allotted

			Rs.
(2)	Money received on allotment		
	Money due on 20,000 shares @ Rs. 5	=	1,00,000
Less	Excess application money on 4,000 shares @ Rs. 2		8,000
			92,000
Less	Money not paid by Ramesh*3		1,840
			90,160

(3) Shares allotted to Ramesh 400

			Rs.
	He must have applied for $\left(400 \times \frac{6}{5}\right)$ = 480 Shares		
	Hence money paid by him on allotment = 480 × 2		960
Less	money adjusted on application 400 × 2		800
	Excess application money to be adjusted on allotment		160
	Money due from Ramesh on allotment = 400 × 5	=	2,000
Less	Excess application money paid by him		160
	Money due not paid by Ramesh		1,840

		Rs.
(4)	Calculation of Capital Reserve	
	Amount Forfeited on Ramesh's Shares (400 shares)	960
	Amount Forfeited on Mohan's Shares (600 Shares)	3,000
	Shares reissued 800 shares	
	Whole lot of Ramesh's 400 Shares	960
	Balance form Mohan's lot 400 $\left(\frac{3,000}{600} \times 400\right)$	2,000
		2,960
Less	discount on re issue	800
	Profit on re issue transferred to Capital reserve	2,160

(5) Securities premium has been received on (20,000 – 400) 19,600 Shares @ Rs. 2 = Rs. 39,200

Illustration (7)

(Over-Subscription, full and pro-rata allotment, forfeiture and re issue)

New-Comers Ltd. issued 2,00,000 equity shares of Rs. 10 each at 10% discount payable Rs. 3 on application, Rs. 4 on allotment and Rs. 2 on call. Applications were received for 3,20,000 shares out of which letter of regrets were issued for 60,000 shares. Full allotment was made to applications for 80,000 shares and allotment balance was made on the balance. A holder of 200 shares to whom full allotment was made failed to pay allotment money. Another shareholder holding 400 shares to whom pro-rata allotment was made also failed to pay allotment money. On call there was further default on 600 shares.

All these shares were forfeited. The first lot of 600 (200 + 400) shares was reissued at Rs. 8 per share. Pass journal entries in the books of Company to record the above transactions. Also prepare Bank A/c and Balance Sheet.

I.C.W.A. (Inter) - Adapted

Solution (7)

JOURNAL ENTRIES

			Rs.	Rs.
	Bank A/c	Dr.	9,60,000	
	To Share Application A/c			9,60,000
	(Being application money on 3,20,000 shares received)			
	Share Application A/c	Dr.	9,60,000	
	To Share Capital A/c			6,00,000
	To Share Allotment A/c			1,80,000
	To Bank A/c			1,80,000
	(Being application money on 2,00,000 shares transferred to Share Capital A/c, on 60,000 shares adjusted against allotment and balance refunded.)			
	Share Allotment A/c	Dr.	8,00,000	
	Discount on Shares A/c	Dr.	2,00,000	
	To Share Capital A/c			10,00,000
	(Being money on allotment become due)			

Contd.

			Rs.	Rs.
	Bank A/c (2) Dr. To Share Allotment A/c (Being money on 1,99,400 shares received)		6,18,200	6,18,200
	Share Call A/c Dr. To Share Capital A/c (Being money on first & final call due)		4,00,000	4,00,000
	Bank A/c Dr. To Share Call A/c (Being call money on 1,98,800 shares received)		3,97,600	3,97,600
	Share Capital A/c Dr. To Discount on Shares A/c To Share Allotment A/c (3) To Share Call A/c To Share Forfeited A/c (4) (Being 1,200 shares forfeited)		12,000	 1,200 1,800 2,400 6,600
	Bank A/c Dr. Discount on Shares A/c Dr. Share Forfeited A/c Dr. To Share Capital A/c (Being first lot of 600 shares reissued)		4,800 600 600	 6,000
	Share Forfeited A/c Dr. To Capital Reserve A/c (5) (Being profit on re-issue of shares transferred to Capital Reserve)		1,800	1,800

BANK A/C

	Rs.		Rs.
To Share Application A/c	9,60,000	By Share Application A/c	1,80,000
To Share Allotment A/c	6,18,200	By Balance c/d	18,00,600
To Share Call A/c	3,97,600		
To Share Capital A/c (Re issue)	4,800		
	19,80,600		19,80,600

BALANCE SHEET OF NEW COMERS LTD.
As on.....

Liabilities	Rs.	Assets	Rs.
Authorised Capital	—	Cash at Bank	18,00,600
— shares of Rs. 10 each		Discount on Shares	1,99,400
Issued Capital	—		
— shares of Rs. 10 each			
Subscribed & Paid up Capital			
1,99,400 shares of Rs. 10 each			
fully paid	19,94,000		
Share Forfeited Account	4,200		
Capital Reserve	1,800		
	20,00,000		20,00,000

Working notes :

		No. of Shares Issued		No. of Shares applied for
(1)		2,00,000		3,20,000
Less	Rejected	—		60,000
		2,00,000		2,60,000
Less	Full Allotment	80,000		80,000
	Pro-rata Ratio	1,20,000		1,80,000
		12	:	18
		2	:	3

For every three shares applied for 2 shares have been allotted.

		Rs.
(2)	Money Received on Allotment	
	2,00,000 shares @ Rs. 4	8,00,000
Less	Excess application money due to pro-rata allotment (1,80,000 – 1,20,000) × 3	1,80,000
		6,20,000
Less	Money not received on 600 shares*	1,800
	Money Received on allotment	6,18,200

(3) * Money due but not paid by Holders of 600 shares

Holder of 200 Shares (100% allottee) @ Rs. 4 — 800

Holder of 400 shares (pro-rata allottee)

He must have applied for $\left(400 \times \frac{3}{2}\right) = 600$ shares

	and paid application money	Rs. 1,800
Less	Application money adjusted (400 × 3)	1,200
	Excess Application money	600
	On allotment he was required to pay 400 × 4 =	Rs. 1,600
Less	Excess Appolication money =	Rs. 600

Amount not paid by holder of 400 shares	1,000
Therefore total amount not received by company on allotment :	
on 200 shares	800
and on 400 shares	1000
	1,800

(4) Amount forfeited by the Company

On 200 shares (100% allottee) (i.e. application money)	600
On 400 shares (Pro-rata allottee) (application money on 600 shares)	1,800
On 600 and further shares (application & allotment money)	
@ Rs. (3 + 4) Rs. 7 per share	4,200
Total amount forfeited	6,600

(5) Capital Reserve

Since only first lot has been re issued thus the Capital Reserve will be total amount forfeited on first lot (200 + 400) shares less discount on reissue *i.e.* (2,400 – 600) = 1,800

> It should be remembered that if shares were originally issued at discoiunt, then while reissuing forfeited shares the discount account will always be debited first & balancing figure will be adjusted against Share Forfeited A/c if reissue price still falls short.

Illustration (8) (Various Scales of Allotment)

A Ltd. issued 40,000 shares of Rs. 10 each at 25% premium. The money was payable as follows:

	Rs.
On Application	2
On Allotment	4.5 (including premium)
On First Call	4
On Final Call	Balance

96,400 shares were applied for and owing to heavy over-subscription, allotment was made as under :

Applicants for 23,000 shares (in respect of applications for 2,000 or more shares) were allotted 10,560 shares.

Applicants for 48,000 shares (in respect of applications for 1,000 or more shares) were allotted 14,200 shares.

Applicants for 25,400 shares were allotted 15,240 shares pro-rata.

It was decided that the excess amount received on application would be utilised in payment of allotment money and surplus, if any, would be refunded.

P - an applicant of 500 shares but allotted on pro-rata basis failed to pay allotment money. R the holder of 450 shares who was also allotted on pro-rata basis failed to pay both the calls. Their shares were forfeited after the final call was made. Of these 500 shares were reissued @ Rs. 9 per share credited as fully paid the whole of P's share being included. Pass journal entries and show the Bank Account.

C.A. (Inter) Adapted

Solution (8)

JOURNAL ENTRIES

			Rs.	Rs.
	Bank A/c	Dr.	1,92,800	
	To Share Application A/c			1,92,800
	(Being appliation money received on 96,400 shares)			
	Share Application A/c	Dr.	1,92,800	
	To Equity Share Capital A/c			80,000
	To Share Allotment A/c (1)			1,09,100
	To Bank A/c (1)			3,700
	(Being application money transferred to Share Capital A/c, and excess application money adjusted on allotment and surplus thereafter refunded)			
	Share Allotment A/c	Dr.	1,80,000	
	To Share Capital A/c			80,000
	To Securities Premium A/c			1,00,000
	(Being allotment money become due)			
	Bank A/c (2)	Dr.	69,950	
	To Share Allotment A/c			69,950
	(Being money received on allotment)			
	Share First Call A/c	Dr.	1,60,000	
	To Share Capital A/c			1,60,000
	(Being first call money become due)			
	Bank A/c	Dr.	1,57,000	
	To Share First Call A/c			1,57,000
	(Being first call money received on 39,250 shares)			
	Share Second and final A/c	Dr.	80,000	
	To Share Capital A/c			80,000
	(Being final call money due)			
	Bank A/c	Dr.	78,500	
	To Share Second & Final Call A/c			78,500
	(Being final call received on 39,250 shares)			
	Share Capital A/c	Dr.	7,500	
	Securities Premium A/c	Dr.	750	
	To Share Allotment A/c (3)			950
	To Share First Call A/c			3,000
	To Share Final Call A/c			1,500
	To Share Forfeited A/c (4)			2,800
	(Being 750 shares forfeited)			

Contd.

			Rs.	Rs.
	Bank A/c	Dr.	4,500	
	Share Forfeited A/c	Dr.	500	
	To Share Capital A/c			5,000
	(Being 500 shares reissued @ 9 per share)			
	Share Forfeited A/c	Dr.	1,300	
	To Capital Reserve A/c (5)			1,300
	(Being profit on reissue transferred to Capital Reserve)			

BANK ACCOUNT

	Rs.		Rs.
To Share Application A/c	1,92,800	By Share Application A/c	3,700
To Share Allotment A/c	69,950	By Balance c/d	4,99,050
To Share First Call A/c	1,57,000		
To Share Final Call A/c	78,500		
To Share Capital A/c	4,500		
	5,02,750		5,02,750

BALANCE SHEET OF A LTD.
As on....

Liabilities	Rs.	Assets	Rs.
Authorised Capital		Cash at Bank	4,99,050
— Shares —— of Rs. —			
Issued Capital			
—Shares of Rs. —			
Subscribed & Paid up Capital			
39,750 shares of Rs. 10 each fully paid up	3,97,500		
Share Forfeited Account (6)	1,000		
Securities Premium (7)	99,250		
Capital Reserve	1,300		
	4,99,050		4,99,050

Working notes : (1) Table showing adjustment and reund of application money.

Category	Shares Applied for	Shares Allotted	Application Money received	Application money Adjusted		Excess/ Refund
				On Application	On Allotment	
			Rs.	Rs.	Rs.	Rs.
I	23,000	10,560	46,000	21,120	24,880	—
II	48,000	14,200	96,000	28,400	63,900	3,700
III	25,400	15,240	50,800	30,480	20,320	—
	96,400	40,000	1,92,800	80,000	1,09,100	3,700

		Rs.
(2)	Amount received on allotment	
	Total amount due on 40,000 shares @ 4.50	1,80,000
Less	Excess appliation Money to be adjusted on allotment	1,09,100
		70,900
Less	Amount not paid by defaulter*	950
	Amount received	69,950

(3) Amount not paid by a defaulter on allotment.

Applicant of 500 shares allotted on pro-rata basis

		Rs.
	means allottee of 300 shares $\left(500 \times \frac{15{,}240}{25{,}400}\right)$	
	On application he paid 500 × 2 =	1,000
	Money adjusted on application 300 × 2 =	600
	Excess Application money	400
	On allotment he was required to pay 300 × 4.50 =	1,350
Less	Exces application money =	400
	Amount not paid by him	950

		Rs.
(4)	Amount forfeited	
P -	Applicant of 500 Shares (or allottee of 300 shares) paid only application money	1,000
R -	Allottee of 450 Shares who paid application and allotment money *i.e.* (2 + 4.50) = 6.50 Since as a rule premium is transferred to securities premium account & hence cannot be forfeited	
	Thus amount forfeited is Rs. 6.50 – 250 = 4 per share 450 × 4 =	1,800
	Total amount forfeited	2,800

(5)	Capital Reserve on reissue of 500 shares	
	300 (Whole lot of P's Shares re issued)	1,000
	and 200 from R's shares = 200 × 4	800
	Total amount available for concession	1,800
Less	Discount on re issue	500
	Capital Reserve	1,300

		Rs.
(6)	Shares Forfeited Account (Shares forfeited but not reissued)	
	250 Shares @ Rs. 4	1,000
(7)	40,000 Shares @ Rs. 2.50 =	Rs. 1,00,000
Less	Premium not paid by P on 300 Shares @ Rs. 2.50	750
	Securities Premium Received	99,250

Illustration (9) (Different lots of applications and Allotments)

A B C Ltd. issued 50,000 equity shares of Rs. 10 each at 20% premium. Under terms of issue money was payable as under :

		Rs.
On application	:	5 (including premium)
On allotment	:	5
On First and Final Call	:	balance

The issue was over-subscribed. The details are as under:

Category	No. of Applicants	No. of Shares applied for by each applicant	No. of shares allotted to each applicant
I	400	100	50
II	200	1,000	100
III	10	4,000	1,000

As per the terms of issue amount overpaid on application was to be retained and adjusted against the further sums due on shares allotted Surplus, if any, was to be refunded.

Some holders who had subscribed Rs. 5,000 on applications of 100 shares were unable to pay money due on first & final call, the directors forfeited their shares. The directors reissued the forfeited shares as fully paid for Rs. 5,200.

You are required to prepare a statement showing the over-payments, under payments in respect of each category of applicants and pass journal entries, prepare cash book (Bank column) and a Balance Sheet. Working should form part of your answer.

C.A. (Inter) Adapted

Solution (9)

STATEMENT SHOWING APPLICATION MONEY RECEIVED ADJUSTED AND REFUNDED

Category	Number of Applicants	Number of Shares Applied for by each applicant	No. of shares allotted to each applicant	Total No. of Shares applied for in each category	Total Shares Allotted for each Category	Application money received @ Rs. 5	Aplication Money Adjusted			Refund
							On Application @ Rs. 5	On Allotment @ Rs. 5	On First & Final @ 2	
I	400	100	50	40,000	20,000	2,00,000	1,00,000	1,00,000	—	—
II	200	1,000	100	2,00,000	20,000	10,00,000	1,00,000	1,00,000	40,000	7,60,000
III	10	4,000	1,000	40,000	10,000	2,00,000	50,000	50,000	20,000	80,000
				2,80,000	50,000	14,00,000	2,50,000	2,50,000	60,000	8,40,000

JOURNAL ENTRIES

		Rs.	Rs.
Bank A/c	Dr.	14,00,000	
To Share Application A/c			14,00,000
(Being application money received on 2,80,000 Shares @ Rs. 5 each)			
Share Aplication A/c	Dr.	14,00,000	
To Share Capital A/c			1,50,000
To Securities Premium A/c			1,00,000
To Share Allotment A/c			2,50,000
To Calls-in-Advance A/c			60,000
To Bank A/c			8,40,000
(Being application money transferred to Share Capital A/c, Securities Premium, and adjusted against sums due on allotment and Call-the surplus being refunded.)			
Share Allotment A/c	Dr.	2,50,000	
To Share Capital A/c			2,50,000
(Being allotment money transferred to Share Capital A/c)			
Share First & Final Call A/c	Dr.	1,00,000	
To Share Capital A/c			1,00,000
(Being Call money due)			
Bank A/c	Dr.	39,000	
Calls-in-Advance A/c	Dr.	60,000	
To Share First & Final Call A/c			99,000
(Being Call money on 49,500 shares received & adjusted against calls-in-advance)			
Share Capital A/c	Dr.	5,000	
To Share First & Final Call A/c			1,000
To Share Forfeited A/c			4,000
(Being 500 shares of first category forfeited for non-payment non-payment of call money)			
Bank A/c	Dr.	5,200	
To Share Capital A/c			5,000
To Securities Premium A/c			200
(Being 500 shares reissued for Rs. 5,200)			
Share Forfeited A/c	Dr.	4,000	
To Capital Reserve A/c			4,000
(Being amount of forfeiture transferred to Capital reserve)			

CASH BOOK (BANK COLUMN ONLY)

	Rs.		Rs.
To Share Application A/c	14,00,000	By Share Application A/c	8,40,000
To Share Allotment A/c	—	By Balance c/d	6,04,200
To Share First & Final A/c	39,000		
To Share Capital A/c	5,200		
	14,44,200		14,44,200

BALANCE SHEET OF ABC LTD

As on....

Liabilities	Rs.	Assets	Rs.
Authorised Capital	—	Cash at Bank	6,04,200
— Shares of Rs. — each			
Issued Capital			
— Shares of Rs. — each	—		
Subscribed & Paid up Capital			
50,000 shares of Rs. 10 each fully paid	5,00,000		
Securities Premium	1,00,200		
Capital Reserve	4,000		
	6,04,200		6,04,200

Working notes :

(1) Number of Shares forfeited

Amount paid on application Rs. 5,000 @ Rs. 5 = Shares applied for 1,000 since shares applied for on each application are of 100 shares category the shares allotted will be 500 shares $\left(1{,}000 \times \frac{50}{100}\right)$

(2) Since premium has been paid along with application money, an amount of Rs. 1,000 (500 × 2) has been transferred to securities premium account and balance of Rs. 4,000 (5,000 – 1,000) to Share Forfeited Account.

(3) On reissue, shares have been issued at premium of Rs. 200 hence entire amount of Rs. 4,000 on accoiunt of forfeiture has been transferred to Capital Reserve.

ISSUE OF SHARES FOR CONSIDERATION OTHER THAN CASH

(a) Issue of shares to Vendors

When a company aquires some assets from other company or from any vendor and in lieu of purchase price the purchasing company issues shares rather than making cash payment, then such a issue of shares is called "issue of shares for a consideration other than cash". The shares are issued as per terms of agreement between the purchasing company and vendor company. The issue may be made at par, at discoiunt or at premium. The number of shares to be issued is calculated by dividing the purchase consideration by the agreed value of share i.e. by issue price which may either be par value, discounted value or premium value.

The puchase price may be a lump sum consideration or is based on net assets value. In case liabilities are also assumed by the purchasing company, then the same must be deducted out of the agreed value of assets which may be either the book value or market value. The following journal entries are recorded :

(1) When assets are acquired

Sundry Assets A/c	Dr.	(Individually as per agreed value)
To Vendor's A/c	—	with the purchase price* as agreed

* In case purchase price is morethan or less than the net value of assets the same may be transferred to Goodwill or Capital Reserve as the case may be. [Debit Goodwill or Credit Capital Reserve]

(2) When liabilities and assets - both are takenover

Sundry Assets A/c	Dr.	Value of assets
To Vendor's A/c		Purchase price
To S. liabilities		Value of liabilities

(3) When shares are issued

(a) If at Par

Vendor's A/c	Dr.	Purchase price
To Share Capital A/c		
(Being shares issued to vendors)		

(b) If at discount

Vendor's A/c	Dr.	with the amount of purchase consideration
Discount on Shares A/c	Dr.	Amount of discount
To Share Capital A/c		with Total

(c) If at Premium

Vendor's A/c	Dr.	with the purchase price
To Share Capital A/c		with the nominal value of shares
To Securities Premium A/c		with the amount of premium

Illustration (10)

(When purchase price is not given)

X Ltd. acquired assets worth Rs. 5,20,000 and liabilities worth Rs. 1,24,000 for a purchase price payable in shares. X Ltd. allotted equity shares of Rs. 10 each fully paid in satisfaction of purchase price. Pass journal entries in the books of X Ltd. assuming that

(i) Shares are issued at par

(ii) Share are issued at premium of 10%

(iii) Share are issued at a discount of 10%

Solution (10)

JOURNAL ENTRIES

			Rs.	Rs.
	Sundry Assets A/c Dr.		5,20,000	
	To Vendor's A/c (Balancing figure)			3,96,000
	To liabilities			1,24,000
	(Being assets and liabilities taken over)			
(i)	If shares are issued at par:			
	Vendor's A/c Dr.		3,96,000	
	To Equity Share Capital A/c			3,96,000
	(Being 39,600 shares of Rs. 10 each issued to vendor's in satisfaction of purchase price)			
(iii)	If shares are issued at premium of 10%			
	Vendor's A/c Dr.		3,96,000	
	To Equity Share Capital A/c			3,60,000
	To Securities Premium A/c			36,000
	(Being 36,000 shares of Rs. 10 each issued at a premium of 10% to vendors in satisfaction of purchase price)			
(iv)	If shares are issued at 10% discount			
	Vendor's A/c Dr.		3,96,000	
	Discount on Issue A/c Dr.		44,000	
	To Equity Share Capital A/c			4,40,000
	(Being 44,000 shares of Rs. 10 each issued at a discount of 10% in satisfaction of purchase price.)			

Working note :

The number of shares has been worked as under : Purchase Price ÷ Agreed Value of share.

(i) Issue at par = Rs. $\frac{3,96,000}{10}$ = 39,600 shares

(ii) Issue at premium of 10% = Rs. $\frac{3,96,000}{11}$ = 36,000 shares

(iii) Issue at discount of 10% = Rs. $\frac{3,96,000}{9}$ = 44,000 shares

Illustration (11) (When purchase price is given)

Z Ltd. purchased from X Y Ltd the following assets :

		Rs.
Computers	—	62,000
Motor Vehicles	—	1,28,000
Tools & Equipments	—	30,000
Stock	—	1,25,000
Investments	(Book value Rs. 80,000)	(Market Value Rs. 70,000)

Sundry Creditors of Rs. 65,000 were also asumed by Z Ltd. The purchase price was agreed at Rs. 3,15,000 which was to be paid in fully paid equity shares. Pass journal entries in the books of Z Ltd. if (a) Shares are issued at par (b) Shares are issued at 10% discount (c) Shares are issued at 20% premium.

Solution (11)

JOURNAL ENTRIES IN THE BOOKS OF Z LTD.

			Rs.	Rs.
	Computers A/c	Dr.	62,000	
	Motor vehicles A/c	Dr.	1,28,000	
	Tools & Equipments A/c	Dr.	30,000	
	Stock A/c	Dr.	1,25,000	
	Investments A/c	Dr.	70,000	
	To S. Creditors A/c			65,000
	To X Y Ltd. A/c			3,15,000
	To Capital Reserve A/c (Balancing figure)			35,000
	(Being assets and liabilities takenover)			
(a)	If shares are issued at Par			
	X Y Ltd. A/c	Dr.	3,15,000	
	To Equity Share Capital A/c			3,15,000
	(Being 31,500 shares issued in satifaction of purchase price)			
(b)	If shares are issued at 10% Discount			
	X Y Ltd. A/c	Dr.	3,15,000	
	Discount on shares A/c	Dr.	35,000	
	To Equity Share Capital A/c			3,50,000
	(Being 35,000 shares of Rs. 10 issued to Vendors at 10% disocount)			
(c)	If Shares are issued at 20% premium			
	X Y Ltd. A/c	Dr.	3,15,000	
	To Equity Share Capital A/c			2,62,500
	To Securities Premium A/c			52,500
	(Being 26,250 equity shares of Rs. 10 each issued to vendors at 20% premium)			

(b) Issue of Shares to Promoters

A company may issue fully paid or partly paid shares to the promoters of the company. Such shares form the part of consideration for the services rendered by them to the company. The services may include furnishing technical information, engineering services, plant layout, drawing and designing or any other managerial knowhow. Such a payment in cash or shares is treated as capital expenditure. However, while issuing shares to promoters in part or full satisfaction of purchase consideration the following entry is recorded.

Goodwill A/c Dr.
To Share Capital A/c
(Being shares issued to promoters for a consideration other than cash)

Note: Shares may be issued at par, at discount or at premium to the promoters and accordingly entry will be recorded as discussed earlier.

(c) Issue of shares to Underwriters or brokers

When a company avails the services of underwriters or brokers in connection with raising money from public subscription, it may issue shares to them in satisfaction of their claims for commission or brokerage. Underwriters are those persons who give guarantee to the company that a public issue made by the company will be fully subscribed. In case of poor public response, where shares subscribed by public fall short of shares offered for public subscription the remaining shares (unsubscribed) will be taken up by them. For this they are paid commission by the company in form of fully paid or partly paid shares. Similarly brokers also help company in the share sale process by striking deals with the public on behalf of the company. Hence, a company may issue shares for a consideration other than cash to the underwriters and brokers also. When shares are issued to discharge underwriting commission or brokerage, the following entries are recorded.

(1) Under writing Commission A/c Dr.
To Underwriters A/c
(Being underwriting commission payable to underwriters credited to their account)

(2) Brokerage A/c Dr.
To Brokers A/c
(Being brokerage credited to Brokers A/c)

(3) Underwriters A/c Dr.
Brokers A/c Dr.
To Equity Share Capital A/c
(Being shares isued to underwriters and brokers for a consideration other than cash)

Illustration (12) (Issue of shares to promoters and vendors)

New Company Ltd. was registered with an authorised capital of Rs. 20,00,000 divided into equity shares of Rs. 10 each. New Ltd. acquired the following assets at the values stated below.

	Rs.
Plant and Machinery	3,50,000
Computers & Printers	85,000
Stock	1,65,000
Investments	60,000

The purchase price was to be discharged by issue of 62,000 shares of Rs. 10 each @ Rs. 11 per share in full satisfaction of the purchase price. The company also issued 1800 shares at par to the promoters as a payment of their remuneration for their services.

The company offered to public 1,00,000 shares at a premium of 10%. The issue was underwritten by M/s. Financial Services. As per terms of agreement New Company Ltd. had to pay a commission @ 2% of the issue price in the form of equity shares at par. The issue was fully subscribed by public.

Pass journal entries and prepare a Cash Book, Share Capital A/c, Vendors A/c and a Balance Sheet of the Company.

Solution (12)

JOURNAL ENTRIES

			Rs.	Rs.
	Goodwill A/c (Balancing figure)	Dr.	22,000	
	Plant and Machinery A/c	Dr.	3,50,000	
	Computers and Printers A/c	Dr.	85,000	
	Investments A/c	Dr.	60,000	
	Stock A/c	Dr.	1,65,000	
	To Vendor's A/c			6,82,000
	(Being assets acquired at an agreed price of Rs. 6,82,000)			
	Vendor's A/c	Dr.	6,82,000	
	To Equity Shares Capital A/c			6,20,000
	To Securities Premium A/c			62,000
	(Being 62,000 equity shares allotted to Vendors in full satisfaction of purchase price at 10% premium)			
	Goodwill A/c	Dr.	18,000	
	To Equity Share Capital A/c			18,000
	(Being 1,800 shares issued at par to promoters in consideration for their services)			
	Equity Share application & allotment A/c	Dr.	11,00,000	
	To Equity Share Capital A/c	Dr.		10,00,000
	To Securities Premium A/c			1,00,000
	(Being 1,00,000 shares allotted to public at a premium of 10%)			
	Underwriting Commission A/c	Dr.	22,000	
	To M/s. Financial Services A/c			22,000
	(Being underwriting commission credited to underwriter's account @ 2% or Rs. 11,00,000			
	M/s. Financial Services A/c	Dr.	22,000	
	To Equity Share Capital A/c			22,000
	(Being 2,200 equity shares issued at par to underwriters)			

CASH BOOK (BANK COLUMN ONLY)

	Rs.		Rs.
To Equity Share Application and Allotment A/c	11,00,000	By Balance c/d	11,00,000
	11,00,000		11,00,000

EQUITY SHARE CAPITAL ACCOUNT

	Rs.		Rs.
To Balance c/d	16,60,000	By Vendor's A/c	6,20,000
		By Goodwill A/c	18,000
		By M/s Financial Services A/c	22,000
		By Equity Share application and allotment A/c	10,00,000
	16,60,000		16,60,000

VENDOR'S ACCOUNT

	Rs.		Rs.
To Equity Share Capital A/c	6,20,000	By Goodwill A/c (B. F.)	22,000
To Securities Premium A/c	62,000	By Plant & Machinery A/c	3,50,000
		By Computers & Printers A/c	85,000
		By Investments A/c	60,000
		By Stock A/c	1,65,000
	6,82,000		6,82,000

BALANCE SHEET OF NEW COMPANY LTD.
As on........

Liabilities	Rs.	Assets	Rs.
Authorised Capital		**Fixed Assets :**	
...... Shares of Rs.....each		Goodwill	40,000
Issued Capital		Plant & Machinery	3,50,000
..... Share of Rs. each		Computers & Printers	85,000
Subscribed & Paid up Capital		**Current Assets, Advances**	
1,66,000 Shares of Rs. 10 each		**& Investments :**	
		Investments	60,000
fully paid	16,60,000	Stock	1,65,000
Securities Premium Accoiunt(1)	1,62,000	Cash at Bank	11,00,000
		Miscellaneous Expenditure :	
		Underwriting Commission (2)	22,000
	18,22,000		18,22,000

Working notes :

(1) Securities premium has been calculated on 1,62,000 shares (Public Subscription + Shares to Vendors)

(2) Goodwill has been debited on account of consideration to promoters Rs. 18,000 and Excess of purchase consideration over assets takenover which is Rs. 22,000.

RIGHTS ISSUE

According to Section 81 of Companies Act 1956, "Where a company decides to increase it's Subscribed Capital by issue of shares at any time after the expiry of two (2) years from the date of incorporation or one (1) year from the date of first allotment of shares whichever is earlier, such shares must be offered first to existing shareholders of the company on pro-rata basis. Hence, shareholders have the legal right to subscribe for such shares and the Company is bound to make first offer to existing shareholders on subsequent issue. Such an issue of shares is known as "rights issues. However the company is not legally bound to make an offer to existing shares in the following cases:

1. If a special resolution has been passed in the general meeting or an ordinary resolution has been passed and which has been duly approved by Central Government to this effect.
2. The provision does not apply to a private company.
3. Increase in subscribed capital due to conversion of debentures in to shares as per the legal provisions as stated therein.

Any how, the shareholders are not bound to accept the offer of the company they may accept the offer or reject the offer or renounce (transfer) in favour of any third person. The offer price of any right issue is always less than the market price of the shares. In case any shareholder does not accept the offer or does not renounce in favour of any third party within stipulated time, the company may dispose off such shares in any manner it may deem fit. *i.e.* the same may be offered to outsiders. (general public)

Argument in favour of Rights Issue

(1) Company may save shares issue expenses including commission or brokerage to underwriters and brokers.

(2) Existing share holders are able to retain control in their hands as the right issue is made on pro-rata basis. Their proportionate share in the interests of the company remain unaffected.

(3) It improves the image (goodwill) of the company and develops better under-standing, trust and ties between members and management.

(4) Chances of manipulation or discrimination by directors are totally eliminated because they cannot offer shares to their friends or relatives at a low price or in any number. All existing shareholders get shares on the basis of their present holdings.

(5) Element of uncertaintly relating to public response is minimised and company's programmes of modernisation, diversification or expansion are not hampered.

Calculation of Value of Right

Value of right is the gain an existing holder makes while exercising his right. It is calculated by the difference between the market price of share and average price after right. The following procedure is adopted to get the value of right.

(1) Findout the ratio of right issue *i.e.* whether it is 1 : 4 , 1 : 3 or 1 : 2 or any other basis. This shows that for every 4 shares or 3 shares or two (2) shares, one share will be offered to existing share holder at a price which is usually lower than the market price.

(2) Findout the total price (market price) of number of shares which will entitle the holder to avail right. It may be 4, 3 or 2 as illustrated above.

(3) Add to the above total price the offer price of share/shares the company is offering.

(4) Calculate the average price by dividing the total (as per 3) by the total number of shares including right.

(5) Find out the difference between market price and average price of a share.

This difference represents value of right.

Example :

A Ltd. made a right issue and offered to the existing share holders to buy one share of Rs. 100 at Rs. 120 for every four shares held. The prevailing market price (cum right) of the share is Rs. 160. Findout value of right.

Answer : Rights Ratio = 1 : 4

It means to get one share at "right offer price" of Rs. 120 you have to buy four shares from the market.

		Rs.
	Thus market price (cum right) of 4 shares @ 160 each	640
Add	Right's offer price of one share	120
	Total price of 5 shares	760
	Average price Rs. 760 ÷ 5 =	152
Less	Right's offer price =	120
	Value of right	32

Illustration (13)

(Issue on Rights basis)

S Ltd. had Share Capital of Rs. 5,00,000 divided in to equity shares of Rs. 10 each fully paid up. On 1.1.2006 the Company offered to the holders shares on rights basis in the ratio of 1 : 2 at a premium of Rs. 5 per share. The money was payable as under.

	On application	On allotment
	Rs.	Rs.
Share Capital	4	6
Share premium	3	2

The offer was accepted by all the shareholders. R - a shareholder holding 200 shares paid the full offer price with the application whereas V, another shareholder of 300 shares failed to pay the allotment moneyand as a consequene her shares were forfeited. These shares were reissued at the minimum reissue price. Pass journal entries and prepare other relevant ledger accounts and Balance Sheet (b) Also calculate the value of right if share price is quoted in the market at Rs. 20.

Solution (13)

JOURNAL ENTRIES

		Rs.	Rs.
	Bank A/c Dr.	1,76,600	
	To Share Application A/c		1,76,600
	(Being application money received) (25,000 – 200) @ Rs. 7 + on 200 shares @ Rs. 15		
	Share Application A/c Dr.	1,76,600	
	To Share Capital A/c (25,000 × 4)		1,00,000
	To Securities Premium A/c (25,000 × 3)		75,000
	To Share Allotment A/c (200 × 8)		1,600
	(Being application amount transferred to relevant accounts)		
	Share Allotment A/c Dr.	2,00,000	
	To Share Capital A/c		1,50,000
	To Securities Premium A/c		50,000
	(Being allotment money due)		
	Bank A/c Dr.	1,96,000	
	To Share Allotment		1,96,000
	(Being money on 24,500 shares @ Rs. 8 received on allotment)		
	Share Capital A/c Dr.	3,000	
	Securities Premium A/c Dr.	600	
	To Share Allotment A/c		2,400
	To Share Forfeited A/c		1,200
	(Being 300 shares of V forfeited)		
	Bank A/c (Balancing figure) Dr.	1,800	
	Share Forfeited A/c Dr.	1,200	
	To Share Capital A/c		3,000
	(Being 300 shares reissued at the minimum price)		

CASH BOOK (BANK COLUMN)

	Rs.		Rs.
To Share Aplication A/c	1,76,600	By Balance c/d	3,74,400
To Share Allotment A/c	1,96,000		
To Share Capital A/c	1,800		
	3,74,400		3,74,400

SHARE APPLICATION A/C

	Rs.		Rs.
To Share Capital A/c	1,00,000	By Bank A/c	1,76,600
To Share Allotment A/c	1,600		
To Securities Premium A/c	75,000		
	1,76,600		1,76,600

SHARE ALLOTMENT A/C

	Rs.		Rs.
To Share Capital A/c	1,50,000	By Share Application A/c	1,600
To Securities Premium A/c	50,000	By Bank A/c	1,96,000
		By Share Capital A/c	1,800
		By Securities Premium A/c	600
	2,00,000		2,00,000

SHARE CAPITAL A/C

	Rs.		Rs.
To Share Allotment A/c	1,800	By Share Application A/c	1,00,000
To Share Forfeited A/c	1,200	By Share Allotment A/c	1,50,000
To Balance c/d	2,50,000	By Bank A/c	1,800
		By Share Forfeited A/c	1,200
	2,53,000		2,53,000

SECURITIES PREMIUM A/C

	Rs.		Rs.
To Share Allotment A/c	600	By Share Application A/c	75,000
To Balance c/d	1,24,400	By Share Allotment A/c	50,000
	1,25,000		1,25,000

SHARE FORFEITED A/C

	Rs.		Rs.
To Share Capital A/c	1,200	By Share Capital A/c	1,200
	1,200		1,200

BALANCE SHEET
As on ......

Liabilities	Rs.	Assets	Rs.
Authorised Capital		S. Assets	5,00,000
..... Shares of Rs. ... each		Cash at Bank	3,74,400
Issued and Subscribed Capital			
75,000 shares of Rs. 10 each	7,50,000		
Called up & Paid up Capital			
75,000 shares of Rs. 10 each			
fully paid	7,50,000		
Securities Premium	1,24,400		
	8,74,400		8,74,400

			Rs.
(b)	Calculation of Value of right		
	Right Ratio 1 : 2		
	Market Value of 2 shares to avail right offer @ Rs. 20		40
Add	Right offer price		15
			55
	Average price 55 ÷ 3 =	18.33	

Value of Right = Market price – Average price
= Rs. 20 – 18.33 = Rs. 1.67

Working notes :

(1) The Company had Share Capital of Rs. 5,00,000 before right issue i.e. 50,000 fully paid shares. Since right offer was made in the ratio of 1 : 2 company made a right issue of 25,000 shares

(2) Since V has not paid allotment money on 300 shares @ Rs. 8 (6 + 2) an amount of Rs. 600 has been debited to securities premium account.

(3) Minimum reissue price is the difference between paid up value of share and amount forfeited per shares *i.e.* Rs. (10 – 4) Rs. 6 per share.

ISSUE OF BONUS SHARES

Meaning

Bonus shares simply means shares offered by a company to it's existing shareholders free of cost without any charge or as gift on pro-rata basis. When a company has accumulated a large amount of undistributed profits, the real share capital employed in the busines tends to be obscured. To bring the issued capital into a truer relationship with the capital actually employed, the accumulation can be capitalised and used to pay up the amount due on shares to be issued to the members as bonus shares. Bonus shares issue implies an increase in share capital and distribution of accumulated profits to the members without any release of company's assets. However, the Companies Act permits that the securities premium amount can be used by the company in paying up un-issued shares of the company to be issued to it's members as fully paid bonus shares. However, following points may be noted in connection with the bonus shares.

1. The bonus shares are issued to the existing shareholders and not to the outsiders.
2. Issue of bonus shares are made out of accumulated profits.
3. Such profits are converted into share capital which implies capitalisation of accumulated profits.
4. Since shares are distributed (allotted) free of cost no cash passes between company and it's members.

Thus a bonus issue adds nothing to the net assets of the company and it's effect, therefore, is merely to divide the capital employed in the business into larger number of shares. The SEBI (Securities Exchanges Board of India) has issued certain guidelines in connection with issue of bonus shares.

1. These guide lines are applicable to existing listed companies who shall forward a certificate duly signed by the issuer and duly countersigned by it's statutory auditor or by a company secretary in practice to the effect that the terms and conditions for issue of bonus shares as laid down in these guide lines have been complied with.
2. Issue of bonus shares after any public/right issue is subject to the condition that no bonus issue shall be made which will dilute the value of rights of the holders of debentures convertible fully or partly.
3. The bonus issue is made out of "free reserves" built out of the genuine profits or securities premium collected in cash only.
4. Reserves created out of revaluation of fixed assets are not capitalised.
5. The declaration of bonus issue in lieu of dividend, is not made.
6. The bonus issue is not made unless the partly paid shares, if any existing, are made fully paid up.
7. The Company
   (i) has not defaulted in payment of interest or principal in respect of fixed deposits and interest on existing debentures or principal on redemption thereof, and
   (ii) has sufficient reason to belive that it has not defaulted in respect of the payment of statutory dues of the employees such as contribution to provident fund, gratuity, bonus etc.
8. A company which announces the bonus shares after the approval of Board of Directors must implement the proposals within six months from the date of such approval and shall not have the option of changing the decision.
9. There shall be a provision in the Articles of Association of the company for capitalisation of reserves etc. and if not, the company shall pass a resolution at it's General Body Meeting making provisions in the Articles of Association of capitalisation.
10. Consequent to issue of bonus shares if the subscribed and paid up Capital exceeds the authorised capital, a resolution shall be passed by the company at it's General Body Meeting for increasing the authorised capital.

Accounting Treatment

Bonus issue may be made to allot fully paid shares to the existing share holders on pro-rata basis or for converting the existing partly paid shares into fully paid up. However, following points must be remembered at the time of recording journal entries.

1. Utilise the Capital Reserve (before the Revenue Reserve) as far as legally permissible, if choice is made between Captal & Revenue.
2. Capital Reserve created out of Revaluation of fixed assets can not be utilised for issuing bonus shares.
3. Securities Premium, if not realised in cash, cannot be utilised for issuing bonus shares.
4. Capital Redemption Reserve and Securities Premium cannot be utilised for converting the partly paid shares into fully paid shares.

It is to be noted that when bonus issue is made to convert the partly paid shares in to fully paid shares, it is termed as "partly paid up bonus shares.

JOURNAL ENTRIES

1. *For Converting the partly paid shares into fully paid up shares i.e. for issuing partly paid bonus shares.*

(i) Equity Share Final Call A/c Dr.
  To Equity Share Capital A/c
(Being final money due @ Rs.... per share)

(ii) Profit and Loss A/c Dr.
Profit & Loss Appropriation A/c Dr.
General Reserve A/c Dr.
or Other Revenue Reserves A/c Dr.
Capital Reserve A/c (if required) Dr.
  To Bonus to Equity Shareholders A/c
(Being bonus declared)

(iii) Bonus to Equity Shareholders A/c Dr.
  To Equity Share Final Call A/c
(Being bonus utilised for converting the partly paid up shares in to fully paid up)

2. *For issuing Fully paid bonus shares*

(i) Capital Redemption Reserve A/c Dr.
Securities Premium A/c Dr.
Capital Reserve A/c Dr.
Revenue Reserve A/c (Free Reserve) Dr.
  To Bonus to Equity share holders A/c
(Being bonus issue declared in the ratio of ......)

(ii) Bonus to Equity shareholders A/c Dr.
  To Equity Share Capital A/c
(Being bonus issue made)

Sources of Bonus Issue = At a Glance : priority-wise.

For Partly paid up Bonus Shares	For Fully paid up Bonus Shares
Only from free reserves (in the following order of utilisation)	
1. Profit & Loss or P & L Appropriation A/c	1. Capital Redemption Reserve
2. General Reserve	2. Securities Premium (if collected in cash)
3. Capital Reserve (if realised in cash)	3. Profit & Loss or P & L Appropriation A/c
4. Sinking Fund (After debenture redemption)	4. General Reserve
	5. Capital Reserve (if realised in cash)
	6. Sinking Fund (After debenture redemption)

Illustration (14) (Partly paid & Fully paid Bonus Shares)

PQ Ltd. had Equity Capital of Rs. 7,00,000 dividend into shares of Rs. 10 each Rs. 7 paid up. It resolvd to declare bonus to shareholders in the form of payment of final call. The Directors also decided to utilise Securities Premium Account to issue fully paid bonus shares in the ratio of 1 : 5. Pass journal Entries presuming that there is sufficient balance to the credit of concerned account.

Solution (14)

JOURNAL ENTRIES

			Rs.	Rs.
	Equity Share Final Call A/c Dr. To Equity Share Captal A/c (Being Final Call @ Rs. 3 per share due)		3,00,000	3,00,000
	Free Reserves A/c Dr. To Bonus to Equity Share holders A/c (Being bonus payable on 1,00,000 shares @ Rs. 3 per share)		3,00,000	3,00,000
	Bonus to Equity Shareholders A/c Dr. To Equity Share Final Call A/c (Being bonus utilised towards final Call)		3,00,000	3,00,000
	Securities Premium A/c Dr. To Bonus to Equity Shareholders (Being bonus shares declared in the ratio of 1 : 5)		2,00,000	2,00,000
	Bonus to Equity Share holders A/c Dr. To Equity Share Capital A/c (Being 20,000 bonus shares issued out of securities premium)		2,00,000	2,00,000

Working notes :

(1) No. of equity shares $= \dfrac{\text{Paid up Capital}}{\text{Paid up Value per share}} = \dfrac{\text{Rs. } 7{,}00{,}000}{\text{Rs. } 7} = 10{,}000$ Shares

(2) Amount required for partly paid up bonus shares

No. of shares X unpaid amount per share

= 1,00,000 × 3 = Rs. 3,00,000 to be adjusted against free reserves only.

(3) Amount required for fully paid up bonus shares :

Total number of fully paid shares × Bonus Issue Ratio

= 1,00,000 × 1/5 = 20,000 shares to be issued at par.

Hence an amount of Rs. 2,00,000 is to be adjusted against securities premium A/c (as per instruction given in the question.)

Illustration (15) (Issue of Bonus Shares at premium)

X Ltd. had the following balances as on 31st December, 2005

	Rs.
9% Preference Share Capital	
Shares of Rs. 100 each fully paid up	2,00,000
Equity Share Capital	
(Shares of Rs. 10 each fully paid up)	3,00,000
Capital Redemption Reserve	50,000
General Reserve	5,00,000

The directors of the Company declared bonus issue in the ratio of 4 fully paid bonus shares of Rs. 10 each at Rs. 12 per share for every 5 fully paid shares held.

Pass journal entries to record above transactions.

Solution (15)

JOURNAL ENTRIES

				Rs.	Rs.
	Capital Redemption Reserve A/c	Dr.		50,000	
	General Reserve A/c	Dr.		1,38,000	
	To Bonus to Equity Shareholders' A/c				2,88,000
	(Being bonus issue declared in the 4 : 5 ratio)				
	Bonus to Equity Shareholders' A/c	Dr.		2,88,000	
	To Equity Share Capital A/c				2,40,000
	To Securities Premium A/c				48,000
	(Being issue of 24,000 bonus shares of Rs. 10 each at Rs. 12 per share)				

Working notes :

(1) No. of bonus shares to be issued 30,000 share × 4/5 = 24,000 shares

(2) Amount to be utilised

24,000 × Rs. 12 per share = 2,88,000

(Share Capital = 24,000 × 10 = Rs. 2,40,000

Securities Premium = 24,000 × 2 Rs. 40,000)

Illustration (16)

(Issue of Fully Paid Bonus Shares)

Following is the Balance Sheet of A Ltd. as on 31st March, 2006

Liabilities	Rs.	Assets	Rs.
Authorised Capital :		Fixed Assets	10,00,000
11% Preference Share Capital		Current Assets	3,75,000
2000 Shares of Rs. 100 each	2,00,000		
Equity Share Capital :			
80,000 Shares of Rs. 10 each	8,00,000		
Issued and Subscribed Capital :			
1,000 11% Preference Shares of Rs. 100 each fully paid	1,00,000		
70,000 Equity Shares of Rs. 10 each Rs. 8 paid	5,60,000		
Reserve & Surplus :			
General Reserve	80,000		
Capital Reserve	60,000		
Securities Premium	30,000		
Profit & Loss Account	1,70,000		
Secured Loans :			
9% Debentures	1,50,000		
Current liabilities provisions and Reserves :			
S. Creditors	1,50,000		
Provision for Taxation	75,000		
	13,75,000		13,75,000

On 1st April 2006, the directors decided,

(i) To make a final Call.

(ii) To capitalise reserve by way of bonus issue in the ratio of 2 : 5.

These decisions were implemented and process of money collection and bonus issue was completed on 30th June, 2006. Securities premium include a premium of Rs. 10,000 on shares issued to a vendor for acquiring certain assets. Capital Reserve of Rs. 60,000 includes Rs. 35,000 being profit on sale of Motor Vehicle and the balance from revaluation of Building. On 1st July one third of the debentures were converted into equity shares of Rs. 10 each at par.

Pass journal entries and prepare a Balance Sheet as on 30th June, 2006 after bonus issue but before conversion of debentures. Are the Convertibile Debenture holders entitled to bonus share?

Solution (16)

JOURNAL ENTRIES

			Rs.	Rs.
2002				
April	Equity Share Final Call A/c	Dr.	1,40,000	
	To Equity Share Capital A/c			1,40,000
	(Being final call money due on 70,000 shares @ Rs. 2 per share)			
June	Bank A/c	Dr.	1,40,000	
	To Equity Share Final Call A/c			1,40,000
	(Being final call money received)			
	Capital Reserve A/c	Dr.	35,000	
	Securities Premium A/c	Dr.	20,000	
	General Reserve A/c	Dr.	80,000	
	Profit & Loss A/c	Dr.	1,45,000	
	To Bonus to Equity Share holders A/c			2,80,000
	(Being bonus issue in the ratio of 2 : 5 was made and utilised reserves as per SEBI's guidelines)			
	Bonus to Equity Shareholders A/c	Dr.	2,80,000	
	To Equity Share Capital A/c			2,80,000
	(Being reserve capitalised)			

BALANCE SHEET OF A LTD.
As on 30th June, 2006

Liabilities	Rs.	Assets	Rs.
Authorised Capital:		Fixed Assets	10,00,000
1000, 11% Preference Share Capital		Current Assets	5,15,000
2000 shares of Rs. 100 each	2,00,000		
80,000 Equity Shares of Rs. 10 each	8,00,000		
Issued & Subscribed Capital			
11% Preference Shares of			
Rs. 100 each fully paid	1,00,000		
98,000 Equity Shares of Rs. 10			
each fully paid	9,80,000		
Reserve & Surplus:			
Capital Reserve	25,000		
Securities Premium	10,000		
Profit & Loss Account	25,000		
Secured Loans:			
9% Debentures	1,50,000		

Contd.

Current Liabilities, Provisions and Reserves:			
S. Creditors	1,50,000		
Provision for Taxation	75,000		
	15,15,000		15,15,000

Working notes:

(1) As per SEBI's guide lines Securities premium and Capital Reserve if realised in cash, can be used for paying up fully paid bonus shares. Hence premium on shares issued to vendors and revaluation profits have not been utilised.

(2) With the bonus issue, the issued, subscribed and paid up capital has exceeded the authorised capital, it is assumed that the company has passed a necessary resolution at it's general body meeting for increasing the authorised capital.

(3) As per SEBI's guide lines no company can issue bonus shares without extending the benefit to convertisble (Partly/Fully) Debenture holders. Hence, convertible debenture holders are also entitled to bonus shares.

BUY BACK OF SECURITIES (SHARES)

According to Companies (Amedment) Act 1999, Section 77A a company is permitted to buy it's own shares and other securities subject to fulfilment of certain conditions & provisions as laid down by SEBI. The salient features of buyback provisions are as under.

(1) A Company may purchase it's own shares or other securities out of

  (i) It's free reserves or

  (ii) Securities Premium or

  (iii) Proceeds of any shares or specified securities.

  Provided that no buy back shall be made out of the proceeds of an earlier issue of same kind of shares/securities.

(2) Buy back is duly authorised by Articles of Association.

(3) A special resolution has been passed in general meeting of the company authorising buy back.

(4) The buy back is of less than 25% of the total paid up capital and free reserves and does not exceed 25% of paid up Capital in any financial year.

(5) The debt equity ratio after such buyback does not exceed 2 : 1.
However Central Government may prescribe higher limit in certain cases.

(6) The shares or specified sucurities for buy back are fully paid up and are listed in any recognised stock exchange.

(7) Such buy back is compled with in twelve months from the date of passing the special resolution.

(8) Where a company has passed a special resolution to buy back it's own shares or other securities, the company must file with the Registrar and SEBI, a "declaration of solvency" in the prescribed form and an "Affidavit" to the effect that Board has made a full enquiry in to the affairs of the company and that it will not be rendered insolvent. This should be signed by the managing director and a director.

(9) The buy back may be

(i) from the existing holders on a pro-rata basis, or

(ii) from open market, or

(iii) from odd lots

(iv) by purchasing the securities issued to employees under the scheme of stock-option or sweat equity.

(10) The shares or securities so bought back, shall be physically destroyed within seven (7) days from the last date of completion of buy back.

(11) The Company shall not make further issue of same kind of shares or securities within a period of 24 months. However, company may issue bonus shares, sweat equity or under the scheme of stock-option, or in lieu of conversion of warrants, or preference shares or debentures into equity shares.

(12) No company shall purchase, directly or indirectly, it's own shares or other specified securities through.

(i) any subsidiary company (including it's own subsidiary)

(ii) any investment company or group thereof.

(iii) or any company which has defaulted in respect of payment of interest, deposit, dividend term loan redemption amount of preference shares or debentures etc. is subsisting.

(13) A notice of general meeting must be accompanied by an Explanatory Statement giving:

(i) Full disclosure of all material facts.

(ii) Necessity of buy back.

(iii) Class of security intended to be bought back.

(iv) Amount to be invested under buyback and

(v) Time limit for completion of buy back.

(14) No Company shall directly or indirectly purchase it's own share or other specified securities unless it complies with the provisions of sections 159, 207 and 211 of the Companies Act 1956.

(15) SEBI requires that the Company must open an "Escrow Account" before any buyback, and deposit a specified percentage of total consideration payable for the buyback. Escrow Account is a account which is opened and held until a specific duty is performed. In this case of buyback it involves payment of consideration to shareholders on buy back.

Thus, the Companies who have adequate accumulated profits may intend to buyback it's own shares. The buyback results in an increase in earnings per share which may in turn, push the share price upward. The buyback provides an opportunity to restructure the company's financial sources. Depending upon the circumstances debt-equity ratio may be adjusted according to company's requirements. The buy back also helps to retain control and prevents the company from going out of control due to hostile takeover. It also helps to avoid corporate dividend tax as cash resources are utilised to buy back shares rather than paying dividend. However, the buyback may increase the risk of manipuation by management for inside trading may be a decisive factor for such buybacks.

It should be noted that buy back shall not result in reduction of Share Capital, or Capital gains in the hands of shareholders. Further, it cannot be treated as 'deemed dividend'. Redemption of preference shares, forfeiture of shares and surrender of shares are not to be treated as 'buy back'.

Accounting Treatment

As per Section 77 AA of the Companies (Amendment) Act 1999, if shares are bought back out of free reserves, then a sum equal to the nominal value of shares so purchased shall be transferred to 'Capital Redemption Reserve Account'. The Capital Redemption Reserves so created shall be utilised for isuing fully paid bonus shares. These guidelines are issued by SEBI & the same are applicable in case of redemption of preference shares out of free reserves or divisible profits. The following points should be remembered.

(i) Only fully paid securities can be bought back. In case of partly paid securities, the same should be made fully paid up by making final call.

(ii) Sufficient balance must be standing to the credit of free reserves if buy back is to be made out of it.

(iii) An amount equal to face value of shares so bought back out of fee reserves must be transferred to Capital Redemption Reserve. Premium, if any, so paid on buyback must be adjusted against free reserves or securities premium. or

(v) Discount on buyback, if any, must be transferred to Capital Reserve.

(vi) Capital Redemption Reserve may be utilised for the purpose of issuing fully paid bonus shares.

JOURNAL ENTRIES

There are two steps for completing the transaction of buy back First relates to purchase of it's own shares either at par, premium or discount (depending upon the prevailing share price) Secondly transfer to Capital Redemption Reserve an amount equal to facevalue of shares so purchased, out of divisible profits (free reserves). However, no transfer to Captial Redemption Reserve shall be made if shares are boiught back out of the proceeds of 'fresh issue'. In that case only entry relating to 'issue' shall be recorded. Following entries shall be recorded.

1. (a) *Buy back at Par*

Equity Share Capital A/c	Dr.	with the face value of shares bought back
To Bank A/c		

(b) *Buyback at Premium*

Equity Share Capital A/c	Dr.	with the face value
Free Reserves/Securities Premium A/c	Dr.	With the Excess of purchase price over face value
To Bank A/c		Amount paid

(c) *Buy back at Discount*

Equity Share Capital A/c	Dr.	With the face value
To Bank A/c		With the amount paid
To Capital Reserve A/c		With the Excess of Face Value over purchase price

2. Divisible profits/Free Reserves A/c Dr.
To Capital Redemption Reserve

Illustration (17)

Following was the Balance Sheet of Z Ltd. as on 31st March, 2004.

	Rs.			Rs.
9% Preference Share Capital	5,00,000	Gross Block	22,50,000	
Equity Share	12,00,000	*Less* Dep.	2,50,000	20,00,000
Securities	2,50,000	Investments		2,50,000
General Reserve	4,50,000	Current Assets		7,50,000
Profit & Loss Account	1,75,000	(Other than Cash & Bank)		
10% Debentures	3,50,000	Cash & Bank Balance		1,50,000
S. Creditors	2,25,000			
	31,50,000			31,50,000

On 1st April 2004, the Company decided to buyback 25% of it's equity shares @ Rs. 14 per share. To meet the cash resources the ompany made the following arrangement

(a) To issue Rs. 1,00,000 9% Preference Shares at par

(b) To sell investments at 98%.

The issue was fully subscribed & investments realised. Record journal entries to effect above transactions and prepare a Balance Sheet as on that date.

Solution (17)

JOURNAL ENTRIES

			Rs.	Rs.
2004				
April1.	Bank A/c	Dr.	1,00,000	
	To 9% Preference Share Capital A/c			1,00,000
	(Being shares isued at par)			
	Bank A/c	Dr.	2,45,000	
	Profit & Loss A/c	Dr.	5,000	
	To Investments A/c			2,50,000
	(Being investments sold)			
	Equity Share Capital A/c	Dr.	3,00,000	
	Securities Premium A/c	Dr.	1,20,000	
	To Bank A/c			4,20,000
	(Being 30,000 Equity Shares bought back @ Rs. 14 each)			
	General Resrve A/c	Dr.	2,00,000	
	To Capital Redemption Reserve A/c			2,00,000
	(Being CRR created equivalent to the face value of shares so repurchased out of free (general) reserve)			

I Underwriting

It is an agreement between a company issuing shares or debentures and an individual or firm of individuals who guarantee that the whole issue will be subscribed by the public. In case there is a poor response on the part of public, the remaining shares will be subscribed by them. In other words, when a public company invites applications from public to subscribe it's shares or debentures, wants to make sure that the whole isue of shares or debentures will be subscribed. For this purpose the company enters into agreement with an individual or group individuals who undertake that the issue will be fully subscribed by the public, if not, the remaining shall be purchased by them at the offer price. For this they charge some commission which is known as underwriting commission. Thus underwiting is in the nature of an insurance against the under-subscription. The payment of commission must be authorised by the Articles. The rate of commission should not exceed 5% of the issue price of shares which may be issued at par, discount or at premium. However, in case of debentures the commission shall not exceed 2.5% of issue price. Bankers or stock-brokers usually act as underwriters. For example a company issues 1,00,000 shares of Rs. 10 each at par which is underwritten by X. In case public subscribes 90,000 shares, the remaining 10,000 shares shall be subscribed by X at the offer price of Rs. 10 each. If however, issue is fully subscribed X need not to subscribe any number of shares.

II A 'Firm Underwriting' is different from pure or simple underwriting. Under 'firm underwriting', certain number of shares/debentures are reserved for the underwriters and reamining are issued to public. Say, out of a issue of 50,000 shares, 10,000 shares may be kept for the underwriters and remaining 40,000 shares are issued to public. It simply means, the underwriters get preference with regard to allotment of shares but they do not give any guarantee in case of any undersubscription. It simply means they get priority over general public with regard to allotment in case an issue is over-subscribed.

Accounting Treatment

(i) When Commission is due :

Underwriting Commission A/c	Dr.
To Underwriters A/c	

(ii) When Commission is paid :

(a) If paid in shares

Underwriter's A/c	Dr.
To Share Capital A/c	

Partial Underwriting

(a) When an issue is not underwritten wholly it is known as partial underwriting. For example a compay issues 20,000 shares out of which underwriters guarantee subscription of only 15,000 shares, this will be treated a case of partial underwriting. The liability of underwriters will arise only if when public subscription falls short of 15,000 shares.

(b) If there are more than one underwriters, the liability shal be determined in the ratio of number of shares underwritten by them. For example, A, B & C underwrite an issue of 60,000 shares to the extent of 15,000, 25,000 and 10,000 shares (Total 50,000 shares). If public subscribes only 45,000 shares the short fall of 5,000 shares (50,000 – 45,000) shall be taken by A, B & C in the ratio of 3 : 5 : 2 (15,000 : 25,000: 10,000). Thus the liability of A, B & C will be

1,500 shares $\left(\frac{3}{10}\times 5{,}000\right)$ 2,500 shares $\left(\frac{5}{10}\times 5{,}000\right)$ and 1,000 shares $\left(\frac{2}{10}\times 5{,}000\right)$ respectively.

Marked & Unmarked Applications

When an issue is underwritten by several underwriters, as stated above, each of them tries to sell securities through him to reduce his risk undertaken by him. These individual underwriters put their own stamp on the prescribed application forms so that the number of shares subscribed by the public through each of them can be ascertained easily. Such application forms are known as 'marked application'. Applications forms not bearing the stamp of any underwriter are known as 'unmarked aplications'. *i.e.* shares application forms made directly to the company without any underwriter.

II 'Firm' Underwriting

Under 'firm' underwriting the gross liability is calculated on the basis of agreed ratio i.e. in the ratio of number of shares underwritten by them individually. Out of this, respective "marked application forms number is deducted. Unmarked application forms are also given credit in the ratio of gross liability. Credit is also given for firm underwriting in the ratio of gross liability or their individual commitment. In case there is a surplus (minus figure) for any underwriter, the same is transferred to other underwriters in the ratio of gross liability. There after liability in respect of firm underwriting is added to get the total liability of each underwriter. This can be illustrated as follows.

		A	B	C
	Gross liability (in % age)	50%	30%	20%
Less	Marked Appliations (as per public response)	----	----	----
Less	Unmarked Applications in the 5 : 3 : 2 ratio	----	----	----
Less	Firm underwriting (5 : 3 : 2 or Commitment ratio, if any)	----	----	----
	Mutual Adjustment in respect of surplus if any in the gross liability ratio			
Add	Firm underwriting	----	----	----
	Total Liability	***	***	***

Illustration (18)

Z Ltd. issued 50,000 shares of Rs. 10 each at par. The issue was underwritten as follows :

P 30,000 Shares
Q 12,500 Shares
R 7,500 Shares

The total subscriptions excluding firm underwriting but including marked applications which were for 25,000 shares. The marked applications were as under:

P 5,000 Shares
Q 10,000 Shares
R 2,500 Shares

The underwriters made applications for firm underwriting as follows:

P 4,000 shares
Q 1,500 Shares
R 5,000 Shares

Determine liability of underwriters. *C.S. (I) Adapted*

Solution (18)

STATEMENT SHOWING UNDER-WRITER'S LIABILITY

	P	Q	R	Total
	Rs.	Rs.	Rs.	Rs.
Gross liability	3,00,000	1,25,000	75,000	5,00,000
Less Marked Applications	50,000	1,00,000	25,000	1,75,000
	2,50,000	25,000	50,000	3,25,000
Less Firm underwriting	40,000	15,000	50,000	1,05,000
	2,10,000	10,000	—	2,20,000
Less Unmarked Applications*	45,000	18,750	11,250	75,000
(in the ratio of gross liability)	1,65,000	(8,750)	(11,250)	1,45,000
Surplus of Q & R adjusted	20,000	8,750	11,250	—
	1,45,000	—	—	1,45,000
Add Firm Underwriting	40,000	15,000	50,000	1,05,000
Total liability	1,85,000	15,000	50,000	2,50,000

*25,000 – (5,000 + 10,000 + 2,500) = 7,500 shares × 10 = Rs. 75,000

Shares subscribed excluding firm underwriting but including marked applications – Marked applications = Unmarked applications.

Illustration (19)

Sony Ltd. made a public issue of 5,00,000 hares of Rs. 10 each, Rs. 5 was payable on application. The entire issue was underwritten by O, P, Q & R in the proportion of 30%, 25%, 25% and 20% respectively. Under the terms, a commission of 2% was pauyable on the amount underwritten.

O, P, Q & R had also agreed on firm underwriting of 16,000, 24,000 Nil & 60,000 shares respectively. The total subscriptions, excluding firm underwriting but including marked applications were for 3,60,000 shares. Marked applications received were as under.

O — 96,000; Shares	P — 80,000; Shares	Q 48,000; Shares	R — 96,000 Shares

Ascertain the liability of the individual underwriters and record the journal entries in the books of the Company.

C.A. (I) Adapted

Solution (19)

STATEMENT SHOWING LIABILITY OF THE UNDERWRITERS

	O	P	Q	R	Total
Gross liability (in shares)	1,50,000	1,25,000	1,25,000	1,00,000	5,00,000
Less Marked Application	96,000	80,000	48,000	96,000	3,20,000
	54,000	45,000	77,000	4,000	1,80,000
Less Unmarked applications	12,000	10,000	10,000	8,000	40,000
(Gross liability ratio)	42,000	35,000	67,000	(4,000)	1,40,000
Less Firm Underwriting	16,000	24,000	—	(60,000)	1,00,000
	26,000	11,000	67,000	(64,000)	40,000

Balance b/d (in shares	26,000	11,000	67,000	(64,000)	40,000
R's Surplus Adjusted in the O, P, Q A/cs in the Gross	24,000	20,000	20,000	(64,000)	—
Liability ratio	2,000	(9,000)	47,000	—	40,000
Surplus of P Adjusted	2,000	9,000	7,000	—	—
	—	—	40,000	—	40,000
Add Firm Underwriting	16,000	24,000	—	60,000	1,00,000
Total liability in shares	16,000	24,000	40,000	60,000	1,40,000
	Rs.	Rs.	Rs.	Rs.	Rs.
Amount due @ Rs. 5 per share	80,000	1,20,000	2,00,000	3,00,000	7,00,000
Less Commission @ 2% on nominal value of shares	30,000	25,000	25,000	20,000	1,00,000
(in gross liability ratio)	50,000	95,000	1,75,000	2,80,000	60,000

JOURNAL ENTRIES

			Rs.	Rs.
	Bank A/c	Dr.	18,00,000	
	To Share Application A/c			18,00,000
	(Being application money received)			
	Share Application A/c	Dr.	18,00,000	
	To Share Capital A/c			18,00,000
	(Being application money transferred to share Capital A/c)			
	O's A/c	Dr.	80,000	
	P's A/c	Dr.	1,20,000	
	Q's A/c	Dr.	2,00,000	
	R's A/c	Dr.	3,00,000	
	To Share Capital A/c			7,00,000
	(Being application money due from under writers)			
	Underwriting Commission A/c	Dr.	1,00,000	
	To O's A/c			30,000
	To P's A/c			25,000
	To Q's A/c			25,000
	To R's A/c			20,000
	(Being underwriter's commission due)			
	Bank A/c	Dr.	6,00,000	
	To O's A/c			50,000
	To P's A/c			95,000
	To Q's A/c			1,75,000
	To R's A/c			2,80,000
	(Being share application money received from underwriter after adjustment of commission)			

CONCEPT OF BOOK-BUILDING

Stock market is considered as vital for long term economic growth and there is a strong positive correlation between the level of standard (sophistication) of a country's stock market and the level of economic growth. Countries with well developed stock market generally tend to enjoy higher economic growth than those with under developed stock markets. There was a vital need to strengthen the capital market, which could only be achieved through structural modifications, introducing new market mechanism, instruments and by taking steps for safeguarding the interest of the investors.

In this context, an important mechanisms named as "Book Building" in the system of Initial Public Offerings (IPOs) was introduced by SEBI in India on the basis of recommendations of the committee constituted under the chairmanship of YH Malegam in October 1995. It is the most practical mechanism for the quick and efficient management of mega issues.

Meaning

Book Building involves sale of securities to the public and institutional bidders on the basis of predetermined price range. It is an innovative method of marketing securities involving price determination and quantum of securities on the basis of demand from the prospective investors (Shareholders).

SEBI's Guidelines 1995 defined Book Building as "a process undertaken by which a demand for the securities proposed to be issued by a body corporate is elicited and built up and the price for such securities is assessed for the determination of the quantum of such securities to be issued by means of a notice, circular, advertisement, document or information memoranda or offer document. In general, the word "Book Building" is a method of marketing the shares of a company where by the quantum and the price of the securities to be issued will be decided on the basis of the bids received from the prospective shareholders by the lead merchant bankers. According to this method, share prices are determined on the basis of real demand for the shares at various price levels in the market.

The issue of securities in the Book Building process is generally bifurcated into two parts i.e. (i) Placement and (ii) Net offer to the public. As per SEBI's Guidelines, the book building process may be adopted for the placement portion and net offer to the public may be made at "Fixed Price Method". The securities are offered to the public under the net offer at the same price as applicable to the placement portion under the Book Building process. However, as per SEBI's guidelines 1997, the Book Building process may be applied to 100 percent of the issue if the issue size is 100 crores or more.

SEBI's Guidelines & Book Building Process

The regulator - SEBI has issued various guidelines for control and regulation of Book-Building process in India. These guidelines relating to book building process may be summarised as under:

(1) The option of Book-Building is available to all body corporates which are otherwise eligible to make an issue of capital to the public.

(2) The issuer company has an option of either reserving the securities for firm allotment or issuing the securities through book building process.

(3) The issue of securities through book-building process will be separately identified as "placement portion category" in the prospectus.

(4) The Companies are bound to adhere to the SEBI's guidelines for book building offers in the following manner :

(a) **75% Book Building Process :** Under this process 25% of the issue is to be sold at a fixed price and the balance of 75% through the Book. Building process.

(b) **Offer to Public through Book Building :** The process specifies that an issuer company may make an issue of securities to the public through prospectus in the following manner.

(i) 100 percent of the net offer to the public through book building process.

or

(ii) 75 percent of the net offer to the public through Book Building process and 25 percent of the net offer to the public at a price determined through book building process.

(5) In case the "Book Building Option" is availed of underwriting may be undertaken to the extent of the net offer to the public.

(6) The draft prospectus containing all the information except the information regarding the price at which the securities are offered shall be filed with SEBI as per the existing guidelines.

(7) One of the lead merchant bankers to the issue shall be nominated by the issuing company as a Book Runner whose name shall be mentioned in the draft prospectus submitted to SEBI.

(8) The copy of the draft prospectus filed with the SEBI may be circulated by the Book Runner to the institutional buyers who are eligible for firm allotment as per the existing SEBI's Guidelines and to the eligible underwriters inviting offers for subscribing to the securities provided that the draft prospectus to be circulated shall indicate the price band within the securities offered for public subscription.

(9) The Book Runner on receipt of offers shall maintain a record of the names and number of securities ordered and the price at which the institutional buyer or underwriter is willing to subscribe to securities under the placement portion.

(10) The underwriters shall maintain a record of the orders received by them for subscribing the issue out of placement portion

(11) The underwriters shall aggregate the offers so received for subscribing to the issue and intimate to the "Book Runner" the aggregate amount of the orders received by him. The institutional investors shall also forward their orders to the Book Runner.

(12) On receipt of above information the Book Runner and Issuer Company shall determine the price at which the securities will be offered to the public. Provided that the issue price for the placement portion and offer to the public (IPO) shall be the same.

(13) On determination of the price, the underwriter shall enter into an underwriting agreement with the issuer indicating the number of securities as well as the price at which the underwriter would subscribe to the securities. Provided that the Book Runner will have an option of requiring the underwriters to the net offer to the public to pay in advance all money required to be paid in respect of their underwriting commitment.

(14) The acknowledgement card will be issued by SEBI without mentioning the issue price or the price band. On receipt of the acknowledgement and determination of the issue price within two days, thereafter the prospectus will be filed with the Registrar of Companies.

(15) The issuer company shall open two different accounts for collection of application money - one for the private placement portion and other for the public subscription.

(16) One day prior to the opening of the issue to the public, the Book Runner shall collect from the institutional buyers and the underwriters the application forms along with the application money to the extent of the securities proposed to be allotted to them/subscribed by them.

(17) Allotment for the private placement portion shall be made on the second day from the closure of the issue.

(18) In case the Book Runner has exercised the option requiring the underwriter to the net offer to the public to pay in advance all money required to be paid by the underwriter in respect of their commitment by the 11th day of the closure of the issue of shares allotted as per the private placement category, shall be eligible to be listed. The Allotment of securities under the public category shall be made as per the existing statutory requirements.

(19) The Book Runner and other intermediaries involved in the "Book Building Process" shall maintain records of the Book Building process. SEBI has the right to inspect such records.

(20) In case of under subscription in the net offer to public spilled over to the extent of under-subscription shall be permitted from the placement portion to the net offer to the public portion subject to the condition that preference shall be given to the individual investors.

(21) It shall be permissible for the issuer company to pay interest on the application money till the date of allotment or the deemed date of allotment provided that payment of interest is made uniformly to all the applicants.

Recent Changes in Book Building Machanism

The SEBI on March 29, 2005 announced sweeping changes in initial public offer (IPO) norms, which are as follows:

1. Increased allocation for retail investors in book building issue from 25 percent to 35 percent and also has changed the definition of the retail category.
2. The market regulator has now permitted retail investors to apply for Rs. 1,00,000 worth of shares in a Book Building issue against Rs. 50,000 earlier. For this purpose SEBI has redefined the retail investor (individual) as one who applies or bids for securities for a value not exceeding Rs. 1,00,000.
3. It has reduced the non-institutional category (popularly known as high net worth individuals) allocation from 25 percent to 15 percent.
4. Institutional investors include Foreign Financial Institutions (FIIs) Banks, Mutual Funds and Indian Financial Institutions like LIC or IDBI.
5. The changes have been made in the SEBI (DIP) Guidelines 2,000, on the basis of recommendations made by SEBI's primary market advisory committee.
6. The new norms will be applicable to all public issues whose draft offers documents are filed with SEBI on or after April 4, 2005.
7. SEBI has decided to reduce the bidding period from the current 5 to 10 days (including holidays) to 3 to 7 working days.
8. It has also provided more flexibility for listed companies to disclose price band/floor price for public issues one day before bid opening.

9. SEBI has decided to give an option to listed issuers to either disclose price band in RHP/ application form/ abridged prospectus (current practice) or to disclose the price band/floor price at least one day before the bid opening.
10. It is proposed to amend the guidelines to improve the contents and ensure uniformity in data display on the websites of the stock exchanges. The data will be made available for a further period of three days after the closure of bid/issue.

Book Building Process in India

The principal parties/intermediaries involve in Book-Building process are:

(1) The issuer company.

(2) The Book Running Lead Manager (BRLM) who is a category I Merchant Banker registered with SEBI.

(3) The Syndicate Members who are intermediaries registered with SEBI and who are permitted to carry on activities as underwriters. Syndicate Members are appointed by Book Running Lead Manager.

Steps for Book Building Process

(i) Preparation of draft prospectus.

(ii) Formation of Syndicate

(iii) Record of orders

(iv) Consolidation

(v) Closure of order Book

(vi) Determination of price

(vii) Agreement with Syndicate Members

(viii) Payment in advance

(ix) Filing of prospectus.

(x) Opening of two separate accounts by the issuer company for collection of application money.

(xi) Collection of application for securities.

(xii) Allotment of placement and public portion

(xiii) The adjustment of under-subscription, if any, against placement portion.

(xiv) Rate of allotment

(xv) Maintenance of records

Recent Trends in Book Building Issues in India

The Book Building process in India is very transparent. All investors (including small investors) can see on an hourly basis where the book is being built before applying. Therefore, no asymmetry as far as information dissemination is concerned. The practice of Book-Building is new to the Indian Capital market and the procedure is still evolving. ICICI was the first company to use the Book-Building method for it's Rs. 1000 crore bond issue in April 1996 followed by Rs. 4,323 crore Larsen and Toubro issue and Rs. 5,879 crore TISCO bond issue for the placement portion.

The recent issue of Hughes Software made history in more than one way. It was the first Indian IPO in IT Industries to adopt the Book-Building process and the issue was highly over subscribed.

In November 1999 the HCL Technologies has raised capital through IPO Book-Building method. The issue was oversubscribed by 27 times. This was despite the fact that the company revised its share price band of Rs. 450-540 to 500-580. The final price offered was Rs. 580 for the share. Of the 112 mega issues raised Rs. 51,823 crores forming 92.3% of total capital mobilised through public issue in the year 2003-04. The share of mega issues in total capital mobilised through public issues increase more than two time from 45.25% in 1992-93 to 92.3% in 2003-04.

The types of issues are consisting of voluntary offer for sale and public issue. The contribution of voluntary offer for sale is significantly higher than the public offer. Further types of instruments issued by the companies are equity and bonds Amount contributed by equity is 80.5% as compared to 19.5% of bonds. The Kotak Mahendra Capital Services Company followed by DSP Merril Lynch Ltd. have become prominent Book Running Lead Managers (BRLM) of mega issues.

IPO of Bharat Shipyard Ltd. was over-subscribed by 72 times, Indoco Remedies Ltd. 68 times, Power Trading Corporation of India, Dishman Pharmaceuticals and Chemicals Ltd. by 38 times each NDTV 37 times, Biocon Ltd. 32 times and other mega issues 6 to 30 times. It may be noted that some of the mega issues were over subscribed by many times with in couple of minutes from opening of issue due to enormous support from corporate enterprises, financial institutions and high net worth investors.

An Evaluation of Book Building System

The Book-Building system has various limitations which may be summarised as follows:

1. Book-Building is suitable for mega issues only. In case of the potential investors, the companies can adjust the attributes of the offer according to the preferences of the potential, investors. It may be possible in big issues since the risk return preference of the investors cannot be estimated easily.
2. The issuer company should be fundamentally strong and well known to the investors.
3. The Book-Building system works very efficiently in matured market conditions. In such circumstances the investors are aware of the various parameters affecting the market price of the securities. But such conditions are not commonly found in practice.
4. There is a possibility of price rigging on listing as promoters may try to bailout syndicate members.

In spite of these limitations the process of Book-Building is most economical sure shot way of raising capital in the shortest time span. It provides transparency and offers shares at a reasonable price which can easily be compared with the NAV (Net Assets Value) of the issuer company since demand of securities is known before the issue closes, the issue can be deferred and rescheduled after having realised the temper or mood of the market.

The spirit behind the introduction of Book-Building mechanism in India is to discover the right price for a public issue which in turn would eliminate unreasonable issue pricing by greedy promoters. The success of Book-Building system depends on co-operation among the Book Runner Lead Manager, Issuing Company, SEBI and the investors.

Green Shoe Option : It is an option that allows the underwriting of an IPO to sell additional shares if the demand is high and issue is oversubscribed. In other words, if a company making an initial offer (IPO) of equity shares through book building process can avail GSO for stabilising the post-listing price of it's shares. GSO means an option of allocating shares in excess of shares included in the public issue and operating a post listing price stabilising mechanism through a stabilising agent. GSO was recognised by SEBI in August 2003 in the system of IPO using Book Building method. According to SEBI's Guidelines a company desirous of availing a GSO shall in the resolution of the General Meeting authorising the public issue, seeks authorisation for the possibility of allotment of additional shares to the management team as the SA who will be responsible for the price stabilisation process. IDBI, ICICI and Infosys Technologies have exercised the GSO.

Demat Shares (Dematerialisation)

Financial markets, consisting of capital market and money market, constitute one of the major elements of the corporates operating environment. All corporate entities have an inevitable relationship with the capital market. In the primary market segment of capital market, a company issues various types of securities to raise funds where as in the secondary market, the securities already issued, are traded. The Indian capital market, a growing one, has been undergoing through the various process of reforms in the light of globalisation and liberalisation policies initiated by the Government since 1991. The formation of SEBI in 1992 and consequent sweeping changes brought about in view of increasing number of market participants including foreign players, unwarranted delay in transfer of securities, problem of duplicate or forged shares, bad delivery, loss or theft of share certificates, the SEBI has issued a number of rules and regulations for the supervision, monitoring and control of activities of market participants. So that interest of all those concerned could be protected. The traditional method of settlement which was based upon physical delivery of securities certificates has been replaced by computerised on line trading (paper less trading) or depository system of securities to ensure safety, security, transparency and promptness in clearing and settlement system.

Meaning

Shares which are held in electronic form instead of physical form are termed as demat shares. Trading in shares of the company is compulsory in dematerialised form for all investors. The depositories system enables the conversion of physical securities certificates in to electronic form through a process of dematerialisation of certificates. At present there are two Depositories viz National Securities Depository Limited (NSDL) and Central Depository Services (I) Limited (CDSL) registered with SEBI.

What is Dematerialisation?

Dematerialisation ("Demat" in short form) signifies conversion of a share certificate from its physical form to electronic form for the same number of holding which is credited to your demat account which you open with a Depository Participant (DP).

Dematerialisation is a process by which the physical share certificates of an investor are taken back by the Company and an equivalent number of securities are credited in electronic form at the request of the investor. An investor will have to first open an account with a Depository Participant and then request for the dematerialisation of his share certificates through the Depository Participant so that the dematerialised holdings can be credited into that account. This is very similar to opening a Bank Account.

Dematerialisation of shares is optional and an investor can still hold shares in physical form. However, he/she has to demat the shares if he/she wishes to sell the same through the Stock Exchanges. Similarly, if an investor purchases shares, he/she will get delivery of the shares in demat form.

What is a Depository?

A Depository (NSDL & CDSL) is an organisation like a Central Bank where the securities of a shareholder are held in the electronic form at the request of the shareholder through the medium of a Depository Participant.

If an investor wants to utilise the services offered by a Depository, the investor has to open an account with the Depository through a Depository Participant.

So a depository is just another form of a custodial service, the only difference being that the securities are held in an electronic form.

The Depository can legally transfer beneficial ownership which a custodian cannot. The main objective of a Depository is to minimize the paper work involved with the ownership, trading and transfer of securities.

Who is a Depository Participant?

Similar to the brokers who trade on your behalf in and outside the Stock Exchange; a Depository Participant (DP) is your representative (agent) in the depository system providing the link between the Company and you through the Depository. Your Depository Participant will maintain your securities account balances and intimate to you the status of your holding from time to time. According to SEBI guidelines, Financial Institutions like banks, custodians, stockbrokers etc. can become participants in the depository. A DP is one with whom you need to open an account to deal in electronic form. While the Depository can be compared to a Bank, DP is like a branch of your bank with whom you can have an account.

How does the Depository System operate?

The Depository System functions very much like the banking system. A bank holds funds in accounts whereas a Depository holds securities in accounts for its clients. A Bank transfers funds between accounts whereas a Depository transfers securities between accounts. In both systems, the transfer of funds or securities happens without the actual handling of funds or securities. Both the Banks and the Depository are accountable for the safe keeping of funds and securities respectively.

What are the benefits of having a demat account?

a. Trading in the shares of the Company is now under the compulsory demat segment. With SEBI making demat mandatory on most of the traded scrips, electronic transaction will be the only way everyone will trade.

b. No stamp duty for transfer of securities in the electronic form. In case of transfer of physical shares, stamp duty of 0.5 percent is payable on the market value of shares being transferred.

c. All risks associated with physical certificates such as delays, loss, in transit, theft, mutilation, bad deliveries, etc. eliminated. Your shares can be kept in the "Frozen Mode" by your Depository Participant under your specific instructions.

d. The concept of an "odd lot" in respect of dematerialized shares stands abolished, i.e. in the demat mode, market lot becomes one share.

e. Dematerialised securities are most preferred by banks and other financiers for providing credit facility against securities. Generally, demat securities attract lower margin and lower rates of interest compared to physical securities.

f. Even in the electronic mode of trading, the payment mechanism (usually through a broker) between the buyer and seller continues to be as before. Also the usual brokerage charges would have to be incurred. However, after the settlement, pay in and pay out are on the same day for scripless trading which means you get your securities as well as cash immediately.

g. Shares bought or sold are transferred in your name on the very next day of pay out. In case of physical shares, transfer of ownership takes 30 days or sometimes even more.

h. No courier/postal charges for sending share certificates/transfer deeds.

i. Facility for freezing/locking of investor accounts, which enables you to make your account non-operational, for instance if you are abroad.

j. Facility to pledge and hypothicate your securities available.

k. As the Depository System becomes popular, brokers will be increasingly reluctant to deal with physical shares.

l. Investors prefer to buy shares which are already in dematerialised form.

SOME QUERIES

Why should investors prefer to buy shares in the depository mode?

When you buy shares already in the depository mode, you will become the owner of those shares in the depository within a day of the settlement being completed. You will not have to apply to the Company for registering the shares in your name. Thus, there will be no possibility of loss or theft when the share certificates are posted to the company. You will have no fear that any fake or stolen shares may have been delivered to you.

Why should brokers become reluctant to deal with physical shares?

Apart from the risk arising out of having to deal with the paper work and keeping account of the share certificates, the brokers are exposed to the risk of bad deliveries in the present system. It may take upto one year for the broker to discover that such a risk exists. As against this in the depository mode the broker will be free from the worries of bad deliveries. The broker's only risk will be that the investor does not own the shares which the investor has sold. But this will be known within the settlement period (10-15 days). The broker will thus prefer to sell securities that are in the depository mode.

How do you demat your shares?

The process of opening an account with a Depository Participant is similar to the opening of a bank account. First, you will have to open an account with a Depository Participant (DP) of your choice by filling up an Account Opening Form and signing a "Participant-Client Agreement". You will be then given a unique client ID number, which must be quoted in all correspondence with the DP.

Thereafter, you will have to fill up and submit a Dematerialisation Request Form (DRF) provided by the DP duly signed by all the holders and surrender the physical shares intended to be dematted to the DP. The DP upon receipt of the shares and the DRF, will issue you an acknowledgement and will send an electronic request to the Company/Registrars and Transfer Agents of the Company through the Depository for confirmation of demat. The DP will simultaneously surrender the DRF and the shares to the Company/Registrars and Transfer Agents of the Company with a covering letter requesting the Company to confirm demat. The Registrars and Transfer Agents of the Company, after necessary verification of the documents received from the DP, will cancel the physical shares and confirm demat to the Depository. This confirmation will be passed on by the Depository to the DP which holds your account. After receiving this confirmation from the Depository, the DP will credit your account with the number of shares dematerialized. The DP will hold the shares in the dematerialized form thereafter on your behalf. And you will become the beneficial owner of these dematerialized shares.

Do not send the share certificates/ documents for dematerialisation to the company or its registrars and transfer agents.

When you submit the shares for dematerialisation, your DP will deface the share certificates with the stamp "Surrendered for dematerialisation". This ensures that your shares are not lost in transit or misused till credit is received by you in your demat account.

What are the charges to be paid for opening an account and to demat one's physical shares? Will there be any charges for each transaction?

Each DP can levy charges by way of account opening fees, transaction fees, custody fees and so on. The charges differ from Depository Participant to Depository Participant and therefore you will have to contact your DP for the same.

I have purchased some shares in paper form. Can I directly give the share certificates to my Depository Participant for dematting them in my favour?

Prior to dematting your shares, they have to be registered in your favour. Hence, you have to necessarily lodge the share certificates with a duly executed transfer deed with the Registrars and Transfer Agents of the Company. Once the share transfer is processed, an option letter for dematting your shares will be sent to you. You can then give us your Demat Account No. with the Demat Request form for the dematting process through your DP and the shares will be directly credited to your Demat Account.

Is it a fact that Syngenta shares are to be traded compulsorily in Demat Form? Do I have the option of holding them in physical form?

Yes. The shares of the company are to be compulsorily traded in demat form. However you can still buy shares in physical form upto 500 (through odd lot window facilities provided by Stock Exchanges) and send the same for transfer to the Registrars and Transfer Agents of the Company. You may indicate your desire to return the shares in physical form, while loading the same for transfer. After the transfer is registered in your favour, the share certificates will be returned to you in physical form.

How do I get my dividends on dematted shares? Will I get the Annual Report after I demat my shares and would I be able to attend the AGM?

The Depositories will give the list of demat account holders and the number of shares held by them in electronic form on the Record date to the Registrars and Transfer Agents of the Company (known as Benpos). On the basis of Benpos, the Company will issue dividend warrants in favour of the demat account holders.

The rights of the shareholders holding shares in demat form are at par with the holders in physical form. Hence you will be eligible to get the Annual Report and will have the right to attend the AGM as a shareholder.

What are the chances of any fraud/disputes in using a demat account? Whom should I approach in such cases?

Common risk factors applicable to trading in physical shares like mismatch in signatures, loss in postal transit, etc., are absent since the dematted shares are traded scripless.

However, in the unlikely event of any other dispute, the concerned Stock Exchange and/or Depository Custodian viz. NSDL/CDSL or SEBI would have to be approached for resolving such issues.

Can I pledge my shares in demat form for the purpose of availing any funding/loan arrangement with my bankers?

Yes. You will have to contact your DP for this.

Can your dematted shares be converted back into physical shares?

Yes, definitely. If you wish to get your securities in the physical form all you have to do is to submit a Rematerialisation Request Form (RRF) trough your DP in the same manner as Dematerialisation. Your Depository Participant will forward your request to the Depository after verifying that you have the necessary securities in balance. The Depository in turn will intimate the Registrar and Transfer Agents of the Company Who will print and despatch to you the share certificates for the number of shares so rematerialised and your account will be debited by the Depository and credited with the Company.

Will you get back the same certificates after rematerialisation?

It does not really matter at all. The Registrars and Transfer Agents will print new certificates with a new range of certificate numbers. You will be allotted a new folio number; however if you already have an existing folio number you may be allotted the same.

How will I know that my Depository Participant has updated my account after each transaction.

Here again just a Bank, the Depository Participant will give you a Pass Book or a Statement of Holdings. The Statement of Holdings will be despatched to you periodically by the Depository Participant; however the Statement of Holdings can be sent to you as and when requested for a fee.

What if there are any discrepancies in the share holding statement or the pass book entries?

In case of any discrepancy in the Statement of Holdings, you can contact your Depository Participant. If the discrepancy cannot be solved at the Depository Participants level, you should approach the Depository concerned for clarification.

What happens if you lose your share holding statement or depository pass book?

Inform your Depository Participant and obtain a duplicate share holding statement or depository passbook. Your holding statement or passbook cannot be used by any body else for trading in your account.

Are you restricted to having accounts with only one depository participant?

There are absolutely no restrictions on the number of DPs you can open accounts with. Opening an account with a DP is very similar to opening a bank account. Just as you can have savings or current accounts with more than one bank, you can open accounts with more than one Depository Participant.

However, you would need to open accounts in the same sequence of names in which the shares are held by you. For example, if you hold some shares jointly in the names in which the shares are held by you. For example, if you hold some shares jointly in the names A, B, C and some shares also in the names A, C, B you would need to open 2 DP accounts.

Do you have to keep any minimum balance of securities in your account?

No, the Depository has not prescribed any minimum balance. In fact, you can have zero balance in your account. However, the DPs may fix some minimum limits.

What security do you have if the only proof of your holdings in your depository is merely a piece of paper indicating your account balance?

When you open an account with a DP, you sign an agreement with the Depository Participant, in which the DP indemnifies you for any misuse of your holdings. The Depository will also ensure that the interests of the investors are protected, so that your grievances, if any, against your DP will be resolved by the Depository.

Are there any additional security features which depository participants will offer you to protect your account?

Yes, every transaction in your account will be authorised by you. You can authorise any transaction either by affixing your signature or by using any smart card similar to the use of an ATM or a credit card. Your Depository Participant will advertise its facilities and you should go through them carefully.

There is a facility by which you can lock your account so that the Depository Participant will not be able to carry out any transactions in your absence without your authorisation.

Is it possible for you to get the securities allotted to you in public offerings credited to your account directly in electronic form?

Definitely. In fact, in the public issue application form itself there will be a provision for you to indicate the manner in which you want the securities allotted to you. All you have to do is to mention your client account number and the name of the DP and any allotment due to you will be credited into that account.

Who will give you the benefits arising out of your holdings, say bonus rights or dividend?

When any corporate event such as rights or bonus or dividend is announced for a particular security, the Depositories will give all the details of the clients having electronic holdings of that security as of record date/book closure to the Registrars and Transfer Agents of the Company who will then calculate the corporate benefits due to all the share holders. The disbursement of cash benefits such as dividend/ interest will be done by the Company whereas the distribution of securities/ entitlements will be done by the Depositories based on the information provided by the Registrars and Transfer Agents of the Company. Thus, bonus/ rights shares, if any, will be credited to your account electronically.

REFERENCES

1. The Chartered Accountant; November 2005, pp. 676-683
2. Chartered Secretary, May 2002, pp. 198-2002
3. SEBI website on Demat shares.

QUESTIONS

1. Define company. Explain the difference between a company limited by shares, a company limited by guarantee and an unlimited company.
2. Distinguish between 'Share Capital', 'Reserve Capital' & 'Capital Reserve'.
3. What are preference shares? Explain the nature of
   (i) Cumulative and Non-Cumulative preference shares
   (ii) Participating and Non-participating preference shares.
   (iii) Redeemable & Irredeemable preference shares.
   (iv) Convertible and non-convertible preference shares.
4. Draw distinction between shares and stock.
5. Explain the SEBI's guidelines on issue of shares.
6. Can a company issue shares at premium, or at a discount? Explain the conditions.
7. What is minimum subscription? How is it different from 'undersubscription' and 'over subscription'?
8. Write a note on 'sweat equity shares'.
9. How a surrender of shares is different from forfeiture of shares?
10. Can Company buy it's own shares? Mention it's salient features.
11. Write short note on :
    prorata allotment
    Rights Issue
    Bonus Issue

PROBLEMS

1. A Ltd. issued 10,000 equity shares of Rs. 10 each at a premium of 10% payable as follows:

	Rs.
On application	3 per share
On allotment (including premium)	3 per share
First Call	2 per share

The application and allotment money was received in full. Member holding 1,000 shares failed to pay call money and as a consequence the shares were forfeited. Subsequently 500 of these shares were reisued as fully paid @ Rs. 8 per share.

Record journal entries & prepare ledger accounts.

Ans: Share Capital — Rs. 63,000; Share Captial — Rs. 5,000; Share Forfeiture — Rs. 2,500 &
(Partly paid) (Fully paid) Capital Reserve — Rs. 1,500

2. Z Ltd. with an authorised capital of Rs. 5,00,000 in shares of Rs. 10 each. Of these 5,000 shares were issued as fully paid up, as a part of consideration of Building purchased, to the vendor. 8,000 shares were subscribed for by the public. The money was payable as under :

On application	Rs. 2
On allotment	Re. 1
On first call	Re. 1
On Second Call	Re. 1

The amount received in respect of these shares was as follows:

On 6,000 shares	Full amount
On 1,250 shares	Rs. 4 per share
On 500 shares	Rs. 3 per share
On 250 shares	Rs. 2 per share

The directors forfeited the shares on which less than Rs. 4 per share had been paid.

Record journal entries, prepare Cash Book and the Balance Sheet giving relevant information.

C.S. (I): ICWA (I) Modified

Ans: Paid up Capital — Rs. 85,000; Share forfeited A/c — Rs. 2,000; Bank Balance — Rs. 37,000; Balance Sheet Total — Rs. 87,000.

(3) Record journal entries:

(a) X Ltd. forfeited 100 equity shares of Rs. 10 each for non-payment of First Call of Rs. 2 per share and Final Call of Rs. 3 per share. These shares were reissued at a discount of Rs. 3.50 per share.

(b) X Ltd. forfeited 200 equity shares of Rs. 10 each, issued at a premium of 50% for non-payment of Final Call of Rs. 3 per share. These shares were reissued at a discount of Rs. 4 per share.

(c) X Ltd. forfeited 150 equity shares of Rs. 10 each issued at a premium of Rs. 5 per share for non-payment of allotment money of Rs. 8 per share (including Rs. 5 for premium), First Call of Rs. 2 per share and the Final Call of Rs. 3 per share. Of these, 100 equity shares were reissued @ Rs. 14 per share.

(d) X Ltd. forfeited 100 equity shares of Rs. 10 each at a discount of 10% for non-payment of First call of Rs. 2 per share, & Final Call of Rs. 3 per share. Of these 50 shares were reissued @ Rs. 8 per share and remaining @ Rs. 7 per share credited as fully paid up.

Ans: Capital Reserve (a) Rs. 150; (b) Rs. 600; (c) Rs. 200; (d) Rs. 250 Share Forfeited A/c (c) Rs. 100

(4) X Ltd. invited applications for 50,000 Equity Shares of Rs. 10 each at a premium of 20%, payable Rs. 3 on application, Rs. 7 on allotment including premium and the balance on first & final call.

Application for 62,500 shares wre received. It was decided:

(i) To refuse allotment to the applicants for 2,500 shares,

(ii) To allot in full to the applicants for 10,000 shares.

(iii) To allot the balance of the available shares on pro-rata basis, and

(iv) To utilise excess application money against allotment.

Vyoma holding 500 shares to whom shares had been allotted on pro-rata basis failed to pay the amount due on allotment and call. Shalini, holding 250 shares, to whom full allotment was made, failed to pay the amount due on call only. These shares were forfeited. Of these 300 shares of Vyoma and 100 shares of Shalini were reissued at a discount of Re. 1 per share.

Record journal entries.

I.C.W.A. (Adapted)

Ans: Capital Reserve - Rs. 1,800; Prorata ratio 5 : 4

5. A Ltd. issued a prospectus offering 1,00,000 equity shares of Rs. 10 each on the following terms :

Payable on Application	Rs. 2 per share
Payable on Allotment	Rs. 5 per share (including premium of Re. 1)
Payable on First Call	Rs. 3 per share
Payable on Final Call	Re. 1 per share

Subscriptions were received for 1,35,000 shares and the allotment was made as under:

	Shares Allotted
(i) Allotment in full	75,000
(ii) Allotment of one half shares applied for	25,000

Cash received on remaining appications was returned. Money overpaid on accepted applications was employed on account of sums due on allotment. P who was allotted 1,000 shares paid in full on allotment.

Q to whom 500 shares were allotted (who applied for the same) failed to pay the allotment money and on his subsequent failure to pay the first call, his shares were forfeited. R, the holder of 1,000 shares failed to pay the two calls and his shares were forfeited after the final call.

Of the shares forfeited 1,000 shares were reissued @ Rs. 9.50 per share credited as fully paid, the whole of Q's shares being included.

Record transactions in the ledgers & prepare Balance Sheet.

C.A. (I) Adapted

Ans: Allotment money received - Rs. 4,47,500 (excluding calls - in-advance Rs. 4,000)

First Call Money received -	Rs. 2,92,500
Share Capital -	Rs. 9,95,000
Securities Premium -	Rs. 99,500
Share Forfeited -	Rs. 3,000
Capital Reserve -	Rs. 3,500
Cash at Bank -	Rs. 11,01,000

(6) Z Ltd. issued 60,000 shares of Rs. 10 each at a premium of 25% payable on application. The amount payable on allotment was Rs. 4 per share and an equal amount was due on call to be made.

Total applications received were for 1,10,000 shares. The directors scaled down the allotment as follows :

Category	A	B	C
Grouping of Shares	1-100	101-500	Over 500

No. of applications received	1,200	175	5
No. of shares applied for	70,000	35,000	5,000
No. of shares allotted	42,000	14,000	4,000

It was decided that the excess amount received on application would be utilised in payment of allotment money and surplus if any, would be refunded to applicants.

Anjali who was one of the applicants (under 'A' category) and had applied for 100 shares defaulted in payment of allotment money. Yogesh (an applicant under category (C) who had been allotted 800 shares failed to pay the call money. Their shares were forfeited after the respective calls were made and reisued as fully paid up for Rs. 8 and Rs. 6 per share respectively.

Show the necessary journal entries in the books of the copany to record the above transactions.

[C.A. (Inter) Modified]

Ans: Share Forfeited Account - Rs. 5,100 (Rs. 300 + 4,800)
Capital Reserve - Rs. 1,780

(7) A Ltd. made a rights issue in the proprotion of 1 : 2. Calculate the value of right if the market price of share at the time of annoncement of rights issue is Rs. 250. The Company decided to give a share of Rs. 100 each at a premium of Rs. 25 each.

Calculate Value of right.

Ans: Value of right - Rs. 41.67.

(8) PQR Ltd. invited applications for 20,000 shares of Rs. 100 each at 5% discount. The money was payable as under :

Rs. 20 - on appliation
Rs. 40 - on allotment
Rs. 35 - On call.

The applications received were for 18,000 shares and all of these were accepted. All money due were received except the first and final call on 200 shares which were forfeited. Of these 100 shares were reissued at the rate of Rs. 90 per share credited as fully paid up.

Record journal entries and prepare Cash book and balance sheet.

Ans:

Balance at Bank	Rs. 17,12,000
Share Forfeited	Rs. 6,000
Capital Reserve	Rs. 5,500
Share Discount	Rs. 89,500
Total - B/s	Rs. 18,01,500

(9) From the following information determine the maximum amount that can be capitalised for the bonus issue.

	Rs.
Equity Capital	75,00,000
(75,000 Shares of Rs. 100 each fully paid up)	
Securities Premium	10,00,000
General Reserve	50,00,000

Capital Redemption Reserve	5,00,000
Development Rebate Reserve	2,50,000
Profit and Loss A/c	15,00,000
Gratuity	7,50,000
Income Tax	2,25,000
Sales Tax	75,000
Investment Allowance Reserve	1,10,000
Claims against company disputed	60,000
Revaluation Reserve	12,00,000

Ans: Rs. 80,00,000.

(10) Cyma Ltd. resolved to utilise Rs. 4,50,000 out of general reserve to declare bonus in the form of payment of final call of Rs. 3 per share on 1,50,000 Equity shares of Rs. 10 each and to utilise balance of securities premium to issue fully paid bonus shares in the ratio 1 : 5. Record journal entries in the books of Cyma Ltd.

Ans: Amount to be utilised from Securitie Premium- Rs. 3,00,000.

(11) Adnan Corporation Ltd. decided to declare bonus shares out of divisible profits standing to the credit of General Reserve Rs. 7,50,000; Profit & Loss A/c - Rs. 2,50,000 and Securities Premium Rs. 50,000, by making 20,000 partly paid shares of Rs. 10 each Rs. 6 paid up as fully paid up and to issue fully paid bonus shares of Rs. 10 each at Rs. 12 per share in the ratio of 4 : 5 to the holders of 40,000 shares.

Give entries.

Ans: Fully paid bonus Issue :

Share Captial — Rs. 3,20,000

Securities Premium — Rs. 64,000

2

Redemption of Preference Shares

Section 80 of Companies Act 1956 deals with the provisions of issue and redemption of preference shares. As per the provisions of this section a Company limited by shares if authorised by it's Articles, may issue preference shares. Such shares are liable to be redeemed at the option of the Company. The Act lays down certain conditions which should be fulfilled before redemption and further compliance of some other conditions in the process of redemption.

These conditions are :

(i) No preference shares can be redeemed unless those are fully paid up.

(ii) Such preference shares can be redeemed either

(a) Out of the "divisible profits" of the company or

(b) Out of the "proceeds" of the fresh issue of shares made for the purpose of redemption.

(c) Or out of both.

(iii) If such shares are redeemed out of the divisible profits, then an amount equivalent to the nominal value of preference shares so redeemed out of such profits shall be transferred to Capital Redemption Reserve Account.

(iv) In case redemption is made at premium, the same should be met out of 'Securities Premium or divisible profits of the company or both.

(v) Capital Redemption Reserve so created is available only for issuing fully paid bonus shares.

*** Explanation and Clarification**

(i) **"Divisible profits"** are those profits which are available for distribution as dividend. These profits include.

- General Reserve/Reserve Fund
- Profit & Loss Account/ Profit & Loss Appropriation A/c.
- Dividend Equalisation Fund
- Insurance Fund
- Workmen's Compensation Fund/Accident Compensation Fund (after actual liability, if any)
- Any other fund/reserve created voluntarily out of profits-such as sinking fund or debenture redemption fund created voluntarily.

(ii) "Proceeds" of fresh issue

"Proceeds" means the amount actually received by the company, on making an issue of shares only for the purpose of redemption, *excluding securities premium.* Securities premium once received is transferred to "securities premium" account which can be utilised as per the guide lines of section 78.

Hence, 'proceeds' of fresh issue is the '*Nominal Value*' if shares are issued at *par* or at *premium*, and if shares are issued at *discount*, it is the "*net amount received*".

This can be summed up as follows :

Fresh Issue	**Proceeds**
At Par	Nominal Value
At Premium	Nominal Value
At Discount	Net amount received

(iii) Capital Redemption Reserve

As required under the provisions of Companies Act 1956, any redemption of preference shares out of divisible profits will make it obligatory on the part of company to create Capital Redemption Reserve by transferring an amount equal to the face value of preference shares so redeemed out of profits.

The main purpose of making a "fresh issue" of equity shares is to meet the long-term/ permanent financial requirements of the Company and to reduce the burden of fixed commitment in terms of dividend on preference shares. The Company resorts to fresh issue to make funds available for redemption purposes without affecting or disturbing the liquidity position. Sometimes accumulated divisible profits are not sufficient to redeem preference shares out of it.

It should be noted that redemption of preference shares does not result in reduction of Share Capital. (Authorised)

(iv) "Premium on Redemption of Preference Shares"

As per Companies Act 1956 - section 80 (i) (c) the premium on redemption of Preference Shares, if any, is to be adjusted against " Securities Premium Account" (securities premium as per Balance Sheet plus securities premium on fresh issue) or against the profits of the Company.

Steps for Redemption — Accounting Treatment

1. Making redemption due /showing the amount due to Preference Shareholders.

Preference Share Capital A/c	Dr.	Face Value
Premium on Redemption A/c	Dr.	Premium amount
To Preference Shareholders A/c		Total

2. Making " Fresh Issue"

(i) *at par*

Bank A/c	Dr.
To Equity Share Capital A/c	

(ii) *or at premium*

Bank A/c	Dr.
To Equity Share Capital A/c	
To Securities Premium A/c	

(iii) *or at Discount*

Bank A/c Dr.

Discount on Issue of Shares A/c Dr.

To Equity Share Capital A/c

3. Providing for *Premium on Redemption Account* :

Securities Premium A/c Dr.

Or Profit & Loss A/c* Dr.

To Premium on Redemption A/c

(*or any other divisible Profit)

4. Transfer to *Capital Redemption Reserve* :

General Reserve A/c Dr.

Profit & Loss A/c Dr.

Or Other free reserves or divisible profit A/c Dr.

To Capital Redemption Reserve A/c*

(CRR* = Nominal Value of Pref. Share Capital – Proceeds of Fresh Issue)

5. Making *payment to Preference Shareholders*.

Preference Shareholders A/c Dr.

To Bank A/c

6. Making bonus issue, if any.

Capital Redemption Reserve A/c Dr.

General Reserve A/c Dr.

Securities Premium A/c Dr.

Profit & Loss A/c Dr.

To Bonus to Equity Shareholders A/c

Bonus to Equity Shareholders A/c Dr.

To Equity Share Capital A/c

Illustration (1)

Calculate the amount to be transferred to Capital Redemption Reserve under each of the following cases.

(a) 9% 5,000 Preference Shares of Rs. 100 each to be redeemed at Par & if "Fresh Issue" of 20,000 Equity Shares of Rs. 10 each is to be made :

(i) at par

(ii) at 10% Discount

(iii) at 10 % Premium

(b) 9% 5,000 Preference Shares of Rs. 100 each to be redeemed at 5% Premium and if "Fresh Issue" of 20,000 equity shares of Rs. 10 each is to be made :

(i) at par

(ii) at 10% Discount

(iii) at 10 % Premium

Solution : 1

(a) Pref. Share Capital – Proceeds of Fresh Issue = CRR

(i) Rs. 5,00,000 – Rs. 2,00,000 = Rs. 3,00,000

(ii) Rs. 5,00,000 – Rs. 1,80,000 = Rs. 3,20,000

(iii) Rs. 5,00,000 – Rs. 2,00,000 = Rs. 3,00,000

(b) (i) Rs. 5,00,000 – Rs. 2,00,000 = Rs. 3,00,000

(ii) Rs. 5,00,000 – Rs. 1,80,000 = Rs. 3,20,000

(iii) Rs. 5,00,000 – Rs. 2,00,000 = Rs. 3,00,000

It is to be noted that for calculating CRR the "Premium on Redemption Account" and 'Securities Premium' are totally ignored.

Illustration : 2 Calculation of ' Fresh Issue'

From the following information calculate the fresh issue in each of the following cases.

(a) Free reserve Rs. 75,000, Securities Premium Rs 25,000 and. 9% Rs. 5,00,000 Preference shares are to be redeemed :

(i) at par

(ii) at 10 % Premium.

(b) Revenue reserves Rs. 1,25,000, Securities Premium Rs. 20,000 Dividend Equalisation Fund Rs. 1,25,000 and 9% Rs. 5,00,000 Preference Shares are to be redeemed.

(i) at par

(ii) at 10% Premium.

Solution : 2

(a) Fresh Issue = Nominal Value of Pref.. Shares – Free Reserves available

(i) Rs 4,25,000 = 5,00,000 – 75,000

(ii)

Premium on Redemption A/c	Rs. 50,000
Less Premium available	Rs. 25,000
To be adjusted against free reserves	Rs. 25,000
Hence, Free Reserves available	Rs. 75,000
Less Premium on Redemption A/c to be adjusted	Rs. 25,000
	50,000

Proceeds of Fresh Issue = Rs. 5,00,000 – 50,000
Rs. 4,50,000

(b) (i) Proceeds of
Fresh Issue = Rs. 5,00,000 – (1,25,000 + 1,25,000)
Rs. 2,50,000

(ii)

Premium on Redemption required :	Rs. 50,000
Less available (Sec. Premium)	Rs. 20,000
To be adjusted against free reserves	30,000

Free Reserves :

	Rs.
Revenue Reserves	Rs. 1,25,000
Dividend Equalisation Fund	Rs. 1,25,000
	2,50,000
Less Premium to be adjusted	Rs. 30,000
	2,20,000

Proceeds of Fresh Issue = Rs. 5,00,000 – 2,20,000 = Rs. 2,80,000

To calculate the number of equity shares to be issued for the purpose of redemption the " Proceeds from Fresh Issue" (as calculated above) may be divided by par value or discount value per share of the fresh issue, as the case may be.

Illustration : 3 (Redemption out of profits)

N Ltd. redeemed 5,000 9% Preference Shares of Rs. 100 each at a premium of 5%. On that date the following balances appeared on the liabilities side of Balance Sheet.

	Rs.
9 % 5,000 Preference Shares of Rs. 100 each Rs. 80 paid	4,00,000
70,000 Equity Shares of Rs. 10 each fully paid	7,00,000
General Reserve	3,75,000
Securities Premium	70,000
Profit & Loss Account	1,25,000
Capital Reserve	75,000

The Company had sufficient Cash & Bank balance to pay off Preference Share holders.

Show journal entries. Give the extracts (liabilities side) of the Balance Sheet after redemption.

Solution : 3

JOURNAL ENTRIES

			Rs.	Rs.
	Preference Share Final Call A/c	Dr.	1,00,000	
	To 9% Preference Share Capital			1,00,000
	(Being final call due on preference share Capital)			
	Bank A/c	Dr.	1,00,000	
	To Preference Share Final Call A/c			1,00,000
	(Being final call amount received)			
	9% Preference Share Capital A/c	Dr.	5,00,000	
	Premium on Redemption A/c	Dr.	25,000	
	To Preference Shareholders A /c			5,75,000
	(Being amount due on redemption)			

Contd.

		Rs.	Rs.
	Securities Premium A/c Dr.	25,000	
	To Premium on Redemption A/c		25,000
	(Being Premium on Redemption adjusted against Securities Premium)		
	General Reserve A/c Dr.	3,75,000	
	Profit & Loss A/c Dr.	1,25,000	
	To Capital Redemption Reserve A/c		5,00,000
	(Being CRR created as per the legal requirements)		
	9% Preference Share holders A/c Dr.	5,50,000	
	To Bank A/c		5,50,000
	(Being amount paid to Preference shareholders)		

BALANCE SHEET (EXTRACT LIABILITIES SIDE)

	Rs.
70,000 Equity Shares of Rs. 10 each fully paid	7,00,000
Securities Premium	45,000
Capital Redemption Reserve	5,00,000
Capital Reserve	75,000

Working notes :

(1) As per the legal provisions, only fully paid preference shares can be redeemed, hence the final call was made and amount due collected.

(2) Premium on Redemption has been met out of "Securities Premium Account".

(3) Capital Redemption Reserve is created to the extent of nominal value of preference shares because the same are redeemed out of profits.

Illustration (4) (Redemption out of proceeds of fresh issue)

Following balances are extracted from the books of Adu Ltd.

	Rs.
8% 2500 Preference Shares of Rs. 100 each fully paid	2,50,000
50,000 Equity Shares of Rs. 10 each fully paid	5,00,000
Securities Premium	7,500
Development Rebate Reserve	2,00,000
General Reserve	50,000
Profit & Loss Account	35,000

The Company decided to redeem preference shares at a premium of 10%. For this purpose a fresh issue of 25,000 equity shares of Rs. 10 each at 5% premium was made. The issue was fully subscribed and paid for in cash and 8% preference shares were redeemed.

Record journal entries and show the extracts of liabilities side of Balance Sheet after the redemption.

Solution : 4

JOURNAL ENTRIES

			Rs.	Rs.
1.	Bank A/c	Dr.	2,62,500	
	To Share Application & Allotment A/c			2,62,500
	(Being amount received on 25,000 Rs. 10.5 per share)			
2.	Share Application & Allotment A/c	Dr.	2,62,500	
	To Equity Share Capital A/c			2,50,000
	To Securities Premium A/c			12,500
	(Being amount transferred to Equity share Capital and Securities Premium A/c)			
3.	8 % Preference Share Capital A/c	Dr.	2,50,000	
	Premium on Redemption A/c	Dr.	25,000	
	To 8% Preference Shareholders A/c			2,75,000
	(Being amount due to Preference Shareholders)			
4.	8% Preference Share Capital A/c	Dr.	2,50,000	
	Premium on Redemption A/c	Dr.	25,000	
	To 8% Preference Shareholders A/c			2,75,000
	(Being amount paid to Pref. Shareholders)			
5.	Securities Premium A/c	Dr.	20,000	
	General Reserve A/c		5,000	
	To Premium on Redemption A/c			25,000
	(Being Premium on Redemption met out of securities Premium & General Reserve)			
6.	6% Preference Shareholders A/c	Dr.	2,75,000	
	To Bank A/c			2,75,000
	(Being amount paid to Pref. Shareholders)			

BALANCE SHEET (EXTRACT OF LIABILITIES SIDE)

	Rs.
75,000 Equity Shares of Rs. 10 each fully paid	7,50,000
Development Rebate Reserve	2,00,000
General Reserve	45,000
Profit & Loss A/c	35,000

Working notes :

(i) Rs. 20,000 from Securities Premium (Rs. 7500 + 12,500) and Rs. 5,000 from General Reserve have been utilised against Premium on Redemption A/c.

(ii) Since the redemption is made wholly out of proceeds of fresh issue, no CRR is created.

Illustration (5) (Redemption out of proceeds of fresh issue & Divisible profits both)

N.P. Ltd. had 7 % 4,000 preference shares of Rs. 100 each due for redemption on 31.3,2004. For this purpose the company made an issue of 30,000 Equity shares of Rs. 10 each at a premium of 15 %. The issue was immediately subscribed. The issue expenses amounted to Rs. 10,000. The company had Rs. 5,50,000 in General Reserve and Rs. 85,000 in profit & Loss A/c on that date. The redemption was carried out at 8% premium except the holders of 500 shares who could not be traced.

Record Journal entries. Use revenue reserve to the minimum possible extent.

Solution (5)

JOURNAL ENTRIES

			Rs.	Rs.
	Bank A/c	Dr.	3,45,000	
	To Equity Share Capital A/c			3,00,000
	To Securities Premium A/c			45,000
	(Being 30,000 equity shares issued)			
	Share Issue Expenses A/c	Dr.	10,000	
	To Bank A/c			10,000
	(Being issue expenses paid)			
	7% Preference Share Capital A/c	Dr.	4,00,000	
	Premium Redemption A/c	Dr.	32,000	
	To Preference Shareholders A/c			4,32,000
	(Being amount due on redemption)			
	Securities Premium A/c	Dr.	42,000	
	To Premium on Redemption A/c			32,000
	To Share Issue Expenses A/c			10,000
	(Being Premium on Redemption & share issue expenses W/o)			
	General Reserve A/c	Dr.	1,00,000	
	To Capital Redemption Reserve A/c			1,00,000
	(Being CRR created out of General Reserve)			
	Preference Shareholders A/c	Dr.	3,78,000	
	To Bank A/c			3,78,000
	(Being amount due on redemption paid to Preference Shareholders of 3500 shares)			

Illustration (6) (Sale of Investments & Issue of Bonus Shares)

Following is the Balance Sheet of SRK Ltd. as on 31st March, 2004.

Liabilities	Rs.
8% Redeemable Preference Shares of Rs 100 each fully paid	1,50,000
Equity Shares of Rs. 10 each fully paid	3,00,000
Securities Premium	1,45,000
General Reserve	2,00,000
Profit & Loss Account	1,25,000

	Rs.	Rs.
S. Creditors		95,000
		10,15,000
Assets	Rs.	
Gross Block	7,50,000	
Less Accumulated Depreciation	2,50,000	5,00,000
6 % Investment (face value 1,00,000)		1,05,000
Current Assets other than Bank Balance		3,00,000
Bank Balance		1,10,000
		10,15,000

On the above date the Company exercised its option to redeem the preference shares at a premium of 5%. To bridge the shortfall in cash resources, the investments were sold at a discount of 2.5 %. It was further resolved to issue 7 bonus shares for every 6 equity shares held on that date.

These transactions were effected in the books of the company. You are required o pass journal entries end prepare a Balance Sheet as on that date.

Solution (6)

JOURNAL ENTRIES

	Particulars		Rs.	Rs.
	8% Red. Pref. Share Capital A/c	Dr.	1,50,000	
	Premium on Redemption A/c	Dr.	7,500	
	To Preference Share holders A/c			1,57,500
	(Being amount due on redemption)			
	Bank A/c	Dr.	97,500	
	Profit & Loss A/c	Dr.	7,500	
	To Investments A/c			1,05,000
	(Being Investments sold)			
	Securities Premium A/c	Dr.	7,500	
	To Premium on Redemption A/c			7,500
	(Being Premium on Redemption adjusted)			
	General Reserve A/c	Dr.	1,50,000	
	To Capital Redemption Reserve A/c			1,50,000
	(Being amount transferred to CRR)			
	Preference Shareholders A/c	Dr.	1,57,500	
	To Bank A/c			1,57,500
	(Being amount paid to Pref. Shareholders)			
	Capital Redemption Reserve A/c	Dr.	1,50,000	
	General Reserve A/c	Dr.	50,000	
	Securities Premium A/c	Dr.	1,37,500	
	Profit & Loss A/c	Dr.	12,500	
	To Bonus to Equity Shareholders A/c*			3,50,000
	(Being 3,500 bonus shares issued)			

	Bonus to Equity Shareholders A/c Dr.		3,50,000	
	To Equity Share Capital A/c			3,50,000
	(Being bonus shares transferred to Eq. Share Capital A/c)			

BALANCE SHEET OF SRK LTD.
As on 31st March 2004 (post - Redemption)

Liabilities	Rs.	Assets		Rs.
65,000 Equity Shares of Rs. 10 each		Gross Block	7,50,000	
fully paid	6,50,000	*Less* Acc. Depreciation	2,50,000	5,00,000
		Current Assets (other than Bank		3,00,000
Profit & Loss A/c	1,05,000	Balance)		
S. Creditors	95,000	Bank Balance		50,000
	8,50,000			8,50,000

Working notes :

(1) Discount on sale of Investments is calculated on face value and not at the Cost of Investments which is shown in Balance Sheet.

(2) Bonus issue in the ratio of 7 : 6 has been met in the order* as per the provisions of Act.

1. MINIMUM FRESH ISSUE AND REDEMPTION AT PAR

As already discussed and illustrated earlier that the 'minimum fresh issue' is the difference between "Nominal value of preference shares to be redeemed" and the "divisible profits available for redemption". The amount so worked out is simply divided by the issue price (par value, or Discount value) to arrive at the number of equity shares to be issued for the purpose of redemption only when redemption is made at **Par**.

Example (1)

		Rs.
Nominal Value of Preference Shares to be redeemed		6,00,000
Divisible Profits or free reserve available for redemption		4,02,000
Amount of Fresh issue		1,98,000
(i) If issue is to be made at par (Shares of Rs. 10 each)	$= \text{Rs. } \frac{1,98,000}{10}$	19,800 shares
(ii) If issue is to be made at 10% at discount	$= \text{Rs. } \frac{1,98,000}{9}$	22,000 shares
(iii) If issue is to be made at 10% premium	$= \text{Rs. } \frac{1,98,000}{10}$	19,800 shares

II MINIMUM FRESH ISSUE AND REDEMPTION AT PREMIUM

When preference shares are to be redeemed at premium, the students should cheek the amount of securities premium "available for writing off the Premium on Redemption Account" There may be two situations.

(a) "Securities Premium" before the fresh issue is more than the amount required to write- off the " Premium on Redemption Account".

(b) "Securities Premium before the fresh issue is less than the amount required to write off the "Premium on Redemption Account or "Securities Premium" is not at all appearing in the Balance Sheet.

In the first case the fresh issue shall be worked out as discussed under I method as if shares are redeemed at par. Because the Premium on Redemption account shall be met out of "Securities Premium Account." and under second situation use of algebric equation is a must when minimum fresh issue is to be made.

When Preference shares are to be redeemed at premium and the fresh issue is to be made either at premium or at discount and the " Premium on Redemption Account is more than the amount of "Securities Premium (taken together with existing securities premium & premium from fresh issue) then the amount of fresh issue shall be worked out by the following equation :

Nominal Value of Preference Shares + Premium on Redemption = Divisible Profits or Free Reserve + Securities Premium (as per Balance Sheet + Fresh issue) – Discount on issue or + Premium on Fresh issue

Example (2)

	Rs.
Nominal Values of Preference Shares to be redeemed	5,00,000
Premium on Redemption (10%)	50,000
Free Reserves/Divisible Profits available	3,72,000
Securities Premium as per Balance Sheet	13,000

Find out amount of minimum fresh issue if the same is issued at 10% premium.

Let "fresh issue" be X

on applying the equation :

$$\text{Preference Share Capital} + \text{Premium on Redemption} = \text{Divisible Profit} + \text{Securities Premium} + x + \frac{10x}{100}$$

$$\text{Rs. } 5{,}00{,}000 + 50{,}000 = 3{,}72{,}000 + 13{,}000 + x + \frac{x}{10}$$

$$= 5{,}50{,}000 = 3{,}95{,}000 + \frac{11x}{10}$$

$$= 5{,}50{,}000 - 3{,}95{,}000 \neq \frac{11x}{10}$$

$$1{,}65{,}000 \times 10 = 11x$$

$$16{,}50{,}000 = 11x$$

$$1{,}50{,}000 = x$$

Hence fresh issue of Rs. 1,50,000 will be made on which Rs. 15,000 shall be on account of premium.

Verification :

	Rs.
Nominal value of Pref. Shares	5,00,000
Premium on Redemption at 10%	50,000

The Premium on Redemption shall be written off Rs. 28,000 (Rs. 13,000 + 15,000) out of Securities Premium Account and balance Rs. 22,000 out of divisible Profits. Thus leaving a balance of Rs. 3,50,000 for Capital Redemption Reserve (CRR).

Rs. 5,00,000 – 3,50,000 = Rs. 1,50,000 being the face value of fresh issue

Notes : The use of equation shall be made if the following conditions are satisfied :

(i) Redemption is to be made at Premium

(ii) Fresh issue is to be made either at Premium or at discount.

(iii) Premium on Redemption exceeds the amount available as "securities premium" (including both existing and from fresh issue)

(iv) Fresh issue is necessary because divisible profit are not sufficient to meet redemption amount

It should be noted that premium on fresh issue cannot be ascertained (in terms of actual amount) because the exact amount of fresh issue is not given. Since there is a shortfall between the Premium on Redemption and "Securities Premium" some part of divisible profits has to be used to write off Premium on Redemption Account. This makes again unclear as to how much amount shall be transferred to Capital Redemption Reserve. That's why the equation is used to find out exact amount of fresh issue to be made.

Illustration (7) (Use of equation)

Following is the Balance Sheet of H. A. R. Ltd. as on 31st March, 2004.

Liabilities	Rs.	Assets	Rs.
9% Preference Share Capital		Net Block	8,50,000
Shares of Rs. 50 each	3,00,000	Investment	87,500
Equity Share Capital		(Face Value Rs. 1,00,000)	
Shares of Rs. 10 each)	10,00,000	Current Assets	8,12,500
Securities Premium	5,000		
General Reserve	67,500		
Profit & Loss A/c	50,000		
Development Rebate Reserve	52,500		
Current Liabilities	2,75,000		
	17,50,000		17,50,000

Additional Information :

(i) Preference Shares are redeemed on 1.4.2004 at 10% premium

(ii) To provide cash for redemption, investments were sold at 75%

(iii) Minimum number of equity shares are issued at 10% premium for the purpose of redemption.

Pass Journal entries and prepare Balance Sheet just after redemption.

Solution (7)

	Rs.
Premium on Redemption Required	30,000
where as premium as per Balance Sheet	5,000
Premium required from fresh issue	25,000

Fresh Issue = Nominal Value of Pref. Shares – Divisible Profits available

Fresh Issue = 3,00,000 – (67,500 + 50,000 – 12,500*) = 1,95,000

* Loss on sale of Investments.

Hence on issue of Rs. 1,95,000 the premium on issue could be Rs. 19,500 and not Rs. 25,000 as required. Since Premium on redemption is more than the Securities Premium, the following equation will be used :

Pref. Share Capital + Premium on Redemption = Divisible Profit + Securities Premium + Nominal Amount of fresh issue + Premium on Fresh Issue

*Let nominal value of fresh issue be x

$$\text{Pref. Share Capital} + \text{Premium on Redemption} = \text{Divisible profit} + \text{Securities Premium} + x + \frac{10x}{100}$$

$$\text{Rs. } 3{,}00{,}000 + 30{,}000 = 1{,}05{,}000 + 5{,}000 + x + \frac{x}{10}$$

$$= \text{Rs. } 3{,}30{,}000 = 1{,}10{,}000 + \frac{11x}{10}$$

$$= \text{Rs } 3{,}30{,}000 - 1{,}10{,}000 \neq \frac{11x}{10}$$

$$= \text{Rs. } 2{,}20{,}000 \times 10 = 11x$$

$$\text{Rs } 22{,}00{,}000 = 11x$$

$$\text{Rs. } 2{,}00{,}000 = x$$

Hence 'Fresh issue' of the face Value of Rs. 2,00,000 will be made at 10% premium of Rs. 20,000

JOURNAL ENTRIES

				Rs.	Rs.
	9% Preference Share Capital A/c	Dr.		3,00,000	
	Premium on Redemption A/c	Dr.		30,000	
	To Preference Share holders A/c				3,30,000
	(Being amount due on redemption)				
	Bank A/c	Dr.		75,000	
	Profit & Loss A/c	Dr.		12,500	
	To Investments A/c				87,500
	(Being investments sold at a loss)				
	Bank A/c	Dr.		2,20,000	
	To Share Application A/c				2,20,000
	(Being application money received)				
	Share Application A/c	Dr.		2,20,000	
	To Equity Share Capital A/c				2,00,000
	To Securities Premium A/c				20,000
	(Being amount transferred to Equity Share Capital A/c and Securities Premium A/c)				

Contd.

			Rs.	Rs.
	Securities Premium A/c	Dr.	25,000	
	Profit & Loss A/c	Dr.	5,000	
	To Premium on Redemption A/c			30,000
	(Being Premium on Redemption written off)			
	General Reserve A/c	Dr.	67,500	
	Profit & Loss A/c	Dr.	32,500	
	To Capital Redemption Reserve A/c			1,00,000
	(Being amount transferred to CRR as per the provisions of the Act.)			
	Preference share holders A/c	Dr.	3,30,000	
	To Bank A/c			3,30,000
	(Being Preference Shareholders paid)			

BALANCE SHEET OF HAR LTD.
(after redemption)

Liabilities	Rs.	Assets	Rs.
Equity Share Capital	12,00,000	Net Block	8,50,000
Development Rebate Reserve	52,500	Current Assets	7,77,500
Capital Redemption Reserve	1,00,000		
Current Liabilities	2,75,000		
	16,27,500		16,27,500

CURRENT ASSETS A/C

	Rs.		Rs.
To Balance b/d	8,12,500	By Preference Shareholders A/c	3,30,000
To Investments A/c	75,000	By Balance c/d	7,77,500
To Share Application A/c	2,20,000		
	11,07,500		11,07,500

Illustration (8) (Arranging funds)

Following is the Balance Sheet of Grey Ltd. as on 31st December, 2005.

Liabilities	Rs.
7% Redeemable Preference Shares of Rs. 100 each	3,00,000
50,000 Equity Shares of Rs. 10 each	5,00,000
Securities Premium	50,000
Debenture Redemption Reserve	1,50,000
Revenue Reserve	2,10,000
6% Debentures	2,50,000
Current Liabilities	1,40,000
	16,00,000

Assets	Rs.	
Gross Block	10,00,000	
Less Depreciation	2,00,000	8,00,000
Investments		1,00,000
Cash & Bank balance		2,00,000
Other Current Assets		5,00,000
		16,00,000

Both the redeemable preference shares and debentures were due for redemption on 15th January 2006. The Directors took the following steps in this regard.

(i) Issued 20,000 Equity Shares of Rs. 10 each at a premium of 10%. These shares were fully subscribed and paid for.

(ii) Sold Investments at 10% loss..

(iii) Arranged overdraft to the extent necessary after keeping the minimum cash balance of Rs. 20,000

The redemption was duly carried out. Record journal entries and prepare Balance Sheet after redemption

B.Com. (D.U.) Adapted

Solution (8)

JOURNAL ENTRIES

			Rs.	Rs.
	7% Redeemable Pref. Share Capital A/c	Dr.	3,00,000	
	6% Debentures A/c	Dr.	2,50,000	
	To 7% Preference Shareholders A/c			3,00,000
	To 6% Debenture holders A/c			2,50,000
	(Being amount due on redemption)			
	Bank A/c	Dr.	90,000	
	Revenue Reserve (Loss on sale) A/c	Dr.	10,000	
	To Investments A/c			1,00,000
	(Being investments sold at loss)			
	Bank A/c	Dr.	2,20,000	
	To Share Application A/c			2,20,000
	(Being shares issued at premium)			
	Share Application A/c	Dr.	2,20,000	
	To Share Capital A/c			2,00,000
	To Securities Premium A/c			20,000
	(Being share application money transferred)			
	Revenue Reserves A/c	Dr.	1,00,000	
	To Capital Redemption Reserve A/c			1,00,000
	(Being capital Redemption Researve created)			

Contd.

		Rs.	Rs.
Revenue Reserves A/c	Dr.	1,00,000	
To Debenture Redemption Reserve A/c			1,00,000
(Being revenue reserves transferred to Debenture Redemption Reserve)			
Debenture Redemption Reserves A/c	Dr.	2,50,000	
To General Reserve A/c			2,50,000
(Being DRR closed by transferring the same to General Reserve)			
Bank A/c	Dr.	1,50,000	
To Bank Overdraft A/c			1,50,000
(Being overdraft arranged)			
7% Preference Share holders A/c	Dr.	3,00,000	
6% Debenture holders A/c	Dr.	2,50,000	
To Bank A/c			5,50,000
(Being payment made)			

BALANCE SHEET OF GREY LTD.
As on 1st April, 2004

Liabilities	Rs.	Assets		Rs.
70,000 Equity Shares of Rs. 10 each fully paid	7,00,000	Gross Block	10,00,000	
		Less Depreciation	2,00,000	8,00,000
Securities Premium	70,000	Current Assets other than Cash at Bank		5,00,000
Capital Redemption Reserve	1,00,000			
General Reserve	2,50,000	Cash and Bank Balance		20,000
Bank overdraft	60,000			
Current liabilities	1,40,000			
	13,20,000			13,20,000

Working notes :

(1) Loss on sale of investments has been charged to Revenue Reserves.

(2) As per SEBI's guidelines, the debentures can be redeemed only when an amount equal to 50% of nominal value of debentures to be redeemed, is transferred to Debenture Redemption Reserve. Since the amount stood at more than 50% of the nominal value of debentures, the same have been redeemed. Further, DRR no more required has been transferred to General Reserve which can be used for issuing fully paid bonus shares.

Illustration (9) (Partly paid Shares and Redemption)

Following is the Balance Sheet of S. Ltd. as on 31st March, 2006.

Liabilities		Rs.
6% 15,000 Preference Shares of Rs. 10 each Rs. 8 paid		1,20,000
25,000 Equity Shares of Rs. 10 each fully paid		2,50,000
Securities Premium		4,000
General Reserve		75,000
Investment Allowance Reserve		10,000
Profit & Loss Account		15,000
S. Creditors		1,26,000
		6,00,000
Assets		
Gross Block	5,75,000	
Less Acc. Depreciation	1,75,000	4,00,000
Current Assets (including Rs. 30,000 Cash at Bank)		2,00,000
		6,00,000

Additional Information

Preference shares are to be redeemed at a premium of 10%. A final call of Rs. 2 per share was made. 50 holders holding 3500 shares failed to pay the call money. Directors went on redemption utilising the un-distributed profits and reserves. New equity shares of Rs. 10 each were issued to the public to the extent necessary to comply with the requirements of law. At the time of redemption 5 holders holding 1600 shares were not traceable.

The Directors decided to maintain a minimum Cash & Bank balance of Rs. 75,000 and a balance of General Reserve Rs. 25,000. Out of Investment Allowance Reserve Rs. 6,000 was not free for distribution as dividend. A bank loan necessary for redemption was arranged. Record journal entries & prepare necessary ledger accounts and a Balance Sheet.

ICWA (1) Adapted.

Solution (9)

JOURNAL ENTRIES

			Rs.	Rs.
	Preference Share Final Call A/c	Dr.	30,000	
	To Preference Share Capital A/c			30,000
	(Being Final Call made)			
	Calls in Arrears A/c	Dr.	7,000	
	Bank A/c	Dr.	23,000	
	To Pref. Share Final Call A/c			30,000
	(Being final Call on 11,500 Shares received)			
	6% Preference Share Capital A/c	Dr.	1,15,000	
	Premium on Redemption A/c	Dr.	11,500	
	To Pref. Shares holders A/c			1,26,500
	(Being amount due on redemption)			

		Rs.	Rs.
Bank A/c	Dr.	53,500	
To Equity Share Application A/c			53,500
(Being 5350 shares issued)			
Equity Share Application A/c	Dr.	53,500	
To Equity Share Capital A/c			53,500
(Being application money transferred to Share Capital A/c)			
Securities Premium A/c	Dr.	4,000	
P & L A/c	Dr.	7,500	
To Premium on Redemption A/c			11,500
(Being Premium on Redemption adjusted)			
General Reserve A/c	Dr.	50,000	
Profit & Loss A/c	Dr.	7,500	
Investment Allowance Reserve A/c	Dr.	4,000	
To Capital Redemption Reserve A/c			61,500
(Being amount transferred to CRR)			
Bank A/c	Dr.	77,400	
To Bank Loan A/c			77,400
(Being Bank Loan arranged)			
Preference Shareholders A/c	Dr.	1,08,900	
To Bank A/c			1,08,900
(Being amount paid to Preference Shareholders)			

6% PREFERENCE SHARE CAPITAL A/C

	Rs.		Rs.
To Preference Share holders A/c	1,15,000	By Balance b/d	1,20,000
To Calls-in-Arrears A/c	7,000	By Share Final Call A/c	30,000
To Balance c/d	28,000		
	1,50,000		1,50,000

PREFERENCE SHARE HOLDERS A/C

	Rs.		Rs.
To Bank A/c	1,08,900	By Pref. Share Capital A/c	1,15,000
To Balance c/d	17,600	By Premium on Redemption A/c	11,500
	1,26,500		1,26,500

CASH & BANK A/C

	Rs.		Rs.
To Balance b/d	30,000	By Pref. Shareholders A/c	1,08,900
To Share Final Call A/c	23,000	By Balance c/d	75,000
To Equity Share Application A/c	53,500	(minimum required)	
To Bank Loan A/c (Balancing figure)	77,400		
	1,83,900		1,83,900

BALANCE SHEET AS ON 1.4.2004
(after redemption)

		Rs.			Rs.
30350 Equity Shares of Rs. 10 each fully paid		3,03,500	Gross Block	5,75,000	
			Acc. Depreciation	1,75,000	4,00,000
			Current Assets other than Cash and Bank		1,70,000
6% Pref. Share Capital 3500 Shares of Rs. 10 each	35,000		Cash & Bank		75,000
Less Calls in Arrears	7,000	28,000			
General Reserve		25,000			
Capital Redemption Reserve		61,500			
Investment Allowance Reserve		6,000			
Preference Shareholders		17,600			
Bank Loan		77,400			
S. Creditors		1,26,000			
		6,45,000			6,45,000

Working notes :

(1) Only fully paid shares are redeemed Shares on which final call has not been paid are shown in the Balance Sheet at their paid up value. Amount due to Preference shareholders, who could not be traced, has been shown as a liability.

(2) Investment Allowance Reserve has been utilised to the extent it was available for distribution by way of dividend.

(3) Fress issue has been worked out as under :

Free Reserves :

	Rs.
General Reserve (75,000 – 25,000)	50,000
Profit & Loss A/c (15,000 – 7,500)	7,500
Investment Allowance Reserve (to the extent available)	4,000
Transferred to CRR	61,500

		Rs.
	Pref. Share Capital (Fully Paid)	
	11,500 Shares (15,000 Shares – 3500 Shares on which call money not received)	1,15,000
Less	Free Reserves (as above)	61,500
	Fresh issue to be made	53,500

(4) Premium on Redemption has been adjusted as follows :

	Premium on Redemption Required	11,500
Less	Securities Premium	4,000
	Adjusted against P & L A/c	7500

Illustration (10) (Forfeiture & Redemption)

Following is the Balance Sheet of P Ltd. as on 31st March, 2006.

Liabilities			Rs.
	8% 6000 Preference Shares of Rs. 100 each6,00,000		
Less	Calls in Arrears Rs. 20 per Share	10,000	5,90,000
	50,000 Equity Shares of Rs. 10 each fully paid		5,00,000
	Securities Premium		30,000
	General Reserve		3,70,000
	Current Liabilities		1,60,000
			16,50,000
Assets			
	Gross Block	13,50,000	
Less	Acumulated Depreciation	3,00,000	10,50,000
	Current Assets (except Cash and Bank Balance)		3,50,000
	Cash & Bank Balance		2,50,000
			16,50,000

The 8% Preference Shares were issued at 10% discount which was written off in first three years. The reminders were sent to those preference shareholders who had to pay the arrears of their final call. On failure to comply with the final reminder, these preference shares were forfeited and cancelled. Remaining preference shares were redeemed at 5% premium. For the purpose of redemption it was decided to issue minimum number of equity shares of Rs. 10 each at a discount of 10%. The issue was fully subscribed and preference shares were redeemed after arranging for a overdraft. Pass journal entries to record the above transactions and give a Balance Sheet.

Solution (10)

JOURNAL ENTRIES

			Rs.	Rs.
	8% Preference Share Capital A/c	Dr.	50,000	
	To Share Discount A/c			5,000
	To Share forfeited A/c			35,000
	To Calls-in-Arrears A/c			10,000
	(Being Preference Shares forfeited for non-payment of arrears)			

Particulars		Rs.	Rs.
Share forfeited A/c	Dr.	35,000	
To Capital Reserve A/c			35,000
(Being forfeited amount transferred to Capital Reserve)			
8% Preference Share Capital A/c	Dr.	5,50,000	
Premium on Redemption A/c	Dr.	27,500	
To Preference Share holders A/c			5,77,500
(Being amount due on redemption)			
Bank A/c	Dr.	1,80,000	
To Share Application A/c			1,80,000
(Being application money on 20,000 shares received)			
Share Application A/c	Dr.	1,80,000	
Share Discount A/c	Dr.	20,000	
To Equity Share Capital A/c			2,00,000
(Being application money transferred to Share Discount A/c)			
Securities Premium A/c	Dr.	27,500	
To Premium on Redemption A/c			27,500
(Being Premium on Redemption written off)			
General Reserve A/c	Dr.	3,70,000	
To Capital Redemption Reserve A/c			3,70,000
(Being amount transferred to CRR)			
Bank A/c	Dr.	1,45,500	
To Bank Overdraft A/c			1,45,500
(Being overdraft arranged)			
Preference Share holders A/c	Dr.	5,77,500	
To Bank A/c			5,77,500
(Being amount paid to Preference Shareholders on redemption)			
Capital Reserve A/c	Dr.	15,000	
To Share Discount A/c			15,000
(Being Share Discount written off against Capital Reserve)			

BALANCE SHEET OF P LTD. AS ON 1.4.2006
(after Redemption)

Liabilities	Rs.
70,000 Equity Shares of Rs. 10 each	7,00,000
Securities Premium (Rs. 30,000 – 27,500)	2,500
Capital Reserve (35,000 – 15,000)	20,000
Capital Redemption Reserve	3,70,000
Current Liabilities	1,60,000
Bank Overdraft	1,47,500
	14,00,000

Assets

		Rs.
Gross Block	13,50,000	
Acc. Depreciation	3,00,000	10,50,000
Current Assets		3,50,000
		14,00,000

Working notes :

(1) Share discount on shares forfeited has been adjusted against discount on fresh issue which has been written off against Capital Reserve.

(2) Fresh issue has been worked out as follows :

Nominal value of preference shares redeemed	5,50,000
Less General Reserve	3,70,000
Fresh Issue	1,80,000

No. of shares issued 20,000 i.e. Rs. 1,80,000 / 9

Illustration (11) (Forfeiture, Reissue and Redemption)

Following is the Balance Sheet of Z Ltd. as on 31st March, 2006.

Liabilities

			Rs.
	55,000 Equity Shares of Rs. 10 each fully paid		5,50,000
	7% 2000 Preference Shares of Rs. 100 each	2,00,000	
Less	Calls in Arrears @ Rs. 20 per share	2,000	1,98,000
	Securities Premium		40,000
	General Reserve		1,40,000
	Profit & Loss Account		1,20,000
	S Creditors		1,52,000
			12,00,000

Assets

	Gross Block	9,75,000	
Less	Accumulated Depreciation	3,75,000	6,00,000
	Bank Balance		1,80,000
	Other Current Asserts		4,20,000
			12,00,000

On the above date the preference shares were due for redemption. The Directors redeemed the preference shares on the following basis :

(i) 9000 Equity shares of Rs. 10 each were issued at a premium of 10% Share issue expenses amounted to Rs. 8000.

(ii) Final reminder was sent to the holders of preference shares who have not paid final call money. Of these, holders of 80 shares paid their arrears On failure to pay final call money the remaining shares were forfeited. Subsequently these were reissued for Rs. 1000 as fully paid up.

(iii) Preference shares were redeemed at a premium of 10% and "securities premium" was utilised in full for this purpose.

Pass Journal Entries and prepare Balance Sheet after redemption.

Solution (11)

JOURNAL ENTRIES

	Particulars		Rs.	Rs.
	Bank A/c	Dr.	99,000	
	To Share Application A/c			99,000
	(Being application money received)			
	Share Application A/c	Dr.	99,000	
	To Equity Share Capital A/c			90,000
	To Securities Premium A/c			9,000
	(Being application amount transferred)			
	Shares Issue Expenses A/c	Dr.	8000	
	To Bank A/c			8,000
	(Being expenses on share issue paid)			
	Bank A/c	Dr.	1600	
	To Calls in Arrears A/c			1600
	(Being arrears received on 80 shares)			
	7% Preference Share Capital A/c	Dr.	2000	
	To Share forfeited A/c			1600
	To Calls-in-Arrears A/c			400
	(Being 20 shares forfeited)			
	Bank A/c	Dr.	1,000	
	Shares forfeited A/c	Dr.	1,000	
	To $7^1/_2$% Red. Pref. Share Capital A/c			2,000
	(Being forfeited shares reissued)			
	Shares forfeited A/c	Dr.	600	
	To Capital Reserve A/c			600
	(Being Profit on reissue transferred to Capital Reserve)			
	$7^1/_2$ Red. Preference Share Capital A/c	Dr.	2,00,000	
	Premium on Redemption A/c	Dr.	20,000	
	To Pref. Share holders A/c			2,20,000
	(Being amount due on Redemption)			
	Securities Premium A/c	Dr.	28,000	
	To Premium on Redemption A/c			20,000
	To Share Issue Expenses A/c			8,000
	(Being Premium on Redemption and Share Issue expenses written off)			

Contd.

			Rs.	Rs.
	General Reserve A/c To Capital Redemption Reserve A/c (Being amount transferred to CRR)	Dr.	1,10,000	1,10,000
	Preference Share holders A/c To Bank A/c (Being amount paid to Preference Shareholders)	Dr.	2,20,000	2,20,000

BALANCE SHEET OF Z LTD.
As on 1st April, 2006

Liabilities			Rs.
	64,000 Equity Shares of Rs. 10 each		6,40,000
	Securities premium (Rs. 49,000 – 20,000 – 8,000)		21,000
	General Reserve		30,000
	Profit & Loss Account		1,20,000
	Capital Redemption Reserve		1,10,000
	Capital Reserve		600
	S. Creditors		1,52,000
			10,73,600
Assets			
	Gross Block	9,75,000	
Less	Acc. Depreciation	3,75,000	6,00,000
	Bank Balance		53,600
	Other Current Assets		4,20,000
			10,73,600

Illustration (12) (Redemption & Rights and Bonus Issue)

Following is the Balance Sheet A B C Ltd. as on 31st March, 2006.

Liabilities			
	11% Cumulative Redeemable Preference Shares of Rs. 100 each fully paid		2,50,000
	Equity Shares of Rs. 10 each fully paid		5,00,000
	Securities Premium		20,000
	General Reserve		1,00,000
	Profit & Loss Account		1,25,000
	Current liabilities		1,05,000
			11,00,000
Assets			
	Gross Block	9,00,000	
Less	Acc. Depreciation	2,70,000	6,30,000
	Investments		1,80,000
	Current Assets		2,90,000
			11,00,000

The Directors decided to redeem preference shares at 10% premium on 1st April 2004. For this purpose certain investments whose book value and market value was Rs. 1,00,000 and Rs. 1,25,000 respectively were sold. It was also resolved to utilise free reserves to the minimum extent and issue rights equity shares at a premium of 20% in 1 : 4 ratio to finance redemption.

After redemption , the Board made a bonus issue in 2:5 ratio. The holders of 25 preference shares could not be traced. The redemption was duly carried out.

Record journal Entries and prepare Balance sheet.

Solution (12)

JOURNAL ENTRIES

			Rs.	Rs.
	11% Cum. Red. Pref. Share Capital A/c Dr.		2,50,000	
	Premium on Redemption A/c Dr.		25,000	
	To Preference Share holders A/c			2,75,000
	(Being Preference Shares become due for redemption)			
	Bank A/c Dr.		1,25,000	
	To Investments A/c			1,00,000
	To Profit & Loss A/c			25,000
	(Being Investments sold at profit)			
	Bank A/c Dr.		1,50,000	
	To Equity Share Capital A/c			1,25,000
	To Securities Premium A/c			25,000
	(Being rights issue made in 1.4 ratio)			
	Securities Premium A/c Dr.		25,000	
	To Premium on Redemption A/c			25,000
	(Being Premium on Redemption written off)			
	General Reserve A/c Dr.		1,00,000	
	Profit & Loss A/c Dr.		25,000	
	To Capital Redemption Reserve A/c			1,25,000
	(Being required amount transferred to Capital Red. Reserve)			
	Preference Share holders A/c Dr.		2,72,250	
	To Bank A/c			2,72,250
	(Being amount paid to Pref. Shareholders except those untraced)			
	Capital Redemption Reserve A/c Dr.		1,25,000	
	Profit & Loss A/c Dr.		1,25,000	
	To Bonus to Equity Shareholders A/c			2,50,000
	(Being bonus issue of 2 : 5 made)			
	Bonus to Equity Shareholders A/c Dr.		2,50,000	
	To Equity Share Capital A/c			2,50,000
	(Being Bonus Shares transferred to share Capital A/c)			

BALANCE SHEET OF A B C LTD.
As on 1.4.2006 (after redemption)

Liabilities			Rs.
	87,500 Equity Shares of Rs. 10 each fully paid		8,75,000
	Securities Premium		20,000
	Preference Share holders		2,750
	Current liabilities		1,05,000
			10,02,750
Assets			
	Gross Block	9,00,000	
Less	Acc. Depreciation	2,70,000	6,30,000
	Investments		80,000
	Current Assets		2,90,000
	Cash Bank Balance		2,750
			10,02,750

Working notes :

(1) Rights issue (1 : 4) $= \frac{5,00,000}{10} \times \frac{1}{4} = 12,500$ Shares of Rs. 10 each at 20% Premium

(2) Bonus issue (2 : 5)

Opening Capital	50,000 Shares
Add Rights Issue	12,500 Shares
Total	62,500 Shares

Bonus issue $= 62,500 \times \frac{2}{5} = 25,000$ Shares .

(3) **EQUITY SHARE CAPITAL A/C**

	Rs.		Rs.
To Balance c/d	8,75,000	By Balance b/d	5,00,000
		By Bank A/c (Rights Issue)	1,25,000
		By Bonus to S/H A/c	2,50,000
	8,75,000		8,75,000

(4) **CASH AND BANK A/C**

	Rs.		Rs.
To Balance b/d	—	By Pref. Share holders A/c	2,72,250
To Investments A/c	1,25,000	By Balance c/d	2,750
To Equity Share Capital A/c (Ri)	1,25,000		
To Securities Premium A/c	25,000		
	2,75,000		2,75,000

Illustration (13) (Sale of Fixed Assets and Investments and the Bonus Issue)

Following is the Balance Sheet of Nadia Ltd. as on 31st March, 2006

Liabilities		Rs.
9% 7500 Preference Shares of Rs. 100 each	7,50,000	
7500 Equity Shares of Rs. 10 each Rs. 8 paid		6,00,000
Securities Premium		1,47,000
General Reserve		1,35,000
Profit & Loss Account		1,68,000
Current liabilities		2,50,000
		20,50,000
Assets		
Gross Block	12,00,000	
Less Acc. Depreciation	3,00,000	9,00,000
Investments		3,00,000
Bank & Cash Balance		4,50,000
Other Current Assets		4,00,000
		20,50,000

The Board resolved :

(i) To convert partly paid equity shares into fully paid up without requiring the share holders to pay for the same.

(ii) To redeem the preference shares at a premium of 7.5% and for this purpose to issue 4500 10% preference shares at a premium of 10% payable full on application.

(iii) To sell fixed assets (Book value Rs. 4,50,000) for Rs. 5,73,750 and all investments for Rs. 3,90,000.

These resolutions were carried into effect and materialised.

All payments were made on redemption except to the holders of 300 shares whose whereabouts could not be known.

On 30th April, 2006 the Directors issued fully paid bonus shares at the rate of three for every five shares held at a premium of 5%.

Pass journal entries and prepare Balance Sheet.

[ICWA (i) Adapted]

Solution (13)

JOURNAL ENTRIES

			Rs.	Rs.
	Share Final Call A/c	Dr.	1,50,000	
	To Equity Share Capital A/c			1,50,000
	(Being final call made)			
	General Reserve A/c	Dr.	1,35,000	
	Profit & Loss A/c	Dr.	15,000	
	To Share Final Call A/c			1,50,000
	(Being General Reserve and Profit & Loss Account adjusted against final call)			

Contd.

		Rs.	Rs.
Bank A/c	Dr.	9,63,750	
To Fixed Assets A/c			4,50,000
To Investments A/c			3,00,000
To Profit & Loss A/c			2,13,750
(Being fixed assets and Investments sold at profit)			
Bank A/c	Dr.	4,95,000	
To Pref. Share Application A/c			4,95,000
(Being Pref. share application money received)			
Pref. Share Application A/c	Dr.	4,95,000	
To 10% Preference Share Capital A/c			4,50,000
To Securities Premium A/c			45,000
(Being application money transferred to Pref. Share Capital A/c and Securities Premium A/c)			
9% Preference Share Capital A/c	Dr.	7,50,000	
Premium on Redemption A/c	Dr.	56,250	
To Preference Share holders A/c			8,06,250
(Being Preference shares become due for redemption)			
Securities Premium A/c	Dr.	56,250	
To Premium on Redemption A/c			56,250
(Being Premium on redemption adjusted)			
Profit & Loss A/c	Dr.	3,00,000	
To Capital Redemption Reserve A/c			3,00,000
(Being CRR created)			
Preference Share holders A/c		7,74,000	
To Bank A/c			7,74,000
(Being amount due on redemption paid except to the holders of 500 shares)			
Capital Redemption Reserve A/c	Dr.	3,00,000	
Securities premium A/c	Dr.	1,35,750	
Profit & Loss A/c	Dr.	36,750	
To Bonus to Equity Shareholders A/c			4,72,500
(Being bonus issue declared)			
Bonus to Equity Share holders A/c	Dr.	4,72,500	
To Equity Share Capital A/c			4,50,000
To Securities Premium A/c			22,500
(Being bonus shares issued at 5% premium)			

BALANCE SHEET OF NADIA LTD.
As on 30th April, 2006

Liabilities			Rs.
	10% Preference Share Capital (4500 shares of Rs. 100 each)		4,50,000
	Equity Share Capital (1,20,000 Shares of Rs. 10 each)		12,00,000
	Securities Premium		22,500
	Profit & Loss Account		30,000
	Preference Share holders		32,250
	Current Liabilities		2,50,000
			19,84,750
Assets			
	Gross Block	6,00,000	
Less	Acc. Depreciation	1,50,000	4,50,000
	Bank Balance		11,34,750
	Other Current Assets		4,00,000
			19,84,750

Working notes :

(1) **PROFIT & LOSS A/C**

	Rs.		Rs.
To Share Final Call A/c	15,000	By Balance b/d	1,68,000
To Capital Redemption Reserve A/c	3,00,000	By Profit on Sale of Fixed Assets	
To Bonus to Share holders A/c	36,750	and Investments	2,13,750
To Balance c/d	30,000		
	3,81,750		3,81,750

(2) **GENERAL RESERVE A/C**

	Rs.		Rs.
To Share Final Call A/c	1,35,000	By Balance b/d	1,35,000
	1,35,000		1,35,000

(3) **SECURITIES PREMIUM A/C**

	Rs.		Rs.
To Premium on Redemption A/c	56,250	By Balance b/d	1,47,000
To Bonus to Shareholders A/c	1,35,750	By Preference Share App. A/c	45,000
To Balance c/d	22,500	By Bonus to Shareholders A/c	22,500
	2,14,500		2,14,500

(4) CRR = Nominal value of Preference Shares redeemed – Proceeds of Fresh Issue
CRR = Rs. 7,50,000 – Rs. 4,50,000 = 3,00,000

(5) Profit on sale of fixed assets may be transferred to Capital Reserve Account instead of Profit & Loss Account. However, such transfer will not affect the amount of CRR on Bonus Issue as these profits are realised in cash.

Illustration (14) (Fully Paid, partly paid Preference Shares and Fresh Issue at discount)

Jalan India Ltd. decided to redeem all their preference shares as on 31st March, 2006 on which date their position was as under :

Liabilities		Rs.
8% 2,500 Redeemable Preference Shares of Rs. 100 each fully paid		2,50,000
9% 5,000 Red. Preference Shares of Rs. 50 each Rs. 25 paid		1,25,000
50,000 Equity Shares of Rs. 10 each fully paid		5,00,000
Reserve & Surplus		
Securities Premium		12,500
Capital Redemption Reserve		1,12,500
Dividend Equalisation Fund		1,34,500
Current liabilities		1,15,500
		12,50,000
Assets		
Gross Block	7,70,000	
Less Acc. Depreciation	2,30,000	5,40,000
Cash & Bank Balance		1,75,000
Other Current Assets		5,35,000
		12,50,000

Additional Information :

(a) Capital Redemption Reserve is the result of redemption made in the year 1999.

(b) The preference shares are to be redeemed at a premium of 5 %

(c) To enable redemption, the Directors, decided to issue sufficient number of equity shares at a discount of 10%

Pass journal entries to give effect to these transactions

Solution (14)

JOURNAL ENTRIES

			Rs.	Rs.
	9% Pref. Share Final Call A/c	Dr.	1,25,000	
	To 9% Pref. Share Capital A/c			1,25,000
	(Being final call due)			
	Bank A/c	Dr.	1,25,000	
	To 9% Pref. Share Final Call A/c			1,25,000
	(Being call amount received)			*Contd.*

		Rs.	Rs.
8% Red. Preference Share Capital A/c	Dr.	2,50,000	
9% Red. Preference Share Capital A/c	Dr.	2,50,000	
Premium on Redemption A/c	Dr.	25,000	
To 8% Red. Pref. Share holders A/c			2,62,500
To 9% Red. Pref. Share holders A/c			2,62,500
(Being amount due on redemption)			
Bank A/c	Dr.	3,78,000	
To Share Application A/c			3,78,000
(Being application money received on fresh issue of 42,000 shares)			
Share Application A/c	Dr.	3,78,000	
Share Discount A/c	Dr.	42,000	
To Equity Share Capital A/c			4,20,000
(Being amount transferred to Share Capital & Share Discount A/c)			
Securities Premium A/c	Dr.	12,500	
Dividend Equalisation Fund A/c	Dr.	12,500	
To Premium on Redemption A/c			25,000
(Being premium on redemption written off)			
Dividend Equalisation Fund A/c	Dr.	1,22,000	
To Capital Redemption Reserve A/c			1,22,000
(Being required amount transferred to CRR)			
8% Red. Preference Share holders A/c	Dr.	2,62,500	
9% Red. Preference Share holders A/c	Dr.	2,62,500	
To Bank A/c			5,25,000
(Being amount due on redemption paid to Pref. Share holders)			

Balance Sheet of Jalan India Ltd. As on 1st April, 2006

			Rs.
Liabilities			
	92,000 Equity Shares of Rs. 10 each fully paid		9,20,000
Reserve & Surplus			
	Capital Redemption Reserve		2,34,500
	Current liabilities		1,15,500
			12,70,000
Assets			
	Gross Block	7,70,000	
Less	Acc. Depreciation	2,30,000	5,40,000
	Cash and Bank Balance		1,53,000
	Other Current Assets		5,35,000
	Discount on Issue of Shares		42,000
			12,70,000

CASH & BANK A/C

	Rs.		Rs.
To Balance b/d	1,75,000	By 8% Pref. Share holders	2,62,500
To 9% Pref. Share Final call	1,25,000	By 9% Pref. Share holders	2,62,500
To Share Application	3,78,000	By Balance c/d	1,53,000
	6,78,000		6,78,000

Working notes :

(1) Fresh issue has been worked out as follows. Let fresh issue be 'X'

$$\text{Preference Share Capital} + \text{Premium on Redemption} = \text{Divisible profits} + \text{Securities Premium} + x - \frac{10x}{100}$$

$$\text{Rs. } 5{,}00{,}000 + 25{,}000 = 1{,}34{,}500 + 12{,}500 + x - \frac{10x}{100}$$

$$\text{Rs. } 5{,}25{,}000 = 1{,}47{,}000 + x - \frac{x}{10}$$

$$\text{Rs. } 5{,}25{,}000 - 1{,}47{,}000 = \frac{9x}{10}$$

$$\text{Rs. } 3{,}78{,}000 \times 10 = 9x$$

$$\text{Rs. } 4{,}20{,}000 = x$$

Illustration (15) (Ascertaining divisible Profit and Redemption)

Zoya Ltd. had issued 5,000 9% Redeemable Preference Shares of Rs. 100 each. Now these are due for redemption as on 1st April, 2006 at a premium of 5%. The Balance Sheet of Zoya Ltd. as on 31st March, 2005 was as follows :

Liabilities	Rs.
Red. Preference Shares of Rs. 100 each	5,00,000
50,000 Equity shares of Rs. 10 each	5,00,000
Securities Premium	10,000
General Reserve	3,50,000
Profit & Loss Account	50,000
	14,10,000
Assets	
Building	4,00,000
Plant & Machinery	5,00,000
Furniture	1,00,000
Debtors	1,50,000
Stock	2,00,000
Bank Balance	60,000
	14,10,000

On 1.4.2006 the assets and liabilities were as under :

	Rs.	
Building	4,00,000	(Depreciation @ 2.5% p.a.)
Plant & Machinery	5,00,000	(Depreciation @ 10% p.a.)
Furniture	1,00,000	(Depreciation @ 10% p.a.)
Investments	50,000	
Debtors	2,60,000	(Provision @ 5%)
Stock	3,00,000	
Bank Balance	40,000	
S. Creditors	65,000	

Market value of Building is Rs. 5,25,000 and that of Investments Rs. 75,000.

You are required to record journal entries for redemption of preference shares on 1st April, 2006. No fresh issue of shares is made for redemption of preference shares. Also prepare Balance Sheet.

Solution (15)

Since fresh issue is not to be made, the total divisible profit have to be ascertained.

Total amount of profit and premium required (Rs. 5,00,000 + 25,000) =	5,25,000
Less Available (Rs. 10,000 + 3,50,000 + 50,000) =	4,10,000
Short fall as on 1.4.2005	1,15,000

Profit earned during the year can be ascertained as follows :

Increase in Current Assets + Decrease in Current liabilities – Increase in Current liabilities – decrease in Current assets – Depreciation on fixed assets – Provisions for doubtful debts.

Increase in Investment		50,000
Increase in Debtors		1,10,000
Increase in Stock		1,00,000
		2,60,000
Less Decrease in Bank Balance	20,000	
Increase in Creditors	65,000	
Provision for Doubtful debt.	13,000	
Depreciation on Building	10,000	
Depreciation on P/M	50,000	
Depreciation on Furniture	10,000	1,68,000
Profit for the current year		92,000
Add Profit on sale of Investment		25,000
Current years' profits available		1,17,000

JOURNAL ENTRIES

		Rs.	Rs.
9% Red. Preference Share Capital A/c	Dr.	5,00,000	
Premium on Redemption A/c	Dr.	25,000	
To Preference Share holders A/c			5,25,000
(Being amount due on redemption)			
Securities Premium A/c	Dr.	10,000	
General Reserve A/c	Dr.	15,000	
To Premium on Redemption A/c			25,000
(Being Premium on redemption written off)			
Bank A/c	Dr.	75,000	
To Investments A/c			50,000
To Profit & Loss A/c			25,000
(Being Investments sold)			
General Reserve A/c	Dr.	3,35,000	
Profit & Loss A/c	Dr.	1,65,000	
To Capital Redemption Reserve A/c			5,00,000
(Being amount transferred to CRR)			
Bank A/c	Dr.	4,10,000	
To Bank Loan A/c			4,10,000
(Being Bank Loan arranged to pay off Preference Share holders)			
Preference Share holders A/c	Dr.	5,25,000	
To Bank A/c			5,25,000
(Being amount paid to Preference Shareholder)			

Working Notes :

CASH & BANK A/C

	Rs.		Rs.
To Balance b/d	40,000	By Preference Shareholders A/c	5,25,000
To Investment	75,000		
To Bank Loan (Bal. figure)	4,10,000		
	5,25,000		5,25,000

(2) The Company had the option to sell Building to arrange the necessary funds for redemption purposes. However, in the absence of any clear instruction, the bank-loan has been arranged.

BALANCE SHEET OF ZOYA LTD.
As on 1st April, 2006

Liabilities		Rs.
50,000 Equity Shares of Rs. 10 each		5,00,000
Capital Redemption Reserve		5,00,000
Profit & Loss Account		2,000
Bank Loan		4,10,000
S. Creditors		65,000
		14,77,000
Assets		
Building (4,00,000 – 10,000)	3,90,000	
Plant & Machinery (5,00,000 – 50,000)		4,50,000
Furniture (1,00,000 – 10,000)		90,000
Debtors (2,60,000 – 13,000)		2,47,000
Stock		3,00,000
		14,77,000

Illustration (16) (Redemption adjustments & effect on future profit)

On 31st March, 2004 the Balance Sheet of Ara Ltd. was as follows :

Liabilities		Rs.
9% Redeemable Preference Share Capital (4000 Shares of Rs. 100 each)		4,00,000
75,000 Shares of Rs. 10 each		7,50,000
Securities Premium		25,000
Profit & Loss Account		5,60,000
8% Debentures (Secured against mortgage of Freehold Properties)		6,00,000
S. Creditors		1,65,000
		25,00,000
Assets		
Freehold Property at cost	15,00,000	
Less Accumulated Depreciation @ 2%	3,00,000	12,00,000
Computers and Equipments at Cost.	6,00,000	
Less Accumulated Depreciation @ 10%	2,00,000	4,00,000
Bank Balance		40,000
Other Current Assets		8,60,000
		25,00,000

Additional Information — The Directors resolved that :

(i) Preference Shares be redeemed at 10% Premium.

(ii) Freehold property should be used to provide additional working capital. For this purpose it was sold for Rs.16,50,000 to an Insurance Company who leased them back to Ara Ltd. for 33 years at an annual rental of Rs.1,20,000. The expenses of repairs and insurance are to be borne by Ara Ltd.

(3) To discharge 8% Debentures at par by issuing necessary number of equity shares @ Rs. 12 per share.

The Directors estimated that in addition to the effect of the above transactions the increased working capital available will improve profit by Rs. 85,000 p.a.

You are required to pass journal entries necessary to record the above transactions. Also work-out the effect on the future annual profits (before tax) available for distribution to equity shareholders.

Solution (16)

JOURNAL ENTRIES

			Rs.	Rs.
	9% Redeemable Preference Share Capital A/c	Dr.	4,00,000	
	Premium on Redemption A/c	Dr.	40,000	
	To Preference Share holders A/c			4,40,000
	(Being Pref. share due for redemption)			
	Securities Premium A/c	Dr.	25,000	
	Profit & Loss A/c	Dr.	15,000	
	To Premium on Redemption A/c			40,000
	(Being Premium on Redemption written off)			
	Bank A/c	Dr.	16,50,000	
	To Free hold Property A/c			12,00,000
	To Profit & Loss A/c			4,50,000
	(Being property sold at profit)			
	Preference Share holders A/c	Dr.	4,40,000	
	To Bank A/c			4,40,000
	(Being preference shareholders paid off)			
	Profit & Loss A/c	Dr.	4,00,000	
	To Capital Redemption Reserve A/c			4,00,000
	(Being required amount transferred to CRR)			
	8% Debentures A/c	Dr.	6,00,000	
	To Debenture holders A/c			6,00,000
	(Being amount transferred to Debenture holders)			
	Debenture holders A/c	Dr.	6,00,000	
	To Equity Share Capital A/c			5,00,000
	To Securities Premium A/c			1,00,000
	(Being Equity Shares issued to Debenture holders on redemption)			

BALANCE SHEET OF AVA LTD.
As on 1st April, 2006

Liabilities		Rs.
1,25,000 Equity Shares of Rs. 10 each		12,50,000
Securities Premium		1,00,000
Profit & Loss Account (3)		5,95,000
Capital Redemption Reserve		4,00,000
S. Creditors		1,65,000
		25,10,000
Assets		
Computers & Equipments	6,00,000	
Less Acc. Depreciation	2,00,000	4,00,000
Bank Balance (2)		12,50,000
Other Current Assets		8,60,000
		25,10,000

Working notes :

(1) Computation of Net increase/decrease in future profits

Increase in profits :

	Rs.
Depreciation on freehold property (no more required)	30,000
Debenture- Interest (now not payable)	48,000
Preference Dividend (now not payable)	32,000
Improvement in profit due to increase in Working Capital	85,000
	1,95,000
Less Annual Rental (now payable)	85,000
Increase in future profits	1,10,000

(2) **BANK A/C**

	Rs.		Rs.
To Balance b/d	40,000	By Pref. Shareholders	4,40,000
To Freehold property	16,50,000	By Balance c/d	12,50,000
	16,90,000		16,90,000

(3) **PROFIT & LOSS A/C**

	Rs.		Rs.
To Premium on Redemption A/c	15,000	By Balance b/d	5,60,000
To Capita Redemption A/c	4,00,000	By Bank A/c	4,50,000
To Balance c/d	5,95,000	(Profit on sale of property)	
	10,10,000		10,10,000

Illustration (17) (Calculation of shares reissued)

The following figures have been extracted from the books of P P Ltd.

	31st March, 2001	31st March, 2002
	Rs.	Rs.
Equity Share Capital (shares of Rs. 10 each)	5,80,000	6,70,000
Less Calls-in-arrears @ Rs. 2 per share	6,000	2,000
	5,74,000	6,68,000
Add Share Forfeited Account	16,000	8,000
	5,90,000	6,76,000
6% Preference Share Capital (Shares of Rs. 100 each)	2,00,000	1,00,000
Securities Premium Account	24,000	4,000
General Reserve	2,40,000	1,60,000
Capital Redemption Reserve	—	1,20,000
Capital Reserve	14,000	35,000

Additional Information :

During the year 2001-02, 8000 Equity Shares of Rs. 10 each and 1000 6% Preference Shares of Rs. 100 each were issued at par which were fully subscribed and paid for. Reissue of forfeited shares, if made, was @ Rs. 9 per share. Capital Reserve Account balance on 31st March, 2001 and on 31st March, 2002 indicated only profit arising out of reissue of forfeited shares.

Record necessary entries for the transactions which took place during the year 2001-2002.

ICWA (1) Adapted

Solution (17)

JOURNAL ENTRIES

			Rs.	Rs.
	Bank A/c	Dr.	1,80,000	
	To Equity Share Capital A/c			80,000
	To Preference Share Capital A/c			1,00,000
	(Being Equity & Preference Shares issued at par)			
	6% Preference Share Capital A/c	Dr.	2,00,000	
	Premium on Redemption A/c	Dr.	20,000	
	To Preference Share holders A/c			2,20,000
	(Being amount payable on redemption)			
	Equity Share Capital A/c	Dr.	20,000	
	To Calls-in-Arrears A/c			4,000
	To Share Forfeited A/c			16,000
	(Being 2000 shares[(1)] forfeited)			
	Bank A/c	Dr.	27,000	
	Share Forfeited A/c	Dr.	3,000	
	To Equity Share Capital A/c			30,000
	(Being 3000* Shares[(2)] reissued)			

Contd.

		Rs.	Rs.
	Share Forfeited A/c Dr.	21,000	
	To Capital Reserve A/c		21,000
	(Being Profit on reissue transferred to Capital Reserve)		
	Securities Premium A/c Dr.	20,000	
	To Premium on Redemption A/c		20,000
	(Being Premium on Redemption adjusted out of Securities Premium A/c)		
	Profit & Loss Appropriation A/c(3) Dr.	40,000	
	To General Reserve A/c		40,000
	(Being amount transferred to General Reserve)		
	General Reserve A/c Dr.	1,20,000	
	To Capital Redemption Reserve A/c		1,20,000
	(Being amount transferred to CRR out of General Reserve)		
	Preference Shareholders A/c Dr.	2,20,000	
	To Bank A/c		2,20,000
	(Being amount paid on redemption)		

Working notes :

(1) No. of shares forfeited is worked out as under :

	Calls-in-Arrears as on 31.3.2001	6,000*
Less	Calls- in-Arrears as on 31.3.02	2,000
	Represents amount of Calls-in-Arrears relating to share forfeiture	4,000
	Hence number of shares forfeited	$\frac{4000}{2^*}$
	(denominator being Calls in Arrear per share)	2,000 shares

(2) Calculation showing number of shares reissued :

Capital Reserve as on 31.3.2002	35,000
Capital Reserve as on 31.3.2001	14,000
Profit on reissue	21,000

Since shares have been reissued @ Rs. 9 per share, a discount or concession of Re. 1 per share has been allowed.

	Total Amount paid per share	Rs. 8
Less	Concession per share	1
	Profit per share transferred to Capital Reserve	7
	Since the total amount transferred during the year to Capital Reserve is	Rs. 21,000
	The number of shares reissued	$= \frac{21,000}{7}$
		3000 shares

(3) An increase in general reserve of Rs. 40,000 has been presumed to be made out of Profit and Loss Appropriation A/c

It is to be noted that the number of shares forfeited during the current year is 2000 only as against the shares reissued 3000. This clearly indicates that 1000 shares have been reissued out of the shares forfeited last year.

Illustration (18) (Fresh Issue- Partly paid and CRR)

The following is the extract of the Balance Sheet of PQR Ltd. as on 31st March, 2006.

	(Rs. '000)
50,000, 8% Preference Shares of Rs. 100 each, Rs. 70 paid up	3,500
1,00,000 Equity Shares of Rs. 100 each fully paid up	10,000
Securities Premium	500
Capital Redemption Reserve	2,000
General Reserve	5,000

Under the terms, the preference shares are to be redeemed on 30th June 2006. To finance redemption the Company made a rights issue of 50,000 Equity shares of Rs. 100 each at Rs. 110 per share. The money was payable as under :

On application	Rs. 20
On allotment (including premium)	Rs. 35
And the first and final call : (on 1.4.2007)	the balance

The issue was fully subscribed and money due on allotment was received in time after fulfilling the necessary conditions of section 80 of Companies Act 1956. The Company decided to make minimum utilisation of general reserves you are required to show necessary journal entries and relevant extracts from the Balance Sheet as on 30.6.2006 with corresponding figures of last year.

C.A (1) Nov., 1999 (Modified)

Solution (18)

JOURNAL ENTRIES

			Rs. ('000)	Rs. ('000)
	8% Pref. Share Final Call A/c To 8% Pref. Share Capital A/c (Being final call made)	Dr.	1,500	1,500
	Bank A/c To 8% Pref. Share Final Call A/c (Being final call amount received)	Dr.	1,500	1,500
	Bank A/c To Equity Share Application A/c (Being application money on Equity Shares received)	Dr.	1,000	1,000
	Equity Share Application A/c To Equity Share Capital A/c (Being application money transferred to Share Capital A/c	Dr.	1,000	1,000

Contd.

		Rs. ('000)	Rs. ('000)
Equity Share Allotment A/c	Dr.	1,750	
To Equity Share Capital A/c			1,250
To Securities Premium A/c			500
(Being allotment money due)			
Bank A/c	Dr.	1,750	
To Equity Share Allotment A/c			1,750
(Being allotment money received)			
8% Preference Share Capital A/c	Dr.	5,000	
Premium on Redemption A/c		250	
To Preference Shareholders A/c			5,250
(Being amount due on redemption)			
Securities Premium A/c	Dr.	250	
To Premium on Redemption A/c			250
(Being premium redemption adjusted against securities premium)			
General Reserve A/c	Dr.	2,750	
To Capital Redemption Reserve A/c			2,750
(Being amount transferred to CRR)			
Preference Shareholders A/c	Dr.	5,250	
To Bank A/c			5,250
(Being amount paid to Preference Shareholders)			

EXTRACTS OF LIABILITIES SIDE OF THE BALANCE SHEET
As on 30.6.2006 (after redemption)

31.3.2006 Rs.('000)	Liabilities	30.6.2006 Rs. ('000)
	8% Preference Share Capital	
3,500	50,000 Shares of Rs. 100 each Rs. 70 Paid up	—
	Equity Share Capital	
10,000	1,00,000 Equity Shares of Rs. 100 each fully paid	10,000
—	50,000 Equity Shares of Rs. 100 each Rs. 45 paid up.	2,250
	Reserve & Surplus	
500	Securities Premium	750
2,000	Capital Redemption Reserve	4,750
5,000	General Reserve	2,250

Working notes :

Amount transferred to Capital Redemption Reserve

(1) CRR = Nominal value of Pref. Shares – proceeds of fresh issue

CRR = Rs. 50,00,000 – 22,50,000*

= 27,50,000

* 50,000 shares × Application and allotment money (20 + 25)

(2)	Securities Premium (Op. Balance)	5,00,000
Add	Premium from fresh issue	5,00,000
		10,00,000
Less	Premium on Redemption Account	2,50,000
		7,50,000

(3) Since the final call has not been made till the date of Balance Sheet after redemption the final call amount has been ignored for the purpose of calculating the amount of proceeds of fresh issue.

Illustration (19) (Redemption by Conversion)

The Balance Sheet of Omar Ltd. As on 31st March, 2005 was as follows :

Liabilities		Rs.
12% Redeemable Preference Shares of Rs. 100 each		5,00,000
Equity Shares of Rs. 10 each	10,00,000	
11% Debentures		7,50,000
Revenue Reserve		6,25,000
Bank Loan		1,25,000
S. Creditors		2,00,000
		32,00,000
Assets		
Gross Block		20,00,000
Less Depreciation		6,00,000
Net Block		14,00,000
Current Assets		17,70,000
Discount on Debentures		30,000
		32,00,000

For the purpose of redemption of preference shares and debentures the Directors offered Preference shareholders and Debentures holders the option to convert their holdings into equity shares of Rs. 10 each @ Rs. 12.50 per share. One half of the preference shareholders and one-third of the debentureholders accepted the offer. The company also issued 75,000 equity shares at a premium of 25% to the public for cash. The Directors redeemed the remaining preference shares and debentures, and also paid off the bank Loan.

Record necessary entries to show the above transactions. Also prepare a Balance Sheet after redemption.

Solution (19)

JOURNAL ENTRIES

			Rs.	Rs.
	12% Red. Preference Share Capital A/c	Dr.	5,00,000	
	To Preference Shareholders A/c			5,00,000
	(Being amount due on redemption)			
	Preference Shareholders A/c	Dr.	2,50,000	
	To Equity Share Capital A/c			2,00,000
	To Securities Premium A/c			50,000
	(Being Equity shares issued to Preference Shareholders at their option)			
	11% Debentures A/c	Dr.	7,50,000	
	To Debentureholders A/c			7,50,000
	(Being amount due on redemption)			
	Debentureholders A/c	Dr.	2,50,000	
	To Equity Share Capital A/c			2,00,000
	To Securities Premium A/c			50,000
	(Being Equity Shares issued to debentureholders at their option)			
	Bank A/c	Dr.	9,37,500	
	To Equity Share Capital A/c			7,50,000
	To Securities Premium A/c			1,87,500
	(Being equity shares issued for cash at 25% Premium)			
	Securities Premium A/c	Dr.	30,000	
	To Discount on Debentures A/c			30,000
	(Being Discount on debentures adjusted against securities premium)			
	Revenue Reserve A/c	Dr.	5,00,000	
	To Debenture Redemption Reserve A/c			5,00,000
	(Being required amount transferred to CRR)			
	Preference Shareholders A/c	Dr.	2,50,000	
	Debentureholders A/c	Dr.	5,00,000	
	To Bank A/c			7,50,000
	(Being preference Shareholders and debentureholders are paid the amount on redemption)			
	Bank Loan A/c	Dr.	1,25,000	
	To Bank A/c			1,25,000
	(Being bank loan paid off)			

BALANCE SHEET OF OMAR LTD.

As on 31st March, 2005

Liabilities		Rs.
Equity Share Capital		
2,15,000 Shares of Rs. 10 each fully paid		21,50,000
Securities Premium (3)		2,57,500
Debenture Redemption Reserve General Reserve		5,00,000
Revenue Reserve		1,25,000
S. Creditors		2,00,000
		32,32,500
Assets		
Gross Block	20,00,000	
Less Depreciation	6,00,000	14,00,000
Current Assets		17,70,000
Cash at Bank		62,500
		32,32,500

Working notes :

(1) Since redemption of preference shares has been made by conversion method and out of the proceeds of fresh issue, no CRR is required to be created. It should be remembered that CRR is to be created only when redemption is made out of profits.

(2) An amount equivalent to the face value of the Debentures so redeemed out of profits, has been transferred to "Debenture Redemption Reserve". Of the Debentures of Rs. 7,50,000, 1/3 (Rs. 2,50,000) have opted for equity shares and remaining have been redeemed out of the profits of the company. Hence DRR of Rs. 5,00,000 is created, which may directly be transferred to General Reserve.

(3) **SECURITIES PREMIUM A/C**

	Rs.		Rs.
To Discount on Debentures* A/c	30,000	By Pref. Shareholders A/c	50,000
To Balance c/d	2,57,500	By Debentureholders A/c	50,000
		By Bank A/c	1,87,500
	2,87,500		2,87,500

*Since all the debentures have been redeemed the discount on issue of debentures has been written off.

(4) **CASH AT BANK A/C**

	Rs.		Rs.
To Balance b/d	—	By Pref. Shareholders A/c	2,50,000
To Equity Share Capital A/c	7,50,000	By Debentureholders A/c	5,00,000
To Securities Premium A/c	1,87,500	By Bank Loan A/c	1,25,000
		By Balance c/d	62,500
	9,37,500		9,37,500

Illustration (20) (Preference Dividend, Cash flow from operation & Redemption)

The following is the Balance Sheet of Trinity Ltd. as on 31st March, 2004

Liabilities		Rs.
9% 10,000 Redeemable Preference Shares of Rs. 10 each		1,00,000
10,000 Equity Shares of Rs.10 each		1,00,000
Reserves and Surplus :		
General Reserve		1,20,000
Securities Premium		70,000
Profit & Loss Account		18,500
Current liabilities & Provisions		11,500
		4,20,000
Assets		
Gross Block	3,00,000	
Less Depreciation	1,00,000	2,00,000
Investments		1,00,000
Current Assets, Loans & Advances :		
Inventory	25,000	
Debtors	25,000	
Cash & Bank Balance	50,000	1,00,000
Miscellaneous Expenditure		20,000
		4,20,000

For the year ended 31st March, 2005 the Company made a net profit of Rs. 15,000 after providing depreciation of Rs. 20,000 and writing off the miscellaneous expenditure of Rs. 20,000.

The following additional information is available with regard to Company's operation :

1. The preference dividend for the year ended 31st March, 2005 was paid before 31st March, 2005.
2. Except cash & bank balance other current assets and current liabilities as on 31.3.2005 were the same as on 31.3.2004.
3. The company redeemed the preference shares at a premium of 10%.
4. The company issued bonus shares in the ratio of one share for every equity share held as on 31.3.2005.
5. To meet the cash requirements of redemption the company sold a portion of investments so as to leave a minimum balance of Rs. 30,000 after such redemption.
6. Investments were sold at 90% of cost on 31st March, 2005.

You are required to –

(1) Prepare necessary journal entries.

(2) Prepare Cash and Bank Account.

(3) Prepare Balance sheet as on 31.3.2005 incorporating the above transactions.

C.A (1) Nov.1996-Modified

JOURNAL ENTRIES

Particulars		Rs.	Rs.
Preference Dividend A/c	Dr.	10,000	
To Bank A/c			10,000
(Being preference dividend paid)			
Profit & Loss A/c	Dr.	10,000	
To Preference Dividend A/c			10,000
(Being dividend charged to P & L A/c)			
9% Red. Pref. Share Capital A/c	Dr.	1,00,000	
Premium on Redemption A/c	Dr.	10,000	
To Pref. Shareholders A/c			1,10,000
(Being amount due on Redemption)			
Bank A/c	Dr.	45,000	
Profit & Loss A/c	Dr.	5,000	
To Investments A/c			50,000
(Being investments sold at 10% loss)			
Securities Premium A/c	Dr.	10,000	
To Premium on Redemption A/c			10,000
(Being Premium on redemption adjusted against securities premium)			
General Reserve A/c	Dr.	1,00,000	
To Capital Redemption Reserve A/c			1,00,000
(Being CRR created out of general reserve)			
Preference Shareholders A/c	Dr.	1,10,000	
To Bank A/c			1,10,000
(Being amount due on redemption paid off)			
Capital Redemption Reserve A/c	Dr.	1,00,000	
To Bonus to Equity Shareholders A/c			1,00,000
(Being bonus declared)			
Bonus to Equity Shareholders A/c	Dr.	1,00,000	
To Equity Share Capital A/c			1,00,000
(Being bonus shares issued)			

BALANCE SHEET OF TRINITY LTD.
As on 31st March, 2005

			Rs.
Liabilities			
	20,000 Equity Shares of Rs. 10 each		2,00,000
	Reserves & Surplus		
	General Reserve		20,000
	Securities Premium		60,000
	Profit & Loss Account		18,500
	Current liabilities & Provisions		11,500
			3,10,000
Assets			
	Gross Block	3,00,000	
Less	Depreciation (3)	1,20,000	1,80,000
	Investments (2)		50,000
	Current Assets Loans & Advances :		
	Inventory	25,000	
	Debtors	25,000	
	Cash Bank Balance (1)	30,000	80,000
			3,10,000

Working notes :

(1) **CASH AND BANK A/C**

	Rs.		Rs.
To Balance b/d	50,000	By Pref. Dividend	10,000
To Flow from Operation*	55,000	By Pref. Shareholders	1,10,000
To Sale of Investment (Balancing figure)	45,000	By Balance c/d (as required)	30,000
	1,50,000		1,50,000

* Net Profit + Depreciation + Misc. Expenses w/o

= Rs. 15,000 + 20,000 + 20,000

= Rs. 55,000

(2) Cost of Investment sold = Sale proceeds $\times \frac{100}{90}$

$= 45{,}000 \times \frac{100}{90} = \text{Rs. } 50{,}000$

(3) Accumulated Depreciation = Rs. 1,00,000 + 20,000 = Rs. 1,20,000

Illustration (21) (General)

The Financial position of P Ltd. as on 31st December, 2004 was as follows :

Liabilities	Rs.
Share Capital :	
8% 40,000 Preference Shares of Rs. 10 each fully paid	4,00,000
20,000 Equity Shares of Rs. 10 each fully paid	2,00,000
Reserves & Surplus :	
Securities Premium Account	50,000
Profit & Loss Account	2,80,000
Current liabilities & provisions	
S. Creditors	2,10,000
	11,40,000
Assets	
Net Block	5,40,000
Current Assets other than Cash & Bank	3,00,000
Cash and Bank balance	3,00,000
	11,40,000

As per the terms of issue the Preferences Shares were redeemable at 105% on 1.2.2005.

It was decided to arrange this, as far as possible, out of company's resources subject to leaving a balance of Rs. 50,000 to the credit of Profit & Loss Account. It was also decided to raise the balance amount by issue of sufficient number of Equity Shares of Rs. 10 each at 10 % premium.

Prepare necessary leader accounts and Balance Sheet on that date.

C.A. (1) May 2002 Adapted

Solution (21)

8% RED. PREF. SHARE CAPITAL A/C

	Rs.		Rs.
To Pref. Share holders' A/c	4,00,000	By Balance b/d	4,00,000

PREF. SHARE HOLDERS' A/C

	Rs.		Rs.
To Bank A/c	4,20,000	By 8% Pref. Share Capital A/c	4,00,000
		By Premium on Redemption A/c	20,000
	4,20,000		4,20,000

PREMIUM ON REDEMPTION A/C

	Rs.		Rs.
To Pref. Shareholders' A/c	20,000	By Securities Premium A/c	20,000

EQUITY SHARE CAPITAL A/C

	Rs.		Rs.
To Balance c/d	3,70,000	By Balance b/d	2,00,000
		By Bank A/c	1,70,000
	3,70,000		3,70,000

SECURITIES PREMIUM A/C

	Rs.		Rs.
To Premium on Redemption A/c	20,000	By Balance b/d	50,000
To Balance c/d	47,000	By Bank A/c	17,000
	67,000		67,000

PROFIT & LOSS ACCOUNT

	Rs.		Rs.
To Capital Redemption Reserve A/c	2,30,000	By Balance b/d	2,80,000
To Balance c/d	50,000		
	2,80,000		2,80,000

CASH & BANK A/C

	Rs.		Rs.
To Balance b/d	3,00,000	By Preference Shareholders A/c	4,20,000
To Equity Share Capital A/c	1,70,000	By Balance c/d	67,000
To Securities Premium A/c	17,000		
	4,87,000		4,87,000

BALANCE SHEET OF P LTD.
As on 1st February, 2005

Liabilities	Rs.
Share Capital	
37,000 Equity Shares of Rs. 10 each fully paid	3,70,000
Reserve & Surplus	
Securities Premium	47,000
Capital Redemption Reserve	2,30,000
Profit & Loss A/c	50,000
Current liabilities & Provisions	
S. Creditors	2,10,000
	9,07,000
Assets	
Net Block	5,40,000
Current Assets other than Cash & Bank	3,00,000
Cash & Bank Balance	67,000
	9,07,000

Working notes :

Nominal Value of Pref. Shares	4,00,000
Less Amount available out of Profit Less minimum balance required (2,80,000 – 50,000)	2,30,000
Proceeds from fresh Issue	1,70,000
Hence CRR	2,30,000

QUESTIONS

1. State the conditions which must be satisfied for redemption of preference shares.
2. Explain the provisions of the Companies Act regarding redemption of preference shares.
3. Explain in the following terms :
   "Proceeds from fresh issue"
   "Capital Redemption Reserve"
   "Divisible Profits".
4. Can a company create CRR by increasing the debit balance of Profit & Loss Account? Explain.
5. Pin point the profits which are available for dividend or out of which Capital Redemption Reserve may be created.
   (a) Securities Premium
   (b) Profit & Loss Account
   (c) Share Forfeited Account
   (d) Reserve Fund
   (e) Capital Reserve
   (f) Dividend Equalization fund
   (g) Insurance Fund
   (h) Workmen's Compensation fund
   (i) Pre-incorporation profit
   (j) Development Rebate Reserve
   (k) Debenture Redemption Reserve
   (l) Sinking Fund
   (m) Investment Allowance Reserve.

Ans : b, d, f, g, j, h, k, l.

6. State the circumstances when the equation is used for calculating the minimum fresh issue.

PROBLEMS

1. Find the amount to be transferred to Capital Redemption Reserve (CRR) in each of the following cases :

Preference Shares to be redeemed	Fresh Issue
(a) 2,500 shares of Rs. 100 each	(a) 10,000 shares of Rs. 10 each
(i) at Par	(i) at Par
(ii) at 10 % Premium	(ii) at Par
(iii) at Par	(iii) at 10% Premium
(iv) at Par	(iv) at 10% Discount
(v) at 10% Premium	(v) at 10% Premium

Ans : (i), (ii), (iii), & (v) = Rs. 1,50,000 (iv) = Rs. 1,60,000

(2) Find out the amount of minimum fresh issue in the following cases

Preference shares to be redeemed	Reserve & Surplus as per Balance Sheet
3,000 Pref. Shares of Rs. 100 each	
(a) at Par	(a) Divisible Profits = Rs. 1,80,000 Securities premium = Rs. 12,000
(b) at 10 % Premium	(b) General Reserve = Rs. 1,80,000 Securities Premium = Rs. 12,000
(c) at 10 % Premium	(c) Profit & Loss A/c Rs. 1,80,000 General Reserve Rs. 30,000 Capital Reserve Rs. 30,000 Securities Premium Rs. 60,000 Dividend Equalisation Fund 30,000

Ans. : (a) Rs.1,20,000; (b) Rs. 1,38,000; (c) Rs. 60,000

(3) Determine the number of shares of fresh issue and amount of CRR. Also record the necessary journal entries on the redemption of preference shares.

	Rs.
(a) 9% 2,500 Preference Shares of R. 100 each	2,50,000
Revenue Reserves	45,000
Securities Premium	9,500

Preference shares are to be redeemed at 10% premium and fresh issue of equity shares of Rs. 10 each is to be made at 5% premium.

	Rs.
(b) 8 % 3,000 Preference Shares of Rs. 100 each	3,00,000
Profit & Loss A/c (Cr.)	52,000
General Reserve	75,000
Securities Premium	8,000

Fresh issue is to be made at 10% discount and Preference shares are to be redeemed at 5% premium.

(c) 10% 4,000 Preference Shares of Rs. 100 each	4,00,000
Profit & Loss A/c (Cr.)	55,000
General Reserve	1,00,000
Securities Premium	15,000

Preference shares are to be redeemed at 10% premium and fresh issue is to be made at 10% discount.

Ans. : CRR = (a) Rs. 40,000 (b) Rs. 1,20,000 (c) Rs. 1,30,000
Fresh Issue (a) 21,000 shares (b) 20,000 Shares (c) 30,000 shares.

(4) The following balances have been extracted from the books of NRI Ltd. when the preference shares were due for redemption.

	Rs.
9% 4,500 Red. Pref. Shares of Rs. 100 each	4,50,000
General Reserve	5,25,000
Profit & Loss Account	90,000

The company made an issue of 30,000 Equity Shares of Rs. 10 each at a premium of 20% The issue was immediately subscribed and paid for in full. Share issue expenses amounted to Rs. 15,000.

Record journal entries. Revenue reserves are to be used to the minimum extent possible.

Ans. : CRR = Rs. 1,50,000

Hint : Write off share issue expenses out of securities premium.

(5) The following is the Balance Sheet of S R Ltd. as on 31st March, 2004.

Liabilities	Rs.
9% 4,000 Red. Preference shares of Rs. 100 each	4,00,000
12,000 Equity Shares of Rs. 10 each	7,20,000
Reserves & Surplus	
Securities Premium	80,000
General Reserve	1,60,000
Profit & Loss Account	2,00,000
Current liabilities	2,40,000
	18,00,000
Assets	
Net Block	10,56,000
Investments at cost (F.V. Rs. 2,50,000)	2,24,000
Current Assets	5,20,000
	18,00,000

The Company decides to redeem its preference shares at a premium of 5%. A fresh issue of 8,000 shares of Rs. 10 each was made at 20% premium. The shares were fully subscribed and paid for in full on application. Investments were sold for Rs. 2,16,000. The Directors intend to make minimum reductions in revenue reserves.

Required : Journal Entries & Balance Sheet after redemption

C.A. (1) adapted

Ans. : CRR : Rs. 3,20,000; B/S Total Rs. 14,68,000

(6) The ledger accounts of M Ltd. disclosed the following balances on the date of redemption of preference shares.

	Rs.
10% Red. Preference Share Capital (3,000 shares of Rs. 100 each)	3,00,000
Reserves & Surplus	
Securities Premium	20,000
General Reserve	80,000
Profit & Loss Account	38,000
Investment Allowance Reserve	50,000

The company redeems preference shares at a premium of 10%. For the purpose of redemption a fresh issue is made at 20% premium in lots of 100 shares for such amount as is necessary after utilising the available sources to the extent. Record journal entries.

Ans. : Fresh Issue : 18,200 shares; CRR : Rs. 1,18,000.

(7) The following balances appeared in the books of N N Ltd.

9% Redeemable Preference shares of Rs. 100 each	4,00,000
Less Calls in Arrears	8,000
	3,92,000
50,000 Equity Shares of Rs. 10 each	5,00,000
General Reserve	2,40,000
Securities Premium	32,000
Development Rebate Reserve	1,60,000

Preference shares are due for immediate redemption at a premium of 10 %. Calls-in-Arrears are on account of final call of Rs. 20 pre share. The holders of these shares are not traceable. Rs. 40,000 of the Development Rebate Reserve is free for distribution as dividend. Make fresh issue of equity shares at par, if required.

Ans. : CRR = Rs. 2,76,000 Fresh Issue : Rs. 84,000

(8) The following balances were extracted from the books S A Ltd. as on 31st March, 2004.

	Rs.
10% 2,000 Red. Preference Shares of Rs. 100 each	2,00,000
Less Calls-in-Arrears @ Rs. 20 Per share	6,000
	1,94,000
General Reserve	50,000
Capital Reserve	10,000

The preference shares were redeemed on 1st May, 2004 at a premium of 5%. The company issued such number of equity shares of Rs. 10 each as were necessary for the purpose of redeeming preference shares. The Equity shares were fully subscribed & paid for in full.

Record journal entries and show the relevant extracts of liabilities side of the Balance Sheet.

Ans. : CRR : Rs. 40,000 Fresh Issue : Rs. 1,30,000

C A (i) Modified

(9) Global Computers Ltd. issued 9% 10,000 Preference shares of Rs. 100 each at par. On 31st March, 2004 these shares are to be redeemed at 110%. For the purpose of redemption 60,000 Equity Shares of Rs. 10 each were issued at par. On the above date, 400 redeemable preference shares were forfeited for non payment of final call of Rs. 25. Of these 320 shares had been reissued as fully paid for Rs. 60 per share. The balance of the Profit & Loss account was Rs. 4,84,000 and general reserve Rs. 1,20,000

The redemption was completed on 30th April, 2004. A bonus share dividend was declared of Rs. 5,00,000

Prepare necessary ledger accounts.

ICWA (i) Adapted

Ans. : CRR : Rs. 4,00,000
Capital Reserve : Rs. 17,200
General Reserve (Balance) : Rs. 4,800

(10) The following is the Balance Sheet of Somu Ltd. as on 31st March, 2004.

Liabilities		Rs.
9% 5,000 Preference Shares of Rs. 100 each		5,00,000
1,25,000 Equity Shares of Rs. 10 each		12,50,000
Reserves & Surplus :		
General Reserve		2,00,000
Profit & Loss A/c		1,00,000
Current Liabilities :		
S. Creditors		3,50,000
Bills Payable		2,50,000
Provision for Taxation		1,50,000
		28,00,000
Assets		
Gross Block	20,00,000	
Less Depreciation	2,00,000	18,00,000
Current Assets excluding Cash at Bank		6,50,000
Cash & Bank Balance		3,50,000
		28,00,000

The preference shares are due for redemption at 5% premium. The profits available being not sufficient to redeem the whole issue, the company issued 2,500, 9.5% Redeemable Preference shares of Rs. 100 each at par. These shares were taken up and paid for Redemption process was completed on due date.

On 1st July, 2004 the Company decided to utilise Capital Redemption Reserve (CRR) by issuing fully paid bonus shares to the old equity shareholders.

Pass Journal entries.

ICWA (1) Adapted.

Ans. : CRR Rs. 2,50,000 Bonus Issue Rs. 2,50,000

(11) The following is the Balance Sheet of Addu Ltd. as on 31st March, 2004.

Liabilities	Rs.
9% Preference Share Capital	
6,000 shares of Rs. 100 each	6,00,000
Less Final Call of Rs. 20 per Share	4,800
	5,95,200
72,000 Equity Shares of Rs.10 each	7,20,000
Reservers & Surplus	
Securities Premium	36,000
Profit & Loss Account	3,60,000
Current liabilities	64,800
	17,76,000

Assets

		Rs.
Gross Block	19,00,000	
Less Depreciation	4,60,000	14,40,000
Investments		1,20,000
Cash & Bank Balance		2,16,000
		17,76,000

On the above date the Directors decided to redeem the preference shares at a premium of 20% and to sell the investments at its marke value of Rs. 96,000. It was resolved to issue sufficient number of equity shares of Rs. 10 each at premium of 10 % required after utilising the profit & Loss account but leaving a balance of Rs.1,20,000. Premium on redemption is required to be set off against securities premium account.

Repayments on redemption were made in full except to one shareholder holding 120 shares whose where about were not known.

Pass Journal entries and prepare a Balance Sheet.

Ans. : CRR : Rs. 2,16,000; Fresh issue (Proceed) : Rs. 3,36,000; Balance Sheet : Rs. 15,27,600

Hint : Redeem only fully paid shares

(12) Following is the Balance Sheet of Z Ltd. as on 31st March, 2004.

Liabilities

	Rs.
13% 5,000 Red. Preference Shares of Rs. 10 each	5,00,000
50,000 Equity Shares of Rs. 10 each Rs. 8 paid	4,00,000
Securities Premium	98,000
General Reserve	90,000
Profit & Less Account	1,12,000
S. Creditors	3,00,000
	15,00,000

Assets

Fixed Assets	6,00,000
Investments	2,00,000
Current Assets excluding Bank Balance	4,00,000
Cash at Bank	3,00,000
	15,00,000

The company resolved :

(i) To convert the partly paid up Equity shares in to fully paid up without requiring the shareholders to pay for the same.

(ii) Redeem the preference shares at a premium of 7.5% and for this purpose to issue 3,000 12% Preference Shares of Rs. 100 each at a premium of 10% payable in full on application.

These resolutions were carried into effect. For the purpose of the above redemption the company sold its' Fixed Assets costing Rs. 3,00,000 for Rs. 3,82,500 and all investments for Rs. 2,60,000.

All payments were made by 31st May, 2004 except to holders of 200 shares who could not be traced.

On 30th June, 2004, the Directors issued fully paid bonus shares to the shareholders at the rate of 3 for 5 held at a premium of 5%.

Pass necessary journal entries.

Ans. : CRR : Rs. 2,00,000 Bonus Shares : 30,000 shares

Premium on Bonus issue : Rs. 15,000

Hint : Use securities premium for the purpose of issuing bonus shares after writing off premium on redemption account.

(13) Following balances appeared in the books of Pooja Ltd. as on 31.3.2004.

	8% Redeemable Pref. Shares (Cumulative) 5,000 shares of Rs. 100 each	5,00,000
Less	Calls-in-Arrears @ Rs. 25 per share	2,500
		4,97,500
	Securities Premium Account	70,000
	General Reserve	1,17,000
	Proposed dividend on cumulative preference shares (since sanctioned)	39,200
	Cash & Bank Balance	2,75,000

The directors redeemed the preference shares at a premium of 10% and for the purpose made a fresh issue of equity shares for such amount as was necessary for the purpose after utilising the available sources to the maximum extent possible and satisfied the amount of preference dividend.

Journalise the transaction including those of Cash. Also show the relevant extracts.

C.A. (1) adapted

Ans. : CRR : 1,60,000 Fresh issue : 3,30,000

Hint : Redeem only fully paid preference shares (4900 shares) excluding 100 shares on which final call is not paid.

(14) On 31st March, 2004, the following balances appeared in the books of A Ltd.

	Rs.
7,500 7% Redeemable Preference Shares of Rs. 100 each	7,50,000
1,50,000 Equity Shares of Rs. 10 each	15,00,000
Profit and Loss Account	6,00,000
General Reserve	7,50,000

The company resolved :

(a) To make a bonus issue of one share for every two shares held by the existing ordinary shareholders from the General reserve.

(b) To redeem the preference shares.

(c) To issue 45,000 ordinary shares of Rs. 10 each at Rs. 11.25 per share in order to provide part of the funds for the redemption of the preference shares.

The resolutions were carried into effect. You are required to prepare necessary ledger accounts in the books of A Ltd. along with the relevant extracts of Balance Sheet.

C.A (1) Adapted

Ans. : CRR : Rs. 3,00,000 Fresh issue : Rs. 4,50,000 Bonus issue Rs. 7,50,000

(15) The following is the Balance Sheet of A Ltd. as on 31st March, 2004

Liabilities			Rs.
	9% 6,000 Red. Preference Shares of Rs. 100 each		6,00,000
	1,20,000 Equity Shares of Rs. 10 each		12,00,000
Reserve & Surplus :			
	Capital Reserves		1,20,000
	Securities Premium		1,20,000
	General Reserve		2,40,000
	Profit & Loss A/c		1,20,000
	Current Liabilities		12,00,000
Assets			36,00,000
	Gross Block	28,50,000	
Less	Depreciation	3,50,000	25,00,000
	Current Assets excluding Cash at Bank		10,40,000
	Cash Bank		60,000
			36,00,000

The preference shares are to be redeemed on 1st April at 10% premium. The company made fresh issue of equity shares to the extent it is required under the Companies Act. for the purpose of redemption of preference shares.

The short fall in cash resources for the purpose of redemption, after utilising the proceeds of fresh issue was made by raising a bank loan, the bank balance of Rs. 60,000 being the minimum the company requires for it's trading operation.

Record Entries and prepare a Balance Sheet.

[B.Com (H) (Adapted)]

Ans. : CRR : Rs. 3,60,000 Balance Sheet Total : Rs. 36,00,000

(16) On 31st March, 2004, the financial position of YAS Ltd. was as under :

Liabilities		Rs.
	11% 5,000 Red. Preference Shares of Rs. 100 each	5,00,000
Less	Calls-in-Arrears @ Rs. 20 per share	4,000
		4,96,000
	60,000 Equity Shares of Rs. 10 each	6,00,000
	Securities Premium	30,000
	Profit & Loss Account	3,00,000
	Current liabilities	1,54,000
		15,80,000
Assets		
	Net Block	13,00,000
	Investments at Cost	1,00,000
	Bank	1,80,000
		15,80,000

On the above date the directors decided to redeem the preference shares at a premium of 10 % and to sell the investments at its market price which was 20 % less than its cost price. It was further resolved to issue sufficient number of equity shares of Rs. 10 each at a premium of 10% required after utilising the profit & Loss Account leaving a balance of Rs. 1,00,000. Premium on redemption is required to be set off against Securities Premium Account. All payments were made except to one shareholder holding 100 shares who could not be traced. Calls-in-Arrears, however realised in full. Pass Journal Entries and prepare a Balance Sheet.

C.S. (i) Adapted

Ans. : Fresh issue : 32,000 Shares; CRR : Rs. 1,80,000

(17) Resham Ltd. disclosed the following balances as on 31st March, 2004.

			Rs.
Liabilities			
	8% 75,000 Preference Shares of Rs. 10 each Rs. 8 paid		6,00,000
	1,25,000 Equity Shares of Rs. 10 each		12,50,000
Reserves & Surplus			
	Capital Reserve		2,50,000
	Securities Premium		1,50,000
	General Reserve		3,12,500
	Profit & Loss Account		5,00,000
	Current Liabilities		2,50,000
			33,12,500
Assets			
	Gross Block	15,00,000	
Less	Depreciation	2,50,000	12,50,000
	Investments		5,00,000
	Current Assets other than Cash Bank		15,37,500
	Cash at Bank		25,000
			33,12,500

On 1.4.2004 the Company made a final call on its preference shares which was july received. The preference shares were redeemed at 10% premium. For this purpose the company sold its investments at 110% and issued 9% 2,500. Redeemable preference shares of Rs. 100 each which were fully subscribed and paid for in full on application. Thereafter, the company issued fully paid bonus shares in the ratio of 1 : 2.

Record Journal entries and prepare a Balance Sheet.

B.Com. (H) (Adapted)

Ans. : CRR : Rs. 5,00,000 Total of Balance Sheet : Rs. 29,37,500

(18) The following is the Balance Sheet of Vyoma Ltd. as on 31.3.2004.

			Rs.
Liabilities			
	6% Redeemable Preference Shares of Rs. 100 each		5,00,000
Less	Call-in-Arrear @ Rs. 25 per share		5,000
			4,95,000
	Equity Shares of Rs. 10 each	7,50,000	

Reserves & Surplus		
Securities Premium		1,00,000
Capital Reserve		1,00,000
General Reserve		2,00,000
Profit & Loss A/c		3,00,000
Secured Loan		
10% Debentures		2,00,000
Current liabilities		4,50,000
		25,95,000
Assets		
Gross Block	20,00,000	
Less Depreciation	5,00,000	15,00,000
Investments		1,95,000
Current Assets other than Cash & Bank		3,00,000
Cash & Bank Balance		6,00,000
		25,95,000

The Preference Shares and debentures were due for redemption on 1.4.2004. The company took the following steps :

(i) For the half year ending 31st March, 2004, the company paid debenture interest and preference dividend.

(ii) Debentureholders agreed to accept 12% New Debentures at par in exchange for old debentures. The redemption was made at 10% premium.

(iii) A fresh issue of 10,000 Equity shares of Rs. 10 each was made at a premium Rs. 5 per share. These were subscribed in full and all money received.

(iv) Redemption of preference shares was made at 25% premium.

Record Journal Entries and prepare a Balance Sheet just after redemption.

Ans. : CRR : Rs. 4,00,000

3

Issue and Redemption of Debentures

There are two main sources of funds on which a joint stock company relies most. These are : (i) ownership securities or shares and (ii) creditorship securities viz bonds or debentures. When a Company's financial requirements are met by issuing shares, the money so collected is termed as "Owned Capital" and when financial requirements are met by issuing bonds debentures, the money so raised is called "Borrowed Capital". Companies Act 1956 empowers Board of Directors to borrow funds to supplement its resources especially to meet Company's long term financial requirements such as expansion, modernisation, acquisition of fixed assets, setting up of a new unit, and to meet the long term working capital requirements.

Meaning

Debenture is an instrument of acknowledgement of debt. According to Section 2 (12) of the Companies Act 1956 "Debenture includes debenture stock, bonds or any other securities of the Company whether constituting a charge on the assets of the company or not"

Bond like debenture is an acknowledgement of debt which was used for the debt instruments issued by Government. But now a days bonds are synonyms of debentures. In Indian and British terminology, there is no distinction between a bond and a debenture. However, in American terminology a "bond" may be secured or unsecured where as debenture is treated as an unsecured bond.

Ordinarily "debenture represents a document of evidence acknowledging a debt and securing repayment thereof by a mortgage or charge on the company's property and providing that until repayment, interest will be paid thereon at a fixed rate on specific dates either half yearly or annually.

Thus a debenture may be defined as an instrument of acknowledgement of debt issued by a company under seal. **It is to be noted that a certificate signed by two directors and without bearing the company's seal is a valid debenture.**

To sum up, a debenture is an acknowledgement of debt by a company. A debentureholder, being a creditor has no voting rights. It usually specifies the date of redemption (repayment of principal amount). The interest is payable at regular interval yearly or half yearly. A debenture creates "charge on the undertaking or properties of the Company.

KINDS OF DEBENTURES

The debentures may be classified according to their characteristics as shown in the Chart.

Debentures' Classification on the basis of

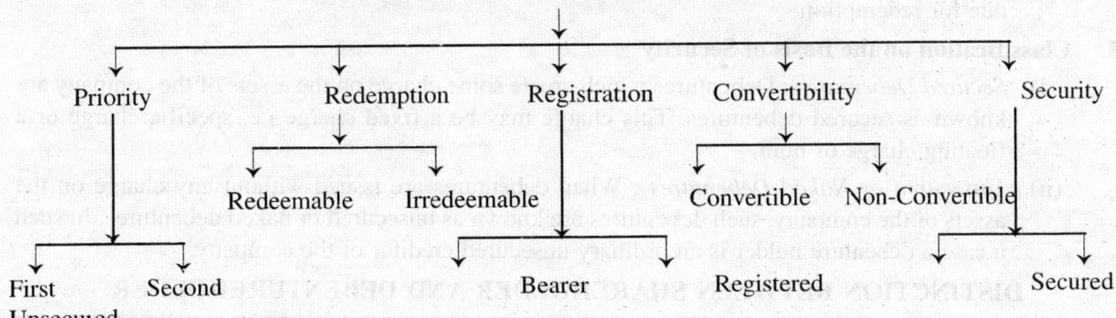

1. Classification According to Priority :

(i) *First Debentures* : These are the debentures which are to be repaid in priority to other debentures.

(ii) *Second Debentures* : Debentures which are to be redeemed after the first debentures have been paid off.

2. Classification on the Basis of redemption

(i) *Redeemable Debentures* : Redeemable Debentures are those debentures which are issued for a specified period of time. On the expiry of such period the debentures are paid off and property released from charge. These debentures are known as redeemable.

(ii) *Irredeemable Debentures* : The debentures which are not to be redeemed during the life time of the company, are known as irredeemable or perpetual debentures.

3. Classification on the Basis of Registration

(i) *Bearer Debentures or Unregistered Debentures* : These debentures are payable to its bearer and regarded as negotiable instruments which are transferable by delivery. The transferee of a bearer debenture becomes its holder and is entitled to principal and interest when due. Interest is payable by coupons attached.

(ii) *Registered Debentures* : A debenture which is registered in the name of a holder in the books of the Company. The principal amount and the interest is payable to the person whose name appears in the register of debenture holders. It is transferable in the same manner as shares or in accordance with the conditions endorsed on its back.

4. Classification on the Basis of Convertibility

(i) *Convertible Debentures* : When a Company issues debentures which gives the option to the holders to convert them into equity or preference shares at stated rate of exchange after a certain period, such debentures are known as convertible debentures. These convertible debentures can be

(a) Fully Convertible Debentures (FCDS)

(b) Partly Convertible Debentures (PCDS)

It is to be noted that debentures once converted into shares cannot be reconverted into debentures.

(ii) *Non-Convertible Debentures* : These debentures do not give any option to their holders to convert them into preference or equity shares. These are to be duly paid as and when become due for redemption.

5. Classification on the Basis of Security

(i) *Secured Debentures* : Debentures which create some charge on the assets of the company are known as secured debentures. This charge may be a fixed charge i.e. specific charge or a floating charge or both.

(ii) *Unsecured or Naked Debentures* : When debentures are issued without any charge on the assets of the company, such debentures are known as unsecured or naked debentures. In such a case a debenture holder is an ordinary unsecured creditor of the company.

DISTINCTION BETWEEN SHAREHOLDER AND DEBENTUREHOLDER

Basis	Shareholder	Debentureholder
(1) Status	A share holder is a member or **owner** of the company.	A debentureholder is a **creditor** of the company.
(2) Votings and other rights & privileges	Rights and privileges of shareholders are governed by Articles which include right to attend and vote at company meetings.	A debenture holder has no such rights and privileges. They can attend and participate in the meetings of creditors on winding up only.
(3) Conditions of issue at discount	Shares can be issued at discount only when certain conditions as laid down by Companies Act are fulfilled.	There is no restriction regarding the terms of issue of debentures at discount.
(4) Return	A shareholder is entitled to a part of profit as dividend if declared. The rate of dividend varies from year to year depending upon the amount of profits earned.	A debentureholder is entitled to interest at a fixed rate as per the terms of issue. Interest is payable irrespective of amount of profit or loss.
(5) Security	There is no security to shareholder hence there cannot be secured or mortgaged shares. They are not secured by any specific or general charge Shares cannot be used as collateral securities	There can be mortgaged or secured debentures. They are secured by a floating charge on the assets of the company. Debentures can be issued as collateral security
(6) Convertibility	There are no convertible shares and hence these cannot be converted into debentures.	As per the terms of issue the debenture holders can get their holdings converted into shares.
(7) Redemption	Except in case of redeemable Preference Shares or when Company is wound-up the shares are not redeemable in the lifetime of the company. Equity Shares have no preference or priority over preference shares or debentures.	The amount of debentures must be paid as per the terms of issue or on winding up whichever is earlier. The debenture holders have priority over both equity and preference shareholders.

Debenture Stock

A company instead of issuing individual debentures may consolidate borrowed money into one single unit which is capable of being divided and transferred into small fractional amounts. The company issues to each lender a certificate known as debenture stock certificate showing the fraction of the debt which the company owes to holder of certificate. A debenture stock may be created for any amount of money by consolidation of serval debenture amounts and a single certificate is issued covering several debentures. A debenture may or may not be fully paid. Again, a debenture may create a separate charge while in case of debenture stock the charge is usually created through a trust deed executed between trustees (Debenture stockholders) and the company. A debenture is transferable in it's entirety as against the debenture stock which may be transferable in fractions/parts if articles so permit.

Debenture Trust Deed

When debentures are issued to public involving large number of debenture holders, it is not feasible to create separate charge in favour of thousands of debenture holders. Likewise nor do these debentureholders have the time and necessary expertise to look after their interest in the property mortgaged or secured by a charge. Hence, in order to protect and safeguard their interest the debentureholders appoint among themselves a few persons as trustees. A trust deed is executed conveying the property of company to trustees. Thus the trustees have a legal mortgage of the property of the company. This gives an advantage to the debentureholders or priority over subsequent lenders of money to the company.

Under the terms of deed the company undertakes to pay to the debentureholders their principal and interest and normally charges it's property to the trustees as security. The trust deed contains the terms and conditions endorsed on the debentures and defines the rights of debentureholders and the company. It usually empowers the trustees to appoint a receiver to protect their interest. It also contains the other provisions concerning meetings of the debentureholders supervision of the assets charged and keeping the register of debentureholders. Whenever there is a default by the company action may be taken by the trustees on behalf of all debentureholders.

Who can be Trustees?

When the debentures with maturity of more than 18 months are issued the issuing company appoints Debenture Trustees out of the following :

(i) A Scheduled Bank carrying business actively.

(ii) An Insurance Company

(iii) A Public Financial Institution such as ICICI, IFCI, IDBI & UTI etc.

(iv) A body Corporate

However the following cannot be appointed as Trustees.

(i) A person beneficially holding shares in the issuing company.

(ii) A person who is beneficially entitled to receive money which is to be paid by the company to the debenture trustee.

(iii) A person who has entered into any guarantee in respect of principal debts secured by debentures or interest thereon.

"Duties of Trustees"

(i) To call for periodic reports from the debenture issuing company.

(ii) To take possession of trust property in accordance with the provisions of 'Trust deed.'

(iii) To enforce security and to protect the interest of the debentureholders.

(iv) To expedite the process of taking charge created against the assets under debenture trust deed. As a rule this should be completed with in 30 days of the issue of allotment letter and despatch of debenture certificate.

A debenture trustee who fails to comply with any condition or contravenes with any of the provisions of the Act, rules, regulation, the Companies Act or rules made thereunder may disqualify him to act as trustee.

Coupon Rate *Vs.* Deep Discount Bonds (Zero Coupon Bond)

As already explained, the debentures are issued with a specified or "predetermined rate of interest". This pre-determined rate of interest is known as *'coupon rate'*, which may either be fixed or floating (variable)

The floating interest rate is linked with the "bank rate" and yield on treasury bonds/securities plus a reward for risk. Since *'bank rate'* and yield on treasury bonds' keep on fluctuating, any change is compensated with the risk premium. The coupon rate may be 'Prime Landing Rate' (PLR) plus a certain percentage calculated on the basis of risk factor. If PLR is 8% and reward for the risk is 1% (say 100 basis point = 1%) The rate of interest would be 9% and if PLR is 8.5% then interest rate will be 9.5% on 100 basis point. It is to be noted that basis points are determined keeping in view of the degree of risk involved in the investment.

A *Zero coupon* bond/deep discount bond does not carry any specific rate of interest. Thus in order to compensate the investors, these bonds are issued at a substantial discount, The difference between the nominal and value issue price is treated as total amount of interest for the period for which such bonds are issued. However, the periodic interest can be calculated by using the following formula.

$$BO = \frac{MV}{(1+i)^n}$$

Where :

BO = Value of Zero Coupon Bond

MV = Maturity Value of Zero Coupon Bond

i = Required rate of return (Interest)

n = Life of Zero Coupon Bond.

The value of $(1 + i)^n$ is computed by *dividing issue price* by the maturity value of the bond. To find out the interest rate applicable to such bonds, a reference to "Present Value Interest Factor" table across the period equal to 'n' is made which is near the above computed value. The interest rate in that column will be the interest on bonds. Thus, if interest rate, 'years to maturity and issue price' are known then the maturity value can be computed and similarly if interest rate, years to maturity and maturity value are known, then the issue price can be calculated.

Hence

$$BO = MV \times (PVIF \times i \times n)$$

If a Company issues a Zero coupon bond with maturity value of Rs. 1,000 redeemable after 10 Years. If required rate of return is 9% the issue price of the bond will be :

BO = MV × (PVIF, i, n)

= Rs. 1,000 × (PVIF, 0.09, 0.10)

= Rs. 1,000 × 0.422* = Rs. 422

The issue price will be Rs. 422

* Please refer to PVIF table.

Charge

The power of a company to borrow includes the power to create a charge upon its assets. A company like any other person, when it borrows money gives its creditors security. Often it mortgages or charges its property to its debenture holders. That is a charge includes mortgage Secured debentures are issued by creating a "charge" on the assets of the company which may be either (i) a fixed charge or (ii) a floating charge.

(i) Fixed Charge : A fixed charge is one which is created on some specific and definite property of the company, e.g. a charge on land and building. A fixed charge prevents the company from dealing with the property charged without the consent of the holder of charge. Under fixed charge, the security of the debenture holders is confined to the asset under "charge" or mortgage, they cannot proceed against other assets of the company

(ii) Floating Charge : A floating charge is an equitable charge which is created on some class of property/assets which are constantly changing such as stock-in-trade, debtors. The company can deal in such property/assets in its normal course of business until the charge becomes fixed on the happening of an event, such as

(i) Company goes into liquidation, or

(ii) Company ceases to carry on business, or

(iii) a receiver is appointed, or

(iv) a default is made in paying the principal/interest

Debentures usually create a floating charge on the assets of the company.

Priority of Charges

(1) A Fixed Charge over the same property has priority over the floating charge

(2) When a fixed charge is created on the same property, the fixed charge which is created first, takes priority over the second.

(3) A company cannot create mortgages ranking in priority of the floating charge after it has been crystallised. On crystallisation the floating charge becomes a specific mortgage.

(4) A company is allowed to create a second floating charge over its assets but the second floating charge cannot have priority over the first floating charge.

Debentures with "PARI PASSU" clause

Usually the terms of issue include "Parri Passu" clause which means all debentures of a particular series will rank together with regard to the security irrespective of different timings of issue. It means that all debentures of a series are to be paid rateably and proportionately in case of shortfall

If terms of issue do not mention "Parri Passu" the debentures would be payable according to the date of issue or if these were all issued on the same day, then according to their numerical order.

SEBI'S Guidelines relating to issue of debentures.

1. Requirement of credit rating

(i) No public or rights issue of debentures without credit rating from a credit rating agency.

(ii) If a public/rights issue is equal to or greater than Rs. 100 crore, two ratings from two different credit rating agencies shall be obtained. In this case all credit ratings of last 3 years including un-accepted credit ratings shall be disclosed in the offer document.

2. Requirement in respect of Debenture Trustee

(i) The issuing company shall appoint a Debenture Trustee in case the debentures are redeemable for more than 18 months.

(ii) A trust deed shall be executed with in six months of the closure of issue.

(iii) The names of the trustees must be stated in the offer document.

(iv) The debenture trustees shall be vested with the requisite powers for protecting the interest of debentureholders.

(v) Trustees shall ensure compliance with regard to investment of funds, monitor the progress, replenishing of funds and shall supervise implementation of conditions regarding creation of security for the debentures and Debenture Redemption Reserve.

3. Creation of Debenture Redemption Reserve (DRR)

(i) A company is required to create a DRR in case debentures are redeemable after 18 months. Hence no DRR is required for debentures with maturity period of not exceeding 18 months.

(ii) If debentures are issued for project finance the DRR can be created up to the date of commercial production. No DRR is required for infrastructure companies.

(iii) The DRR may be created either in equal instalments or higher amounts if profits so permit.

(iv) A company shall create DRR equivalent to 50% of the amount of debenture issue before redemption commences. Drawl from DRR is permissible for redemption purposes only after 10%, of the debenture liability has been actually redeemed by the company.

(v) In case of partly convertible debentures, DRR should be created in respect of non-convertible portion. In case of convertible issue by new companies, DRR shall be created from the year company earns profits for the remaining life of debentures.

(vi) DRR will be treated as a part of General Reserve for the purpose of issuing bonus shares.

4. Distribution of Dividends

(i) In case of a new company distribution of dividend shall require approval of trustees.

(ii) In case of an existing company prior permission of lead institution for declaring dividend exceeding 20% or as per the loan covenant is necessary if the company does not comply with the institutional condition regarding interest and debt service coverage ratio.

(iii) Dividends may be distributed out of profits of particular years only after transfer of the requisite amount in the DRR.

(iv) The company may distribute dividends out of general reserve if residual profits, after transfer to DRR are inadequate.

5. Redemption and Other disclosure requirements

(i) Issues of FCD having a conversion period of more than 36 months will not be permissible unless conversion is made optional with "put" or "call" option.

"Put Option" refers to *option to sell* a fixed amount of securities on a certain day and at certain price.

"Call Option" means an *option to buy* a fixed amount of securities on a certain day at a certain price.

(ii) The premium amount and time of conversion shall be determined by the issuer company and disclosed.

(iii) In case of PCDs/NCDs redemption amount, period of maturity, yield on redemption of PCD/NCD.

(iv) The discount at which such offer is made and the effective price for the investor as a result of such discount.

(v) The existing and future equity and long term debt ratio.

(vi) The company shall make adequate disclosures regarding the terms and conditions, redemption, security conversion and any other relevant features of the instruments, such as "Deep Discount Bonds" Debentures with warrants, Secured premium Notes etc. so that an investor can make reasonable determination of the risks, returns, safety and liquidity of instruments.

ISSUE OF DEBENTURES

There is no difference between the issue of shares and issue of debentures, as far as the procedure and methodology of issue is concerned. Debentures are issued in the same manner as the shares are issued. The money payable by the allottees of debentures may be received either in various steps, such as on application, allotment and on calls or the entire amount may be collected in lump sum *i.e.* on application or on application and allotment. This depends purely at the discretion of directors who, in view of the financial requirements of the company, decide the mode & timings of receipt of money on issue of debentures. The only difference is that the word 'debenture is used in place of "share," and in lieu of "share capital" term 9%* Debenture is used.

Like shares, the debentures may be issued at par, at premium or at discount. However, there is no maximum limit of discount on issue of debentures as applicable in case of shares. The premium on issue of debentures may be transferred to "securities premium" account because now "share premium" is termed as Securities premium for debentures are also securities. In this case premium shall be utilised as per the legal provisions of the Companies Act : Alternatively premium on issue of debentures represents capital profit and should be transferred to Capital Reserve, which can be used for writing off :

- Discount on issue of shares and debentures
- Preliminary Expenses
- Underwriting commission
- Amortisation of Goodwill

* any rate of interest which the debentures carry as per Company's policy.

- Fictitious assets
- Cost of issue of debentures
- Loss on issue/ expenses on issue or
- Any other capital losses.

It should be noted that once the premium on issue of debentures is transferred to 'Securities Premium Account' then the restrictions relating to the use of premium on issue of shares will be applicable to the premium on issue of debentures also.

ACCOUNTING TREATMENT OF ISSUE OF DEBENTURES

There are three basis which govern the accounting treatment of issue of debentures :

(1) "Consideration" as the basis of accounting entries

(2) "Price" as the basis of accounting entries

(3) "Terms" (of issue and redemption) as the basis of accounting entries.

1. 'Consideration' aspect

Again from consideration point of view the debentures may be issued :

(a) for Cash

(b) for Consideration other than cash (*i.e.* kind)

(c) as Collateral security.

(a) When debentures are issued for cash

(i) *When money is received in instalments :*

Bank A/c	Dr.	with the actual amount
To 9% Debentures Application A/c		
(Application money received)		
9% Debentures Application A/c	Dr.	
To 9% Debentures A/c		
(Application money transferred to Debentures A/c)		
9% Debentures Allotment A/c	Dr.	
To 9% Debentures A/c		
(Allotment money due)		
Bank A/c	Dr.	
To Debentures Allotment A/c		
(Allotment money received)		

If the debentures are issued at discount :

9% Debentures Allotment A/c	Dr.	with amount due
Discount on issue of Debenture A/c	Dr.	with discount
To 9% Debentures A/c		with total

If debentures are issued at premium

9% Debentures Allotment A/c Dr.

To 9% Debentures A/c

To Securities Premium A/c / Debenture Premium A/c

9% Debentures Call A/c Dr.

To 9% Debentures A/c

(Call money falling due)

Bank A/c Dr.

To 9% Debentures Call A/c

(Call money received)

It is to be noted that "Debentures A/c" is a Debenture Capital A/c" which is like "Share Capital" for accounting purposes.

In case of **"over subscription"** the company has the option to refund excess application money or adjust it against allotment money and call money.

On calls-in-advance and on calls-in-Arrear the company may allow interest or charge interest which is debited and credited respectively to Profit & Loss Account. In case of default, like shares the debentures may also be forfeited and reissued.

The Debentures should be prefixed with the rate of interest. If the rate of interest is 9%, then these will be known as 9% Debentures, and if rate is 12%, then 12% Debentures

(ii) *When money is received in lump sum :*

* If *issued at par*

Bank A/c Dr.

To 9% (say) Debentures A/c

* If *issued at Discount*

Bank A/c Dr.

Discount on Issue of Debentures A/c Dr.

To 9% Debentures A/c

* If *issued at Premium*

Bank A/c Dr.

To 9% Debentures A/c

To Securities Premium/Debenture Premium A/c

(b) Issue of Debentures for consideration other than Cash :

When a company allots debentures against the payment of purchase price of the assets acquired, it is treated as issue of debentures for consideration other than cash. It happens in case of takeover or acquisition of business. The following entries are recorded :

(i) ***When assets are acquired :***

Sundry Assets A/c Dr.

To Vendors A/c

(ii) ***When debentures are issued :***

* If *issued at par* :

Vendors A/c Dr.

To (say) 9% Debentures A/c

* If *issued at Discount :*

Vendors' A/c Dr.

Discounts issue of Debentures A/c Dr.

To 9% Debentures A/c

* If *issued at Premium :*

Vendors' A/c Dr.

To 9% Debentures A/c

To Securities Premium/debenture Premium A/c

It should be noted that :

(i) Debentures Account will always be credited with the par value and

(ii) Vendor's Account will be debited or credited with the amount of net purchase price of the assets acquired.

Illustration (1)

Cyma Ltd. acquired the assets worth Rs. 14,30,000 and took over the liabilities of Rs. 2,20,000 from Shyama Co. Ltd. for a purchase consideration of Rs. 12,60,000. Record Journal entries if Cyma Ltd. issues 11% debentures of Rs. 100 each against the purchase consideration to Shyama Co. Ltd. when :

(a) Debentures are issued at par

(b) Debentures are issued at 10% discount

(c) Debentures are issued at 5% premium.

Solution (1)

In the Book of Cyma Ltd.

JOURNAL ENTRIES

		Rs.	Rs.
	Goodwill A/c (Bal. figure) Dr.	50,000	
	Sundry Assets A/c Dr.	14,30,000	
	To Liabilities A/c		2,20,000
	To Shyama Co. Ltd. A/c		12,60,000
	(Being assets and liabilities takenover)		

Contd.

			Rs.	Rs.
(a)	Shyama Co. Ltd. A/c	Dr.	12,60,000	
	To 11% Debentures A/c			12,60,000
	(Being 12,600, 11% Debentures issued)			
(b)	Shyama Co. Ltd.	Dr.	12,60,000	
	Discount on Issue of Debentures A/c	Dr.	1,40,000	
	To 11% Debentures A/c			14,00,000
	(Being debentures issued at 10% discount)			
(c)	Shyama Co. Ltd. A/c	Dr.	12,60,000	
	To 11% Debentures A/c			12,00,000
	To Securities Premium /Debentures Premium A/c			60,000
	(Being debentures issued at 5% premium			

Working notes :

(1) The excess of Purchase Consideration over Net Assets has been transferred to Goodwill A/c.

(2) The number of debentures should be calculated by dividing the purchase consideration by the agreed value of a debentures to be credited to Debentures Account. It is to be noted that "Debentures Account" will always be shown at its *'nominal value'*.

(a) $\frac{\text{Rs.}12{,}60{,}000}{100}$ = 12,600 Debentures of Rs. 100 each issued at par

(b) $\frac{\text{Rs.}\ 12{,}60{,}000}{90}$ = 14,000 Debentures of Rs. 100 each at 10% discount

(c) $\frac{\text{Rs.}12{,}60{,}000}{105}$ = 12,000 Debentures of Rs. 100 each at 5% premium

Illustration (2)

A Ltd. took over the assets Rs. 8,85,000 and liabilities worth Rs. 75,000 at a purchase price of Rs. 7,92,000 from CV Ltd. It was agreed that purchase consideration be paid by issuing 12% Debentures of Rs. 100 each Pass journal entries of :

(a) Debentures are issued at par

(b) Debentures are issued at 10 % Discount

(c) Debentures are issued at 10 % Premium.

Solution (2)

JOURNAL ENTRIES

		Rs.	Rs.
Sundry Assets A/c	Dr.	8,85,000	
To Liabilities A/c			75,000
To N Ltd. A/c			7,92,000
To Capital Reserve A/c (B.F.)			18,000
(Being assets and liabilities takenover)			

Contd.

			Rs.	Rs.
(a)	N Ltd. A/c	Dr.	7,92,000	
	To 12% Debentures A/c			7,92,000
	(Being Purchase Consideration paid in Debentures of Rs. 100 each par)			
(b)	N Ltd. A/c	Dr.	7,92,000	
	Discount on issue of Debentures A/c	Dr.	88,000	
	To 12% Debentures A/c			8,80,000
	(Being purchase consideration paid in Debentures of Rs. 100 each at 10% Discount)			
(c)	N Ltd. A/c	Dr.	7,92,000	
	To 12% Debentures A/c			7,20,000
	To Securities Premium/Debenture Premium A/c			72,000
	(Being debentures issued at 10% premium)			

Working note :

(1) The excess of net assets (Sundry Assets – liabilities) over purchase consideration has been transferred to capital reserve.

(c) Issue of Debentures as a Collateral Security)

When a Loan is raised against the mortgage of any asset, and if the lender considers that the asset (main security) may not cover the entire risk, he may demand or insist on additional (subsidiary or secondary) security. Under these circumstances, the company (borrower) may issue its own debentures to the lender as additional security so that the amount of loan could be realised in full in case the main/principal security (mortgaged asset) fails to fetch the required amount if there is a default. Such an issue of debentures is known as "issue of debentures as collateral security"

The debentures so issued remain dormant until and unless there is a default with regard to the repayment of loan along with interest on the due date. These debentures can be realised if (i) There is shortfall between the amount due (principal plus interest) and the value of mortgaged asset (principal security) and (ii) There is a default on the part of borrowing company.

In case the amount is repaid in full by the borrowing company, the lender is bound to return debentures and the asset mortgaged immediately.

ACCOUNTING TREATMENT

There are two methods :

First Method

No entry is made in the books under first method. Only a note is given under the heading "Secured Loan" on the liabilities side of the Balance Sheet stating the number of debentures issued as collateral security as shown below :

BALANCE SHEET OF ...(AN EXTRACT)
AS ON...

Liabilities	Rs.
Share Capital	--
Reserves & Surplus	---

Secured Loans	
9% Debentures*	5,00,000
Loan from SBI	4,00,000
(Secured by mortgage of Office Building and 9% 1000 Debentures of Rs. 100 each issued as collateral security)	
* 1000 Debentures are not included.	
(Figures shown in the Balance Sheet are imaginary.	

Second Method

The following entry is recorded :

Debentures Suspense A/c Dr. with the nominal value
To (say) 9% Debentures A/c
(Being debentures issued as collateral security)

These debentures are shown on the liabilities side of the Balance Sheet along with the corresponding entry on assets side of the Balance Sheet under the heading "Miscellaneous Expenditure" as "Debenture Suspense Account"

BALANCE SHEET OF----------(AN EXTRACT)

Liabilities		**Rs.**
Shares Capital		------
Reserves and Surplus		----
Secured Loan		----
9% Debentures		6,00,000*
Loan from SBI		4,00,000
(Secured by mortgage of office Building and 9%. 1000 Debentures of Rs. 100 each issued as collateral security)		
* includes debentures issued as collateral security.		
Assets		Rs
Fixed Assets		......
Investments		......
Current Assets loans & Advances		......
Miscellaneous Expenditure		......
Debenture Suspense Account	100,000	
(Debentures issued as collateral security as per contra)		....

When the loan is repaid and the debentures are released, the following entry is recorded :

9% Debentures A/c Dr.
To Debentures Suspense A/c
(Being debentures issued as collateral security cancelled)

2. Issue of Debentures : From "Price" point of view

As already explained, there are three methods of issuing debentures from price point of view. Like shares, the debentures may be issued :

(a) at par
(b) at discount or
(c) at premium

When a company collects/demands amount equal to the face value of debentures issued, it is known as issue at **par**.

Debentures are said to be issued at discount when amount demanded/collected by the company is less than the nominal value of the debentures issued.

When price charged by the company for the debentures issued exceeds its nominal value, the debentures are said to be issued at premium.

It is to be noted that the impact of "price factor" is seen in all the methods of issue of debentures.

3. From "Terms" (of issue and Redemption) point of view.

Since debentures are invariably redeemable securities these are issued in according with the terms of redemption along with the terms of issue. In fact almost all companies issue debentures with reference to terms of redemption which to a greater extent, affect the accounting treatment of issue of debentures.

There are five possible cases on the basis of terms of issue and redemption of debentures. These are :

1. Issued at **Par** Redeemable at **Par**
2. Issued at **Discount** Redeemable at **Par**
3. Issued at **Premium** Redeemable at **Par**
4. Issued at **Par** Redeemable at **Premium**
5. Issued at **Discount** Redeemable at **Premium**

It is to be noted that the debentures are redeemed at **Par** or at **Premium** but not at discount. This is because of the fact that no person will pay Rs. 100 now to receive Rs. 95 in future — say after 3 or 5 years. However, a company has the option to buy it's own debentures in the open market, let the price falls below the nominal value and thus making profits on redemption. However, this should not be termed as redemption at discount because price fall does not come within the terms of redemption.

ACCOUNTING TREATMENT

Case 1. Issued at **Par** Redeemable at **Par**

Bank A/c	Dr.	with nominal value
To Debentures A/c		

Case 2. Issued at **Discount** Redeemable at **Par**

Bank A/c	Dr.	With Actual Cash Received
Discount on Issue of Debentures A/c	Dr.	With Discount
To Debentures A/c		With Nominal Value

Case 3. Issued at **Premium** Redeemable at **Par**

Bank A/c	Dr.	With actual case
To Debentures A/c		With Nominal Value
To Securities Premium/Debentures Premium A/c		With Premium

Case 4. Issued at **Par** Redeemable at **Premium**

Bank A/c	Dr.	Actual Cash Received
Loss on Issue of Debentures A/c	Dr.	*
To Debentures A/c		Nominal Value
To Premium on Redemption A/c		*

* Note (Loss on issue is equal to Premium on Redemption)

Case 5. Issued at Discount Redeemable at Premium

Bank A/c	Dr.	Actual Cash Received
* Discount on issue of Debentures A/c	Dr.	Amount of discount
* Loss on Issue of Debentures A/c	Dr.	*Premium on Redemption
To Debentures A/c		Nominal Value
To Premium on Redemption A/c		*

* Both may be shown under loss on issue of Debentures.

TREATMENT IN THE BALANCE SHEET (AN EXTRACT)

Liabilities	Rs.	Assets	Rs.
Case No. 1			
(say) 9% Debentures	Nominal Value	Cash at Bank (equal to Nominal value)	Actual Cash received
Case No. 2			
9% Debentures	Nominal Value	Cash at Bank (equal to Nominal Value – discount)	Actual Cash
		Discount on issue of Deb.	----
Case No. 3			
9% Debentures	Nominal Value	Cash at Bank (Nominal value plus Premium on issue)	Actual Cash
Securities Premium	----		
Case No. 4			
9% Debentures	Nominal value	Cash at Bank (equal to nominal value)	Actual Cash
Premium on Redemption A/c*		Loss on issue of Deb. (equal to premium on redemption)	
Case No. 5			
9% Debentures	Nominal value	Cash at bank (Nominal Value less discount)	Actual Cash
Premium on Redemption A/c	....	* Discount on Issue of Deb.---	----
		* Loss on Issue of Deb	----

It is to be noted that "Premium on Redemption A/c" is a liability which will be paid by the company at the time of redemption. Since it is a loss it is also shown as "Loss on issue of Debentures" on the assets side of the Balance Sheet. This Loss on issue is written off either gradually or at the time of redemption of debentures.

Illustration (3)

Record journal entries in the books of Rana Ltd. in the following cases.

(i) Issued 12% 1000 Debentures of Rs. 100 each at par and redeemable at par.

(ii) Issued 10% 800 debentures of Rs. 100 each at 5% discount and redeemable at par.

(iii) Issued 9% 1,500 Debentures of Rs. 100 each at 10% premium and redeemable at par.

(iv) Issued 11% 2,000 Debentures of Rs. 100 each at par and redeemable at 5% premium.

(v) Issued 9.5% 2,500 Debentures of Rs. 100 each at 4% discount and redeemable at 5% premium.

Also show the relevant extract of Balance Sheet.

Solution (3)

JOURNAL ENTRIES

			Rs.	Rs.
(i)	Bank A/c	Dr.	1,00,000	
	To 12% Debentures A/c			1,00,000
	(Being 12% debentures issued at par and redeemable at par)			
(ii)	Bank A/c	Dr.	76,000	
	Discount on issue of Debentures A/c	Dr.	4,000	
	To 10% Debentures A/c			80,000
	(Being 10% debentures issued at discount redeemable at par)			
(iii)	Bank A/c	Dr.	1,65,000	
	To 9% Debentures A/c			1,50,000
	To Securities Premium A/c			15,000
	(Being 9% Debentures issued at premium redeemable at par)			
(iv)	Bank A/c	Dr.	2,00,000	
	Loss on issue of debentures A/c	Dr.	10,000	
	To 11% Debentures A/c			2,00,000
	To Premium on Redemption A/c			10,000
	(Being 11% Debentures issued at par redeemable at premium)			
(v)	Bank A/c	Dr.	2,40,000	
	* Discount on issue of Debentures A/c	Dr.	10,000	
	* Loss on issue of Debentures A/c	Dr.	12,500	
	To 9.5% Debentures A/c			2,50,000
	To Premium on Redemption A/c			12,500
	(Being 9.5% Debenture issued at discount redeemable at premium)			

* Both may be shown under the Loss on issue of Debentures A/c.

BALANCE SHEET OF ---- (AN EXTRACT)

AS ON ---------

	Liabilities	Rs.	Assets	Rs.
(i)	12% Debentures	1,00,000	Cash at Bank	1,00,000
(ii)	10% Debentures	80,000	Cash at Bank	76,000
			Discount on Issue of Deb.	4,000
(iii)	Securities Premium	15,000	Cash at Bank	1,65,000
	9% Debenture	1,50,000		
(iv)	11% Debentures	2,00,000	Cash at Bank	2,00,000
	Premium on Redemption	10,000	Loss on Issue	10,000
(v)	9.5% Debentures	2,50,000	Cash at Bank	2,40,000
	Premium on Redemption	12,500	* Discount on issue of Debentures	10,000
			* Loss on Issue of Debentures	12,500

* Both may be shown under Loss on issue of Debentures

It is to be noted that : Loss on issue is equal to premium on redemption and if discount is clubbed then, Loss on Issue will be = Discount on issue plus Premium on Redemption A/c

DISCOUNT AND LOSS ON ISSUE OF DEBENTURES

Discount on issue of debentures and the "loss on issue of debentures (which is Premium on redemption account) are capital losses which are shown in the Balance Sheet under the heading "Miscellaneous Expenditure" as fictitious assets. Although the writing off discount/Loss on issue is not a legal compulsion but sound and prudent accounting principles require that such discount/loss should be written off during the life span of debentures at least if not earlier. Such loss being a capital loss may be adjusted against the Capital Profits/Capital Reserve/ Securities Premium. In case capital profits are not available then such loss should be written off against revenue profits on a rational basis

Accounting Treatment

(i) If Discount/ Loss on issue of Debentures is to be written off against Capital profits/ Capital Reserves/Securities Premium.

Capital Profits/ Capital Reserves/Securities Premium A/c Dr.

To Discount/Loss on Issue of Debentures A/c

(Being discount/Loss on issue written off)

(ii) If the company decides to treat it as deferred revenue expenditure and to write off against the revenue profits, the following entry shall be recorded

Profit & Loss A/c Dr.

To Discount/Loss on Issue of Debentures A/c

(Being discount/Loss on issue written off)

Now the problem arises as to how much and in how many instalments the discount or loss on issue should be written off. However, there are two methods of writing off the discount/loss on issue of debentures out of revenue incomes.

(i) Fixed Instalment Method

When debentures are redeemed after the expiry of a stipulated period of time, the total amount of discount/ Loss on issue is written off equally over the life span of the debentures.

For example amount to be written off is Rs. 60,000 and the debentures issued are redeemable after 10 years. Then the annual amount to be charged to Profit & Loss Account will be Rs. 6,000

i.e. $\left(\text{Rs. } \frac{60,000}{10}\right)$

This method is based on equity in the sense that the benefit of debentures funds throughout the life span of the debentures remains same each year.

(ii) Proportionate benefit Method or Fluctuating Instalment Method

When the debentures are to be redeemed in instalments then the total amount of discount/Loss on issue **is written off in the proportion of debentures amount remaining outstanding at** the beginning of each year. This method is again based on benefits received, from debentures funds each year. The debentures funds each year go on decreasing and therefore discount/loss on issue of debentures is spread over the years in the ratio of amount of debentures fund outstanding at the beginning of each year.

Illustration (4)

X Ltd. issued 9% 2000 Debentures of Rs. 100 each at a discount of 4% redeemable at 2% premium. What method of writing off discount/loss on issue, you will adopt if :

(a) Debentures are redeemable at the and of five years.

(b) The debentures of Rs. 50,000 are to be redeemed each year.

Required : (i) Journal entry recording issue of debentures

(ii) Discount/ Loss on Issue of Debentures A/c.

Solution (4)

Bank A/c	Dr.	1,92,000	
Discount on Issue of Debentures A/c	Dr.	8,000	
Loss on Issue of Debentures A/c	Dr.	4,000	
To 9% Debentures A/c			2,00,000
To Premium on Redemption A/c			4,000
(Being 9% Debentures issued)			

(a) Total amount to be written off — Rs.

Discount on Issue of Debentures — 8,000

Loss on Issue (Premium on redemption) — 4,000

Amount to be written off annually $\frac{12,000}{5}$ = Rs. 2,400

DISCOUNT/LOSS ON ISSUE OF DEBENTURES A/C

Year		Rs.	Year		Rs.
I	To 9% Debentures A/c	8,000	I	By Profit & Loss A/c	2,400
	To Premium on Redemption A/c	4,000		By Balance c/d	9,600
		12,000			12,000
II	To Balance b/d	9,600	II	By Profit & Loss A/c	2,400
				By Balance c/d	7,200
		9,600			9,600
III	To Balance b/d	7,200	III	By Profit & Loss A/c	2,400
				By Balance c/d	4,800
		7,200			7,200
IV	To Balance b/d	4,800	IV	By Profit & Loss A/c	2,400
				By Balance c/d	2,400
		4,800			4,800
V	To Balance b/d	2,400	V	By Profit & Loss A/c	2,400
		2,400			2,400

(b)

Year	O/s Debentures in the beginning of year	Ratio	Amount to be written off
Ist yr.	2,00,000	4	12,000 × 4/10 = 4,800
IInd yr.	1,50,000	3	12,000 × 3/10 = 3,600
IIIrd yr.	1,00,000	2	12,000 × 2/10 = 2,400
IVth yr.	50,000	1	12,000 × 1/10 = 1,200
		10	

DISCOUNT/LOSS ON ISSUE OF DEBENTURES A/C

Year		Rs.	Year		Rs.
Ist yr.	To 9% debentures A/c	8,000	Ist yr.	By Profit & Loss A/c	4,800
	To Premium on Redemption A/c	4,000		By Balance c/d	7,200
		12,000			12,000
IInd yr.	To Balance b/d	7,200	IInd yr.	By Profit & Loss A/c	3,600
				By Balance c/d	3,600
		7,200			7,200
IIIrd.yr.	To Balance b/d	3,600	IIIrd yr.	By Profit & Loss A/c	2,400
				By Balance c/d	1,200
		3,600			3,600
IVth yr.	To Balance b/d	1,200	IVth yr.	By Profit & Loss A/c	1,200
		1,200			1,200

Illustration (5)

(Proportionate benefit Method)

Solomen Ltd. issued 9% Debentures at 6% discount for Rs. 10,00,000 on 1.7.1998 repayable by five equal instalments of Rs. 2,00,000 by drawing a lot at par. The company closes it's accounts on calendar year basis.

Prepare a discount on issue of Debentures account assuming that company writes off debentures discount during the life span of the debentures.

Solution (5)

Table showing ratio of allocation

Year ended 31st Dec.	Product = (Amount of deb. × duration of use) Rs.	Ratio
1998	10,00,000 × 6 = 60,00,000	60 = 5
1999	10,00,000 × 6 = 60,00,000 8,00,000 × 6 = 48,00,000	108 = 9
2000	8,00,000 × 6 = 48,00,000 6,00,000 × 6 = 36,00,000	84 =7
2001	6,00,000 × 6 = 36,00,000 4,00,000 × 6 = 24,00,000	60 = 5
2002	4,00,000 × 6 = 24,00,000 2,00,000 × 6 = 12,00,000	36 = 3
2003	2,00,000 × 6 = 12 00 000	12 = 1

Hence, the amount of discount on issue of debentures Rs. 60,000 will be written off in the ratio of 5 : 9 : 7 : 5 : 3 : 1 as shown below :

$$1998 = \frac{60,000 \times 5}{30} = 10,000$$

$$1999 = \frac{60,000 \times 9}{30} = 18,000$$

$$2000 = \frac{60,000 \times 7}{30} = 14,000$$

$$2001 = \frac{60,000 \times 5}{30} = 10,000$$

$$2002 = \frac{60,000 \times 3}{30} = 6,000$$

$$2003 = \frac{60,000 \times 1}{30} = 2,000$$

Note : Since Debentures are issued on 1st July and the books of accounts are closed on 31st December each year, the usage period in each celender year is bifurcated between 1st July to 31st December (6 months) in the first year and then 1st January to 30th June & July to 31st December in each subsequent year.

DISCOUNT ON ISSUE OF DEBENTURES A/C

		Rs.			Rs.
1st July 1998	To 12% Debentures A/c	60,000	31st Dec. 1998	By Profit & Loss A/c	10,000
				By Balance c/d	50,000
		60,000			60,000
1st Jan. 1999	To Balance b/d	50,000	31st Dec. 1999	By Profit & Loss A/c	18,000
				By Balance c/d	32,000
		50,000			50,000
1st Jan. 2000	To Balance b/d	32,000	31st Dec. 2000	By Profit & Loss A/c	14,000
				By Balance c/d	18,000
		32,000			32,000
1st Jan. 2001	To Balance b/d	18,000	31st Dec. 2001	By Profit & Loss A/c	10,000
				By Balance c/d	8,000
		18,000			18,000
1st Jan. 2002	To Balance b/d	8,000	31st Dec. 2002	By Profit & Loss A/c	6,000
				By Balance c/d	2,000
		8,000			8,000
1st Jan. 2003	To Balance c/d	2,000	31st Dec. 2003	By Profit & Loss A/c	2,000
		2,000			2,000

Debenture Interest

Interest on debentures is paid at a fixed rate as per the terms of issue of debentures. Interest on debentures is a charge against the profits of the company and is debited to Profit & Loss A/c on accrual basis. Interest is normally payable six monthly. However, Companies are required to deduct tax at source (T.D.S.) as per the provisions of Income Tax Act 1961. The following entries are recorded :

(i) *When interest is due :*

Debenture Interest A/c	Dr.	Gross interest
To Income Tax Payable A/c		T.D.S.
To Debentureholders' A/c	Dr.	Net amount of interest (Gross — T.D.S.)

(ii) *When Interest is paid**

Debentureholders' A/c	Dr.	Net amount of Interest
To Bank A/c		

(iii) *When TDS is paid**

Income Tax payable A/c	Dr.	
To Bank A/c		

(iv) *On the date of closing of Books*:

Profit & Loss A/c	Dr.	With Gross interest for the accounting year
To Debentures Interest A/c		

* If net interest to debentureholders and T.D.S. to Tax authorities is paid concurrently, a combined entry may be recorded.

However, in case T.D.S. is not paid till the date of closing of Books it will be shown as "Income Tax Payable" under the heading "Current liabilities and provisions" on the liabilities side of Balance Sheet.

Debenture Interest Accrued but Outstanding

It is to be noted that interest is payable on specific dates say 31st December and 30th June each year. If the interest on these dates is not paid, then it will be treated interest accrued and due or outstanding. This amount if remains unpaid on the date of Balance Sheet, will be shown on the liabilities side of Balance Sheet under the heading "Secured Loans".

Debenture Interest Accrued but not due*

Interest Accrued means interest earned by Debentureholders by virtue of their holding but the same has not fallen due because interest falls due only on specific dates. If the Books of Accounts are closed on 31st March then the interest for three months (Jan to March) will be treated as "Interest accrued but not due" on the date of Balance Sheet and will be shown as current liability.

* (Presumed to be 30th June and 31st Dec.)

Illustration (6)

On 1.1.2004 X Ltd. issued 9% 5,000 Debentures of Rs. 100 each at 6% discount redeemable at 5% premium after the expiry of 5 years Interest is payable on 30th June and 31st December every year. Presume 10% TDS.

Pass Journal entries for the accounting year ending on 31st December, 2004.

(b) Will it make any difference if Interest and Tax remain unpaid on 31.12.2004

JOURNAL ENTRIES

2004			Rs.	Rs.
1. 1.	Bank A/c	Dr.	4,70,000	
	Discount on issue of Debentures A/c	Dr.	30,000	
	Loss on Issue of Debentures A/c	Dr.	25,000	
	To 9% Debentures A/c			5,00,000
	To Premium on Redemption A/c			25,000
	(Being debentures issued)			
30.6	Debenture Interest A/c	Dr.	22,500	
	To Debentureholders' A/c			20,250
	To Income Tax Payable A/c			2,250
	(Being interest payable for 6 months)			
	Debentureholders' A/c	Dr.	20,250	
	Income Tax Payable A/c	Dr.	2,250	
	To Bank A/c			22,500
	(Being interest & Tax paid)			

Contd.

2004			Rs.	Rs.
31.12	Debenture Interest A/c	Dr.	22,500	
	To Debentureholders' A/c			20,250
	To Income Tax Payable A/c			2,250
	(Being interest due for six month)			
	Debenture holders A/c	Dr.	20,250	
	Income Tax Payable A/c	Dr.	2,250	
	To Bank A/c			22,500
	(Being interest and Tax paid)			
	Profit & Loss A/c	Dr.	45,000	
	To Debenture Interest A/c			45,000
	(Being interest for the year charged to Profit & Loss A/c)			
	Profit & Loss A/c	Dr.	11,000	
	To Discount on issue of Debentures A/c			6,000
	To Loss on issue of Debentures A/c			5,000
	(Being discount & loss on issue written off equally over five years)			
(b)	In this case entries for the interest due and payment will not be recorded but the following entry shall be recorded.			
	Debenture Interest A/c	Dr.	22,500	
	To Debenture Interest o/s			20,250
	To Income Tax Payable A/c			2,250
	(Being interest due but not paid)			

Debenture Interest o/s will be shown under the heading **"secured loans"** and Income Tax payable under the heading **"Current liabilities** and provisions" on the liabilities side of the Balance Sheet.

DEBENTURE INTEREST AND DEEP DISCOUNT BONDS OR DEBENTURES

With out coupon (interest) rate

Also known as zero coupon bonds. Usually debentures are issued with a specific interest rate but some times these bonds or debentures are issued without any prefix interest rate but having a definite maturity value. Under such a situation bonds/debentures are issued at a heavily or substantially discounted price. These debentures are known as Deep Discount Bonds/Debentures as explained earlier also. The difference between maturity value and issue price (a notional discount) is treated as **"deferred interest expense"** which is written off proportionately over the life span of the debentures like general interest expense. The following entries are recorded :

1st Year *When debentures/bonds are issued :*

* Bank A/c	Dr.	
Deferred Interest Expense A/c	Dr.	
To Debentures A/c		

At the end of subsequent Years

* Debenture Interest A/c Dr.

To Deferred Interest Expense A/c

(Being deferred interest charged to debenture interest A/c)

*Profit & Loss A/c Dr.

To Debenture Interest A/c

(Being debenture interest transferred to P & L A/c)

* Last Year - *When amount is due on maturity :*

Debentures A/c Dr.

To Debentureholders' A/c

* *When amount is paid* :

Debentureholders' A/c Dr.

To Bank A/c

Computation of periodic interest

There are two methods for computing interest on deep discount bonds/debentures :

(i) Present Value based on discounting

(ii) Future Value based on compounding.

Under first method the following formula is used :

$$PV = FV\left(\frac{1}{1+i}\right)^n$$

PV = Issue price

FV = Maturity Value

i = Interest rate

n = number of years (period of redemption)

Under second method, for calculating FV (Future Value) based on compounding the following equation will be used.

$$FV = PV\ (1+i)^n$$

A company issues deep discount bond at a price of Rs. 713 and pays you Rs. 1,000 after 5 Years. Find out rate of interest with the help of present value and future value.

Applying the First Method (Discounted Value)

$$PV = FV\left(\frac{1}{(1+i)}\right)^n$$

$$\text{PVIF*} = \frac{\text{Issue Price}}{\text{Maturity Value}}$$

$$713 = 1000\left(\frac{1}{(1+i)}\right)^n$$

PVIF = 0.713*

If refer to PVIF table, the present Value of Rupee 1 which is 0.713 in five years period falls in 7% and similarly if we apply the second formula.

We get :

$$FV = PV (1+i)^n$$

$$Rs\ 1,000 = 713\ (1+i)^n$$

$$Rs.\ 1,000 = 713\ (FVIF\ .\ i\ .5)$$

$$FVIF\ i\ .5 = \frac{1000}{713} = 1.4025$$

If we locate 1.4025 in FVIF table

We find it under 7% rate

$$\text{Hence in short } FVIF = \frac{\text{Maturity Value}}{\text{Issue Price}}$$

Illustration (6A)

A Limited company issued 5000 Zero coupon bonds of the face value of Rs 1000 each maturing after 5 years at an issue price of Rs. 650 Record necessary entries in the books of company.

Ist year			Rs	Rs.
1.1	Bank A/c	Dr.	32,50,000	
	Deferred Interest Expense A/c	Dr.	17,50,000	
	To Bonds A/c			50,00,000
	(Being Zero coupon bonds issued)			
31.12	Bond Interest A/c	Dr.	2,92,400	
	To Deferred Interest Expense A/c			2,92,400
	(Being Def. Int. Exp. Charged to bond interest)			
	Profit & Loss A/c	Dr.	2,92,400	
	To Bond Interest A/c			2,92,400
	(Being bond interest charged to P & L A/c)			
IInd Year	Bond Interest A/c	Dr.	3,18,700	
	To Deferred Interest Expenses A/c			3,18,700
	(Being Def. Interest. Exp. charged to bond interest)			
	Profit & Loss A/c	Dr.	3,18,700	
	To Bond Interest A/c			3,18,700
	(Being bond interest charge to P & L A/c)			
IIIrd Year	Bond Interest A/c	Dr.	3,47,400	
	To Deferred Interest Expense A/c			3,47,400
	(Being Def. Interest Exp. charged to bond interest A/c)			
	Profit & Loss A/c	Dr.	3,47,400	
	To Bond Interest A/c			3,47,400
	(Being bond interest charge to PEC A/c)			

Contd.

IVth Year	Bond Interest A/c	Dr.	3,78,700	
	To Deferred Interest Expense A/c			3,78,700
	(Being Interest Expense charged to bond interest.)			
	Profit & Loss A/c	Dr.	3,78,700	
	To Bank Interest A/c			3,78,700
	(Being bond interest Charged to P & L A/c)			
Vth Year	Bond Interest A/c	Dr.	4,12,800	
	To Deferred interest Expense A/c			4,12,800
	(Being Def. Interest Exp. charge to bond interest.)			
	Profit & Loss A/c	Dr.	4,12,800	
	To Bond Interest			4,12,800
	(Being bond interest charge P & L A/c)			

Table showing Computation of Interest

1 Year	2 FV(Rs.)	3 Interest (Rs.)*	4 (2-3) PV(Rs)
5th	1000	$1000 = \frac{9}{109} = 82.568$	917.431
4th	917.431	$917.431 = \frac{9}{109} = 75.751$	841.679
3rd	841.679	$841.679 = \frac{9}{109} = 69.496$	772.182
2nd	772.182	$772.182 = \frac{9}{109} = 63.758$	708.423
1st	708.423	$708.423 = \frac{9}{109} = 58.493$	649.929 App. 650%

* Represents interest on one bond for the Year. While calculating total yearly interest, figures have been multiplied by the number of bonds issued, (*i.e.* by 5,000 bonds). However, interest figures have been approximated due to multiple digits.

REDEMPTION OF DEBENTURES

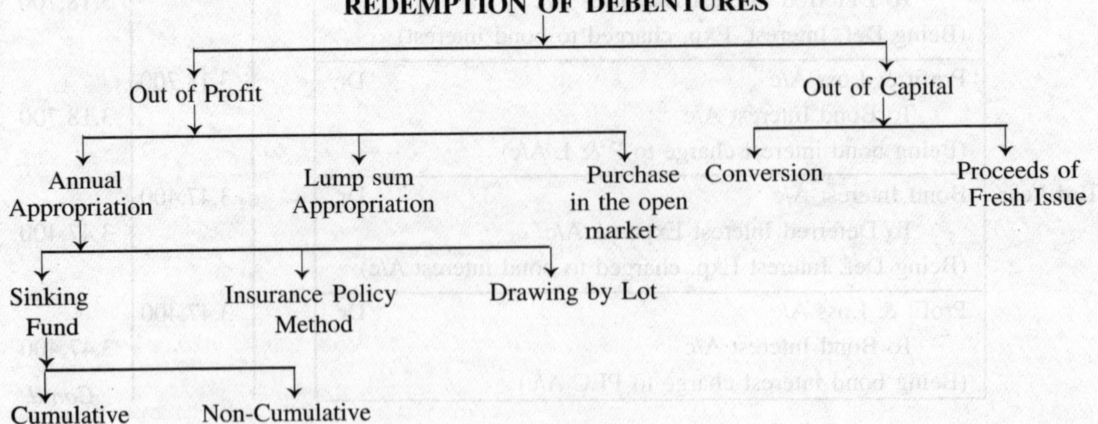

REDEMPTION OF DEBENTURES

Redemption implies repayment of money raised through debentures. In other words it refers to discharge of an obligation created through the Debenture Trust Deed after the debentures have been issued. The Companies Act does not contain any specific guidelines relating to term and conditions for the redemption of debentures. Invariably debentures are redeemed after the expiry of the period for which the debentures were issued. But the company may, if authorised by Articles of Association and terms of issue, redeem the debentures even before the date of maturity. The debentures may be redeemed either out of profits or out of capital. In both these cases the following methods may be adopted.

1. Redemption after the stipulated period of time (Lump Sum)
2. Redemption by drawing by lot.
3. Redemption by conversion or out of proceeds of fresh issue
4. Redemption by purchase in the open market.

It is to be noted that when debentures are redeemed out of profits, an amount equivalent to nominal value of debentures so redeemed has to be transferred to General Reserve. Further as per SEBI'S guidelines, there must be a balance equal to 50% of the nominal value of debentures issued, to the credit of DRR before redemption commences. When all debentures are redeemed, the balance of DRR is transferred to General Reserve.

It should be remembered that when redemption is made out of capital, no transfer to DRR/GR is required to be made.

DRR = Debenture Redemption Reserve

GR = General Reserve

METHODS OF REDEMPTION

1. Redemption after the expiry of stipulated period of time

Under this method, a company redeems its debentures after the expiry of the specified period of time as per the terms of issue or even before the date of maturity/redemption of such debentures. Usually, the debentures are redeemed in one lot under this method. Since the company is well aware of the date of maturity/redemption in-advance, it makes necessary arrangement to provide funds for **the purpose of redemption of debentures in such a way so as to carry out redemption** without affecting the financial position of the company. Hence, a company may opt for one of the following methods by appropriating profits annually or otherwise. Such methods are known as redemption out of profits.

(a) Sinking Fund Method/Debenture Redemption Fund Method
  (i) Cumulative
  (ii) Non-cumulative

(b) Insurance Policy Method.

(c) Redemption (without annual appropriation) in one lot

Redemption by creating a Sinking Fund or by taking a Insurance Policy is known as **"redemption out of profits"**

(a) (i) Sinking Fund/Debenture Redemption Fund Method

Sinking Fund (or Debenture Redemption fund) is a fund created out of divisible profits appropriated annually and invested outside in marketetable securities/first class securities with the object of providing necessary funds as and when required i.e. on specified date. It enables the company to redeem debentures without affecting its working capital or liquidity position.

Under this method following steps are required :

(i) Work out total amount required at the time of redemption of debentures which is usually equal to the nominal value of debentures to be redeemed plus premium on redemption, if any.

(ii) Calculation of amount to be appropriated annually out of the profits of the company. This can be worked out as follows.

Total amount required × Reference to Sinking Fund Table.

In case Sinking Fund table is not available the following formula may be used to ascertain the annual appropriation

$$\text{Annual Appropriation} = P \times \left(\frac{i}{(1+i)^{n-1}} \right)$$

Where : i = rate of interest

n = number of years

p = Amount required on redemptio

It should be noted that reference to Sinking fund table may state that if Rs. 0.2155 invested @ 10% p.a. for 5 years will accumulate Re. 1. The reference to S.F. Table 0.2155 will be multiplied by the amount required. If, however, it is stated in the question that if Re. 1 invested @ 5% for 5 years total amount required will be divided by reference to Sinking Fund Table to get the amount of annual appropriation.

(iii) Purchase the marketable securities such as Government bonds or other readily marketable securities.

(iv) In the second & subsequent years (except. Final year) annual appropriation along with the interest is invested in outside securities.

(v) Sell the securities in the last year. Do not invest or purchase the securities in the final year when redemption is due.

Sinking Fund to "Replace an Asset. Vs. *Sinking Fund to "Repay a liability"*

1. Sinking Fund created to replace an asset is treated as a "charge" and debited to Profit & loss Account like any other expense. However, Sinking Fund created to repay a liability is an "appropriation" and as such debited to Profit & Loss Appropriation Account.

2. S.F. to replace an asset represents accumulated depreciation which is closed by transferring to Asset Account whereas S.F. to repay a liability represents accumulated profits and hence transferred to General Reserve after debentures are redeemed.

Accounting Treatment

JOURNAL ENTRIES

At the end of first accounting year

1. Profit & Loss Appropriation A/c Dr.
   To Sinking Fund A/c
   (Being amount set-aside for S. Fund)
2. Sinking Fund Investments A/c Dr.
   To Bank A/c
   (Being amount invested)

At the end of Second & Subsequent Years

1. Bank A/c Dr.
   To Interest on S. F. Investments A/c
   (Being interest on S.F. Investments received)
2. Interest on S.F. Investments A/c Dr.
   To Sinking Fund A/c
   (Being Interest on S.F. Investments transferred to S. F. Account)
3. Profit & Loss Appropriation A/c Dr.
   To Sinking Fund A/c
   (Being annual appropriation made)
4. Sinking Fund Investments A/c Dr.
   To Bank A/c
   (Being amount of annual appropriation and interest invested)

At the end of Last year when redemption is due

1. Bank A/c Dr.
   To Interest on S.F. Investments A/c
   (Being interest on S.F. Investments received)
2. Interest on S.F. Investments A/c Dr.
   To Sinking Fund A/c
   (Being Interest on S.F. Investments transferred to Sinking Fund Account)
3. Profit & Loss Appropriation A/c Dr.
   To Sinking Fund A/c
   (Being annual appropriation made)
4. Bank A/c Dr.
   To Sinking Fund Investments A/c
   (Being S.F. Investments sold at Cost *i.e.* no profit and no loss)

(a) *If sold at profits*

Bank A/c	Dr.	....	Sale Proceed
To Sinking Fund Investments A/c		....	Cost
To Sinking Fund A/c		....	Profit

(b) *If sold at loss*

Bank A/c Dr.. ..... Sale Proceeds

Sinking Fund A/c Dr. ..... Loss

To S.F. Investments A/c ..... Cost.

5. Sinking Fund A/c Dr.

To General Reserve A/c

(Being S. F. A/c closed by transferring to General Reserve)

Illustration (7)

S Ltd. issued 9% 5000 Debentures of Rs. 100 each redeemable after three years at 6% premium for the purpose of redemption a Sinking Fund was created. Sinking Fund table shows that if Re. 0.31720856 invested at 5% compound interest will accumulate Re. 1 at the end of third year.

You are required to pass journal entries and open necessary ledger accounts.

Solution (7)

JOURNAL ENTRIES

			Rs.	Rs.
1st Year	Bank A/c	Dr.	5,00,000	
	Loss on Issue A/c	Dr.	50,000	
	To 9% Debentures A/c			5,00,000
	To Premium on Redemption A/c			50,000
	(Being 9% Debentures issued redeemable at premium)			
1st year at the end	Profit & Loss Appropriation A/c	Dr.	1,74,465	
	To Sinking Fund A/c			1,74,465
	(Being amount transferred to Sinking Fund)			
	Sinking Fund Investments A/c	Dr.	1,74,465	
	To Bank A/c			1,74,465
	(Being amount invested)			
IInd Yr. at the end	Bank A/c	Dr.	8,723	
	To Interest on S.F. Investment A/c			8,723
	(Being Interest on S.F. Investments received)			
	Interest on S.F. Investments A/c	Dr.	8,723	
	To Sinking Fund A/c			8,723
	(Being Interest on S.F. investments transferred to S. Fund A/c)			
	Profit and Loss Appropriation A/c	Dr.	1,74,465	
	To Sinking Fund A/c			1,74,465
	(Being annual appropriation made)			

Contd.

			Rs.	Rs.
IIIrd. yr. at the end	Bank A/c To Interest on S.F. Investments A/c (Being Interest on S.F. Investments received)	Dr.	17,882	17,882
	Interest on S.F. Investments A/c To Sinking Fund A/c (Being Interest on S.F. Investments transferred to S. Fund. A/c)	Dr.	17,882	17,882
	Profit & Loss Appropriation A/c To Sinking Fund A/c (Being annual appropriation made to S. Fund A/c)	Dr.	1,74,465	1,74,465
	Bank A/c To Sinking Fund Investments A/c (Being S.F. Investments sold at Cost)	Dr.	3,57,653	3,57,653

9% DEBENTURES ACCOUNT

		Rs.			Rs.
Ist Yr.	To Balance c/d	5,00,000	Ist Yr.	By Bank A/c	5,00,000
IInd Yr.	To Balance c/d	5,00,000	IInd Yr.	By Balance b/d	5,00,000
III rd Yr.	To Debentureholders' A/c	5,00,000	III rd Yr.	By Balance b/d	5,00,000

SINKING FUND A/C

		Rs.			Rs.
Ist yr.	To Balance c/d	1,74,465	Ist yr.	By P & L Appropriation A/c	1,74,465
IInd Yr.	To Balance c/d	3,57,653	II nd yr.	By Balance b/d	1,74,465
				By Interest on S.F.I.	8723
				By P & L App. A/c	1,74,465
		3,57,653			3,57,653
III rd yr.	To Loss on Issue A/c	50,000	III rd Yr.	By Balance b/d	3,57,653
	To General Reserve A/c	5,00,000		By Interest on S.F. Investments	17,882
				By P & L App. A/c	1,74,465
		5,50,000			5,50,000

SINKING FUND INVESTMENTS A/C

		Rs.			Rs.
Ist yr.	To Bank A/c	1,74,465	I st	By Balance c/d	1,74,465
II nd yr.	To Balance b/d	1,74,465	II nd yr.	By Balance c/d	3,57,653
	To Bank A/c	1,83,188			
		3,57,653			3,57,653
IIIrd Yr.	To Balance b/d	3,57,653	IIIrd Yr.	By Bank A/c	3,57,653
		3,57,653			3,57,653

Points to Remember :

* Sinking Fund Investments A/c should always be shown at cost. However, a separate column may be prepared to show the nominai value of investments made in securities, if so desired.
* Interest on investments should be calculated on the nominal value of securities and not at the cost of investments.
* In case balance standing to the credit of Sinking Fund is given without any corresponding balance of S. F. Investments, then credit balance of Sinking Fund A/c will be equal to debit balance of S.F. Investments Account.
* Premium on Redemption Account which represents "Loss on issue of debentures" should be debited to Sinking Fund Account at the time of redemption of debentures proportionate to the debentures redeemed.
* If debentures are redeemed in instalments, an amount equal to face value of debentures so redeemed should be transferred to General Reserve. If all the debentures are redeemed at one time the balancing figure should be transferred to General Reserve.
* Loss on sale of S.F. Investments, if any, should be charged to Sinking Fund Account whereas profit on sale of S.F. Investments be credited to Sinking Fund Account and therefrom it may be transferred either to capital reserve or general reserve.
  There is no hard and fast rule as to the treatment of profit on sale of sinking fund investments. Some authorities prefer to transfer to General Reserve where as others to Capital Reserve.

Illustration (8)

The following balances appeared in the books of Vyoma Ltd. as on 31st March, 2004.

9% Debentures	4,00,000
9% Debentures Redemption Fund	3,00,000
9% Debentures Redemption Fund Investments	3,00,000
(represented by 10% Government. Bonds Rs. 3,60,000)	

Annual contribution to Debentures Redemption Fund was Rs. 64,000 made on 31st March each year. On 31st March, 2005 bank balance before the receipt of interest was Rs. 2,00,000. The company sold the investments at 80% and paid the amount due to the debentureholders.

Journalise the transactions and prepare necessary ledger accounts.

ICWA (1) (Adapted)

Solution (8)

JOURNAL ENTRIES

				Rs.	Rs.
31.3.2005	Bank A/c	Dr.		36,000	
	To Interest on D.R.F. Investments A/c				36,000
	(Being interest on DRF Investments received)				
	Interest on D.R.F. Investments A/c	Dr.		36,000	
	To D.R. Fund A/c				36,000
	(Being interest or D.R.F. Investments transferred to D. R. Fund Account)				
	Profit & Loss Appropriation A/c	Dr.		64,000	
	To D. R. Fund A/c				64,000
	(Being annual appropriation to D.R. Fund made)				
	Bank A/c	Dr.		2,88,000	
	Deb. Red. Fund A/c	Dr.		12,000	
	To D. R. F. Investments A/c				3,00,000
	(Being investments sold and Loss transferred to D.R. Fund A/c)				
	9% Debentures A/c	Dr.		4,00,000	
	To Debentureholders A/c				4,00,000
	(Being amount due on redemption)				
	Debentureholders A/c	Dr.		4,00,000	
	To Bank A/c				4,00,000
	(Being amount paid on redemption)				
	Debenture Redemption Fund A/c	Dr.		3,88,000	
	To General Reserve A/c				3,88,000
	(Being balance of D.R. Fund A/c transferred to General Reserve after redemption)				

9% DEBENTURES A/C

		Rs.			Rs.
31.03.05	To Debentureholders A/c	4,00,000	1. 4. 04	By Balance b/d	4,00,000

DEBENTURE REDEMPTION FUND A/C

		Rs.			Rs.
31. 3. 05	To D.R.F. Investments A/c (Loss on sale)	12,000	1. 4. 04	By Balance b/d	3,00,000
	To General Reserve	3,88,000	31.03.05	By Interest on D.R. F. Investments	36,000
				By P& L Appropriation A/c	64,000
		4,00,000			4,00,000

DEBENTURE REDEMPTION FUND INVESTMENTS A/C

		Rs.			Rs.
1.4.2004	To Balance b/d	3,00,000	31.03.05	By Bank A/c	2,88,000
				By D.R. Fund A/c (Loss on Sale)	12,000
		3,00,000			3,00,000

BANK A/C

		Rs.			Rs.
1.4.2004	To Balance b/d	2,00,000	31.03.05	By Debenturers	4,00,000
	To Intrest of DRFI	36,000		By Balance c/d	1,24,000
	To Deb. Red. Fund Investment	2,88,000			
		5,24,000			5,24,000

Working notes :

(i) Interest on D.R.F. Investments has been calculated @ 10% on the face value of investments of Rs. 3,60,000

(ii) Sale proceeds $= \frac{3,60,000 \times 80}{100} =$ Rs.2,88,000

Illustration (9) (Loss on sale of S.F. Investments)

The following balances appeared in the books of S. Adnan Ltd. as on 1st April, 2004.

9% Debentures	6,00,000.
Debenture Redemption Fund Account	5,00,000
(Represented by Rs. 5,90,000 5% Government bonds)	

The annual contribution to Debenture Redemption Fund was Rs. 82,300.

On 31st March, 2005 the Bank Balance after the receipt of interest was Rs. 1,50,000.

The D.R.F. Investments was sold at 17% less than the face value. The debentures were paid off. Prepare necessary ledger accounts for the year ended 31st March, 2005.

9% DEBENTURES A/C

31.03.05	To Debentureholders A/c	6,00,000	1.4.04	By Balance b/d	6,00,000

DEBENTURE REDEMPTION FUND A/C

		Rs.			Rs.
31.03.05	To Deb. Redem. Fund A/c Investment A/c	10,300	1.4.04	By Balance b/d	5,00,000
	To General Reserve A/c	6,01,500	31.3.05	By Interest on Deb. Redem. Investments A/c	29,500
				By P & L Appropriation A/c	82,300
		6,11,800			6,11,800

DEBENTURE REDEMPTION FUND INVESTMENT A/C

		Rs.			Rs.
1.4.04	To Balance b/d	5,00,000	31.3.05	By Bank A/c	4,89,700
				By Deb. Red. Fund A/c (loss on sale)	10,300
		5,00,000			5,00,000

BANK A/C

		Rs.			Rs.
31.3.05	To Balance b/d	1,50,000	31,03,05	By Debentureholders' A/c	6,00,000
	To D.R.F. investments A/c	4,89,700		By Balance c/d	39,700
		6,39,700			6,39,700

Working notes :

(i) Interest on D.R.F. Investments

Rs. $\dfrac{5,90,000 \times 5}{100}$ = Rs. 29,500

(ii) Sale Proceeds of D.R.F. Investments

Rs. $\dfrac{5,90,000 \times 83}{100}$ = Rs.4,89,700

(iii) Loss = Cost – Sale Proceeds (Rs. 5,00,000 – 4,89,700) = Rs. 11,300

Illustration (10) (Profit on Sale of S.F. Investments and Premium on Redemption A/c.

The following balances appeared in the books of Prosperous Ltd. as on 31st March, 2004.

	Rs.
6% Debentures	2,50,000
Debenture Redemption Fund	2,82,500
Represented by :	
Rs.80,000 3.5% Government Loan	85,000
Rs.90,000 4% U.P. Govt. Loan	86,000
Rs. 30,000 6% Debentures	28,000
Rs. 83,500 7% Preference Shares	83,500

These investments were sold on the above date as under :

3.5% Government Loan	at Cost
4% U.P. Govt. Loan	at 96%
6% Debentures	at Rs. 90
7% Preference Shares	at Rs.105

On 1st April, 2004, the company redeemed the Debentures at a premium of 10%. The Bank balance after the receipt of interest but before the sale of investments stood at Rs. 47,500.

You are required to prepare :
6% Debentures A/c
6% Debentures holders A/c
Debenture Redemption Fund A/c
Debenture Redemption Fund Investments A/c & Bank A/c

ICWA (1) Adapted.

6% DEBENTURES ACCOUNT

		Rs.			Rs.
1.4.2004	To Debentureholders' A/c	2,50,000	1.4.04	By Balance b/d	2,50,000
		2,50,000			2,75,000

DEBENTUREHOLDERS' A/C

		Rs.			Rs.
1.4.2004	To Debentureholders' A/c	2,50,000	1.4.04	By Balance b/d	2,50,000
				By Premium on Redemp. A/c	25,000
		2,75,000			2,75,000

DEBENTURE REDEMPTION FUND A/C

		Rs.			Rs.
1.4.2004	To Loss on Issue	25,000	1.4.04	By Balance b/d	2,82,500
	To Capital Reserve A/c*	3,575		By D.R.F. Investments A/c	3,575
	To General Reserve A/c	2,57,500		(Profit on Sale)	
		2,86,075			2,86,075

DEBENTURE RED. FUND INVESTMENTS A/C

		Rs.			Rs.
1.4.2004	To Balance b/d	2,82,500	1.4.04	By Bank:	
	To D.R. Fund A/c	3575		3.5% Govt. Loan	85,000
	(Profit on Sale)			4% U.P. Govt. Loan	86,400
				6% Debentures	27,000
				7% Pref. Shares	87,675
		2,86,075			2,86,075

BANK A/C

		Rs.			Rs.
1.4.2004	To Balance b/d	47,500	1.4.04	By Debentureholders' A/c	2,75,000
	To D.R.F. Investments A/c	2,86,075		By Balance c/d	58,575
		3,33,575			3,33,575

* Alternatively, it could been merged with General Reserve

(II) NON-CUM ʼLATIVE SINKING FUND

Under non-cumulative sinking fund method interest on Sinking Fund Investment is neither reinvested nor transferred to Sinking Fund but credited to Profit & Loss Account as non-operating income.

However, since amount required at the time of redemption determines the amount of annual appropriation, thus the amount needed to be appropriated annually is bound to be more in case of Non- cumulative Sinking Fund as compared to cumulative Sinking Fund. It is because of the fact that the interest reinvested annually has cumulative effect on the amount available for redemption.

As far as profit on sale of Sinking Fund Investments is concerned, being a capital profit it is transferred to Capital Reserve whereas loss on sale of investments is charged to Profit & Loss Account.

Illustration (11) (N. C. Sinking Fund)

On 1.1.2000 X Ltd. issued 9% 10,000 Debentures of Rs. 100 each redeemable at par. As per the terms of issue, the company is required to maintain a Non- Cumulative Sinking Fund. The annual contribution to Sinking Fund amounted to Rs. 50,000. It was decided to invest annual contribution in 6% Government Loans.

On 31st December, 2002, the Company decided to redeem 9% 1000 Debentures. For this purpose Rs. 1,00,000 6% Govt. Loans were sold at a loss of 1%.

You are required to prepare necessary ledger accounts up to 31st December, 2002.

Solution (11)

6% DEBENTURES A/C

		Rs.			Rs.
31.12.2000	To Balance c/d	10,00,000	1.1.2000	By Bank A/c	10,00,000
31.12.2001	To Balance c/d	10,00,000	1.1.2001	By Balance b/d	10,00,000
31.12.2002	To Debentureholders' A/c	100,000	1.1.2002	By Balance b/d	10,00,000
	To Balance c/d	9,00,000			
		10,00,000			10,00,000

SINKING FUND A/C (NON-CUMULATIVE)

		Rs.			Rs.
31.12.00	To Balance c/d	50,000	31.12.00	By P&L Appropriation A/c	50,000
31.12.01	To Balance c/d	100,000	1.1.01	By Balance b/d	50,000
			31.12.01	By P& L Appropriation A/c	50,000
		1,00,000			1,00,000
31.12.02	To General Reserve	1,00,000	1.1.02	By Balance b/d	1,00,000
	To Balance c/d	50,000	31.12.02	By P&L Appropriation A/c	50,000
		1,50,000			1,50,000

SINKING FUND INVESTMENTS A/C (6% GOVT. LOANS)

		Rs.			Rs.
31.12.2000	To Bank A/c	50,000	31.12.00	By Balance c/d	50,000
1.1.2001	To Balance b/d	50,000	31.12.01	By Balance c/d	1,00,000
31.12.01	To Bank A/c	50,000			
		1,00,000			1,00,000
1.1.2002	To Balance b/d	1,00,000	31.12.02	By Bank A/c	99,000
31.12.2002	To Bank A/c	50,000		By P & L A/c (Loss)*	1000
				By Balance c/d	50,000
		1,50,000			1,50,000

* Had there been a profit, it would have been transferred to Capital Reserve.

(B) INSURANCE POLICY METHOD

Under this method a specified sum is paid by way of premium to an insurance company. The amount of premium so paid annually depends upon the amount required on redemption and the duration or period of redemption. In consideration of annual premium paid by the company, the insurer undertakes to make the required sum available for redemption purpose. It is to be noted that insurance company does not pay any interest on the premium paid by the company.

This method is similar to that non-cumulative sinking fund where interest received is not reinvested. However, there is no risk involved due to wide fluctuation in prices of investments and company is quite confident and assured of the sum required for redemption of debentures on its due date.

Accounting Treatment

First Year and subsequent years

(i) *On making annual appropriation to pay premium*

Profit & Loss Appropriation A/c Dr.

To Debenture Redemption Fund A//c

(ii) *On paying the annual premium*

Debenture Redemption Fund Policy A/c Dr.

To Bank A/c

Last Year : Beside above two entries following entries will also be recorded.

(i) *On the maturity of policy/ date of redemption*

Bank A/c Dr.

To Debenture Redemption Fund Policy A/c

(ii) *On closing the Debenture Redemption Fund Account*

Debenture Redemption Fund A/c Dr.

To General Reserve A/c

* **In case Debentures are to be redeemed at Premium** then premium on redemption account should be transferred to Debenture Redemption Fund Account in the same manner as shown under Sinking Fund Method.
* The difference between the total amount paid by way of insurance premium (which is treated as an asset) and the lump sum amount received on the date of maturity is transferred to Deb. Redemption Fund Account.

Illustration (12) (Insurance Policy)

On 1.1.2000 S & A Ltd. issued 9% 2,000 Debentures of Rs. 100 each redeemable at 5% premium after 4 years. The Company decided to take out an insurance policy to provide necessary funds for the redemption of debentures. The annual premium on the policy payable on 1st April each year was Rs. 47,750.

You are required to prepare necessary ledger accounts in the books of the Company.

Solution (12)

9% DEBENTURES A/C

		Rs.			Rs.
31.12.00	To Balance c/d	2,00,000	1.1.00	By Bank A/c	2,00,000
31.12.01	To Balance c/d	2,00,000	1.1.01	By Balance c/d	2,00,000
31.12.02	To Balance c/d	2,00,000	1.1.02	By Balance b/d	2,00,000
31.12.03	To Debentureholders' A/c	2,00,000	1.1.03	By Balance b/d	2,00,000

DEBENTURE REDEMPTION FUND POLICY A/C

		Rs.			Rs.
1.4.2000	To Bank A/c	47,750	31.12.00	By Balance c/d	47,750
1.1.2001	To Balance b/d	47,750	31.12.01	By Balance c/d	95,500
1.4.2001	To Bank A/c	47,750			
		95,500			95,500
1.1.2002	To balance b/d	95,500	31.12.02	By Balance c/d	1,43,250
1.4.2002	To Bank A/c	47,750			
		1,43,250			1,43,250
1.1.2003	To Balance b/d	1,43,250	31.12.03	By Bank A/c	2,10,000
1.4.2003	To Bank A/c	47,750			
31.12.03	To Deb. Red. Fund A/c (B.F.)	19,000			
		2,10,000			2,10,000

DEBENTURE REDEMPTION FUND A/C

		Rs.			Rs.
31.12.00	To Balance c/d	47,750	31.12.00	By P & L Appropriation A/c	47,750
31.12.01	To Balance c/d	95,500	1.1.01	By Balance b/d	47,750
			31.12.01	By P & L Appropriation A/c	47,750
		95,500			95,500
31.12.02	To Balance c/d	1,43,250	1.1.2002	By Balance b/d	95,500
			31.12.02	By P & L Appropriation A/c	47,750
		1,43,250			1,43,250
31.12.03	To Loss on issue of Debentures	10,000	1.1.03	By Balance b/d	1,43,250
	To General Reserve	2,00,000	31.12.03	By P & L Appropriation A/c	47,750
			31.12.03	By Deb. Red, Fund Policy A/c	19,000
		2,10,000			2,10,000

(C) REDEMPTION (OUT OF PROFITS) WITHOUT ANNUAL APPROPRIATION

Under this method there is no annual systematic appropriation of profits to any specific fund for the purpose of redemption of debentures. When a company accumulates sufficient divisible profits out of routine business operations over the years, such profits may be utilised to carry out redemption of debentures. An amount equal to paid up value of debentures redeemed is transferred to "Debenture Redemption Reserve (DRR) Account. Thus profits are neither earmarked for redemption nor are invested outside business but retained in the business. Once all the debentures of a particular series are redeemed the amount standing to the credit of DRR Account is transferred to General Reserve Account.

It is to be noted that any appropriation out of profits, if invested outside business, for the purpose of redemption, will be a transfer under "Debenture Redemption Fund" Where as if such appropriations retained in the business, they will be treated under "Debenture Redemption Reserve."

Accounting Treatment

(1) ***When debentures are due for redemption*** :

(a) *If at par* :

Debentures A/c Dr.

To Debentureholders' A/c

(b) *If at premium :*

Debentures A/c Dr.

Premium on Redemption A/c Dr.

To Debentureholders' A/c

(2) ***On transfer to DRR (Equal to paid up value of debentures)***

Profit & Loss Appropriation A/c Dr.

To Debenture Redemption Reserve A/c

(3) ***On Payment to Debenture holders***

Debentureholders' A/c Dr.

To Bank A/c

(4) On Completion of Redemption of Debentures

Debenture Redemption Reserve A/c Dr.

To General Reserve A/c

(DRR no more required, transferred to General Reserve)

Illustration (13)

On 1.1.2001 Z Ltd. issued 9% 5,000 Debentures of Rs. 100 each redeemable at 5% premium.

On 1.1.2005 the company decided to redeem debentures out of profits of the company. The Debenture Redemption Reserve stood at Rs. 1,75,000 on that date.

Pass necessary journal entries relating to issue and redemption of debentures.

Solution (13)

JOURNAL ENTRIES

			Rs.	Rs.
2001 Jan. 1	Bank A/c	Dr.	5,00,000	
	Loss on issue of debentures A/c	Dr.	25,000	
	To 9% Debentures A/c			5,00,000
	To Premium on Redemption A/c			25,000
	(Being debentures issued)			
2005 Jan. 1	9% Debentures A/c	Dr.	5,00,000	
	Premium on Redemption A/c	Dr.	25,000	
	To Debentureholders' A/c			5,25,000
	(Being amount due on redemption)			
	Profit & Loss Appropriation A/c	Dr.	75,000	
	To Debentures Redemption Reserve A/c			75,000
	(Being transfer to DRR made to the extent of 50% of paid value of debentures redeemed as per SEBI's guidelines)			
	Debenture Redemption Reserve A/c	Dr.	2,50,000	
	Profit & Loss Appropriation A/c	Dr.	2,50,000	
	To General Reserve A/c			5,00,000
	(Being required amount equal to normal value of debentures redeemed transferred to General Reserve)			
	Debentureholders' A/c	Dr.	5,25,000	
	To Bank A/c			5,25,000
	(Being payment made)			
	Profit and Loss A/c	Dr.	25,000	
	To Loss on Issue of Debentures A/c			25,000
	(Being Loss on issue written off)			

Working notes :

(1) As per SEBI's guidelines an amount equal to 50% of the nominal value of debentures to be redeemed, should be transferred to DRR before redemption starts. Hence an amount of Rs. 75,000 has been transferred to DRR to make balance equal to 50% of Rs. 5,00,000 = (Rs. 1,75,000 + 75,000) = Rs. 2,50,000.

(2) The appropriation of Rs. 2,50,000 (being remaining amount) could have been transferred to first DRR and there after to General Reserve.

(3) Premium on Redemption being Loss on issue of debentures has been written off completely. Alternatively it would have been written off over a period of four years equally or otherwise *i.e.* (from 2000 to 2004)

(2) REDEMPTION BY DRAWING BY LOT

Under this method debentures are redeemed in instalments at regular intervals usually every year during the life span of the debentures issued. A certain amount of debentures which are to be redeemed each year is worked out by dividing the total liability of debentures by the life span in years. However, amount of debentures to be redeemed may be equal or unequal depending upon the company's policy. The serial number of debentures to be redeemed are takenout by drawing by lot each year out of a box containing serial numbers of all debentures issued.

Usually such type of redemption is made out of the profit appropriated annually at the time of redemption by creating Debenture Redemption Reserve equivalent to nominal value of debentures redeemed

Illustration (14) (Drawing by lot)

On 1.1.2000 SN. Ltd. issued 9% 10,000 debentures @ Rs. 98, redeemable at Rs. 104 by annual drawing of Rs. 2,00,000 by annual appropriation of profits. Interest is payable yearly on 31st December after 20% tax deducted at source. It is decided to write of discount and loss on issue of debentures equally over a period of 5 years.

Pass necessary journal entries.

Solution (14)

JOURNAL ENTRIES

			Rs.	Rs.
2000	Bank A/c	Dr.	9,80,000	
Jan. 1	Discount on issue of Debentures A/c	Dr.	20,000	
	Loss on issue of Debentures A/c	Dr.	40,000	
	To 9% Debentures A/c			10,00,000
	To Premium on Redemption A/c			40,000
	(Being debentures issued)			
Dec. 31	Interest on Debentures A/c	Dr.	90,000	
	To Debentureholders' A/c			72,000
	To Tax Deducted at Source A/c			18,000
	(Being interest due)			

Contd.

2000			Rs.	Rs.
Dec. 31	9% Debentures A/c	Dr.	2,00,000	
	Premium on Redemption A/c	Dr.	8,000	
	To Debentureholders' A/c			2,08,000
	(Being amount due on redemption)			
" "	Debentureholders' A/c	Dr.	2,80,000	
	Tax Deducted at Source A/c	Dr.	18,000	
	To Bank A/c			2,98,000
	(Being amount of interest, redemption and T.D.S. paid)			
" "	Profit and Loss A/c	Dr.	1,02,000	
	To Interest on Debentures A/c			90,000
	To Loss on issue of Debentures A/c			8,000
	To Discount on issue of Debentures A/c			4,000
	(Being interest, loss and discount on issue written off)			
Dec. 31	Profit and Loss Appropriation A/c	Dr.	2,00,000	
	To Debenture Redemption Reserve A/c			2,00,000
	(Being required amount transferred to DRR.)			
2001	Interest on Debentures A/c	Dr.	72,000	
Dec. 31	To Debentureholders' A/c			57,600
	To Tax Deducted at Source A/c			14,400
	(Being interest due)			
" "	9% Debentures A/c	Dr.	2,00,000	
	Premium on Redemption A/c	Dr.	8,000	
	To Debentureholders' A/c			2,08,000
	(Being amount due or redemption)			
" "	Debentureholders' A/c	Dr.	2,65,600	
	Tax Deducted at Source A/c	Dr.	14,400	
	To Bank A/c			2,80,000
	(Being amount due paid)			
" "	Profit & Loss A/c	Dr.	84,000	
	To Interest on Debentures A/c			72,000
	To Loss on Issue of debentures A/c			8,000
	To Discount on issue of debentures A/c			4,000
	(Being amount written off)			
" "	Profit & Loss Appropriation A/c	Dr.	2,00,000	
	To Debenture Redemption Reserve A/c			2,00,000
	(Being amount transferred to DRR)			

Contd.

			Rs.	Rs.
2002 Dec. 31	Interest on Debentures A/c	Dr.	54,000	
	To Debentureholders' A/c			43,200
	To Tax Deducted at Source A/c			10,800
	(Being interest due)			
" "	9% Debentures A/c	Dr.	2,00,000	
	Premium on Redemption A/c	Dr.	8,000	
	To Debentureholders' A/c			2,08,000
	(Being amount due on redemption)			
Dec. 31	Debentureholders' A/c	Dr.	2,51,200	
	Tax Deducted at Source A/c	Dr.	10,800	
	To Bank A/c			2,62,000
	(Being amount due to Debentureholders and for tax paid)			
" "	Profit & Loss A/c	Dr.	66,000	
	To Interest in Debentures A/c			54,000
	To Loss on Issue of Debentures			8,000
	To Discount on issue of Debentures A/c			4,000
	(Being amount written off)			
" "	Profit & Loss Appropriation A/c	Dr.	2,00,000	
	To Debenture Redemption Reserve A/c			2,00,000
	(Being amount transferred to DRR)			
2003 Dec. 31	Interest on Debentures A/c	Dr.	36,000	
	To Debentureholders' A/c			28,800
	To Tax Deducted at Source A/c			7,200
	(Being interest due)			
" "	9% Debentures A/c	Dr.	2,00,000	
	Premium on Redemption A/c	Dr.	8,000	
	To Debentureholders' A/c			2,08,000
	(Being amount due on redemption)			
" "	Debentureholders' A/c	Dr.	2,36,800	
	Tax Deducted at Source A/c	Dr.	7,200	
	To Bank A/c			2,44,000
	(Being amount due paid)			
" "	Profit & Loss A/c	Dr.	48,000	
	To Interest on Debentures A/c			36,000
	To Loss on issue of debentures A/c			8,000
	To Discount on Issue of Debentures A/c			4,000
	(Being amount written off)			

Contd.

2004			Rs.	Rs.
Dec. 31	Profit & Loss Appropriation A/c	Dr.	2,00,000	
	To Debenture Redemption Reserve A/c			2,00,000
	(Being amount transferred to DRR)			
2004	Interest on Debentures A/c	Dr.	18,000	
Dec. 31	To Debentureholders' A/c			14,400
	To Tax Deducted at Source A/c			3,600
	(Being interest due)			
Dec. 31	9% Debentures A/c	Dr.	2,00,000	
	Premium on Redemption A/c	Dr.	8,000	
	To Debentureholders A/c			2,08,000
	(Being amount due on redemption)			
" "	Debentureholders' A/c	Dr.	2,22,400	
	Tax Deducted at Source A/c	Dr.	3,600	
	To Bank A/c			2,26,000
	(Being amount due paid)			
2004	Profit & Loss A/c	Dr.	30,000	
Dec. 31	To Interest on Debentures A/c			18,000
	To Loss on issue of Debentures A/c			8,000
	To Discount on issue of Debentures A/c			4,000
	(Being amount written off)			
" "	Profit & Loss Appropriation A/c	Dr.	2,00,000	
	To Debenture Redemption Reserve A/c			2,00,000
	(Being amount transferred to DRR)			
" "	Debenture Redemption Reserve A/c	Dr.	10,00,000	
	To General Reserve A/c			10,00,000
	(Being DRR transferred to General Reserve)			

3 REDEMPTION BY "CONVERSION"

Subject to terms of issue, the redemption of debentures may take form of conversion. The terms of issue may give the debentureholders the option to get their holdings converted in to equity shares preference shares or new debentures.

If the terms of issue do not provide any provision relating to conversion, the company may give such an option to its debentureholders. Such offer may be accepted by the debenture holders or turned down by them. The new securities offered may be issued at par, premium or at discount.

It is to be noted that where the debentures were originally issued at discount, such debentures cannot be converted into fully paid shares of the **same nominal value** except at discount as per the provisions of section 79 of the Companies Act. However, shares with paid up value equal to amount received on debentures can be issued in exchange for such debentures. *e.g.* A debenture of Rs. 100 each issued at 10 % discount can be converted into a share of Rs. 100 each Rs. 90 paid or 9 fully paid shares of Rs. 10 each. It means **paid up value of shares issued** in lieu of debentures **should not exceed amount actually received on debentures.**

As per SEBI's Guidelines no company shall issue fully convertible debentures (FCD's) having a conversion period of more than 36 months. However, if a company makes conversion optional with "Put" or 'Call option' then the debentures with a conversion period of more than 36 months can be issued.

Any conversion of debentures having a period of 18 months or more but less than 36 months shall be optional on the part of debentureholders. The premium and time of conversion is to be determined by the issuing company.

In case of listed company issuing convertible debentures (FCD's & PCD'S) of the value of exceeding Rs. 50 lakhs, the holder of such debentures shall be given a compulsory option of not converting into equity shares if the conversion price was not fixed at the time of issue.

Redemption by Conversion or redemption out of sale proceeds of a fresh issue made for the purpose of redemption refer to "redemption out of Capital" and hence no amount is required to be transferred to DRR.

Illustration (15) (Redemption of Convertible debentures originally issued at discount)

N Ltd. issued 9% 50,000 Debentures of Rs. 100 each at a discount of 10% redeemable after 7 years by converting them into equity shares of Rs. 10 each.

Pass necessary journal entries for the issue and redemption of debentures

Solution (15)

JOURNAL ENTRIES

			Rs.	Rs.
Ist Yr.	Bank A/c	Dr.	45,00,000	
	Discount on Issue of Debentures A/c	Dr.	5,00,000	
	To 9% Debentures A/c			50,00,000
	(Being debentures issued at discount)			
at the end of 7th yr.	9% Debentures A/c	Dr.	50,00,000	
	To Discount on Issue of debentures A/c			5,00,000
	To Debentureholders' A/c			45,00,000
	(Being amount due on redemption transferred to Debentureholders A/c which is equal to amount of actually received from debentures)			
	Debentureholders' A/c	Dr.	45,00,000	
	To Equity Share Capital A/c			45,00,000
	(Being debentures redeemed by conversion)			

(CONVERSION)

Illustration (16)

A Company issued 8% 1,000 Debentures of Rs. 1000 each at 10 % discount redeemable after seven years. However, the company gave the option to the debentureholders to get their debentures converted into equity shares of Rs. 100 each at a premium of 25% at any time after the expiry of two years.

Holders of 250 debentures notified their intention to exercise the option. The Company accepted their request and converted their holdings in to equity shares.

Pass necessary journal entries for the issue and redemption of debentures.

Solution (16)

JOURNAL ENTRIES

			Rs.	Rs.
1st Yr.	Bank A/c	Dr.	9,00,000	
	Discount on Issue of Debentures A/c	Dr.	1,00,000	
	To 8% Debentures A/c			10,00,000
	(Being debentures issued at discount)			
At the end of Third year	8% Debentures A/c	Dr.	2,50,000	
	To Discount on issue of Debentures A/c			25,000
	To Debentureholders A/c			2,25,000
	(Being amount due on redemption)			
	Debentureholders' A/c	Dr.	2,25,000	
	To Equity Share Capital A/c			1,80,000
	To Securities Premium A/c			45,000
	(Being debentures converted into shares)			

Working notes :

(1) Debentureholders' A/c will be credited with an amount equal to an amount actually received from them at the time of issue of debentures at discount which will now be adjusted against debentures.

(2) The amount so due shall be divided by the agreed value of new security to find out number of new securities to be issued on conversion.

Amount due to Debentureholders	
250 debentures @ Rs. 1000 each	2,50,000
Less discount @ 10% (Originally allowed)	25,000
	2,25,000
Amount due to Debentureholders	2,25,000
Agreed value of equity share (Rs. 100 + 25 Premium)	125

No. of Equity Shares = Rs. $\frac{2,25,000}{125}$ = 1,800 Shares

Illustration (17) (Conversion)

Following is the summarised Balance Sheet of Blue Ltd. as on 31st March, 2004.

Liabilities			Rs.
	50,000 Equity Shares of Rs. 10 each		5,00,000
	General Reserve		7,50,000
	Debenture Redemption Fund		5,00,000
	9% 10,000 Debentures of Rs. 100 each		10,00,000
	Unsecured Loans		5,00,000
	Current Liabilities & Provisions		12,50,000
			45,00,000
Assets			
	Gross Block	20,00,000	
Less	Depreciation	4,00,000	16,00,000
	Debenture Redemption Fund Investments	4,00,000	
	Cash & Bank balance		5,00,000
	Current assets		20,00,000
			45,00,000

The debentures are due for redemption on 1st April, 2004. The terms of issue provided redemption of debentures at a premium of 5% with an option to convert 20% of their holdings into equity shares at a predetermined price of Rs. 15.75 per share and the balance in cash. Assuming that :

(i) Except the holders of 2,500 debentures, other exercised their option for conversion.

(ii) Investments were sold for Rs. 4,40,000.

Pass journal entries for redemption and prepare a balance sheet as on that date.

C.A. (1) Adapted.

Solution (17)

JOURNAL ENTRIES

			Rs.	Rs.
2004	9% Debentures A/c	Dr.	10,00,000	
1st April	Premium on Redemption A/c	Dr.	50,000	
	To Debentureholders' A/c			10,50,000
	(Being debentures due for redemption)			
	Debentureholders' A/c	Dr.	1,57,500	
	To Equity Share Capital A/c			1,00,000
	To Securities Premium A/c			57,500
	(Being holders of 1,500 debentures opted for the conversion)			
	Debentureholders' A/c	Dr.	8,92,500	
	To Bank A/c			8,92,500
	(Being remaining debentures redeemed for cash)			

Contd.

	Bank A/c Dr.		4,40,000	
	To Investments (DRF)			4,00,000
	To Debenture Red. Fund A/c			40,000
	(Being investments sold & profit thereon transferred to D. R. fund)			
	Securities Premium A/c Dr.		50,000	
	To Premium on Redemption A/c			50,000
	(Being premium on redemption written off against securities Premium A/c)			
	Debenture Redemption Fund A/c Dr.		5,40,000	
	To General Reserve A/c			5,40,000
	(Being balance of DRF transferred to General Reserve)			

BALANCE SHEET OF BLUE BIRD LTD.
As on 1. 4. 2004

Liabilities		Rs.
60,000 Equity Shares of Rs. 10 each		6,00,000
Reserve & Surplus :		
General Reserve (3)		12,90,000
Securities Premium (4)		7,500
Unsecured Loans		5,00,000
Current liabilities & Provisions		12,50,000
		36,47,500
Assets		
Gross Block	20,00,000	
Less Depreciation	4,00,000	16,00,000
Current Assets, Loans & Advances :		
Other current Assets		20,00,000
Cash & Bank balance (2)		47,500
		36,47,500

Working notes :

(1)	No. of Debentures o/s for redemption	10,000
Less	holders of 2,500 not opting for Conversion	2,500
	20% of 7,500 = 1,500 debentures	7,500
	Holders of 1,500 debentures exercised option =	1,50,000
Add	Premium on Redemption	7,500
		1,57,500

No. of shares to be issued = $\frac{1,57,500}{15.75}$ = 10,000 shares

Equity Share Capital (10,000 ×10) =	1,00,000
Securities Premium (10,000 × 5.75)	57,500
Amount due to Debentureholders who exercised the option	1,57,500

(2) **CASH & BANK A/C**

	Rs.		Rs.
To Balance b/d	5,00,000	By Debentureholders' A/c	8,92,500
To DRF Investments A/c	4,40,000	By Balance c/d	47,500
	9,40,000		9,40,000

(3) **GENERAL RESERVE A/C**

	Rs.		Rs.
To Balance c/d	12,90,000	By Balance b/d	7,50,000
		By Deb. Red. Fund A/c	5,40,000*
	12,90,000		12,90,000

* Existing Rs. 5,00,000 plus Rs. 40,000 being profit on sale of Deb. Redemption Fund Investment.

(4) **SECURITIES PREMIUM A/C**

	Rs.		Rs.
To Premium on Redemption A/c	50,000	By Debentureholders' A/c	57,500
To Balance c/d	7,500		
	57,500		57,500

REDEMPTION OUT OF PROCEEDS OF FRESH ISSUE

Under this method, the Company, instead of allotting shares or new debentures to the existing debentureholders (as explained under conversion) makes a fresh issue for the purpose of redemption of debentures. The proceeds of such fresh issue is utilised for making payment to debentureholders.

Illustration (18) (Redemption out of proceeds of Fress Issue)

N.M. Ltd. had 11% 5,000 Debentures of Rs. 100 each due for redemption on 1.4.2005. The debenture trust deed provided that the company may redeem the debentures at a premium of 5% at any time before maturity. The directors decided to exercise this option and issued 40,000. Equity Shares of Rs. 10 each at 10% premium and 1000 9% Debentures of Rs. 100 each at par for the purpose of redemption. Record journal entries to give effect to above transactions.

Solution (18)

JOURNAL ENTRIES

Particulars		Rs.	Rs.
11% Debentures A/c	Dr.	5,00,000	
Premium on Redemption A/c	Dr.	25,000	
To Debentureholders' A/c			5,25,000
(Being 11% Debentures due for redemption)			
Bank A/c	Dr.	4,40,000	
To Equity Share Application A/c			4,40,000
(Being application money received)			

Contd.

		Rs.	Rs.
Equity Share Application A/c	Dr.	4,40,000	
To Equity Share Capital A/c			4,00,000
To Securities Premium A/c			40,000
(Being application money transferred to Equity Share Capital and Securities Premium Account)			
Bank A/c	Dr.	1,00,000	
To 9% Debenture Application A/c			1,00,000
(Being debenture application money received)			
9% Debenture Application A/c	Dr.	1,00,000	
To 9% Debentures A/c			1,00,000
(Being debenture application transferred to 9% Debentures Account)			
Debentureholders' A/c	Dr.	5,25,000	
To Bank A/c			5,25,000
(Being amount paid on redemption)			
Securities Premium A/c	Dr.	25,000	
To Premium on Redemption A/c			25,000
(Being premium on redemption account written off against securities premium account)			

The amount due on redemption may be transferred to Debenture Redemption Account instead of Debentureholder' Account. The Debenture Redemption Account should be opened only if it is specifically asked in the question.

(4) REDEMPTION BY PURCHASE IN THE OPEN MARKET

If terms of issue so provide a company can buy its own debentures and thus discharge the liability in full or in part before the date of redemption. The Company applies this method of redemption if

(i) it has surplus funds or

(ii) market price of the debentures is less than the amount payable on redemption or

(iii) existing debentures carry higher rate of interest as compared to current interest rate prevailing in the market.

Thus in order to minimise the interest burden, to utilise the surplus funds or/and to make profits on cancellation or on redemption, the Company may buy its own debentures from the open market :

either for –

(a) Immediate cancellation or

(b) to be held as investment for the time being and for subsequent cancellation.

Accounting Treatment

(a) *When debentures are purchased for immediate Cancellation*

(1) *Where sinking fund does not exist.*

* *On purchase* of own debentures (if price is less than the face value)

Debentures A/c	Dr.	face value
To Bank A/c		Amount paid
To Profit on Cancellation A/c		difference.

* *On transfer of profit* on cancellation to *Capital Reserve*

Profit on Cancellation A/c	Dr.
To Capital Reserve A/c	

Or (alternatively) only one entry can be recorded

Debentures A/c	Dr.
To Bank A/c	
To Capital Reserve	

Illustration (19)

X Ltd. purchased its Rs. 9% 2000 debentures of Rs. 100 each @ Rs. 97 for immediate cancellation. Pass journal entries, when (a) Sinking Fund does not exist (b) Sinking Fund Exists.

Solution (19)

(a)	9% Debentures A/c	Dr.	2,00,000	
	To Bank A/c			1,94,000
	To Profit on Cancellation A/c			6,000
	(Being 2000 debentures purchased & cancelled)			
	Profit on Cancellation A/c *	Dr.	6,000	
	To Capital Reserve A/c			6,000
	(Being profit on cancellation transferred to Capital Reserve)			

* alternatively it can be utilised to write of discount/Loss on issue of debentures.

(b) Where *sinking fund exists* :

* On purchase of own debentures : same entry (No change)

* On *transfer of profit on cancellation.*

Profit on cancellation A/c	Dr.
To Sinking Fund A/c	

Or *alternatively a combined entry*

Debentures A/c	Dr.
To Bank A/c	
To Sinking Fund A/c	

It is to be noted that if price paid for its own debentures is equal to nominal value of debentures there will neither be profit nor loss on cancellation. If price paid exceeds the nominal value of debentures purchased the resultant shall be the loss and accordingly will be adjusted against Capital profit (reserve) or transferred to Sinking Fund A/c as the case may be.

Illustration (20)

Using the figures of illustration 19 there shall be no change in the first entry.

The other entries will be recorded as under :

(ii) Profit on cancellation A/c	Dr.	6000	
To Sinking Fund A/c			6,000
(Being profit transferred to Sinking Fund)			
(iii) Sinking Fund A/c	Dr.	6,000	
To Capital Reserve A/c			6,000

(b) *Purchase of own "debentures as investments"*

Some time a company purchases its own debentures which are held as investments to be sold or cancelled on any subsequent date. There may be again two situations :

(i) Where Sinking Fund does not exist.

(ii) Where Sinking Fund exists.

Accounting Treatment

(I) ***Where Sinking fund does not exist :***

* *When own debentures are purchased as investments* :

Own Debentures A/c	Dr.	Actual amount paid
To Bank A/c		

* *When Investments (own debentures) are sold :*

Bank A/c	Dr.	Sale proceeds
* Loss on sale of own debentures A/c	Dr.	Excess of C.P. over S.P.
To Own Debentures A/c		Cost of own Debentures
* To Profit on sale of own Debentures A/c		Excess of S.P. over C.P.

* Profit or Loss on sale of own debentures will be transferred to profit & Loss Account.

or if debentures are cancelled.

Debentures A/c	Dr.
To Own Debentures A/c	
To Profit on Cancellation A/c#	

\# may be transferred to Capital reserve or discount/Loss on issue may be adjusted against such profits.

II. *Where Sinking Fund exists*

Under such situation journal entries relating to purchase of own debentures (held as investments) and sale there of will be the same as explained under first method. However profit or loss arising therefrom will be transferred to Sinking Fund Account.

Important Points :

* **Where sinking fund does not exist, it is presumed that Company has sufficient amount standing to the credit of DRR to satisfy the condition of redemption as per SEBI's guidelines.**
* **Where sinking fund exists an amount equal to nominal value of debentures so cancelled is transferred to General Reserve.**
* **As long as investments in own debentures are not cancelled the same shall be shown on the assets side of Balance Sheet without any change in the amount of Debentures appearing on the liabilities side.**

Interest on Own Debentures

When a company purchases its own debentures as investments, the Company continues to save interest on its own debentures till the date of cancellation Otherwise, the interest would have been paid to outsiders. Hence, debenture interest payable is divided in two parts.

(i) Interest payable to outsiders

(ii) Interest on own debentures

The following entry is recorded :

*	Debenture Interest A/c	Dr.	Total interest
	To Interest on own debentures A/c		
	To Debentureholders' A/c		Interest payable to outsiders
	(Being interest due on debentures)		
*	Debentureholders' A/c	Dr.	
	To Bank A/c		
	(Being interest paid)		
*	Profit & Loss A/c	Dr.	Total interest
	To Debenture Interest A/c		" "
	(Being interest charged to P&L A/c)		
*	Interest on Own Debentures A/c	Dr.	
	To Profit & Loss A/c		
	(Being interest on own debentures transferred to P & L A/c)		

It should be noted that when Sinking Fund exists, then the *"interest on own debentures"* is transferred to Sinking Fund A/c and *not* to the Profit & Loss Account.

Illustration (21) (Interest on own debentures)

On 1.1.2004 Nahid Ltd. had a balance of Rs. 5,00,000 to the credit of 9% Debentures. Interest on these debentures was payable on 30th June and 31st December every year. On 1.1.2004 the Company purchased 500 own debentures of Rs. 100 each @ Rs. 97 to be cancelled immediately. On 1.7.2004 Company again purchased 400 own debentures @ Rs. 96. These debentures were cancelled on 31st December, 2004.

Pass journal entries. Ignore tax.

Solution (21)

JOURNAL ENTRIES

Date	Particulars		Rs.	Rs.
1.1.2004	Own Debentures A/c Dr.		48,500	
	To Bank A/c			48,500
	(Being 500 debentures purchased @ Rs. 97)			
1.1.2004	9% Debentures A/c Dr.		50,000	
	To Own Debentures A/c			48,500
	To Profit on Cancellation A/c			1,500
	(Being own debentures cancelled).			
30.6.04	Debenture Interest A/c Dr.		20,250	
	To Debentureholders' A/c			20,250
	(Being interest due on 4500 debentures for six month)			
	Debentureholders' A/c Dr.		20,250	
	To Bank A/c			20,250
	(Being interest paid to Debentureholders)			
1.7.04	Own Debentures A/c Dr.		38,400	
	To Bank A/c			38,400
	(Being 400 Debentures purchased)			
31.12.04	9% Debentures A/c Dr.		40,000	
	To Own Debentures A/c			38,400
	To Profit on Cancellation A/c			1,600
	(Being 400 own debentures cancelled)			
	Debenture Interest A/c Dr.		20,250	
	To Debentureholders' A/c			18,450
	To Interest on own Debentures A/c			1,800
	(Being interest due on debentures)			
	Debentureholders' A/c Dr.		18,450	
	To Bank A/c			18,450
	(Being interest to debentureholders paid)			
	Profit on Cancellation A/c Dr.		3,100	
	To Capital Reserve A/c			3,100
	(Being profit on cancellation transferred to Capital reserve)			
	Profit & Loss A/c Dr.		40,500	
	To Debenture Interest A/c			40,500
	(Being interest on debentures changed to P & L A/c)			
	Interest on own Debentures A/c Dr.		1,800	
	To Profit & Loss A/c			1,800
	(Being interest on own debentures transferred to P & L A/c)			

EX-INTEREST CUM-INTEREST QUOTATIONS

In the proceding part the date of purchase of it's own debentures was taken to be the date when interest fell due or the next day thereof. Hence the interest on debentures was totally ignored at the time of recording entry for the purchase of own debentures either meant for immediate cancellation or held as investments. It is to be noted that interest on debentures is payable on fixed dates generally with six monthly intervals. The interest accrued up to the date of purchase of debentures will be payable to debentureholder. Thus such transactions do not create any problem relating to interest accrued and due, because it is received by them separately. However, in actual practice, it does not happen. The Company can buy its own debentures from the open market at any time during the year. In such a case the problem arises to the treatment of interest for the expired period *i.e.* the interest for the period the debentures were held by the debentureholders *i.e.* from the last date of payment of interest upto the date of purchase of debentures. The interest accrued but not due for this period has to be paid by the Company to the debentureholder. Thus interest portion paid with price is treated as revenue expenditure and the balance as capital expenditure being actual cost of debentures purchased.

Ex-Interest Price : When price of a debenture does not include interest for the expired period, the price is said to be Ex-Interest. It means the company has to pay interest for the expired period extra *i.e.* in addition to the cost of debentures. Hence total payment will be price as quoted plus interest occrued. Thus price = cost of debenture.

Cum-Interest Price : It means interest for the expired period is included in the price of debenture. Cost of debentures is equal to price paid less interest for the expired period. Thus Price Less Interest = cost of debenture.

Accounting Treatment :

When debentures are purchased :

Own Debentures A/c	Dr.
Interest on Debentures A/c*	Dr.
To Bank A/c	

Illustration (22) Ex- Interest & Cum-Interest

On 1.9.2004 X Ltd. Purchased its own 12% Debentures of Rs. 100 each as follows :

300 12% Debentures @ Rs. 97 Cum-Interest; 200 12% Debentures @ Rs. 96 Ex-Interest Interest is payable on 30th June & 31st December every year. Record Entries.

Solution : (22)

Cum-Interest

Own Debentures A/c (B.F.)	Dr.	28,500	
Interest on Debentures A/c	Dr.	600	
To Bank A/c (300 × 97)			29,100
(Being 300 debentures purchased)			

* Interest $= 30{,}000 \times \frac{12}{100} \times \frac{2}{12}$ = Rs. 600 {Interest accrued for July and August}

Ex-Interest

Own Debentures A/c (200 × 96)	Dr.	19,200	
* Interest on Debentures A/c	Dr.	400	
To Bank A/c (Total)			19,600
(Being 200 debentures purchased)			

$* \ 20{,}000 \times \frac{12}{100} \times \frac{2}{12} = \text{Rs. } 400$ {Interest accrued for July & August}

Illustration (23)

On 1.4.2003 SRK Ltd. issued 12% 5,000 Debentures of Rs. 100 each. Interest is payable on 30th September and 31st March every year. As per the terms of issue the Company had the option to buy its own debentures from the open market at any time after one year.

On 1.5.2004 Rs. 30,000 own debentures were purchased by the company @ Rs. 95 Cum- interest and cancelled immediately.

On 1.12.2004 Rs. 50,000 own debentures were purchased @ Rs.96 ex-interest. On 01.02.2005 the company again purchased Rs. 60,000 own debentures @ Rs. 97 Cum-interest.

On 31st March, 2005 the debentures purchased by the Company were cancelled.

Record necessary journal entries. Books are closed on 31st March every year. Ignore Income Tax.

Solution (23)

JOURNAL ENTRIES

			Rs.	Rs.
2003 1.4	Bank A/c To 12% Debentures A/c (Being 12% debentures issued)	Dr.	5,00,000	5,00,000
30.9	Debenture Interest A/c To Bank A/c (Being interest for six months paid)	Dr.	30,000	30,000
2004 31.3	Debenture Interest A/c To Bank A/c (Being interest paid for six months)	Dr.	30,000	30,000
”	Profit & Loss A/c To Debenture Interest A/c (Being interest charged to Profit & Loss Account)	Dr.	60,000	60,000
1.5	12% Debentures A/c Debenture Interest A/c To Bank A/c To Profit on cancellation A/c (Being debentures purchased and cancelled)	Dr. Dr.	30,000 300	 28,500 1,800

Contd.

			Rs.	Rs.
2004 30.9	Debenture Interest A/c To Bank A/c (Being debentures interest paid)	Dr.	28,200	28,200
2004 1.12	Own Debentures A/c Debenture Interest A/c To Bank A/c (Being own debentures purchased @ 96 ex-interest)	Dr. Dr.	48,000 1000	49,000
2005 1.2	Own Debentures A/c Debentures Interest A/c To Bank A/c (Being own debentures purchased @ Rs. 97 Cum-Interest)	Dr. Dr.	55,800 2,400	58,200
31.3	Debenture Interest A/c To Bank A/c To Interest on own Debentures A/c (Being interest paid & interest on own debentures credited)		24,800	21,600 3200
2005 31.3	12% Debentures A/c To Own Debenture A/c To Profit on Cancellation A/c (Being debentures cancelled)	Dr.	1,10,000	10,3800 6,200
"	Profit on Cancellation A/c To Capital Reserve A/c (Being profit on cancellation transferred to Capital reserve)	Dr.	8,000	8,000
"	Profit & Loss A/c To Debenture Interest A/c (Being interest transferred to P & L A/c)	Dr.	56,700	56,700
"	Interest on own Debentures A/c To Profit & Loss A/c (Being interest on own debentures transferred to P & L A/c)	Dr.	3,200	3,200

Working notes

(1) Interest on Debentures purchased on 1.5.2004

$$\text{Rs. } 30{,}000 \times \frac{12}{100} \times \frac{1}{12} = \text{Rs. } 300$$

(2) Amount paid for debentures purchased on 1.5.2004

$$\text{Rs. } 30{,}000 \times \frac{95}{100} = \text{Rs. } 28{,}500$$

(3) Interest on Debentures purchased on 1.12. 2004

$$\text{Rs. } 50{,}000 \times \frac{12}{100} \times \frac{2}{12} = \text{Rs. } 1{,}000$$

(4) Cost of own Debentures purchased on 1.12.2004

$$\text{Rs. } 50{,}000 \times \frac{96}{100} = \text{Rs. } 48{,}000$$

(Ex-Interest Price = Cost of debenture.)

(5) Interest on own Debentures purchased on 1.2.2005

$$\text{Rs. } 60{,}000 \times \frac{12}{100} \times \frac{4}{12} = \text{Rs. } 2{,}400$$

(6) Cost of own Debentures purchased on 1.2.2005

$$\text{Rs. } 60{,}000 \times \frac{97}{100} = \text{Rs. } 58{,}200$$

Less Interest	Rs. 2,400
	55,800

(Cum Interest Price – Interest = Cost of debenture)

DEBENTURES OR BONDS WITH *PUT* OR *CALL* OPTION

Put Option : As already discussed companies may issue bonds/debentures with put or call option.

Under "Put Option" the holder has the option to sell his holdings to the issuing company against cash payment. When the rate of interest is showing an increasing trend the debentureholders would like to return the debentures to the company in anticipation of investing this money at a higher rate of interest. Thus "Put Option" is exercised by the holder under increasing interest rate tendencies. This option is beneficial to debentureholders.

Call Option : Debentures with Call option authorises the Company to redeem its debentures before the date of maturity at a call price which is usually higher than the face value but may decrease over a period of time. Call option benefits the company as it reduces the interest burden. After redemption the company may issue new debentures carrying low interest rate. This option is exercised by the Company when interest rate is showing decreasing trend.

Illustration (24)

("Put Option")

Cyma Ltd. issued 30,000 7% Debentures of Rs. 100 each redeemable after 10 years. Debentureholders are given option to get their holdings redeemed at Rs. 105 per debenture at any time after 5 years. At the end of sixth year debentureholders holding 5,000 debentures and in the begining of eighth year holders of 10,000 debentures exercised their option.

Pass necessary journal entries, ignore interest.

Solution (24) **Journal Entries**

			Rs.	Rs.
1st Year	Bank A/c	Dr.	30,00,000	
	To 7% Debentures A/c			30,00,000
	(Being debentures issued for cash)			
VIth year	7% Debentures A/c	Dr.	5,00,000	
	Loss on Redemption of Debentures A/c	Dr.	25,000	
	To Bank A/c			5,25,000
	(Being debentures redeemed under "Put Option")			
	Profit & Loss A/c	Dr.	25,000	
	To Loss on Redemption of Debentures A/c			25,000
	(Being loss on redemption charged to P & L A/c)			
	Profit & Loss Appropriation A/c	Dr.	15,00,000	
	To Deb. Red. Reserve A/c			15,00,000
	(Transfer to DRR as per SEBI's guidelines)			
VIIIth year	7% Debentures A/c	Dr.	10,00,000	
	Loss on Redemption of Debentures A/c	Dr.	50,000	
	To Bank A/c			10,50,000
	(Being debentures redeemed under "Put option")			
"	Profit & Loss A/c	Dr.	50,000	
	To Loss on Redemption A/c			50,000
	(Being Loss on redemption charged to P& L A/c)			

Illustration (25) (Call Option)

Adnan Ltd. issued 12% 10,000 Debentures of Rs; 100 each redeemable after 7 years. The terms of issue provide that the debentures carry call option which the company can exercise at any time after 5 years at a call price of Rs. 103.

At the and of sixth year the company exercised it's call option and redeemed 5,000 debentures. Pass necessary journal entries ignore interest.

Solution (25)

JOURNAL ENTRIES

			Rs.	Rs.
1st Year	Bank A/c	Dr.	10,00,000	
	To 12% Debentures A/c			10,00,000
	(Being debentures issued for cash)			
	12% Debentures A/c	Dr.	5,00,000	
	Loss on Redemption of debentures A/c	Dr.	15,000	
	To Bank A/c			5,15,000
	(Being debentures redeemed under call option)			

Profit & Loss A/c Dr.		15,000	
To Loss on Redemption of Debentures A/c			15,000
(Being loss on redemption charged to P & L A/c)			
Profit & Loss Appropriation A/c Dr.		5,00,000	
To Deb. Redemption Reserve A/c			5,00,000
(Being an amount equivalent to 50% of Nominal value of debentures issued transferred to DRR-as per SEBI's guidelines)			

GRADED ILLUSTRATIONS

Illustration (1) (Sinking Fund & Redemption at premium)

The following balances appeared in the books of Z Ltd. as on 1st January 2004.

11% Debentures (Rs. 100 each)	25,00,000
Debenture Redemption Fund	16,25,690
5% Debenture Redemption Fund Investments	16,25,500

The annual instalment added to the Debenture Redemption Fund is Rs. 7,93,535

On 31st December, 2004 the Company redeemed the debentures at 105%. For this purpose D.R.F. Investments were sold for Rs. 16,40,000. The Bank balance on that day before the receipt of interest was Rs. 10,50,000

Prepare necessary ledger accounts.

Solution (1)

11% DEBENTURES A/C

2004		Rs.	2004		Rs.
Dec. 31	To Debentureholders' A/c	25,00,000	Jan. 1	By Balance b/d	25,00,000

DEBENTUREHOLDERS' A/C

2004		Rs.	2004		Rs.
Dec. 31	To Bank A/c	26,25,000	Dec. 31	By 11% Debentures A/c	25,00,000
				By Premium on Redem. A/c	1,25,000
		26,25,000			26,25,000

DEBENTURE REDEMPTION FUND A/C

2004		Rs.	2004		Rs.
Dec. 31	To Loss on issue of Deben. (Premium on Red. A/c)	1,25000	Jan.1	By Balance b/d	16,25,690
"	To Capital Reserve*	14,500	Dec. 31	By Interest on DRFI @ 5% on 16,25,500	81,275
"	To General Reserve (Transfer)	23,75,500	"	By P & L Appropriation A/c	7,93,535
			"	By DRF Investment (Profit or sale)	14,500
		25,15,000			25,15,000

* Alternatively, this may be ignored and transferred to General Reserve.

DEBENTURE REDEMPTION FUND INVESTMENTS A/C

2004		Rs.	2004		Rs.
Jan. 1	To Balance b/d	16,25,500	Dec.31	By Bank A/c	16,40,000
Dec., 31	To Deb. Red. Fund A/c (Profit on sale)	14,500			
		16,40,000			16,40,000

BANK A/C

2004		Rs.	2004		Rs.
Jan. 1	To Balance b/d	10,50,000	Dec.31	By Debentureholders' A/c	26,25,000
Dec. 31	To Interest on DRFI A/c	81,275	"	By Balance c/d	1,46,275
"	To Deb. Red. Fund Invest. A/c	16,40,000			
		27,71,275			27,71,275

Illustration (2)

(Cost & nominal value of S.F. Investments)

The following balances appeared in the books of P Ltd. as on 31st March, 2004. Rs.

	Rs.
9% Debentures	5,00,000
Debenture Redemption Fund	5,65,000
Represented by :	
Rs. 1,60,000 3.5% Punjab Govt. Loan	1,70,000
Rs. 1,80,000 4% Delhi Govt. Loan	1,72,000
Rs. 60,000 6% Debentures of Reliance Ltd.	56,000
Rs. 16,70,000 7% Preference Shares of T Ltd.	1,67,000

These investments were sold on the above date as under :

3.5% Punjab Govt. Loan	at par
4% Delhi Govt. Loan	at Rs. 96
6% Debentures of Reliance Ltd.	at Rs. 90
7% Preference Shares	at Rs.105

On 1st April, 2004, the Company redeemed the debentures at a premium of 10%

You are required to prepare :

(i) 9% Debentures Account.

(ii) Debenture Redemption Fund Account

(iii) Debenture Redemption Fund Investment Account

(iv) Debenture Redemption Account

ICWA (1) Adapted

9% DEBENTURES A/C

2004		Rs.	2004		Rs.
Mar. 31	To Debenture Redemption A/c	5,00,000	Mar. 31	By Balance b/d	5,00,000

DEBENTURE REDEMPTION FUND A/C

2004		Rs.	2004		Rs.
Mar. 31	To Loss on Issue (Premium on Red. A/c)	50,000	Mar. 31	By Balance b/d	5,65,000
" "	To Deb. Redemption Fund Investments A/c (Loss on sale)	2,850			
" "	To General Reserve A/c	5,12,150			
		5,65,000			5,65,000

DEBENTURE REDEMPTION FUND INVESTMENT A/C

2004		Rs.	2004		Rs.
Mar. 31	To Balance b/d	5,65,000	Mar. 31	By Bank A/c	
				Punjab Govt. Loan	1,60,000
				Delhi Govt. Loan	1,72,800
				6% Debentures	54,000
				7% Preference Shares	1,75,350
				By Deb. Red. Fund A/c (Loss on sale)	2,850
		5,65,000			5,65,000

DEBENTURE REDEMPTION A/C

2004		Rs.	2004		Rs.
Mar. 31	To Bank A/c	5,50,000	Mar. 31	By 9% Debentures A/c	5,00,000
				By Deb. Red. Fund A/c (Prem. on Red.)	50,000
		5,50,000			5,50,000

Working notes :

(1) Debenture Redemption Fund Investment A/c has been shown at total cost of investments. Nominal value is taken for the purpose of calculating income on investments and sale proceeds thereof. Since investments have been sold the same day, income on such investments has been ignored.

(2) Debenture Redemption Account is another version or equivalent to own debentures account.

Illustration (3)

(Sinking Fund and Partial Redemption)

On 1.4.04 the Debenture Redemption Fund of A Ltd. stood at Rs. 3,20,000 represented by 5% Rs. 4,00,000 nominal investments in Central Securities. 8% Debentures had a balance of Rs. 10,00,000

The annual contribution to Debenture Redemption Fund amounted to Rs. 60,000. On 31st March, 2005 the Company sold the investments of the nominal value Rs. 2,40,000 @ Rs. 84 and redeemed Rs. 2,00,000 debentures at a premium of 2%. The bank balance before the receipt of interest and sale of investments stood at Rs. 45,500. During the year Rs. 1,00,000 5% Central Securities were purchased at Rs. 80,000.

Prepare :

8% Debentures A/c, Debenture Redemption Fund A/c, Debentures Redemption Fund Investments A/c and Debentureholders A/c

8% DEBENTURES A/C

2005		Rs.	2004		Rs.
Mar. 31	To Debentureholders' A/c	2,00,000	April 1	By Balance b/d	10,00,000
	To Balance c/d	8,00,000			
		10,00,000			10,00,000

DEBENTURE REDEMPTION FUND A/C

2005		Rs.	2004		Rs.
Mar. 31	To Loss on Issue (Premium on Red. A/c)	2,000	April 1	By Balance b/d	3,20,000
" "	To General Reserve A/c	2,00,000	2005	By Interest on Deb. Red. Fund Investment A/c	20,000
	To Balance c/d	2,07,600	" "	By Profit & Loss Appro. A/c	60,000
			" "	By Deb. Red. Fund Investments A/c (Profit on sale)	9,600
		4,09,600			4,09,600

DEBENTURE REDEMPTION FUND INVESTMENTS A/C

2004		Rs.	2005		Rs.
April 1	To Balance b/d	3,20,000	Mar. 31	By Bank A/c	2,01,600
2005				By Balance c/d	2,08,000
March 31	To Bank A/c	80,000			
	To D. R. Fund A/c (Profit or Sale)	9,600			
		4,09,600			4,09,600

DEBENTUREHOLDERS' A/C

2005		Rs.	2005		Rs.
March 31	To Bank A/c	2,02,000	Mar. 31	By 8% Debentures A/c	2,00,000
			"	By Premium on Redem. A/c	2,000
		2,02,000			2,02,000

BANK A/C

2004		Rs.	2005		Rs.
April 1	To Balance b/d	45,500	Mar. 31	By Debentureholders' A/c	2,02,000
2005	To Interest on D.R.F			By Balance c/d	65,100
March	Investment A/c	20,000			
" "	To D.R.F. Investment	2,01,600			
		2,67,100			2,67,100

Working notes :

(1) Op. Balance of DRF Investments (at Nominal value) 4,00,000
Less Nominal Value of Investments sold 2,40,000
1,60,000
Add Nominal Value of Investments purchased 1,00,000
Nominal Value of Investments at the end 2,60,000

(2) Profit on sale of investments has not been transferred to Capital Reserve. It is prudent to transfer only when all investments are sold and all debentures redeemed.

(3) Profit on Sale of investments :

Sale Proceeds of investments $\frac{2,40,000 \times 84}{100}$ = Rs. 2,01,600

Less Cost of Investments $\left(\frac{2,40,000 \times 3,20,000}{4,00,000}\right)$ = Rs. 1,92,000

9,600

(4) An amount equal to nominal value of debentures redeemed has been transferred to General Reserve.

Illustration (4)

(Sinking Fund and purchase of own debentures out of proceeds of investments)

On 1.1.2004 A B C Ltd. had 9% Rs. 5,00,000 Debentures outstanding. On the same day a balance of Rs. 2,00,000 standing to the credit of Debenture Redemption Fund which was represented by 8% Rs. 2,50,000 (Nominal Value) Investments.

On 1.10.2004 it sold investments of the face value of Rs. 50,000 @ Rs. 90 and purchased own debentures of face value of Rs. 50,000 for cancellation out of net proceeds.

The interest dates for both debentures and investments are 30th June and 31st December. All transactions are cum-interest.

Prepare Debenture Redemption Fund A/c, Debenture Redemption Fund Investments A/c and 12% Debentures A/c.

ICWA (Adapted)

Solution (4)

DEBENTURE REDEMPTION FUND A/C

2004		Rs.	2004		Rs.
Dec. 31	To General Reserve	50,000	Jan. 1	By Balance b/d	2,00,000
	To Capital Reserve	6,125	June 30	By Interest on DRF Investments A/c	10,000
" "	To Balance c/d	1,73,000	Oct. 1	By Deb. Red. Fund Investments A/c	4,000
			Oct. 1	By Interest on DRF Investments A/c (Accrued)	1,000
			" "	By Debentures A/c	6,125
			Dec. 31	By Interest on DRF Investment s A/c	8,000
		2,29,125			2,29,125

DEBENTURE REDEMPTION FUND INVESTMENTS A/C

2004		Rs.	2004		Rs.
Jan. 1	To Balance b/d (F.V. Rs. 2,50,000)	2,00,000	Oct. 1	By Bank A/c	44,000
	To Deb. Red. Fund A/c (Profit)	4,000		By Balance c/d (F.V. 2,00,000)	1,60,000
		2,04,000			2,04,000

9% DEBENTURES A/C

2004		Rs.	2004		Rs.
Oct. 1	To Bank b/d	43,875	Jan. 1	By Balance b/d	5,00,000
	To Profit on Cancellation transferred to DRF A/c	6,125			
Dec. 31	To Balance c/d	4,50,000			
		5,00,000			5,00,000

Working notes:

(1) Interest on D.R.F. Investments (1.1.2004 to 30.6.2004)

$$\text{Rs.}2,50,000 \times \frac{8}{100} \times \frac{6}{12} = \text{Rs.}10,000$$

(2) Interest in DRF Investments (1.07 2004 to 1.10.2004)

$$\text{Rs. } 50,000 \times \frac{8}{100} \times \frac{3}{12} \quad \text{Rs. } 1000\ *$$

	Rs.
(3) Sale Proceeds of Investments Rs. 50,000 × 90% =	45,000
* *Less* Interest for the holding period	1000
	44,000

	Rs.
Less Cost of Investments $\left(\frac{2,00,000}{2,50,000} \times 50,000\right)$	40,000
Profit	4,000

(5) Profit on Cancellation of Debentures

	Rs.
Nominal value of Debentures Cancelled	50,000
* *Less* Net Proceeds of DRF Investments	43,875
Profit on Cancellation	6,125

(6) Interest for the holding period (being interest accrued but not due) which is included in the sale proceeds has been excluded because of Cum- interest Price.

(7) An amount equivalent to face value of the debentures cancelled (Redeemed) has been transferred to General Reserve.

(8) Interest on Debentures (1.7.04 to 1.10.04)

$$\text{Rs. } 50,000 \times \frac{9}{100} \times \frac{3}{12} = \text{Rs. } 1,125$$

	Rs.
Sales proceeds of Investments	45,000
Less Interest on Debentures (Cum- interest)	1,125
* Cost of own Debentures purchased	* 43,875

It is to be noted that the interest accrued for the holding period will be deducted from the amount paid for the debentures if price is Cum-interest. No interest shall be deduced if it is Ex-interest Price.

Illustration (5) (Cancellation of Own debentures and Sinking Fund)

A Ltd. had Rs. 8,60,000 14% Debentures outstanding on April 1, 2004. On that date Sinking Fund stood at Rs. 7,49,000 represented by Rs. 1,50,000 own debentures purchased on an average at Rs. 90 and Rs. 7,00,000 10% Government Loan. The annual contribution to the Sinking Fund was Rs. 20,000.

On 31st March, 2005 the investments were realised at 90% and the debentures were redeemed at a premium of 4%. The own debentures were also cancelled on the above date.

You are required to prepare necessary ledger accounts in the books of A Ltd. The bank balance stood at Rs. 2,45,000 as on 1st April, 2004.

C.A. (1) Modified

Solution (5)

14% DEBENTURES A/C

2005		Rs.	2004		Rs.
March 31	To Own Debentures A/c	1,50,000	April 1	By Balance b/d	8,60,000
" "	To Debentureholders' A/c	7,10,000			
		8,60,000			8,60,000

OWN DEBENTURES A/C

2004		Rs.	2005		Rs.
April 1	To Balance b/d (Rs. 1,50,000 @ 90%)	1,35,000	Mar. 31	By 14% Debentures A/c	1,50,000
	To Sinking Fund A/c (Profit on cancellation)	15,000			
		1,50,000			1,50,000

DEBENTUREHOLDERS' A/C

2005		Rs.	2005		Rs.
Mar. 31	To Bank A/c	7,38,400	Mar. 31	By 14% Debentures A/c	7,10,000
				By Premium on Red. A/c	28,400
		7,38,400			7,38,400

SINKING FUND A/C

2005		Rs.	2004		Rs.
March 31	To Loss on Issue A/c (Premium on Redem. A/c)	28,400	April 1	By Balance b/d	7,49,000
	To Capital Reserve A/c	31,000	2005 Mar. 31	By Interest on S. F. Investments A/c	70,000
	To General Reserve A/c	8,31,600		By Interest on Own Debentures A/c	21,000
				By Profit & Loss App. A/c	20,000
				By Own Debentures A/c	15,000
				By S. F. Investments A/c	16,000
		8,91,000			8,91,000

SINKING FUND INVESTMENTS A/C (10% GOVT. LOAN)

2004		Rs.	2005		Rs.
April 1	To Balance b/d (7,49,000 – 1,35,000)	6,14,000	Mar. 31	By Bank A/c (90% of Rs. 7,00,000)	6,30,000
	To Sinking Fund A/c (Profit)	16,000			
		6,30,000			6,30,000

BANK A/C

2004		Rs.	2005		Rs.
April 1	To Balance b/d	2,45,000	Mar. 31	By Debentureholders' A/c	7,38,400
	To Interest on S.F. Invest. A/c	70,000	" "	By Interest on Debentures A/c	99,400
Mar. 31	To S. F. Investment A/c	6,30,000	" "	By Balance c/d	1,07,200
		9,45,000			9,45,000

Working notes :

		Rs.
(1)	Interest on Investments	
	On own debentures @ 14% on Rs. 1,50,000	21,000
	On S.F. Investments @ 10% on Rs. 7,00,000	70,000
(2)	Capital Reserve (Rs. 15,000 + 16,000)	31,000

Illustration (6)

(Immediate Cancellation of Own debentures & Sinking fund)

The following balances appeared in the books of a limited Company as on 31st March, 2004.

12% 2,000 Debentures of Rs. 100 each	2,00,000
Debenture Redemption Fund	1,25,000
Debenture Redemption Fund Investments	1,25,000
(Represented by 8% Government Bonds of Rs. 1,50,000)	

Interest on debentures and Govt. Bonds was payable on 30th September and 31st March.

On 31.5.2004, the Company purchased for immediate cancellation 250 debentures from the open market @ Rs. 96 Cum-interest. The amount required for this was raised by selling 8% Govt. Bonds of the face value of Rs. 27,000 Cum-interest.

On 31st March, 2005 Rs. 20,800 was appropriated for the Sinking Fund and on the same date 8% Government Bonds were purchased for the amount plus interest on investment. The face value of the Government Bonds purchased was Rs. 37,200.

You are required to show :

(i) 12% Debentures A/c

(ii) Debenture Redemption Fund Investments A/c

(iii) Debenture Redemption Fund A/c

(iv) Debenture Interest A/c

(v) Interest on D. R. F. Investments A/c

C.S. (i) Modified

12% DEBENTURES A/C

2004		Rs.	2004		Rs.
May 31	To Bank A/c	23,500	April 1	By Balance b/d	2,00,000
	To Deb. Red. Fund A/c(1)	1,500			
2005	(Profit on Cancellation)				
March 31	To Balance c/d	1,75,000			
		2,00,000			2,00,000

DEBENTURE REDEMPTION FUND A/C

2004		Rs.	2004		Rs.
May 31	To Capital Reserve A/c (1,500 + 1,140)	2,640	April 1	By Balance b/d	1,25,000
" "	To General Reserve A/c	25,000	May 31	By 12% Debentures A/c (Profit on Cancellation)	1,500
2005			" "	By Debenture Redemption Fund Investments A/c (Profit on sale)	1,140
Mar. 31	To Balance c/d	1,31,000	2005		
			Mar. 31	By Interest on DRFI A/c	10,200
				By Profit & Loss App. A/c	20,800
		1,58,640			1,58,640

DEBENTURE REDEMPTION FUND INVESTMENTS A/C (8% GOVT. BONDS)

2004		Rs.	2004		Rs.
April 1	To Balance b/d	1,25,000	May 31	By Bank A/c	23,640
May 31	To Deb. Red. Fund A/c (2) (Profit on sale)	1140	2005 March 31	By Balance c/d	1,33,500
2005 Mar. 31	To Bank A/c (3)	31,000			
		1,57,140			1,57,140

DEBENTURE INTEREST A/C

2004		Rs.	2005		Rs.
May 31	To Bank A/c	500	Mar. 31	By Profit & Loss A/c	21,500
Sept.. 30	To Bank A/c	10,500			
2005 Mar. 31	To Bank A/c	10,500			
		21,500			21,500

INTEREST ON DEB. RED. FUND INVESTMENTS A/C

2005			2004		
Mar. 31	To Deb. Redemp. Fund A/c	10,200	May 31	By Bank A/c	360
			Sept.. 30	By Bank A/c	4,920
			2005 Mar. 31	By Bank A/c	4,920
		10,200			10,200

Working notes :

(1) Profit on Cancellation

	Rs.
Amount paid for the Debentures including interest 250 Deb. × Rs. 96	24,000
Less Interest Accrued for 2 months $\left(25{,}000 \times \frac{12}{100} \times \frac{2}{12}\right)$	500
Actual price paid for Debentures	23,500
Face Value of Debentures	25,000
Profit on Cancellation	1,500

(2) Profit on Sale of D.R.F. Investments (8% Govt. Bonds)

Interest Accrued for April and May $\left(27{,}000 \times \frac{8}{100} \times \frac{2}{12}\right)$	360
Amount received on sale of Investments Cum-Interest (Being price for Debentures including interest)	24,000
Hence Amount realised on sale of Investments excluding interest (24,000 – 360)	23,640
Cost of Investments sold $\left(27{,}000 \times \frac{1{,}25{,}000}{1{,}50{,}000}\right)$	22,500
Profit on sale of Investments	1,140

(3) Purchase of 8% Govt. Bonds on 31.3.2005

	Rs.
Annual Appropriation	20,800
Add Interest Received on Investments (8% Bonds)	
On 31.5.2004 for 2 month on Rs. 27,000	360
On 30.9.2004 for 6 months on Rs. 1,23,000	4,920
On 31.3.2005 for 6 months on Rs. 1,23,000	4,920
	31,000

(4) Debenture Interest paid @ 12% p.a.

	Rs.
On 31.5.2004 for 2 months on Rs. 25,000	500
On 30.9.2004 for 6 months on Rs. 1,75,000	10,500
On 31.3.2005 for 6 months on Rs. 1,75,000	10,500
	21,500

(5) Alternatively the profit on sale of investments may be transferred to General Reserve instead to Capital reserve. However profit on cancellation should always be transferred to Capital Reserve

Illustration (7) (Purchase of own Debentures and half-yearly investments in Sinking Fund)

A Ltd. had issued 9% 5,000 Debentures of Rs. 100 each at par. A Sinking Fund was created to provide for redemption. Under the terms of issue, the Company had an option to purchase it's own debentures from the open market for cancellation

On 1st January, 2004, 3,800 Debentures were outstanding and the Sinking Fund balance stood at Rs. 2,50,000. The Sinking Fund Investments on that date consisted of Rs. 1,24,000, 5% Government Loans at a Cost of Rs. 1,20,000.

On 1st January 2004, the Company purchased Rs. 20,000 of the Debentures for Rs. 19,300 realising 5% Govt. Loans at 96.5% to raise the necessary funds Interest on 5% Govt. Loans was received on 30th June. and 31st December and was invested forthwith in further purchase of 5% Govt. Loans at par. On 31st December, 2004 a sum of Rs. 20,000 was credited to the Sinking Fund Account and invested in 5% Govt. Loans, Rs. 19,850 of which was purchased.

Pass journal entries and prepare necessary ledger accounts. Interest on debentures is payable on 31st December each year.

B. Com (H) D.U. 1995-Modified

JOURNAL ENTRIES

2004			Rs.	Rs.
Jan. 1	Bank A/c	Dr.	19,300	
	Sinking Fund A/c	Dr.	55	
	To Sinking Fund Investments A/c			19,355
	(Being S.F. Investments sold & loss transferred to Sinking Fund A/c)			
"	Own Debentures A/c	Dr.	19,300	
	To Bank A/c			19,300
	(Being Rs. 20,000 debentures purchased)			
June, 30	Bank A/c	Dr.	2,600	
	To Interest on S. F. Investments A/c			2,600
	(Being interest on 5% Govt. Loan of Rs. 1,04,000 received)			
" "	Interest on S.F. Investments A/c	Dr.	2,600	
	To Sinking Fund A/c			2,600
	(Being interest transferred to S. Fund A/c)			
" "	Sinking Fund Investments A/c	Dr.	2,600	
	To Bank A/c			2,600
	(Being 5% Govt. Loans purchased at par)			
Dec. 31	Bank A/c	Dr.	2,665	
	To Interest on S.F. Investments A/c			2,665
	(Being interest on 5% Govt. Loans of Rs. 1,06,400)			
Dec. 31	Interest on S.F. Investments A/c	Dr.	2,665	
	To Sinking Fund A/c			2,665
	(Being interest transferred to Sinking Fund A/c)			
"	Sinking Fund Investments A/c	Dr.	2,665	
	To Bank A/c			2,665
	(Being 5% Govt. Loans purchased at par)			
" "	Profit & Loss Appropriation A/c	Dr.	20,000	
	To Sinking Fund A/c			20,000
	(Being annual appropriation made to Sinking fund)			*Contd.*

2004			Rs.	Rs.
" "	Sinking Fund Investments A/c	Dr.	20,000	
	To Bank A/c			20,000
	(Being 5% Govt. Loan of the face value of Rs. 19,850 purchased at a cost of 20,000.			
Dec.31	Debenture Interest A/c	Dr.	34,200	
	To Bank A/c			32,400
	To Interest on own Deb. A/c			1,800
	(Being interest paid and transferred to Interest on own debenture A/c)			
	Profit & Loss A/c	Dr.	34,200	
	To Debenture Interest A/c			34,200
	(Being Deb. Interest charged to Profit & Loss A/c)			
	Interest on Own Debenture A/c	Dr.	1,800	
	To Profit & Loss A/c			1,800
	(Being interest on Own debentures transferred to P & L A/c			

9% DEBENTURES A/C

2004		Rs.	2004		Rs.
Dec.31	To Balance c/d	3,80,000	Jan. 1	By Balance b/d	3,80,000

OWN DEBENTURES A/C

2004		Rs.	2004		Rs.
Jan. 1	To Bank A/c	19,300	Dec.31	By Balance c/d	19,300

SINKING FUND ACCOUNT

2004		Rs.	2004		Rs.
Jan. 1	To S. Fund Investments A/c (Loss on sale)	55	Jan. 1	By Balance b/d	2,50,000
Dec. 31	To Balance c/d	2,75,210	June, 30	By Interest on S.F. Investments A/c	2,600
			Dec. 31	By Interest on S.F. Investments A/c	2,665
				By Profit & Loss App. A/c	20,000
		2,75,265			2,75,265

SINKING FUND INVESTMENTS A/C (5% GOVT. LOANS)

2004		Rs.	2004		Rs.
Jan. 1	To Balance b/d	1,20,000	Jan. 1	By Bank A/c	19,300
June 30	To Bank A/c	2,600		By Sinking Fund A/c	55
Dec. 31	To Bank A/c	22,665		(Loss on sale)	
	(2,665 + 20,000)		Dec. 31	By Balance c/d	1,25,910
		1,45,265			1,45,265

INTEREST ON INVESTMENTS A/C

2004		Rs.	2004		Rs.
June 30	To Sinking Fund A/c	2,600	June, 30	By Bank A/c	2,600
Dec. 31	To Sinking Fund A/c	2,665	Dec. 31	By Bank A/c	2,665

9% DEBENTURE INTEREST A/C

2004		Rs.	2004		Rs.
Dec. 31	To Bank A/c	32,400	Dec. 31	By Profit & Loss A/c	34,200
	To Interest on Own Debentures	1,800			
		34,200			34,200

INTEREST ON OWN DEBENTURES A/C

2004		Rs.	2004		Rs.
Dec. 31	To Profit & Loss A/c	1,800	Dec. 31	By Debenture Interest	1,800

Working notes :

(1) Loss on sale of Investments : Rs.

	Rs.
Nominal value of Investments sold $\left(19{,}300 \times \frac{100}{96.5}\right)$	20,000
Cost of Investments sold. $\left(20{,}000 \times \frac{1{,}20{,}000}{1{,}24{,}000}\right)$	19,355
Sale proceeds (used to buy own debentures)	19,300
Loss on Sale of Investments	55

(2) Interest on S. F. Investments On 30.6 2004 $\left(1{,}04{,}000 \times \frac{5}{100} \times \frac{6}{12}\right)$ 2,600

On 31.12. 2004 $\left(1{,}06{,}600^{*} \times \frac{5}{100} \times \frac{6}{12}\right)$ 2,665

*(1,04,000 + 2,600)

(3) 5% Govt. Loans have been purchased at par on 30th June and on 31st December, interest of Rs. 2,600 and Interest of Rs. 2,665 has been invested at par while annual appropriation of Rs. 20,000 could fetch nominal investments worth Rs. 19,850 only.

Illustration (8) (Purchase of own debentures when no Sinking Fund exists)

On 1.1.2004 S.G. Ltd. had 6% 5,000 Debentures of Rs. 100 each. As per the terms of redemption the Company purchased its own debentures from the open market for immediate cancellation as follows:

March 1	250 Debentures @ Rs. 98 Cum-interest
Aug.1	500 Debentures @ Rs. 100.25 Cum-interest
Dec. 15	120 Debentures @ Rs. 98.5 Ex- Interest

Debenture interest is payable on 30th June and 31st December every year.

Prepare necessary ledger accounts.

Solution (8)

6% DEBENTURES ACCOUNT

2004		Rs.	2004		Rs.
Mar. 1	To Bank A/c	24,250	Jan. 1	By Balance b/d	5,00,000
	To Capital Reserve A/c (Profit on Cancellation)	750			
Aug. 1	To Bank A/c	49,875			
	To Capital Reserve A/c Profit on Cancellation)	125			
Dec. 15	To Bank A/c	11,820			
	To Capital Reserve A/c (Profit on Cancellation)	180			
Dec. 31	To Balance c/d	4,13,000			
		5,00,000			5,00,000

DEBENTURE INTEREST A/C

2004		Rs.	2004		Rs.
Mar. 1	To Bank A/c	250	Dec. 31	By Profit & Loss A/c	27,470
June 30	To Bank A/c	14,250			
Aug. 1	To Bank A/c	250			
Dec. 15	To Bank A/c	330			
Dec. 31	To Bank A/c	12,390			
		27,470			27,470

Working notes

(1) Calculation of interest : (Paid at the time of purchase of Debentures)

* On 250 debentures purchased on March 1 (for two months) $\left(25{,}000 \times \frac{6}{100} \times \frac{2}{12}\right)$ Rs. 250

* On 500 debentures purchased on August 1 (for one month) $\left(50{,}000 \times \frac{6}{100} \times \frac{1}{12}\right)$ Rs. 250

* On 120 Debentures purchased on December 15, ($5\frac{1}{2}$ month) $\left(12{,}000 \times \frac{6}{100} \times \frac{11}{2 \times 12}\right)$

Rs. 330.

(2) Calculation of interest paid on due dates :

On 30th June 2004 (Rs. 5,00,000 – 25,000) – $\left(4{,}75{,}000 \times \frac{6}{100} \times \frac{6}{12}\right) =$ Rs. 14,250

On 31st December 2004

(Rs. 4,75,000 – 50,000 – 12,000) = $\left(4{,}13{,}000 \times \frac{6}{100} \times \frac{6}{12}\right) =$ Rs. 12,390

(3) Profit on cancellation : On March 1,

		Rs.
Nominal value of debentures cancelled		25,000
Cum-interest Price paid for debentures	Rs. 24,500	
Less Interest Accrued	Rs. 250	24,250
		750
On August 1 Nominal Value of debentures Cancelled		50,000
Cum-Interest price paid for debentures	50,125	
Less Interest Accrued	250	49,875
		125
On December 15 Nominal Value of debentures Cancelled		12,000
Ex. Interest price paid for debentures		11,820
		180

The working shows that profit on Cancellation is equal to Nominal Value less Ex- Interest price. That's why interest has been deducted from the Cum- Interest price.

Illustration (9) (Purchase of own debentures as investments and subsequent Cancellation Where no sinking fund exists.)

Sillycon Ltd. had 6% Rs. 10,00,000 Debentures outstanding on which interest is payable on 31st March and 30th September each year. The Company has option to purchase debentures from the open market to be cancelled subsequently.

During the year ended 31st December, 2004, the Directors purchased the Debentures as follows:

March 1	Rs. 50,000 Debentures for Rs. 49,450 Ex- Interest
September 1	Rs. 40,000 Debentures for Rs. 40,250 Cum-Interest
November 1	Rs. 10,000 Debentures for Rs. 9,950 Cum- Interest

All these debentures were cancelled on 31st March, 2005.

Prepare following ledger accounts upto the date of cancellation.

(i) 6% Debentures Account

(ii) Own Debentures Account

(iii) Debenture Interest Account

(iv) Interest on Own debentures A/c

Solution (9)

6% DEBENTURES ACCOUNT

2004		Rs.	2004		Rs.
Dec. 31	To Balance c/d	10,00,000	Jan. 1	By Balance b/d	10,00,000
		10,00,000			10,00,000
2005	To Own Debentures A/c	1,00,000	2005	by Balance b/d	10,00,000
Mar. 31	To Balance c/d	9,00,000	Jan. 1		
		10,00,000			10,00,000

OWN DEBENTURES A/C

2004			2004		Rs.
March 1	To Bank A/c	49,450	Dec. 31	By Balance c/d	98,600
Sept.. 1	To Bank A/c	39,250			
Nov. 1	To Bank A/c	9,900			
		98,600			98,600
2005			2005		
Jan. 1	To Balance b/d	98,600	Mar. 31	By 6% Debentures A/c	1,00,000
	To Capital Reserve A/c (Profit on Cancellation)	1,400			
		1,00,000			1,00,000

DEBENTURE INTEREST A/C

2004		Rs.	2004		Rs.
March 1	To Bank A/c (Interest on Rs. 50,000 for 5 months)	1,250	Dec.	By Profit & Loss A/c	60,000
				By Accrued Interest A/c	15,000
Mar. 31	To Bank A/c (Interest on Rs. 9,50,000 for 6 months)	28,500			
" "	To Interest on Own Debentures (For one month)	250			
Sept. 1	To Bank A/c (Interest on (Rs. 40,000 for 5 months)	1000			
Sept. 30	To Bank A/c (On Rs. 9,10,000 for 6 Months)	27,300			
" "	To Interest on Own Debentures (On Rs. 50,000 for 6 months & Rs. 40,000 for one month)	1,700			
Nov. 1	To Bank A/c (On Rs. 10,000 for one month)	50			
Dec. 31	To Interest Accrued (on Rs. 9,00,000 for 3 months)	13,500			
					Contd.

2004		Rs.			Rs.
Dec. 31	To Interest Accrued on Own debentures A/c (On Rs. 90,000 for 3 months & on Rs. 10,000 for 2 months)	1,450			
		75,000			75,000
2005	To Bank A/c (on Rs. 9,00,000 for 6 months)	27,000	2005	By Interest Accrued A/c	13,500
" "	To Interest on Own debentures A/c (on Rs. 1,00,000 for 3 months)	1,500	Mar. 1	By Balance c/d	15,000
		28,500			28,500

INTEREST ON OWN DEBENTURES A/C

2004		Rs.	2004		Rs.
Dec. 31	To Profit & Loss A/c	3,400	Mar. 31	By Debenture Interest A/c	250
			Sept. 30	By Deb. Interest A/c	1,700
			Dec. 31	By Deb. Interest A/c	1,450
		3,400			3,400
2005			2005		
Mar. 31	To Balance c/d	1,500	Mar. 31	By Deb. Interest A/c	1,500

Working notes :

(1) Interest on debentures has been charged to Profit on Loss Account on accrual basis.

(ii) It is to be noted that interest on debentures of Rs. 10,00,000 @ 6% p.a. should not exceed Rs. 60,000 in any year, Rs. 30,000 for 6 months, and Rs. 15,000 for 3 months period including interest on own debentures and debenture interest paid at the time of purchase from the open market.

Verification : *(see Debenture interest A/c)*

	Rs.
Interest for 1st half	1,250 *
ending on 31st March 2004	28,500**
	30,000
Interest for the second half	1,000 *
ending 30th Sept. 2004	27,300 **
	1,700***
	30,000

Interest (Accrued) for 3 months (due up to the date of closing) (1.10. 2004 to 31.12.2004)

	Rs.
*Paid at the time of purchase of debenture	50
**Accrued till the date of closing	13,500
***Accrued on own debentures	1,450
	15,000

Interest for next 3 months (1.1.2005 to 31.3.2005)	
(Paid Rs. 27,000 – 13,500 (Accrued))	13,500
Interest on own debenture.	1,500

It should be noted that debenture interest is Charged to Profit & Loss Account on the date of closing of books of accounts.

Illustration (10) Conversion or purchase of own debentures as investments with subsequent cancellation where no sinking fund exists.)

On 1.4.2000 Z Ltd. issued 13.5 % 10,000 Debentures of Rs. 100 each at Rs. 99 on the following terms :

(i) payment of half yearly interest on 30th September and 31st March.

(ii) Automatic conversion of three fifth of the debentures into fully paid up 40,000 equity shares of Rs. 10 each on 1.4.2001.

(iii) Redemption of remaining debentures in two equal instalments on 31st March, 2002 and 1st April, 2004 by drawings or/and purchase of own debentures from the open market.

On 1.4.2001 Rs. 2,00,000 Govt. Bonds were acquired at 80% and sold at 95% on 1.10.2001 to purchase immediately own debentures at Rs. 95 for cancellation on 31.3.2002.

Show with working the amount of discount on issue of debentures that should be written off during 2000-01 and 2001-02.

Pass journal entries and prepare relevant ledger accounts for the year 2000-01 and 2001-02.

Solution (10)

JOURNAL ENTRIES

2000			Rs.	Rs.
April 1	Bank A/c	Dr.	9,90,000	
	Discount on Issue of Debentures A/c	Dr.	10,000	
	To 13.5% Debentures A/c			10,00,000
	(Being debentures issued at discount)			
Sept. 30	Debenture Interest A/c	Dr.	67,500	
	To Bank A/c			67,500
	(Being interest on debentures paid)			
2001				
March 31	Debenture Interest A/c	Dr.	67,500	
	To Bank A/c			67,500
	(Being interest on debentures paid)			
	Profit & Loss A/c	Dr.	1,40,000	
	To Debenture Interest A/c			1,35,000
	To Discount on Issue of Debentures A/c			5,000
	Being interest and discount charged to P & L A/c			
April 11	13.5% Debentures A/c	Dr.	6,00,000	
	To Debentureholders' A/c			6,00,000
	(Being debentures due for conversion)			*Contd.*

April 1	Debentureholders' A/c Dr. To Equity Share Capital A/c To Securities Premium A/c (Being debentures converted into shares)	6,00,000	 4,00,000 2,00,000
April 1	Govt. Bonds (Investments) A/c Dr. To Bank A/c (Being Govt. Bonds purchased)	1,60,000	 1,60,000
Sept. 30	Debenture Interest A/c Dr. To Bank A/c (Being debenture interest paid)	27,000	 27,000
Oct. 1	Bank A/c Dr. To Investments A/c To Profit on Sale of Investments A/c (Being investment sold at profit)	1,90,000	 1,60,000 30,000
" "	Own Debentures A/c Dr. To Bank A/c (Being own debentures purchased)	1,95,000	 1,95,000
March, 31	Debenture Interest A/c Dr. To Bank A/c To Interest on own Debentures A/c (Being interest due, paid & transferred to interest on own debentures A/c	27,000	 13,500 13,500
	Profit & Loss A/c Dr. To Debenture Interest A/c To Discount on Issue of Debentures A/c (Being interest & discount on issue charged to P & L A/c)	56,000	 54,000 2,000
	Interest on Own Debentures A/c Dr. To Profit & Loss A/c (Being interest on own debentures transferred)	13,500	 13,500
	13.5 % Debentures A/c Dr. To Own Debentures A/c To Profit on Cancellation A/c (Being debentures cancelled)	2,00,000	 1,90,000 10,000
	Profit on Cancellation A/c Dr. To Capital Reserve A/c (Being profit on Cancellation transferred to Capital Reserve)	10,000	 10,000
	Profit & Loss Appropriation A/c Dr. To General Reserve A/c (Being an amount equal to nominal value of debentures redeemed transferred to General Reserve)	2,00,000	 2,00,000

13.5% DEBENTURES A/C

2001		Rs.	2000		Rs.
Mar. 31	To Balance c/d	10,00,000	April 1	By Bank A/c	9,90,000
				By Discount on Issue	10,000
		10,00,000			10,00,000
2001			2001		
April 1	To Debentureholders' A/c	6,00,000	April 1	By Balance b/d	10,00,000
2002	To Own Debentures A/c	2,00,000			
March 31	To Balance c/d	2,00,000			
		10,00,000			10,00,000

OWN DEBENTURES A/C

2001		Rs.	2002		Rs.
Oct. 1	To Bank A/c	1,90,000	Mar. 31	By 13.5% Debentures A/c	2,00,000
2002	To Profit on Cancellation	10,000			
Mar., 31		2,00,000			2,00,000

DEBENTUREHOLDERS' A/C

2001		Rs.	2001		Rs.
April 1	To Equity Share Capital A/c	4,00,000	April 1	By 13.5% Debentures	6,00,000
	To Securities Premium A/c	2,00,000			
		6,00,000			6,00,000

DEBENTURE INTEREST A/C

2000		Rs.	2001		Rs.
Sept.	To Bank A/c	67,500	Mar. 31	By Profit & Loss A/c	1,35,000
2001					
March 31	To Bank A/c	67,500			
		1,35,000			1,35,000
2001			2002		
Sept. 30	To Bank A/c	27,000	Mar. 31	By Profit & Loss A/c	54,000
2002					
March 31	To Bank	13,500			
" "	To Interest on Own Debentures	13,500			
		54,000			54,000

INTEREST ON OWN DEBENTURES A/C

2002		Rs.	2002		Rs.
Mar. 31	To Profit & Loss A/c	13,500	Mar. 31	By Debenture Interest	13,500

Working notes :

(1) Discount on issue of debentures has been charged to Profit & Loss Account in the ratio of amount of debentures outstanding in the beginning of the year. However, the amount could have been written-off against the profit on cancellation as well.

(2) Working showing the amount of discount to be written off.

April 1	Amount of debentures Outstanding	Ratio	Discount to be w/o
2000	10,00,000	5 or 5/10	5,000
2001	4,00,000	2 or 2/10	2,000
2002	2,00,000	1 or 1/10	1,000
2003	2,00,000	1 or 1/10	1,000
2004	2,00,000	1 or 1/10	1,000
		10	10,000

Illustration (11)

(Redemption by Conversion)

On 1.1.2000 S Ltd. issued 10,000 fifteen years debentures of Rs. 100 each bearing interest at 10% p.a. The terms of issue include that the company could redeem the debentures by giving six months notice at any time after five years, at a premium of 4% either by payment in Cash or by allotment of preference shares and/or other debentures at the option of the debentureholders.

On 1st April, 2005, the Company gave notice to the debentureholders of the intention to redeem the debentures on 1st October, 2005 either by payment in Cash or by allotment of 11% Preference Shares of Rs. 100 each at Rs. 130 per share or 11% Second Debentures of Rs. 100 each at Rs. 96 per debenture.

Holders of 4,000 debentures accepted the offer of preference shares, holders of 4,800 debentures accepted the offer of 11% Second debentures and the rest demanded Cash on 1st October, 2005.

Give journal entries to give effect to the above as on 1st October, 2005. Suggest how discount on issue of debentures can be death with in the accounts.

C.A. (1) Modified

Solution (11)

JOURNAL ENTRIES

2005			Rs.	Rs.
Oct. 1	10% Debentures A/c	Dr.	10,00,000	
	Premium on Redemption A/c	Dr.	40,000	
	To Debenturesholders' A/c			10,40,000
	(Being debentures due for redemption)			
	Debentureholders' A/c	Dr.	4,16,000	
	To 11% Preference Share Capital A/c			3,20,000
	To Securities Premium A/c			96,000
	(Being preference shares issued to debentureholders)			

Contd.

		Rs.	Rs.
Debentureholders' A/c	Dr.	4,99,200	
Discount on Issue of Debentures A/c	Dr.	20,800	
To 11% Second Debentures			5,20,000
(Being 11% Second Debentures issued at 4% discount)			
Debentureholders' A/c	Dr.	1,24,800	
To Bank A/c			1,24,800
(Being debentures redeemed for Cash)			
Profit & Loss Appropriation A/c	Dr.	1,20,000	
To General Reserve A/c			1,20,000
(Being amount equal to face value of debentures redeemed out of profit transferred to General Reserve)			

Working note :

	Ist option 11% Pref. Shares Rs.	IInd option 11% Second Deb. Rs.	IIIrd option Cash Rs.
Nominal Value of Debentures to be redeemed	4,00,000	4,80,000	1,20,000
Add Premium on Redemption @ 4%	16,000	19,200	4,800
	4,16,000	4,99,200	1,24,800
Agreed Value of New security	÷ 130	÷ 96	
No. of securities- to be issued	= 3,200	= 5,200	
	Pref. Shares of Rs. 100 each	Debentures of Rs. 100 each	
Face Value of Pref. Shares / Deb.	3,20,000	5,20,000	
Premium (Discount)	96,000	(20,800)	

Illustration (12) (Redemption by Conversion)

A Ltd. Issued 9% 80,000 Debentures to the public as per the following conditions.

(i) The 9% debentures of Rs. 100 each issued at par which are partly convertible.

(ii) Convertible portion per debenture is 60% and date of conversion six months from the date of closing of issue.

(iii) Date of closure of subscription list 1.7.2004
Date of allotment — 1.8.2004

(iv) Interest is payable from the date of allotment.

(v) Value of equity share for the purpose of conversion : Rs. 60 for the equity share of Rs. 10 each.

(vi) Underwriting Commission — 2%

(vii) Public subscribed 60,000 debentures only.

(viii) Interest is payable half yearly on 30th September and 31st March.

Pass Journal entries to record above transactions for the year ended 31st March, 2005.

C.A. (1) (Modified)

Solution (12)

JOURNAL ENTRIES

2004			Rs.	Rs.
July, 1st	Bank A/c	Dr.	60,00,000	
	To Debenture Application A/c			60,00,000
	(Being application money received)			
Aug.1	Debenture Application A/c	Dr.	60,00,000	
	To 9% Debentures A/c			60,00,000
	(Being allotment of debentures made)			
	Underwriters' A/c	Dr.	20,00,000	
	To 9% Debentures A/c			20,00,000
	(Being allotment of debentures to underwriters on account of under-subscription)			
	Bank A/c	Dr.	18,40,000	
	Underwriters' Commission A/c	Dr.	1,60,000	
	To Underwriters' A/c			20,00,000
	(Being money received from underwriters after adjusting their commission)			
Sept. 30	Debenture Interest A/c	Dr.	1,20,000	
	To Bank A/c			1,20,000
	(Being payment of interest for two months only)			
2005				
Feb.	9% Debentures A/c	Dr.	48,00,000	
	To Debentureholders' A/c			48,00,000
	(Being 60% debentures are due for conversion)			
	Debentureholders' A/c	Dr.	48,00,000	
	To Equity Share Capital A/c			8,00,000
	To Securities Premium A/c			40,00,000
	(Being debentures converted into equity shares of Rs. 10 each at Rs. 50 per shares as premium)			
Mar. 31	Debenture Interest A/c	Dr.	2,88,000	
	To Bank A/c			2,88,000
	(Being debenture Interest paid)			
	Profit & Loss A/c	Dr.	4,08,000	
	To Debenture Interest A/c			4,08,000
	(Being debenture Interest transferred to P & L A/c)			

Working notes :

(1) Interest paid on 30. 9. 2004

* Interest on Rs. 80,00,000 @ 9% p.a. for two months — Rs. 1,20,000
i.e. from date of allotment to 30th September, 2004.

(2) Interest paid on 31st March, 2005

		Rs.
On Rs. 80,00,000 @ for 4 months (before conversion)	=	2,40,000
and on Rs. 32,00,000 @ 9% for 2 months (after conversion)		48,000
		2,88,000

(3) Amount Charged to profit & Loss A/c

Being interest paid during the year (Rs. 1,20,000 + 2,88,000) = 4,08,000

(4) As per the terms of underwriting agreement the underwriters are required to buy the unsubscribed securities. Hence, the remaining Rs. 20,00,000 debentures have been bought by the underwriters.

(5) Commission on underwriting is to be calculated on the total face value of the issue undertaken by them.

Illustration (13) (Redemption by Conversion/Cancellation out of proceeds of issue)

S Ltd. has an authorised Capital of Rs. 10,00,000 divided into equity shares of Rs. 10 each. It's Balance Sheet as on 31st December, 2004 stood as follows :

Liabilities :	Rs.
40,000 Equity Shares of Rs. 10 each	4,00,000
Capital Reserve	1,00,000
General Reserve	1,50,000
Profit & Loss Account	4,00,000
6% Debentures	4,00,000
S. Creditors	2,50,000
	17,00,000
Assets :	
Fixed Assets	11,40,000
Current Assets	4,00,000
Investments in Own debentures (Nominal value Rs. 1,00,000)	85,000
Bank Balance	75,000
	17,00,000

The 6% Debentures were due for payment on 30th June, 2005 at a premium of 5%. The Company decided :

(1) To issue to the public 25,000 equity shares of Rs. 10 each at Rs. 15 per share. The issue was underwritten and the amount due on shares was received on 1.6.2005. The underwriting commission was 5%.

(2) To redeem out of profits the debentures on 30th June, 2005 together with interest for six months.

(3) To give the debentureholders an option to receive either cash in repayment of the amount due or New 9% Debentures at par.

The holders of Rs. 1,00,000 of the old debentures accepted new debentures. The debentures which the company held as an investment were cancelled.

Pass journal entries and prepare a revised Balance Sheet.

C.A. (1) Modified

Solution (13)

JOURNAL ENTRIES

2005			Rs.	Rs.
June 1	Bank A/c	Dr.	3,75,000	
	To Share Application A/c			3,75,000
	(Being application money received)			
" "	Share Application A/c	Dr.	3,75,000	
	To Equity Share Capital A/c			2,50,000
	To Securities Premium A/c			1,25,000
	(Being application money transferred to Equity Share Capital and Securities Premium Account)			
	Underwriting Commission A/c	Dr.	12,500	
	To Underwriters' A/c			12,500
	(Being underwriting Commission due)			
	Underwriters' A/c	Dr.	12,500	
	To Bank A/c			12,500
	(Being Commission Paid)			
June 30	6% Debentures A/c	Dr.	3,00,000	
	Premium on Redemption A/c	Dr.	15,000	
	To Debentureholders' A/c			3,15,000
	(Being amount of debentures due on redemption)			
	Debenture Interest A/c	Dr.	12,000	
	To Debentureholders' A/c			9,000
	To Interest on own debentures A/c			3,000
	(Being interest transferred to debentureholders and interest on own debentures account)			
	Debentureholders' A/c	Dr.	2,16,000	
	To Bank A/c			2,16,000
	(Being payment made to Debentureholder with premium and interest)			
	6% Debentures A/c	Dr.	1,00,000	
	To Own Debentures A/c			85,000
	To Profit Cancellation A/c			15,000
	(Being own debentures cancelled)			

Contd.

		Rs.	Rs.
Debentureholders' A/c Dr. To 9% Debentures A/c (Being new 8% debentures issued to debenturesholders)		1,08,000	1,08,000
Profit & Loss A/c Dr. To Debenture Interest A/c (Being interest charged to P & L)		12,000	12,000
Interest on Own Debentures A/c Dr. To Profit & Loss A/c (Being interest on own debentures credited to P & L A/c)		3,000	3,000
Profit on Cancellation A/c Dr. To Premium on Redemption A/c (Being premium on redemption adjusted)		15,000	15,000
Profit & Loss A/c Dr. To General Reserve A/c (Being amount transferred to General Reserve)		3,00,000	3,00,000

BALANCE SHEET OF S LTD.
As on 30 the June, 2005

	Rs.
Liabilities	
65,000 Equity Shares of Rs. 10 each fully paid	6,50,000
Securities Premium	1,25,000
Capital Reserve	1,00,000
General Reserve	4,50,000
Profit & Loss Account	91,000
9% Debentures (New)	1,08,000
S. Creditors	2,50,000
	17,74,000
Assets	
Fixed Assets	11,40,000
Current Assets	4,00,000
Bank balance	2,21,500
Underwriting Commission	12,500
	17,74,000

Working notes :

(1) An amount equal to nominal value of debentures redeemed out of profits Rs. 3,00,000 (4,00,000 – 1,00,000) has been transferred to General Reserve.

(2) Equity shares have not been issued for the purpose of redemption.

(3) Underwriting commission may be written off against Profit & Loss A/c

(4) Bank Balance Rs. 2,21,500 = (75,000 + 3,75,000 – 2,16,000 – 12,500)

Illustration (14) (Purchase and resale of own debentures)

(i) S Ltd. issued 10,000 12% Debentures of Rs. 100 each on 1.4.2000 redeemable at par after three years Interest is payable annually.

(ii) On 1.1.2002 S Ltd. purchased 1,500 Debentures @ Rs. 98. These were resold on 30.9.2002 @ Rs. 105.

(iii) On April 1, 2002 S Ltd. purchased 1000 debentures @ Rs. 104. These were cancelled on July 1,2002.

(iv) On 1st January, 2003 S Ltd. purchased 2000 debentures @ Rs. 106. These debentures along with other debentures were redeemed on 31st March, 2003.

Pass Journal entries and prepare relevant ledger accounts. Ignore debenture redemption reserve. All transactions are ex-interest.

CA (1) Modified.

Solution (14)

JOURNAL ENTRIES

2000			Rs.	Rs.
April 1	Bank A/c	Dr.	10,00.000	
	To 12% Debentures A/c			10,00,000
	(Being debentures issued for cash)			
2001	Debenture Interest A/c	Dr.	1,20,000	
Mar. 31	To Bank A/c			1,20,000
	(Being debenture interest paid)			
	Profit & Loss account	Dr.	1,20,000	
	To Debentures Interest A/c			1,20,000
	(Being interest charged to P & L A/c)			
2002	Own debentures A/c	Dr.	1,47,000	
Jan. 1	Debenture Interest A/c	Dr.	13,500	
	To Bank A/c			1,60,500
	(Being own debentures purchased)			
Mar. 31	Debenture Interest A/c	Dr.	1,06,500	
	To Bank A/c			1,02,000
	To Interest on Own Debentures A/c			4,500
	(Being interest to debentureholders paid and interest on debentures held by company transferred to interest on own debentures)			
	Profit & Loss A/c	Dr.	1,20,000	
	To Debenture Interest A/c			1,20,000
	(Being interest charged to profit & Loss Account)			
	Interest on Debentures A/c	Dr.	4,500	
	To Profit & Loss A/c			4,500
	(Being Interest on own debentures transferred to P & L A/c)			*Contd.*

2002			Rs.	Rs.
April 1	Own Debentures A/c	Dr.	1,04,000	
	To Bank A/c			1,04,000
	(Being own debentures purchased @ Rs. 104)			
July 1	12% Debentures A/c	Dr.	1,00,000	
	Loss on Cancellation A/c	Dr.	4,000	
	To Own Debentures A/c			1,04,000
	(Being debentures purchased on 1st April cancelled)			
" "	Debenture Interest A/c	Dr.	3,000	
	To Interest on own debentures A/c			3,000
	(Being interest accrued on own debentures for 3 months)			
Sept. 30	Bank A/c	Dr.	1,66,500	
	To Interest on own debentures A/c			9,000
	To Own Debenture A/c			1,57,500
	(Being 1,500 debentures purchased on 1st January, 2002 sold)			
" "	Own Debentures A/c	Dr.	10,500	
	To Profit on resale of own Deb. A/c			10,500
	(Being profit on resale of debentures made)			
2003				
Jan. 1	Own Debentures A/c	Dr.	2,12,000	
	Debenture Interest A/c	Dr.	18,000	
	To Bank A/c			2,30,000
	(Being 2000 debentures @ Rs. 106 purchased - Ex-interest)			
Mar. 31	12% Debentures A/c	Dr.	2,00,000	
	Loss on Cancellation of debentures A/c	Dr.	12,000	
	To Own Debentures A/c			2,12,000
	(Being 2000 Debentures cancelled)			
May 31	Debenture Interest A/c	Dr.	6,000	
	To Interest on Own Debentures A/c			6,000
	(Being interest accrued on own debentures from the date of purchase to the date of cancellation)			
" "	Debenture Interest A/c	Dr.	84,000	
	To Bank A/c			84,000
	(Being interest paid to Debentureholder)			
	12% Debentures A/c	Dr.	5,50,000	
	To Bank A/c			5,50,000
	(Being debentures redeemed)			

Contd.

2002			Rs.	Rs.
March 31	Profit & Loss A/c	Dr.	1,27,000	
	To Debenture Interest A/c			1,11,000
	To Loss on Cancellation A/c			16,000
	(Being debenture interest & Loss on cancellation charged to P & L A/c)			
" "	Profit on resale of Debentures A/c	Dr.	10,500	
	Interest on Own Debentures A./c	Dr.	18,000	
	To Profit & Loss A/c			28,500
	(Being profit on resale of debentures and interest on own debentures credited to P & L A/c)			

12% DEBENTURES A/C

2001		Rs	2000		Rs.
Mar. 31	To Balance c/d	10,00,000	April 1	By Bank A/c	10,00,000
2002			2001		
Mar. 1	To Balance c/d	10,00,000	April 1	By Balance b/d	10,00,000
2002			2002		
July 1	To Own Debentures A/c	1,00,000	April 1	By Balance b/d	10,00,000
2003	To Own Debentures A/c	2,00,000			
March	To Debentureholders' A/c	7,00,000			
		10,00,000			10,00,000

OWN DEBENTURES A/C

2002		Rs.	2002		Rs.
Jan. 1	To Bank A/c	1,47,000	Mar. 31	By Balance c/d	1,47,000
Apr. 1	To Balance b/d	1,47,000	July 1	By 12% Debentures A/c	1,00,000
" "	To Bank A/c	1,04,000	"	By Loss on Cancellation A/c	4,000
Sept. 30	To Profit on Resale of debentures A/c	10,500	Sept. 30	By Bank A/c	1,57,500
2003			2003		
Jan. 1	To Bank A/c	2,12,000	Mar. 31	By 12% Debentures A/c	2,00,000
				By Loss on Cancellation A/c	12,000
		4,73,500			4,73,500

DEBENTURE INTEREST A/C

2001		Rs.	2001		Rs.
Mar. 31	To Bank A/c	1,20,000	Mar. 31	By Profit & Loss A/c	1,20,000
Jan 1,2002	To Bank A/c	13,500	2002		
Mar. 31	To Bank A/c	1,02,000	Mar. 31	By Profit & Loss A/c	1,20,000
" "	To Interest on own Debentures A/c	4,500			
		1,20,000			1,20,000
2002 July	To Interest on own Debentures A/c	3,000	2003 Mar. 31	By Profit & Loss A/c	1,11,000
2003 Jan.1	To Bank A/c	18,000			
Mar. 31	To Interest on own Debentures A/c	6,000			
" "	To Bank A/c	84,000			
		1,11,000			1,11,000

INTEREST ON OWN DEBENTURES A/C

2002		Rs.	2002		Rs.
Mar. 31	To Profit & Loss A/c	4,500	Mar. 31	By Debenture Interest	4,500
2003			July 1	By Debenture Interest A/c	3,000
Mar. 31	To Profit & :Loss A/c	18,000	Sept 30	By Bank A/c	9,000
			Mar. 31	By Debenture Interest A/c	6,000
		18,000			18,000

Working notes :

(1) Interest on debentures purchased on 1.1.2002 Rs. $1,50,000 \times \frac{12}{100} \times \frac{9}{12}$ = Rs. 13,500

(2) Interest payable on 31st March, 2002 :

Interest on Rs. 8,50,000 @ 12% for one year	1,02,000
Interest on own debentures (1.1.2002 to 31.3.2002)	
On Rs. 1,50,000 @ 12% for 3 months	4,500
	1,06,500

(3) Interest on debentures resoled Rs. 1,50,000 @ 12% for 6 months = 9,000

(4) Profit on resale of debentures :

Rs. 1,57,500 – Rs. 1,47,000 10,500

(Sale proceeds – Cost of purchase) excluding interest.

(5) Loss on Cancellation represents excess of Cost paid for debentures less nominal value of debentures cancelled.

Illustration (15) (Redemption by Debenture Trustees)

S. Ltd. had 6% Rs. 10,00,000 Debentures as on 1st April, 2004. Interest is paid annually on 31st March. The terms of issue provide that the Company should pay to the trustees Rs. 1,20,000 each year to be applied by the trustees in redemption of debentures by purchase below par in the open market. It is also provided that one fifth of the outstanding balance is to be redeemed from this year. If redemption by purchase is below the required amount the balance is redeemable at par by drawing lots on 31st March.

On 1.4.2004 the trustees had Rs. 1,69,000 represented by 5% investments (Cost Rs. 1,60,000; Face Value – Rs. 1,70,000) and Rs. 9000 Cash. The trustees purchased Rs. 1,30,000 debentures at Rs. 96 Cum-interest on 30.9.2004 and the balance required was redeemed by lot. For this purpose Rs. 1,27,500, 5% Investments were sold for Rs. 1,17,500, balance being met from cash-in-hand. Surplus Cash in hand was invested to acquire a investment of the face value of Rs. 60,000.

Prepare, 6% Debentures A/c, Debenture Trustees Fund A/c, Debenture Trustees Investments A/c Debenture Trustee Cash A/c and Debenture Interest A/c.

C.S. (1) Modified.

Solution (15)

6% DEBENTURES A/C

2004		Rs.	2004		Rs.
Sept. 30	To Deb. Trustees Cash A/c	1,20,900	April 1	By Balance b/d	10,00,000
" "	To Debenture Trustees Fund A/c (Profit on Cancellation)[(1)]	9,100			
2005 Mar. 31	To Debenture Trustees Cash A/c [(3)]	70,000			
" "	To Balance c/d	8,00,000			
		10,00,000			10,00,000

DEBENTURE TRUSTEES FUND A/C

2004		Rs.	2004		Rs.
Sept. 30	To General Reserve A/c	1,30,000	April 1	By Balance b/d	1,69,000
" "	To Debenture Trustees Investments A/c	2,500	Sept. 30	By 6% Debentures (Profit)	9,100
2005 Mar. 31	To General Reserve A/c	70,000	" "	By Deb.Trustees Cash A/c (Interest on Investment)	3,188
" "	To Balance c/d	1,00,913	2005 Mar. 31	By Deb.Trustees Cash A/c (Interest on Investment)	2,125
			" "	By Profit & Loss App. A/c	1,20,000
		3,03,413			3,03,413

DEBENTURE TRUSTEES INVESTMENTS A/C

2004		Rs.	2004		Rs.
April 1	To Balance b/d (F.V. 1,70,000)	1,60,000	Sept.30	By Deb. Trustees Cash A/c (F.V. 1,27,500)	1,17,500
2005			"	By Deb. Trustees Fund A/c (Loss on sale)	2,500
March	To Deb. Trustees Cash A/c (FV. 60,000)	60,913	2005 March	By Balance c/d (F.V. 1,02,500)	1,00,913
		2,20,913			2,20,913

DEBENTURE TRUSTEES CASH A/C

2004		Rs.	2004		Rs.
April 1	To Balance b/d	9,000	Sept. 30	By 6% Debentures A/c	1,20,900
Sept. 30	To Debenture Trustee Investments A/c	1,17,500	2005 Mar. 31	By 6% Debentures A/c (Redeemed by lot at par)	70,000
" "	To Deb. Trustees Fund A/c (Interest)	3,188		By Debenture Trustees Investments A/c	60,913
Mar. 31	To Deb. Trustee Fund A/c (Interest)	2,125		(Balancing figure invested in Deb. Trustees Investments)	
" "	To Bank A/c (Annual Contribution)	1,20,000			
		2,51,813			2,51,813

DEBENTURE INTEREST A/C

2004		Rs.	2005		Rs.
Sept. 30	To Bank A/c	3,900	Mar. 31	By Profit & Loss A/c	56,100
2005 March 31	To Bank A/c	52,200			
		56,100			56,100

Working notes :

(1) Profit on Cancellation

			Rs.
	Nominal Value of Debentures Cancelled		1,30,000
Less	Cost of Debentures (Price less interest accrued)		
	Rs. $1,30,000 \times \frac{96}{100} =$	1,24,800	
	Less interest*	3,900	1,20,900
			9,100

$* \left(\text{Rs. } 1,30,000 \times \frac{6}{100} \times \frac{6}{12}\right)$

			Rs.
(2)	Remaining amount of debentures to be Cancelled at par:		
	(1/5th of Rs. 10,00,000)	2,00,000	
Less	Cancelled	1,30,000	70,000

(3) Interest on Investments

Sept. 30 $\left(\text{Rs. } 1{,}27{,}000 \times \frac{5}{100} \times \frac{6}{12}\right) =$ 3,188

Mar. 31 (Rs. 1,70,000 – 1,27,500) = $42{,}500 \times \frac{5}{100} =$ 2,125

(4) "Loss on Sale of Investments"

		Rs.
Cost of Investments	$\text{Rs. } 1{,}27{,}000 \times \frac{1{,}60{,}000}{1{,}70{,}000} =$	1,20,000
Sale proceeds		1,17,500
		2,500

Students should note that Redemption by Trustees method is simply a procedure adopted under Sinking Fund Method. Instead of using the Sinking Fund Account and Sinking Fund Investments A/c, we use the terms Debenture Trustees Fund A/c. The only difference is in Debenture Trustees Cash A/c where an agreed amount is transferred every year for the purpose of purchasing of investment and redemption of debentures.

Illustration (16) (Redemption by Trustees)

Progressive Ltd. issued Rs. 10,00,000 6% Debenture stock at par on 1.1.2002 Interest was payable on 30th June and 31st December each year.

Under the terms of the debenture trust deed, the stock is redeemable at par. The trust deed obliges the company to pay to the trustees on 31st December on 2002 and thereafter, the sum of Rs. 1,00,000 to be utilised for the redemption and cancellation of an equivalent amount of stock, which is to be selected by drawing lots. Alternatively the Company is empowered as from 1st January, 2003 to purchase its own debentures in the open market. These debentures must be surrendered to the trustees for cancellation and any adjustments for accrued interest and recorded in the books of accounts. If in any year, the nominal amount of stock surrendered does not amount to Rs. 1,00,000 then the shortfall is to be paid by the Company to the trustees in Cash on 31st December.

The following purchases of stock were made by the Company :

	Nominal Value of stock purchased (Rs.)	Purchase price per Rs. 100 of stock (Rs.)
30th Sept., 2003	1,20,000	98
31st May, 2004	75,000	95 Ex-Interest
31st July, 2005	1,15,000	92

The company fulfilled all its obligations under the trust deed.

You are required to prepare : Debenture Stock A/c, Debenture Redemption A/c, Debenture Interest A/c.

Ignore Costs & Taxation

C.A. (i) Modified.

Solution (16)

6% DEBENTURE STOCK A/C

2002		Rs.	2002		Rs.
Dec. 31	To Balance c/d	10,00,000	Jan. 1	By Bank A/c	10,00,000
2003			2003		
Sept. 30	To Debenture Redemp. A/c	1,20,000	Jan. 1	By Balance b/d	10,00,000
Dec. 31	To Balance c/d	8,80,000			
		10,00,000			10,00,000
2004			2004		
May 31	To Debenture Redemp. A/c	75,000	Jan. 1	By Balance b/d	8,80,000
Dec. 31	To Debenture Redemp. A/c	25,000			
Dec. 31	To Balance c/d	7,80,000			
		8,80,000			8,80,000
2005			2005		
July 31	To Debenture Redemp. A/c	1,15,000	Jan. 1	By Balance b/d	7,80,000
Dec. 31	To Balance c/d	6,65,000			
		7,80,000			7,80,000

DEBENTURE REDEMPTION A/C

2003		Rs.	2003		Rs.
Sept. 30	To Bank A/c (1)	1,15,800	Sept. 30	By 6% Debenture Stock A/c	1,20,000
" "	To Capital Reserve A/c	4,200			
		1,20,000			1,20,000
2004			2004		
May 31	To Bank A/c(2)	71,250	May 31	By 6% Debenture Stock A/c	75,000
	To Capital Reserve A/c	3,750	Dec. 31	By 6% Deb. Stock A/c	25,000
Dec. 31	To Bank A/c	25,000			
		1,00,000			1,00,000
2005			2005		
July 31	To Bank A/c(3)	1,05,225	July 31	By 6% Debenture Stock A/c	1,15,000
" "	To Capital Reserve A/c	9,775			
		1,15,000			1,15,000

DEBENTURE INTEREST A/C

2002		Rs.	2000		Rs.
June, 30	To Bank A/c	30,000	Dec. 31	By Profit & Loss A/c	60,000
Dec. 31	To Bank A/c	30,000			
		60,000			60,000
2003			2003		
June 30	To Bank A/c	30,000	Dec. 31	Profit & Loss A/c	58,200
Sept. 30	To Bank A/c	1,800			
Dec. 31	To Bank A/c	26,400			
		58,200			58,200
2004			2004		
May 31	To Bank A/c	1,875	Dec. 31	By Profit & Loss A/c	50,175
June 30	To Bank A/c	24,150			
Dec.31	To Bank A/c	24,150			
		50,175			50,175
2005			2005		
June 30	To Bank A/c	23,400	Dec. 31	By Profit & Loss A/c	43,925
July 31	To Bank A/c	575			
Dec. 31	To Bank A/c	19,950			
		43,925			43,925

Working notes :

(i) Calculation of Capital Reserve:

Nominal Value of debentures purchased on 30.9.2003 for immediate Cancellation		1,20,000
Less Cost of Debentures purchased Rs. $1,20,000 \times \frac{98}{100} =$	1,17,600	
Less Interest Accrued (July to Sept.) $\left(\text{Rs.}1,20,000 \times \frac{6}{100} \times \frac{3}{12}\right) =$	1,800	1,15,800
		4,200

(2)

Nominal Value of debentures purchased on 31.5.2004 for immediate Cancellation		75,000
Less Cost of debentures purchased Rs.$75,000 \times \frac{95}{100} =$		71,250*
* Since price paid is ex-interest, no interest has been deducted.		3,750

(3)

Nominal Value of debentures purchased on 31,7.2005		1,15,000
Rs. $1,15,000 \times \frac{92}{100}$	1,05,800	
Less Interest for July	575	1,05,225
		9,775

Illustration (17) (Miscellaneous)

X Ltd. had issued 9% Debentures of Rs. 1000 each redeemable at par. Interest on which is to be paid half yearly on 30th June & 31st December each year. Under the terms of issue it was permitted to acquire its own debentures from the market with option to resale them or cancel them in redemption of outstanding debenture liability

On 1. 4. 2004, the debentures account showed a credit balance of Rs. 40,60,000 and Sinking Fund Rs. 4,90,000. The annual set- aside to sinking fund was to be Rs. 1,00,000. During the year to March 31st 2005, it's transactions in its own debentures were as under :

April 1 2004	Opening balance of uncancelled own debentures (FIFO basis) 10 Debentures @ Rs. 990, 20 Debentures @ Rs.1000
April 30	Sold 16 debentures @ Rs. 1005
July 1	Purchased 10 debentures @ Rs. 985
Nov. 1	Purchased 10 debentures @ Rs. 990
March 31,2005	After retaining 14 debentures the remaining own debentures were cancelled in part redemption of outstanding debenture liability.

All transactions of sale and purchase are *Cum-Interest*. Show own debentures account and debenture interest account Ignore tax.

C.A. (F) Modified.

Solution (17)

OWN DEBENTURES A/C

2004		Rs.	2004		Rs.
April 1	To Balance b/d 10 Deb. @ Rs. 990 20 Deb. @ Rs 1,000	29,900	April 30	By Bank A/c 16% Deb. @ Rs. 1005 *Less* Interest	15,600
July 1	To Bank A/c 10 Deb. @ Rs. 985	9850		By Loss on Debenture A/c	300
Nov. 1	To Bank A/c 10 Deb. @ Rs. 990 *Less* interest (Actual rate Rs. 960)	9,600	2005 Mar. 31	By 9% Debentures (Cancellation of 20 debentures)	20,000
Nov. 1	To Profit on Cancellation	90	Mar. 31	By Balance c/d	13,540
		49,440			49,440

DEBENTURE INTEREST A/C

2004		Rs.	2004		Rs.
June 30	To Bank A/c	1,82.070	April 1	By Interest Accrued (on 40,60,000 – 30,000)	90,765
" "	To Interest on Own Deb.	435			
Nov. 1	To Bank A/c	300	April 30	By Bank A/c (Interest on deb. sold)	480
Dec.. 31	To Bank A/c	1,81,170			
Dec. 31	To Interest on Own Deb.	1,230	July 1	By Bank A/c	90
2005 Mar. 31	To Interest accrued	90,585	2005 Mar. 31	By Profit & Loss A/c	3,65,400
	To Interest on Own Deb.	765			
		4,56,555			4,56,555

Working notes :

(1) Cost of the debentures purchased should always be taken ex- interest. If the Cum-interest price is given the interest should be deducted therefrom. Similarly selling price should be taken ex-interest. If it is Cum-interest, interest accrued should be deducted.

> It is to be noted that if a Company after purchasing it's own debentures, resells them before the due date, then the new holder will be entitled interest for the whole intervening period i.e. from the last due date to the current due date.

(2) **Calculation of Interest**

(i) Interest on Debentures paid on 30. 6. 2004

Rs. 40,60,000 – Rs. 30,000 (Own debentures uncancelled) + Rs. 16,000 debenture sold before due date, hence these become active and are entitled interest for full six months.

Rs. 40,46,000 $\times \frac{9}{100} \times \frac{6}{12} =$ 1,82,070

* Interest on own debentures/or Interest saved

On Rs. 30,000 for April = 225

On Rs. 14,000 for May & June = 210

435

(ii) Interest paid on 31. 12. 2004

Rs. 40,46,000 – Rs. 10,000* — 10,000*

* Purchase of own debentures Rs. 40,26,000 $\times \frac{9}{100} \times \frac{6}{12} =$ 1,81,170

* Interest on own debentures/interest saved

Rs. 14,000 + Rs. 10,000 = Rs. 24,000 $\times \frac{9}{100} \times \frac{6}{12} =$ 1,080

Rs. 10,000 $\times \frac{9}{100} \times \frac{6}{12}$ (Nov. Dec.) = 150

(iii) Interest Accrued (Jan. to March)

* Rs. 40,26,000 $\times \frac{9}{100} \times \frac{3}{12} =$ 90,585

* Interest on own debentures /interest saved

Rs. 34,000 $\times \frac{9}{100} \times \frac{3}{12} =$ 765

(3) Loss on sale of debentures

16 Debentures @ Rs. 1005 16,080

Less Interest for 4 months (Jan. to April) 480

15,600

	Less Cost of Debentures (FIFO)		
	10 Deb. @ Rs. 990	9,900	
	6 Deb. @ Rs. 1,000	6,000	15,900
			300
(4)	Profit on Cancellation :		
	Nominal Value of Debentures Cancelled		
	20 Debentures		20,000
	Less Cost of Debentures (FIFO)		
	14 Deb. (balance remaining from the opening lot of 20 Deb.)	Rs. 14,000	
	6 Deb. from the July lot @ Rs. 985	5910	19,910
			90
(5)	Closing Balance of Own Debentures		
	4 Debentures from July lot @ Rs. 985		3,940
	10 Debentures from November lot @ Rs. 960 (actual Cost)		9,600
			13,540

QUESTIONS

1. Define debenture and distinguish it from share and stock.
2. Briefly explain the various types of debentures a company can issue.
3. What is the accounting treatment of loss/ discount on issue of debentures?
4. Write short note on debentures issued as collateral security.
5. What do you understand by fixed and floating charge?
6. Explain the various methods of redemption of debentures.
7. Distinguish between "Interest Accrued and due" and Interest Accrued and not due.
8. Can a company purchase its own debentures ? Explain giving its accounting treatment.
9. Explain the terms Ex- interest " and Cum-interest price. Give suitable examples.
10. Write short notes on: Debentures Redemption Reserve, Deep Discount Bonds, Put option and Call option.
11. Distinguish between Sinking Fund to repay a liability and Sinking Fund to replace an asset.

PROBLEMS

(1) Record Journal entries

(i) Issue of 9% Rs. 5,00,000 debentures at par redeemable at par.

(ii) Issue of 9% Rs. 4,00,000 Debentures at 10% discount, redeemable at par.

(iii) Issue of 9% Rs. 3,00,000 Debentures at 5% premium, redeemable at par.

(iv) Issue of 9% Rs. 5,00,000 Debentures at par, redeemable at 4% premium.

(v) Issue of 9% Rs. 4,00,000 Debentures at 10% discount, redeemable at 4% premium.

(2) On 1.1.2004 X Ltd. issued 9% 5,000 debentures of Rs. 100 each at discount of 6%. The debentures were repayable by annual drawings of Rs. 1,00,000 made on 31st December each year.

The directors decided to write off discount over the period of debentures in such a way so as to charge each year with an amount proportionate to debentures outstanding in that year.

Ans. : Rs. 10,000, Rs. 8,000, Rs. 6,000, Rs. 4,000, Rs. 2000.

(3) S Ltd. issued Rs. 10,00,000 9% debentures @ 94% on 1.4.2000, repayable in 5 equal instalments of Rs. 2,00,000 each. The Company closes its accounts on calendar year basis. Assuming that the Company decides to write off the debenture discount during the life of debentures show the amount of discount that should be written off in each accounting year.

Ans. : Rs. 15,000, Rs. 17,000, Rs. 13,000, Rs. 9,000, Rs. 5,000 & Rs. 1,000 during the calendar years 2,000 to 2005 respectively.

(4) X Ltd. had 9% Rs. 20,00,000 Debentures outstanding in the Balance Sheet as on 31st December, 2004. The Company has not paid six monthly interest after 31st March, 2004. State the amount of interest on debentures "Accrued and due" and "Accrued but not due

Ans. : Rs. 90,000 Accrued & due

Rs. 45,000 Accrued but not due.

(5) On 1.1.2004 A Ltd. issued 9% 5,000 Debentures of Rs. 100 each at 4% discount. Under the terms of issue the debenture interest is payable on 30th June & 31st December each year and 1/5 th of the debentures are annually redeemable by drawings starting from 31st December, 2001. Show 9% Debentures Account and Discount on Issue of Debentures A/c.

Ans. : Amount of Discount to be written off in 5 : 5 : 4 : 3 : 2 : 1 ratio.

(6) On 1.1.2002 Atlantic Ltd. issued 9% 5,000 Debentures of Rs. 100 each at par redeemable on 31.12.2004 A sinking fund was created for redemption of these debentures. The sinking fund table shows that Re. 0.317208 invested at 5% interest. p. a. amounts to Re 1 at the end of three years. On 31.12.2004, the investments were sold for Rs 3,28,000. The bank balance on that date before the receipt of interest amount to Rs 2,15,000.

Investments are made in the multiples of Rs 100. Prepare :

9% Debentures A/c

Sinking fund A/c

Sinking fund investments A/c

Ans. : Profit on sale of investment. Rs.2,850

(7) The following balances appeared in the books of Z Ltd. as on 31 March, 2003.

9% Debentures	8,50,000
Debenture Redemption Fund	5,81,800
Debenture Redemption Fund Investments represented by :	
10% Government Loans at par	5,81,500

The annual contribution to the Debenture Redemption Fund was Rs. 69535. The debentures fell due for redemption on 31st March, 2005. The Govt. Loans were disposed of for Rs. 7,05,000.

It is to be noted that investments in Govt. Loans were made in the multiples of Rs. 100

Ans. : Loss on sale of Govt. Loans Rs. 4,500.

(8) A Company had Rs 800,000 5% Debentures out standing on 1.1.2004, redeemable on 31st December, 2004. On that date, the Sinking Fund Stood at Rs. 7,49,000 represented by Rs. 100,000 Own debentures purchased at an average price of Rs. 99 and Rs. 6,60,000 4% Government securities. The annual contribution to Sinking fund was Rs.22,800. On 31st December, 2004 the investments were realised at 98% and debentures were redeemed prepare necessary ledger accounts.

B.Com. (H) DU Adapted

Ans. : Profit on Cancellation of Debentures Rs 1,000

Transfer to General Reserve Rs. 800,000

Loss on sale of investments Rs. 3,200

(9) X Ltd. issued 9% 2,000 debentures of Rs. 100 each at par on 1st April, 2002. The debentures are redeemable after 5 years from the date of issue at 10% premium. The Directors decided to create Sinking fund which is to be invested in 10% Government Bonds of Rs. 100 each. Interest on bonds is payable on 31st March every year. It was further decided to appropriate Rs. 36,080 to be transferred to Sinking fund annually on 31st March 10% Govt. Bonds of the required amount were purchased as follows :

On 31st March 2003 @ Rs. 80

On 31st March 2004 @ Rs. 90

On 31st March 2004 @ Rs. 100

You are required to prepare Debenture Redemption Fund Account and Debenture Redemption Fund Investment Account for the first three years. Books of accounts are closed 31st March each year.

B.Com (H) DU Modified

Ans. : The Company will purchase 10% 451 Govt. Bonds each year.

Interest : IInd year 4,510; IIIrd Year 9,020

Balance at the end of IIIrd year

To Deb. Red. Fund A/c 1,21,770

(Face Value of 10% Bonds) = 1,35,300

(10) A Ltd. has Rs. 4,50,000 14% Debentures outstanding on 1st April, 2004. The debentures are redeemable on 31st March, 2005. On that date the Sinking Fund stood at Rs. 3,74,500 represented by Rs. 50,000 own debentures purchased at an average rate of Rs. 99 per debenture and Rs. 3,30,000 10% Stock. The annual instalment was Rs. 35,500. On 31st March, 2005, the investments were realised at cost and the debentures were redeemed.

Record journal entries and prepare necessary ledger accounts.

ASC (1) Modified.

Ans. : Profit on Cancellation of debentures transferred to Capital reserve : Rs. 500.

Transferred to General Reserve : Rs. 4,50,000

(11) The following ledger balances extracted from the books of S Ltd. as on 30th September 2004.

	Rs.
9% Debentures issued @ Rs. 95	9,50,000
Discount on Issue of Debentures	26,000
Debenture Redemption Fund	9,37,000
Debenture Redemption Fund Investments	9,37,000

Additional Information :

(i) Investments include debentures of the face value of Rs. 2,00,000 purchased on 1.8.2004 @ Rs. 99

(ii) Interest on debentures is payable on 30th June and 31st December.

(iii) Income from outside investments of Redemption Fund from 1.10.2004 to 31.12.2004 amounted to Rs. 45,000. All outside investments were sold at a gain of 10% over cost.

Prepare ledger accounts.

C.A. (1) Modified

Ans. : Profit on Cancellation of own Deb. : Rs. 3,500

Profit on sale of Investment : Rs. 74,050

Hint : Discount is to be charged to Sinking Fund A/c.,

(12) A Ltd. had issued 5,000 7% Debentures of Rs. 1000 each at par. The debentures were redeemable at any time by the Company after giving three months notice. Under the terms of issue the Company had the power to purchase in the open market it's own debentures which could be cancelled or resold. From the following particulars prepare relevant ledger accounts.

	Rs.
7% Debentures	48,20,000
Own Debentures	4,200
(Nominal value Rs. 5,000)	
Debenture Redemption Fund A/c	6,50,000
Debenture Redemption Fund Investments A/c	6,50,000

During the year ending 31st December, 2004, the following were the transactions :

- Purchased 3 own debentures	3,100
- Resold own debentures held at the beginning of the year	5,000
- Interest received on Debenture Redemption Fund Investments	26,000
- Annual Contribution to Debenture Redemption Fund	50,000
- Investment of Debenture Redemption Fund	76,000

Own debentures purchased during the year were cancelled.

B Com. (D.U.) Adapted.

Ans. : 7% Debentures balance :	Rs.	48,17,000
Deb. Redemption Fund Balance :	Rs.	7,22,900
Deb. Red. Fund Investments :	Rs.	7,26,000

(13) A B Ltd. disclosed the following balances as on 1st January, 2003.

	Rs.
11% Debentures (Rs. 100 each)	50,00,000
Sinking Fund A/c	45,00,000
13.5 % Debentures in Z Ltd. (Rs. 100 each) (face Value Rs. 20,00,000)	19,50,000
Own Debentures A/c (Face Value 20,00,000)	18,50,000

On 31st December, the Debentures were due for redemption. During the year the following purchases were made.

February 1, 2003 Own debentures @ Rs. 98 Cum-Interest June 1 2003 Own Debentures @ Rs. 99 Ex-Interest; Interest is payable half Yearly on 30 June and 31st December each year incase of both companies.

On 31st December, 2003, the debentures of Z Ltd. were sold @ Rs. 95 each Ex Interest. A B Ltd. redeemed debentures by payment and by cancellation.

Prepare :

(i) Sinking Fund Account

(ii) Own Debentures A/c

C.A. (1) Modified

Ans. : Loss on sale of Investments	Rs.	50,000
Transfer to General Reserve-	Rs.	49,73,000
Profit on Cancellation	Rs.	1,57,833
Interest on Debentures of Z Ltd.	Rs.	2,70,000
Interest on own debentures	Rs.	2,53,000

(14) B Ltd. had issued Rs. 6,00,000 debentures on the following terms:

(i) A Sinking Fund is to be created by yearly appropriation of profit and similar amount to be invested outside.

(ii) The Company will have the right to purchase for cancellation, the debentures from the market if available below par value.

(iii) The debentures are to be redeemed of 31st December, 2004 at a premium of 2%. The following balances appeared as on 1st January, 2004.

	Rs.
Debenture Account	4,50,000
Sinking Fund A/c	4,43,250

The following transactions took place during the year.

(a) On 1.7. 2004 Rs. 30,000 debentures were purchased for Rs. 26,664 and cancelled immediately, the amount being provided out of sale proceeds of investments of the book value of Rs. 34,800 at Rs. 33,900.

(b) The income from "Sinking fund" investments amounted to Rs. 22,200

(c) The remaining investments were sold for Rs. 4,02,300

(d) On 31st December 2004, the remaining debentures were redeemed.

Prepare necessary ledger accounts.

C.S. (1) Adapted

Ans. : Profit Cancellation - Rs. 3,336
Loss sale of Investments - Rs. 900 & Rs. 6,150
Transfer to General Reserve - Rs. 4,50,000

(15) On 1.4.2004 Megha Ltd. had 9% Rs. 6,00,000 debentures of Rs. 100 each which were due for immediate redemption. The Company gave the notice of it's intention to redeem its outstanding debentures at 5% premium. The following options were given :

(1) To accept 9% Preference Shares of Rs. 20 each at 25% premium , or

(2) To opt for 8% Debentures at 90 percent.

(3) To get their holdings redeemed for Cash.

Holders of Rs. 2,00,000 Debentures accepted preference shares and holders of Rs. 2,70,000 opted for the new 8% debentures and remaining debentureholders gave their acceptance for Cash payment.

Record Journal entries to give effect to above transactions.

Ans. : Transfer to General Reserve Rs. 1,30,000; 8,400 Preference Shares and 3,150 8% new Debentures issued by the Company.

(16) H Ltd. disclosed the following balances as on 1st January 2004.

	Rs.
6% Debentures of Rs. 100 each	4,67,000
Sinking Fund	1,31,680

Represented by :

6% State Loans (Nominal Value Rs. 80,000)	74,000
Sinking Fund Cash A/c	57,680

(Includes annual appropriation of Rs. 50,000 which was invested in 6% State Loan. The Loan Bonds purchased cum-interest had a face value of Rs. 60,000)

On 1.9.2004, the company sold State loans of the face value of Rs. 40,000 out of loans held on 1st January 2004 for Rs. 38,000 (ex-interest) and proceeds were applied in purchasing own debentures (face value Rs. 45,000 ex-interest).

The Debentures purchased were Cancelled on 31st December.

Interest on State Loans is received on 31st March and 30th September, whereas interest on debentures is paid on 30th June and 31st December. Prepare necessary ledger accounts in the books of H Ltd. interest income credited to Sinking Fund amounted to Rs. 8,500

Ans. : Profit on sale of investments = Rs. 1000

Profit on Cancellation of Deb. = Rs. 6,450

Transfer to General Reserve = Rs 45,000

(17) On 1. 4. 2004 Z Ltd. disclosed the following balances :

	Rs.
12% 5,000 debentures of Rs. 100 each	5,00,000
Debenture Redemption Reserve	3,00,000

On 1.8.2004, the Company purchased 1000 of it's own debentures @ Rs. 98 as investment ex-interest. However, on 31st March, 2005, the Company cancelled all these debentures.

Interest on debentures is payable on 30th September and 31st March every year.

Record Journal entries & prepare 12% Debentures A/c, Own debentures A/c, Debentures Redemption Reserve A/c, Debenture Interest A/c & Interest on own Debentures A/c for the year 2004-05.

C. S. (1) Adapted.

Ans. : 12% Debentures A/c balance Rs 4,00,000

Deb. Redemption Reserve- Rs. 2,00,000

Profit on Cancellation Rs. 2,000

Debenture interest charged to P and L A/c Rs. 60,000 Interest on Own Debentures credited to P & L A/c Rs. 8,000.

4

Final Accounts of Companies

(CORPORATE FINANCIAL STATEMENTS)

The process of preparation of financial statements of companies is similar to that of non-corporate entities except for certain peculiar items and legal requirements. The corporate reporting has assumed great importance in recent years. The Company Law Board, The Institute of Chartered Accountants of India and whole corporate world are trying to bring about a total transparency in the matter of reporting. The fundamental objective of corporate reporting is to communicate economic information about the resources and performance of the reporting entity to the users of financial statements. The professional bodies have also developed several (till date - 29) Accounting Standards for the purpose of preparing and disclosing accounting information in order

(i) To serve the varied needs of users of accounting information for decision making purposes

(ii) To harmonise the diverse accounting practices

(iii) To ensure transparency consistency, comparability, adequacy and reliability of information - contents.

(iv) To make accounting information more meaningful & useful

(v) And to improve overall quality of presentation and reporting.

Since every interested party has a right to information which is merely not the outcome of statue but is based on the principle of public accountability. The financial statements which are prepared on the basis of various accounting postulates, concepts and conventions, are supposed to be endowed with many qualitative characteristics viz understandability, relevance, materiality reliability, faithful representation, substance-over-form, neutrality, prudence, completeness and comparability.

General & legal Requirements

Sections 209 to 223 of the Companies Act 1956 deal with provisions governing maintenance and preparation of financial statements.

Section 209 deals with the maintenance of proper books of accounts in respect of

(i) Receipts and disbursements of money

(ii) Sales and purchases of raw-materials/goods

(iii) Description pertaining to usage of raw-materials & labour etc. and

(iv) All assets and liabilities.

Section 209 also requires that books of accounts must show the "True and fair" view of state of affairs of the company. Section 211 requires that the Balance Sheet must give "true and fair" view of the state of affairs and Profit and Loss Account must give "true and fair" view of the results of operations. It simply implies that financial statements should disclose every material information without any concealment of facts and figures and in such a manner that working results and financial position of the reporting enterprise, may correctly be interpreted in true sprits. It should be free from personal biases and mis-statements. It will be possible only if financial statements are prepared in acordance with generally accepted accounting principles and in conformity with the various accounting standards as applicable to the reporting enterprise. Companies (Amendment) Act 1999 has made it mandatory for companies to comply with accounting standards set by ICAI. In case company fails to comply with any of generally accepted accounting assumptions or standards, the fact should be disclosed.

Section 210 requires that financial statements should be presented to shareholders at every Annual General Meeting along with the Auditor's and Director's Reports. Every Balance Sheet and Profit & Loss Account must be duly authenticated. These statements must be signed by Manager or Secretary and by two directors at least - one of whom must be managing director. (Section 215)

PREPARATION AND PRESENTATION OF CORPORATE FINANCIAL STATEMENTS

As already stated, the Board of Directors of the Company shall present the following at the annual general meeting.

(i) a Balance Sheet as at the end of the period;

(ii) a Profit and Loss Account for that period; and also

(iii) a Statement of Changes in Financial Position (SCFP/Cash Flow Statement)

In case of a company not carrying on business for profit, an Income and Expenditure Account shall be laid at the annual general meeting instead of Profit and Loss Account.

Every Profit and Loss Account shall also give a "true and fair" view of profit or loss of the company for the financial year and shall comply with the requirements of schedule VI. Every Insurance or Banking company or any company engaged in the generation of electricity or any other class of company for which the Profit and Loss Account has been specified under the Act governing such class of company need not follow the Form given in schedule VI to this Act.

Similarly every Balance Sheet shall give a "true and fair" view of the state of affairs of the company as per schedule VI. Any Insurance or Banking Company or any company engaged in generation or supply of electricity or any other class of company for which a form of Balance Sheet has been prescribed under the Act governing such class of company need not to follow such form.

Recently, the Companies (Amendment) Act 1999 has made the compliance of accounting standards mandatory. Accordingly every Profit and Los Account and Balance Sheet of the Company shall comply with the "Accounting Standards". However, in case of non-compliance the company must disclose the "deviation" from the accounting standards, "reasons" for such deviation; and "financial effect" if any due to such deviation.

If the company does not disclose any change in policy, the fundamental assumptions such as going concern, consistency and prudence have been adhered to.

On the basis of requirements of Schedule VI and accounting standards following is the proforma of Profit and Loss Account of a company.

PROFIT AND LOSS ACCOUNT OF .... (CONVENTIONAL FORM)

For the year ended 31st March.......

Figures for the Previous year Rs.		Figures for the current year Rs.	Figures for the previous year Rs.		Figures for the Current year Rs.
....	To Opening Stocks :		....	By Sales Less Returns	....
....	Raw Materials	....	....	By Income from Services	....
....	Work-in-Progress	....	....	By Closing Stocks	
....	Finished Goods	....	....	Raw Materials	....
....	To Purchases (Raw materials)	....	....	Work-in- Progress	....
	Less Returns	....	....	Finished Goods	....
....	To Stores & Spares (Consumed)	....			
....	To Power and Fuel	....			
....	To Wages (Productive)	....			
....	To Manufacturing Expenses	....			
....	To Gross Profit c/d	....			
		....			....
....	To Rent	....			
....	To Repairs to Building	....	....	By Gross Profit b/d	....
....	To Repairs to Machinery	....	....	By Income from Investments	....
....	To Salaries & Bonus	....		By Profit on Sale of Investment	....
....	To Contribution to Provident Fund	....		By Dividend Income	
....	To Staff Welfare Expenses			By Miscellaneous Incomes	
....	To Contribution to Pension/ Gratuity Fund	....			
....	To Insurance	....			
....	To Rates & Taxes	....			
....	To Printing & Stationery	....			
....	To Postage, Telegrams, Fax & Telephones	....			
....	To Commission, Brokerage & Discounts	....			
....	To Bank Charges & Interest	....			
....	To Depreciation	....			
....	To Loss on sale of Investments	....			
	To Remuneration payable to Directors & other Managerial Personel	....			
	To Provision for Taxation	....			
	To Net Profit transferred to Profit & Loss Account	....			
....		....	....		....

SCHEDULE VI
(SECTION 211)
(PART I - FORM OF BALANCE SHEET)
(Conventional Format)
Balance Sheet of —
As on 31st March, ——

Figures for the Previous year Rs.		Figures for the current year Rs.	Figures for the previous year Rs.		Figures for the Current year Rs.
	Share Capital			**Fixed Assets**	
	Authorised*— shares of			Goodwill	
	Rs.—— each			Land	
	Issued*— shares of Rs.— each			Building	
	Subscribed** — shares of			Leasehold	
	Rs. —each			Railway sidings	
	*(Various classes of shares/capital)			Plant and Machinery	
	(**Various classes of shares and			Furniture and Fittings	
	their called up amount including			Development of Property	
	details of			Patents, Trade Marks	
	— Shares issued for consideration			and designs	
	other than cash			Live Stock & Vehicles etc.	
	— Bonus Issue made, if any			**Investments**	
	Less Call unpaid			Showing nature of Investments	
	(i) By Directors			and mode of valuation- cost or	
	(ii) By Others			Market Value, & distinguishing	
	Add Forfeited shares			between :	
	(amount actually paid)			1. Investment in Government	
	Reserves & Surplus			or Trust Securities.	
	(1) Capital Reserve			2. Investments in Shares,	
	(2) Capital Redemption Reserve			Debentures or bonds	
	(3) Securities Premium			(Giving details of classes of shares	
	(4) Other Reserves specifying the			along with their paid up value)	
	nature of each reserve & amount			3. Immovable Properties	
	in respect thereof			4. Investments in Capital	
	Less Debit Balance of P & L A/c			of Partnership firms.	
	(5) Surplus-Balance in			**Current Assets, Loans & Advances**	
	Profit & Loss Account			*A Current Assets*	
	after providing for proposed			1. Interest Accrued on Investments	
	allocations-namely			2. Stores and Spares parts*	
	Dividend-Bonus or Reserves			3. Loose Tools	
	(6) Proposed Addition to Reserves			4. Stock in-Trade*	
	(7) Sinking Fund			5. Work-in-Progress*	
				*Mode of Valuation and Amount in case of raw materials.	

Figures for the Previous year Rs.		Figures for the current year Rs.	Figures for the previous year Rs.		Figures for the Current year Rs.
	Secured Loans* (1) Debentures (2) Loans & Advances from Banks (3) Loans & Advances from Subsidiaries (4) Other loans & Advances *Interest accrued and due should be included in the respective sub-head) *Nature of security to be specified in each case *Terms of redemption or conversion of debentures to be stated together with earliest date of conversion/redemption. **Unsecured Loans** (1) Fixed Deposits (2) Loans & Advances from Subsidiaries (3) Short-term loans & advances (a) From Banks (b) From Others (4) Other loans and advances (a) From Banks (b) From Others **Current Liabilities & Provisions** *A. Current Liabilities* (i) Acceptances (ii) Sundry Creditors (iii) Subsidiary Companies (iv) Advance payments and unexpired discounts for the portion for which value has still to be given *e.g.* in the following classes of companies Newspapers, Fire-Insurance, Theatres, Clubs, Banking and and Steamship companies. (v) Unclaimed Dividends (vi) Other Liabilities, if any (vii) Interest accrued but not due on loans *B. Provision* (viii) Provision for taxation			(6) Sundry Debtors (a) Debts outstanding for a period exceeding six months (b) Other debts (Less Provision) In regard to sundry debtors, particulars to be given separately (i) Debts considered good & inrespect of which company is fully secured (ii) Debts considered good for which company holds no security other than the debtor's personal security. (iii) Debts considered doubtful or bad. (iv) Debts due by directors or other officers or any of them either severally or jointly with any other person or debts due by firms or private companies respectively in which any director is a partner or director or a member - to be separately stated. (7a) Cash Balance at hand (7b) Bank Balances (i) With Scheduled banks & (ii) With Others **(B) Loans and Advances** (8) (a) Advances & loans to subsidiaries. (b) Advances and loans to partnership firms in which company or any of it's subsidiaries is a partner. (9) Bills of Exchange (10) Advance receivable in cash or in kind or for value to be received e.g. rates, taxes, insurance etc. (11) Balance on Current Account with Managing Agents, secretaries and Treasurers. (12) Balances with customs port trust (where payable on demand)	

	(ix) Proposed dividends (x) For contingencies (xi) For Provident Fund Scheme (xii) For Insurance, pension and similar staff benefit schemes (13) Other provisions			**Miscellaneous Expenditure** (1) Preliminary Expenses (2) Expenses including commission, or brokerage or underwriting or subscription of shares or debentures. (3) Discount on issue of shares Similar Staff benefit schemes (4) Interest paid out of capital during construction period. (5) Development Expenditure not adjusted (6) Other items (specifying nature) **Profit & Loss Account** (Debit balance of P & L A/c carried forward after adjusting uncommitted (free) reserves, if any.
....		....	....		....

Foot note: to be shown separately such as

(1) Claims against the company not acknowledged as debts.

(2) Uncalled liability on shares partly paid.

(3) Arrears of cumulative dividends.

(4) Estimated amount of contract remaining to be executed on capital account and not provided for.

(5) Other money for which company is contingently liable.

Vertical Format of Corporate Financial Statements

Under vertical form, a Balance Sheet is prepared under single column divided in two sections. First section shows the "Sources of Funds" which includes Share Capital, Reserves and Surplus, Secured and Unsecured loans. The second section is represented by "Application of funds" in the form of Fixed Assets, Investments, Net Current Assets. (Current assets-Current liabilities) and Miscellaneous Expenditure. A Format is given below :

BALANCE SHEET OF
AS ON ______

	Schedule No.	Figures for the Current year	Figures for Previous year
I Sources of Funds :			
1. Shareholders' Funds			
(a) Share Capital	1	....	....
(b) Reserves and Surplus	2	....	....
		....	....
2. Loan Funds	3	....	....
(a) Secured Loans		....	....
(b) Unsecured Loans		....	....
Total		....	....

	Schedule No.	Figures for the Current year	Figures for Previous year
II Application of Funds:			
1. Fixed Assets	4	—	—
(a) Gross Block		—	—
(b) Less Depreciation		—	—
(c) Net Block		—	—
(d) Capital work-in-progress		—	—
2. Investments	5	—	—
3. Current Assets, Loans and Advances	6	—	—
(a) Investments		—	—
(b) Sundry Debtors		—	—
(c) Cash and Bank balances		—	—
(d) Other Current assets		—	—
(e) Loans and Advances		—	—
Less Current Liabilities and Provisions			
(a) Liabilities	7	—	—
(b) Provisions			
Net Current Assets		—	—
4. (a) Miscellaneous Expenditure	—		
(Amount not written off)			
(b) Profit & Loss Account		—	—
(*Less* balance in general reserve as per contra)		—	—
Total	15	—	—

Significant Accounting Policies and Notes on Accounts

Various schedules as mentioned above, will provide necessary details of items and information as required to be given as per schedule VI of Companies Act 1956. The figures in the amount column may be rounded off to the nearest thousand ('000') or hundred ('00') as may be decided by the management. These schedules, significant accounting policies and explanatory notes form an integral part of the Balance Sheet as required by applicable "Accounting Standards" regarding disclosure of accounting policies. Contingent liabilities are shown by means of footnote to the Balance Sheet.

Vertical Format of Profit and Loss Account: Almost all the companies prepare and present their Income Statement (Profit and Loss Account) in vertical form. Infact the information relating to activities (operating, investing, financing) of the Companies are arranged in vertical order rather than in conventional (Horizontal or 'T') form.

A FORMAT OF PROFIT AND LOSS IN VERTICAL FORM IS GIVEN BELOW.

	Particulars	Schedule No.	Figures at the end of Current year	Figures for Previous year
I	**Income**			
	Sales			
	Services			
	Dividend			
	Interest			
	Other Income	8		
	Total		—	—
II	**Expenditure**			
	Cost of goods sold/raw material consumed	9		
	Selling & other Expenses	10		
	Depreciation	11		
	Financial Expenses	12		
	Total		—	—
	Profit before Taxation, Extraordinary and Prior Period Items		—	—
	Provision for Taxation		—	—
	Net Profit before Extra ordinary and Prior Period items		—	—
	Extraordinary items (Net of Tax)	13	—	—
	Prior Period items (Net of Tax)	14	—	—
	Net Profit		—	—
	Balance Brought forward from previous year		—	—
	Profits available for appropriation		—	—
Appropriations:				
	Interim Dividend			
	Dividend on Preference Shares		—	—
	Proposed final dividend	—	—	—
	Corporate Dividend Tax		—	—
	Transfer to Debenture Redemption Reserve		—	—
	Transfer to Capital Redemption Reserve		—	—
	Transfer to General Reserve		—	—
	Balance taken to Balance Sheet			—
	Significant Accounting policies and notes on accounts	15	******	******

(For details of schedules please refer to Horizontal (Conventional) form of Balance Sheet).

A list of significant accounting policies and notes is as follows :

1. Basis of Accounting
2. Revenue Recognition
3. Fixed Assets
4. Depreciation and Amortisation
5. Investments
6. Foreign Currency transactions
7. Retirement Benefits
8. Deferred Revenue Expenditure
9. Hire purchase lease rental income
10. Product Warranty Expenses
11. Provision for Contingencies
12. Research and Development
13. Taxation
14. Investment in debt and equity shares
15. Long term contracts and property development activity
16. Government grants
17. Amortisation of licence fee
18. Changes in accounting policies
19. Provision for reinvesting the company
20. Employees stock option scheme
21. Amalgamation
22. Changes in provisions of retirement benefits of employees
23. Investment in sick units
24. Contingencies
25. Approval of managerial remuneration
26. Extraordinary items.

REQUIREMENTS FOR CORPORATE FINANCIAL STATEMENTS AS PER SCHEDULE VI

Requirements as to Profit and Loss Account — "Salient Features"

(i) The Profit & Loss Account shall be so made out as clearly to disclose the result of the working of the company during the period covered by the P & L Accounts and shall disclose every material feature, including credits or receipts and debits or expenses in respect of non-recurring transactions or transactions of an exceptional nature.

(ii) The Income Statement is not required to be split in three parts, such as Trading Account, Profit & Loss Account and Profit and Loss Appropriation. Account to show the profit earned and appropriated Schedule VI only recommends to disclose gross profit, net profit and it's appropriation thereof. This may be shown under one head of Income statement or

Profit and Loss Account. Chargeable items are shown above the line whereas appropriations below the line.

(iii) Figures relating to previous year should also be shown along with the current year's figure in a separate column.

(iv) As far as possible information given in the statement must be complete in all respects. Such as the details of "turnover" made by the company should disclose sales in respect of each class of goods & their quantities separately. Like-wise commission paid to sole selling agents and to other agents should be shown along with the brokerage or discount or sales other than the usual trade discount.

(v) The Account should disclose quantities and values of various types of raw-material purchased and quantities and values of various products produced/ purchased including opening and closing balances thereof and that of work-in-progress.

(vi) The amount provided for depreciation, renewals or diminution in value of fixed assets and the method adopted for making such provisions. If no such provision has been made- the fact should be disclosed by way of note including arrears of depreciation.

(vii) The amount of interest on company's debentures and on other fixed period loans be stated separately, including interest paid or payable to directors.

(viii) The amount of Income Tax on profits as per Income Tax Act 1961 at the prescribed rate including other taxes if any, should be shown separately.

(ix) Expenditure incurred on each of the following items be disclosed separately.

(a) Consumption of stores and spare parts

(b) Power and fuel

(c) Rent

(d) Repairs to Building

(e) Repairs to Machinery

(f) (i) Salaries, wages and bonus

(ii) Contribution to provident and other funds

(iii) Workmen and staff welfare expenses

(g) Insurance

(h) Rates and Taxes (excluding income tax)

(i) Miscellaneous expenses provided any item exceeds 1% of revenue or Rs. 5,000 whichever is higher be shown separately.

(g) Payment to Auditor

(a) — as auditor

(b) — as advisor in respect of

(i) Taxation matter

(ii) Company Law matters

(iii) Management services

(k) Remuneration received by managing directors or managers either from the company or it's subsidiaries should be indicated separately including it's computation.

(l) The Profit and Loss Account should disclose the various items of incomes arranged under appropriate heads

(a) Turnover - giving details in respect of each class of goods indicating quantities of such sales for each class separately.

(b) Amount of income from interest specifying the nature of the income

(c) Income from investments — stating from trade investments & other investments

(d) Profit or losses on investments

(e) Dividends — including dividends from subsidiary companies

(f) Miscellaneous incomes such as royalty fees etc.

(g) Foreign exchange earnings, if any.

The Profit & Loss Account must be made out in such a manner that it discloses "true and fair" view of the profit or loss of the company for the current accounting year. This means that items of extraordinary nature or those unrelated to company's business or items relating to previous years (Prior Period items) should be separately stated, if these are material.

Similarly amount drawn from reserves, profits from revaluation of assets or profits arising due to change in method of accounting or major policy change in the method of valuation of inventories or charging of depreciation, should be stated separately. It means that showing higher operating efficiency or position much better that it actually is - would be contrary to the spirit of law.

Explanation of basic principles governing the preparation of Financial Statements

(1) *Materiality*

It is a relative term. What is material for one company may be immaterial for other. According to American Accounting Association (AAA) an item should be regarded as material if there is reason to believe that knowledge of it would influence the decision of informed investors, bankers creditors & other interested parties. IAS-5 states that all material information and items should be disclosed which are necessary & vital to make the financial statements more clear and understandable - operating efficiency-wise and financial - position-wise. Treatment of certain expenditure as capital by one company and revenue by the other is a clear example of it. Hence materiality is purely matter of personal judgment which is guided by size and nature of enterprise.

(2) *Prior Period Items: (AS - 5)*

As a matter of fact the Profit and Loss Account should disclose the profit or loss for the period for which accounts are prepared, that is for the reported (current) period. If, however, some items were omitted to be accounted for in the preparation of financial statements then it is not possible to reopen the accounts for the previous year after it has been adopted by the shareholders in the annual general meeting. The ICAI defines "Prior Period Items" as incomes or expenses which arise in the current period as a result of errors or omissions in the preparation of financial statements of one or more periods". The errors may occur as a result of mathematical mistakes oversight (omissions), misinterpretation of facts and wrong application of accounting policies or a wrong or inaccurate estimate. Hence these items should be shown "below the line" i.e. in the Profit and Loss Appropriation Account. However, prior period adjustments do not cover-

- Minor omissions of accruals and prepayments
- Prior period's revenue which was not accounted for on the ground of prudential practice
- Recovery of bad debts written off earlier
- Adjustments to the useful life of the depreciable assets.

(3) *Extra - ordinary Items (AS - 5)*

Extraordinary items are income or expenses that arise from events or transactions that are clearly distinct from the ordinary activities of the enterprise and therefore, are not expected to recur frequently and regularly. (AS-5). These items are shown in the Profit and Loss Account for the period but the nature of such items should be disclosed separately. These include

- Write down of inventories to "net realisable value"
- Profit or Loss on sale of fixed assets or long term investments.
- Reversals of provisions
- Reversals of writing off of the fixed assets
- Losses sustained on account of an earth quake or any other natural clamity

(4) *Change in Accounting Policies (AS-5)*

Accounting policies are the specific accounting principles and the methods of applying those principles adopted by an enterprise in the preparation and presentation of financial statements. A change in accounting policy should be made only if the adoption of a different accounting policy is required by statue or by the accounting standard setting body or if it is considered that the change will result in a more appropriate presentation of the financial statements of the enterprise. Any material effect of such a change in the current or subsequent periods should be quantified and disclosed together with the reasons for the change. Following are the change in policy.

- A change in the method of charging depreciation from written down value (WDV) to straight line Method (SLM) and vice versa
- A change in the method of valuation of inventories.

However, a change in the estimated life of a machine is not a change in policy but a change in estimate.

ITEMS PECULIAR TO CORPORATE FINANCIAL STATEMENTS

A-Balance Sheet

(1) "Share Capital"

Under this head following details are required to be disclosed —

(i) Details of Authorised, Issued and Subscribed Capital along with number and nominal value of the shares with respect to preference and equity shares.

(ii) Calls-in-Arrears must be deducted from Called-up Capital. However, Calls-in-arrears on shares held by directors are to be shown separately. Similarly Calls-in-Advance should be treated as a separate item and shown accordingly.

(iii) Forfeited shares Account, if any, should be added to Paid-up Capital which forms the part of total of Balance Sheet. It is to be noted that the Authorised, Issued and Subscribed Capital. are not considered for the purpose of total of Balance Sheet.

(iv) Shares issued for consideration other than cash-must be disclosed such as

- shares allotted to transferor company under the agreement of takeover/merger.
- Issue of bonus shares and the source there of

(v) If preference shares have been issued, the terms of redemption or conversion along with the earliest date of redemption/conversion must be specified.

(vi) Excess application money on account of over-subscription not requiring any adjustment, should be refunded. If not, the money refundable must be shown as part of current liabilities.

(2) Reserves & Surplus

This may be in the following forms.

(i) Capital Reserves— It refers to those profits which are not earned from normal business operations. Such profits are not available for the purpose of distribution as dividend. It is created out of profit on sale of fixed assets or investments held as asset, profit on reissue of forfeited shares, pre-incorporation profit, profit on revaluation of fixed assets, profit on, purchase/acquisition of asset or business (excess of net assets over purchase price)

(ii) Capital Redemption Reserve— It is created when fully paid preference shares are redeemed out of divisible profits of the company. This reserve may be utilised for the purpose of issuing fully paid bonus shares to the members of the company.

(iii) Securities Premium— When a company issues shares/or debentures at a price which is more than it's face value, it is said to have issued shares/debentures at a premium. The premium so received is transferred to "Securities Premium Account. According to section 78 of Companies Act, the premium may be utilised for

- Issuing fully paid bonus shares
- Writing off preliminary expenses, discount on issue of shares or debentures
- Providing premium on redemption of preference shares or debentures.

(iv) Revenue Reserves— These may be in the form of specific reserves or free reserves and are created out of revenue profits of the company. Usually such reserves are formed from annual appropriation.

Specific reserves are created for specific purpose. For example Dividend Equalisation Reserve is created to meet the short fall in the divisible profits if the company intends to follow a stable dividend policy, or to redeem the debentures a sinking fund or a debenture redemption reserve may be created. Other specific reserves are Development Rebate Reserve, Investment Allowance Reserve, Export Incentive Reserve.

The term "Fund" is used when the money earmarked for any specific purpose is invested in outside securities. For example if money appropriated for the purpose of redemption of debentures is invested outside the business is termed as Debenture Redemption Fund, if not invested outside but retained or ploughed back in the business, it is called Debenture Redemption Reserve

Surplus

The Credit balance of Profit & Loss Account or P & L Appropriation Account (*i.e.* after making necessary transfer to reserves, & appropriating for proposed, interim or final dividend including bonus, if any) is shown under the heading as surplus. If a company has a debit balance of Profit & Loss Account, the same should be adjusted under this head.

(3) Secured Loans

This refers to mortgaged loan or other loans, which are fully secured either by a fixed or floating charge on the assets of the company. It includes loans from banks, financial institutions or from other companies provided these are secured against the specific or all assets of the company. Debentures are assumed to have first floating charge on the assets of the company. It is to be noted that interest accrued and due on secured loans is to be treated as and shown under Secured Loans. Loan from or guaranteed by directors should be disclosed and shown separately. In case of debentures the terms of redemption/conversion and it's earliest date of redemption/conversion be stated.

(4) Unsecured Loans

These are the loans against which no security stands as pledged or mortgaged. It also includes amount not covered by the value of security provided in respect of partly secured loans. It covers all loans which are not at all secured such as

- Fixed Deposits from public
- Loans and Advances from Subsidiaries
- Short-Term loans & Advances from Banks & others
- Other Loans & Advances.

It may include creditors for purchase of an asset.

(5) Current Liabilities and Provisions

This heading is split in two sub-headings

(A) *Current Liabilities*

It refers to those liabilities which are to be paid or payable with in a period of twelve months. It includes

- Sundry Creditors
- Bills Payable
- Outstanding Expenses
- Income Received in Advance
- Amount payable to subsidiaries

> It is to be noted that short-term loans and Interest o/s thereon are to be shown under "Secured" or "Unsecured Loans" to which these relate to as the case may be and not under Current Liabilities."

(B) ***Provisions***

Such provisions are shown separately from Current Liabilities. This includes

- Proposed Dividend
- Provision for Taxation
- Provision for Depreciation, Repairs & Renewals.
- Provision for Doubtful Debts
- Investment Fluctuation Reserve

- Provident Fund
- Pension Fund

*Provision for Depreciation and Provision for Doubtful Debts may be shown on the 'Assets' side as deduction from the asset concerned.

Contingent liabilities

As explained earlier, these liabilities are shown as foot note and include

- Liability for bills discounted
- Claims against the company not acknowledged as debt
- Uncalled liability on partly paid shares
- Arrears of fixed cumulative preference dividends
- Guarantee given by the company on behalf of directors or other officers of the company
- Estimated amount of contracts remaining to be executed on capital account not provided for and
- Other money for which company is contingently liable :

It is to be noted that if any provision is made against any contingent liability, the same is to be shown under the head provisions.

(6) Fixed Assets

Under this head there are eleven types of fixed assets* starting from goodwill to vehicles. According to AS-10 a fixed asset is an "asset held with the intention of being used for the purpose of producing or providing goods or services and is not held for sale in the normal course of business". Even assets which are not legally owned but held for the purpose of production are treated and shown under this head. These include assets acquired under hire-purchase agreement and assets taken on lease. Valuation of fixed asses is made at cost less depreciation after considering the addition & disposal if any.

It is worth remembering that "goodwill" should be shown in the books only when it is acquired for some consideration. According to AS - 26 internally generated goodwill should not be recognised as an asset.

***As per Schedule VI the fixed assets are classified as follows:**

1. Goodwill
2. Land
3. Building
4. Leasehold
5. Railway Slidings
6. Plant & Machinery
7. Furniture & Fittings
8. Development of property
9. Patents, Trade-marks & Designs
10. Live Stock
11. Vehicles

In case of revaluation of fixed assets, every Balance Sheet subsequent to such revaluation must show the revised figures with the date of increase or decrease in place of original cost.

In ascertaining the cost of an asset all expenditures incurred in bringing the asset to it's working condition should be included. This includes costs of transportation expenditure on trial runs. In case of Land & Building stamp duty, registration fee & architects fee should be capitalised.

(7) Investments

As per AS - 13 (Accounting for Investments), " Investments are assets held by an enterprise for earning income by way of dividends, interest and rental, for capital appreciation or for other benefits to the investing enterprise". Assets held as stock-in-trade are not investments. Money invested outside business is termed as investments which may be long-term, current investment or an investment property.

According to AS-13, a "Current investment by it's nature are readily realisable is intended to be held for not more than one year, where as an investment property is an investment in land or buildings that are not intended to be occupied substantially for use by the enterprise. Schedule VI requires investments to be shown as follows—

(i) Investments in Government or Trust Securities

(ii) Investments in shares, debentures or bonds, fully paid up & partly paid up and also different classes of shares.

(iii) Immovable properties.

(iv) Investments in the Capital of partnership firms.

The following details must be given :

1. Nature of Investment
2. Mode of valuation of Investments
3. Aggregate amount of company's quoted investments and it's market value
4. Aggregate amount of company's unquoted investments
5. Amount of fully paid and partly paid shares.
6. Investment in subsidiary companies.

(8) Current Assets, Loans and Advances

This is subdivided in two sub-headings :

(a) *Current Assets*

As per the Guidance note issued by ICAI, "Current assets means cash and other assets that are expected to be converted into cash or consumed in the production of goods or rendering of services in the normal course of business and include.

(1) *Stock-in-trade* (inventories of raw-materials, work-in-progress finished goods, stores and spare parts to be shown separately) including mode of valuation. Debtors should show the age-wise, and security-wise classification such as.

- Debts outstanding for a period of more than six-months and other debts
- Debts considered good in respect of which the company is fully secured
- Debts considered good in respect of which company holds no security other than the debtor's personal security.

- Debts considered doubtful or bad.
- Debts due by directors or other officers
- Debts due from other companies (subsidiaries)
- Maximum amount due by directors or other officers of the company (through footnote)
- Provision for doubtful debts is required to be deducted from sundry debtors. Provision should not exceed the amount considered doubtful or bad. Any excess provision be shown under "Reserve & Surplus".

(iii) *Cash and Bank balance should be shown separately.* Bank balances should be classified into balances with scheduled banks and other banks along with details of current account, saving bank and fixed deposits. Bank Overdraft, if any, should be shown under sundry creditors. This information of inclusion be disclosed in a footnote that the sundry creditors include bank overdraft amounting to Rs. ————.

(B) *Loans & Advances*

The disclosing rules which are applicable to sundry debtors, the same should be applied to "Loans and Advances". *i.e.* These should be shown in age-wise security wise and realisability wise classification. In addition the following should be shown.

- Advances and loans to subsidiaries.
- Advances and Loans to partnership firms in which the company or subsidiary is a partner
- Bills of Exchange
- Advances recoverable in cash or kind or for value (Rent, Rates & Insurance)
- Balance with customers, port trust etc. which are payable on demand.

(9) Miscellaneous Expenditure

These are the expenses incurred in earlier years but not written off. These include.

(i) Preliminary Expenses (Formation expenses incurred on preparation of Memorandum and Articles of Association, legal fees, registration fee etc.

(ii) Shares & Debentures issue expenses such as brokerage, underwriting commission, discount on issue of shares and debentures

(iii) Interest paid out of capital during construction

Such miscellaneous expenditure is written off over a period for which benefit is available.

(10) Profit and Loss Account (Debit balance)

This represents past unwritten off losses. These are adjusted and written off against the free reserves (divisible profits/revenue profits) to the available extent. Unabsorbed amount is shown under this head.

B- INCOME STATEMENT/PROFIT & LOSS ACCOUNT

Salient features

Though the procedure and the process of preparation of "Income Statement" of a company and that of non-corporate entities are similar in principles yet, there are some differences in the method of presentation and some additional items which form the part of a corporate Income Statement. These differences are as under :

1. **Heading :** Non-corporate entities name income statement as "Trading and Profit and Loss Account, while companies call it "Income Statement" or Profit and Loss Account only. The items of Trading Account become the part of "Income Statement " No separate Trading Account is prepared.
2. **Appropriations :** Sole Trader does not prepare any appropriation account, while partnership firms and Companies do. A company 's Profit and Loss Account is split up in to two parts - "above the line" and "below the line". All items of appropriations are shown "below the line" and the remaining balance is transferred to the liabilities side of the Balance Sheet. A Partnership firm prepares a separate Profit & Loss Appropriation Account.
3. **As per AS - 5 extraordinary items** (abnormal nature) **prior period items** are shown separately where as in case of non-corporate entities such items are stated along with the normal and routine items.
4. **Requirements :** The Profit & Loss Account of a company should confirm to the requirements of schedule VI of Companies Act 1956 and adhere to AS - 1; AS-4 & AS - 5 recommendations, where as non-corporate enterprises are not required to do so.
5. **Income Tax** is treated as an expense for the companies while for firms and sole trade enterprise, it is treated as drawings.
6. Companies Profit & Loss Account should disclose the figures for the previous year along with the current year's where as non-company enterprises are not required to show figures relating to previous year.

TREATMENT OF SPECIAL ITEMS OF PROFIT & LOSS ACCOUNT

1. Interest on Debentures and Loans

This item includes interest paid and payable for the financial period for which accounts are prepared and shown to the debit side of Profit and Loss Account. Likewise, interest due but remaining outstanding is taken to the liability side of the Balance Sheet. Interest on Debentures and interest on secured loans outstanding if any, is shown under the heading "Secured Loans" whereas interest O/s on unsecured loan is shown under "unsecured loans".

It is to be noted that interest on loan for the construction period should be capitalised and added to the cost of the asset concerned.

2. Tax on interest on Debentures

As per the Income Tax Act 1961, every company must deduct tax at source (TDS) while paying interest to the debenture holders. The amount so deducted shall be deposited with the Government treasury. The current rate for TDS are as follows.

Debentures (listed)	10.2% including Education cess
Debentures (unlisted)	20.4% including Education cess

If A Ltd. has to pay interest on it's 9% debentures (listed) of the face value of Rs. 5,00,000 then gross interest will be Rs. 45,000 while tax deducted at source Rs. 4,590 and balance shall be paid to the Debentureholder Rs. 40,410. The following entry is recorded :

Interest on Debentures A/c	Dr.	45,000	
To Debenture holders A/c			40,410
To Income Tax Payable A/c			4,590

Income tax deducted but not deposited with the Government is to be shown in the Balance Sheet under the heading "Current Liabilities".

> It should be remembered that Profit and Loss Account will always be debited with the gross amount of interest.

3. Discount on Debentures/ Loss on Issue/ Debenture Issue Expenses.

Discount on issue of debentures, debenture issue expenses such as commission, brokerage etc. or premium payable on redemption (treated as loss on issue which may include discount also) are to be written off as early as possible, or over the life span of the debentures, depending upon the policy of the company. In the absence of any specific instructions in the question, such amount should be written off on the basis of debentures outstanding. The unwritten off balance is to be shown on the assets side of the Balance Sheet under the heading of "Miscellaneous Expenditure".

> **Note :** Only written off * amount is charged to Profit and Loss Account.

4. Preliminary Expenses

As already explained under Balance Sheet items, it appears on the assets side of the Balance Sheet under the heading "Miscellaneous Expenditure" as long as it is not written off. The amount written off* is charged to Profit and Loss Account. If there is no specific instruction relating to the amount to be written off, then the entire amount should be shown in the Balance Sheet.

5. Corporate Income Tax

This is shown under three stages.

(i) *Advance Income Tax*

As per Income Tax Act 1961, the companies are required to pay income tax on the profits earned. They have to deposit advance tax under PAYE (Pay As You Earn) scheme on specific dates during the financial year. The advance tax so paid is adjusted against income tax liability. The unadjusted amount of advance income tax is shown as an asset under the heading Current Assets, Loans and Advances.

(ii) *Provision for Taxation*

While preparing Profit and Loss Account, a provision for income tax is created on the basis of current year's profit to meet the actual tax liability. The amount so provided depends on the prevailing tax rate. The Current rate of corporate tax is 30% plus 10% surcharge and 2 % education less for domestic companies and 40% plus 2.5% surcharge and 2% education cess for foreign companies. The following entry is recorded.

Profit & Loss Account Dr.

To Provision for Taxation A/c

AS-22 "Accounting for Taxes on Income" recommends that the net balance i.e. excess of "Advance Tax" over "Provision for Taxation" or excess of "Provision for Taxation" over Advance Tax" may be shown on the assets side or liabilities side of the Balance Sheet as the case may be, till the final assessment is made and actual tax liability determined by the tax authorities.

* Students are advised to update themselves with the latest amendment in the tax rate.

(iii) *Determination of actual tax liability*

As per Income Tax rules, Income (Profits) for the previous year is assessed and taxed in the assessment year. When the assessment is completed the provision for taxation so created may either fall short of actual tax liability or may exceed the tax liability. Such a shortfall or excess is treated as prior period item (AS-5) and therefore it's adjustment is made in the Profit and Loss Account but "below the line", either to the debit side (for short fall) or to the credit side (for excess).

On the other hand, the actual tax liability is compered with advance income tax paid. In case actual tax liability is more than the amount of advance tax paid the same may be paid or shown as a current liability in the Balance Sheet and if advance tax paid exceeds, the difference being refund should be stated under "Current Assets" loans and Advances in the Balance Sheet.

Example (1)

EXTRACTS FROM A TRIAL BALANCE OF A COMPANY
As on 31st March, 2003

	Dr. (Rs.)	Cr. (Rs.)
Provision for Taxation (2001-02)		2,50,000
Advance Income Tax (for 2001-02)	2,60,000	
Advance Income Tax (for 2002-03)	3,00,000	

Additional Information

(i) The actual tax liability for the year 2001-02 amounted to Rs. 2,75,000.

(ii) Provision for Taxation for the year 2002-03 of Rs. 2,85,000 is required to be made.

Show the relevant information in the relevant ledgers.

PROFIT AND LOSS ACCOUNT (EXTRACTS)
for the year ended 31st March 2003

	Rs.		
To Provision for Taxation (2002-03)	2,85,000	above the line	
To Provision for Taxation (2001-02) (Rs. 2,75,000 – 2,50,000) Tax liability – Provision	25,000	below the line	

BALANCE SHEET (EXTRACTS)
As on 31st March 2003

(Liabilities)	Rs.	(Assets)		Rs.
Income Tax Payable (Tax liability – Advance Tax) for 2001-02 2,75,000 – 2,60,000	15,000	Loans & Advances Advance Tax (Current year) Provision for Taxation Current Year	 3,00,000 2,85,000	 15,000

* relates to last year

PROVISION FOR TAXATION (2001-02)

	Rs.		Rs.
To Income Tax (Tax liability)	2,75,000	By Balance b/d	2,50,000
		By Profit & Loss A/c (below the line)	25,000
	2,75,000		2,75,000

PROVISION FOR TAXATION (2002-03)

	Rs.		Rs.
To Balance c/d	2,85,000	By Profit and Loss A/c (above the line)	2,85,000
	2,85,000		2,85,000

Example (2)

From the following extract of a Trial Balance and the additional information, show the treatment of taxation in the relevant ledger accounts.

TRIAL BALANCE (EXTRACTS)

As on 31st March, 2002

	Dr. (Rs.)	Cr. (Rs.)
Provision for Taxation		1,20,000
Income Tax	1,10,000	

Additional Information

Provide Rs. 1,50,000 for provision for taxation.

Solution :

PROVISION FOR TAXATION A/C (OLD)

	Rs.		Rs.
To Income Tax	1,10,000	By Balance b/d	1,20,000
To Profit and Loss A/c (below the line)	10,000		
	1,20,000		1,20,000

PROVISION FOR TAXATION A/C (NEW)

	Rs.		Rs.
To Balance c/d (To taken to liabilities side of B/s) (above the line	1,50,000	By Profit and Loss A/c	1,50,000
	1,50,000		1,50,000

PROFIT AND LOSS ACCOUNT (EXTRACTS)

	Rs.		Rs.
To Provision for Taxation (New)	1,50,000		Above the line
			below the line
		By Provision for Taxation	10,000

BALANCE SHEET (EXTRACTS)
As on 31st March, 2002

Liabilities	Rs.	Assets	Rs.
Current liabilities & Provisions			
B. Provisions			
Provision for Taxation	1,50,000		

Example (3)

From the following information show the treatment of taxation in the relevant accounts.

TRIAL BALANCE (EXTRACTS)
As on 31st March, 2003

	Dr. (Rs.)	Cr. (Rs.)
Provision for Taxation		1,40,000
Advance Payment of Income Tax	95,000	
Tax deducted at source	15,000	

Additional information:

(i) Income tax for the year 2001-02 has been assessed at Rs. 1,55,000 against which the advance tax and the deducted at source are to be adjusted.

(ii) Provide Rs. 1,70,000 for taxation for the year 2002-03

Solution:

PROVISION FOR TAXATION ACCOUNT (OLD)

	Rs.		Rs.
To Income Tax (Tax liability)	1,55,000	By Balance b/d	1,40,000
		By Profit & Loss A/c (below the line)	15,000
	1,55,000		1,55,000

PROVISION FOR TAXATION ACCOUNT (NEW)

	Rs.		Rs.
To Balanec c/d	1,70,000	By Profit & Loss A/c (above the line)	1,70,000

BALANCE SHEET (EXTRACTS)
As on 31st March, 2003

Liabilities	Rs.	Assets	Rs.
Current Liabilities & Provisions			
A: Current Liabilities			
Income Tax Payable	45,000*		
B: Provisions:			
Provision for Taxation	1,70,000		

*Being the difference between actual tax liability (assessed) Rs. 1,55,000 and advance income including the tax deducted at source (Rs. 95,000 + 15,000)

Example (5)

From the following particulars prepare necessary accounts for the year ending 31st March, 2003

TRIAL BALANCE (EXTRACTS)
as on 31st March, 2003

	Dr. (Rs.)	Cr. (Rs.)
Provision for Taxation (1. 4. 2002)		4,50,000
Advance Tax Paid (1. 4. 2002)	4,20,000	
Tax Deducted at Source (1. 4. 2002)	3,500	

On 1.1.2003 the assessment was completed with a tax liability of Rs. 5,30,000. Advance payment of tax for the year 2002-03 amounted to Rs. 5,10,000. A provision for taxation is to be made for Rs. 5,10,000. A provision for taxation is to be made for Rs. 5,75,000 for the year ended 31st March, 2003.

Solution:

PROVISION FOR TAXATION ACCOUNT

	Rs.		Rs.
To Income Tax A/c (Tax liability)	5,30,000	By Balance b/d	4,50,000
		By Profit & Loss A/c (below the line)	80,000
	5,30,0000		5,30,000
To Balance c/d	5,75,000	By Profit & Loss A/c (above the line)	5,75,000

ADVANCE INCOME TAX ACCOUNT

	Rs.		Rs.
To Balance b/d	4,20,000	By Income Tax A/c	4,20,000
	4,20,000		4,20,000

TAX DEDUCTED AT SOURCE ACCOUNT

	Rs.		Rs.
To Balance b/d	3,500	By Income Tax A/c	3,500
	3,500		3,500

INCOME TAX ACCOUNT (TAX LIABILITY)

	Rs.		Rs.
To Advance Income Tax A/c	4,20,000	By Provision for Taxation A/c	5,30,000
To Tax Deducted at Source A/c	3,500		
To Bank A/c (Balance paid)	1,06,500		
	5,30,000		5,30,000

PROFIT AND LOSS ACCOUNT
For the year ended 31st March, 2003

	Rs.		Rs.
To Provision for Taxation (2002-03)	5,75,000	Above the line	
To Provision for Taxation (2001-02)	80,000	Below the line	

Managerial Remuneration

The payment of managerial remuneration is governed by the provisions of sections 198 and 309 either by the Articles or by a ordinary/special resolution passed by the company in general meeting.

Managerial personnel refers to managing director, whole-time-director, part-time director and manager. The provision of Companies Act shall apply to a public company and a private company which is a subsidiary of a public company but to no other private company.

Managerial Personnel	Maximum limit
1. A whole time director or a managing director who may be paid remuneration either by way of a 6 monthly payment or specified percentage of the net profits of the company or partly by one way and partly by the other	(a) 5 %* of the net profits for one such director. (b) 10%* of the net profits if there is more than one such director-for all of them together.
2. Any other type of director (par-time-director) who may be paid remuneration either (i) by way of a monthly, quarterly or annual payment with the approval of Central Government or (ii) by way of commission if the company by special resolution authorises such payment	(a) 1%* of the net profit if the company has a managing or whole-time director or a manager (b) 3%* of the net profits in any other case.

*The rates can be increased by the company in general meeting with the approval of the Central Government.

If any director receives any sum by way of remuneration in excess of prescribed limit without the prior sanction of the Central Government, he shall refund such sum to the Company. The Company cannot waive the recovery of such sum.

A whole-time director or a managing director who receives a commission from the company shall not be entitled to receive a commission or remuneration from any subsidiary of the company.

The **overall** managerial remuneration payable by a public company or a private company which is a subsidiary of a public company to it's managerial personnel shall not exceed 11% of the net profits for that financial year **Remuneration limit does not include fees.**

Fees

A director may receive remuneration by way of fee for each meeting attended by him. But the sitting fees for attending the meetings of the Board cannot be paid on monthly basis.

What is included in managerial remuneration?

Managerial remuneration includes, in addition to usual salary, commission & allowance the following perquisites:-

(i) Rent free accommodation or any other benefit or amenity in respect of accommodation free of charge.

(ii) Any other benefit or amenity free of charge or at concessional rate

(iii) Obligations met by the company, which otherwise would have been incurred by the managerial personnel.

(iv) Amount paid by the company to effect any insurance policy, or to provide any pension, amenity or gratuity for any managerial personnel or his/her spouse or child.

Computation of Managerial Remuneration u/s 349 & 350

In computing the net-profit of a Company the following sums are to included.

*Subsidies received from any Government or any public authority constituted or authorised in this behalf by any Government.

***Items not to be included :**

- Profits by way of premium on shares or debentures issued or sold
- Profits on reissue of forfeited shares.
- Capital profits* from sale of fixed assets (Excess of sale price over original cost)
- Capital profits from sale of undertakings.

*** What is to be deducted**

While computing the net profits of a company the following sums shall be deducted.

- All the normal working charges
- Bonus or commission to employees
- Any tax notified by the Central Government as being in the nature of a tax on abnormal profits (excess)
- Any tax on business profits imposed for special reasons or in special circumstances and notified by the Central Government in this behalf.
- Director's remuneration

- Interest on debentures issued by company
- Interest on secured loans & advances
- Interest on unsecured loans and advances
- Expenses on repairs
- Contribution to charitable and other funds not directly relating to business not exceeding Rs. 50,000 or 5% of the average net profits during the financial years immediately preceding the current accounting year, which ever is greater.
- Depreciation to the extent specified U/s 350
- Past losses not yet adjusted so far
- Any compensation and damages to be paid due to any legal liability including liability arising from breach of contract.
- Bad debts adjusted or written off.

*** What is not to be deducted**

- Income tax and super tax paid by the company
- Any other tax on the income of the company (other than the tax on abnormal profits or tax imposed for special reasons)
- Any compensation, damages or payments made voluntarily.
- Capital Losses.

(B) Remuneration Payable by Companies having no profits or inadequate profits. The monthly remuneration payable shall not exceed as per the following table

Where the effective Capital is Rs.	A Not exceeding the ceiling limit of Rs. 24,00,000 p. a. Rs. (p.m.)	B Not exceeding the ceiling limit of Rs. 48,00,000 p. a. Rs.(p.m)	C Exceeding the ceiling limit of Rs. 48,00,000 p. a. per annum Rs. (p.m.)
(i) Less than 1 crore	75,000	1,50,000	1,50,000
(ii) 1 crore to 5 crores	1,00,000	2,00,000	2,00,000
(iii) 5 crores to 25 crores	1,25,000	2,50,000	2,50,000
(iv) 25 crores to 50 crores	1,50,000	3,00,000	3,00,000
(v) 50 crores to 100 crores	1,75,000	3,50,000	3,50,000
(vi) 100 crores or more	2,00,000	4,00,000	4,00,000

Example (4)

The following is the Profit and Loss Account of X Ltd. for the year ended 31st March 2003.

	Rs.		Rs.
To Office & Administration Expenses	3,10,000	By Balance b/d	3,43,200
To Selling & Distribution	1,92,000	By Gross Profit b/d	24,15,000
To Director's Fees	39,500	By Subsidies	1,39,300
To Managerial Remuneration	1,70,000	By Interest on Investments	9,500
To Interest on debentures	18,500	By Transfer fees	1,000
To Donation to charitable trust	15,000	By Profit on sale of Machinery	25,000
To Compensation for breach of contract	27,000	(W.D.V Rs. 30,000)	
To Depreciation on fixed assets	3,12,000		
To Investment Revaluation Reserve	12,500		
To Provision for Taxation	7,40,000		
To General Reserve	2,50,000		
To Balance c/d	8,46,500		
	29,33,000		29,33,000

Additional Information:

(1) Original Cost of the machinery sold was Rs. 40,000

(2) Depreciation on fixed assets as per schedule XIV of the Companies Act 1956 was Rs. 3,42,000.

You are required to calculate managerial remuneration in the following situations.

(i) When there is only whole time director

(ii) When there are two whole time directors

(iii) When there are two whole time directors, a managing director and a part-time director.

Solution:

Calculation of net profit U/s 340 of the Companies Act 1956

			Rs.
	Gross Profit as per P & L A/c		24,15,000
Add	Subsidies	1,39,300	
Add	Interest on Investment	9,500	
Add	Transfer fees	1,000	
Add	Profit on sale if machinery (Cost-W.D.V) (40,000 – 30,000)	10,000	1,59,800
			25,74,800
Less	Office & Administrative Expenses	3,10,000	
Less	Directors Fees	39,500	
Less	Selling & Distribution Expenses	1,92,000	
Less	Interest on debentures	18,500	
Less	Compensation for breach of contract	27,000	
Less	Depreciation as per schedule XIV	3,42,000	(9,29,000)
	Profit U/s 349		16,45,800

Computation of remuneration

(i)	When there is only whole time director 5% of Rs. 16,45,800	82,290
(ii)	When there are two whole time directors 10% of Rs. 16,45,800	1,64,580
(iii)	When there are two whole time directors a part-time director, and a manager 11% of Rs. 16,45,800	1,81,038

In situations (i) & (ii) actual remuneration as per P & L A/c Rs. 1,70,000 exceeds the maximum amount payable, the company must obtain permission U/s 309 for such excess payment.

Fees:

It is to be noted that fee is not to be included in the managerial remuneration for the purpose of over all limit. However, fee for attending the meeting of the board is payable on the basis of companies paid up capital as shown below.

Paid up Share Capital (Rs.)	Maximum fee per meeting (Rs.)
Up to Rs. 50 lacs	250
Rs. 50 lacs to Rs. 5 crores	500
Rs. 5 crores to Rs. 10 crores	750
Above Rs. 10 crores	1,000

Contribution/donation to a Political party

Any contribution or donation to any political party must be disclosed separately in the Profit and Loss Account. According to section 293 Government companies and companies with less than three years are not allowed to make any political contribution or donation. Those allowed can make such contribution up to 5% of it's average profits.

Prior Period Items

The nature and amount of prior period items should be separately disclosed in the Profit and Loss Account in a manner that their impact on the current profit or loss can be perceived. In case accounts are adopted in the annual general meeting and if some adjustments relating to previous year are to be made, these should be stated below the line, i.e. in the Profit and Loss Appropriation Account as per AS-5.

Extra-Ordinary Items

Extra-Ordinary items are incomes or expenses that arise from events or transactions which are clearly distinct from the ordinary activities of the enterprise and therefore are not expected to recur frequently or regularly. These items should be disclosed in the statement of profit and loss as a part of net-profit or loss for the period (AS-5). "Fixed assets destroyed in an earthquake" is an example of Extraordinary items.

Contingencies and Events occurring after Balance Sheet Date

As per AS-4, the amount of a contingent loss should be provided for by a charge in the statement of Profit and loss if.

(i) It is possible that future events will confirm that on assets has been impaired or a liability has been incurred as at the Balance Sheet date and

(ii) A reasonable estimate of the amount of the resulting loss can be made.

The existence of a contingent loss should be disclosed in the financial statements if either of the above condition is not met, unless the possibility of loss is remote.

Contingent gains should not be disclosed in the financial statements. Only virtually certain gains should be recognised.

Appropriation and Disposition of Profits

Once the profits have been ascertained as per the statement of profit and loss, the next step is the appropriation and disposition of the available profits. It includes.

- Transfer to general reserve and other reserves such as capital redemption reserve, development rebate reserve etc.
- Transfer to sinking fund
- Transfer to Dividend Equalisation fund
- Providing for Corporate Dividend Tax, interim or final dividend and
- Paying bonus to shareholders etc.

All these items are treated below the line or a separate Profit and Loss Appropriation Account is prepared.

Divisible Profit

All the profits of the company are not divisible profits. Only those profits which can be legally made available to shareholders by way of dividend. In other words divisible profits are that part of profits which can be distributed among shareholders in the form of dividend.

It is to be noted that divisible profits do not include "profit on revaluation" of fixed assets and other profits of "Capital nature" (Extraordinary)

Section 205 of the Companies Act 1956 lays down the rules for ascertaining the "divisible profits".

(i) Dividend out of the current year's profits can be declared only after providing for depreciation as per the provisions of the Companies Act. Similarly
Dividend out of previous year's profits can be declared only after providing for such depreciation. It means dividend can be paid out of current year's or previous year's profits or out of both.

(ii) Dividend can be paid put of subsidy provided by the Central or state Government in pursuance of guarantee given by the Government.

(iii) A company which fails to redeem the preference shares in accordance with the provisions of section 80A, can not declare any dividend on its equity shares.

(iv) Current profits cannot be distributed without making good the past losses However, it is not necessary to write off preliminary expenses and other deferred revenue expenditure for the purpose of determining the amount of divisible profits.

(v) Profits of subsidiary companies should not be included in the divisible profits unless the subsidiary company has actually declared the dividend. The losses of subsidiary companies need not be provided for, however it is desirable to do so in view of convention of conservatism.

(vi) Profits from writing back of the fixed assets, preferably, should not be included in the divisible profits. However, the provisions of the Act do not prohibit such inclusion. A reasonable amount of such revision may be included in the divisible profits.

Computation of Divisible Profits

Steps

(1) First provide for current year's depreciation

(2) Arrears of depreciation must be made good (if these fall after 28. 12. 1960) before declaring dividend out of the profit of such previous years.

(3) Past losses: If a company incurs loss in any financial year (after 28. 12. 1960) then the amount of such loss or an amount equivalent to depreciation provided for that year or years, which ever is less, must be set-off against ;

(a) the profits of the company after providing for the depreciation of that year for which dividend is to be declared or proposed or

(b) the profits of the company for the previous year or years after charging relevant year/years depreciation or

(c) the aggregate of (a) and (b) together.

Example (5)

From the following figures calculate divisible profits for the year ended 31st March 2003.

PROFITS FOR THE YEAR ENDING 31ST MARCH

	2001 (Rs.)	2002 (Rs.)	2003 (Rs.)
1. Net profit/or less before depreciation	(6,00,000) (Loss)	(3,00,000) (Loss)	15,00,000 (Profit)
2. Depreciation as per books of accounts	60,000	60,000	1,80,000
3. Depreciation as per section 205	4,80,000	4,20,000	3,60,000

***Computation of divisible profits**

			Rs.
(i)	Profit for the year ending 31st March, 2003		15,00,000
Less	Depreciation for the year 2003		1,80,000
			13,20,000
(ii)	Arrears of Depreciation		
	Dep. as per section 205 – Dep. as per Books		
	Rs. 4,80,000 – 60,000	= 4,20,000	
	Rs. 4,20,000 – 60,000	= 3,60,000	
	Rs. 3,60,000 – 1,80,000	= 1,80,000	9,60,000
		9,60,000	3,60,000

(iii) **Arrears of loss** or
amount equal to depreciation
provided during the years
of losses — which ever is less

(a)	Past losses before Depreciation	6,00,000 + 3,00,000	
Add	Depreciation	60,000 + 60,000	
	Total Losses	= Rs. 10,20,000 or	
(b)	Amount of Depreciation = 60,000 + 60,000 = 1,20,000		
	which ever is less		1,20,000
	Divisible Profits		2,40,000

Alternatively the divisible profits can be ascertained as under :

		Rs.
	Current year's profit before depreciation	15,00,000
Less	Depreciation as per section 205 for all these years (Rs. 4,80,000 + 4,20,000 + 3,60,000)	12,60,000
	Divisible Profits	2,40,000

Students should note that while calculating divisible profits the depreciation calculated for all these years as per section 205, must be adjusted against the current year's profits rather than the past losses.

DIVIDENDS

Dividend refers to that amount of divisible profits which is distributed among the shareholders of the company. A member (shareholder) is entitled to receive dividend when it is declared by the Board of Directors as per the provisions of the Article. The Board has absolute right to recommend the rate of dividend to be declared subject to the approval of shareholders and provisions of Articles of Association. However, the shareholders cannot compel the Board to recommend & declare dividend. It is to be noted that dividend is always declared for the working of one financial year at the annual general meeting. In case the dividend could not be declared at the annual general meeting the same can be declared at the Extraordinary meeting. The power to declare dividend is implied and does not require express authority either in the Articles or Memorandum of Association. It should be remembered that where a dividend has been declared at the Annual General Meeting neither the company nor the directors can declare a further dividend for the same year at the subsequent general meeting. It is knows as Final Dividend.

Legal Provisions Relating to Dividends

The payment of dividends is governed by two basic principles, first-that dividend must not be paid out of capital and secondly it must be paid out of profits only. Other provisions are stated below.

1. Dividends cannot be declared on equity shares of a company which fails to redeem it's preference shares in accordance with the provisions of section 80A so long as failure continues. It is to be noted that now no company can issue irredeemable shares, after the commencement of companies (Amendment) Act 1988. The duration of redemption is terms of issue or 10 years whichever is earlier.

(1) Sources of Dividends (Section 205)

Dividends can be declared and paid by a company for any financial year out of:

(a) Profits of the company for "that year" (Current year) or accumulated revenue profits (previous year's profits) of the company arrived at after providing for depreciation in accordance with the provision of the act and after transferring to the reserve an amount as prescribed under the section 205 (2A). or

(b) Accumulated revenue reserves : Such declaration of dividend shall not be made except in accordance with such rules as may be prescribed by the Central Government in this behalf where any such declaration shall not be made except with the prior approval of the Central Government.

(c) Money provided by Central or State Government for the payment of dividend in pursuance of a guarantee given by that Government.

(d) Capital Profits, subject to following conditions :

(i) It is authorized by the Article of Association and Memorandum of Association.

(ii) Such capital profits are realized in cash.

(iii) These remains as profits after revaluation of all the assets and liabilities of the company.

2. Dividends not to be paid out of Capital

Payment of dividend out of capital is unlawful return of capital to its shareholders. It will lead to unauthorized reduction in share capital. Where, however, the shareholders received dividends with the knowledge that these were paid out of capital, the same may be required to return the amount so received.

3. Payment of Dividend in proportion of Amount paid up on shares

Dividends shall be paid in proportion to the amount paid up on each share. However, no dividends shall be payable on call-in-advance unless authorized by the Articles.

4. Dividends in Cash only

No dividends shall be payable except in Cash except when these are adjusted towards paying up unpaid amount on shares or where bonus shares are issued. Any dividend payable in Cash may be paid by the cheque or dividend warrant.

5. Transfer to Dividend Bank and Unclaimed Dividend Account

The dividend declared must be deposited in a separate bank account within 5 days of declaration for the purpose of paying dividend where any amount remains unclaimed or unpaid after the expiry of 30 days of it's declaration, the company shall transfer the balance to unclaimed dividend account within 7 days after the expiry of above said 30 days.

Preference Dividend

The Preference Dividend is paid to Preference shareholders at a predetermined fixed rate on priority basis. These holders are entitled dividend in preference to (before) equity shareholders. However, the preference shareholders can claim dividend only out of profits and if it is declared at the Annual General meeting. If preference shares are of cumulative nature, the arrears of preference dividend if any, shall be payable to preference shareholders before equity dividend. It should be noted that preference shareholders cannot force the company to pay all the dividends including arrears. If equity shareholder are not paid any dividend, preference shareholders cannot claim any dividend from the company.

It is to be noted that the arrears of preference dividend are treated as a contingent liability which appears as a footnote under the Balance sheet.

Non-cumulative preference shares are not entitled to any arrears resulting from non-payment of dividend due to losses or inadequate profits. If a company has issued participating preference shares with a right to participate in the balance of profits, left after paying fixed preference dividend a certain percentage out of the balance (residual) profit as per the terms of issue is paid to participating shareholders.

For example 9% preference shares may be issued with a further right to 40% of the excess dividend over 20% paid to equity shareholders. If a company declares 25% dividend to equity shareholders, the preference shareholders will get 11% dividend. (9% plus 40% of (25% – 20%) *i.e.* 2%).

Unclaimed Dividend

According to the section 205A of the Companies Act 1956 dividends remaining unpaid must be deposited in the "Unpaid or Unclaimed Dividend Account within 42 days of declaration of dividend. Any claim thereafter, must be met out of the unclaimed dividend account. Money so transferred to the aforesaid account which remain unpaid on unclaimed for a period of seven years from the date of such transfer, shall be transferred to "Investor Education and Protection Fund" maintained u/s 205 of Companies (Amendment) Act 1999.

Unclaimed dividend appears on the liabilities side of Balance Sheet under the head Current Liabilities and Provisions.

Proposed Dividend

Dividend recommended by the directors to be paid to shareholders for any accounting period on or after the close of books of accounts but before the Annual General Meeting is known as proposed dividend. Once it is approved by the shareholders in the General Meeting, it becomes final dividend. It is to be noted that rate of dividend declared cannot exceed the proposed dividend. Proposed dividend is an appropriation of profit, hence it is shown to the debit side of Profit and Appropriation Account and on the liabilities side of Balance Sheet under the heading "Current liabilities and Provisions".

Final Dividend

It is a dividend which is declared at the annual general meeting of the shareholders. Such dividend is declared only after the close of books of accounts. The shareholders may reduce the rate of final dividend but cannot increase it. Once the final dividend is declared it becomes the liability of the company. It should be noted that when a final dividend is declared then interim dividend is not adjusted unless there is any specific resolution for such adjustment. Final dividend is paid on paid up capital for the whole year as against the interim dividend which is usually paid only for six months. For example N Ltd. has 5,00,000 shares of 10 each Rs. 8 paid, declares 5% p.a. interim dividend and final dividend @ 10%, then the total dividend will be Rs. 5,00,000 *i.e.* (Rs. 1,00,000 interim dividend + Rs. 4,00,000 final dividend)

$$\text{Interim Dividend} = \left(40,00,000 \times \frac{5}{100} \times \frac{6}{12} = 1,00,000\right) + \text{Final Dividend} = \left(40,00,000 \times \frac{10}{100}\right) = 4,00,000$$

$$= \text{Rs. } 5,00,000$$

Interim Dividend

A dividend declared by the Directors between two annual general meetings of the company is known as interim dividend. Where the directors believe that the company will have sufficient profits available for dividends at the end of the year, they may distribute a part of the profit as a part payment on account. Payment so made in anticipation and on account of total dividend to be paid for the year is treated as interim dividend. However, such payment must be authorized by the Articles. Interim dividend should be declared only when the company has made substantial profits during the first half of the year and it is expected that the company has even a better prospects for the second half as well. Regulation 86 of Table – A provides that "Board may from time to time pay to the members such interim dividend as it appears to be justified by the profits of the company". Thus, there is no limit on the number of interim dividend the company may pay in a year. The payment of interim dividend does not require approval of general meeting.

Companies (Amendment) Act 2,000 has granted statutory recognition to the right of directors to declare interim dividend. The term "dividend" now includes interim dividend also. **All provisions of the Companies Act which apply to dividends have now become applicable to interim dividends also.** A company cannot declare any interim dividend unless it has made :

(i) necessary provision for depreciation for the whole year,

(ii) prior adjustment of accumulated losses, if any, and,

(iii) transfer to general reserve as required U/s 205 (2A).

Once an interim dividend is declared it becomes legally enforceable debt against the company. Prior to the Amendment Act 2000 the interim dividend was not an enforceable debt and Board had the right to rescind the resolution already passed.

The period, for which an interim dividend is paid, is usually six months. However students should note that whether the rate of dividend includes the words "per annum" or not. For example the directors of a company declare an interim dividend @ 12% per annum the interim dividend shall be calculated only for six months. If the rate declared by directors is 12% and the words "per annum" are not mentioned, then the dividend shall be calculated @ 12% without reference to time *i.e.* 12% X amount of paid up capital. If the capital of the company is Rs. 10,00,000 then in the first case interim dividend will amount to Rs. 60,000 and in the second case Rs. 1,20,000.

CORPORATE DIVIDEND TAX

Finance Act 1997 had exempted the dividend in the hands of shareholders and introduced corporate dividend tax to be paid by the dividend paying company. Thereafter, the corporate dividend tax was withdrawn by the Finance Act 2002 and the burden of tax was shifted on the shareholders and hence company was not liable to pay any tax on dividend declared, distributed or paid between 1.4.2002 to 31.3.2003.

The Finance Act 2003 had again shifted the liability of such tax on the domestic companies who shall be liable to pay additional tax on the amount declared, distributed or paid by way of dividends on or after 1.4.2003. The rate of tax being 12.5% plus surcharge @ 10% and 2% Education Cess. Thus the effective rate is equal to 14.025%. This rate is applicable for the financial year 2004-05 onwards. Now w.e.f. financial year 2006-07 the rate is 15% + 10% surcharge + 3% Education Cess = 16.995%.

Note : Students should verify the rate applicable because this rate may be changed by the subsequent Finance Act. It is further to be noted that dividends from domestic companies in the hands of shareholders are totally exempt. As per guidance note it is be treated as appropriation.

Transfer to General Reserve

According to section 205 (2A) no company shall declare or pay dividend for any financial year out of the profit of company for that year unless a certain percentage of profits as prescribed by the Central Government not exceeding 10% has been transferred to reserve. However, a company may voluntarily transfer a higher percentage of it's profits to reserve as discussed below :

The Central Government has prescribed the following rules under the Companies (Transfer of profits to reserves) Rules 1975 as amended in 1976.

Rate of Dividend	Percentage of profits* to be transferred to reserve
(i) More than 10% to 12.5%	2.5%
(ii) More than 12.5% to 15%	5%
(iii) More than 15% to 20%	7.5%
(iv) More than 20%	10%

Voluntary Transfer of a Higher Percentage

A company may transfer a percentage higher than 10% to it's reserves as per the following rules :

(i) Where a dividend is declared, a minimum distribution sufficient for the maintenance of dividend to shareholders at a rate equal to the average of rates at which dividends declared by it over the three years immediately preceding the financial year is ensured. However, where the net-profits after tax are lower by 20 percent or more than the average net profits after tax of the two financial years immediately preceding the current financial year, it shall not be necessary to ensure such minimum distribution.

(ii) Where bonus shares have been issued during the financial year then the average of last three years amount of dividend and not the rate shall be ensured.

(iii) Where no dividend is declared, the amount proposed to be transferred to it's reserves from the current profits shall be lower than the average amount of the dividends to it's shareholders declared by it over the three years immediately preceding the financial year.

However, these provisions do not apply to a newly incorporated company. Such a company is prohibited to transfer more than 10 percent of the profits to reserves for the initial three years.

Declaration of Dividend Out of Reserves

In the event of inadequate or no profits a company may declare dividend out of it's accumulated profits earned during the previous years and transferred to reserves. To maintain a stable rate of dividend during the lean years some companies maintain "dividend equalization reserve" by means of transfer from the profits when company earned sufficiently large amount. However, Secton 205 A (3) of The Companies (Declaration of Dividend out of Reserves) Rules 1975 states that a company can declare dividend out of reserves subject to following conditions

(i) The rate of dividend declared shall not exceed the average rate of dividend declared during the last five years immediately preceding that year or ten percent (10%) of it's paid up capital, whichever is less;

(ii) The total amount to be drawn from the accumulated profits earned in the previous years and transferred to reserves shall not exceed an amount equal to one-tenth (1/10th) of the sum of it's paid up capital and free reserves and the amount so drawn shall first be utilized to set-off the losses incurred in the financial year before any dividend in respect of preference or equity shares is declared.

(iii) That the balance of reserves after such withdrawal shall not fall below fifteen percent (15%) of it's paid up share capital.

Explanation : For the purpose of this rule, "Profits earned by a company in previous years and transferred to the reserves" means "total amount of net profits after tax," transferred to reserves" as at the beginning of the year for which dividend is to be declared and in computing the said amount the appropriation out of the amount transferred from Development Rebate Reserve at the expiry of the period specified under the Income Tax Act 1961, shall be included and all items of Capital Reserves (including revaluation reserves) shall be excluded.

Illustration (1)

From the following particulars of X Ltd. You are required to ascertain the amount that can be withdrawn for the purpose of declaring dividend out of reserves under the Rules 1975.

	Rs.
5,000 9% Preference Shares of Rs. 100 each fully paid	5,00,000
5,00,000 Equity Shares of Rs. 10 each Rs. 8 paid	40,00,000
Securities Premium	2,50,000
Revaluation Reserve (Revaluation of Building)	4,00,000
General Reserves	12,50,000
Profit and Loss Account (Cr.)	50,000
Net Profit for the Current year ending 31st March 2003	1,80,000

Equity Dividend paid by the company during the last five years is as under :

Year	Rate of Equity dividend
1997-98	12%
1998-99	15%
1999-00	13%
2000-01	17%
2001-02	18%

Solution :

Average rate of dividend for the last five years preceding the current year

$$= \frac{12 + 15 + 13 + 17 + 18}{5} = 15\%$$

* According to first condition either average rate or 10% whichever is less - shall be the rate of dividend to be declared, and secondly
* Maximum amount to be drawn should not exceed 1/10th of paid capital and free reserves. *i.e.* (Rs. 5,00,000 + 40,00,000 + 12,50,000) = 5,75,000 and,
* According to third condition that minimum balance to be left after such withdrawal should not be less than 15% of paid up capital.

  Therefore 15% of paid up capital = Rs. 45,00,000 = 6,75,000

  Thus maximum amount that can be withdrawn = Rs. 12,50,000 – 6,75,000 = 5,75,000

Since rate of dividend can not exceed 10% the total amount required is

	10% of Rs. 40,00,000 =		Rs. 4,00,000

Profits available

	Opening balance of P & L A/c	Rs. 50,000	
Add	Current year's profit	Rs. 1,80,000	
		Rs. 2,30,000	
Less	Preference Dividend @ 9% on Rs. 5,00,000	Rs. 45,000	Rs. 1,85,000
			Rs. 2,15,000

(Shortfall) Amount to be withdrawn from reserves to declare a dividend of 10%

Since Rs. 2,15,000 is less than the amount as per second and third condition, a dividend @ 10% can be declared.

Illustration (2)

A Ltd. closes it's books of accounts on 31st December each year. Due to loss suffered by the company during the year the Directors propose to declare dividend out of reserves. From the following particulars ascertain the amount that can be utilised out of reserves for the purpose of declaring dividend under Companies (Declaration of dividend out of Reserves) Rules 1975.

	Rs.
10% 1,50,000 Preference shares of Rs. 10 each fully paid	15,00,000
6,00,000 Shares (Equity) of Rs. 10 each fully paid	60,00,000
General Reserves	15,80,000
Loss for the year	(65,000)
Capital Reserves	5,25,000
Profit & Loss Appropriation Account (Op. Balance)	1,25,000

The dividend paid on equity and preference shares during the last years was as follows :

Years	Total Dividend paid (Rs.)
1998	8,10,000
1999	9,30,000
2,000	9,60,000
2001	10,80,000
2002	7,20,000

Solution :

Step : Calculation of average rate of equity dividend for the last five years

Year	Total Dividend (Rs.)	Preference Dividend (Rs.)	Equity Dividend (Rs.)
1998	8,10,000	1,50,000	6,60,000
1999	9,30,000	1,50,000	7,80,000
2000	9,60,000	1,50,000	8,10,000
2001	10,80,000	1,50,000	9,30,000
2002	7,20,000	1,50,000	5,70,000
Total Equity Dividend			37,50,000

Average Dividend= 37,50,000/5 = 7,50,000

Average rate = $\frac{7,50,000}{60,00,000} \times 100$ = 12.5%

But as per rules company cannot pay more than 10%

Step : 2 Determination of amount to be withdrawn from reserves. The amount that can be withdrawn being 1/10th of (paid up capital & free reserves) subject to the remaining balance of reserves to be 15% of paid up Capital 1/10 (75,00,000 + 15,80,000) = 9,08,000

Balance to remain to the credit of reserves being 15% of paid up Capital

$= \frac{75,00,000 \times 15}{100} = 11,25,000$

Hence amount available for withdrawal

Rs. 15,80,000 – 11,25,000 = 4,55,000

But the Current loss has to be adjusted before paying any dividend

Rs. 4,55,000 – 65,000 = 3,90,000

	Total Amount available for dividend	Rs. 3,90,000
Less	Preference dividend	1,50,000
	Amount available for equity dividend	2,40,000
	Rate of dividend to be declared (2,40,000/60,00,000 × 100)	= 4%

Hence Company can declare only 4% dividend

Exercise Due to inadequacy of the profits A Ltd. intends to declare dividend out of reserve. From the following particulars, you are required to work-out the amount that can be withdrawn from the reserves for the purpose of declaring dividend for the year ending 31st March, 2003

	Rs.
8% Preference Share Capital	2,00,000
Equity Share Capital	28,00,000
Revenue Reserves	7,00,000
Capital Reserve	1,25,000
Revaluation Reserve	3,75,000
Profit & Loss Account (1. 4. 2002)	25,000
Profit for the Current year	71,000
Average rate of dividend of the last five years	13%

Ans. : Dividend @ 10% can be declared on Equity Capital

Amount to be drawn from reserves to pay preference and equity dividend is Rs. 2,00,000.

PAYMENT OF INTEREST OUT OF CAPITAL (SECTION 208)

A company may pay interest out of capital under the following two circumstances.

(1) On Calls-in-Advance at the rate not exceeding 6% p.a

(2) On shares issued for raising money to defray expenses and on construction works, erection of building or installation of any plant which can be made profit able after a long gestation period. But the payment of such interest is subject to following conditions.

(i) The payment is authorised by Articles or by a special resolution.

(ii) Prior sanction of the Central Government is obtained.

(iii) The interest shall be paid only for such period as may be sanctioned by the Central Government and that period shall in no case extend beyond the close of the half year next, after the half year during which the construction has been actually completed or the plant provided.

(iv) The rate of interest shall in no case, exceed 4% per annum or such other rate as the Central Government may notify in the official Gazette.

The payment of such interest does not tantamount to reduction of share Capital. However, the Central Government can order an enquiry at the company's cost before according it's sanction the company can treat the interest so paid as part of the cost of construction.

Capital Profits

Profits arising from other than the normal business activity or profits which are not revenue profits are capital profits. These arise under special circumstances in connection with acquisition of fixed assets, purchase of business or discharge of long term liabilities. Following are the instances of capital profits.

(i) Profits prior to incorporation.

(ii) Securities Premium

(iii) Profit on reissue of forfeited shares

(iv) Profits on redemption of debentures

(v) Profit on sale of fixed assets

(vi) Capital Redemption Reserve (Created on redemption of Preference Shares)

(vii) Profits on acquisition of fixed assets or business as a whole.

(viii) The credit balance in the Capital Reduction Account, where there has been a reduction of capital with the consent of the court.

Generally the capital profits are not available for the purpose of distribution by way of dividend. These profits can be utilised for writing off capital losses including revaluation loss, preliminary expenses, discount on issue of shares and debentures, goodwill or may be utilised for the purpose of issuing bonus shares or providing premium on redemption of preference shares and debentures.

As stated earlier under certain circumstances, the capital profits may be utilised for paying dividend only if.

(i) It is authorised by Articles

(ii) such profits are realised in cash

(iii) balance remains after revaluation and

(iv) capital losses have been written off.

However, the following capital profits are never available for the purpose of distribution of dividends. These are

(i) Securities Premium

(ii) Profit on reissue of forfeited shares and

(iii) Capital Redemption Reserve

It is to be noted that once capital profits are transferred to capital reserves then such profits cease to be available for dividend.

Accounting Treatment of Dividend

Illustration (3)

X Ltd. has a paid up capital of Rs. 30,00,000 divided into 2,00,000 equity shares of Rs. 10 each and 10% 1,00,000 Preference shares of Rs. 10 each. Other particulars were as under :

	Rs.
Opening balance of Profit and Loss Appropriation Account	57,500
Net profit earned during the year (after Tax)	7,50,000
Dividend declared for the year	22%

Prepare Profit & Loss Appropriation Account. Comply with necessary statutory provisions.

Solution :

PROFIT AND LOSS APPROPRIATION ACCOUNT

	Rs.		Rs.
To General Reserve[(1)]	75,000	By Balance b/d	57,500
To Preference Dividend[(2)]	1,00,000	By Net Profit	7,50,000
To Equity Dividend	4,40,000		
To Corporate Dividend[(3)] Tax	75,735		
To Balance c/d	1,16,765		
	8,07,500		8,07,500

Working notes

(1) As per the provisions of the section 205 on a dividend of 22% a statutory transfer of 10% on the net profit is to be made.

(2) Declaration of equity dividend will automatically make the company liable to pay preference dividend. No equity dividend can be paid without paying preference dividend.

(3) A Corporate Dividend Tax (C.D.T.) @ 12.5% including a surcharge of 10% and 2% Education Cess. Thus the effective rate of C.D.T. is 14.025% including surcharge and education cess.

Illustration (4)

Victor Ltd. disclosed the following particulars.

	Rs.
9% 80,000 Preference Shares of Rs. 10 each fully paid	8,00,000
5,00,000 Equity shares of Rs. 10 each fully paid	5,00,000
3,00,000 Equity shares of Rs. 10 each Rs. 8 paid up	2,40,000
2,00,000 Equity shares of Rs. 10 each Rs. 6 paid up	1,20,000

The directors proposed a dividend of 15% on equity shares and resolve to make the following appropriations :

— Transfer to general reserve as per the provisions of the section 205
— Transfer to dividend equalisation fund Rs. 1,75,000
— Transfer to Debenture Redemption Fund Rs. 1,00,000
— Transfer to Investment Allowance Reserve Rs. 1,25,000

The net-profit (before tax) for the year amounted to Rs. 12,50,000. You are required to prepare Profit and Loss Appropriation Account. Provide for income tax @ 50% and Corporate Dividend Tax as applicable.

PROFIT AND LOSS APPROPRIATION ACCOUNT

	Rs.		Rs.
To General Reserve (1)	31,250	By Net Profit (after tax)	6,25,000
To Dividend Equalisation Fund	75,000		
To Debenture Redemption Fund	1,00,000		
To Investment Allowance Reserve	1,25,000		
To Proposed Dividend			
— Preference Dividend	72,000		
— Equity Dividend	1,29,000		
To Corporate Dividend Tax (2) on Rs. (72,000 + 1,29,000)	28,190		
To Balance c/d	64,560		
	6,25,000		6,25,000

Working notes :

(1) As per the statutory requirements, a transfer of 5% of the net profit after tax" has been made to General Reserve.

(2) Corporate dividend tax has been provided on the total dividend @ 14.025%

Illustration (4)

X Ltd. has issued 25,000 8% Cumulative Preference Shares of Rs. 100 each fully paid and 2,50,000 Equity shares of Rs. 10 each fully paid. The profit for the year 2002-03 amounted to Rs 13,75,000 before tax which was to be provided @ 40%. The Articles of Association provided that-

(i) An amount equal to 10% of equity dividend shall be set aside for bonus to staff.

(ii) 10% of the profits of each year shall be transferred to Reserve Fund

(iii) The balance so available shall be applied as follows-

(a) To pay dividend on Cumulative Preference Shares

(b) To pay 10% to equity shareholders

(c) One-third of the balance available as additional dividend on preference shares and two-thirds as additional equity dividend.

(d) That carry forward balance should not be less than 5% of equity share Capital plus Rs. 500.

(e) Ignore - Corporate Dividend Tax (CDT)

Prepare Profit & Loss Appropriation Account.

Solution (5)

Let the additional dividend to equity shareholders be x,

the preference share holders will get = $x / 2$

and Bonus to staff = $x / 10$

The minimum balance required to be carried forward is Rs. 1,25,500 *i.e.*

5% of (Rs. 25,00,000) + Rs. 500

			Rs.
	Profit before Tax		13,75,000
Less	Tax @ 40%		5,50,000
			8,25,000
	Transfer to Reserves @ 10%		82,500
			7,42,500
Less	Preference Dividend @ 8%	2,00,000	
	Equity Dividend @ 10%	2,50,000	4,50,000
			2,92,500
Less	Bonus to Staff 10% of Equity dividend		25,000
			2,67,500
Thus	and Less minimum balance required		1,25,500
	Amount available for additional Equity dividend, preference dividend and additional bonus to staff		1,42,000

$$x + \frac{x}{2} + \frac{x}{10} = 1,42,000$$

$$10x + 5x + x = 14,20,000$$

$$16x = 14,20,000$$

$$x = 88,750$$

Hence additional Equity dividend =	88,750
and additional Preference dividend =	44,375
and additional Bonus (10% of additional equity dividend	8,875
	1,42,000

PROFIT & LOSS APPROPRIATION ACCOUNT

	Rs.		Rs.
To General Reserve	82,500	By Net Profit (after tax)	8,25,000
To Provision for Bonus to staff (Rs. 25,000 + 8,875)	33,875		
To Preference Dividend (Rs. 2,00,000 + 44,375)	2,44,375		
To Equity Dividend (Rs. 2,50,000 + 88,750)	3,38,750		
To Balance c/d	1,25,500		
	8,25,000		8,25,000

CAPITALISATION OF PROFITS - "ISSUE OF BONUS SHARES"

As per section 205 (3) the company must pay dividend in cash, but some time shareholders are given a share in profits not as "dividend in cash" but in the form of shares. Such shares are known as bonus shares. Bonus shares simply means shares offered by a company to it's existing shareholders free of cost or without any charge as a gift on pro-rata basis. When a company has accumulated a large amount of accumulated profits the real capital employed in the business tends to be obscured. To bring the issued capital into a truer relationship with the capital actually employed in the business, the accumulations can be capitalised and used to pay up amount due on shares to be issued to members as bonus shares.

Bonus shares may also imply an extra-dividend to shareholders of a company. Bonus shares are issued by the company when it wants to pay extra-dividend by issuing shares without incurring any cash outflow or creating the problem of cash crunch. Bonus shares issue implies an increase in share capital and distribution of accumulated profits to the members without any release of company's assets. Thus the following points may be noted in connection with the bonus shares.

(i) Bonus shares are issued to the existing shareholders and not to the out siders out of accumulated profits.

(ii) Such profits are coverted into share capital which implies capitalisation of accumulated profits.

(iii) Shares are issued free of cost and no cash passes between the company and it's members.

Hence bonus shares are generally issued when the company's cash resources are inadequate or it intends to use it's cash resources for expansion, modernisation or diversification programme or repay a debt. A bonus issue can be made out of the following balances standing to the credit of-

(i) Profit and loss Account/Profit and Loss Appropriation Account

(ii) General reserves or other revenue reserves.

(iii) Sinking Fund/ Debenture Redemption Fund (after the redemption of debentures)

(iv) Capital Redemption Reserve* (created after the redemption of preference shares)

(v) Securities Premium*(if realised in cash)

However, it is to be noted that Capital Redemption Reserve and Securities Premium are used for the purpose of issuing "fully paid" bonus shares only. This cannot be utilised in making partly paid shares into fully paid up.

SEBI's Guidelines for Issuing Bonus Shares

(i) These guidelines are applicable only to listed public companies who shall forward a certificate duly signed by the issuing company and countersigned by the Auditor/Secretary stating that terms and conditions for issue of bonus shares as laid down in these guidelines have been complied with.

(ii) No bonus issue shall be made within twelve months of public/rights issue. Issue of bonus shares after any public/ rights issue is subject to condition that no bonus issue shall be made which will dilute the value or rights of the holders of debentures which are convertible either fully or partly.

(iii) The bonus issue is made out of free reserves built out of genuine profits or securities premium collected in cash only.

(iv) Reserves created by revaluation of fixed assets are not capitalised.

(v) The declaration of bonus issue, in lieu of dividend, is not made.

(vi) The bonus issue is not made unless partly paid shares if any, are made fully paid up.

(vii) The Company-

(a) has not defaulted in payment of interest or principal in respect of fixed deposits and interest on existing debentures or principal on redemption there of.

(b) has sufficient reason to believe that it has not defaulted in respect of payment of statutory dues of employees such as contribution to provident fund, gratuity, bonus etc.

(viii) A Company which announces the bonus issue after the approval of Board of Directors must implement the proposal within a period of six months from the date of such approval and shall not have the option of changing the decision.

(ix) There should be a provision in the Articles of Association of the company for capitalisation of reserves and if not, the company shall pass a resolution at its General Body Meeting making provisions in the articles for capitalisation of reserves etc.

(x) Consequent to issue of bonus shares, if the subscribed and paid up capital exceeds the authorised capital, a resolution shall be passed by the company at it's General Body Meeting for increasing the authorised share Capital.

Accounting Treatment

Capitalisation of profits may take either of the two forms

(a) by making the partly paid shares in to fully paid up. and

(b) by issuing fully paid bonus shares

The accounting treatment in each case is different

(a) *When partly paid shares are made fully paid up.*

JOURNAL ENTRIES

(i) *When bonus issue is sanctioned*

Profit & Loss A/c Dr.

General Reserve A/c Dr.

or Other Revenue Reserve A/c Dr.

To Bonus to Shareholders' A/c

(ii) *When bonus is adjusted against called up amount*

Share Final Call A/c Dr.

To Share Capital A/c

(iii) Bonus to Shareholders' A/c Dr.

To Share Final Call A/c

(b) *When fully paid bonus shares are issued*

First entry will be recorded as above and Second entry will be as follows :

Bonus to Shareholders' A/c Dr.

To Share Capital A/c

Illustration (6)

Following is the Balance Sheet of Y Ltd. as on 31st March, 2006

Liabilities	Rs.	Assets	Rs.
9% Preference Share Capital		Fixed Assets (Net)	6,50,000
15,000 Share of Rs. 10 each	1,50,000	Current Assets	4,20,000
Equity Share Capital			
50,000 Shares of Rs. 10 each			
Rs. 8 paid up	4,00,000		
Reserves & Surplus:			
General Reserve	75,000		
Capital Reserve	50,000		
Securities Premium	25,000		
Profit and Loss Account	1,20,000		
Secured Loan			
10% Debentures (Convertible)	2,50,000		
	10,70,000		10,70,000

On 1.4.2006 the company resolved

(i) that the profit be used in making the partly paid up shares fully paid.

(ii) to issue fully paid bonus shares in the ratio of 1: 5 by capitalising reserves.

Securities Premium includes a premium of Rs. 5,000 for shares issued to Z Ltd. in pursuant of an amalgamation scheme. Capital Reserve includes Rs. 20,000 being profit on sale of plant.

Record journal entries and prepare a Balance Sheet immediately after bonus issue.

JOURNAL ENTRIES

			Rs.	Rs.
	Equity Share Final Call A/c	Dr.	1,00,000	
	To Equity Share Capital A/c			1,00,000
	(Being final call of Rs. 2 per share due as per Board's resolution —dated)			
	Profit & Loss A/c	Dr.	1,00,000	
	To Bonus to Equity Shareholders' A/c			1,00,000
	(Being bonus amount set aside)			
	Bonus to Equity Shareholders' A/c	Dr.	1,00,000	
	To Equity Share Final Call A/c			1,00,000
	(Being bonus amount adjusted against the final call amount due)			
	Capital Reserve A/c	Dr.	20,000	
	Securities Premium A/c	Dr.	20,000	
	General Reserve A/c	Dr.	60,000	
	To Bonus to Equity Shareholders' A/c			1,00,000
	(Being bonus issue in the ratio of 1 : 5 made)			
	Bonus to Equity Shareholders' A/c	Dr.	1,00,000	
	To Equity Share Capital A/c			1,00,000
	(Being profits capitalised)			

BALANCE SHEET OF Y LTD.
As on 1st April, 2003 (after bonus issue)

	Rs.		Rs.
9% Preference Share Capital		Fixed Assets	6,50,000
15,000 Shares of Rs. 10 each	1,50,000	Current Assets	4,20,000
Equity Share Capital			
60,000 Shares of Rs. 10 each	6,00,000		
Reserves & Surplus			
Capital Reserve	30,000		
Securities Premium	5,000		
General Reserve	15,000		
Profit & Loss Account	20,000		
Secured Loan			
10% Convertible Debentures	2,50,000		
	10,70,000		10,70,000

Working Notes :

(i) As per SEBI's guidelines securities premium collected in cash can only be utilised for the purpose of issuing bonus shares.

(ii) Similarly Capital profits realised in cash can be used for issuing bonus shares.

(iii) Bonus shares are issued to Equity shareholders only.

Exercise : 1

Following is the extract of a Balance Sheet of Z Ltd. as on 31st March, 2003.

11% Preference Shares of Capital	5,00,000
50,000 Equity shares of Rs. 10 each fully paid up	6,00,000
40,000 Equity shares of Rs. 10 each 60% paid up	2,40,000
Securities Premium	3,75,000
10% Debentures	10,00,000

Profit before interest on debentures and tax @ 40% is Rs. 7,50,000 for the year ended 31st March 2006.

The Directors profits for making partly shares fully paid up.

Pass journal entries and prepare Profit and Loss Appropriation Account and show how those items would appear in the Balance Sheet. The rate of Corporate Dividend tax is 12.5%.

Ans. : Total Equity Capital Rs. 10,00,000; Total Dividend Rs. 1,81,000 Corporate Dividend Tax Rs. 25,385.

Balance of P & L App. A/c Rs. 4,115.

Exercise : 2

Due to inadequacy of profit during the year, the Company proposes to declare dividend out of general reserves. From the following particulars, you are required to ascertain the amount that can be withdrawn under the Companies (Declaration of Dividend out of Reserves) Rules 1975.

8% 9000 Preference Share Capital (Shares of Rs. 100 each)	9,00,000
35,000 Equity shares of Rs. 100 each	35,00,000
General Reserve	7,50,000
Securities Premium	1,50,000
Capital Reserve	1,75,000
Profit & Loss App. A/c 1.4.2003	50,000
Net Profit for the year	1,80,000

Ans. : Rs. 90,000

GRADED ILLUSTRATIONS

Illustration (1) (General)

The following balance have been extracted from the books of Exe Ltd. for the year ended 31st March, 2006.

(Rs. in '000')

Particulars	Dr. Rs.	Cr. Rs.
Share Capital (Rs. 10)		4,000
12% Debentures		3,000
Profit & Loss Account		262
Land & Building	3,072	
Plant & Machinery	3,300	
Stock	750	
Bills Payable		370
Creditors		400
Debtors	880	
Goodwill	240	
Cash and Bank	406	
Calls in Arrears	75	
Sales		4,150
General Reserve		250
Provision for Bad Debt (1. 4. 2005)		35
Interim Dividend paid including corporate dividend tax	393	
Purchases	1,850	
Preliminary Expenses	50	
Wages	980	
General Expenses	68	
Salaries	202	
Bad debts	21	
Interest on Debentures	180	
	12,467	12,467

Additional Information:

(a) Stock on 31st March, 2006 was Rs. 9,50,000

(b) Write off Rs. 5,000 from Preliminary Expenses.

(c) Half year's debenture interest is due

(d) A claim of Rs. 25,000 for workmen's compensation is being disputed by the company.

(e) Create 5% provision for doubtful debts.

(f) Depreciate Plant & Machinery by 15%

(g) Provide for provision for taxation @ 40%

Prepare Final Accounts of the Exe Ltd.

[B. Com. (H) DU 1993 Modified]

Solution :

EXE LTD.

Profit and Loss Account for the year ended 31st March, 2006.

		(Rs. in '000')		(Rs. in '000')
To Opening Stock		750	By Sales	4,150
To Purchases		1,850	By Closing Stock	950
To Wages		980		
To Gross Profit c/d		1,520		
		5,100		5,100
To Salaries		202	By Gross Profit b/d	1,520
To Debenture Interest	180			
Add Outstanding	180	360		
To General Expenses		68		
To Preliminary Expenses		05		
To Bad debts		21		
To Provision for Doubtful debts*		09		
To Depreciation on Plant		495		
To Provision for Taxation		144		
To Net Profit c/d		216		
		1,520		1,520
To Interim Dividend including Corporate Dividend Tax		393	By Balance b/d	262
			By Net Profit b/d	216
To Balance c/d		85		
		478		478

(*5% of Debtors Less Provision as on 1. 4. 2005)

BALANCE SHEET AS ON 31ST MARCH, 2006

Liabilities		(Rs. '000')	Assets		(Rs. '000')
Share Capital :			**Fixed Assets :**		
Authorised			Goodwill		240.00
-----		-------	Land & Building		3,072.00
Issued & Subscribed :			Plant & Machinery	3,300	
Share of Rs. 10 each	4,000		*Less* Dep.	495	2,805.00
Less Calls in Arrears	75	3,925.00	Investments		Nil
Reserve & Surplus:			**Current Assets Loans & Advances**		
General Reserve		250.00			
Profit & Loss Account		85.00	*(A) Current Assets:*		
Secured Loans :			Stock		950.00
12% Debentures		3,000.00	Debtors	880	
Accrued Interest		180.00	*Less* Provision	44	836.00

Unsecured Loans	Nil	Cash & Bank	406.00
Current Liabilities &		(B) Loans and Advances	Nil
Provisions:		**Miscellaneous Expenditure**	
(A) Current Liabilities :		Preliminary Expenses	45.00
Creditors	400.00		
Bills Payable	370.00		
(B) *Provisions :*			
Provision for Taxation	144.00		
Corporate Dividend Tax	Nil		
	8,354.00		8,354.00

Note: There is a contingent liability for workmen's Compensation to the extent of Rs. 2,500.

Illustration (2) (Provision for Managerial Remuneration)

The following is the Trial Balance of Zen Ltd. as on 31st March 2006.

	Rs.		Rs.
Stock (1. 4. 05)	75,000	Sales	3,40,000
Purchases	2,45,000	Purchases Returns	10,000
Wages	30,000	Discount	3,000
Debtors	37,500	Creditors	17,500
Carriage Inward	900	Profit & Loss App. A/c	15,000
Furniture	17,000	(1. 4. 2005)	
Salaries	7,500	Share Capital	1,00,000
Rent	4,000	General Reserve	15,500
General Expenses	7,100	Bills Payable	7,000
Dividend paid (2004-05) including CTD	9,000		
Computers	29,000		
Cash at Bank	36,200		
Patents	4,800		
Bills Receivable	5,000		
	5,08,000		5,08,000

Prepare Trading and Profit & Loss Account and Profit & Loss Appropriation Account for the year ended 31st March, 2006 and a Balance Sheet as on that date after taking into account the following adjustments :

(i) Stock on 31st March, 2006 was valued at Rs. 88,000.

(ii) Depreciate Computer @ 15% Furniture @ 10% and Patents @ 5%.

(iii) Make a provision for doubtful debts amounting to Rs. 210.

(iv) On 31st March, 2006, the Salaries and Rents were outstanding to the extent of Rs. 1,000 each.

(v) Make a provision for taxation @ 40%

(vi) The Directors proposed a dividend @ 15% per annum for the year ended 31st March 2006 after the minimum transfer to General Reserve.

(vii) Provide for managerial remuneration at 10% of net profits before tax.

[B. Com (H) DU 1990. Modified]

Solution :

ZEN LTD.
Profit & Loss Account for the year ended 31st March, 2006

		Rs.		Rs.
To Opening Stock		75,000	By Sales	3,40,000
To Purchases	2,45,000		By Closing Stock	88,000
Less Return	10,000	2,35,000		
To Wages		30,000		
To Carriage Inward		900		
To Gross Profit C/d		87,100		
		4,28,000		4,28,000
To Salaries	7,500		By Gross Profit b/d	87,100
Add Outstanding	1,000	8,500	By Discount	3,000
To Rent	4,000			
Add outstanding	1,000	5,000		
To General Expenses		7,100		
To Provision for Doubtful debts		210		
To Depreciation on:				
Computer		4,350		
Furniture		1,700		
Patents		240		
To Managerial Remuneration*		6,300		
To Provision for Taxation		22,680		
To Net Profit c/d		34,020		
		90,100		90,100
To Dividend (2004-05)		9,000	By Balance b/d	15,000
To General Reserve (5% of Rs. 34,020)		1,701	By Net Profit b/d	34,020
To Proposed Dividend		15,000		
To Corporate Dividend Tax [(1)]		2,366		
To Balance c/d		20,953		
		49,020		49,020

(*10% of Rs. 63,000 being profit before tax)

BALANCE SHEET OF ZEN LTD.

As on 31st March, 2006

Liabilities	Rs.	Assets		Rs.
Share Capital:		**Fixed Assets:**		
Authorised Capital		Computers	29,000	
--- Shares of Rs.--	—	*Less* Depreciation	4,350	24,650
Issued & Subscribed Capital		Furniture	17,000	
Shares of Rs. 10 each	1,00,000	*Less* Depreciation	1,700	15,300
Reserve & Surplus		Patents	4,800	
General Reserve	17,201	*Less* Depreciation	240	4,560
Profit & Loss A/c	20,953	Investments		Nil
Secured Loans	Nil	**Current Assets Loans &**		
Unsecured Loans	Nil	**Advances:**		
Current Liabilities Provisions		**Current Assets**		
(A) *Current Liabilities:*		Stock		88,000
Trade Creditors	17,500	Debtors	37,500	
Bills Payable	7,000	*Less* Provision	210	37,290
Managerial Remuneration	6,300	Cash at Bank		36,200
Outstanding Expenses	2,000	**Loans & Advances**		
(Salaries & Rent)		Bills Receivable		5,000
(B) *Provisions:*				
Provision for Taxation	22,680			
Corporate Dividend Tax	2,366			
Proposed Dividend	15,000			
	2,11,000			2,11,000

(1) Corporate Dividend Tax has been calculated as under :

Tax rate	12.50	
Surcharge 10%	1.25	
	13.75	= 14.025%
Education cess 2%	0.275	

Illustration (3) (Corporate dividend Tax and Provision)

From the following particulars relating to PQR Ltd. prepare Balance Sheet as on 31st March, 2006.

Rs. in "000"

		Dr.	Cr.
Equity Share Capital			
Shares of 10 each fully paid up			4,000
Calls in Arrears		4	
Land & Building		2,200	
Plant & Machinery		2,100	
Furniture		200	
General Reserve			840
Loan from ICICI			600
Stock :			
Finished Goods	800		
Raw-materials	200	1,000	
Provision for Taxation			248
Sundry Debtors		800	
Advances		172	
Proposed Dividend			240
Provision for Corporate Dividend Tax			24
Profit & Loss Account			400
Cash and Bank Balance		1,108	
Preliminary Expenses		52	
Loans (unsecured)			484
Sundry Creditors			800
		7,636	7,636

Additional Information:

(i) 8,000 Equity shares were issued for consideration other than cash.

(ii) The Cost of Fixed assets are :

Land & Building	Rs. 25,00,000
Plant & Machinery	Rs. 28,00,000
Furniture	Rs. 2,50,000

(iii) Debtors of Rs. 2,00,000 are due for more than six months.

(iv) The balance of Loan from ICICI is inclusive of Rs. 30,000 for interest accrued but not due. The loan is secured by hypothecation of Plant and Machinery.

(v) Cash & Balance at Bank includes Rs. 10,000 with Zed Bank Ltd. which is not a scheduled Bank and Rs. 8,000 cash in hand.

(vi) Bills Receivable for Rs. 2,50,000 maturing on 30th September 2006 have been discounted

(vii) The Company had contract for the erection of machinery at Rs. 5,00,000 which is still incomplete.

[C.A. (I) May 89 Adapted]

BALANCE SHEET OF PQR LTD.
As on 31st March, 2006

Liabilities		Rs. in "000"	Assets		Rs. in "000"
Share Capital			**Fixed Assets**		
Authorised			Land & Building at cost	2,500	
--- shares of Rs. 10 each		---	*Less* Dep. Acc.	300	2,200
Issued & Subscribed			Plant & Machinery at cost	2,800	
4,00,000 shares of Rs. 10			*Less* Acc. Dep.	700	2,100
each fully paid		4,000	Furniture	250	
(of the above 8,000 shares are			*Less* Acc. Dep.	50	200
allotted as fully paid under a			**Current Assets Loans**		
contract at cost without payment			**and Advances**		
received in cash)			(A) *Current Assets*:		
Less Calls in Arrears		4	Stock: (FG)	800	
		3,996	(RM)	200	1,000
Reserves & Surplus			**Sundry Debtors**		
General Reserve		840	(a) Debts Outstanding		
Profit & Loss A/c		400	for more than 6 months	200	
Secured Loans			(b) Other debts	600	800
Loan from ICICI	570		Bank balance		
Add Interest Accrued but not due	30	600	(a) With Scheduled Bank	1,090	
(Secured by hypothecation			(b) With other Bank	10	1,100
of Plant & Machinery)			Cash in hand		8
Unsecured Loans		484	**(B) Loans & Advances :**		
Current liabilities and Provisions			Advances		172
(A) *Current liabilities :*			Miscellaneous Expenses		
Sundry Creditors		800	Preliminary Expenses		52
(B) *Provisions :*					
Provision for Tax		248			
Provision for Corporate Dividend Tax		24			
Proposed Dividend		240			
		7,632			7,632

Note :

Provision for corporate Dividend Tax must be made at the rate of 14.025%. Since it is given in the question, no change has been made. Otherwise the liability for corporate dividend tax will be 2,40,000 14.025% Rs. 33,660 and balance of Profit and Loss Account will be reduced by additional tax liability of Rs. 9,660.

Illustration (4) (Share forfeiture and Share Suspense Account)

The following balances have been extracted from the books of SJ Ltd. for the year ended 31st March, 2006.

	Rs.
Authorised & Issued Capital	8,00,000
(Shares of Rs. 10 each)	
Properties at cost	16,00,000
Motor Van	50,000
Provision for Depreciation (1.4.2005)	
On Properties (Leasehold)	42,000
On Properties (Freehold)	1,00,000
On Motor Van	20,000
Administration & Selling Expenses	3,53,000
Opening Stock	2,40,000
Purchases	27,75,000
Sales	41,30,000
Directors Remuneration	1,00,000
Rent Received	72,000
Investments at cost	1,35,000
Investment Income (Gross)	9,400
7% Debentures	3,00,000
Debenture Interest	21,000
Bank Interest	11,800
Bank Overdraft	14,600
Debtors	6,20,000
Creditors	3,02,000
Interim Dividend	1,50,000
Profit & Loss A/c (1.4.2005)	2,28,800
Calls in Arrears	2,000
General Reserves (1.4.2005)	2,40,000
Share Suspense A/c (Cr.)	6,000
Unclaimed dividend	3,000
Cash in hand	30,000
Cash at Bank	1,80,000

Additional Information :

(i) Closing stock at cost was Rs. 3,34,000

(ii) No effect has been given to the following : Forfeiture of 1,000 shares for non-payment of call of Rs. 2,000 which were reissued for Rs. 6,000. This amount is lying in the Share Suspense A/c.

(iii) The Directors have recommended the following appropriations.

(a) Final dividend @ Rs. 5 per share including interim dividend.

(b) Transfer to General Reserve as per the provisions of Companies Act.

(iv) Depreciation to be provided on :

Motor Van 20% (on W.D.V.)

Freehold property 3% (on W.D.V.)

Lease-hold Property at cost of Rs. 2,80,000 on 1.4.1999 for a period of 40 years.

(v) Directors are entitled to a remuneration of 10% of Net-profit subject to a minimum of Rs. 1,00,000.

(vi) Provide for income tax @ 40%

(vii) Of the book debts Rs. 1,20,000 are outstanding for more than 6 months.

Prepare Trading and Profit & Loss Account for the year ended 31st March, 2006 and a Balance Sheet as on 31st March, 2006

[C.A. (I) Adapted]

S J LTD.

TRADING & PROFIT AND LOSS ACCOUNT
for the year ended 31st March, 2006

	Rs.		Rs.
To Opening Stock	2,40,000	By Sales	41,30,000
To Purchases	27,75,000	By Closing Stock	3,34,000
To Gross Profit c/d	14,49,000		
	44,64,000		44,64,000
To Administrative and Selling Expenses	3,53,000	By Gross Profit b/d	14,49,000
To Debenture Interest	21,000	By Rent Received	72,000
To Bank Interest	11,800	By Income from Investment	9,400
To Depreciation on:			
Motor Van	6,000		
Leasehold Properties	7,000		
Free hold Properties	36,600		
To Remuneration	1,09,500		
To Provision for Taxation	3,94,200		
To Net Profit c/d	5,91,300		
	15,30,400		15,30,400
To Interim Dividend	1,50,000	By Gross Profit b/d	5,91,300
To Proposed Dividend	2,50,000	By Balance b/d	2,28,800
To General Reserve	59,130		
To Corporate Dividend* Tax	56,100		
To Balance c/d	3,04,870		
	8,20,100		8,20,100

		%
	*Corporate Dividend Tax	12.5
Add	Surcharge @ 10%	1.25
		13.75
Add	2% Education Less	0,275
		14.025

BALANCE SHEET OF SJ LTD.
As on 31st March, 2006

Liabilities		Rs.	Assets		Rs.
Share Capital:			**Fixed Assets:**		
Authorised Issued & Subscribed Capital			Freehold Properties		
Shares of Rs. 10 each		8,00,000	at cost	13,20,000	
Reserve & Surplus:			*Less* Acc. Dep.	1,36,600	11,83,400
Capital Reserve		4,000	Leasehold Properties		
General Reserve	2,40,000		at cost	2,80,000	
Add Transfer	59,130	2,99,130	*Less* Acc. Dep.	49,000	2,31,000
Profit & Loss A/c		3,04,870	Motor Van at cost	50,000	
Secured Loans :			*Less* Acc. Dep.	26,000	24,000
7% Debentures		3,00,000	Investments at cost		1,35,000
Unsecured Loans:			(Market Value Rs. 1,40,800)		
Bank overdraft		14,600	**Current Assets Loans & Advances**		
Current Liabilities & Provisions:					
(A) *Current liabilities*			(A) *Current Assets*		
Sundry Creditors*		3,11,500	Stock at cost		3,34,000
Unclaimed dividend		3,000	Debtors :		
(b) Provisions:			Due for more than 6 months		1,20,000
Proposed dividend		2,50,000	Other Debts		5,00,000
Provision for Taxation		3,94,200	Cash at Bank		1,80,000
Corporate dividend Tax		56,100	Cash in hand		30,000
		27,37,400			27,37,400

*Sundry creditors include Rs. 9,500 being Directors remuneration due but not paid.

Working notes :

(1) Depreciation has been calculated as under :

	Total properties at cost	16,00,000
Less	Lease hold at cost	2,80,000
	Freehold at cost	13,20,000

(*) Depreciation on Leasehold :

Cost of Leasehold on 1.4.1999	2,80,000
Depreciation already charged	42,000
Written down value	2,38,000

	Balance b/d	2,38,000
	Depreciation for the Current year	7,000
	@ 2% (100 / 40 yrs.)	2,31,000

(*) Depreciation on Freehold Properties :

	Free hold at cost	13,20,000
Less	Accumulated Depreciation	1,00,000
	Written down value	12,20,000
Less	Depreciation @ 3%	36,600
		11,83,400

(*) Depreciation on Motor Van :

	Motor Van at Cost	50,000
Less	Accumulated Depreciation	20,000
	Written down value	30,000
Less	Depreciation @ 20%	6,000
		24,000

(2)	Director's remuneration	
	Net profit before Tax & Remuneration	10,95,000
	Remuneration @ 10%	1,09,500
Less	Remuneration already paid	1,00,000
	Due but not paid	9,500
(3)	Capital Reserve: Calls in Arrears	2,000
	Amount Received on Reissue	6,000
	Profit on reissue transferred to Capital Reserve.	4,000

Illustration (5) (Prior period items)

Following balances have been extracted from the books of Vyoma Ltd. as on 31st March, 2006.

Particulars	Rs.
Share Capital : Shares of Rs. 10 each	12,00,000
Rent	15,900
Prepaid expenses	13,800
Advances from Customers	1,50,000
Cash in hand	18,600
Repairs and Maintenance	25,800
General Reserve	5,00,000
Capital Redemption Reserve	4,00,000
Raw materials at cost	8,01,000
Plant and Machinery	12,90,000
Sundry Creditors	10,20,000
Investments at cost (31. 3. 2006)	90,000

Raw-materials consumed	85,80,000
Sales	1,26,90,000
Development Rebate Reserve	3,00,000
Building	2,22,300
Salaries and Wages	34,80,000
Cash Credit from Bank	37,500
Power	26,500
Miscellaneous Expenses	12,300
Printing and Stationery	4,500
Cash at Bank	24,000
Provision for Taxation	6,30,000
Staff Advances	15,900
Miscellaneous Income	1,63,800
Furniture	36,600
Debtors	4,20,000
Finished Stock	9,30,000
Advance Income Tax	9,00,000
Other Administrative, Selling and Distribution Overheads	1,50,000
Preliminary Expenses w/o	19,200
Auditors Fees	15,000

Additional Information :

(i) The Authorised Capital of the Company is Rs. 24,00,000 divided in shares of Rs. 10 each. Half of which has been issued, subscribed fully and paid in full.

(ii) A dividend of 30% has been recommended by the Board.

(iii) The closing stock of finished goods was valued at Rs. 16,80,000.

(iv) The development rebate reserve is no longer required.

(v) Depreciation on Plant & Machinery of Rs. 1,29,000 is included in Administrative, Selling and Distribution overheads, where as depreciation on Furniture amounting to Rs. 3,900 and on Building 11,400 has been debited to Preliminary Expenses Account.

(vi) Surplus in Profit and Loss Account, if any, is to be transferred to General Reserve.

(vii) Income tax assessment for the last year has been completed with a net tax liability of Rs. 4,65,000 against which a provision of Rs. 2,40,000 and advance of income tax of Rs. 2,10,000 exists in the books.

(viii) Provide for income Tax @ 50% and Corporate Dividend Tax as applicable.

Prepare Final Accounts .

[C.S. (I) June 1993 Adapted]

Solution :

VYOMA LTD.
PROFIT AND LOSS ACCOUNT
For the year ended 31st March, 2006

	Rs.		Rs.
To Opening Stock	9,30,000	By Sales	1,26,90,000
To Raw materials consumed	85,80,000	By Closing Stock	16,80,000
To Power consumed	26,400	(Finished Goods)	
To Salaries & wages	34,80,000	By Miscellaneous Income	1,63,800
To Rent	15,900		
To Repairs & Maintenance	25,800		
To Auditors Fees	15,000		
To Other Administrative, Selling & Distribution O/H	21,000		
To Depreciation on :			
Plant & Machinery	1,29,000		
Furniture	3,900		
Building	11,400		
To Preliminary Expenses w/o	3,900		
To Miscellaneous Expenses	12,300		
To Printing & Stationery	4,500		
To Provision for Taxation	6,37,350		
To Net Profit c/d	6,37,350		
	1,45,33,800		1,45,33,800
To Provision for Taxation (for last year)	2,25,000	By Net Profit b/d	6,37,350
To General Reserve (Statutory Transfer)	63,735	By Development Rebate Reserve (Not required)	3,00,000
To Proposed Dividend	3,60,000		
To Corporate Dividend Tax	50,490		
To General Reserve (Residual transfer as required)	2,38,125		
	9,37,350		9,37,350

BALANCE SHEET OF VYOMA LTD.

As on 31st March, 2006

Liabilities	Rs.	Assets		Rs.
Share Capital :		**Fixed Assets :**		
Authorised		Building	2,33,700	
2,40,000 shares of Rs. 10 each	24,00,000	*Less* Dep.	11,400	2,22,300
Issued & Subscribed:		Plant & Machinery	14,19,000	
1,20,000 Shares of Rs. 10 each fully paid up	12,00,000	*Less* Dep.	1,29,000	12,90,000
		Furniture	40,500	
Reserves & Surplus		*Less* Dep.	3,900	36,600
General Reserve	8,01,860	**Investments**		90,000
(5,00,000 + 63,735 + 2,38,125)		**Current Assets**		
Capital Reserve	4,00,000	**Loans & Advances:**		
Development Rebate Reserve	Nil	(A) Current Assets:		
Secured Loans		Raw materials		8,01,000
Cash Credit from Bank	37,500	Finished Goods		16,80,000
Unsecured Loans	Nil	Sundry Debtors		4,20,000
Current liabilities & Provisions:		Cash at Bank		24,000
		Cash in hand		18,600
(A) Current liabilities		(B) Loans & Advances:		
Sundry Creditors	10,20,000	Staff Advances		15,900
Income Tax Payable	2,55,000	Prepaid Expenses		13,800
Advance from Customers	1,50,000	Advance Income Tax		6,90,000
(B) Provisions:				
Provision for Taxation	10,27,350			
Proposed Dividend	3,60,000			
Corporate Dividend Tax	50,490			
	53,02,200			53,02,200

Working notes:

(i) A statutory transfer of 10% of Net profit after tax has been made to General Reserve which is in accordance with the provisions of Companies Act.

(ii) The residual transfer (balance left in the Profit & Loss Account) has been made as per the instruction in the question.

(iii) Development Rebate Reserve (no longer required) has been credited to Profit & Loss Appropriation Account as it represents profit of last years.

(iv) Provision for Taxation has been worked out as under :

		Rs.
	* Provision as per Trial Balance	6,30,000
Less	Last year's provision	2,40,000
		3,90,000
Add	Current year's provision (as per P & L A/c)	6,37,350
	Total provision taken to Balance Sheet	10,27,350

***Adjustment for last year's Provision**

		Rs.
	Provision of tax for the last year	2,40,000
Less	Actual Tax liability	4,65,000
	Short fall charged to P & L App. A/c (out of last year's balance)	2,25,000

*** Income Tax Payable (for the last year)**

		Rs.
	Actual Tax liability	4,65,000
Less	Advance tax paid (last for year)	2,10,000
	Tax payable	2,55,000

		Rs.
	*** Advance Tax as per Trial Balance**	9,00,000
Less	Last year's advance tax	2,10,000
		6,90,000

Illustration (6) (Bills discounted and dishonoured)

The authorised capital of Exe Ltd. is Rs. 5,00,000 consisting of 6% 2,000 Preference shares of Rs. 100 each ad 30,000 Equity shares of Rs. 10 each. The following was the Trial Balance of Exe Ltd. as on 31st March, 2006.

	Rs.		Rs.
Investments at cost	50,000	Creditors	87,850
Purchases	4,90,500	6% Preference Capital	2,00,000
Selling Expenses	79,100	Equity Capital	2,00,000
Stock (1.4.2005)	1,45,200	5% Mortgaged Debentures	1,50,000
Salaries & Wages	52,000	(secured on property)	
Cash in Hand	12,000	Dividends	4,250
Interim Preference Dividend	6,000	Profit & Loss A/c (1. 4. 2005)	28,500
(for 6 months)		Sales (Net)	6,70,350
Discount on Debentures	2,000	Bank overdraft	1,50,000
Preliminary Expenses	1,000	(Secured by hypothecation of	
Bills Receivable	41,500	Stock and Debtors)	
Interest on Overdraft	7,800		
Interest on Debentures (upto 30.9.2005)	3,750		
Debtors	50,100		
Freehold Property at cost	3,50,000		
Furniture at cost	35,000		
(Less depreciation 15,000)			*Contd.*

	Rs.		Rs.
Income Tax paid in Advance (for 2005-06)	10,000		
Technical Know-how fees paid during the year	1,50,000		
Audit Fees	5,000		
	14,90,950		14,90,950

You are required to prepare the Profit & Loss Account for the year ended 31st March, 2006 and the Balance Sheet as on that date after taking into account the following :

(a) Closing stock was valued at Rs. 1,42,500

(b) Purchases include Rs. 5,000 worth of goods and articles distributed as samples.

(c) Salaries and wages include Rs. 2,000 being wages incurred on installation of electrical fittings which were recorded under "Furniture".

(d) Bills Receivable include Rs. 1,500 being dishonoured bills, 50% of which had been considered irrecoverable.

(e) Bills Receivable of Rs. 2,000 maturing after 31st March 2006 was discounted.

(f) Rs. 1,000 of Discount on issue of debentures to be written off.

(g) Interest on Debentures for the half year ending on 31st March 2006 was due on that date.

(h) Depreciation on furniture to be charged at 10% on written down value.

(i) Technical know-how fees is to be written off over a period of 10 years. Half of the preliminary expenses to be written off.

(j) Salaries and wages include Rs. 10,000 being the Director's remuneration.

(k) Sundry Debtors include Rs. 6,000 which are due for more than 6 months.

(l) An amount of Rs. 3,050 will be sufficient for provision of taxation to meet the tax liability.

[C A (I) May 1992 Modified']

Solution:

EXE LTD.
PROFIT & LOSS ACCOUNT
For the year ended 31st March, 2006

		Rs.		Rs.
To Opening Stock		1,45,200	By Sales	6 ,70,350
To Purchases		4,85,500	By Closing Stock	1,42,500
(*Less* Value of goods* given as samples)			By Dividends	4,250
To Salaries & Wages	52,000			
Less Director's Remuneration	10,000			
	42,000			
Less Installation wages to be capitalised	2,000	40,000		

Contd.

		Rs.		Rs.
To Director's Remuneration		10,000		
To Discount on issue of debentures		1,000		
To Interest on Overdraft		7,800		
To Selling Expenses		79,100		
To Interest on Debentures	3,750			
Add outstanding	3,750	7,500		
To Audit Fees		5,000		
To Bad debts		750		
To Advertisement*		5,000		
T o Preliminary Expenses w/o		500		
To Technical know-how w/o		15,000		
To Depreciation on:				
Furniture		3,700[(2)]		
To Provision for Taxation		3,050		
To Net Profit c/d		8,000		
		8,17,100		8,17,100
To Interim Dividend (Pref.)		6,000	By Balance b/d	28,500
To Corporate Dividend Tax		842[(1)]	By Net Profit b/d	8,000
To Balance c/d		29,658		
		36,500		36,500

BALANCE SHEET OF EXE LTD.
As on 31st March, 2006

Liabilities	Rs.	Assets		Rs.
Share Capital :		**Fixed Assets :**		
Authorised		Freehold Property at cost		3,50,000
6% 2,000 Preference	2,00,000	Furniture at cost	52,000	
Shares of Rs. 100 each		*Less* Acc. Dep.	18,700	33,300
30,000 Equity Shares of Rs. 10 each	3,00,000	Technical know-how		1,35,000
Issued & Subscribed Capital		Investments at cost		50,000
6% 2,000 Preference Shares of Rs. 10		**Current Assets, Loans & Advances:**		
each fully paid	2,00,000	*(A) Current Assets:*		
20,000 Equity Shares of Rs. 10		Stock-in-Trade		1,42,500
each fully paid	2,00,000	Sundry Debtors		
Reserves & Surplus :		(a) Debts outstanding for more		6,000
Profit & Loss Account	29,658	than 6 months		
Secured Loans :		(b) Other Debts		44,850[(3)]
5% Mortgaged Debentures	1,50,000	Cash in hand		12,000
(Secured on Freehold property)				

Contd.

Liabilities	Rs.	Assets	Rs.
		Loans & Advances :	
Interest Outstanding	3,750	Bills Receivable	40,000[(4)]
Bank Overdraft	1,50,000	Advance Tax	10,000
(Secured by hypothecation of stock and Debtors)		**Miscellaneous Expenses**	
		Preliminary Expenses	500
Unsecured Loans	Nil	Discount on Issue of Debentures	1,000
Current Liabilities and Provisions :			
(A) Current Liabilities			
Sundry Creditors	87,850		
(B) Provisions:			
Provision for Taxation	3,050		
Corporate dividend Tax	842		
	8,25,150		8,25,150

Note : There is a contingent liability for bills discounted for Rs. 2,000.

Working Notes :

(1) Since preference (interim) dividend has been paid, the corporate dividend tax at the rate of 14.025 has been provided in the books. The rate has been work-out as under :

	%
Corporate dividend Tax	12.50
Surcharge @ 10%	1.25
	13.75
Education cess @ 2% thereon	0.275
Effective rate	14.025

(2) Depreciation on Furniture :

	Furniture	Cost Rs.	Acc. Dep. Rs.	W.D.V. Rs.
	As per Trial Balance	50,000	15,000	35,000
Add	Installation charges Capitalised	2,000	—	2,000
		52,000		37,000
	10% Depreciation on W.D.V.	—	3,700	3,700
		52,000	18,700	33,300

(3)

		Rs.
(3)	Sundry Debtors as per Trial Balance	50,100
Less	Debts due for more than 6 months	6,000
		44,100
Add	Bills Dishonoured	1,500
		45,600
Less	Provision (50% of Rs. 1,500) Considered irrecoverable	750
		44,850

(4)	Bills Receivable	41,500
Less	Dishonoured	1,500
		40,000

Illustration (7) (Manager's Commission)

The following balances have been extracted from the books of N.N. Ltd. for the year ended 31st March, 2006.

Particulars	Rs.
Share Capital	
50,000 Equity shares of Rs. 10 each	5,00,000
General Reserve (1.4.2005)	1,50,000
Furniture (including addition during the year)	35,000
Office computer (1.4.2005)	32,000
Sundry Debtors (Unsecured)	30,000
Advances to staff (Unsecured)	8,50,000
Balance with Post office in Savings A/c (31. 3. 06)	20,000
Cash in hand	2,000
Balance with Canara Bank (including fixed deposits of Rs. 1,00,000)	1,20,000
Loan from Directors (Unsecured)	2,00,000
Liability for expenses and goods supplied	2,67,000
Provision for Taxation (1.4.2005)	1,00,000
Profit & Loss A/c (1.4.2005)	3,000
Closing Stock	3,00,000
Advance Income Tax paid	1,90,000
Depreciation written off up to 31. 3. 2005	
On Furniture	5,000
On Computer	12,000
Opening Stock	1,50,000
Legal Charges including Rs. 3,000 paid to Auditor for tax representation	10,000
Salary to staff	50,000
Miscellaneous expenses including travelling expenses : Rs. 4,000 in India and Rs. 36,000 by managing director for visit abroad for export promotion.	2,00,000
Motor Car (Purchased on 31. 3. 2006)	30,000
Purchases	30,39,000
Audit Fees	4,000
Interest on Fixed Deposits with Bank	5,000
Sales (including export sales of Rs. 10,00,000)	35,00,000

Additional Information :

(i) Sundry Debtors include Rs. 1,50,000 outstanding for more than 6 months. Out of this Rs. 20,000 is considered doubtful for which provision is to be made in the books.

(ii) Rates of depreciation for Computer, Furniture and Motor are 15%, 10% and 20% respectively.

(iii) Managing Director is entitled to commission @10% on net profit before tax and provision for bad debts.

(iv) The provision for tax liability for the year 2005-06 is to be provided @ 50%

(vi) The Directors have decided to transfer Rs. 50,000 out of net profit to general reserve and to propose to pay 10% dividend.

You are required to prepare Profit & Loss Account for the year ended 31st March 2006 and the Balance Sheet as on that date.

[C.S. (I) Dec. 1988, Modified]

Solution :

PROFIT AND LOSS ACCOUNT OF N N LTD.
For the year ended 31st March, 2006

	Rs.		Rs.
To Opening Stock	1,50,000	By Sales	35,00,000
To Purchases	30,39,000	By Closing Stock	3,00,000
To Salaries	50,000	By Interest on Fixed Deposits	5,000
To Legal Charges	10,000		
To Audit Fee	4,000		
To Travelling Expenses	40,000		
To Provision for Doubtful debts	20,000		
To Miscellaneous Expenses	1,60,000		
To Depreciation	6,000		
To Managing Director's Commission	34,600		
To Provision for Taxation	1,45,700		
To Net Profit c/d	1,45,700		
	38,05,000		38,05,000
To General Reserve	50,000	By Balance b/d	3,000
To Proposed Dividend	50,000	By Net Profit b/d	1,45,700
To Corporate Dividend Tax @ 14.025%*	7,013		
To Balance c/d	41,687		
	1,48,700		1,48,700

* 12.5% + 10% there of + 2% of total

Dividend Tax + Surcharge + Education cess.

BALANCE SHEET OF NN LTD.
As on 31st March, 2006

Liabilities	Rs.	Assets		Rs.
Share Capital :		**Fixed Assets :**		
Authorised		Computer at cost	22,000	
---Shares of Rs. 10 each		*Less* Acc. Depreciation	5,000	17,000
Issued, Subscribed and Paid up Capital		Furniture at cost	30,000	
50,000 Equity Shares of Rs. 10 each	5,00,000	Addition	5,000	
Reserves & Surplus			35,000	
General Reserve	2,00,000	*Less* Acc. Depreciation	8,000	27,000
Profit & Loss Account	41,687	Motor Car at cost		30,000
Secured Loan	Nil	**Investments**		Nil
Unsecured Loans :		**Current Assets, Loans & Advances**		
Loan from Director	2,00,000	*(A) Current Assets:*		
Current Liabilities & Provisions		Stock		3,00,000
(A) Current Liabilities :		Debtors		
Sundry creditors	2,67,000	More than 6 months	1,50,000	
Commission Payable	34,600	Others	7,00,000	
(B) *Provisions :*			8,50,000	
Provision for Taxation	2,45,700	*Less* Provision	20,000	8,30,000
Corporate Dividend Tax	7,013	Cash at Bank		20,000
Proposed Dividend	50,000	Post office (S.B. A/c)		20,000
		Fixed Deposits		1,00,000
		Cash in hand		2,000
		(B) Loans & Advances		
		Advance to staff		10,000
		Advance Tax		1,90,000
	15,46,000			15,46,000

Working Notes :

(1) No depreciation has been charged on Motor Car as it has been acquired on the date of closing of books of accounts. Income Tax rules permit availing of full depreciation, however, accounting rules allow depreciation only on usage basis.

(2) Opening balance of Provision for Taxation has been added to current year's provision. No adjustment has been made for advance tax. Conversely the advance tax would have been deducted out of total provision.

(3) Managerial Remuneration has been calculated as under:

Net Profit before Tax, Commission and Provision for Bad debts.	1,45,700
	1,45,700
	34,600
	20,000
	Rs. 3,46,000
10% of Rs. 3,46,000	= Rs. 34,600

Illustration (8) (Net loss and Proposed dividend)

The following balances have been extracted from the books of CC Ltd. for the year ended 31st March 2006.

		Rs.
Equity Share Capital (Shares of Rs. 10 each)		40,00,000
6% Preference Share Capital (Shares of Rs. 100 each)		10,00,000
Plant and Machinery		86,00,000
Furniture and Fittings	73,750	
Less Depreciation	15,000	58,750
Unexpired Insurance		40,000
Dividend Equalisation Reserve		14,55,375
Loan to Director		37,500
Provision for Doubtful debts		1,33,000
General Reserve		13,50,000
Book Debts (of Rs. 1,43,500 are doubtful)		24,05,000
Management Expenses		8,90,000
Unclaimed dividend		44,500
Sundry Creditors		2,05,625
Investment in shares		4,25,000
Final call unpaid on 12,500 shares		31,250
Dividend accrued on investment		13,250
Dividend from investments		39,450
Cash and Bank balance		3,40,425
Sales		55,94,725
Depreciation on Plant & Machinery		18,50,000
Profit & Loss Account (Cr.)		64,500
Purchases		28,96,000

Additional Information :

(1) The depreciation is charged on original cost @ 25% on Plant and Machinery and @ 10% on Furniture.

(2) Additional machinery was acquired at a cost of Rs. 16,00,000 on 1. 10. 2002. It is fully destroyed by fire on 30. 9. 2005. The Insurance company agreed to settle the claim for Rs. 5,00,000.

(3) The equity shares on which final call was in arrears were forfeited by the Board during the year and have not been reissued.

(4) In the Profit & Loss Account of 2004-05 a provision of Rs. 50,000 was made in respect of damages. The claim was settled for Rs. 45,000 and the balance was transferred to creditors.

(5) The Articles of Association of the company provides that in the event of inadequacy of profits, the dividend equalisation reserve should be used to the extent it is necessary to make good the deficiency in the proposed amount of dividend.

(6) Directors propose to pay preference dividend and equity dividend @ 5%

(7) Provide @ 35% for Taxation.

[C S (I) Dec. 1991 Adapted]

Solution:

CC LTD.
PROFIT AND LOSS ACCOUNT
For the year ended 31st March, 2006

	Rs.		Rs.
To Purchases	28,96,000	By Sales	55,94,725
To Management Expenses	8,90,000	By Dividend Received	39,450
To Depreciation on :		By Profit on Machinery	1,00,000
Plant & Machinery	19,50,000	By Net Loss c/d	9,200
Furniture	7,375		
	57,43,375		57,43,375
To Net Loss b/d	9,200	By Balance b/d	64,500
To Proposed dividend :		By Provision for damages not required	5,000
Preference	60,000	By Dividend Equalisation Reserve	2,19,838
Equity	1,93,750	By Balance c/d	9,200
To Corporate Dividend Tax	35,588		
	2,98,538		2,98,538

BALANCE SHEET OF CC LTD.
As on 31st March, 2006

Liabilities		Rs.	Assets		Rs.
Share Capital:			**Fixed Assets:**		
Authorised			Plant & Machinery		44,00,000
-- Equity Shares of Rs. 10 each		***	Furniture		51,375
-- 6% Preference Shares			Investments		4,25,000
of Rs. 100 each		**	**Current Assets Loans & Advances**		
Issued & Subscribed :			*(A) Current Assets:*		
4,00,000 Equity Shares of			Dividend Accrued		13,250
Rs. 10 each	40,00,000		Book Debts:		
6% 10,000 Preference Shares			Due for more than 6 months		—
of Rs. 100 each	10,00,000	50,00,000	Others	24,05,000	
Paid up			*Less* Provision	1,33,000	22,72,000
3,87,500 shares of Rs. 10 each		38,75,000	Cash & Bank Balance		3,40,425
Share Forfeited		93,750	*(B) Loans & Advances*		
6% 10,000 Preference Shares of			Loan to Director		37,500
Rs. 100 each		10,00,000	Insurance claims		5,00,000
Reserves & Surplus			Unexpired Insurance		40,000
General Reserve	13,50,000				
Less Net Loss	9,200	13,40,800			

Contd.

Contd.

Liabilities		Rs.	Assets	Rs.
Dividend Equalisation				
Reserve	14,55,375			
Less Transfer to				
P & L A/c	2,19,838	12,35,537		
Secured Loans		—		
Unsecured Loans		—		
Current Liabilities & Provisions				
(A) Current Liabilities				
Sundry Creditors	2,05,625			
Less Provision not required	5,000	2,00,625		
Unclaimed Dividend		44,500		
(B) Provisions:				
Proposed Dividend:				
Preference		60,000		
Equity		1,93,750		
Corporate Dividend Tax		35,588		
		80,79,550		80,79,550

Working Notes :

			Rs.
(1)	Plant and Machinery		
	Cost of Plant & Machinery		86,00,000
Less	Cost of Machine destroyed by fire		16,00,000
			70,00,000
Less:	Accumulated Depreciation :		
	(18,50,000 Less Dep. on Machine destroyed Rs. 10,00,000*)	8,50,000	
Add	Depreciation on Rs. 70,00,000 @ 25%	17,50,000	26,00,000
	W.D.V. shown in the Balance Sheet		44,00,000

*Depreciation on Machine destroyed

	Rs.
Cost of Machine destroyed as on 1. 10. 2002	16,00,000
Depreciation from 1.10.2002 to 31.3.05) *i.e.* for 2 year & 6 months @ 25% p.a.	10,00,000
	6,00,000
Depreciation for the current year for 6 months. *i.e.* (1.4.2005 to 30.9.2005)	2,00,000
	4,00,000
Insurance claim	5,00,000
Profit on Machinery	1,00,000

Total Depreciation on Plant & Machinery charged to Profit & Loss A/c
Rs. 17,50,000 + 2,00,000 = Rs. 19,50,000.

(2) An amount equivalent to proposed dividend and corporate dividend tax there on has been charged to Dividend Equalisation Reserve as per the provisions of Articles of Association:

(3) The Net loss of the current year has been adjusted against the General Reserve.

Illustration (9) (Tax free interest & Provision for Taxation)

The following balances have been extracted from the books of Greenway Ltd. for the year ended 31st March, 2006.

Particulars	Dr. Rs.	Cr. Rs.
Share Capital		8,00,000
Land and Building	3,40,000	
Plant & Machinery	6,60,000	
Computer	40,000	
Preliminary Expenses	20,000	
Furniture	29,000	
Calls-in-Arrears	6,000	
Cash in hand & at Bank	12,000	
Sundry creditors		1,20,000
Reserve Fund		60,000
Profit & Loss Account (1.4.2005)		45,400
Purchases and Returns O/W	9,60,000	20,000
Sales and Return I/W	28,000	12,31,200
5% Tax Free Government Bonds (Face value - Rs. 40,000)	36,000	
Bills Receivable	58,000	
Goodwill	36,000	
Motor Vehicles	40,000	
Sundry Debtors	83,000	
Interim Dividend	38,000	
Repairs	3,000	
Advertisement	10,000	
Audit Fees	4,000	
Carriage	15,000	
Wages	92,000	
Insurance	20,000	
Stock (1. 4. 2005)	1,90,000	
General Expenses	17,000	
6% Debentures of Rs. 100 each		4,00,000
Bank Overdraft		70,000
Debenture Interest (less Tax @ 20%)	9,600	
	27,46,600	27,46,600

Additional Information

(1) Stock as on 31st March 2006 valued at Rs. 1,80,000

(2) Create reserve for bad debts at 5% on debtors.

(3) Provide Depreciation on :

Plant and Machinery @ 5%

Furniture @ 10%

Computer @ 15%

Motor Vehicle @ 20%

(4) Prepaid insurance Rs. 2,000

(5) Reserve Fund to be increased by Rs. 3,000.

(6) Directors declared on 31st December, 2005 an interim dividend for six moths ending on 30th September, 2005 @ 10%. Calls in Arrears are realised in full.

(7) Wages outstanding Rs. 3,000.

(8) Debenture interest is outstanding for the second half.

(9) Provide for income tax 50%.

Prepare Profit and Loss Account for the year ended 31st March, 2006 and a Balance Sheet as on that date.

[I.C.W.A. (I) Modified]

Solution:

PROFIT AND LOSS ACCOUNT OF GREENWAY LTD.

For the year ended 31st March, 2006

		Rs.			Rs.
To Opening Stock		1,90,000	By Sales	12,31,200	
To Purchases	9,60,000		*Less* Returns	28,000	12,03,200
Less Return	20,000	9,40,000	By Closing Stock		1,80,000
To Wages	92,000		By Interest on Tax-free		
Add outstanding	3,000	95,000	Government Bonds		2,000
To Carriage		15,000			
To Repairs		3,000			
To Insurance	20,000				
Less Prepaid	2,000	18,000			
To Advertising		10,000			
To Audit Fees		4,000			
To General Expenses		17,000			
To Debenture Interest		24,000			
To Provision for doubtful debts		4,150			
To Depreciation on:					
Plant & Machinery		33,000			*Contd.*

	Rs.		Rs.
Computer	6,000		
Furniture	2,900		
Motor Vehicle	8,000		
To Provision for Taxation (1)	6,575		
To Net Profit c/d	8,575		
	13,85,200		13,85,200
To General Reserve	3,000	By Balance b/d	45,400
To Interim Dividend	40,000	By Net Profit b/d	8,575
To Corporate Dividend Tax	5,610		
To Balance c/d	5,365		
	53,975		53,975

BALANCE SHEET OF GREENWAY LTD.
As on 31st March, 2006

Liabilities	Rs.	Assets		Rs.
Share Capital:		**Fixed Assets**		
Authorised ----	----------	Goodwill		36,000
Subscribed & Paid up:		Land & Building		3,40,000
80,000 shares of Rs. 10 each fully paid	8,00,000	Plant & Machinery (Less Dep.)		6,27,000
Reserves & Surplus:		Furniture (Less Dep.)		26,100
Reserve Fund	63,000	Computer (Less Dep.)		34,000
Profit & Loss Account	5,365	Motor Vehicle (Less Dep.)		32,000
Secured Loans:		**Investments**		
6% Debentures	4,00,000	5% Govt. Bonds (F.V. 40,000)		36,000
Debenture Interest o/s	9,600	**Current Assets, Loans & Advances**		
Bank Overdraft	70,000	Closing Stock		1,80,000
Unsecured Loans	Nil	Debtors	83,000	
Current Liabilities & Provisions		*Less* Provision	4,150	78,850
(A) Current liabilities		Interest on Bonds o/s		2,000
Wages outstanding	3,000	Cash & Bank		18,000
Tax Deducted at Source	4,800	*Loans & Advances*		
Unclaimed dividend	2,000	Prepaid Insurance		2,000
(40,000 – 38,000)		Bills Receivable		58,000
S. Creditors	1,20,000	**Miscellaneous Expenditure**		
(B) Provisions		Preliminary Expenses		20,000
Provision for Taxation	6,575			
Corporate Dividend Tax	5,610			
	14,89,950			14,89,950

Working notes:

(1) Interest on Tax free Government Bonds has been excluded for the purpose of calculating provision for taxation.

(2) Debenture interest @ 6% on Rs. 4,00,000, Rs. 24,000 has been debited to Profit and Loss Account and Tax deducted at source (TDS) @ 20% has been shown on the liability side of Balance Sheet as current liability. Since interest for first half (excluding TDS) has been paid the interest for the second half is still outstanding.

(3) Calls in Arrears received have been debited to Cash and Bank Account

Illustration (10) (Past losses, and dividend per share)

The following information has been extracted from the books of Zara Ltd. for the year ended 31st March 2006.

	Rs.
Sales	50,00,000
Motor Car	37,500
Furniture & Fixtures	50,000
Plant & Machinery	2,50,000
Preliminary Expenses	25,000
Profit and Loss Account (Dr.) 1.4. 2005	5,00,000
Miscellaneous Receipts	3,00,000
Opening stock of Finished Goods	7,50,000
Consumption of Raw material	22,50,000
Closing stock of Raw-material	12,50,000
Bank Overdraft	2,50,000
Securities Premium	9,00,000
Share Capital	15,00,000
Unsecured loans	7,50,000
Sundry Debtors (including Rs. 2,50,000 over six months)	17,50,000
Salaries & Wages	5,00,000
Office overheads	10,00,000
Selling & Distribution overheads	3,75,000
Advance Income Tax	7,50,000
Miscellaneous Advances	1,00,000
Interim Dividend	1,50,000
Sundry Creditors	10,37,500

Additional Information :

(i) Closing stock of finished goods at cost is Rs. 15,00,000

(ii) The original cost of fixed assets was as under:

	Rs.
Plant and Machinery	5,00,000
Furniture and Fixtures	75,000
Motor Car	62,500

Depreciation is to be charged on the written down value @ 10% on Plant and Machinery and Furniture & Fixtures, and 20% on Motor Car. There were no additions or disposals during the year.

(iii) The entire authorised capital which consists of equity shares of Rs. 10 each has been issued and subscribed. The share capital is paid up to the extent of 60%. There are no calls in arrears.

(iv) The unsecured loan was taken on 1. 1. 2006 @ 12% interest p.a. The interest is payable half yearly and necessary provisions are to be made in accounts

(v) Preliminary Expenses are to be written off.

(vi) Office overheads include.

	Rs.
Auditor's Fees (including Rs. 2,500 for tax consultancy)	12,500
Director's Fees	7,500

(vii) Provision for Taxation is to be made @ 40%

(viii) The directors have proposed a final dividend of Re. 1 per share in addition to interim dividend already paid.

[C. S (I) Dec. 89 Modified]

Solution:

PROFIT AND LOSS ACCOUNT OF ZARA LTD.
for the year ended 31st March 2006

	Rs.		Rs.
To Opening Stock (F.G.)	7,50,000	By Sales	50,00,000
To Raw Material Consumed	22,50,000	By Closing Stock of	
To Salaries & Wages	5,00,000	Finished Goods	15,00,000
To Office Overheads	9,80,000	By Miscellaneous Income	3,00,000
To Director's Fees	7,500		
To Selling & Distribution overheads	3,75,000		
To Interest on Unsecured Loans	22,500		
To Depreciation on:			
Plant & Machinery	25,000		
Furniture & Fixtures	5,000		
Motor Car	7,500		
To Auditors Fees	12,500		
(including consultancy charges)			
To Preliminary Expenses	25,000		
To Provision for Taxation	7,36,000		
To Net Profit c/d	11,04,000		
	68,00,000		68,00,000

Contd.

	Rs.		Rs.
To Balance b/d	5,00,000		
To Interim Dividend	1,50,000	By Net Profit b/d	11,04,000
To Final Dividend (Proposed)	2,50,000		
To Corporate Dividend Tax			
@ 14.025% on 4,00,000)	56,100		
To General Reserve	1,10,400		
To Balance c/d	37,500		
	11,04,000		11,04,000

BALANCE SHEET OF ZARA LTD.
As on 31st March, 2006

Liabilities	Rs.	Assets		Rs.
Share Capital:		**Fixed Assets:**		
Authorised:		Plant & Machinery		
2,50,000 Equity Shares of		*Less* Depreciation	5,00,000	
Rs. 10 each	25,00,000		2,75,000	2,25,000
2,50,000 Equity Shares of		Furniture & Fixture	75,000	
Rs. 10 each Rs. 6 paid up	15,00,000	*Less* Depreciation	30,000	45,000
Reserves & Surplus		Motor Car	62,500	
General Reserve	1,10,400	*Less* Depreciation	32,500	30,000
Securities Premium	9,00,000	Investments		Nil
Profit & Loss Account	37,500	**Current Assets Loans &**		
Secured Loans :		**Advances**		
Bank overdraft	2,50,000	*(A) Current Assets*		
Unsecured Loans	7,50,000	Stock (F.G.)		15,00,000
Current Liabilities and Provisions:		Stock (R. M)		12,50,000
(A) Current Liabilities:		Sundry Debtors:		
Sundry Creditors	10,37,500	More than 6 months		2,50,000
Interest accrued		Others		15,00,000
on unsecured loans	22,500	*(B) Loans & Advances:*		
(B) Provisions:		Miscellaneous Advances		1,00,000
Provision for Taxation	7,36,000	Income Tax Advance		7,50,000
Proposed Dividend	2,50,000			
Corporate Dividend	56,100			
	56,50,000			56,50,000

Working note:

(1) Since dividend declared and paid exceeds 20% (Rs. 4,00,000 on Rs. 15,00,000 paid up capital works out to be 26.67%) a statutory transfer of 10% of current year's profit has been made to General Reserve.

Illustration (11) (Apportionment of Expenses)

ABC Ltd. has an authorised capital of Rs. 10,00,000 comprising 2,500 Preference shares of Rs. 100 each and 75,000 Equity shares of Rs. 10 each. Issued and subscribed share capital of the company is 50,000 Equity shares of Rs. 10 each and 1,000 6% Preference shares of Rs. 100 each. From the following particulars, prepare Manufacturing, Trading and Profit and Loss Account for the year ended on 31st March, 2006 and a Balance Sheet as on that date.

	Rs.		Rs.
Opening Stock:		Sales	17,00,000
Raw-material	2,70,000	Miscellaneous Receipts	17,500
Work-in-progress	30,000	Issued & Subscribed Capital:	
Finished Goods	2,40,000	50,000 Equity Shares of Rs. 10	
Purchases of Materials	12,00,000	each fully called	5,00,000
Freight & duty	1,05,000	1,000 6% Preference Shares of	
Electricity, Power and Fuel	30,000	Rs. 100 each fully called	1,00,000
Wages, salaries & bonus	3,00,000	Dividend Equalisation Reserve	30,000
Rent, Rates & Taxes	15,000	Secured Loans	2,00,000
Insurance (factory)	7,500	(against Fixed Assets)	
Director's Remuneration	13,000	Bank Overdraft	3,50,000
Interest	30,000	Sundry Creditors	1,00,000
Sundry Expenses	1,25,000	Provision for Taxation	19,500
Calls-in-Arrears:		Unpaid dividend	85,000
On Equity Shares	6,000	Profit & Loss Account (Cr.)	18,000
On Preference Shares	1,500	General Reserve	1,00,000
Sundry Debtors	2,60,000		
Cash & Bank	1,32,000		
Land & Building (1.4.2005)	75,000		
Plant & Machinery	2,90,000		
Other Assets	75,000		
Office Furniture	15,000		
	32,20,000		32,20,000

Additional Information :

	Rs.
(1) Closing Stock :	
Raw material	3,30,000
Work-in-progress	40,000
Finished Goods	4,00,000
(2) Depreciation is to be provided on:	
Land and Building	@ 2%
Plant & Machinery	@ 10%
Other Assets (Factory)	@ 3%
Furniture	@ 15%

(3) Outstanding and accrued expenses: Rs.

	Rs.
Interest on Secured Loans	4,000
Rent, Rates and Taxes	3,000
Audit Fee	8,000

(4) Insurance paid in advance 1,500

(5) Expenses on Electricity and Salaries, Wages and Bonus should be apportioned between factory and the office in 2 : 1 ratio.

(6) The Board of Directors recommended the following appropriations.

(a) Proposed dividend on Equity shares and Preference shares @ 6% on respective nominal value.

(b) Transfer to General Reserve Rs. 11,000

(c) Provision for Taxation @ 40%

(7) Out of total sundry debtors Rs. 9,000 are considered doubtful and rest considered good. It is decided to provide for bad and doubtful debts @ 4%

(8) There was a pending law suit against the company for a sum of Rs. 5,000.

[C.S. (I) June 89 Modified]

Solution :

ABC LTD.

MANUFACTURING, TRADING AND PROFIT & LOSS ACCOUNT

for the year ended on 31st March, 2006

		Rs.		Rs.
To Opening stock:			By Cost of goods Manufactured	
Raw materials		2,70,000	transferred to Trading A/c	14,61,000
Work-in-progress		30,000	By Closing Stock:	
To Purchases		12,00,000	Raw-Material	3,30,000
To Freight & Duty		1,05,000	Work-in-progress	40,000
To Insurance (Factory)	7,500			
Less Prepaid	1,500	6,000		
To Electricity Power and Fuel (2/3)		20,000		
To Wages, Salaries & Bonus (2/3)		2,00,000		
		18,31,000		18,31,000
To Opening Stock (F.G.)		2,40,000	By Sales	17,00,000
To Cost of goods transferred			By Closing Stock (F.G.)	4,00,000
from Manufacturing A/c		14,61,000		
To Gross Profit c/d		3,99,000		
		21,00,000		21,00,000

Contd.

	Rs.		Rs.
To Wages & Salaries & Bonus (1/3)	1,00,000	By Gross Profit b/d	3,99,000
To Electricity Power and Fuel	10,000	By Miscellaneous Receipts	17,500
To Rent, Rates & Taxes (15,000 + 3,000 o/s)	18,000		
To Interest (30,000 + 4,000 o/s)	34,000		
To Directors Remuneration	13,000		
To Sundry Expenses	1,25,000		
To Audit Fees	8,000		
To Depreciation on:			
Land & Building	1,500		
Plant & Machinery	29,000		
Furniture	2,250		
Other Assets	2,250		
To Provision for Doubtful debts	10,400		
To Provision for Taxation	25,240		
To Net Profit c/d	37,860		
	4,16,500		4,16,500
To General Reserve	11,000	By Balance b/d	18,000
To Proposed Dividend		By Net Profit b/d	37,860
Preference	6,000		
Equity	30,000		
To Corporate Dividend Tax (@ 14.025% on 36,000)	5,049		
To Balance c/d	3,811		
	55,860		55,860

BALANCE SHEET OF ABC LTD.
As on 31st March, 2006

Liabilities		Rs.	Assets		Rs.
Share Capital:			**Fixed Assets:**		
Authorised:			Land & Building	75,000	
@ 2,500 Preference Shares			*Less* Depreciation	1,500	73,500
of Rs. 100 each		2,50,000	Plant & Machinery	2,90,000	
75,000 Equity Shares			*Less* Depreciation	29,000	2,61,000
of Rs. 10 each		7,50,000	Furniture	15,000	
Issued & Subscribed			*Less* Depreciation	2,250	12,750
6% 1,000 Preference Shares			Other Assets	75,000	
of Rs. 100 each	1,00,000		*Less* Depreciation	2,250	72,750
Less Calls in Arrears	1,500	98,500	**Investments**		Nil

Contd.

Liabilities		Rs.	Assets		Rs.
50,000 Equity Shares			Current Assets		
of Rs. 10 each	5,00,000		**Loans & Advances:**		
Less Calls in Arrears	6,000	4,94,000	*(A) Current Assets:*		
Reserves & Surplus:			Stock Raw materials		3,30,000
General Reserve	1,00,000		Work-in-progress		40,000
Add Transfer	11,000	1,11,000	Finished Goods		4,00,000
Profit & Loss Account		3,811	Sundry Debtors		
Dividend Equalisation Reserve		30,000	(a) Debts considered		
Secured Loans:			good	2,51,000	
(Against Fixed Assets)	2,00,000		(B) Doubtful	9,000	
O/s Interest	4,000	2,04,000		2,60,000	
Unsecured Loans:			(c) Provision		
Bank Overdraft		3,50,000	for D. Debts	10,400	2,49,600
Current liabilities & Provision:			Cash & Bank Balance		1,32,000
(A) Current Liabilities			*(B) Loans & Advances:*		
Sundry Creditors		1,00,000	Prepaid Insurance		1,500
Unpaid Dividend		85,000			
Outstanding Expenses		11,000			
(8,000 + 3,000)					
(B) Provisions					
Provision for Taxation		44,740			
(19,500 + 25,240)					
Corporate Dividend Tax		5,049			
Proposed Dividend		36,000			
		15,73,100			15,73,100

Note: There is a Contingent liability for a pending law suit against the company for a sum of Rs. 5,000.

Illustration (12) (Consignment & Interest on calls in Arrears)

Trial Balance of XYZ Ltd. as on 31. 3. 2006

	Rs. (Dr.)	Rs. (Cr.)
Share Capital:		
50,000 Shares of Rs. 10 each		
Issued: 40,000 shares of Rs. 10 each		
Rs. 7.50 per share called		3,00,000
Calls in Arrears (in respect of 2,000 shares)	5,000	
Stock	27,200	
Purchase and Sales	2,91,200	4,23,100
Other expenses	38,400	
Salaries and Wages	41,000	

Investments:		
Quoted	80,000	
Unquoted	10,000	
General Reserve		1,00,000
Plant & Machinery	80,000	
Debtors and Creditors	1,42,000	20,300
Goods sent on Consignment	7,200	
Cash at Bank	2,17,300	
Provision for Taxation		1,00,000
Investment Income (after 20% TDS)		6,400
Tax paid in Advance	91,000	
Profit & Loss Account		80,500
	10,30,300	10,30,300

You are required to prepare Trading and Profit and Loss Account for the year ended 31st March 2005 and a Balance Sheet as on that date after taking into account the following:

(i) Closing stock is valued at Rs. 40,900.

(ii) Included in sales are Rs. 32,000 being Goods on sale or return. The cost price of such goods is Rs. 25,000.

(iii) Provision for Bad debts @ 20% is to be created.

(iv) Provision for taxation on the year's profit is Rs. 30,050. Tax deducted from investment is Rs. 1,600 and from interest on calls in arrears is Rs. 50.

(v) A dividend of 10% is proposed.

(vi) Interest on calls in arrears to be charged at 5% p.a. (due date is 30th September 2005)

(vii) Provisions of Table A apply to dividends

(viii) Depreciation @ 10% is to be provided

(ix) The manager is entitled to 10% of the net profits of the company as commission after charging such commission excluding income from investments and before charging taxation.

(x) Transfer Rs. 7,136 to General Reserve.

(xi) All goods sent on consignment have been sold for Rs. 9,000 subject to agent's commission of 5%

(xii) Creditors include Rs. 12,000 outstanding for plant purchased on hire-purchase on 1.10.2005. Purchase price being payable in four equal quarterly instalments commencing on 01.01.2006 (Cash value of plant is Rs. 10,400) against which a deposit of Rs. 2,000 was paid on 1.10.2005, included in the debtors.

(xiii) Interest to be distributed in proportion to time.

[ICWA (F) Adapted]

Solution:

XYZ LTD.
PROFIT AND LOSS ACCOUNT
for the year ended 31st March 2006

	Rs.			Rs.
To Opening Stock	27,200	By Sales		3,91,100
To Purchases	2,91,200	(4,23,100 – 32,000)		
To Goods Sent on Consignment	7,200	By Goods sent on Consignment		9,000
To Salaries & wages	41,000	(Sold)		
To Other Expenses	38,400	By Closing Stock	40,900	
To Provision for Bad debts	21,600	*Add* Cost of Goods sent		
To Interest on hire-purchase	800	for sale/Return	25,000	65,900
To Agent's Commission	450			
To Manager's Commission	2,232	By Investment Income (Gross)		8,000
To Provision for Taxation	30,050	By Interest on Calls in arrears		125
To Depreciation	7,320	(for six months)		
To Net Profit	6,673			
	4,74,125			4,74,125
To General Reserve	7,136			
To Proposed Dividend	29,500	By Balance b/d		80,500
To Corporate Dividend Tax	4,137	By Net Profit		6,673
To Balance c/d	46,400			
	87,173			87,173

BALANCE SHEET OF XYZ LTD.
As on 31st March, 2006

Liabilities		Rs.	Assets		Rs.
Share Capital:			**Fixed Assets:**		
Authorised:			Plant & Machinery	68,000	
50,000 Equity Shares of			*Less* Depreciation	6,800	61,200
Rs. 10 each		5,00,000	Plant on Hire Purchase	10,400	
Issued & Subscribed			*Less* Depreciation	520	9,880
40,000 Equity Shares			**Investments:**		
of Rs. 10 each		4,00,000	Quoted		80,000
Called up & Paid up			Unquoted		10,000
40,000 Shares of Rs. 10 each			**Current Assets Loans & Advances:**		
Rs. 7.50 per share called	3,00,000		**Current Assets:**		
Less Calls in Arrear	5,000	2,95,000	Closing Stock		65,900
Reserves & Surplus			Debtors	1,08,000	
General Reserve		1,07,136	*Less* Provision	21,600	86,400

Contd.

Liabilities	Rs.	Assets	Rs.
Profit & Loss A/c	46,400	Consignee's A/c (9,000 – 450)	8,550
Secured Loans	Nil	Interest on Calls on Arrears	125
Unsecured Loans	Nil	Interest on H. P. Instalments	800
Current liabilities & Provisions		(1,600 – 800)	
(A) Current liabilities:		Cash at Bank	2,17,300
Creditors (20,300 – 12,000)	8,300	**Loans & Advances:**	
Hire Purchase Creditors	10,000	Advance Income Tax	91,000
(12,000 – 2,000)		Tax Deducted at sources	1,600
Manager's Commission	2,232		
(B) Provisions			
Provision for Taxation	1,30,050		
Proposed Dividend	29,500		
Corporate Dividend Tax	4,137		
(on Investment Income)			
	6,32,755		6,32,755

Working Notes:

(1) Since goods sent on sale/return basis, have been treated as sale, the rectification has been effected with the help of following entries.

(i) Sales A/c	Dr.	32,000	
To Debtors A/c			32,000
(ii) Cl. Stock A/c	Dr.	25,000	
To Trading A/c			25,000

i.e. Sales and Debtors have been reduced with the sales value while closing stock has been increased with the cost of goods.

(2) Provision for doubtful debts has been created on Rs. 1,08,000 (Rs. 1,42,000 – 2,000 H.P. down payment – 32,000 goods sent on approval)

(3) Income on investment has been grossed up and TDS has been shown on the assets side of Balance Sheet = Rs. 8,000

(4) Interest payable on hire purchase transaction Rs. 1,600 (Hire purchase price – Cash price *i.e.* 12,000 – 10,400) has been apportioned on time basis. Since out of four quarterly instalments, two fall due in the current year, thus half of the interest Rs. 800 has been treated as advance payment.

(5) Creditors for hire purchase has been taken at (12,000 – 2,000) Rs. 10,000 as there is no clue as to the quarterly payment.

(6) Since goods sent on consignment has been shown to the debit of Trial Balance, it shows that the same have been deducted from the purchases, hence debited to Profit & Loss A/c. The sale price has been credited to Profit & Loss A/c and commission there on debited. The net amount has been debited to consignee's A/c.

(7) Depreciation on plant purchased on hire purchase basis has been calculated for 6 months. (1.10.2005 to 31.3.2006)

(8) Manager's commission has been calculated before investment income & tax but after such commission. (Profit before investment income and tax) $24,555 \times \frac{10}{110} = 2,232.$

Illustration (13)

(Gross Profit & Valuation of closing Stock)

The following balances were extracted from the books of EC Ltd. for the year ended 31st March 2006.

	Rs.
Building	6,00,000
Furniture	60,000
Motor Vehicles	60,000
Equity Shares of Companies	4,00,000
Stock in trade at cost	4,00,000
Sundry Debtors, Unsecured considered good	2,80,000
Cash at Bank	1,72,000
Advance against construction of Building	1,30,000
Share Capital:	
1,00,000 Equity Shares of Rs. 10 each	10,00,000
Sundry creditors	3,50,000
Profit & Loss Account (Cr.)	20,000
Gross Profit	10,00,000
Dividend received on investments	10,000
Salaries and wages	2,20,000
Directors Fees	8,000
Electricity Charges	25,000
Rates, Taxes and Insurance	10,000
Auditors Fees	15,000

Prepare Profit and Loss Account of the Company for the year ended 31st March, 2006 and a Balance Sheet as on that date. Provide depreciation @ 10% p.a. Stock has been revalued at Rs. 3,60,000. This has not been considered yet. Debtors of Rs. 80,000 are due for more than 6 months Provide for Taxation @ 40% and 20% for dividend.

(ICWA (I) Modified]

Solution:

E C LTD.
PROFIT & LOSS ACCOUNT
for the year ended 31st March, 2006

	Rs.		Rs.
To Salaries & Wages	2,20,000	By Gross Profit b/d	10,00,000
To Electricity charges	25,000	By Dividend Received on	
To Rates, Taxes & Insurance	10,000	Investments	10,000
To Director's Fees	8,000		
To Auditor's Fees	15,000		
To Loss on Revaluation* of Stock (4,00,000 – 3,60,000)	40,000		
To Depreciation on:			
Building	60,000		
Furniture	6,000		
Motor Vehicles	6,000		
To Provision for Taxation	2,48,000		
To Net Profit c/d	3,72,000		
	10,10,000		10,10,000
To General Reserve	37,200	By Balance b/d	20,000
To Proposed Dividend	2,50,000	By Net Profit	3,72,000
To Corporate Dividend Tax @ 14.025%	35,063		
To Balance c/d	69,737		
	3,92,000		3,92,000

*Since Loss on revaluation of stock has not been considered while calculating gross profit, the same has been debited in the Profit and Loss Account.

BALANCE SHEET OF EC LTD.
As on 31st March, 2006

Liabilities	Rs.	Assets		Rs.
Share Capital:		**Fixed Assets:**		
Authorised		Building	6,00,000	
---	---	*Less* Depreciation	60,000	5,40,000
Issued, Subscribed and Paid up:		Furniture	60,000	
1,00,000 Equity Shares of Rs. 10 each		*Less* Depreciation	6,000	54,000
fully paid	10,00,000	Motor Vehicles	60,000	
Reserves & Surplus		*Less* Depreciation	6,000	54,000
General Reserve	37,200	**Investments:**		
Profit & Loss Account	69,737	Equity Shares of Companies		4,00,000
Secured Loans	Nil	**Current Assets Loans & Advances:**		
Unsecured Loans	Nil	*(A) Current Assets:*		
		Stock (cost Rs. 4,00,000)		3,60,000

Current Liabilities:		Debtors (Unsecured Considered good:	
Sundry Creditors	3,50,000	More than 6 months	80,000
Provisions		Other Debts	2,00,000
Provision for Taxation	2,48,000	Cash at Bank	1,72,000
Proposed Dividend	2,50,000	**Loans & Advances:**	
Corporate Dividend Tax	35,063	Advances for Construction of Building	1,30,000
	19,90,000		19,90,000

Illustration (14) (Leasing Company & Excess Tax provision)

HH Co. Ltd. is engaged in leasing houses. It also invests in land development. The following balances appeared in the books of the Company on 31st March, 2006.

	Rs.
Credit Balances	
Share Capital (50,000 Shares of Rs. 100 each)	50,00,000
Provision for Taxation (1. 4. 2005)	25,75,750
Lease Receipts	3,25,070
Deposits from Public	15,20,250
Deposits from Lessees	3,250
Advances from Members	3,07,050
Dividends Refundable	1,850
Suspense Account	23,160
Fees from Subsidiary	2,100
Rent Received	1,21,235
Dividends Received	13,81,950
Interest Received	97,350
Land Rent Payable	1,490
Bank	12,01,850
Profit & Loss Account	2,420
General Reserve	20,50,000
Debit Balances:	
Building	14,50,850
Land	17,850
Furniture	18,350
Motor Car	6,550
Interim Dividend including corporate dividend Tax	5,64,000
Investments in Shares	82,41,650
Arrears of Dividend	9,375
Meter Security Deposit	4,525
Advance Payment of Income Tax	17,77,875
Dues from Tenants for water & Electricity	450
Sundry Debtors	21,01,300
Advance to employees	6,500

Interest paid	2,01,900
Fees to Directors	58,200
Salary to Staff	33,350
Printing and Stationery	900
Ground Rent	11,700
Municipal Tax	10,800
Motor Car Expenses	6,000
Travelling and Conveyance	1,700
Guest House Expenses	2,200
Bank Charges	250
House Rent for Staff	3,600
Repairs to Building	15,750
Legal Expenses	650
Insurance Premium	5,000
Type writer	3,900
Miscellaneous Expenses	3,700
Water & Electricity	1,600
Cash in hand	13,500

Additional Information:

(a) Authorised Capital is 50,000 Equity Shares of Rs. 100 each.

(b) The Original cost of motor car was Rs. 54,990. Depreciation provided upto the previous year was Rs. 8,440. Provide depreciation Rs. 4,000 for the year.

(c) Income tax assessment was completed for the previous year and the tax liability has been assessed at Rs. 25,50,000. For the current year provide 50% for taxation, charity Rs. 80,000 and proposed final dividend @ 8%.

(d) Provide depreciation on Typewriter Rs. 425

(e) The Bank overdraft was secured

(f) Sundry Debtors more than 6 months old are unsecured but considered good Rs. 20,94,800 Debts considered doubtful Rs. 6,500 are over 9 months old.

(g) Suspense Account represents credits for cheques received from Sundry Debtors but not collected.

(h) Details of investments in shares are as follows :

Shares in subsidiary companies:	Rs.
Equity Shares fully paid up	6,93,000
Equity Shares partly paid up (80%)	8,07,000
Debentures fully paid up	54,000
	15,54,000
Shares in Other Companies:	
Equity Shares fully paid up	41,58,000
Preference Shares fully paid up	22,07,000

Preference Shares partly paid up (50%)	3,22,650
	82,41,650

Prepare Final Accounts

[ICWA (F) Adapted]

Solution:

H.H. CO. LTD.
PROFIT AND LOSS ACCOUNT
for the year ended 31st March, 2006

	Rs.		Rs.
To Salary to Staff	33,350	By Lease Receipts	3,25,070
To Ground Rent	11,700	By Fees from Subsidiary	2,100
To Municipal Tax	10,800	By Rent Received	1,21,235
To Printing & Stationery	900	By Dividend Received	13,81,950
To Postage & Telegrams	800	By Interest Received	97,350
To Motor Car Expenses	6,000		
To Travelling & Conveyance	1,700		
To Guest House Expenses	2,200		
To Bank Charges	250		
To Repairs to Building	15,750		
To Legal Expenses	650		
To Insurance Premium	5,000		
To Water & Electricity	1,600		
To Interest paid	2,01,900		
To Directors Fees	58,200		
To House Rent for staff	3,600		
To Miscellaneous Expenses	3,700		
To Depreciation on:			
Motor Car	4,000		
Typewriter	425		
To Provision for bad debts	6,500		
To Provision for Charity	80,000		
To Provision for Taxation	7,39,340		
To Net Profit c/d	7,39,340		
	19,27,705		19,27,705
To Interim Dividend	5,64,000	By Balance b/d	2,420
To Proposed Dividend	4,00,000	By Net Profit b/c	7,39,340
To Corporate dividend Tax	56,100	By Provision for Income Tax	25,750
		By Transfer from Reserve	2,52,290
	10,20,100		10,20,100

*Since Corporate dividend tax on intrim dividend has already been paid the provision for corporate dividend tax has been made on proposed dividend only

BALANCE SHEET OF HH CO. LTD.
As on 31st March, 2006

	Rs.			Rs.
Share Capital:		**Fixed Assets:**		
Authorised Capital		Land		17,850
50,000 Equity Shares		Building		14,50,850
of Rs. 100 each	50,00,000	Furniture		18,350
Issued, Subscribed & Paid up Capital		Motor Car	54,990	
50,000 Equity Shares of Rs. 100		*Less* Acc Depreciation	12,440	42,550
each fully paid	50,00,000	Typewriter	3,900	
Reserves & Surplus:		*Less* Depreciation	425	3,475
General Reserve (20,50,000–2,52,590)	17,97,410	**Investments**		82,41,650
Profit & Loss A/c	Nil	**Current Assets:**		
Secured Loans :		Arrears of Dividend		9,375
Bank Overdraft	12,01,850	Dues from Tenants		450
(Secured against equity shares		Sundry Debtors		
of joint stock companies)		More than 6 months old	21,01,300	
Unsecured Loans:		*Less* Provision	6,500	
Deposits from public	15,20,250	Debts Considered good	20,94,800	
Current liabilities		*Less* Cheques not collected		
Deposits from Tenants	3,250	(Suspense A/c)	23,160	20,71,640
Advances from Members	3,07,050	Cash in hand		13,500
Dividends-refundable	1,850	**Loans & Advances**		
Land Rent Payable	1,490	Meter Security Deposits		4,525
Income Tax payable	7,72,125	Advance to Employees		6,500
Provisions:				
Provision for Taxation	7,39,340			
Provision for Charity	80,000			
Provision Final Dividend	4,00,000			
Corporate Dividend Tax	56,100			
	1,18,80,715			1,18,80,715

Working Note: (1)

PROVISION FOR TAXATION A/C

	Rs.		Rs.
To Liability for Taxation (Actual)	25,50,000	By Balance b/d	25,75,750
To Profit & Loss A/c (below the line)	25,750		
	25,75,750		25,75,750
To Balance c/d	7,39,340	By Profit & Loss A/c	7,39,340
	7,39,340		7,39,340

LIABILITY FOR TAXATION

	Rs.		Rs.
To Advance Tax	17,77,875	By Provision for Taxation	25,50,000
To Balance c/d	7,72,125		
	25,50,000		25,50,000

ADVANCE TAX A/C

To Balance c/d	17,77,875	By Liability for Taxation	17,77,875

Alternatively

PROVISION FOR TAXATION

	Rs.		Rs.
To Advance Tax	17,77,875	By Balance c/d	25,75,750
To Liability for Taxation	7,72,125		
To Profit & Loss A/c (below the line)	25,750		
	25,75,750		25,75,750
To Balance c/d	7,39,340	By Profit & Loss A/c	7,39,340

LIABILITY FOR TAXATION A/C

To Balance c/d	7,72,125	By Provision for Taxation	7,72,125

ADVANCE TAX A/C

To Balance b/d	17,77,875	By Provision for Taxation	17,77,875

Illustration (15) (Profit & Loss Adjustment A/c)

From the following balances taken from the books of PT Ltd. prepare Profit and Loss Adjustment Account for the year ended 31st March, 2006 and the Balance Sheet as on that date.

	Rs.
Share Capital	
1,50,000 Shares of Rs. 30 each fully paid	45,00,000
1,200 8% Redeemable Preference Shares	1,20,000
Securities Premium	75,000
General Reserve	3,00,000
Preference Share Redemption	1,44,000
Net Block (Gross Block Rs. 40,00,000)	28,65,000
Trading Profit-net profit for the year (before tax)	12,63,000
Current Assets	18,00,000
Creditors for goods	6,76,800
Profit and Loss A/c (1. 4. 2005)	30,000
Interim Dividend	2,29,800
Unpaid Dividend	6,000

Investments (at cost)	12,00,000
Outstanding Expenses	18,000
Income Tax paid under dispute (for the year 2004-05)	3,00,000
Provision for Taxation (1. 4. 05)	2,10,000
Advance payment of Tax	6,60,000

Other information:

(i) Depreciation charged in the accounts amounts to Rs. 4,00,000 for the year where as the depreciation under section 350 of the Companies Act works out to Rs. 4,50,000

(ii) Interim dividend paid includes prorata dividend paid on preference shares on redemption.

(iii) Proposed final dividend is equal to the amount of interim dividend.

(iv) Profit was calculated after charging and paying Rs. 47,000 to Managing Director as minimum remuneration. He is entitled to a remuneration of 5% on the net profits after charging his remuneration but before taxation.

(v) Preference shares were redeemed on 30th September, 2005 at a premium of 20% but no entries were passed for giving effect there of except for the payment standing to the debit of preference share redemption account.

(vi) Income tax demand for the year ended 31st March, 2005 of Rs. 3,00,000 has not been provided in full against which an appeal is pending.

(vii) Market value of investments is equal to the book value.

(viii) Income tax for the year is to be provided @ 50%.

(ix) Current assets include inventory at cost Rs. 12,00,000; Debtors all considered good Rs. 5,00,000 (including Rs. 2,00,000 outstanding for more than six months); and Bank balance Rs. 1,00,000.

[C.S. (I) Modified]

Solution:

PROFIT & LOSS ADJUSTMENT ACCOUNT
for the year ended 31st March 2006

	Rs.		Rs.
To Managerial Remuneration	60,000*	By Trading Profit	13,10,000
To Provision for Taxation	6,25,000	before managerial remuneration	
To Net Profit c/d	6 ,25,000	(Rs. 12,63,000 + 47,000)	
	13,10,000		13,10,000
To Preference dividend (for 6 months)	4,800	By Balance b/d	30,000
To Interim Dividend (2,29,800 – 4,800)	2,25,000	By Net profit b/d	6,25,000
To Final Dividend	2,25,000		
To Corporate Dividend Tax	63,786		
To Balance c/d	1,36,414		
	6,55,000		6,55,000

*** Managerial Remuneration**

	Net Profit before Tax and remuneration	12,63,000
Add	Remuneration already paid	47,000
		13,10,000
Less	Excess of Depreciation U/s 350 over depreciation allowed (4,50,000 – 4,00,000)	50,000
		12,60,000

Remuneration @ 5% of net profit after charging such commission $\frac{12,60,000 \times 5}{105} = 60,000$

BALANCE SHEET OF PT LTD.
As on 31st March, 2006

Liabilities	Rs.	Assets		Rs.
Share Capital:		**Fixed Assets**		
Authorised:		Gross –	40,00,000	
1,50,000 Equity Shares of Rs. 30 each	45,00,000	*Less* Depreciation	11,35,000	28,65,000
8% 1,200 Redeemable Preference	1,20,000	**Investments at cost**		12,00,000
Shares of Rs. 100 each	46,20,000	(Market Value 12,00,000)		
Issued & Subscribed		**Current Assets, loans & Advances**		
1,50,000 Equity Shares of Rs. 30	45,00,000	(A) Current Assets		
each fully paid		Inventory		12,00,000
Reserves & Surplus		Debtors:		
Capital Redemption Reserve	1,20,000	More than 6 months		2,00,000
Securities Premium	51,000	Others (All considered good)		3,00,000
(75,000 – 24,000)		Bank balance		1,00,000
General Reserve	1,80,000	*(B) Loans and Advances:*		
Profit & Loss A/c	1,36,414	Advance Income Tax		9,60,000
Secured Loans	Nil	Miscellaneous Expenditure		Nil
Unsecured Loans	Nil			
Current liabilities:				
Creditors for Goods	6,76,800			
Unpaid Dividend	6,000			
O/s Expenses	18,000			
Managerial Remuneration o/s (60,0000 – 47,000)	13,000			
Provisions:				
Provision for Taxation	8,35,000			
Proposed Dividend	2,25,000			
Corporate Dividend	63,786			
	68,25,000			68,25,000

Working notes:

(1) Income tax paid under dispute for the last year has been shown under Advance Income Tax.

(2) Provision for taxation of last year has been added to the current year's provision for taxation.

(3) Corporate dividend tax has been calculated @ 14.025% on the total dividends - Preference and Equity, paid and proposed (4,800 + 2,25,000 + 2,25,000)

(4) An amount equivalent to the face value of preference shares redeemed out of profits has been transferred to Capital Redemption Reserve out of General Reserve.
General Reserve = (3,00,000 – 1,20,000) Rs. 1,80,000

(5) Premium on Redemption Account has been charged to Securities Premium account.

Illustration (16) (Consignment and Investment in Subsidiaries)

From the following particulars relating to P.V. Ltd. prepare final accounts for the year ended 31st March, 2006.

Debit balances	Rs.
Furniture at cost less depreciation	3,90,000
Go down, at cost	13,00,000
Building	11,05,000
Debtors	3,90,000
Technical Know how at cost	91,000
Debenture Interest for the half year to 30 th September 2005	26,000
Income Tax Account balance	91,000
Cash at Bank	3,09,000
Cash in hand	1,20,000
Discount on issue of Debentures (1. 4. 2005)	13,000
Preference Dividend for the half year to 30th September 2005	39,000
Final dividend for 2004-05	48,750
Bill paid against pending consignments	3,90,000
Bills Receivable	26,000
Charges paid against unsold consignments	10,400
Stock as on 31. 3. 2006	1,95,000
Investments at cost in subsidiaries	6,76,000
	52,20,150
Sales ex-consignments not closed	3,25,000
Reserve Fund	2,60,000
6% Preference Shares of Rs. 1000 each	13,00,000
Equity shares of Rs. 10 each Rs. 7.50 paid	9,75,000
Sundry Consignor's balances	1,30,000
5% Debentures with general charge	10,40,000
Current Account Balances of Subsidiaries	52,000

Trade Creditors	4,55,000
Commission on sales ex-consignments	52,000
Profit and Loss Account (1.4.2005)	1,95,000
Trading Profits	4,36,150
	52,20,150

Other information

(i) Provide 5% for Doubtful debts and 5% Depreciation on Furniture. Writer off discount on issue of debentures Rs. 6,500.

(ii) Create provision for Taxation @ 40%

(iii) Bills receivable for Rs. 9,750 maturing after 31st March 2006 has been discounted.

(iv) Stock includes Rs. 39,000 in respect of unsold stock in stores, ex-sundry consignments invoiced proforma at that figure.

(v) Investments in subsidiaries include 13,000 equity shares of Y Ltd. of Rs. 10 each Rs. 6.25 per share paid up.

(vi) All subsidiary companies close their Accounts on 31st March each year and have made profits for the year ended 31st March 2006.

[ICWA (F) Adapted]

Solution:

PV LTD.
PROFIT AND LOSS ACCOUNT
for the year ended 31st March, 2006

	Rs.			Rs.
To Debenture Interest	52,000	By Gross Profit b/d	4,36,150	
To Provision for Doubtful debts	19,500	Less Stock of Unsold		
To Depreciation on Furniture	19,500	goods adjusted	39,000	3,97,150
To Discount on Issue of Debentures w/o	6,500	By Commission on Sales		52,000
To Provision for Income Tax	1,40,660	ex-consignments		
(including Rs. 91,000)				
To Net Profit c/d	2,10,990			
	4,49,150			4,49,150
To Final Dividend for 2004-05:	48,750	By Balance b/d		1,95,000
Preference Dividend	78,000	By Net Profit b/d		2,10,990
(39,000 + 39,000)				
(Interim + Final)				
To Corporate Dividend Tax*	17,777			
To Balance c/d	2,61,463			
	4,05,990			4,05,990

*Calculated on Rs. 1,26,750 @ 14.025%

BALANCE SHEET OF PV LTD.
As on 31st March, 2006

	Rs.			Rs.
Share Capital:		**Fixed Assets:**		
Authorised Capital		Godown at cost		13,00,000
---	---	Building at cost		11,05,000
Issued, Subscribed &		Furniture at cost		
Paid up Capital		*Less* Depreciation		3,70,500
13,000 6% Preference Shares		**Investments**		
of Rs. 100 each fully paid	13,00,000	Investments at cost in		6,76,000
1,30,000 Equity Shares of		Subsidiaries		
Rs. 10 each Rs. 7.50 paid up	9,75,000	**Current Assets, Loans**		
Reserves & Surplus		**& Advances:**		
Reserve Fund	2,60,000	*(A) Current Assets*		
Profit & Loss Account	2,61,463	Debtors	3,90,000	
Secured Loans		*Less* Provision	19,500	3,70,500
5% Debentures	10,40,000	Stock		1,56,000
(with general charge)		(1,95,000 – 2,39,000)		
Unsecured Loans	Nil	Cash at Bank		3,09,000
Current Liabilities & Provisions:		Cash in hand		1,20,000
(A) Current liabilities		*(B) Loans & Advances*		
Trade Creditors	4,55,000	Bills Receivable		26,000
O/s Debentures Interest	26,000	**Miscellaneous Expenditure**		
Current Account (Subsidiaries)	52,000	Discount on Issue of		
Due to consignor (1)	54,600	Debentures		6,500
(B) Provisions:		Technical know		91,000
Preference dividend	39,000			
Provision for Taxation	49,660			
(Rs. 1,40,660 – 91,000)				
Corporate Dividend Tax	17,777			
	45,30,500			45,30,500

There is contingent liability for bills discounted for Rs. 9,750 and for partly paid shares in subsidiaries Rs. 48,750.

Working Notes:

		Rs.
(1) Sales ex-consignments not closed		3,25,000
Add Sundry Consignors balances		1,30,000
		4,55,000
Less Bills paid	3,90,000	
Charges paid	10,400	4,00,400
Due to consignor		54,600

(2) Dividends already paid whether relating to last year or interim dividend for the current year are not shown in the Balance Sheet.

Illustration (17) (Vertical Statements)

The following is the Trial Balance of S Ltd. as on 31st March, 2006.

Debit	Rs. '000'	Credit	Rs. '000'
Land at cost	110	Equity Capital (Rs. 10)	150
Plant & Machinery at cost	385	10% Debentures	100
Debtors	48	General Reserve	65
Stock (31. 3. 06)	43	Profit & Loss Account	36
Bank	10	Securities Premium	20
Adjusted Purchases	160	Sales	350
Factory Expenses	30	Creditors	26
Administration Expenses	15	Provision for Depreciation	86
Selling Expenses	15	Suspense A/c	2
Debenture Interest	10		
Interim Dividend Paid	9		
	835		835

Additional Information:

(i) On 31st March, 2006 the company issued bonus shares to the shareholders on 1:3 basis. No entry relating to this has yet been made.

(ii) The authorised share capital of the company is 25,000 shares of Rs. 10 each.

(iii) The company on the advice of an independent valuer wishes to revalue the land at Rs. 1,80,000.

(iv) Proposed final dividend 10%

(v) Suspense Account represents cash received for the sale of some of the machinery on 1. 4. 2005. The cost of the machinery was Rs. 5,000 and the accumulated depreciation there on being Rs. 5,000.

(vi) Depreciation is to be provided on Plant and Machinery at 10% on cost.

You are required to prepare Profit and Loss Account for the year ended 31st March 2006 and a Balance Sheet on that date in vertical form as per the provisions of Schedule VI of the Companies Act 1956. Your answer to include schedules only for the following.

(1) Share Capital (2) Reserves & Surplus (3) Fixed Assets.

Provide 50% for taxation. Ignore Corporate dividend tax. *[C.A. (I) May 1997 Modified]*

Solution:

S LTD.

BALANCE SHEET AS ON 31ST MARCH, 2006

I Sources of Funds	Schedule No.		Rs. '000'
(1) Shareholders' Funds			
(a) Capital	1	200	
(b) Reserve and Surplus	2	159	359
(2) Loan Funds			
10% Debentures			100
			459

II Application of Funds

(1) Fixed Assets:	3			
Land			180	
Gross Block (385 – 5)		380		
Less Depreciation (86 + 38 – 5)		119	261	441
(2) Current Assets				
Stock		43		
Debtors		48		
Cash		10	101	
Less Current liabilities & Provisions				
Creditors		26		
Proposed dividend		15		
Provision for Taxation		42	83	18
				459

PROFIT AND LOSS ACCOUNT
for the year ended 31st March, 2006

		Rs. '000'
Sales		350
Other Income (Profit on sale of machine)		2
Total Income		352
Less Expenses:		
Purchases	160	
Factory Expenses	30	
Administrative Expenses	15	
Selling Expenses	15	
Depreciation	38	
Interest on Debentures	10	268
Net Profit before Tax		84
Less Provision for Taxation @ 50%		42
Net profit after Tax		42
Less Dividend: Interim	9	
Final	15	24
Balance carried to Balance Sheet		18

SCHEDULES

Schedule 1:

	Rs.
Share Capital	
Authorised Capital	
25,000 Equity Shares of Rs. 10 each	2,50,000
Issued, Subscribed and Paid up Capital	
20,000* Equity Shares of Rs. 10 each fully paid up	2,00,000

(*15,000 + 5,000 Bonus Issue)

Schedule 2:

Reserves & Surplus	
Securities Premium	20,000
Revaluation Reserve	70,000
General Reserve	15,000
Profit & Loss Account (36,000 + 18,000)	54,000
	1,59,000

Working notes:

General Reserve	
General Reserve as per T/B	65,000
Less Bonus Issue (1,50,000/3)	50,000
	15,000

Revaluation Reserve	
Revised Value of Land	1,80,000
Less Land at cost as per T/B	1,10,000
Appreciation	70,000

Schedule 3: Fixed Assets

Op. Balance	1.4.2005	Appreciation	Deletion	Depreciation	Net Value 31.3.06
Land	1,10,000	70,000	—	—	1,80,000
Plant & Machinery	3,85,000	—	5,000	1,19,000*	2,61,000
	4,95,000	70,000	5,000	1,19,000	4,41,000

* 86,000 – 5,000 + 38,000

Illustration (18) (Final Accounts and Missing figures)

Following is the abridged Balance Sheet of Everest Co. Ltd. as on 31st March, 2005.

Liabilities	Rs.	Assets		Rs.
Paid up Share Capital	5,00,000	Freehold Property		4,00,000
Profit & Loss Account	85,000	Plant & Machinery	2,50,000	
Current liabilities	2,00,000	*Less* Depreciation	75,000	1,75,000
		Stock		1,05,000
		Debtors		1,00,000
		Bank		5,000
	7,85,000			7,85,000

From the following information you are required to prepare Profit & Loss Account and Balance Sheet as on 31st March, 2006.

(a) The Composition of the total 'Liabilities side' of the company's Balance Sheet as at 31st March, 2006 (the paid up Capital remaining the same as at 31st March, 2005) was:

Share Capital	50 percent
Profit & Loss Account	15 percent

7% Debentures	10 percent
Creditors	25 percent

The Debentures were issued on 1st April, 2005, interest being paid on 30th September, 2005 and 31st March, 2006.

(b) During the year ended on 31st March, 2006 additional plant had been bought and a further Rs. 25,000 depreciation written off. Freehold property remained unchanged. The total fixed assets then constituted 60 percent of the total fixed and current assets.

(c) The Current ratio was 1.6 : 1. The quick assets ratio was 1 : 1.

(d) The debtors (four fifth of the quick assets) to sales ratio revealed a credit period of two months.

(e) Gross profit was at the rate of 15% of selling price and Return on Net worth as at 31st March, 2006 was 10%.

Ignore taxation.

[C.A. (I) Nov. 1997 Modified]

BALANCE SHEET OF EVEREST CO. LTD.
As on 31st March, 2006

Liabilities	Rs.	Assets		Rs.
Share Capital		**Fixed Assets**		
Authorised -----	-----	Freehold Property		4,00,000
Issued, Subscribed & Paid up		Plant & Machinery	3,00,000	
--- Shares of Rs. ---	5,00,000	*Less* Depreciation	1,00,000	2,00,000
Reserves & Surplus		**Investments**		Nil
Profit & Loss A/c	1,50,000	**Current Assets, Loans & Advances :**		
Secured Loans:		*(A) Current Assets*		
7% Debentures	1,00,000	Stock		1,50,000
Unsecured Loans	Nil	Debtors		2,00,000
Current Liabilities and Provisions:		Bank		50,000
Creditors	2,50,000	*(B) Loans & Advances*		Nil
		Miscellaneous Expenditure		Nil
	10,00,000			10,00,000

PROFIT AND LOSS ACCOUNT
for the year ended 31st March, 2006

	Rs.		Rs.
To Opening Stock	1,05,000	By Sales	12,00,000
To Purchases (Bal. figure)	10,65,000	By Closing Stock	1,50,000
To Gross Profit c/d	1,80,000		
	13,50,000		13,50,000

	Rs.		Rs.
To Expenses (Bal. figure)	83,000	By Gross Profit b/d	1,80,000
To Debenture Interest	7,000		
To Depreciation	25,000		
To Net Profit	65,000		
	1,80,000		1,80,000

Working Notes:

(1) Since there is no change in paid up Capital which is Rs. 5,00,000 the total of liabilities side of Balance Sheet will be Rs. 10,00,000

			Rs.
	Thus, Profit & Loss A/c	(15% of Total) =	1,50,000
	7% Debentures	(10% of total) =	1,00,000
	Creditors	(25% of total) =	2,50,000
(2)	Total value of Fixed Assets (60%)	=	6,00,000
Less	Freehold property		4,00,000
	Plant & Machinery (Net)		2,00,000
(3)	Total Depreciation = Rs. 75,000 + 25,000	=	1,00,000
(4)	Gross value of Plant & Machinery	=	3,00,000
(5)	Debtors turn over ratio = $\frac{12}{2}$	=	6 times
	Thus the sales = 2,00,000 × 6 =		Rs. 12,00,000
(6)	Gross Profit 15% of Rs. 12,00,000 =		Rs. 1,80,000

(7) Net Profit = Return on Networth

Net worth = Total Assets – liabilities

Rs. 10,00,000 – 3,50,000 = 6,50,000

10% of Rs. 6,50,000 = Rs. 65,000

(8) Total current liabilities = Rs. 2,50,000

Total current Assets = 1.6 times

= 2,50,000 1.6 = Rs. 4,00,000

Liquid Assets are equal to **Current Liabilities**

(9) Stock = Total current Assets – liquid assets

= 4,00,000 – 2,50,000 = Rs. 1,50,000

(10) Debtors are 4/5th of total liquid Assets

= 2,50,000 × 4/5 = Rs. 2,00,000

The balancing figure Rs. 50,000 is treated as Bank balance

Illustration (19) (Change of method of depreciation and final accounts)

ABC Ltd. is a manufacturing company, having authorised share capital comprising 60,000 Equity Shares of Rs. 10 each and 3,000 5% preference shares of Rs. 100 each.

Following is the Trial Balance as on 31.3.06

	Dr. (Rs.)	Cr. (Rs.)
Equity Share Capital		
30,000 Shares of Rs. 10 each		3,00,000
Preference Share Capital		
3,000 shares of Rs. 100 each		3,00,000
General Reserve		2,00,000
Profit & Loss Account		20,000
Purchases	3,00,000	
Bought ledger balances		50,000
Sales		5,50,000
Wages	30,000	
Salaries	40,000	
Commission paid to M.D. on account	10,000	
Factory Expenses	3,800	
Carriage Inward	10,000	
Opening Stock :		
Finished Goods	40,000	
Raw-materials	20,000	
Other Administrative Expenses	20,000	
Sales Ledger balances	25,000	
Plant & Machinery (including motor car)	4,50,000	
Furniture	70,000	
Dividend Unpaid		500
Preliminary Expenses	30,000	
Preference Share dividend for the year paid	15,000	
Cash and Bank balance	48,000	
Bad debts Reserve		1,400
Miscellaneous Income		4,900
Land & Building	3,15,000	
	14,26,800	14,26,800

You are required to prepare Trading and Profit and Loss Account for the year ended 31st March, 2006 and a Balance Sheet as on that date after considering the following:

	Rs.
(i) Closing Stock :	
Finished Goods	50,000
Raw-material	25,000

(ii) Depreciation:

Plant	15%
Furniture	10%

(iii) Write off 1/5th of preliminary expenses.

(iv) Reserve for doubtful debts at 5%

(v) Managing Director would get commission of net profit after charging such commission. 10%

(vi) Motor Car purchased three years back costing Rs. 20,000 has been written off at 10% on straight line basis. Now it is decided to write it off at 10% on written down value basis with retrospective effect.

(vii) Rs. 500. received from a customer which had been written off last year as bad debt wrongly credited to creditors Account

(viii) Income tax is to be provided at 50%.

(ix) Proposed dividend on equity shares is 11%

(x) Profit & Loss Account balance is to be retained after making statutory transfer.

[C.S. (I) Modified]

Solution :

TRADING & PROFIT & LOSS ACCOUNT
for the year ending 31st March, 2006

		Rs.		Rs.
To Opening Stock (F.G.)		40,000	By Sales	5,50,000
To Opening Stock (R.M)	20,000		By Closing Stock	
Add Purchases	3,00,000		(finished goods)	50,000
	3,20,000			
Less Closing Stock	25,000			
To Raw-material Consumed		2,95,000		
To Wages		30,000		
To Carriage Inward		10,000		
To Factory Expenses		3,800		
To Gross Profit c/d		2,21,200		
		6,00,000		6,00,000
To Salaries		40,000	By Gross Profit b/d	2,21,200
To Other Administrative Expenses		26,000	By Miscellaneous Income	4,900
To Preliminary Expenses		6,000	By Bad debts recovered	500
To Depreciation on :			By Provision for Bad debts (Excess)	150
Plant & Machinery (2)		65,400	By Depreciation (Written back)	580
Motor Car (1)		1,458		
Furniture		7,000		

Contd.

	Rs.		Rs.
To Managing Director's Commission(3)	7,952		
To Provision for Income Tax	39,760		
To Net Profit c/d	39,760		
	2,27,330		2,27,330
To Preference dividend	15,000	By Balance b/d	20,000
To Equity Dividend	33,000	By Net Profit b/d	39,760
To General Reserve	994		
To Corporate Dividend Tax	6,732		
To Balance c/d	4,034		
	59,760		59,760

*@ 14.025% on Total dividend.

BALANCE SHEET OF ABC LTD.
As on 31st March 2005

Liabilities	Rs.	Assets		Rs.
Share Capital:		**Fixed Assets:**		
Authorised:		Land & Building		3,15,000
5% 3,000 Preference shares of	3,00,000	Plant & Machinery	4,36,000	
Rs. 100 each		*Less* Depreciation	65,400	3,70,600
60,000 Equity Shares of Rs. 10 each	6,00,000	Motor Car	20,000	
	9,00,000	*Less* Depreciation	6,878	13,122
Issued, Subscribed and Paid up:		(5,420 + 1,458)		
3,000 5% Preference Shares of	3,00,000	Furniture	70,000	
Rs. 100 each fully paid up		*Less* Depreciation	7,000	63,000
30,000 Equity Shares of Rs. 10 each	3,00,000	**Investments:**		Nil
fully paid up		**Current Assets:**		
Reserves & Surplus:		Closing stock		
General Reserve	2,00,994	Raw material		25,000
Profit & Loss A/c	4,034	Finished Goods		50,000
Secured Loans	Nil	Debtors	25,000	
Unsecured Loans	Nil	*Less* Provision	1,250	23,750
Current Liabilities:		Cash at Bank		48,000
Creditors (50,000 – 500)	49,500	**Loans & Advances:**		
Dividend Unpaid	500	Advance Commission to M.D.		2,048
Provisions:		(10,000 – 7,952)		
Provision for Income Tax	39,760	**Miscellaneous Expenditure**		
Proposed Dividend	33,000	Preliminary Exp.(30,000 – 6,000)		24,000
Corporate Dividend Tax	6,732			
	9,34,520			9,34,520

Working Notes :

		Rs.
(1)	Motor Car	
	Depreciation on S.L.M.	
	Cost of Motor Car	20,000
	Depreciation @ 10% for 3 years at straight line Method	6,000
	W.D.V.	14,000
	Depreciation on W.D.V. basis @ 10%	
	Cost of the Car	20,000
	Depreciation for Ist Yr	2,000
		18,000
	Depreciation for IInd yr	1,800
		16,200
	Depreciation for IIIrd yr	1,620
		14,580
	Total Depreciation Charged under W.D.V. Method for 3 years	5,420
	Depreciation Charged under S.L.M. for 3 years	6,000
	Excess Depreciation to be written back	580
	Depreciation for the current year on W.D.V. basis @ 10% (10% of Rs. 14,580)	1,458
(2)	Plant and Machinery (W.D.V) (1.4.2005)	4,50,000
Less	W.D.V. of Car (included in P/M)	14,000
		4,36,000
	Depreciation @ 15%	65,400
(3)	Net Profit before Managing Director's Commission and Tax (2,27,330 – 1,39,858)	= 87,472
	Commission = $8{,}7472 \times \frac{10}{110}$	= 7,952

MISCELLANEOUS ILLUSTRATIONS

Illustration (20) (Tax Adjustments)

The Trial Balance of C Ltd. as on 31st March 2006 shows the following items in respect of taxation.

	Dr. (Rs.)	Cr. (Rs.)
Advance Payment of Tax	2,20,000	
Provision for Taxation for the year ended 31st March, 2005		1,20,000

The following further information is available.

(i) Advance payment of income tax includes Rs. 1,40,000 for 2004-05

(ii) Actual tax liability for 2004-05 amount to Rs. 1,52,000 and no effect for the same has so far been given in accounts.

(iii) Provision for Income Tax for year 2005-06 to be provided Rs. 1,60,000

Prepare a Provision for Income Tax Account; (b) Advance Payment of Tax Account and, (c) Liabilities for Taxation Account and how these items will appear in the Profit & Loss Account and Balance Sheet of the Company.

[C.A. (I) Nov. 1998 Modified]

Solution :

PROVISION FOR TAXATION A/C

		Rs.			Rs.
31.3.06	To Advance Payment	1,40,000	1.4.05	By Balance b/d	1,20,000
	To Liability for Taxation A/c	12,000	31.3.06	By Profit & Loss A/c (below the line)	32,000
		1,52,000			1,52,000
31.3.06	To Balance c/d	1,60,000	31.3.98	By Profit & Loss A/c	1,60,000

LIABILITY FOR TAXATION A/C

To Balance c/d	12,000	By Provision for Taxation A/c	12,000

ADVANCE PAYMENT OF TAX A/C

		Rs.			Rs.
31.3.06	To Balance b/d	2,20,000	31.03.06	By Provision for Taxation A/c	1,40,000
				By Balance c/d	80,000
		2,20,000			2,20,000

PROFIT & LOSS ACCOUNT (EXTRACT)
for the year ended 31st March, 2006

	Rs.		Rs.
To Provision for Taxation	1,60,000		
To Net Profit c/d			
To Provision for Taxation (for the previous year)	32,000	By Balance b/d	---
		By Net Profit b/d	---

BALANCE SHEET OF C LTD. (EXTRACT)
As on 31st March, 2006

Liabilities	Rs.	Assets	Rs.
Current liabilities and Provisions:		**Current Assets**	
(A) Current liabilities		**Loans & Advances**	
Liability for Taxation	12,000	*(B) Loans & Advances:*	
(for the previous year)		Advances Income Tax	80,000
(B) Provisions:			
Provisions for Taxation	1,60,000		
(for the current year)			

Students should note that the difference between Actual Tax liability and provision for tax made for that year will result either in short fall or excess provision which should be debited or credited respectively below the line as these items always relate to last year.

Whereas the difference between the Actual Tax liability and the Advance Payment of Tax for that year will result either in income tax payable (liability for taxation) if advance tax is less than the actual tax liability or refund if Advance Tax for that year exceeds actual tax liability of that year.

Illustration (21)

The following balances have been extracted from the books of B.P. Ltd. as on 31st March 2006

	Debit Rs.	Credit Rs.
Provision for Taxation (2004-05)		20,000
Advance Tax Paid for (2004-05)	18,000	
Advance Tax Paid for (2005-06)	10,000	
Tax Deducted at Source (2005-06)	1,000	
Profit & Loss Account balance (1.4.2005)	—	20,000

Assessment for the year 2004-05 was finalised during the year 2005-06. The total tax liability for that year was fixed at Rs. 22,000. The net profit earned by the company during the current year 2005-06 before tax amounts to Rs. 40,000. The company is in 35% tax bracket.

Pass journal entries and show how various items will appear in the company's Balance Sheet and Profit & Loss A/c.

[B.Com (H) DU 2002 Modified]

Solution:

JOURNAL ENTRIES

			Rs.	Rs.
	Profit & Loss Appropriation A/c Dr. To Provision for Taxation A/c (Being additional provision required to meet the actual tax liability)		2,000	2,000
	Provision for Taxation A/c Dr. To Advance Tax Paid A/c To Liability for Taxation A/c (Being unpaid balance transferred to LFT A/c)		22,000	18,000 4,000
	Profit & Loss A/c Dr. To Provision for Taxation A/c (Being provision for taxation made on the net profit of Rs. 40,000 @ 35%)		14,000	14,000

PROFIT & LOSS A/C

	Rs.		Rs.
To Provision for Taxation	14,000	By Profit before Tax	40,000
To Net Profit	26,000		
	40,000		40,000
To Provision for Taxation	2,000	By Balance b/d	20,000
To Balance c/d	44,000	By Net Profit b/d	26,000
	46,000		46,000

BALANCE SHEET (EXTRACT)
As on 31st March, 2006

Liabilities	Rs.	Assets	Rs.
Reserves & Surplus		**Loans & Advances**	
Profit & Loss Account	44,000	Advances Tax Paid	10,000
Provision :		Tax Deducted at Source	1,000
Provision for Taxation	14,000		

Illustration (22) (Appropriation of Profits)

The Balance Sheet of PN Ltd. as on 31st March, 2006 was as under.

Liabilities	Rs.	Assets	Rs.
Issued and Paid up Capital		Freehold Property	20,00,000
20,000 Equity Shares of Rs. 10 each	20,00,000	Stock-in-Trade	12,00,000
Profit & Loss A/c	18,00,000	S. Debtors	10,00,000
12% Debentures	12,00,000	Cash & Bank	18,00,000
S. Creditors	10,00,000		
	60,00,000		60,00,000

It was resolved in the Annual General Meeting:

(i) To pay a dividend of 10%

(ii) To issue one bonus share for every four held.

(iii) To give existing shareholders the option to buy one Rs. 100 share @ Rs. 125 for every four shares held prior to distribution of bonus.

(iv) To repay debentures at premium of 5% All shareholders exercise the option (iii) above. Pass journal entries and draw up the Balance Sheet. Also prepare Profit and Loss Appropriation Account. Ignore income tax. All the transactions have been given effect.

[B.Com (H) DU 2004 Modified]

PN LTD.
JOURNAL ENTRIES

			Debit (Rs.)	Credit (Rs.)
1.	Profit and Loss Appropriation A/c	Dr.	2,28,050	
	To Dividend Payable A/c			2,00,000
	To Corporate Dividend Tax Payable A/c			28,050
	(Being profits set aside for Dividend and corporate dividend tax as applicable)			
2.	Dividend Bank A/c	Dr.	2,00,000	
	To Bank A/c			2,00,000
	(Being amount of dividend transferred to separate account)			

Contd.

			Rs.	Rs.
3.	Dividend Payable A/c	Dr.	2,00,000	
	To Dividend Bank A/c			2,00,000
	(Being dividend paid)			
4.	Corporate Dividend Tax Payable A/c	Dr.	28,050	
	To Bank A/c			28,050
	(Being corporate Dividend Tax paid)			
5.	Profit & Loss Appropriation A/c	Dr.	5,00,000	
	To Bonus Issue A/c			5,00,000
	(Being profits appropriated)			
6.	Bonus Issue A/c	Dr.	5,00,000	
	To Equity Share Capital A/c			5,00,000
	(Being Bonus shares allotted)			
7.	Bank A/c	Dr.	6,25,000	
	To Equity Share Application & Allotment A/c			6,25,000
	(Being application money on rights issue received)			
8.	Equity Share Application and Allotment A/c	Dr.	6,25,000	
	To Equity Share Capital A/c			5,00,000
	To Securities Premium A/c			1,25,000
	(Being amount of rights issue transferred to Share Capital and securities premium A/c)			
9.	12% Debentures A/c	Dr.	12,00,000	
	Premium on Redemption A/c	Dr.	60,000	
	To Debentureholders' A/c			12,60,000
	(Being amount due on redemption)			
10.	Debentureholders' A/c	Dr.	12,60,000	
	To Bank A/c			12,60,000
	(Being amount paid to Debentureholders)			
11.	Securities Premium A/c	Dr.	60,000	
	To Premium on Redemption A/c			60,000
	(Being premium on redemption written off against securities premium Account)			
12.	Profit and Loss A/c*	Dr.	12,00,000	
	To General Reserve A/c			12,00,000
	(Being on amount equal to face value of debentures redeemed out of profits transferred to General Reserve)			

* As per SEBI's Guidelines a company must create Debenture Redemption Reserve before the commencement of redemption.

PROFIT AND LOSS APPROPRIATION A/C

	Rs.		Rs.
To Dividend Payable	2,00,000	By Balance b/d	18,00,000
To Corporate Dividend Tax	28,050	(Net Profit)	
To Bonus Issue	5,00,000		
To Balance c/d	10,71,950		
	18,00,000		18,00,000

CASH AT BANK A/C

	Rs.		Rs.
To Balance b/d	18,00,000	By Dividend Bank A/c	2,00,000
To Equity Share Application &		By Corporate Dividend Tax A/c	28,050
Allotment A/c	6,25,000	By Debentureholders A/c	12,60,000
		By Balance c/d	9,36,950
	24,25,000		24,25,000

BALANCE SHEET AS ON 31ST MARCH, 2006

Liabilities	Rs.	Assets	Rs.
Share Capital:		**Fixed Assets:**	
30,000 Equity Shares* of Rs. 100 each	30,00,000	Freehold Property	20,00,000
Reserves & Surplus		**Current Assets:**	
Securities Premium	65,000	Stock	12,00,000
Profit & Loss A/c	10,71,950	S. Debentures	10,00,000
Current Liabilities:		Cash at Bank	9,36,950
S. Creditors	10,00,000		
	51,36,950		51,36,950

*of the 30,000 shares, 5,000 shares have been issued as bonus i.e. share issued for a consideration other than cash.

Illustration (23) (Appropriation of Profits)

The following items appear on the liabilities side of the Balance Sheet of a limited company as on 31st March, 2005.

		Rs.
(i)	13.5% Preference Share Capital	4,00,000
(ii)	Equity Share Capital-Fully paid	5,00,000
(iii)	Equity Share Capital-Partly Paid (60%)	3,00,000
(iv)	Securities Premium Account	7,00,000
(v)	15% Debentures	10,00,000

Profit before interest on debentures and tax @ 40% is Rs. 11,50,000 for the accounting year 2005-06. The recommendation of the company's Board of Directors include equity dividend of 20% and capitalisation of profits for making partly paid shares as fully paid up.

Pass journal entries to incorporate Board's recommendation and present the aforesaid items on the liabilities side of Balance Sheet.

[B. Com (H) DU 1995, 1996 Adapted]

Solution:

JOURNAL ENTRIES

			Rs.	Rs.
1.	Debenture Interest A/c Dr. To Debenture Interest O/s A/c (Being interest debentures falls due)		1,50,000	1,50,000
2.	Profit & Loss A/c Dr. To Debenture Interest A/c (Being debenture interest transferred to Profit & Loss A/c)		1,50,000	1,50,000
3.	Profit & Loss A/c Dr. To Provision for Taxation A/c (Being provision for tax made)		4,00,000	4,00,000
4.	Profit & Loss A/c Dr. To Profit & Loss Appropriation A/c (Being net profit for the year transferred to Profit & Loss Appropriation A/c)		6,00,000	6,00,000
5.	Profit & Loss Appropriation A/c Dr. To General Reserve A/c (Being statutory transfer of 7.5% made to General reserve)		45,000	45,000
6.	Profit & Loss Appropriation A/c Dr. To Proposed Preference Dividend A/c To Proposed Equity Dividend A/c (Being provision for preference and equity dividend made)		2,14,000	54,000 1,60,000
7.	Equity Share Final Call A/c Dr. To Equity Share Capital A/c (Being final call due on partly paid shares)		2,00,000	2,00,000
8.	Profit & Loss Appropriation A/c Dr. To Equity Share final Call A/c (Being final call adjusted out of P & L Appropriation A/c)		2,00,000	2,00,000
9.	Profit & Loss Appropriation A/c Dr. To Corporate Dividend Tax A/c (Being provision for corporate dividend tax made @ 14.025%)		30,014	30,014

BALANCE SHEET AS ON 31ST MARCH, 2006 (EXTRACT)

Liabilities	
	zRs.
Share Capital:	
13.5% Preference Share Capital	4,00,000
Equity Share Capital	10,00,000
Reserves & Surplus	
Securities Premium	7,00,000
General Reserve	45,000
Profit & Appropriation Account	1,10,986
Secured Loans	
15% Debentures	10,00,000
Debenture Interest o/s	1,50,000
Unsecured Loans	Nil
Current Liabilities and Provisions:	
(A) Current Liabilities	Nil
(B) Provision	
Provision for Taxation	4,00,000
Proposed Dividend:	
Preference	54,000
Equity	1,60,000
Corporate Dividend Tax	30,014

Illustration (24) (Adjustments & Appropriation)

The Articles of Association of ABC Ltd. provide for the following:

(1) That 10 percent of the profits of each year shall be transferred to Reserve fund

(2) That an amount equal to 10% of Equity dividend shall be set aside for bonus to staff.

(3) That the balance available for distribution shall be applied;

(i) in paying 9% dividend on cumulative preference shares,

(ii) One third of the balance available as additional dividend on preference shares and 2/3rd as additional equity dividend.

A further condition was also imposed by the Articles that the minimum balance carried forward should be equal to 6% of Preference share capital.

The company has issued 25,000 9% Cumulative participating preference shares of Rs. 100 each fully paid; and 2,50,000 Equity Shares of Rs. 10 each fully paid. The profit for the year 2005-06 amounted to Rs. 12,90,000 and balance brought forward from the previous year Rs. 1,90,000.

You are required to provide Rs. 90,000 for depreciation, 50% for taxation before making other appropriations. Ignore corporate dividend tax.

Prepare Profit & Loss Appropriation Account

C.A. (F) Adapted.

Solution :

PROFIT AND LOSS APPROPRIATION ACCOUNT

	Rs.		Rs.
To Reserve Fund (10% 6,00,000)	60,000	By Balance b/d	1,90,000
To Provision for Bonus to staff	30,000	By Net Profit b/d	6,00,000
To Preference dividend	2,50,000	(12,90,000–90,000–60,000)	
To Equity Dividend	3,00,000	(Tax and Depreciation)	
To Balance c/d	1,50,000		
	7,90,000		7,90,000

Working Notes:

	Equity Dividend	Preference Dividend	Bonus to Staff
Normal Dividend/Bonus	2,50,000	2,25,000	25,000
Additional Dividend/Bonus	50,000	25,000	5,000
	3,00,000	2,50,000	30,000

Additional dividend/Bonus has been worked out as under :

	Let the additional Bonus to staff be	x (10% of Equity Div.)
	Additional Equity Dividend and Additional Preference Dividend	$10x$, $5x$ } The ratio is 2 : 1
	Total Profits Available	7,90,000
Less:	Minimum Balance Required (6% of Preference Capital)	(1,50,000)
	Transfer to General Reserve	(60,000)
	Normal Bonus to Staff 10% of Normal Equity Dividend	(25,000)
	Normal Preference Dividend @ 9%	(2,25,000)
	Normal Equity Dividend @ 10%	(2,50,000)
		(6,10,000)
	Balance Available	80,000

$5x + 10x + x = 80,000$

$16x = 80,000$

$x = 5,000$

Hence Additional Bonus to Staff	5,000
Additional Equity Dividend =	50,000
Additional Preference Dividend =	25,000

Alternatively equation may be worked out as under :

Let Additional Equity dividend be x

the additional Preference Dividend $= \frac{x}{2}$

& Additional Bonus to Staff $= \frac{x}{10}$

(10% of Equity dividend)

Hence $x + \frac{x}{2} + \frac{x}{10} = 80,000$

$x + .5x + .1x = 80,000$

$1.6x = 80,000$

$x = 50,000$

Thus Equity shareholders will get Rs. 50,000 as additional equity dividend and preference shareholders 50% there of i.e Rs. 25,000 as additional preference dividend and 10% of additional equity dividend will given to staff (Rs. 5,000) as additional bonus because it is linked with equity dividend.

QUESTIONS

1. What are the statutory provisions relating to transfer of profit to general reserve?
2. Draw up a proforma Balance Sheet in horizontal form as per the provisions of Companies Act 1956 (Schedule VI).
3. Distinguish between interim dividend and final dividend.
4. A company cannot make payment of dividend out of current profits without making good the past losses. Comment.
5. What are contingent liabilities? How these are treated in the final accounts of a joint stock company?
6. What are divisible profits? How are these profits capitalised?
7. What are capital profits? Can a Company make payment of dividend out of capital profits?
8. Write short notes on the following
   (a) Provision for Taxation
   (b) Miscellaneous Expenditure
   (c) Payment of interest out of capital

PROBLEMS

(1) The balance in Profit and Loss Account as per Balance Sheet as on 31st March, 2005 is Rs. 32,600 where as the balance on Balance Sheet as on 31st March, 2006 is Rs. 38,100. The following information is available.

(a) Rs. 8,500 depreciation has been charged

(b) A dividend of Rs. 15,000 has been provided.

(c) An amount of Rs. 4,500 has been transferred to General Reserve.

(d) A dividend of Rs. 1,000 (gross) received from X Ltd. has been credited.

(e) A Loss on sale of Fixed Asset amounting to Rs. 2,300 has been debited.

(f) Indirect expenses charged to Profit and Loss Account amounted to Rs. 30,500.

Calculate Gross Profit, Trading Profit and Net Profit.

[ICWA (I) Adapted]

Ans.: Gross Profit: Rs. 65,300 Trading Profit (operating) Rs. 34,800

Net Profit Rs. 25,000

(2) The Balance Sheet of Z Ltd. as on 31st March, 2005 was as under:

Liabilities	Rs.	Assets	Rs.
50,000 Equity Shares of Rs. 10 each	5,00,000	Freehold Property	5,00,000
Profit & Loss Account	4,50,000	Stock	3,00,000
6% Debentures	3,00,000	Debtors	2,50,000
S. Creditors	2,50,000	Cash & Bank balance	4,50,000
	15,00,000		15,00,000

The Directors resolved that :

(a) To pay a dividend of 10%

(b) To issue one bonus share for every four held.

(c) To give existing shareholders the option to buy one Rs. 10 share of Rs. 14 for every four shares held prior to bonus issue and

(d) To redeem debentures at a premium of 4%

All the shareholders exercised the option 'C' above. Pass journal entries and draw up the Balance Sheet after the above transactions have been given effect. Ignore taxation but provide for Corporate dividend Tax.

[B.Com (H) DU 1982 Adapted]

Ans. : Total of Balance Sheet - Rs. 13,13,000

Hint : CDT 12.5%
Surcharge 10%
Education cess 2%

Hence effective rate = 14.025%

i.e. CDT	12.5
Surcharge 10%	1.25
	13.75
E. Cess 2%	0.225

(3) APJ Ltd. was registered with an authorised capital of Rs. 20,00,000 dividend into shares of Rs. 10 each.

TRIAL BALANCE OF APJ LTD.
as on 31st March, 2006

	Debit (Rs.)	Credit (Rs.)
Stock	1,86,420	
Purchases and Sales	7,18,210	11,69,900
Returns	12,680	9,850
Manufacturing Wages	1,09,740	
Carriage Inward	4,910	
18% Bank Loan (Secured)	—	50,000
Interest on Bank Loan	4,500	
Office Salaries & Expenses	17,870	
Auditor's Fees	8,600	
Directors remuneration	26,250	
Preliminary Expenses	6,000	

Freehold premises	1,64,210	
Plant & Machinery	1,28,400	
Furniture	5,000	
Loose Tools	12,500	
Debtors and Creditors	1,05,400	62,220
Cash in hand	19,530	
Cash at Bank	96,860	
Advance Payment of Tax	84,290	
Profit & Loss Account	—	
(1. 4. 2005)		38,640
Share Capital	—	4,00,000
Sundry Manufacturing Expenses	19,240	
	17,30,610	17,30,610

You are required to prepare Trading and Profit & Loss Account for the year ended 31st March, 2006 and a Balance Sheet as on that date after taking into account the following adjustments:

(i) On 31st March, 2006, Outstanding manufacturing wages and outstanding office salaries stood at Rs. 1,890 and Rs. 1,200 respectively. On the same date stock was valued at Rs. 1,24,840 and Loose Tools at Rs. 10,000.

(ii) Provide for interest on Bank Loan for 6 months.

(iii) Depreciation on Plant & Machinery is to be provided at 15% while on office furniture @ 10%.

(iv) Write off 1/3rd of preliminary expenses.

(v) Make a provision of Income Tax at 50%.

(vi) The Directors recommended a maiden dividend of 15% for the year ending 31st March 2006.

[B.Com (H) DU 1991]

Ans: Gross Profit Rs. 2,51,500

Net Profit Rs. 82,160

Total of Balance Sheet - Rs. 6,40,160

(4) The following is the Trial Balance of E.L. Ltd. as on 31st March, 2006

Debit Balances :	Rs.
Advance Tax for 2005-06	2,50,000
Interim Dividend	50,000
Capital Redemption Account	2,20,000
Discount on Issue of Debentures	6,000
Share Reissue Account	2,000
Fixed Assets	10,00,000
Investments	3,00,000
Current Assets	1,60,000
	19,88,000

Credit Balances

Share Forfeiture Account	6,000
10% Preference Share Capital	2,00,000
Equity Share Capital	5,00,000
General Reserve	2,00,000
Securities Premium Account	20,000
Profit & Loss Account	1,50,000
Operating Profit for 2005-06 (before tax)	6,02,000
13% Debentures	1,00,000
Current Liabilities	2,10,000
	19,88,000

Additional Information:

(a) On 31st March, 2006, the issued Share Capital consists of 50,000 equity shares of Rs. 10 each fully paid up. Share reissue account represents discount allowed at the time of reissue of 1,000 forfeited equity shares which were earlier forfeited for the non-payment of the final call.

(b) Subsequent to above, the preference share capital was redeemed out of profits otherwise available for dividend, the directors deciding to pay a premium of 10% to the preference shareholders. The company also issued bonus shares to equity shareholders in the ratio of 2:5 out of Capital Redemption Reserve Account. Both the redemption of preference shares and the issue of bonus shares have not been recorded in the books except that the amount paid to the preference share holders has been debited to the Capital Redemption Account.

(c) Provision for taxation is required at 50%

(d) The Board of Directors has proposed a final dividend of 20% on equity shares after appropriating profits as per law.

(e) The Board of Directors has decided to record the upward revaluation of fixed assets by 25%

(f) Rs. 2,000 out of discount on debentures account, is yet to be written off against the profit for the current year.

Prepare Profit & Loss Account for the year ended 31st March 2006 and a Balance Sheet as on that date after incorporating the above.

[C.S. (I) June 1997]

Ans: Net Profit - Rs. 3,00,000
Corporate Dividend Tax Rs. 19,635
Total B/s - Rs. 19,64,000. **Hint :** Pay preference dividend on Rs. 4,00,000.

(5) A Ltd. has a paid up capital of Rs. 15,00,000 dividend into 1,50,000 shares of Rs. 10 each and 11% Preference Share Capital of Rs. 5,00,000 divided into 5,000 shares of Rs. 100 each. The balance of profit brought forward from the previous year was Rs. 38,000.

The profit for the year 2005-06 amounted to Rs. 9,50,000 before tax which has to be provided @ 40%. The Directors proposed a dividend of 25% on Equity Share Capital after the following provisions.

(a) A statutory minimum transfer to general reserve and

(b) Providing for Preference dividend.

Prepare Profit and Loss Appropriation Account.

[B.Com (H) DU Adapted 1998]

Ans: Balance of Profit & Loss Appropriation Account taken to Balance Sheet - Rs. 60,692

Hint - Provide for Corporate Dividend Tax @ 14.025%

(6) Following is the summarised Balance Sheet of SRK Ltd. as on 31st March, 2006.

Liabilities	Rs.	Assets	Rs.
Share Capital (Rs. 10)	2,50,000	Fixed Assets	4,50,000
General Reserve	50,000	Current Assets	2,50,000
Profit & Loss A/c	2,50,000		
14% Debentures	50,000		
S. Creditors	1,00,000		
	7,00,000		7,00,000

Other Information :

The Fixed assets include Freehold Property which the company got professionally valued at Rs. 4,00,000 as against it's book value of Rs. 2,50,000.

At the same time it is proposed to:

(a) Capitalise part of the undistributed profits by making a bonus issue in the ratio of 1:5.

(b) Create a reserve of Rs. 25,000 for the replacement of fixed assets in addition to aggregate depreciation of Rs. 50,000 already provided, and

(c) Redeem one half of the outstanding debentures at a premium of 5%.

Assume that the appropriate resolutions were adopted to give effect of the above.

Pass journal entries and prepare a Balance Sheet as on that date.

[B.Com (H) DU 1986 Modified]

Ans: Capital Reserve - Rs. 1,50,000
Profit & Loss A/c (Balance) Rs. 1,48,750
Assets Replacement Reserve - Rs. 25,000
Total of Balance Sheet - Rs. 8,23,750

(7) The following balances have been extracted from the books of X Ltd. as on 31st March, 2006.

	Rs.
Profit & Loss Account-debit balance as on 1.4.2005	2,00,000
Preliminary expenses	10,000
Plant and machinery	1,00,000
Furniture and fixtures	20,000
Motor car	15,000
Sales	20,00,000

Miscellaneous receipts	1,20,000
Opening stock of finished goods	3,00,000
Consumption of raw material	9,00,000
Closing stock of raw material at cost	5,00,000
Bank overdraft	1,00,000
Securities premium	3,60,000
Share Capital	6,00,000
Unsecured loan	3,00,000
Sundry debtors (including Rs. 1,00,000 over six months)	7,00,000
Salaries and wages	2,00,000
Office administration expenses	4,00,000
Selling and distribution expenses	1,50,000
Sundry creditors	4,15,000
Advance payment of income tax	3,00,000
Misc. advances	40,000
Interim dividends	60,000

The following further information is given:

(i) Closing Stock of finished goods at cost is Rs. 6,00,000

(ii) The original cost of fixed assets was:

Plant and machinery	2,00,000
Furniture and Fixture	30,000
Motor Car	25,000

Depreciation is to be charged on the written down value @ 10% on Plant & Machinery and Furniture & fixtures and 20% on motor car. There were no additions or disposals during the year.

(iii) The entire authorised capital which consists of equity shares of Rs. 100 each has been issued and subscribed. The share capital is paid up to the extent of 30% and there are no calls-in-arrears.

(iv) The unsecured loan was taken on 1. 1. 2006 @ 18% interest per annum. Interest is payable half yearly and necessary provisions are to be made in accounts.

(v) Office administration expenses include auditor's fee: Rs. 5,000 (including fee for taxation services: Rs. 1,000) and directors fee: Rs. 3,000.

(vi) Provision for taxation to be made @ 40% and corporate dividend tax as applicable.

(vii) Preliminary expenses are to be written off.

(viii) The directors have proposed a final dividend of Rs. 6 on each equity share in addition to the interim dividend already declared.

You are required to prepare Profit & Loss Account for the year ended 31st March, 2006 and balance sheet as on that date.

[C.S. (I) Dec. 89 Modified]

Ans: Net Profit after Tax - Rs. 4,38,900

Total of Balance Sheet - Rs. 22,60,000

(8) S Ltd. has authorised capital of Rs. 50,00,000 divided in to 5,00,000 Equity Shares of Rs. 10 each. Their books disclosed the following balances as on 31st March, 2006.

Particulars	Rs.	Particulars	Rs.
Stock 1. 4. 2005	6,65,000	Bank Current A/c	20,000
Discounts & rebates	30,000	Cash in hand	8,000
Carriage inwards	57,500	Debenture interest	
Patterns	3,75,000	(for half year 30.09.05)	10,000
Rates, taxes and insurance	55,000	Interest (Banks)	91,000
Furniture and fixtures	1,50,000	Preliminary expenses	10,000
Material purchased	12,32,500	Calls in arrears	10,000
Wages	13,05,000	Equity share capital	
Coal and coke	63,000	(2,00,000 shares of Rs. 10 each)	20,00,000
Freehold land	12,50,000	4% Debentures (repayable	
Plant & machinery	7,50,000	after 10 years)	5,00,000
Engineering tools	1,50,000	Bank overdraft	7,57,000
Goodwill	3,75,000	Sundry creditors (for goods)	2,40,500
Sundry debtors	2,66,000	Sales	36,17,000
Bills receivables	1,34,500	Rent (Cr.)	30,000
Advertisement	15,000	Transfer fees	6,500
Commission and brokerage	67,500	Profit & Loss A/c (Cr.)	67,000
Business expenses	56,000		
Repairs	46,500		
Bad debts	25,500		

The stock (valued at cost or market value, which is lower) as on 31st March 2006 was Rs. 7,08,000. Outstanding liabilities for wages Rs. 25,000 and business expenses Rs. 25,000. Dividend declared @ 10% on paid-up capital.

Charge depreciation: Plant and Machinery @ 5% Engineering Tools @ 20%; Patterns @ 10%; and Furniture & Fixtures @ 10%. Provide 2% on debtors as doubtful debts after writing off Rs. 21,500 as bad debts. Write off preliminary expenses Rs. 5,000 and create debenture redemption reserve Rs. 50,000. Provide 40% for income tax and corporate dividend tax as applicable.

You are required to prepare:

(i) Profit & Loss Account for the year ended 31st March 2006 and a

(ii) Balance sheet as on that date in vertical form.

(C.S. (I) Dec. 1990 Modified)

Ans: Net Profit after Tax - R. 2,58,366

Total of Balance Sheet - Rs. 33,15,610

(9) The following balances have been extracted from the books of Premier Ltd. as on 31st March, 2006.

Debit	Rs.	Credit		Rs.
Freehold Land	2,50,000	Income from investment		12,000
Building	1,00,000	Provision for Bad debts		
Furniture	30,000	(1. 4. 2005)		2,000
Debtors	50,000	Creditors		30,000
Stock (31. 3. 2006)	40,000	Provision for depreciation:		
Cash at bank	15,000	(1. 4. 2005)		
Cash in hand	1,000	Building	5,000	
Cost of goods sold	3,00,000	Furniture	5,000	10,000
Salaries and wages	15,000	Suspense A/c		2,500
Miscellaneous Expenses	8,000	Equity Share Capital		3,67,500
Investment in shares	2,00,000	6% Cum. Preference Share Capital		80,000
Interest	3,000	Securities Premium		20,000
Bad debts	1,000	Bank overdraft		1,00,000
Repairs and maintenance	1,500	Sales		4,00,000
Advance payment of Income tax	16,000	Profit & Loss A/c (1.4.2005)		6,500
	10,30,500			10, 30,500

The following further particulars are available:

(i) The land was revalued on 1st January, 2006 at Rs. 3,50,000 by an expert valuer but no effect given in the books although the directors have decided to adjust the revalued amount.

(ii) Provision for bad debts is to be adjusted to 5% on the amount of debtors.

(iii) Equity share capital consists of 36,900 equity hares of Rs. 10 each, out of which 36,400 shares are fully paid-up, and on 500 shares final call of Rs. 3 remains unpaid.

(iv) Suspense account represents money received from the new allottee for reissue of 500 shares forfeited during the year for non-payment of the final call, but no entry thereof has been passed.

(v) Provision for taxation is to be made at 35%

(vi) Market value of investments was Rs. 1,85,000 on 31st March, 2006.

(vii) The company is managed by the directors who are entitled to a remuneration calculated at 3% of the annual net profits.

(viii) Depreciation is to be charged on:
(a) Building @ 2%; and
(b) Furniture @ 10%.

(ix) The land and building of the company are mortgaged in favour of the bank as security for overdraft sanctioned upto a limit of Rs. 3,00,000.

(x) Dividends on cumulative preference shares were in arrear for 5 years upto 31st March, 2006. The directors have recommended payment of dividend for 4 years.

(xi) Bills receivable for Rs. 6,500 maturing after 31st March, 2006 had been discounted.

You are required to prepare the profit and loss account for the year ended on 31st March, 2006 and the balance sheet as on that date after making such assumptions as may be considered necessary. Ignore previous year's figures.

[C.S. (I) June 1990 Modified]

Ans: Net Profit after Tax - Rs. 49,548
Total of Balance Sheet - Rs. 7,85,100

(10) Given below is the trial balance and additional information relating to Bharat Implements Ltd. as at the end of their financial year 2005-06. Prepare the final accounts in proper form:

TRIAL BALANCE AS ON 31ST MARCH, 2006

(Rs. in thousands)

	Dr.	Cr.
Stock (1. 4. 2005):		
Raw materials and stores	50,020	
Work-in-progress	20,080	
Finished goods	99,900	
Purchases	4,48,400	
Sales		6,69,700
Salaries and wages	29,710	
Other Expenses	1,17,640	
Other income		2,880
Depreciation	3,550	
Investments	190	
Fixed assets at cost	63,870	
Interest accrued	25	
Sundry Debtors	59,000	
Cash at Bank	320	
Loans and Advances	580	
Share Capital		20,000
Development rebate reserve		2,340
Investment allowance reserve		4,250
General reserve		25,800
Secured Loans		13,480
Fixed Deposits		16,000
Depreciation reserve		28,000
Provision for doubtful debts		60
Sundry Creditors		1,10,775
	8,93,285	8,93,285

Additional information:

(a) Stocks at the end of 31st March, 2006 (Rs. In thousands)

Raw materials and stores	30,010
Work-in-process	25,040

	Finished goods	75,950
(b)	Depreciation allowable under income-tax rules for the year.	4,250
(c)	Market value of investments	150

(d) Sundry debtors include Rs 121 thousands due for more than six months of which provision has been made for doubtful debts at Rs. 45 thousands during the year.

(e) Included in other expenses are—

(i) Fees to auditors Rs. 65 thousands, out of which Rs. 15 thousands are in other capacities; and

(ii) Interest on fixed loans Rs. 620 thousands and other interest Rs. 1,000 thousands.

(f) Rs. 340 thousands are to be re-transferred from development rebate reserve account.

(g) Provision is to be made for managing director's remuneration at 5% of net profits as provided under law, subject to a maximum of Rs. 120 thousands per annum and Income tax @ 40%

(h) Balance of profit is to be transferred to general reserve after providing for dividend at 25% on capital and corporate dividend tax as applicable.

(i) The authorised capital of the company is 20 lakhs equity shares of Rs. 10 each.

[C.S. (I) Dec. 87 Modified]

Ans. : Profit after Tax - Rs. 20,496 Thousands

Total of Balance Sheet - Rs. 2,26,925 Thousands.

(11) S. Kanad & Co. Ltd., have an authorised capital of rupees one lakh comprising 250 preference shares of Rs. 100 each and 7,500 equity shares of Rs. 10 each. From the following particulars prepare manufacturing account and profit and loss account for the year ended on 31st March, 2006 and also the balance sheet as at that date :

Debit balances (in Rs.): Opening stock of raw materials & stores — 27,000: Opening W. I. P. — 3,000; Opening finished goods — 24,000; Purchase of materials & stores — 1,20,000; Inward freight & duty — 10,500; Electricity, power and fuel — 3,000; salaries, wages & Bonus — 30,000; Rent, rates & taxes — 1,500; Insurance — 750; Directors' remuneration — 1,300; Interest — 3,000; Sundry expenses — 12,500; Calls-in-arrears (equity shares) — 600; Calls-in-arrears (Preference shares) — 150; Sundry debtors — 26,000; Cash and bank balances — 13,200; Land & Building — 7,500 (1. 4. 2005); Plant and Machinery (1. 4. 2005) — 29,000; Other miscellaneous factory assets (1. 4. 2005) — 7,500; Office furniture (1. 4. 2005) — 1,500.

Credit Balances (in Rs.): Net sales — 1,70,000; Miscellaneous receipts 1,750; Issued & subscribed capital — 5,000 Equity shares of Rs. 10 each fully called — 50,000 ; 100 6% Preference shares of Rs. 100 each fully called — 10,000 General reserve — 10,000; Dividend equalisation fund 3,000; Secured loans (against fixed assets) — 20,000; Bank Overdraft — 35,000; Sundry creditors — 10,000; Provision for taxation — 1,950; Unpaid dividend — 8,500; Profit and loss account — 1,800.

The following additional information were also available:

(a) Closing stock — raw materials & stores Rs. 33,000; work-in-progress Rs. 4,000; and finished goods — Rs. 40,000.

(b) Depreciation to be provided @ 2% on land and buildings; 10% on plant and machinery; 3% on other factory assets; and 15% on furniture.

(c) Outstanding & accrued expenses: interest an secured loans Rs. 400; rent, rates and taxes — Rs. 300; audit fees Rs. 800.

(d) Insurance paid in advance — Rs. 150.

(e) Expenses on electricity, etc. and salary, wages, etc. should be apportioned between factory and office in the ratio of 2:1.

(f) Out of the figure of sundry debtors of Rs. 900 was considered doubtful and the rest was considered good for which there was no security other than the Director's personal security. It was decided to provide a bad and doubtful debts reserve @ 4%. There was no debt due from directors and officers or any other company under the same management.

(g) The Board of directors recommended the following appropriations of profit, which are to be incorporated in the final accounts:

Provision for taxation Rs. 50; transfer to general reserve Rs. 1,100; proposed dividend on equity shares @ 10% and on preference shares @ 6% to the extent of the amount paid-up. Provide for corporate dividend tax as applicable.

(h) No calls on shares were due from directors of the company.

(i) There was a pending law suit against the company for a sum of Rs. 500.

[C.S. (I) June 86 Modified]

Ans: Net profit after tax - Rs. 6,260

Total of Balance Sheet Rs. 1,57,310

(12) The following balances relate to Himalaya Company Ltd. as on 31st March, 2006.

Particulars	Dr. Rs.	Particulars	Cr. Rs.
Motor car (cost less depreciation)	8,000	Share forfeiture account	500
Sundry debtors	60,000	Share capital	1,00,000
Furniture (cost less depreciation)	4,000	Profit and loss (31.3.2005)	1,500
Plant (cost less depreciation)	15,000	Gross Profit	54,150
Compensation to Employees	2,000	Development rebate reserve	1,350
Closing stock	35,000	Bank overdraft-UCO	25,000
Rent and taxes	8,000	Sundry creditors	11,000
Selling expenses	10,000	Liabilities for expenses	3,500
Office expenses, etc.	12,000		
Security deposit	4,000		
Advance income-tax	9,000		
Cash in hand	2,500		
Cash in bank	27,500		
	1,97,000		1,97,000

The following additional information is available:

(i) Share capital consists of :

(a) 15,000 10% cumulative preference shares of Rs. 100 each, out of which 500 shares are fully called up and paid-up.

(b) 15,000 equity shares of Rs. 10 each, out of which 5,000 shares are fully called up and paid-up.

(ii) Transfer Rs. 900 to the development rebate reserve account on 31st March, 2006

(iii) Bank overdraft is secured by the hypothecation of stock.

(iv) The manager is entitled to 5% commission on the net profit of the company.

(v) Addition made to plant during the year ended 31st March, 2006 was Rs. 8,000.

(vi) Depreciation written off upto of 31st March, 2005 and **rates** against each are as under :

	Amount Rs.	Rate (%)
Plant	2,000	15
Furniture	1,000	10
Motor car	10,000	20

(vii) Provision for taxation to be made at 40%

(viii) The amount shown against forfeited account represents unadjusted profit on reissue of forfeited shares made during the year.

(ix) Sundry debtors include outstanding Rs. 1,000 for more than six months.

(x) Office expenses include Rs. 1,500 as audit fee and Rs. 500 as audit expenses.

You are required to draw:

(a) the profit and loss account for the year ended on 31st March, 2006 and

(b) The balance sheet (in Schedule VI - Form) as on that date.

[C.S. (I) June 92 Modified]

Ans: Net Profit after Tax Rs. 9,663

Balance Sheet Total - Rs. 1,60,750

(13) On 31st March, 2006 the following balances appear in the books of the Alfa Hotels Ltd.:

Particulars	Rs.	Particulars	Rs.
Interest on debentures	60,000	12% Mortgage debentures	5,00,000
Rates and taxes	18,000	Share Capital	40,00,000
Stock of provisions on 1.4.2005	2,50,000	General reserve	5,00,000
		Unclaimed dividends	50,000
Purchase of provisions	25,00,000	Prov. for bad debts	50,000
Salaries and wages	7,50,000	Trade creditors	2,50,000
Provident fund contribution	30,000	Expenses owing	80,000
Misc. expenses	50,000	Visitors' credit Balances	10,000
Directors fees	24,000	Staff Provident fund	7,50,000

Managing Director's salary	2,15,000	Profit & loss A/c	81,000
Land	15,00,000	Income from boarding and lodging	51,00,000
Buildings	50,00,000	Misc. receipts	65,000
Furniture and fittings	15,00,000	Depreciation A/c:	
Linen, Crockery, Glassware,		Buildings	20,00,000
cutlery and utensils	3,20,000	Furniture, etc.	10,00,000
Sundry debtors	3,50,000	Linen, crockery etc.	1,80,000
Prepaid Expenses	25,000		
Advance against purchase of Buildings	15,00,000		
Cash in hand	15,000		
Balance at bank	4,74,000		
	1,45,81,000		1,45,81,000

After taking the following information into account, prepare the company's balance sheet as on 31st March, 2006 and its profit and loss account for the year ended:

(i) Stock of provisions on 31st March, 2006 was valued at Rs. 3,00,000.

(ii) Provide Rs. 1,00,000 for depreciation of furniture and fittings: Rs. 20,000 for depreciation of linen, crockery, glassware, etc.

(iii) Make a provision for taxation @ 35%.

(iv) The directors decide to recommend a dividend @ 10% on the paid up capital of the company and transfer the remaining balance in profit and loss account to general reserve.

(v) The entire paid up share capital of the company consists of fully paid equity shares of Rs. 10 each.

(vi) Provide for corporate dividend tax as applicable.

[C.S. (I) June 1995 Modified]

Ans: Net profit after tax - Rs. 9,41,200

Total of Balance Sheet - Rs. 76,34,000

(14) The Trial Balance of Pradeep Constructions Ltd., as on 31st March, 2006 is as follows :

	Dr. Rs.	Cr. Rs.
Capital: authorised and issued		
(42,000 equity shares of Rs. 20 each)		8,40,000
Provision for depreciation (as on 1. 4. 2005)		
Leasehold property		42,000
Other properties		1,00,000
Motor van		20,000
Cash in hand	30,200	
Cash at bank	1,80,000	
Motor van	50,000	
Properties (at cost)	16,00,000	

Opening Stock	2,40,000	
Administrative and selling expenses	3,53,000	
Purchases and sales	27,75,000	41,30,000
Managing Director's remuneration	1,00,000	
Rent received		72,000
Investments at cost	1,35,000	
(Tax deducted at source 10%) income on investments		6,800
9% debentures		3,00,000
Debentures interest	21,000	
Bank interest	11,640	
Bank overdraft		14,600
Debtors and creditors	6,20,000	3,02,000
Interim dividend	33,600	
P & L A/c, as on 1.4.2005		1,15,000
Calls-in-arrears	2,000	
General reserve as on 1.1.2005		2,00,000
Share suspense		6,000
Unclaimed dividend		3,000
	61,51,440	61,51,440

The following further information is available :

(a) Closing stock at or under cost was Rs. 3,34,000.

(b) No effect has been given to the following resolution of the Board :

(i) dated July 15, 2005 forfeiting 1,000 shares on which calls amounting to Rs. 2,000 remained unpaid;

(ii) dated 18th September, reissuing the 1,000 forfeited shares for Rs. 6,000 as fully paid. The amount received was credited to share suspense a/c.

(c) The directors have recommended a final dividend of Rs. 10 per share including the interim dividend already on 25th December, 2005 and also to transfer Rs. 20,000 to general reserve.

(d) Depreciation to be provided as follows:

— Motor van 20 per cent on written down value.

— Properties other than leasehold 3 per cent on written down value.

— Leasehold property was purchased on April 1, 1999 for Rs. 2,80,000 for a period of 40 years.

(e) Managing directors are entitled to a remuneration of 10% of the net profits subject to a minimum of Rs. 50,000.

(f) Provision for taxation is to be made @ 40 per cent and corporate dividend tax as applicable

Ignoring figures for the previous year, prepare the profit and loss account for the year ended 31st March, 2006 and the balance sheet as on that date.

Ans: Net Profit after Tax Rs. 5,87,150

Total of Balance Sheet Rs. 27,38,356

[C.S. (I) June 1985 Modified]

(15) Prepare the Profit and Loss Account for the year ended 31st March, 2006 and a Balance Sheet as on that date from the following ledger balances:-

Debit.	Rs.	Credit	Rs.
Opening Stock finished	1,20,000	Sales	16,50,000
Goods in process	55,000	Export subsidy & Draw Back	50,000
Raw materials Consumed	3,50,000	Share Capital	4,90,000
Stores consumed	1,75,000	General Reserve	75,000
Wages	6,20,000	Profit & Loss A/c (as on 1.4.2005)	10,000
Closing stock:-		Secured Loan	3,85,000
Raw materials	2,00,000	Sundry Creditors	1,35,000
Stores	15,000	Outstanding expenses	82,000
Staff salary	20,000	Proposed dividend	30,000
Audit fee	5,000	Motor Car Sales A/c	9,000
Sundry Debtors	2,55,100	Reserve for Bad debts	15,000
Bad debts	8,000	Interest received	8,000
Cash and Bank Balances	1,56,200		
Fixed Deposit	1,35,000		
Income tax, advance payment	2,00,000		
Fixed Assets	3,50,000		
Managing Directors remuneration	12,000		
General expenses	2,31,500		
Directors fee	1,200		
Dividend paid	23,100		
Payment of tax deducted from Dividend	6,900		
	29,39,000		29,39,000

Further available information are as follows:-

(i) Closing stock valued at cost:

Finished goods Rs. 67,000

Goods in process Rs. 95,000

(ii) 5% of Profits as per Companies Act, subject to minimum of Rs. 1,000/- per month.

(iii) Details of Fixed Assets:-

	Original Cost upto last year	Depreciation upto last year	Addition on 1.4.2005	Rate of Depreciation
(a) Machinery	3,50,000	50,000	—	15%
(b) Furniture	30,000	18,000	—	10%
(c) Motor Cars	33,000	25,000	30,000	20%

(iv) Depreciation allowed under Income tax rule is Rs. 45,000/-

(v) An old motor car having original cost of Rs. 18,000/- and depreciation allowed Rs. 15,000/- upto last year was sold on 30. 9. 05 for Rs. 9,000/- and proceeds were credited to Motor Car Sales A/c. without any adjustment,

(vi) Provision for taxation to be made @ 50% and corporate dividend Tax as applicable

(vii) Directors recommend payment of dividend @ 10% on paid up capital,

(viii) Excess Provision for doubtful debts is no longer required.

[ICWA (F) June 1984 Modified]

Ans. : Net Profit after Tax - Rs. 1,16,317

Balance Sheet Total - Rs. 14,17,100

Hint: While calculating managerial remuneration add depreciation of Rs. 53,200 (Calculated as per accounting rules) and deduct Rs. 45,000 depreciation (Calculated as per Income Tax rules) and Rs. 8,000 for Bad debts being actual bad debts which have been deducted only out of provision created last year. Thus the provision for taxation will be Rs. 1,16,518.

(16) The summarised Balance Sheet of Vasudha Ltd. as on 30th September, 2006 was as follows:

Liabilities	Rs.	Assets	Rs.
Share Capital:		**Fixed assets**	15,00,000
Issued and fully paid		**Investments**	
5,000 Equity shares of Rs. 100		(Own Debentures of nominal value	
each fully paid	5,00,000	of nominal value of Rs. 1,00,000)	95,000
Redeemable Preference Shares of		Other securities	1,00,000
Rs. 100 each		**Current Assets:**	
(less calls in arrears on 200 shares	4,95,000	Stock	2,00,000
Reserve and Surplus:		Debtors	1,00,000
Share premium	1,00,000	Cash at bank	6,00,000
Capital Reserve	1,00,000		
General Reserve	2,00,000		
Profit & Loss A/c	3,00,000		
Secured Loans:			
10% Debentures	2,00,000		
Current Liabilities			
Creditors	7,00,000		
	25,95,000		25,95,000

On 30th September, 2006 the following were due for redemption:

(i) 5,000 6% Redeemable Preference Shares at a premium of Rs. 25 per share.

(ii) 2,000 10% Redeemable Debentures at a premium of 10%.

The redemption was made on that date or subsequently thus:

(a) For the half year ending 30th September, 2006 the debenture interest and preference dividend were paid out of the profits of the company.

(b) On an offer made to the 10% debenture-holders, the outsiders agreed to take new 12% Debentures at par in exchange of old debentures: The company also decided to assume the new debentures.

(c) A fresh issue of 1,000 equity shares of Rs. 100 each were made at a premium of Rs. 50 per share and subscribed in full. All moneys due were received forthwith.

(d) Redemption of all preference shares were made on 10th October, 2006.

You are required to show all journal entries for the above transactions and to give the company's opening Balance Sheet after giving effect to them.

[C.A. (I) May 1994 Modified]

Ans: Closing Bank Balance - Rs. 1,10,150
P & L A/c - Rs. 95,150
Total of Balance Sheet - Rs. 21,20,150

(17) From the following information relating to M.C.R. Ltd. prepare Final Accounts.

(a) Closing Stock was valued at Rs. 42,800.

(b) Depreciation to be provided on plant and machinery and furniture at 10%.

(c) The provision for reserve on sundry debtors for doubtful debts to maintain at 5% and that for discount at 1%.

(d) Income-tax to be provided at 40% and corporate dividend tax as applicable.

(e) Proposed dividend at 12%.

(f) Managing Director's commission to provide at 5% on net profit after charging his commission.

(g) Outstanding expenses:

Salary	Rs. 800
Wages	Rs. 500
Rent	Rs. 300

(h) Rs. 250 in respect of premises sublet is yet to be received. Insurance paid is for the period upto 30. 9. 06.

TRIAL BALANCE AS AT 31. 03. 2006

	Dr. Rs.	Cr. Rs.
Paid-up equity capital		2,00,000
Opening stock	85,600	
Discount		350
Advertising	4,700	
Goodwill	9,500	
Bad-debt reserve		1,800
Bills payable		1,200
Wages	7,500	
Duty and clearing charges	1,200	
Factory rent	1,600	
Carriage inwards	3,300	

	Dr. Rs.	Cr. Rs.
Returns inwards	4,500	
Salaries	15,000	
Interest		400
Plant and Machinery	40,000	
Sales		5,00,000
Gas and Water	700	
Returns outwards		1,900
Office rent	1,500	
Purchases of raw materials	3,02,700	
Bills receivable	2,000	
Cash at Bank	56,660	
Cash in hand	1,025	
Office furniture	2,500	
Sundry Creditors		8,450
Investment	1,00,000	
Rates and taxes	300	
Printing and Stationary	475	
Sundry debtors	68,000	
Advances	12,500	
General expenses	1,360	
Insurance	420	
General reserve		7,940
Profit & Loss Account balance		1,000
	7,23,040	7,23,040

[C.S. (I) June 1983 Modified]

Ans: Net profit after tax - Rs. 61,120

Total of Balance Sheet - Rs. 3,27,150

(18) The following is the Trial Balance of RV Ltd. as on 31st March, 2006.

	Debit Rs.	Credit Rs.
Opening Stock	3,00,000	
Sales		14,00,000
Purchases	9,80,000	
Productive Wages	2,00,000	
Discounts	28,000	20,000
Salaries	30,000	
Rent	19,800	
General Expenses	68,200	
Profit & Loss A/c (1.4.2005)		60,120

	Cr. Rs.	Cr. Rs.
Dividend paid	36,000	
Capital - 40,000 shares of Rs. 10 each		4,00,000
Debtors & Creditors	1,50,000	70,000
Plant & Machinery	1,16,000	
Cash & Bank	64,800	
General Reserve		62,000
Bad Debts	19,320	
	20,12,120	20,12,120

Other Information:

(a) Stock on 31st March 2006- Rs. 3,28,000
(b) Depreciation Machinery @ 15% p.a.
(c) Provide 5% discount on Debtors and 2.5% discount on creditors.
(d) One month's rent @ 21,600 p.a. was due on 31st March 2006.
(e) Six month's insurance was unexpired at Rs. 3,000 per annum.
(f) Make a provision for income tax @ 40%
(g) Provide Managing Directors Commission @ 5% on the net profits before charging his commission.

Prepare Final Accounts.

B.Com. (DU) Adapted

Ans: Net profit before commission and I. Tax = Rs. 79,230
Commission = Rs. 3,962
Net Profit after Tax and Commission = Rs. 45,161
Total of Balance Sheet = Rs. 6,35,400

(19) XYZ Ltd. has an Authorised Capital of Rs. 20,00,000 made up of 5000 6% Preference shares of Rs. 100 each and 1,50,000 Equity shares of Rs. 10 each. The Trial Balance as on 31st March 2006 was as under :

	Debit Rs.	Credit Rs.
6% Preference Shares of Rs. 100 each Fully Paid up		2,50,000
Equity Shares of Rs. 10 each Fully Called up		5,00,000
Securities Premium		50,000
General Reserve		2,00,000
Suspense Account		11,500
Calls in Arrears (@ Rs. 2 per share)	4,000	
8% Mortgaged Debentures (issued on 1.4. 2005)		3,50,000
Bank-Overdraft		91,000
Creditors		1,30.950
Interim Dividend	20,000	
Preference Dividend	15,000	

Patents & Trademarks	25,000	
Land & Building	6,72,500	
Depreciation on Land & Building		27,500
Plant & Machinery	3,62,250	
Depreciation on Plant & Machinery		1,56,200
Trade Investments at cost	96,800	
Quoted Investments at cost	1,04,000	
Work-in-progress	99,200	
Stock (1. 4. 2005)	3,37,100	
Debtors	5,35,300	
Cash in hand	5,600	
Preliminary Expenses	3,750	
Discount on Debentures	8,000	
Provision for Doubtful debts		2,350
Profit & Loss A/c (1. 4. 2005)		67,500
Provision for Taxation (for the year ending 31st March 2005)		86,000
Debenture Interest	21,000	
Sales Less Returns		23,78,000
Overhead Expenditure (50% works)	8,53,250	
Direct Material purchases	9,47,400	
Advertising	32,000	
Bank Interest	6,650	
Director's fees	2,000	
Direct Labour	3,55,950	
Loan to Employees	13,500	
Income from Trade Investments		10,600
Income from quoted Investments		8,650
	43,20,250	43,20,250

Other Information :

1. The following provisions are required to be made

		Rs.
(a)	Depreciation on : Land & Building	4,500
	Plant & Machinery	31,150
	(But the amount under schedule XIV would be Rs. 3,750 and Rs. 28,000 respectively)	
(b)	Directors Fees	2,000
(c)	Additional Provision for doubtful debts	1,050
(d)	Possible loss on a contract not yet invoiced (Work-in-progress)	6,850
(e)	Debenture Interest for 3 months	
(f)	Provision for Taxation for the year	50%
(g)	Advertising Expenses	1,300
(h)	Auditors Fees	825

2. Stock on 31st March, 2006 was valued at 1,12,500
3. Work-in-progress on 31st March, 2006 stood at Rs. 8,74,350 against which progress claims of Rs. 5,60,000 had been invoiced to customers to be included in the sales figures.
4. On 31st March 2006 the Company's Land and Building was professionally valued to be appreciated by Rs. 2,87,500.
5. Tax liability for the year ended 31st March 2006 had been agreed at Rs. 81,500.
6. Preliminary expenses and discount on debentures to be written off against profits.
7. Overhead expenditure includes remuneration of Managing Director of Rs. 13,500.
8. The directors recommended a final dividend on Equity Shares @ 9% and propose to transfer Rs. 50,000 to General Reserve.
9. Capital Expenditure commitments on 31st March 2005 amounted to Rs. 23,250 of which firm contract have been placed for Rs. 15,000.
10. The market value of quoted investments on 31st March 2006 was Rs. 1,08,750.
11. Suspense Account represents the proceed of reissue of 1,000 shares subsequent to forfeiture. No entries were passed on the forfeiture.

You are required to prepare.

(i) Profit and Loss Account and

(ii) Balance Sheet in the prescribed form.

[C.A. (I) Adapted]

Ans: Net profit after tax - Rs. 94,681

Total of Balance Sheet - Rs. 22,01,587

Hint: Calculation of Managerial Remuneration:

		Rs.
	Net profit before tax & Remuneration	2,16,625
Add	Excess of Depreciation Charged over depreciation allowed as per schedule XIV (35,650 – 31,750)	3,900
Add	Preliminary Expenses, Discount on Debentures (not to be deducted for Calculating remuneration)	11,750
		2,32,275
	Remuneration @ 5%	11,614
		2,20,661
	Tax @ 50%	1,10,330

Net profit for the year:

	Profit before tax & Remuneration (as calculated before)	2,16,625
Less	Remuneration	11,614
		2,05,011
Less	Tax	1,10,330
		94,681

5

Valuation of Goodwill and Shares

Goodwill is an intangible asset. Enterprises often pay for the acquisition of intangible assets. An intangible asset is an identifiable non-monetary asset, without physical identity and held for use in operations, for rentals or for administrative purpose. According to AS-26 Intangible assets include:

- Goodwill, trade marks, copyrights, design & system.
- Intellectual property, licences, scientific and/ or technical knowledge, market knowledge or marketing rights, customers lists & market share
- Brand names, publishing titles, computer software
- Motion picture films, mortgage servicing rights, Import quotas etc.

There are three basic features of intangible assets:

(i) Indentifiability : *i.e.* it could be distinguished and separated from other assets & that it could be rented or exchanged.

(ii) Future Economic benefits: An intangible asset must result in future flow of economic benefits from sale of goods or services or saving of cost. i.e. it should either increase the revenue or reduce cost of operation.

(iii) Control : An enterprise should have a control over the intangible asset. It means that the enterprise has the power to obtain the future economic benefits from the intangible asset and also to restrict others to avail these benefits.

What is "Goodwill"?

Goodwill may be defined as the value of reputation, location, position or a business connection which an enterprise enjoy over other firms, which helps them to earn extra (super normal) profit. According to Lord Macnaghten, "goodwill is the benefit or advantage of the good name, reputation and connection of a business. It is the attractive force which brings in customers. And it is the one thing which distinguishes an old established business from a new business at it's first start".

In theory, Goodwill is the excess earning power of the (acquired) company and in practice goodwill represents the premium paid to acquire control. In fact, goodwill is viewed in accounting as the combination of those factors that permit an enterprise to earn above average profit. According to AS-26, goodwill should be based at actual cost to the purchaser, where objectively determinable. Many of the expenditures made by a company may or may not enhance the earning power, because expenditure on self generated goodwill often are not distinguishable from current operating costs.

When goodwill is purchased, the amount of expenditure is viewed as objectively determinable and is capitalised. In case of amalgamation/acquisition the cost of goodwill purchased is measured as the excess of total price over fair value of the net identifiable assets acquired. If a company purchases another enterprise at a price in excess of the total fair value of the vendor company's net identifiable assets, the additional amount generally is considered to be the payment for the excess earning power of the acquired company, referred to as goodwill. Thus once the identifiable assets of the vendor company are restated to their fair values, any remaining differential is allocated to goodwill. Hence, goodwill appears in the books of accounts only when an enterprise has purchased some intangible and valuable property right. The amount by which the purchase-price exceeds the value of the net tangible assets is called goodwill, representing the value of the name, the reputation, the location or other intangible possessions of the vendor company. Unless the business has actually purchased such intangibles, no goodwill account appear in the books. If item does appear, it is shown at purchase price.

Salient characteristics

(i) Goodwill is an intangible real asset.

(ii) Goodwill is inherent in business. It cannot be separated or sold in part or isolation.

(iii) The value of goodwill (self generated) has no relation to the amount incurred.

(iv) It is difficult to calculate the exact cost of self generated goodwill.

(v) Goodwill represents payment for the future anticipated extra earnings.

(vi) Goodwill is shown in the books only when some payment has been made or acquired at some cost.

(vii) It is valuable only if it is transferable. The professionals cannot transfer their professional expertise, hence no goodwill.

(viii) Goodwill may be negative also. It happens when purchase price of an acquired company is less than the fair value of it's net assets.

(ix) Valuation of goodwill depends upon several factors.

(x) Intangible long-lived assets including goodwill are usually converted to expenses over a number of accounting periods. The periodic write off is specifically called amortisation.

(xi) Internally generated goodwill is not recognised as an asset because it is not an identifiable resource controlled by the enterprise that can be reliably measured. (AS-26)

(xii) The difference between the market value of the enterprise and the carrying amount of net assets may be due to many factors and hence this difference cannot be treated as goodwill. (AS-26)

(xiii) Goodwill cannot be sold in isolation. The old firm must cease to exist.

Need for Valuation of Goodwill

The need for valuation of goodwill arises on various occasions depending upon the form of business enterprise. In case of sole trade, the need for valuation of goodwill arises only when the business is to be disposed off or converted into partnership firm. Whereas, in case of partnership firm the need for valuation arises under the following circumstances :

(i) When a new partner is admitted,

(ii) When a partner is retired or expired

(iii) When the firm is sold or converted into private limited company.

(iv) When it is amalgamated with another firm.

(v) When a change in existing profit sharing ratio is to be effected.

In case of joint stock company the question of valuation of goodwill arises on:

(i) Amalgamation/Merger

(ii) Acquisition of controlling interest in another company i.e. a case of holding company.

(iii) Valuation of shares, when stock exchange quotations are not available.

(iv) When Government acquires the company under any scheme.

(v) or when one class of shares are converted into another class of shares.

Factors affecting Valuation of goodwill

The list of factors which determine the value of goodwill include every thing that contribute to an attractive earnings result. These include suitable location, quality of the product, better customers relations, satisfactory employees relations, marketing or production "know how", ineffective or absence of competition, managerial skill, degree of risk involved in the business, favourable contracts, Government's patronage etc.

Although every enterprise customarily spend considerable amount for the purpose of goodwill. It is generally impossible to establish whether any goodwill was infact created. Therefore, amount incurred in an attempt to create goodwill are expensed. The only goodwill given recognition in the books of accounts is that amount which specifically paid for it, in connection with the purchase of a business, a product line or some group of assets. But the question arises that how the amount of goodwill is determined? However, the estimate for the amount to be paid for goodwill will depend upon host of factors which are as under.

(1) Suitable Location

A suitable location of an enterprise contributes to profitability through cost savings by availing the various economies of manufacturing and distribution which in turn affects the value of goodwill. A good location may contribute heavily toward a favourable cost position, whereas a poor location may just have the opposite effect. Thus a favourable location enhances the value of goodwill. A location may be favourable if it provides necessary infrastructure for smooth running of business.

(2) Nature of business

It refers to the type of industry, the type of product, the state of business conditions, investment opportunities, expansion or future prospects, amount of capital required, the velocity of turnover, debt-collection period etc. which govern the value of goodwill. It is to be noted that the value of goodwill does not depend only on past profits but on the future prospects of the business to earn more. The greater the excess-earning-power, the greater shall be the value of goodwill. A proper evaluation of each factor and its pros & cons will determine the value of goodwill.

(3) Past record and trend in profitability

The value of goodwill depends on earnings potential which is estimated by the past performance of the business. If the past record shows an upward trend in the profits, naturally it refers to continued prosperity and reputation with the expectation that the same trend will be continued in the future also. Obviously it reflects a higher value for the goodwill. On the other hand if the past profitability is exhibiting a downward trend, this will simply be an indicator of low or no goodwill.

(4) Managerial Skill

An efficient and competent management is the backbone of business. The survival, growth, expansion, diversification and modernisation depends upon the managerial ability to cope with the new challenges. It always strives to excel in terms of cost, sales, profitability, production & distribution. Thus goodwill depends wholly upon the reputation of the management for its farsightedness, dynamism, proficiency and integrity. If the company earns fairly high average return per unit of capital employed, the raising of finances will not be a problem. The extent to which the funds may be obtained cheaply and promptly will contribute to super profit which, again, in turn, enhance the value of goodwill.

(5) Favourable Contracts

Exceptionally favourable contracts for supply of goods and services to customers enhance the value of goodwill. Similarly, favourable contracts with suppliers will have the same effect. Even the bulk of export orders and huge quota for scarce material will definitely, especially during import restriction period, have valuable goodwill. Similarly the import and export licences for a long duration will definitely contribute to the higher value of goodwill.

(6) Special Advantages

These include technical know how, protection or possession of patents, copyrights, or trade mark and the reputation which has been built up by an enterprise over the years. These serve as benchmark for customers, bankers, creditors, investors and others who provide the necessary base for augmenting value of goodwill. The more adherent the customers are to the trademarks, the larger shall be the volume of sales and the super profits. Consequently, the greater will be the value of goodwill.

(7) Dedicated labour force

The value of goodwill also rests on the willingness of the employees (especially skilled and semi-skilled) to work sincerely and efficiently. It is a well known fact that for a successful enterprise, there must be healthy industrial relations *i.e.* employer (management) and employees (trade union) relation is a sign of prosperity or adversity of a business. If the company is able to keep its labour force satisfied by providing them better working conditions, attractive pay packages job and economic security, retirement and fringe benefits, this will definitely motivate workers to work harder with great devotion and dedication. This expenditure is ultimately reflected in an increased output & efficiency thereby reducing the cost of production, administration & distribution per unit of labour which will increase the profits and hence value of goodwill.

(8) Degree of risk involved and monopoly power

The value of goodwill has inverse relation with degree of risk while direct positive relation with the monopoly power. When the degree of risk Involved is less, it has more goodwill and if the risk is more the value of goodwill is less. Whereas when an enterprise is enjoying monopoly power, it has ability to command higher value for goodwill as compared to a firm which does not enjoy monopoly power at all but subject to open competition. Thus while evaluating goodwill the possibility of future competition and attitudes, plans & programmes of the rivals should properly be analysed.

(9) Government's policy

A review of Government policy will also provide necessary input for the proper valuation of goodwill. An insight into the Government's attitude toward that particular type of business will determine the future prospects and its earnings potentials which has a direct bearing on the valuation of goodwill. If the Industrial policy of the Government provides soap for promotion and encourage. It by giving preferential allotment of licences, land for expansion, concessional power, water, tarrif or tax holidays, the business will enjoy higher value of goodwill. On the other hand if the Government policy imposes any sort of restriction, this is bound have adverse effect on the value of goodwill.

(10) Miscellaneous Factors

There are many other factors which affect the value of goodwill. These include socio-economic conditions, money market conditions, capital requirements, trade cycle, political stability and access to raw-materials.

It is to be noted that if the firm enjoys better reputation due to personal factors involved in management or technical know-how, then the continuity or discontinuity of the personal involved must be discounted while valuing goodwill.

METHODS OF VALUATION OF GOODWILL

From foregoing analysis of factors affecting the value of goodwill, it is evident that "centre" of all factors focuses on excess earnings or profits potentials. Each and every factor, individually and/or collectively, contribute to expected future profits which in turn governs the value of goodwill. However, the following methods are used for the purpose of valuation of goodwill.

(i) Average Profit Method
(ii) Super Profit Method
(iii) Capitalisation Method
(iv) Annuity Method

I Average Profit Method

Average profit means average of actual profits of past three, four or five years depending upon the nature of business. This average of actual profits must be adjusted in the light of future events that may affect the future profits. It should be noted that the payment for goodwill is made for the future expected profits. However, the estimate for future is guided by the past performance coupled with future possibilities of maintaining the expected level of profits. Hence, average profits should always mean "Future Maintainable Profits". Under this method, goodwill is calculated by multiplying the average future maintainable profits by certain number of years. This is done with reference to probability of new business to catch up with an existing business within the period span of 2,3,4, or 5 years. This period span differs from business to business and industry to industry. Computation of "Future Maintainable Profits" while calculating future maintainable profits, the following adjustments must be made in the past years profits.

(i) All such expenses which are not likely to be incurred in future must be added back.
(ii) All expenses which are likely to arise in future must be deducted.
(iii) Any additional profit or income that may accrue in future must be added back.
(iv) Any possible loss which may arise in future must be deducted.
(v) The actual past profits must be adjusted on account of abnormal, exceptional or non-recurring events & transactions, such as losses due to fire, theft, flood, lock-out, strike, riots, famine, earthquake or any other natural calamity, must be eliminated-added back.
(vi) Non-operating incomes and non-operating expenses must be excluded from the past actual profits.

(vii) Due adjustments must be made for capital receipts and capital losses if credited/charged to Profit & Loss Account of any year.

(viii) Due adjustments must also be made for the various provisions required to be made in future. Excess or shortfall, if any, as compared to existing ones should be adjusted. i.e. their effects on future profits to be taken care of. Any additional provision required to be made should be deducted while excess should be added back.

(ix) Adjustments should also be made with reference to undervaluation or over-valuation of closing stock, if any.

(x) Actual profits must also be adjusted in view of tax provisions of the relevant Finance Act to arrive at profits after tax.

(xi) The impact of managerial remuneration on the future anticipated profits must be properly considered. Any increase in future remuneration will reduce the future maintainable profits while a decrease will increase the profit expectancy. Any remuneration, fees or commission foregone by directors must be added back while any enhanced remuneration or commission should be deducted.

(xii) If the company intends to change the method of charging depreciation either with immediate effect or with retrospective effect, due adjustments must be made in the profits.

(xiii) Similarly, the impact of any major change in company's policy relating to dropping of any particular product, discontinuation of any part of business, or expansion or diversification programme which may affect the future profits, must be property accounted for while ascertaining the future maintainable profits.

Simple Average Vs. Weighted Average

While averaging past profits, an attempt must be made to arrive at a realistic figure. It is possible only when we know the trend of profits earned in the past. It is easy to calculate average profits when there are no wide fluctuations in the profits earned for the period under consideration. Under such a situation the simple average profit will give a realistic figure. However, if there are wide fluctuations from year to year, a simple average will fail to ascertain the future trend. Thus, to arrive at a true figure of future maintainable profits, the weighted average must be applied. Under this method the profits are arranged chronologically and multiplied by their respective number *i.e.* 1, 2, 3, 4, 5 & so on giving highest weightage to the most recent past year's profits and the least weightage to the earliest year's profits.

Thus to calculate goodwill, following steps are required.

(A) For simple average

1. Find out the actual profits of the past years. Take the average.
2. Make necessary adjustments with reference to past and provide for the future events and adjustments having a bearing on future profits to ascertain future maintainable profits.
3. Multiply by the number of year's purchase, as required in the question.
4. Resultant is the value of goodwill.

(B) For Weighted Average

(1) Fund out the past years' actual profits.

(2) Make necessary adjustment in respective year's of profits with reference to past events.

(3) Provide for the future adjustments.

(4) Calculate average profit by giving weightage in chronological order.

(5) Find out the weighted Average

(6) Multiply by the number of years' purchase as required in the question.

(7) Resultant is the value of goodwill.

Illustration (1) (Simple Average Method)

X Ltd. purchased a running business of Mr. Y on 1st January 2006. The profits earned by Mr. Y for the last four years were as under.

	Rs.
Year ending 31st December, 2002	2,20,000
Year ending 31st December, 2003	2,10,000
Year ending 31st December, 2004	2,30,000
Year ending 31st December, 2005	2,40,000

Additional Information

(i) Included in the profits of the year 2005, a non-recurring item of profit of Rs. 25,000.

(ii) Profit for the year ending 31st December 2003 are affected by loss by fire of Rs. 20,000.

(iii) The closing stock for the year ending 31st December 2004 was over-valued by Rs. 10,000.

(iv) Acquisition of this business will require replacement of existing manager who was getting a salary of Rs. 10,000 p.m. The new manager is to be employed at a monthly salary of Rs. 12,000.

(v) Additional insurance premium is required to be made at Rs. 500 p.m.

Calculate goodwill at 2 year's purchase of average profit.

Solution:

			Rs.
	Profits for the year 2002		2,20,000
	Profits for the year 2003	2,10,000	
Add	Abnormal Loss (Loss by fire)	20,000	2,30,000
	Profits for the year 2004	2,30,000	
Less	Over Valuation of closing stock	(10,000)	2,20,000
	Profits for the year 2005	2,40,000	
Add	Under Valuation of opening stock	10,000	
		2,50,000	
Less	Non-recurring profits (Non-operating)	(25,000)	2,25,000
		Total profits	8,95,000
	Average Profits (8,95,000 ÷ 4)		2,23,750
Less	Additional Remuneration of the Manager (Rs. 2,000 × 12)		(24,000)
Less	Additional Insurance Premium (Rs. 500 × 12)		(6,000)
	Future Maintainable Profits		1,93,750
	Goodwill at 2 year's Purchase (Rs. 1,93,750 × 2)		3,87,500

Illustration (2) (Simple Average Method)

Following information relates to X Ltd. who closes its books of accounts on 31st March, each year.

Year	PAT	Tax	Director's Remuneration	Transfer to Reserves
	Rs.	Rs.	Rs.	Rs.
2001-02	1,25,000	55,000	25,000	12,500
2002-03	1,10,000	42,000	25,000	11,000
2003-04	93,000	35,000	25,000	9,300
2004-05	1,15,000	40,000	35,000	11,500
2005-06	1,40,000	45,000	35,000	14,000

Y Ltd. is willing to acquire X Ltd. The Directors of Y Ltd. have appointed you to calculate the value of goodwill at two year's purchase after taking into account the following information.

(i) X Ltd's paid up capital is Rs. 5,00,000 on which dividend @ 15% has been paid through out the five year period.

(ii) X Ltd.'s has been transferring to General Reserve @ 10% whereas Y Ltd. has been transferring to General Reserve as per the provisions of Section 205 (A) of the Companies Act 1956. The same policy will be continued after the acquisition.

(iii) Depreciation on fixed assets has been provided @ 10% p.a. Y Ltd. has revalued the fixed assets of X Ltd. by Rs. 2,00,000.

(iv) The profits for the year 2003-04 include profits from sale of investment of Rs. 10,000 and loss from sale of an obsolete plant of Rs. 20,000.

(v) Director's remuneration has been paid ignoring the provisions of the Act. The total remuneration not to exceed 10% as per the present strength of the directors.

(vi) The Current rate of taxation is 30%.

Solution :

			Rs.
	Profit Before Tax (PBT) and Remuneration		
	2001-02 Profit After Tax	1,25,000	
Add	Tax	55,000	
Add	Remuneration	25,000	2,05,000
	2002-03 PAT	1,10,000	
Add	Tax	42,000	
Add	Remuneration	25,000	1,77,000
	2003-04 PAT	93,000	
Add	Tax	35,000	
Add	Remuneration	25,000	
		1,53,000	
Less	Non-operating Profit	(10,000)	
Add	Non-operating Loss	20,000	1,63,000

	2004-05 PAT	1,15,000	
Add	Tax	40,000	
Add	Remuneration	35,000	1,90,000
	2005-06 PAT	1,40,000	
Add	Tax	45,000	
Add	Remuneration	35,000	2,20,000
	Total Profit before Tax and Remuneration		9,55,000
	Average Profit before Tax and Remuneration		1,91,000
Less	Additional Depreciation on revaluation of Fixed Assets		(20,000)
	Average Profit before Remuneration and Tax		1,71,000
Less	Managerial Remuneration @ 10% on Rs. 1,71,000		17,100
	Average Profit before Tax		1,53,900
Less	Income Tax @ 30%		46,170
	Future Maintainable Profits		1,07,730
	Goodwill at two year's purchase		2,15,460

Note : Payment of dividend and transfer to General Reserve will not affect future maintainable profit.

Illustration (3) (Weighted Average Method)

On 1st April, 2006 A Ltd. proposed to purchase the business of B Ltd. Goodwill for this purpose is agreed to be valued at three years' purchase of the weighted average profits of the past four years. The appropriate weights were as under :

Year	Weight	Profit Rs.
2002-03	1	1,01,000
2003-04	2	1,24,000
2004-05	3	1,00,000
2005-06	4	1,40,000

On scrutiny of the accounts, the following facts were revealed.

(i) On 1st December, 2004, a major repair was made in respect of the plant incurring Rs. 30,000 which was charged to revenue. The said sum is agreed to be capitalised for goodwill calculation subject to adjustment of depreciation of 10% p.a. on reducing balancing method.

(ii) Closing stock for the year 2003-04 was over-valued by Rs. 12,000.

(iii) To cover the management cost, an annual charge of Rs. 24,000 should be made for the purpose of valuation of goodwill.

Compute Value of goodwill

[B. Com. (H), DU 2000 Modified]

Solution :

	Computation of Adjusted Profits	Rs.
2002-03	Profits as reported	1,01,000
Less	Managerial Cost	(24,000)
		77,000
2003-04	Profits as reported	1,24,000
Less	Over Valuation of Stock	(12,000)
Less	Managerial Cost	(24,000)
		88,000
2004-05	Profits as reported	1,00,000
Add	Over Valuation of Opening Stock	12,000
Add	Repairs to be Capitalised	30,000
		1,42,000
Less	Depreciation on Capitalised amount @ 10% p.a. for 4 months.	(1,000)
Less	Managerial Cost	(24,000)
		1,17,000
2005-06	Profits as reported	1,40,000
Less	Depreciation @ 10% on Rs. 29,000 (being W.D.V. of capitalised repair)	(2,900)
Less	Managerial Cost	(24,000)
		1,13,100

CALCULATION OF WEIGHTED AVERAGE PROFITS

Year	Adjusted Profits Rs.	Weightage	Amount Rs.
2002-03	77,000	1	77,000
2003-04	88,000	2	1,76,000
2004-05	1,17,000	3	3,51,000
2005-06	1,13,100	4	4,52,400
		10	10,56,400

Weighted Average Profits = (10,56,400 ÷ 10) = 1,05,640

Goodwill at 3 year's Purchase = (1,05,640 × 3) = 3,16,920

II SUPER PROFIT METHOD

Super profit refers to excess of adjusted average profit (Future Maintainable profit) over the normal profit. Normal profit represents profits based on normal rate of return (NRR) and the normal rate of return (NRR) is the rate of earnings which investors in general expect on their investments in any given industry. The NRR differs from industry to industry and depends upon many factors such as bank rate general economic conditions prevailing in the country, degree of risk attached to the investment and the duration or period of investment. To get normal profit the average capital employed is multiplied by the normal rate of return (NRR).

> **Thus remember :**
> Super Profit = Adjusted Average Profit – Normal Profit, and Normal Profit = Average Capital Employed × NRR. Adjusted Average Profits = Future Maintainable Profits

Illustration (4) (Super Profit Method)

From the following particulars, calculate value of goodwill on the basis of three years' purchase of super profit. The actual profits for the last four years were as under :

		Rs.
2002-03	Profit	1,83,000
2003-04	Profit	2,25,000
2004-05	Loss	(30,000)
2005-06	Profit	3,15,000

Other information

(i) Capital employed (Average) Rs. 7,50,000

(ii) Market rate of return on investment 8%

(iii) Rate of risk attached to such investment 2%

(iv) Remuneration from alternative employment of the proprietor, if not engaged in business, Rs. 90,000 p.a.

(v) Salary of manager who is not required in new set up. Rs. 60,000 p.a.

Solution:

CALCULATION OF AVERAGE ADJUSTED PROFITS OR SAY FUTURE MAINTAINABLE PROFITS

Profits of the last four years :

		Rs.
	2002-03	1,82,000
	2003-04	2,25,000
	2004-05	– (30,000)
	2005-06	3,15,000
		6,92,000
	Average Profits (6,92,000 ÷ 4)	1,73,000
Less	Proprietor's salary from alternative employment	(90,000)
		83,000
Add	Manager's salary not to be paid in new set-up	60,000
	Future Maintainable Profits	1,43,000

Normal Profits :

8% + 2% = 10% of Rs. 7,50,000	75,000
Super Profits = 1,43,000 – 75,000 =	68,000
Goodwill at 3 years' purchase of Super profits = 68,000 × 3 =	2,04,000

Illustration (5) (Super profit based on Weighted Average)

Mr. X is interested to acquire the business of Mr. Z, the details of which are as under :

Profits for the last four years	Rs.
2002-03	1,55,000
2003-04	1,85,000
2004-05	1,75,000
2005-06	2,20,000

Scrutining of the books of accounts revealed the following :

(i) The profits are before managerial remuneration of Rs. 30,000 p.a.

(ii) Closing stock for the year 2005-06 was overvalued by Rs. 20,000.

(iii) Profits for the year 2004-05 are affected by speculation loss of Rs. 15,000.

(iv) To cover inventory risk, an annual fire insurance policy is to be undertaken. The annual premium payable will amount to Rs. 5,000.

(v) The amount of average capital employed is Rs. 9,00,000. Compute value of goodwill on the basis of 2 years' purchase of super profits calculated by weighted average profits. The Normal Rate of Return is 10%.

Solution :

COMPUTATION OF WEIGHTED AVERAGE PROFITS

Year	Reported Profits Rs.	Managerial Remuneration Rs.	Adjustment for errors Rs.	Fire insurance Premium Rs.	Adjusted Profits Rs.	Weight	Product Rs.
2002-03	1,50,000	– 30,000	—	–5,000	1,20,000	1	1,20,000
2003-04	1,85,000	– 30,000	—	–5,000	1,50,000	2	3,00,000
2004-05	1,75,000	– 30,000	+ 15,000	–5,000	1,55,000	3	4,65,000
2005-06	2,20,000	– 30,000	– (20,000)	–5,000	1,65,000	4	6,60,000
						10	15,45,000

Weighted Average Profits (15,45,000 ÷ 10)	1,54,500
Normal Profits (10% of Rs. 9,00,000)	90,000
Super Profit	64,500
Goodwill at two year's purchase (64,500 × 2)	1,29,000

III CAPITALISATION METHOD

There are two methods of calculating value of goodwill by capitalisation method.

(a) Capitalisation of super Profit

(b) Capitalisation of Average Profits.

Under capitalisation of super profit method goodwill is calculated by ascertaining the capitalised value of the super profit on the basis of normal rate of return. This method is based on the assumption that the business so acquired will continue to yield constant return.

$$\text{Thus value of goodwill} = \frac{\text{SuperProfit}}{\text{NRR}} \times 100$$

Assuming super profits of Rs. 12,500 and normal rate of return at 10%, the value of goodwill will be = $\left(\frac{12{,}500 \times 100}{10}\right)$ = Rs. 1,25,000

However, under **Capitalisation of Average Profits**, the value of goodwill is calculated by taking the difference between **capitalised value of adjusted average profits** (future maintainable profits) and **actual capital employed** in that business.

Goodwill = Normal Capital Employed – Actual Capital employed

Capital Employed

There are two approaches for calculating the amount of capital employed :

(i) ***Net Assets Approach***

Under this the capital employed is worked out by adding the current values of assets except :

- Non-trading (Non-business) assets such as investments made outside business.
- Goodwill appearing in the Balance Sheet or otherwise including Patents, copyrights & Trademarks.
- Fictitious Assets-such as debit balance of Profit & Loss A/c, Discount on Issue of shares/ debentures and Preliminary Expenses and deducting therefrom:
- All liabilities due to outsiders, long term or short term loans & current liabilities.

(ii) ***Reserves & Surplus Approach***

The Capital employed may, also be obtained by adding Capital, Reserves, Accumulated Profits, Profits on Revaluation of Assets/liabilities and deducting there from :

- Accumulated losses (Dr. balance of P & L A/c)
- Fictitious assets such as Preliminary Expenses, Discount on issue of shares debentures.
- Loss on revaluation of assets/liabilities
- and other intangibles such as patents, copyrights, trademarks etc.

Average Capital Employed

Average capital employed means capital employed throughout the year which can be obtained by averaging the opening and closing capitals.

$$\text{Average capital Employed} = \frac{\text{Opening Capital} + \text{Closing Capital}}{2}$$

In other words the average capital employed is calculated by adding capital employed in the beginning of the year and capital employed at the end of the year and by dividing the total by two.

In case the opening capital of any year is not given, the Average capital Employed can be ascertained by deducting half of the current year's profit from the closing balance of capital employed. This is done on the presumption that profit has been earned uniformly throughout the year. It is to be noted that Normal Profits should be ascertained by multiplying the Average capital Employed by the Normal Rate of Return.

Illustration (6) (Capitalisation Method)

The following is the Balance Sheet of Addu & Somu Ltd. as on 31st March 2006

Liabilities:	Rs.
9% Preference Shares of Rs. 100 each	2,50,000
Equity Share Capital - Shares of Rs. 10 each	5,00,000
General Reserve	3,00,000
Profit & Loss Appropriation A/c	1,50,000
9% Debentures	2,00,000
Provision for taxation	50,000
Accounts Payable	1,75,000
	16,25,000
Assets	
Goodwill	50,000
Net Blocks	9,00,000
6% Government Securities	1,00,000
Stock	2,70,000
Debtors	1,95,000
Cash & Bank balance	35,000
Preliminary Expenses	55,000
Discount on Issue of Debentures	20,000
	16,25,000

Additional Information:

1. Net Blocks are considered worth Rs. 10,00,000
2. The average profits of the company are estimated to be Rs. 1,56,000. The normal rate of return of the industry is 10%. Calculate the value of goodwill by
   (a) Capitalisation of average profit and
   (b) Capitalisation of super-profit.

Solution:

CALCULATION OF AVERAGE CAPITAL EMPLOYED

			Rs.
	Net Blocks		10,00,000
	Stock		2,70,000
	Debtors		1,95,000
	Cash & Bank balance		35,000
			15,00,000
Less	Liabilities		
	9% Debentures	2,00,000	
	Provision for Taxation	50,000	
	Accounts Payable	1,75,000	(4,25,000)
	Actual Capital Employed		10,75,000

	Balance d/d	10,75,000
Less	Half of the Profit of the current year 1/2 (Rs. 1,56,000 – 6,000)	75,000
	Average Capital Employed	10,00,000
	Normal Profits (Rs. 10,00,000 × NRR)	1,00,000
	Adjusted Average Profit	1,50,000
	Super profit	50,000
	(Average Adjusted Profits – Normal Profits)	

(a) Goodwill by Capitalisation of Average Profit – Capitalised Value of Average Profit.

$$= \frac{1,50,000 \times 100}{\text{NRR}}$$

$$= \frac{1,50,000 \times 100}{10} = 15,00,000$$

Average Capital Employed	= 10,00,000
Value of Goodwill	= 5,00,000
(Capital Value of Average Profits – Actual Capital employed)	

(b) Goodwill by Capitalisation of Super Profit

$$= \text{Super Profit} \times \frac{100}{\text{NRR}} = 50,000 \times \frac{100}{10} = 5,00,000$$

Average Capital Employed may also be worked as under :

		Rs.
	Share Capital : Equity	5,00,000
	Preference	2,50,000
	General Reserve	3,00,000
	Profit & Loss App. A/c	1,50,000
		12,00,000
Add	Appreciation in Net Blocks	1,00,000
		13,00,000
Less	Non Trading Asset (Investment)	(1,00,000)
	Goodwill (Intangible)	(50,000)
	Fictitious Assets (55,000 + 20,000)	(75,000)
	Capital Employed	10,75,000
Less	Half of the profit of the current year	75,000
	Average Capital Employed	10,00,000

Working Note :

While calculating Capital Employed non-business assets, intangibles and fictitious assets have been excluded. Similarly income from the non-business asset (6% Government Securities) has been excluded from the current year's profit.

(IV) ANNUITY METHOD

Goodwill is always paid in anticipation of earning excess (additional/abnormal) profits in future which are termed as 'Super Profit'. The goodwill as per annuity method is calculated by multiplying the super profit by the 'Reference to Annuity Table. It means value of goodwill is the present value of an annuity of the annual super profit which the purchaser will recover over a period of time gradually. Since payment of goodwill is made immediately in lumpsum in anticipation of future super profits, the purchaser bears the loss of interest. Hence goodwill is considered equal to present value of future returns. In other words goodwill is the discounted value of the total amount calculated as per purchase method. The expected extra (super) profits are discounted at normal rate of return. In the absence of reference to Annuity Table, the following formula should be applied for the purpose of calculating value of goodwill.

$$\text{Reference to Annuity Table} = A = \frac{1-\left(1+\frac{r}{100}\right)^{-n}}{\frac{r}{100}}$$

Where A = Present Value of Annuity for Re. 1.

r = Normal rate of return (Interest rate)

n = Number of years over which the goodwill will be recovered in the form of super (extra) profits.

Taking normal rate of return (NRR) at 10%, the present value of Re. 1 for 3 years will be calculated as under.

$$A = \frac{1-\left(1+\frac{r}{100}\right)^{-3}}{\frac{10}{100}}$$

$$= \frac{1-\frac{110}{100}\times\frac{110}{100}\times\frac{110}{100}}{\frac{10}{100}} = \frac{1-\frac{1331}{1000}}{\frac{1}{10}}$$

$$= \left(1-\frac{1000}{1331}\right)\times\frac{10}{1}$$

$$= 2.4868$$

Illustration (7) (Annuity Method)

From the following particulars calculate the value of goodwill by Annuity Method.

(i) Net profits after tax for the last five years – Rs. 1,60,000, Rs. 1,66,000, Rs. 1,80,000, Rs. 1,94,000 and Rs. 2,10,000.

(ii) Capital employed in the business Rs. 10,00,000

(iii) Normal rate of return 10%

(iv) Present value of annuity for Re. 1 for five years at 10% interest is 3.78

The profits include interest on investments in Government Bonds on an average basis of Rs. 7,000.

Solution:

Average Profits for the last five years

$$= \frac{\text{Rs. } 1,60,000 + 1,66,000 + 1,80,000 + 1,94,000 + 2,10,000}{5}$$

= 9,10,000 ÷ 5

Average Profits = 1,82,000

Less Non-business income (7,000)

Average Adjusted Profits 1,75,000

Normal Profits = Capital Employed × NRR

= Rs. 10,00,000 10%

= 1,00,000

Super Profit = Adjusted Profits – Normal Profit

= Rs. 1,75,000 – 1,00,000

= Rs. 75,000

Value of Goodwill = Super Profit Reference to Annuity Table

= 75,000 × 3.78

= Rs. 2,83,500

GRADED ILLUSTRATIONS

Illustration (1) (Super Profit & Capitalisation Methods)

From the following information, calculate the value of goodwill by

(a) Three years' purchase of 'Super Profit', and

(b) Capitalisation Method

		Rs.
(i)	Average Capital employed	6,00,000
(ii)	Net Assets (excluding goodwill)	7,50,000
(iii)	Net Profits for the last three years:	1,48,000
		1,50,000
		1,49,000
(iv)	Expected Rate of Return	20%
(v)	Partners' salary p.a.	10,000

[B. Com (H) DU 2002]

Solution :

(a) Average Profits = $\dfrac{1,48,000 + 1,50,000 + 1,49,000}{3}$

= Rs. 1,49,000

Normal Profits = Rs. 6,00,000 × 20%

(Average Capital Employed × NRR) Rs. 1,20,000

Super Profit = (Rs. 1,49,000 – 1,20,000) = Rs. 29,000

Goodwill at 3 year's purchase = Rs. 29,000 × 3

Value of Goodwill = Rs. 87,000

(b) Capitalisation of Average Profit :

$$\text{Normal Capital Employed} = \frac{\text{AverageProfit}}{\text{NRR}}$$

$$= \frac{\text{Rs. } 1,49,000}{20\%} = \text{Rs. } 7,45,000$$

Goodwill = Rs. 7,45,000 – 6,00,000 (Normal Capital Employed – Average (Actual Capital employed)

Goodwill 1,45,000

(b) Capitalisation of super Profit.

$$\text{Capitalised Value of super profit} = \frac{\text{Rs. } 29,000 \times 100}{20}$$

Value of goodwill = Rs. 1,45,000

Illustration (2) (Weighted Average Method)

X Ltd. proposes to purchase of business of Mr. Z. Goodwill for this purpose is agreed to be valued at three years' purchase of super profits calculated on the basis of weighted average profits of past three years. The profits for the last three years were as under.

	Rs.
2003-04	1,63,000
2004-05	1,75,000
2005-06	2,15,000

The above profits include income from investments Rs. 9,000 which is withdrawn in full immediately by Mr. Z.

The Balance Sheet of X Ltd. as 31st March, 2006 was as under :

	Rs.		Rs.
Capital	8,00,000	Fixed Assets	8,00,000
General Reserve	2,00,000	9% Investments	1,00,000
Current liabilities	1,75,000	Current Assets	2,75,000
	11,75,000		11,75,000

The standard rate of return on capital employed in such type of business is 10%. The average capital employed may be taken at Rs. 10,00,000.

Solution:

Calculation of Super Profit

Average Profits of last three years

Trading Profits – Income on Investment

	Rs. Rs.		Rs.
2003-04	1,63,000 – 9,000	=	1,54,000
2004-05	1,75,000 – 9,000	=	1,66,000
2005-06	2,15,000 – 9,000	=	2,06,000

Weighted Average :

	Rs.		
2003-2004	1,54,000	1	= 1,54,000
2004-2005	1,66,000	2	3,32,000
2005-2006	2,06,000	3	6,18,000
		6	11,04,000

Weighted Average Profits	1,84,000
Normal Profits (Capital employed × NRR) (10% of Rs. 10,00,000)	1,00,000
Super profit	84,000
Goodwill at 3 years' purchase (Rs. 84,000 × 3)	2,52,000

Illustration (3) (Super Profit and Capitalisation Methods)

From the following information relating to business of Somu and Addu Enterprises Calculate value of goodwill at four years' purchase of super profit and by capitalisation of average profits.

		Rs.
(i)	Average Capital employed	7,00,000
(ii)	Expected Rate of Return	18%
(iii)	Sundry Assets (Excluding goodwill)	7,54,760
(iv)	Sundry liabilities	29,205
(v)	Fair Remuneration to partners	12,000
(vi)	Net trading profits for the last 3 years : Rs. 1,47,000; Rs. 1,48,000; Rs. 1,49,000	

[B. Com (H) DU Modified]

Solution :

Super Profit Method

		Rs.
	Average Profits = Rs. 4,44,000 ÷ 3	1,48,000
Less	Fair Remuneration to partners	(12,000)
	Average Adjusted Profits	1,36,000
Less	Normal Profit	
	(Average Capital Employed × NRR) Rs. 7,00,000 × 18%	(1,26,000)
	Super Profit	10,000
	Goodwill at 4 Years' purchase (Rs. 10,000 × 4)	40,000

Capitalisation of Average Profits

Capitalised Value of Average Profits $\left(\text{Rs.}1{,}36{,}000 \times \dfrac{100}{18}\right)$	= 7,55,555
Actual Capital Employed (Rs. 7,54,760 – 29,205)	7,25,555
Value of Goodwill	30,000

> **It is to be noted that to get :**
> Normal profit, the NRR is multiplied by Average Capital Employed and while calculating value of goodwill the Actual Capital Employed is deducted from the Capitalised valued of Average Adjusted profits (or say Normal Capital Employed)

Illustration (4) (Super Profit & Capitalisation Methods)

From the following Balance Sheet and additional information calculate

(a) Value of goodwill at 5 years' purchase of super profit and

(b) by capitalising average profits

BALANCE SHEET OF T.R. LTD. AS ON 31ST MARCH, 2006

Liabilities	Rs.	Assets	Rs.
Share Capital	3,00,000	Goodwill at Cost	30,000
General Reserve	60,000	Fixed Assets	2,65,000
Profit & Loss A/c	26,000	Stock	1,15,000
S. Creditors	71,000	Debtors	95,000
Provision for Taxation	55,000	Cash & Bank	7,000
	5,12,000		5,12,000

Additional Information :

(i) The reasonable rate on capital invested in such type of business is 12%

(ii) Adequate provision has been made for income tax and depreciation.

(iii) The rate of tax is 50%

(iv) The average rate of dividend declared by the company for the past five years is 15%

[C.A. (P) Adapted]

Solution :

(a) Super Profit Method

			Rs.
Calculation of Capital Employed			
	Fixed Assets		2,65,000
	Stock		1,15,000
	Debtors		95,000
	Cash & Bank		7,000
			4,82,000
Less	Creditors	71,000	
	Provision for Taxation	55,000	(1,26,000)
			3,56,000

		Rs.
	Capital Employed	3,56,000
Less	Half of the profits of the Current year	(27,500)
	Average Capital Employed	3,28,500
	Actual Profit after Tax	55,000
	(Equal to Provision for Tax being 50% Tax rate)	
Less	Normal Profit	(39,420)
	(Average Capital Employed X NRR)	
	(Rs. 3,28,500 × 12%)	
	Super Profit	15,580
	Goodwill at 5 years' purchase	77,900
(b)	Capitalisation Method	
	Capitalised Value of Average Profits	4,58,333
Less	Actual Capital Employed	3,56,000
	Value of Goodwill	1,02,333

Illustration (5) (Goodwill on Amalgamation)

X Ltd. and Y Ltd. agreed to amalgamate as on 31st March 2006 when their Balance Sheets were as under :

Liabilities	X Ltd.	Y Ltd.
	Rs.	Rs.
Equity Share Capital	5,00,000	2,50,000
General Reserve	2,00,000	25,000
Profit & Loss A/c	1,50,000	37,500
Current liabilities	1,50,000	62,500
	10,00,000	3,75,000
Assets		
Fixed Assets	5,00,000	2,25,000
Investments in 6% Bonds (Face value Rs. 1,00,000)	1,00,000	
Current Assets	4,00,000	1,50,000
	10,00,000	3,75,000

Profits after tax for the last three years were as under :

	X Ltd.	Y Ltd.
2003-04	1,65,000	50,000
2004-05	1,60,000	60,000
2005-06	1,70,000	70,000

Goodwill for the purpose of amalgamation may be taken at 4 years' purchase of average super profits on the basis of 15% normal profit on closing capital invested. The current assets of both the companies are valued 10% more than the book value.

Calculate value of goodwill of both the companies.

[C.A. (F) Adapted]

Solution :

Calculation of Capital Employed :

		Y Ltd.	X Ltd.
		Rs.	Rs.
	Fixed Assets	5,00,000	2,25,000
	Current Assets	4,40,000	1,65,000
		9,40,000	3,90,000
Less	Liabilities	1,50,000	62,500
		7,90,000	3,27,500

Calculation of Average Profits :

		X Ltd.	Y Ltd.
		Rs.	Rs.
	2003-04	1,65,000	50,000
	2004-05	1,60,000	60,000
	2005-06	1,70,000	70,000
		4,95,000	1,80,000
	Average Profits	1,65,000	60,000
Less	Non-Trading Income (Interest on Bonds)	6,000	—
	Average Adjusted Profits	1,59,000	60,000
Less	Normal Profits* (15% on Capital Employed)	1,18,500	49,125
	Super Profits	40,500	10,875
	Goodwill at 4 years' Purchase	= 1,62,000	43,500

***Note:** Normal profits have been calculated on the basis of closing capital employed and not on average capital employed as per the instruction in the question.

Illustration (6) (Super Profit Method)

Following is the Balance Sheet of Z H Ltd. as on 31st March, 2006.

Liabilities	Rs.	Assets	Rs.
Share Capital	10,00,000	Goodwill	1,00,000
Shares of Rs. 10 each		Fixed Assets	11,00,000
Reserve & Surplus	4,00,000	Investments	1,00,000
S. Creditors	3,00,000	Current Assets	4,00,000
	17,00,000		17,00,000

Negotiations are going on to transfer business of Z H Ltd. to MS Ltd. The Goodwill is to be worked out on the basis of 2 years' purchase of super profit after considering the following:

(i) Profit before tax for the current year amounted to Rs. 6,00,000 including Rs. 10,000 as interest on investments.

(ii) The market value of fixed assets is estimated at Rs. 19,00,000.

(iii) In order to match the above figures further depreciation to the extent of Rs. 40,000 should be taken into consideration.

(iv) Income tax may be taken at 30%

(v) Return on Capital before tax @ 20% is taken to be normal.

(vi) For the purpose of determining rate of return, profit for the current year after aforesaid adjustments may be taken as expected average profit. Similarly average trading capital employed is also to be considered on the basis of the position in this year. An additional amount of Rs. 50,000 is required to be spent for smooth running of the business. Calculate value of goodwill.

[C.A. (F) Modified]

Solution:

Calculation of Capital Employed:		Rs.
Fixed Assets		19,00,000
Current Assets		4,00,000
		23,00,000
Less Sundry Creditors		(3,00,000)
Capital employed at the end		20,00,000
Less Half the Profits of the Current year*		(1,75,000)
Average Capital Employed		18,25,000
Calculation of Average Adjusted Profits		
(Future Maintainable Profits)		
Net-Profit before tax		6,00,000
Less Additional Depreciation	40,000	
Non-operating Income	10,000	
Additional Expenses required	50,000	(1,00,000)
Profit before tax		5,00,000
Less Tax @ 30%		1,50,000
Profit after Tax* (Av. M. Profit)		3,50,000
Calculation of Super Profit		
Average maintainable Profits		3,50,000
Less Normal Profits (14% of Average Capital employed)		2,55,500
(20% before tax means 14% after tax *i.e.* 20% – 30% of 20% = 6%)		
Super Profit		94,500
Goodwill at 2 years purchase		= 1,89,000

Illustration (7) (Super Profit & Capitalisation Methods)

Balance Sheet of S Ltd. as on 31st March, 2006 is as follows :

Liabilities	Rs.	Assets	Rs.
Share Capital	6,00,000	Fixed Assets	3,70,000
Reserve & Surplus	50,000	Current Assets	5,20,000
Bank Over draft	10,000		
Creditors	60,000		
Provision for Taxation	1,10,000		
Proposed Dividend	60,000		
	8,90,000		8,90,000

The net profits of the company after deducting usual working expenses but before providing for tax, were as under :

Year	Rs.
2003-04	2,18,000
2004-05	2,40,000
2005-06	2,12,000

On 31st March, 2006, Fixed Assets were valued at Rs. 4,50,000. Sundry Debtors, on the same date, included Rs. 10,000 as irrecoverable. Having regard to nature of the business a 10% return on net tangible capital employed is considered reasonable. Valuation of goodwill may be based upon three years' purchase of annual super profits. Also calculate goodwill by capitalisation of average maintainable profits. Depreciation on fixed assets is charged @ 10% p.a. and the rate of income tax is 30%

[C.A. (F) Modified]

Solution :

Calculation of Capital Employed

			Rs.
	Fixed Assets		4,50,000
	Current Assets (5,20,000 – 10,000)		5,10,000
			9,60,000
Less	Bank Over draft	10,000	
	Creditors	60,000	
	Provision for Taxation	1,10,000	(1,80,000)
			7,80,000
	Capital Employed		7,80,000
Less	Half of the Profit after tax of the Current year*		74,200
	Average Capital Employed		7,05,800

Calculation of Average Adjusted Profits

		Rs.
	Total Profits for last 3 years	6,70,000
Less	Provision for Bad debts	10,000
		6,60,000
	Average Profit	2,20,000
Less	Depreciation on revaluation of fixed assets 10% (4,50,000 – 3,70,000)	(8,000)
		2,12,000
Less	Income Tax @ 30%	(63,600)
	Average Maintainable Profit	1,48,400
Less	Normal Profits 10% of 7,05,800	(70,580)
	Super profit	77,820
	Goodwill at 3 years purchase	2,33,460

* 1/2 (2,12,000 – Tax @ 30% Rs. 63,600)

Capitalisation Method

		Rs.
	Capitalised Value of Average Maintainable profits	14,84,000
Less	Actual Capital Employed	7,80,000
		7,04,000

Illustration (8) (Super-profit Method)

From the following information ascertain the value of goodwill of Appu Ltd. under :
(a) Super Profit Method (b) Capitalisation of Super profit Method.

BALANCE SHEET OF APPU LTD.
As on 31st March, 2006

Liabilities	Rs.	Assets	Rs.
Share Capital	5,00,000	Goodwill	50,000
Profits & Loss App. A/c	1,13,000	Fixed Assets	4,50,000
Bank Over draft	1,18,000	Current Assets	4,50,000
S. Creditors	1,80,000		
Provision for Taxation	39,000		
	9,50,000		9,50,000

The Company commenced operations in April 1991 with a paid up capital of Rs. 5,00,000. Profits for the recent year's (after taxation) have been as follows :

Year		Rs.
2001-02	Loss	(40,000)
2002-03	Profit	88,000
2003-04	Profit	1,08,000
2004-05	Profit	1,20,000
2005-06	Profit	1,26,000

The Loss 2001-2002 occurred due to prolonged strike. The tax has been paid so far @ 35% but now it is likely to be 30% from now onwards. Profits till now have been ascertained after debiting Rs. 40,000 as remuneration to the managing director. The Government has approved a remuneration of Rs. 72,000 with effect from 1st April 2006. The company has been able to secure a contract for supply of materials at advantageous prices which has been valued at Rs. 62,000 per annum for the next five years. The NRR is estimated to be 12%.

[C.A. (F) Adapted]

Solution:

Calculation of Capital employed

			Rs.
	Fixed Assets		4,50,000
	Current Assets		4,50,000
			9,00,000
Less	Liabilities :		
	Bank Overdraft	1,18,000	
	S. Creditors	1,80,000	
	Provision for Tax	39,000	(3,37,000)
	Capital employed		5,63,000

		Rs.
	Balance b/d	5,63,000
Less	Half of the profits of the current year	63,000
	Average Capital Employed	5,00,000

Calculation of Future Maintainable Profits

		Rs.
	2001-02 Loss due to strike to be ignored	
	2002-03	88,000
	2003-04	1,08,000
	2004-05	1,20,000
	2005-06	1,26,000
	Total Profits	4,42,000
	Average Profits after Tax	1,10,500
	Average Profits before Tax $\left(1{,}10{,}500 \times \dfrac{100}{65^*}\right)$	1,70,000

*(100 – Tax rate 35)

	Average Profits before Tax	1,70,000
Less	Increase in remuneration	(32,000)
Add	Savings in cost of materials	42,000
		1,80,000
Less	Tax @ 30%	54,000
	Future Maintainable Profits after tax	1,26,000
Less	Normal Profits (12% on Rs. 5,00,000)	60,000
	Super Profits	66,000
	Goodwill at (say) 3 years' purchase	1,98,000

(b) Goodwill by Capitalisation of Super profits $\left(66{,}000 \times \dfrac{100}{12}\right)$ = 5,50,000

Value of Goodwill = Rs. 5,50,000

Illustration (9) (Super profit Method and Adjustments)

Following is the Balance Sheet of SN Ltd. as on 31st March, 2006

Liabilities	Rs.	Assets	Rs.
Equity Share Capital	8,00,000	Goodwill	80,000
(Shares of Rs. 10 each)		Building	4,80,000
11% Preference Share Capital	4,00,000	Machinery	4,40,000
(Shares of Rs. 100 each)		Furniture	2,00,000
General Reserve	3,20,000	Vehicles	3,60,000
Profit & Loss A/c	64,000	Investments	3,20,000
Bank Loan		Stock	2,20,000
(Secured against fixed Assets)	2,40,000	Debtors	3,60,000
Bills Payable	1,20,000	Bank Balance	64,000
Creditors	6,20,000	Preliminary Expenses	40,000
	25,64,000		25,64,000

Additional Information

(i) Return on Capital employed is 20% in similar business.

(ii) Fixed assets are worth 30% more than book value, stock is overvalued by Rs. 20,000. Debtors are to be reduced by Rs. 4,000. Trade investments which constitute 10% of the total investments are to be valued at 10% below cost.

(iii) Trade investments are purchased on 1.4.2005 50% of non-trade investments were purchased on 1.4.2004 and rest on 1.4.2003. Non-Trade investments yielded 15% return on cost.

(iv) In 2003-04 new machinery costing Rs. 40,000 was purchased but wrongly charged to revenue. This amount should be adjusted taking depreciation at 10% on reducing value method.

(v) In 2004-05 furniture with a book value of Rs. 20,000 was sold for Rs. 12,000.

(vi) For calculating goodwill two years' purchase of super profits based on simple average profit of last four years are to be considered. Profits of the last four years are:

	Rs.
2002-03	3,20,000
2003-04	3,60,000
2004-05	4,20,000
2005-06	4,40,000

(vii) Additional depreciation provision at the rate of 10% on the additional value of Plant and Machinery alone may be considered for arriving at average profits.

Find out value of Goodwill

[C.A. (F) May 2003-Modified]

Solution:

I CALCULATION OF FUTURE MAINTAINABLE PROFIT

	2002-03 Rs.	2003-04 Rs.	2004-05 Rs.	2005-06 Rs.
Profits reported	3,20,000	3,60,000	4,20,000	4,40,000
Add Purchase of Machinery Charged to Repairs	—	40,000	—	—
Add Loss on sale of Furniture	—	—	8,000	—
Less Depreciation on Machinery	—	(4,000)	(3,600)	(3,240)
Less Non-operating income: (on non-trade-investments)	—	(21,600)	(43,200)	(43,200)
Less Value of Stock Adjusted	—	—	—	(20,000)
Less Bad debits	—	—	—	(4,000)
Adjusted Profits	3,20,000	3,74,400	3,81,200	3,69,560

		Rs.	Rs.
	Total Adjusted Profits		14,45,160
	Average Adjusted Profits		3,61,290
	(Rs. 14,45,160 4)		
Less	Depreciation on Appreciated Value (2)		(14,075)
	Average Adjusted Profits		3,47,215

II Calculation of Capital Employed:

Fixed Assets:			
	Building		4,80,000
	Machinery (1)		4,69,160
	Furniture		2,00,000
	Vehicles		3,60,000
			15,09,160
Add	Appreciation (30%)		4,52,748
			19,61,908
	Trade Investments (3,20,000 × 10/100 × 90/100)		28,800
	Stock (Rs. 2,20,000 – 20,000)		2,00,000
	Debtors (Rs. 3,60,000 – 4,000)		3,56,000
	Bank Balance		64,000
			26,10,708
Less	Liabilities:		
	Bank Loan	2,40,000	
	Bills Payable	1,20,000	
	Creditors	6,20,000	(9,80,000)
	Capital Employed		16 ,30,708
Less	Half of the Current Year's Profit		(1,84,780)
	Average Capital Employed		14,45,928

III Calculation of Goodwill:

Normal Profits (Average Capital employed NRR) 20% on Rs. 14,45,928 = 2,89,185

Super Profit = (Average Adjusted Profits – Normal Profits)

(Rs. 3,47,215 – 2,89,185) = 58,030

Goodwill at 2 years' purchase = Rs. 58,030 × 2 = 1,16,060

Working notes:

(1) Value of Plant & Machinery and the additional depreciation has been worked out as follows:

	W.D.V. as per Balance Sheet		4,40,000
Add	Cost of machinery charged to repairs:		
	now Capitalised:	40,000	
Less	Depreciation (4,000 + 3,600 + 3,240)	10,840	29,160
			4,69,160

(2)	Depreciation on Appreciated Value of Machinery	Rs.
	Book Value as on 31.3.2006	4,69,160
	Appreciation 30%	1,40,748
	Depreciation on Appreciated Value @10%	= 14,075

Illustration (10) (Super Profit Method & Value of Business)

The Balance Sheets of SRK Ltd. for the y ear ended on 31st March 2004, 2005, & 2006 were as follows :

	Year ending as on 31st March		
Liabilities	2004	2005	2006
	Rs.	Rs.	Rs.
Equity Share Capital (Shares of Rs. 10 each)	3,20,000	3,20,000	3,20,000
General Reserve	2,40,000	2,80,000	3,20,000
Profit & Loss A/c	28,000	32,000	48,000
S. Creditors	1,20,000	1,60,000	2,00,000
	7,08,000	7,92,000	8,88,000
Assets			
Goodwill	2,00,000	1,60,000	1,20,000
Fixed Assets	2,80,000	3,20,000	3,20,000
Stock	2,00,000	2,40,000	2,80,000
Debtors	4,000	32,000	88,000
Bank Balance	24,000	40,000	80,000
	7,08,000	7,92,000	8,88,000
Actual Valuation were as under:			
Fixed Assets	3,60,000	4,00,000	4,40,000
Stock	2,40,000	2,80,000	3,20,000
Net Profit (including opening balance) (after writing off depreciation Goodwill, Tax provision and transfer to General Reserve.	84,000	1,24,000	1,64,000

Capital employed in the business at market values at the beginning of 2003-04 was Rs. 7,32,000 which included cost of goodwill. The normal return on Average Capital Employed in this line of business is 12.5%. The balance in the General Reserve on 1st April, 2003 was Rs. 2,00,000.

The Goodwill shown on 31.3.2004 was purchased on 1.4.2003 for Rs. 2,00,000 on which date the balance in the Profit & Loss A/c was Rs. 24,000.

Calculate value of goodwill at 5 years' purchase of super profits (simple average method). Also calculate total value of business.

[C.A. (F) Nov. 2003- Modified]

Solution :

Calculation of Capital Employed

	31.3.2004	31.3.05	31.3.06
	Rs.	Rs.	Rs.
Goodwill	2,00,000	1,60,000	1,20,000
Fixed Assets	3,60,000	4,00,000	4,40,000
Stock	2,40,000	2,80,000	3,20,000
Debtors	4,000	32,000	88,000
Bank Balance	24,000	40,000	80,000
	8,28,000	9,12,000	10,48,000
Less Creditors	1,20,000	1,60,000	2,00,000
Capital employed at the end	7,08,000	7,52,000	8,48,000
Capital Employed in the beginning	7,32,000	7,08,000	7,52,000
	14,40,000	14,60,000	16,00,000
Average Capital Employed	7,20,000	7,30,000	8,00,000

Calculation of Future Maintainable Profits

	31.3.2004	31.3.05	31.3.06
	Rs.	Rs.	Rs.
Net Profit	84,000	1,24,000	1,64,000
Less Opening balance	24,000	28,000	32,000
	60,000	9,60,000	1,32,000
Add Under valuation of closing stock	40,000	40,000	40,000
	1,00,000	1,36,000	1,72,000
Less Adjustment for Valuation of opening stock	—	40,000	40,000
	1,00,000	96,000	1,32,000
Add Goodwill w/o	—	40,000	40,000
	1,00,000	1,36,000	1,72,000
Add Transfer to Reserve	40,000	40,000	40,000
	1,40,000	1,76,000	2,12,000
Less Normal Profits*	90,000	91,250	1,00,000
Super Profits	50,000	84,750	1,12,000
Average Super Profits			

Average Super Profits $\frac{50,000 + 84,750 + 1,12,000}{3} = 82,250$

Goodwill at 5 years' purchase = Rs. 82,250 × 5   Rs. 4,11,250

*Normal Profits = Average Capital Employed × Normal Rate of Return

	31.3.04	31.3.05	31.3.06
	Rs.	Rs.	Rs.
Average Capital Employed	7,20,000	7,30,000	8,00,000
	X	X	X
Normal Rate of Return	12.5%	12.5%	12.5%
Normal Profits	90,000	91,250	1,00,000

Value of Business:

	Rs.
Net Assets as on 31.3.06 (Capital Employed)	8,48,000
Less Goodwill as per B/s	1,20,000
	7,28,000
Add Value of Goodwill as computed	4,11,250
	11,39,250

Note: For the purpose of calculating capital employed the value of goodwill as per Balance Sheet has been included because the same has been acquired against a payment.

Illustration (11)

On the basis of following information, calculate the value of goodwill of X Ltd. at three years purchase of super profits, if any, earned by the company during the last four previous years.

BALANCE SHEET OF X LTD.

As on 31st March 2005

Liabilities	Rs.	Assets	Rs.
Share Capital:		Goodwill	31,000
Authorised	7,50,000	Land & Building	1,85,000
Issued & Subscribed		Plant & Machinery	3,76,000
(Shares of Rs. 10 each)	5,00,000	Furniture	1,01,500
Capital Reserve	26,000	Patents	3,200
General Reserve	2,54,300	9% Non-Trading Investments	60,000
Profit & Loss App. A/c	47,700	Stock	87,300
Trade Creditors	56,800	Debtors	61,400
Provision for Taxation (Net)	2,200	Cash & Bank	54,600
Proposed dividend (for 2003-04)	75,000	Preliminary Expenses	2,000
	9,62,000		9,62,000

The profits before tax of the four years have been as follows :

	Rs.
2000-01	3,19,000
2001-02	2,50,000
2002-03	3,10,800
2003-04	2,90,000

The rate of income tax for the accounting year 2000-01 was 40%. Thereafter it had been 35% for the years so far but for year 2004-05 will be 30%.

During the year 2000-01, the company made an extraordinary income of Rs. 10,000 due to special foreign contract. In August 2001 there was an earthquake due to which the company lost property worth Rs. 5,000 and the insurance policy did not cover the loss due to earth quake or riots.

9% Non-trading investments appearing in the above Balance Sheet were purchased at par by company on 1st April 2002. The Normal Rate of Return (NRR) for the industry is 20%. Also note that the shareholders of the company have passed a resolution in the general meeting sanctioning the directors an additional remuneration of Rs. 5,000 every year beginning from the accounting year 2004-05.

[C.A. (F) May 2004- Modified]

Solution:

I Calculation of Future Maintainable Profits

	2000-01	2001-02	2002-03	2003-04
	Rs.	Rs.	Rs.	Rs.
Profit before Tax	3,19,000	2,50,000	3,10,800	2,90,000
Less Extra-Ordinary Income	(10,000)			
Add Extra-Ordinary Loss)		5,000		
Less Non-Operating Incomes	—	—	(5,400)	5,400
Adjusted Profits	3,09,000	2,55,000	3,05,400	2,84,600

	Rs.
Total adjusted Profits (3,09,000 + 2,55,000 + 3,05,400 + 2,84,600	= Rs. 11,54,000
Average Profits = (11,54,000/4)	= Rs. 2,88,500
Less Additional Remuneration	(5,000)
	2,83,500
Less Income Tax @ 30%	(85,050)
Future Maintainable Profits	1,98,450

II Calculation of Capital Employed

		Rs.
Land & Building		1,85,000
Plant & Machinery		3,76,000
Furniture		1,07,500
Patents		3,200
Stock		87,300
Debtors		61,400
Cash & Bank		54,600
		8,69,000
Less Trade Creditors	56,800	
Provision for Tax (Net)	2,200	(59,000)
		8,10,000

III Calculation of Super profits

		Rs.
	Future Maintainable Profits	1,98,450
Less	Normal Profit (Rs. 8,10,000 20%)	1,62,000
	Super Profits	36,450
	Goodwill at 3 years' purchase (Rs. 36,450 × 3)	= 1,09,350

Note: Normal profits have been worked out on the basis of capital employed at the end rather than "Average Capital Employed", because in the absence of current year's profits the Average Capital Employed cannot be calculated.

Illustration (12) (Super Profit Method & Weighted Average)

The following is the Balance Sheet of Z Ltd. as on 31st March, 2006.

Liabilities	Rs.	Assets	Rs.
Equity Share Capital	5,00,000	Goodwill	40,000
(Shares of Rs. 10 each)		Land & Building at cost	3,20,000
Bank overdraft	1,86,000	Plant & Machinery at cost	2,80,000
Creditors	2,11,000	Stock	3,20,000
Provision for Taxation	51,000	Debtors (Good)	2,00,000
Profit & Loss Appropriation A/c	2,12,000		
	11,60,000		11,60,000

In 1985 when the company commenced operation the paid up capital was same. The profit and Loss Account for the last five years discloses the following results:

2001-02	Loss (Strike)	(55,000)
2002-03	Profit	98,200
2003-04	Profit	1,17,000
2004-05	Profit	1,45,000
2005-06	Profit	1,70,000

Although income tax has so far been paid @ 40% and the above profits have been arrived at on the basis of such rate. Now with effect from the year 2005-06 the income tax rate will be 30% plus 2% Education cess. Dividend @ 10% in 2002-03 and 2003-04 and 15% dividend in 2004-05 and 2005-06 has been paid. Market price of share of the company on 31st March 2006 was Rs. 125. With effect from 1st April 2006 the Managing Director's remuneration has been approved to be Rs. 80,000 in place of Rs. 60,000. The company has been able to secure a contract for supply of materials at advantageous prices. The advantage has been valued at Rs. 40,000 per annum for the next five years.

Ascertain goodwill at three years purchase of super profit (for calculation of future maintenance profit, weighted average is to be taken into account.)

[C.A. (F) May 2005-Adapted]

Solution :

I Calculation of Future Maintainable Profit

Year	Profit Rs.	Weight	Product Rs.
2002-03	98,200	1	98,200
2003-04	1,17,000	2	2,34,000
2004-05	1,45,000	3	4,35,000
2005-06	1,70,000	4	6,80,000
		10	14,47,200

*Abnormal year's result has been ignored.

		Rs.
	Total weighted Profits after Tax	14,47,200
	Average Weighted Profits after Tax	1,44,720
	Average Weighted Profits before Tax $\left(\frac{1,44,720 \times 100}{60}\right)$	Rs. 2,41,200
Less	Increase in Remuneration	(20,000)
		2,21,200
Add	Economy in cost of Raw-materials	40,000
		2,61,200
Less	Income Tax @ 30.6% including Education cess	77,927
	Future Maintainable Profits	1,81,273

II Calculation of Capital Employed

			Rs.
	Land & Building		3,20,000
	Plant & Machinery		2,80,000
	Stock		3,20,000
	Sundry Debtors		2,00,000
			11,20,000
Less	Liabilities:		
	Bank Overdraft	1,86,000	
	Creditors	2,11,000	
	Provision for Taxation	51,000	(4,48,000)
	Capital employed at the end		6,72,000
Add	Dividend @ 15%		75,000
			7,47,000
Less	Half of the profits of the current year		85,000
	Average capital employed		6,62,000

III Calculation of Normal Rate of Return

$$\text{NRR} = \frac{\text{Average dividend}}{\text{Market price of share}} \times 100$$

Average Dividend = Average dividend = $\frac{10+10+15+15}{4} = 12.5\%$

$$\text{NRR} = \frac{12.5}{125} \times 100 = 10\%$$

Normal Profits = Average Capital Employed × NRR
= Rs. 6,62,000 × 10% = 66,200

Super Profit = Future Maintainable Profits – Normal Profits
= Rs. 1,81,273 – 66,200
= Rs. 1,15,073

Goodwill at 3 years' purchase = Rs. 3,45,219
(say) = Rs. 3,45,220

Points to Remember:

1. Average Profits means Future Maintainable profits
2. Normal Profits are worked out as under:
   Average Capital Employed × NRR
3. NRR (Normal Rate of Return) is calculated as under :

$$\frac{\text{Average dividend for last 3,4 or 5 years}}{\text{Market price of share}} \times 100$$

Add additional risk, if any.

4. Weighted Average should be calculated only when it is mentioned in the question or the profits are showing an increasing trend. The highest weight should be given to the most recent year's profit in an ascending order
5. Average Capital Employed = Capital Employed at the end less half of the current year's profits after adjusting for errors & omissions but before adjusting for future events.

VALUATION OF SHARES

Shares are traded in the stock exchange where forces of demand and supply determine the price of various securities. The prices at which transactions take place are recorded and made public in the form of market quotations which help the investors and other to know current market prices of shares. But this information is available only in respect of public limited companies whose shares are listed in any stock exchange. The private limited companies shares however, cannot be quoted in the stock exchange. Further, stock exchange quotations do not hold good for a very large lot. In addition to this, the valuation of shares is required under following situations :

1. In case of amalgamation, acquisition absorption or reconstruction etc.
2. In case of purchase or sale of shares of a private company.
3. Acquisition of controlling interest in the company.
4. Conversion of debentures/preference shares into equity shares
5. On pledging the shares as collateral security.
6. On assessment of estate duty or wealth tax.

7. For ascertaining payment to any dissentient shareholders under any scheme of takeover or reconstruction.
8. For ascertaining compensation to shareholders under the scheme of nationalisation.
9. In case of trust finance or investment trust finance companies.

As stated earlier the price quoted in the stock exchange does not represent the actual worth or true value of shares. The prevailing price is not the conclusive proof of efficiency or inefficiency of the concerned company. The net worth or net assets value of (NAV) cannot be worked out with the help of stock exchange price. All authorities agree that the price mechanism does not function purely on the basis of fundamentals but greatly affected by speculative forces, rumours and unhealthy practices. Therefore, the stock market quotation cannot form a fair, equitable or rational basis of valuation of shares.

Factors Affecting Valuation of shares

The factors affecting value of shares are almost, similar to the factors which affect the value of goodwill. These include nature of business, past record and trend in profitability, managerial efficiency, earning capacity, dividend declared by the company in the past, nature of competition, future plan of expansion and diversification, trading on equity, composition of capital structure pattern of investment in fixed and current assets, price level changes, general economic conditions, political condition in the region, basic fundamentals of the company, the capital employed and the Government policy with regard to industry in which the company operates.

Weinberg and Blank in the book Takeovers and Mergers, have stated that some of the following factors will have to be taken into account while determining the value of shares for exchange ratio.

1. Stock exchange prices of the shares of the two companies before the commencement of negotiations or the announcement of the bid.
2. The dividends presently paid on the shares of the two companies. It is often difficult to induce a shareholder, particularly an institution to agree to a share to share bid if it involves a reduction in dividend income.
3. The relative growth prospects of the two companies.
4. The cover (ratio of after tax earnings to dividends paid during the year) for the present dividends of the two companies. The fact that dividend of one company is better covered than that of the other is a factor that has to be compensated for, at least, to some extent.
5. In the case of equity shares the relative gearing of the shares of the two companies. The gearing of an ordinary share is the ratio of borrowings to the equity capital.
6. The values of net assets of the two companies. Where the transaction is a thorough going merger, this may be more of a talking point rather than a matter of substance, since what is relevant is the relative values of the two undertakings as going concerns.
7. The voting strength in the merged enterprise of the shareholders of the two companies.
8. Past history of the prices of the shares of the two companies.

The Department of Companies Affairs appointed a Expert Committee in October, 2002, to recommend comprehensive rules governing valuation of shares under the Companies Act. This committee submitted it's report in January, 2003. The Committee observed that whereas one method may be more or less applicable to particular case, they are often used in conjunction to arrive at the fair value. It felt that the key criteria for valuation must ensure in objectivity, consistency, credibility, reliability and practicability.

METHODS OF VALUATION OF SHARES

The methods of valuation of shares depend upon the purpose and factors affecting valuation of shares as explained earlier. There are certain judicial decisions with regard to valuation of shares. The Bombay High Court (ITR 799) concluded that in a company which is a running concern, the market value of a share is determined mainly on the basis of the yield method because a person who holds the shares or who wants to purchase shares does it in the hope of getting adequate return on his investments. The Supreme Court (ITR 38) held that where the shares of a public limited company are not quoted on any stock exchange or the shares of a private company, the proper method of valuation of shares would be the profit earning method. The Court has laid down the following principles for share valuation:

(1) Where the shares in a public limited company are quoted on the stock exchange, the price prevailing on the valuation date is the value of shares.

(2) Where shares are of a private company (which cannot be quoted) or of a public company which are not quoted, the value is determined by reference to the dividend reflecting the profit earning capacity on a reasonable commercial basis. Otherwise the amount of yield would determine the value of shares.

(3) Where the total yield and earning method breakdown by reason of company's inability to earn profits and declare dividends. In that case value would be discounted by the percentage corresponding to proportionate fall in the quoted prices.

(4) Where expenses are incurred out of proportion to the commercial venture these would be added back to the profits while computing yield. In case of private companies the restriction on transfer of shares would be taken into account in arriving at the value of shares.

The court has pointed out that among the factors which govern the consideration of buyer and seller of the shares of a going concern, the factor of break up value of a share as on liquidation hardly enters into consideration. It is only where a company is ripe for winding up or the situation is such that the fluctuation of profits and uncertainty of conditions at the date of valuation prevent any reasonable estimate of it's profit earning capacity that the valuation by the break up method would be justified. Broadly speaking, there are five methods of valuation of shares.

(I) Net Assets Value (NAV) Method

This method is also called Intrinsic value Method or Break up Value Method or Asset Backing Method. Under this method the net assets (Assets – liabilities) are calculated and divided by the number of shares to get the "net assets value" per share. Efforts must be made to find out a more realistic NAV (Net Assets Value). For this purpose adjustments must be made for adherence to accounting policies, provision for adequate depreciation, gratuity liability and other employee related payments etc. as also a realistic values of all assets and liabilities including receivables and payables and contingent liabilities. Further the value of intangibles such as goodwill, patents, trademarks, & copyrights has to be considered in a realistic valuation. In short the following should be taken into account.

1. Fixed assets to be taken at realisable values (In case market values cannot be ascertained) then adequate provision for depreciation must be made out of book values)

2. The value of intangible assets such as goodwill, copyrights, patents and trademarks must properly be valued. In case these are considered worthless, the same should be ignored.
3. Investments in shares or debentures (whether trading or non-trading) should be taken at their market values.
4. Stock of finished goods to be valued at market value, whereas stock of raw-material be valued at cost.
5. Debtors and other receivables at their realisable values i.e. after providing for reasonable amount for bad and doubtful debts.
6. Contingent assets, if any, be valued on a conservative basis, such as claims for damages/ insurance.
7. All fictitious assets are to be be ignored.
8. Ascertain the amount payable to outsiders such as Debentureholders, creditors, provision for taxation and outstanding expenses.

Proposed Dividend should be treated as a liability for Ex-dividend value of equity shares while it should be excluded from liabilities for cum-dividend value of equity share.

9. The difference between the total assets and the total liabilities so arrived at represent "Net Assets" available for Preference share holders and Equity shareholders.

To determine the 'Intrinsic Value' (Net Assets Value) of equity shares the claims of Preference shareholders must be deducted. The claims of Preference shareholders include the paid up value of preference shares and arrears of dividend there-on (for cumulative preference shares). If preference shares have a right to participate in the surplus (as it happens in case of liquidation) the amount so attributable should also be deducted and included in the preference shareholders' claims.

The whole procedure may be surnmed up as follows :

Assets at realisable value/market value :

	Rs.
Goodwill	---
Land & Building	---
Plant & Machinery	---
Furniture & Fixtures	---
Investments	---
Patents	---
Copyrights	---
Trade marks	---
Stock	---
Debtors	---
Bills Receivable	---
Cash & Bank Balance	---
Any other contingent assets	---
	****

Less

Debenture holders' claims (Debentures plus interest)	----	
Creditors	----	
Bills Payable	----	
Provision for Taxation	----	
Other liabilities		(****)
Total Net Asset Available for Preference and Equity Shareholders		****
Less Claims of Preference Shareholders		(***)
Net Assets available for Equity Shareholders		***

$$\text{Value of Equity Share} = \frac{\text{Net Assets Available for Equity shareholders}}{\text{No. of Equity shares}}$$

Illustration: (1) (Net Assets Method)

The following is the Balance Sheet of X Ltd. as on 31st March, 2006.

Liabilities	Rs.	Assets	Rs.
50,000 Equity Shares		Goodwill	70,000
of Rs. 10 each	5,00,000	Land & Building	3,30,000
9% Preference Shares		Plant & Machinery	1,70,000
of Rs. 100 each	2,50,000	Computers	70,000
General Reserve	75,000	Motor Vehicles	60,000
Profit & Loss A/c	25,000	Stock	1,80,000
9% Debentures	1,00,000	Debtors	80,000
S. Creditors	50,000	Cash & Bank	20,000
		Preliminary Expenses	20,000
	10,00,000		10,00,000

Additional Information:

(1) The value of Land & Building and Stock to be taken at Rs. 5,00,000 and Rs. 2,00,000 respectively.

(2) Plant & Machinery, Computers and Motor Vehicles subject to 10% depreciation.

(3) Debtors : Good Rs. 70,000

Doubtful Rs. 10,000

(50% likely to realise)

(4) Goodwill is valued at Rs. 1,00,000.

(5) Preference dividend has not been paid for last two years.

(6) The liability for bills discounted likely to arise is estimated at Rs. 15,000.

Calculate value of equity shares by Net Assets Method.

Solution :

Calculation of Net Assets

			Rs.
Sundry Assets:			
	Goodwill		1,00,000
	Land & Building		5,00,000
	Plant & Machinery	1,70,000	
	Computers	70,000	
	Motor Vehicles	60,000	
		3,00,000	
Less	10%	(30,000)	2,70,000
	Stock		2,00,000
	Debtors (Good)	70,000	
	50% of Rs. 10,000	5,000	75,000
	Cash & Bank		20,000
	Total Assets		11,65,000
Less **Liabilities**:			
	9% Debentures	1,00,000	
	S. Creditors	50,000	1,50,000
			10,15,000
Less	Liability for Bills discounted		(15,000)
	Net Assets		10,00,000
Less	Claims of Preference Shareholders		(2,50,000)
	Net Assets available for Equity Shareholders		7,50,000

$$\text{Value of Equity Share} = \frac{\text{Rs. } 7,50,000}{50,000 \text{ Shares}}$$

Rs. 15 per share

Equity Shares with different paid up Values

There may be two possibilities :

(i) The company has issued shares with different face values (denominations)

(ii) The company has issued shares with only one face value (denomination) but with different paid up value.

When the share capital of a company consists of shares in different number lots and are of different denominations with different paid up values, then the value of equity share shall be calculated on the basis of 'unit value' of capital. *i.e.* To Calculate value of equity shares, the per unit value of capital shall be calculated first. (see illustration no. 2) The unit value will be multiplied by the paid up value of different lots to get the intrinsic value per share.

When shares are of same denomination (face value) but of different paid up values, the value of equity shares shall be determined after the notional call (see illustration 3). The total net assets will be divided by the total number of equity shares. This will give the value of each fully paid equity share. Unpaid amount of each share will be deducted from each value to ascertain the value of partly paid up shares.

Illustration (2) (Fully paid, partly paid shares with different denominations)

The following is the Balance Sheet of SS Ltd. as on 31st March 2006.

Liabilities	Rs.	Assets	Rs.
10,000 Equity Shares of Rs. 100 each fully paid	10,00,000	Goodwill	88,000
20,000 Equity Shares of Rs. 50 each Rs. 40 paid	8,00,000	Land & Building	7,00,000
30,000 Equity Shares of Rs. 10 each Rs. 5 paid	1,50,000	Plant & Machinery	5,62,000
General Reserve	5,00,000	Investments	2,00,000
Profit & Loss App. A/c	2,50,000	Stock	6,50,000
10% Debentures	2,00,000	Debtors	4,50,000
Provision for Tax	80,000	Bills Receivable	1,75,000
S. Creditors	1,20,000	Bank Balance	2,45,000
		Preliminary Expenses	30,000
	31,00,000		31,00,000

Additional Information:

For the purpose of valuation of shares, the following should be taken into consideration :

(i) Land & Building is valued at Rs. 20,00,000, Machinery at Rs. 5,00,000 and investments at Rs. 2,50,000.

(ii) Stock is considered Rs. 50,000 less than the book value and Debtors are estimated to realise Rs. 20,000 less.

(iii) Goodwill is agreed to be valued at Rs. 1,00,000

Calculate value of different class of shares.

Solution:

Calculation of Net Assets

Assets:		Rs.
Goodwill		1,00,000
Land & Building		20,00,000
Plant & Machinery		5,00,000
Investments		2,50,000
Stock		6,00,000
Debtors		4,30,000
Bills Receivable		1,75,000
Bank Balance		2,45,000
		43,00,000
Less Liabilities :		
6% Debentures	2,00,000	
S. Creditors	1,20,000	
Provision for Tax	80,000	(4,00,000)
Net Assets		39,00,000

$$\text{Unit Value of Capital} = \frac{\text{Net Assets}}{\text{Total paid up Capital}}$$

$$= \frac{\text{Rs.}39{,}00{,}000}{\text{Rs.}10{,}00{,}000 + 8{,}00{,}000 + 1{,}50{,}000}$$

$$= \frac{\text{Rs.}39{,}00{,}000}{\text{Rs.}19{,}50{,}000} = \text{Rs. } 2$$

Value of Share = Unit Value × Paid up Value of Share

Equity Shares of Rs. 100 each fully paid	= 2 × 100 = Rs. 200 per share
Equity Shares of Rs. 50 each Rs. 40 paid	= 2 × 40 = Rs. 80 per share
Equity Shares of Rs. 10 each Rs. 5 paid	= 2 × 5 = Rs. 10 per share

Illustration (3) (Fully paid, partly paid shares of the same denomination)

Following is the Balance Sheet of Everest Ltd. as on 31st March, 2006.

Liabilities	Rs.	Assets	Rs.
25,000 Equity Shares of Rs. 10 each fully paid up	2,50,000	Fixed Assets	6,00,000
15,000, Equity Shares of Rs. 10 each Rs. 8 paid up	1,20,000	Current Assets	2,30,000
10,000 Equity Shares of Rs. 10 each Rs. 5 paid up	50,000	Deferred Revenue Expenditure	20,000
Reserves	2,80,000		
Current Liabilities	1,50,000		
	8,50,000		8,50,000

Additional Information:

1. Goodwill for the purpose of valuation of shares is valued at Rs. 50,000
2. Fixed assets are valued at Rs. 6,30,000
3. Included in the debtors an amount of Rs. 20,000 due from Z who became insolvent. A dividend of 50 paisa in a rupee is likely to be recovered from him.

Calculate value of equity shares.

Solution:

Calculation of Net Assets

		Rs.
	Goodwill	50,000
	Fixed Assets	6,30,000
	Current Assets (Rs. 2,30,000 – 10,000)	2,20,000
		9,00,000
Less	Liabilities	(1,50,000)
	Net Assets	7,50,000

	Balance b/d	7,50,000
Add	Notional Call*	
	15,000 Shares @ Rs. 2 each	30,000
	10,000 Shares @ Rs. 5 each	50,000
		8,30,000
	Total number of shares	50,000 Shares

$$\text{Value of fully paid share} = \frac{\text{Rs.}8,30,000}{50,000 \text{ Shares}} = \text{Rs. } 16.60 \text{ each}$$

Value of Rs. 8 paid up share = Rs. 16.60 – 2 = Rs. 14.60

Value of Rs. 5 paid up share = Rs. 16.60 – 5 = Rs. 11.60

* Unpaid amount per share.

VALUATION OF PREFERENCE SHARES

The valuation of preference shares depends upon the nature or terms and conditions of the preference shares issued by a company. A preference shareholder is particularly interested in the security of capital and consistency of returns. That is why he is anxious for a priority of repayment of his capital/dividend or both. The following points must be kept in mind while calculating the value of preference shares.

(i) If preference shares are non-cumulative and non-participating the value of each preference share shall be equal to it's paid up value.

(ii) If preference shares are cumulative and non-participating, the value will be determined after arrears of preference dividend are added back to their paid up capital.

(iii) In case preference shares are cumulative and participating, then besides arrears they will also be entitled to share in the surplus of the company, left after returning equity capital. (presuming liquidation)

It should be noted that the preference share holders are entitled arrears only if the dividend was declared and surplus is available.

(iv) However, if the preference shares do not have ay preference (priority) with regard to repayment of capital and dividend, the value of preference shares shall be calculated as if these are equity shares.

Illustration (4) (Valuation of Equity and Preference Shares)

Following is the Balance Sheet of NP Ltd. as on 31st March, 2006.

Liabilities	Rs.	Assets	Rs.
9% Preference Shares		Fixed Assets	12,00,000
of Rs. 100 each fully paid	2,00,000	Goodwill	50,000
Equity Shares		Current Assets	5,50,000
of Rs. 100 each fully paid	8,00,000		
Capital Reserve	1,00,000		
Revenue Reserve	3,00,000		
9% Debentures	2,00,000		
Current liabilities	2,00,000		
	18,00,000		18,00,000

Additional Information

(i) Goodwill is considered worthless

(ii) Fixed assets are valued at 90% of their book value

(iii) Included in the Current assets are:
Stock valued Rs. 10,000 more than book value, Debtors requiring provision of Rs. 5,000 for doubtful debts, other assets are considered woth book value.

(iv) The debenture interest and preference dividends are in arrears for one and two years respectively. Liability for bills discounted Rs. 17,000. Calculate value of Shares if:

(a) Preference shares have no priority as to repayment of Capital or dividend.

(b) Preference shares have priority as to the payment of capital and arrears of dividend.

Solution:

Calculation of "Net Assets"

			Rs.
	Fixed Assets (at 90%)		10,80,000
	Current Assets	5,50,000	
Add	Increase in Stock	10,000	
Less	Provision for doubtful debts	(5,000)	5,55,000
			16,35,000
Less	9% Debentures	2,00,000	
	Interest o/s	18,000	(2,18,000)
			14,17,000
Less	Current Liabilities	2,00,000	
	Liability for Bills-discounted	17,000	(2,17,000)
	Net assets available For Preference and Equity shareholders		12,00,000

(a) When preference shares have no priority

$$\text{Value of Equity and Preference share } \frac{12,00,000}{8000 + 2000\text{ shares}} = \text{Rs. } 120 \text{ each}$$

Alternatively

$$\begin{array}{l}\text{Share of Preference Shareholders} \\ \text{In the net assets of the company}\end{array} = \frac{12,00,000 \times 2000}{10,000} = \text{Rs. } 2,40,000$$

$$\text{Value of Preference Share} = \frac{2,40,000}{2,000} = \text{Rs. } 120 \text{ per share}$$

$$\text{Value of Equity Shares} = \frac{12,00,000 \times 8,000}{10,000} = \text{Rs. } 9,60,000$$

Rs. 9,60,000/ 8,000 shares
= Rs. 120 per share

(b) When preference shares have priority as to repayment of Capital and dividend both.

			Rs.
	Total Net Assets		12,00,000
Less	Preference Share Capital	2,00,000	
	Dividend for 2 years	18,000	(2,18,000)
	Assets available for Equity Shareholders		9,82,000

$$\text{Value of preference share} = \frac{2,18,000}{2,000} = \text{Rs. } 109$$

$$\text{Value of Equity Share} = \frac{9,82,000}{8,000} = \text{Rs. } 122.75$$

It is to be noted that the value of preference and Equity Shares depends upon the "net assets" available for preference shareholders and equity shareholders. This totally depends upon the terms of issue of preference shares.

Net Assets Method: An Appraisal

Net assets method is useful in case of amalgamation, merger, acquisition or any other form of liquidation of a company. This method determines the rights of various types of shares in an unambiguous manner. Since all the assets and liabilities are valued properly including intangibles, this method creates no problem for valuation of preference or equity shares.

However, it is difficult to make proper valuation of goodwill and estimate net realisable value of various other assets of the company. Such estimates are likely to be influenced by personal factors of the valuers.

This method is suitable in case of companies likely to be liquidated in near future or where future maintainable profits cannot be estimated properly, or when valuation of shares by this method is required statutorily. e.g. Under mutual funds scheme, the finance and investments companies are required to show their Net Assets Value (NAV) per unit.

II Yield Method

This method takes into account the future prospects in terms of return on investment. Yield means the possible return an investor expects from his investment. Under this method the valuation of shares is done on the basis of expected rate of return which is calculated from future maintainable profits or by taking the average of last four or five years' of dividend (rate) declared by the company. The formula for ascertaining the value of share is as follows :

$$\text{Value of share} = \frac{\text{Expected Rate of Dividend}}{\text{Normal Rate of Return}} \times \text{Paid up value of share}$$

The Expected Rate of dividend can be :

(A) Calculated by any of the two methods :

(i) Calculate future maintainable profits as explained under valuation of goodwill

(ii) Provide for taxes

(iii) Transfer to general reserve

(iv) Transfer to Debenture Redemption Fund or any other statutory transfers

(v) Provide for preference dividend, if any.

The balance available will be treated as profits available for equity share holders. Thus Expected Rate of Dividend will be calculated as under :

$$\text{ERR} = \frac{\text{Profit available for Equity Shareholders}}{\text{Equity Capital}} \times 100$$

(B) Alternatively, if expected profits available for equity share holders cannot be ascertained, then the dividend paid by the company during the last four or five years may be averaged. Such average rate of dividend will represent expected rate of dividend.

The market value of share can also be calculated by the following formula :

$$= \frac{\text{Dividend per share (Amount)}}{\text{Normal Rate of Return}} \times 100 \quad \text{and NRR} = \frac{\text{Dividend Per share}}{\text{Market Value}} \times 100$$

or Dividend per share × Price Earnings Ratio*

$$\text{*Price Earnings Ratio} = \frac{\text{Market Value of share}}{\text{Earnings per share}}$$

$$\text{or P. E. Ratio} = \frac{100}{\text{NRR}}$$

For example : the market price of a share of X Ltd. is Rs. 250. The Company has declared a dividend of 40% on it's paid up value of Rs. 100. Then the NRR and Price Earnings Ratio will be as under :

$$\text{NRR} = \frac{40 \times 100}{250} = 16\%$$

$$\text{P.E. Ratio} = \frac{250}{40} = 6.25$$

$$\text{or} = \frac{100}{16} = 6.25$$

It shows that higher the NRR lower shall be price earnings ratio and vice versa.

Illustration (5) (Yield Method)

From the following information calculate value of share by Yield Method.

	Rs.
50,000 Equity Shares of Rs. 10 each	5,00,000
10% Preference Shares of Rs. 100 each	2,00,000

The company transfers 20% of profits to General Reserve. If the future maintainable profits before tax are Rs. 2,50,000 and the rate of tax is 40%, calculate value of equity share. The normal rate of return may be taken at 15%.

Solution :

		Rs.
	Future maintainable profits	2,50,000
Less	Tax @ 40%	(1,00,000)
		1,50,000
Less	Transfer to General Reserve @ 20%	(30,000)
		1,20,000
Less	Preference dividend	(20,000)
	Profits available for equity shareholders	1,00,000

$$\text{Expected Rate of Return} = \frac{1,00,000}{5,00,000} \times 100 = 20\%$$

$$\text{Value of Equity Share} = \frac{\text{Expected Rate of Return}}{\text{Normal Rate of Return}} \times \text{Paid up Value}$$

$$= \frac{20}{15} \times 100 = \text{Rs. } 150$$

Valuation of Preference shares under Yield Method

Preference shares are valued on the basis of "dividend" under Yield Method as against "Net Assets" under first method Generally preference shares enjoy priority with regard to repayment of capital and payment of dividend at the predetermined rate. If the pre-determined rate is more than the normal rate of return (NRR) the value of preference shares will be higher. In case it is less than the normal rate of return (NRR) the value of preference shares shall be lower than the paid value. If both are equal the yield value and paid up value will be the same. The formula for calculating yield value is as under:

$$\text{Value of Preference Share} = \frac{\text{Rate of Preference dividend}}{\text{Normal rate of return}} \times \text{Paid up Value}$$

However, in case of participating preference shares, the value of preference share under yield method will depend upon additional dividend the preference shareholders are likely to receive after satisfying the claims of equity shareholders.

Illustration (6) (Participating Preference Shares under Yield Method)

From the following information calculate,

(i) Value of Equity Shares

(ii) Value of preference shares

	Rs.
1,00,000 Equity Shares of Rs. 10 each	10,00,000
9% Preference Shares of Rs. 100 each	2,00,000
Average annual profits before tax	4,80,000
Rate of Tax	40%
Transfer to General Reserve	10%
Normal rate of return	10%

The preference shares are entitled to participate in the profits of the company upto 3% after payment of dividend @ 10% on equity shares.

Find out value of preference and equity shares.

Solution:

		Rs.
	Profits before Tax	4,80,000
Less	Tax @ 40%	1,92,000
		2,88,000
Less	Transfer to General Reserve	28,800
		2,59,200
Less	Preference dividend @ 9%	18,000
		2,41,200
Less	Equity dividend @ 10%	1,00,000
		1,41,200
Less	Additional dividend for participating Preference shares @ 3%	6,000
	Available for Equity shareholders	1,35,200

I Value of Preference Share

$$= \frac{\text{Actual dividend rate}}{\text{Normal rate of return}} \times \text{Paid up Value}$$

$$= \frac{9+3}{10} \times 100 = \frac{12}{10} \times 100 = \text{Rs. } 120$$

II Valuation of Equity Share

$$\text{ERR} = \frac{\text{Total Profits available for Equity shareholders}}{\text{Equity Capital}} \times 100$$

$$= \frac{1{,}00{,}000 + 1{,}35{,}200}{10{,}00{,}000} = \frac{2{,}35{,}200}{10{,}00{,}000} \times 100 = 23.52\%$$

$$\text{Value} = \frac{\text{ERR}}{\text{NRR}} \times \text{Paid up Value}$$

$$= \frac{23.52}{10} \times 10 = 23.52\%$$

Size of lot and Valuation of Shares

The valuation of equity shares is also affected by the size of lot under transaction. If the lot size is big *i.e.* a person holding 20% or more voting power is in a position to control the affairs of the company, makes a deal, the capitalisation method will be the most suitable method of valuation of big lot. If however, it is a small lot, the yield method will be applied.

Yield Method : An Appraisal

The "Net Assets Value" method is based on the assumption that the company is going under liquidation whereas under yield method the it is assumed that the company is a going concern having perpetual succession *i.e.* the company will continue to operate. An investor is always interested in the consistent, steady, higher and regular return rather than what he will get on liquidation. The market sentiments go by the immediate return and not on what is there in store in the long run. It is easier and more rational to calculate NRR or ERR rather than estimating the market values of all assets. The chances of subjectivity are greater in case of Net Assets method. The necessary information relating to NRR and ERR is available along with the financial statements. Hence, this method is more rational & reliable.

However, this method suffers from certain limitations.

While calculating ERR the profits available for equity shareholders are to be ascertained. This in turn depends upon the company's policy to transfer to general reserve. If a company is transferring to general reserve at a higher rate than the statutorily required u/s 205, the ERR is bound to be low and so the yield value of the share.

Similarly, it is very difficult to determine NRR. One has to be very skilled & conversant with the industry situations and practices.

This method is suitable in case of growing and expanding companies having no sign of winding up in near future, and those declaring consistently regular dividend with relatively smaller capital employed. For valuing small lots this method is most appropriate method of valuation of shares.

III Earning Capacity Method

The yield method is considered inappropriate for valuing large lots of equity shares i.e. for acquiring controlling interest.

This method takes into account the earnings potentials of a company rather than the return of shareholders. A company with high potential earnings may not be able to declare high rate of dividend due to prudent and shrewd policy. It is quite possible that a large amount of earnings have gone to wipe out outstanding balance of losses.

Further, it is quite possible a large amount has been transferred to general reserve and thus leaving a small amount of profits for equity share holders. Usually growing and expanding companies do resort to ploughing back of profits. Hence, shares valued under other methods may not reflect the actual worth (market value).

Thus Earning Capacity Method takes into account total earnings of the company before any appropriations. This method involves the following steps.

1. Calculation of future maintainable profits
2. Calculation of Capital employed.
3. Ascertaining the rate of earnings
4. Determining the normal rate of return.
5. Determination of value of shares.

The computation of "Future Maintainable Profits" has already been discussed under the valuation of goodwill.

However, there are two views of the authorities as far as determination of capital employed is concerned.

According to some authorities, the Capital employed should mean Equity capital employed as explained under valuation of goodwill *i.e.* Equity Capital plus retained earnings. The preference share Capital, the long term borrowings and Debentures were to be excluded.

The second view states that the 'Earnings rate' should be calculated on the basis of equity, preference and total long term borrowings and profits should mean profits before interest but after tax. However, in this book, in view of a more rational approach that sounds more prudent, only first view has been taken into account for calculating the value of equity shares. Since problem under consideration is the valuation of equity shares, the capital employed belonging to equity shareholders has been taken into account. Similarly profits after interest, tax and preference dividend but before any other appropriation has been taken as profits for equity shareholders. Thus rate of earnings can be calculated as under:

$$\text{Rate of Earnings} = \frac{\text{Profits after interest, tax \& Preference dividend}}{\text{Equity Capital Employed}} \times 100$$

$$\text{Value of Equity Share} = \frac{\text{Earning Rate}}{\text{Normal Rate of Return}} \times \text{Paid up Value}$$

Illustration (7) (Earning Capacity and Yield Method)

From the following particulars calculate the value of a equity share of Rs. 10 under:

(a) Earning Capacity Method

(b) Yield Method.

Year	Capital Employed Rs.	Profits after Tax Rs.	Dividend %
2001-02	5,00,000	80,000	12
2002-03	8,00,000	1,60,000	15
2003-04	10,00,000	2,20,000	18
2004-05	15,00,000	3,75,000	20

The normal rate of return is 10%

Solution: (a) (Earning Capacity Mathod)

Year		Rate of Earnings
2001-02	$\frac{80,000}{5,00,000} \times 100$	= 16%
2002-03	$\frac{1,60,000}{8,00,000} \times 100$	= 20%
2003-04	$\frac{2,20,000}{10,00,000} \times 100$	= 22%
2004-05	$\frac{3,75,000}{15,00,000} \times 100$	= 25%

$$\text{Average Earning rate*} = \frac{16 + 20 + 22 + 25}{4} \times 20.75\%$$

Hence Future maintainable earning rate = 20.75

$$\text{Value of Share} = \frac{\text{Expected Rate of Earning}}{\text{Normal Rate of Return}} \times \text{Paid up Value}$$

$$= \frac{20.75}{10} \times 10 = \text{Rs. } 20.75$$

(b) Yield Method

$$\text{Average rate of dividend} = \frac{12 + 15 + 18 + 20}{4}$$

Expected rate of dividend = 16.25%

$$\text{Value of Share} = \frac{\text{Expected Rate of Return}}{\text{Normal Rate of Return}} \times \text{Paid up Value}$$

$$= \frac{16.25}{10} \times 10 = \text{Rs.} 16.25$$

***Since earnings of last four years are given, it is better to take average to determine future maintainable earnings.**

(IV) Capitalisation of Earning Capacity Method

There is an alternative method of calculating the market value of share based on the earning capacity of the company. Under this method profits available for equity shareholders, as calculated under capitalisation method, are capitalised on the basis of normal rate of return. Then the value of equity share is ascertained by dividing the capitalised profits by the number of equity shares, as shown under :

$$\text{Capitalised Value of Profits} = \frac{\text{Future Maintainable Profits}}{\text{Normal Rate of Return}} \times 100$$

$$\text{Value of Equity Share} = \frac{\text{Capitalised Value of Profits}}{\text{No. of Equity Shares}}$$

Illustration (8) (Capitalisation Method)

From the following particulars, calculate value of equity share by capitalisation of earnings method.

	Sales Rs.	Operating Cost Rs.	Interest on Bank Loan Rs.
2001-02	6,00,000	3,45,000	25,000
2002-03	7,00,000	3,95,000	25,000
2003-04	8,00,000	4,45,000	25,000
2004-05	5,00,000	2,95,000	25,000
2005-06	9,00,000	4,95,000	25,000

BALANCE SHEET AS ON 31ST MARCH, 2006

Liabilities	Rs.	Assets	Rs.
Equity Share Capital	2,50,000	Fixed Assets	5,00,000
(Shares of Rs. 10 each)		Current Assets	3,00,000
Reserves	1,00,000	Preliminary Expenses	25,000
12% Debentures (1999)	2,50,000		
Other Liabilities	2,25,000		
	8,25,000		8,25,000

The rate of taxation may be as follows :

2001-02	50%
2002-03	40%
2003-04	40%
2004-05	35%
2005-06	35%
The Normal Rate of Earnings	10%

[B.Com. (H) DU - Adapted]

Solution:

CAPITALISATION OF EARNINGS METHOD

	2001-02 Rs.	2002-03 Rs.	2003-04 Rs.	2004-05 Rs.	2005-06 Rs.
Sales	6,00,000	7,00,000	8,00,000	5,00,000	9,00,000
Less Operating Cost	(3,45,000)	(3,95,000)	(4,45,000)	(2,95,000)	(4,95,000)
PBIT	2,55,000	3,05,000	3,55,000	2,05,000	4,05,000
Less Interest*	(55,000)	(55,000)	(55,000)	(55,000)	(55,000)
PBT	2,00,000	2,50,000	3,00,000	1,50,000	3,50,000
Less Tax	(1,00,000)	(1,00,000)	(1,20,000)	(52,500)	(1,22,500)
PAT	1,00,000	1,50,000	1,80,000	97,500	2,27,500

*Including debenture interest.

Average Profits of last five years:

$$= \frac{1,00,000 + 1,50,000 + 1,80,000 + 97,500 + 2,27,500}{5}$$

$= \text{Rs. } 7,55,000/5 \;=\; \text{Rs. } 1,51,000$

$$\text{Capitalised Value of Profits} = \frac{1,51,000 \times 100}{10} = \text{Rs. } 15,10,000$$

$$\text{Value of Equity Share} = \frac{15,10,000}{25,000} = \text{Rs. } 60.40$$

Working note

Since debenture interest of Rs. 30,000 has not been shown in the Income Statement, the same has been added with Interest on bank loan.

Earning Capacity: An Appraisal

This method is suited only when future maintainable profits and Normal Rate of Return (NRR) can be ascertained correctly. It is possible only when market information is easily available. However, while calculating NRR the risk factor should be taken into account. This method is different from the Yield method which is purely based on the return (dividend) to investors whereas earning capacity shows the overall earnings potentials of a company in view of capital employed.

(V) Fair Value Method

In order to overcome the shortcomings of any one single method of valuation of shares, the Fair Value Method of valuation of shares is considered as the most appropriate method Fair value is simply an average of 'Intrinsic Value' and Yield Value or Earning Capacity method. For valuing shares of investment companies for wealth tax purposes, the fair value method has been recognised by the Government. It is suited to manufacturing and other organisations. The Fair value can be worked out as under :

$$\text{Fair Value of Share} = \frac{\text{Intrinsic Value + Yield Value}}{2}$$

$$\text{or} = \frac{\text{Intrinsic Value + CapitalisedValue / Earning Capicity}}{2}$$

Illustration (9) (Fair Value Method)

From the following particulars calculate value of equity share by "Fair Value Method".

	Rs.
10% 50,000 Preference Shares of Rs. 10 each	5,00,000
1,00,000 Equity shares of Rs. 10 each	10,00,000
Reserves & Surplus	4,50,000
Liability to outsiders	2,50,000
Fictitious Assets	1,50,000
Average normal profits after tax	8,50,000
Normal profit earned on the market value of fully paid equity shares of similar companies	16%
Transfer to General Reserve	10%

[C.S. (I) June 2001 - Adapted]

Solution:

CALCULATION OF INTRINSIC VALUE OF SHARES

Calculation of Gross Assets

Liabilities	Rs.	Assets	Rs.
10% 50,000 Pref. Shares	5,00,000	S. Assets (B.F.)	20,50,000
1,00,000 Equity Shares	10,00,000	Fictitious-Assets	1,50,000
Reserves & Surplus	4,50,000		
Liabilities	2,50,000		
	22,00,000		22,00,000

	Gross Assets	20,50,000
Less	Liabilities	(2,50,000)
	Assets available for Equity & Preference S/H	18,00,000
Less	Preference Share Capital	(5,00,000)
	Amount available for Equity shareholders	13,00,000

$$\text{Intrinsic Value} = \frac{13,00,000}{1,00,000} = \text{Rs. } 13$$

Yield Method

		Rs.
	Average Profits	5,00,000
Less	Transfer to General Reserve @ 10% on 5,00,000	(50,000)
		4,50,000
Less	Preference dividend	(50,000)
	Profits available for Equity Shareholders	4,00,000

$$\text{Expected Rate of Return} = \frac{4,00,000 \times 100}{1,00,000} = 40\%$$

$$\text{Value of Share} = \frac{\text{Expected Rate of Return}}{\text{Normal Rate of Return}} = \text{Paid up Value} = \frac{40}{16} \times 10 = \text{Rs. } 25$$

$$\text{Fair Value} = \frac{\text{Intrinsic Value + Yield Value}}{2}$$

$$= \frac{13 + 25}{2} = \frac{38}{2} = \text{Rs. } 19$$

GRADED ILLUSTRATIONS

Illustration (1) (Fair Value Method)

Mr. X intends to invest Rs. 52,200 in equity shares of Zed Ltd. and seeks your advice as to the maximum number of shares he can expect to purchase based on a fair value of the shares. The following information is available:

	Rs.
9% Preference Shares of Rs. 100 each fully paid	3,00,000
Equity Shares of Rs. 10 each fully paid	5,00,000
Average net profits of the company	1,27,000
Expected Normal Yield on Equity	10%

It is observed that net assets on revaluation are Rs. 50,000 more than the amount as per Balance Sheet figures.

Goodwill is to be calculated at 2 years' purchase of super profits. Ignore tax.

(ICWA (F) Modified)

Solution:

CALCULATION OF GOODWILL

		Rs.
	Average net profits	1,27,000
Less	Preference dividend	(27,000)
		1,00,000
Less	Normal Profits (5,50,000* 10%)	55,000
	Super Profits	45,000
	Goodwill at 2 years purchase (45,000 × 2)	90,000

Equity Capital Employed

Equity Share Capital	5,00,000
Reserve & Surplus	—
Appreciation in S. Assets	50,000
	5,50,000

Since current year's profits are not given, the capital employed has been treated as 'Average Capital Employed'.

Net Assets for Equity Shareholders

Capital employed = Net Assets

Equity Capital Employed = Net Assets for Equity Shareholders

		Rs.
	Net Assets for Equity Shareholders (before goodwill)	5,50,000
Add	Goodwill	90,000
	Value of 50,000 Equity Shares	6,40,000

$$\text{Net Assets or Intrinsic Value per share} = \frac{6,40,000}{500,000} = \text{Rs. } 14.80$$

Value on Yield Basis

		Rs.
	Average Profits (Future maintainable)	1,27,000
Less	Preference dividend	(27,000)
	Profits available for Equity Shareholders	1,00,000

$$\text{Expected rate of return} = \frac{1,00,000}{5,00,000} \times 100 = 20\%$$

$$\text{Yield Value} = \frac{\text{ERR}}{\text{NRR}} \times \text{Paid up Value} = \frac{20}{10} \times 10 = \text{Rs. } 20$$

or $$\text{Yield Value per share} = \frac{1,00,000}{5,00,000} \times 10 = \text{Rs. } 20$$

$$\text{Fair Value per share} = \frac{\text{Intrinsic Value + Yield Value}}{2}$$

$$= \frac{14.80 + 20}{2} = \frac{34.80}{2} = \text{Rs. } 17.40$$

$$\text{Mr. X Can buy } \left(\frac{\text{Rs. } 52{,}200}{14.80}\right) = 3527 \text{ shares under Intrinsic Value Method.}$$

$$\frac{\text{Rs. } 52{,}200}{17.40} = 3{,}000 \text{ shares under Fair Value Method}$$

$$\frac{\text{Rs. } 52{,}200}{20} = 2{,}610 \text{ shares under Yield Method}$$

Working note :

Since rate of dividend and general reserve are not given, the amount to be transferred to general reserve as required U/s 205 has been ignored.

Illustration (2) (Value for Controlling and non-controlling shares)

The Balance Sheet of Somu Ltd. as on 31st March, 2006 was as under :

Liabilities	Rs.	Assets	Rs.
10% Preference Share Capital Shares of Rs. 100 each	2,00,000	Land & Building	8,00,000
		Plant & Machinery	4,00,000
Equity Share Capital :		Stock	5,00,000
Shares of Rs. 10 each fully paid	6,00,000	S. Debtors	4,20,000
Shares of Rs. 10 each Rs. 5 paid	4,00,000	Cash & Bank	80,000
Reserve & Surplus	6,00,000		
Current liabilities	4,00,000		
	22,00,000		22,00,000

Profits and dividends during the last 3 years were as under :

	Profit (Rs.)	Equity Dividend %
2003-04	4,40,000	12%
2004-05	5,00,000	15%
2005-06	6,40,000	18%

Land and Building are worth Rs. 10,00,000. The managerial remuneration is likely to go up by Rs. 60,000 per annum. Income Tax may be provided at 40%. The equity shares of companies in the same industry with dividend rate of 10% are quoted at par.

Find out most appropriate value of an equity share. If (a) Controlling interest is to be acquired.

(b) Only a few shares are to be acquired. Ignore goodwill value, depreciation adjustment for revaluation and need of transfer to general reserve.

[C.A. (F) - Modified]

Solution :

I Calculation of Future Maintainable Profits

	Profit (Rs.)	Weight	Product (Rs.)
2003-04	4,40,000	1	4,40,000
2004-05	5,00,000	2	10,00,000
2005-06	6,40,000	3	19,20,000
		6	33,60,000

	Average Profits (32,60,000/6)	5,60,000
Less	Increase in Remuneration	(60,000)
		5,00,000
Less	Tax @ 40%	(2,00,000)
	Profit after Tax	3,00,000
Less	Preference dividend	(20,000)
	Maintainable profits for Equity Shareholders	2,80,000

(a) **When controlling interest is to be acquired then capitalisation of maintainable Profits will be applied.**

	Capitalised Value of profits (2,80,000 × 100/10	28,00,000
Add	Notional Call on partly Paid shares	4,00,000
		32,00,000

Value of fully paid share $\frac{32,00,000}{1,00,000 \text{ Shares}}$ = Rs. 32

Value of Partly paid share Rs. 32 – 5 = Rs. 27

or Shares may acquired on **Fair Value basis**

Second Method : Net Assets Method

	Sundry Assets	22,00,000
Add	Profit on Revaluation	2,00,000
		24,00,000
Add	Notional Call on partly paid share	4,00,000
		28,00,000
Less	Current liabilities	(4,00,000)
		24,00,000
Less	Preference Share Capital	(2,00,000)
		22,00,000

Value of fully paid Equity Share = 22,00,000/ 10,00,000 = Rs. 22

Value of partly paid share Rs. 22 – 5 = Rs. 17

Fair Value of Fully paid Share = $\frac{32 + 22}{2}$ = Rs. 27

Fair Value of Partly paid Share = $\frac{27 + 17}{2}$ = Rs. 22

or Rs. 27 – 5 = Rs. 22

(b) When only few shares are acquired. Yield Method will be applied.

$$\text{Average Yield (Dividend) Rate} = \frac{12+15+18}{3} = 15\% = 15\%$$

$$\text{Value of Fully Paid Share} = \frac{\text{ERR}}{\text{NRR}} \times \text{Paid up Value}$$

$$= \frac{15}{10} \times 10 = 15$$

$$\text{Value of Partly paid share} = \frac{15}{10} \times 5 = \text{Rs. } 7.50$$

Note: Fair Value for smaller lots will be $= \frac{\text{Intrinsic Value + Yield Value}}{2}$

$$\text{For Fully paid share} = \frac{22+15}{2} = \frac{37}{2} = \text{Rs. } 18.50$$

$$\text{For Partly paid share} = \frac{17+7.50}{2} = \frac{24.50}{2} = \text{Rs. } 12.25$$

It is to be noted that when profits earned over the years show a definite trend, the weighted average is worked out for the purpose of calculating future maintainable profits.

Illustration (3) (Ex-Dividend & Cum-Dividend value of share)

From the following particulars calculate value of equity share Ex-dividend and Cum-dividend

BALANCE SHEET OF P LTD.
As on 31st March, 2006

Liabilities	Rs.	Assets	Rs.
50,000 Equity Shares of Rs. 10 each	5,00,000	Land & Building	2,70,000
Profit & Loss A/c	1,40,000	Plant & Machinery	1,00,000
Bank-Overdraft	10,000	Stock	3,60,000
Creditors	80,000	S. Debtors	1,60,000
Provision for Taxation	1,00,000		
Proposed dividend	60,000		
	8,90,000		8,90,000

The net profits of the company after deducting usual working expenses but before providing for taxation were as under :

Year	Profit Rs.
2001-02	1,72,500
2002-03	2,10,000
2003-04	1,80,000
2004-05	2,20,000
2005-06	2,00,000

On 31st March 2006, the Land and Building were valued at Rs. 2,80,000 Plant and Machinery at Rs. 1,20,000, Sundry Debtors included Rs. 4,000 as irrecoverable.

Keeping in mind the nature of business, 10% return is considered reasonable. The goodwill is to be valued at 2 years purchase of the annual super profits. The company charges 5% depreciation on Land & Building and 10% on Plant & Machinery. The tax rate may be taken at 40%.

[C.A. (F) Adapted]

Solution :

COMPUTATION OF NET ASSETS

			Rs.
	Goodwill		2,37,000
	Land & Building		2,80,000
	Plant & Machinery		1,20,000
	Stock		3,60,000
	Debtors		1,56,000
Less	Liabilities		11,53,000
	Bank overdraft	10,000	
	Creditors	80,000	
	Provision for Taxation	1,00,000	
	Proposed Dividend	60,000	2,50,000
			9,03,000

Intrinsic Value of Share = Rs. 9,03,000/50,000 shares = Rs. 18.60

(Ex-dividend) (- -)

II Calculation of Capital Employed

	Land & Building		2,80,000
	Plant & Machinery		1,20,000
	Stock		3,60,000
	Debtors		1,56,000
			9,16,000
Less	Liabilities:		
	Bank Overdraft	10,000	
	Creditors	80,000	
	Provision for Taxation	1,00,000	(1,90,000)
			7,26,000
Less	Half of the profits after Tax		60,000
	1/2 (2,00,000 – 80,000)		
	Average Capital Employed		6,66,000
(iii)	**Value of Goodwill**		
	Total Profits before Tax		9,82,500
	Average Profits (9,82,500/5)		1,96,500
Less	Adjustments :		
	Provision for Debts	4,000	

	Depreciation on Appreciated Value of Land & Building	500	
	Plant & Machinery	2,000	(6,500)
			1,90,000
Less	Tax @ 40%		(76,000)
	Average Annual Profits		1,14,000
Less	Normal Profits (10% of Average Capital Employed)		(66,600)
	Super profits		47,400
	Goodwill at 5 years' purchase (47,400 × 5)		2,37,000

(b) While calculating Cum-dividend value the "proposed dividend" will not be treated as a liability.

Thus Net Assets will increase by	Rs. 60,000
Total Net Assets (Cum-dividend)	9,63,000
Intrinsic Value of Share Cum-dividend = 9,63,000/ 50,000 Rs. 19.26	

Illustration (4) (Valuation of Share & P/E Ratio)

The Capital structure of a company is as follows :

10% Preference shares of Rs. 100 each	5,00,000
Equity Shares of Rs. 10 each	10,00,000
Reserves & Surplus	5,00,000
9% Debentures	5,00,000
10% Bank Loan	5,00,000

The average annual profits before interest & tax is Rs. 5,95,000. The income tax rate is 40%. Calculate value of equity shares if price earning ratio is 8.

[C.S. (I) Adapted]

Solution:

CALCULATION OF EARNINGS PER SHARE

			Rs.
	Profit before Interest & Tax		5,95,000
Less	Interest on:		
	9% Debentures	45,000	
	10% Bank Loan	50,000	(95,000)
	Profit before Tax		5,00,000
Less	Tax @ 40%		(2,00,000)
	Profit after Tax		3,00,000
Less	Preference Dividend		(50,000)
	Profit available for Equity Shareholders		2,50,000
	Earnings per share (Rs. 2,50,000/1,00,000 Shares)		= Rs. 2.50

$$\text{Price Earnings Ratio} = \frac{\text{Market Price per share}}{\text{Earning per share}}$$

$$8 = \frac{\text{Market Price per share}}{2.5}$$

Market price per share = 2.5 × 8 = Rs. 20

Illustration (5) (Valuation of assets and fair value)

Following is the Balance Sheet of Addu Ltd. as on 31st March, 2006.

Liabilities	Rs.	Assets	Rs.
50,000 Equity Shares of Rs. 10 each	5,00,000	Land & Building	2,50,000
		Plant & Machinery	3,00,000
Reserves & Surplus	1,80,000	Patents & Trade Marks	50,000
S. Creditors	2,20,000	Current Assets	3,80,000
Income Tax	1,00,000	Preliminary Expenses	20,000
	10,00,000		10,00,000

The valuers valued the assets as under :

	Rs.
Land & Machinery	5,00,000
Plant & Machinery	2,50,000
Debtors subject to Provision for Doubtful Debts	8,000
Goodwill	1,48,000
Other assets at Book value	

The profits (after tax) of the company were as follows :

	Rs.
2003-04	1,90,000
2004-05	2,05,000
2005-06	2,18,000

The Company follows the practice of transferring 25% of profits to general reserve. Similar type of companies earn at 12% of the value of their shares, Ascertain the value of shares under fair value method. Depreciation on Land & Building and Plant and Machinery is charged @ 4% and 10% respectively.

[C.S. (I) Adapted]

Solution:

I CALCULATION OF INTRINSIC VALUE

Assets:

			Rs.
	Goodwill		1,48,000
	Land & Building		5,00,000
	Plant & Machinery		2,50,000
	Patents & Trademarks		50,000
	Current Assets (3,80,000 – 8,000)		3,72,000
	Gross Assets		13,20,000
Less	Liabilities:		
	S. Creditors	2,20,000	
	Income Tax	1,00,000	(3,20,000)
	Net Assets		10,00,000

Intrinsic Value per share = Rs. 10,00,000/ 50,000 shares = Rs. 20. per share.

II CALCULATION OF YIELD VALUE

	Profits	Weight	Product
2003-04	1,90,000	1	1,90,000
2004-05	2,05,000	2	4,10,000
2005-06	2,10,000*	3	6,30,000
**Less* for Doubtful debts*		6	12,30,000

		Rs.
	Weighted Average Profits	2,05,000
Less	Depreciation on Appreciated Value on Land & Building Rs. 2,50,000 4%)	(10,000)
		1,95,000
Add	Depreciation on Plant & Machinery 50,000 @ 10%	5,000
	Average Profits	2,00,000
	Future maintainable profits	2,00,000
Less	Transfer to Reserve @ 25%	(50,000)
	Profits available for Equity Shareholders	1,50,000

Expected rate of return $= \frac{1,50,000 \times 100}{5,00,000} = 30\%$

Yield Value $= \frac{\text{ERR}}{\text{NRR}} \times$ Paid up Value of Share

$= \frac{30 \times 10}{12} =$ Rs. 25 per Share

Fair Value $= \frac{\text{Intrinsic Value + Yield Value}}{2}$

$= \frac{20 + 25}{2} = \frac{45}{2} =$ Rs. 22.50 per share

Note: Since profits show a definite trend the same have been averaged on weighted average basis.

Illustration (6) (Value of smaller lots and larger lots)

Following is the Balance Sheet of A Ltd. as on 31st March, 2006

Liabilities	Rs.	Assets	Rs.
Equity Share Capital Shares of Rs. 10 each fully paid	5,00,000	Goodwill at cost	50,000
		Fixed Assets	8,30,000
Equity Share Capital Shares of Rs. 5 each fully paid	5,00,000	Current Assets	8,60,000
		Preliminary Expenses	10,000
General Reserve	2,50,000		
Profit & Loss A/c	1,50,000		
Gratuity Fund	50,000		
Workmen Compensation Fund	45,000		
Depreciation Fund	50,000		
Trade Creditors	1,55,000		
Expenses Creditors	10,000		
Bank Overdraft	40,000		
	17,50,000		17,50,000

A Shareholder holding 500 shares of Rs. 10 each and 1,000 shares of Rs. 5 each want to dispose off all the shares. Dividends paid for last three years were 12%, 11% & 13% Normal expectation is 8%.

Fixed assets are worth Rs. 6,50,000 Goodwill is to be increased by an amount equal to average of book value and a valuation made at 5 years' purchase of average super profits for the last three years. Debtors worth Rs. 10,000 considered doubtful and Trade Creditors of Rs. 5,000 are outstanding for many years and it is estimated that this amount will not be payable. On the other hand Rs. 15,000 being disputed bonus claim has not been provided in the accounts but it is likely that the amount shall have to be paid.

Profits for the last three years after taxation are Rs. 1,35,000, Rs. 1,55,000 and Rs. 1,15,000 respectively.

(a) Find out the break-up value market value and fair value of both types of equity shares.

(b) What should be the fair value of the shares if controlling interest of the Managing Director is being sold.

[ICWA (F) Adapted]

Solution

Calculation of Average Capital Employed:

			Rs.
Assets :			
	Goodwill at Cost		50,000
	Fixed Assets		6,50,000
	Current Assets - Provision for Bad debts		8,50,000
			15,50,000
Less	Liabilities:		
	Creditors	1,50,000	
	Creditors for expenses	10,000	
	Bank overdraft	40,000	2,00,000
	Capital Employed		13,50,000
Less	1/2 of the profit of the Current year		
	(1/2 × 1,15,000 – 15,000 for Bonus)		(50,000)
	Average Capital employed		13,00,000

II Calculation of Super profits

	Total profits of last three years	
	(Rs. 1,35,000 + 1,55,000 + (1,15,000 – 15,000) = Rs. 3,90,000	
	Average Profits	1,30,000
Less	Normal Profits (Rs. 13,00,000 × 8%)	(1,04,000)
	Super profits	26,000

Value of Goodwill Rs. 26,000 × 5 = Rs. 1,30,000

$$\text{Average Value of goodwill} = \frac{50,000 + 1,30,000}{2} = \text{Rs. } 90,000$$

	Capital Employed (Net Assets)	13,50,000
Add	Increase in goodwill	90,000
		14,40,000
	Total Paid up Capital	10,00,000
	Unit Value of Re. 1 of paid up Capital	1.44

(a) (i) Break up/Intrinsic Value of Shares of Rs. 10 each 1.44 × 10 = Rs. 14.40

Share of Rs. 5 each 1.44 × 5 = Rs. 7.20

(ii) Market Value or Yield Value of share

$$= \frac{\text{Expected Rate of Return}}{\text{Normal Rate of Return}} \times \text{Paid up Value of Share}$$

= Expected Rate of Return = Average Dividend

$$= \text{Average Dividend} = \frac{12 + 11 + 13}{3} \times \frac{36}{3} = 12\%$$

$$\text{Yield Value of Rs. 10 share} = \frac{12}{8} \times 10 = \text{Rs. } 15$$

$$\text{Yield Value of Rs. 5 share} = \frac{12}{8} \times 5 = \text{Rs. } 7.50$$

(b) If Controlling interest of Managing Director is to be sold the Earnings of Capitalisation or Earnings Capacity Method of valuation will be applied to get the Fair Value of share. Thus

$$\text{Capitalised Value of profits} = \frac{\text{Profits available for Equity Shareholders}}{\text{Normal Rate of Return}} \times 100$$

$$= \frac{1{,}30{,}000}{8} \times 100 = \text{Rs. } 16{,}25{,}000$$

Since shares of Rs. 10 each and Rs. 5 each have equal contribution i.e. Rs. 5,00,000 each, the capitalised value of the profits will be divided equally among both the categories.

Rs. 16,25,000 ÷ 2 = 8,12,500

$$\text{Value of Rs. 10 share} = \frac{8{,}12{,}500}{50{,}000} = \text{Rs. } 16.25$$

$$\text{Value of Rs. 5 share} = \frac{8{,}12{,}500}{1{,}00{,}000} = \text{Rs. } 8.125$$

$$\text{Fair Value of Rs. 10 share} = \frac{14.40 + 16.25}{2} = \text{Rs. } 15.325$$

$$\text{Value of Rs. 5 share} = \frac{7.20 + 8.125}{2} = \text{Rs. } 7.66$$

Note: In the absence of any information relating to Gratuity and workmen's compensation fund, these have been treated as accumulated profits.

Illustration (7) (Yield on distributed and Undistributed profits)

The Capital structure of A Ltd. as on 31st March, 2006 was as follows :

	Rs.
Equity Share Capital	18,00,000
Shares of Rs. 100 each fully paid	
12% Preference Share Capital Shares of Rs. 100 each	5,00,000
12% Secured Debentures	5,00,000
Reserves & Surplus	5,00,000
Profit earned before interest and taxes during the year (Tax rate 40%)	7,60,000
General rate of return on equity shares in this type of industry is	15%

Yield on shares is calculated at 60% of distributed profits and 12% on undistributed profits.

The Company has been paying regularly an equity dividend of 15%. The risk premium for dividends is generally assumed at 1%.

Find out value of equity shares of the company.

C.A. (F) Nov. 2004, Modified]

Solution:

I. Calculation of Distributed and undistributed Profits of the Company.

			Rs.
	Profit before Interest & Tax		7,60,000
Less	Interest on Debentures		(60,000)
	Profit before tax		7,00,000
Less	Tax @ 40%		(2,80,000)
			4,20,000
Less	Preference dividend	60,000	
	Equity dividend* (15% on Rs. 18,00,000)	2,70,000	3,30,000
	Undistributed Profits		90,000

*Distributed Profits

II Calculation of Yield on Equity Shares

60% of distributed profits (Rs. 2,70,000 × 60/100)	1,62,000
12% of undistributed profits (90,000 × 12%)	10,800
	1,72,800

Rate of Yield = $\frac{1,72,800}{18,00,000} \times 100$ = 9.6%

	Normal Rate of Return	= 15%
Add	Risk	1%
	NRR	16%

Value of Equity Shares = $\frac{\text{ERR}}{\text{NRR}} \times \text{Paid up Value}$

$= \frac{9.6}{16} \times 100$

= Rs. 60

Illustration (8) (Value of Equity and Preference Shares)

The financial position of Zed Ltd. as on 31st March, 2006 was as under :

Liabilities	Rs.	Assets	Rs.
10,000 12% Preference Shares of Rs. 100 each	10,00,000	Goodwill	1,50,000
15,000 Equity Shares of Rs. 100 each	15,00,000	Land & Building	10,00,000
25,000 Equity Shares of Rs. 100 each Rs. 60 paid	15,00,000	Plant & Machinery	25,00,000
General Reserve	4,50,000	Stock	30,00,000
Profits of Current year	7,50,000	Book-Debts	7,50,000
5% Debentures	10,00,000	Cash & Bank	40,000
S. Creditors	12,50,000	Preliminary Expenses	10,000
	74,50,000		74,50,000

The assets were revalued as under :

	Rs.
Land & Building	22,75,000
Plant & Machinery	22,50,000
Stock	27,10,000

Normal return for valuation of goodwill is 8.75% Profits for the last three years have shown an increase of Rs. 1,50,000 annually. The basis of valuation of goodwill is Five years purchase of super profits. Preference dividend for the year was in arrear and was included in Sundry Creditors. Similar companies are paying 12% dividend on equity shares.

Find out the value of Equity and Preference Shares. Ignore depreciation and tax.

[ICWA (F) Modified]

Solution:

I Calculation of Capital Employed

Assets		Rs.
Land & Building		28,75,000
Plant & Machinery		22,50,000
Stock		27,10,000
Book Debts		7,50,000
Cash & Bank		40,000
		86,25,000
Less Liabilities		
5% Debentures	10,00,000	
S. Creditors	12,50,000	22,50,000
Net Assets (Capital Employed)		63,75,000
Less Half of the profits of the current year		3,75,000
Average Capital Employed		60,00,000

II Calculation of Super Profits & Valuation of goodwill

Computation of "Average Profits" or Future maintainable profits		Rs.
Profits for the year	2005-06	7,50,000
Profits for the year	2004-05	6,00,000
Profits for the year	2003-04	4,50,000

Since profits show a definite trend, the weightage has to be given.

Year	Profits Rs.	Weight	Product Rs.
2003-04	4,50,000	1	4,50,000
2004-05	6,00,000	2	12,00,000
2005-06	7,50,000	3	22,50,000
		6	39,00,000

		Rs.
	Weighted Average Profits or Future maintainable Profits	6,50,000
Less	Normal Profits 8.75% of Rs. 60,00,000	5,25,000
	Super Profits	1,25,000
	Goodwill at 5 years purchase	6,25,000

III Valuation of Shares

	Net Assets before Goodwill	63,75,000
Add	Value of goodwill	6,25,000
	Total net assets	70,00,000
Less	Preference Share Capital	(10,00,000)
	Assets available for Equity Shareholders	60,00,000
Add	Notional Call on Partly paid Shares	10,00,000
	Total Net Assets	70,00,000
	Value of fully paid 40,000 Equity Shares (15,000 + 25,000 shares)	= Rs. 70,00,000
	Intrinsic Value	= Rs. 175 per share
	Value of partly paid share = Rs. 175 – 40	= Rs. 135 per share
IV	**Value of Preference Share** Rs. 100 + Rs. 12 arrear of dividend	= Rs. 112
V	**Yield Method** :	Rs.
	Average Profits	6,50,000
Less	Preference dividend	(1,20,000)
		5,30,000
Less	Transfer to General Reserve (say 10%)	53,000
	Profits available for Equity Shareholders	4,77,000

$$\text{Expected Rate of Return} = \frac{4,77,000}{30,00,000} \times 100 = 15.9\%$$

$$\text{Yield Value of fully paid share} = \frac{ERR}{NRR} \times \text{Paid up Value}$$

$$= \frac{15.9}{12} \times 100 = \text{Rs. } 132.50$$

$$\text{Yield Value of Partly paid share} = \frac{15.9}{12} \times 60 = \text{Rs. } 79.50$$

VI $$\text{Fair Value of fully paid share} = \frac{\text{Intrinsic Value + Yield Value}}{2}$$

$$= \frac{175 + 132.50}{2} = \frac{307.50}{2} = \text{Rs. } 153.75$$

$$\text{Fair Value of Partly paid share} = \frac{112 + 79.50}{2} = \frac{191.50}{2} = \text{Rs. } 95.75$$

Illustration (9) (Valuation of goodwill and fair value of shares)

The Balance Sheet of NN Ltd. as on 31st March, 2006 was as under :

Liabilities	Rs.	Assets	Rs.
Equity Share Capital	50,00,000	Fixed Assets (Net)	35,50,000
Shares of Rs. 100 each		Current Assets	42,00,000
Reserves & Surplus	12,50,000		
Bank Loan	10,00,000		
Current Liabilities	5,00,000		
	77,50,000		77,50,000

The Net profits after charging interest and taxes amounted to Rs. 3,00,000, Rs. 3,00,000 and Rs. 5,00,000 during the year 2003-04, 2004-05 and 2005-06 respectively.

For the purpose of share valuation the fixed assets and current assets are considered worth Rs. 50,00,000 and Rs. 40,00,000 respectively.

Goodwill was agreed to be valued at a years' purchase of super profits, arrived at as excess of weighted average net profits of past three years over 4% of revised net worth. (Assign weight 1,2 & 3 for the year 2003-04, 2004-05 and 2005-06 respectively)

Assign fair value for the equity shares on the basis of "Intrinsic Value" and capitalised value of future profits. The Capitalisation rate being 5%.

[C.S. (F) Modified]

Solution:

I : Computation of Weighted Average Profits

Year	Profits Rs.	Weight	Product Rs.
2003-04	3,00,000	1	3,00,000
2004-05	3,00,000	2	6,00,000
2005-06	5,00,000	3	15,00,000
		6	24,00,000

Weighted Average 4,00,000

II Calculation of Revised Net worth

			Rs.
	Net fixed Assets		50,00,000
	Current Assets		40,00,000
			90,00,000
Less	Liabilities:		
	Bank Loan	10,00,000	
	Current Liabilities	5,00,000	(15,00,000)
	Revised Net worth		75,00,000

Calculation of Goodwill

	Goodwill = Weighted Average Profits	4,00,000
Less	4% of Revised Net worth	(3,00,000)
	Goodwill	1,00,000

III Intrinsic Value of Share

	Goodwill		1,00,000
	Fixed Assets		50,00,000
	Current Assets		40,00,000
			91,00,000
Less	Liabilities:		
	Bank Loan	10,00,000	
	Current Liabilities	5,00,000	(15,00,000)
	Net Assets		76,00,000

$$\text{Intrinsic Value per share} = \frac{76,00,000}{50,000} = \text{Rs. } 152$$

IV Capitalised Value

	Rs.
Future Maintainable Profits (Weighted Average Profits)	4,00,000
Capitalisation rate	5%

$$\text{Capitalised Value} = \frac{4,00,000}{5\%} = \text{Rs. } 80,00,000$$

$$\text{Capitalised Value per share} = \frac{80,00,000}{50,000} = \text{Rs. } 160$$

V **Fair Value** $= \frac{\text{Intrinsic Value + Capitalised Value}}{2}$

$$= \frac{152 + 160}{2} = \text{Rs. } 156 \text{ per share.}$$

Illustration (10) (Bonus Shares and Valuation of Equity Shares and Preference shares)

Following is the Balance Sheet of Evergreen Ltd. as on 31st March, 2006.

Liabilities	Rs.	Assets	Rs.
Equity Share Capital		**Fixed Assets**	4,00,000
20,000 shares of Rs. 10 each fully paid	2,00,000	Investments of 5% Government Bonds	1,00,000
15,000 Shares of Rs. 10 each Rs. 8 paid	1,20,000	**Current Assets :**	
		Stock	2,50,000
10,000 Shares of Rs. 10 each Rs. 5 paid 10% Preference Shares	50,000	Debtors	1,50,000
	2,00,000	Bank	60,000
General Reserve	2,00,000	**Loans & Advances:**	
Profit & Loss A/c	40,000	Staff	70,000
Secured Loans:		Others	50,000
On Building	60,000		
On Stock	60,000		
Deposits	20,000		
Current Liability	80,000		
Provision for Taxation	40,000		
Unclaimed dividend	10,000		
	10,80,000		10,80,000

Fixed Assets were revalued at Rs. 4,80,000 Bonus shares issued for Rs. 1,50,000. Dividends declared at Annual General Meeting before bonus issue at 20%. Income Tax in dispute on appeal Rs. 90,000.

You are required to value each one of the class of equity shares and preference shares by

(a) Assets Backing Method

(b) Yield Method assuming normal rate of return is 10%.

[ICWA (F) Adapted]

Solution:

I. Assets Backing or Net Assets Method

Calculation of Net Assets

	Rs.
Fixed Assets	4,80,000
Investments	1,00,000
Stock	2,50,000
Debtors	1,50,000
Bank	60,000
Loans & Advances	1,20,000
	11,60,000

		Rs.	Rs.
	Balance b/d		11,60,000
Less	Liabilities		
	Secured Loans	1,20,000	
	Deposits	20,000	
	Current Liability	80,000	
	Provision for Taxation	90,000	
	Unclaimed Dividend	10,000	(3,20,000)
	Net Assets		8,40,000
Less	Preference Share Capital		2,00,000
	Net Assets for Equity Shareholders		6,40,000
Add	Notional Call on partly paid shares:		
	15,000 shares @ Rs. 2		30,000
	10,000 shares @ Rs. 5		50,000
			7,20,000
	Intrinsic Value of fully paid share		7,20,000
	(Cum-Bonus)		Rs. 7,20,00/45,000 shares = Rs. 16 per share
	(Ex-Bonus)		$\frac{\text{Rs. } 7,20,000}{45,000 + 15,000}$ = Rs. 12 per share

For Partly paid share : (Rs. 8 paid)

Cum-Bonus = Rs. 16 – 2 = Rs. 14 per share

Ex-Bonus = Rs. 12 – 2 = Rs. 10 per share

For Partly paid share : (Rs. 5 paid)

Cum-Bonus = Rs. 16 – 5 = Rs. 11 per share

Ex-Bonus = Rs. 12 – 5 = Rs. 7 per share

10% Preference Share (non-participating) Rs. 100

II Yield Method $\left[\frac{\text{ERR*}}{\text{NRR}} \times \text{Paid up value}\right]$

Value of Equity Shares: Fully paid share = $\frac{20}{10} \times 10$ = Rs. 20

Partly paid (Rs. 8) = $\frac{20}{10} \times 8$ = Rs. 16

Partly paid (Rs. 5) = $\frac{20}{10} \times 5$ = Rs. 10

Preference Shares = $\frac{10}{10} \times 100$ = Rs. 100

***ERR is based on the dividend rate**

Illustration (11) (Past Adjustments, Goodwill and Valuation of Shares)

The following is the Balance Sheet of SJ Ltd. as on 31st March, 2006.

Liabilities	Rs.	Assets	Rs.
Equity Shares of Rs. 100 each	10,00,000	Goodwill	1,00,000
Less Calls in Arrears (@ Rs. 20 for final call)	1,00,000	Factory	5,50,000
		Machinery	5,00,000
	9,00,000	Motor Vehicles	1,50,000
10% Preference Shares		Furniture	50,000
of Rs. 100 each	4,00,000	Investments	2,00,000
General Reserve	4,00,000	Stock	4,00,000
Profits & Loss A/c	3,00,000	S. Debtors	7,00,000
Bank Loan	2,00,000	Cash & Bank	1,00,000
S. Creditors	6,00,000	Preliminary Expenses	50,000
	28,00,000		28,00,000

Additional Information

(1) Fixed Assets are worth 25% above their book value. Depreciation on appreciated value of fixed assets not to be considered for valuation of goodwill.

(2) Of the investments, 60% is non-trading and the balance is trading. All trade investments are to be valued at 25% above cost. A uniform rate of dividend at 15% is earned on all investments.

(3) For the purpose of valuation of shares, goodwill is to be considered on the basis of 2 $^1/_2$ years' purchase of the super profits based on the simple average profit (after tax) of the last three years. The profits (after tax 50%) were as follows :

	Rs.
2003-04	4,00,000
2004-05	4,30,000
2005-06	4,50,000

In a similar business return on capital employed is 15% (after tax).

(4) During 2003-04 a new machinery costing Rs. 20,000 was purchased but was wrongly debited to Profit & Loss A/c (No effect has yet been given for rectifying the same).

(5) Depreciation charged on machinery was 10% on Straight Line Method.

Calculate value of each class of shares.

[C.A. (F) Modified]

Solution:

I Calculation of Average Profits

	2003-04	2004-05	2005-06
	Rs.	Rs.	Rs.
Profits after Tax	4,00,000	4,30,000	4,50,000
Add Machinery Charged to P & L A/c*(1)	10,000	—	—
Less Depreciation on the above(2)	(1,000)	(1,000)	(1,000)

Less Income from [3]			
Non-trading Investments	(9,000)	(9,000)	(9,000)
Annual Profits	4,00,000	4,20,000	4,40,000
Average Profits (Rs. 12,60,000/3)			4,20,000

II Calculation of Capital Employed

		Rs.
	Fixed Assets:	
	Factory	5,50,000
	Machinery [4]	5,14,000
	Motor Vehicles	1,50,000
	Furniture	50,000
		12,64,000
Add	Appreciation @ 25%	3,16,000
	Trade Investments (5)	80,000
	Current Assets	12,00,000
	Total Assets	28,60,000
Less Liabilities:		
	(Bank Loan + Creditors)	8,00,000
	Capital employed	20,60,000
Less	Half of the profits of the current year	(2,20,000)
	Average Capital Employed	18,40,000

III Calculation of Goodwill

	Future Maintainable Profits (Average Profits)	4,20,000
Less	Normal Profits (Average Capital Employed × NRR)	(2,76,000)
	Super Profits	1,44,000
	Goodwill at 2 1/2 years purchase (1,44,000 × 2 1/2	3,60,000

IV Valuation of Shares

	Capital Employed or Net operating Assets (as calculated above)	20,60,000
Add	Non Trading Investment at cost	1,20,000
Add	Goodwill	3,60,000
	Total Net Assets	25,40,000
Less	Preference Share Capital	(4,00,000)
	Net Assets for Equity Shareholders	21,40,000
Add	Notional Calls in Arrears	1,00,000
		22,40,000

Value of fully paid Equity Share = 22,40,000/10,000 shares

Rs. 224 per share

Value of partly paid Equity Share = Rs. 224 – 20 = 204 per share

Working notes:

(1) The rectification of capital expenditure (purchase of machinery) charged to P & L A/c will increase the profits before tax by Rs. 20,000 (Cost of machinery) where as by Rs. 10,000 to profits after tax – the tax rate being 50%)

(2) Similarly Depreciation on the above amount will decrease the profit before tax by Rs. 2,000 where as by Rs. 1,000 to profits after tax

(3) Income from non-trading investments is calculated as under.

60% of Rs. 2,00,000	Rs. 1,20,000
Interest @ 15% (before tax 18,000)	
Interest after tax @ 50%	9,000

(4) The revised value of machinery has been arrived at as under

		Rs.
	Book Value as per Balance Sheet	5,00,000
Add	Cost of machinery	20,000
		5,20,000
Less	Depreciation @ 10% for 3 yrs. (20,000)	6,000
		5,14,000

(5) Trade Investments 40% (at cost)

Rs. 2,00,000 40%	80,000

Illustration (12) (Assets backing and Pay out ratio)

Following is the Balance Sheet of ZH Corporation Ltd. as on 31st March, 2006.

Liabilities	Rs.	Assets	Rs.
9% Preference Shares		Land & Building	3,50,000
of Rs. 100 each	2,00,000	Plant & Machinery	3,00,000
5,000 Equity Shares		Patents	1,00,000
of Rs. 100 each	5,00,000	S. Debtors	1,50,000
Reserves & Surplus	2,00,000	Stock	2,50,000
6% Debentures	1,00,000	Cash & Bank	50,000
S. Creditors	2,00,000		
	12,00,000		12,00,000

The Land & Building acquired long ago was considered worth Rs. 6,50,000. The Company earned the profits as under

Year	Profits before Tax Rs.	Tax paid Rs.
2001-02	1,50,000	40,000
2002-03	2,00,000	80,000
2003-04	50,000 (Strike)	20,000
2004-05	2,50,000	1,15,000
2005-06	2,75,000	1,50,000

The tax rate applicable for the company is 40%. The company paid a remuneration of Rs. 60,000 to managerial personnel but in future it will be paying Rs. 1,00,000. There has been no substantial change in capital employed. The company has paid a dividend of Rs. 9 per share consistently and proposes to stick to this rate in future. The company proposes to create plant rehabilitation reserve @ 15%. In the class of business to which the company belongs, the dividend rates have been fluctuating and assets backing of equity shares is about 1 1/2 times. The equity shares with an average dividend of 8% with pay out ratio of 80% sell at par. Calculate value of equity share on Assets backing method, Yield basis and Earnings per share.

[C.S. (F) Modified]

Solution:

I Calculation of Future Maintainable Profits

Year	Profits Rs.	Weight	Product Rs.
2001-02	1,50,000	1	1,50,000
2002-03	2,00,000	2	4,00,000
2003-04	Abnormal year	—	—
2004-05	2,50,000	3	7,50,000
2005-06	2,75,000	4	11,00,000
		10	24,00,000

		Rs.
	Weighted Average Profits	2,40,000
Less	Increase in managerial remuneration	(40,000)
		2,00,000
Less	Tax @ 40%	80,000
	Future maintainable profits	1,20,000
Less	Plant Rehabilitation Reserve @ 15% on Rs. 1,20,000	(18,000)
		1,02,000
Less	Preference dividend	(18,000)
	Profits available for Equity Shareholders	84,000

EPS = = Rs. 16.80 per share [Rs. 84,000 ÷ 5,000 shares)

II Yield Value = $\frac{\text{ERR}}{\text{NRR}} \times$ Paid up Value [ERR is based on dividend rate]

$= \frac{9}{8} \times 100$ = Rs. 112.50 per share

II Assets Backing (Intrinsic Value)

Calculation of Net Assets

Assets	Rs.
Land & Building	6,50,000
Plant & Machinery	3,00,000
Patents	1,00,000
S. Debtors	1,50,000

	Stock		2,50,000
	Cash at Bank		50,000
			15,00,000
Less	liabilities:		
	6% Debentures	1,00,000	
	S. Creditors	2,00,000	3,00,000
			12,00,000
Less	Preference Share Capital		2,00,000
	Net Assets available for equity shareholders		10,00,000

$$\text{Intrinsic Value (Net Assets per share)} = \frac{10,00,000}{5,000 \text{ Shares}} = \text{Rs. } 200$$

or 2 times of the paid up value.

$$\text{Thus value of Equity Share by Assets backing method} = \frac{2 \text{ Times}}{1\frac{1}{2} \text{ Times}} \times 100 = \text{Rs. } 133.33$$

Points to Remember

(1) Yield Method and Earnings Capacity are two different methods of valuation of shares. Yield means dividend expressed in relation to market value of share. Hence it is known as Market Value method also. Yield again refers to return to investors. It is calculated on the basis of profits available to equity shareholders as dividend.

(2) Earnings Capacity refers to earnings to company on it's equity fund. Hence out of future maintainable profits (Average Profits) dividend payable to preference shareholder is deducted. The transfer of any sum to General Reserve is ignored.

(3) Weighted Average of profits is calculated only when it is required in the question or when profits show an increasing trend.

(4) Fair Value is the simple average of Intrinsic Value and Yield value or Intrinsic Value and Value calculated under Capitalisation/Earning capacity method.

QUESTIONS

Valuation of Goodwill

(1) What is goodwill? Explain the various factors that affect the value of goodwill.

(2) Describe the various methods of valuation of goodwill.

(3) Explain the 'Super Profits Method' valuation of goodwill. How will you calculate goodwill by capitalisation of super profit method ?

(4) Explain the methods applicable for valuation of small lots and large lots of shares.

(5) Distinguish between :

(a) Current year's Profits and Future maintainable profits

(b) Simple Average profits and Weighted Average profits.

(c) Capital Employed and Average Capital Employed

(d) Capitalisation of Average Profits and Capitalisation of Super Profits.

PROBLEMS : VALUATION OF GOODWILL

1. The following information is available in respect of business carried on by a trader:

(i) Profits earned for the years :

	Rs.
1997-98	50,000
1998-99	60,000
1999-00	55,000

(ii) Normal rate of return 10%

(iii) Capital employed Rs. 3,00,000

(iv) Present Value of an annuity of one rupee for five year's at 10% = Rs. 3.78

(v) Profits included non-recurring profits on an average basis of Rs. 3,000.

You are required to calculate the value of goodwill:

(a) As per five years' purchase of super profits

(b) As per capitalisation of super profits method

(c) As per Annuity Method.

B.Com (H) DU 2001

Ans : (a) Rs. 1,10,000 (b) Rs. 2,20,000 (c) Rs. 83,160

Hint : Treat Capital employed as average capital employed

2. The Balance Sheet of A Ltd. as on 31st March, 2006.

Liabilities	Rs.	Assets	Rs.
Equity Share Capital	6,00,000	Fixed Assets	3,60,000
General Reserve	2,16,000	Current Assets	4,88,000
Current Liabilities	1,52,000	Investments	1,20,000
	9,68,000		9,68,000

The Normal Rate of Return (NRR) is 10%. The profits earned during the last four years including interest of Rs. 8,000 on investment were as under:

Year ending 31st March	Rs.
2002-03	1,28,000
2003-04	1,44,000
2004-05	1,72,000
2005-06	1,80,000

Compute the amount of goodwill at two years' purchase of average super profits of four years presuming that each year's profit was fully distributed as dividend to shareholders.

[CA (I) Adapted]

Ans : Weighted Average Profits — Rs. 1,57,200

Average Capital Employed — 7,80,000

Goodwill at 2 years' purchase — 2,37,600

Hint : Since all the profits are distributed as dividend, add half of the current year's operating profits to the capital employed to find out the average capital employed.

3. The Balance Sheet of X Ltd. as on 31. 3. 2006 was as under :

Liabilities	Rs.	Assets	Rs.
Share Capital	4,50,000	Land & Building	3,60,000
Reserve	50,000	Plant & Machinery	2,20,000
Current liabilities	2,00,000	Furniture	40,000
		Stock	70,000
		Cash	10,000
	7,00,000		7,00,000

The profits for the last five years ending 31st March were as under :

	Rs.
2001-02	80,000
2002-03	82,000
2003-04	90,000
2004-05	1,00,000
2005-06	1,06,000

The assets were revalued as under:

Land & Building	4,24,000
Plant & Machinery	2,00,000
Furniture	38,000

The reasonable return on capital employed is 10%. The managerial remuneration is expected to be increased by Rs. 12,000 p.a. with effect from 1.4.2006. Find out value of goodwill by capitalisation method. Apply simple average.

Ans: Value of goodwill - Rs. 2,58,000

4. The following is the Balance Sheet of SJF Ltd. as on 31st March, 2006

Liabilities	Rs.	Assets	Rs.
Equity Share Capital	25,00,000	Goodwill at cost	2,50,000
Shares of Rs. 10 each		Fixed Assets	27,50,000
Reserves	10,00,000	Investments	2,50,000
Liabilities	7,50,000	Current Assets	10,00,000
	42,50,000		42,50,000

Additional Information:

(1) Profits before tax for the year 2005-06 amounted to Rs. 15,00,000 including Rs. 25,000 as interest on investment. However, an additional amount of Rs. 1,25,000 p.a. shall be required to be spent for smooth running of the business.

(2) Fixed assets are considered worth Rs. 47,50,000 subject to a depreciation of Rs. 1,00,000.

(3) The rate of income tax may be taken at 50%

(4) The Normal rate of return before tax is 20% in such type of business.

Calculate value of goodwill at 2 years' purchase of super profits.

[C.A. (F) Adapted]

Ans : Value of goodwill Rs. 3,12,500.

(5) From the following information ascertain the value of goodwill at 3 years' purchase of super profits.

BALANCE SHEET AS ON 31ST MARCH, 2006

Liabilities	Rs.	Assets	Rs.
Equity Share Capital	10,00,000	Goodwill at Cost	1,00,000
Shares of Rs. 10 each		Fixed Assets	8,40,000
Profit & Loss App. A/c	2,26,600	Stock	6,00,000
Current liabilities	5,95,400	Debtors	3,60,000
Provision for Tax	78,000		
	19,00,000		19,00,000

The profits earned by the company during the last five years were as under :

Year	Rs.
2001-02	Strike (80,000) Loss
2002-03	1,77,600
2003-04	2,06,000
2004-05	2,32,000
2005-06	2,60,000

The income tax has been @ 40% so far but it is likely to be 50% from 2006-07 onwards. The managerial remuneration is expected to be increased by Rs. 40,000 p.a. with effect from 1st April 2006. The company has secured contract for supply of materials at a concessional price the value of which is estimated at Rs. 80,000 for next five years. The NRR is 10%

Ans: Super Profits - Rs. 50,170 Goodwill - Rs. 1,50,510

Hint: Apply weighted Average

(6) Following is the Balance Sheet of Cyma Ltd. as on 31st March, 2006

Liabilities	Rs.	Assets	Rs.
Equity Share Capital	5,00,000	Goodwill at Cost	50,000
Shares of Rs. 10 each		Fixed Assets	4,20,000
Profit & Loss A/c	1,20,000	Current Assets	4,92,000
Current Liabilities	2,57,000		
Provision for Taxation	85,000		
	9,62,000		9,62,000

The financial results for the last five years were as under:

Year ended 31st March	Profits before Tax
	Rs.
2001-02	1,20,000
2002-03	1,50,000
2003-04	1,70,000
2004-05	1,90,000
2005-06	1,70,000

The rate of taxation is 40%. The Fixed Assets are valued at Rs. 5,00,000. The dividends have been distributed out of profits @ 10% for the first three years' and @ 15% for the next two years.

ICWA (F) Adapted

Ans: Value of Goodwill = Rs. 1,50,000

Hint: NRR = Average dividend paid.

(7) X Ltd. acquires the business of Mr. Z. For this purpose goodwill is valued at two years' purchase of the weighted average profits of the past four years. The profits for the last four years were as under:

	Rs.
2002-03	1,01,000
2003-04	1,24,000
2004-05	1,00,000
2005-06	1,50,000

On scrutining of the accounts the following was revealed.

(i) On 1st December, 2004 a major repair was made in respect of the plant for Rs. 30,000 which was charged to revenue. This sum is agreed to be capitalised for the purpose of calculating goodwill subject to adjustment of depreciation @ 10% p.a. on reducing balance method

(ii) The closing stock for the year 2003-04 was over-valued by Rs. 12,000.

(iii) To cover extra management cost an annual charge of Rs. 24,000 should be made for the purpose of valuation of goodwill.

Compute the value of goodwill.

Ans: Value of goodwill - Rs. 2,19,280

(8) Following is the Balance Sheet of Everest Ltd. as on 31st March 2006.

Liabilities	Rs.	Assets	Rs.
6% Preference Shares		Goodwill	2,00,000
of Rs. 100 each	6,00,000	Land & Building	15,00,000
Equity Shares		Plant & Machinery	14,00,000
of Rs. 10 each	26,00,000	Stock	14,80,000
Profit & Loss A/c	18,00,000	Debtors (Net)	15,97,000
5% Debentures (1990)	12,00,000	Bank	9,80,000
Creditors	9,57,000		
	71,57,000		71,57,000

Additional Information

(i) The profits after tax for the last three years were as follows :

	Rs.
2003-04	8,82,000
2004-05	12,90,000
2005-06	9,60,000

(ii) The Normal Rate of Return is 10%

(iii) The value of Land & Building is to be ascertained on the basis of 8% return. The current rental value is Rs. 2,01,600

(iv) 10% of profits for the year 2004-05 are of non-recurring nature.

(v) A provision of Rs. 63,000 on Sundry Debtors was made in 2005-06 which is no longer required. The profit for the year 2005-06 is to be adjusted for this item.

(vi) A claim of Rs. 33,000 against the company is to be provided and adjusted against profit for the year 2005-06.

(vii) Goodwill is to be calculated at three times adjusted average super profits of the three years. The present value of Re. 1 is 2.487.

(viii) The rate of tax applicable is 50%.

Ascertain the value of goodwill. The capital employed may be taken as on 31st March 2006.

Ans: Capital employed Rs. 58,50,000
Future Maintainable Profits Rs. 10,06,000
Super Profits Rs. 4,21,000

Hint: Deduct tax on the net increase in profits Net increase in profit is Rs. 30,000 (Rs. 63,000 – 33,000)

(9) The following particulars are available in respect of the business curried on by a trader.

(i) Profits earned for the years:

	Rs.
2003-04	2,50,000
2004-05	3,00,000
2005-06	2,75,000

(ii) Normal rate of return 10%

(iii) Capital employed 15,00,000

(iv) Present Value of an annuity of one rupee for five years at 10% = 3.78

(v) Profits included non-recurring profits on an average basis = 15,000

Calculate value of goodwill at five years' purchase of super profits and as per Annuity Method.

Ans: (a) Rs. 5,50,000
(b) Rs. 4,15,800

(10) From the following particulars ascertain the value of goodwill of S. Ltd.

BALANCE SHEET AS ON 31ST MARCH, 2006

Liabilities	Rs.	Assets	Rs.
Equity Share Capital	25,00,000	Goodwill at cost	2,50,000
Shares of Rs. 10 each		Land & Building	11,00,000
Profit & Loss App. A/c	6,00,000	Plant & Machinery	10,00,000
Bank-over draft	8,05,000	Stock	15,00,000
Creditors	4,80,000	Book-Debts	9,60,000
Provision for Taxation	4,25,000		
	48,10,000		48,10,000

The Company started operations in 1990 with a paid up capital of Rs. 25,00,000. The profits earned before providing for taxation are:

	Rs.
2001-02	6,00,000
2002-03	7,50,000
2003-04	8,50,000
2004-05	9,50,000
2005-06	8,50,000

Income tax @ 50% has been payable on these profits. The dividends have been distributed @ 10% and 15% for the first three years and next two years respectively.

Calculate value of goodwill by capitalisation method.

[ICWA (F) Modified]

Ans: Value of goodwill - Rs. 4,83,333

(11) Mr. X runs a chemist's shop. His net assets on 31st March, 2006 amounted to Rs. 20,00,000. After paying rent of Rs. 15,000 p.a. to the landlord for the premises valued Rs. 1,00,000 and a salary of Rs. 20,000 to the chemist salesperson he earns a profit of Rs. 1,50,000. His landlord incidentally is the chemist salesman of the shop is keen to purchase the business. 12% is considered to be a reasonable return on capital employed for this type of business.

What can Mr. X expect as payment for goodwill?

[ICWA (F) Modified]

Ans : Value of goodwill - Nil (Negative)

under all the three methods.

VALUATION OF SHARES

Questions :

(1) Explain in brief the various methods of valuation of shares.

(2) Differentiate between Yield Method and Earnings Capacity Method of valuation of shares.

(3) Explain the methods which are applicable for buying a small lot and large lot of shares.

(4) What are the circumstances in which there may be a need for valuation of shares of a joint stock company.

(5) Explain briefly the steps involved in valuing shares under each of the follow..ig methods:

(i) Intrinsic Value Method

(ii) Yield Method

(iii) Fair Value

(6) Write short notes on :

Valuation of preference shares

Factors affecting value of shares

Notional call

Capitalisation of Earnings Method.

Price-earnings ratio

Normal Rate of Return (NRR)

Expected Rate of Return (ERR)

PROBLEMS

(1) From the following particulars calculate the intrinsic value and Yield Value of share.

(i) 9,000 6% Preference shares of Rs. 100 each fully paid.

(ii) 90,000 Equity shares of Rs. 10 each fully paid.

(iii) External liabilities - Rs. 75,000

(iv) Reserves Rs. 70,000

(v) Preliminary Expenses Rs. 7,000

(vi) Average normal profits earned every year by the company Rs. 1,70,000

(vii) The normal profits earned on the market-value of equity shares of the same type of business is 9%.

(viii) Transfer to general reserve Rs. 8,000

Ans. : Intrinsic Value = Rs. 10.70
Yield Value - Rs. 13.33

(2) The following is the Balance Sheet of X Ltd. as on 31st March, 2006.

Liabilities	Rs.	Assets	Rs.
Equity Shares of Rs. 10 each	20,00,000	Goodwill	2,00,000
		Furniture	3,00,000
General Reserve	7,00,000	Investments at Cost	6,00,000
Profit & Loss A/c	4,50,000	(Market Value Rs. 5,50,000)	
12% Debentures	5,00,000	Stock	22,00,000
S. Creditors	8,50,000	Debtors	6,00,000
Provision for Taxation	5,50,000	Bank	11,00,000
		Debenture Discount	50,000
	50,50,000		50,50,000

Goodwill is to be valued at Rs. 2,60,000. Debtors are subject to a provision for bad debts @ 5% Calculate value of equity share.

[B.Com (H) DU 1996]

Ans: Intrinsic Value - Rs. 15.40

(3) Following is the Balance Sheet of KKS Ltd. as on 31st March 2006.

Liabilities	Rs.	Assets	Rs.
Equity Share Capital:		Goodwill	70,000
30,000 Shares of Rs. 10 each	3,00,000	Fixed Assets	4,50,000
10,000 Shares of Rs. 10 each		Current Assets	2,20,000
Rs. 8 paid	80,000	Preliminary Expenses	10,000
Revenue Reserve	1,80,000		
9% Debentures	1,00,000		
S. Creditors	90,000		
	7,50,000		7,50,000

The goodwill is independently valued at Rs. 50,000 and Fixed Assets at Rs. 4,80,000. There was a contingent liability of Rs. 20,000 which has become payable.

Determine the value of both the shares under net assets method.

[B.Com (H) DU 1997 Modified]

Ans : Value of fully paid share - Rs. 14.00
Value of partly paid share - Rs. 12.00

(4) Following is the Balance Sheet of A Ltd. as on 31st March, 2006

Liabilities	Rs.	Assets	Rs.
Equity Share Capital		Building at Cost	7,60,000
Shares of Rs. 10 each	10,00,000	Furniture	6,000
Reserve Fund	2,25,000	Investments	1,60,000
Depreciation Fund :		Stock (at market price)	8,50,000
Building	80,000	S. Debtors (Good)	6,50,000
Investments	20,000	Bank	1,40,000
Profit & Loss A/c :			
Balance (1.4.05)	1,60,000		
Current year's Profit	8,60,000		
S. Creditors	96,000		
Provision for Doubtful debts	40,000		
Provision for Taxation	85,000		
	25,66,000		25,66,000

It is now ascertained that :

(i) Company's prospects for 2006-07 are equally good.
(ii) Profit for the past three years have shown an average increase of Rs. 40,000 annually.
(iii) The Building is worth Rs. 7,96,000 and Furniture Rs. 10,000
(iv) Companies of similar nature are showing a profit earning capacity of 10% on market value of shares.

Ascertain fair value of each share. Ignore goodwill.

[B.Com (H) DU Modified]

Ans: Intrinsic Value Rs. 25.10
Yield Value Rs. 81] Fair Value = Rs. 53.05

Hint:	Profit for the year	Rs. 8,60,000
Add	Increase (Annual)	40,000
	Future Maintainable Profits	9,00,000
Less	Transfer to Reserve (Say 10%)	(90,000)
		8,10,000

Note : Earning capacity in relation to market value of shares refers to yield value of share.

(5) Following is the Balance Sheet of N Ltd. as on 31st March, 2006.

Liabilities	Rs.	Assets	Rs.
15,000 Equity Shares of Rs. 10 each fully paid up	1,50,000	S. Fixed Assets	2,20,000
		Investments	40,000
20,000 Equity Shares of Rs. 10 each Rs. 6 paid up	1,20,000	Stock	80,000
		Debtors	40,000
9% Cumulative Preference Shares		Cash & Bank	40,000
of Rs. 100 each	60,000	P & L A/c	1,30,000
Long Term Loan	1,40,000		
S. Creditors	80,000		
	5,50,000		5,50,000

Other Information :

(i) Current cost of Sundry Fixed Assets is Rs. 3,70,000 and that of Stock is Rs. 1,00,000.

(ii) Investments could fetch only Rs. 10,000.

(iii) 50% Debtors are doubtful.

(iv) Preference dividend is in arrears for the last five years.

Find out intrinsic value of per share.

[B.Com (H) 2001]

Ans. : Value of Fully paid share = Rs. 8.94
Value of share Rs. 6 paid = Rs. 4.94

Hint : Make notional call and pay preference dividend arrears.

(6) The Balance Sheet of Zed Ltd. as on 31st March, 2006 was as under :

Liabilities	Rs.	Assets	Rs.
20,000 Equity Shares		Factory Premises	11,50,000
of Rs. 100 each	20,00,000	Plant & Machinery	10,00,000
Reserves	6,00,000	Stock	15,00,000
Profit & Loss A/c	3,50,000	Debtors	5,00,000
Creditors	4,00,000		
Bank overdraft	3,00,000		
Provision for Taxation	5,00,000		
	41,50,000		41,50,000

The net profits of the company for the five years before providing for taxation were: Rs. 4,10,000; Rs. 7,40,000; Rs. 6,00,000; Rs. 8,50,000; Rs. 9,00,000. The managerial remuneration of Rs. 6,000 has been charged for each year. The market value of assets were as follows: Stock- Rs. 15,50,000; Plant - Rs. 10,40,000; Factory Premises - Rs. 12,60,000. Taxation may be considered at 50%. The Normal rate of return on actual capital employed at the end is 10%. Goodwill may be calculated as three year's purchase of super profits.

Calculate intrinsic value of shares.

[ICWA (F) Adapted]

Ans: Value of goodwill - Rs. 1,05,000
Intrinsic Value of Share - Rs. 162.75

Hint: Use simple average

(7) The following information relates to a company.

	Rs.
6% 4,500 Preference Share Capital Shares of Rs. 100 each fully paid	4,50,000
45,000 Equity Shares of Rs. 10 each fully paid	4,50,000
Reserves & Surplus	35,000
External Liabilities	75,000
Average Profit (after Tax)	85,000
Normal rate of return	10%
Transfer to general reserve	10%

Calculate intrinsic value of equity share and the value as per Yield method. The assets are considered Rs. 58,500 more than the book value. There are fictitious assets worth Rs. 3,500.

Ans : Intrinsic Value = Rs. 12 Yield Value = Rs. 11

(8) Following is the Balance Sheet of Y Ltd. as on 31st March, 2006.

Liabilities	Rs.	Assets	Rs.
Equity Share Capital Share of Rs. 10 each	10,00,000	Goodwill Fixed Assets	1,00,000 12,50,000
General Reserve	4,75,000	Current Assets	10,00,000
Profit & Loss A/c	3,00,000		
9% Debentures	2,50,000		
Current Liabilities	3,25,000		
	23,50,000		23,50,000

On the above date fixed assets were valued at Rs. 12,00,000 and goodwill at Rs. 1,25,000. The profits for three years were Rs. 1,00,000; Rs. 90,000 and Rs. 1,10,000 of which 20% was transferred to general reserve. Fair return on investment may be taken at 10%. Compute the value of share by net assets and yield method. Ignore taxation.

[CA (I) Adapted]

Ans: Intrinsic Value = Rs. 17.50
Yield Method = Rs. 20.00

(9) B Ltd. and C Ltd. propose to sell their business to a new company. Their Balance Sheets as on 31st March 2006 were as under.

Liabilities	B Ltd. Rs.	C Ltd. Rs.
Equity Shares of Rs. 10 each	6,00,000	2,50,000
Reserves	3,90,000	2,70,000
Profit & Loss A/c	1,10,000	1,60,000
Creditors	2,15,800	1,26,800
	13,15,800	8,06 ,800

Assets

Free hold Property	7,60,000	3,20,000
Plant & Machinery	3,20,000	1,80,000
Investments at cost	—	1,00,000
Stock-in-Trade	1,11,000	89,500
Debtors	88,000	64,000
Bank Balance	36,800	53,300
	13,15,800	8,06,800

Additional Information

(i) Net Profits for the year end 31st March

	2004	2005	2006
	Rs.	Rs.	Rs.
B Ltd.	1,93,400	1,74,500	2,14,700
C Ltd.	1,22,900	1,44,500	1,07,600

(ii) The Freehold property and Plant & Machinery are to be revalued as under :

	B Ltd.	C Ltd.
Freehold property	8,48,000	3,44,000
Plant & Machinery	3,05,700	1,70,950

(iii) The value of stocks be reduced by 10% and a provision of 12.5% be made on debtors for bad and doubtful debts.

(iv) The Goodwill be valued at two years purchase of the average annual trading profits, of the past three years after deducting a standard profit of 10%, on the trading assets, before revaluation or adjustment on 31st March 2006.

(v) Profits of C Ltd. include Rs. 6,000 income from investments in each of the three years. The market value of the investments as on 31st March 2006 was Rs. 1,00,000.

Calculate value of equity shares of both companies by Net Assets Method.

[CS (I) Adapted]

	B Ltd.	C Ltd.
Ans : Value of Share -	Rs. 22	Rs. 32
Goodwill	Rs. 1,68,400	1,22,000
Hint : Standard Profit on net assets (Trading)	1,10,000	58,000

Deduct standard (Normal Profit) out of average adjusted profits.

(10) A Ltd. and it's subsidiary B Ltd. get their supply from C Ltd. To co-ordinate their production A Ltd. and C Ltd. agree between themselves each to acquire a quarter of shares in others Authorised share capital by means of exchange of shares as per the following terms.

(a) A Ltd.'s shares are quoted at Rs. 140 but for the purpose of exchange, the value is to be taken at the higher of the two values, i.e. quoted price and value on the basis of Balance Sheet.

(b) C Ltd.'s Shares which are unquoted are to be at the higher of the value as per Yield basis and Balance Sheet basis.

(c) The future profits are estimated at Rs. 1,35,000 subject to one-third to be retained for development purpose. Shares of similar companies yield 10%.

(d) Freehold premises of C Ltd. are to be taken at Rs. 4,30,000.

SUMMARISED BALANCE SHEET OF COMPANIES

	A Ltd. Rs.	B Ltd. Rs.	C Ltd. Rs.
Authorised Share Capital	12,00,000	5,00,000	10,00,000
Equity Share Capital (Shares of Rs. 100 each)	8,00,000	5,00,000	7,50,000
Securities Premium	80,000	—	—
Profit & Loss A/c	2,30,000	2,10,000	2,00,000
7% Debentures	3,00,000	—	—
Current Liabilities	2,80,000	1,80,000	2,10,000
Proposed Dividend	1,00,000	50,000	—
	17,90,000	9,40,000	11,60,000
Assets			
Freehold Premises	6,60,000	2,90,000	3,30,000
Plant & Machinery	4,50,000	4,10,000	4,40,000
Investment in 4,000 shares of B Ltd.	4,70,000	—	—
Current Assets	2,10,000	2,40,000	3,90,000
	17,90,000	9,40,000	11,60,000

You are required to compute the value of shares according to the terms of agreement.

[ICWA (F) Modified]

Ans :

Value of Shares	A Ltd. Rs.	C Ltd. Rs.
Balance Sheet basis (Intrinsic Value)	156	140
Yield Basis (Quoted)	140	120

Hint : Deduct 1/3rd out of Rs. 1,35,000 to get future maintainable profits in case of C Ltd.

(11) The Capital structure of a company as on 31st March 2006 was under:

	Rs.
Equity Share Capital	10,00,000
10% Preference Share Capital	6,00,000
10% Secured Debentures	8,00,000
Reserves	6,00,000

The Company on an average earns a profit of Rs. 10,80,000 annually before deduction of interest on debentures and income tax @ 40%. The normal rate of return on equity shares of such type companies is 15% provided.

(i) The profit after tax covers the fixed interest and fixed dividends at least 4 times.

(ii) Equity capital and reserves are 150% of debentures and preference capital

(iii) Yield on shares is calculated at 60% of profits distributed and 20% undistributed.

(iv) The Company has been paying dividend regularly an equity dividend of 18%.

Ascertain the value of each equity share of the company.

[C.A. (F) Adapted]

Ans: Yield Value = Rs. 112.50

Hint: Add 1% for additional risk.

ERR has been calculated as under :

			Rs.
	Profit before interest and tax		10,80,000
Less	Interest on 10% debentures		(80,000)
			10,00,000
Less	Tax @ 40%		(4,00,000)
			6,00,000
Less	Preference dividend	60,000	
	Equity dividend	1,80,000	(2,40,000)
	Undistributed Profits		3,60,000
	60% Distributed Profits (60% of Rs. 1,80,000)	1,08,000	
	20% of Undistributed Profits (20% of 3,60,000)	72,000	1,80,000

$$\text{ERR} = \frac{1,80,000}{10,00,000} \times 100 = 18\%$$

$$\text{Yield Value} = \frac{18}{16} \times 100 = \text{Rs. } 112.50$$

Note : Distributed profits refer to equity dividend only.

6

Accounting for the Amalgamation

Meaning

Amalgamation refers to a situation where two or more existing companies are joined to form a third company or where an existing company takes over the other existing company. Thus amalgamation entails two kinds of situations :

(i) Two or more companies join to form a new company or

(ii) One company absorbs other company. Thus amalgamation includes absorption.

The Companies Act 1956 does not define amalgamation. However, it may be noted that under amalgamation two companies go into liquidation to form a new company where as in absorption there is no formation of a new company, only absorbed company goes into liquidation while absorbing or purchasing company continues to retain it's legal entity.

According to AS-14– Accounting for Amalgamation, issued by Institute of Chartered Accountants of India, amalgamation means an amalgamation in pursuant to the provisions of the Companies Act 1956 or any other statute applicable to companies. This standard is mandatory in nature and is applicable w.e.f. 1.4.1995. AS-14 recognises amalgamation in two forms.

(i) Amalgamation in the nature of merger and

(ii) Amalgamation in the nature of purchase.

An amalgamation in the nature of merger is an amalgamation which satisfies all the following conditions :

(i) **All assets and liabilities** of the **transferor** Company become, after amalgamation, the assets and liabilities of the **transferee** company.

(ii) **Shareholders** holding not less than **90% of the face value** of the equity shares of the transferor company (other than the equity shares already held there in, immediately before amalgamation, by the transferee company or its subsidiary or their nominees) become equity shareholders of the transferee company **by virtue of the amalgamation.**

(iii) The **consideration** for the amalgamation receivable by those equity shareholders who agree to become equity shareholders of transferee company, is discharged wholly by the issue of **equity shares** in the transferee company except that cash may be paid in respect of any fractional shares.

(iv) The business of the transferor company is intended to be carried on, after the amalgamation, by the transferee company.

(v) No adjustment is intended to be made to the book values of the assets and liabilities of the transferor company when they are incorporated in the financial statements of the transferee company except to ensure uniformity of accounting policies.

If any one or more of the above conditions are not satisfied in an amalgamation, such amalgamation is called amalgamation in the nature of purchase.

Explanation & Clarification

- **Transferor Company** means the company which is amalgamated into another company i.e. the one which went into liquidation.
- **Transferee Company** means the company into which a transferor company is amalgamated. This company does not go into liquidation but retains it's legal entity.
- **Consideration** means the aggregate of shares and other securities issued and the payment made in the form of cash by the transferee company to the **shareholders** of the transferor company.

Hence purchase consideration does not include the sum which the transferee company will pay directly to the creditors of the transferor company. Even the expenses on winding up paid by the transferee company will not form part of purchase consideration.

In essence it is the payment meant only for shareholders- equity and preference. Therefore, purchase consideration does not include any payment to outsiders including debenture holders.

It is to be noted that liabilities are presumed to be taken over by the transferee company and discharged by the transferee company except when expressly mentioned that these liabilities have not been takenover and the same shall be paid by the transferor company.

CALCULATION OF PURCHASE CONSIDERATION

There are three methods of calculation of purchase consideration :

1. Net Assets Method
2. Share Exchange Method
3. Net Payment Method

1. Net Assets Method

Under this method the purchase consideration is ascertained as follows :

Agreed Values of assets takenover*	***
Less Agreed Values of liabilities takenover**	**
	Purchase Consideration

* *Assets do not include*

Preliminary Expenses

Debit balance of Profit & Loss Account

Discount on issue of shares or debentures

Miscellaneous Expenditure or any other fictitious asset.

***** Liabilities do not include***

Reserves and Surplus which are in the form of :

Profit & Loss Account (credit balance)

General Reserve or Reserve fund

Dividend Equalisation Reserve/Fund

Sinking Fund

Development Rebate Reserve

Capital Redemption Reserve

Debenture Redemption Reserve/Fund

Workmen's Compensation Fund

Share Forfeited Account

Securities Premium, Share Forfeiture, Capital Reserve, Insurance Fund and Workmen's Accident Compensation Fund etc.

*but includes Provisions** such as :

Provision for Bad & Doubtful debts

Provision for repairs and renewals

Provision against fluctuation in Investment (Investment Fluctuation Fund)

Provision for Taxation

Provision for Depreciation and

Proposed Dividend

Liabilities Vs. Trade Liabilities

"Liabilities" refer to amount payable to third parties whether incurred in connection with operating activities, financing or investing activities and includes :

Trade Creditors

Bills Payable

*Provisions (as mentioned above)

Creditors for expenses

Bank Overdraft

Employees' Provident Fund

Employees' Profit Sharing fund

Employees' Saving Deposits

Employees' Pension Fund

Employees' Superannuation Fund

Loans

Debentures and Unclaimed dividends etc.

However, "Trade Liabilities" are incurred in connection with operating activities of the enterprise, such as purchase of goods or raw-materials in which the company deals in *i.e.* **Creditors** and **Bills Payable** are treated as trade liabilities.

Important note: When "question mentions that "business" is takenover, it refers to all assets and all liabilities. Thus, purchase consideration = Total Assets - Total Liabilities.

Illustration (1) (Net Assets Method)

A Ltd. and B Ltd. decided to amalgamate and form a New Company called A B Ltd. as on 1st April, 2004 when their Balance Sheets were as follows :

BALANCE SHEET OF A LTD.

Liabilities	Rs.	Assets	Rs.
50,000 Equity Shares of Rs. 10 each fully paid	5,00,000	Plant & Machinery	3,75,000
		Computers	1,25,000
Securities Premium	50,000	Motor Van	85,000
General Reserve	60,000	Stock	2,15,000
Capital Reserve	10,000	Debtors	1,50,000
Dividend Equalisation Fund	30,000	Cash at Bank	25,000
9% Debentures	2,00,000	Preliminary Expenses	20,000
Trade Creditors	80,000		
Employees Profits Sharing Fund	25,000		
Provident Fund	40,000		
	9,95,000		9,95,000

BALANCE SHEET OF B LTD.

Liabilities	Rs.	Assets	Rs.
30,000 Equity Shares of Rs. 10 each fully paid	3,00,000	Goodwill	20,000
		Plant & Machinery	2,30,000
General Reserve	25,000	Stock	1,20,000
Profit & Loss Account	75,000	Debtors	80,000
10% Debentures	50,000	Bills Receivable	10,000
Sundry Creditors	20,000	Cash at Bank	13,000
Bills Payable	10,000	Cash in hand	2,000
		Discount on Issue of Debentures	5,000
	4,80,000		4,80,000

A B Ltd. took over the assets and liabilities of both the Companies as follows :

	A Ltd.	**B Ltd.**
Plant & Machinery at	10% less	20% less
Computers at	Rs. 1,20,000	—
Motor Van at	Rs. 75,000	—
Debtors	Subject to 5% Provision against bad & doubtful debts.	
Stock	20% higher than the Book values.	

An amount equal to 10% of net assets is to be paid for goodwill. Remainings were taken at their book values. Calculate purchase consideration.

Solution : 1

Calculation of Purchase Consideration

	A Ltd.	**B Ltd.**
	Rs.	Rs.
Plant & Machinery	3,37,500	1,84,000
Computers	1,20,000	—
Motor Van	75,000	—
Stock	2,58,000	1,44,000
Debtors	1,42,500	76,000
Bills Receivable	—	10,000
Cash at Bank	25,000	13,000
Cash in hand	—	2,000
	9,58,000	4,29,000
Less Liabilities		
Debentures	(2,00,000)	(50,000)
Creditors	(80,000)	(20,000)
Bills Payable	-	(10,000)
Employees Profit Sharing Fund	(25,000)	-
Provident Fund	(40,000)	-
Net Assets before goodwill	6,13,000	3,49,000
Add Goodwill (10% of net assets)	61,300	34,900
Purchase Consideration	**6,74,300**	**3,83,900**

2. SHARE EXCHANGE METHOD

Sometime, purchase consideration is to be discharged in shares based on certain ratio which is determined by their respective intrinsic values. The purchase consideration is arrived at by multiplying the number of shares to be issued to shareholders of transferor company by the agreed value of the share which may either be face value, market value or the intrinsic value itself. Fractional shares should be valued at market price unless otherwise stated. Following steps are taken.

(i) Calculate the net assets of the transferor company and divide the same by the number of equity shares to asertain the intrinsic value of share of transferor company.

(ii) Calculate the net assets of the transferee company and ascertain the intrinsic value as per step first.

(iii) Determine the ratio of exchange between the shares of transferor and transferee company.

Suppose intrinsic values of A Ltd. and B Ltd. are Rs. 80 and Rs. 60 respectively. Then the ratio of exchange will be determined as follows :

	A Ltd.		B Ltd.
Intrinsic Value	Rs. 80		Rs. 60
Ratio of intrinsic Value	4	:	3

It means 3 shares of A Ltd. are equal to 4 shares of B Ltd.

A Ltd.'s 3 shares @ Rs. 80 = B Ltd.'s 4 shares @ Rs. 60

Rs. 240 = Rs. 240

Alternatively the Net assets of Transferor company may be divided by intrinsic value of Transferee company to get the number of shares to be issued to transferor company and multiplied by the agreed value of share.

Illustration (2) (Share Exchange Ratio Method)

Following are the Balance Sheets of P Ltd. and Q Ltd. as on 31st March, 2004.

Liabilities	P Ltd. Rs.	Q Ltd. Rs.
Equity Share Capital (Shares of Rs. 10 each)	5,00,000	4,00,000
Revenue Reserve	1,75,000	25,000
9% Debentures	1,00,000	50,000
Current Liabilities :		
S. Creditors	60,000	45,000
Provision for Taxation	40,000	25,000
	8,75,000	5,45,000
Assets		
Net Block	3,75,000	2,45,000
Investments	1,00,000	50,000
Current Assets :		
Stock	2,15,000	1,40,000
Debtors	1,50,000	85,000
Bank Balance	35,000	25,000
	8,75,000	5,45,000

P Ltd. takes over the business of Q Ltd. on the following terms :

(i) Fixed assets of P Ltd. and Q Ltd. are to be considered worth Rs. 5,00,000 and Rs. 3,00,000 respectively.

(ii) P Ltd. agreed to discharge 9% Debentures of Q Ltd.

(iii) Shares of both the companies are to be valued on the basis of its' intrinsic value. Determine the ratio of exchange and calculate purchase consideration if :

(a) Shares are to be issued at par

(b) Shares are to be issued on the basis of it's intrinsic value.

(c) Shares are issued on the basis of it's market price of Rs. 20 each.

Solution : 2

Calculation of ratio of exchange of shares

	P Ltd. Rs.	Q Ltd. Rs.
Net Block	5,00,000	3,00,000
Investments	1,00,000	50,000
Stock	2,15,000	1,40,000
Debtors	1,50,000	85,000
Bank Balance	35,000	25,000
	10,00,000	6,00,000
Less Liabilities		
9% Debentures	(1,00,000)	(50,000)
S. Creditors	(60,000)	(45,000)
Provision for Taxation	(40,000)	(25,000)
Net Assets	8,00,000	4,80,000
	16	12
$\left(\text{Intrinsic Value} = \dfrac{\text{Net Assets}}{\text{No. of Shares}}\right)$	4 :	3

On the basis of intrinsic value 3 shares of P Ltd. will be equal to 4 shares of Q Ltd. Therefore, ratio of exchange will be 3 : 4.

Therefore P Ltd. will issue to the shareholders of Q Ltd. $40{,}000 \times \dfrac{3}{4} = 30{,}000$ shares

(a) Now if P Ltd. issues shares at par purchase consideration will be 30,000 shares @ Rs. 10 = Rs. 3,00,000

(b) If shares are issued by P Ltd. at it's intrinsic value then purchase consideration will be Rs. 4,80,000 i.e. 30,000 @ Rs. 16 and P Ltd. will issue 30,000 shares of Rs. 10 each at Rs. 6 per share as premium.

(c) If P Ltd. issues shares at the market value of Rs. 20 per share, then the purchase consideration will be Rs. 6,00,000 i.e. 30,000 @ Rs. 20 each. Thus P Ltd. will issue 30,000 shares of Rs 10 each at Rs. 10 per share as premium.

Important Note : **It is to be noted that number of shares are to be calculated on the basis of intrinsic value of shares which is to be multiplied by the value at which these are to be *recorded* in the books of accounts.**

3. NET PAYMENT METHOD

According to AS-14 purchase consideration means all payments made by the transferee company only to the "share holders" of the transferor company irrespective of their form of payment. Thus, payments may be made by the transferee company in the form of shares, debentures or any other securities and cash to the shareholders of transferor company.

Therefore, any payment made by the transferee company to any other party (creditors or Debentureholders or Bank etc.) will not form part of purchase consideration. And similarly, payment of liquidation or Realisation expenses will not be included in the purchase consideration even if these are expressly stated to be paid by Transferee company.

Market Value Vs. Par Value

While calculating the amount of purchase consideration the main problem the students face as to which value should be taken into consideration once the number of shares to be issued is ascertained by the exchange ratio. Whether it is the market value or par value? *In accordance with world wide practice and in the spirit of AS-14, the shares should be valued at par in case of merger and at marked price in case of amalgamation in the nature of purchase.*

However, as already stated that the intention of Transferee and Transferor company should also be taken into account. The shares may be valued at market price but recorded at par value if so agreed upon. (see illustration no. 4)

Share Fraction Vs Fractional Shares

These two terms seem to be similar in nature but the accounting treatment is different.

Share fraction is the fraction of one share which arises due to exchange ratio. Since "share cannot be issued in fraction", it has to be paid in cash on the basis of market value of share if not otherwise stated.

Fractional Shares represent sum total of share fractions and hence these are expressed in absolute figures, such as total sum of fractions is 100, 50 or 200. In such a case the fractional shares may be paid either on the basis of par value or market value as per the mutual agreement between the transferor and transferee company.

Important note : Students should note that if *shares are issued of Rs. ......at the market value of .....* stated in the question the market value should be taken into account because 'at' is directed towards market value. The phrase ("quoted in market") has no relevance for the use of market price.

Illustration (3) (Net Payment)

X Ltd. agrees to takeover business of Y Ltd. as on 31st March 2004 on which date the Balance Sheet of Y Ltd. was as follows

Liabilities	Rs.	Assets	Rs.
50,000 Equity shares of Rs. 10 each	5,00,000	Sundry Assets	10,00,000
Reserves & Surplus	2,50,000		
9% Debentures	1,00,000		
Current Liabilities	1,50,000		
	10,00,000		10,00,000

The purchase consideration was agreed as follows :

1. X Ltd. to issue 4 shares of Rs. 10 each for every 5 shares held in Y Ltd. at the market price of Rs. 15 each.
2. A cash payment of Rs. 2 per share for every share in Y Ltd.
3. Issue of such an amount of fully paid 8% Debentures in X Ltd. at 96% as is sufficient to discharge 9%. Debentures in Y Ltd. at a premium of 20%.
4. To pay liquidation expenses of Rs. 10,000.

Calculate purchase consideration

Solution :

		Rs.
Equity Shares	$\left(50{,}000 \times \frac{4}{5} \times \text{Rs. } 15\right)$	6,00,000
Cash	(50,000 Shares × Rs. 2)	1,00,000
	Purchase Consideration	7,00,000

As per AS-14 payment to debentureholders and liquidation expenses will not form part of purchase consideration.

Illustration (4)

(Calculation and Recording at different prices)

Following is the Balance Sheet of Z Ltd. as on 31st March, 2004

Liabilities	Rs.	Assets		Rs.
9% Preference Shares		Gross Block	12,00,000	
of Rs. 100 each	2,00,000	*Less* Depreciation	2,00,000	10,00,000
60,000 Equity Shares of Rs. 10 each	6,00,000	Current Assets		5,00,000
Reserves	1,50,000			
Profit & Loss A/c	90,000			
10% Debentures	2,50,000			
Accounts Payable	2,10,000			
	15,00,000			15,00,000

A Ltd. takesover the business of Z Ltd. on the following terms.

(i) A Ltd. to issue necessary number of 11% Preference shares to discharge 9% Preference shares at 20% premium.

(ii) A Ltd. to issue equity shares on the basis of intrinsic value to the shareholders of Z Ltd. However, the entry to be made at par. The intrinsic value of share of A Ltd. is Rs. 15.

(iii) Debentureholders of Z Ltd. are discharged by A Ltd. by issuing 12% Debentures.

(iv) Realisation expenses of Rs. 5,000 are to be met by A Ltd. Calculate purchase consideration.

Solution :

Intrinsic value of Equity share of Z Ltd.

		Rs.
Sundry Assets		15,00,000
Less Liabilities		
10% Debentures	2,50,000	
Accounts Payable	2,10,000	4,60,000
		10,40,000
Less Preference Share Capital		2,00,000
Net assets for Equity Shareholders		8,40,000
Intrinsic Value = Rs. 8,40,000/60,000 Shares	=	14

Calculation of Purchase Consideration

		Rs.
11% Preference Shares	Rs. 2,50,000	
Add Premium 20%	50,000	3,00,000
Equity Shares		5,60,000
		8,60,000

A Ltd. will issue $60{,}000 \times \frac{14}{15} = 56{,}000$ shares based on it's intrinsic value. Since it is desired to record the same at par value 56,000 shares have been multiplied by the par value (Rs. 10) of share.

Illustration (5) (Share fraction)

Following is the Balance Sheet of A Ltd. Rs. on 31st March, 2004.

Liabilities	Rs.	Assets	Rs.
50,000 Equity Shares of Rs. 10 each	5,00,000	Net Block	7,50,000
Reserve Fund	1,00,000	Investments	1,00,000
Sinking Fund	50,000	Current Assets	2,50,000
Dividend Equalisation Fund	40,000		
Workmen Compensation Fund	10,000		
9% Debentures	2,00,000		
Provision for Taxation	60,000		
Sundry Creditors	1,40,000		
	11,00,000		11,00,000

B Ltd. takes over the business of A Ltd. on the following terms:

(i) B Ltd. will issue to the shareholders of A Ltd. 4 shares of Rs. 10 each for every 3 shares held by them. The price quoted in the market is Rs. 30 each for the shares of B Ltd.

(ii) B Ltd. to issue necessary number of New 10% Debentures to the Debenture holders of A Ltd. so as to redeem them at a premium of 10%.

(iii) B Ltd. agrees to bear cost of absorption to the extent of Rs. 10,000. However, actual expenses amounted to Rs. 7,000.

Calculate purchase consideration.

Solution :

Calculation of Purchase Consideration

	Rs.
Equity Shares $50,000 \times \frac{4}{3} = 66,666.67$	
66,666 Shares of Rs. 10 each	6,66,660
Cash for fraction of share Rs. 30 × .67 share	20
	6,66,680

Since share cannot be issued in fraction it has to be paid in cash on the basis of it's market price.

Illustration (6) (Fractional Shares)

Balance Sheet of Atlantic Ltd. as on 31st March, 2004 was us under :

Liabilities	Rs.	Assets		Rs.
50,000 Equity Shares of Rs. 10 each	5,00,000	Gross Block	12,00,000	
Retained Earnings	2,50,000	Less Depreciation	3,00,000	9,00,000
12% Debentures	2,00,000	Current Assets		2,80,000
Employees Fund	75,000	Preliminary Expenses		20,000
Proposed Dividend	50,000			
S. Creditors	1,25,000			
	12,00,000			12,00,000

Atlantic Ltd. is absorbed by Antartica Ltd. as on the above date on the following terms.

1. That, the shareholders of Atlantic Ltd. to receive 5 shares of Rs. 10 each in Antartica Ltd. for every 8 shares held by them in Atlantic Ltd. The total number of fractional shares came to 50. The market price of the share of Antartica Ltd. was Rs. 25.
2. Liabilities are to be discharged by the Antartica Ltd. Debentures are to be redeemed at 5% premium by issue of 9% Debentures.

Calculate Purchase Consideration.

Solution :

Calculation of Purchase Consideration.

		Rs.
Equity Shares	$50,000 \times \frac{5}{8} = 31,250$	
Less Fractional Shares	50	
	31,200 shares	
31,200 Shares of Rs. 10 each		3,12,000
Cash to deal with fractions 50 × Rs. 25		1,250
		3,13,250

ACCOUNTING TREATMENT

I Books of Transferor Company

Transferor company goes into liquidation because assets and liabilities are taken over by the transferee company, and the same are transferred to Transferee company. In case, if some of the assets or liabilities are not taken over the same are realised or discharged by the transferor company.

The account of shareholders is settled after the receipt of purchase consideration from transferee company. For this purpose accumulated profits or losses in whatever form these may be, including fictitious assets are transferred to Shareholders Account. It is to be noted that besides share capital the profit or loss arising from transfer of assets and liabilities takenover including disposal or discharge of assets or liabilities not takenover, are transferred to Shareholders' Account. Thus the transferor company prepares mainly :

1. Realisation Account
2. Shareholders' Account
3. Transferee Company's Account

The accounting treatment can be studied under two stages:

(a) Journalisation of Transactions.

(b) Preparation of relevant ledger Accounts.

Journal Entries

1. *On transfer of assets :*

Realisation A/c	Dr.	Total
To Sundry Assets		*with book value of all individual assets.

* In case Cash or Bank balance is not taken over by the Transferee company the same shall not be transferred to Realisation Account. Similarly fictitious assets will not form part of Sundry Assets but these will be transferred to Shareholders Account.

2. *On transfer of liabilities*

Sundry Liabilities A/c	Dr.	with book value of individual liability
To Realisation A/c		(Total)

3. *On recording the purchase consideration receivable*

Transferee Company's A/c	Dr.	with total P.C.
To Realisation A/c		

4. *On realisation of assets not taken over*

Bank A/c	Dr.	with sale proceeds
To Realisation A/c		

5. *On payment of liabilities not taken over*

Realisation A/c	Dr.	with book value*
To Bank A/c		Amount paid*

*It is to be noted that if liabilities not takenover are not transferred to Realisation A/c then the difference between book value of the liability and the amount paid is transferred to Realisation A/c.

6. *Realisation expenses borne by Transferee company*

   No Entry. If however, actual expenses exceed the amount paid by the Transferee Company the excess will be debited to Realisation Account.

7. *Realisation expenses paid by Transferor Company*

   Realisation A/c Dr. with amount of expenses

   To Bank A/c

8. *When Preference shares are redeemed at premium*

   Realisation A/c Dr. Amount of premium

   To Preference Shareholders' A/c

9. *If preference shareholders are paid less than the nominal (book) value of shares*:

   Preference Shareholders' A/c Dr. with Difference

   To Realisation A/c

10. *For Profit on realisation*

    Realisation A/c Dr.

    To Equity Shareholders' A/c

11. *For Loss on realisation :*

    Equity Shareholders' A/c

    To Realisation A/c

12. *On transfer of equity capital & Accumulated profits* :

    Equity Share Capital A/c Dr.

    Accumulated Profit– (such as General Reserves, P & L A/c etc.) Dr.

    To Equity Shareholders' A/c

13. *On transfer of accumulated losses and fictitious assets.*

    Equity Shareholders' A/c Dr.

    To Profit & Loss A/c

    To Preliminary Expenses A/c

    To Discount on Issue of Shares/Debentures A/c

14. *On receipt of Purchase Consideration*

    Shares in Transferee Co. A/c Dr.

    Debentures in Transferee Co. A/c Dr.

    Bank A/c Dr.

    To Transferee Company A/c

15. *On Payment to Preference Shareholders*

    Preference Shareholders' A/c Dr.

    To Shares in Transferee Co. A/c

    To Debentures in Transferee Co. A/c

    To Bank A/c

    } as the form of payment may be

16. Equity Shareholders' A/c Dr.

    To Shares in Transferee Co. A/c

    To Debentures in Transferee Co. A/c

    To Bank A/c

LEDGER ACCOUNTS

Realisation A/c (A Format)

	Rs.		Rs.
To Sundry Assets (Each individual asset except : Fictitious assets Cash & bank balance, if not taken over.)	at Book value	By Sundry Liabilities (Each individual liability)	at Book value
		By Transferee Company	Purchase Consideration
*To Bank (Liability not takenover)		By Bank (Disposal of assets not taken over)	
To Bank (Expenses) If paid by Transferor Company			
*To Liability (Loss on discharge of liability not taken over)	← or →	*By Liability (Profit on discharge of liability not takenover)	
To Preference Shareholders' Account (Premium on Redemption)	← or →	By Preference Shareholders' A/c (Discount on redemption, if any.)	
To Equity Shareholders' A/c (Profit)	← or →	By Equity Shareholders' A/c (Loss)	
	***		***

* Only one entry.

EQUITY SHAREHOLDERS' A/C

	Rs.		Rs.
To Fictitious Assets	—	By Equity Share Capital	—
To Realisation A/c (Loss)	—	By Revenue Reserves	—
To Shares in Transferee Co.	—	By Capital Reserves	—
To Other Securities in Transferee Co.	—	By Other accumulated Profits	—
To Bank A/c	—	By Realisation A/c (Profit)	—
	***		***

TRANSFEREE COMPANY'S A/C

	Rs.		Rs.
To Realisation A/c	P.C.	By Shares in Transferee Co.	—
		By Debentures in Transferee Co.	—
		By Bank A/c	
	**		**

*All those securities which are issued by Transferee Company to discharge purchase consideration i.e. amount payable to equity shareholders and preference shareholders only.

Illustration : 7

The Balance Sheets of A Ltd. and B Ltd. are as follows :

Liabilities	A Ltd. Rs.	B Ltd. Rs.
9% Preference Share Capital (Shares of Rs. 100 each)	4,00,000	—
Equity Share Capital (Shares of Rs. 10 each)	8,00,000	4,00,000
Reserves	1,60,000	1,00,000
Profit & Loss A/c	2,00,000	40,000
Creditors	40,000	20,000
	16,00,000	5,60,000
Assets		
Goodwill	2,80,000	—
Building (office)	4,00,000	2,00,000
Plant & Machinery	3,00,000	1,20,000
Furniture & Fixtures	1,40,000	80,000
Investments	2,00,000	—
Stock	1,60,000	80,000
Debtors	80,000	60,000
Bank Balance	40,000	20,000
	16,00,000	5,60,000

A new Company called A B Ltd. was formed to takeover both the companies on the following terms:

(i) A Ltd. was valued worth Rs. 20,00,000 and purchase consideration was paid by issue of equity shares of Rs. 10 each at a premium of Rs. 6 per share.

(ii) B Ltd. was considered worth Rs. 8,00,000 to be paid in equity shares of Rs. 10 @ Rs. 16 per share.

(iii) Liquidation expenses amounted to Rs. 8,000 and Rs. 4,000 for A Ltd. & B Ltd. respectively which were paid by AB Ltd.

Record journal entries & prepare necessary ledger accounts to close the books of A Ltd. & B Ltd.

In the books of A Ltd.

JOURNAL ENTRIES

	Particulars		L.F.	Rs.	Rs.
	Realisation A/c	Dr.		16,00,000	
	To Goodwill				2,80,000
	To Building (office)				4,00,000
	To Plant & Machinery				3,00,000
	To Furniture & Fixtures				1,40,000
	To Investments				2,00,000
	To Stock				1,60,000
	To Debtors				80,000
	To Bank Balance				40,000
	(Being assets transferred to Realisation A/c)				

Contd.

Particulars		Dr.	Cr.
Creditors A/c	Dr.	40,000	
To Realisation A/c			40,000
(Being liabilities transferred)			
AB Ltd. A/c	Dr.	20,00,000	
To Realisation A/c			20,00,000
(Being Purchase Consideration due)			
Realisation A/c	Dr.	4,40,000	
To Shareholders' A/c			4,40,000
(Being profit on realisation transferred to shareholders' A/c)			
9% Preference Share Capital A/c	Dr.	4,00,000	
To Preference Shareholders' A/c			4,00,000
(Being preference share Capital transferred to preference shareholders' account.			
Equity Share Capital A/c	Dr.	8,00,000	
Reserves A/c	Dr.	1,60,000	
Profit & Loss A/c	Dr.	2,00,000	
To Equity Shareholders' A/c			11,60,000
(Being capital and accumulated profits transferred to shareholders' account)			
Shares in A B Ltd. A/c	Dr.	20,00,000	
To A B Ltd. A/c			20,00,000
(Being purchase consideration received.)			
Preference Shareholders' A/c	Dr.	4,00,000	
Equity Shareholders' A/c	Dr.	16,00,000	
To Shares in AB Ltd.			20,00,000
(Being claims of shareholders' mat)			

REALISATION A/C

	Rs.		Rs.
To Goodwill	2,80,000	By Creditors	40,000
To Building	4,00,000	By AB Ltd.	20,00,000
To Plant & Machinery	3,00,000		
To Furniture & Fixtures	1,40,000		
To Investments	2,00,000		
To Stock	1,60,000		
To Debtors	80,000		
To Bank Balance	40,000		
To Shareholders A/c (Profit)	4,40,000		
	20,40,000		20,40,000

EQUITY SHAREHOLDERS' A/C

	Rs.		Rs.
To Shares in AB Ltd.	16,00,000	By Share Capital	8,00,000
		By Reserves	1,60,000
		By Profit & Loss A/c	2,00,000
		By Realisation A/c	4,40,000
	16,00,000		16,00,000

PREFERENCE SHAREHOLDERS' A/C

	Rs.		Rs.
To Shares in AB Ltd.	4,00,000	By Preference Share Capital	4,00,000
	4,00,000		4,00,000

AB LTD.'S A/C

	Rs.		Rs.
To Realisation A/c	20,00,000	By Shares in AB Ltd.	20,00,000
	20,00,000		20,00,000

SHARES IN AB LTD. A/C

	Rs.		Rs.
To AB Ltd.	20,00,000	By Equity Shareholders' A/c	16,00,000
		By Preference Shareholders' A/c	4,00,000
	20,00,000		20,00,000

IN THE BOOKS OF B LTD.
JOURNAL ENTRIES

			Rs.	Rs.
	Realisation, A/c	Dr.	5,60,000	
	To Building			2,00,000
	To Plant and Machinery			1,20,000
	To Furniture & Fixtures			80,000
	To Stock			80,000
	To Debtors			60,000
	To Bank balance			20,000
	(Being assets transferred to Realisation A/c)			
	Creditors A/c	Dr.	20,000	
	To Realisation A/c			20,000
	(Being liabilities transferred to Realisation A/c)			

Contd.

	Particulars		Dr. (Rs.)	Cr. (Rs.)
	AB Ltd. A/c	Dr.	8,00,000	
	To Realisation A/c			8,00,000
	(Being purchase consideration due)			
	Realisation A/c	Dr.	2,60,000	
	To Shareholders' A/c			2,60,000
	(Being profit transferred to shareholders' A/c)			
	Share Capital A/c	Dr.	4,00,000	
	Reserves A/c	Dr.	1,00,000	
	Profit & Loss A/c	Dr.	40,000	
	To Equity Shareholders' A/c			5,40,000
	(Being Capital and accumulated profits transferred to shareholders' A/c)			
	Shares in A B Ltd. A/c	Dr.	8,00,000	
	To A B Ltd. A/c			8,00,000
	(Being purchase consideration received)			
	Equity Shareholders' A/c	Dr.	8,00,000	
	To Shares in A B Ltd.			8,00,000
	(Being shares in A B Ltd. given to equity shareholders.)			

LEDGER ACCOUNTS
REALISATION A/C

	Rs.		Rs.
To Building	2,00,000	By Creditors	20,000
To Plant & Machinery	1,20,000	By AB Ltd.	8,00,000
To Furniture & Fixtures	80,000		
To Stock	80,000		
To Debtors	60,000		
To Bank Balance	20,000		
To Shareholders' A/c (Profit)	2,60,000		
	8,20,000		8,20,000

SHAREHOLDERS' A/C

	Rs.		Rs.
To Shares in A B Ltd.	8,00,000	By Share Capital	4,00,000
		By Reserves	1,00,000
		By Profit & Loss A/c	40,000
		By Realisation A/c	2,60,000
	8,00,000		8,00,000

A B LTD. A/C

	Rs.		Rs.
To Realisation A/c	8,00,000	By Shares in A B Ltd.	8,00,000
	8,00,000		8,00,000

SHARES IN A B LTD.

	Rs.		Rs.
To A B Ltd.	8,00,000	By Shareholders' A/c	8,00,000
	8,00,000		8,00,000

II BOOKS OF TRANSFEREE COMPANY

As per AS 14 there are two methods of accounting for amalgamation :

(a) The Pooling of Interest Method

(b) The Purchase Method.

(a) The Pooling of Interest Method

(i) This Method is applicable in case of amalgamation in the nature of merger.

Under pooling of interest method the assets, liabilities and reserves of the transferor company are recorded by the transferee company at their existing amounts and in the same form as on that date of amalgamations. However, changes/adjustment in the values, if any, should be made to ensure uniformity in policy.

(ii) Profit and Loss of transferor company should be aggregated with the corresponding balance of the transferee company or transferred to the General Reserve; if any.

(iii) If at the time of amalgamation, the transferor and transferee companies have conflicting accounting policies, an uniform set of accounting policies should be adopted following the amalgamation. The effects on the financial statements of any changes in accounting policies should be reported in accordance with AS-5.

(iv) The identity of the reserves is preserved and these appear in the financial statements of the transferee company in the same form in which these appeared in the financial statements of transferor company.

For example, the General Reserve of transferor company becomes the General Reserve of the transferee company, the Capital Reserve of transferee Company becomes the Capital Reserve of the transferee company and like wise Revaluation Reserve of transferor company becomes the Revaluation Reserve of transferee Company.

(v) The difference between the amount recorded as share capital issued (plus any additional consideration in the form of cash or other assets) and the amount of share capital of the transferor company is adjusted in reserves in the financial statements of the transferee Company.

Clarification: If there is excess of share capital and accumulated profits of Transferor company over purchase consideration the difference should be transferred to General Reserve. If however, the purchase consideration is more than the Share Capital and accumulated profits the difference should be adjusted against the Reserves of Transferee company or shown as debit balance of P & L A/c.

Share Capital and Accumulated Profits	* * *
Less Purchase Consideration	* *
Add to the General Reserve of Transferee Co.	* *

If purchase consideration exceeds then the difference is treated as Profit & Loss A/c (Dr.)

JOURNAL ENTRIES

(1) *When business is takenover & purchase consideration due*

Business Purchase A/c Dr.

To Liquidator of Transferor Co.

(2) *When assets & liabilities are transferred*

Sundry Assets (individually) (Takenover)	Dr.	(with respective book values)
To Sundry Liabilities (individually)		(with respective book values)
To Provisions (individually)		(with respective book values)
To Profit & Loss A/c		(with respective book values)
To Reserves A/c (Individually)		(with respective book values)
To Business Purchase A/c		(with purchase consideration)

(The difference between the debit side and credit side is adjusted in the reserves of the transferee Company. However the excess of debits over credits of above entry will be transferred to Reserves or may be shown as debit balance of Profit & Loss A/c on the assets side of Balance Sheet in case there are no reserves of the transferor Company. However, such a debit balance be adjusted against the reserves of transferee Company.)

(3) *On payment of Purchase Consideration.*

Liquidator of Transferor Company A/c	Dr.	
To Share Capital A/c		(with face value)
To Preference Share Capital A/c		(with face value)
To Securities Premium A/c		(Amount of premium)
*To other assets (if any)		(with fair value)
*To Bank A/c		(to deal with fractions)

(*may be required for dissenting shareholders)

(4) *On payment of liquidation expenses.*

Liquidation Expenses A/c Dr.

To Bank A/c

and

Profit & Loss A/c Dr.

To Liquidation Expenses A/c

(5) *On payment of formation expenses.*

Preliminary Expenses A/c Dr.

To Bank A/c

(6) *On discharge of any liability takenover*

Liability (Creditors/Debentures/other liability) A/c Dr.

To New Debentures A/c (if debenture are issued)

To Share Capital A/c (if shares are issued)

To Bank A/c (if paid in cash)

Note : Discount/premium on issue of new securities against the discharge of any liability will be debited/ credited as the case may be.

(b) The Purchase Method

It is applied in case of amalgamation in the nature of purchase.

(i) Under Purchase Method the assets and liabilities of the Transferor Company should be incorporated at their existing carrying amounts (Book Values) or at their fair values (Revised Values) on the date of amalgamation.

(ii) The identity of reserves (Whether Capital reserve, revenue reserve or revaluation reserve) of the transferor company, other than the "statutory reserves" is not maintained and hence not included in the financial statements of transferee company.

Statutory reserves are those reserves which are required to be maintained as per the legal provisions, and there is a restriction on it's usage. For example, to avail benefits under Income Tax Act 1961, Development Allowance Reserve or Investment Allowance Reserve has to be maintained. Thus if a statutory reserve is appearing in the balance sheet of a transferor company, the same should appear in the financial statements of the transferee company. For this purpose Amalgamation Adjustment A/c is debited and Statutory Reserve A/c is credited, which are shown on the assets side under the heading Miscellaneous Expenditure and on the liabilities side under the heading Reserves & Surplus respectively as shown below :

BALANCE SHEET OF TRANSFEREE CO.

Liabilities	Rs.	Assets	Rs.
Reserve & Surplus		Miscellaneous Exp.	
Name of Statutory Reserve	***	Amalgamation Adjustment A/c	***

After the expiry of required time limit when statutory reserves are not required to be maintained a reverse entry is required cancelling both the accounts.

Statutory Reserves A/c Dr.

To Amalgamation Adjustment A/c

(iii) The purchase consideration is allocated to individual assets & liabilities on the basis of their fair value at the date of amalgamation. In other words the purchase consideration is to be valued at the market price of the shares issued by the transferee company.

(iv) Any excess of purchase consideration over net assets of the transferor company should be recognised as goodwill in the financial statements of transferee company. While excess of net assets over purchase consideration should be treated as capital reserve.

(v) The goodwill so arising on amalgamation should be amortised systematically over it's useful life. The period of amortisation, however, should not exceed five years unless a somewhat longer period is justified.

Note : There is no difference, as for as recording of journal entries is concerned, between the two methods viz Pooling of Interest and Purchase method except the second entry where resultant is transferred to Reserves A/c and Goodwill/or Capital Reserve A/c respectively.

Difference between Pooling of Interest Method and The Purchase Method

Basis	Pooling of Interest	Purchase Method
(1) Applicability:	It is applicable in case of merger.	It is used in case of amalgamation in the nature of purchase.
(2) Transfer of assets and liabilities	Under this methods the assets and liabilities are transferred at their respective book values.	Assets and liabilities are transferred at fair values.
(3) Identity of reserves	Under pooling of interest methods the identity of reserves is maintained and these are incorporated in the financial statements of the transferee company.	Under purchase method the identity of reserves and profits is not maintained except that of statutory reserves.
(4) Purchase Consideration	Purchase consideration is payable only in shares under this method. Cash is paid only to deal with fractions and dissenting shareholders, if any.	Purchase consideration may be paid in shares, debentures or Cash or in a combination there of.
(5) Resultant of Net assets and purchase consideration	The excess of net assets over purchase consideration and vice versa is adjusted against the general reserve.	The excess of "net assets" over purchase consideration is transferred to Capital reserve, where as excess of purchase consideration over net assets is treated as goodwill.
(6) Amalgamation Adjustment Account	Under pooling of interest method 'Amalgamation Adjustment A/c is not required to be opened.	Amalgamation Adjustment A/c is to be maintained under this method.

AMALGAMATION IN THE NATURE OF MERGER
(Pooling of Interest Method)

Illustration (8) (Merger Simple)

Following are the Balance Sheets of X Ltd. and Y Ltd. as on 31st March, 2004.

Liabilities	X Ltd. Rs.	Y Ltd. Rs.
Equity Share Capital (Share of Rs. 10 each)	6,00,000	15,00,000
General Reserve	2,00,000	6,50,000
Profit & Loss Account	15,000	35,000
Creditors	35,000	65,000
	8,50,000	22,50,000

Assets :		
Fixed Assets	5,50,000	15,50,000
Current Assets (other than Cash and bank balance)	2,50,000	5,50,000
Cash & bank balance	50,000	1,50,000
	8,50,000	22,50,000

X Ltd. is absorbed by Y Ltd. The holder of every 12 shares in X Ltd. were to receive 11 shares in Y Ltd. Pass journal entries in the books of both companies and prepare a Balance Sheet of Y Ltd. after merger.

Solution

In the books of X Ltd.

JOURNAL ENTRIES

			Rs.	Rs.
	Realisation A/c	Dr.	8,50,000	
	To Fixed Assets			5,50,000
	To Current Assets			2,50,000
	To Cash & bank balance			50,000
	(Being assets taken over by Y Ltd.)			
	Creditors A/c	Dr.	35,000	
	To Realisation A/c			35,000
	(Being liabilities takenover by Y Ltd.)			
	Y Ltd. A/c	Dr.	5,50,000	
	To Realisation A/c			5,50,000
	(Being purchase consideration due from Y Ltd.)			
	Share Capital A/c	Dr.	6,00,000	
	General Reserve A/c	Dr.	2,00,000	
	Profit & Loss A/c	Dr.	15,000	
	To Shareholders' A/c			8,15,000
	(Being amount due to shareholders)			
	Shareholders' A/c	Dr.	2,65,000	
	To Realisation A/c			2,65,000
	(Being loss on Realisation transferred to Shareholders)			
	Equity Shares in Y Ltd.		5,50,000	
	To Y Ltd. A/c			5,50,000
	(Being 55,000 Shares received)			
	Shareholders' A/c	Dr.	5,50,000	
	To Equity Shares in Y Ltd.			5,50,000
	(Being Shares in Y Ltd. distributed)			

Books of Y Ltd.
JOURNAL ENTRIES

			Rs.	Rs.
	Business Purchase A/c	Dr.	5,50,000	
	To Liquidator of X Ltd.			5,50,000
	(Being purchase of business of X Ltd. for a consideration)			
	Fixed Assets A/c	Dr.	5,50,000	
	Current Assets A/c	Dr.	2,50,000	
	Cash & bank balance A/c	Dr.	50,000	
	To Creditors A/c			35,000
	** [To Profit & Loss A/c			15,000
	** [To General Reserve A/c		*(B.F)	2,50,000
	To Business Purchase A/c			5,50,000
	(Being assets & liabilities takenover)			
	Liquidator of X Ltd. A/c	Dr.	5,50,000	
	To Share Capital A/c			5,50,000
	(Being shares issued to liquidator of X Ltd.)			

* Share Capital Rs. 6,00,000 less Rs. 5,50,000 purchase consideration plus General Reserve of X Ltd.

**Alternatively Rs. 2,50,000 (being balancing figure) could have been transferred to General Reserve only or Rs. 2,65,000 including P & L A/c.

BALANCE SHEET OF Y LTD.
As on 31st March 2004

Liabilities		Rs.	Assets		Rs.
2,05,000 Equity shares of Rs. 10 each		20,50,000	Fixed Assets		
			X Ltd.	5,50,000	
			Y Ltd.	15,50,000	21,00,000
General Reserve			Current Assets		
X Ltd.	2,50,000		X Ltd.	2,50,000	
Y Ltd.	6,50,000	9,00,000	Y Ltd.	5,50,000	8,00,000
Profit & Loss A/c			Cash & Bank balance		
X Ltd.	15,000		X Ltd.	50,000	
Y Ltd.	35,000	50,000	Y Ltd.	1,50,000	2,00,000
Creditors					
X Ltd.	35,000				
Y Ltd.	65,000	1,00,000			
		31,00,000			31,00,000

Illustration : 9 (Merger & Purchase)

Following are the Balance Sheets of A Ltd. & B Ltd. as on 31st March 2004.

Liabilities :	A Ltd. Rs.	B Ltd. Rs.
9% Preference Share Capital (Shares of Rs. 100 each)	2,50,000	2,00,000
Equity Share Capital (Shares of Rs. 10 each)	5,00,000	3,00,000
General Reserve	50,000	25,000
Export Profit Reserve	30,000	20,000
Investment Allowance Reserve	—	10,000
Profit & Loss A/c	75,000	50,000
10% Debentures	3,00,000	2,00,000
Current liabilities	65,000	50,000
	12,70,000	8,55,000
Assets :		
Gross Block	9,50,000	7,00,000
Less Depreciation	(2,50,000)	(1,80,000)
Net Block	7,00,000	5,20,000
Investments	1,00,000	80,000
Stock	2,25,000	1,10,000
Debtors	1,75,000	90,000
Bank Balance	70,000	55,000
	12,70,000	8,55,000

A Ltd. takesover B Ltd. as on the above date on the following terms:

(i) A Ltd. to issue to the holders of equity shares in B Ltd. 5 shares for every 4 shares held.

(ii) Preference shares of B Ltd. are to be redeemed at a premium of 10% by issue of 9% Preference Shares.

(iii) The debentures of B Ltd. are to be converted into equivalent number of debentures of A Ltd. The statutory reserves of B Ltd. are to be maintained for two more years.

Record journal entries and prepare Balance Sheet in the books of A Ltd. on the assumption that:

(a) It is amalgamation in the nature of merger

(b) It is amalgamation in the nature of purchase

Solution : (a) Amalgamation in the nature of merger

Working notes.

(1) Calculation of Purchase Consideration

		Rs.
Equity Shares $30,000 \times \frac{5}{4}$ @ Rs. 10 each		3,75,000
Preference Shares	Rs. 2,00,000	
Add 10% Premium	Rs. 20,000	2,20,000
Purchase Consideration		5,95,000

(2) Purchase Consideration		5,95,000
Less Share Capital (Preference + Equity)		5,00,000
	Difference	95,000
Less Accumulated Profits (Rs. 25,000 + 20,000 + 10,000 + 50,000)		1,05,000
Excess of Acc. profits to be added to General Reserve of Transferee Co.		10,000

Since statutory reserves are required to be maintained for 2 years more, thus Export Profit Reserve Rs. 20,000 and Investment Allowance Reserve Rs. 10,000 have to be adjusted against general reserve.

	Rs.
General Reserve of transferee Company	50,000
Add Excess of Share Capital and accumulated profits over purchase consideration	10,000
	60,000
Less Statutory Reserves required to be maintained adjusted	30,000
To be shown in the Balance Sheet	30,000

JOURNAL ENTRIES

				Rs.	Rs.
	Business Purchase A/c	Dr.		5,95,000	
	To Liquidator of B Ltd.				5,95,000
	(Being B Ltd. acquired)				
	Gross Block A/c	Dr.		7,00,000	
	Investments A/c	Dr.		80,000	
	Stock A/c	Dr.		1,10,000	
	Debtors A/c	Dr.		90,000	
	Bank balance A/c	Dr.		55,000	
	To Provision for Depreciation				1,80,000
	To 10% Debentures				2,00,000
	To Current Liabilities				50,000
	To Business Purchase A/c				5,95,000
	To General Reserve (B.F.)				10,000
	(Being assets & liabilities taken over)				
	Liquidator's of B Ltd. A/c	Dr.		5,95,000	
	To Equity Share Capital				3,75,000
	To Preference Share Capital				2,20,000
	(Being shares issued to liquidators of B Ltd.)				
	10% Debentures (old) A/c	Dr.		2,00,000	
	To 10% New Debentures				2,00,000
	(Being new debentures issued to Debentureholders)				

BALANCE SHEET OF A LTD. (AFTER MERGER)
As on 31st March, 2004

Liabilities	Rs.	Assets		Rs.
10% Preference Share Capital	2,20,000	Gross Block	16,50,000	
(Shares of Rs. 100 each)		*Less* Depreciation	4,30,000	
9% Preferences share Capital	2,50,000			12,20,000
(Shares of Rs. 100 each)		Investments		1,80,000
Equity Share Capital	8,75,000	Stock		3,35,000
(Shares of Rs. 10 each)		Debtors		2,65,000
General Reserve (2)	30,000	Bank balance		1,25,000
Export Profit Reserve	50,000			
Investment Allowance Reserve	10,000			
Profit & Loss A/c	75,000			
10% Debentures	5,00,000			
Current liabilities	1,15,000			
	21,25,000			21,25,000

(b) Amalgamation in the nature of purchase.

			Rs.	Rs.
	Business Purchase A/c	Dr.	5,95,000	
	To Liquidator of B Ltd.			5,95,000
	(Being B Ltd. takenover)			
	Gross Block A/c	Dr.	7,00,000	
	Investment A/c	Dr.	80,000	
	Stock A/c	Dr.	1,10,000	
	Debtors A/c	Dr.	90,000	
	Bank A/c	Dr.	55,000	
	To Provision for Depreciation			1,80,000
	To Current liabilities			50,000
	To Business Purchase A/c			5,95,000
	To 10% Debentures A/c			2,00,000
	To Capital Reserve (B.F.)			10,000
	(Being assets & liabilities takenover)			
	Liquidator of B Ltd. A/c	Dr.	5,95,000	
	To Equity Share Capital			3,75,000
	To 9% Preference Share Capital			2,20,000
	(Being Shares issued to liquidators of B Ltd.)			*Contd.*

		Dr.	Cr.
10% Debentures (old) A/c	Dr.	2,00,000	
To 10% New Debentures A/c			2,00,000
(Being New Debentures issued to Debentureholders of B Ltd.)			
Amalgamation Adjustment A/c	Dr.	30,000	
To Export Profit Reserve			20,000
To Investment Allowance Reserve			10,000
(Being statutory reserves maintained)			

BALANCE SHEET OF A LTD.
As on 31st March 2004

Liabilities	Rs.	Assets		Rs.
10% Preference Share Capital	2,20,000	Gross Block	16,50,000	
(Share of Rs. 100 each)		*Less* Depreciation	4,30,000	
9% Preferences share Capital	2,50,000			12,20,000
(Share of Rs. 100 each)		Investments		1,80,000
Equity Share Capital	8,75,000	Stock		3,35,000
(Shares of Rs. 10 each)		Debtors		2,65,000
General Reserve	50,000	Bank balance		1,25,000
Capital Reserve	10,000	Amalgamation Adjustment A/c		30,000
Export Profit Reserve	50,000			
Investment Allowance Reserve	10,000			
Profit & Loss A/c	75,000			
10% Debentures	5,00,000			
Current liabilities	1,15,000			
	21,55,000			21,55,000

Illustration (10) (Merger and Adjustment in General Reserve)

Exe Ltd. takes over Wye Ltd. as on 1st April, 2004 when their Balance Sheets stood as under:

Liabilities	Exe Ltd. Rs.	Wye Ltd. Rs.
11% Preference Share Capital (Shares of Rs. 100 each)	11,00,000	8,50,000
Equity Share Capital (Shares of Rs. 10 each)	25,00,000	15,00,000
General Reserve	2,50,000	1,25,000
Investment Allowance Reserves	1,50,000	1,50,000
Profit and Loss A/c	3,75,000	2,50,000
12% Debentures (Rs. 100 each)	2,50,000	1,75,000
Trade Creditors	2,25,000	1,75,000
Other Current liabilities	1,00,000	75,000
	49,50,000	33,00,000

Assets

Land & Building	12,50,000	7,75,000
Plant & Machinery	16,25,000	8,50,000
Furniture and Fittings	2,87,500	1,75,000
Computers & Printers	3,50,000	2,50,000
Stock	6,25,000	4,75,000
Debtors	4,50,000	5,15,000
Cash at Bank	3,62,500	2,60,000
	49,50,000	33,00,000

The purchase consideration was discharged as follows :

(i) Exe Ltd. issued 1,75,000 equity shares of Rs. 10 each to the equity shareholders of Wye Ltd. and

(ii) Issued 13% Preference Shares of Rs. 100 each to discharge the preference shareholders of Wye Ltd. at 10% premium.

The debentures of Wye Ltd. will be converted into debentures of Exe Ltd.

Close the books of Wye Ltd. and record opening entries and prepare a Balance Sheet in the Books of Exe Ltd.

Solution : 10

Calculation of Purchase Consideration

		Rs.
Equity Shares 1,75,000 Shares @ Rs. 10		17,50,000
13% Preference Shares	Rs. 8,50,000	
Add Premium	85,000	9,35,000
Purchase Consideration		26,85,000

In the books of Wye Ltd.

REALISATION A/C

	Rs.		Rs.
To Land & Building	7,75,000	By 12% Debentures	1,75,000
To Plant & Machinery	8,50,000	By Trade Creditors	1,75,000
To Furniture & Fixtures	1,75,000	By Other Current Liabilities	75,000
To Computers & Printers	2,50,000	By Exe Ltd.	26,85,000
To Stock	4,75,000	By Shareholders A/c (Loss)	2,75,000
To Debtors	5,15,000		
To Cash at Bank	2,60,000		
To Preference Shareholders A/c	85,000		
	33,85,000		33,85,000

11% PREFERENCE SHARE CAPITAL A/C

	Rs.		Rs.
To Pref. Shareholder's A/c	8,50,000	By Balance b/d	8,50,000

PREFERENCE SHAREHOLDERS' A/C

	Rs.		Rs.
To 13% Pref. Shares in Exe Ltd.	9,35,000	By 11% Pref. Share Capital A/c	8,50,000
		By Realisation A/c (Premium)	85,000
	9,35,000		9,35,000

EQUITY SHAREHOLDERS' A/C

	Rs.		Rs.
To Realisation A/c (Loss)	2,75,000	By Equity Share Capital A/c	15,00,000
To Shares in Exe. Ltd.	17,50,000	By General Reserve	1,25,000
		By Investment Allowance Reserve	1,50,000
		By Profit & Loss A/c	2,50,000
	20,25,000		20,25,000

EXE LTD. A/C

	Rs.		Rs.
To Realisation A/c	26,85,000	By Shares in Exe Ltd.	17,50,000
		By Pref. Shares in Exe Ltd.	9,35,000
	26,85,000		26,85,000

BOOK OF EXE LTD.
JOURNAL ENTRIES

			Rs.	Rs.
	Business Purchase A/c	Dr.	26,85,000	
	To Liquidator of Wye Ltd.			26,85,000
	(Being Wye Ltd. takenover)			
	General Reserve A/c (B.F.)	Dr.	2,10,000	
	Land & Building A/c	Dr.	7,75,000	
	Plant & Machinery A/c	Dr.	8,50,000	
	Furniture & Fittings A/c	Dr.	1,75,000	
	Computers & Printers A/c	Dr.	2,50,000	
	Stock A/c	Dr.	4,75,000	
	Debtors A/c	Dr.	5,15,000	
	Cash at Bank A/c	Dr.	2,60,000	

Contd.

		Rs.	Rs.
To 12% Debentures			1,75,000
To Trade Creditors			1,75,000
To Other Current liabilities			75,000
To Profit & Loss A/c			2,50,000
To Investment Allowance Reserve			1,50,000
To Business Purchase A/c			26,85,000
(Being assets and liabilities takenover)			
Liquidator of Wye Ltd. A/c	Dr.	26,85,000	
To 13% Preference Share Capital A/c			9,35,000
To Equity Share Capital A/c			17,50,000
(Being shares issued to liquidators of Wye Ltd.)			
12% Debentures A/c	Dr.	1,75,000	
To 12% Debentures (New)			1,75,000
(Being 12% debentures converted into 13% Deb.)			

BALANCE SHEET OF EXE LTD.

As on 31st April, 2004

Liabilities	Rs.	Assets	Rs.
11% Preference Share Capital (Shares of Rs. 100 each)	11,00,000	Land & Building	20,25,000
13% Preference Share Capital (Shares of Rs. 100 each)	9,35,000	Plant & Machinery	24,75,000
Equity Share Capital (Shares of Rs. 10 each)	42,50,000	Furniture & Fittings	4,62,500
General Reserve*	40,000	Computers & Printers	6,00,000
Investment Allowance Reserve	3,00,000	Stock	11,00,000
Profit & Loss A/c	6,25,000	Debtors	9,65,000
12% Debentures	4,25,000	Cash at Bank	6,22,500
Trade Creditors	4,00,000		
Other liabilities	1,75,000		
	82,50,000		82,50,000

*** Working Note.**

		Rs.
	Purchase Consideration	26,85,000
Less	Capital of Wye Ltd. (Equity & Preference)	23,50,000
	Difference	3,35,000
	Accumulated Profits of Wye Ltd. (General Reserve only because other accumulated profits are transferred at the same amount)	1,25,000
	To be adjusted against general reserve of Exe Ltd.	2,10,000**
	General Reserve of Exe Ltd.	2,50,000
	To be shown in the Balance Sheet	40,000

** Students are advised to verify the figure with the balancing figure of second opening entry.

Illustration 11 (Merger and Debit balance of P & L A/c)

On 1.4.04 the Balance Sheets of Radha Ltd. and Shyam Ltd. were as follows :

Liabilities	Radha Ltd. Rs.	Shyam Ltd. Rs.
11% Preference Share Capital (Shares of Rs. 100 each)	3,00,000	1,00,000
Equity Share Capital (Shares of Rs. 10 each)	10,00,000	4,00,000
General Reserve	5,00,000	50,000
Profit & Loss Account	4,50,000	2,50,000
Export Allowance Reserve	1,50,000	20,000
9% Debentures	2,00,000	80,000
Current liabilities	2,50,000	50,000
	28,50,000	9,50,000
Assets :		
Land & Building	8,50,000	—
Plant & Machinery	2,75,000	3,50,000
Computers	1,25,000	1,00,000
Furniture & Fixtures	2,50,000	75,000
Motor Vehicles	4,00,000	1,25,000
Intangibles	3,20,000	—
Investments	1,30,000	50,000
Current Assets	5,00,000	2,50,000
	28,50,000	9,50,000

Radhey Shyam Ltd. was formed to takeover the business of both the companies as per the following terms :

(i) The purchase consideration of Radha Ltd. and Shyam Ltd. was fixed Rs. 30,00,000 and Rs. 10,00,000 payable in shares of Rs. 10 each

(ii) Intangibles include goodwill, copyrights and patents.

(iii) The Authorised Capital of Radhey Shyam Ltd. was Rs. 50,00,000 divisible in equity shares of Rs. 10 each. Half of the remaining Shares were issued to public @ Rs. 10 payable on application. These shares were subscribed and paid for in full.

(iv) Cost of winding-up of Radha Ltd. came to Rs. 10,000 and that of Shyam Ltd. Rs. 5,000 which was met by Radhey Shyam Ltd.

(v) The New Company incurred Rs. 25,000 as cost of formation.

(vi) Export Allowance Reserve is no more required. Close the books of Radha Ltd. & Shyam Ltd. and record opening entries and prepare a Balance Sheet as on that date in the books of Radhey Shyam Ltd.

Solution : 11

Books of Radha Ltd.

REALISATION A/C

	Rs.		Rs.
To Land & Building	8,50,000	By 9% Debentures	2,00,000
To Plant & Machinery	2,75,000	By Current liabilities	2,50,000
To Computers	1,25,000	By Radhey Shyam Ltd.	30,00,000
To Furniture & Fixture	2,50,000		
To Motor Vehicles	4,00,000		
To Intangibles	3,20,000		
To Investments	1,30,000		
To Current Assets	5,00,000		
To Shareholders' A/c (Profit)	6,00,000		
	34,50,000		34,50,000

EQUITY SHAREHOLDERS' A/C

	Rs.		Rs.
To Shares in Radhey Shyam Ltd.	27,00,000	By Equity Share Capital A/c	10,00,000
		By General Reserve	5,00,000
		By Profit & Loss A/c	4,50,000
		By Export Allowance Reserve	1,50,000
		By Realisation A/c (Profit)	6,00,000
	27,00,000		27,00,000

11% PREFERENCE SHAREHOLDERS' A/C

	Rs.		Rs.
To Shares in Radhey Shyam Ltd.	3,00,000	By Preference Share Capital	3,00,000

Books of Shyam Ltd.

REALISATION A/C

	Rs.		Rs.
To Plant & Machinery	3,50,000	By 9% Debentures	80,000
To Computers	1,00,000	By Current liabilities	50,000
To Furniture & Fixtures	75,000	By Radhey Shyam Ltd.	10,00,000
To Motor Vehicles	1,25,000		
To Investments	50,000		
To Current Assets	2,50,000		
To Shareholders' A/c (Profit)	1,80,000		
	11,30,000		11,30,000

EQUITY SHAREHOLDERS' A/C

	Rs.		Rs.
Shares in Radhey Shyam Ltd.	9,00,000	By Equity Share Capital	4,00,000
		By General Reserve	50,000
		By Profit & Loss A/c	2,50,000
		By Export Allowance Reserve	20,000
		By Realisation A/c	1,80,000
	9,00,000		9,00,000

11% PREFERENCE SHAREHOLDERS' A/C

	Rs.		Rs.
To Shares in Radhey Shyam Ltd.	1,00,000	By 11% Preference Share Capital A/c	1,00,000

Books of Radhey Shyam Ltd.

JOURNAL ENTRIES

			Rs.	Rs.
	Business Purchase A/c	Dr.	40,00,000	
	To Liquidator of Radha Ltd.			30,00,000
	To Liquidator of Shyam Ltd.			10,00,000
	(Being business of Radha Ltd & Shyam Ltd. takenover)			
	Profit and Loss A/c (B.F.)	Dr.	7,80,000	
	Land & Buildings A/c	Dr.	8,50,000	
	Plant & Machinery A/c	Dr.	6,25,000	
	Computers A/c	Dr.	2,25,000	
	Furniture & Fixture A/c	Dr.	3,25,000	
	Motor Vehicles A/c	Dr.	5,25,000	
	Intangibles A/c	Dr.	3,20,000	

Contd.

		Rs.	Rs.
Investments A/c	Dr.	1,80,000	
Current Assets A/c	Dr.	7,50,000	
To 9% Debentures			2,80,000
To Current Liabilities			3,00,000
To Business Purchase A/c			40,00,000
(Being assets & Liabilities transferred and the difference adjusted against Profit & Loss A/c)			
Liquidator of Radha Ltd. A/c	Dr.	30,00,000	
Liquidator of Shyam Ltd. A/c	Dr.	10,00,000	
To Equity Share Capital A/c			40,00,000
(Being Shares allotted to liquidators)			
Bank A/c	Dr.	5,00,000	
To Equity Share Application A/c			5,00,000
(Being application money received on 50,000 Shares)			
Equity Share Application A/c	Dr.	5,00,000	
To Equity Share Capital A/c			5,00,000
(Being application money transferred to Share Capital A/c)			
Liquidation (winding up) Exp. A/c	Dr.	15,000	
Preliminary (formation) Exp. A/c	Dr.	25,000	
To Bank A/c			40,000
(Being liquidation and formation expenses met)			
Profit & Loss A/c	Dr.	15,000	
To Liquidation Expenses A/c			15,000
(Being liquidation expenses Charged to P & L A/c)			

BALANCE SHEET OF RADHEY, SHYAM LTD.
As on 1st April 2004

Liabilities	Rs.	Assets	Rs.
Authorised Capital		Fixed Assets :	
5,00,000 Shares of Rs. 10 each	50,00,000	Land & Building	8,50,000
Issued & Subscribed Capital		Plant & Machinery	6,25,000
4,50,000 Shares of Rs. 10 each	4,50,000	Computers	2,25,000
fully paid		Furniture & Fixtures	3,25,000
Secured Loans :		Motor Vehicles	5,25,000
9% Debentures	2,80,000	Intangibles	3,20,000
Current liabilities	3,00,000	Investments	1,80,000

Contd.

BALANCE SHEET *(Contd.)*

Liabilities	Rs.	Assets	Rs.
		Current Assets	750,000
		Cash at Bank (5,00,000 – 40,000)	4,60,000
		Preliminary Expenses	25,000
		Profit & Loss A/c* (7,80,000 + 15,000)	7,95,000
	50,80,000		50,80,000

*** Working Note (Verification)**

(1)

	Radha Ltd.	Shyam Ltd.
Purchase Consideration	30,00,000	10,00,000
Less Share Capital (Equity + Preference)	13,00,000	5,00,000
Difference (Excess)	17,00,000	5,00,000
Accumulated Profits (General Reserve + Profit & Loss A/c + Export Allowance Reserve)	11,00,000	3,20,000
Balancing figure	6,00,000	1,80,000

= 7,80,000

Add Liquidation Expenses = 15,000

7,95,000

(2) Since Export Allowance Reserve is no more required it has not been carried forward.

Illustration (12) (Apportionment of purchase consideration —Merger and Purchase)

On 1st April 2005 the Balance Sheets of R Ltd. and S Ltd. were as under :

Liabilities	R Ltd. Rs.	S Ltd. Rs.
12% Preference Share Capital (Shares of Rs. 100 each)	2,50,000	—
Equity Share Capital (Shares of Rs. 10 each)	12,50,000	9,00,000
General Reserve	40,000	90,000
Export Profit Reserve	60,000	40,000
Investment Allowance Reserve	—	20,000
Profit & Loss A/c	1,50,000	1,20,000
13% Debentures	1,00,000	70,000
Sundry Creditors	1,30,000	1,00,000
	19,80,000	13,40,000
Assets :		
Fixed Assets	11,50,000	6,50,000
Current Assets	830,000	6,70,000
Preliminary Expenses	—	20,000
	19,80,000	13,40,000

A new Company RS Ltd. was formed to takeover the business of R Ltd. and S Ltd. on the following terms :

(i) RS Ltd. to takeover both the companies at a total price of Rs. 24,00,000 to be discharged by issue of equity shares of Rs. 10 each at a premium of 20%.

(ii) The Shareholders of R Ltd. and S Ltd. to get shares in RS Ltd. in the ratio of net assets value of their respective shares.

(iii) The debentures of both companies are to be converted into equivalent number of 12% Debentures in RS Ltd.

(iv) Statutory Reserves are to be maintained for 3 more years.

(v) The Fixed assets of R Ltd. & S Ltd. are valued at Rs. 12,00,000 and Rs. 7,00,000 respectively.

Record journal entries in the books of RS Ltd. and prepare a Balance Sheet if :

(a) It is a case of amalgamation in nature of merger.

(b) It is an amalgamation in nature of purchase.

[B.Com. (H) D.U. Adapted]

Solution : 12

(a) Amalgamation in the nature of merger.

Calculation of Purchase Consideration

		R Ltd.	S Ltd.
Fixed Assets (Revised Value)		12,00,000	7,00,000
Current Assets		8,30,000	6,70,000
		20,30,000	13,70,000
Less Liabilities		2,30,000	1,70,000
	Net Assets	18,00,000	12,00,000
	Ratio	18 :	12

Hence total purchase consideration of Rs. 24,00,000 to be divided in the ratio of 3 : 2

Purchase Consideration for R Ltd. = Rs. 14,40,000

$\left(\text{Rs. } 24,00,000 \times \frac{3}{5}\right)$

No. of shares to be issued = 1,20,000 Shares

(Rs. 14,40,000 ÷ 12)

Purchase consideration for S Ltd. = Rs. 9,60,000

$\left(\text{Rs. } 24,00,000 \times \frac{2}{5}\right)$

No. of Shares to be issued = 80,000 Shares

(Rs. 9,60,000 ÷ 12)

Books of RS Ltd.
JOURNAL ENTRIES

		Rs.	Rs.
Business Purchase A/c	Dr.	24,00,000	
To Liquidator of R Ltd.			14,40,000
To Liquidator of S Ltd.			9,60,000
(Being purchase consideration payable on takeover)			
Fixed Assets A/c	Dr.	18,00,000	
Current Assets A/c	Dr.	15,00,000	
Preliminary Expenses A/c	Dr.	20,000	
To 13% Debentures			1,70,000
To Sunday Creditors			2,30,000
To Export Profit Reserve			1,00,000
To Investment Allowance Reserve			20,000
To Profit & Loss A/c			2,70,000
To General Reserve (B. F.)			1,30,000
To Business Purchase A/c			24,00,000
(Being assets and liabilities takenover at book values)			
Liquidator of R Ltd. A/c	Dr.	14,40,000	
Liquidator of S Ltd. A/c	Dr.	9,60,000	
To Equity Share Capital A/c			20,00,000
To Securities Premium A/c			4,00,000
(Being shares allotted to liquidators)			
13% Debentures A/c	Dr.	1,70,000	
To 12% Debentures			1,70,000
(Being 13% Debentures Converted into 12% Debentures)			

BALANCE SHEET OF RS LTD.
As on 1st April, 2005

Liabilities	Rs.	Assets	Rs.
Authorised Capital		Fixed Assets	18,00,000
Issued & Subscribed Capital		Current Assets	15,00,000
2,00,000 Shares of Rs. 10 each	20,00,000	Miscellaneous Expenditures :	
Reserve & Surplus :		Preliminary Expenses	20,000
Securities Premium	4,00,000		
Export Profit Reserve	1,00,000		
Investment Allowance Reserve	20,000		
General Reserve*	1,30,000		
Profit & Loss A/c	2,70,000		

Contd.

BALANCE SHEET OF RS LTD. (*Contd.*)

	Rs.		Rs
Secured Loans :			
12% Debentures	1,70,000		
Current liabilities :			
Trade Creditors	2,30,000		
	33,20,000		33,20,000

* Verification	Rs.
Total Purchase consideration	24,00,000
Total Share Capital (Rs. 2,50,000 + 12,50,000 + 9,00,000)	24,00,000
Difference	Nil

Hence accumulated profits are not be affected and will be maintained in the same form as before.

(b) Amalgamation in the nature of purchase

JOURNAL ENTRIES

			Rs.	Rs.
	Business Purchase A/c Dr.		24,00,000	
	To Liquidator of R Ltd.			14,40,000
	To Liquidator of S Ltd.			9,60,000
	(Being purchase consideration payable to liquidators)			
	Fixed Assets A/c Dr.		19,00,000	
	Current Assets A/c Dr.		15,00,000	
	To 13% Debentures			1,70,000
	To Sundry Creditors			2,30,000
	To Business Purchase			24,00,000
	To Capital Reserve (B.F.)			6,00,000
	(Being assets and liabilities takenover at revised values)			
	Liquidator of R Ltd. A/c Dr.		14,40,000	
	Liquidator of S Ltd. A/c Dr.		9,60,000	
	To Equity Share Capital A/c			20,00,000
	To Securities Premium A/c			4,00,000
	(Being shares allotted to liquidators at premium)			
	Amalgamation Adjustment A/c Dr.		1,20,000	
	To Export Profit Reserve A/c			1,00,000
	To Investment Allowance Reserve A/c			20,000
	(Being statutory reserves maintained)			
	13% Debentures A/c Dr.		1,70,000	
	To 12% Debentures			1,70,000
	(Being 13% Debentures Converted into 12% Debentres)			

BALANCE SHEET OF R S LTD.
As on 1st April, 2005

Liabilities	Rs.	Assets	Rs.
Authorised Capital :	....	Fixed Assets	19,00,000
Issued & Subscribed Capital		Current Assets	15,00,000
2,00,000 Shares of Rs. 10 each	20,00,000	Miscellaneous Expenditure :	
Reserves & Surplus :		Amalgamation Adjustment A/c	1,20,000
Securities Premium	4,00,000		
Capital Reserve	6,00,000		
Export Profit Reserve	1,00,000		
Investment Allowance Reserve	20,000		
Secured Loans :			
12% Debentures	1,70,000		
Current Liabilities			
Sundry Creditors	2,30,000		
	35,20,000		35,20,000

Illustration (13) (Merger : P.C. at intrinsic Value but recording at par)

Following is the Balance Sheet of Resham Ltd. as on 1st April, 2005.

Liabilities	Rs.	Assets	Rs.
12% Preference Share Capital		Fixed Assets	15,00,000
(Shares of Rs. 100 each)	3,00,000	Investments	2,50,000
Equity Share Capital		Current Assets	7,50,000
(Shares of Rs. 10 each)	12,00,000	(Other than Cash & Bank)	
Foreign Project Reserve	1,50,000	Cash & Bank balance	2,00,000
(Statutory Reserve)			
General Reserve	3,50,000		
11% Debentures	5,00,000		
Current Liabilities	2,00,000		
	27,00,000		27,00,000

Rashmi Ltd. takesover Resham Ltd. on the following terms :

(1) Preference Shareholders of Resham Ltd. are to be discharged at a premium of 25% by issuing the necessary number of 13% preference shares of Rs. 100 each.

(2) Equity Shareholders of Resham Ltd. are to be issued on the basis of intrinsic values of shares of both the Companies. The intrinsic value of Resham Ltd. was Rs. 20 per share and of Rashmi Ltd. was Rs. 30 each. However, it was agreed to record the entry on the basis of par value only. The nominal value of Rashmi Ltd. was Rs. 10 per share.

(3) The debentures of Resham Ltd. are to be redeemed by Rashmi Ltd. by issuing 13% own debenture of Rs. 100 each at Rs. 120 per debenture.

Record entries in the books of Rashmi Ltd.

Solution :

CALCULATION OF PURCHASE CONSIDERATION

	Rs.	Rs.
12% Preference shares	3,00,000	
Add Premium @20%	60,000	3,60,000
Equity Shares $\left(\text{Rs. } 12,00,000 \times \frac{20}{30} \text{ @ Rs. } 10\right)$		8,00,000
		11,60,000

			Rs.	Rs.
	Business Purchase A/c	Dr.	11,60,000	
	To Liquidator of Resham Ltd.			11,60,000
	(Being business of Resham Ltd. taken over)			
	Fixed Assets A/c	Dr.	15,00,000	
	Investment A/c	Dr.	2,50,000	
	Current Assets A/c	Dr.	7,50,000	
	Cash & Bank balance A/c	Dr.	2,00,000	
	To Current Liabilities			2,00,000
	To 11% Debentures			5,00,000
	To Foreign Project Reserve			1,50,000
	To Business Purchase A/c			11,60,000
	*To General Reserve (B.F.)			6,90,000
	(Being assets and liabilities incorporated)			
	Liquidator of Resham Ltd. A/c	Dr.	11,60,000	
	To 13% Preference Share Capital A/c			3,60,000
	To Equity Share Capital A/c			8,00,000
	(Being shares issued to liquidator of Resham Ltd.)			
	11% Debentures A/c	Dr.	5,00,000	
	To 13% Debentures A/c			4,00,000
	To Securities Premium A/c			1,00,000

***Verification :**

	Rs.
Purchase Consideration	11,60,000
Less Share Capital (Preference & Equity)	15,00,000
Add to General Reserve	3,40,000
General Reserve as per B/s	3,50,000
	6,90,000

Illustration (14) (Merger : P.C Adjustment based on intrinsic value but recording at par)

Exe Ltd. is absorbed by Wye Ltd. Given below are the Balance Sheets of two companies prepared after revaluation of their assets on a uniform basis.

Liabilities	Exe Ltd. Rs.	Wye Ltd. Rs.
Authorised Share Capital :		
9,000 Equity Shares of Rs. 150 each	13,50,000	—
60,000 Equity Shares of Rs. 75 each	—	45,00,000
Paid up Share Capital :		
9,000 Equity Shares of Rs. 150 each Rs. 135 paid up	12,15,000	—
40,000 Equity Shares of Rs. 75 each fully paid up	—	30,00,000
General Reserve	4,03,500	12,85,000
Profit & Loss Account	15,000	35,000
Sundry Creditors	55,000	65,000
	16,88,500	43,85,000
Assets :		
Sundry Assets	16,85,000	43,57,500
Cash in hand	3,500	27,500
	16,88,500	43,85,000

The holder of every three shares in Exe Ltd. was to receive five shares in Wye Ltd. plus as much cash as is necessary to adjust the rights of shareholders of both the companies in accordance with the intrinsic values of the shares as per respective Balance Sheets.

Pass necessary journal entries in the books of Wye Ltd. assuming it to be an amalgamation in the nature of merger and prepare a Balance Sheet giving effect to the above scheme. Entries are to be made at par value only.

C.A. (I)

Solution : 14

CALCULATION OF PURCHASE CONSIDERATION

(i) computation of Intrinsic value of shares.

	Exe Ltd. Rs.	Wye Ltd. Rs.
Total Assets	16,88,500	43,85,000
Less liabilities	55,000	65,000
Net Assets	16,33,500	43,20,000
divided by	÷	÷
No. of Shares	9,000	40,000
Intrinsic Value per Share	181.50	108

The Shareholders of Exe Ltd. to receive 5 shares of Wye Ltd. for every 3 shares held.

Therefore,	Rs.
3 Shares of Exe Ltd. (181.5 × 3) =	544.50
5 Shares of Wye Ltd. (108 × 5) =	540.00
Difference (To be paid in cash for every 3 shares)	*4.50
Thus Purchase Consideration will be :	Rs.
$\frac{9{,}000 \times 5}{3}$ = 15,000 shares @ Rs. 75	11,25,000
Cash $\frac{9{,}000 \times 4.5}{3}$	13,500
	11,38,500

Books of Wye Ltd.

JOURNAL ENTRIES

			Rs.	Rs.
	Business Purchase A/c Dr. To Liquidator of Exe Ltd. (Being business of Exe Ltd. takenover and purchase consideration payable)		11,38,500	11,38,500
	Sundry Assets A/c Dr. Cash A/c Dr. To Sundry Creditors A/c To Profit & Loss A/c To Business Purchase A/c To General Reserve A/c (B.F.) (1) (Being assets and liabilities incorporated)		16,85,000 3,500	 55,000 15,000 11,38,500 4,80,000
	Liquidator of Exe Ltd. Dr. To Equity Share Capital A/c To Bank A/c (Being purchase consideration paid to liquidators)		11,38,500	 11,25,000 13,500

BALANCE SHEET OF WYE LTD.

As on .....

Liabilities	Rs.	Assets	Rs.
Authorised Capital	45,00,000	Sundry Assets	60,42,500
60,000 Shares of Rs. 75 each		Cash (2)	17,500
Issued and Subscribed Capital			
55,000 shares of Rs. 75 each	41,25,000		
Reserves & Surplus			
General Reserve	17,65,000		
Profit & Loss A/c	50,000		
Current Liabilities			
Sundry Creditors	1,20,000		
	60,60,000		60,60,000

	Rs.
(1) Verification of General Reserve	
Purchase consideration	11,38,500
Less Share Capital	12,15,000
Excess of Share Capital over purchase-	
Consideration to be added to General Reserve	76,500
General Reserve as per Balance Sheet of Exe Ltd.	4,03,500
General Reserve on merger	4,80,000
Total General Reserve (Rs. 12,85,000 + 4,80,000) =	17,65,000

(2) **CASH A/C**

To Balance b/d	27,500	By Liquidator of Exe Ltd.	13,500
To Transfer from Exe Ltd.	3,500	By Balance c/d	17,500
	31,000		31,000

Illustration (15) (Merger : P.C. at intrinsic value and recording at I.V.)

Following are the Balance Sheets of A Ltd. & B Ltd. as on 31st March, 2005.

Liabilities	A Ltd. Rs.	B Ltd. Rs.
Share Capital :		
5,000 shares of Rs. 100 each	5,00,000	—
80,000 shares of Rs. 10 each	—	8,00,000
Capital Reserve	1,00,000	—
General Reserve	3,60,000	10,00,000
Secured Loans	—	4,00,000
Unsecured Loans	2,20,000	—
Creditors	4,20,000	4,60,000
Provision for Tax	1,10,000	5,20,000
Proposed Dividend	—	1,00,000
	17,10,000	32,80,000
Assets :		
Fixed Assets	8,30,000	16,00,000
Current Assets	6,90,000	16,80,000
Investments	1,70,000	—
Goodwill	20,000	—
	17,10,000	32,80,000

A Ltd. is amalgamated with B Ltd. as on the above date. For the purpose of amalgamation the goodwill of A Ltd. is considered valueless. There are arrears of depreciation in A Ltd. amounting to Rs. 40,000.

The Shareholders of A Ltd. are allotted, in full satisfaction of their claims, shares in B Ltd. in the same proportion as the respective intrinsic values of the shares of the two companies bear to each other.

Prepare the necessary ledger accounts in the books of A Ltd. and pass journal entries and prepare a Balance Sheet in the books of B Ltd.

[B.Com (H) D.U., Modified]

Solution :

Calculation of Purchase Consideration and Computation of Intrinsic value

	A Ltd.	B Ltd.
	Rs.	Rs.
Fixed Assets (8,30,000 – 40,000)	7,90,000	16,00,000
(*Less* Arrears of depreciation)		
Investments	1,70,000	—
Current Assets	6,90,000	16,80,000
	16,50,000	32,80,000
Less Liabilities		
Secured Loans	—	(4,00,000)
Unsecured Loans	(2,20,000)	—
Creditors	(4,20,000)	(4,60,000)
Provision for Tax	(1,10,000)	(5,20,000)
Proposed dividend	—	(1,00,000)
Net Assets	9,00,000	18,00,000
divided by	÷	÷
No. of shares	5,000	80,000
Intrinsic Value per share	180	22.50
Rate of exchange	1 :	8

B Ltd. will issue 8 Shares for every share held in A Ltd. Therefore the liquidator of A Ltd. will receive 5,000 × 8 = 40,000 shares of Rs. 10 each @ Rs. 22.50 per share. Since question is silent on the recording of price, the shares shall be recorded at it's intrinsic value. Hence B Ltd. will issue 40,000 shares of Rs. 10 each at a premium of Rs. 12.50 per share.

Books of A Ltd.

REALISATION A/C

	Rs.		Rs.
To Fixed Assets	8,30,000	By Unsecured Loans	2,20,000
To Investments	1,70,000	By Creditors	4,20,000
To Current Assets	6,90,000	By Provision for Tax	1,10,000
To Goodwill	20,000	By B Ltd.	9,00,000
		By Shareholders' A/c (Loss)	60,000
	17,10,000		17,10,000

SHAREHOLDERS A/C

	Rs.		Rs.
To Realisation A/c (Loss)	60,000	By Share Capital	5,00,000
		By General Reserve	3,60,000
To Shares in B Ltd. A/c	9,00,000	By Capital Reserve	1,00,000
	9,60,000		9,60,000

B LTD. A/C

	Rs.		Rs.
To Realisation A/c	9,00,000	By Shares in B Ltd.	9,00,000

SHARES IN B LTD. A/C

	Rs.		Rs.
To B Ltd.	9,00,000	By Shareholders A/c	9,00,000

Books of B Ltd.
JOURNAL ENTRIES

				Rs.	Rs.
	Business Purchase A/c	Dr.		9,00,000	
	To Liquidator of A Ltd.				9,00,000
	(Being business of A Ltd. acquired)				
	Fixed Assets A/c	Dr.		7,90,000	
	Current Assets A/c	Dr.		6,90,000	
	Investments A/c	Dr.		1,70,000	
	To Unsecured Loans				2,20,000
	To Creditors				4,20,000
	To Provision for Tax				1,10,000
	To Business Purchase A/c				9,00,000
	(Being assets and liabilities of A Ltd. incorporated)				
	Liquidator of A Ltd. A/c	Dr.		9,00,000	
	To Share Capital A/c				4,00,000
	To Securities Premium A/c				5,00,000
	(Being shares allotted to liquidator of A Ltd.)				

Working note :

Since purchase consideration is equal to net assets there is no transfer /Adjustment to/in General Reserve.

	Purchase Consideration	9,00,000
Less	Share Capital	5,00,000
		4,00,000
Less	Accumulated Profits after deducting for depreciation and valueless goodwill.	4,00,000
	(Capital Reserve + General Reserve) Rs. 4,60,000 — (Rs. 40,000 + 20,000)	Nil

BALANCE SHEET OF B LTD.
As on 1st April, 2005

Liabilities	Rs.	Assets	Rs.
Share Capital		Fixed Assets	23,90,000
1,20,000 Shares of Rs. 10 each	12,00,000	Investments	1,70,000
Reserves & Surplus :		Current Assets	23,70,000
Securities Premium	5,00,000		
General Reserve	10,00,000		
Secured Loans	4,00,000		
Unsecured Loans	2,20,000		
Current liabilities & Provisions :			
Creditors	8,80,000		
Provision for tax	6,30,000		
Proposed dividend	1,00,000		
	49,30,000		49,30,000

II Amalgamation in the nature of purchase (Purchase Method)

Illustration (16) (General)

The summarised Balance Sheet of Gunjan Ltd. as on 31st March, 2005 was as follows :

Liabilities	Rs.	Assets	Rs.
Share Capital		Goodwill	1,00,000
60,000 Shares of Rs. 10 each	6,00,000	Land, Building & Plant	6,40,000
General Reserve	1,70,000	Stock	1,68,000
Profit & Loss A/c	1,10,000	Debtors	36,000
12% Debentures	1,00,000	Cash & bank balance	56,000
Creditors	20,000		
	10,00,000		10,00,000

Konark Ltd. agreed to absorb the business of Gunjan Ltd. with effect from 1st April, 2005 the purchase consideration payable by Konark Ltd. was agreed as follows :

(a) A cash payment equivalent to Rs. 2.50 for every Rs. 10 share in Gunjan Ltd.

(b) The issue of 90,000 Equity Shares of Rs. 10 each fully paid in Konark Ltd. having an agreed value of Rs. 15 per share.

(c) The issue of such an amount of fully paid 10% Debentures in Konark Ltd. at 96 percent as is sufficient to discharge 12% Debentures in Gunjan Ltd. at a premium of 20 percent.

While computing purchase consideration Konark Ltd. valued Land, Building and Plant at Rs. 12,00,000, Stock at Rs. 1,42,000 and Debtors at their face value subject to a reserve of 5 percent for doubtful debts. The cost of liquidation of Gunjan Ltd. was Rs. 5,000.

You are required : (i) To close the books of Gunjan Ltd. by preparing Realisation A/c, Konark Ltd. A/c, Shareholders' A/c, and Debentureholders' A/c and

(ii) To pass journal entries in the books of Konark Ltd. regarding acquisition of business.

[B.Com (H) D.U., Modified]

Solution :

CALCULATION OF PURCHASE CONSIDERATION

	Rs.
90,000 Equity Shares @ Rs. 15	13,50,000
Cash @ Rs. 2.50 per Share (60,000 × 2.5)	1,50,000
	15,00,000

Books of Gunjan Ltd.

REALISATION A/C

	Rs.		Rs.
To Goodwill	1,00,000	By Creditors	20,000
To Land, Building & Plant	6,40,000	By 12% Debentures	1,00,000
To Stock	1,68,000	By Konark Ltd.	15,00,000
To Debtors	36,000		
To Cash & bank balance	56,000		
To Cash (Exp.)	5,000		
To Shareholders A/c (Profit)	6,15,000		
	16,20,000		16,20,000

KONARK LTD. A/C

	Rs.		Rs.
To Realisation A/c	15,00,000	By Bank	1,50,000
		By Equity Shares in Konark Ltd.	13,50,000
	15,00,000		15,00,000

SHAREHOLDERS' A/C

	Rs.		Rs.
To Equity Shares in Konark Ltd.	13,50,000	By Share Capital	6,00,000
To Bank	1,45,000*	By General Reserve	1,70,000
		By Profit & Loss A/c	1,10,000
		By Realisation A/c	6,15,000
	14,95,000		14,95,000

12% DEBENTURES A/C

	Rs.		Rs.
To Realisation A/c	1,00,000	By Balance b/d	1,00,000

* Cash received from Konark Ltd. Rs. 1,50,000 less expenses Rs. 5,000 which are borne by Gunjan Ltd., (as the entire Cash and bank balance has been transferred to Konark Ltd.)

Books of Konark Ltd.
JOURNAL ENTRIES

			Rs.	Rs.
	Business Purchase A/c	Dr.	15,00,000	
	To Liquidator of Gunjan Ltd.			15,00,000
	(Being business of Gunjan Ltd. takenover)			
	Goodwill A/c (B.F.)	Dr.	2,07,800	
	Land, Building & Plant	Dr.	12,00,000	
	Stock	Dr.	1,42,000	
	Debtors	Dr.	36,000	
	Cash & bank balance	Dr.	56,000	
	To Creditors			20,000
	To Provision for doubtful debts			1,800
	To 12% Debentures			1,20,000
	To Business Purchase A/c			15,00,000
	(Being assets & liabilities incorporated)			
	Liquidator of Gunjan Ltd. A/c	Dr.	15,00,000	
	To Equity Share Capital A/c			9,00,000
	To Securities Premium A/c			4,50,000
	To Bank A/c			1,50,000
	Being purchase consideration paid to liquidatior of Gunjan Ltd.			
	12% Debentures A/c	Dr.	1,20,000	
	Discount on Issue of Deb. A/c	Dr.	5,000	
	To 14% Debentures			1,25,000
	(Being 14% Debentures issued at 4% discount)			

It is to be noted that in case of purchase method the revised values of assets and liabilities are taken into account.

Illustration (17) (Unpaid Calls & bad debts)

Following are the Balance Sheets of Divya Ltd. and Pranav Ltd. as on 1st April 2005.

	Divya Ltd. Rs.	Pranav Ltd. Rs.
Issued & Subscribed Capital	15,00,000	5,00,000
Shares of Rs. 10 each		
Profit & Loss Account balances	98,800	26,900
10% Debentures	5,00,000	1,00,000
Creditors	83,400	43,600
Bank Overdraft	—	20,000
	21,82,200	6,90,500

Unpaid Calls	5,000	1,000
Land & Building	10,33,300	3,56,800
Goodwill	3,00,000	50,000
Plant & Machinery	3,87,650	1,64,350
Stock	1,79,250	78,500
Debtors	72,400	39,850
Bank	1,68,400	-
Bills Receivable	36,200	-
	21,82,200	6,90,500

With a view to reducing establishment expenses and generally to effect economy in working, Divya Ltd. agreed to takeover the Pranav Ltd. as a going concern, both companies being engaged in the same trade. Divya Ltd. was to pay the debentures and liabilities of Pranav Ltd. and takeover the assets, the consideration being the issue of 40,000 shares of Rs. 10 each fully paid and the payment of Rs. 30,000 in cash to the Pranav Ltd. Divya Ltd. was to pay the liquidation expenses which amounted to Rs. 14,000.

Assume that the absorption was duty effected but the unpaid calls and a book debt of Rs. 4,000 due to Pranav Ltd. proved irrecoverable.

Close the books of Pranav Ltd. and prepare a Balance Sheet after absorption.

[C.A. (F) Modified]

Solution : 17

Books of Pranav Ltd.
REALISATION A/C

	Rs.		Rs.
To Goodwill	50,000	By 10% Debentures	1,00,000
To Land & Building	3,56,800	By Creditors	43,600
To Plant & Machinery	1,64,350	By Bank Overdraft	20,000
To Stock	78,500	By Divya Ltd.*	4,30,000
To Debtors	39,850	By Shareholders A/c (Loss)	95,900
	6,89,500		6,89,500

*** Purchase Consideration.**	Rs.
40,000 Equity Shares of Rs. 10 each	4,00,000
Cash	30,000
	4,30,000

SHAREHOLDERS' A/C

	Rs.		Rs.
To Unpaid Calls	1,000	By Share Capital A/c	5,00,000
To Realisation A/c (Loss)	95,900	By Profit & Loss A/c	26,900
To Shares in Divya Ltd.	4,00,000		
To Bank	30,000		
	5,26,900		5,26,900

DIVYA LTD. A/C

	Rs.		Rs.
To Realisation A/c	4,30,000	By Shares in Divya Ltd.	4,00,000
		By Bank	30,000
	4,30,000		4,30,000

Books of Divya Ltd.

JOURNAL ENTRIES

			Rs.	Rs.
	Business Purchase A/c	Dr.	4,30,000	
	To Liquidator of Pranav Ltd.			4,30,000
	(Being business of Pranav Ltd. absorbed)			
	Land & Building A/c	Dr.	3,56,800	
	Plant & Machinery A/c	Dr.	1,64,350	
	Stock A/c	Dr.	78,500	
	Debtors A/c (Less Provision)	Dr.	35,850	
	To 10% Debentures			1,00,000
	To Creditors			43,600
	To Bank Overdraft			20,000
	To Business Purchase A/c			4,30,000
	To Capital Reserve (B.F.)			41,900
	(Being assets & liabilities of Pranav Ltd. incorporated)			
	Liquidator of Pranav Ltd. A/c	Dr.	4,30,000	
	To Equity Share Capital A/c			4,00,000
	To Bank A/c			30,000
	(Being purchase consideration paid)			
	Liquidation Expenses A/c	Dr.	14,000	
	To Bank A/c			14,000
	(Being liquidation expenses of Pranab Ltd. paid)			
	Goodwill A/c	Dr.	14,000	
	To Liquidation Expenses A/c			14,000
	(Being liquidation expenses adjusted against goodwill)			

BALANCE SHEET OF DIVYA LTD.
As on 1st April, 2005

Liabilities	Rs.	Assets	Rs.
Issued & Subscribed Capital	19,00,000	Fixed Assets :	
1,90,000 Shares of Rs. 10 each		Goodwill (1)	2,72,100
Less Unpaid Calls	5,000	Land & Building	13,90,100
	18,95,000	Plant & Machinery	5,52,000
Reserves & Surplus :		Current Assets, Loans & Advances :	
Profit & Loss Account	98,800	Stock	2,57,750
Secured Loans		Debtors	1,08,250
10% Debentures	6,00,000	Bank (2)	1,24,400
Current liabilities and Provisions :		Bills Receivable	36,200
Creditors	1,27,000		
Bank Overdraft	20,000		
	27,40,800		27,40,800

Working notes :

		Rs.
(1)	Goodwill of Divya Ltd.	3,00,000
	Add liquidation expenses charged to Goodwill	14,000
		3,14,000
	Less Capital Reserve on incorporation of assets & liabilities of Pranav Ltd.	41,900
		2,72,100
(2)	Bank balance	1,68,400
	Less Paid to Pranav Ltd.	30,000
		1,38,400
	Less Liquidation Expenses	14,000
		1,24,400

Illustration : 18 (Intrinsic Value and adjustments of rights)

A Ltd. and B Ltd. amalgamate to form a new Company AB Ltd. as on 31st March, 2005 when their Balance Sheets were as follows :

Liabilities	A Ltd. Rs.	B Ltd. Rs.
9% Preference Share Capital (Shares of Rs. 100 each)	3,50,000	2,50,000
Equity Share Capital (Shares of Rs. 100 each)	7,00,000	3,00,000
Profit & Loss A/c	3,87,000	85,500
General Reserve	—	90,000
6% Debentures	1,80,000	—
Secured Loans	—	1,80,000
Sundry Creditors	90,000	1,90,000
	17,07,000	10,95,500

Assets :	Rs.	Rs.
Goodwill	72,000	
Land & Building	4,00,000	2,80,000
Plant & Machinery	5,50,000	4,50,000
Computers	54,000	30,000
Stock & Stores	2,00,000	1,25,000
Sundry Debtors	2,50,000	1,50,000
Cash at Bank	1,08,000	45,000
Cash in hand	33,000	15,500
Preliminary Expenses	40,000	-
	17,07,000	10,95,500

The terms of amalgamation are as under :

(i) The assumption of liabilities of both companies.

(ii) Issue of 5 preference shares of Rs. 20 each in AB Ltd. Rs. 18 paid up at a premium of Rs. 4 per share for each preference share held in both the companies.

(iii) Issue of 6 equity shares of Rs. 20 each in AB Ltd. Rs. 18 paid up at a premium of Rs. 4 per share for each equity share held in both the companies. In addition, necessary cash should be paid to equity shareholders of both companies as is required to adjust the rights of shareholders of both the companies in accordance with the intrinsic value of shares of both the companies.

(iv) Issue of such amounts of fully paid 7% Debentures in AB Ltd. at a discount of 4% as is sufficient to discharge 6% debentures after takeover.

(v) The assets and liabilities are to be taken at book values except Stock & Debtors on which provision @2% is to be made.

(vi) Sundry debtors of A Ltd. include Rs. 30,000 due from B Ltd.

(vii) AB Ltd. is to issue 10,000 equity shares of Rs. 20 each Rs. 18 paid up at a premium of Rs. 4 per share so as to have sufficient working capital.

Prepare necessary ledger accounts to close the books of A Ltd. & B Ltd. and record journal entries in the books of AB Ltd. and a Balance Sheet as on that date.

[C.A. (F) Modified]

Solution : 18

Calculation of Purchase Consideration

	A Ltd. Rs.	B Ltd. Rs.
Goodwill	72,000	—
Land & Building	4,00,000	2,80,000
Plant & Machinery	5,50,000	4,50,000
Computers	54,000	30,000
Stock & Stores (Less 2%)	1,96,000	1,22,500
Debtors (Less 2%)	2,45,000	1,47,000
Cash at Bank	1,08,000	45,000
Cash in hand	33,000	15,500

Total Assets :	16,58,000	10,90,000
Less Liabilities:		
6% Debentures	(1,80,000)	—
Sundry Creditors	(90,000)	(1,90,000)
Secured Loans		(1,80,000)
Net assets (Purchase Consideration)	13,88,000	7,20,000
*Payable in Shares	13,09,000	6,71,000
Payable in Cash (Balancing figure)	79,000	49,000
* Preference Shares		
3,500 × 5 × 22	3,85,000	—
2,500 × 5 × 22	—	2,75,000
Equity Shares		
7,000 × 6 × 22	9,24,000	
3,000 × 6 × 22	—	3,96,000
	13,09,000	6,71,000

Books of A Ltd.

REALISATION A/C

	Rs.		Rs.
To Goodwill	72,000	By 6% Debentures	1,80,000
To Land & Building	4,00,000	By Sundry Creditors	90,000
To Plant & Machinery	5,50,000	By AB Ltd.	13,88,000
To Computers	54,000	By Equity Shareholders' A/c	44,000
To Stock & Stores	2,00,000	(Loss)	
To Sundry Debtors	2,50,000		
To Cash at Bank	1,08,000		
To Cash in hand	33,000		
To Preference Shareholders' A/c	35,000		
	17,02,000		17,02,000

9% PREFERENCE SHAREHOLDERS' A/C

	Rs.		Rs.
To Preference Shares in AB Ltd.	3,85,000	By Pref. Share Capital A/c	3,50,000
		By Realisation A/c	35,000
	3,85,000		3,85,000

EQUITY SHAREHOLDERS' A/C

	Rs.		Rs.
To Preliminary Expenses	40,000	By Equity Share Capital A/c	7,00,000
To Realisation A/c (Loss)	44,000	By General Reserve	—
To Shares in AB Ltd.	9,24,000	By Profit & Loss A/c	3,87,000
To Bank	79,000		
	10,87,000		10,87,000

AB LTD. A/C

	Rs.		Rs.
To Realisation A/c	13,88,000	By Preference Shares in AB Ltd.	3,85,000
		By Equity Shares in AB Ltd.	9,24,000
		By Bank	79,000
	13,88,000		13,88,000

Books of B Ltd.

REALISATION A/C

	Rs.		Rs.
To Land & Building	2,80,000	By Secured Loans	1,80,000
To Plant & Machinery	4,50,000	By Sundry Creditors	1,90,000
To Computers	30,000	By A B Ltd.	7,20,000
To Stock & Stores	1,25,000	By Equity Shareholders' A/c	30,500
To Debtors	1,50,000		
To Cash at Bank	45,000		
To Cash in hand	15,500		
To Preference Shareholders' A/c	25,000		
	11,20,500		11,20,500

PREFERENCE SHAREHOLDERS' A/C

	Rs.		Rs.
To Preference Shares in AB Ltd.	2,75,000	By Pref. Share Capital	2,50,000
		By Realisation A/c	25,000
	2,75,000		2,75,000

EQUITY SHAREHOLDERS' A/C

	Rs.		Rs.
To Realisation A/c (Loss)	30,500	By Equity Share Capital	3,00,000
To Equity Shares in AB Ltd.	3,96,000	By General Reserve	90,000
To Bank	49,000	By Profit & Loss A/c	85,500
	4,75,500		4,75,500

AB LTD. A/C

	Rs.		Rs.
To Realisation A/c	7,20,000	By Pref. shares in AB Ltd.	2,75,000
		By Equity Shares in AB Ltd.	3,96,000
		By Bank A/c	49,000
	7,20,000		7,20,000

Books of AB Ltd.
JOURNAL ENTRIES

			Rs.	Rs.
	Business Purchase A/c	Dr.	21,08,000	
	To Liquidator of A Ltd.			13,88,000
	To Liquidator of B Ltd.			7,20,000
	(Being purchase consideration settled on acquisition)			
	Goodwill A/c	Dr.	72,000	
	Land & Building A/c	Dr.	6,80,000	
	Plant & Machinery A/c	Dr.	10,00,000	
	Computers A/c	Dr.	84,000	
	Stock & Stores A/c	Dr.	3,18,500	
	Debtors A/c	Dr.	3,92,000	
	Cash at Bank A/c	Dr.	1,53,000	
	Cash in hand A/c	Dr.	48,500	
	To 6% Debentures			1,80,000
	To Secured loans			1,80,000
	To Sundry Creditors			2,70,000
	To Business Purchase A/c			21,08,000
	(Being assets & liabilities of A Ltd. & B Ltd. incorporated)			
	Liquidator of A Ltd. A/c	Dr.	13,88,000	
	Liquidator of B Ltd. A/c	Dr.	7,20,000	
	To Preference Share Capital			5,40,000
	To Equity Share Capital			10,80,000
	To Securities Premium			3,60,000
	To Bank			1,28,000
	(Being purchase consideration discharged)			
	Sundry Creditors A/c	Dr.	30,000	
	To Sundry Debtors			30,000
	(Being Common transactions eliminated)			

Contd.

		Rs.	Rs.
Bank A/c	Dr.	2,20,000	
To Equity Share Application A/c			2,20,000
(Being 10,000 equity shares issued)			
Equity Share Application A/c	Dr.	2,20,000	
To Equity Share Capital			1,80,000
To Securities Premium			40,000
(Being application money transferred to share Capital and Securities Premium A/c)			
6% Debentures A/c	Dr.	1,80,000	
Discount on Issue of Debentures A/c	Dr.	7,500	
To 7% Debentures			1,87,500
(Being 7% Debentures issued at 4% discount to discharge 6% Debentures of A Ltd.)			

BALANCE SHEET OF AB LTD.
As on 1st April, 2005

Liabilities	Rs.	Assets	Rs.
Authorised Capital :		Fixed Assets :	
.... Preference Shares	....	Goodwill	72,000
.... Equity Shares	....	Land & Building	6,80,000
Issued Capital :		Plant & Machinery	10,00,000
30,000 Pref. Shares of Rs. 20 each	6,00,000	Computers	84,000
70,000 Equity Shares of Rs. 20 each	14,00,000	Current Assets :	
30,000 Preference Shares of Rs. 20 each, Rs. 18 paid	5,40,000	Stock & Stores	3,18,500
		Debtors	3,62,000
70,000 Equity Shares of Rs. 20 each, Rs. 18 paid	12,60,000	Cash at Bank*	2,45,000
		Cash-in-hand	48,500
Reserves & Surplus :		Miscellaneous Exp.:	
Securities Premium	4,00,000	Discount on issue of debentures	7,500
Secured Loans :			
7% Debentures	1,87,500		
Secured Loans	1,80,000		
Current liabilities :			
Sundry Creditors	2,50,000		
	28,17,500		28,17,500

*(Rs. 1,53,000 – 1,28,000 + 2,20,000)

Illustration (19) (Purchase Consideration based on Share Value)

Following are the Balance Sheets of Addu Ltd. & Somu Ltd. as on 1st April, 2005.

Liabilities	Addu Ltd. Rs.	Somu Ltd. Rs.
Share Capital		
Shares of Rs. 10 each	4,00,000	6,00,000
Profit & Loss A/c		1,20,000
9% Debentures	1,00,000	
Creditors	2,20,000	1,60,000
	7,20,000	8,80,000
Assets :		
Goodwill	80,000	3,00,000
Fixed Assets	2,40,000	4,00,000
Current Assets	2,80,000	1,00,000
Profit & Loss A/c	1,20,000	80,000
	7,20,000	8,80,000

Somu Ltd. agreed to takeover Addu Ltd. on the following terms :

(i) Shares of Addu Ltd. are considered worth Rs. 7 each and that of Somu Ltd. Rs. 12 each. The Shareholders of Addu Ltd. are to be paid one-quarter in Cash and balance in shares at it's agreed worth.

(ii) The debentureholders of Addu Ltd. agreed to take Rs. 95 of 12% Debentures in Somu Ltd. for every Rs. 100 of 9% Debentures held in Addu Ltd.

(iii) Addu Ltd. is to be wound up.

Pass journal entries in the books of Somu Ltd. and draw up a Balance Sheet after amalgamation. Liquidation expenses amounted to Rs. 5,000 which were paid by Somu Ltd.

Solution : 19

Calculation of Purchase Consideration

40,000 Shares of Addu Ltd. @ Rs. 7 =	2,80,000
Payment in Equity Shares (3/4 of Rs. 2,80,000)	2,10,000
Payment in Cash	70,000
	2,80,000

Somu Ltd. will issue 17,500 Shares (Rs. 2,10,000 ÷ 12) of Rs. 10 each @ Rs. 12 per Share

Books of Somu Ltd.
JOURNAL ENTRIES

			Rs.	Rs.
Business Purchase A/c	Dr.		2,80,000	
To Liquidator of Addu Ltd.				2,80,000
(Being business of Addu Ltd. takenover)				
Goodwill A/c (B. F)	Dr.		75,000	
Fixed Assets A/c	Dr.		2,40,000	
Current Assets A/c	Dr.		2,80,000	
To Creditors				2,20,000
To 9% Debentures				95,000
To Business Purchase A/c				2,80,000
(Being assets & liabilities incorporated)				
Liquidator of Addu Ltd. A/c	Dr.		2,80,000	
To Share Capital				1,75,000
To Securities Premium				35,000
To Bank				70,000
(Being purchase consideration discharged)				
9% Debentures A/c (Addu Ltd.)	Dr.		95,000	
To 12% Debentures A/c (New)				95,000
(Being 9% Debentures redeemed by conversion)				
Liquidation Expenses A/c	Dr.		5,000	
To Bank A/c				5,000
(Being winding up expanses paid)				
Goodwill A/c	Dr.		5,000	
To Liquidation Expenses				5,000
(Being Cost of winding up charged to Goodwill)				

BALANCE SHEET OF SOMU LTD.
As on 1st April, 2005

Liabilities	Rs.	Assets	Rs.
Share Capital		Fixed Assets :	
77,500 Shares of Rs. 10 each.	7,75,000	Goodwill	3,80,000
Reserves & Surplus :		Fixed Assets	6,40,000
Profit & Loss A/c	1,20,000	Current Assets*	3,05,000
Securities Premium	35,000	Miscellaneous Exp.:	
Secured Loans :		Profit & Loss A/c	80,000
12% Debentures	95,000		
Current liabilities :			
Creditors	3,80,000		
	14,05,000		14,05,000

		Rs.	Rs.
	* Current Assets balance		1,00,000
	Transfer from Addu Ltd.		2,80,000
			3,80,000
Less	Expenses	5,000	
	Paid to Addu Ltd.	70,000	75,000
			3,05,000

Illustration (20) (Maintaining Intrinsic Net-worth)

Following are the Balance Sheets of B Ltd. and C Ltd. as on 31st March, 2005.

	B Ltd. Rs.	C Ltd. Rs.
9% Preference Share Capital Shares of Rs. 100 each	—	15,00,000
Equity Share Capital Shares of Rs. 10 each	12,50,000	10,00,000
Reserves & Surplus	50,00,000	37,50,000
Secured Loans	25,00,000	25,00,000
Current Liabilities	2,50,000	2,50,000
	90,00,000	90,00,000
Net Block	37,50,000	37,50,000
Current Assets	52,50,000	52,50,000
	90,00,000	90,00,000

The present worth of "Net Block" of B Ltd. is Rs. 50,00,000 and that of C Ltd. is Rs. 107,25,000 Goodwill of B Ltd. is valued at Rs. 10,00,000 and that of C Ltd. 18,75,000.

C Ltd. absorbs B Ltd. by issuing equity shares **at par** in such a way that intrinsic net worth is maintained. Goodwill is not to appear in the books and the fixed assets are to be shown at pre-amalgamation amount.

Record journal entries in the books of C Ltd. and prepare a Balance Sheet after amalgamation.

[C.A. (F) Adapted]

Solution : 20

Calculation of purchase consideration

		Rs.	Rs.
	Goodwill		10,00,000
	Net Block (Fixed Assets)		50,00,000
	Current Assets		52,50,000
			112,50,000
Less Liabilities :			
	Secured Loans	25,00,000	
	Current liabilities	2,50,000	27,50,000
	Net worth		85,00,000

Intrinsic net worth per share Rs. $\frac{85,00,000}{1,25,000}$ 68

Net Worth of C Ltd.

		Rs.
	Net Block (Fixed Assets)	107,25,000
	Goodwill	18,75,000
	Current Assets	52,50,000
		178,50,000
Less	Liabilities (Secured Loans + Current liabilities)	27,50,000
	Total Net Worth	1,51,00,000
Less	Preference Share Capital	15,00,000
	Net worth of Equity Shares	136,00,000

Intrinsic net worth per share Rs. $\frac{136,00,000}{1,00,000}$ 136

Hence ratio is 1 : 2. The C Ltd. will issue 1 equity share of Rs. 10 each **at par** for every 2 shares held in B Ltd.

Thus the purchase consideration will be Rs.1,25,000 $\times \frac{1}{2}$ = 62,500 shares of Rs. 10 each at par Rs. 6,25,000

JOURNAL ENTRIES

			Rs.	Rs.
	Business Purchase A/c	Dr.	6,25,000	
	To Liquidator of B Ltd.			6,25,000
	(Being business of B Ltd. takenover)			
	Net Block (Fixed Assets) A/c	Dr.	37,50,000	
	Current Assets A/c	Dr.	52,50,000	
	To Current liabilities			2,50,000
	To Secured Loans			25,00,000
	To Business Purchase A/c			6,25,000
	To Capital Reserve (B.F.)			56,25,000
	(Being assets & liabilities of B Ltd. incorporated)			
	Liquidator of B Ltd. A/c	Dr.	6,25,000	
	To Equity Share Capital			6,25,000
	(Being 62,500 shares issued to the liquidator of B Ltd.)			

Note : Since it is decided to show old values of assets and liabilities in the Balance Sheet after amalgamation, the assets & liabilities have not been incorporated as revised values.

However, for the purpose of determining the exchange ratio on the basic of intrinsic values of equity shares of respective Companies the revised values have been accounted for the purpose.

BALANCE SHEET OF C LTD.
As on 31st March, 2005

Liabilities	Rs.	Assets	Rs.
Share Capital :		Net Block	75,00,000
9% Preference Share Capital	15,00,000	Current Assets	105,00,000
Shares of Rs. 100 each			
Equity share Capital			
1,62,500 Shares of Rs. 10 each	16,25,000		
Reserves & Surplus :			
Capital Reserve	56,25,000		
Other Reserves	37,50,000		
Secured Loan	50,00,000		
Current liabilities	5,00,000		
	180,00,000		180,00,000

Illustration (21) (Share Exchange at premium)

X Ltd. and Y Ltd. are to be amalgamated into XY Ltd. which will takeover the assets and liabilities of both the companies.

Assets and liabilities of X Ltd. are to be takenover at book values in exchange of shares in XY Ltd. Three shares in the new company are to be issued at a premium of 20% for every two shares of X Ltd. The consideration for Y Ltd. was agreed as follows :

(i) 11% Preference Shareholders are to be allotted three 12% Preference Shares of Rs. 100 each in XY Ltd. for four Preference Shares held in Y Ltd.

(ii) The debentures of Y Ltd. are to be paid off by the issue of same number of debentures at 5% discount by XY Ltd.

(iii) The Equity Shareholders of Y Ltd. are to be allotted as many shares in XY Ltd. as will cover the balance on their account and for this purpose plant & machinery to be valued at 10% less and obsolete stock forming 10% of overall stock value is to be treated as worth less.

The Balance Sheets of X Ltd. & Y Ltd. as on 1st April, 2005 were as under :

Liabilities	X Ltd. Rs.	Y Ltd. Rs.
Share Capital :		
11% Preference Share Capital	—	5,00,000
Shares of Rs. 100 each		
Equity Share Capital	4,50,000	9,00,000
Shares of Rs. 10 each		
9% Debentures	—	4,00,000
General Reserve	6,00,000	—
Sundry Creditors	50,000	1,00,000
	11,00,000	19,00,000

Assets :	Rs.	Rs.
Plant & Machinery	8,50,000	13,50,000
Stock	70,000	1,00,000
Sundry Debtors	1,00,000	90,000
Cash & Bank balance	80,000	60,000
Profit & Loss A/c	—	3,00,000
	11,00,000	19,00,000

Pass journal entries in the books of XY Ltd. and prepare Balance Sheet after amalgamation.

[ICWA (F) Adopted]

Solution : 21

Calculation of Purchase Consideration

For X Ltd.

		Rs.
45,000 Shares $\times \frac{3}{2}$ @ Rs. 12		8,10,000
67,500 Shares of Rs. 10 each at a premium of Rs. 2 per share.		

For Y Ltd.

			Rs.
	Plant & Machinery (13,50,000 – 10%)		12,15,000
	Stock Less 10%		90,000
	Debtors		90,000
	Cash & Bank balance		60,000
			14,55,000
Less	Liabilities :		
	Sundry Creditors	1,00,000	
	Debentures at 5% discount	3,80,000	4,80,000
	Purchase Consideration		9,75,000

Mode of payment

Preference Shares $\left(5{,}000 \times \frac{3}{4}\right)$ Rs. 100 =	3,75,000
Equity Shares (Balancing figure)	6,00,000
(6,00,000/12) 50,000 Shares	9,75,000

Thus XY Ltd. will issue 1,17,500(67,500 + 50,000) Equity Shares of Rs. 10 each at 20% premium and 3,750 Preference shares of Rs. 100 each at par.

Books of XY Ltd.
JOURNAL ENTRIES

			Rs.	Rs.
	Business Purchase A/c	Dr.	17,85,000	
	To Liquidator of X Ltd.			8,10,000
	To Liquidator of Y Ltd.			9,75,000
	(Being purchase consideration due to liquidators on takeover)			*Contd.*

		Rs.	Rs.
Plant & Machinery A/c	Dr.	20,65,000	
Stock A/c	Dr.	1,60,000	
Debtors A/c	Dr.	1,90,000	
Cash & bank balance A/c	Dr.	1,40,000	
To Sundry Creditors			1,50,000
To 9% Debentures			3,80,000
To Business Purchase A/c			17,85,000
To Capital Reserve (B.F.)			2,40,000
(Being assets & liabilities incorporated)			
Liquidator of X Ltd.	Dr.	8,10,000	
Liquidator of Y Ltd.	Dr.	9,75,000	
To Equity Share Capital			11,75,000
To Securities Premium			2,35,000
To Preference Share Capital			3,75,000
(Being 1,17,500 Equity Shares @ Rs. 12 per share and preference shares @ Rs. 100 were allotted to liquidators of X Ltd. & Y Ltd.			
9% Debentures (Y Ltd.) A/c	Dr.	3,80,000	
Discount on Issue of debentures		20,000	
To 9% Debentures (New)			4,00,000
(Being new debentures issued)			

BALANCE SHEET OF XY LTD.
As on 1st April 2005

Liabilities	Rs.	Assets	Rs.
Share Capital :		**Fixed Assets :**	
12% Preference Share Capital	3,75,000	Plant & Machinery	20,65,000
(Shares of Rs. 100 each)		**Current Assets :**	
Equity Share Capital	11,75,000	Stock	1,60,000
1,17,500 shares of Rs. 10 each		Debtors	1,90,000
Reserve & Surplus :		Cash & bank balance	1,40,000
Capital Reserve	2,40,000	**Miscellaneous Expenditure :**	
Securities Premium	2,35,000	Discount on issue of Debentures	20,000
Secured Loans :			
9% Debentures	4,00,000		
Current liabilities :			
Sundry Creditors	1,50,000		
	25,75,000		25,75,000

Illustration (22) (Valuation of goodwill)

S Ltd. was formed on 1st January, 2005 with an Authorised Capital of Rs. 50,00,000 divided in to equity shares of Rs. 10 each. On 1st April, 2005 the Company issued for cash 1,00,000 equity shares at a premium of Rs. 2 per share. On the same date S Ltd. agreed to buy the assets including goodwill and assume the liabilities of T Ltd. & R Ltd. for a total of 4,00,000 shares.

For the purpose of determining the premium at which the shares of S Ltd. were to be issued, the fixed assets, current assets and liabilities are to be taken at book values and goodwill is to be determined on the basis of two times of super profits. The NRR is 10%. The profits for the last three years are as under :

	T Ltd.	R Ltd.
Year ending 31st March, 2003	3,50,000	2,85,500
Year ending 31st March, 2004	4,15,000	3,05,000
Year ending 31st March, 2005	4,20,000	3,24,500

Whereas their summarised Balance Sheets were as follows :

Liabilities	T Ltd. Rs.	R Ltd. Rs.
Equity Share Capital	15,50,000	16,75,000
Shares of Rs. 10 each		
Profit & Loss Account	9,50,000	75,000
Sundry Creditors	10,00,000	27,50,000
	35,00,000	45,00,000
Assets :		
Fixed Assets	22,50,000	14,50,000
Current Assets	12,50,000	30,50,000
	35,00,000	45,00,000

You are required to calculate the number of shares to be issued by S Ltd. to the shareholders of T Ltd. and R Ltd. respectively and prepare a Balance Sheet of S Ltd.

[ICWA (F) Adopted]

Solution :

Computation of Goodwill

	T Ltd.	R Ltd.
Fixed Assets	22,50,000	14,50,000
Current Assets	12,50,000	30,50,000
	35,00,000	45,00,000
Less Sundry Creditors	10,00,000	27,50,000
Net Assets (Capital Employed)	25,00,000	17,50,000
Normal Profits (10% of Capital employed)	2,50,000	1,75,000
Average profits of last three years	3,95,000	3,05,000
Super profits*	1,45,000	1,30,000
Goodwill (2 times of super profit)	= 2,90,000	2,60,000

*Actual (Average) Profits – Normal Profits)

Calculation of Purchase Consideration

	T Ltd.	R Ltd.
	Rs.	Rs.
Net assets before Goodwill	25,00,000	17,50,000
Add Goodwill	2,90,000	2,60,000
Total Net assets	2,7,90,000	20,10,000
Intrinsic Value per Share	18 :	12
(Net assets divided by No. of Shares)		

Since S Ltd. is issuing shares at a premium of Rs. 2 per share the ratio of exchange will be :

T Ltd.	R Ltd.
18 : 12	12 : 12
3 : 2	1 : 1

S Ltd. will issue 3 shares for every 2 shares held in T Ltd. and one share for every one share held in R Ltd.

Thus shareholders of T Ltd. will get 1,55,000 shares $\times \frac{3}{2}$ =	2,32,500	shares
and that of R Ltd.	1,67,500	Shares
Total	4,00,000	Shares

BALANCE SHEET
As on 1st April, 2005

Liabilities	Rs.	Assets	Rs.
Authorised Capital :		**Fixed Assets :**	
5,00,000 Equity Shares of		Goodwill	5,50,000
Rs. 10 each	50,00,000	Other fixed assets	37,00,000
Issued & Subscribed Capital	50,00,000	**Current Assets :**	
5,00,000* Shares of Rs. 10 each		Cash at Bank (1)	12,00,000
Reserves & Surplus :		Other Current Assets	43,00,000
Securities Premium (2)	10,00,000		
Current liabilities & Provisions :			
Sundry Creditors	37,50,000		
	97,50,000		97,50,000

Working note:

(1) 1,00,000 Shares have been issued for Cash @ Rs. 12 each.

(2) Securities premium @ 2 per share on 5,00,000 share.

* Total Shares issued 5,00,000 (*i.e.* 1,00,000 + 4,00,000)

Illustration (23)

(Commission on realisation of debtors & payment to creditors)

X Ltd. a newly formed Company took over the business of Y Ltd. with effect from 1st April, 2005. On 31st March, 2005 the Balance Sheet of Y Ltd. was as follows :

Liabilities	Rs.	Assets	Rs.
Share Capital		Fixed Assets	11,80,000
50,000 Equity Shares of Rs. 10 each	5,00,000	Current Assets :	
Loan Creditor	6,00,000	Stock	70,000
Trade Creditors	3,60,000	Debtors	2,10,000
	14,60,000		14,60,000

X Ltd. tookover the business of Y Ltd. on the following terms:

(i) Fixed assets to be taken over at 90% of their book values.

(ii) Stock be valued at Rs. 58,000

(iii) The X Ltd. would realise Trade debtors and pay Trade creditors on behalf of Y Ltd. for a commission @ 3% on the amount collected and 2% on the amount paid.

X Ltd. realised Rs. 1,90,000 from debtors as the agent of vendor in full settlement and discharged all the Trade Creditors by paying Rs. 3,40,000 only. Necessary bank over draft was arranged.

The Loan Creditor accepted from X Ltd. fully paid 12% Preference Shares of Rs. 100 each at 20% premium in full settlement of claim.

After realisation of debtors and payment of liabilities, the amount due to Y Ltd. was discharged by allotment of 35,000 fully paid equity shares of Rs. 10 each at par and the balance was paid in cash.

Pass journal entries and prepare a Balance Sheet of X Ltd.

[C.S. (I) Modified]

Solution : 23

Calculation of Purchase Consideration

		Rs.	Rs.
	Fixed Assets	11,80,000	
Less	10%	1,18,000	10,62,000
	Current Assets (Stock)		58,000
			11,20,000
Less	Loan Creditor		6,00,000
	Purchase Consideration		5,20,000

JOURNAL ENTRIES

			Rs.	Rs.
	Business Purchase A/c	Dr.	5,20,000	
	To Liquidator of Y Ltd.			5,20,000
	(Being business of Y Ltd. acquired)			
	Fixed Assets A/c	Dr.	10,62,000	
	Stock A/c	Dr.	58,000	
	To Loan Creditor A/c			6,00,000
	To Business Purchase A/c			5,20,000
	(Being assets and liabilities of Y Ltd. incorporated)			
	Vendor's Debtors A/c	Dr.	2,10,000	
	Vendor's A/c	Dr.	1,50,000	
	To Vendor's Creditors A/c			3,60,000
	(Being debtors and creditors of Vendors to be realised and paid on its behalf)			
	Bank A/c	Dr.	1,90,000	
	Vendor's A/c (B.F)	Dr.	20,000	
	To Vendor's Debtors A/c			2,10,000
	(Being Vendor's debtors realised)			
	Vendor's Creditors A/c	Dr.	3,60,000	
	To Bank A/c			3,40,000
	To Vendor's A/c			20,000
	(Being Vendor's Creditors paid off)			
	Vendor's A/c	Dr.	12,500	
	To Commission A/c			12,500
	(Being Commission due)			
	Loan Creditor A/c	Dr.	6,00,000	
	To 12% Preference Share Capital			5,00,000
	To Securities Premium A/c			1,00,000
	(Being preference shares issued to loan creditor)			
	Liquidator of Y Ltd.	Dr.	5,20,000	
	To Vendor's A/c*			1,62,500
	To Share Capital A/c			3,50,000
	To Bank A/c			7,500
	(Being purchase consideration settled)			
	Commission A/c	Dr.	12,500	
	To P & L A/c			12,500
	(Being Commission transferred to P & L A/c)			

VENDOR'S A/C

	Rs.		Rs.
To Vendor's Creditors	3,60,000	By Vendor's Debtors	2,10,000
To Vendor's Debtors (Loss)	20,000	By Vendor's Creditors (Gain)	20,000
To Commission	12,500	By Liquidator's A/c (Bal. figure)	1,62,500
	3,92,500		3,92,500

BANK A/C

	Rs.		Rs.
To Vendor's Debtors	1,90,000	By Vendor's Creditors	3,40,000
To Balance c/d (Overdraft)	1,57,500	By Liquidators A/c	7,500
	3,47,500		3,47,500

BALANCE SHEET OF X LTD.
As on 1st April, 2005

Liabilities	Rs.	Assets	Rs.
Authorised Capital	....	Fixed Assets	10,62,000
Issued & Subscribed Capital		Stock	58,000
35,000 Shares of Rs. 10 each	3,50,000		
12% 5,000 Preference Share Capital	5,00,000		
Securities Premium	1,00,000		
Profit & Loss A/c (Commission)	12,500		
Bank Overdraft	1,57,500		
	11,20,000		11,20,000

Illustration (24) (Payment of Dividend before absorption)

The Balance Sheets of X Ltd. and Y Ltd. as on 31st March, 2004 were as under :

Liabilities	X Ltd.	Y Ltd.
Share Capital	Rs.	Rs.
Authorised Capital		
Equity Shares of Rs. 100 each	60,00,000	20,00,000
Issued & Subscribed Capital		
Shares of Rs. 100 each fully paid	60,00,000	20,00,000
Reserves & Surplus		
General Reserve	8,00,000	1,00,000
Capital Reserve	—	2,00,000
Profit & Loss Account	4,80,000	1,40,000
Unsecured Loans :		
12% Debentures	—	12,00,000

Current Liabilities & Provisions :		
S. Creditors	9,60,000	3,80,000
	82,40,000	40,20,000
Fixed Assets :		
Goodwill		4,00,000
Fixed Assets		
Building	20,00,000	—
Machineries	26,00,000	16,80,000
Furniture	40,000	20,000
Current Assets :		
Stock	16,00,000	7,20,000
Debtors	9,20,000	7,20,000
Cash in hand	2,80,000	20,000
Bank balance	8,00,000	1,60,000
Expenditure on New Project	—	3,00,000
	82,40,000	40,20,000

Y Ltd. was absorbed by X Ltd. on 1st April 2005 on the following terms :

(i) Fixed assets other than Goodwill to be valued at Rs. 20,00,000 including Rs. 24,000 for furniture.

(ii) Stock to be reduced by Rs. 80,000 and Debtors by 5%.

(iii) X Ltd. to assume liabilities and to discharge the 12% Debentures by issue of 11% Debentures of the same value and in addition a premium of 6% was paid in cash.

(iv) The New project to be valued at Rs. 3,80,000.

(v) The Shareholders of Y Ltd. to receive cash payment of Rs. 30 per share plus four equity shares in X Ltd. for every five shares held in Y Ltd.

(vi) Both the companies to declare and pay dividend of 6% prior to absorption.

(vii) Expenses of liquidation of Y Ltd. are to be reimbursed by X Ltd. to the extent of Rs. 20,000. The actual expenses amounted to Rs. 24,000.

Draft journal entries recording the scheme in the books of Y Ltd. and give opening entries and a Balance Sheet of X Ltd. after absorption.

[C.A. (I) Modified]

Solution :

Books of Y Ltd.
JOURNAL ENTRIES

			Rs.	Rs.
	Profit & Loss A/c	Dr.	1,20,000	
	To Dividend Payable A/c			1,20,000
	(Being dividend declared @ 6%)			
	Dividend Payable A/c	Dr.	1,20,000	
	To Bank A/c			1,20,000
	(Being dividend paid)			

Contd.

Particulars		Dr. (Rs.)	Cr. (Rs.)
Realisation A/c	Dr.	38,96,000	
To Goodwill			4,00,000
To Machineries			16,80,000
To Furniture			20,000
To Stock			7,20,000
To Debtors			7,20,000
To Cash in hand			*16,000
To Bank			40,000
To Expenditure on New Project			3,00,000
(Being assets transferred to Realisation A/c)			
S. Creditors A/c	Dr.	3,80,000	
12% Debentures A/c	Dr.	12,00,000	
To Realisation A/c			15,80,000
(Being liabilities transferred)			
X Ltd. A/c*	Dr.	22,00,000	
To Realisation A/c			22,00,000
(Being purchase consideration due)			
X Ltd. A/c	Dr.	20,000	
Realisation A/c	Dr.	4,000	
To Bank A/c			24,000
(Being realisation expenses paid)			
Bank A/c	Dr.	20,000	
To X Ltd.			20,000
(Being realisation expenses reimbursed by X Ltd.)			
Shareholders' A/c	Dr.	1,20,000	
To Realisation A/c			1,20,000
(Being loss on realisation transferred to shareholders A/c)			
Equity Shares in X Ltd. A/c	Dr.	16,00,000	
Bank A/c	Dr.	6,00,000	
To X Ltd.			22,00,000
(Being purchase consideration received)			
Equity Share Capital A/c	Dr.	20,00,000	
Capital Reserve A/c	Dr.	2,00,000	
General Reserve A/c	Dr.	1,00,000	
Profit & Loss A/c	Dr.	20,000	
To Equity Shareholders' A/c			23,20,000
(Being amount due to equity shareholders transferred to their Account)			

Contd.

Equity Shareholders' A/c	Dr.		22,00,000	
To Equity Shares in X Ltd.				16,00,000
To Bank A/c				6,00,000
(Being Shareholders' paid off)				

Calculation of Purchase Consideration*

	Rs.
Cash 20,000 Shares @ Rs. 30 each	6,00,000
Equity Shares	16,00,000
	22,00,000

Books of X Ltd.
JOURNAL ENTRIES

			Rs.	Rs.
	Business Purchase A/c	Dr.	22,00,000	
	To Liquidator of Y Ltd.			22,00,000
	(Being business of Y Ltd. takenover)			
	Goodwill A/c (Balancing Figure)	Dr.	92,000	
	Machineries A/c	Dr.	19,76,000	
	Furniture A/c	Dr.	24,000	
	Stock A/c	Dr.	6,40,000	
	Debtors A/c	Dr.	6,84,000	
	Cash in hand A/c	Dr.	16,000	
	Cash at Bank A/c	Dr.	40,000	
	New Project A/c	Dr.	3,80,000	
	To 12% Debentures			12,72,000
	To Sundry Creditors			3,80,000
	To Business Purchase A/c			22,00,000
	(Being assets and liabilities of Y Ltd. incorporated)			
	Liquidator of Y Ltd. A/c	Dr.	22,00,000	
	To Share Capital A/c			16,00,000
	To Bank A/c			6,00,000
	(Being purchase consideration discharged)			
	12% Debentures A/c	Dr.	12,72,000	
	To 11% Debentures A/c			12,00,000
	To Bank A/c			72,000
	(Being 12% debentures discharged)			
	Goodwill A/c		20,000	
	To Bank			20,000
	(Being liquidation expenses paid)			

Contd.

Profit and Loss A/c	Dr.	3,60,000	
To Dividend Payable A/c			3,60,000
(Being dividend provided)			
Dividend Payable A/c		3,60,000	
To Bank A/c			3,60,000
Being Dividend paid)			

BALANCE SHEET OF X LTD.
As on 1st April 2005

Liabilities	Rs.	Assets	Rs.
Share Capital :		Fixed Assets :	
Authorised Share Capital		Goodwill	1,12,000
80,000 Equity Shares	80,00,000	Building	20,00,000
of Rs. 100 each		Machineries	45,76,000
Issued & Subscribed Capital		Furniture	64,000
76,000 Equity Shares		Capital Work in Progress	3,80,000
of Rs. 100 each	76,00,000	Current Assets :	
Reserves & Surplus :		Stock	22,40,000
General Reserve	8,00,000	Debtors	16,04,000
Profit & Loss A/c	1,20,000	Cash at Bank*	40,000
Secured Loans :		Cash in hand*	44,000
11% Debentures	12,00,000		
Current liabilities & Provisions :			
Sundry Creditors	13,40,000		
	1,10,60,000		1,10,60,000

***BANK A/C**

	Rs.		Rs.
To Balance b/d	8,00,000	By Dividend	3,60,000
To Cash A/c (Shortfall)	2,52,000	By Liquidator of Y Ltd.	6,00,000
(deposited)		By Debentureholders	72,000
To Y Ltd.	40,000	By Realisation Expenses	20,000
		By Balance c/d	40,000
	10,92,000		10,92,000

***CASH IN HAND**

	Rs.		Rs.
To Balance b/d	2,80,000	By Bank (Transfer)	2,52,000
To Y Ltd.	16,000	By Balance c/d	44,000
	2,96,000		2,96,000

Illustration (25)

(Adjustment of depreciation and computation of Goodwill)

XYZ Ltd. was formed to takeover X Ltd. , Y Ltd. and Z Ltd. on the basis of their respective Balance Sheets as on 1st April, 2005 subject to the following terms :

(a) Goodwill is to be valued at three years' purchase of average super profit of last three years. Such average is to be calculated after adjustment of depreciation at 10% on the amount of increase/decrease on the revaluation of fixed assets.

(b) Assets are to be revalued as under :

	X Ltd.	Y Ltd.	Z Ltd.
	Rs.	Rs.	Rs.
Tangible Fixed Assets	10,00,000	5,00,000	6,00,000
Current Assets	3,50,000	1,40,000	80,000
(c) The average profit for three years are :	1,60,000	1,50,000	70,000

(d) Normal profits on Capital employed to be taken at 10% Capital employed being considered on the basis of revaluation amount of assets.

(e) Equity shares of Rs. 10 each fully paid up in XYZ Ltd. are to be distributed in the ratio of average profits after adjustment of depreciation on the revalued assets.

(f) XYZ Ltd. will issue equity shares and debentures in the ratio of 3:1.

(g) 10% Debentures of Rs. 100 each fully paid are to be issued by XYZ Ltd. for the balance due.

The summarised Balance Sheets of X Ltd., Y Ltd. & Z Ltd. were as under :

Assets :	X Ltd.	Y Ltd.	Z Ltd.
	Rs.	Rs.	Rs.
Net Tangible Fixed Assets	8,00,000	6,00,000	5,00,000
Goodwill	—	50,000	—
Current Assets	3,00,000	2,50,000	1,00,000
	11,00,000	9,00,000	6,00,000
Liabilities :			
Equity Shares of Rs. 10 each	6,00,000	7,00,000	3,00,000
Reserves & Surplus	1,00,000	50,000	1,00,000
10% Debentures	2,00,000	—	1,00,000
Trade Creditors	2,00,000	1,50,000	1,00,000
	11,00,000	9,00,000	6,00,000

You are required to :

(i) Calculate number of equity shares and debentures to be issued to each company.

(ii) Prepare a Balance Sheet of XYZ Ltd. immediately after amalgamation assuming that amounts required for Preliminary Expenses of Rs. 50,000 and payment to existing debentures was provided by issue of equity shares of Rs. 10 each.

[ICWA (F) Adapted]

Solution :

(i) Computation of Capital Employed and Normal profit.

	X Ltd.	Y Ltd.	Z Ltd.
	Rs.	Rs.	Rs.
Net Tangible Fixed Assets	10,00,000	5,00,000	6,00,000
Currents Assets	3,50,000	1,40,000	80,000
	13,50,000	6,40,000	6,80,000
Less Liabilities			
(Creditors & Debentures)	4,00,000	1,50,000	2,00,000
Net Assets (Capital employed)	9,50,000	4,90,000	4,80,000
*Normal profit @10% of Capital employed.	95,000	49,000	48,000

(ii) Calculation of Goodwill

	X Ltd.	Y Ltd.	Z Ltd.
	Rs.	Rs.	Rs.
Average Profits	1,60,000	1,50,000	70,000
Adjustment for Depreciation on increase/decrease of Fixed Assets	(– 20,000)	+10,000	(– 10,000)
	1,40,000	1,60,000	60,000
Less *Normal Profits	95,000	49,000	48,000
Super profits	45,000	1,11,000	12,000
Goodwill at 3 Year's Purchase	1,35,000	3,33,000	36,000

(iii) Calculation of Purchase Consideration

	X Ltd.	Y Ltd.	Z Ltd.
Net Assets + Goodwill =	10,85,000	8,23,000	5,16,000
Purchase consideration in the form of Equity Shares (in the ratio of 14 : 16 : 6 *i.e.* Adjusted Profits)	7,07,000	8,08,000	3,03,000
10% Debentures (bal. fig.)	3,78,000	15,000	2,13,000
No. of Equity Shares	70,700	80,800	30,3000
No. of Debentures	3,780	150	2,130

Total Purchase Consideration :	Rs.
X Ltd.	10,85,000
Y Ltd.	8,23,000
Z Ltd.	5,16,000
	24,24,000
To be discharged in Equity Shares $\left(24,24,000 \times \frac{3}{4}\right)$	18,18,000
To be paid in Debentures $\left(24,24,000 \times \frac{1}{4}\right)$	6,06,000

As per the terms of amalgamation the Equity Shares are to be issued in the ratio of average adjusted profits which are in the ratio of 14: 16 : 6 or 7 : 8 : 3 and the balance has been paid in debentures.

(iv) Total Share Capital :

	Rs.
Issued to Liquidators	18,18,000
Issued to redeem Debentures of Rs. 3,00,000 and to pay preliminary expenses of Rs. 50,000	3,50,000
	21,68,000

BALANCE SHEET OF XYZ

As on 31st March, 2005

Liabilities	Rs.	Assets	Rs.
Share Capital :		Fixed Assets	
2,16,800 Shares of Rs. 10 each	21,68,000	Goodwill	5,04,000
Secured Loans :		T. Fixed Assets	21,00,000
12% Debentures	6,06,000	Current Assets	5,70,000
Current Liabilities		**Miscell. Expenditure**	
Trade Creditors	4,50,000	Preliminary Expenses	50,000
	32,24,000		32,24,000

Illustration (26)

(Dividend and Estimated Profits)

The Balance Sheets of P Ltd. and Q Ltd. as on 30th September 2004 were as follows :

Liabilities	P Ltd. Rs.	Q Ltd. Rs.
Share Capital		
Equity Shares of Rs. 100 each	10,00,000	6,00,000
Reserve	80,000	40,000
Profit & Loss A/c	1,20,000	80,000
Sundry Creditors	1,00,000	60,000
	13,00,000	7,80,000
Assets :		
Fixed Assets	6,00,000	4,00,000
Stock	1,60,000	1,20,000
Debtors	2,80,000	1,80,000
Cash & Bank	2,40,000	70,000
Miscellaneous Expenditure	20,000	10,000
	13,00,000	7,80,000

Q Ltd. was taken over by P Ltd. as on 1st January 2005. No Balance Sheets of the companies were prepared as at that date. But it is estimated that Q Ltd. made a profit of Rs. 50,000 in the period, after charging 10% per annum depreciation on fixed assets. Profits of P Ltd. during that period on the same basis were Rs. 90,000.

Both the companies declared and paid a dividend of 10% of their Capital in November 2004. Purchase consideration is to be satisfied by issue of fully paid shares by P Ltd. at par after revaluing goodwill and fixed assets of Q Ltd. at Rs. 40,000 (book value- Nil) and at a premium of Rs. 30,000 over book value respectively.

Record entries and prepare a Balance Sheet of P Ltd. after absorption of Q Ltd.

[ICWA (F) Modified]

Solution : 26

Calculation of Purchase Consideration

		Rs.
	Goodwill	40,000
	Fixed Assets	4,30,000
	Stock	1,20,000
	Debtors	1,80,000
	Cash and bank after dividend & Profits for* three month (70,000 – 60,000 + 50,000)	60,000
		8,30,000
Less	Liabilities (creditors)	60,000
		7,70,000

P Ltd. will issue 7,700 share of Rs. 100 each.

* Presumed to be realised in Cash.

BALANCE SHEET OF P LTD.
As on 1st January, 2005

Liabilities	Rs.	Assets	Rs.
Share Capital:		Goodwill	40,000
17,700 shares of Rs. 100 each.	17,70,000	Fixed Assets (2)	10,05,000
Reserves & Surplus		**Current Assets**	
General Reserve	80,000	Stock	2,80,000
Profit & Loss A/c (1)	1,10,000	Debtors	4,60,000
Current liabilities		Cash & Bank (3)	3,15,000
Sundry Creditors	1,60,000	Miscellenious Expenditure	20,000
	21,20,000		21,20,000

Working notes :

(1) **PROFIT & LOSS A/C**

	Rs.		Rs.
To Dividend	1,00,000	By Balance b/d	1,20,000
To Balance c/d	1,10,000	By Profits for 3 months	90,000
	2,10,000		2,10,000

(2) **FIXED ASSETS A/C**

	Rs.		Rs.
To Balance b/d	6,00,000	By Depreciation* for three months	25,000
To Q Ltd.	4,30,000	(15,000 + 10,000)	
		By Balance c/d	10,05,000
	10,30,000		10,30,000

On Rs. 6,00,000 & Rs. 4,00,000 respectively.

(3) **CASH & BANK**

	Rs.		Rs.
To Balance b/d	2,40,000	By Dividend	1,00,000
To Net Profit before depreciation (90,000 + 15,000)	1,05,000	By Balance c/d	3,15,000
To Q Ltd.	70,000		
	4,15,000		4,15,000

Illustration (27) (Share Fractions and Profit Adjustments)

A Ltd. agreed to absorb the business of B Ltd. as on 31st March 2005. On that date the Balance Sheet of B Ltd. was as under:

Liabilities	Rs.	Assets	Rs.
Share Capital		Goodwill	75,000
45,000 Shares of Rs. 10 each	4,50,000	Other Fixed Assets	4,80,000
General Reserve	1,20,000	Stock	1,26,000
Profit & Loss A/c	90,000	Debtors	27,000
6% Debentures	75,000	Cash & Bank balance	42,000
Creditors	15,000		
	7,50,000		7,50,000

The debentureholders agreed to receive such 9% Debentures issued at Rs. 90 each as would discharge the debentures in B Ltd. at a premium of 20%. The shareholders in B Ltd. were to receive Rs. 2.50 in cash per share and 3 shares in A Ltd. for 2 shares held. The shares of A Ltd. were quoted in market at Rs. 12.50 each. There were fractions equal to 60 shares for which cash was paid. The directors of A Ltd. valued assets as follows :

	Rs.
Fixed Assets	9,00,000
Stock	1,20,000
Debtors	27,000

A Ltd. paid the cost of liquidation of B Ltd. amounting to Rs. 5,000. Due to certain unavoidable circumstances the deal could be completed only on 30th June 2005 during which B Ltd. earned a profit of Rs. 30,000 after providing Rs. 10,000 as depreciation. There was no change in the fixed assets. However the changes in the current assets and current liabilities were as follows :

	Rs.
Stock	1,45,000
Debtors	37,500
Creditors	22,500

Cash & Bank balance could not be ascertained. Prepare Realisation A/c and Shareholders' A/c in the books of B Ltd. and pass journal entries in the books of A Ltd.

[C.A. (F) Adapted]

Solution : 27

(1) Calculation of Purchase Consideration :

Cash 45,000 Shares @ Rs. 2.50	1,12,500
Equity Shares $\left(45{,}000 \times \frac{3}{2}\right)$ = 67,500 – 60 = 67,440 @ Rs. 10 each	6,74,400
Cash to deal with fractions 60 shares @ Rs.12.50	750
	7,87,650

Note : In the absence of any specific instructions, the phrase "quoted" has no relevance but for fractions of shares whose value has to be paid in cash.

Books of B Ltd.
REALISATION A/C

	Rs.		Rs.
To Goodwill	75,000	By Creditors*	22,500
To Fixed Assets	4,80,000	By 6% Debentures	75,000
To Stock*	1,45,000	By A Ltd.	7,87,650
To Debtors*	37,500	By Provision for Depreciation	10,000
To Cash & Bank[(1)]*	60,000		
To Shareholders A/c (Profit)	97,650		
	8,95,150		8,95,150

SHAREHOLDERS' A/C

	Rs.		Rs.
To Shares in A Ltd.	6,74,400	By Share Capital	4,50,000
To Cash (1,12,500 + 750)	1,13,250	By General Reserve	1,20,000
		By Profit & Loss A/c**	1,20,000
		By Realisation A/c	97,650
	7,87,650		7,87,650

* Figures as on 30th June, 2005 after changes.

** Including profit earned during 1.4.2005 to 30th June, 2005.

				Rs.
(1)	Cash & Bank Balance as on 31.3.2005			42,000
Add	Cash from operations : (In flow)			
	Net Profit		30,000	
	Depreciation (A Non Cash charge)		10,000	40,000
				82,000
Less	Increase in working Capital (outflow).			
	Stock	19,000		
	Debtors	10,500	29,500	
	Increase in creditors		– 7,500	22,000
				60,000

Books of A Ltd.
JOURNAL ENTRIES

			Rs.	Rs.
	Business Purchase A/c	Dr.	7,87,650	
	To Liquidator of B Ltd.			7,87,650
	(Being business of B Ltd. takenover)			
	Fixed Assets A/c	Dr.	9,00,000	
	Stock A/c (Less fall on revaluation)	Dr.	1,39,000[(2)]	
	Debtors A/c	Dr.	37,500	
	Cash & bank balance A/c	Dr.	60,000	
	To Provision for Depreciation			10,000
	To Creditors			22,500
	To 6% Debentures			90,000
	To Business Purchase A/c			7,87,650
	To Capital Reserve (Bal. fig.)			2,26,350
	(Being assets and liabilities of B Ltd. incorporated)			
	Liquidator of B Ltd. A/c	Dr.	7,87,650	
	To Share Capital			6,74,400
	To Bank			1,13,250
	(Being purchase consideration discharged)			
	6% Debentures A/c	Dr.	90,000	
	Discount on Issue of debentures A/c	Dr.	10,000	
	To 9% Debentures			1,00,000
	(Being 6% debentures discharged)			
	Capital Reserve A/c	Dr.	5,000	
	To Bank			5,000
	(Being liquidation expenses charged to capital Reserve)			

Working note :

(2) It is assumed that reduction in value still applies, because stock has been taken at Rs. 1,39,000 which is Rs. 6,000 less than the value of Stock given on 30th June 2005. This is due to adjustment of loss on earlier revaluation on 1st April 2005 when stock stood at Rs. 1,26,000 was valued at Rs. 1,20,000.

(3) There has been no change in the value of Debtors on revaluation.

(4) Changes in current assets and current liabilities are worked out as under:

Book Values

	As on 31.3.2005	As on 30.6.2005	+/– in W.C
Stock	1,26,000	1,45,000	+19,000
Debtors	27,000	37,500	+10,500
			29,500
Creditors	15,000	22,500	– 7,500
Net increase in working Capital or (out flow)			22,000

Illustration (28) (Miscellaneous)

A One Ltd. was formed to takeover the assets and liabilities of B. Gone Ltd. as on 1st April, 2005 when it's Balance Sheet was as under :

BALANCE SHEET OF B. GONE LTD.

Liabilities	Rs.	Assets	Rs.
Share Capital :		Goodwill	1,00,000
10,000 Equity Shares of Rs. 100 each	10,00,000	Land & Building	3,00,000
9% 6,000 Preference shares		Plant & Machinery	4,00,000
of Rs. 100 each	6,00,000	Furniture	50,000
10% Debentures of Rs. 100 each	4,00,000	Patents	1,00,000
Unsecured Loan	2,00,000	Investments	2,00,000
Sundry Creditors	1,00,000	Stock	2,00,000
		Debtors	1,50,000
		Cash at Bank	50,000
		Profit & Loss A/c	6,50,000
		Preliminary Expenses	1,00,000
	23,00,000		23,00,000

Dividend on preference shares are in arrears for two years and interest on debentures has not been paid for last two years. The purchase consideration was agreed as follows:

(i) Preference Shareholders waived the dividend and accepted one equity share in new company for every two shares held by them in the old company.

(ii) Debenture holders accepted one equity share of Rs. 100 each for one debenture of Rs. 100 and also for interest due to them by way of equity shares.

(iii) Loan creditors agreed to waive interest for next year.

(iv) Sundry creditors accepted to receive half in cash in full settlement of their dues.

(v) Equity Shareholders accepted one equity share of Rs. 100 each Rs. 50 paid for every four shares held by them in old company and agreed to bring Rs. 50 per share to be used for paying creditors.

(vi) Land and Building taken at 1/3 more in value while Plant & Machinery 25% less, stock at Rs. 1,00,000 Debtors at Rs. 1,00,000. Investment at book value, Furniture at 50%.

You are required to close the books of B Gone Ltd. and prepare a Balance Sheet of A One Ltd. after takeover.

[ICWA (F) Modified]

Solution :

Calculation of Purchase Consideration

	Rs.
For Preference Shareholders :	
$\left(6,000 \times \frac{1}{2}\right)$ 3,000 Equity Shares @ Rs. 100 each =	3,00,000
For Equity Shareholders	
10,000 Shares $\times \frac{1}{4} =$ 2,500 Equity shares of Rs. 100 each Rs. 50 paid.	1,25,000
	4,25,000

REALISATION A/C

	Rs.		Rs.
To Goodwill	1,00,000	By S. Creditors	1,00,000
To Land & Building	3,00,000	By 10% Debentures	4,00,000
To Plant & Machinery	4,00,000	By Unsecured Loans	2,00,000
To Furniture	50,000	By Business Purchase A/c	4,25,000
To Patents	1,00,000	By Preference Shareholders' A/c	3,00,000
To Investments	2,00,000	By Loss transferred to	
To Stock	2,00,000	Equity Shareholders' A/c	1,25,000
To Debtors	1,50,000		
To Cash & bank	50,000		
	15,50,000		15,50,000

PREFERENCE SHAREHOLDERS' A/C

	Rs.		Rs.
To Equity Shares in A One Ltd.	3,00,000	By Pref. Share Capital	6,00,000
To Realisation A/c (B.F.)	3,00,000		
	6,00,000		6,00,000

EQUITY SHAREHOLDERS' A/C

	Rs.		Rs.
To Realisation A/c (Loss)	1,25,000	By Share Capital A/c	10,00,000
To Profit & Loss	6,50,000		
To Preliminary Expenses	1,00,000		
To Shares in A One Ltd.	1,25,000		
	10,00,000		10,00,000

JOURNAL ENTRIES

			Rs.	Rs.
	Business Purchase A/c	Dr.	4,25,000	
	To Liquidator of B Gone Ltd.			4,25,000
	(Being B. Gone Ltd. acquired)			
	Land & Building A/c	Dr.	4,00,000	
	Plant & Machinery A/c	Dr.	3,00,000	
	Furniture A/c	Dr.	25,000	
	Investments A/c	Dr.	2,00,000	
	Stock A/c	Dr.	1,00,000	
	Debtors A/c	Dr.	1,00,000	
	Cash & bank A/c	Dr.	50,000	
	To Sundry Creditors			50,000
	To Loan (Unsecured)			2,00,000
	To 10% Debentures			4,80,000
	To Business Purchase A/c			4,25,000
	To Capital Reserve (B.F.)			20,000
	(Being assets & liabilities of B. Gone Ltd. incorporated)			
	Liquidator of B. Gone Ltd. A/c	Dr.	4,25,000	
	To Share Capital A/c			4,25,000
	(Being purchase consideration discharged)			
	10% Debentures A/c	Dr.	4,80,000	
	To Equity Share Capital			4,80,000
	(Being debentureholders allotted equity shares)			
	Bank A/c	Dr.	1,25,000	
	To Equity Share Capital			1,25,000
	(Being cash received from shareholders to make shares fully paid)			
	Sundry Creditors A/c	Dr.	50,000	
	To Bank A/c			50,000
	(Being creditors settled)			

BALANCE SHEET OF A ONE LTD.
As on 1st April, 2005

Liabilities	Rs.	Assets	Rs.
Authorised Capital :	....	**Fixed Assets :**	
Issued & Subscribed Capital		Land & Building	4,00,000
10,300 shares of Rs. 100		Plant & Machinery	3,00,000
each fully paid	10,30,000	Furniture	25,000
Capital Reserve	20,000	**Investments**	2,00,000
Unsecured Loan	2,00,000	**Current Assets**	
		Stock	1,00,000
		Debtors	1,00,000
		Cash & Bank*	1,25,000
	12,50,000		12,50,000

*Cash at Bank. 50,000 + 1,25,000 – 50,000

Op. Balance + Received from shareholders – paid to creditors.

Dissenting Shareholders

These are the shareholders who do not approve the scheme of amalgamation and refuse to transfer their shares. They constitute an insignificant number as compared to total number of shareholdings. Since majority of shareholders agree, there is no legal hitch or hurdle in implementing the scheme of amalgamation whether that of merger or purchase. However, section 395 of Companies Act 1956 states that the shares of dissenting shareholders may be acquired by the amalgamated company in any of the manners :

(i) As per the terms and conditions as set by dissenting shareholders or

(ii) As per mutual agreement between the dissenting shareholders and amalgamated company, or

(iii) As per the terms set or ordered by the court on an application moved by the amalgamated company or by the dissenting shareholders.

Accounting Treatment

(i) The Share Capital held by the dissenting shareholders is transferred to a separate account known as "Dissenting shareholders" Account. The sum so agreed upon between the amalgamated company and dissenting shareholders is paid to them. The difference between the amount so paid and the amount of share capital held by them is transferred to Realisation Account. It is to be noted that these dissenting shareholders do not have any share/claim in the accumulated profits or losses including loss or profit arising from Realisation Account.

(ii) While calculating purchase consideration the shares held by dissenting shareholders are deducted out of the total shares of vendor company before calculating the number of shares to be issued by purchasing company.

Illustration (29) (Dissenting Shareholders)

Vyoma Ltd. agrees to acquire Shyam Ltd. as on 31st March, 2005 when it's Balance Sheet stood as follows :

Liabilities	Rs.	Assets	Rs.
Share Capital		Fixed Assets	7,50,000
1,50,000 Equity Shares of	15,00,000	Investments	2,50,000
Rs. 10 each		Stock	5,25,000
Reserve & Surplus :		Debtors	3,75,000
General Reserve	2,50,000	Bills Receivable	1,75,000
Dividend Equalisation Fund	62,500	Cash & Bank	75,000
Profit & Loss A/c	1,50,000		
Current liabilities			
Sundry Creditors	1,87,500		
	21,50,000		21,50,000

Vyoma Ltd. tookover all the assets and liabilities of the Shyama Ltd. subject to Rs. 15,000 cash to provide for cost of liquidation and to pay dissenting shareholders, if any.

Vyoma Ltd. to issue 2 shares of Rs. 10 each Rs. 7 paid for every share held in Shyama Ltd. The shares of Shyama Ltd. were quoted in the market at Rs. 25. The liquidator paid Rs. 2,500 towards cost of liquidation and Rs. 12,500 to the dissenting shareholders holding 500 shares @ Rs. 25 each as per the mutual agreement.

Prepare necessary ledger accounts in the books of Shyama Ltd. and pass journal entries in the books of Vyoma Ltd.

Solution : 29

Calculation of Purchase consideration

	Total No. of shares of Shyama Ltd.	1,50,000
Less	Shares held by Dissenting shareholders	500
		1,49,500
	Vyoma Ltd. to issue 1,49,500 × 2/1	= 2,99,000 Shares
	2,99,000 shares of Rs. 10 each Rs. 7 paid	= Rs. 20,93,000

Books of Shyama Ltd.

REALISATION A/C

	Rs.		Rs.
To Fixed Assets	7,50,000	By S. Creditors	1,87,500
To Investments	2,50,000	By Vyoma Ltd.	20,93,000
To Stock	5,25,000		
To Debtors	3,75,000		
To Bills Receivable	1,75,000		
To Cash & Bank	60,000		
To Cash (Exp.)	2,500		
To Dissenting Shareholders	7,500		
To Shareholders' A/c (Profit)	1,35,500		
	22,80,500		22,80,000

SHARE CAPITAL A/C

	Rs.		Rs.
To Dissenting Shareholders' A/c	5,000	By Balance b/d	15,00,000
To Shareholders' A/c (willing)	14,95,000		
	15,00,000		15,00,000

DISSENTING SHAREHOLDERS' A/C

	Rs.		Rs.
To Cash A/c	12,500	By Share Capital A/c	5,000
		By Realisation A/c	7,500
	12,500		12,500

SHAREHOLDERS' A/C

	Rs.		Rs.
To Shares in Vyoma Ltd.	20,93,000	By Share Capital	14,95,000
		By General Reserve	2,50,000
		By Dividend Equalisation Fund	62,500
		By Profit & Loss A/c	1,50,000
		By Realisation A/c (Profit)	1,35,500
	20,93,000		20,93,000

Books of Vyoma Ltd.
JOURNAL ENTRIES

			Rs.	Rs.
	Business Purchase A/c	Dr.	20,93,000	
	To Liquidator of Shyama Ltd.			20,93,000
	(Being business of Shyama Ltd. takenover)			
	Goodwill A/c (B.F.)	Dr.	1,45,500	
	Fixed Assets A/c	Dr.	7,50,000	
	Investment A/c	Dr.	2,50,000	
	StockA/c	Dr.	5,25,000	
	Debtors A/c	Dr.	3,75,000	
	Bills Receivable A/c	Dr.	1,75,000	
	Cash & Bank A/c	Dr.	60,000	
	To Sundry Creditors A/c			1,87,500
	To Business Purchase A/c			20,93,000
	(Being Assets & liabilities of Shyama Ltd. incorporated)			
	Liquidator of Shyama Ltd. A/c	Dr.	20,93,000	
	To Share Capital A/c			20,93,000
	(Being shares allotted to liquidator)			

INTER COMPANY "OWINGS"/ "TRANSACTIONS"

Quite often there may be unsettled transactions between the amalgamated and amalgamating companies at the time of amalgamation. The transferor company may be a debtor or creditor of the transferee company or vice versa. This may be the result of

(i) Loan given by one company to other company

(ii) Bills accepted by one company, drawn by other company and vice versa

(iii) Goods purchased from other Co.

(iv) Goods sold to one company by other company.

These owings or transactions if remain unsettled, require adjustments which can be explained under two heads.

(1) Elimination of common debts.

(2) Cancellation of unrealised profits.

It is to be noted that no adjustment is required in the books of Transferor Company in any of the circumstances mentioned above.

BOOKS OF TRANSFEREE COMPANY

(1) Elimination of Common debts

There is no effect of such transactions on the entries relating to purchases of business, calculation of purchase consideration, incorporation of assets and liabilities and payment of purchase consideration. After recording the usual routine entries the following additional entry will also be recorded to eliminate the common debts In case of Loan:

Loan from (one Company) A/c Dr.

To Loan to (Other Company) A/c

In case of bills **:**

Bills Payable (of one Company) A/c Dr.

To Bills Receivable (of other Company) A/c Dr.

In Case of debtors & Creditors

Creditors (of one company) A/c Dr.

To Debtors (of other company)

It should be noted that for cancellation credit items will be debited and debit items will be credited.

(2) Cancellation of un-realised profits

When goods purchased by the transferor company from the transferee company remain unsold at the time of takeover of business then the unsold stock of transferor company become the part of stock of the transferee company. Since transferee company had sold the goods at "Cost plus profit" the same cannot be taken back or included in the stock at this price. Hence the profit element which is included in the unsold stock of transferor company is treated as unrealised profit and has to be excluded there from. For this the following entry is recorded :

(i)	Profit & Loss A/c	Dr.	In Case of merger
	To Stock		
(ii)	Goodwill A/c	Dr.	In case of amalgamation
	To Stock *or*		
	Capital Reserve A/c	Dr.	In the nature of purchase
	To Stock		

Students are required to recall the second entry in the books of transferee company which shows the balancing figure as "goodwill" or "Capital reserve" in case of purchase (and Profit & Loss or General reserve in case of merger). Since unrealised profit reduces the value of stock there by reducing the net assets which will result either in increase in goodwill or decrease in Capital reserve.

Illustration (30) (Inter-company owings and unrealised profit)

The following is the Balance Sheet of Z Ltd. as on 31st March, 2005

Liabilities	Rs.	Assets	Rs.
Share Capital		Goodwill	62,500
50,000 Shares of Rs. 10 each	5,00,000	Fixed Assets	6,12,500
General Reserve	50,000	Stock	1,37,500
Loan from Bank	1,00,000	Debtors	1,62,500
10% Debentures	2,50,000	Cash at Bank	1,05,000
Sundry Creditors	2,00,000	Preliminary Expenses	20,000
	11,00,000		11,00,000

The business of Z Ltd. is takenover by N Ltd. on the following terms.

(i) All assets except Cash at Bank and goodwill are takenover at book value less 10%

(ii) Goodwill is to be valued at four years' purchase of the excess of average profits of last five years over 8% of the combined amount of Share Capital and General reserve.

(iii) Debentures are takenover by N Ltd. and paid off in cash. Trade creditors are to be takenover subject to a discount of 5%.

(iv) Loan from bank is to be repaid by Z Ltd.

(v) The purchase consideration is to be discharged by Cash Rs. 1,31,650 and the balance in fully paid equity shares of Rs. 10 each valued at Rs. 12.50 per share.

The average of the five year's profit is Rs. 75,250. The expenses of liquidation amount to Rs. 5,000 which were borne by Z Ltd. During the month of March 2005 goods costing Rs. 75,000 were sold to Z Ltd. for Rs. 1,00,000. On the date of absorption Rs. 60,000 worth of goods were still in the stock of Z Ltd. Debtors include Rs. 50,000 still due from Z Ltd.

You are required to

(i) Prepare Realisation Account, Bank Account, Shareholders' Account and Shares in N Ltd.

(ii) Journal entries in the books of N Ltd.

[B. Com (Hons.) D.U. Adapted]

Solution : 30

(i) Calculation of Goodwill

			Rs.
	Super Profit = Average Profit – Normal Profit		
	Average Profit (as given)		75,250
Less	Normal Profit [8% of (5,00,000 + 50,000) Capital & Reserve]		44,000
	Super profit		31,250
	Goodwill at 4 years' purchase		1,25,000

(ii) Calculation of Purchase Consideration

	Fixed Assets		6,12,500
	Stock		1,37,500
	Debtors		1,62,500
			9,12,500
Less	10%		91,250
			8,21,250
	Goodwill (as Calculated above)		1,25,000
	Gross assets		9,46,250
Less	Creditors less 5%	1,90,000	
	10% Debentures	2,50,000	4,40,000
	Purchase Consideration		5,06,250

Mode of Payment :

Cash	1,31,250
30,000 Shares @ Rs. 12.50	3,75,000
	5,06,250

Books of Z Ltd.

REALISATION A/C

	Rs.		Rs.
To Goodwill	62,500	By Sundry Creditors	2,00,000
To Fixed Assets	6,12,500	By 10% Debentures	2,50,000
To Stock	1,37,500	By Loan from Bank	1,00,000
To Debtors	1,62,500	By N Ltd.	5,06,250
To Bank (Loan from Bank)	1,00,000	By Shareholders' A/c	23,750
To Cash (Expenses)	5,000	(Loss)	
	10,80,000		10,80,000

SHAREHOLDERS' A/C

	Rs.		Rs.
To Realisation A/c	23,750	By Share Capital	5,00,000
To Preliminary Expenses	20,000	By General Reserve	50,000
To Shares in N Ltd.	3,75,000		
To Bank	1,31,250		
	5,50,000		5,50,000

BANK A/C

	Rs.		Rs.
To Balance b/d	1,05,000	By Realisation A/c (Exp.)	5,000
To N Ltd.	1,31,250	By Realisation A/c (Loan)	1,00,000
		By Shareholders' A/c	1,31,250
	2,36,250		2,36,250

SHARES IN N LTD. A/C

	Rs.		Rs.
To N Ltd.	3,75,000	By Shareholders' A/c	3,75,000
	3,75,000		3,75,000

Books of N Ltd.
JOURNAL ENTRIES

			Rs.	Rs.
	Business Purchase A/c	Dr.	5,06,250	
	To Liquidator of Z Ltd.			5,06,250
	(Being business of Z Ltd. takenover)			
	Goodwill A/c	Dr.	1,25,000	
	Fixed Assets A/c	Dr.	5,51,250	
	Stock A/c	Dr.	1,23,750	
	Debtors A/c	Dr.	1,46,250	
	To S. Creditors			1,90,000
	To 10% Debentures			2,50,000
	To Business Purchase A/c			5,06,250
	(Being assets & liabilities takenover)			
	Liquidator of Z Ltd. A/c	Dr.	5,06,250	
	To Equity Share Capital A/c			3,00,000
	To Securities Premium A/c			75,000
	To Bank A/c			1,31,250
	10% Debentures A/c	Dr.	2,50,000	
	To Bank A/c			2,50,000
	(Being debentures paid off)			
	Sundry Creditors A/c	Dr.	50,000	
	To Debtors			50,000
	(Being Common debts eliminated)			
	Goodwill A/c	Dr.	15,000	
	To Stock			15,000
	(Being unrealised profit eliminated)			

$$* \left(\text{Rs. } \frac{25,000}{1,00,000} \times 60,000 \right) = \text{Rs. } 15,000$$

Working note :

Unrealised profit has been debited to Goodwill A/c and credited to stock because stock which includes goods sold on profit, cannot be shown at the same figure hence such profit element has to be adjusted against stock. This reduction in the value of stock will automatically either increase the goodwill or reduce the capital reserve.

RECONSTRUCTION

Reconstruction refers to a process by which affairs of a Company are reorganised by :

- Revaluation of assets.
- Reassessment of liabilities including arrangement with creditors,
- Writing off the losses & fictitious assets,
- Reorganise or restructure capital to effect economies or make company financially viable. Such a process is called **internal reconstruction** which does not involve liquidation of an existing company or formation of a new company. It is in essence an internal arrangement made as per the provisions of the Companies Act.

However, external reconstruction involves liquidation of an existing company and takingover it's business by a new company which is formed for the purpose. In other words under external reconstruction the business of an existing company is in substance transferred not to outsiders, but to another company consisting substantially the same shareholders.

External Reconstruction is similar to the amalgamation in the nature of purchase as far as it's accounting treatment is concerned. The books of the transferor company are closed by preparing Realisation Account and Shareholders' Account and that in the books of transferee company opening entries are recorded and a Balance Sheet is prepared. Otherwise external reconstruction differs from amalgamation on certain grounds :

DISTINCTION BETWEEN AMALGAMATION AND RECONSTRUCTION

(a) In an amalgamation there are at least two existing companies involved where as in external reconstruction there is only one existing company which gets a new lease of life.

(b) In amalgamation one existing company may absorb or takeover the other existing company or a new company may be formed to takeover the business of both existing companies. Where as in an external reconstruction a new company has to be formed.

(c) An amalgamation scheme is mooted to eliminate competition or to avail economies of large scale operation where as an external reconstruction aims to cure the evils of poor financial structure and to wipe out accumulated losses & fictitious assets to give a new look to the Company.

(d) In an amalgamation the number and composition of shareholders changes because the shareholders of transferor Company become the shareholders of transferee Company, whereas in external reconstruction the number and composition of shareholders is substantially the same.

Illustration (31) (External Reconstruction)

The Balance Sheet of H Ltd. was as follows :

BALANCE SHEET OF H LTD.
As on 31st March, 2005

	Rs.		Rs.
Share Capital :		Goodwill	40,000
12% 5,000 Preference shares of		Plant & Machinery	70,000
Rs. 10 each	50,000	Furniture & Fixtures	20,000
15,000 Equity Shares of Rs. 10 each	1,50,000	Patents	15,000
15% Debentures	30,000	Stock	49,000
Creditors	20,000	Debtors	25,500
		Bank	500
		Preliminary Expenses	800
		Discount on Issue of Debentures	1,200
		Profit & Loss A/c	28,000
	2,50,000		2,50,000

Note : Preference dividends are in arrears for 3 years.

The following scheme of reconstruction was agreed upon :

(i) A New Company to be formed called J Ltd. with an authorised capital of Rs. 3,25,000 divided into equity shares of Rs. 10 each.

(ii) One equity share of Rs. 5 paid up in the new company to be allotted for each equity share in the old company.

(iii) Two equity shares Rs. 5 paid up, in the new company to be issued for each preference share in the old company.

(iv) Arrears of preference dividends to be cancelled.

(v) Debenture-holders to receive 3,000 equity shares in the new company credited as fully paid.

(vi) The remaining unissued shares to be taken up and paid for in full by the directors.

(vii) The new company to takeover the old company's assets except patents, subject to writing down plant & machinery by Rs. 29,000 and stock by Rs. 6,000.

(viii) The Patents were realised by H Ltd. for Rs. 1,000.

Prepare necessary ledger accounts in the books of H Ltd. and open the books of J Ltd. by means of journal entries and give the initial Balance Sheet of J Ltd. Expenses of H Ltd. came to Rs. 1,000.

[B. Com (H) D.U. Modified]

Solution :

Calculation of Purchase Consideration

	Rs.
For Preference Shareholders	
5,000 × 2/1 = 10,000 Shares Rs. 5 paid	50,000
For Equity Shareholders	
15,000 × 1/1 = 15,000 Shares Rs. 5 paid	75,000
	1,25,000

Books of H Ltd.

REALISATION A/C

	Rs.		Rs.
To Goodwill	40,000	By 10% Debentures	30,000
To Plant & Machinery	70,000	By Creditors	20,000
To Furniture & Fixtures	20,000	By J Ltd.	1,25,000
To Patents	15,000	By Cash (Patents)	1,000
To Stock	49,000	By Equity Shareholders A/c	45,000
To Debtors	25,500	(Loss)	
To Bank	500		
To Cash (Expenses)	1,000		
	2,21,000		2,21,000

12% PREFERENCE SHAREHOLDERS' A/C

	Rs.		Rs.
To Equity Shares in J Ltd.	50,000	By Pref. Share Capital	50,000
	50,000		50,000

EQUITY SHAREHOLDERS' A/C

	Rs.		Rs.
To Profit & Loss A/c	28,000	By Share Capital A/c	1,50,000
To Discount on Issue of Debentures		1,200	
To Preliminary Expenses	800		
To Realisation A/c (Loss)	45,000		
To Shares in J Ltd.	75,000		
	1,50,000		1,50,000

Books of J Ltd.

JOURNAL ENTRIES

			Rs.	Rs.
	Business Purchase A/c	Dr.	1,25,000	
	To Liquidator of H Ltd.			1,25,000
	(Being H Ltd. acquired)			
	Goodwill A/c (B.F)	Dr.	45,000	
	Plant & Machinery A/c	Dr.	41,000	
	Furniture & Fixtures A/c	Dr.	20,000	
	Stock A/c	Dr.	43,000	
	Debtors A/c	Dr.	25,500	
	Bank A/c	Dr.	500	
	To Creditors			20,000
	To 10% Debentures			30,000
	To Business Purchase A/c			1,25,000
	(Being assets & Liabilities of H Ltd. incorporated)			
	Liquidator of H Ltd. A/c	Dr.	1,25,000	
	To Equity Share Capital A/c			1,25,000
	(Being shares allotted to liquidator)			
	10% Debentures A/c	Dr.	30,000	
	To Equity Share Capital A/c			30,000
	(Being 10% Debentures discharged)			
	Bank A/c	Dr.	45,000	
	To Equity Share Capital A/c			45,000
	(Being Shares issued for cash to directors)			

BALANCE SHEET OF J LTD.

As on 31st March, 2005

Liabilities	Rs.	Assets	Rs.
Authorised Share Capital		Fixed Assets :	
32,500 Shares of Rs. 10 each	3,25,000	Goodwill	45,000
Issued subscribed and paid up Capital		Plant & Machinery	41,000
7,500 Equity Shares of	75,000	Furniture & Fixture	20,000
Rs. 10 each fully paid		Current Assets, Loans & Advances :	
25,000 Equity Shares of		Stock	43,000
Rs. 10 each Rs. 5 paid up.	1,25,000	Debtors	25,500
Reserves & Surplus	—	Cash at Bank	45,500
Current liabilities and Provisions :			
Creditors	20,000		
	2,20,000		2,20,000

Working Notes

(1) Shares issued for cash

	Total No. of shares	32,500
Less	Shares allotted to Preference Shareholders	(10,000)
	Shares allotted to Equity Shareholders	(15,000)
	Shares allotted to Debentureholders	(3,000)
		28,000
	Balance (Shares allotted to Directors)	4,500

(2) **CASH & BANK A/C**

	Rs.		Rs.
To Business Purchase A/c (Transfer from H Ltd.)	500	By Balance c/d	45,500
To Share Capital A/c	45,000		
	45,500		45,000

(3) Cancellation of unrecorded arrears of Preference dividend will not affect any item of asset/liability.

Illustration (32) (External Reconstruction)

The following is the Balance Sheet of Samson Ltd. as on 31st March 2005

Liabilities	Rs.	Assets	Rs.
13% 2,500 Preference Shares of Rs. 100 each	2,50,000	Building Plant & Machinery	3,00,000
30,000 Equity Shares of Rs. 10 each	3,00,000	Patents	1,22,500
10% Debentures	50,000	Stock	90,000
Debenture Interest o/s	10,000	Debtors	60,000
Creditors	40,000	Cash & Bank	2,500
		Profit & Loss A/c	75,000
	6,50,000		6,50,000

The following scheme of reconstruction was duly approved.

(i) Ramson Ltd. to be formed with authorised capital of Rs. 2,50,000 to takeover the business of Samson Ltd.

(ii) One share of Rs. 10 each fully paid in the new company to be issued for every six equity shares in the old company.

(iii) Three shares of Rs. 10 each fully paid in the new company to be issued for every preference share in the old company.

(iv) Debentureholders are to be paid in full by Ramson Ltd.

(v) The creditors to receive 80% of the amount due to them in fully paid equity shares in the new company in full settlement.

(vi) Patents and debit balance of Profit & Loss A/c is to be written off.

(vii) Arrears of preference dividend to be cleared by issuing one Rs. 10 fully paid equity share in Ramson Ltd. for every four shares held, and

(viii) Any balance available by the scheme to be used in writing down Building, Plant & Machinery.

Close the books of Samson Ltd. and give opening entries and prepare Balance Sheet of Ramson Ltd.

[C.S. (I) Adapted]

Solution : 32

Calculation of Purchase Consideration

For Preference Shareholders :

	Rs.
(i) For Capital	
2,500 × 3/1 = 7,500 shares of Rs. 10 each	75,000
(ii) For Arrears of preference dividend	
$2{,}500 \times \frac{1}{4}$ = 625 shares of Rs. 10 each	6,250
For Equity Shareholders :	
$30{,}000 \times \frac{1}{6}$ = 5,000 Shares of Rs. 10 each	50,000
	1,31,250

Books of Samson Ltd.

REALISATION A/C

	Rs.		Rs.
To Building Plant & Machinery	3,00,000	By 10% Debentures	50,000
To Patents	1,22,500	By Creditors	40,000
To Stock	90,000	By Debenture Interest%	10,000
To Debtors	60,000	By Preference Shareholders A/c	1,68,750
To Cash & Bank	2,500	By Ramson Ltd.	1,31,250
		By Equity Shareholders A/c	1,75,000
	5,75,000		5,75,000

PREFERENCE SHAREHOLDERS' A/C

	Rs.		Rs.
To Equity Shares in Ramson Ltd.	81,250	By Preference Share Capital A/c	2,50,000
To Realisation A/c	1,68,750		
	2,50,000		2,50,000

EQUITY SHAREHOLDERS' A/C

	Rs.		Rs.
To Profit & Loss A/c	75,000	By Share Capital A/c	3,00,000
To Realisation A/c	1,75,000		
To Shares in Ramson Ltd.	50,000		
	3,00,000		3,00,000

Books of Ramson Ltd.

JOURNAL ENTRIES

			Rs.	Rs.
	Business Purchase A/c	Dr.	1,31,250	
	To Liquidator of Samson Ltd.			1,31,250
	(Being business of Samson Ltd. takenover)			
	Building, Plant & Machinery A/c* (B.F)	Dr.	70,750	
	Stock	Dr.	90,000	
	Debtors	Dr.	60,000	
	Cash & Bank	Dr.	2,500	
	To 10% Debentures			50,000
	To Creditors			32,000
	To Debenture Interest o/s			10,000
	To Business Purchase A/c			1,31,250
	(Being assets and liabilities of Samson Ltd. incorporated)			
	Creditors A/c	Dr.	32,000	
	To Equity Share Capital			32,000
	(Being creditors discharged by issue of shares)			
	Liquidator of Samson Ltd. A/c	Dr.	1,31,250	
	To Equity Share Capital			1,31,250
	(Being purchase consideration paid in shares)			

* As per the terms of scheme, the excess of credit balances has been adjusted against Building Plant & Machinery, instead of transferring the amount to goodwill or Capital reserve.

BALANCE SHEET OF RAMSON LTD.

As 31st March, 2005

Liabilities	Rs.	Assets	Rs.
Authorised Capital		Fixed Assets:	
25,000 Shares of Rs. 10 each	2,50,000	Building, Plant & Machinery	70,750
Issued & Subscribed Capital	1,63,250	Current Assets :	
16,325 Shares of Rs. 10 each		Stock	90,000
Fully paid		Debtors	60,000
Reserves & Surplus	—	Cash & Bank	2,500
Secured Loans :			
10% Debentures	50,000		
Debenture Interest o/s	10,000		
Current liabilities & Provisions	—		
	2,23,250		2,23,250

Illustration (33)

(External Reconstruction)

The following is the Balance Sheet of Nancy Ltd. as on 31st March, 2005

Liabilities	Rs.	Assets	Rs.
8% 2,500 Preference Shares of		Goodwill	25,000
Rs. 100 each	2,50,000	Fixed Assets	12,85,000
1,20,000 Equity Shares of	12,00,000	Stock	2,50,000
Rs. 10 each		Debtors	3,00,000
8% Debentures	5,00,000	Bank	5,000
Debenture Interest o/s	40,000	Preliminary Expenses	15,000
S. Creditors	5,00,000	Profit & Loss A/c	6,10,000
	24,90,000		24,90,000

The following scheme is sanctioned by the court :

(i) A New Company called Simonancy Ltd. is formed with an Authorised Capital of Rs. 15,00,000 divided into shares of Rs. 10 each.

(ii) The New Company will acquire the assets and liabilities of Nancy Ltd. on the following terms :

(a) Preference Sharesholders to get 10 equity shares for every share held in the old company. For arrears of preference dividend amounting to Rs. 60,000, 5 shares are issued at par for each Rs. 100 in full satisfaction.

(b) Equity shareholders are to be issued one share for three shares held.

(c) Debenture holders are to be paid similar debentures in New Company and for outstanding debenture interest shares of equal amount are issued at par.

(d) The creditors are paid for every Rs. 100 Rs. 16 in cash and 10 shares issued at par.

(e) Expenses Rs. 20,000 are to be borne by the New Company as part of purchase consideration.

(iii) Current assets are to be taken at book value (except stock which is to be reduced by Rs. 15,000) Goodwill is to be eliminated, balance of purchase consideration being attributed to fixed assets.

(iv) Remaining shares of the new company are to be issued at par for cash.

You are required to show in the books of old company.

(i) New Company's Account (ii) Realisation A/c and in the books of New Company

(i) Bank A/c & (ii) Summarised Balance Sheet.

[C.A. (F) Adapted]

Solution : 33

Calculation of Purchase Consideration

	Rs.
For Preference Shareholders :	
For Capital 2,500 × 10/1 = 25,000 Equity Shares of Rs. 10 each at par	2,50,000
For arrears of dividend	
$60,000 \times \frac{5}{100}$ = 3,000 Shares of Rs. 10 each at par	30,000
For Equity Shareholders :	
$1,20,000 \times \frac{1}{3}$ = 40,000 Shares of Rs. 10 each at par	4,00,000
	6,80,000

Book of Nancy Ltd.
REALISATION A/C

	Rs.		Rs.
To Goodwill	25,000	By 8% Debentures	5,00,000
To Fixed Assets	12,85,000	By Debenture Interest o/s	40,000
To Stock	2,50,000	By Creditors	5,00,000
To Debtors	3,00,000	By Simonancy Ltd.	6,80,000
To Bank	5,000	By Equity Share holders A/c	1,75,000
To Preference Shareholders' A/c	30,000		
	18,95,000		18,95,000

SIMONANCY LTD.

	Rs.		Rs.
To Realisation A/c	6,80,000	By Equity Shares in Simonancy Ltd.	6,80,000
	6,80,000		6,80,000

PREFERENCE SHAREHOLDERS' A/C

	Rs.		Rs.
To Equity Shares in Simonancy Ltd.	2,80,000	By Pref. Share Capital	2,50,000
		By Realisation A/c	30,000
	2,80,000		2,80,000

EQUITY SHAREHOLDERS' A/C

	Rs.		Rs.
To Realisation A/c (Loss)	1,75,000	By Share Capital	12,00,000
To Profit & Loss A/c	6,10,000		
To Preliminary Expenses	15,000		
To Shares in Simonancy Ltd.	4,00,000		
	12,00,000		12,00,000

Books of Simonancy Ltd.
BANK A/C

	Rs.		Rs.
To Business Purchase A/c	5,000	By Creditors	80,000
(Transfer from Nancy Ltd.)		By Liquidation Expenses	20,000
To Equity Share Capital[(1)]	2,80,000	By Balance c/d	1,85,000
	2,85,000		2,85,000

BALANCE SHEET OF SIMONANCY LTD.
As on 31st March, 2005

Liabilities	Rs.	Assets	Rs.
Authorised Capital	15,00,000	Fixed Assets	12,85,000
1,50,000 Shares of Rs. 10 each		Stock	2,35,000
Issued, Subscribed & Paid up Capital	15,00,000	Debtors	3,00,000
1,50,000 Shares of Rs. 10 each		Bank	1,85,000
Reserves & Surplus :			
Capital Reserve[(2)]	5,000		
Secured Loans :			
8% Debentures (New)	5,00,000		
Current liabilities & Provisions	—		
	20,05,000		20,05,000

Working note:

(1) Issued Capital and Shares issued for cash.

		Rs.
Equity Shares allotted to Preference Shareholders		2,80,000
Equity Shares allotted to Equity Shareholders		4,00,000
Equity Shares allotted to Creditors $\left(\frac{5,00,000}{100} \times 10 \times 10\right)$		5,00,000
Equity Shares allotted to Debenture holders in lieu of interest o/s		40,000
		12,20,000
Authorised Capital		15,00,000
Balance issued for cash		2,80,000

Capital Reserve

		Rs.
Fixed Assets		12,85,000
Stock		2,35,000
Debtors		3,00,000
Bank		5,000
		18,25,000
Less Liabilities 8% Debentures	5,00,000	
Deb. Interest	40,000	
Creditors	5,80,000	11,20,000

	Net Assets		7,05,000
Less	Purchase Consideration		6,80,000
		Capital Reserve	25,000
Less	Expenses of liquidation		20,000
	Balance to be taken to B/s		5,000

Illustration (34) (External Reconstruction)

P Ltd. incurred exceptional losses and a scheme of reconstruction was approved and sanctioned by the count. The Balance Sheet of P Ltd. as on 31st March, 2005 stood as follows :

Liabilities	Rs.	Assets	Rs.
12% Cumulative Preference Shares of Rs. 100 each	4,80,000	Fixed Assets	18,00,000
Equity Shares of Rs. 100 each	12,00,000	Stock at cost	7,20,000
Bank Overdraft (Secured)	12,00,000	Trade Debitors	9,60,000
Creditors (Preferential)	60,000	Profit & Loss A/c	9,00,000
Other Creditors	14,40,000		
	43,80,000		43,80,000

The scheme of reconstruction provided :

(a) A new company called PB Ltd. will be formed to takeover the assets and liabilities of P Ltd.

(b) 24,000 equity shares of Rs. 10 each in PB Ltd. credited as Rs. 5 paid to be issued to the shareholders of P Ltd. who had agreed to pay up the balance of Rs. 5 per share immediately.

(c) 4,800 Preference Shares of Rs. 100 each in PB Ltd. credited as Rs. 75 per share paid up to be issued to the preference shareholders of P Ltd. who have agreed to pay Rs. 25 per share immediately. In addition, Rs. 57,600 in 14% debentures (redeemable after 5 years) are to be issued as compensation for arrears of preference dividends.

(d) PB Ltd. to imburse liquidation expenses of P Ltd. for Rs. 12,000.

(e) PB Ltd. decided to value of tangible assets acquired as follows.

	Rs.
Fixed assets	16,80,000
Stock	6,00,000
Trade debtors	9,60,000

(f) PB Ltd. to discharge preferential creditors in cash immediately.

(g) PB Ltd. to fully satisfy other creditors as under :
Rs. 7,20,000 in cash
Rs. 3,60,000 in Bills of Exchange
Rs. 3,60,000 in 14% Debentures

(h) The Authorised Capital of New Company will be Rs. 30,00,000 divided into 15,000, 12% Cumulative Preference shares of Rs. 100 each and 1,50,000 Equity Shares of Rs. 10 each.

(i) Directors of PB Ltd. have agreed to subscribe for 84,000 shares of Rs. 10 each payable in full with application.

(j) PB Ltd. decided to pay off bank overdraft to the extent of Rs. 2,40,000 and the balance to be secured against fixed assets.

(k) Preliminary expenses of PB Ltd. amounted to Rs. 24,000.

You are required to prepare :

(i) Realisation A/c and Sundry Members A/c in the books of P Ltd. and

(ii) Journal entries and opening Balance Sheet of PB Ltd.

[ICWA (F) Modified]

Solution :

Calculation of Purchase Consideration

	Rs.
For Preference Shareholders :	
For Capital : 4,800 Preference Shares of Rs. 100 each Rs. 75 paid up	3,60,000
For Arrears of dividend : 14% Debentures	57,600
For Equity Shareholders :	
24,000 Shares of Rs. 10 each Rs. 5 paid up.	1,20,000
	5,37,600

REALISATION A/C

	Rs.		Rs.
To Fixed Assets	18,00,000	By Creditors (Pref.)	60,000
To Stock	7,20,000	By Other Creditors	14,40,000
To Trade debtors	9,60,000	By Bank Overdraft	12,00,000
		By PB Ltd.	5,37,600
		By Preference Shareholders' A/c	62,400
		By Equity Shareholders A/c	1,80,000
	34,80,000		34,80,000

PREFERENCE SHAREHOLDERS' A/C

	Rs.		Rs.
To Shares in PB Ltd.	3,60,000	By Preference Share Capital	4,80,000
To 14% Debentures	57,600		
To Realisation A/c (B.F.)	62,400		
	4,80,000		4,80,000

SUNDRY MEMBERS' A/C

	Rs.		Rs.
To Realisation A/c (Loss)	1,80,000	By Equity Share Capital A/c	12,00,000
To Profit & Loss A/c	9,00,000		
To Shares in PB Ltd.	1,20,000		
	12,00,000		12,00,000

Books of PB Ltd.
JOURNAL ENTRIES

Particulars		Rs.	Rs.
Business Purchase A/c	Dr.	5,37,600	
To Liquidator of P Ltd.			5,37,600
(Being purchase consideration payable)			
Fixed Assets A/c	Dr.	16,80,000	
Stock A/c	Dr.	6,00,000	
Trade Debtors A/c	Dr.	9,60,000	
To Bank Overdraft			12,00,000
To S. Creditors			15,00,000
To Business Purchase A/c			5,37,600
To Capital Reserve (B.F)			2,400
(Being assets & liabilities of PB Ltd. incorporated)			
Liquidator of P Ltd. A/c	Dr.	5,37,600	
To 12% Preference Share Capital			3,60,000
To Equity Share Capital			1,20,000
To 14% Debentures			57,600
(Being purchase consideration paid)			
Liquidation Expenses A/c	Dr.	12,000	
To Bank			12,000
(Being expenses paid)			
Capital Reserve A/c	Dr.	2,400	
Goodwill A/c (B.F)	Dr.	9,600	
To Liquidation Expenses			12,000
(Being liquidation expenses charged to capital reserve and goodwill)			
Bank A/c	Dr.	2,40,000	
To Equity Share Capital			1,20,000
To 12% Preference Share Capital			1,20,000
(Being balance received on partly paid shares)			
Bank A/c	Dr.	8,40,000	
To Equity Share Capital			8,40,000
(Being equity shares issued for cash)			
Sundry Creditors (Pref.) A/c	Dr.	60,000	
To Bank			60,000
(Being preferential creditors discharged)			

Contd.

			Rs.	Rs.
	Sundry Creditors A/c To Bank To Bills Payable To 14% Debentures (Being other creditors also discharged as per terms)	Dr.	14,40,000	 7,20,000 3,60,000 3,60,000
	Bank Overdraft A/c To Bank (Being overdraft paid off)	Dr.	2,40,000	 2,40,000
	Preliminary Expenses A/c To Bank (Being formation expenses paid)	Dr.	24,000	 24,000

BALANCE SHEET OF PB LTD.
As on 31st March, 2005

Liabilities	Rs.	Assets	Rs.
Authorised Capital :		**Fixed Assets :**	
15,000 12% Preference Shares of Rs. 100 each	15,00,000	Goodwill	9,600
1,50,000 Equity Shares of Rs. 10 each	15,00,000	Other Fixed Assets	16,80,000
Issued & Subscribed Capital		**Investments Loans & Advances**	—
12% 4,800 Preference Shares of Rs. 100 each fully paid up	4,80,000	**Current Assets**	
1,08,000 Equity shares of Rs. 10 each fully paid	10,80,000	Stock in trade	6,00,000
Secured Loans :		Sundry Debtors	9,60,000
Bank Overdraft	9,60,000	Cash at Bank	24,000
14% Debentures	4,17,600	**Miscellaneous Expenses**	
Current Liabilities & Provisions :		Preliminary Expenses	24,000
Bills Payable	3,60,000		
	32,97,600		32,97,600

Working note

BANK A/C

	Rs.		Rs.
To Equity Share Capital	1,20,000	By Liquidation Expenses	12,000
To Pref. Share Capital	1,20,000	By Preliminary Expenses	24,000
To Equity Share Capital	8,40,000	By S. Creditors	7,80,000
		By Bank Overdraft	2,40,000
		By Balance c/d	24,000
	10,80,000		10,80,000

Illustration (35) (External Reconstruction)

The following is the Balance Sheet of Upset India Ltd. as on 31st March, 2005.

Liabilities	Rs.	Assets	Rs.
Authorised Capital :	25,00,000	Goodwill	2,00,000
Issued & Subscribed Capital		Other Fixed Assets	15,00,000
10% 5,000 Preference Shares of		Stock	1,10,000
of Rs. 100 each fully paid	5,00,000	Debtors	50,000
1,20,000 Equity Shares of		Cash & Bank	12,000
of Rs. 10 each fully paid	12,00,000	Preliminary Expenses	30,000
12% Debentures	2,00,000	Profit & Loss A/c	2,50,000
Debenture Interest o/s	12,000		
Creditors	2,40,000		
	21,52,000		21,52,000

Note : Preference dividend arrears amount to Rs. 90,000. A scheme of reconstruction was approved as follows :

(1) A new Company called Set up India Ltd. to be formed with an authorised capital of Rs. 10,00,000 divided into shares of Rs. 5 each.

(2) The new Company to issue twenty fully paid shares for every preference share in the old company and arrears of preference dividend to be satisfied by the issue of one fully paid share in the new company for every Rs. 10.

(3) The equity shareholders in the old company to receive one fully paid shares in the new company for every 3 shares held.

(4) Debentureholders in the old company to receive equal number of debentures carrying 9% interest in the New Company together with two fully paid shares in the new company for every Rs. 10 of debenture interest outstanding.

(5) The creditors of old company to accept Rs. 2.5 in cash and 2 fully paid shares in the new company for every Rs. 10 due.

(6) Cost of reconstruction of Rs. 5,000 to be borne by the New Company.

(7) Current assets to be taken at book values except stock which is to be taken at Rs. 1,00,000.

(8) Goodwill to be eliminated and other fixed assets valued at Rs. 11,31,000.

(9) Remaining shares were taken up by a director for cash.

(10) Short fall may be arranged by "loan from" directors'.

You are required to prepare :

(i) Realisation A/c, New Company's A/c and Sundry Shareholders' A/c, in the books of old Co.

(ii) Equity Share Capital A/c, Bank A/c and Opening Balance Sheet in the books of New Company.

C.A. (F) Adapted.

Books of Upset India Ltd.

REALISATION A/C

	Rs.		Rs.
To Goodwill	2,00,000	By 12% Debentures	2,00,000
To Other Fixed Assets	15,00,000	By Debenture Interest o/s	12,000
To Stock	1,10,000	By Creditors	2,40,000
To Debtors	50,000	By Setup India Ltd.	7,45,000*
To Bank & Cash	12,000	By Equity Shareholders' A/c	7,20,000
To Preference Shareholders' A/c	45,000	(Loss)	
	19,17,000		19,17,000

10% PREFERENCE SHARE HOLDERS' A/C

	Rs.		Rs.
To Equity Shares in Setup India Ltd.	5,45,000	By Preference Share Capital	5,00,000
		By Realisation A/c	45,000
	5,45,000		5,45,000

EQUITY SHAREHOLDERS' A/C

	Rs.		Rs.
To Profit & Loss A/c	2,50,000	By Share Capital	12,00,000
To Preliminary Exp.	30,000		
To Realisation A/c	7,20,000		
To Shares in Setup India Ltd.	2,00,000		
	12,00,000		12,00,000

SETUP INDIA LTD.

	Rs.		Rs.
To Realisation A/c	7,45,000	By Equity Shares in	
(Purchase Consideration)		Setup India Ltd.	7,45,000
	7,45,000		7,45,000

* Calculation of Purchase Consideration

For Preference Shareholders :

For Capital 5,000 × 20/1 = 1,00,000 Shares of Rs. 5 each	5,00,000
For Divided Arrears Rs. 90,000 = 9,000 Shares Rs 10 of Rs. 5 each	45,000

For Equity Shareholders :

1,20,000 × $^{1}/_{3}$ = 40,000 Shares of Rs. 5 each	2,00,000
	7,45,000

Books of Setup India Ltd.

EQUITY SHARE CAPITAL A/C

	Rs.		Rs.
To Balance c/d	10,00,000	By Liquidator of Setup India Ltd.	7,45,000
		By Debentureholders (For Interest o/s)	12,000
		By Creditors	2,40,000
		By Bank	3,000
	10,00,000		10,00,000

BANK A/C

	Rs.		Rs.
To Business Purchase A/c (Transfer from Upset India Ltd.)	12,000	By Creditors	60,000
To Share Capital	3,000	By Reconstruction Expenses	5,000
To Loan from Director	50,000		
	65,000		65,000

BALANCE SHEET OF SETUP INDIA
As on 31st March, 2005

	Rs.		Rs.
Authorised Capital		Fixed Assets	11,00,000
2,00,000 Equity Shares of Rs. 5 each	10,00,000	**Current Assets:**	
Issued & Subscribed		Stock	1,00,000
2,00,000 Shares of Rs. 5 each fully paid	10,00,000	Debtors	50,000
Reserves & Surplus	—		
Secured Loans			
9% Debentures	2,00,000		
Unsecured Loans			
Loan from Director	50,000		
	12,50,000		12,50,000

Verification working note :

(1) Balance Sheet figures can be verified by recording following entry :

Fixed Assets A/c	Dr.	11,00,000	
Stock A/c	Dr.	1,00,000	
Debtors A/c	Dr.	50,000	
Bank A/c	Dr.	12,000	
To 12% Debentures			2,00,000

To Debenture Interest o/s	12,000
To Creditors	3,00,000
To Business Purchase A/c	7,45,000
To Capital Reserve (Bal. figure)	5,000

(2) Reconstruction expenses of Rs. 5,000 have been adjusted against the Capital Reserve.

(3) Debenture Interest O/s has been discharged by issuing equity shares.

QUESTIONS

1. Define amalgamation, absorption & reconstruction.
2. Distinguish between, "amalgamation in the nature of merger" and "amalgamation in the nature of purchase."
3. Explain the conditions to be satisfied in amalgamation in the nature of merger as per AS-14.
4. Define purchase consideration as per AS-14.
5. Write a note on treatment of realisation expenses.
6. When amalgamation adjustment account is opened and why?
7. Write a note on "pooling of interest method" and "purchase method".
8. Write short notes :

   Statutory Reserves Vs. Capital Reserve; Transferor Vs. Transferee Company; External Reconstruction Vs. Amalgamation; Book Value Vs. Intrinsic Value.

ASSIGNMENTS

1. A Ltd. is absorbed by B Ltd. on that date the Balance Sheet of A Ltd. was as follows:

Liabilities	Rs.	Assets	Rs.
12% Preference Shares of Rs. 100 each	5,00,000	Sundry Assets	20,00,000
7,500 Equity Shares of Rs. 100 each	7,50,000		
General Reserve	3,00,000		
Profit & Loss A/c	1,50,000		
6% Debentures	2,00,000		
Sundry Creditors	1,00,000		
	20,00,000		20,00,000

B Ltd. agrees to

(i) Issue 9% Preference Shares of Rs. 100 each in the ratio of 3:4 to preference shareholders.

(ii) Issue to the debenture holders of AS Ltd. 9% Debentures at Rs. 96 in lieu of 6% Debentures in the old company.

(iii) Pay Rs. 10 per share in Cash and to issue six equity shares of Rs. 100 each at the market price of Rs. 125 in exchange for every 5 shares held in A Ltd. and

(iv) Assume liability to creditors.

Calculate Purchase Consideration.

Ans. : Rs. 15,75,000

2. X Ltd. absorbs Y Ltd. as on 31st March, 2005 when its Balance Sheet was as follows :

Liabilities	Rs.	Assets	Rs..
70,000 Equity Shares of Rs. 10 each	7,00,000	S. Net Assets	6,80,000
9% Preference Shares of Rs. 100 each	1,00,000	Profit & Loss A/c	1,20,000
	8,00,000		8,00,000

X Ltd. agrees to takeover assets of X Ltd. An equity share in Y Ltd. is valued at Rs. 7 for the purpose of absorption. X Ltd. agrees to pay Rs. 1,00,000 cash to preference shareholders and the balance in the form of equity shares valued at Rs. 12.50 each.

Calculate Purchase consideration.

Ans. : Rs. 5,90,000

Hint : Rs. 1,00,000 Cash to Preference Shareholders and Equity Shares worth Rs. 4,90,000 to Equity Shareholders.

3. The two Companies Abad Ltd. and Nabad Ltd. amalgamate and form a new company called Kamyab Ltd. The position of two Companies was as under :

Liabilities:	Abad Ltd. Rs.	Nabad Ltd. Rs.
Paid-up Capital		
Shares of Rs. 10 each fully paid	3,00,000	2,00,000
Profit & Loss A/c	50,000	42,000
5% Debentures	70,000	—
Sundry Creditors	30,000	58,000
	4,50,000	3,00,000

Assets :	Rs.	Rs.
Goodwill	70,000	—
Stock	1,80,000	80,000
Debtors	2,00,000	2,20,000
	4,50,000	3,00,000

The average profits of Abad Ltd. and Nabad Ltd. have been Rs. 30,000 and Rs. 20,000 respectively. Kamyab Ltd. agrees with the two companies to takeover both the companies for the sum of Rs. 6,00,000 and in addition to discharge all liabilities; Rs. 1,00,000 to be paid in cash and the balance in shares at face value.

It is further agreed that the Debtors of both the companies before being taken over by Kamyab Ltd. will be written off to the extent of 10% of their respective book figures. The profit on conversion is to be divided between the shareholders of Abad Ltd. and Nabad Ltd. in the same proportion as to profits previously earned by them.

Calculate purchase consideration and prepare, Realisation A/c and Shareholders' A/c in the books of Abad Ltd. and Nabad Ltd. and prepare Business Purchase A/c in the books of Kamyab Ltd.

C.A. (I) Modified.

	Abad Ltd.	Nabad Ltd.
	Rs.	Rs.
Ans : Purchase Consideration (Rs.)	3,60,000	2,40,000
Profit (Loss) on Realisation A/c	10,000	(2,000)
Profit on Conversion	30,000	20,000

Goodwill arising from Business Purchase A/c Rs. 1,20,000

4. A Ltd. was absorbed by B Ltd. as on 31st March, 2005. The purchase consideration was agreed at Rs. 3,36,600 to be discharged in fully paid equity shares of Rs. 10 each Balance Sheets of both the companies were as under :

Liabilities :	A Ltd.	B Ltd.
	Rs.	Rs.
Share Capital (Issued & Subscribed)		
Shares of Rs. 10 each	2,00,000	7,50,000
General Reserve	50,000	1,50,000
Profit & Loss A/c	12,900	20,500
Workmen Compensation Fund	9,000	12,000
Sundry Creditors	30,460	58,570
Staff Provident Fund	4,000	10,000
Provision for Taxation	5,000	12,000
	3,11,360	10,13,070
Assets :		
Goodwill	60,000	2,00,000
Plant & Machinery	1,00,000	3,12,000
Stock	80,000	2,65,000
Debtors	56,000	2,21,200
Prepaid Insurance	700	—
Income Tax Refund Claim	6,000	—
Cash at Bank	8,300	14,000
Cash in hand	360	870
	3,11,360	10,13,070

Prepare necessary ledger accounts in the books of A Ltd. and pass journal entries in the books of B Ltd. Also prepare a Balance Sheet after amalgamation.

C.S. (I) Modified.

Ans : Realisation A/c Profit = Rs. 64,700

General Reserve (Dr.) Rs. 73,700 after Adjustment 76,300

5. The following are the Balance Sheets of P Ltd. and S Ltd. as 31st March, 2005

Liabilities :	P Ltd.	S Ltd.
	Rs.	Rs.
Equity Share Capital (Rs. 10 each)	5,00,000	3,00,000
14% Preference Share Capital (Rs. 100 each)	2,20,000	1,70,000
General Reserve	50,000	25,000
Export Profit Reserve	30,000	20,000
Investment Allowance Reserve	—	10,000
Profit & Loss A/c	75,000	50,000
13% Debentures (Rs. 100 each)	50,000	35,000
Current liabilities	65,000	50,000
	9,90,000	6,60,000
Assets :		
Land & Building	2,50,000	1,55,000
Plant & Machinery	3,25,000	1,70,000
Furniture & Fittings	57,500	35,000
Investments	1,25,000	95,000
Stock	90,000	1,03,000
Debtors	72,500	52,000
Cash & Bank	70,000	50,000
	9,90,000	6,60,000

P Ltd. takesover S Ltd. as on 1st April 2005 P Ltd. discharges the purchase consideration as below :

(i) Issued 35,000 equity shares of Rs. 10 each at par to the equity shareholders of S Ltd.

(ii) Issued 15% preference shares of Rs. 100 each to discharge the preference shareholders of S Ltd. at 10% premium.

(iii) The debentures of S Ltd. will be converted into equivalent number of debentures of P Ltd.

(iv) The Statutory Reserves of S Ltd. are to be maintained for three more years.

You are required to show the Balance Sheet of P Ltd. assuming that :

(a) It is amalgamation in the nature of merger.

(b) It is amalgamation in the nature of purchase.

[B.Com (H) D.U. Modified]

Ans : Purchase Consideration : Rs. 5,37,000

Total of Balance Sheet : Rs. 16,50,000 (Merger)

Rs. 16,80,000 (Purchase)

General Reserve Rs. 8,000 (Merger)

Capital Reserve Rs. 38,000 (Purchase)

6. The Balance Sheets of Star Ltd. and Moon Ltd. as on 31st March 2005 were as under :

Liabilities :	Star Ltd. Rs.	Moon Ltd. Rs.
Share Capital :		
9% Redeemable Preference Shares of Rs. 100 each	1,80,000	—
Equity Shares of Rs. 10 each	4,20,000	3,00,000
Securities Premium	21,000	—
Capital Redemption Reserve	1,20,000	—
General Reserve	99,000	1,50,000
8% Debentures	1,20,000	1,80,000
Sundry Creditors	2,40,000	2,70,000
	12,00,000	9,00,000
Assets :		
Goodwill	30,000	—
Land & Building		2,10,000
Plant	6,00,000	2,70,000
Fixtures	10,000	30,000
Motor Vehicles	20,000	30,000
Stock	2,40,000	1,50,000
Debtors	1,60,000	1,00,000
Advances	1,00,000	70,000
Cash & Bank	40,000	40,000
	12,00,000	9,00,000

On 1st April 2005 Sun Ltd. was formed by amalgamating Star Ltd. & Moon Ltd. on the following terms :

1. Sun Ltd. to issue 120-10%. Debentures of Rs. 1000 each to debentureholders of Star Ltd.
2. The debentureholders of Moon Ltd. insisted that they should be allotted equity shares in Sun Ltd. Accordingly they were allotted 15,000 equity shares of Rs. 10 each @Rs. 12 per share.
3. Preference shareholders of Star Ltd. insisted for allotment of 1,800-11% Redeemable preference shares of Rs. 100 each.
4. The equity shareholders of Star Ltd. are to be allotted 10 equity shares at par for every 7 equity shares held by them.
5. The assets of the Star Ltd. are takenover at book value. The assets of Moon Ltd. are valued as under :

Goodwill	60,000
Land & Building	3,90,000
Plant	2,40,000
Other Fixed Assets	30,000
All Current Assets	3,00,000
All Current Liabilities	3,00,000

The balance of consideration is to be paid by allotment of equity shares at par to Moon Ltd.

You are required to show :

1. Purchase consideration payable to Star Ltd. & Moon Ltd. & necessary ledger accounts to close the books.
2. Opening entries and Balance Sheet of Sun Ltd.

[ICWA (F) Adapted]

Ans : Purchase Consideration : Star Ltd. = Rs. 7,80,000; Moon Ltd. = Rs. 5,40,000

Total of Balance Sheet : Rs. 21,90,000

7. A Ltd. and B Ltd. decided to amalgamate their business and to form a new company called N Ltd. having an authorised capital of Rs. 25,00,000 divided into equity shares of Rs. 10 each. Equity Shares of N Ltd. are to be allotted at par to the shareholders of A Ltd. and B Ltd. in exchange for their shares.

The Balance Sheets of A Ltd. & B Ltd. as on 31st March, 2005 were as follows:

	A Ltd. Rs.	B Ltd. Rs.
Fixed Assets :		
Free hold Property at Cost	2,50,000	70,000
Plant & Machinery (at Cost less depreciation)	4,20,000	1,40,000
Trade Investment	1,50,000	—
	8,20,000	2,10,000
Current Assets :		
Stock	4,00,000	1,60,000
Debtors	1,04,000	57,000
Bank balance	49,000	33,000
	5,53,000	2,50,000
Total Assets	13,73,000	4,60,000
Less Current liabilities	3,52,000	1,20,000
	10,21,000	3,40,000
Representing :		
Equity Share Capital (Shares of Rs. 10 each)	4,00,000	1,60,000
General Reserve	5,00,000	1,00,000
Profit & Loss A/c	1,21,000	80,000
	10,21,000	3,40,000

It was agreed that :

(i) Fixed Assets be valued as follows :

	A Ltd.	B Ltd.
Freehold Property	3,00,000	80,000
Plant & Machinery	3,64,400	1,05,700
Trade Investments	2,00,000	—

(ii) A Provision for doubtful debts to be created @ 10% on debtors.

(iii) Value of stock be reduced by 12.5% and

(iv) Goodwill of A Ltd. be valued at Rs. 5,95,000 and B Ltd. Rs. 1,10,000.

After amalgamation N Ltd. issued for each additional equity share by means of rights issue in the ratio of 1 : 4. The issue was made at Rs. 12.50 per share which was paid in full on application. At the same time company also issued Rs. 10,00,000 10% debentures at Rs. 99 payable in full on application. Both the issues were fully subscribed and paid for in full.

You are required to calculate :

(i) The number of shares in N Ltd. to be issued to shareholders of A Ltd. and B Ltd. respectively indicating the ratio thereof to their former holdings.

(ii) Pass journal entries in the books of N Ltd.

(iii) Prepare a Balance Sheet of N Ltd.

[ICWA (F) Modified]

Ans :

	A Ltd.	B Ltd.
Purchase Consideration (Rs.)	16,00,000	4,00,000
No. of Shares issued	1,60,000	40,000
Ratio of former holding	4 : 1	5 : 2

Total of Balance Sheet Rs. 40,97,000

Hint : Rights issue of 50,000 Shares.

8. Anna Ltd. agreed to takeover the business of Panna Ltd. as on 31st March 2005 when the Balance Sheet of Panna Ltd. was as under :

Liabilities	Rs.	Assets	Rs.
Share Capital :		Goodwill	1,25,000
Equity Shares of Rs. 10 each	7,50,000	Fixed Assets	8,00,000
General Reserve	2,00,000	Stock	2,10,000
Profit & Loss A/c	1,50,000	Debtors	45,000
6% Debentures	1,25,000	Cash & Bank	70,000
Creditors	25,000		
	12,50,000		12,50,000

The consideration payable by Anna Ltd. was as follows :

(i) Issue of 1,12,500 shares of Rs. 10 each in Anna Ltd. having an agreed value of Rs. 15 per Share.

(ii) Cash payment equivalent to Rs. 2.50 for every share of Rs. 10 in Panna Ltd.

(iii) Issue of such an amount of fully paid 7% Debentures of Anna Ltd. at 96% as is sufficient to discharge 6% Debentures of Panna Ltd. at a premium of 20%.

(iv) The directors of Anna Ltd. valued Fixed Assets at Rs. 15,00,000

Stock at Rs. 1,77,500

Debtors subject to 5% for doubtful debts.

The cost of liquidation amounted to Rs. 6,250 Anna Ltd. also issued 12,500 shares of Rs. 10 each at Rs. 15 per share. The issue was fully subscribed and paid for.

You are required to prepare ledger accounts in the books of Panna Ltd. and prepare opening Balance Sheet of Anna Ltd.

[C.S. (I) Adapted]

Ans : Purchase Consideration — Rs. 18,75,000
Profit on Realisation — Rs. 7,68,750
Total of Balance Sheet — Rs. 20,56,250

9. Thick Ltd. agreed to absorb Thin Ltd. as on 31st March, 2005 when it's Balance Sheet was as follows :

Liabilities	Rs.	Assets	Rs.
Share Capital		**Fixed Assets :**	
2,000 6% Preference Shares of Rs. 100 each	2,00,000	Land & Building	4,00,000
		Plant & Machinery	2,00,000
40,000 Equity Shares of Rs. 10 each	4,00,000	**Current Assets :**	
General Reserve	40,000	Stock	4,00,000
Profit & Loss A/c	60,000	Debtors	1,00,000
8% Debentures	2,00,000	Cash & bank	70,000
Current liabilities	3,00,000	**Miscellaneous Expenses :**	
		Preliminary Expenses	20,000
		Discount on Issue of Debentures	10,000
	12,00,000		12,00,000

The consideration was payable as under :

(i) Preference shareholders of Thin Ltd. were to be allotted 9% Preference shares so as to redeem 6% Preference shares at 10% premium.

(ii) Equity shareholders of Thin Ltd. to be allotted six equity shares of Rs. 10 each issued at a premium of 10% and Rs. 3 cash against every five shares held.

(iii) 8% debentureholders of Thin Ltd. to be paid at 8% premium by 9% debenture at 10% discount. While arriving at the agreed consideration the directors of Thick Ltd. valued land & building at Rs. 5,00,000 stock at Rs. 4,40,000 and debtors at book value subject to an allowance of 4% to cover doubtful debts. Debtors of Thin company include Rs. 20,000 due from Thick Ltd. The machinery was taken at book figure.

It was agreed that before acquisition Thin Ltd. will pay a dividend of 10% on equity shares only because preference dividend has already been paid.

Liquidation expenses of Rs. 10,000 to be borne by Thin Ltd.

Pass journal entries to close the books of Thin Ltd. and opening entries in the books of Thick Ltd.

C.S. (I) Adapted.

Ans : Purchase Consideration— Rs. 7,72,000; Goodwill — Rs. 32,000

10. The following are the Balance Sheets of P Ltd. and N Ltd. as on 31st March, 2005.

Liabilities	P Ltd. Rs.	N Ltd. Rs.
Share Capital :		
Equity shares of Rs. 10 each	2,00,000	90,000
General Reserve	2,50,000	50,000
Profit & Loss A/c	1,50,000	40,000
Debentures	1,75,000	—
Current liabilities	1,25,000	70,000
	9,00,000	2,50,000
Assets :		
Fixed Assets	3,50,000	1,50,000
Investments	2,50,000	—
Current Assets	3,00,000	1,00,000
	9,00,000	2,50,000

(a) P Ltd. agrees to take over N Ltd. Findout the ratio of exchange of shares on the basis of intrinsic value.

(b) Calculate purchase consideration if :

(i) Shares are issued to liquidator of N Ltd. at intrinsic value.

(ii) Shares are issued at par.

[B.Com (H) Adapted]

Ans : (a) Ratio of exchange = 2 : 3

Intrinsic Value — P Ltd. Rs. 30; N Ltd. — Rs. 20

(b) Purchase consideration (i) Rs. 1,80,000

(Shares to be issued 6,000) (ii) Rs. 60,000

11. A Ltd. is absorbed by B. Ltd. On that date the Balance Sheet of A Ltd. was as follows :

Liabilities	Rs.	Assets		Rs.
20,000 Equity shares of Rs. 100 each	20,00,000	Machinery		30,00,000
General Reserve	14,00,000	Patents		3,50,000
12% Debentures	4,00,000	Investments		2,50,000
Creditors	1,40,000	Stock		2,00,000
Staff Provident Fund	2,00,000	Debtors	4,00,000	
Workmen's Accident Compensation		*Less* Provision	40,000	3,60,000
Fund (Estimated liability Rs. 10,000)	50,000	Bank		30,000
	41,90,000			41,90,000

The consideration for absorption is as follows :

(i) Payment of Rs. 15 per equity share in cash.

(ii) Allotment of one 14% Preference Share of Rs. 100 each in B Ltd. for every 4 equity shares held in A Ltd.

(iii) Allotment of 5 equity shares of Rs. 100 each in B Ltd. for every 4 equity shares held in A Ltd.

(iv) The creditors of A Ltd. include Rs. 50,000 due to B Ltd. The cost of liquidation amounts to Rs. 10,000

Close the books of A Ltd. and give opening entries in the books of B Ltd.

[B.Com (H) D.U. 2002]

Ans : Purchase Consideration — Rs. 33,00,000
Loss on Realisation — Rs. 1,50,000
Capital Reserve — Rs. 1,40,000

12. The following is the Balance Sheet of Black & White Company Ltd. as an 31st March, 2005.

Liabilities	Rs.	Assets	Rs.
Share Capital :		Land & Building	1,50,000
30,000 Shares of Rs. 10 each	3,00,000	Plant & Machinery	2,25,000
Reserve Fund	37,500	Furniture	3,750
Dividend Equalisation Fund	30,000	Stock	1,35,000
Profit & Loss A/c	7,500	S. Debtors	37,500
9% Debentures	1,50,000	Cash & Bank	18,750
S. Creditors	45,000		
	5,70,000		5,70,000

Due to some technical reasons the company could not operate and as such it was takenover by Evergreen Ltd. on the above date. The consideration was payable as follows :

(i) Payment of Rs. 4 in cash and one share of Rs. 5 in the Evergreen Ltd. at the market value of Rs. 8 per share in exchange for one share in the Black & White Ltd.

(ii) Discharge of debentures at a premium of 5%.

(iii) Taking over of sundry creditors.

(iv) Cost of liquidation amounted to Rs. 750 to be borne by the purchasing Company.

Prepare necessary ledger accounts in the books of absorbed Company and opening Balance Sheet in the books of absorbing Company.

[C.S. (I) Adapted]

Ans : Purchase consideration — Rs. 3,60,000
Realisation Loss — Rs. 7,500
Total of Balance Sheet — Rs. 5,51,250
Capital Reserve — Rs. 6,750
Bank Loan for paying P.C. — Rs. 2,59,500

13. Following are the Balance Sheets of S Ltd. and N Ltd. as on 31st March, 2005.

Liabilities	S Ltd. Rs.	N Ltd. Rs.
10% Preference Share Capital (Shares of Rs. 100 each)	1,50,000	1,50,000
Equity Share Capital (Shares of Rs. 10 each)	7,50,000	3,00,000
Reserve & Surplus	3,00,000	2,25,000
12% Debentures	1,50,000	1,50,000
Current liabilities		
S. Creditors	5,10,000	2,40,000
Bills Payable	30,000	30,000
	18,90,000	10,95,000

Note : Contingent liability for bills discounted Rs. 30,000

Assets	S. Ltd.	N Ltd.
Fixed Assets	9,00,000	5,25,000
Investments	90,000	1,20,000
Stock	4,50,000	2,55,000
Debtors	2,40,000	1,35,000
Bills Receivable	75,000	15,000
Cash & Bank	1,35,000	45,000
	18,90,000	10,95,000

Fixed assets of both the companies are to be valued at 20% above book value. Both the companies are to pay 10% equity dividend, preference dividend having already been paid.

After above transactions are given effect to, S Ltd. will absorb N Ltd. on the following terms :

(1) 6 Equity shares of Rs. 10 each are to be issued by S Ltd. at par against 5 shares of N Ltd.

(2) 10% Preference Shareholders of N Ltd. are to be paid at 10% discount by issue of 11% Preference shares of Rs. 100 each at par in S Ltd.

(3) 12% Debentureholders of N Ltd. are to be paid at 8% premium by 11% Debentures in S Ltd. issued at 10% discount.

(4) Liquidation expenses amounted to Rs. 30,000.

(5) Sundry Creditors of N Ltd. include Rs. 45,000 due from S Ltd. Bills Receivable discounted by S Ltd. were all accepted by N Ltd. Prepare.

(i) Realisation A/c, Shareholders' A/c and S Ltd. A/c in the books of N Ltd.

(ii) Opening entries and a Balance Sheet in the books of S Ltd.

[C.S.(F) Adapted]

Ans : Purchase Consideration — Rs. 4,95,000
Realisation Loss — Rs. 2,85,000
Capital Reserve — Rs. 2,43,000
Total of Balance Sheet — Rs. 30,90,000

Hint : Transfer fixed assets to Realisation A/c after revaluation because absorption is effected after the revaluation.

14. Aara Ltd. and Zara Ltd. are engaged in similar line of business. They decided to amalgamate their business as on 31st March, 2005 by forming Azra Ltd. with an Authorised Capital of Rs. 60,00,000 divided into 5,00,000 equity shares of Rs. 10 each and balance in preference shares of Rs. 100 each. The Balance Sheets of both the Companies were as under :

Liabilities	Aara Ltd. Rs.	Zara Ltd. Rs.
8% Preference Share Capital	10,00,000	—
Equity Share Capital	30,00,000	8,00,000
General Reserve	16,00,000	—
Profit & Loss A/c	1,80,000	64,000
Sundry Creditors	1,00,000	42,000
	58,80,000	9,06,000
Assets		
Goodwill	—	1,40,000
Land & Building	12,00,000	—
Plant	31,00,000	—
Furniture	—	50,000
Vehicles		80,000
Patents	4,00,000	
Stock	7,00,000	4,78,000
Debtors	1,60,000	1,24,000
Cash & Bank	3,20,000	34,000
	58,80,000	9,06,000

The terms of amalgamation were agreed upon as under :

(i) Azra Ltd. to allot 3,60,000 Equity shares @Rs. 12.50 to Aara Ltd. and pay cash Rs. 10,90,000 as consideration of whole of assets except cash & bank.

(ii) Zara Ltd. is to receive 60,000 equity shares @Rs. 12.50 as consideration for whole of the assets except Cash & Bank and a cash of Rs. 12,000.

(iii) Assets - except goodwill, taken at book value.

(iv) Azra Ltd. is to issue remaining Equity Shares at Rs. 12.50 each and Preference Shares at par for cash. The entire issue was fully subscribed and paid for.

(v) Both Aara Ltd. and Zara Ltd. are to pay liabilities and preference shareholders individually.

(vi) Azra Ltd. is to pay and bear liquidation expenses of Rs. 10,000 for Aara Ltd. and Rs. 4,000 for Zara Ltd. The formation expenses of Azra Ltd. amounted to Rs. 36,000 and Capital issue expenses Rs. 48,000.

You are required to close the books of Aara Ltd. & Zara Ltd. and opening entries and a Balance Sheet after amalgamation in the books of Azra Ltd.

[ICWA (F) Modified]

Ans. : Purchase Consideration — Aara Ltd. Rs. 55,90,000; Zara Ltd. Rs. 7,62,000
Realisation Account 1,30,000 (Profit) 68,000 (Loss)
Total of Balance Sheet Rs. 72,50,000 ; Goodwill Rs. 74,000

15. Strong Ltd. and Weak Ltd. doing similar business decided to merge with each other and form a New Company called Prosperous Ltd. with an Authorised Capital of Rs. 15,00,000 divided in equity shares of Rs. 10 each. Their Balance Sheets as on 31st March, 2005.

Liabilities	Strong Ltd.	Weak Ltd.
Share Capital :	Rs.	Rs.
Equity Shares of Rs. 10 each	6,00,000	2,25,000
General Reserve	2,70,000	22,500
Profit & Loss A/c	90,000	34,500
Current Liabilities	1,56,750	36,750
	11,16,750	3,18,750
Assets		
Fixed Assets	4,95,000	1,50,000
4% Government Notes @ Rs. 90	1,08,000	—
Inventory	2,40,000	60,750
Receivable	1,40,250	75,000
Cash & Bank	1,33,500	33,000
	11,16,750	3,18,750

Additional Information :

(i) Net profits for past three years :

Year ended 31st March, 2005	1,84,500	62,250
Year ended 31st March, 2004	1,64,250	47,100
Year ended 31st March, 2003	1,48,500	43,050

(ii) Goodwill is to be valued at 4 years average super profits based on the weighted average. The weights being as follows :

Year ended 31st March, 2005 — 3
Year ended 31st March, 2004 — 2
Year ended 31st March, 2003 — 1

(iii) Normal rate of return being 10% on operating capital employed as on 31st March, 2005.

(iv) Investments of Strong Ltd. to be disposed of at book value.

(v) Prosperous Ltd. agreed to allot 20 shares for holders of 10 shares in Strong Ltd. and 15 shares for holders of 10 shares in Weak Ltd. and to pay balance consideration in cash.

(vi) The expenses of formation came to Rs.7,800.

(vii) Prosperous Ltd. acquired a new computer costing Rs. 1,20,000. against cash.

Calculate purchase consideration Pass journal to close the books of both companies and prepare Balance Sheet of Prosperous Ltd.

[ICWA (F) Adopted]

Ans :

	Strong Ltd.	Weak Ltd.
Purchase Consideration	Rs. 12,87,000	Rs. 3,85,200

Balance Sheet (Total) Rs. 17,31,000; Goodwill in the Balance Sheet Rs. 4,30,200

Hint : For Calculating goodwill : Investments are to be treated as non-business asset and income therefrom as non-operating income. Hence exclude investment for calculating operating Capital employed and deduct Rs. 4,800 interest on investment from net profits given. Value of Goodwill Rs. 3,27,000 and Rs. 1,03,200 for Strong Ltd. & Weak Ltd. respectively.

(16) A Ltd. and B Ltd. were amalgamated on and from 1st April, 2005. A new company called C Ltd. was formed to takeover the business of existing companies. The Balance Sheets of A Ltd. and B Ltd. on that date were as follows :

Liabilities	A Ltd. Rs.	B Ltd. Rs.
Share Capital :		
12% Preference Share Capital (Shares of Rs. 100 each)	3,00,000	2,00,000
Equity Share Capital (Shares of Rs. 100 each)	8,00,000	7,50,000
Reserves & Surplus ;		
Revaluation Reserve	1,50,000	1,00,000
General Reserve	1,70,000	1,50,000
Investment Allowance Reserve	50,000	50,000
Profit & Loss A/c	50,000	30,000
Secured Loans :		
10% Debentures (Rs. 100)	60,000	30,000
Current liabilities & Provisions :		
Sundry Creditors	2,70,000	1,20,000
Bills Payable	1,50,000	70,000
	20,00,000	15,00,000
Assets		
Fixed Assets :		
Land & Building	5,50,000	4,00,000
Plant & Machinery	3,50,000	2,50,000
Investments	1,50,000	50,000
Current Assets :		
Stock	3,50,000	2,50,000
Sundry debtors	2,50,000	3,00,000
Bills Receivable	50,000	50,000
Cash & Bank	3,00,000	2,00,000
	20,00,000	15,00,000

Additional Information :

(i) C Ltd. will issue 5 equity shares for each equity share of A Ltd. and 4 equity shares for each equity share of B Ltd. The shares are to be issued @ Rs. 30 each having a face value of Rs. 10 per share.

(ii) Preference Shareholders of both the companies are issued equivalent number of 11% Preference shares of C Ltd. at a price of Rs. 150 per share having a face value of Rs. 100 each.

(iii) 10% Debentures of A Ltd. & B Ltd. are discharged by C Ltd. by issuing such number of it's 12% Debentures of Rs. 100 each so as to maintain same amount of interest.

(iv) Investment allowance reserve is to be maintained for 2 more years.

Record journal entries and prepare a Balance Sheet of C Ltd. as on 1st April 2005 assuming that it is amalgamation in the nature of purchase.

[C.A. (F) Modified]

Ans :	A Ltd.	B Ltd.
Purchase consideration :	Rs. 16,50,000	Rs. 12,00,000
Total of Balance Sheet :	Rs. 36,05,000	

Hint : Calculate debentures by dividing interest by the new coupon rate debentures.

(17) On 31st March, 2005. The Balance Sheets of N Ltd. and P Ltd. were as under :

Liabilities	N Ltd. Rs.	P Ltd. Rs.
Share Capital :		
12% 2,500 Preference Shares of Rs. 100 each	2,50,000	—
Equity Shares of Rs. 10 each	7,50,000	2,00,000
General Reserve	4,00,000	—
Profit & Loss A/c	16,000	
Investment Allowance Reserve	29,000	16,000
Creditors	25,000	10,500
	14,70,000	2,26,500
Assets		
Goodwill	—	35,000
Patents	1,00,000	—
Land & Building	3,00,000	—
Plant & Machinery	7,75,000	—
Motor Vehicles	—	20,000
Furniture	—	12,500
Investments	57,500	—
Stock	1,75,000	1,19,500
Debtors	40,000	31,000
Cash & Bank	22,500	8,500
	14,70,000	2,26,500

A new Company, R Ltd. was formed to acquire the assets and liabilities of N Ltd. & P Ltd. on the following terms :

(i) R Ltd. to have an Authorised Capital of Rs. 17,50,000 divided in 2,500 11% Preference Shares of Rs. 100 each and 1,50,000 Equity shares of Rs. 10 each.

(ii) Business of N Ltd. was valued at Rs. 15,00,000, settlement being Rs. 3,00,000 cash and the balance by issue of fully paid equity shares at Rs. 12 per share.

(iii) Business of P Ltd. valued at Rs. 2,40,000, to be satisfied by issue of fully paid equity shares at Rs. 12 each.

(iv) Preference Shares of N Ltd. were redeemed.

(v) R Ltd. made a public issue of 1,500 preference shares at par and 15,000 equity shares at Rs. 12 The issue was under written at the commission allowed by Law. The issue was fully subscribed. All obligations were met.

(vi) Lodha who promoted the scheme was allotted 2,000 equity shares credited as fully paid at Rs. 12 per share in consideration of his services.

Pass journal entries in the books of R Ltd. and it's Balance Sheet.

[C.S. (F) Adapted]

Ans. : Goodwill on acquisition — Rs. 94,000
Total of Balance Sheet — Rs. 18,74,500

(18) The following are the Balance Sheets of Radha Ltd. & Meera Ltd. as on 31st March, 2005.

Liabilities	Radha Ltd. Rs.	Meera Ltd. Rs.
Share Capital :		
Equity Shares of Rs. 10 each	8,00,000	6,00,000
Reserves & Surplus :		
Capital Reserve	20,000	50,000
Securities Premium	40,000	—
Reserve fund	60,000	1,00,000
Dividend Equalisation Fund	—	10,000
S. Creditors	80,000	60,000
	10,00,000	8,20,000
Assets		
Goodwill	60,000	20,000
Building	3,00,000	2,00,000
Stock	80,000	1,44,000
Debtors	4,20,000	2,40,000
Bank	1,20,000	1,80,000
Preliminary Expenses	20,000	36,000
	10,00,000	8,20,000

The goodwill of the two companies is to be valued at Rs. 80,000 and Rs. 1,00,000. respectively. Building of Radha Ltd. is worth Rs.5,80,000 and of Meera Ltd. Rs.2,80,000. Stock of Meera Ltd. has been shown at 90% of it's cost. The revised values of Radha Ltd. are not to be recorded and are given only for ascertaining the intrinsic values of the shares of both companies.

Pass journal entries in the books of the Radha Ltd. and show Balance Sheet after absorption of Meera Ltd.

[C.A. (F) Adapted]

Ans. :

		Radha Ltd. Rs.	Meera Ltd. Rs.
Intrinsic Value per share		15	15
Purchase Consideration	—	Rs. 9,00,000	
Total of Balance Sheet	—	Rs. 19,60,000	

(19) With a view to effecting economy in working the United Mills Limited agrees to takeover the business of the Bharat Hosiery Limited as on 31st March, 2005.

Liabilities	Rs.	Assets	Rs.
Share Capital		Land & Building	1,80,000
12,000 Shares of Rs. 50 each	6,00,000	Plant & Machinery	1,25,000
Reserve Fund	1,20,000	Stock	2,50,000
Reserve for doubtful debts	10,000	Debtors	2,90,000
Profit & Loss A/c	65,000	Cash & Bank	25,000
S. Creditors	75,000		
	8,70,000		8,70,000

The purchasers took over all assets and liabilities of the vendor company excepting a sum of Rs.10,000 to provide for cost of liquidation and payment to any dissentient shareholders. The purchase price was to be discharged by the allotment to the shareholders of the Vendor Company of the share of Rs. 100 (Rs. 90 paid up) of the United Mills Ltd. for every two shares in the Bharat Hosiery Ltd. The expenses of liquidation amount to Rs. 3,000. Dissentient shareholders of 100 shares are paid out at Rs. 70 per share.

Pass journal entries in the books of respective companies to give effect so the above transactions. Also prepare Balance Sheet after absorption.

[B.Com (H) D.U. Modified]

Ans. : Purchase Consideration — Rs. 5,35,500
Loss on Realisation — Rs. 2,44,500
Capital Reserve — Rs. 2,39,500
Balance Sheet Total — Rs. 8,60,000

EXTERNAL RECONSTRUCTION

(20) Ess Ltd. is taken-over by, Zed Ltd., newly formed Company. The Balance Sheet of Ess Ltd. as on 31st March, 2004 was as follows :

Liabilities	Rs.	Assets	Rs.
9% Preference Share Capital	9,00,000	Freehold Property	6,00,000
Shares of Rs. 100 each		Plant & Machinery	3,00,000
Equity Share Capital	12,00,000	Stock	1,50,000
Shares of Rs. 10 each		S. Debtors	2,25,000
Current liabilities	3,00,000	Profit & Loss A/c	11,25,000
	24,00,000		24,00,000

There was a contingent liability of Rs. 45,000 on account of legal dispute. Zed Ltd. agrees to take over the assets as follows :

Freehold property	90% of book value
Plant & Machinery	60% of book value
Stock	30% of book value
S. Debtors are considered	40% bad.

The purchase consideration was satisfied by issuing equal number of equity shares and preference shares in Zed Ltd., both having a face value of Rs. 10 each. The contingent liability materialised only to the extent of Rs. 30,000 It was takenover by Zed Ltd. and settled by issue of equity shares.

Record journal entries in the books of Ess Ltd. & Zed Ltd.

[ICWA (F) Adapted]

Ans. : Realisation Profit — Rs. 2,10,000
Purchase Consideration — Rs. 5,70,000

(21) The following is the Balance Sheet of Frank Ltd. on 31st March, 2005. The Company went into voluntary liquidation on 1.4.2005 and a new Company was formed to takeover the assets and liabilities of the old Company.

Liabilities	Rs.	Assets	Rs.
9% Preference Shares Capital		Goodwill	1,50,000
Shares of Rs. 100 each	9,00,000	Building	4,50,000
Equity Share Capital		Plant & Machinery	6,00,000
Shares of Rs. 100 each	15,00,000	Furniture	75,000
10% Debentures (Rs. 100)	6,00,000	Patents	1,50,000
Unsecured Loans	3,00,000	Investments	3,00,000
S. Creditors	1,50,000	Stock	3,00,000
		S. Debtors	2,25,000
		Cash & Bank	75,000
		Profit & Loss A/c	9,75,000
		Preliminary Expenses	1,50,000
	34,50,000		34,50,000

Preference dividend is in arrear for three years. Debenture interest has not been paid for last two years.

A company named Franklin Corporation was formed with an authorised capital of Rs. 18,00,000 divided into equity shares of Rs. 100 each. The New Company and stakeholders of old company agreed on the following terms :

(1) Preference shareholders waived the dividend and accepted one equity share in the new company for two shares held by them in old company.

(2) Equity shareholders accepted one equity share of Rs. 100 each Rs. 50 paid for every four shares held by them in the old company and agreed to bring Rs. 50 per share to be used for paying creditors.

(3) Debentureholders accepted one equity share of Rs. 100 for one debenture of Rs. 100 and also for interest due to them by way of equity shares.

(4) Loan creditors agreed to waive interest for next two years.

(5) S. Creditors accepted to receive half in cash in full settlement of their claims.

(6) Building is taken at 1/3rd more in value, Plant & machinery 25% less Furniture 50% less, Stock at Rs. 1,50,000 Investment at book value and Cash & Bank.

Prepare opening Balance Sheet.

[ICWA (F) Adapted]

Ans. : Purchase Consideration — Rs. 6,37,500
Capital Reserve — Rs. 30,000
Balance Sheet (Total) — Rs.19,50,000

(22) Unable to meet liabilities the court sanctioned a scheme of reconstruction as on 31st March, 2005 when the assets and liabilities of C Ltd. were as under :

Liabilities	Rs.	Assets	Rs.
Equity Share Capital	19,20,000	Land & Building	6,91,200
Shares of Rs. 10 each		Plant & Machinery	6,56,000
12% Debentures	17,60,000	Stock	9,72,800
Sundry Creditors	3,48,800	S. Debtors	14,40,000
o/s Liabilities	6,40,000	Bank	14,700
		Profit & Loss A/c	8,94,100
	46,68,800		46,68,800

Note : Debenture interest for one year had not been paid and is included in the figures of outstanding liabilities shown in the Balance Sheet.

The broad features of the sanctioned scheme are as under:

(i) CEE Ltd. will have a share capital of Rs. 25,00,000 divided into equity shares of Rs. 10 each.

(ii) Arrears of debenture interest will be satisfied by issue of fully paid up equity shares.

(iii) For every Rs. 100 due to creditors an immediate cash payment of Rs. 50 be made. In addition they would be allotted 3 equity shares in the company as fully paid up. Creditors will not have any other claims against the company.

(iv) Outstanding liabilities other than interest on debentures, would receive 75 paise in the rupee in full settlement.

(v) For every two equity shares in the company the holders will receive one share fully paid up.

(vi) 12% debentures will be replaced by 8% debentures.

(vii) Balance of equity shares will be fully paid up in cash by the holders.

(viii) Sundry debtors would be written off to the extent of Rs.12,00,000. Any balance on adjustment under the scheme of reconstruction, will be utilised to adjust the value of land & Building.

Close the books of C Ltd. and pass opening entries and give effect to the above in the Balance Sheet of CEE Ltd.

[ICWA (F) Modified]

Ans. : Purchase Consideration — Rs. 9,60,000
Realisation A/c (Loss) — Rs. 65,900
Balance Sheet — Rs. 42,60,000

(23) The following is the Balance Sheet of Sunset Ltd. as on 31st March, 2005.

Liabilities	Rs.	Assets	Rs.
Share Capital :		Goodwill at Cost	1,60,000
9% Preference Shares of	8,00,000	Plant & Machinery	14,40,000
Rs. 100 each		Stock	2,40,000
Equity Share Capital	16,00,000	Debtors	3,60,000
Shares of Rs. 50 each		Cash & Bank	1,20,000
6% Debentures	2,40,000	Preliminary Expenses	80,000
S. Creditors	3,20,000	Profit & Loss A/c	8,00,000
Bank Overdraft	2,40,000		
	32,00,000		32,00,000

Note : Preference dividends are in arrears for three years. In order to revitalise and revamp the company the following scheme of reconstruction was approved.

A Company named Sunrise Ltd.. is to be formed who will takeover the assets and liabilities as follows :

(i) Preference share holders to forgo their claim for arrears of dividend and claim in capital by 20% in consideration of 9% preference shares.

(ii) Creditors to forgo Rs. 40,000

(iii) Bank to convert the overdraft to a term loan.

(iv) Debentures will be exchanged according to existing terms and denomination.

(v) Plant & Machinery to be revalued at Rs. 12,00,000.

(vi) Debtors are considered bad up to Rs. 40,000.

(vii) Equity shares will be exchanged for the same number of equity shares in the new company at a reduced denomination as would be warrant under the circumstances.

Close the books of Sunset Ltd. and give opening balance sheet of Sunrise Ltd.

[C.A. (F) Adapted]

Ans. : Purchase Consideration — Rs. 11,20,000
Loss on Realisation — Rs. 2,40,000
Payment to Equity Shareholders — Rs. 4,80,000
Total of Balance Sheet — Rs. 18,80,000

Hint : Equity shareholders are to be paid the balance remaining after adjusting all accumulated losses including realisation loss, which amounts to Rs. 4,80,000. Since they are to be paid in same number but at reduced denomination which will be Rs. 15. (Rs. 4,80,000/ 32,000 shares)

(24) Following is the Balance Sheet of Dee Ltd. as on 31st March, 2005.

Liabilities	Rs.	Assets	Rs.
5,000 Equity Shares of Rs. 100 each	5,00,000	Fixed Assets	4,50,000
8% Debentures	2,00,000	Current Assets	2,00,000
S. Creditors	30,000	Cash	20,000
		Profit & Loss A/c	60,000
	7,30,000		7,30,000

It is decided to reconstruct the company and for this purpose a new company called Eee Ltd. is to be formed with nominal capital of Rs. 5,00,000 divided into 2,500 9% Preference Shares of Rs. 100 each and 25,000 equity shares of Rs. 10 each to takeover the assets and liabilities of Dee Ltd. on the following terms.

(i) Shareholders of Dee Ltd. are to receive 10 equity shares in Eee Ltd. for every two shares held by them.

(ii) The debenture holders in Dee Ltd. are to accept 2,000 preference shares.

(iii) Cost of liquidation amounting to Rs. 3,000 is paid by the new company. The balance of preference shares has been issued and takenup by the public.

Close the books of Dee Ltd. and pass journal entries in the books of Eee Ltd.

Ans. : Purchase Consideration — Rs. 2,50,000
Loss on Realisation — Rs. 1,90,000
Capital Reserve — Rs. 1,87,000

(25) A Ltd. incurred huge trading losses. Fail to improve the image and goodwill it went to into voluntary liquidation. It's balance sheet on that date was under :

Liabilities	Rs.	Assets	Rs.
9% Preference Shares of Rs. 100 each	5,00,000	Freehold Properties	2,12,000
		Other Fixed Assets	4,22,000
Equity Shares of Rs. 10 each	8,00,000	Current Assets	2,80,000
Pre Incorporation Profit	15,000	Profit & Loss A/c	5,36,000
Liabilities	1,35,000		
(There is a contingent liability in respect of a pending suit Rs. 18,500)			
	14,50,000		14,50,000

Z Ltd. was incorporated on 1st April 2005 to takeover some of the assets of A Ltd. at an agreed valuation as under :

	Rs.
Freehold property	3,00,000
Plant & Machinery	1,50,000
Stock	50,000
Furniture & Fixture	20,000

The total purchase consideration was satisfied by the allotment of preference and equity shares in the new Company in the ratio of 3 : 2. The preference shares carried 7% dividend where as equity shares of Rs. 30 each were issued as partly paid to the extent of Rs. 20 per share. New Company also agreed to takeover the contingent liability which ultimately materialised. The claimant was allotted equity shares as fully paid. The Book Debts of the old Company realised Rs. 1,65,000 and Trade creditors were settled for Rs. 1,14,000. The liabilities were discharged. The cost of winding up came to Rs. 13,000. The preference shareholders of the old Company agreed to accept in full satisfaction of their claims, the preference shares in the new Company and all the available cash.

Close the books of A Ltd. and give the Balance Sheet of Z Ltd.

[ICWA (F) Adapted]

Ans. : Purchase Consideration — Rs. 5,20,000 (Equity Shares Rs. 2,08,000
Preference Shares — Rs. 3,12,000)

Loss on Realisation — Rs. 71,000
Sacrifice by Preference Shareholders — Rs. 1,50,000

Preference Shareholders are paid Rs. 38,000 cash which is the balance available after discharging liabilities including contingent.

Total of Balance Sheet — Rs. 5,20,000

7

Internal Reconstruction

Internal reconstruction denotes reorganisation of capital structure of a company with out it's liquidation. Hence, no new company is formed and an existing company takes over another existing company. In fact it refers to an internal arrangement that gives a new look to the capital structure, adjusts the rights of various stakeholders viz shareholders, debentureholders and creditors along with the adjustments in the values of assets and eliminates fictitious assets forming part of Balance Sheet.

Legal Provisions

Sections 100 to 105 of the Companies Act 1956 contain the legal provisions relating to internal reconstruction which involves in essence an alteration of the Share Capital and adjustments in the values of assets and liabilities. An alteration of share capital may be done in any of the ways :

- Reduction in Share Capital
- Consolidation
- Sub-division
- Conversion and
- Cancellation or Surrender

However the following conditions must be satisfied.

(i) The scheme is authorised by Articles of Association and passed by a special resolution of the general meeting and confirmed by the Court.

(ii) The Scheme does not affect the creditors interest in any way. If the proposed scheme affects the interests of the creditors, the Court/Government (Company Law Board) shall confirm the scheme only after consulting the creditors.

(iii) The Government (CLB) shall pass the order of confirmation of internal reconstruction on such terms and conditions as it may think proper and just after consulting the creditors. If some of the creditors are unwilling the company will have to settle their claims. The court may sanction scheme if the company secures whole of the debts or amount fixed by the court.

(iv) The court may order the use of word "and reduced" after the name the company and may order the company to publish the reason of such reduction.

(v) The order of the court has to be filed with the registrar.

(vi) Capital reduction may involve variation of rights of different classes of shares. In such a case the consent of the holders of three fourth shares should be obtained.

(vii) Holders of at least one - tenth of the issued capital affected by variation may apply to court, within 21 days after the consent is obtained or resolution is passed, for cancellation of such variation. However, the decision of court shall be final.

ACCOUNTING TREATMENT

Internal reconstruction involving alteration of capital results in reduction of Capital by any of the following ways :

I. Cancellation or extinguishing the uncalled capital

A company may extinguish the uncalled amount of partly paid shares. This reduces the liability of the shareholders because shares are treated as fully paid. Simultaneously the security of creditors is also reduced to the extent of cancellation of uncalled capital. The following entry is recorded.

Share Capital A/c (Face Value)	Dr.	
To Share Capital A/c (Called up value)		(Now becomes the new face value)

Example (1)

A Ltd. has an issued capital of 50,000 shares of Rs. 10 each Rs. 8 called up & paid up. The company decides to write off uncalled liability in respect of shares. Pass journal entry.

Share Capital (Rs. 10) A/c	Dr.	4,00,000	
To Share Capital (Rs. 8) A/c			4,00,000

It simply implies that share of Rs. 10 each has been converted into Rs. 8 fully paid share. The entry cancels the old capital having a face values of Rs. 10 and creates new share capital account having a share value of Rs. 8.

II. Reduction through Refund of excess Capital

When a company finds surplus or idle capital due to recessionary tendencies it may return the excess capital to its shareholders Refund may be made (a) either by reducing the liability of members (b) or by without reducing the liability of members.

(a) (i)	Share Capital A/c	Dr.	(Total amount of old Capital)
	To Share Capital A/c		(Total amount of New Capital)
	To Shareholders' A/c		(Amount to be refunded)
(ii)	Shareholders' A/c	Dr.	
	To Bank A/c		

Example (2) (Refund through reduction in liability)

B Ltd. has an issued Capital of Rs. 10,00,000 divided in shares of Rs. 10 each fully paid. The Company decides to refund Rs. 2 per share by making the shares Rs. 8 fully paid up. Record journal entries.

(i)	Share Capital A/c (Rs. 10)	Dr.	10,00,000	
	To Share Capital A/c (Rs. 8)			8,00,000
	To Shareholders' A/c (Rs. 2)			2,00,000
(ii)	Shareholders' A/c	Dr.	2,00,000	
	To Bank A/c			2,00,000

(b) If the company decides **not to reduce the liability** of the members then the following entries are to be recorded :

(i) Share Capital A/c Dr. With the amount of reduction
To Shareholders' A/c

(ii) Shareholders' A/c Dr.
To Bank A/c

Taking the above example, the entries will be :

		Dr.		
(i)	Share Capital A/c	Dr.	2,00,000	
	To Shareholders' A/c			2,00,000
(ii)	Shareholders' A/c	Dr.	2,00,000	
	To Bank A/c			2,00,000

III. Reduction of Paid up Capital

A reduction in paid up capital is resorted to write off accumulated losses incurred by the company over the past years or to write off fictitious assets such as preliminary expenses, discount on issue of shares or debentures etc. All these items if appearing in the Balance Sheet are the proof of inept management resulting in continued losses because company could not write off such losses in the past. Even the goodwill appearing in the Balance Sheet is valueless. Further fixed assets are charged minimum possible depreciation in order to give the impression of better financial position. In other words company resorts to window dressing which is not a desirable way of presentation of facts and figures because it leads to a distorted picture about the affairs of business enterprise. Hence a capital reduction is aimed to eliminate such accumulated losses & fictitious assets and to make necessary adjustment in the value of fixed assets. For this purpose "Capital Reduction" A/c or Reconstruction A/c is opened which is credited with the amount of reduction in capital representing sacrifice by the shareholders. The amount so credited is utilised to reduce overvalued assets and to wipe out accumulated losses including fictitious assets.

Following entries are recorded :

(1) Reduction in capital without reducing the liability of the holder. (There is no change in the nominal value of share).

Share Capital A/c Dr. The amount of reduction
To Capital Reduction A/c
or
Reconstruction A/c

(2) Reduction in Capital and in liability of the holder. (Nominal value changed after reduction)

Share Capital A/c (Old Value) Dr.
To Share Capital A/c (New Value)
To Capital Reduction A/c
or
Reconstruction A/c

(3) In case the debentureholders or creditors also agree to forgo or reduce their claims against the Company.

Debentures A/c Dr. (With the amount waived or
Creditors A/c Dr. for gone by them)
To Reconstruction A/c

(4) If the debentureholders agree to accept new debentures of lower amount.

(Old) Debentures A/c	Dr.	(Total paid up value)
To (New) Debentures A/c		(Paid up amount of New Deb.)
To Reconstruction A/c		(Difference)

(5) To record an appreciation in land & building if any.

Land & Building A/c	Dr.	(Amount of appreciation)
To Reconstruction A/c		

(6) When accumulated losses and fictitious assets are written off.

Reconstruction A/c Dr.

To Profit & Loss A/c

To Preliminary Expenses

To Discount on Issue of shares/debentures

(7) When valueless intangibles are written off

Reconstruction A/c Dr.

To Goodwill

To Patents, Copyrights and Trademarks

(8) When over-valued assets and unrecorded liability are adjusted :

Reconstruction A/c Dr.

To Plant & Machinery

To Furniture

To Other Fixed Assets

To unrecorded Liability

(9) When expenses are incurred:

Reconstruction A/c Dr.

To Bank

(10) Balance of Reconstruction A/c remaining after above adjustment is transferred to Capital Reserve.

Reconstruction A/c Dr.

To Capital Reserve

(11) If there is a short fall *i.e.* the amount required to be adjusted against Reconstruction A/c is more than the amount standing to the credit of Reconstruction Account, accumulated profit in any form such as General Reserve, Profit & Loss A/c (Cr.) or Profit & Loss Appropriation A/c or ay un-utilised provision may be used.

General Reserve/Reserve Fund or

Profit & Loss/ Profit & Loss Appropriation A/c or Dr.

Provision A/c (Name)

To Reconstruction A/c

RECONSTRUCTION A/C (A FORMAT)

	Rs.		Rs.
To Profit & Loss A/c (Dr.)		By Preference Share Capital A/c	
To Preliminary Expenses		By Equity Share Capital A/c	
To Discount on Issue of Shares		By Debentures A/c	
To Discount or Issue of Debentures		By S. Creditors A/c	
To Goodwill		By Any Provision or	
To Patents		accumulated profit (B.F)*	
To Copyrights			
To Trade marks			
To Plant & Machinery			
To Furniture			
To Any other asset			
To Unrecorded liab.			
To Capital Reserve (B.F.)*			

* Only one balancing figure will appear.

IV. Sub-division of Shares

Sub-division of shares refers to conversion of shares of larger denomination into shares of smaller denominations, Sub division does not result in reduction of Capital but it simply changes the face value along with the number of shares. The total paid up capital remaining unchanged.

Journal Entry :

Share Capital A/c	(Shares of big denomination/Face value)
To Share Capital A/c	(Shares of small denomination or face value)

Example (3)

X Ltd. has 10,000 shares of Rs. 50 each. It decides to subdivide shares into shares of Rs. 10 each. Record entry.

Share Capital (Rs. 50) A/c	Dr.	5,00,000	
To Share Capital (Rs. 10) A/c			5,00,000
(Being 10,000 Shares of Rs. 50 each sub-divided into 50,000 shares of Rs. 10 each)			

V. Consolidation of Shares.

It refers to conversion of shares of smaller denomination (Face value) into shares of larger (face value) denomination.

Example (4) X Ltd. has 1,00,000 shares of Rs. 10 each. It decides to consolidate it's shares into shares of Rs. 100 each. Pass entry.

Share Capital A/c (Rs. 10 each)	Dr.
To Share Capital A/c (Rs. 100 each)	

(Being 1,00,000 shares of Rs. 10 each consolidated into 10,000 shares of Rs. 100 each)

VI. Conversion of Shares

In an internal reconstruction usually the preference shares, which carry fixed rate of dividend, may be converted in to equity shares. Thus company is able to minimise it's fixed commitment (burden) at the initial stage of reconstruction. Generally preference share holders accept the equity shares which are of smaller value.

Preference Share Capital A/c Dr.
  To Equity Share Capital A/c
  To Reconstruction A/c (difference)

VII. Surrender of Shares

Sometime reduction of share capital is effected through surrender of shares. For this purpose shares are sub-divided into shares of smaller denominations and the shareholders are made to surrender some of these subdivided shares. These shares so surrendered facilitate reconstruction of company through reorganisation. The debenture holders' and creditors' claims are settled through issue of surrendered shares. The amount forgone by these claimants is transferred to Reconstruction Account. Similarly the unissued surrendered shares are transferred to Reconstruction Account to be utilised to write off accumulated losses and fictitious assets etc.

(*Please see the illustrations no.* 15, 16, 17)

Illustration (1)

The following is the Balance Sheet of Oris Ltd. before reconstruction.

Liabilities	Rs.	Assets	Rs.
7% 12,000 Preference Shares of Rs. 100 each	12,00,000	Land & Building	8,00,000
15,000 Equity Shares of Rs. 100 each	15,00,000	Plant & machinery	5,36,000
6% Debentures (Including interest o/s)	11,46,000	Intangibles	6,36,000
S. Creditors	4,14,000	Stock	8,00,000
Other liabilities	70,000	Debtors	6,56,000
		Preliminary Expenses	22,000
		Profit & Loss A/c	8,80,000
	43,30,000		43,30,000

Preference dividend is in arrears for three years. The company is now earning profit but is short of working capital and a scheme of reconstruction is approved and sanctioned by the court.

(i) The preference shareholders have agreed to cancel arrears of dividend and to accept for each preference share four 6% preference shares of Rs. 20 each and to buy 6* new equity shares of Rs. 5 each fully paid.

(ii) The equity shareholders have agreed that their share of Rs. 100 be reduced to Rs. 5. They also agreed to subscribe in cash three new equity shares of Rs. 5 each.

(iii) Debentureholders of Rs. 3,00,000 have agreed to convert their debentures into preference shares of Rs. 20 each and 12,000 equity share of Rs. 5 each.

(iv) The directors have agreed to subscribe in cash for additional 40,000 new equity shares of Rs. 5 each.

(v) Of the cash received by the issue of new equity shares Rs. 3,46,000 is to be used to pay the debenture holders.

(vi) The amount available is to be applied to write off preliminary expenses, debit balance of Profit & Loss A/c and to write off Plant & Machinery by Rs. 70,000 the balance is to be used to write off the value of intangibles which include Copyrights, Trademarks & goodwill.

Pass journal entries prepare Reconstruction A/c and Balance Sheet after reconstruction.

B.Com. (D.U.) Adapted

Solution : 1

JOURNAL ENTRIES

Particulars		Rs.	Rs.
Equity Share Capital (old) A/c	Dr.	15,00,000	
To Equity Share Capital (New) A/c			75,000
To Reconstruction A/c			14,25,000
(Being equity shares reduced to Rs. 5 per share)			
Bank A/c	Dr.	2,25,000	
To Equity Share Capital A/c (New)			2,25,000
(Being Shareholders paid for 3 new equity shares for each share held) (15,000 × 3 × 5)			
7% Preference Share Capital A/c	Dr.	12,00,000	
To 6% Preference Share Capital A/c			9,60,000
To Reconstruction A/c			2,40,000
(Being preference Shares reduced to Rs. 20 per and balance transferred to Reconstruction A/c)			
Bank A/c	Dr.	3,60,000	
To Equity Share Capital A/c (New)			3,60,000
(Being preference shares paid for 6 equity shares for each share held) (12,000 × 6 × 5)			
6% Debentures A/c	Dr.	6,46,000	
To 6% Preference Share Capital (New) A/c			2,40,000
To Equity Share Capital (New) A/c			60,000
To Bank A/c			3,46,000
(Being 6% debentures converted in to shares and paid cash)			
Bank A/c	Dr.	2,00,000	
To Equity Share Capital (New) A/c			2,00,000
(Being 40,000 equity shares issued to directors for cash)			

Contd.

			Rs.	Rs.
	Reconstruction A/c	Dr.	16,65,000	
	To Preliminary Expenses A/c			22,000
	To Profit & Loss A/c			8,80,000
	To Plant & Machinery A/c			70,000
	To Intangibles A/c			6,36,000
	To Capital Reserve A/c (B.F.)			57,000
	(Being writing off fictitious assets writing down of other assets)			

BALANCE SHEET OF ORIS LTD. (... and reduced)
As on (after reconstruction)

Liabilities	Rs.	Assets	Rs.
Share Capital :		**Fixed Assets :**	
6% 60,000 Preference shares of Rs. 20 each	12,00,000	Land & Building	8,00,000
		Plant & Machinery	4,66,000
1,84,000 Equity shares of Rs. 5 each	9,20,000	**Current Assets :**	
		Stock	8,00,000
Reserve & Surplus :		Debtors	6,56,000
Capital Reserve	57,000	Bank	4,39,000
Secured Loan :			
6% Debentures	5,00,000		
Current liabilities :			
S. Creditors	4,14,000		
Other liabilities	70,000		
	31,61,000		31,61,000

BANK A/C

	Rs.		Rs.
To Balance b/d	—	By 6% Debentures	3,46,000
To Equity Share Capital	2,25,000	By Balance c/d	4,39,000
To Equity Share Capital	3,60,000		
To Equity Share Capital	2,00,000		
	7,85,000		7,85,000

Illustration (2)

The following in the Balance Sheet of Weak Ltd. as on 31st March 2005.

Liabilities	Rs.	Assets	Rs.
6% Preference Share Capital	5,00,000	Goodwill	4,20,000
5,000 Shares of Rs. 100 each		Building	6,20,000
Equity Share Capital		Plant & Machinery	5,25,000
90,000 Share of Rs. 10 each	9,00,000	Loose Tools	1,50,000
6% Debentures	3,60,000	Stock	1,20,000
Current liabilities	6,00,000	Debtors	1,80,000
(Creditors)		Cash & Bank	75,000
		Profits & Loss A/c	2,70,000
	23,60,000		23,60,000

A scheme of reconstruction was agreed to by the court and the creditors on the following terms:

(i) Creditors to accept 6% Debentures to the extent of half of their claims, the balance being payable in cash.

(ii) Preference shares to be reduced to Rs. 40 per share.

(iii) Equity shares to be reduced to Rs. 2 per share.

(iv) That the goodwill is worthless and assets are found overvalued to the following extent :

	Rs.
Building	1,50,000
Plant & Machinery	75,000
Loose Tools	90,000
Debtors	15,000

Record journal entries and prepare a Balance Sheet after reconstruction.

Solution : 2

JOURNAL ENTRIES

			Rs.	Rs.
	6% Preference Share Capital A/c (Rs. 100)	Dr.	5,00,000	
	To 6% Preference Share Capital (Rs. 40) A/c			2,00,000
	To Reconstruction A/c			3,00,000
	(Being preference shares reduced to Rs. 40 each)			
	Equity Share Capital A/c (Rs. 10)		9,00,000	
	To Equity Share Capital A/c (Rs. 2)			1,80,000
	To Reconstruction A/c			7,20,000
	(Being equity shares reduced to Rs. 2)			
	Current liabilities A/c	Dr.	6,00,000	
	To 6% Debentures			3,00,000
	To Bank A/c			3,00,000
	(Being creditors settled)			*Contd.*

			Rs.	Rs.
	Reconstruction A/c	Dr.	6,90,000	
	To Profit & Loss A/c			2,70,000
	To Goodwill			4,20,000
	(Being fictitious & intangibles written off)			
	Reconstruction A/c	Dr.	3,30,000	
	To Building			1,50,000
	To Plant & Machinery			75,000
	To Loose Tools			90,000
	To Debtors			15,000
	(Being assets written down)			

BALANCE SHEET OF WEAK LTD. (... and reduced)

As an 31st March, 2005

Liabilities	Rs.	Assets	Rs.
6% Preference Share Capital	2,00,000	Fixed Assets :	
Shares of Rs. 50 each		Building	4,70,000
Equity Share Capital	1,80,000	Plant & Machinery	4,50,000
Shares of Rs. 2 each		Loose Tools	60,000
6% Debentures	6,60,000	**Current Assets:**	
Bank Overdraft	2,25,000	Stock	1,20,000
		Debtors	1,65,000
	12,65,000		12,65,000

Illustration (3)

The Balance Sheet of Vyoma Ltd. as on 31st March, 2004 was as under :

Liabilities	Rs.	Assets	Rs.
6% 15,000 Preference Shares	15,00,000	Leaseholds	2,61,600
of Rs. 100 each		Plant & Machinery	84,400
1,00,000 Equity Shares	10,00,000	Patents & Goodwill	17,00,000
of Rs. 10 each		S. Debtors	1,53,000
S. Creditors	60,000	Stock	1,10,000
Bank Overdraft	40,000	Cash	1,000
		Preliminary Expenses	24,000
		Discount on Issue of Shares	36,000
		Profit & Loss A/c	2,30,000
	26,00,000		26,00,000

A scheme of reconstruction was sanctioned by the court. The accountant prepared the following Reconstruction Account as per proposed scheme.

RECONSTRUCTION ACCOUNT

	Rs.		Rs.
To Profit & Loss A/c	2,30,000	By 6% Preference Share Capital	7,50,000
To Preliminary Expenses	24,000	By Equity Share Capital	7,50,000
To Discount on issue of Shares	36,000		
To Patents & Goodwill	10,00,000		
To Debtors	30,600		
To Stock	30,000		
To Leaseholds	61,600		
To Plant & Machinery	16,880		
To Capital Reserve	70,920		
	15,00,000		15,00,000

Prepare Balance Sheet after implementation of scheme.

Solution : 3

BALANCE SHEET OF VYOMA LTD. (... and reduced)

As on 31st March, 2004

Liabilities	Rs.	Assets	Rs.
6% Preference Share Capital		Fixed Assets :	
15,000 shares of Rs. 50 each	7,50,000	Leaseholds	2,00,000
Equity Share Capital		Plant & Machinery	67,520
1,00,000 Share of Rs. 2.50 each	2,50,000	Patents & Goodwill	7,00,000
Reserve & Surplus :		**Current Assets :**	
Capital Reserve	70,920	Stock	80,000
Current liabilities:		Debtors	1,22,400
S. Creditors	60,000	Cash	1,000
Bank Overdraft	40,000		
	11,70,920		11,70,920

Illustration (4)

The following ledger balances are extracted from the books of Zed Ltd. as on 31st March, 2005.

	Rs.
Fixed Assets	7,00,000
7% Investments	10,000
Stock	3,90,000
Debtors	4,60,000

	Rs.
Preliminary Expenses	20,000
Sundry Creditors (including Y for Rs. 8,50,000)	11,50,000
10% First Debentures	2,00,000
12% Second Debentures	5,00,000
Bank Overdraft	50,000
Interest on Debentures o/s for one year	80,000
Equity Share Capital	6,00,000
(Shares of Rs. 10 each - 60% paid)	

Due to heavy and continued losses a scheme of reconstruction was agreed as follows:

(i) Equity shares to be made fully paid up and reduced to Rs. 2 each.

(ii) First Debentureholders' claims to be settled by issuing 11% 2000 Debentures of Rs. 100 each.

(iii) The claims of second Debentures are to be settled by issuing 13% Debentures of Rs. 100 each.

(iv) To pay Rs. 3,00,000 to Y in full settlement of his claim.

(v) To allot 1,50,000 Equity Shares of Rs. 2 each to discharge remaining creditors.

(vi) To write off the fictitious assets and to reduce the fixed assets.

Pass journal entries to give effect to reconstruction scheme and show the Balance Sheet after reconstruction.

[B.Com (H) D.U. Modified]

Solution : 4

Since heavy losses incurred in the past have not been given in the question, it is necessary to prepare opening balance sheet to determine the amount of losses incurred by the company.

Opening Balance Sheet (Just before Reconstruction)

Liabilities	Rs.	Assets	Rs.
Equity Share Capital	6,00,000	Fixed Assets	7,00,000
(Shares of Rs. 10 each		Investments	10,000
Rs. 6 paid up)		Stock	3,90,000
10% Debentures	2,00,000	Debtors	4,60,000
12% Debentures	5,00,000	Preliminary Expenses	20,000
S. Creditors	11,50,000	Profit Loss A/c	10,00,000
(including Y for Rs. 8,50,000)		(Bal. Figure)	
Bank Overdraft	50,000		
Debenture Interest o/s	80,000		
(One Year)			
	25,80,000		25,80,000

JOURNAL ENTRIES

		Rs.	Rs.
Share Final Call A/c	Dr.	4,00,000	
To Share Capital A/c			4,00,000
(Being final call made)			
Bank A/c	Dr.	4,00,000	
To Share Final Call A/c			4,00,000
(Being final call amount received)			
Equity Share Capital A/c (Rs. 10)	Dr.	10,00,000	
To Equity Share Capital (Rs. 2) A/c			2,00,000
To Reconstruction A/c			8,00,000
(Being equity share reduced to Rs. 2 each)			
10% First Debentures A/c	Dr.	2,00,000	
Interest on Debentures A/c	Dr.	20,000	
To Debenture holders A/c			2,20,000
(Being redemption due)			
Debenture holders' A/c	Dr.	2,20,000	
To 11% Debentures			2,00,000
To Reconstruction A/c			20,000
(Being debentureholders issued 11% debentures)			
12% Debentures A/c	Dr.	5,00,000	
Interest on Debentures A/c	Dr.	60,000	
To Debentureholders A/c			5,60,000
(Being redemption due)			
Debentureholders A/c	Dr.	5,60,000	
To 13% Debentures A/c			4,00,000
To Reconstruction A/c			1,60,000
S. Creditors A/c	Dr.	11,50,000	
To Bank A/c			3,00,000
To Equity Share Capital A/c			3,00,000
To Reconstruction A/c			5,50,000
(Being creditors discharged)			
Reconstruction A/c	Dr.	15,30,000	
To Profit & Loss A/c			10,00,000
To Preliminary Expenses A/c			20,000
To Fixed Assets A/c			5,10,000
(Being writing off fictitious assets & writing down fixed assets)			

BALANCE SHEET OF ZED LTD. (... and reduced)
As on 31st March, 2005

Liabilities	Rs.	Assets	Rs.
Share Capital :		Fixed Assets:	1,90,000
Equity Share Capital	5,00,000	Investments	10,000
Shares of Rs. 2 each		Current Assets :	
Reserve & Surplus :	—	Stock	3,90,000
Secured Loans :	—	Debtors	4,60,000
11% Debentures	2,00,000	Bank	50,000
13% Debentures	4,00,000		
Current liabilities & Provisions :	—		
	11,00,000		11,00,000

Illustration (5)

The following is the Balance Sheet of Sick Ltd. as on 31st March, 2005.

Liabilities	Rs.	Assets	Rs.
13% Cum-Preference Shares of Rs. 100 each	1,00,000	Fixed Assets	15,00,000
		Current Assets	35,00,000
Equity Shares of Rs. 10 each	7,00,000	Profit & Loss A/c	3,00,000
8% Debentures	3,00,000		
Current liabilities	39,00,000		
Provision for Taxation	3,00,000		
	53,00,000		53,00,000

The following scheme of reconstruction is sanctioned :

(a) Fixed assets are to be written down by 33 $^1/_3$%.

(b) Current assets are to be valued at Rs. 27,00,000.

(c) Preference shareholders decide to forego their right to arrears of dividend which are in arrears for three years.

(d) The tax liability of the company is settled at Rs. 4,00,000 and the same is paid immediately.

(e) One of the creditors of the company, to whom the company owes Rs. 25,00,000 decides to forgo 50% of his claim. He is allotted 1,00,000 equity shares of Rs. 5 each in part satisfaction of the balance of his claim.

(f) The rate of interest on debentures is increased to 11%. The debentureholders surrender their debentures of Rs. 100 each in exchange for fresh debentures of Rs. 75 each.

(g) The existing equity and preference shares are reduced to Rs. 5 each and Rs. 75 each respectively.

Pass journal entries and show the new balance sheet of the company.

[C.S. (I) & B. Com. (H) Modified]

Solution : 5

JOURNAL ENTRIES

			Rs.	Rs.
	Equity Share Capital A/c (Rs. 10)	Dr.	7,00,000	
	To Equity Share Capital A/c (Rs. 5)			3,50,000
	To Reconstruction A/c			3,50,000
	(Being equity shares reduced to Rs. 5 each)			
	13% Preference Share Capital A/c (Rs. 100)	Dr.	1,00,000	
	To 13% Preference Share Capital A/c (Rs. 75)			75,000
	To Reconstruction A/c			25,000
	(Being preference shares reduced to Rs. 75 each)			
	Current Liabilities A/c	Dr.	17,50,000	
	To Equity Share Capital A/c			5,00,000
	To Reconstruction A/c			12,50,000
	(Being creditors settled)			
	8% Debentures A/c	Dr.	3,00,000	
	To 11% Debentures A/c			2,25,000
	To Reconstruction A/c			75,000
	(Being 8% Debentures of Rs. 100 each converted in to debentures of Rs. 75 each)			
	Reconstruction A/c	Dr.	17,00,000	
	To Profit & Loss A/c			3,00,000
	To Fixed Assets			5,00,000
	To Current Assets			8,00,000
	To Provision for Taxation			1,00,000
	(Being adjustments made in the assets & liabilities as per the provisions of scheme)			
	Provision for Taxation A/c	Dr.	4,00,000	
	To Current Assets			4,00,000
	(Being tax liability paid)			

BALANCE SHEET AS ON 31ST MARCH, 2005 (... and reduced)

Liabilities	Rs.	Assets	Rs.
13% Cum Preference Shares		Fixed Assets	10,00,000
of Rs. 75 each	75,000	Current Assets*	23,00,000
Equity Shares of Rs. 5 each	8,50,000		
11% Debentures	2,25,000		
Current liabilities	21,50,000		
	33,00,000		33,00,000

* Includes Cash and Bank balance also.

Cancellation of arrears of preference dividend does not require any entry unless the same is not shown in the liabilities side of Balance Sheet.

Illustration (6)

Following was the Balance Sheet of Grand Ltd. as on 31st March, 2005

Liabilities		Rs.	Assets		Rs.
Share Capital :			Goodwill		1,00,000
1,20,000 Equity Shares			Machinery		5,09,000
of 10 each	12,00,000		Furniture		1,13,000
Less Calls in Arrears	90,000	11,10,000	Stock		2,05,000
@ Rs. 3 per share			Debtors		1,50,000
S. Creditors		1,55,000	Cash & Bank		15,000
Provision for Taxation		50,000	Preliminary Expenses		15,000
			Profit & Loss A/c	2,20,000	
			Less Profit for the current year	12,000	2,08,000
		13,15,000			13,15,000

The directors found machinery over valued by Rs. 1,00,000. It is proposed to write down machinery to its true value and to extinguish the deficiency in the Profit & Loss A/c and to write off goodwill and preliminary expenses by adopting the following scheme :

(i) Forfeit the shares on which the call is outstanding.

(ii) Reduce the paid up capital by Rs. 3 per share.

(iii) Reissue the forfeited shares as fully paid share of Rs. 7 each at Rs. 5 per share.

(iv) Utilise the provision for taxation, if necessary.

The shares on which the calls were in arrears were duly forfeited and reissued on payment of Rs. 5 per share.

Pass journal entries, prepare Reconstruction Account and draw Balance Sheet after the implementation of scheme of reconstruction.

[B. Com (H) D.U. Modified]

Solution : 6

JOURNAL ENTRIES

		Rs.	Rs.
	Reconstruction A/c Dr.	4,23,000	
	To Machinery A/c		1,00,000
	To Profit & Loss A/c		2,08,000
	To Preliminary Expenses		15,000
	To Goodwill		1,00,000
	(Being reconstruction scheme implemented)		
	Share Capital A/c Dr.	3,00,000	
	To Share Forfeited A/c		2,10,000
	To Calls-in-Arrears		90,000
	(Being shares forfeited)		

Contd.

		Rs.	Rs.
Bank A/c	Dr.	1,50,000	
Share Forfeited A/c	Dr.	60,000	
To Share Capital A/c			2,10,000
(Being forfeited shares issued @Rs. 5 per share credited @ Rs. 7 per share as fully paid)			
Share forfeited A/c	Dr.	1,50,000	
To Capital Reserve A/c			1,50,000
(Being balance of share forfeited account transferred to Capital Reserve)			
Share Capital A/c	Dr.	2,70,000	
To Reconstruction A/c			2,70,000
(Being remaining 90,000 shares reduced to Rs. 7 per share)			
Capital Reserve A/c	Dr.	1,50,000	
Provision for Taxation A/c	Dr.	3,000	
To Reconstruction A/c			1,53,000
(Being short full of reconstruction met out of capital reserve and Provision for taxation)			

RECONSTRUCTION A/C

	Rs.		Rs.
To Machinery A/c	1,00,000	By Share Capital A/c	2,70,000
To Profit & Loss A/c	2,08,000	By Capital Reserve A/c	1,50,000
To Goodwill A/c	1,00,000	By Provision for Taxation (B.F.)	3,000
To Preliminary Expenses	15,000		
	4,23,000		4,23,000

BALANCE SHEET OF GRAND LTD. (... and reduced)
As on 31st March, 2005

Liabilities	Rs.	Assets	Rs.
Share Capital :		Machinery	4,09,000
1,20,000 Shares of Rs. 10 each		Furniture	1,03,000
Rs. 7 paid up	8,40,000	Stock	2,05,000
S. Creditors	1,55,000	Debtors	1,50,000
Provision for Taxation	37,000	Cash & Bank balance*	1,65,000
	10,32,000		10,32,000

* Rs. 15,000 + 1,50,000 (Balance + Reissue)

Illustration (7)

The following is the Balance Sheet of Damodar Ltd. as on 31st March, 2005.

	Rs.		Rs.
Share Capital :		Goodwill	2,50,000
20,000 Equity Shares of		Plant & Machinery	3,80,000
Rs. 100 each	20,00,000	Land & Building	1,50,000
12% Debentures	5,00,000	Stock	2,70,000
Debentures Interest o/s	1,20,000	Debtors	60,000
S. Creditors	3,00,000	Cash & Bank	35,000
		Profit & Loss A/c	17,55,000
		Preliminary Expenses	20,000
	29,20,000		29,20,000

The following scheme of reconstruction is executed :

(i) Equity shares are reduced by Rs. 95 per share and then consolidated into 10,000 equity shares of Rs. 10 each.

(ii) Debentureholders agree to forgo outstanding debenture interest. As a compensation 12% Debentures are converted into 14% Debentures.

(iii) S. Creditors are given the option to either accept 50% of their claims in cash in full settlement or to convert their claims into equity shares of Rs. 10 each. Creditors for Rs. 2,00,000 opt for shares and the remaining for cash.

(iv) To make payment to creditors opting for cash payment and to augment working capital the company issued 50,000 equity shares of Rs. 10 each at par. The issue by was fully subscribed and paid for in full on application.

(v) Following revaluations were made :

		Rs.
Land and Building	—	2,00,000
Plant & Machinery	—	2,90,000
Debtors	—	Subject to provision of Rs. 5,000

Pass journal entries, prepare reconstruction account & draw a Balance Sheet after reconstruction.

[B.Com (H) D.U. Modified]

Solution : 7

JOURNAL ENTRIES

		Rs.	Rs.
Equity Share Capital A/c (Rs. 100)	Dr.	20,00,000	
To Equity Share Capital A/c (Rs. 5)			1,00,000
To Reconstruction A/c			19,00,000
(Being shares reduced to Rs. 5 per share)			
Equity Share Capital A/c (Rs. 5)	Dr.	1,00,000	
To Equity Share Capital A/c (Rs. 10)			1,00,000
(Being 20,000 shares of Rs. 5 each consolidated into 10,000 shares of Rs. 10 each)			

Contd.

Particulars		Rs.	Rs.
Debenture Interest o/s A/c	Dr.	1,20,000	
To Reconstruction A/c			1,20,000
(Being debenture Interest forgone by debenture holders)			
12% Debentures A/c	Dr.	5,00,000	
To 14% Debentures A/c			5,00,000
(Being 12% debentures converted into 14% debentures)			
S. Creditors A/c	Dr.	3,00,000	
To Equity Share Capital A/c			2,00,000
To Bank A/c			50,000
To Reconstruction A/c			50,000
(Being creditors account settled)			
Bank A/c	Dr.	5,00,000	
To Equity Share Application A/c			5,00,000
(Being share issued)			
Equity Share Application A/c	Dr.	5,00,000	
To Equity Share Capital A/c			5,00,000
(Being application transferred to Share Capital A/c)			
Land & Building A/c	Dr.	50,000	
To Reconstruction A/c			50,000
(Being land and building revalued)			
Reconstruction A/c	Dr.	21,20,000	
To Goodwill A/c			2,50,000
To Plant & Machinery A/c			90,000
To Provision for doubtful debts A/c			5,000
To Preliminary Expenses A/c			20,000
To Profit & Loss A/c			17,55,000
(Being fictitious assets written off & other assets adjusted to it's true values)			

RECONSTRUCTION A/C

	Rs.		Rs.
To Goodwill A/c	2,50,000	By Share Capital A/c	19,00,000
To Plant & Machinery A/c	90,000	By Land & Building A/c	50,000
To Provision for Bad debts	5,000	By Debenture Interest o/s	1,20,000
To Preliminary Expenses	20,000	By S. Creditors	50,000
To Profit & Loss A/c	17,55,000		
	21,20,000		21,20,000

BALANCE SHEET OF DAMODAR LTD. (... and reduced)
As on 31st March, 2005

	Rs.			Rs.
Share Capital :		Fixed Assets:		
80,000 Shares of* Rs. 10 each	8,00,000	Land & Building		2,00,000
Secured Loans :		Plant & Machinery		2,90,000
14% Debentures	5,00,000	Current Assets		
		Stock		2,70,000
		Debtors	60,000	
		Less Provision	5,000	55,000
		Bank balance		4,85,000
	13,00,000			13,00,000

Working notes

*10,000 Shares (Original Capital after reduction)
20,000 Shares issued to creditors
50,000 Shares issued to public.
80,000 Shares.

CASH & BANK A/C

	Rs.		Rs.
To Balance b/d	35,000	By S. Creditors	50,000
To Equity Share Application	5,00,000	By Balance c/d	4,85,000
	5,35,000		5,35,000

Illustration (8)

The following is the Balance Sheet of H Ltd. as on 1st April 2005

Liabilities	Rs.	Assets	Rs.
Authorised Share Capital :		Goodwill	20,000
80,000 Equity Shares of Rs. 10 each	8,00,000	Land & Building	1,60,000
		Plant & Machinery	1,20,000
9% 2,000 Preference shares of Rs. 100 each	2,00,000	Investments	24,000
		Stock	54,000
Issued & Paid up Capital :		Debtors	1,18,000
40,000 Equity Shares of		Cash & Bank	6,000
Rs. 10 each Rs. 7.50 paid up	3,00,000	Profit & Loss A/c	1,48,000
9% 2,000 Preference Shares of Rs. 100 each fully paid	2,00,000		
Unsecured Loans	80,000		
Trade Creditors	48,000		
Bank Overdraft	22,000		
	6,50,000		6,50,000

Preference dividend has not been declared for last two years. No provision has been made for sales tax liability of Rs. 9,600. A scheme of reconstruction initiated by members and creditors has been approved by the court on the following lines :

(i) Uncalled capital is to be called up in full and equity shares are to be reduced to Rs. 5 per share.
(ii) Sales Tax Liability of Rs. 9,000 is to be paid immediately.
(iii) Land & Building is to be shown in the Balance Sheet at full market value of Rs. 2,20,000 and goodwill is to be written off.
(iv) Trade creditors have consented for 25% of remission of liability on a condition that 25% of net liability after remission is paid forth with and the balance is paid within one year.
(v) The investments are takenover by the bank in full settlement of the overdraft balance.
(iv) Preference shareholders have agreed to give up their right for the arrears of dividend and accept 12 fully paid equity shares of Rs. 5 each for each preference share held.

You are required to :

(i) Draft journal entries, (ii) Prepare Reconstruction Account and (iii) Draw up Balance Sheet after reconstruction scheme is implemented.

[C.A. (I) Modified]

Solution : 8

JOURNAL ENTRIES

			Rs.	Rs.
	Share Final Call A/c	Dr.	1,00,000	
	To Equity Share Capital A/c			1,00,000
	(Being final call become due)			
	Bank A/c	Dr.	1,00,000	
	To Share final Call A/c			1,00,000
	(Being final call money received)			
	Equity Share Capital A/c (Rs. 10)	Dr.	4,00,000	
	To Equity Share Capital A/c (Rs. 5)			2,00,000
	To Reconstruction A/c			2,00,000
	(Being equity shares reduced to Rs. 5 per share)			
	Sales Tax Payable A/c	Dr.	9,000	
	To Bank A/c			9,000
	(Being sales tax liability met)			
	Land & Building A/c	Dr.	60,000	
	To Reconstruction A/c			60,000
	(Being appreciation of Land & Building transferred to Reconstruction A/c)			
	Trade Creditors A/c	Dr.	21,000	
	To Reconstruction A/c			12,000
	To Bank A/c			9,000
	(Being creditors claims adjusted)			

Contd.

Particulars		Rs.	Rs.
Bank Overdraft A/c	Dr.	22,000	
Reconstruction A/c	Dr.	2,000	
To Investments A/c			24,000
(Being Bank over draft discharged against investments)			
9% Preference Share Capital A/c	Dr.	2,00,000	
To Equity Share Capital A/c			1,20,000
To Reconstruction A/c			80,000
(Being Pref. Shares converted into Equity Shares of Rs. 5 each)			
Reconstruction A/c	Dr.	1,77,000	
To Goodwill A/c			20,000
To Profit & Loss A/c			1,48,000
To Sale Tax Payable A/c			9,000
(Being items adjusted against reconstruction A/c)			
Reconstruction A/c	Dr.	1,73,000	
To Capital Reserve A/c			1,73,000
(Being balance of reconstruction A/c transferred to Capital reserve)			

RECONSTRUCTION A/C

	Rs.		Rs.
To Goodwill A/c	20,000	By Equity Share Capital A/c	2,00,000
To Profit & Loss A/c	1,48,000	By Preference Share Capital A/c	80,000
To Sales Tax Payable A/c	9,000	By Land & Building A/c	60,000
To Investments A/c	2,000	By Trade Creditors A/c	12,000
To Capital Reserve (Bal. Figure)	1,73,000		
	3,52,000		3,52,000

BALANCE SHEET OF H LTD. (... and reduced)
As on 1st April, 2005

Liabilities	Rs.	Assets	Rs.
Authorised Capital :		**Fixed Assets:**	
80,000 Equity Shares of Rs. 5 each	4,00,000	Land & Building	2,20,000
Issued, Subscribed & Paid up Capital :		Plant & Machinery	1,20,000
64,000 Equity Shares of Rs. 5		**Current Assets:**	
each fully paid	3,20,000	Stock	54,000
Reserve & Surplus :		S. Debtors	1,18,000
Capital Reserve	1,73,000	Cash & Bank	88,000
Unsecured Loan	80,000		
Current liabilities :			
S. Creditors	27,000		
	6,00,000		6,00,000

Illustration (9)

The following is the Balance Sheet of P Ltd. as on 31st March, 2005.

Liabilities	Rs.	Assets	Rs.
Share Capital :		Goodwill	60,000
6% Preference Shares of Rs. 100 each	3,00,000	Patents (Estimated value Rs. 30,000)	80,000
Equity Shares of Rs. 100 each	2,00,000	Building at Cost	1,30,000
6% Debentures	1,00,000	Plant & Machinery at Cost	2,60,000
(Secured by floating charge)		Stock	80,000
Debenture Interest o/s	12,000	(Market Value)	
S. Creditors	1,00,000	Debtors (Good)	40,000
Bank Overdraft (Limit Rs. 25,000)	24,000	Profit & Loss A/c	86,000
	7,36,000		7,36,000

Dividend on preference shares has been in arrears for two years. The directors are of the opinion that if additional plant is installed at a cost of Rs. 1,00,000 and working capital requirement are fully met, the company will earn enough profit to pay equity @10% subject to suitable scheme of reconstruction being put through. The existing Building and Plant & Machinery are considered as being worth Rs. 1,52,000 and Rs. 2,00,000 on a going concern basis.

Debenture holders are anxious to be paid the interest due to them but are willing to provide one-half of the additional capital required on a suitable basis Preference shareholders are willing to accept a reasonable sacrifice provided they are given an interest in equity capital. An scheme of reconstruction was sanctioned as follows :

(i) Preference shareholders to accept sufficient number of 9% cum preference shares so as to maintain their interest. Arrears of dividend to be cancelled.

(ii) Equity shareholders to get same number of shares of Rs. 30 each.

(iii) Working Capital is required to be maintained on the basis of standard current ratio.

(iv) To augment working capital and to meet cost of plant the company issued 9% Preference shares of Rs. 100 each and equity shares of Rs. 30 each in equal proportion, besides the agreed proportion of 8% Debentures of Rs. 100 each at par. Interest due to debentureholders was paid in cash.

Pass journal entries and prepare Balance Sheet after reconstruction.

[ICWA (F) Adapted]

Solution : 9

JOURNAL ENTRIES

			Rs.	Rs.
	6% Preference Share Capital A/c	Dr.	3,00,000	
	To 9% Preference Share Capital A/c			2,00,000
	To Reconstruction A/c			1,00,000
	(Being 6% Pref. Shares converted in to 9% Pref. Shares)			

Contd.

Particulars		Rs.	Rs.
Equity Share Capital A/c (Rs. 100)	Dr.	2,00,000	
To Equity Share Capital A/c (Rs. 30)			60,000
To Reconstruction A/c			1,40,000
(Being equity shares reduced to Rs. 30 each as fully paid)			
Bank A/c	Dr.	2,40,000	
To 9% Preference Share Capital A/c			60,000
To Equity Share Capital A/c			60,000
To 6% Debentures A/c			1,20,000
(Being Preference Shares, Equity Shares and Debentures issued for cash)			
Debenture Interest o/s A/c	Dr.	12,000	
To Bank A/c			12,000
(Being o/s Debenture Interest paid)			
Building A/c	Dr.	22,000	
To Reconstruction A/c			22,000
(Being building revalued)			
Machinery A/c	Dr.	1,00,000	
To Bank A/c			1,00,000
(Being machinery acquired)			
Reconstruction A/c	Dr.	2,56,000	
To Goodwill A/c			60,000
To Patents A/c			50,000
To Profit & Loss A/c			86,000
To Plant & Machinery A/c			60,000
(Being accumulated Losses intangibles written off and plant & Machinery revalued)			
Reconstruction A/c	Dr.	6,000	
To Capital Reserve A/c			6,000
(Being balance of Reconstruction A/c transferred to Capital Reserve)			

Working notes

(1) 9% Preference shares to be issued in lieu of 6% Preference shares to maintain same return.

$$\frac{18,000 \times 100}{9}$$ Rs. 2,00,000

(2) Amount required to be raised

	Rs.
Purchase of additional plant	1,00,000
O/s Interest on Debentures to be paid	12,000
Working Capital required*	1,28,000
Total	2,40,000

* Since standard current ratio is 2 : 1 the current assets have to be double of current liabilities.

Current liabilities (after o/s debenture interest) (S. Creditors + Bank Overdraft)	Rs. 1,24,000
Hence Current Assets to be	Rs. 2,48,000
Where as existing current Assets are	Rs. 1,20,000
Working Capital or additional net Current Assets required	Rs. 1,28,000

Since debentureholders are willing to provide one-half of the additional capital requirements the debentures worth Rs. 1,20,000 ($^1/_2$ of Rs. 2,40,000) to be issued, and remaining Rs. 1,20,000 to be raised by issue of preference shares and equity shares in equal proportion i.e. Rs. 60,000 each.

BALANCE SHEET (After Reconstruction)
As on 31st March, 2005

Liabilities	Rs.	Assets	Rs.
Share Capital :		**Fixed Assets :**	
9% Preference Share Capital		Building	1,52,000
2,600 shares of Rs. 100 each		Machinery	
fully paid	2,60,000	(including addition)	3,00,000
Equity Share Capital		Patents	30,000
4,000 Shares of Rs. 30 each	1,20,000	**Current Assets :**	
fully paid		Stock	80,000
Reserve & Surplus :		Debentures	40,000
Capital Reserve	6,000	Bank Balance*	1,28,000
Secured Loan			
6% Debentures	2,20,000		
Current Liabilities			
S. Creditors	1,00,000		
Bank Overdraft	24,000		
	7,30,000		7,30,000

* Rs. 2,40,000 – Rs. 12,000 – Rs. 1,00,000

Illustration : (10)

The following is the Balance Sheet of Zed Ltd. as on 31st March, 2005

Liabilities	Rs.	Assets	Rs.
Share Capital :		Freehold Property	3,50,000
6% 2,000 Cumulative Preference		Plant	50,000
Shares of Rs. 100 each	2,00,000	Trade Investments	60,000
75,000 Equity Shares of Rs. 10 each	7,50,000	Stock	2,00,000
6% Debentures (secured on property)	3,75,000	Debtors	4,00,000
Accrued Interest on Debentures	22,500	Deferred Advertisement Expenses	1,50,000
Director's Loan	2,00,000	Profit & Loss A/c	3,50,000
S. Creditors	12,500		
	15,60,000		15,60,000

The following scheme of Reconstruction was approved by the court.

(i) Preference shares to be written down to Rs. 75 each and equity shares to Rs. 2 each.

(ii) For Preference dividend in arrears for four years, 75% to be waived and equity shares of Rs. 2 end to be allotted for the remaining quarter.

(iii) Accrued debenture interest to be paid in cash.

(iv) Debentureholders agreed to takeover property (Book value- Rs. 1,00,000) at a valuation of Rs. 1,50,000 in part payment of their holding and to provide additional cash of Rs. 1,30,000 secured by a floating charge of the company's assets at an interest rate of 10% p.a.

(v) Deferred Advertisement expenses to be written off.

(vi) Stock to be written off fully.

(vii) Rs. 2,33,000 to be provided for bad debts.

(viii) Remaining property to be valued at Rs. 4,00,000.

(ix) Investments sold out at Rs. 1,50,000.

(x) Directors to accept equity shares of Rs. 2 each for 90% of their loans, waiving 10% of the balance of their loan amount.

(xi) Capital commitments contracts totalling Rs. 3,00,000 are to be cancelled by payment of penalty @ 5% of contract value.

(xii) Taxation & cost of scheme to be ignored.

Pass journal entries and draw Balance Sheet implementing the scheme.

[ICWA (F) Modified]

Solution : 10

JOURNAL ENTRIES

		Rs.	Rs.
	6% Preference Share Capital A/c Dr.	50,000	
	To Reconstruction A/c		50,000
	(Being Preference shares paid up amount reduced to Rs. 75)		
	Equity Share Capital A/c Dr.	6,00,000	
	To Reconstruction A/c		6,00,000
	(Being paid up value of equity shares reduced to Rs. 2)		
	Accrued Debenture Interest A/c Dr.	22,500	
	To Bank A/c		22,500
	(Being accrued debenture interest paid)		
	Freehold Property A/c Dr.	2,00,000	
	To Reconstruction A/c		2,00,000
	(Being appreciation of Freehold property transferred to Reconstruction A/c)		
	6% Debentures A/c Dr.	1,50,000	
	To Freehold property		1,50,000
	(Being takeover of freehold property in part settlement of claims of debentureholders)		

Contd.

		Rs.	Rs.
Reconstruction A/c	Dr.	12,000	
To Equity Share Capital A/c			12,000
(Being 6,000 equity shares allotted in full settlement of preference dividend)			
Bank A/c	Dr.	1,30,000	
To 10% Debentures A/c			1,30,000
(Being 10% debentures issued for cash)			
Bank A/c	Dr.	1,50,000	
To Investments A/c			60,000
To Reconstruction A/c			90,000
(Being investments sold)			
Director's Loan A/c	Dr.	2,00,000	
To Equity Share Capital A/c			1,80,000
To Reconstruction A/c			20,000
(Being director's loan settled)			
Reconstruction A/c	Dr.	15,000	
To Bank A/c			15,000
(Being 5% penalty paid)			
Reconstruction A/c	Dr.	9,13,000	
To Profit & Loss A/c			3,50,000
To Deferred Advertisement Exp. A/c			1,50,000
To Stock A/c			2,00,000
To Provision for bad debts A/c			2,33,000
(Being fictitious assets and losses on revaluation writing off)			

BALANCE SHEET OF ZED LTD.
As on 31st March, 2005

Liabilities	Rs.	Assets		Rs.
Share Capital :		Fixed Assets :		
6% Preference Shares of Rs. 100 each Rs. 75 paid up.	1,50,000	Freehold Property		4,00,000
Equity Shares of Rs. 10 each Rs. 2 paid up	3,42,000	Plant		50,000
Secured Loans :		**Current Assets :**		
10% Debentures	1,30,000	Debtors	4,00,000	
6% Debentures	2,25,000	*Less* Provision	2,33,000	1,67,000
S. Creditors	12,500	Bank Balance		2,42,500
	8,59,500			8,59,500

Working note:

Arrears of preference dividend for 4 years Rs. 2,00,000 @ 6% × 4	48,000
Less 75% waived	36,000
Paid in Equity Shares	12,000

Illustration (11)

The financial position of Ahuja Ltd. as on 31st March 2005 was as under:

Liabilities	Rs.	Assets	Rs.
6% Preference Shares of Rs. 100 each	10,00,000	Freehold Property	3,40,000
Equity Shares of Rs. 100 each	15,00,000	Plant & Machinery	9,60,000
7% Secured Debentures	6,00,000	Tools & Dies	2,73,000
Interest thereon o/s	42,000	Investments	1,50,000
Secured Loan	2,00,000	Stock	4,25,000
S. Creditors	5,00,000	Debtors	5,34,000
		Research & Development Expenses	1,80,000
		Profit & Loss A/c	9,80,000
	38,42,000		38,42,000

A Scheme of reconstruction sanctioned by the court, was as follows :

(a) Assets to be revalued as under :

	Rs.
Plant & Machinery	5,90,000
Tools & Dies	1,50,000
Stock	3,00,000
Debtors	4,87,000

(b) Research & Development Expenses and Profit & Loss Account to be written off.

(c) Land at book value of Rs. 60,000, valued at Rs. 1,40,000 to be takenover by debentureholders in part payment. The remaining property is valued at Rs. 4,00,000.

(d) Investments valued at Rs. 2,20,000 to be taken over by Loan Creditors, Rs. 20,000 to be refunded to company.

(e) The Creditors for Rs. 1,80,000 have agreed to accept new 10% debentures secured by second floating charge in settlement of Rs. 1,55,000. Creditors of Rs. 1,00,000 agreed to accept cash at a discount of 15%.

(f) Preference Shares are to be reduced to Rs. 80 each & equity shares to Rs. 10 each Equity shareholders to subscribe and pay for two new equity shares of Rs. 10 each for every share held.

(g) The cost of scheme amounted to Rs. 35,000 to be paid & written off.

Draft journal entries, prepare Reconstruction A/c and resultant Balance Sheet.

[ICWA (F) Modified]

Solution : 11

JOURNAL ENTRIES

		Rs.	Rs.
6% Preference Share Capital A/c (Rs. 100)	Dr.	10,00,000	
To 6% Preference Share Capital A/c (Rs. 80)			8,00,000
To Reconstruction A/c			2,00,000
(Being preference shares reduced to Rs. 80 as fully paid)			
Equity Share Capital A/c (Rs. 100)	Dr.	15,00,000	
To Equity Share Capital A/c (Rs. 10)			1,50,000
To Reconstruction A/c			13,50,000
(Being equity shares reduced to Rs. 10 as fully paid)			
Freehold Property A/c	Dr.	2,00,000	
To Reconstruction A/c			2,00,000
(Being Freehold property revalued)			
Investments A/c	Dr.	70,000	
To Reconstruction A/c			70,000
(Being appreciation recorded)			
S. Creditors A/c	Dr.	2,80,000	
To 10% Debentures A/c			1,55,000
To Bank A/c			85,000
To Reconstruction A/c			40,000
(Being creditors settled)			
Loans (Secured) A/c	Dr.	2,00,000	
Bank A/c	Dr.	20,000	
To Investments A/c			2,20,000
(Being investments takenover by the loan creditor)			
7% Debentures (Secured) A/c	Dr.	1,40,000	
To Freehold Property A/c			1,40,000
(Being Freehold property taken over by debentureholders)			
Reconstruction A/c	Dr.	18,25,000	
To Profit & Loss A/c			9,80,000
To Research & Development Exp. A/c			1,80,000
To Plant & Machinery A/c			3,70,000
To Tools & Dies A/c			1,23,000
To Stock A/c			1,25,000
To Debtors A/c			47,000
(Being fictitious assets written off & other assets adjusted at revised figures)			

Contd.

			Rs.	Rs.
	Reconstruction A/c To Bank A/c (Being payment of expenses made)	Dr.	35,000	35,000
	Bank A/c To Equity Share Capital A/c (Being shares issued for cash)	Dr.	3,00,000	3,00,000

RECONSTRUCTION A/C

	Rs.		Rs.
To Profit & Loss A/c	9,80,000	By Preference Share Capital A/c	2,00,000
To Research & Development A/c	1,80,000	By Equity Share Capital A/c	13,50,000
To Plant & Machinery A/c	3,70,000	By Freehold Property A/c	2,00,000
To Tools & Dies a/c	1,23,000	By Investment A/c	70,000
To Stock A/c	1,25,000	By S. Creditors A/c	40,000
To Debtors A/c	47,000		
To Bank (Exp.)	35,000		
	18,60,000		18,60,000

BANK A/C

	Rs.		Rs.
To Equity Share Capital A/c	3,00,000	By S. Creditors	85,000
To Investments A/c	20,000	By Reconst. Expenses	35,000
		By Balance c/d	2,00,000
	3,20,000		3,20,000

BALANCE SHEET OF AHUJA LTD. (... and reduced)
As on 31st March, 2005

Liabilities	Rs.	Assets	Rs.
Share Capital :		**Fixed Assets :**	
6% Pref. Shares of Rs. 80 each	8,00,000	Freehold Property	4,00,000
Equity Shares of Rs. 10 each	4,50,000	Plant & Machinery	5,90,000
7% Secured Debentures	4,60,000	Tools & Dies	1,50,000
10% Debentures (Secured by floating charge)	1,55,000	**Current Assets :**	
		Stock	3,00,000
Debenture Interest o/s	42,000	Debtors	4,87,000
S. Creditors	2,20,000	Bank	2,00,000
	21,27,000		21,27,000

Illustration (12)

The following is the Balance Sheet of Rocky Ltd. as on 31st March, 2005.

Liabilities	Rs. in '000'	Assets	Rs. in '000'
Equity Share Capital		Goodwill	15
Shares of Rs. 10 each	500	Land & Building	184
Capital Reserve	6	Plant & Machinery	286
12% Debentures	400	Furniture & Fixtures	41
Debenture Interest O/s	48	Stock	142
Trade Creditors	165	Debtors	80
Director's Remuneration O/s	10	Cash & Bank	27
Other o/s Expenses	11	Discount on Issue of debentures	8
Provisions	33	Profit & Loss A/c	390
	11,73		11,73

The following scheme of internal reconstruction was framed, approved by the court and all concerned parties and implemented :

(i) All the equity shares be converted into same number of equity shares of Rs. 2.50 each.

(ii) Directors agree to forgo their outstanding remuneration.

(iii) The debentureholders also agreed to forgo outstanding interest in return of their 12% debentures being converted into 13% debentures.

(iv) The existing shareholders agree to subscribe for cash fully paid equity shares of Rs. 2.50 each for Rs. 1,25,000.

(v) Trade creditors are given the option of either to accept fully paid equity shares of Rs. 2.50 each for the amount due to them or to accept 80% of the amount due in cash. Creditors for Rs. 65,000 accept equity shares where as those for Rs. 1,00,000 accept Rs. 80,000 in cash in full settlement.

(vi) The assets are revalued as under :

	(Rs. '000')
Land and Building	230
Plant & Machinery	220
Stock	120
Debtors	76

Pass journal entries and draft company's Balance Sheet immediately after reconstruction.

[C.A. (I) May 2000, Modified]

Solution : 12

JOURNAL ENTRIES

			Rs.	Rs.
	Equity Share Capital A/c (Rs. 10)	Dr.	5,00,000	
	To Equity Share Capital A/c (Rs. 2.50)			1,25,000
	To Reconstruction A/c			3,75,000
	(Being equity shares converted into shares of Rs. 2.50 each)			
	O/s Directors' Remuneration A/c	Dr.	10,000	
	To Reconstruction A/c			10,000
	(Being remuneration forgone by directors)			
	12% Debentures A/c	Dr.	4,00,000	
	Debenture Interest o/s	Dr.	48,000	
	To 13% Debentures A/c			4,00,000
	To Reconstruction A/c			48,000
	(Being 12% debentures converted into 13% debentures)			
	Trade Creditors A/c	Dr.	1,65,000	
	To Equity Share Capital A/c			65,000
	To Bank A/c			80,000
	To Reconstruction A/c			20,000
	(Being Creditors Claims settled)			
	Land & Building A/c	Dr.	46,000	
	To Reconstruction A/c			46,000
	(Being appreciation of Land and Building transferred to Reconstruction A/c)			
	Reconstruction A/c	Dr.	4,99,000	
	Capital Reserve A/c (B.F.)	Dr.	6,000	
	To Goodwill A/c			15,000
	To Plant & Machinery A/c			66,000
	To Stock A/c			22,000
	To Debtors A/c			4,000
	To Discount on Issue of Deb.			8,000
	To Profit & Loss A/c			3,90,000
	(Being fictitious assets written off and other assets adjusted as per reconstruction scheme)			
	Bank A/c	Dr.	1,25,000	
	To Equity Share Capital A/c			1,25,000
	(Being equity shares issued for cash)			

BALANCE SHEET OF ROCKY LTD. (... and reduced)
As on 31st March, 2005

Liabilities	Rs.	Assets	Rs.
Equity Share Capital*	3,15,000	**Fixed Assets:**	
1,26,000 Shares of Rs. 2.50 each		Goodwill	—
Secured Loans :		Land & Building	2,30,000
13% Debentures	4,00,000	Plant & Machinery	2,20,000
Current Liabilities & Provisions :		Furniture & Fixtures	41,000
O/s Expenses		**Current Assets :**	
Provisions	11,000	Stock	1,20,000
	33,000	Debtors	76,000
		Cash & Bank	72,000
	7,59,000		7,59,000

*Equity Shares : Op. Balance	50,000
+ Issued to Creditors	26,000
+ Issued to public for cash	50,000
Total No. of Shares	1,26,000

Illustration (13)

Green Ltd. had decided to reconstruct the Balance Sheet since it had accumulated huge losses. The following is the Balance Sheet of the Company on 31st March, 2005 before reconstruction :

Liabilities	Rs.	Assets	Rs.
Share Capital :		**Fixed Assets :**	
Authorised:		Goodwill	20,00,000
1,50,000 Equity Shares of		Building	10,00,000
Rs. 50 each	75,00,000	Plant	10,00,000
Subscribed & Paid up Capital:		Computers	25,00,000
50,000 Equity Shares of		Investments	Nil
Rs. 50 each fully paid up	25,00,000	Current Assets	Nil
1,00,000 Equity Shares of		Profit & Loss A/c	20,00,000
Rs. 50 each Rs. 40 paid up	40,00,000		
Secured Loans :			
12% First Debentures	5,00,000		
12% Second Debentures	10,00,000		
Current Liabilities :			
S. Creditors	5,00,000		
	85,00,000		85,00,000

The following is the interest of Mr. X & Mr. Y in Green Ltd.:

	Mr. X	Mr. Y
12% First Debentures	3,00,000	2,00,000
12% Second Debentures	7,00,000	3,00,000
Sundry Creditors	2,00,000	1,00,000
	12,00,000	6,00,000
Fully Paid up Rs. 50 Shares	3,00,000	2,00,000
Partly Paid up (Rs. 40 paid up)	5,00,000	5,00,000

The following scheme of reconstruction is approved by all parties having interest and by the court.

(a) Un called capital is to be called up in full and such shares and fully paid up shares be converted into equity shares of Rs. 20 each.

(b) Mr. X is to cancel Rs. 7,00,000 of his total debt (other than the share amount) and to pay Rs. 2,00,000 to company and to receive new 14% First Debentures for the balance amount.

(c) Mr. Y is to cancel Rs. 3,00,000 of his total debt (other than the share amount) and to accept new 14% First Debentures for the balance.

(d) The amount thus rendered available by the scheme shall be utilised in writing off Goodwill, Profit & Loss Account and the balance to write off value of Computers.

Pass journal entries and draw Balance Sheet of the reconstructed company.

[C.A. (I) Nov. 2000 Modified]

Solution : 13

JOURNAL ENTRIES

			Rs.	Rs.
	Share Final Call A/c	Dr.	10,00,000	
	To Equity Share Capital A/c			10,00,000
	(Being final call of Rs. 10 per share made on 1,00,000 shares)			
	Bank A/c	Dr.	10,00,000	
	To Share Final Call A/c			10,00,000
	(Being final call amount received)			
	Equity Share Capital A/c (Rs. 50)	Dr.	75,00,000	
	To Equity Share Capital A/c (Rs. 20)			30,00,000
	To Reconstruction A/c			45,00,000
	(Being equity shares reduced to Rs. 20 as fully paid)			
	12% First Debentures A/c	Dr.	3,00,000	
	12% Second Debentures A/c	Dr.	7,00,000	
	S. Creditors A/c	Dr.	2,00,000	
	Bank A/c	Dr.	2,00,000	
	To 14% First Debentures A/c			7,00,000
	To Reconstruction A/c			7,00,000
	(Being issue of 14% Debentures against cash payment of Rs. 2,00,000 and discharge of debt of Mr. X)			

Contd.

		Rs.	Rs.
12% First Debentures A/c	Dr.	2,00,000	
12% Second Debenture A/c	Dr.	3,00,000	
Sundry Creditors A/c	Dr.	1,00,000	
To 14% First Debentures A/c			3,00,000
To Reconstruction A/c			3,00,000
(Being 14% First debentures issued against total debts of Y)			
Reconstruction A/c	Dr.	55,00,000	
To Profit & Loss A/c			20,00,000
To Goodwill A/c			20,00,000
To Computers A/c			15,00,000
(Being accumulated losses and goodwill written off and the computers to the extent of available balance)			

BALANCE SHEET OF GREEN LTD. (AFTER RECONSTRUCTION)

Liabilities	Rs.	Assets	Rs.
Share Capital :		**Fixed Assets:**	
1,50,000 Equity Shares Rs. 20 each	30,00,000	Building	10,00,000
Secured Loans :		Plant	10,00,000
14% First Debentures	10,00,000	Computers	10,00,000
Current Liabilities :		**Current Assets :**	
Sundry Creditors	2,00,000	Cash & Bank	12,00,000
	42,00,000		42,00,000

Illustration (14)

The Balance Sheet of Y Ltd. as on 31st March 2005 was as follows:

Liabilities	Rs.	Assets	Rs.
9% Preference Shares of Rs. 100 each fully paid	20,00,000	Goodwill	10,00,000
		Patents	5,00,000
Equity Shares of Rs. 10 each fully paid	50,00,000	Land & Building	30,00,000
10% First Debentures	6,00,000	Plant & Machinery	10,00,000
10% Second Debentures	10,00,000	Furniture & Fixture	2,00,000
Debenture Interest o/s	1,60,000	Computers	3,00,000
Director's Loan	1,00,000	Trade Investments	5,00,000
Trade Creditors	5,00,000	Debtors	5,00,000
Bank overdraft	1,00,000	Stock	10,00,000
Outstanding liabilities	40,000	Discount on Issue of debentures	1,00,000
Provision for Tax	1,00,000	Profit & Loss A/c	15,00,000
	96,00,000		96,00,000

Note : Preference dividend is in arrears for last 3 years 'A' holds 10% First Debentures for Rs. 4,00,000 and 10% Second Debentures for Rs. 6,00,000. He is also a creditor for Rs. 1,00,000.

'B' holds 10% First Debentures for Rs. 2,00,000 and 10% Second Debentures for Rs. 4,00,000 and is also a creditor for Rs. 50,000.

The following scheme of reconstruction has been agreed upon and duly approved by the court :

(i) All the equity shares be converted in fully paid shares of Rs. 5 each.

(ii) The preference shares be reduced to Rs. 50 each and the preference share holders agree to forego arrears of preference dividend in consideration of which 9% preference shares are to be converted into 10% preference shares.

(iii) Mr. 'A' is to cancel Rs. 6,00,000 of his total debt including interest on debentures and to pay Rs. 1,00,000 to the company and to receive new 12% Debentures for the balance amount.

(iv) Mr. 'B' is to cancel Rs. 3,00,000 of his total debt including interest on debentures and to accept new 12% Debentures for the balance amount.

(v) Trade creditors (other than A & B) agreed to forgo 50% of their claims.

(vi) Directors to accept settlement of their loans as to 60% thereof by allotment of equity shares and the balance being waived.

(vii) Directors refund Rs. 1,10,000 of the fees previously received by them.

(viii) Reconstruction expenses paid Rs. 10,000.

(ix) Capital commitment contract of Rs. 2,00,000 is to be cancelled by payment of penalty @ 7.5% of the contract value .

(x) The taxation liability of the company is settled at Rs. 80,000 and the same is paid immediately.

(xi) The assets are revalued as under :

	Rs.
Land & Building	28,00,000
Plant & Machinery	4,00,000
Stock	7,00,000
Debtors	3,00,000
Computers	1,80,000
Furniture & Fixtures	1,00,000
Trade Investments	4,00,000

Pass journal entries for all the above mentioned transactions including amounts to be written off of Goodwill, Patents, Loss in Profit & Loss A/c and Discount on Issue of debentures. Prepare Bank A/c, and working of allocation of interest on debentures between A & B. Also draw the Balance Sheet.

[C.A. (I) Nov., 2003 Modified]

Solution : 14

JOURNAL ENTRIES

Particulars		Rs.	Rs.
Equity Share Capital A/c (Rs. 10)	Dr.	50,00,000	
To Equity Share Capital A/c (Rs. 5)			25,00,000
To Reconstruction A/c			25,00,000
(Being equity shares converted into fully paid shares of Rs. 5 each)			
9% Preference Share Capital A/c (Rs. 100)	Dr.	20,00,000	
To 10% Preference Share Capital A/c (Rs. 50)			10,00,000
To Reconstruction A/c			10,00,000
(Being 9% Preference Shares Converted into 10% Preference Shares of Rs. 50 each as fully paid)			
10% First Debentures A/c	Dr.	4,00,000	
10% Second Debentures A/c	Dr.	6,00,000	
Debenture Interest o/s A/c	Dr.	1,00,000	
Trade Creditors A/c	Dr.	1,00,000	
Bank A/c	Dr.	1,00,000	
To 12% New Debentures A/c			7,00,000
To Reconstruction A/c			6,00,000
(Being 12% New Debentures issued to 'A' against cancellation of his debts and cash payment of Rs. 1,00,000)			
10% First Debentures A/c	Dr.	2,00,000	
10% Second Debentures A/c	Dr.	4,00,000	
O/s Interest on Debentures A/c	Dr.	50,000	
Trade Creditors A/c	Dr.	60,000	
To 12% New Debentures A/c			4,10,000
To Reconstruction A/c			3,00,000
(Being 12% New Debentures issued to B against his total debts)			
Directors' Loan A/c	Dr.	1,00,000	
To Equity Share Capital A/c			60,000
To Reconstruction A/c			40,000
(Being equity shares issued against directors' loans)			
Trade Creditors A/c	Dr.	1,75,000	
To Reconstruction A/c			1,75,000
(Being creditors forgone 50% of their claims)			
Bank A/c	Dr.	1,10,000	
To Reconstruction A/c			1,10,000
(Being fees refunded by the directors)			*Contd.*

		Rs.	Rs.
Reconstruction A/c	Dr.	25,000	
To Bank A/c			25,000
(Being amount paid for cancellation of capital commitment Rs. 15,000 and reconstruction expenses of Rs. 10,000)			
Provision for Tax A/c	Dr.	1,00,000	
To Bank A/c			80,000
To Reconstruction A/c			20,000
(Being tax liability settled at 80%)			
Reconstruction A/c	Dr.	47,20,000	
To Profit & Loss A/c			15,00,000
To Discount on Issue of debentures A/c			1,00,000
To Goodwill A/c			10,00,000
To Patents A/c			5,00,000
To Land & Building A/c			2,00,000
To Plant & Machinery A/c			6,00,000
To Furniture & Fixtures			1,00,000
To Computers A/c			1,20,000
To Trade Investments A/c			1,00,000
To Stock A/c			3,00,000
To Debtors A/c			2,00,000
(Being of losses and reduction in the value of assets writing off)			

BALANCE SHEET (After Reconstruction)
As on 31st March, 2005

Liabilities	Rs.	Assets	Rs.
Share Capital		**Fixed Assets :**	
10% Preference Shares of Rs. 50		Land & Building	28,00,000
each fully paid	10,00,000	Plant & Machinery	4,00,000
Equity Share Capital	25,60,000	Computers	1,80,000
Shares of Rs. 5 each fully paid		Furniture	1,00,000
Secured Loans:		Trade Investments	4,00,000
12% New Debentures	11,10,000	**Current Assets :**	
Current Liabilities :		Stock	7,00,000
Trade Creditors	1,75,000	Debtors	3,00,000
Outstanding liabilities	40,000	Cash & Bank	5,000
	48,85,000		48,85,000

Working notes :

(1) **CASH & BANK A/C**

	Rs.		Rs.
To A (Reconstruction A/c)	1,00,000	By Balance b/d (Overdraft)	1,00,000
To Reconstruction A/c (Director's fees refund)	1,10,000	By Reconstruction (Expenses & penalty)	25,000
		By Provision for Tax (Paid)	80,000
		By Balance c/d	5,000
	2,10,000		2,10,000

(2) Interest has been apportioned on the basis of holdings of A & B.

"Re-organisation or Reconstruction through Surrender of Shares"

Illustration (15)

The following is the Balance Sheet of Zed Ltd. as on 31st March, 2005.

Liabilities	Rs.	Assets	Rs.
Share Capital :		Goodwill	5,00,000
30,000 Equity Shares of Rs. 100 each	30,00,000	Fixed Assets	30,00,000
10% 10,000 Preference Shares of Rs. 100 each	10,00,000	Current Assets	10,90,000
15% Debentures	10,00,000	Profit & Loss A/c	15,50,000
Debenture Interest o/s	3,00,000		
Sundry Creditors	8,40,000		
	61,40,000		61,40,000

Following scheme of reconstruction has been passed and approved by the court :

(i) The equity shares are to be sub-divided into shares of Rs. 10 each and each shareholder shall surrender 70% of his holding.

(ii) Out of surrendered shares 50,000 shares shall be issued to preference shareholders in full settlement of their claims.

(iii) Debentureholders' total claim shall be reduced to Rs. 7,00,000 and shall be satisfied by issue of 70,000 equity shares out of surrendered shares.

(iv) Creditors claims are to be reduced by 50 per cent and in consideration the creditors shall receive 20,000 equity shares out of the surrendered shares.

(v) The remaining surrendered shares shall be cancelled.

(vi) Goodwill and Profit & Loss Account to be written off completely and Fixed Assets are to be depreciated by Rs. 10,00,000.

Pass journal entries and prepare a Balance Sheet just after reconstruction.

[B. Com. (H) D.U. 1998 Modified]

Solution : 15

JOURNAL ENTRIES

	Particulars		Rs.	Rs.
	Equity Share Capital A/c (Rs. 100)	Dr.	30,00,000	
	To Equity Share Capital A/c (Rs. 10)			30,00,000
	(Being Equity Shares of Rs. 100 each sub-divided in to shares of Rs. 10 each)			
	Equity Share Capital A/c	Dr.	21,00,000	
	To Shares Surrendered A/c			21,00,000
	(Being 70% of shares surrendered)			
	Shares Surrendered A/c	Dr.	5,00,000	
	To Equity Share Capital A/c			5,00,000
	(Being Equity Shares issued to Preference Shareholders out of shares surrendered)			
	11% Preference Share Capital A/c	Dr.	1,00,000	
	To Reconstruction A/c			1,00,000
	(Being Preference Shareholder's claims cancelled)			
	Shares Surrendered A/c	Dr.	7,00,000	
	To Equity Share Capital A/c			7,00,000
	(Being Equity Shares issued to Debentureholders out of shares surrendered)			
	15% Debentures A/c	Dr.	10,00,000	
	O/s Debenture Interest A/c	Dr.	3,00,000	
	To Reconstruction A/c			13,00,000
	(Being claims of Debentureholders cancelled)			
	Share Surrendered A/c	Dr.	2,00,000	
	To Equity Share Capital A/c			2,00,000
	(Being Equity Shares issued to creditors out of shares surrendered)			
	Sundry Creditors A/c	Dr.	4,20,000	
	To Reconstruction A/c			4,20,000
	(Being claims of creditors reduced by 50%)			
	Shares Surrendered A/c	Dr.	7,00,000	
	To Reconstruction A/c			7,00,000
	(Being remaining unissued surrendered shares cancelled)			
	Reconstruction A/c	Dr.	34,20,000	
	To Profit & Loss A/c			15,50,000
	To Goodwill A/c			5,00,000
	To Fixed Assets A/c			10,00,000
	To Capital Reserve (Bal. figure)			3,70,000
	(Being accumulated losses, goodwill & fixed assets written off)			

BALANCE SHEET OF ZED LTD.
As on 31st March, 2005

Liabilities	Rs.	Assets	Rs.
Share Capital :		Fixed Assets	20,00,000
2,30,000 Equity Shares of		Current Assets	10,90,000
Rs. 10 each	23,00,000		
Reserve & Surplus :			
Capital Reserve	3,70,000		
Secured Loans	—		
Current liabilities			
Sundry Creditors	4,20,000		
	30,90,000		30,90,000

Important notes :

(1) It is to be noted that when surrendered shares are issued in lieu of balance of claim (after reduction of liability) the entire amount of claimant is transferred to Reconstruction A/c (Preference Shareholder's and Debenture-holders claims in the above example).

(2) In case surrendered shares, if issued, in lieu of reduction of claim, then only reduced amount shall be transferred to Reconstruction A/c (S. Creditors in the above example)

Illustration (16)

The Balance Sheet of R Ltd. as on 31st March, 2005 was as under :

Liabilities	Rs.	Assets	Rs.
Authorised and Subscribed Capital		**Fixed Assets :**	
10,000 Equity Shares of		Machineries	1,00,000
Rs. 100 each	10,00,000	**Current Assets**	
Unsecured Loans :		Stock	3,20,000
12% Debentures	2,00,000	Debtors	2,70,000
Accrued Interest	24,000	Bank	30,000
Current liabilities	72,000	Profit & Loss A/c	6,00,000
Provision for Income Tax	24,000		
	13,20,000		13,20,000

It was decided to reconstruct the company for which necessary resolution was passed and the sanctions were obtained from appropriate authorities. Accordingly it was decided that :

(i) Each share be subdivided into ten fully paid up equity shares of Rs. 10 each.

(ii) After sub-division, each shareholder shall surrender to the company 50% of his holding for the purpose of reissue to debentureholders and creditors as necessary.

(iii) Out of shares surrendered, 10,000 shares of Rs. 10 each shall be converted into 12% Preference shares of Rs. 10 each fully paid up.

(iv) The claims of debentureholders shall be reduced by 75%. In consideration of reduction, the debentureholders shall receive preference shares of Rs. 1,00,000 which are converted out of shares surrendered.

(v) Creditors claims shall be reduced to 50%, it is to be settled by issue of equity shares out of share surrendered.

(vi) Balance of Profit & Loss A/c is to be written off.

(vii) The shares surrendered not reissued shall be cancelled.

You are required to show the journal entries giving effect to the above and the resultant Balance Sheet.

[C.A. (I) Modified]

Solution : 16

JOURNAL ENTRIES

			Rs.	Rs.
	Equity Share Capital A/c (Rs. 100) Dr. To Equity Share Capital A/c (Rs. 10) (Being Shares of Rs. 100 each sub-divided into shares of Rs. 10 each)		10,00,000	10,00,000
	Equity Share Capital A/c Dr. To Share Surrendered A/c (Being 50% of holdings surrendered)		5,00,000	5,00,000
	12% Debentures A/c Dr. Accrued Interest A/c Dr. To Reconstruction A/c (Being 75% of claims of debentureholders reduced)		1,50,000 18,000	1,68,000
	Shares Surrendered A/c Dr. To Preference Share Capital A/c (Being Pref. Shares Converted out of shares surrendered, issued to debentureholders)		1,00,000	1,00,000
	Creditors A/c Dr. To Reconstruction A/c (Being claims of creditors cancelled)		72,000	72,000
	Shares Surrendered A/c Dr. To Equity Share Capital A/c (Being Equity Shares issued to creditors out of surrendered shares)		36,000	36,000
	Shares Surrendered A/c Dr. To Reconstruction A/c (Being unissued surrendered shares cancelled and transferred to Reconstruction A/c)		3,64,000	3,64,000
	Reconstruction A/c Dr. To Profit & Loss A/c To Capital Reserve A/c (Being accumulated losses written off & the balance of Reconstruction A/c transferred to capital reserve)		6,04,000	6,00,000 4,000

BALANCE SHEET OF R LTD.
As on 31st March, 2005

Liabilities	Rs.	Assets	Rs.
Share Capital :		**Fixed Assets :**	
53,600 Equity Shares of Rs. 100 each	5,36,000	Machineries	1,00,000
12% Preference Shares of Rs. 10 each	1,00,000	**Current Assets Loans & Advances :**	
Reserve & Surplus :		Stock	3,20,000
Capital Reserve	4,000	Debtors	2,70,000
Unsecured Loans :		Bank balance	30,000
12% Debentures	50,000		
Accrued Interest	6,000		
Current Liabilities & Provisions:			
Provision for Income Tax	24,000		
	7,20,000		7,20,000

Note : Mere conversion of shares out of shares surrendered will not result in any entry, unless these shares so converted are issued to any claimant or stakeholders.

Illustration (17)

The following is the Balance Sheet of Exe Ltd. as on 31st March 2005

Liabilities	Rs.	Assets	Rs.
10% 10,000 Preference Shares of Rs. 100 each	10,00,000	Goodwill	2,50,000
		Land & Building	5,00,000
1,50,000 Equity Share of Rs. 10 each	15,00,000	Plant & Machinery	10,00,000
		Furniture	50,000
Securities Premium	2,25,000	Debtors	10,00,000
Capital Reserve	2,25,000	Stock	10,00,000
Unsecured Loan (from a Director)	2,50,000	Cash at Bank	2,25,000
Sundry Creditors	15,00,000	Preliminary Exp.	25,000
Outstanding Expenses (including Manager's commission Rs. 1,00,000)	3,50,000	Profit & Loss A/c	10,00,000
	50,50,000		50,50,000

The following scheme of reconstruction has been agreed upon and duly approved by the court:

(i) Equity shares are to be converted in to 3,00,000 shares of Rs. 5 each and each shareholder shall surrender 90% of his/her holdings.

(ii) Dividends on preference shares are in arrears for three years and preference shareholders agree to forgo their claims in consideration of being conversion of 10% Preference Shares into 11% Preference Shares.

(iii) Creditors agree to reduce their claims by 20% for consideration of getting Rs. 1,75,000 shares out of shares surrendered.

(iv) Manager and Director forgo their claims.

(v) Assets are to be revalued as follows :

		Rs.
Goodwill		Nil
Plant		7,50,000
Furniture		10,000
Debtors	Subject to provision of	Rs. 1,75,000
Land & Building		Rs. 5,50,000

(vi) Reconstruction Expenses - Rs. 50,000

(vii) 13% 2,500 Debentures of Rs. 100 each are issued for increasing working capital.

Pass journal entries, prepare Reconstruction Account and a Balance Sheet after reconstruction.

[B.Com (H) D.U. Adapted]

Solution : 17

JOURNAL ENTRIES

	Particulars		Rs.	Rs.
	Equity Share Capital A/c (Rs. 10)	Dr.	15,00,000	
	To Equity Share Capital A/c (Rs. 5)			15,00,000
	(Being equity shares of Rs. 10 each sub-divided into shares of Rs. 5 each)			
	Equity Share Capital A/c	Dr.	13,50,000	
	To Shares Surrendered A/c			13,50,000
	(Being 90% of holding surrendered)			
	10% Preference Share Capital A/c	Dr.	10,00,000	
	To 11% Preference Share Capital A/c			10,00,000
	(Being 10% Preference Shares converted into 11% Preference shares)			
	Shares Surrendered A/c	Dr.	1,75,000	
	To Equity Share Capital A/c			1,75,000
	(Being equity shares reissued to creditors out of shares surrendered)			
	Share Surrendered A/c	Dr.	11,75,000	
	To Reconstruction A/c			11,75,000
	(Being unissued surrendered shares cancelled)			
	Outstanding Expenses A/c	Dr.	1,00,000	
	Unsecured Loan A/c	Dr.	2,50,000	
	S. Creditors A/c	Dr.	3,00,000	
	To Reconstruction A/c			6,50,000
	(Being liabilities forgone transferred to Reconstruction A/c)			

Contd.

Particulars			Rs.	Rs.
	Land & Building A/c	Dr.	50,000	
	To Reconstruction A/c			50,000
	(Being appreciation in land & building transferred to Reconstruction A/c)			
	Reconstruction A/c	Dr.	50,000	
	To Bank A/c			50,000
	(Being expenses charged to Reconstruction A/c)			
	Reconstruction A/c	Dr.	18,25,000	
	To Profit & Loss A/c			10,00,000
	To Preliminary Expenses A/c			25,000
	To Goodwill A/c			2,50,000
	To Plant & Machinery A/c			2,50,000
	To Furniture A/c			40,000
	To Debtors A/c			1,75,000
	To Capital Reserve A/c (Bal. Figure)			85,000
	(Being assets & losses written off & balance transferred to Capital Reserve A/c)			
	Bank A/c	Dr.	2,50,000	
	To 13% Debentures			2,50,000
	(Being debentures issued for cash)			

BANK A/C

	Rs.		Rs.
To Balance b/d	2,25,000	By Reconstruction A/c	50,000
To 13% Debentures	2,50,000	By Balance c/d	4,25,000
	4,75,000		4,75,000

RECONSTRUCTION A/C

	Rs.		Rs.
To Profit & Loss A/c	10,00,000	By Share Surrendered A/c	11,75,000
To Preliminary Expenses A/c	25,000	By Outstanding Expenses A/c	1,00,000
To Goodwill A/c	2,50,000	By Unsecured Loans A/c	2,50,000
To Plant & Machinery A/c	2,50,000	By S. Creditors A/c	3,00,000
To Furniture A/c	40,000	By Land & Building A/c	50,000
To Debtors A/c	1,75,000		
To Bank A/c (Expenses)	50,000		
To Capital Reserve (B.F.)	85,000		
	18,75,000		18,75,000

BALANCE SHEET OF EXE LTD. (After Reconstruction)
As on 31st March, 2005

Liabilities	Rs.	Assets		Rs.
Share Capital :		**Fixed Assets :**		
65,000 Equity Shares of		Land & Building		5,50,000
Rs. 5 each	3,25,000	Plant & Machinery		7,50,000
11% Preference Shares of		Furniture		10,000
Rs. 100 each	10,00,000	Current Assets		
Reserve & Surplus :		Stock		10,00,000
Securities Premium	2,25,000	Debtors	10,00,000	
Capital Reserve	3,10,000	*Less* Provision	1,75,000	8,25,000
Unsecured Loans :	—	Cash at Bank		4,25,000
Secured Loans :				
13% Debentures	2,50,000			
Current Liabilities :				
S. Creditors	12,00,000			
O/s Expenses	2,50,000			
	35,60,000			35,60,000

ASSIGNMENTS

(1) What do you understand by term "Reconstruction"? How for internal reconstruction is different from external reconstruction?

(2) Write a note relating to legal provisions governing the internal reconstruction.

(3) Write short notes on :
Sub-division & consolidation of shares
Shares Surrendered Account
Reconstruction Account

(4) The following is the Balance Sheet of Weak and Freak Ltd. as on 31st March, 2003.

Liabilities	Rs.	Assets	Rs.
Share Capital :		Building	4,00,000
9% Cumulative Preference Shares		Plant	2,60,000
of Rs. 100 each	1,00,000	Patents	80,000
Equity Shares of Rs. 10 each	4,00,000	Stock	1,60,000
9% Debentures	2,00,000	Debtors	1,10,000
Trade Creditors	6,60,000	Preliminary Expenses	20,000
O/s Expenses	40,000	Profit & Loss A/c	3,70,000
	14,00,000		14,00,000

A scheme of reconstruction, approved by the court was as under :

(a) To reduce equity shares by Rs. 9 each, preference shares by Rs. 40 each, Debentures by 10%, Trade creditors by 33 $^1/_3$%, Machinery to Rs. 1,40,000 and stock by Rs. 20,000.

(b) To provide Rs. 30,000 for bad debts.

(c) To write off intangible assets and

(d) To raise the rate of preference dividend to 11% and rate of debenture interest to 10%.

Record journal entries to give effect to above proposals and prepare Balance Sheet immediately after reconstruction.

[B.Com (H) D.U. Adapted]

Ans. : Total of Balance Sheet — Rs. 7,60,000
Amount transferred to Reconstruction A/c — Rs. 6,40,000

(5) The paid up capital of Pooja Ltd. consisted of 2,50,000 Equity Shares of Rs. 10 each. Due to continued losses, the directors prepared a scheme of reconstruction which was duly approved by the court. The terms of reconstruction were as follows :

(a) In lieu of their present holdings the share holders are to receive:

(i) Fully paid equity shares of Rs. 10 each equal to 2/5th of their holdings.

(ii) 6% Preference Shares of Rs. 100 each fully paid to the extent of 20% of the above new equity shares.

(iii) 3,000 7% Debentures of Rs. 100 each.

(b) An issue of 2,500, 6% Debentures of Rs. 100 each was made and fully subscribed in cash.

(c) The Assets were reduced as follows :
Goodwill from Rs. 15,00,000 to Rs. 7,50,000
Machinery from Rs. 5,00,000 to Rs. 3,75,000
Computers from Rs. 7,50,000 to Rs. 6,25,000

Pass journal entries and prepare Reconstruction A/c

[C.A. (I) Adapted]

Ans. : Reconstruction A/c Rs. 10,00,000

(6) A Ltd. decided to implement a scheme of internal reconstruction when it's Balance Sheet was as under :

Liabilities		Rs.	Assets	Rs.
8% Preference Share Capital			**Fixed Assets:**	
Shares of Rs. 100 each		10,00,000	Goodwill	2,75,000
Equity Share Capital			Property	3,00,000
Shares of Rs. 10 each		7,50,000	Plant & Machinery	8,00,000
Securities Premium		25,000	Investments	6,10,000
9% Debentures	3,00,000		**Current Assets**	
(Secured on property)			Stock	1,50,000
Add Accrued Interest	13,500	3,13,500	Debtors	3,00,000
S. Creditors		4,25,000	Other Current Assets	2,00,000
Bank Overdraft		4,80,000	Preliminary Expenses	12,500
			Profit & Loss A/c	3,46,000
		29,93,500		29,93,500

Note : Preference dividends are in arrears for four years.

The following scheme was approved by court.

(i) Preference shares are reduced to Rs. 75 each and equity shares to Rs. 2 per share. After reduction these shares are consolidated into Rs. 10 shares. However, authorised Capital was restored.

(ii) One new equity share of Rs. 10 each issued for every Rs. 40 of gross preference dividend in arrears.

(iii) The balance of securities premium account was utilised.

(iv) The debenture holders tookover the property at an agreed value of Rs. 3,75,000 and paid the balance after deducting the balance due to them.

(v) Plant & Machinery was written down to Rs. 7,00,000.

(vi) Other current assets realised Rs. 1,60,000.

(vii) Goodwill, preliminary expenses, book debts of Rs. 43,000 and obsolete stock of Rs. 50,000 were written off.

(viii) Contingent liability for which no provision was made has been settled for Rs. 35,000 and of the amount of Rs. 31,500 was recovered from Insurance company.

(ix) Available cash is deposited in Overdraft account.

Pass journal entries, show Reconstruction A/c Cash Account and Balance Sheet just after reconstruction.

[C.A. (I) Adapted]

Ans. : Reconstruction A/c Rs. 9,50,000; Cash A/c (Total) Rs. 2,53,000
Balance Sheet (Total) Rs. 16,67,000

(7) The Balance Sheet of Maria Ltd. as on 31st March, 2005 was as under :

Liabilities	Rs.	Amount		Rs.
Share Capital:		Fixed Assets:		
11% Cumulative Preference Shares of Rs. 100 each	4,00,000	Goodwill at Cost:	40,000	
Equity Shares of Rs. 100 each Rs. 50 paid up	4,00,000	Other Fixed Assets	8,50,000	
			8,90,000	
		Less Depreciation	2,70,000	6,20,000
Securities Premium (received on preference Shares)	40,000	Investments		25,000
General Reserve	60,000	Stock		2,10,000
Current liabilities	3,10,000	Debtors		2,55,000
		Bank		1,00,000
(Contingent liability not provided for : Preference dividends are in arrears for three years including the year ended 31st March, 2005.)				
	12,10,000			12,10,000

The funds of the company are sufficient to discharge it's liabilities including preference dividends in arrears. However, the company does not want to deplete its resources. It would also like to reflect the value of some of it's assets in a realistic manner. The Board of Directors of the company propose the following scheme of reconstruction.

(i) The cumulative Preference Shareholders are to be issued in exchange for their holdings, 10% Debentures of Rs. 100 each at premium of 10% Fractions if any, to be paid in cash.

(ii) Arrears of Pref. dividends to be converted into equity shares of Rs. 100 each, Rs. 50 paid up.

(iii) After the issue of equity shares in lieu of arrears of Preference dividend, the paid up value of equity shares to be reduced to Rs. 25 each.

(iv) The face value of all equity shares to be reduced to Rs. 50 each and balance of unpaid portion is to be called up fully.

(v) Goodwill has lost it's value and has to be written off. Market value of other fixed assets is determined at Rs. 5,00,000 as on 31st March, 2005.

(vi) Investments have no market value and have to be written off.

(vii) Stock is to be valued at 110% of its book value and Debtors are to be discounted by 5%.

The above scheme was duly approved by court and implemented accordingly.

During the working for the first half, after reconstruction, it is noticed that the trading for the period ending 30th September, 2005, has resulted in an increase of bank balance by Rs. 55,100 Debtors by Rs. 40,000, Creditors by Rs. 26,000 and a decrease in stock by Rs. 8,000. Depreciation for the period on fixed assets is to be provided. The increase in bank balance was prior to the company paying half yearly interest on debentures and redeeming one-half of the debentures on 30th September, 2005.

Pass journal entries, prepare relevant ledger accounts and show the Balance Sheet as on 30th September, 2005.

[C.A. (F) Modified]

Ans. : Balance Sheet after reconstruction — Rs. 13,39,210
Balance Sheet as on 30.9.2005 — Rs. 12,01,330, Reconstruction Account — Rs. 2,89,750

Hint : Profit for First half (after reconstruction)

	Increase in Bank Balance and Debtors (55,100 + 40,000)		95,100
Less	Decrease in Stock	8,000	
	Increase in creditors	26,000	34,000
	Profit before Dep. & Interest.		61,100
Less	Interest for six months @ 10% or Rs. 3,63,600 Debentures*	18,180	
	Depreciation @ 10% on Rs. 5,00,000	25,000	43,180
	Net profit for the first half		17,920

Cash & Bank Balance :

	Op. Balance b/d	1,00,000
	Equity Share Capital (made fully paid)	2,66,000
		3,66,000
Less	Cash paid for fraction on redemption of Preference Shares	40
		3,65,960
Add	Increase in Bank balance	55,100
		4,21,060
Less	Interest paid	(18,180)
	Redemption of 10% Debentures ($^1/_2$ of Rs. 3,63,600)	(1,81,800)
	Balance as on 30. 9. 2005	2,21,080

* Preference Shares Rs. 4,00,000 ÷ 110 (agreed value of Debentures) 3,636.4 Debentures.
Hence Company issued 10% Debentures for Rs. 3,63,600 and .4 × Rs. 100 Rs. 40 paid in cash.

(8) Growing Concern Ltd. is in the hands of a Receiver of Debentureholders who holds a charge on all assets except uncalled capital. The following statement shows the position as on 31st March, 2005.

Liabilities	Rs.	Assets	Rs.
Share Capital		Property Machinery &	
6,000 Equity Shares of		Plant at Cost	3,90,000
Rs. 60 each Rs. 30 paid	1,80,000	Cash & Bank	2,70,000
First Debentures	3,00,000	Deficiency (Profit & Loss A/c)	8,70,000
Second Debentures	6,00,000		
Unsecured Creditors	4,50,000		
	15,30,000		15,30,000

A holds the First Debentures for Rs. 3,00,000 and Second Debentures for Rs. 3,00,000. He is also an unsecured creditor for Rs. 90,000. 'B' holds second Debentures for Rs. 3,00,000 and unsecured creditors for Rs. 60,000.

The following scheme of reconstruction is proposed and approved:

(i) A is to cancel Rs. 2,10,000 of the total debt owing to him, to advance Rs. 30,000 in cash and to take New First Debentures for Rs. 5,10,000 in full settlement of all his claims.

(ii) B is to accept Rs. 90,000 in cash in satisfaction of all claims by him.

(iii) Unsecured Creditors (other than A & B) are to accept four shares of Rs. 7.50 each fully paid in satisfaction of 75% of every Rs. 60 of their claim. The balance of 25% is to be postponed and to be payable at the end of three years. Uncalled capital is to be called up in full and Rs. 52.50 per share cancelled, thus making the shares of Rs. 7.50 each.

Pass journal entries & prepare a Balance Sheet immediately after reconstruction.

[C.A. (F) Adapted]

Ans. : Balance Sheet total — Rs. 7,80,000 Reconstruction A/c — Rs. 8,70,000
Claims forgone by A — Rs. 2,10,000 Claims forgone by B — Rs. 2,70,000
Sacrifice by creditors — Rs. 75,000 Sacrifice by Equity Shareholders —Rs. 3,15,000

(9) Following is the Balance Sheet of Zeenath Ltd. as on 31st March, 2005.

Liabilities	Rs.	Assets	Rs.
Share Capital		**Fixed Assets :**	
11% Cumulative Pref. Shares	3,00,000	Goodwill	1,00,000
of Rs. 100 each		Other Fixed Assets	9,80,000
Equity Shares of Rs. 100 each	7,50,000	Investments	20,000
Securities Premium	12,000	**Current Assets :**	
General Reserve	80,000	Stock	2,00,000
Trade Creditors	3,75,000	Cash & Bank	62,500
		Debtors	1,54,500
	15,17,000		15,17,000

Note : Preference dividend is in arrears for 2 years. A scheme of reconstruction duly drafted by the Board was approved by the court.

(i) The preference shares are to be converted into unsecured 13% Debentures of Rs. 100 each with regard to 80% of their dues (including arrears of dividend) and for the balance, equity shares of Rs. 50 paid up would be issued.

(ii) Equity shares are to be reduced to shares of Rs. 50 each.

(iii) All equity shareholders agreed to pay the balance in cash.

(iv) Goodwill is considered worth less and is to be written off. Investments are to reflect their market value of Rs. 30,000 Obsolete items of stock are to be written off Rs. 50,000. Bad debts @ 5% is to be provided. Fixed assets to be written off by Rs. 1,50,000.

The company carried on trading for six months and after providing depreciation @ 20% p.a on the revised value of fixed assets, made a net profit of Rs. 80,000. The half yearly working resulted in an increase in Debtors by Rs. 60,000, stock by Rs. 80,000 & Cash by Rs. 40,000.

Pass journal entries and draw a Balance Sheet as on 30th September, 2005.

[C.A. (I) Modified]

Ans. : Balance Sheet total (30. 9. 2005) — Rs. 17,64,475
Bank Balance - 5,50,700
Capital Reserve - 11,275

(10) The following is the Balance Sheet of Hard Luck Ltd.

Liabilities	Rs.	Assets	Rs.
Authorised Share Capital :		**Fixed Assets :**	
1,00,000 Equity of Rs. 20 each	20,00,000	Goodwill at Cost	4,52,000
Issued Capital		Property	8,30,000
85,000 shares of Rs. 20 each	17,00,000	Plant	12,00,000
Securities Premium	3,00,000	Investments	9,20,000
Loan from Bank	12,00,000	**Current Assets:**	
Bank Over draft	11,30,000	Stock	4,60,000
Trade Creditors	12,90,000	Debtors	3,92,000
		Profit & Loss A/c	13,66,000
	56,20,000		56,20,000

A scheme of reconstruction was approved and sanctioned by the court.

(i) Ordinary shares are to be reduced to Re. 1 per share. The unpaid value of share was subsequently called by the company and paid by all the shareholders.

(ii) The balance of unissued capital was allotted to the Bank in part discharge of the Loan and the balance was paid in cash.

(iii) The authorised capital of the company is to be increased by another 50,000 shares and these are issued to the existing shareholders as rights issue. The amount due from shareholders was realised in full.

(iv) Trade Creditors to give up 25% of their claims and balance due to them to be converted into 12% Secured Debentures of Rs. 100 each.

(v) Interest of Rs. 1,30,000 on overdraft to be waived by the Bank and balance to be paid forthwith.

(vi) All amounts available including securities premium to be utilised to write off losses, goodwill and value of investments.

Show journal entries and draw a Balance Sheet of the company after implementation of scheme.

[C.A. (I) Adapted]

Ans : Reconstruction (Capital Reduction)
Amount available — Rs. 23,67,500
Balance Sheet (Total) — Rs. 39,67,500
Bank and Cash Balance — Rs. 7,15,000

(11) Following is the Balance Sheet of Manasee Ltd. as on 31st March 2005

Liabilities	Rs.	Assets	Rs.
8% Preference Shares of Rs. 100 each	7,50,000	Fixed Assets	1,75,000
Equity Shares of Rs. 10 each Rs. 5 paid up	12,50,000	Patents and Copyrights	1,00,000
9% Debentures	7,50,000	Investments (Market Value Rs. 68,750)	81,250
Debenture Interest o/s	1,35,000	**Current Assets:**	
Bank Overdraft	1,87,500	Stock	17,50,000
O/s Interest on Overdraft	18,750	Debtors	5,48,750
Creditors	86,250	Bank	12,500
		Profit & Loss A/c	5,10,000
	31,77,500		31,77,500

Note : Preference dividend is in arrears for one year.

Due to continued losses, a scheme of reconstruction was prepared which was approved and sanctioned by the court.

(i) Preference shareholders to give up their claims, inclusive of dividends to the extent of 30% and desire to be paid off.

(ii) Debentureholders agree to give up their claims of interest in consideration of their interest being enhanced to 11%.

(iii) Bank agrees to give up 50% of it's interest outstanding in consideration of it's overdraft and balance of interest being paid at once.

(iv) Creditors to allow a discount of Rs. 4,375 if they are paid immediately.

(v) Balance of Profit and Loss A/c, Patents and Copyrights and Debtors of Rs. 30,000 to be written off.

(vi) Fixed assets to be written down by Rs. 42,500

(vii) Investments are to reflect their market value.

(viii) To the extent not specifically stated, equity shareholders suffer on reduction of their rights. Cost of reconstruction amounted to Rs. 3,400.

Record journal entries show the Balance Sheet assuming that scheme has been implemented fully and the equity shareholders bringing in necessary cash to pay off the parties and leave a working capital of Rs. 25,000.

[C.A. (I) Adapted]

Ans. : Reconstruction A/c — Rs. 7,48,750

Cash Brought in Equity Shareholders — Rs. 8,75,000

(12) A Ltd. has become a loss incurring entity. The management intends to prepare a reconstruction scheme to be implemented. It's Balance Sheet as on 31st March, 2005 was as under :

Liabilities	Rs.	Assets	Rs.
Share Capital		**Fixed Assets:**	
Equity Shares of Rs. 10 each	15,00,000	Land & Building	2,50,000
6% Pref. Shares of Rs. 100 each	5,00,000	Plant & Machinery	5,00,000
9% Debentures of R. 300 each	7,50,000	**Current Assets:**	
Trade Creditors	10,00,000	Stock	5,00,000
O/s Expenses	1,25,000	Debtors	5,00,000
		Cash & Bank	75,000
		Profit & Loss A/c	20,50,000
	38,75,000		38,75,000

The scheme of reconstruction was under :

(i) Land & Building to be valued at real worth of Rs. 10,00,000.

(ii) Stock and Debtors are expected to fetch 20% Less.

(iii) Equity Shares to be reduced to Rs. 2.50 as fully paid up.

(iv) Debentures are to be reduced to Rs. 200 each fully paid up and rate of interest being raised proportionately.

(v) Trade creditors and creditors for expenses may wait for payment provided 20% of their dues are paid forthwith.

(vi) Directors are willing to bring in Rs. 2,50,000 in form of equity Capital. Rs. 50,000 is estimated to be the actual cost of reconstruction.

Pass journal entries and show the Reconstruction Account & a Balance Sheet immediately after reconstruction.

[C.A. (F) Adapted]

Ans. : Reconstruction A/c — Rs. 23,75,000

Capital Reserve — Rs. 75,000

Balance Sheet — Rs. 23,50,000

(13) The Balance Sheet of Adnan- Ahad Ltd. was as under :

Liabilities	Rs.	Assets	Rs.
Share Capital :		Fixed Assets	1,00,000
30,000 Equity Shares of		Stock	1,20,000
Rs. 10 each	3,00,000	Debtors	2,90,000
1,000 11% Preference Shares		Other Current Assets	40,000
of Rs. 100 each	1,00,000	Profit & Loss A/c	3,28,000
Secured Loans :			
11% Debentures	1,00,000		
Interest Accrued on Deb.	22,000		
Overdraft	1,26,000		
Unsecured Loans :			
Bank Loan	1,00,000		
Interest there on	30,000		
Current liabilities	1,00,000		
	8,78,000		8,78,000

The following scheme of reconstruction has been agreed amongst the shareholders and creditors.

(i) 11% Preference Shareholders rights are to be reduced to 50% and converted into 12% Debentures of Rs. 100 each.

(ii) 50% of the interest due on the debentures is waived.

(iii) Interest due on unsecured loans is waived.

(iv) Current liabilities would be reduced by Rs. 10,000 on account of provisions no longer required.

(v) The Bank agrees to the arrangement and to increase the cash credit/overdraft limit by Rs. 20,000 upon the shareholders agreeing to bring-in a like amount by way of new equity.

(vi) Besides, the equity shareholders also agreed to convert existing equity shares into new 10 rupee-shares of total value of Rs. 1,00,000.

(vii) The debit balance in the profit & Loss A/c is to be wiped out. Rs. 52,000 are to be provided for doubtful debts and the value of fixed assets is to be increased by Rs. 80,000.

Pass entries and redraft Balance Sheet after the implementation of scheme.

[C.A. (I) Adapted]

Ans. : Capital Reserve — Rs. 1,000
Balance Sheet — Rs. 5,78,000

SHARE SURRENDER

(14) The following is the Balance Sheet of Sushma Ltd. as on 31st March 2005.

Liabilities	Rs.	Assets	Rs.
Share Capital :		**Fixed Assets :**	
11% Preference Shares of		Goodwill	50,000
Rs. 100 each	3,00,000	Land & Buildind	3,00,000
Equity Shares of Rs. 100 each			
Rs. 90 called	9,00,000	Furniture & Fixtures	50,000
Secured Loans		**Current Assets Loans and**	
9% Debentures	2,50,000	**Advances :**	
Unsecured Loans:	1,00,000	Stock	2,95,000
Current liabilities and Provisions		Debtors	1,50,000
S. Creditors	40,000	Cash & Bank	4,000
Provident Fund	14,000	Profit & Loss A/c	3,55,000
	16,04,000		16,04,000

The following scheme of reconstruction has been approved by the court.

(i) Uncalled capital is to be called in full.

(ii) Every equity share of Rs. 100 is to be sub-divided into equity shares of Rs. 10 each.

(iii) After sub-division, equity shareholders are to surrender 50% of their holding for immediate cancellation.

(iv) Preference shareholders have agreed to accept identical number of fully paid 11% preference shares of Rs. 75 each in lieu of their present holding.

(v) 9% debentureholders have agreed to accept 10% Rs. 2,25,000 debentures in full satisfaction of their claims.

(vi) Unsecured loans of Rs. 1,00,000 are to be converted into 11% Debentures of Rs. 80,000.

(vii) Sundry creditors have agreed to surrender 30% of their claims in consideration of balance being paid forth with.

(viii) Stock is found over-valued by Rs. 60,000 while machinery is to be depreciated by Rs. 1,50,000.

(ix) Provision for bad debts is to be made for Rs. 15,000.

Pass journal entries, show Reconstruction A/c and a Balance Sheet immediately after reconstruction.

[B.Com (H) D.U. Adapted]

Ans. : Capital Reserve — Rs. 2,000

Total of Balance Sheet — Rs. 10,46,000

(15) Gloria & Swanson Ltd. has to pass to the hands of a Receiver for Debentureholders who held charge on all assets except uncalled capital. The following is the position as prepared by the Receiver.

	Rs.
Share Capital :	
20,000 Shares of Rs. 50 each fully paid up	10,00,000
1,00,000 Shares of Rs. 50 each Rs. 25 paid up	25,00,000
First Debentures	25,00,000
Second Debentures	50,00,000
Unsecured Creditors	40,00,000
Bank Balance	30,00,000
Building, Plant & Machinery	40,00,000
(Estimated to realise Rs. 15,00,000)	

The following is the interest of Gloria and Swanson in the company.

	Gloria	Swanson
	Rs.	Rs.
First Debentures	20,00,000	5,00,000
Second Debentures	30,00,000	20,00,000
Unsecured Creditors	6,00,000	9,00,000
	56,00,000	34,00,000
Share Capital : Fully Paid up	5,00,000	5,00,000
Partly Paid up	10,00,000	10,00,000

The following scheme of reconstruction is proposed.

(a) Gloria is to cancel Rs. 31,00,000 of his total debt, pay cash Rs. 5,00,000 and he would be issued Rs. 30,00,000 12% Debentures in lieu of First and Second Debentures to be cancelled.

(b) (i) Swanson is to cancel his total debt by accepting Rs. 5,00,000 in cash and Rs. 5,00,000 in 12% Debentures.

(ii) Swanson is to surrender for cancellation Rs. 5,00,000 worth of fully paid up shares.

(c) Unsecured creditors, other than Gloria and Swanson, agree to reduce their debt by 20% and accept in lieu there of 1,00,000 shares of Rs. 10 each fully paid up and balance in cash payable in five equal annual instalments.

(d) Uncalled Capital is to be called up in full and Rs. 40 per share to be cancelled thus making Share of Rs. 10 each.

Assuming the scheme is duly approved by all parties interested by the court, show the Reconstruction A/c and Balance Sheet.

[C.A. (F) Modified]

Ans. : Balance Sheet — Rs. 70,00,000

(16) Following is the Balance Sheet of Texla Ltd. as on 31st March, 2005.

Liabilities	Rs.	Assets		Rs.
8% Cumulative Preference Shares		Goodwill		75,000
of Rs. 100 each	3,00,000	Plant	4,50,000	
Equity Shares		Tools		15,000
of Rs. 10 each	4,50,000	Stock		2,25,000
Securities Premium	1,35,000	Debtors		3,75,000
(Unsecured) Loan from a Director	75,000	Cash		15,000
S. Creditors	4,50,000	Bank	52,500	
o/s Expenses	1,05,000	Preliminary Expenses		7,500
(including directors remuneration Rs. 30,000)		Profit & Loss A/c		3,00,000
	15,15,000			15,15,000

Note : Preference dividends are in arrears for three years.

The following scheme of reconstruction has been agreed upon and duly approved by court.

(i) Equity shares to be converted into 2,25,000 shares of Rs. 2 each.

(ii) Equity shareholders to surrender 90% of their holdings.

(iii) Preference shareholders agree to forgo their right to arrears of dividends in consideration of which 8% Preference shares are to be converted into 9% Preference shares.

(iv) Sundry Creditors to reduce their claims by one-fifth in consideration of their getting shares of Rs. 52,500 out of surrendered shares.

(v) Directors agree to forgo the amount due on account of unsecured loan and directors remuneration.

(vi) Surrendered Shares not otherwise utilised to be cancelled.

(vii) Assets to be reduced as under :

Goodwill by — Rs. 75,000, Plant by — Rs. 60,000, Tools by — Rs. 12,000, Debtors by — Rs. 22,500 and Stock by — Rs. 30,000.

(viii) Any Surplus after meeting the losses should be utilised in writing down the value of plant further.

(ix) Expenses of reconstruction amounted to Rs. 15,000.

(x) Further Equity Shares are issued to the existing members in the 1:3 ratio for increasing the working capital. The issue was fully subscribed and paid for in full.

Record journal entries and give a resultant Balance Sheet of the Company.

[C.A. (F) Adapted]

Ans. : Reconstruction A/c — Rs. 5,34,000

Balance Sheet — Rs. 11,17,500

(17) Following is the Balance Sheet of Adaish Ltd. as on 31st March 2005.

Liabilities	Rs.	Assets	Rs.
Share Capital :		Fixed Assets	21,45,000
12,000 Equity Shares		Investments	25,500
of Rs. 100 each	12,00,000	Stock	1,20,000
Secured Loans		Debtors	45,000
6% Debentures	21,00,000	Bank	1,54,500
Accrued Interest	1,05,000	Profit & Loss A/c	16,05,000
Current liabilities			
Trade Creditors	6,75,000		
Income Tax	15,000		
	40,95,000		40,95,000

A Scheme of reconstruction duly approved and confirmed by the court was as under :

(i) Each share to be subdivided into twenty fully paid equity shares of Rs. 5 each.

(ii) Each shareholder to surrender 95% of his holding after subdivision for the purpose of reissue to debentureholders and creditors so far as required and otherwise for cancellation.

(iii) Of the shares surrendered 69,000 shares shall be converted into 8% preference shares of Rs. 5 each fully paid.

(iv) Debentureholders total claim to be reduced to Rs. 3,45,000.

(v) Liabilities for income tax to be paid in full.

(vi) The claims of unsecured creditors shall be reduced by 80% and the balance shall be satisfied by allotment of equity shares of Rs. 5 each fully paid from shares surrendered.

(vii) Shares surrendered and not issued shall be cancelled .

Pass entries & prepare Balance Sheet.

Ans. : Capital Reserve — Rs. 19,35,000,
Balance Sheet — Rs. 24,90,000.

8

Accounting of Holding Companies

(CONSOLIDATED FINANCIAL STATEMENTS)

A business enterprise is an entity which has inherent urge to surrive, expand and grow. Infact growth is a precondition for the survival of a business firm. Sometimes it becomes necessary to avail economies of large scale, to avoid cut-throat competition, to control market or to attain self sufficiency At present in view of globalisation and liberalisation policies initiated by the Government since 1991, the Indian corporate world is facing stiff competition from top world corporate leaders who are showing keen interest in acquiring the controlling shares in Indian companies. Thus accounting for holding companies has assumed a special significance in the light of partial acquisitions and take-overs by the national and multinational companies. Under holding companies device each company retains its identity and carries on the business activity in it's own name.

Holding company is an integrated form of combination whereby control of several companies is vested in one company through transfer of ownership rights. It controls the majority composition of the Board of Directors of another company or which holds more than half of the equity share capital. The company in which controlling interest is acquired is known as subsidiary company.

According to AS-21,"A" holding company is a parent company that has one or more subsidiaries.

A "subsidiary" is an enterprise that is controlled by another enterprise (known as the parent (holding) Company)

A "Group" is a parent and all its subsidiaries.

"Control" is the ownership, directly or indirectly through subsidiary (ies) of more than half of the voting power of an enterprise or control of the composition of the Board of Directors.

Definition

A holding company may be defined as a company which controls one or more other companies by means of holding more than 50% shares in that company or companies or by having power to appoint (directly or indirectly) whole or majority of directors/of that company or companies. The Company which is controlled by the holding (parent) Company is known as "subsidiary company".

Companies Act 1956 and Holding and Subsidiary Company (Section-4)

As per the provisions of Section 4 of the Companies Act 1956

(i) A Company is known as the holding company of another company if it has control over that other company;

(ii) A Company is deemed to be a holding company of another if, but only if, that other company is its subsidiary.

A Company is known as **subsidiary** of another company in the following 3 cases :

(a) Where a holding company controls the composition of Board of Directors of another company latter company becomes its **subsidiary**.

The term controls means the right of holding company in respect of appointment and removal of directors of subsidiary company.

(b) Where a holding company holds more than half in **nominal value** of equity shares of another Company, the latter company becomes its subsidiary.

(c) Where a company is a subsidiary of another company which is itself a subsidiary of controlling company the former company becomes the subsidiary of the controlling company.

For example : Y Ltd. is a subsidiary X Ltd. and Z Ltd. is a subsidiary of Y Ltd. Z Ltd. becomes the subsidiary of X Ltd. by virtue of clause (c) above.

A holding Company and its subsidiaries are separate legal entities and each has a separate corporate veil. The fact that a company is a holding company does not means that holding and subsidiary companies constitute one company.

However, provisions of sections 212 to 214 require a holding company to attach the accounts and the Board's report of its subsidiary with its own accounts.

As per Companies (Amendment) Act, 2000 a private company which is a subsidiary of a public company, shall be included in the definition of a public company. This means once a private Company becomes a subsidiary of a public company, it shall be regulated exactly like a public company. These amended provisions extend to even existing private companies which are subsidiaries of public companies.

EXPLANATION & CLARIFICATION

(a) Control of composition of Board of Directors

A Company is considered to have control over the composition of the Board of Directors, if the Company has the power to appoint or remove all majority directors of subsidiary company without the consent of any other person. Control over the composition of the subsidiary's Board of Directors is enjoyed invariably because of holding majority shares in that company. In case of a Company limited by guarantee or an unlimited company without share capital, the Articles of Association may empower the holding company to appoint directors in the subsidiary company. Thus relationship of a holding company and a subsidiary company may exist even where there is no share capital. The holding company here shall, control the subsidiary by controlling the majority composition of its Board of Directors.

(b) Holding More than half of the Total Voting Power

Some companies incorporated before the commencement of Companies Act, 1956 had the preference shares with same voting rights as equity shares. In such companies the holding company must enjoy more than half of the total voting for the purpose of control. However, Section 80 A prohibits the issue of irredeemable preference shares. A period of five years was given from 15th June 1988 to redeem such shares. Thus, now no preference shares with voting right exist.

(c) Subsidiary of another subsidiary

As already explained, if a holding company's subsidiary becomes the holding company of "some other Company' then the "some other Company" becomes the subsidiary of first holding company and so on.

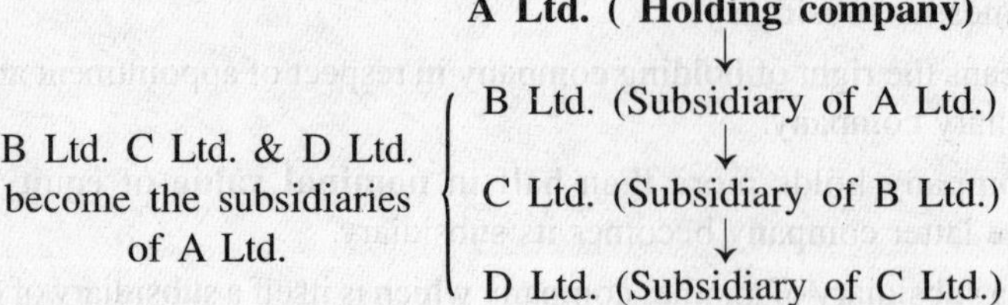

However, in determining whether one company is a subsidiary of another, the following shall be disregarded.

(i) Any shares held or power exercisable by the company in a fiduciary capacity.

(ii) Where shares are held or power exercisable by a lending company merely as a security for transactions, entered into the ordinary course of business.

(iii) Any shares held or power exercisable by any person by virtue of the provisions of any debentures, or of a trust deed for securing any issue of such debentures of other company.

It is to be noted that Section 77B dealing with buy back of shares restricts a company from buying back its shares through any subsidiary company including its own shares.

LEGAL REQUIREMENTS AS PER COMPANIES ACT, 1956

Accounting for the Holding Companies

Section 212 to 214 of the Companies Act, 1956, govern the preparation and presentation of accounts of subsidiary companies by the holding Companies. It should be noted that a holding company and its subsidiary maintain separate entity as such the financial statements of each are prepared separately by themselves.

(1) Section 212 requires that following documents must be attached to the Balance Sheet of a holding Company.

(a) A copy of the Balance Sheet of the subsidiary.

(b) A copy of its Profit and Loss Account.

(c) A Copy of the report of Board of Directors.

(d) A copy of the report of its auditors.

(e) A Statement showing holding company's interest in the subsidiary at the end of the financial year and the net amount of the profit (earned after acquisition).

(2) The Balance Sheet of the subsidiary shall be made in accordance with the requirements of this Act as at the end of the financial year of the subsidiary (where such financial year coincides with the financial year of holding Co.)

Where the financial year of the subsidiary Co. does not coincide with the financial year of holding company a statement showing the extent of change in the holding company's interest in the subsidiary since the close of the financial year of the subsidiary company is to be made.

(3) The details of any material changes which have occurred between end of the financial year of the subsidiary company and end of the financial year of holding company in respect of - subsidiary's fixed assets, its investments, the money lent by it and the money borrowed by it for any purpose other than that of meeting current liabilities.

(4) The Profit and Loss A/c and the Report of Board of Directors and Auditors, shall be made in accordance with the requirements of this, for the financial year of the subsidiary.

Where the financial year of the subsidiary does not coincide with that of the holding company the financial year of the subsidiary shall not end on a day which precedes the day on which the holding company's financial year ends by more than six months.

Where the financial year of a subsidiary is shorter in duration than that of its holding company, reference to the financial year of the subsidiary (for Balance Sheet, Profit & Loss A/c & Director's Report) be construed as reference to two or more financial years of the subsidiary the duration of which, in aggregate, is not less than the duration of the holding Company's year.

The statement showing the extent of holding company's interest in the net aggregate amount of profits shall apply only to Profits & Losses of subsidiary which may properly be treated in the holding Company's accounts as revenue profits or losses and the profits or losses attributable to any shares in subsidiary.

If for any reason the Board of Directors of holding company are unable to obtain information on the subject of revenue or capital profits a report in writing should be made to that effect.

(5) The documents (as referred above) shall be signed by the persons by whom the Balance Sheet of the holding Company is required to be signed.

(6) The Central Government may on the application or with the consent of the Board, direct that in relation to any subsidiary the provisions of this section shall not apply or shall apply only to such extent as may be specified in the direction.

(7) If any such person fails to take all reasonable steps to comply with the provisions of this section, he shall in respect of such offence, be punishable with imprisonment for a term which may extend to 6 months or fine which may extend to one thousand rupees or with both.

(8) If any person, other than those referred above, having been charged by the Board of Directors with the duty of complying the provisions, makes default in doing so, he shall, in respect of each offence, be punishable with imprisonment for a term which may extend to six months or with fine which may extend to ten thousand rupees or with both.

Provided that no person shall be sentenced to imprisonment for any such offence unless it was committed wilfully.

CONSOLIDATED FINANCIAL STATEMENTS AND AS-21

The objective of AS-21 is to provide guidelines, principles and procedure to prepare consolidated financial statements for a group of enterprises under the control of a holding company. These consolidated Financial Statements are prepared to provide financial information about the economic activities of the "group". (Holding and its subsidiaries).

While preparing consolidated financial statements, a holding company should include all its subsidiaries (domestic and foreign) except where

(i) Control in subsidiary is temporary due to its subsequent disposal in near future or

(ii) the subsidiary operates under severe long term restrictions and cannot transfer funds to its holding (parent) Company.

CONSOLIDATION PROCEDURE AS PER AS -21

Consolidation is mandatory only for listed companies as per the listing agreement. Consolidation is done as per general rules of preparation of financial statements of individual companies. Significant accounting policies and notes which are necessary for presenting a true and fair view of consolidated financial statements should also be disclosed. The following steps are required :

(1) Cost of acquisition to the parent (holding) company in each subsidiary and the parent's (holding company's) portion of net equity of each subsidiary on the date on which investments in each subsidiary is made, should be eliminated from consolidated Balance Sheet.

(2) If **Cost of acquisition is more than** the net equity (proportionate net assets value) of the subsidiary, such excess is treated as goodwill and should be shown in consolidated financial statements.

(3) If **Cost of acquisition (investments) is less than the net equity** of subsidiary company on the date of investment in subsidiary such difference should be treated as capital reserve and shown is the consolidated financial statements.

(4) **In case of chain subsidiaries,** the parent (holding company) should consolidate its subsidiaries as well as subsidiary of the subsidiaries.

(5) **Minority interests** in the net assets of all subsidiaries should be identified and shown in the consolidated Balance Sheet separately, from liabilities and the equity of parent's (holding company) shareholders.

Where as Minority Interest in the net income of all subsidiaries, for the reporting period should be deducted from the income of the group to get the holding company's share.

(6) If a parent (holding company) makes **two or more investments** in its subsidiary at different dates the consolidated financial statements are presented only from the date on which holding- subsidiary relationship comes into existence.

(7) The **intra-group** transactions of inter-company owings or inter-company loans and it's consequent effect (such as unrealised profit on unsold stock or interest on loans etc.) should be eliminated.

(8) **Date of Consolidation** of financial statements for holding & its subsidiaries should be the same. In case it is not practicable, necessary adjustments should be made for effect of events and transactions that occur between two dates.

(9) If a subsidiary has **cumulative preference shares** which are held by outsiders, the share of holding company's profits should be computed after providing for preference dividend, whether or not dividends have been declared.

(10) Accounting for investment in subsidiaries in the financial statements of holding company should be, treated as per As-13 Accounting for Investments.

Disclosure

The following should be disclosed :

(1) A list of all subsidiaries including the name, country of incorporation, proportion of holding (ownership interest) or voting power held.

(2) Nature of relationship between the parent (holding company) and a subsidiary, if the parent does not own more than one-half of the voting power of the subsidiary.

(3) The effect of the acquisition and disposal of subsidiaries on the financial position at the reporting (Balance Sheet) date, the result of reporting period (accounting period) and the corresponding amount of the preceding period : and

(4) Reasons for not consolidating a subsidiary in Consolidated financial statements.

(5) Names of subsidiaries of which reporting dates are different from the date of holding company and the difference in reporting dates.

FORMS OF HOLDING COMPANIES

Holding Companies may take the following forms :

(i) **Apex Holding Company :** It controls the other Companies and is never controlled by other Company. It controls and organises subsidiaries to consolidate its position.

(ii) **Intermediate Holding Company :** It is a holding Company which is also the subsidiary of another holding Company.

(iii) **Off Spring Holding Company :** When the existing companies transfer their controlling number of shares to the newly incorporated company, such a new company becomes holding company and the existing companies are termed as subsidiaries.

(iv) **Pure-Holding Company :** When a holding Company holds the shares of subsidiary Companies and manages their affairs only without engaging itself in production activity.

(v) **Mixed Holding Company :** It is engaged in business in addition to the management of the subsidiary Companies.

(vi) **Finance holding Company :** It finances only the operations of its subsidiaries. It disposes of the shares of its subsidiaries at the earliest opportune time.

Types of Subsidiaries

(i) *Wholly-Owned Subsidiary Company*

A wholly-owned subsidiary company is one, of which all the shares are acquired by the holding company.

(ii) *Partly Owned Subsidiary Company*

When a holding company does not acquire all the shares of a subsidiary Company, it is known as partly owned subsidiary company. The remaining shares are held by outsiders who are treated as minority shareholders. Their share in the net assets is shown as "Minority Interest" on the liabilities side of Balance Sheet.

Merits of Holding Companies

Holding Company has given flip to combination movement in India. Holding companies have become popular because of following advantages :

1. Centralised control of subsidiary companies : Holding companies exercise control over their subsidiaries which helps to eliminate wasteful competition and monopoly profits are an added advantages of holding company. Price warfare becomes unnecessary and better control is secured over the condition of sale and selling price. Risk of loss due to constant price fluctuations is avoided.

On the other hand, subsidiaries, though under centralised control, maintain their identity which helps holding company to derive the benefits of goodwill of any of the subsidiaries.

2. Economies of large scale : Economies of large scale operations (in production, marketing, finance and management) can be achieved and the benefits of cost reduction can be passed on to consumers. Scientific planning of over all manufacturing and marketing operations is possible by a holding company having its control over subsidiaries. Proper planning further helps in optimum utilisation of vast capital resources at its command.

3. Growth and stability : Holding companies devices have higher capacity to withstand the cyclical changes in the demand for their products. Large scale operations & resources provide greater chance of survival in the market. Holding companies command greater financial strength and stability with all the resources of its subsidiaries at their disposal. Holding companies have stakes in different subsidiaries, the risks of loss or impact of failure will be diversified or eliminated by suitable administrative measures.

4. Encouragement of Foreign Trade : The system of holding company can be used for creating subsidiary Companies in foreign countries. Even Indian subsidiary with a foreign holding company is able to complete globally in terms of quality of product. The foreign technical know-how can be used to overcome & beat its rivals.

5. Increase in shareholders wealth : The shareholders of subsidiary Companies may find the worth of their holdings progressively appreciated as the holding Companies keep on seeking control of more & more subsidiaries. Holding companies are potentially strong to float new Companies and make them economically viable.

6. Maintaining Secrecy : Maintaining secrecy is another merit of holding company. Details of assets, operating result, key decisions, future plans for expansion or diversification etc. can be kept confidential although broad particulars are given in financial statements. Operations of group can be cloaked from public scrutiny.

7. Other benefits : Whenever necessary, holding Company can bring about decentralised administration by the subsidiaries and give local character by exploiting regional potentials. The holding company's structure facilitates decentralisation of management whenever it is desirable in the interest of efficiency and avoid undue delays due to overburdened top management.

DEMERITS OF HOLDING COMPANIES

(1) Rise of monopoly power

Holding company may lead to the formation of secret monopolies which is harmful to the interest of consumers. Holding companies develop into a monopoly to swindle excessive profit by manipulated control over the market. The question of economies remain in the background while desire for monopoly power takes in priority in policy formulation. The social interest factors are totally ignored by holding company's craze for dominance and the consumers may be exploited by charging higher price and offering inferior goods.

(2) Absence of Accountability

Holding Companies concerntrate power of control over subsidiaries without any corresponding responsibility for achieving precise operating result. Control without accountability may prove detrimental to the interests of the group. They may even shirk the responsibility and to keep away from the risks by selling their holdings in the subsidiaries at the critical times. Unrestricted authority may lead to its misuse.

(3) Excessive Control

Since control is concentrated in holding company, the management- in -charge of subsidiary may not take keen interest on the affairs. They may not show business initiative as there is no direct incentive for them to put in diligent efforts for managing their units. Thus managerial efficiency at operational level may not be maintained to the expected level. Subsidiary companies may even be forced to appoint inefficient persons as officers/managers/directors of the company at unduly high remuneration.

(4) Internal frictions

Perfect integration of holding and subsidiaries may not become a reality because of persistent internal frictions and tussle among the component subsidiaries. There is always an apprehension that minority shareholders may be oppressed and exploited and failed to get their due shares in earnings of the company.

(5) Over-Capitalisation

With the pooling of capital of different subsidiaries, holding company find itself over- capitalised. Over-Capitalisation leads to under-utilisation of capacity, excessive overhead costs, reduced earnings and lesser dividend leading to low market price of shares. The holding Company can exploit the subsidiaries as to the investments of funds, use of resources for its own benefit and may indulge in speculation of shares.

(6) Other demerits

Inter- Company loans, inter- company transactions or transfer of assets at inflated or very low price are some of the other disadvantages of holding companies. Sometimes, the management of the subsidiaries becomes complicated and creates the problem of effective coordination and communication.

ACCOUNTING TREATMENT

For Consolidation of Financial Statements

In preparing consolidated financial statements, the financial statements of holding and its subsidiaries should be combined on a line by line basis by adding items together like items of assets, liabilities, income and expenses. The following steps should be taken.

(1) The cost of investment in each subsidiary and the holding company's portion in equity of each subsidiary, should be eliminated.

(2) "Excess of cost of investment" over holding Company's portion of equity of the subsidiary should be treated as goodwill (Cost of control)

(3) If the "cost of investment" in a subsidiary is less than the holding company's portion of equity of the subsidiary the difference should be treated as Capital reserve.

(4) The share of minority share holders in the net income of subsidiary for the reporting period should be identified and adjusted.

(5) Similarly shares of minority shareholders in the net assets of the Company (subsidiary) should be identified and presented in the Consolidated Balance Sheet. Minority interest in the net assets consists of—

(i) Amount of equity attributable to minority shareholders on the date of investment. (Share Capital plus Capital profit) and

(ii) Minority shareholders' share in the profit after the date of investment or acquisition of shares (post acquisition Profit)

(6) A Consolidated Balance Sheet is prepared after eliminating the common transactions, because amount due from one company (say S Ltd.) is the amount due to other company (say H. Ltd.) For example, debtors of one company are the creditors for other company or Bills Receivable for one company are the Bills payable for the other Company. Hence such common items are not shown the Balance Sheet.

(7) Similarly if holding Company has also subscribed some of the debentures of subsidiary company (or vice versa) then the such subscribed portion of debentures along with the interest due should not be shown in the consolidated Balance Sheet.

(8) Acquisition of preference shares by the holding company entails same procedure as that of equity except that share in the profit is restricted to the amount of preference dividend.

(9) Likewise if stock of subsidiary company includes goods purchased from holding company (or vice versa) then such portion of unsold stock should be included at cost rather than at the price at which the vendor (holding) Company had transferred. This amount of unrealised profit has to be adjusted out of the Profit & Loss account of holding company also.

(10) Equity share Capital of the holding company should not be changed except when any subsidiary holds some of the shares of holding company. Such portion should be deducted from the issued capital.

(11) Share Capital of subsidiary should never be aggregated with the Share Capital of holding company. It is to be noted that Share Capital (portion) held by holding company is cancelled against the cost of investments in subsidiary company while the remaining amount is shown under "Minority Interest".

(12) Bank balance of one company and overdraft of other company should not be adjusted but should be shown separately.

(13) In case holding company acquires shares of a subsidiary company who revalues its assets, then the effect of such revaluation and consequent impact on depreciation, revenue or Capital profits should be adjusted and shown in the Consolidated Balance Sheet.

(14) The impact of issue of bonus shares by the subsidiary company either out of revenue profits or Capital profits, should be treated before consolidation.

(15) Proposed Dividend or any payment of dividend (interim/ final) should be adjusted on the basis of pre-acquisition or post acquisition profit in the Consolidated Balance Sheet.

(16) Debit balance of Profit and Loss A/c or Preliminary Expenses appearing in the Balance Sheet on the date of acquisition should be treated as Capital (pre-acquisition) losses and should be adjusted against the capital profits. These should not be shown in the consolidated Balance Sheet.

(17) And lastly, the date of the consolidated Balance Sheet and that of the Balance Sheets of the holding and subsidiary companies should be the same.

FORMS AND CONTENTS OF CONSOLIDATED BALANCE SHEET

Companies Act 1956 does not require preparation and presentation of a Consolidated Balance Sheet. Since directors are the agents and trustees of the shareholders, they are accountable to disclose as to how their funds have been invested. Hence a clear picture of various assets including investments be presented before the shareholders. Therefore, a consolidated Balance Sheet is prepared which is in conformity with the schedule VI of Companies Act, 1956.

CONSOLIDATED BALANCE SHEET
(A Format)
As on ....

	Liabilities	Rs.	Rs.
	Share Capital (of H. Ltd. only)		....
	Reserve & Surplus:		
	Revenue Reserves of H Ltd.	......	
Add	Share in Revenue Reserves of S Ltd.	......	......
	Capital Reserve of H Ltd.	......	
Less	Goodwill, if any, as per Contra	......	
	Profit & Loss Account of H Ltd.	......	
Add	Share in Revenue (post-acquisition) profits of S Ltd.		
Less	Holding Company's share in unrealised profits	......	......
	Secured Loans:		
	Secured Loans of H Ltd.	......	
Add	Secured Loans of S Ltd.	......	......
	Unsecured Loans of H Ltd.	......	
Add	Unsecured Loans of S Ltd.	......	
Less	Mutual owings (Inter Company Loans)	......	......
	Current liabilities & Provisions :		
	Of H Ltd.	......	
	Of S Ltd.	......	
Less	Inter Company liabilities	......	
	Minority Interest		
	Assets		
	Fixed Assets		
	Cost of Control (Goodwill)		
	Goodwill of H Ltd. as per Balance Sheet	......	
	Goodwill of S Ltd. as per Balance Sheet	......	
Less	Capital Reserve as per Contra	......	......

	Rs.	Rs.
Other Fixed Assets (Net)		
of H Ltd.	......	
of S Ltd.	......	......
Investments		
of H Ltd. except in subsidiary	......	
of S Ltd.	......	......
Current Assets, Loans & Advances:		
of H Ltd.	......	
of S Ltd.	......	
Less inter Company debts	......	
Less Share of Unrealised profit	......	......
Miscellaneous Expenditure:		
Items such as P & L A/c Preliminary Expenses of Holding Company only		......
		......

H Ltd. = Holding Co./ S Ltd. = Subsidiary

I Wholly Owned subsidiary and Cancellation of Investment Account)

The main and the basic objective of consolidated Balance Sheet is to present and provide financial information about the group (Which Consists of holding and its subsidiaries) The economic activities of the group are shown as the activities of a single economic entity. Hence assets and liabilities represent resources owned and claims payable by the group. While consolidating assets and liabilities of the group, the common items which are the assets for one company and liabilities for other company, are eliminated.

In case of cent- percent holding or wholly owned subsidiary company, the entire share capital (issued) is acquired by the holding company. If S Ltd. has issued capital of Rs. 10,00,000 in shares of Rs. 10 each, then H Ltd. has acquired all 1,00,000 shares of Rs 10 each. If shares are acquired at par then the Cost of investment will be Rs. 10,00,000. While consolidating the Share Capital of S Ltd. (of Rs. 10,00,000) and Investments of H Ltd. costing Rs. 10,00,000 will be eliminated.

Illustration (1) (Wholly owned subsidiary)

BALANCE SHEETS OF H LTD. & S LTD.
As on 31st March, 2005

Liabilities	H Ltd. '000	S Ltd. '000	Assets	H Ltd. '000	S Ltd. '000
Equity Shares Capital Shares of Rs. 10 each	2,500	1,000	Sundry Assets	2,000	1,200
S. Liabilities	500	200	Investments in 1,00,000 shares of S Ltd.	1,000	
	3,000	1,200		3,000	1,200

Prepare Consolidated Balance Sheet.

Solution :

In this problem, the entire issued Capital of S Ltd. is acquired by H Ltd. at par. Thus, while preparing a consolidated Balance Sheet the investment of holding company in equity shares of subsidiary Company is replaced by the assets and liabilities of the subsidiary. It is to be noted that the holding company's interest in the subsidiary company's net assets is 100%. In other words all assets and liabilities of Subsidiary company have become the assets and liabilities of holding company. The financial position of the group can better be understood by eliminating the issued share capital of S Ltd. and Investments in shares of S Ltd. This has been shown below by means of a consolidated Balance Sheet.

CONSOLIDATED BALANCE SHEET

as on ....

Liabilities		Rs.'000	Assets	Rs. '000
Equity Share Capital			S Assets	
Shares of Rs. 10 each		2,500	H Ltd.	2,000
S. Liabilities			S Ltd.	1,200
H Ltd.	500			
S Ltd.	200	700		
		3,200		3,200

II MINORITY INTEREST

When a subsidiary company is not wholly owned by a holding company, then the remaining shares are held by others (outsiders) who are in minority from voting- power point of view. Such outsiders' (shareholders) interest in the subsidiary company is known as "Minority Interest". For example H Ltd. acquires only 8,000 shares in S Ltd. out of total 10,000 shares issued. Thus H Ltd. is holding only 80% of shares in S Ltd. while remaining 20% shares are held by outsiders. Thus the share of minority shareholders in the net assets is restricted to 20% and that of holding company to 80%.

Minority interest represents amount payable to outsiders by virtue of their holdings which is equal to their net value of their holding. These minority sharesholders are entitled to proportionate share in accumulated profits or losses. It is calculated as under :

Minority Interest = Paid up value of equity shares held by outsiders

Add Proportionate share in pre-acquisition profits & reserves.

Add Proportionate share in post-acquisition profits & reserve.

Less Proportionate share in pre/ post acquisition losses

(Such as Debit balance of P& L A/c, Discount on Issue of Debentures/ Shares and Preliminary Expenses)

However, if any change in the value of assets is agreed upon, then the impact of such revaluation should be incorporated in the minority interest also.

The share of minority shareholders so computed is shown on the liabilities side of Balance Sheet under the heading "Minority Interest".

Illustration (2)

Balance Sheets of H Ltd. & S Ltd. As on 31.3.2005

Liabilities	H Ltd. Rs. '000	S.Ltd. Rs. '000	Assets	H Ltd. Rs. '000	S Ltd. Rs. '000
Equity Share Capital Shares of Rs. 100 each	5,000	2000	Sundry Assets	5,400	2,500
S. Liabilities	2,000	500	Investments in 16,000 Shares in S Ltd.	1,600	
	7,000	2,500		7,000	2,500

Prepare Consolidated Balance Sheet.

Solution :

$$\text{Percentage holding} = \frac{1,600}{2000} \times 100 = 80\%$$

In the above illustration H Ltd. has acquired only 80% of shares of S Ltd., the remaining 20% being held by outsiders. The share of outsiders in the net assets of S. Ltd. will be shown under "Minority Interest" as shown below. Net assets = Sundry Assets – S Liabilities (2,500 – 500) 2,000

CONSOLIDATED BALANCE SHEET
As on 31st March, 2005

Liabilities		Rs. '000	Asset		Rs. '000
Equity Share Capital			Sundry Assets :		
Shares of Rs. 100 each		5,000	H Ltd.	5,400	
S. Liabilities			S Ltd.	2,500	7,900
H Ltd.	2,000				
S Ltd.	500	2,500			
Minority Interest		400			
		7,900			7,900

III COST OF CONTROL
(Goodwill or Capital Reserve)

Cost of control represents excess of "Cost of investment in shares of subsidiary" over the " intrinsic value" of shares acquired. It should be remembered that intrinsic value is equal to net assets value of share*

In the preceding illustrations, the investments in shares of subsidiary company was made at par. In the absence of any accumulated profits or losses the "par value" represents "net assets value" and as such there was no cost of control involved there in. However, in actual practice the subsidiary company usually has accumulated profits or losses and the holding company may acquire shares at a price which is either more or less than the paid up (par) value of shares, *i.e.* It may acquire shares either at premium or discount. Thus, if the actual price paid for the shares exceeds the net assets value (intrinsic value) of shares so acquired, it is treated as goodwill. Whereas if the net assets value exceeds the price paid, it is transferred to Capital Reserve For example A Ltd. acquires 80% shares of B Ltd. at a price of Rs. 1,20,000 when it had 10,000 shares of Rs. 10 each fully paid and Rs. 30,000 as accumulated profit, the cost of control will be as under :

			Rs.
	Cost of Investment (8,000 Shares)		1,20,000
Less	Paid Value of Shares	80,000	
	Accumulated Profits (80%)	24,000	1,04,000
	Cost of control (Goodwill)		16,000

If, however, Cost of investment is Rs. 90,000 only then difference shall be transferred to Capital Reserve as shown below :

	Cost of Investment		90,000
Less	Paid up Value of Shares	80,000	
Less	Share in Acc. Profit (80%)	24,000	1,04,000
	Capital Reserve		14,000

* Represent net Assets Value on the date of acquisition

Illustration (3) (Goodwill)

The following are the Balance Sheets of H Ltd. and S.Ltd. as on 31st March, 2005 when H Ltd. acquired 16,000 shares of S Ltd.

	S Ltd.	H Ltd.
Liabilities	Rs.	Rs.
Equity Share Capital (Rs. 10)	10,00,000	2,00,000
Reserves	1,00,000	50,000
Profit & Loss A/c	2,00,000	30,000
Current liabilities	6,00,000	1,00,000
	19,00,000	3,80,000
Assets		
Sundry Assets	16,00,000	3,80,000
Investment in shares of S Ltd. at cost	3,00,000	
	19,00,000	3,80,000

Prepare consolidated Balance Sheet.

Solution :

$$\text{Percentage holding } = \frac{16,000}{20,000} \times 100 = 80\%$$

Calculation of Cost of Control

			Rs.
	Cost of Investment		3,00,000
Less	Net Assets Value i.e.		
	Paid up value of Shares	1,60,000	
	Share in Accumulated profits 80% of (50,000 + 30,000)	64,000	2,24,000
	Cost of control (Goodwill)		76,000

CONSOLIDATED BALANCE SHEET
As On 31st March, 2005

Liabilities		Rs.	Assets		Rs.
Equity Share Capital		10,00,000	S. Assets		
Shares of Rs. 10 each			H Ltd.	16,00,000	
Reserves		1,00,000	S. Ltd.	3,80,000	19,80,000
Profit & Loss A/c		2,00,000	Goodwill		76,000
Current liabilities					
H Ltd.	6,00,000				
S Ltd.	1,00,000	7,00,000			
Minority Interest*		56,000			
		20,56,000			20,56,000

* Share Capital (20%)	40,000
Accumulated Profit (20%) - Reserve	10,000
P & L A/c	6,000
	56,000

Illustration (4) (Capital Reserve)

Following are the Balance Sheets of H Ltd. and S Ltd. as on 31st March, 2005

Liabilities	H Ltd. Rs.	S Ltd. Rs.
Equity Share Capital (Rs. 10)	8,00,000	3,00,000
General Reserve	1,00,000	50,000
Profit & Loss A/c	2,50,000	60,000
Current liabilities	1,50,000	90,000
	13,00,000	5,00,000
Assets		
Sundry Assets	10,20,000	5,00,000
Investment in Shares of S Ltd. (at Cost)	2,80,000	—
	13,00,000	5,00,000

H Ltd. acquired 24,000 shares as on the date of Balance Sheet. Prepare consolidated Balance Sheet.

Solution :

$$\text{Percentage holding} = \frac{24,000}{30,000} \times 100 = 80\%$$

(1) Calculation of Cost of Control\Capital Reserve.

Cost of Investment in Shares of S Ltd.		2,80,000
Less Share Capital 24,000 shares @ 10	2,40,000	
General Reserve (80%)	40,000	
Profit & Loss A/c (80%)	48,000	3,28,000
Capital Reserve		4,8000

* Alternatively intrinsic (Net assets) of the shares can also be worked out as under :

Net assets = Total assets excluding fictitious less liabilities

= 5,00,000 – 9,0000 = 4,10,000

Since H Ltd. holds 24000 shares, the net assets value of 24000 shares will be :

$= \frac{4,10,000}{30,000} \times 24,000 =$ *i.e.* equal to 80% of Total NAV Rs. 3,28,000

> Students should note that "Net Assets Value" approach should be applied only when the shares are acquired on the date of Balance Sheet. In case of time interval the post acquisition profit should not be accounted for while calculating net assets value of shares acquired because NAV of shares has to be calculated on the date of acquisition .

(2) Minority Interest (20%)

Share Capital (6000 shares)	60,000
General Reserve (20%)	10,000
Profit & Loss A/c (20%)	12,000
	8,2000

Alternatively students can prepare cost of control A/c and Minority Interest A/c instead, as shown below :

COST OF CONTROL A/C

	Rs.		Rs.
To Investment in Shares of S Ltd.	2,80,000	By Share Capital	2,40,000
To Capital Reserve (B.F.)	4,8000	By General Reserve	40,000
(To be shown in the B/s)		By Profit & Loss A/c	4,8000
	3,28,000		3,28,000

MINORITY INTEREST A/C

	Rs.		Rs.
To Balance c/d	8,2000	By Share Capital	60,000
(To be shown in the Balance Sheet)		By General Reserve	10,000
		By Profit & Loss A/c	12,000
	82,000		82,000

> **Points to be noted :**
>
> (i) Cost of control A/c considers only pre-acquisition profit equivalent to holding company's share.
>
> (ii) Excess of credit side (Capital + Pre-acquisition profit) over debit side (Cost of investment in Shares in S Ltd.) represents "Capital Reserve" while excess of debit side over credit side 'Goodwill'.

CONSOLIDATED BALANCE SHEET
As on 31st March, 2005

Liabilities		Rs.	Assets		Rs.
Equity Share Capital		8,00,000	Sundry Assets :		
Shares of Rs. 10 each			H Ltd.	10,20,000	
Capital- Reserve		48,000	S Ltd.	5,00,000	15,20,000
General Reserve		1,00,000			
Profit & Loss A/c		2,50,000			
Current liabilities:					
H Ltd.	1,50,000				
S Ltd.	90,000	2,40,000			
Minority Interest		82,000			
		15,20,000			15,20,000

(IV) PRE-ACQUISITION AND POST-ACQUISITION PROFITS

Profits earned by the subsidiary company before the date of acquisition of shares by the holding company are known as pre-acquisition profits. Such profits are treated as Capital profits which may be in the form of General Reserve, Capital Reserve, Profit & Loss Appropriation A/c, Profit & Loss A/c or any other Revenue Reserve. It means all accumulated profits, irrespective of their form, standing on the date of acquisition are pre-acquisition or Capital profits which are taken into account for the purpose of computing cost of control or Capital Reserve as shown in illustration 3 & 4.

On the other hand, profits earned by the subsidiary company after the date of acquisition of shares by the holding company, are treated as post-acquisition or revenue profits. Such revenue profits are ignored while calculating cost of control or Capital reserve. However, the same should be transferred to Profit & Loss A/c General Reserve of the holding company as the case may be. The amount to be transferred should be equivalent to the holding Company's share in such profits (Revenue Profits)

Illustration (5) (Pre-acquisition Profits)

From the following Balance Sheets of H Ltd. and S Ltd., prepare a Consolidated Balance Sheet as on March 2005.

Liabilities	H Ltd. Rs.	S Ltd. Rs.
Share Capital (Rs. 100 Share)	8,00,000	3,00,000
General Reserve	2,00,000	1,50,000
Profit & Loss A/c	2,50,000	75,000
S. Creditors	1,50,000	75,000
	14,00,000	6,00,000
Assets		
Sundry Assets	10,50,000	6,00,000
Investment in Shares of S Ltd.	3,50,000	—
	14,00,000	6,00,000

H Ltd. had acquired 2400 shares in S Ltd. on 1,4,2004 when the General Reserve and Profit & Loss A/c of S Ltd. stood at Rs. 1,00,000 and Rs. 25,000 respectively.

Solution :

$$\text{Percentage holding} = \frac{2,400}{3,000} \times 100 = 80\%$$

Capital Profits	Rs.	Revenue Profits	Rs.
General Reserve (1.4.04)	1,00,000	Profit & Loss A/c	75,000
Profit & Loss A/c (1.4.04)	25,000	(31.3.05)	
	1,25,000	*Less* Balance on 1.4.04	25,000
H Ltd. Share (80%)	1,00,000		50,000
Minority Interest (20%)	25,000	*Add* transfer to General Reserve	50,000
			1,00,000
		H Ltd. Share (80%)	80,000
		Minority Interest (20%)	20,000

COST OF CONTROL A/C

	Rs.		Rs.
To Investments in Shares of S Ltd.	3,50,000	By Share Capital	2,40,000
		By Capital Profit	1,00,000
		By Goodwill (Bal. figure)	10,000
	3,50,000		3,50,000

MINORITY INTEREST A/C*

	Rs.		Rs.
To Balance c/d	1,05,000	By Share Capital	60,000
		By Capital profits	25,000
		By Revenue Profits	20,000
	1,05,000		1,05,000

CONSOLIDATED BALANCE SHEET

Liabilities	Rs.	Assets		Rs.
Share Capital	8,00,000	Goodwill		10,000
General Reserve (1)	2,40,000	Sundry Assets		
Profit & Loss A/c (2)	2,90,000	H Ltd.	10,50,000	
S. Creditors	2,25,000	S Ltd.	6,00,000	16,50,000
Minority Interest	1,05,000			
	16,60,000			16,60,000

* Minority Interest can also be calculated as under :

Share capital	Rs. 60,000	
General Reserve	Rs. 30,000	
P & L A/c	Rs. 15,000	= Rs. 1,05,000

(1) Since S Ltd. has transferred Rs. 50,000 to general reserve out of current year's (Revenue) profits, an amount equivalent to 80% of such amount has been added to General Reserve, being holding company's share in General Reserve.

(2) Of the Rs. 80,000 being holding company's share in the revenue profits, Rs. 40,000 already transferred to general reserve the balance Rs. 40,000 (80,000 – 40,000) has been added to H Ltd. P & L A/c.

Illustration (6) (Shares acquired during the year)

Following are the Balance Sheets of H Ltd. and S Ltd. as on 31st March, 2005.

Liabilities	H Ltd. Rs.	S Ltd. Rs.
Equity Share Capital (Shares of Rs. 100 each)	7,00,000	2,50,000
General Reserve	3,00,000	1,00,000
Profit & Loss A/c	2,00,000	1,00,000
Current liabilities	2,50,000	50,000
	14,50,000	5,00,000
Assets		
Sundry Assets	11,70,000	5,00,000
Investments 2,000 Shares in S Ltd.	2,80,000	
	14,50,000	5,00,000

Shares were acquired by H Ltd. on 30th September, 2004. S Ltd. transferred Rs. 40,000 from profits to General Reserve on 31st March, 2005. Profit & Loss A/c stood at Rs. 20,000 as on 1.4.2004.

Prepare consolidated Balance Sheet.

Solution: Percentage holding $= \dfrac{2,000}{2,500} \times 100 = 80\%$

CALCULATION OF CAPITAL PROFITS & REVENUE PROFITS

	As On 31.3.05 Rs.	As on 1.4.04 Rs.	Profits earned during the year Rs.	Share of Minority as on 31.3.05 Rs.
General Reserve	1,00,000	60,000	40,000	20,000
P&L A/c	1,00,000	20,000	80,000	20,000
		80,000	1,20,000	

Capital Profits	80,000	Revenue Profit :	
Add Half of the Current Year's profit	60,000	Half of the Current year Profit =	60,000
Total	1,40,000		60,000
H Ltd.'s Share (80%)	1,12,000	H Ltd.'s Share	48,000
Minority Interest	28,000	Minority Interest	12,000

COST OF CONTROL A/C

	Rs.		Rs.
To Investments in Shares of S Ltd.	2,80,000	By Share Capital	2,00,000
To Capital Reserve (Bal. figure)	32,000	By Capital Profits	1,12,000
	3,12,000		3,12,000

Since shares are acquired on 30th September 2004, the pre-acquisition & post acquisition period is 6 month each. Hence profits of the current year are apportioned equally.

MINORITY INTEREST A/C

	Rs.		Rs.
To Balance c/d	90,000	By Share Capital	50,000
		By Capital Profit	28,000
		By Revenue Profit	12,000
	90,000		90,000

Alternatively*:

	Rs.		Rs.
To Balance c/d	90,000	By Share Capital	50,000
		By General Reserve	20,000
		By P & L A/c	20,000
	90,000		90,000

*Students are advised to follow only one method. However they should check it by applying alternative method.

CONSOLIDATED BALANCE SHEET.
As on 31st March, 2005

Liabilities		Rs.	Assets		Rs.
Equity Share Capital		7,00,000	Sundry Assets		
Capital Reserve		32,000	H Ltd.	11,70,000	
General Reserve			S Ltd.	5,00,000	16,70,000
H Ltd.	3,00,000				
S Ltd.	32,000	3,32,000			
Profit & Loss A/c					
H Ltd.	2,00,000				
S Ltd.	16,000	2,16,000			
Current Liabilities					
H Ltd.	2,50,000				
S Ltd.	50,000	3,00,000			
Minority Interest		90,000			
		16,70,000			16,70,000

Working Notes :

(1) Holding Company's share in the Revenue (Post - acquisition) profit is Rs. 48,000. Of which Rs. 32,000 has been added to General Reserve because S Ltd. has transferred Rs. 40,000 to General Reserve (H Ltd. share being 32,000) The balance (Rs. 48,000 – 32,000) Rs. 16,000 has been taken to Profit & Loss Account. Alternatively the entire amount of Rs. 48,000 may be taken to Profit & Loss A/c.

(2) It is to be noted that pre-acquisition profits belonging to H Ltd. are adjusted while calculating cost of control/capital Reserve whereas Revenue profits are treated in the Consolidated Balance Sheet.

V Pre-acquisition Losses

In case a subsidiary company has accumulated losses in the form of debit balance of Profit & Loss A/c, Preliminary Expenses, or discount on issue of shares or debentures etc., on the date of acquisition of shares, the same should be treated as Capital losses and an amount equal to holding company's share must be debited to Cost of Control Account and the share of Minority Shareholders' be charged (debited) to Minority Interest A/c.

Illustration (7) (Pre- acquisition Losses)

The Balance Sheets of H Ltd. and S Ltd. as on 31st March, 2005 were as under.

Liabilities	H Ltd.	S Ltd.
Share Capital (Shares of Rs. 100 each)	8,00,000	4,00,000
General Reserve	2,50,000	—
Profit & Loss A/c	1,75,000	1,00,000
Current Liabilities	3,25,000	1,50,000
	15,50,000	6,50,000
Assets		
Sundry Assets	12,50,000	6,30,000
Investment in 3,000 shares of S Ltd.	3,00,000	—
Preliminary Expenses	—	20,000
	15,50,000	6,50,000

H Ltd. acquired shares on 1.4.2004 when S.Ltd. had a debit balance of Profit & Loss A/c of Rs 50,000. Prepare Consolidated Balance Sheet.

Solution :

$$\text{Percentage holding} = \frac{3,000}{4,000} \times 100 = 75\%$$

CALCULATION OF CAPITAL AND REVENUE PROFIT/LOSS

Revenue Profit

		Rs.
	Profit & Loss A/c as on 31.3.2005	1,00,000
Add	Balance (Dr.) of P & L A/c on 1.4.2004	50,000
	Profit earned during the year	1,50,000
	H Ltd.'s Share (3/4)	1,12,500
	Minority Interest (1/4)	37,500

Capital Loss	Rs.
Debit balance of P & L A/c (1.4.2004)	(50,000)
Preliminary Expenses	(20,000)
	(70,000)
H Ltd.'s Share (3/4)	(52,500)
Minority Interest (1/4)	(17,500)

COST OF CONTROL A/C

	Rs.		Rs.
To Capital Loss	52,500	By Share Capital	3,00,000
To Investment in Shares of S Ltd.	3,00,000	By Goodwill (B.F.)	52,500
	3,52,500		3,52,500

MINORITY INTEREST A/C

	Rs.		Rs.
To Capital Loss	17,500	By Share Capital	1,00,000
To Balance c/d	1,20,000	By Revenue Profits	37,500
	1,37,500		1,37,500

Alternatively — Share Capital	1,00,000
P & L A/c	20,000
	1,20,000

CONSOLIDATED BALANCE SHEET
As On 31st March, 2005

Liabilities		Rs.	Assets		Rs.
Share Capital (Shares of Rs. 100 each)		8,00,000	Sundry Assets		
General Reserve		2,50,000	H Ltd.	12,50,000	
Profit & Loss A/c			S Ltd.	6,30,000	18,80,000
H Ltd.	1,75,000		Goodwill		52,500
S Ltd.	1,12,500	2,87,500			
Current liabilities					
H Ltd.	3,25,000				
S Ltd.	1,50,000	4,75,000			
Minority Interest		1,20,000			
		19,32,500			19,32,500

VI Post-acquisition Losses

The loss incurred by a subsidiary company during the post-acquisition period does not affect calculation of goodwill or Capital Reserve, because such losses are treated as revenue losses. Holding company's share of loss is adjusted against the Profit & Loss Account in the Consolidated Balance Sheet while share of loss of minority shareholders is debited to Minority Interest A/c.

Illustration (8) (Post-acquisition Losses)

Following are the Balance Sheet of H Ltd. and S Ltd. as 31st March, 2005.

Liabilities	H Ltd.	S Ltd.
	Rs.	Rs.
Share Capital (Shares of Rs. 10 each)	10,00,000	5,00,000
General Reserve (1.4.2004)	5,00,000	50,000
Profit & Loss A/c	2,50,000	—
Current liabilities	3,50,000	1,50,000
	21,00,000	7,00,000
Assets		
Sundry Assets	17,50,000	6,20,000
Investment in 3000 Shares of S Ltd.	3,50,000	
Profit & Loss A/c	—	80,000
	21,00,000	7,00,000

H Ltd. had acquired shares on 1.4.2004.

There has been no change in the General Reserve since then. During the year S Ltd. incurred loss of Rs. 80,000 after charging depreciation of Rs. 50,000 Interest Rs. 25,000 and preliminary expenses Rs. 20,000.

Prepare Consolidated Balance Sheet as on 31.3.2005.

Solution :

$$\text{Percentage holding} = \frac{30,000}{50,000} \times 100 = 60\%$$

CALCULATION OF COST OF CONTROL

Capital Profit:	Rs.
General Reserve	50,000
Less Preliminary Expenses	(20,000)
	30,000
H Ltd. share	18,000
Minority Interest	12,000

REVENUE PROFITS/LOSSES

Loss incurred by S Ltd.	80,000
Less Preliminary Expenses (Being Capital Loss)	(20,000)
Revenue Loss	60,000
H Ltd. Share	36,000
Minority Interest	24,000

COST OF CAPITAL A/C

	Rs.		Rs.
To Investments in Shares of S Ltd.	3,50,000	By Share Capital	3,00,000
		By Capital Profit	18,000
		By Goodwill (B.F.)	32,000
	3,50,000		3,50,000

MINORITY INTEREST A/C

	Rs.		Rs.
To Revenue Loss	24,000	By Share Capital	2,00,000
To Balance c/d	1,88,000	By Capital Profit	12,000
	2,12,000		2,12,000

CONSOLIDATED BALANCE SHEET
As on 31st March, 2005

Liabilities		Rs.	Assets		Rs.
Share Capital (Shares of Rs. 10 each)		10,00,000	Goodwill		32,000
General Reserve		5,00,000	Sundry Assets		
Profit & Loss A/c			H Ltd.	17,50,000	
H Ltd.	2,50,000		S Ltd.	6,20,000	23,70,000
S Ltd.	(36,000)	2,14,000			
Current liabilities					
H Ltd.	3,50,000				
S Ltd.	1,50,000	5,00,000			
Minority Interest		1,88,000			
		24,02,000			24,02,000

VII Elimination of Common Transactions

As already explained under consolidation procedure as per AS-21, while preparing a consolidated Balance Sheet, the following inter-company owings which appear in both the Balance sheets, should be eliminated.

(a) *Loans advanced by one company to other Company*

Loan advanced by a holding company to subsidiary company or vice versa appear as an asset in the Balance Sheet of lending company and as a liability in the books of borrowing Company. This transaction should be cancelled by means of following entry :

Loan from — Co. A/c Dr.
To Loan to — Co.

Similarly if any interest on such loan remaining outstanding which appear as an asset and a liability in the respective Balance Sheet it should also be cancelled by recording following entry:

Interest Outstanding A/c (Payable) Dr.
To Interest Accrued (Receivable)

> **Note to Remember :**
> To Cancel - always debit the item of liability and credit the item of the asset.

(b) *Goods sold on credit by Holding Company to subsidiary and vice versa*

In case some goods have been sold by one company to an other on credit and the amount remains unpaid, then such amount appears as "Debtors" in the books of the Company who has sold the goods and as "Creditors" in the books of the company who has purchased the goods. This should also be eliminated by means of following entry :

Trade Creditors A/c Dr.
To Trade Debtors

(c) *Bills of Exchange*

Bills drawn by the holding company and accepted by its subsidiary or vice versa and which are appearing in both the Balance Sheets on the date of Consolidation the same should be cancelled. The following entry will be recorded :

Bills Payable A/c Dr.
To Bills Receivable

However, if the bills have been discounted or endorsed, the same should not be eliminated as it becomes a claim of outsider.

Illustration (9) (Elimination of Common transaction)

The Balance Sheets of H Ltd. and its subsidiary S :Ltd. as on 31st March, 2005 were as follows :

	H Ltd.	S Ltd.
Liabilities	Rs.	Rs.
Share Capital (Shares of Rs. 100 each)	12,00,000	3,00,000
General Reserve	2,00,000	60,000
Profit & Loss A/c (1.4.04)	3,00,000	1,20,000
Profit for the year	2,50,000	1,50,000
Sundry Creditors	2,00,000	1,80,000
Bills Payable	50,000	40,000
Provisions for Taxation	1,00,000	50,000
	23,00,000	9,00,000
Assets		
Fixed Assets (Net)	12,80,000	4,00,000
Investment at cost (2100 shares in S Ltd.)	4,00,000	
Current Assets		
Stock	2,50,000	2,50,000
Debtors	1,00,000	1,50,000
Bills Receivable	1,50,000	40,000
Cash & Bank balance	1,20,000	60,000
	23,00,000	9,00,000

H. Ltd. acquired shares in S Ltd. as on 30th September 2004. Bills Receivable held by S Ltd. are all accepted by H Ltd. Included in debtors of S Ltd. is a sum of Rs. 70,000 owing by H Ltd. in respect of goods supplied by S Ltd.

Prepare Consolidated Balance Sheet.

Solution :

$$\text{Percentage holding.} = \frac{2,100}{3,000} \times 100 = 70\%$$

(1) CALCULATION OF CAPITAL PROFIT.

	Rs.
General Reserve	60,000
Profit & Loss A/c (1.4.2004)	1,20,000
Half the Profits of the current year (1.4.2004 to 30.9.2004)	75,000
	2,55,000
H Ltd.'s share (70%)	1,78,500
Minority Interest (30%)	76,500

COST OF CONTROL A/C

	Rs.		Rs.
To Investments in shares of S Ltd.	4,00,000	By Share Capital	2,10,000
		By Capital Profits	1,78,500
		By Goodwill (B.F.)	11,500
	4,00,000		4,00,000

Revenue Profit :	Rs. 75,000
H Ltd.'s Share	Rs. 52,500
Minority Interest	Rs. 22,500

MINORITY INTEREST A/C

	Rs		Rs.
To Balance c/d	1,89,000	By Share Capital	90,000
		By Capital Profit	76,500
		By Revenue Profit	22,500
	1,89,000		1,89,000

Alternatively - Share Capital	90,000
General Reserve	18,000
Profit & Loss A/c (Opening Balance)	36,000
Profit & Loss A/c Current year	45,000
	1,89,000

CONSOLIDATED BALANCE SHEET
As on 31st March, 2005

Liabilities		Rs.	Assets		Rs.
Share Capital (Share of Rs. 100 each)		12,00,000	Goodwill		11,500
General reserve		2,00,000	Fixed Assets		
Profit & Loss A/c			H Ltd.	12,80,000	
H Ltd.	5,50,000		S Ltd.	4,00,000	16,80,000
H Ltd.	52,000	6,02,500	Current Assets:		
S Creditors			Stock		
H Ltd.	2,00,000		H Ltd.	2,50,000	
S Ltd.	1,80,000		S Ltd.	2,50,000	5,00,000
	3,80,000		Debtors: H Ltd.	1,00,000	
Less Mutual owings*	70,000	3,10,000	S Ltd.:	1,50,000	
Bills Payable				2,50,000	
H Ltd.	50,000		*Less* Mutual owings*	70,000	1,80,000
S Ltd.	40,000		Bills Receivable		
	90,000		H Ltd.	1,50,000	
Less Mutual Owing*	40,000	50,000	S Ltd.*	—	1,50,000
Provision for Taxation			Cash & Bank Balance		
H Ltd.	1,00,000		H Ltd.	1,20,000	
S Ltd.	50,000	1,50,000	S Ltd.	60,000	1,80,000
Minority Interest		1,89,000			
		27,01,500			27,01,500

*Adjusted as per contra.

VIII Unrealised Profit

Accounting treatment for unrealised profit arises only when :

(a) Goods have been sold at a profit by one constituent company to another of the same group *i.e.* Holding to its subsidiary and vice-versa, and

(b) Goods (all or portion thereof) remain unsold with the purchasing company on the date of consolidation.

As per the principles of accounting the stock can not be shown at a price higher than its cost price. Hence such intra-group or inter-company profit must be eliminated and necessary adjustments must be made in the closing stock which includes "unsold stock of goods" purchased from the other company of the same group so that stock could be shown at cost in the consolidated Balance Sheet. The following adjustment entry is recorded:

Profit & Loss A/c Dr.
To Closing Stock

It means an amount equal to unrealised profit is deducted from Profit & Loss A/c and the similar amount is adjusted from the closing stock.

Now the question arises whether the entire amount of unrealised profit should be adjusted or only the amount equivalent to holding company's share. There is general consensus that any of the above methods can be applied. However in this book, For the sake of uniformity, the entire amount of such profits is eliminated and that is also the current practice of corporate world. Example : H Ltd.'s stock of Rs. 2,00,000 includes goods of Rs. 50,000 supplied by S Ltd. (subsidiary) at a profit of 25% above cost. H Ltd. holds 80% shares of S Ltd. Show the accounting treatment of unrealised profit in the Consolidated Balance Sheet. H Ltd.'s P & L A/c Rs. 2,50,000.

Solution :

Profit included in the unsold stock of Rs. 50,000 is Rs. 10,,000, *i.e.* (Rs. 50,000 ×25/125) and holding Company's share being Rs. 8,000 (80% Rs. 10,000)

First Approach:

Consolidated Balance Sheet (Skeleton)

Liabilities	Rs.	Assets	Rs.
Profit & Loss A/c	2,50,000	Closing Stock	2,00,000
Less Unrealised Profit*	8,000	*Less* Unrealised Profit*	8,000
(*as per contra)	2,42,000	(*as per contra)	1,92,000

However as per current practice the entire amount of unrealised profits is eliminated as shown below :

Second Approach

Consolidated Balance Sheet

Liabilities	Rs.	Assets	Rs.
Profit & Loss A/c	2,50,000	Closing stock	2,00,000
Less Unrealised Profit* (as per contra)	10,000	*Less* Unrealised Profit* (as per Contra)	10,000
	2,40,000		1,90,000

Illustration (10) (Unrealised Profit)

Following are the Balance Sheets of H Ltd. and S Ltd. as on 31st March, 2005

Liabilities	H Ltd. Rs.	S Ltd. Rs.
Share Capital (Shares of Rs. 100 each)	15,00,000	3,00,000
General Reserve	6,00,000	1,80,000
Profit & Loss A/c	2,50,000	1,00,000
Bills Payable	—	45,000
S Creditors	3,50,000	75,000
	27,00,000	70,00,000
Assets		
Fixed Assets	12,00,000	3,60,000
Stock	8,00,000	1,80,000
Debtors	3,00,000	1,60,000

	Rs.	Rs.
Bills Receivable	60,000	—
Investment in 2400 shares in S Ltd.	3,40,000	
	27,00,000	7,00,000

H Ltd. acquired, shares on 1.4.2004 when S Ltd. had Rs. 1,20,000 to the credit of General Reserve. The bills accepted by S Ltd. are all in favour of H Ltd. The Stock of H Ltd. includes Rs. 75,000 bought from S Ltd. at a profit of 20% on sales.

Prepare Consolidated Balance Sheet as on 31st March, 2005.

Solution :

$$\text{Percentage holding} = \frac{2,400}{3,000} \times 100 = 80\%$$

CALCULATION OF CAPITAL AND REVENUE PROFITS

Capital Profits:

		Rs.
	General Reserve (1.4.2004)	1,20,000
	H Ltd. Share (80%)	96,000
	Minority Interest (20%)	24,000

Revenue Profit:

		Rs.
	Profit as per Balance Sheet	1,00,000
Add	Transfer to Reserve (Rs. 1,80,000 - 1,20,000)	60,000
	Profit earned during the year	1,60,000
	H Ltd.'s Share (80%)	1,28,000
	Minority Interest (20%)	32,000

COST OF CONTROL A/C

	Rs.		Rs.
To Investment in Shares of S Ltd.	3,40,000	By Share Capital	2,40,000
		By Capital Profit	96,000
		By Goodwill (B.F.)	*4,000
	3,40,000		3,40,000

MINORITY INTEREST A/C

	Rs.		Rs.
To Balance c/d	1,16,000	By Share Capital	60,000
		By Capital Profits	24,000
		By Revenue Profits	32,000
	1,16,000		1,16,000

CONSOLIDATED BALANCE SHEET
As on 31st March, 2005

Liabilities		Rs.	Assets		Rs.
Share Capital (Shares of Rs. 100 each)		15,00,000	Goodwill		4,000
General Reserve (1)		6,48,000	Fixed Assets		
Profit & Loss A/c			H Ltd.	12,00,000	
H Ltd.	2,50,000		S Ltd.:	3,40,000	15,60,000
S Ltd.	80,000		Stock :		
	3,30,000		H Ltd.	8,00,000	
Less Unrealised profit	15,000	3,15,000	S Ltd.	1,80,000	
Bills Payable	45,000	—		9,80,000	
Less held by H Ltd.	45,000		*Less* Unrealised Profit	15,000	9,65,000
S. Creditors :			Debtors :		
H Ltd.	3,50,000		H Ltd.	3,00,000	
S Ltd.	75,000	4,25,000	S Ltd.:	1,60,000	4,60,000
Minority Interest		1,16,000	Bills Receivable :		
			H Ltd.	60,000	
			Less Mutual owings as per contra	45,000	15,000
		30,04,000			30,04,000

(1) Since S Ltd. has transferred Rs. 60,000 to General Reserve out of current year's profit the holding company's share Rs. 48,000 has been taken to General Reserve in the Consolidated Balance Sheet and remaining revenue profits Rs. 80,000 (Rs. 1,28,000 — 48,000) have been Credited to H Ltd.'s P & L A/c.

(IX) Contingent liabilities

Contingent liabilities are those liabilities which may or may not arise. The payment of such liabilities depends upon the occurrence of certain events.

(i) **Liability for Bills discounted :** When a company gets some of the bills discounted (cashed) from the bank, the liability for such bill will arise only when bill is not met on maturity by the acceptor on its due date.

(ii) **Liabilities under guarantee :** If company has given guarantee or stands surety in respect of loan/advance taken by other party or payment promised by other person to any third party, such a liability is materialised when the person who has taken loan/advance or promised to make payment on any future date fails to do so.

(iii) **Claim against the company not acknowledged :** When a third party sues the company for any damages and the case is pending in the court of law on the date of consolidation, the liability to pay damages will arise only when court directs the company to make payment.

(vi) **Liability for calls on partly paid shares :** Such liability arises only when company fails to meet unsecured liabilities out of its resources.

(v) **Arrears of dividend on cumulative preference shares :** Such arrears are payable only when there are sufficient profits or there is surplus after refunding equity capital in case of liquidation.

Accounting Treatment

Contingent liabilities appear by way of footnote under the Balance Sheet. However, Contingent liability relating to group (involving holding & subsidiary) is eliminated while external (outsiders) liability is continued to be shown by way of footnote under the consolidated Balance Sheet.

Illustration (11) (Contingent liability)

The Balance Sheets of H Ltd. and S Ltd. as on 31st March, 2005 were as under:

Liabilities	H Ltd. Rs.	S Ltd.. Rs.
Share Capital (Shares of Rs. 10 each)	8,00,000	4,00,000
General Reserve	2,00,000	70,000
Profit & Loss A/c	2,50,000	1,50,000
S Creditors	1,50,000	90,000
Bills Payable	—	30,000
	14,00,000	7,40,000
Assets		
Fixed Assets	6,50,000	4,50,000
Stock	1,50,000	1,00,000
Debtors	1,20,000	1,50,000
Investment in 32,000 Shares in S Ltd.	4,00,000	—
Bills Receivable	50,000	—
Cash & Bank Balance	30,000	40,000
	14,00,000	7,40,000

Note : There is a contingent liability for bills discounted by H Ltd. Rs. 35,000

H Ltd. acquired shares on 1.1.2005 when S Ltd. had Rs. 50,000 and Rs. 30,000 to the credit of General Reserve and Profit and Loss Account respectively.

S Ltd. issued all bills payable to H Ltd. Bills Receivable of H Ltd. include bills of S Ltd. for Rs. 15,000. Sundry debtors of S Ltd. include Rs. 20,000 owing by H Ltd. Stock of H Ltd. includes goods worth Rs. 25,000 purchased from S Ltd. who sold the goods at cost plus 25%.

Prepare a Consolidated Balance Sheet.

Solution :

$$\text{Percentage holding} = \frac{32,000}{40,000} \times 100 = 80\%$$

Capital Profit	Rs.
General Reserve	50,000
Profit & Loss A/c	30,000
Profit for the year (9 months) (1.4.2004 to 1.1.2005)	1,05,000

	Rs.
(Rs. 1,50,000 + Transfer to Reserve Rs. 20,000 – balance of P & L A/c on 1.1.2005 Rs. 30,000) Rs. 1,40,000 × $\frac{9}{12}$)	1,85,000
H Ltd. Share (80%)	1,48,000
Minority Interest (20%)	37,000
Revenue Profit (3 months) (Rs. 1,40,000 – 1,05,000)	35,000
H Ltd. Share	28,000
Minority Interest	7,000

COST OF CONTROL A/C

	Rs.		Rs.
Investments A/c	4,00,000	By Share Capital	3,20,000
Capital Reserve	68,000	By Capital Profit	1,48,000
	4,68,000		4,68,000

MINORITY INTEREST A/C

	Rs.		Rs.
To Balance c/d	1,24,000	By Share Capital	80,000
		By Capital Profits	37,000
		By Revenue Profits	7,000
	1,24,000		1,24,000

Alternatively : -		
	Share Capital	80,000
	General Reserve	14,000
	P & L A/c	30,000
		1,24,000

CONSOLIDATED BALANCE SHEET
As on 31st March, 2005

Liabilities		Rs.	Assets		Rs.
Share Capital (Rs. 10)		8,00,000	Fixed Assets		
Reserve & Surplus :			H Ltd.	6,50,000	
Capital Reserve		68,000	S Ltd.	4,50,000	11,00,000
General Reserve :					
H Ltd.	2,00,000		Current Assets :		
S Ltd.	16,000	2,16,000	Stock		
Profit & Loss A/c			H Ltd.	1,50,000	
H Ltd.	2,50,000		S Ltd.	1,00,000	
S Ltd.	12,000			2,50,000	
(28,000 – 16,000)	2,62,000		*Less* Unrealised Profit	5,000	2,45,000
Less Unrealised Profit	5,000	2,57,000			*Contd.*

CONSOLIDATED BALANCE SHEET (*Contd.*)

		Rs.			Rs.
Current liabilities:			Debtors:		
S Creditors			H Ltd.	1,20,000	
H Ltd.	1,50,000		S Ltd.	1,50,000	
S Ltd.	90,000			2,70,000	
	2,40,000		*Less* Mutual owings	20,000	2,50,000
Less Mutual owings	20,000	2,20,000	Bills Receivable		
Bills Payable			H Ltd.	50,000	
S Ltd.	30,000		*Less* Mutual owings	15,000	35,000
Less Mutual Owings	15,000	15,000	Cash & Bank		
Minority Interest		1,24,000	H Ltd.	30,000	
			S Ltd.	40,000	70,000
		17,00,000			17,00,000

Note : There is a contingent liability of Rs. 20,000 in respect of bills discounted.

Working Note

Bills payable of S Ltd. of Rs. 30,000 are all in favour of H Ltd. who is still holding bills worth Rs. 15,000 relating to S Ltd. It means bills worth Rs. 15,000 (Rs. 30,000 – 15,000) have been discounted which represent an internal contingent liability and hence should be eliminated. Thus contingent liability in respect of bills discounted will appear at Rs. 20,000 (Rs. 35000 – 15000) by way of foot note under consolidated Balance Sheet.

(X) Bonus Shares

Shares allotted by a company to its existing shareholders free of cost on pro-rata basis out of its accumulated profits are known as "Bonus shares". These bonus shares add noting to the net assets of the company but simply increase the number of shares. Thus issue of bonus shares by the subsidiary company increases the number of shares held by a holding company and minority sharesholders. The cost of acquisition (investment) remaining same.

Accounting Treatment

While preparing consolidated Balance Sheet, the accounting treatment of bonus shares depends upon the source out of which these are issued. There are only two sources from "acquisition of shares" point of view.

(a) *Issue of bonus shares out of pre-acquisition profits*

If the subsidiary company issues bonus shares out of pre-acquisition profits, such an issue will not affect or change the cost of control (Goodwill) or Capital Reserve. **It should be noted that issue of bonus shares implies capitalisation of profits.** Since pre-acquisition profits are already in the nature of Capital profits, the proportionate shares of holding company or minority shareholders in the net assets of the company on the date of acquisition or consolidation will not change. On one hand bonus issue increases the number of shares held by a holding company and on the other hand it reduces the share of the holding company in the capital profits (pre-acquisition profits) by the similar amount. The overall net assets value on the date of consolidation remaining unchanged.

Illustration (12)

On 1.4.2005 H Ltd. acquired 4000 shares of Rs. 100 each of S Ltd. at Rs. 5,90,000. S Ltd. had issued capital of Rs. 5,00,000 divided into shares of Rs. 100 each, General Reserve of Rs 1,50,000 and Profit & Loss A/c balance of Rs. 50,000 on that date.

S Ltd. decided to issue bonus shares out of pre-acquisition profit in the ratio of 1 : 5

Calculate cost of control and Minority Interest.

(i) Before the issue of Bonus Shares

(ii) After the issue of Bonus Shares

Percentage holding = $\frac{4,000}{5,000} \times 100 = 80\%$

Solution :

	Capital Profit = (Pre-Acquisition Profits)	
(1)	General Reserve	1,50,000
	Profit & Loss A/c	50,000
		2,00,000
	H Ltd.'s share (80%)	1,60,000
	Minority Interest (20%)	40,000

(1) Before Bonus Issue:

COST OF CONTROL A/C

	Rs.		Rs.
To Investment in shares of S Ltd.	5,90,000	By Share Capital	4,00,000
		By Capital Profits	1,60,000
		By Goodwill (B.F.)	30,000
	5,90,000		5,90,000

MINORITY INTEREST A/C

	Rs.		Rs.
To Balance c/d	1,40,000	By Share Capital	1,00,000
		By Capital Profit	40,000
	1,40,000		1,40,000

(ii) After Bonus Issue

	Capital Profit (Pre-Acquisition Profits)	
	General Reserve	1,50,000
	Profit & Loss A/c	50,000
		2,00,000
Less	Bonus Issue (Rs. 5,00,000 ×1/5)	1,00,000
	Capital Profits	1,00,000
	H Ltd.'s Share	80,000
	Minority Interest	20,000

COST OF CONTROL A/C

	Rs.		Rs.
To Investment in Shares of S Ltd.	5,90,000	By Share Capital	4,00,000
		By Bonus Shares	80,000
		By Capital Profits	80,000
		By Goodwill (B.F.)	30,000
	5,90,000		5,90,000

MINORITY INTEREST A/C

	Rs.		Rs.
To Balance c/d	1,40,000	By Share Capital	1,00,000
		By Bonus Shares	20,000
		By Capital Profits	20,000
	1,40,000		1,40,000

Illustration (13) (Bonus shares out of pre-acquisition profits)

Following are the Balance Sheets of H Ltd. and S Ltd. As on 31st March, 2005.

	H Ltd.	S Ltd.
Liabilities	Rs.	Rs.
Share Capital : Shares of Rs. 10 each	12,00,000	5,00,000
Capital Redemption Reserve	—	3,00,000
General Reserve	6,00,000	—
Profit & Loss A/c	1,50,000	90,000
Bills Payable	—	20,000
S Creditors	1,25,000	25,000
	20,75,000	9,35,000
Assets		
Fixed Assets	10,00,000	7,00,000
Investment in Shares of S Ltd. at cost	7,00,000	—
Stock	2,35,000	1,30,000
Debtors	95,000	80,000
Bills Receivable	35,000	—
Cash & Bank	10,000	25,000
	20,75,000	9,35,000

Additional Information :

(i) On the above date H Ltd. acquired 40,000 shares of Rs. 10 each in S Ltd. On 1.4.2005 S Ltd. made a bonus issue of one equity share of Rs. 10 each for every two shares held by its shareholders.

(ii) S Ltd. has accepted bills of Rs. 10,000 in favour of H Ltd. Bills Receivable of H Ltd. include bills of Rs. 7,500 accepted by S Ltd.

(iii) Sundry creditors of H Ltd. include Rs. 25,000 due to S Ltd.

Prepare Consolidated Balance Sheet as on 1st April, 2005.

Solution :

$$\text{Percentage holding} = \frac{40,000}{50,000} \times 100 = 80\%$$

Capital Profits:

Profit & Loss A/c	90,000
Capital Redemption Reserve*	
(Rs. 3,00,000 – 2,50,000 for Bonus issue)	50,000
(* To be utilised for issuing bonus shares)	1,40,000
H Ltd.'s Share (80%)	1,12,000
Minority Interest (20%)	28,000
Bonus issue (1 : 2)	2,50,000
(Rs. 5,00,000 ×1/2)	
H Ltd.'s Share	2,00,000
Minority Interest	50,000

COST OF CONTROL A/C

	Rs.		Rs.
To Investment In Shares of S Ltd.	7,00,000	By Share Capital	4,00,000
To Capital Reserve (B.F.)	12,000	By Bonus Issue	2,00,000
		By Capital Profits	1,12,000
	7,12,000		7,12,000

MINORITY INTEREST A/C

	Rs.		Rs.
To balance c/d	1,78,000	By Share Capital	1,00,000
		By Bonus Issue	50,000
		By Capital Profits	28,000
	1,78,000		1,78,000

CONSOLIDATED BALANCE SHEET
As On 1st April, 2005

Liabilities		Rs.	Assets		Rs.
Share Capital (Shares of Rs. 10 each)		12,00,000	Fixed Assets		
Reserve & Surplus :			H Ltd.	10,00,000	
General Reserve		6,00,000	S Ltd.	7,00,000	17,00,000
Profit & Loss A/c		1,50,000	Current Assets :		
Capital Reserve		12,000	Stock		
Current Liabilities			H Ltd.	2,35,000	
Bills payable (S Ltd.)	20,000		S Ltd.	1,30,000	3,65,000
Less Mutual owings	7,500	12,500	Debtors : H Ltd.	95,000	
S creditors			S Ltd.	80,000	
H Ltd.	1,25,000			1,75,000	
S Ltd.	25,000		*Less* Mutual owings	25,000	1,50,000
	1,50,000		Bills Receivable		
Less Mutual owings	25,000	1,25,000	H Ltd.	35,000	
Minority Interest		1,78,000	*Less* Mutual owings	7,500	27,500
			Cash & Bank		
			H Ltd.	10,000	
			S Ltd.	25,000	35,000
		22,77,500			22,77,500

Issue of bonus shares out of post-acquisition profit

In case a company issues bonus shares out of its post-acquisition (Revenue) profits it simply capitalises the revenue profits which is turn reduces the cost of control (Goodwill) or increases the Capital Reserve. However, it does not chage the cost of investment or proportionate share of holding company despite the increase in number of shares held but it reduces the share of holding company in the revenue (post-acquisition) profits.

As far as Minority Interest is concerned, the bonus issue out of post-acquisition period does not cause any change (increase or decrease) in their amount. It only changes the composition of minority interest. In lieu of post-acquisition (Revenue profits), the minority shareholders get bonus shares.

Bonus issue out of post acquisition profit simply changes the revenue profits into Capital profits.

Illustration (14) (Bonus issue out of post - acquisition profits)

The following are the Balance Sheets of H Ltd. and S Ltd. as on 31st March 2005.

Liabilities	H Ltd.	S Ltd.
	Rs.	Rs.
Share Capital (Shares of Rs. 10 each)	10,00,000	4,00,000
General Reserve	4,00,000	1,00,000
Profits & Loss A/c	1,50,000	1,25,000

Current liabilities	2,50,000	75,000
	18,00,000	7,00,000
Assets		
Fixed Assets	8,70,000	5,40,000
Investment in 30,000 shares in S Ltd. (at cost)	4,90,000	
Current Assets		
Stock	1,40,000	90,000
Debtors	2,25,000	55,000
Cash & Bank balance	75,000	15,000
	18,00,000	7,00,000

H Ltd. acquired shares on 1.4.2004 when S Ltd. had a credit balance of Rs. 75,000 to General Reserve and Rs. 25,000 to Profit & Loss A/c. S Ltd. issued bonus shares in the ratio of 1 : 5 out of profits earned during the year 2004-05. This is not shown in the above Balance Sheet of S Ltd.

Prepare a Consolidated Balance Sheet as on 31st March, 2005.

Solution :

$$\text{Percentage holding} = \frac{30,000}{40,000} \times 100 = 75\%$$

	Rs.
Capital Profits (Pre-acquisition Profits)	
General Reserve	75,000
Profits & Loss A/c	25,000
	1,00,000
H Ltd.'s Share (75%)	75,000
Minority Interest (25%)	25,000
Revenue Profits (Post- acquisition)	
Profit & Loss A/c (Rs. 1,25,000 – 25,000)	1,00,000
General Reserve (Rs. 1,00,000 – 75,000)	25,000
	1,25,000
Less Capitalised for Bonus Shares (4,00,000 × 1/5)	80,000
Revenue Profits after bonus issue	45,000
H Ltd.'s Share	33,750
Minority Interest	11,250
Bonus Shares	80,000
H Ltd.'s Shares (3/4)	60,000
Minority Interest (1/4)	20,000

COST OF CONTROL A/C

To Investment in Shares of S Ltd. (at cost)	4,90,000	By Share Capital	3,00,000
		By Bonus Issue	60,000
		By Capital Profits	75,000
		By Goodwill (B.F.)	55,000
	4,90,000		4,90,000

MINORITY INTEREST A/C

	Rs.		Rs.
To Balance c/d	1,56,250	By Share Capital	1,00,000
		By Bonus Issue	20,000
		By Capital Profits	25,000
		By Revenue Profit	11,250
	1,56,250		1,56,250

CONSOLIDATED BALANCE SHEET
As on 31st March, 2005

Liabilities		Rs.	Assets		Rs.
Shares Capital Shares of Rs. 10 each		10,00,000	Goodwill		55,000
Reserve & Surplus			**Fixed Assets**		
General Reserve		4,18,750	H Ltd.	8,70,000	
Profit & Loss A/c			S Ltd.	5,40,000	14,10,000
H Ltd.	1,50,000		**Current Assets:**		
S Ltd.	15,000	1,65,000	Stock(2)		
Current liabilities			H Ltd.	1,40,000	
H Ltd.	2,50,000		S Ltd.	90,000	2,30,000
S Ltd..	75,000	3,25,000	Debtors		
Minority Interest		1,56,250	H Ltd.	2,25,000	
			S Ltd.	55,000	2,80,000
			Cash & Bank balance		
			H Ltd.	75,000	
			S Ltd.	15,000	90,000
		20,65,000			20,65,000

Working notes:

(1) General Reserve : H Ltd. - Rs. 4,00,000 + 18,750 (being 75% of Rs. 25,000 transferred to General Reserve by S Ltd.)

(2) P & L A/c : H Ltd. - Rs. 1,50,000 + 15,000 (being Revenue Profit Rs. 33,750- 18,750)

XI Revaluation of Assets & Liabilities

The Holding Company may revalue the assets and liabilities of the subsidiary company at the time of acquisition of shares for the purpose of showing assets and liabilities at its true value and to ascertain the fair price of the shares so acquired. An appreciation in value of assets in treated as capital profit and a fall in value a capital loss. Whereas increase in liability is a Capital loss and a decrease in liability a capital profit. Where such changes in values of assets and liabilities remain unrecorded in the subsidiary books, the same should be incorporated in the consolidated Balance Sheet.

I Accounting Treatment on Revaluation of Assets

(a) Any appreciation or fall in the value of "Non-depreciating asset" on the date of acquisition is treated as a Capital profit/ loss and is adjusted in the cost of control" and Minority Interest like any other Capital profit/Loss, same rule will apply if date of revaluation and consolidation is the same.

(b) If the asset under revaluation is a "Depreciating Asset" then besides making adjustment for Capital profit/loss, necessary adjustment has to be made for depreciation on appreciated value from the date of revaluation to the date of consolidated Balance Sheet *e.g.* if the date of valuation (date of acquisition) is 1.4.2005 and the Consolidated Balance Sheet is required to be prepared on 30th September, 2005, then 6 months **depreciation** on appreciated value will be deducted from the **"Revenue Profits"** of the year. In case of fall in value of depreciating assets, the amount of depreciation on such fall will be added back to revenue profit. It means depreciation had to be charged on the "Revalued price" of the assets from the date of acquisition (date of revaluation) to the date of Consolidation. Any shortfall or excess in depreciation amount has to be adjusted against the revenue profits of the subsidiary company as compared to depreciation already charged for the same period.

II Accounting Treatment in case of revaluation of liabilities

Any change in the value of liability is either a Capital loss or Capital profit and as such adjusted accordingly. It does not require any other adjustment while preparing Consolidated Balance Sheet except that revised values are incorporated in the Consolidated Balance Sheet.

Example (i) H Ltd. acquired 80% of Shares Capital of S Ltd. as on 1.4.2004. The Land & Building appearing in the books of S Ltd. on that date at Rs. 4,50,000 was valued at Rs. 5,00,000.

Solution :

Since date of acquisition and consolidation is the same, the difference in value being appreciation of Rs. 50,000 will be treated like capital (pre-acquisition) profit out of which Rs. 40,000 will be adjusted against cost of control and Rs. 10,000 to minority interest.

Example (ii) H Ltd. acquired 80% of share Capital of S Ltd. as on 1.10.2004. The Plant & Machinery appearing in the Balance Sheet of S Ltd. as on 31.3.2005 at Rs. 1,80,000 after charging depreciation @10% p.a. H Ltd. valued Plant & Machinery at Rs. 2,30,000.

Solution:

Date of acquisition & revaluation : 1.10.2004 Revised Value of Plant & Machinery as on that date Rs. 2,30,000

Value of Plant & Machinery as on 31.3.2005 = Rs. 1,80,000.

Since date of acquisition (revaluation) and date of consolidation is different, we have to calculate.

(i) Appreciation/fall in the value of Plant & Machinery on the date of acquisition &

(ii) Depreciation on appreciated value or depreciation on fall in value.

I Value of P/M as on 31.3.2005		1,80,000
W.D.V. as on 1.4.2004	$\left(1,80,000 \times \frac{100}{90}\right)$	2,00,000
W.D.V. as on 1.10.2004 (Rs. 2,00,000 -Rs. 10,000 Dep.)		1,90,000

Hence actual appreciation (Rs. 2,30,000 – 1,90,000) =	40,000
H Ltd.'s share	32,000
Minority Interest	8,000
II Depreciation on appreciated value $\left(40{,}000 \times \frac{10}{100} \times \frac{6}{12}\right) =$	2,000

Rs. 2,000 will be deducted from the profit of post acquisition period which will reduce the share of holding company & Minority share holders in the revenue of profits proportionately. This will be shown in the consolidated Balance Sheet as follows :

Consolidated Balance Sheet (Skeleton)

Plant & Machinery :		
H Ltd.	xxx	
S Ltd.	1,80,000	
	xxx	
Add appreciation	40,000	
	xxx	
Less Additional Depreciation	2,000	xxx

Illustration (15) (Revaluation of Assets)

Following are the Balance Sheets of H Ltd. and S Ltd. as on 31st March, 2005.

Liabilities	H Ltd.	S Ltd.
	Rs.	Rs.
Share Capital (Shares of Rs. 100 each)	8,00,000	3,00,000
General Reserve (1.4.2004)	2,00,000	1,00,000
Profit & Loss A/c	1,50,000	50,000
S Creditors	1,50,000	50,000
	13,00,000	5,00,000
Assets		
Land & Building	6,60,000	1,90,000
Plant & Machinery	2,40,000	90,000
Investment in Shares of S Ltd.	2,80,000	—
Current Assets	1,20,000	2,20,000
	13,00,000	5,00,000

H Ltd. acquired 2,100 shares in S Ltd.. on 1st April 2004 when Land & Building and Plant & Machinery of S Ltd. were valued at Rs. 2,50,000 and Rs. 85,000 respectively. The changes in values of these assets have not been incorporated. Profit & Loss A/c of S Ltd. shows the profit earned during the current year 2004-05 after charging depreciation on Land & Building @ 5% p.a. and on plant at 10% p.a. There has been no change in the general reserve of S Ltd.

Prepare Consolidated Balance Sheet as on 31st March, 2005.

Solution : Percentage holding = $\frac{2{,}100}{3{,}000} \times 100 = 70\%$

CALCULATION OF CAPITAL PROFITS

		Rs.
	Profit/Loss on Revaluation	
I	Value of Land & Building (Revised)	2,50,000
	Written down value as on 31.3.2005 Rs. 1,90,000	
	Written down value as on 1.4.2004 (1,90,000 × 100/90)	2,00,000
	Capital Profit (Appreciation in Land & Building)	50,000
II	Value of Plant on Machinery (Revised)	85,000
	Written down Value as on 31.3.05 = Rs. 90,000	
	Written down Value as on 1.4.2004 (90,000 × 100/90)	1,00,000
	Capital Loss (Fall in Value)	15,000
Capital Profits:		
	General Reserve	1,00,000
	Profit in Revaluation	50,000
Less	Loss on Revaluation	(15,000)
		1,35,000
	H Ltd. Share (70%)	94,500
	Minority Interest (30%)	40,500
Revenue Profits:		
	Profit for the Current year	50,000
Less	Depreciation on appreciated Value of Land & Building (50,000 × 5/100)	(25,00)
Add	Depreciation on Plant & Machinery being in excess than the required $\left(\frac{15,000 \times 10}{100}\right)$	1,500
		49,000
	H Ltd.'s Share	34,300
	Minority Interest	14,700

COST OF CAPITAL A/C

	Rs.		Rs.
To Investment in 2100 Shares of S Ltd. (at cost)	2,80,000	By Share Capital	2,10,000
		By Capital Profits	94,500
To Capital Reserve (B.F.)	24,500		
	3,04,500		3,04,500

MINORITY INTEREST A/C

	Rs.		Rs.
To Balance c/d	1,45,200	By Share Capital	90,000
		By Capital Profit	40,500
		By Revenue Profits	14,700
	1,45,200		1,45,200

CONSOLIDATED BALANCE SHEET
As on 31st March, 2005

Liabilities		Rs.	Assets		Rs.
Share Capital (Rs.100)		8,00,000	Land & Building		
Reserve & Surplus:			H Ltd.	6,60,000	
Capital Reserve		24,500	S Ltd.	2,37,500	8,97,500
General Reserve		2,00,000	Plant & Machinery		
Profit & Loss A/c			H Ltd.	2,40,000	
H Ltd.	1,50,000		S Ltd.	76,500	3,16,500
S Ltd.	34,300	1,84,300	Current Assets		
Current Liabilities			H Ltd..	1,20,000	
S Creditors			S Ltd.	2,20,000	3,40,000
H Ltd.	1,50,000				
S Ltd.	50,000	2,00,000			
Minority Interest		1,45,200			
		15,54,000			15,54,000

(1)	Land & Building of S Ltd. as on 31.3.2005 as per Balance Sheet (after Depreciation)	1,90,000
	Add Appreciation	50,000
		2,40,000
Less	Depreciation on appreciated value to be charged	(2,500)
		2,37,500

Alternatively:

	Revised Value as on 1.4.2004	2,50,000
Less	Depreciation for one year @ 5% p.a.	12,500
	W.D. V. as on 31.3.2005	2,37,500
(2)	Plant & Machinery of S Ltd.. as on 31.3.2005 (after depreciation)	90,000
Less	fall in value	15,000
		75,000
Add	Depreciation on fall being an excess charge	1,500
		76,500

Alternatively

	Revised Value as on 1.4.2004	85,000
Less	Depreciation @ 10% p.a.	8,500
	W.D.V. as on 31.3. 2005	76,500

XII Preference Shares in Subsidiary Company

Preference shares are those shares which have priority as to payment of dividend and repayment of Capital. (in Case of liquidation). Preference shares are treated as cumulative unless otherwise stated. If a subsidiary company has issued preference shares there may be two situations:

(a) *Preference Shares are held by outsiders*

When preference shares are held by outsiders, the same are included in Minority Interest. The amount to be included consists of paid up value of these shares held by outsiders (Minority shareholders) plus dividend accrued there on up to the date of consolidation.

If the profits of the subsidiary company are sufficient to pay cumulative dividend on preference shares a provision is made from available reserves & surplus and added to minority interest. If the Profit & Loss A/c of subsidiary Company shows a debit balance or there are insufficient profit no provision will be made for arrears of preference dividend. It is to be noted that preference shareholders are not required to bear any loss. The entire amount of loss is apportioned between holding company and minority interest. (Minority shareholders)

(b) Preference Shares are held by the Holding Company

If the preference shares of a subsidiary company are held by its holding company, the paid up value of such preference shares is adjusted in the cost of control Account in the same manner as in case of equity shares. The cost of acquiring these preference shares is debited to Cost of control A/c and the difference (resultant) is either treated as goodwill or capital reserve as the case may be.

Accrued dividend, if relates to pre-acquisition period is treated as capital profits and as such transferred to cost of control A/c *i.e.* Preference dividend accrued on the date of acquisition is included in capital profit whereas preference dividend relating to post acquisition period is credited to Profit & Loss A/c of holding company as a share in revenue profits.

It is to be noted that Preference Share Capital and its cost of investment are cancelled and hence are not shown in the Consolidated Balance Sheet.

Illustration (16) (Preference Shares held by outsiders)

Following are the Balance Sheets of H Ltd. and its subsidiary S Ltd. as on 31st March, 2005

Liabilities	H Ltd.	S Ltd.
	Rs.	Rs.
Share Capital Equity (Share of Rs. 100 each)	12,00,000	5,00,000
9% Preference Shares of Rs. 100 each	3,00,000	2,00,000
General Reserve	1,50,000	75,000
Profit & Loss A/c	1,90,000	1,00,000
S Creditors	2,60,000	1,25,000
	21,00,000	10,00,000
Assets		
Fixed Assets	11,50,000	7,00,000
Investment in 3500 shares in S Ltd. at cost	4,50,000	—
Currents Assets	5,00,000	3,00,000
	21,00,000	10,00,000

H Ltd. acquired shares in S Ltd. on 1.4.2004 when General Reserve and Profit & Loss A/c stood at Rs. 50,000 and Rs. 30,000 respectively. No dividend has been paid or proposed out of current years profits.

Prepare Consolidated Balance Sheet as on 31st March, 2005.

Solution :

Percentage holding $\frac{3,500}{5,000} \times 100 = 70\%$

Calculation of Capital Profits:

	Rs.
General Reserve (1.4.2004)	50,000
Profit & Loss A/c (1.4.2004)	30,000
	80,000
H Ltd. Share (70%)	56,000
Minority Interest (30%)	24,000
Revenue Profits	
Profit and Loss A/c as per Balance Sheet	100,000
Less Opening Balance	30,000
	70,000
Add Transfer to General Reserve (Rs. 75000 — 50,000)	25,000
Profit earned during the year	95,000
Less Preference dividend	18,000
	77,000
H Ltd.'s share (70%)	53,900
Minority Interest (30%)	23,100

COST OF CONTROL A/C

	Rs.		Rs.
Investment in 3,500 shares in S Ltd. at cost	4,50,000	By Equity Share Capital	3,50,000
		By Capital Profit	56,000
		By Goodwill (B.F.)	44,000
	4,50,000		4,50,000

MINORITY INTEREST A/C

	Rs.		Rs.
To Balance c/d	4,15,100	By Preference Share Capital	2,00,000
		By Preference Dividend	18,000
		By Equity Share Capital	1,50,000
		By Capital Profit	24,000
		By Revenue Profit	23,100
	4,15,100		4,15,100

CONSOLIDATED BALANCE SHEET
As on 31st March, 2005

Liabilities		Rs.	Assets		Rs.
Equity Share Capital		12,00,000	Goodwill		44,000
9% Preference Share Capital		3,00,000	Fixed Assets		
General Reserve [(1)]		1,67,500	H Ltd.	11,50,000	
Profit & Loss A/c[(2)]		2,26,400	S Ltd.	7,00,000	18,50,000
S Creditors			Current Assets		
H Ltd. :	2,60,000		H Ltd.	5,00,000	
S Ltd. :	1,25,000	3,85,000	S Ltd.	3,00,000	8,00,000
Minority Interest		4,15,100			
		26,94,000			26,94,000

Working notes :

(1)	General Reserve of H Ltd.	1,50,000	
	70% of General Reserve (Rs. 25,000) transferred by S Ltd	17,500	1,67,500
(2)	Profit & Loss Account of H Ltd.		1,90,000
Add	Revenue Profit	53,900	
Less	Transferred to Reserve*	(17,500)	36,400
			2,26,400

Illustration (17) (Preference Shares held by holding Company)

Following are the Balance Sheets of H Ltd. and S Ltd. as on 31st March, 2005.

Liabilities	Rs.	Rs.
Equity Share Capital Shares of Rs. 10 each	8,00,000	3,00,000
9% Preference Share Capital Shares of Rs. 100 each	2,00,000	1,00,000
General Reserve	2,50,000	1,20,000
Profit & Loss Account	2,00,000	80,000
Current liabilities	1,50,000	75,000
	16,00,000	6,75,000
Assets		
Fixed Assets	7,50,000	4,25,000
Investment in 21,000 Shares of S Ltd.	3,50,000	—
Investment in 400 Preference Shares of S Ltd.	42,000	—
Currents Assets	4,58,000	2,50,000
	16,00,000	6,75,000

H Ltd. acquired Equity and Preference shares of S Ltd. on 1.4.2004 on which date the General Reserve and Profit & Loss A/c balances were Rs. 1,00,000 and Rs. 20,000 respectively.

Prepare consolidated Balance Sheets as on 31.3.2005.

Solution:

Percentage holding = $\frac{21,000}{30,000} \times 100 = 70\%$

Calculation of Capital Profit		Rs.
	General Reserve	1,00,000
	Profit & Loss A/c	20,000
		1,20,000
	H Ltd.'s Share (70%)	84,000
	Minority Interest (30%)	36,000
Revenue Profits		
	Profit & Loss A/c as per B/S (31.3.05)	80,000
Less	Opening balance (1.4.2004)	20,000
		60,000
Add	Transfer to Reserve (1,20,000 — 1,00,000)	20,000
		80,000
Less	Preference Dividend	9,000
		71,000
	H Ltd.'s Share	49,700
	Minority Interest	21,300
Preference Dividend		9,000
	H Ltd.'s Share (40%)	3,600
	Minority Interest (60%)	5,400

COST OF CONTROL A/C

	Rs.		Rs.
To Investment in Equity Shares	3,50,000	By Equity Share Capital	2,10,000
To Investment in Preference Shares	42,000	By Preference Share Capital	40,000
		By Capital Profits	84,000
		By Goodwill (B.F)	58,000
	3,92,000		3,92,000

MINORITY INTEREST A/C

	Rs.		Rs.
To Balance c/d	2,12,700	By Equity Share Capital	90,000
		By Preference Shares Capital	60,000
		By Preference dividend	5400
		By Capital Profits	36,000
		By Revenue Profits	21,300
	2,12,700		2,12,700

CONSOLIDATED BALANCE SHEET
As on 31st March, 2005

Liabilities		Rs.	Assets		Rs.
Equity Share Capital		8,00,000	Goodwill		58,000
Shares of Rs. 10 each			Fixed Assets		
Preference Share Capital		2,00,000	H Ltd.	7,50,000	
Reserve & Surplus :			S Ltd.	4,25,000	11,75,000
			Current Assets		
General Reserve (1)		2,64,000	H Ltd.	4,58,000	
Profit & Loss A/c (2)		2,39,300	S Ltd.	2,50,000	7,08,000
Current liabilities					
H Ltd.	1,50,000				
S Ltd.	75,000	2,25,000			
Minority Interest		2,12,700			
		19,41,000			19,41,000

Working Notes:

(1)	General Reserve of H Ltd.	2,50,000
Add	70% of General Reserve transferred	14,000
	(70% of Rs. 20,000) by S Ltd. out of Current Years profit	2,64,000
(2)	Profit & Loss A/c of H Ltd.	2,00,000
Add	Revenue Profit (49,700 – 14,000)	35,700
Add	Preference dividend	3,600
		2,39,300

(XIII) "Debentures of Subsidiary Company held by its parent Company or vice versa"

Debentures issued by a subsidiary company and held by outsiders (other than the parent company) are shown under secured loans on the liabilities side of the consolidated Balance Sheet. In case debentures are held by its parent company (Holding Co.) then the paid up value of debentures held by the holding Company is cancelled against the cost of investment of such debentures. Difference, if any, is transferred to Cost of Control or Capital reserve. Following entry will make it clear.

Debentures A/c	Dr.	with paid up value of debentures held up a holding Co.
To Investment in Debentures of subsidiary		Cost of Investment

In case debentures of the holding Company are held by its subsidiary, the same (above) treatment will be made. That is debentures issued by any of the Companies (holding or subsidiary) in the group and held as investment by another company of the same group, should be eliminated. "Debenture Interest due but not paid" on the debentures of subsidiary/parent Co. held by either Company should also be cancelled being an item of mutual owings or common transaction. The interest payable by subsidiary parent is equal to interest receivable by parent/subsidiary. The following entry is recorded.

Deb. Interest payable A/c	Dr.
To Debenture Interest Receivable	

Illustration (18) (Debentures in subsidiary Co.)

The following are the balance sheets of H Ltd. and S Ltd. as on 31st March, 2005.

Liabilities	H Ltd. Rs.	S Ltd. Rs.
Equity Share Capital (Shares of Rs. 10 each)	8,00,000	3,00,000
General Reserve	2,50,000	50,000
Profit & Loss A/c	1,75,000	75,000
9% Debentures (Rs. 100 each)	—	1,00,000
Current liabilities	2,25,000	1,25,000
	14,50,000	6,50,000
Assets		
Fixed Assets	7,40,000	3,70,000
Investments in 24,000 shares of S Ltd.	3,00,000	—
Investment in 600 Debentures in S Ltd.	65,000	—
Current assets	3,45,000	2,80,000
	14,50,000	6,50,000

H Ltd. acquired shares on 1.10.2004. The Profit & Loss Account of S Ltd. showed a credit balance of Rs. 20,000 on 1.4.2004. There is no change in the General Reserve.

Prepare Consolidated Balance Sheet as on 31st March, 2005.

Solution :

$$\text{Percentage holding} = \frac{24,000}{30,000} \times 100 = 80\%$$

Calculation of Capital Profits	Rs.
General Reserve as on 1.4.2004	50,000
Profit & Loss A/c as on 1.4.2004	20,000
Current year's profit (1.4.04 to 1.10.04) (75,000 - 20,000) = 55,000 × 6/12	27,500
	97,500
H Ltd.'s share	78,000
Minority Interest	19,500
Revenue Profits (1.10.04 to 31.3.05)	27,500
H Ltd.'s share	22,000
Minority Interest	5500

COST OF CAPITAL A/C

	Rs.		Rs.
To Investments		By Share Capital	2,40,000
in Shares	3,00,000	By Capital Profits	78,000
in Debenture	65,000	By 9% Debentures	60,000
To Capital Reserves (B.F.)	13,000		
	3,78,000		3,78,000

MINORITY INTEREST A/C

	Rs.		Rs.
To Balance c/d	85,000	By Share Capital	60,000
		By Capital Profits	19,500
		By Reserve Profits	5,500
	85,000		85,000

CONSOLIDATED BALANCE SHEET
As on 31st March, 2005

Liabilities		Rs.	Assets		Rs.
Equity Share Capital		8,00,000	Fixed Assets		
Shares of Rs. 10 each			H Ltd.	7,40,000	
Capital Reserve		13,000	S Ltd.	3,70,000	11,10,000
General Reserve		2,50,000	Current Assets		
Profit & Loss A/c			H Ltd.	3,45,000	
H Ltd.	1,75,000		S Ltd.	2,80,000	6,25,000
S Ltd.	22,000	1,97,000			
9% Debentures	1,00,000				
Less Held by H Ltd.	60,000	40,000			
Current Liabilities		3,50,000			
Minority Interest		85,000			
		17,35,000			17,35,000

Illustration (19) (Mutual holding of Debentures)

Following are the Balance Sheets of H Ltd. and its subsidiary S Ltd. as on 31st March, 2005.

	H Ltd.	S Ltd.
Liabilities	Rs.	Rs.
Equity Share Capital (Shares of Rs. 100 each)	15,00,000	5,00,000
General Reserve (1.4.04)	3,00,000	1,00,000
Profit & Loss A/c (1.4.04)	50,000	30,000
Profit earned during the year	2,50,000	1,20,000
9% Debentures (Rs.100)	3,00,000	1,50,000
Interest outstanding thereon	27,000	13,500
Current Liabilities	2,23,000	1,36,500
	26,50,000	10,50,000
Assets		
Fixed Assets	12,50,000	7,50,000
Investment in :		
4000 Shares of S Ltd.	5,50,000	—
1000 Debentures of S Ltd. at par	1,00,000	—
500 Debentures of H Ltd. at par	—	50,000
Current Assets	7,50,000	2,50,000
	26,50,000	10,50,000

H Ltd. acquired shares and debentures in S Ltd. as on 1.4.2004 whereas S Ltd. acquired Debentures of H Ltd. on 1.4.2002. Prepare consolidated Balance Sheet.

Solution :

$$\text{Percentage holding} = \frac{4,000}{5,000} \times 100 = 80\%$$

Calculation of Capital Profits:

	Rs.
General Reserve (1.4.2004)	1,00,000
Profit & Loss A/c (1.4.2004)	30,000
	1,30,000
H Ltd.'s Share (80%)	1,04,000
Minority Interest (20%)	26,000
Revenue Profit	1,20,000
H Ltd.'s Share (80%)	96,000
Minority Interest (20%)	24,000

COST OF CONTROL A/C

	Rs.		Rs.
To Investment in Shares of S Ltd.	5,50,000	By Share Capital	4,00,000
		By Capital Profits	1,04,000
		By Goodwill (B.F.)	46,000
	5,50,000		5,50,000

MINORITY INTEREST A/C

	Rs.		Rs.
To Balance c/d	1,50,000	By Share Capital	1,00,000
		By Capital Profits	26,000
		By Revenue Profits	24,000
	1,50,000		1,50,000

CONSOLIDATED BALANCE SHEET
As on 31st March, 2005

Liabilities		Rs.	Assets		Rs.
Equity Share Capital		15,00,000	Goodwill		46,000
Shares of Rs. 100 each			Fixed Assets:		
Reserve & Surplus :			H Ltd.	12,50,000	
General Reserve		3,00,000	S Ltd.	7,50,000	20,00,000
Profit & Loss A/c			Current Assets:		
H Ltd.	3,00,000		H Ltd.	7,50,000	
S Ltd.	96,000	3,96,000	S Ltd.	2,50,000	
Secured Loans :				10,00,000	
9% Debentures H Ltd.	3,00,000		*Less* Mutual Owings	13,500	9,86,500
Less held by S Ltd.	50,000	2,50,000	(Interest on *debentures) as per Contra		*Contd.*

CONSOLIDATED BALANCE SHEET (*Contd.*)

		Rs.		Rs.
S Ltd.	1,50,000			
Less held by H Ltd.	1,00,000	50,000		
Interest on Debentures o/s				
H Ltd.:	27,000			
Less due to S Ltd.*	4,500	22,500		
S Ltd.	13,500			
Less due to H Ltd.*	9,000	4,500		
Current liabilities:				
H Ltd.	2,23,000			
S Ltd.	1,36,500	3,59,500		
Minority Interest		1,50,000		
		30,32,500		30,32,500

(XIV) Treatment of Dividend

While preparing consolidated Balance Sheet the accounting treatment of dividend depends upon the circumstances, timings and the sources out of which dividend has been paid or proposed to be paid by a subsidiary company.

However, following points should be kept in mind while preparing consolidated Balance Sheet.

(1) Unclaimed Dividend

A part of dividend which is declared by the Company but not claimed by the shareholders is known as unclaimed dividend Usually it appears on the liabilities side of Balance Sheet of the subsidiary Company. If the amount of unclaimed dividend belongs to minority shareholders the same should be added back to "Minority Interest". In case unclaimed dividend belongs to its parent (Holding) Company it should be Cancelled by corresponding unclaimed dividend appearing on the assets side of the Balance Sheet of the holding Company.

(2) Proposed Dividend

When a subsidiary Company proposes the dividend, the Profit and Loss Appropriation A/c is debited and Proposed Dividend A/c is credited.

Accounting treatment of proposed dividend depends upon the nature of profit out of which proposed dvidend has been provided. Usually, it is provided out of current year's (post- acquisition) profit.

There may be two situations.

(a) Proposed dividend appearing in the Balance Sheet.

It implies that proposed dividend has already been deducted out of post acquisition (Current year) profit. In this case, the amount of proposed dividend is added back to the profits to ascertain the actual profit earned during the current year. Then the same are apportioned between the holding company and Minority Shareholders. Holding Company's share is added to profit and Loss Account in the consolidated Balance Sheet, while that of Minority shareholders is added to Minority Interest or alternatively proposed dividend belonging to Minority shareholders may be shown separately under the heading proposed dividend. For this the amount of proposed dividend belonging to minority shareholders is deducted out of total amount of minority interest.

In case proposed dividend has been appropriated out of pre-requisition profit the same should be treated as capital profit and adjusted to the cost of control A/c and Minority Interest A/c.

(b) *Proposed dividend does not appear in the Balance Sheet*

If the directors of a subsidiary company have the intention or simply recommend the proposal for dividend which has not been given any accounting treatment, it will have no effect on the subsidiary company's Current year's profit *i.e.* such amount of proposed dividend will not be added back to profit of current year as there has been no adjustment on account of proposed dividend. Pre or post acquisition profit shall be apportioned between holding company and minority interest as usual.

However, if the directors so desire to show minority shareholders' share of proposed dividend separately, the same should be deducted out of "Minority Interest."

(3) Payment of Dividend

Whenever "subsidiary company pays dividend to its shareholders including its parent (holding) Company the accounting treatment again depends on the nature of profits appropriated for dividend purposes. If the dividend so paid relate to revenue (post-acquisition) profit then the same should be credited to Profit & Loss A/c of holding Company. If the dividend so paid is out of pre-acquisition (Capital Profit) it should be adjusted against Cost of Control A/c. Under no situation it is credited to Profit & Loss Account of the holding company.

In case a holding Company receives dividend out of pre-acquisition profit from it's subsidiary company and credits the same to Profit & Loss Account, the following adjustment entry shall be recorded.

Profit & Loss A/c

To Cost of Control A/c (Or Investment A/c)

Points to note:

(i) It is important to establish the true nature of dividend i.e. whether paid out of pre-acquisition profit or out of post-acquisition profit. It is immaterial whether these are final dividends on interim dividends.

(ii) In case there is no clue as to the true nature of profits, an interim dividend should be treated as paid out of post-acquisition profit and final dividend out of pre-acquisition profit.

(iii) Dividend received by a holding company just after its acquisitions or dividend so paid relate to last year (pre-acquisition period), the same should be treated as if paid out of pre-acquisition profit.

(iv) Dividend paid to minority shareholders out of pre-acquisition profit should be ignored. No accounting treatment is required. However if paid out of post acquisition profit (as interim dividend) the same should be adjusted to calculate current year's profit and deducted from minority interest.

(v) If dividend is paid partly out of pre-acquisition profits and partly out of post-acquisitions profits, the dividend received by holding company is divided in two parts:

(i) dividend received out of pre-acquisition profit

(ii) dividend received out of post-acquisition profit.

The former is credited to Investment A/c (Cost of Control) and the latter Credited to Profit & Loss A/c of the holding company.

Illustration (20) (Proposed dividend shown in the Balance Sheet)

H Ltd. & S Ltd. presented Balance Sheets as on 31st March, 2005.

Liabilities	H Ltd. Rs.	S Ltd. Rs.
Equity Shares Capital (Shares of Rs. 10 each)	8,00,000	4,00,000
General Reserve	1,75,000	60,000
Profit & Loss A/c	1,25,000	75,000
Proposed Dividend	80,000	40,000
Current liabilities	2,20,000	1,25,000
	14,00,000	7,00,000
Assets		
Fixed Assets	6,00,000	4,50,000
30,000 Shares in S Ltd.	3,75,000	—
Current Assets	4,25,000	2,50,000
	14,00,000	7,00,000

H Ltd. acquired Shares in S Ltd. as on 1st April, 2004. The General Reserve of S Ltd. was the same on that date. The Profit & Loss A/c showed a credit balance of Rs. 15,000. Stock of S Ltd. includes goods purchased from H Ltd. for Rs. 20,000 which were sold by H Ltd. at cost plus 25%.

Prepare consolidated Balance Sheet as on 31st March, 2005.

Solution :

$$\text{Percentage holding} = \frac{30,000}{40,000} \times 100 = 75\%$$

Calculation of Capital Profits	Rs.
General Reserve (1.4.2004)	60,000
Profit & Loss A/c (1.4.2004)	15,000
	75,000
H Ltd.'s Shares (3/4)	56,250
Minority Interest (1/4)	18,750
Revenue Profits	
Profit & Loss A/c (31.3.05)	75,000
Less balance on 1.4.2004	15,000
	60,000
Add proposed Dividend	40,000
Profit earned during the year	1,00,000
H Ltd.'s Share (3/4)	75,000
Minority Interest (1/4)	25,000

COST OF CONTROL A/C

	Rs.		Rs.
To Investment in Shares of S Ltd.	3,75,000	By Share Capital	3,00,000
		By Capital Profit	56,250
		By Goodwill (B.F.)	18,750
	3,75,000		3,75,000

MINORITY INTEREST A/C

	Rs.		Rs.
To Balance c/d	1,43,750	By Share Capital	1,00,000
		By Capital Profits	18,750
		By Revenue Profit	25,000
	1,43,750		1,43,750

CONSOLIDATED BALANCE SHEET
As on 31st March, 2005

Liabilities		Rs.	Assets		Rs.
Equity Share Capital		8,00,000	Goodwill		18,750
Shares of Rs. 10 each			Fixed Assets		
Reserve & Surplus :			H Ltd.	6,00,000	
General Reserve		1,75,000	S Ltd.	4,50,000	10,50,000
Profit & Loss A/c			Current Assets		
H Ltd.	1,25,000		H Ltd.	4,25,000	
S Ltd.	75,000		S Ltd.	2,50,000	
	2,00,000			6,75,000	
Less Unrealised Profit	4,000	1,96,000	*Less* Unrealised Profit	4,000	6,71,000
Current liabilities :					
H Ltd.	2,20,000				
S Ltd.	1,25,000	3,45,000			
Minority Interest		1,43,750*			
Proposed Dividend*					
H Ltd.		80,000			
		17,39,750			17,39,750

*** Alternatively the proposed dividend belonging to Minority Shareholders (1/4th of Rs. 40,000)= Rs. 10,000 may be shown under the heading "Proposed Dividend" of S Ltd. and the same should be deducted from the total of minority interest (Rs. 1,43,750 - 10,000) = 1,33,750.**

Illustration (21) (Proposed dividend not shown in the Balance Sheet)

Following are the Balance Sheets of H Ltd. and S Ltd. as on 31st March 2005

Liabilities	H Ltd. Rs.	S Ltd. Rs.
Share Capital Shares of Rs. 10 each	7,00,000	3,00,000
General Reserve	3,00,000	1,00,000
Profit & Loss A./c (1.4.04)	1,00,000	40,000
Profit for the year	2,50,000	80,000
Current liabilities	1,50,000	80,000
	15,00,000	6,00,000

Assets

Fixed Assets	8,00,000	4,00,000
Investment in 27,000 shares of S Ltd.	3,80,000	—
Current Assets	3,20,000	2,00,000
	15,00,000	6,00,000

H Ltd. acquired 27,000 shares of S Ltd. at Rs. 3,80,000 on 1.4.2004. The Directors of both the companies have proposed 10% dividend for 2004-05.

Prepare Consolidated Balance Sheet as on 31st March, 2005.

Solution :

Percentage holding = $\frac{27,000}{30,000} \times 100 = 90\%$

Calculation of Capital Profits	Rs.
General Reserve (1.4.2004)	1,00,000
Profit & Loss A/c (1.4.2004)	40,000
	1,40,000
H Ltd.'s share (90%)	1,26,000
Minority Interest (10%)	14,000
Revenue Profits:	
Profit for the year 2004-05	80,000
H Ltd.'s Share (90%)	72,000
Minority Interest (10%)	8,000

COST OF CONTROL A/C

	Rs.		Rs.
To Investment in S Ltd.	3,80,000	By Share Capital	2,70,000
To Capital Reserve (B.F.)	16,000	By Capital Profits	1,26,000
	3,96,000		3,96,000

MINORITY INTEREST A/C

	Rs.		Rs.
To Proposed dividend*	3,000	By Share Capital	30,000
To Balance c/d	49,000	By Capital Profits	14,000
		By Revenue Profit	8,000
	52,000		52,000

* To be shown separately

CONSOLIDATED BALANCE SHEET
As on 31st March, 2005

Liabilities		Rs.	Assets		Rs.
Equity Share Capital		7,00,000	Fixed Assets		
Shares of Rs. 10 each			H Ltd.	8,00,000	
Reserve & Surplus :			S Ltd.	4,00,000	12,00,000
Capital Reserve		16,000	Current Assets:		
General Reserve		3,00,000	H Ltd.	3,20,000	
Profit & Loss A/c			S Ltd.	2,00,000	5,20,000
Opening Balance.	1,00,000				
Profit for the year	2,50,000				
	3,50,000				
Less Proposed Dividend	70,000				
	2,80,000				
Share in S Ltd.	72,000	3,52,000			
Current liabilities :					
H Ltd.	1,50,000				
S Ltd.	80,000	2,30,000			
Minority Interest		49,000			
Proposed Dividend :					
H Ltd.	70,000				
S Ltd.	3,000	73,000			
		17,20,000			17,20,000

Illustration (22) (Interim dividend paid out of post- acquisition profits)

The following are the summarised Balance Sheets of H Ltd. and S Ltd. as on 31st March, 2005.

	H Ltd.	S Ltd.
Liabilities	Rs.	Rs.
Equity Share Capital : Shares of Rs. 100 each	15,00,000	5,00,000
General Reserve	6,00,000	30,000
Profit and Loss A/c	2,50,000	1,75,000
S Creditors	1,50,000	1,45,000
	25,00,000	8,50,000
Assets:		
Fixed Assets	12,50,000	5,50,000
Investment in 4,000 shares of S Ltd.	5,00,000	
Current Assets	7,50,000	3,00,000
	25,00,000	8,50,000

H Ltd. acquired shares of S Ltd. on 1.4.2004 at total price of Rs. 5,00,000. During the year ending 2004-05 H Ltd. received an interim dividend @ 12% which was credited to Profit & Loss A/c. Sundry Creditor of S Ltd. include Rs. 30,000 for purchase of goods (remaining unsold) and on which latter company made a profit of Rs. 6,000.

On 1.4.2004, the Profit & Loss A/c of S Ltd. stood at Rs. 50,000 and General Reserve at Rs. 30,000.

Prepare Consolidated Balance Sheet as on 31st March, 2005.

Solution :

Capital Profits :

		Rs.
	General Reserve (1.4.2004)	30,000
	Profit & Loss A/c (1.4.2004)	50,000
		80,000
	H Ltd.'s Share (80%)	64,000
	Minority Interest (20%)	16,000

Revenue Profits:

		Rs.
	Profit & Loss A/c as on 31.3.2005	1,75,000
Less	Opening Balance	50,000
		1,25,000
Add	Interim dividend @ 12%	60,000
	Profit earned during the year	1,85,000
	H Ltd.'s Share (80%)	1,48,000
	Minority Interest (20%)	37,000

COST OF CONTROL A/C

	Rs.		Rs.
To Investment in Shares of S Ltd.	5,00,000	By Share Capital	4,00,000
		By Capital Profits	64,000
		By Goodwill (B.F.)	36,000
	5,00,000		5,00,000

MINORITY INTEREST A/C

	Rs.		Rs.
To Interim dividend (paid)	12,000	By Share Capital	1,00,000
To Balance c/d	1,41,000	By Capital Profit	16,000
		By Revenue Profits	37,000
	1,53,000		1,53,000

CONSOLIDATED BALANCE SHEET
As On 31st March, 2005

Liabilities		Rs.	Assets		Rs.
Equity Share Capital		15,00,000	Goodwill		36,000
Minority Interest		1,41,000	Fixed Assets		
Reserve & Surplus			H Ltd.	12,50,000	
General Reserve		6,00,000	S Ltd.	5,50,000	18,00,000
Profit & Loss A/c (1)		3,44,000	Current Assets		
Current liabilities			H Ltd.	7,50,000	
S Creditors			S Ltd.	3,00,000	
H Ltd.	1,50,000			10,50,000	
S Ltd.	1,45,000		*Less* Mutual Debts	30,000	
	2,95,000			10,20,000	
Less Mutual Debts	30,000	2,65,000	*Less* Unrealised Profit	6,000	10,14,000
		28,50,000			28,50,000

Working Notes:

(1) Profit & Loss A/c	Rs.
H Ltd.	2,50,000
S Ltd.	1,48,000
	3,98,000
Less Interim Dividend (already credited to P & L A/c)	48,000
	3,50,000
Less Unrealised Profit	6,000
	3,44,000

Illustration (23) (Dividend out of pre-acquisition profits)

The following are the Balance Sheets of H Ltd. and S Ltd. as on 31st March, 2005.

Liabilities	H Ltd.	S Ltd.
	Rs.	Rs.
Share Capital (Rs 10)	7,50,000	2,50,000
General Reserve	2,75,000	75,000
Profit & Loss A/c	2,25,000	1,25,000
Current liabilities	2,50,000	1,25,000
	15,00,000	5,75,000
Assets		
Fixed Assets	7,90,000	3,75,000
Investment in 20,000 Shares of S Ltd.	2,60,000	—
Current Assets	4,50,000	2,00,000
	15,00,000	5,75,000

H Ltd. acquired shares of S Ltd. on 1.7.2004. S Ltd. paid a dividend @ 12% in July 2004 for the year 2003-04 which was credited to Profit & Loss Account by H Ltd. On 1.4.2004 S Ltd. had Rs. 40,000 to the credit of Profit & Loss Account and Rs. 50,000 to General Reserve.

Prepare Consolidated Balance Sheet as on 31st March, 2005.

Solution : Percentage holding = $\frac{2,000}{2,500} \times 100 = 80\%$

CALCULATION OF REVENUE PROFIT
PROFIT & LOSS APP. A/C

	Rs.		Rs.
To Dividend	30,000	By Balance b/d	40,000
To Balance c/d	10,000		
	40,000		40,000
To General Reserve	25,000	By Balance c/d	10,000*
To Balance c/d	1,25,000	By Net Profit earned during the year	1,40,000
	1,50,000		1,50,000

	Rs.
Profit earned during the year	1,40,000
Revenue Profit (1,40,000 × 9/12)	1,05,000
H Ltd.'s Share (80%)	84,000
Minority Interest (20%)	21,000
Capital Profits:	
General Reserve (1.4.04)	50,000
Profit & Loss A/c (1.4.04) (after dividend for 2003-04)	10,000*
Current year's Profit for 3 months (1,40,000 × 3/12)	35,000
	95,000
H Ltd.'s Share (80%)	76,000
Minority Interest (20%)	19,000

INVESTMENTS A/C

	Rs.		Rs.
To Balance b/d (Shares in S Ltd. at cost)	2,60,000	By Dividend (80% of 30,000)	24,000
		By Cost of Capital A/c	2,36,000
	2,60,000		2,60,000

COST OF CONTROL A/C

	Rs.		Rs.
To Investment A/c	2,36,000	By Share Capital	2,00,000
To Capital Reserve (B.F.)	40,000	By Capital Profit	76,000
	2,76,000		2,76,000

MINORITY INTEREST A/C

	Rs.		Rs.
To Balance c/d	90,000	By Share Capital	50,000
		By Capital Profit	19,000
		By Revenue Profit	21,000
	90,000		90,000

CONSOLIDATED BALANCE SHEET
As on 31st March, 2005

Liabilities		Rs.	Assets		Rs.
Share Capital (Rs. 10)		7,50,000	Fixed Assets		
Capital Reserve		40,000	H Ltd.	7,90,000	
General Reserve			S Ltd.	3,75,000	11,65,000
H Ltd.	2,75,000		Current Assets		
S Ltd.	20,000	2,95,000	H Ltd.	4,50,000	
Minority Interest		90,000	S Ltd.	2,00,000	6,50,000
Profit & Loss A/c					
H Ltd.	2,25,000				
S Ltd. (84,000 – 20,000)	64,000				
	2,89,000				
Less Dividend from pre-acq. profit	24,000	2,65,000			
Current Liabilities					
H Ltd.	2,50,000				
S Ltd.	1,25,000	3,75,000			
		18,15,000			18,15,000

Working Notes :

(1) Out of H Ltd.'s share of revenue profit of Rs. 84,000, Rs. 20,000 (being 80% of Rs. 25,000 transferred to General Reserve by S Ltd.) has been deducted & the balance added to P & L A/c of H Ltd.

(2) Since dividend has been paid out of pre-acquisition profits, the same has been adjusted by means of following entry.

		Dr.	Cr.
Profit & Loss A/c	Dr.	24,000	
To Investment A/c			24,000

(Being dividend received out of pre-acquisition profit which was wrongly credited to profit & Loss A/c now corrected)

Illustration (24) (Dividend from pre-acquisition profit and Corporate dividend tax)

The following are the Balance Sheet of H Ltd. and S Ltd. as on 31st March 2005.

Liabilities	H Ltd.	S Ltd.
	Rs.	Rs.
Share Capital (Rs.100)	7,50,000	3,00,000
General Reserve	1,95,000	75,000
Profit & Loss A/c	2,40,000	90,000
Sundry Creditors	2,15,000	1,35,000
	14,00,000	6,00,000
Assets		
Net Block	7,00,000	4,00,000
Investment in 2,100 shares of S Ltd.	3,00,000	—
Current Assets	4,00,000	2,00,000
	14,00,000	6,00,000

H Ltd. acquired shares in S Ltd. on 1st April, 2004 when Profit & Loss A/c and General Reserve disclosed credit balances of Rs. 51,500 and Rs. 60,000 respectively. S Ltd. declared a dividend @ 15% in May 2004 for the year 2003-04. The dividend was received by H Ltd. and credited to its Profit & Loss A/c S Ltd.. also paid corporate dividend tax @ 10%.

Prepare Consolidated balance Sheet as on 31st March, 2005.

Solution :

$$\text{Percentage holding} = \frac{2,100}{3,000} \times 100 = 70\%$$

Calculation of Current year's profit

PROFIT & LOSS APPROPRIATION A/C

	Rs.		Rs.
To Dividend @ 15%	45,000	By Balance b/d	51,500
To Corporate Dividend Tax @ 10%	4,500		
To Balance e/d	2,000		
	51,500		51,500
To General Reserve	15,000	By Balance b/d	2,000
To balance c/d	90,000	By Profit earned during the year	1,03,000
	1,05,000		1,05,000

Revenue Profits	1,03,000
H Ltd.'s Share (70%)	72,100
Minority Interest (30%)	30,900

Capital Profits

	Rs.
Profit & Loss A/c (after dividend & tax)	2,000
General reserve	60,000
	62,000
H Ltd.'s Share (70%)	43,400
Minority Interest (30%)	18,600

INVESTMENT IN S LTD. A/C

	Rs.		Rs.
To Balance b/d	3,00,000	By Dividend	31,500
		By Balance transferred to Cost of Control A/c	2,68,500
	3,00,000		3,00,000

COST OF CONTROL A/C

	Rs.		Rs.
To Investment A/c	2,68,500	By Share Capital	2,10,000
		By Capital Profits	43,400
		By Goodwill (B.F.)	15,100
	2,68,500		2,68,500

MINORITY INTEREST A/C

	Rs.		Rs.
To Balance c/d	1,39,500	By Share Capital	90,000
		By Capital Profits	18,600
		By Revenue Profit	30,900
	1,39,500		1,39,500

CONSOLIDATED BALANCE SHEET
As on 31st March, 2005

Liabilities		Rs.	Assets		Rs.
Share Capital (Rs.100)		7,50,000	Goodwill		15,100
Reserve & Surplus			Net Block		
General Reserve(1)		2,05,500	H Ltd.	7,00,000	
Profit & Loss A/c(2)		2,70,100	S Ltd.	4,00,000	11,00,000
Current Liabilities :			Current Assets		
Sundry Creditors			H Ltd.	4,00,000	
H Ltd.	2,15,000		S Ltd.	2,00,000	6,00,000
S Ltd.	1,35,000	3,50,000			
Minority Interest		1,39,500			
		17,15,100			17,15,100

Working Notes :

(1)	General Reserve of H Ltd.		1,95,000
Add	Transfer by S Ltd. (70% of Rs. 15,000)		10,500
			2,05,500
(2)	Profit & Loss A/c (H Ltd.)		2,40,000
Add	Revenue Profit	72,000	
Less	Transfer to General Reserve	10,500	61,600
			3,01,600
Less	Dividend from S Ltd. out of pre-acquisition profits credited to P & L A/c		31,500
			2,70,100

Illustration (25) (Interim dividend paid out of pre & post acquisition profits)

H Ltd. acquired 4,000 shares of Rs. 100 each in S Ltd. at Rs. 4,80,000 on 1st October, 2004. On 1.4.2004 S Ltd. had Rs. 45,000 to the Credit of Profit & Loss and Rs. 75,000 in General Reserve. During the year there has been no change in the General Reserve. In January 2005. S Ltd. declared and paid an interim dividend @ 10% to its shareholders. H Ltd. received the dividend on its holdings and credited the same to its Profit and Loss Account.

The Balance Sheet of H Ltd.. and S Ltd. as on 31st March, 2005 were as under :

Liabilities	H Ltd.	S Ltd.
	Rs.	Rs.
Equity Share Capital (Shares of Rs. 100 each)	15,00,000	5,00,000
General Reserve	5,00,000	75,000
Profit & Loss A/c	3,50,000	1,50,000
Current Liabilities	2,50,000	125,000
	26,00,000	8,50,000
Assets		
Net Block	15,00,000	5,50,000
Investments in Shares of S Ltd.	4,80,000	—
Current Assets	6,20,000	3,00,000
	26,00,000	8,50,000

Prepare Consolidated Balance Sheet as on 31st March, 2005

Solution :

$$\text{Percentage holding} = \frac{4,000}{5,000} \times 100 = 80\%$$

Calculation of Revenue & Capital Profits

		Rs.
Current year's Profit :		
	Balance as per Balance Sheet (31.3.2005)	1,50,000
Less	Balance in the beginning (1.4.2004)	45,000
		1,05,000

	Balance b/d		1,05,000
Add	Interim Dividend paid		50,000
	Profits earned during the year		1,55,000
	Revenue Profits (6 months)		77,500
	Capital Profits (6 months)		77,500
Capital Profits			
	General Reserve (1.4.2004)		75,000
	Profit & Loss A/c (1.4.04)		45,000
	1/2 of Current year's profits (1.4.2004 to 01.10.2004)	77,500	
Less	1/2 of Interim dividend	25,000	52,500
			1,72,500
	H Ltd.'s Share (80%)		1,38,000
	Minority Interest (20%)		34,500
Revenue Profits			77,500
	H Ltd.'s Share (80%)		62,000
	Minority Interest (20%)		15,500

INVESTMENT IN SHARES OF S LTD. A/C

	Rs.		Rs.
To Balance b/d	4,80,000	By Dividend (out of pre-acquisition profit) (80% of Rs. 25,000)	20,000
		By Cost of Control A/c	4,60,000
	4,80,000		4,80,000

COST OF CONTROL A/C

	Rs		Rs.
To Investment S Ltd.	4,60,000	By Share Capital	4,00,000
To Capital Reserve (Bal. figure)	78,000	By Capital Profit	1,38,000
	5,38,000		5,38,000

MINORITY INTEREST A/C

	Rs.		Rs.
To Interim Dividend Paid out of post acquisition Period (1)	5,000	By Share Capital	1,00,000
		By Capital Profits	34,500
To balance c/d	1,45,000	By Revenue Profit	15,500
	1,50,000		1,50,000

CONSOLIDATED BALANCE SHEET
as on 31st March, 2005

Liabilities		Rs.	Assets		Rs.
Equity Share Capital		15,00,000	Net Block		
Shares of Rs. 100 each			H Ltd.	15,00,000	
Reserve & surplus:			S Ltd.	5,50,000	20,50,000
Capital Reserve		78,000	Current Assets		
General Reserve		5,00,000	H Ltd.	6,20,000	
Profit & Loss A/c[(2)]		3,72,000	S Ltd.	3,00,000	9,20,000
Current liabilities:					
H Ltd.	2,50,000				
S Ltd.	1,25,000	3,75,000			
Minority Interest		1,45,000			
		29,70,000			29,70,000

(1) Since interim dividend has already been received by Minority shareholders it has been dealt as under :

Dividend out of pre-acquisition profit has been deducted out of profits earned hence ignored whereas dividend paid out of post-acquisition profit has been deducted from the total of minority interest because revenue profits include interim dividend also.

Alternatively revenue profits would have been reduced by Rs. 25,000 & then share of minority could have been calculated.

(2)	Profit & Loss A/c	Rs.
	H Ltd.	3,50,000
Add	Revenue Profits including dividend portion	62,000
		4,12,000
Less	Interim dividend Paid out of Capital (Pre-acquisition) profit	20,000
		3,92,000
Less	Interim dividend out of post-acquisition profit already Credited to P & L A/c but not deducted from Revenue profits	20,000
		3,72,000

Note : It should be remembered that any dividend, whether paid out of pre-acquisition profit or out of post acquisition profit should be deducted out of profits before calculating the share of minority shareholders and holding company's share or their respective share should be debited to Minority Interest A/c and Profit & Loss A/c of holding Company.

(XV) Successive -Acquisition of Shares at Subsequent stages

Successive acquisition of shares means acquiring control in a subsidiary through purchase of shares at different point of interval. It may happen because the controlling interest in a company may not be attained by one time purchase of shares. In such cases of successive purchase of shares, the cost of control has to be calculated by taking into account the cost of shares acquired on different dates. In other words, while calculating cost of control, the capital profits at each point of time of acquisition of shares are calculated. Thus with every successive purchase of shares, cost of control and minority interest keep on changing.

Illustration (26) (Successive Purchase of shares)

On 31st March, 2002 S Ltd. had an issued Capital of Rs. 20,00,000 divided into 20,000 equity shares of Rs. 100 each. H Ltd. aquired shares of S Ltd. on the dates mentioned below :

Date of acquiring Shares	No. of Shares Rs.	Cost of Shares Rs.	Accumulated Profits on the date of acquisition Rs.
1.4.2002	8,000	9,60,000	2,50,000
1.4.2003	4,000	4,80,000	3,40,000
1.4.2004	3,000	3,70,000	4,50,000

You are required to calculate Cost of Control as on different dates of acquisitions of shares in S Ltd.

Solution:

COST OF CONTROL A/C (1.4.2002)

	Rs.		Rs.
To Investment in Shares of S Ltd.	9,60,000	By Share Capital	8,00,000
		By Capital Profits	1,00,000
		(2,50,000 × 8,000/20,000)	
		By Goodwill (B.F.)	60,000
	9,60,000		9,60,000

COST OF CONTROL A/C (1.4.2003)

	Rs.		Rs.
To Investment in Shares of S Ltd.	4,80,000	By Share Capital	4,00,000
		By Capital Profits	68,000
		(3,40,000 × 4,000/20,000)	
		By Goodwill (B.F.)	12,000
	4,80,000		4,80,000

Total Cost of Control as on 1.4.2003 (Rs. 60,000 + 12,000) Rs. 72,000

COST OF CONTROL A/C (1.4.2004)

	Rs.		Rs.
To Investment in Shares of H Ltd.	3,70,000	By Share Capital	3,00,000
		By Capital Profits	67,500
		(Rs. 4,50,000 ×3,000/20,000)	
		By Goodwill (B.F)	2,500
	3,70,000		3,70,000

Total Cost of Control as on 1.4.2004 (72,000 + 2,500) Rs. 74,500

Alternatively Cost of Control A/c may be prepared taking previous balance into account as shown below :

COST OF CONTROL A/C (1.4.2002)

1.4.2002	Rs.		Rs.
To Investments in Shares of S Ltd.	9,60,000	By Share Capital	8,00,000
		By Capital Profits	1,00,000
		By Balance c/d	60,000
	9,60,000		9,60,000
1.4.2003			
To Balance b/d	60,000	By Share Capital	4,00,000
To Investments in Shares of S Ltd.	4,80,000	By Capital Profit c/d	68,000
		By Balance c/d	72,000
	5,40,000		5,40,000
1.4.2004			
To Balance b/d	72,000	By Share Capital	3,00,000
To Investments in Shares of S Ltd.	3,70,000	By Capital Profits	67,500
		By Balance (g.w.)	74,500
	4,42,000		4,42,000

Cost of Control as on 1.4.2004 Rs. 74,500

(XVI) Disposal of Shares

A holding Company may dispose of some of the shares of its subsidiary and thereby reducing the control in it. The sale of such investment in shares may result either in "Loss on Sale" or "profit on sale" In case of loss, it is debited to Cost of Control A/c. Whereas "profit on sale" is credited to it or Investment fluctuation Fund. Cost of Control and Minority Interest are calculated on the basis of actual holdings after the disposal.

The accounting treatment may be summarised as follows :

1. Calculate "sale proceeds" of shares disposed of :
2. Ascertain the Cost of such shares (sold.)
3. Find out the difference of 1 & 2 (above)
4. Debit the Cost of Control A/c with the amount of loss. or
5. Credit the Cost of Control A/c with the amount of profit or transfer to Investment fluctuation Fund.
6. Calculate Minority Interest and Cost of Control on the basis of actual holdings left after disposal.

Illustration (27)

(Disposal of shares held in subsidiary)

Following are the Balance Sheets of H Ltd. and S Ltd. as on 31st March 2005.

Liabilities	H Ltd.	S Ltd.
	Rs.	Rs.
Share Capital Shares of Rs. 10 each	12,00,000	5,00,000
General Reserve	2,50,000	1,25,000
Profit & Loss A/c	2,40,000	1,25,000
Current liabilities	3,10,000	2,50,000
	20,00,000	10,00,000
Net Block	9,50,000	7,50,000
Investment in Shares of S Ltd.	6,75,000	—
Current Assets	3,75,000	2,50,000
	20,00,000	10,00,000

H Ltd. had acquired 45,000 shares of S Ltd. on 1.4.2004 for Rs. 6,75,000 when S Ltd. had Rs. 1,00,000, its General Reserve and Rs. 20,000 to the Credit of Profit & Loss A/c.

On 31st March 2005 H Ltd. sold 10,000 shares of S Ltd. for Rs. 1,80,000. Prepare Consolidated Balance Sheet showing the effect of disposal if :

(a) Profit on sale is transferred to Investment Fluctuation Fund.

(b) Profit on sale is Credited to Cost of Control A/c.

Solution : (a)

Calculation of Profit/Loss on disposal of shares

	Sale proceeds of 10,000 sales	1,80,000
Less	Cost of Acquisition $\left(\frac{6,75,000 \times 10,000}{45,000}\right)$	1,50,000
	Profit on sale transferred to Investment Fluctuation Fund	30,000

COST OF CONTROL A/C

	Rs.		Rs.
To Investment $\left(\frac{6,75,000 \times 35,000}{45,000}\right)$	5,25,000	By Share Capital (35,000 Shares)	3,50,000
		By Capital Profit $\left(\frac{1,20,000 \times 35,000}{50,000}\right)$	84,000
		By Goodwill (B.F.)	91,000
	5,25,000		5,25,000

Revenue Profits

		Rs.
	Profit & Loss A/c as per B/S	1,25,000
Less	Opening balance	20,000
		1,05,000
Add	Transfer to general Reserve	25,000
		1,30,000
	H Ltd.'s share $\left(\frac{1,30,000 \times 35,000}{50,000}\right)$	91,000
	Minority Interest $\left(\frac{1,30,000 \times 15,000}{50,000}\right)$	39,000

Capital Profits :

General Reserve	1,00,000
Profit & Loss A/c	20,000
	1,20,000
H Ltd.'s share 70%	84,000
Minority Interest (30%)	36,000

MINORITY INTEREST A/C (30%)

	Rs.		Rs.
To Balance c/d	2,25,000	By Share Capital	1,50,000
		By Capital Profits	36,000
		By Revenue Profit	39,000
	2,25,000		2,25,000

CONSOLIDATED BALANCE SHEET
As on 31st March, 2005

Liabilities		Rs.	Assets	Rs.	
Shares Capital Shares of Rs. 10 each		12,00,000	Goodwill		91,000
			Net Block		
General Reserve		2,50,000	H Ltd.	9,50,000	
Profit & Loss A/c			S Ltd.	7,50,000	17,00,000
H Ltd.	2,40,000		Current Assets		
S Ltd.	91,000	3,31,000	H Ltd.	3,75,000	
Investments Fluctuation Fund		30,000	*Add* Sale of Shares	1,80,000	
Current liabilities				5,55,000	
H Ltd.	3,10,000		S Ltd.	2,50,000	8,05,000
S Ltd.	2,50,000	5,60,000			
Minority Interest		2,25,000			
		25,96,000			25,96,000

(b) When Profit on sale of shares is Credited to Cost of Control A/c

COST OF CONTROL A/C

	Rs.		Rs.
To Investment in Shares of S Ltd. at Cost	5,25,000	By Share Capital	3,50,000
		By Capital Profits	84,000
		By Profit on Sale of shares	30,000
		By Goodwill (B.F.)	61,000
	5,25,000		5,25,000

CONSOLIDATED BALANCE SHEET
As on 31st March, 2005

Liabilities		Rs.	Amount		Rs.
Share Capital Shares of Rs. 10 each		12,00,000	Goodwill		61,000
General Reserve		2,50,000	Net - Block		
Profit & Loss A/c			H Ltd.:	9,50,000	
H Ltd.	2,40,000		S Ltd.	7,50,000	17,00,000
S Ltd.	91,000	3,31,000	Current Assets		
Current Liabilities			H Ltd.	3,75,000	
H Ltd.	2,40,000		*Add* Sale of Shares	1,80,000	
	2,50,000	5,60,000		5,55,000	
Minority Interest		2,25,000	S Ltd.	2,50,000	8,05,000
		25,66,000			25,66,000

GRADED ILLUSTRATIONS

Illustration (1) (Pre- acquisition Losses)

The following are the Balance Sheets of H Ltd. and S Ltd. as on 31st March, 2005

Liabilities	H Ltd.	S Ltd.
	Rs.	Rs.
Share Capital Shares of Rs. 10 each	10,00,000	6,00,000
General Reserve	4,00,000	—
Profit & Loss A/c	4,00,000	1,80,000
Current liabilities	2,00,000	2,20,000
	20,00,000	10,00,000
Assets		
Sundry assets	16,00,000	10,00,000
Investment in 40,000 Shares in S Ltd.	4,00,000	—
	20,00,000	10,00,000

Shares were purchased by H Ltd. in S Ltd. on 30th September 2004. On 1st April 2004 the Balance Sheet of S Ltd. showed a loss of Rs. 3,00,000 which was written off out of the profits earned during the current year. Profits are assumed to accrue evenly throughout the year. Prepare consolidated Balance Sheet.

[C.S. (1) 1986 Adopted]

Solution:

$$\text{Percentage holding} = \frac{4,000 \times 100}{6,000} = 66.667\% \text{ or } 2/3\text{rd}$$

Calculation of Current year's profits:

		Rs.
	Profits as per Balance Sheet	1,80,000
Add	Loss written off	3,00,000
	Profits earned during the year	4,80,000
	Capital Profits (1.4.04-30.9.04)	2,40,000
	Revenue Profits (1.10.04 - 31.3.05)	2,40,000
	H Ltd.'s Share 2/3rd	1,60,000
	Minority Interest 1/3rd	80,000

Capital profits & Loss

Debit balance of P & L A/c (as on 1.4.2004)	(3,00,000)
Current year's Profits (6 months) (Calculated above)	2,40,000
Capital Loss on the date of acquisition	(60,000)
H Ltd. Share (2/3)	(40,000)
Minority Interest (1/3)	(20,000)

COST OF CONTROL A/C

	Rs.		Rs.
To Capital Loss	40,000	By Share Capital	4,00,000
To Investment in Shares in S Ltd.	4,00,000	By Goodwill (B.F.)	40,000
	4,40,000		4,40,000

MINORITY INTEREST A/C

	Rs.		Rs.
To Capital Loss	20,000	By Share Capital	2,00,000
To Balance c/d	2,60,000	By Revenue Profit	80,000
	2,80,000		2,80,000

CONSOLIDATED BALANCE SHEET
As on 31st March, 2005

Liabilities		Rs.	Assets		Rs.
Share Capital		10,00,000	Sundry Assets		
Shares of Rs. 10 each			H Ltd.	16,00,000	
General Reserve		4,00,000	S Ltd.	10,00,000	26,00,000
Profit & Loss A/c			Goodwill		40,000
H Ltd.	4,00,000				
S Ltd.	1,60,000	5,60,000			
Current liabilities					
H Ltd.	2,00,000				
S Ltd.	2,20,000	4,20,000			
Minority Interest		2,60,000			
		26,40,000			26,40,000

Illustration (2) (Debentures in Subsidiary and Loss by fire during pre-acquisition period)

The following Balance Sheets of H Ltd. & S Ltd. as on 31st March, 2005 are presented to you:

	H Ltd.	S Ltd.
Liabilities	Rs.	Rs.
Share Capital (Shares of Rs. 100 each)	5,00,000	2,00,000
General Reserve	1,00,000	—
Profit & Loss A/c	80,000	—
6% Debentures	—	1,00,000
Trade Creditors	75,000	45,000
	7,55,000	3,45,000
Assets		
Fixed Assets	3,50,000	1,50,000
Stock	90,000	40,000
Debtors	60,000	30,000
6% Debentures in S Ltd. (at Cost)	60,000	—
1500 Shares in S Ltd. (at cost)	1,20,000	—
Cash & Bank balance	75,000	25,000
Profit & Loss A/c	—	1,00,000
	7,55,000	3,45,000

H Ltd. acquired shares on 1st August, 2004. The Profit & Loss A/c of S Ltd. showed a debit balance of Rs. 1,50,000 on 1st April, 2004. During June 2004 goods costing Rs. 6,000 were destroyed by fire against which the Insurance Company paid Rs. 4,000 only. Trade Creditors of S Ltd. include Rs. 20,000 for goods supplied by H Ltd. on which H Ltd. made a profit of Rs. 2,000. Half of the goods were still in stock on 31st March, 2005.

Prepare consolidated Balance Sheet and show the complete working.

[C.S. (1) Dec. 1987Modified][B.Com. (H) DU 1987]

Solution :

$$\text{Percentage holding} = \frac{1,500}{2,000} \times 100 = 75\%$$

Current year's Profits

	Debit balance of P & L A/c as on 31.3.05	1,00,000
	Debit balance of P & L A/c as on 1.4.04	1,50,000
	Profit earned during the year	50,000
Add	Abnormal Loss (Rs. 6,000 – 2,000) (Loss by fire in June 04)	4,000
	Profit before Abnormal Loss	54,000
	Profit for the Pre- acquisition period (1.4.04 to 1.8.04) 4/12	18,000
Less	Loss by fire during (June) pre-acquisition period	4,000
Capital Profits		14,000
	H Ltd.'s Share (75%)	10,500
	Minority Interest (25%)	3,500
	Revenue (Post-Acquisition Period)	36,000
	(1.8.2004) to 31.3.05) for 8 month = $\left(\frac{54,000 \times 8}{12}\right)$	
	H Ltd.'s Share (75%)	27,000
	Minority Interest (25%)	9,000
Pre-acquisition Loss		1,50,000
	H Ltd.'s Share	1,12,500
	Minority Interest	37,500
	Capital Profit (Loss) (1.4.2004)	(1,12,500)
	Capital Profit	10,500
	Capital Loss (Net)	(1,02,000)

COST OF CONTROL A/C

	Rs.		Rs
To Capital Loss (Pre-acquisition Loss)	1,02,000	By Share Capital	1,50,000
		By Goodwill (B.F.)	72,000
To Investment in Shares of S Ltd.	1,20,000		
	2,22,000		2,22,000

MINORITY INTEREST A/C

	Rs.		Rs.
To Pre-acquisition Loss	37,500	By Share Capital	50,000
To Balance c/d	25,000	By Pre-acquisition Profit	3,500
		By Post-acquisition Profit	9,000
	62,500		62,500

CONSOLIDATED BALANCE SHEET
as on 31st March, 2005

Liabilities		Rs.	Assets		Rs.
Share Capital : Shares of Rs. 100 each		5,00,000	Goodwill		72,000
Reserve & Surplus			Fixed Assets		
General Reserve		1,00,000	H Ltd.	3,50,000	
Profit & Loss A/c			S Ltd.	1,50,000	5,00,000
H Ltd.	80,000		Current Assets		
S Ltd.	27,000		Stock H Ltd.	90,000	
	1,07,000		S Ltd.	40,000	
Less Unrealised profit	1,000	1,06,000		1,30,000	
Secured Loans:			*Less* Unrealised Profit	1,000	1,29,000
6% Debentures	1,00,000		Debtors:		
Less held by H Ltd.	60,000	40,000	H Ltd.	60,000	
Minority Interest		25,000	S Ltd.	30,000	
Current Liabilities				90,000	
Trade Creditors			*Less* Mutual owings	20,000	70,000
H Ltd.	75,000		Cash & Bank		
S Ltd.	45,000		H Ltd.	75,000	
	1,20,000		S Ltd.	25,000	1,00,000
Less Mutual owings	20,000	1,00,000			
		8,71,000			8,71,000

Working notes:

(1) Since half of the goods purchased from H Ltd. are still in the stock, an amount equal to half of the profits made by H Ltd. will be treated as unrealised profit i.e. 1/2 of Rs. 2,000 = Rs. 1,000 will be deducted from Profit & Loss A/c and Stock as per contra.

Illustration (3) (Inter Company owings)

The following Balance Sheets of H Ltd. & S Ltd. as on 31st March, 2005 were as under :

Liabilities	H Ltd.	S Ltd.
	Rs.	Rs.
Share Capital Shares of Rs. 100 each	10,00,000	2,50,000
General Reserve	1,50,000	50,000
Profit & Loss A/c Balance on 1.4.2004	2,00,000	1,00,000
Current year's Profit	2,50,000	1,25,000
Creditors	1,50,000	1,50,000
Bank Overdraft	1,00,000	—
Bills Payable	75,000	—
	19,25,000	6,75,000

	Rs.	Rs.
Assets		
Land & Building	3,00,000	—
Plant & Machinery	10,00,000	—
Stock	2,00,000	4,25,000
Investment in 1,500 shares of S Ltd.	3,25,000	—
S Creditors	50,000	1,50,000
Bills Receivable	—	50,000
Cash & Bank balance	50,000	50,000
	19,25,000	6,75,000

Shares were acquired by H Ltd. on 1st October, 2004. Bills Receivable held by S Ltd. are all accepted by H Ltd. Included in the debtors of S Ltd. is Rs. 30,000 owing by H Ltd. in respect of goods supplied.

Prepare Consolidated Balance Sheet.

[CS (1) Dec. 1988 Modified]

Solution :

$$\text{Percentage holding} = \frac{1,500 \times 100}{2,500} = 60\%$$

	Rs.
Pre-acquisition (Capital) profits:	
General Reserve	50,000
Profit & Loss A/c (1.4.2004)	1,00,000
Current year's profits (6 months) (1.4.04 to 1.10.2004)	62,500
	2,12,500
H Ltd.'s Share (60%)	1,27,500
Minority Interest (40%)	85,000
Revenue (Post-acquisition) Profits	
Profit for the Current year (1.10.04 - 31.03.05)	62,500
H Ltd.'s Share (60%)	37,500
Minority Interest (40%)	25,000

COST OF CONTROL A/C

	Rs.		Rs.
To Investment in Shares of S Ltd.	3,25,000	By Share Capital	1,50,000
		By Capital Profits	1,27,500
		By Goodwill (B.F.)	47,500
	3,25,000		3,25,000

MINORITY INTEREST A/C

	Rs.		Rs.
To Balance c/d	2,10,000	By Share Capital	1,00,000
		By Capital Profit	85,000
		By Revenue Profit	25,000
	2,10,000		2,10,000

CONSOLIDATED BALANCE SHEET
As on 31st March, 2005

Liabilities		Rs.	Assets		Rs.
Share Capital Shares of Rs. 100 each		10,00,000	Goodwill		47,500
Reserve & Surplus:			Land & Building		3,00,000
General Reserve		1,50,000	Plant & Machinery		10,00,000
Profit & Loss A/c			Current Assets:		
H Ltd.	4,50,000		Stock		
S Ltd.	37,500	4,87,500	H Ltd.	2,00,000	
Minority Interest		2,10,000	S Ltd.	4,25,000	6,25,000
Current Liabilities :			Debtors :		
Creditors			H Ltd.	50,000	
H Ltd.	1,50,000		S Ltd.	1,50,000	
S Ltd.	1,50,000			2,00,000	
	3,00,000		*Less* Mutual owings	30,000	1,70,000
Less Mutual owing	30,000	2,70,000	Bill Receivable		—
Bills Payable			Cash & Bank Balance		
H Ltd.	75,000		H Ltd.	50,000	
Less Mutual owings	50,000	25,000	S Ltd.	50,000	1,00,000
Bank Overdraft		1,00,000			
		22,42,500			22,42,500

Illustration (4) (Dividend out of pre-acquisition profits and Common transactions)

The Balance Sheet of H Ltd. and S Ltd. are given below :

Balance Sheets as on 30th September, 2005

Liabilities	H Ltd. Rs.	S Ltd. Rs.
Share Capital Shares of Rs. 100 each	10,00,000	3,00,000
General Reserve	3,00,000	1,00,000
Profit & Loss A/c	2,50,000	1,50,000
Trade creditors	1,50,000	1,.20,000
	17,00,000	6,70,000
Assets		
Free-hold Premises	5,50,000	—
Lease-hold Building	—	1,20,000
Plant & Machinery	3,00,000	1,80,000
Investments in Shares in S Ltd.	3,60,000	—
Stock-in-Trade	2,40,000	1,60,000
S Creditors	1,60,000	1,90,000
Cash & Bank balance	90,000	20,000
	17,00,000	6,70,000

H Ltd. holds 60% of issued Capital of S Ltd. and the acquisition was made on 30th June, 2005 when the balances to the accounts of General Reserve and Profit and Loss Account of S Ltd. were Rs. 1,00,000 and Rs. 3,50,000 respectively. S Ltd. distributed dividends @ Rs. 50 per share on 15th July, 2005 out of the whole of 2003-04 profits included in the Profit & Loss A/c balance above. H Ltd. has taken the dividend as part of its current year's profit.

An amount of Rs. 50,000 due to H Ltd. by S Ltd. on trade account and S Ltd. stock on 30th September, 2005 included Rs. 40,000 purchased from H Ltd. on which the seller's margin was 10% on sale value.

Prepare Consolidated Balance Sheet.

[ICWA (F) June 1988 - Adapted]

Solution:

Pre-acquisition (Capital) Profits

	Rs.
General Reserve	1,00,000
Profits and Loss A/c (Rs. 3,50,000 – 1,50,000 Div)	2,00,000
Current year's Profit (9 months) (1.10.04 to 30.6.05) (Loss Rs. 50,000 × 9/12)	– (37,500)
	2,62,500
H Ltd.'s Share	1,57,500
Minority Interest	1,05,000

CURRENT YEAR'S PROFIT/LOSS

P & L A/c (Adjusted)

	Rs.		Rs.
To Dividend	1,50,000	By Balance b/d	3,50,000
To Balance c/d	2,00,000		
	3,50,000		3,50,000
To Loss (B.F.)	50,000	By Balance b/d (after dividend)	2,00,000
To Balance c/d	1,50,000		
	2,00,000		2,00,000

Revenue Profit/Loss

	Rs.
Loss for the year (30.6.05 to 30.9.05) $\left(\frac{50{,}000 \times 3}{12}\right)$	(12,500)
H Ltd.'s Share	(7,500)
Minority Interest	(5,000)

INVESTMENTS A/C (SHARES IN S LTD.)

	Rs.		Rs.
To Balance b/d	3,60,000	By Dividend	90,000
		By Balance transferred to Cost of Control A/c	2,70,000
	3,60,000		3,60,000

COST OF CONTROL A/C

To Investment in Shares A/c	2,70,000	By Shares Capital	1,80,000
To Capital Reserve (B.F.)	67,500	By Capital Profits	1,57,500
	3,37,500		3,37,500

MINORITY INTEREST A/C

	Rs.		Rs.
To Revenue Loss	5,000	By Share Capital	1,20,000
To Balance c/d	2,20,000	By Capital Profits	1,05,000
	2,25,000		2,25,000

CONSOLIDATED BALANCE SHEET
As On 30th September, 2005

Liabilities		Rs.	Assets		Rs.
Shares Capital : Shares of Rs. 100 each		10,00,000	Fixed Assets		
Reserve & Surplus :			Free-hold Premises		5,50,000
Capital Reserve		67,500	Lease-hold Building		1,20,000
General Reserve		3,00,000	Plant & Machinery		
Profit & Loss A/c			H Ltd.	3,00,000	
H Ltd.	2,50,000		S Ltd.	1,80,000	4,80,000
S Ltd. (Loss)	(7,500)		Current Assets:		
	2,42,500		Stock-in-Trade		
Less Dividend Wrongly			H Ltd.	2,40,000	
Credited to P&L A/c	90,000		S Ltd.	1,60,000	
	1,52,500			4,00,000	
Less Unrealised Profits	4,000	1,48,500	*Less* Unrealised Profit	4,000	3,96,000
Current liabilities			S Debtors		
Trade Creditors			H Ltd.	1,60,000	
H Ltd.	1,50,000		S Ltd.	1,90,000	
S Ltd.	1,20,000			3,50,000	
	2,70,000		*Less* Mutual owings	50,000	3,00,000
Less Mutual Owings	50,000	2,20,000	Cash & Bank balance		
Minority Interest		2,20,000	H Ltd.:	90,000	
			S Ltd.:	20,000	1,10,000
		19,56,000			19,56,000

Working Notes:

(1) Since dividend for the year 2003-04 has been paid by S Ltd. out of Pre-acquisition profit the same has been adjusted by means of following entry.

Profit & Loss A/c	Dr.	90,000	
To Investment in Shares of S Ltd.			90,000
(Being dividend by H Ltd. out of pre-acquisition profits)			

(2) Unrealised profits @ 10% on Rs. 40,000 *i.e.* 4,000 have been adjusted by means of following entry :

		Dr.	
Profit & Loss A/c	Dr.	4,000	
To Closing Stock			4,000

Illustration (5) (Two years' comparative Balance Sheets)

The following are the Balance Sheets of H Ltd. and S Ltd. as on 31st March, 2004 and 31st March, 2005.

Balance Sheet of H Ltd. as on

Liabilities	31.03.04	31.03.05
	Rs.	Rs.
Share Capital (Shares of Rs. 10 each)	7,00,000	7,00,000
General Reserve	82,000	114,000
Profit & Loss A/c	1,34,000	1,60,000
Current liabilities	78,000	70,000
	9,94,000	10,44,000
Assets		
Goodwill	1,00,000	1,00,000
Land & Building	2,20,000	2,20,000
Plant & Machinery (Net)	1,60,000	1,50,000
Stock	80,000	94,000
Investments in 18,000 shares of S Ltd.	3,00,000	3,00,000
Debtors	1,10,000	1,20,000
Cash & Bank balance	24,000	60,000
	9,94,000	10,44,000

Balance Sheet of S Ltd. as on

Liabilities	31.03.04	31.03.05
	Rs.	Rs.
Share Capital (Rs. 10)	2,00,000	2,00,000
General Reserve	35,000	41,000
Profit & Loss A/c	24,000	57,000
Current liabilities	20,000	16,000
	2,79,000	3,14,000
Assets		
Goodwill	80,000	80,000
Plant & Machinery (Net)	90,000	85,000
Stock	50,000	60,000
S. Debtors	44,000	64,000
Cash & Bank Balance	15,000	25,000
	2,79,000	3,14,000

The shares in S Ltd. were acquired on 31st March, 2004. Both the companies have proposed dividend @ 10% on paid up capital for the year ending 2004-05 but no effect has given in the above Balance Sheets.

Prepare Consolidated Balance Sheet as on 31st March, 2005

[C.S. (1) June 84 Adapted]

Solution :

$$\text{Percentage holding} = \frac{18,000}{20,000} \times 100 = 90\%$$

Capital (Pre-acquisition) Profits

		Rs.
	General Reserve	35,000
	Profit & Loss A/c	24,000
		59,000
	H Ltd.'s Share (90%)	53,100
	Minority Interest (10%)	5,900

Revenue (Post-acquisition) Profits

	Profit & Loss A/c as on 31.3.05	57,000
Less	Opening Balance	(24,000)
Add	Transfer to General Reserve	6000
		39,000
	H Ltd.'s Share (90%)	35,100
	Minority Interest (10%)	3,900

COST OF CONTROL A/C

	Rs.		Rs.
To Investment in Shares of S Ltd.	3,00,000	By Share Capital	1,80,000
		By Capital Profits	53,100
		By Goodwill (B.F.)	66,900
	3,00,000		3,00,000

MINORITY INTEREST A/C

	Rs.		Rs.
To Proposed Dividend	2,000	By Share Capital	20,000
To Balance C/d	27,800	By Capital Profits	5,900
		By Revenue Profits	3,900
	29,800		29,800

CONSOLIDATED BALANCE SHEET
As on 31st March, 2005

Liabilities		Rs	Assets		Rs.
Share Capital (Shares of Rs. 10 each)		7,00,000	Goodwill		
Reserve & Surplus :			H Ltd.	1,00,000	
General Reserve			S Ltd.	80,000	
H Ltd.	1,14,000		Cost of Control	66,900	2,46,900
S Ltd.	5,400*	1,19,400	Fixed Assets :		
Profit & Loss A/c			Land & Building		2,20,000
H Ltd.	1,60,000		Plant & Machinery		
Less Proposed Dividend	70,000		H Ltd.	1,50,000	
	90,000		S Ltd.	85,000	2,35,000
S Ltd.(35,100-5,400)	29,700	1,19,700	Stock:		
Minority Interest		27,800	H Ltd.	94,000	
Current Liabilities:			S Ltd.	60,000	1,54,000
H Ltd.	70,000		Debtors		
S Ltd.	16,000	86,000	H Ltd.	1,20,000	
Proposed Dividend			S Ltd.	64,000	1,84,000
H Ltd.	70,000		Cash & Bank balance		
S Ltd.	2,000	72,000	H Ltd.:	60,000	
			S Ltd.:	25,000	85,000
		11,24,900			11,24,900

* An amount equal to 90% (H Ltd. Share) of the amount of Rs. 6,000 transferred to General Reserve by S Ltd. has been adjusted against Revenue Profits.

Illustration (6) (Purchase Consideration, Post-acquisition Loss etc.)

The following are the Balance Sheets of H Ltd. and S Ltd. as on 31st March, 2004.

Liabilities	H Ltd. Rs.	S Ltd. Rs.
Share Capital	15,00,000	5,00,000
General Reserve	9,50,000	1,50,000
Profit & Loss A/c	80,000	1,05,000
S Creditors	4,38,000	3,83,000
Provision for Taxation	3,53,000	2,11,000
	33,21,000	13,49,000
Assets		
Land & Building	5,34,000	1,35,000
Plant & Machinery	11,15,000	4,28,000
Stock-in-Trade	6,42,000	3,92,000
Book-Debts	7,80,000	2,70,000

Prepaid Expenses	32,000	6,000
Cash & Bank Balance	2,18,000	1,18,000
	33,21,000	13,49,000

Both Companies have arrangements with their Bankers for overdraft facilities to meet contingencies.

On 01.10.2004 H Ltd. acquired 80% of the shares of S Ltd. To pay, H Ltd. allotted by way of consideration 9% Fully Paid Redeemable Preference Shares of the value of Rs. 6,00,000. These are redeemable after 5 Years.

Trading results for the year 2004-05 disclosed that H Ltd. had earned a profit of Rs. 3,00,000 after writing off 10% depreciation on Plant & Machinery and after providing for taxation. It paid a dividend of 12% on the equity shares.

The Profit and Loss A/c of S Ltd. showed a loss of Rs. 1,20,000 after providing 10% for depreciation on Plant and Machinery. H Ltd. decided to make a provision in its books against its share of the loss of S Ltd.

There was no addition or retirement of fixed asset. The current assets and current liabilities stood as follows on 31st March, 2005.

	H Ltd. Rs.	S Ltd. Rs.
Stock	6,10,000	4,08,000
Book- Debts	7,50,000	2,60,000
Pre-paid Expenses	22,000	6,000
S Ltd.	1,10,000	—
H Ltd.	—	90,000
Bank balance	3,33,500	—
Overdraft	—	2,19,200
Sundry Creditors	4,50,000	2,50,000
Provision for Taxation	2,90,000	—

Prepare the consolidated Balance Sheet.

[ICWA (F) Dec. 1985 Adapted]

Solution :

Capital Profits

	Rs.
General Reserve (1.4.04)	1,50,000
Profit & Loss A/c (1.4.04)	1,05,000
Profit (Loss) during the year (1.4.04 to 1.10.04) $\left(\frac{1,20,000\times 6}{12}\right)$	(60,000)
	1,95,000
H Ltd.'s Share (80%)	1,56,000
Minority Interest (20%)	39,000

Revenue Profit (Loss)	Rs.
Loss during the year (1.10.04 to 31.3.05)	(60,000)
H Ltd.'s Share	(48,000)
Minority Interest	(12,000)

COST OF CONTROL A/C

	Rs.		Rs.
To Investments in Shares of S Ltd.	6,00,000	By Share Capital	4,00,000
		By Capital Profits	1,56,000
		By Goodwill (B.F.)	44,000
	6,00,000		6,00,000

MINORITY INTEREST A/C

	Rs.		Rs.
To Revenue Loss	12,000	By Share Capital	1,00,000
To Balance c/d	1,27,000	By Capital Profits	39,000
	1,39,000		1,39,000

CONSOLIDATED BALANCE SHEET
As on 31st March, 2005

Liabilities	Rs.	Assets		Rs.
Equity Share Capital	15,00,000	Goodwill		44,000
9% Preference Shares Capital	6,00,000	Fixed Assets :		
Reserve & surplus :		Land & Building		
General Reserve	9,50,000	H Ltd.	5,34,000	
Profits & Loss A/c [(1)]	1,25,000	S Ltd.	1,35,000	6,69,000
Minority Interest	1,27,000	Plant & Machinery :[(2)]		
Current liabilities :		H Ltd.	10,03,500	
Bank Overdraft	2,19,200	S Ltd.:	3,85,200	13,88,700
S Creditors	7,00,000	Stock		
Provision for Taxation	2,90,000	H Ltd.	6,10,000	
		S Ltd.	4,08,000	10,18,000
		Book-debts		
		H Ltd.	7,50,000	
		S Ltd.	2,60,000	10,10,000
		Prepaid Expenses		
		H Ltd.	22,000	
		S Ltd.:	6,000	28,000
		Cash & Bank balance		3,33,500
		Cash-in transit[(3)] (1,10,000–90,000)		20,000
	45,11,200			45,11,200

Working notes :

		Rs.	Rs.
(1)	Profit & Loss A/c		
	Profit & Loss A/c (H Ltd.) 1.4.2004		80,000
Add	Profit earned during the year		3,00,000
			3,80,000
Less	Equity Dividend @ 12%	1,80,000	
	9% Preference dividend (for 6 months only)	27,000	2,07,000
			1,73,000
Less	Revenue Loss from S Ltd.		(48,000)
			1,25,000
(2)	Plant & Machinery (H Ltd.)		11,15,000
Less	Depreciation @ 10%		1,11,500
			10,03,500
	Plant & Machinery (S Ltd.)	4,28,000	
Less	Depreciation	42,800	3,85,200
			13,88,700
(3)	Cash-in-Transit (1,10,000 – 90,000)		20,000

Illustration 7 (Dividend Correctly recorded and Different dates of Balance Sheets of holding and it's subsidiary)

H Ltd. purchased 20,000 fully, paid - up shares of Rs. 10 each in S Ltd. paying Rs. 3,00,000. At the time of the purchase of shares, the Balance Sheet of S Ltd. was as follows:

Liabilities	Rs.	Assets	Rs.
Share Capital (Rs. 10 each)	2,50,000	Fixed Assets	2,92,600
General Reserve	50,000	Goodwill	30,000
Profit & Loss App. A/c	86,000	Current Assets	1,98,400
Creditors	36,000		
Bank Over draft	74,000		
Provision for Taxation	25,000		
	5,21,000		5,21,000

Subsequent to purchase, S Ltd. declared a dividend of 10%. At the usual balancing dates (31st March in Case of S Ltd. and 30th June in Case of H Ltd.) the Balance Sheets of the two Companies were as under :

Liabilities

	H Ltd.	S Ltd.
	Rs.	Rs.
Share Capital : Shares of Rs. 10 each	10,00,000	2,50,000
General Reserve	1,25,000	60,000
Profit & Loss App. A/c	97,700	89,000
S. Creditors	85,140	47,000
Bank Overdraft	23,160	29,000
H Ltd.	—	30,000

Provision for Taxation	55,000	30,000
	13,86,000	5,35,000
Assets		
Fixed Assets	5,22,700	2,96,250
Goodwill	50,000	30,000
Investment in Shares of S Ltd.	2,80,000	—
S Ltd.	35,000	—
Current Assets	4,98,300	2,08,750
	13,86,000	5,35,000

You are required to prepare a Consolidated Balance Sheet of H Ltd. and it's subsidiary S Ltd.

[ICWA (F) June 84 Modified]

Solution :

$$\text{Percentage holding} = \frac{20,000}{25,000} \times 100 = 80\%$$

Capital Profits:

			Rs.
	General Reserve		50,000
	Profit & Loss A/c	86,000	
Less	Dividend @ 10% of Rs. 2,50,000	25,000	61,000
			1,11,000
	H Ltd.'s Share (80%)		88,800
	Minority Interest (20%)		22,200

Revenue Profit:

Profit for the Current year	
(Rs. 89,000 – 61,000 + Tr. to Reserve 10,000)	38,000
H Ltd.'s Share (80%)	30,400
Minority Interest (20%)	7,600

INVESTMENT A/C

	Rs.		Rs.
To Balance b/d	3,00,000	By Dividend	20,000
		By Balance transferred to Cost of Control A/c	2,80,000
	3,00,000		3,00,000

COST OF CONTROL A/C

	Rs.		Rs.
To Investment A/c	2,80,000	By Share Capital	2,00,000
To Capital Reserve	8,800	By Capital Profits	88,800
	2,88,800		2,88,800

MINORITY INTEREST A/C

	Rs.		Rs.
To Balance c/d	79,800	By Share Capital	50,000
		By Capital Profits	22,200
		By Revenue Profits	7,600
	79,800		79,800

CONSOLIDATED BALANCE SHEET OF H LTD.
as on 30th June and it's subsidiary S Ltd.
as on 31st March

Liabilities		Rs.	Assets		Rs.
Share Capital (Shares of Rs. 10 each)			10,00,000	Goodwill	
Reserves & Surplus			H Ltd.	50,000	
General Reserve			S Ltd.	30,000	80,000
H Ltd.	1,25,000		Fixed Assets		
S Ltd.	8,000	1,33,000	H Ltd.:	5,22,700	
Profit & Loss A/c (1)		1,20,100	S Ltd.:	2,96,250	8,18,950
Capital Reserve		8,800	Inter Company Owings		
Current liabilities			(35,000 – 30,000)		5,000
S Creditors			Current Assets		
H Ltd.:	85,140		H Ltd.	4,98,300	
S Ltd.	47,000	1,32,140	S Ltd.	2,08,750	7,07,050
Bank overdraft					
H Ltd.:	23,160				
S Ltd.:	29,000	52,160			
Provision for Taxation					
H Ltd.	55,000				
S Ltd.	30,000	85,000			
Minority Interest		79,800			
		16,11,000			16,11,000

Working Note

			Rs.
(1)	Profit & Loss A/c (H Ltd.)		97,700
Add	Revenue Profit	30,400	
Less	Transfer to General Reserve	8,000	22,400
			1,20,100

(2) Since " Dividend" has been correctly recorded, no adjustment has been made in the Profit & Loss A/c of H Ltd. This is evident from the Investments in shares of S Ltd. which stands at Rs. 2,80,000 after the adjustments of dividend receipt.

Illustration (8) (Dividend, Bonus Shares, Unrealised profit and Preference shares)

The following are the Balance Sheets of H Ltd. and S Ltd. as on 30th December, 2005.

Liabilities	H Ltd. Rs.	S Ltd. Rs.
Share Capital : Equity Shares (Rs. 100 each)	5,00,000	2,00,000
12% Preference Shares (Rs. 100 each)	1,00,000	50,000
Reserves & Surplus		
General Reserve	1,00,000	60,000
Profit & Loss Account	1,50,000	90,000
Current liabilities & Provisions:		
Creditors	60,000	70,000
Income Tax	70,000	60,000
	9,80,000	5,30,000
Assets		
Fixed Assets :		
Goodwill	60,000	40,000
Machinery	1,00,000	60,000
Vehicles	1,80,000	70,000
Shares in S Ltd. at Cost	3,80,000	—
Furniture	50,000	30,000
Current Assets		
Stock	70,000	1,40,000
Debtors	1,00,000	1,65,000
Bank Balance	40,000	25,000
	9,80,000	5,30,000

Additional Information:

(i) H Ltd. acquired 1200 Equity shares and 400 Preference shares on 01.10.2004 at a cost of Rs. 2,80,000 and Rs. 1,00,000 respectively.

(ii) The Profit and Loss Account of S Ltd. had a Credit balance of Rs. 30,000 and General Reserve of Rs. 50,000 on 01.10.2004.

(iii) On 31st December S Ltd. declared a dividend out of its pre-acquisition profits of @12% on its share capital. H Ltd. credited the receipt of dividend to it's Profit & Loss Account.

(iv) On 1.4.2005 S Ltd. issued one equity share for every three shares held in as bonus shares at a face value of Rs. 100 per share out of its General Reserve. No entry had been made in the books of H Ltd. for the receipt of bonus shares.

(v) S Ltd. owed H Ltd. Rs. 20,000 for purchase of Stock from H Ltd. The entire stock is held by S Ltd. on 30.9.2005. H Ltd. made a profit of 25% on cost.

Prepare Consolidated Balance Sheet as on 30th September, 2005.

[CA (F) Nov. 1985 Modified

Solution :

PROFIT & LOSS APP. A/C

	Rs.		Rs.
To Preference Dividend (2003-04)	6,000	By Balance b/d	30,000
To Equity Dividend (12% on Rs. 1,50,000)	18,000		
To Balance c/d	6,000		
	30,000		30,000
		By Balance b/d	6,000
To Balance c/d	90,000	By Net Profit (B.F.)	84,000
	90,000		90,000

			Rs.
	Current Years' profit (Revenue Profit)		84,000
Less	Preference dividend (2004-05)		. 6,000
			78,000
	H Ltd.'s Share (80%)		62,400
	Minority Interest (20%)		15,600

Capital Profits:

	General Reserve	50,000	
Less	used for Bonus Issue	50,000	Nil.
	Profit & Loss A/c (after Preference & equity dividend)		6,000
	H Ltd.'s Share (80%)		4,800
	Minority Interest (20%)		1,200
	Revenue Profit (General Reserve)		60,000

H LTD. – 48,000; MI –12000

INVESTMENT IN SHARE IN S LTD.

	Rs.		Rs.
To Balance b/d	3,80,000	By Preference dividend	4,800
		By Equity dividend	14,400
		By Balance transferred to Cost Control A/c	3,60,800
	3,80,000		3,80,000

COST OF CONTROL A/C

	Rs.		Rs.
To Investments in S Ltd..	3,60,800	By Equity Share Capital	1,60,000
		By Preference Share Capital	40,000
		By Capital Profits	4,800
		By Goodwill (B.F.)	1,56,000
	3,60,800		3,60,800

MINORITY INTEREST A/C

	Rs.		Rs.
To Balance c/d	80,000	By Equity Share Capital	40,000
		By Preference Share Capital	10,000
		By Capital Profits	1,200
		By Revenue Profits	15,600
		By General Reserve	12,000
		By Preference dividend	1,200
	80,000		80,000

CONSOLIDATED BALANCE SHEET
As on 30th September, 2005

Liabilities		Rs.	Assets		Rs.
Share Capital :			Fixed Assets :		
Equity Share Capital		5,00,000	Goodwill		2,56,000
12% Preference Share Capital		1,00,000	Machinery		
Reserve & Surplus			H Ltd.	1,00,000	
General Reserve			S Ltd.	60,000	1,60,000
H Ltd.	1,00,000		Vehicles		
S Ltd.	48,000	1,48,000	H Ltd.	1,80,000	
Profit & Loss A/c (1)		1,94,000	S Ltd.	70,000	2,50,000
Current Liabilities :			Furniture		
Creditors			H Ltd.	50,000	
H Ltd.	60,000		S Ltd.	30,000	80,000
S Ltd.	70,000		Current Assets :		
	1,30,000		Stock		
Less Mutual Owings	20,000	1,10,000	H Ltd.	70,000	
Provision for Taxation		1,30,000	S Ltd.	1,40,000	
Minority Interest		80,000		2,10,000	
			Less Unrealised Profit	4,000	2,06,000
			Debtors:		
			H Ltd.	1,00,000	
			S Ltd.	1,65,000	
				2,65,000	
			Less Mutual Owings	20,000	2,45,000
			Bank Balance		
			H Ltd.	40,000	
			S Ltd.	25,000	65,000
		12,62,000			12,62,000

*Since entire opening balance standing to the credit of General Reserve has been utilised for the purpose of issuing bonus shares, the closing balance of Rs. 60,000 represents transfer from Current Year's Profit.

Working Notes :

	(1) P & L A/c of H Ltd.:	Rs.
	Balance as per Balance Sheet	1,50,000
Add	Revenue Profits	62,400
	Preference dividend (2004-05)	4,800
		2,17,200
Less	Dividend Out of Capital Profit Wrongly Credited to P & L A/c	19,200
		1,98,000
Less	Stock Reserve (Unrealised Profit)	4,000
		1,94,000

Illustration (9) (Dividend, Bonus Shares, Unrealised profits on Stock & machinery)

The following are the Balance Sheets of H Ltd. and S Ltd. as on 31st March, 2005.

Liabilities	H Ltd. Rs.	S Ltd. Rs.
Share Capital (Shares of Rs. 100 each)	10,00,000	8,00,000
General Reserve	2,00,000	2,00,000
Profit & Loss Account	4,00,000	3,00,000
Current liabilities	2,00,000	2,00,000
	18,00,000	15,00,000
Assets		
Fixed Assets	5,00,000	4,00,000
Investment in S Ltd.	5,00,000	—
Current Assets	8,00,000	11,00,000
	18,00,000	15,00,000

(i) H Ltd. acquired 3,000 shares in S Ltd. on 1.4.2004 when the reserve and surplus of S Ltd. were as under :

(a) General Reserve — Rs. 5,00,000

(b) Profit & Loss A/c — Rs. 2,00,000

(ii) On 1.10.2004 S Ltd. issued "Three" fully paid shares for every "Five" shares held as bonus shares out of pre-acquisition general reserve. No entry is made in the books of H Ltd. for the receipt of bonus shares.

(iii) On 30th June, 2004 S Ltd. declared 20% dividend out of pre-acquisition profits and H Ltd. credited the receipt of dividend to it's profit & Loss A/c.

(iv) S Ltd. owed H Ltd. on 31st March, 2005 Rs. 1,00,000 for purchase of stock from H Ltd. The entire stock is held by S Ltd. on 31st March, 2005. H Ltd. made profit of 25% on Cost.

(v) H Ltd. transferred against cash payment a machine to S Ltd. for Rs. 80,000. The book value of machine to H Ltd. was Rs. 60,000.

Prepare Consolidated Balance Sheet as at 31st March, 2005. Adjustment for depreciation on machine transferred by H Ltd. to S Ltd. is to be ignored.

[C.S (1) Dec. 1989 Modified]

Solution :

$$\text{Percentage holding} = \frac{3{,}000}{5{,}000} \times 100 = 60\%$$

Capital Profits			Rs.
	General Reserve	5,00,000	
Less	Bonus Issue* (5000 × 3/5) × 100	3,00,000	2,00,000
	Profit & Loss Account	2,00,000	
Less	Dividend (Rs. 5,00,000 × 20%)	1,00,000	1,00,000
			3,00,000
	H Ltd.'s Share		1,80,000
	Minority Interest		1,20,000
Bonus Shares (3 : 5)			3,00,000
	(Rs. 8,00,000 ×3 / 8) H Ltd. Share (60%)		1,80,000
	Minority Interest (40%)		1,20,000
Revenue Profit			
	P & L A/c (31.3.2005)		3,00,000
Less	opening balance after dividend		1,00,000
			2,00,000
Revenue Profits			
	Earned during the year		2,00,000
	H Ltd.'s Share (60%)		1,20,000
	Minority Interest (40%)		80,000

INVESTMENT IN S LTD. A/C

	Rs.		Rs.
To Balance b/d	5,00,000	By Dividend (60%)	60,000
		By Balance transferred to Cost of Control A/c	4,40,000
	5,00,000		5,00,000

COST OF CONTROL A/C

	Rs.		Rs.
To Investment in S Ltd. A/c	4,40,000	By Share Capital	3,00,000
To Capital Reserve (B.F)	2,20,000	By Bonus Issue	1,80,000
		By Capital Profit	1,80,000
	6,60,000		6,60,000

MINORITY INTEREST A/C

	Rs.		Rs.
To Balance c/d	5,20,000	By Share Capital	2,00,000
		By Bonus Issue	1,20,000
		By Capital Profit	1,20,000
		By Revenue Profit	80,000
	5,20,000		5,20,000

CONSOLIDATED BALANCE SHEET
As on 31st March, 2005

Liabilities		Rs.	Assets		Rs.
Share Capital		10,00,000	Fixed Assets		
Shares of Rs. 100 each			H Ltd.		5,00,000
Reserve & Surplus :			S Ltd.	4,00,000	
Capital Reserve		2,20,000	*Less* unrealised Profit	20,000	3,80,000
General Reserve		2,00,000			8,80,000
Profit & Loss A/c[(1)]		4,20,000	Current Assets :		
Current liabilities			H Ltd.:	8,00,000	
H Ltd.	2,00,000		S Ltd.:	11,00,000	
S Ltd.	2,00,000			19,00,000	
	4,00,000		*Less* Unrealised Profit	20,000	
Less Inter Company Owings	1,00,000	3,00,000		18,80,000	
			Less Inter Company		
Minority Interest		5,20,000	Owings	1,00,000	17,80,000
		26,60,000			26,60,000

Working Notes :

	Rs.
(1) Profit & Loss A/c of H Ltd.	4,00,000
Share in the Revenue Profit	1,20,000
	5,20,000
Less Dividend from Pre-acquisition Profit	60,000
	4,60,000
Less Unrealised Profit on Stock	(20,000)
Less Unrealised Profit on Machinery	(20,000)
	4,20,000

Illustration (10) (Proposed dividend, Inter-Company transaction and Unrealised profit)

The following Sheets of H Ltd. and its subsidiary S Ltd. as on 31st March, 2005 are as follows :

Liabilities	H Ltd. Rs.	S Ltd. Rs.
Equity Share Capital (Share of Rs. 100 each)	30,00,000	15,00,000
General Reserve (1.4.04)	8,00,000	4,00,000
Profit & Loss A/c (1.4.04)	2,00,000	2,50,000
Net Profit for the year	6,00,000	4,00,000
15% Debentures	10,00,000	—
S Creditors	4,00,000	2,70,000
Bills Payable	60,000	30,000
	60,60,000	28,50,000
Assets		
Premises	14,00,000	9,00,000
Machinery	12,00,000	7,00,000
Investment in Shares of S Ltd.	17,00,000	—
Inventories	7,00,000	4,50,000
Debtors	5,00,000	4,20,000
Bills Receivable	1,80,000	80,000
Cash and Bank	3,80,000	2,00,000
Miscellaneous Expenditure	—	1,00,000
	60,60,000	28,50,000

The following is the additional information:

(i) H Ltd. acquired 12,000 shares in S Ltd. on 1st April 2004.

(ii) Bills Receivable of H Ltd. include Rs. 30,000 accepted by S Ltd.

(iii) Accounts Receivable of H Ltd. include Rs. 1,00,000 due from S Ltd.

(iv) Inventories of S Ltd. include goods purchased from H Ltd. for Rs. 1,25,000 which were invoiced by H Ltd. at a profit of 25% on Cost.

(v) Both H Ltd. and S Ltd. have proposed 10% dividend for the 2004- 05 but no effect has been given in the Balance Sheet.

Prepare, a Consolidated Balance Sheet giving proper working notes.

[B Com. (H) DU 1999 -Modified]

Solution:

$$\text{Percentage holding} = \frac{12,000}{15,000} \times 100 = 80\%$$

Capital Profits:

		Rs.
	General Reserve (1.4.04)	4,00,000
	Profit & Loss A/c (1.4.04)	2,50,000
Less	Miscellaneous Expenditure (Capital Loss)	(1,00,000)
		5,50,000
	H Ltd.'s Share	4,40,000
	Minority Interest	1,10,000

Revenue Profit:

Profit earned during (2004-05)	4,00,000
H Ltd.'s Share	3,20,000
Minority Interest	80,000

COST OF CONTROL A/C

	Rs.		Rs.
To Investments in Shares in S Ltd.	17,00,000	By Share Capital	12,00,000
		By Capital Profit	4,40,000
		By Goodwill (B.F.)	60,000
	17,00,000		17,00,000

MINORITY INTEREST A/C

	Rs.		Rs.
To Proposed dividend (to be shown separately)	30,000	By Share Capital	3,00,000
		By Capital Profits	1,10,000
To Balance c/d	4,60,000	By Revenue Profits	80,000
	4,90,000		4,90,000

CONSOLIDATED BALANCE SHEET
As on 31st March, 2005

Liabilities		Rs.	Assets		Rs.
Equity Share Capital		30,00,000	Goodwill		60,000
Shares of Rs. 100 each			Fixed Assets		
General Reserve		8,00,000	Premises		
Profit & Loss A/c (1)		7,95,000	H Ltd.	14,00,000	
Secured Loans			S Ltd.	9,00,000	23,00,000
15% Debentures		10,00,000	Machinery		
Current liabilities			H Ltd.	12,00,000	
H Ltd.	4,00,000		S Ltd.	7,00,000	19,00,000
S Ltd.	2,70,000		Inventories		
	6,70,000		H Ltd.	7,00,000	
Less Mutual Owings	1,00,000	5,70,000	S Ltd.	4,50,000	
Bills payable				11,50,000	
H Ltd.:	60,000		*Less* Unrealised Profit	25,000	11,25,000
S Ltd.:	30,000		Debtors:		
	90,000		H Ltd.	5,00,000	
Less Mutual Owings	30,000	60,000	S Ltd.	4,20,000	
				9,20,000	
			Less Mutual Owings	1,00,000	8,20,000

Contd.

CONSOLIDATED BALANCE SHEET (CONTD.)

Liabilities		Rs.	Assets		Rs.
Proposed Dividend			Bills Receivable		
H Ltd.	3,00,000		H Ltd.:	1,80,000	
S Ltd.	30,000	3,30,000	S Ltd.:	80,000	
Minority Interest		4,60,000		2,60,000	
			Less Mutual Owings	30,000	2,30,000
			Cash at Bank		
			H Ltd.:	3,80,000	
			S Ltd.:	2,00,000	5,80,000
		70,15,000			70,15,000

Working Notes:

		Rs.
(1)	Profit & Loss A/c (H Ltd.) as on 1 .4. 2004	2,00,000
	Profit earned during the year	6,00,000
		8,00,000
Less	Proposed Dividend @ 10% on Rs. 30,00,000	3,00,000
		5,00,000
Add	Share of Profit in S Ltd.	3,20,000
		8,20,000
Less	Unrealised Profit Rs. $\frac{1,25,000 \times 25}{125}$	25,000
		7,95,000

Illustration (11) (Dividend, Revaluation & Cheque- in- transit)

On 1.4.2004 S Ltd. issued 10% Preference Shares of Rs. 1,00,000 at par. On this date S Ltd.'s General Reserve and Profit & Loss Account showed balances of Rs. 80,000 and Rs. 50,000 respectively. On 1.7.2004 S Ltd. paid a final dividend of 12% on equity shares for the year ended 31st March, 2004. On 1.4.2004 H Ltd. acquired 80% equity shares in S Ltd. for Rs. 3,00,000. On this date machinery of S Ltd. was revalued at Rs. 2,50,000. No entry for this was made in the books of S Ltd. On 31st March, 2005 the summarised Balance Sheets of H Ltd. and S Ltd. were as follows :

Liabilities	H Ltd. Rs.	S Ltd. Rs.
Equity Share Capital	8,00,000	3,00,000
10% Preference Share Capital	—	1,00,000
General Reserve	4,00,000	1,50,000
Profit & Loss Account	2,00,000	90,000
Loans	1,10,000	—
Creditors	1,70,000	76,000
Bills Payable	—	4,000
	16,80,000	7,20,000

Assets

Machinery	6,25,000	2,70,000
Shares in S Ltd.	3,00,000	—
Furniture	85,000	50,000
Stock	4,00,000	1,90,000
Loans to H Ltd.	—	10,000
Debtors	1,50,000	80,000
Bank Balance	1,20,000	1,10,000
Preliminary Expenses	—	10,000
	16,80,000	7,20,000

Additional Information

(i) S Ltd. provides depreciation on Machinery @ 10% on written down value. No Machine was sold or purchased during the year.

(ii) H Ltd. remitted a cheque of Rs. 10,000 to S Ltd. on 30th March, 2005 for repayment of loans, which was received by S Ltd. on 5th April, 2005.

(iii) No part of preliminary expenses was written off during the year.

Prepare Consolidated Balance Sheet of H Ltd. and S Ltd. as on 31st March, 2005

[B. Com (H) D.U. 1997 Modified

Solution :

Capital Profits :

				Rs.
	General Reserves (1.4.04)			80,000
	Profit & Loss A/c (1.4.04)		50,000	
Less	Dividend (for the year 2003-04) (Rs. 3,00,000 ×12%)		36,000	14,000
				94,000
Less	Capital Losses			
	Fall in the Value of Machinery			
	W. D. V. as on 31.3.05 2,70,000			
	W. D. V. as on 1.4.04 $\frac{2,70,000 \times 100}{90}$	= Rs. 3,00,000		
	Revised Value	Rs. 2,50,000	50,000	
	Preliminary Expenses		10,000	(60,000)
	Net pre-acquisition profits			34,000
	H Ltd.'s Share			27,200
	Minority Interest			6,800

Revenue Profits (Post acquisition Profit)

	Profit & Loss A/c as per B/S	90,000
Less	Opening balance after dividend	14,000
		76,000
Add	Transfer to General Reserve (Rs. 1,50,000 – 80,000)	70,000
		1,46,000

	Balance b/d	1,46,000
Less	Preference Dividend	10,000
		1,36,000
Add	Depreciation (Excess) (to be added back due to fall in the Value of Machinery) on 50,000 @ 10%	5,000
		1,41,000
	H Ltd.'s Share	1,12,800
	Minority Interest	28,200

SHARES (INVESTMENT) IN S LTD. A/C

	Rs.		Rs.
To Balance b/d	3,00,000	By Dividend (80% 36,000)	28,800
		By Cost of Control A/c	2,71,200
	3,00,000		3,00,000

COST OF CONTROL A/C

	Rs.		Rs.
To Shares in S Ltd. A/c	2,71,200	By Share Capital	2,40,000
		By Capital Profit	27,200
		By Goodwill (B.F.)	4,000
	2,71,200		2,71,200

MINORITY INTEREST A/C

	Rs.		Rs.
To Balance c/d	2,05,000	By Equity Share Capital	60,000
		By Preference Share Capital	1,00,000
		By Capital Profits	6,800
		By Revenue Profits	28,200
		By Preference Dividend	10,000
	2,05,000		2,05,000

CONSOLIDATED BALANCE SHEET
As on 31st March, 2005

Liabilities		Rs.	Assets		Rs.
Equity Share Capital		8,00,000	Fixed Assets		
Reserve & Surplus			Goodwill		4,000
General Reserve			Machinery		8,50,000
H Ltd.	400,000		Furniture		
Share in S Ltd.	56,000	4,56000	H Ltd.	85000	
			S Ltd.	50,000	1,35,000

Contd.

CONSOLIDATED BALANCE SHEET(CONTD.)

Liabilities		Rs.	Assets		Rs.
Profit & Loss A/c		2,28,000	Current Assets:		
Unsecured Loans		1,10,000	Stock		
Creditors			H Ltd.:	4,00,000	
H Ltd.	1,70,000		S Ltd.	1,90,000	5,90,000
S Ltd.	76,000	2,46,000	Debtors		
Bills Payable			H Ltd.	1,50,000	
H Ltd.:	-		S Ltd.	80,000	2,30,000
S Ltd.:	4,000	4,000	Bank Balance		
Minority Interest		2,05,000	H Ltd.	1,20,000	
			S Ltd.	1,10,000	2,30,000
			Cheque Transit		10,000
		20,49,000			20,49,000

			Rs.
(1)	Profit & Loss A/c (H Ltd.)		2,00,000
Less	Dividend from Pre-acquisition Profit		28,800
Add	Revenue Profits	1,12,800	1,71,200
Less	Transfer to G. Reserve	56,000	56,800
			2,28,000
	Machinery (S Ltd.)		
	Balance as on 31.3.05		2,70,000
	Written down Value As on 1.4.04		3,00,000
	Revised Value as on 1.4.04		2,50,000
Less	Depreciation for the year 2004-05		25,000
			2,25,000
	Machinery (H Ltd.)		6,25,000
			8,50,000

Illustration (12) (Dividend, dividend tax, Revaluation and unrealised profits)

The Balance Sheets of H Ltd. and S Ltd. as on 31st March, 2005 are as follows :

Liabilities	H Ltd.	S Ltd.
	Rs.	Rs.
9% Preference Share Capital	3,00,000	40,000
Equity Share Capital (Rs. 100)	9,00,000	4,00,000
General Reserve (1.4.2004)	2,00,000	1,20,000
Profit & Loss A/c	2,80,000	1,80,000
Creditors	1,60,000	1,00,000
Bills Payable	—	40,000
	18,40,000	8,80,000

Assets

Goodwill	70,000	60,000
Land & Building	6,00,000	2,60,000
Plant & Machinery	3,30,000	1,80,000
Investment in 3,000 Shares in S Ltd. on 30.9.2004	4,80,000	—
Debtors	40,000	1,50,000
Stock	2,00,000	1,80,000
Cash	1,20,000	40,000
Preliminary Expenses	—	10,000
	18,40,000	8,80,000

Additional Information :

(i) A dividend of 15% was paid by S Ltd. in October 2004 for the year ended 31st March, 2004 which was credited to P & L A/c by H Ltd.

(ii) S Ltd. also paid dividend tax @ 10% on the dividend distributed.

(iii) Plant & Machinery of S Ltd. disclosed a balance of Rs. 2,00,000 on Ist April, 2004 H Ltd. revalued it by Rs. 1,00,000 more at the time of purchase of shares.

(iv) There was a bonus issue of equity shares amounting to Rs. 40,000 out of post-acquisition profits by S Ltd.

(v) Credit balance of Profit & Loss A/c of S Ltd. as on 1.04.04 was Rs. 1,09,960.

(vi) Included in creditors of S Ltd. are Rs. 40,000 for goods supplied by H Ltd. Also included in stock of S Ltd. are goods of the value of Rs. 16,000 which were supplied by H Ltd. at a profit of 25% on sales

Prepare Consolidated Balance Sheet as on 31st March, 2005.

[B. Com. (H) DU 1998 Adapted]

Solution:

PROFIT & LOSS APP. A/C (S LTD.)

	Rs.		Rs.
To Preference dividend	3,600	By Balance b/d	1,09,960
To Equity dividend	60,000	By Net Profit earned during the year (B.F.)	1,40,000
To Dividend Tax	6,360		
To Balance c/d	1,80,000		
	2,49,960		2,49,960

$$\text{Percentage holding} = \frac{3,000}{4,000} \times 100 = 75\%$$

Capital Profits:

	Profit & Loss A/c (1.4.04)		1,09,960
Less	Preference dividend	3,600	
	Equity dividend	60,000	
	Dividend Tax (10% on 63,600)	6,360	69,960
			40,000

		Rs.
	Balance b/d	40,000
	General Reserve (1.4.04)	1,20,000
	Current year's Profit (1.4. 2004 to 30.9.2004) $\left(\frac{1,40,000\times6}{12}\right)$	70,000
	Profit on Revaluation of Machinery	1,00,000
		3,30,000
Less	Preliminary Expenses	10,000
		3,20,000
	H Ltd.'s Share (75%)	2,40,000
	Minority Interest (25%)	80,000
Revenue Profits		
	Current Year's Profit (1.10.04 to 31.3.05)	70,000
Less	Depreciation on appreciated Value of Machinery for 6 Months (Rs. 1,00,000 ×10/100 ×6/12)	5,000
		65,000
Less	Bonus Issue	40,000
		25,000
Bonus Issue		40,000
	H Ltd.'s share	30,000
	Minority Interest	10,000
Revenue Profit		25,000
	H Ltd.'s share (75%)	18,750
	Minority Interest (25%)	6,250

COST OF CONTROL A/C

	Rs.		Rs.
To Investment (Rs. 4,80,000 – 45,000)	4,35,000	By Share Capital	3,00,000
To Capital Reserve (B.F.)	1,35,000	By Capital Profits	2,40,000
		By Bonus Shares	30,000
	5,70,000		5,70,000

MINORITY INTEREST A/C

	Rs.		Rs.
To Balance c/d	2,36,250	By Equity Share Capital	1,00,000
		By Bonus Shares	10,000
		By Preference Shares	40,000
		By Capital Profits	80,000
		By Revenue Profits	6,250
	2,36,250		2,36,250

(1) Profit & Loss A/c of H Ltd.

		Rs.
	Balance as per Balance Sheet	2,80,000
Less	Dividend out of pre-acquisition Profit	45,000
		2,35,000
Add	Share in Revenue Profits	18,750
		2,53,750
Less	Unrealised Profit 25% of Rs. 16,000	4,000
		2,49,750

CONSOLIDATED BALANCE SHEET
As on 31st March, 2005

Liabilities		Rs.	Assets		Rs.
9% Preference Share Capital		3,00,000	Fixed Assets:		
Equity Share Capital		9,00,000	Land & Building		
Reserve & Surplus:			H Ltd.	6,00,000	
Capital Reserve	1,35,000		S Ltd.	2,60,000	8,60,000
Less Goodwill	1,30,000	5,000	Plant & Machinery		
General Reserve		2,00,000	H Ltd.	3,30,000	
Profit & Loss A/c[(1)]		2,49,750	S Ltd.	2,75,000[(2)]	6,05,000
Current liabilities:			Current Assets		
Bills Payable (S Ltd.)		40,000	Stock		
Creditors : H Ltd.	1,60,000		H Ltd.:	2,00,000	
S Ltd.	1,00,000		S Ltd.:	1,80,000	
	2,60,000			3,80,000	
Less mutual Owings	40,000	2,20,000	*Less* Unrealised Profit	4,000	3,76,000
Minority Interest		2,36,250	Debtors		
			H Ltd.	40,000	
			S Ltd.	1,50,000	
				1,90,000	
			Less Mutual Owings	40,000	1,50,000
			Cash at Bank		
			H Ltd.	1,20,000	
			S Ltd.	40,000	1,60,000
		21,51,000			21,51,000

			Rs.
(2)	Plant & Machinery of S Ltd. as on 31.3.05		1,80,000
Add	Appreciation on 30.9.04	1,00,000	
Less	Depreciation there on @ 10% for six months	5,000	95,000
			2,75,000

Illustration (13) (Dividend, Revaluation & Rate of depreciation)

H Ltd. acquired 16,000 shares of Rs. 10 each in S Ltd. 1.10.2004 for Rs. 3,22,800. The Balance Sheets of both the companies as on 31st March, 2005 were as follows :

Liabilities	H Ltd.	S Ltd.
Equity Share Capital (Rs. 10)	5,00,000	2,00,000
General Reserve	2,40,000	1,00,000
Profit & Loss Account	57,200	82,000
Bank-Overdraft	1,00,000	—
Bills Payable	—	13,000
Sundry Creditors	69,800	20,000
	9,67,000	4,15,000
Assets		
Land & Building	1,80,000	1,90,000
Plant & Machinery	2,40,000	1,35,000
Investments	3,60,000	—
Stock	1,14,000	42,000
Debtors	44,000	40,000
Bills Reservable	14,800	—
Cash	14,200	8,000
	9,67,000	4,15,000

Additional Information :

(i) The Profit & Loss Account of S Ltd. showed a balance of Rs. 30,000 on 01.04.2004 out of which a dividend of 10% was paid during November 2004. The dividend, however, was correctly recorded.

(ii) The Plant & Machinery of S Ltd. which stood at Rs. 1,50,000 on 1.4.2004 was valued at Rs. 1,80,000 on the date of acquisition. Prepare Consolidated Balance Sheet.

[C.S. (i) June 93-Modified]

Solution :

Capital Profits : (Pre-acquisition Profit)

	General Reserve		1,00,000
	Profit & Loss A/c (1.4.04)	30,000	
Less	Dividend (2003-04)	20,000	10,000
	Current year's Profits : Balance as on 31.3.05	82,000	
Less	Opening balance	10,000	
		72,000	
	(1.4.04 to 30.9.04) Profits for six month (72,000 × 6/12)		36,000
			1,46,000
	Profit on Revaluation of machinery (Rs. 1,80,000 – 1,42,500)		37,500
			1,83,500
	H Ltd.'s share (80%)		1,46,800
	Minority Interest (20%)		36,700

Revenue Profits : Current year's profits (1.10.04 to 31.3.05)

		Rs.
	(72,000 – 36,000)	36,000
Less	additional depreciation on P/M (on appreciated value)	1,875
		34,125
	H Ltd.'s Share	27,300
	Minority Interest	6,825

COST OF CONTROL A/C

	Rs.		Rs.
To Investment (After dividend) (3,22,800 – 16,000)	3,06,800	By Share Capital	1,60,000
		By Capital Profits	1,46,800
	3,06,800		3,06,800

MINORITY INTEREST A/C

	Rs.		Rs.
To Balance c/d	83,525	By Share Capital	40,000
		By Capital Profits	36,700
		By Revenue Profit	6,825
	83,525		83,525

* Written down Value of Plant & Machinery as on 01.04.04	1,50,000
W. D. V. on 31st March, 2005	1,35,000
Depreciation	15,000

$$\text{Rate of Depreciation} = \frac{15,000}{1,50,000} \times 100 = 10\%$$

Hence, Written down Value of Machinery as on 1.4.2004	1,50,000
W.D.V. on 1.10.2004 $\frac{1,50,000 \times 10}{100} \times \frac{6}{12}$ = 7,500 (1,50,000 – 7,500)	1,42,500
Revised Valued on 1.10.04	1,80,000
Appreciation	37,500
Depreciation on Appreciated Value = $\left(\frac{37,500 \times 10}{100} \times \frac{6}{12}\right)$	1,875

CONSOLIDATED BALANCE SHEET
As on 31st March 2005

Liabilities		Rs.	Assets		Rs.
Equity Share Capital		5,00,000	Fixed Assets :		
Shares of Rs. 10 each			Land and Building		
Reserve & Surplus :			H Ltd.	1,80,000	
General Reserve		2,40,000	S Ltd.	1,90,000	3,70,000
Profit & Loss A/c			Plant & Machinery		
H Ltd.	57,200		H Ltd.	2,40,000	
S Ltd.	27,300	84,500	S Ltd.	1,35,000	
Current Liabilities :				3,75,000	
Bank-Overdraft		1,00,000	*Add* App.	37,500	
Bills payable		13,000		4,12,500	
S Creditors (69,800 + 20,000)		89,800	*Less* Depreciation	1875	4,10,625
Minority Interest		83,525	Investments (3,60,000–3,06,800)		53,200
			Current Assets :		
			Stock		
			H Ltd.	1,14,000	
			S Ltd.	42,000	1,56,000
			Debtors		
			H Ltd.	44,000	
			S Ltd.	40,000	84,000
			Bills Receivable (HO)		
			H Ltd.	14,200	
			S Ltd.	8,000	22,200
			Cash		14,800
		11,10,825			11,10,825

Illustration (14) (Dividend out of pre-acquisition profits, Bonus issue and mutual owings)

The following are the abridged Balance Sheets of H Ltd. and S Ltd. as on 31st March, 2005.

Liabilities	H Ltd.	S Ltd.
Equity Share Capital (Rs. 100)	10,00,000	5,00,000
General Reserve	1,00,000	1,70,000
Profit & Loss A/c	1,60,000	1,30,000
Current Liabilities	4,40,000	2,00,000
	17,00,000	10,00,000
Assets		
Fixed Assets	4,80,000	2,50,000
Investment in Shares of S Ltd.	5,00,000	—
Current Assets	7,20,000	7,50,000
	17,00,000	10,00,000

Additional Information :

(i) H Ltd. acquired 3,000 shares in S Ltd. on 1st July 2004. The Reserves and Surplus position of S Ltd. as on 01.04.2004 was as under:

General Reserve	Rs. 2,50,000
Profit & Loss A/c (Cr)	Rs. 1,20,000

(ii) On 1.10.2004 S Ltd. issued one equity share for every four shares held as 'Bonus shares' out of "General Reserve". No entry has been made in the books of S Ltd. for the issue of bonus shares.

(iii) On 30.9.2004 S Ltd. declared a dividend out of pre-acquisition profits @ 25% on Rs. 4,00,000 its capital on that date. H Ltd. Credited the dividend to its profit & Loss A/c.

(iv) S Ltd. owed H Ltd. Rs. 50,000 for purchase of stock from H Ltd. The entire stock is held by S Ltd. on 31st March 2005. H Ltd. made a profit of 25% on Cost.

Prepare a Consolidated Balance Sheet of H Ltd. ad its subsidiary S Ltd. as on 31st March 2005.

[B. Com (H) DU 2001 and 2005 Modified]

Solution:

Percentage holding $\frac{3,000}{4,000} \times 100 = 75\%$

Since bonus issue has been made in 1: 4 ratio on 1.10.2004 & the post bonus issue capital is Rs. 5,00,000 (or 5,000 shares) the pre-bonus Capital will be = 5,000 × 4/5 or 4,000 shares (Rs. 4,00,000)

Capital Profits (Pre-acquisition profits)			Rs.
	General Reserve (1.4.04)		2,50,000
Less	Bonus issue		1,00,000
			1,50,000*
	Profit & Loss A/c (1.4.04)	1,20,000	
Less	Dividend out of pre-acquisitions profit (25% on Rs. 4,00,000)	1,00,000	20,000
	Profit of Current year (Pre-acquisition) (1.4.2004 to 30.6.2004)*		32,500
			2,02,500
	H Ltd.'s Share		1,51,875
	Minority Interest		50,625
Revenue Profits (1.7.04 to 31.3.05)			
	Profit & Loss A/c 31.3.05		1,30,000
Less	Opening Balance (1,20,000 – 1,00,000)		20,000
			1,10,000
Add	Transfer to Reserve (Rs. 1,70,000 – 1,50,000)		20,000
	Profits earned during the year		1,30,000
	Profit for the pre-acquisition period (Rs. 1,30,000 × 3/12)*		32,500
	Profit for the post-acquisition period (Rs. 1,30,000 ×9/12)		97,500
	H Ltd.* Share (3/4)	=	73,125
	Minority Interest	=	24,375

COST OF CONTROL A/C

	Rs.		Rs.
To Investment*	4,25,000	By Share Capital	3,00,000
(5,00,000 – 75,000)		By Bonus Shares	75,000
To Capital Reserve (B.F.)	1,01,875	By Capital Profits	1,51,875
	5,26,875		5,26,875

* Investment A/c has been credited by the amount of dividend received out of pre-acquisition profit

MINORITY INTEREST A/C

	Rs.		Rs.
To Balance c/d	2,00,000	By Share Capital	1,00,000
		By Bonus Shares	25,000
		By Capital Profits	50,625
		By Revenue Profits	24,375
	2,00,000		2,00,000

CONSOLIDATED BALANCE SHEET
As on 31st March, 2005

Liabilities		Rs.	Assets		Rs.
Share Capital (Shares of Rs. 100 each)		10,00,000	Fixed Assets		
Reserve & Surplus:			H Ltd.:	4,80,000	
Capital Reserve		1,01,875	S Ltd.:	2,50,000	7,30,000
General Reserve		1,00,000	Current Assets:		
Profit & Loss A/c			H Ltd.:	7,20,000	
H Ltd.	1,60,000		S Ltd.:	7,50,000	
Less dividend Wrongly				14,70,000	
Credited	75,000		*Less* Mutual Owings	50,000	
	85,000			14,20,000	
Add Share in Revenue			*Less* Unrealised* Profit	10,000	14,10,000
Profit of S Ltd.	73,125				
	1,58,125				
Less Unrealised profit	10,000	1,48,125			
Current liabilities					
H Ltd.:	4,40,000				
S Ltd.	2,00,000				
	6,40,000				
Less Mutual owings	50,000	5,90,000			
Minority Interest		2,00,000			
		21,40,000			21,40,000

* Unrealised Profit = Rs. 50,000 × 25/125 =10,000

Illustration (15) (Interim dividend out of pre and post acquisition profits)

H Ltd. acquired 80% shares in S Ltd. On 30th September, 2004 at a total cost of Rs. 3,60,000. The Balance Sheets of both the companies as on 31st March, 2005 were as follows:

Liabilities	H Ltd. Rs.	S Ltd. Rs.
Equity Share Capital (Rs. 10)	7,50,000	2,50,000
Securities Premium	50,000	—
General Reserve (1.4.2004)	4,00,000	1,10,000
Profit & Loss A/c	2,40,000	80,000
Creditors	60,000	70,000
	15,00,000	5,10,000
Assets:		
Land & Building	4,15,000	—
Plant & Machinery	2,25,000	1,50,000
Furniture & Fixture	1,50,000	65,000
80% Shares in S Ltd.	3,60,000	—
Stock	1,45,000	1,61,000
Debtors	85,000	79,000
Bank	1,20,000	55,000
	15,00,000	5,10,000

On 1st April, 2004, S Ltd.'s Profit and Loss A/c showed a credit balance of Rs. 40,000. S Ltd. declared an interim dividend of 10% on 1st January, 2005. Assume no taxation.

You are required to prepare a Consolidated Balance Sheet of H Ltd. and it's subsidiary S Ltd. as on 31st March, 2005.

[B Com. (H) DU 2000- Modified [B Com. (H) DU 2004- Modified

Solution:

Capital Profits

	General Reserve (1.4.04)		1,10,000
	Profit & Loss A/c (1.4.04)		40,000
			1,50,000
Add	*Current Profits (1.4.04 to 30.9.04)(Rs. 80,000 + 25,000 – 40,000) = *Rs. 65,000 × 6/12) =	32,500	
Less	1/2 of interim dividend	12500	20,000
			1,70,000
	H Ltd.'s Share (80%)		1,36,000
	Minority Interest (20%)		34,000

***Current year's Profits**

	Balance of P & L A/c as on 31.3.05 =	80,000
Add	Interim dividend paid	25,000
		1,05,000
Less	Opening balancing of P&L A/c	40,000
		65,000

Revenue Profits (1.10.04 to 31.3.05)	20,000
(32,500 – 12,500) H Ltd.'s Share (80%)	16,000
6 Months Profit Less 1/2 of I.D.) Minority Intrest	4,000

COST OF CONTROL A/C

	Rs.		Rs.
**To 80% Shares in S Ltd. Less dividend from pre-acquisition profits) 80% of Rs. 12,500	3,50,000	By Share Capital	2,00,000
		By Capital Profits	1,36,000
		By Goodwill (B.F.)	14,000
	3,50,000		3,50,000

** Cost of Investment	3,60,000
Less 1/2 Interim dividend paid out of pre-acquisition profit 80% (25,000 × 6/12)	10,000
	3,50,000

MINORITY INTEREST A/C

	Rs.		Rs.
To Balance c/d	88,000	By Share Capital	50,000
		By Capital Profit	34,000
		By Revenue Profit	4,000
	88,000		88,000

Alternatively

Share Capital	50,000
General Reserve	22,000
Profit & Loss A/c	16,000
	88,000

CONSOLIDATED BALANCE SHEET
As on 31st March, 2005

Liabilities		Rs.	Assets		Rs.
Equity Share Capital		7,50,000	Fixed Assets :		
Shares of Rs. 10 each			Goodwill		14,000
Reserve & Surplus :			Land & Building		4,15,000
Securities Premium		50,000	Plant & Machinery		
General Reserve		4,00,000	H Ltd.	2,25,000	
Profit & Loss A/c		2,46,000	S Ltd.	1,50,000	3,75,000
Current Liabilities :			Furniture & Fixture		
S Creditors			H Ltd.	1,50,000	
H Ltd.	60,000		S Ltd.	65,000	2,15,000
S Ltd.	70,000	1,30,000	Current Assets :		
			Stock:		
Minority Interest		88,000	H Ltd.	1,45,000	
			S Ltd.	1,61,000	3,06,000

Contd.

CONSOLIDATED BALANCE SHEET (CONTD.)
As on 31st March, 2005

Liabilities	Rs.	Assets		Rs.
		Debtors		
		H Ltd.	85,000	
		S Ltd.	79,000	1,64,000
		Bank.		
		H Ltd.	1,20,000	
		S Ltd.	55,000	1,75,000
	16,64,000			16,64,000

Profit & Loss A/c (H Ltd.) 31.3.05	2,40,000
Less 1/2 Interim dividend paid out of capital profit	10,000
Wrongly Credited	2,30,000
Add Share in Revenue Profit	16,000
	2,46,000

Illustration (16) (Dividend and bonus out of pre-acquisition Profits, effect of which given in the B/S of S Ltd.)

The following are the Balance Sheet of H Ltd. and S Ltd. as on 31st March, 2005.

Liabilities	H Ltd. Rs.	S Ltd. Rs.
Equity Share Capital (Shares of Rs. 100 each)	10,00,000	7,00,000
General Reserve	2,00,000	3,00,000
Profit & Loss Account	3,00,000	3,00,000
Current liabilities	5,00,000	9,00,000
	20,00,000	22,00,000
Assets:		
Fixed Assets	8,00,000	9,00,000
Investment in Shares of S Ltd.	5,00,000	—
Current Assets	7,00,000	13,00,000
	20,00,000	22,00,000

Additional Information:

(i) H Ltd. acquired 3,000 shares of S Ltd. on 1.4.2004 When the Reserve & Surplus position was as under :

(a) General Reserve - Rs. 5,00,000

(b) Profit & Loss A/c-Rs. 2,00,000

(ii) On 1.10.2004 S Ltd. issued 2 shares for every 5 shares held, as bonus shares at a face value of Rs. 100 each. No entry has been in the books of H Ltd. for the receipt of bonus shares.

(iii) On 30th June, 2004 S Ltd. declared a dividend, out of pre-acquisition profits @ 20% and H Ltd. credited the receipt of dividend to it's Profit & Loss Account.

(iv) S Ltd. owed H Ltd. Rs. 1,20,000 for purchase of goods from H Ltd.. The entire stock is held by S Ltd. On 31st March, 2005. H Ltd. made a profit of 20% on Cost.

(v) H Ltd. transferred a machinery to S Ltd. for Rs. 1,00,000, the book value of machinery was Rs. 85,000.

Prepare consolidated Balance Sheet as on 31st March, 2005.

[CA (F) Modified]

Solution :

Percentage holding = $\frac{3,000}{5,000} \times 100 = 60\%$

Capital Profits :

	General Reserve (1.4.04)		5,00,000
Less	Bonus Issue (2 : 5)		2,00,000
	(Post bonus Capital of S Ltd. × 2/5 +2 = $\frac{7,00,000 \times 2}{7}$ = 2,00,000)		3,00,000
	Profit & Loss A/c (1.4.04)	2,00,000	
Less	Dividend out of Pre-acquisition Profit	1,00,000	1,00,000
			4,00,000
	H Ltd.'s Share (60%)		2,40,000
	Minority Interest (40%)		1,60,000

Revenue Profits (S Ltd.)

	Profit & Loss A/c 31.3.05	3,00,000
Less	Balance as on 1.4.04	1,00,000
		2,00,000
	H Ltd.'s Share (60%)	1,20,000
	Minority Interest (40%)	80,000

COST OF CONTROL A/C

	Rs.		Rs.
To Investment* in Shares of S Ltd. after dividend (5,00,000 – 60,000)	4,40,000	By Share Capital	3,00,000
		By Capital Profits	2,40,000
To Capital Reserve (B. F.)	2,20,000	By Bonus Shares**	1,20,000
	6,60,000		6,60,000

* Since dividend has been paid out of pre-acquisition profits, the same has been adjusted against cost of investment.

** Bonus Issue: 2 : 5	2,00,000
H Ltd. Share (60%)	1,20,000
Minority Interest (40%)	80,000

MINORITY INTEREST A/C

	Rs.		
To Balance c/d	5,20,000	By Share Capital	2,00,000
		By Capital Profit	1,60,000
		By Bonus Shares	80,000
		By Revenue Profit	80,000
	5,20,000		5,20,000

CONSOLIDATED BALANCE SHEET
As on 31st March, 2005

Liabilities		Rs.	Assets		Rs.
Equity Share Capital		10,00,000	Fixed Assets		
Share of Rs 100 each			H Ltd.	8,00,000	
Reserves & Surplus :			S Ltd.	9,00,000	
Capital Reserve		2,20,000		17,00,000	
General Reserve		2,00,000	*Less* Unrealised Profit	15,000	16,85,000
Profit & Loss A/c		3,25,000	Current Assets :		
Current liabilities :			H Ltd.	7,00,000	
H Ltd.	5,00,000		S Ltd.	13,00,000	
S Ltd.	9,00,000	14,00,000		20,00,000	
Minority Interest		5,20,000	*Less* Unrealised profit	20,000	19,80,000
		36,65,000			36,65,000

			Rs.
Profit & Loss A/c (H Ltd.) (31.3.05)			3,00,000
Less Dividend wrongly Credited to P & L A/c			60,000
			2,40,000
Add Revenue Profits (Share in S Ltd.)			1,20,000
			3,60,000
Less Unrealised Profits			
(1,20,000 × 20/120)	On Stock-	20,000	
(1,00,000 – 85,000)	On Machinery-	15,000	35,000
			3,25,000

Illustration (17) (Bonus Issue, Revaluation and Charge in the method of depreciation with retrospective effect)

Following are the Balance Sheets of H Ltd. and S Ltd. as on 31st March, 2005.

Liabilities	H Ltd. Rs.	S Ltd. Rs.
Equity Share Capital Shares of Rs. 100 each	12,00,000	6,00,000
General Reserve	5,00,000	2,00,000
Profit & Loss Account	2,75,000	1,85,000
Capital Redemption Reserve	—	2,00,000
Provident Fund	1,25,000	75,000
Payable	4,00,000	1,40,000
	25,00,000	14,00,000

Assets:	H Ltd.	S Ltd.
	Rs.	Rs.
Net Block	12,50,000	9,75,000
Investment in 4,800 Shares in S Ltd.	7,50,000	—
Current liabilities	5,00,000	3,90,000
Preliminary Expenses	—	35,000
	25,00,000	14,00,000

H Ltd. acquired shares on 1.7.2004. On the same date S Ltd. issued bonus shares in the ratio of 1:3 but no entry has been recorded in the books of S Ltd. It was further agreed that a machinery, on which depreciation has been charged @ 10% per annum on written down value basis, be valued at Rs. 50,000. The written down value of machinery as on 1.4.2004 was Rs. 65,610. It was agreed to charge depreciation @ 10% on original cost with retrospective effect when the machinery was installed on 1.4.2000. The Capital Redemption Reserve is the result of redemption of Preference shares carried out during the year 2003-04.

Following was the position of Reserve and Profit & Loss Account as on 1.4.2004.

General Reserve	—	Rs. 1,50,000
Profit & Loss Account	—	Rs. 35,000

Prepare a Consolidated Balance Sheet of H Ltd. and its subsidiary as on 31st March, 2005.

Solution :

$$\text{Percentage holding} = \frac{4,800 \times 100}{6,000} = 80\%$$

Capital Profits

			Rs.
	General Reserve		1,50,000
	Profit & Loss A/c		35,000
	Capital Redemption Reserve	2,00,000	
Less	Bonus Issue	2,00,000	—
Profit for the current year (2,00,000 × 3/12) (1.4.04 to 30.6.04)			50,000
			2,35,000

PROFIT & LOSS APP. A//C

	Rs.		Rs.
To General Reserve (2,00,000–1,50,000)	50,000	By Balance b/d	35,000
To Balance c/d	1,85,000	By Net Profit (B.F.)	2,00,000
	2,35,000		2,35,000

	Total Capital Profits		2,35,000
Less	Preliminary Expenses	35,000	
	Fall in the Value of machinery	7,500	
	Additional depreciation for the pre-acquisition period	5,610	48,110
			1,86,890

Calculation of original cost of Machinery

	Rs.
W.D.V as on 1.4.2004 = 65,610	
W.D.V. as on 1.4.2003 $= 65{,}610 \times \frac{100}{90} =$	72,900
W.D.V. as on 1.4.2002 $= 72{,}900 \times \frac{100}{90} =$	81,000
W.D.V. as on 1.4.2001 $= 81{,}000 \times \frac{100}{90} =$	90,000
W.D.V. as on 1.4.2000 $= 90{,}000 \times \frac{100}{90} =$	1,00,000
Depreciation for 4 years on the basis of original cost $= 1{,}00{,}000 \times \frac{10}{100} \times 4 =$	40,000
Written down value as on 1.4.2004 =	60,000
Depreciation for 3 months	2,500
	57,500
Revised Value	50,000
Capital Loss	7,500

Additional Depreciation

Depreciation on Original Cost for 4 years	40,000
Depreciation already charged on written down value basis (Rs. 1,00,000 – 65,610)	34,390
To be adjusted against pre-acquisition profits as per question.	5,610
Revenue Profits (2,00,000 × 9/12) (1.7.04 to 31.3.2005)	1,50,000
H Ltd.'s Share	1,20,000
Minority Interest	30,000
Capital Profits (Net)	1,86,890
H Ltd.'s Share (80%)	1,49,512
Minority Interest (20%)	37,378

COST OF CONTROL A/C

	Rs.		Rs.
To Investment in Shares of S Ltd.	7,50,000	By Share Capital	4,80,000
To Capital Reserve (B.F.)	39,512	By Capital Profits	1,49,512
		By Bonus Shares	1,60,000
	7,89,512		7,89,512

MINORITY INTEREST A/C

To Balance c/d	2,27,378	By Share Capital	1,20,000
		By Capital Profits	37,378
		By Revenue Profits	30,000
		By Bonus Shares	40,000
	2,27,378		2,27,378

It is to be noted that since the depreciation has been charged on original cost, any change in the written down value of machinery will not affect the amount of depreciation for the current year, hence no adjustment for the depreciation has been made in the current year's profits.

Note: Additional depreciation, if any should be charged to the period to which it relates to.The current year's depreciation however, has been charged on the basis of original cost of machine.

CONSOLIDATED BALANCE SHEET
As on 31st March, 2005

Liabilities		Rs.	Assets		Rs.
Equity Share Capital		12,00,000	Net Block		
Shares of Rs. 10 each			H Ltd.	12,50,000	
Reserve & surplus			S Ltd.	9,75,000	
Capital Reserve		39,512		22,25,000	
General Reserve			*Less* Fall in the value	(7,500)	
H Ltd.:	5,00,000		*Less* Additional Dep.	(5,610)	22,11,890
S Ltd.:	40,000	5,40,000	Current Asset :		
Profit & Loss A/c			H Ltd.	5,00,000	
H Ltd.:	2,75,000		S Ltd.	3,90,000	8,90,000
S Ltd.:	80,000	3,55,000			
Current Liabilities					
Provident Fund					
H Ltd.:	1,25,000				
S Ltd.:	75,000	2,00,000			
Payables					
H Ltd.:	4,00,000				
S Ltd.:	1,40,000	5,40,000			
Minority Interest		2,27,378			
		31,01,890			31,01,890

FIXED ASSETS A/C (S LTD.)

31.03.05	Rs.		Rs.
To Balance b/d	9,75,000	By Fall in the Value of Machinery (Capital Loss)	7,500
		By Additional depreciation	5,610
		By Balance c/d	9,61,890
	9,75,000		9,75,000

Illustration (18) (Dividend, Bonus shares, Revaluation & adjustment for depreciation)

The following are the Balance Sheets of H Ltd. and S Ltd. as on 31st March, 2005.

Liabilities	H Ltd. Rs.	S Ltd. Rs.
Equity Share Capital (Shares of Rs. 100 each)	12,00,000	10,00,000
General Reserve	2,00,000	3,50,000
Profit & Loss A/c	2,20,000	2,10,000
Current Liabilities	2,80,000	1,40,000
	19,00,000	17,00,000
Assets		
Fixed Assets	6,50,000	9,10,000
Investment in 8,000 shares of S Ltd.	9,80,000	7,90,000
Current Assets	2,70,000	—
	19,00,000	17,00,000

Additional Information:

(i) H Ltd. purchased shares on 1.4.2002 when General Reserve and Profit & Loss A/c of S Ltd. stood at Rs. 3,00,000 and Rs. 1,50,000 respectively. Dividend @ 10% has been paid every year after the acquisition of shares, the first dividend being out of pre-acquisition profit. H Ltd. has credited all dividends to Profit & Loss Account.

(ii) On 31st March, 2005 S Ltd. declared bonus shares in the ratio of 1 : 5. No effect has been given to bonus shares which are to be issued out of General Reserve prior to 1.4.2002 period.

(iii) When the shares were purchased the fixed assets were agreed to be valued at Rs. 12,00,000. No effect has been given to revaluation of fixed assets. Depreciation has been charged @ 10% p.a. on the straight line method on the book value as on 1.4.2002. There has been no change (addition or disposal) in the fixed assets since then.

(iv) It was found that H Ltd. has remitted cheque of Rs. 10,000 which has not yet been received by S Ltd. till 31st March 2005.

Prepare consolidated Balance Sheet as on 31st March, 2005

[CA (F) Adapted May 2000.]

Solution:

Percentage holding = 8,000/10,000 × 100 = 80%

Capital Profits:

			Rs.
	General Reserve (1.4.2002)	3,00,000	
Less	Bonus issue (10,000 × 1/5) × 100	2,00,000	1,00,000
	Profit & Loss A/c (1.4.2002)	1,50,000	
Less	dividend out of pre-acquisition profits	1,00,000	50,000
			1,50,000
Less	Loss on Revaluation*		1,00,000
			50,000
	H Ltd.'s Share		40,000
	Minority Interest		10,000

		Rs.
*Book Value as on 31.3.2005		9,10,000
Book Value as on 31.3.2002	$\frac{9,10,000 \times 100}{70} =$	13,00,000
Revised Value on the date of acquisition		12,00,000
Loss on Revaluation		1,00,000
Revenue Profits		
Profit & Loss A/c balance as on 31.3.05		2,10,000
Less opening balance on 1.4.2002 (after dividend)		50,000
		1,60,000
Add transfer to General Reserve		50,000
Add Excess depreciation	$\left(\frac{1,00,000 \times 10 \times 3}{100}\right)$	30,000
		2,40,000
H Ltd.'s Share		1,92,000
Minority Interest		48,000

COST OF CONTROL A/C

	Rs.		Rs.
To Investment		By Share Capital	8,00,000
Less Dividend (9,80,000 – 80,000)	9,00,000	By Bonus Shares	1,60,000
To Capital Reserve (B.F.)	1,00,000	By Capital Profits	40,000
	10,00,000		10,00,000

MINORITY INTEREST A/C

	Rs.		Rs.
To Balance c/d	2,98,000	By Share Capital	2,00,000
		By Bonus Shares	40,000
		By Capital Profits	10,000
		By Revenue Profits	48,000
	2,98,000		2,98,000

CONSOLIDATED BALANCE SHEET
As on 31st March, 2005

Liabilities		Rs.	Assets		Rs.
Equity Share Capital		12,00,000	Fixed Assets		
Shares of Rs. 100 each			H Ltd.		6,50,000
Reserve & Surplus :			S Ltd.	9,10,000	
Capital Reserve		1,00,000	*Less* Loss on Revaluation	1,00,000	
General Reserve				8,10,000	
H Ltd.	2,00,000		*Add* Excess Depreciation	30,000	8,40,000
S Ltd.	40,000	2,40,000			

Contd.

CONSOLIDATED BALANCE SHEET
As on 31st March, 2005

Liabilities		Rs.	Assets		Rs.
Profit & Loss A/c			Current Assets		
H Ltd.	1,40,000*		H Ltd.	2,70,000	
S Ltd.	1,52,000	2,92,000	S Ltd.	7,90,000	
Current Liabilities				10,60,000	
H Ltd.	2,80,000		*Less* Cheque in Transit	10,000	10,50,000
S Ltd.	1,40,000	4,20,000	Cheque in Transit		10,000
Minority Interest		2,98,000			
		25,50,000			25,50,000

* After dividend out of pre-acquisition profit (2,20,000 – 80,000) = Rs. 1,40,000

* After Rs. 40,000 transferred to General Reserve *i.e.* (1,92,000 – 40,000) = 1,52,000

Illustration : (19) (Revaluation, Mutual owings and cheque in transit)

Following are the Balance Sheets of H Ltd. and S Ltd. as on 31st March, 2005.

Liabilities	H Ltd. Rs.	S Ltd. Rs.
Share Capital Shares of Rs. 10 each	5,00,000	1,50,000
General Reserve	1,70,000	25,000
Profit & Loss A/c	55,500	22,000
Bills Payable	45,000	—
Sundry Creditors	2,29,500	76,500
Loan	—	63,000
	10,00,000	3,36,500
Assets:		
Goodwill	70,000	25,000
Land & Building	3,30,000	—
Plant & Machinery	—	1,20,000
Investment	1,45,000	—
Stock	2,55,000	45,000
S Debtors	1,75,000	80,000
Bills receivable	—	30,000
Cash & Bank balance	25,000	36,500
	10,00,000	3,36,500

Additional Information :

(i) The investment consists of 12,000 shares of Rs. 10 each fully paid in S Ltd. which were acquired on 1.7.2004.

(ii) On 1.4.2004 the Plant & Machinery was revalued at Rs. 1,40,000 which should be taken in the consolidated Balance Sheet. Ignore depreciation. There was no addition or deletion to plant during the year.

(iii) Total bills receivable were Rs. 45,000 (all accepted by H Ltd.) of which bills for Rs. 15,000 had been discounted with the bank yet to be matured.

(iv) Cash & Bank balance were arrived at after sending a cheque for Rs. 13,000 to H Ltd. on account of repayment of loan.

(v) Sundry debtors of H Ltd. include loan to S Ltd. Rs. 13,000.

(vi) Balance as on 1.4.2004:

	Rs.
General Reserve	20,000
Profit & Loss A/c	2,000

Prepare Consolidated Balance Sheet. *[CS (1) June 87-Adapted]*

Solution :

$$\text{Percentage holding} = \frac{12{,}000 \times 100}{15{,}000} = 80\%$$

Capital Profits	Rs.
General Reserve (1.4.04)	20,000
Profit & Loss A/c (1.4.04)	2,000
Current year's Profit (1.4.04 to 30.6.04)*	6,250
Profit on Revaluation	20,000
	48,250
Total Capital profit	48,250
H Ltd.'s Share	38,600
Minority Interest	9,650
Revenue Profit	
Profit & Loss A/c (31.3.05)	22,000
Less opening balance (1.4.050)	2,000
	20,000
Add Transfer to General Reserve	5,000
	25,000
Less Capital Profits for 3 months (25,000 ×3/12)*	6,250
	18,750
H Ltd.'s Share (80%)	15,000
Minority Interest (20%)	3,750

COST OF CONTROL A/C

	Rs.		Rs.
To Investments in Shares of S Ltd.	1,45,000	By Share Capital	1,20,000
To Capital Reserve (B.F.)	13,600	By Capital Profits	38,600
	1,58,600		1,58,600

MINORITY INTEREST A/C

	Rs.		Rs.
To Balance c/d	43,400	By Share Capital	30,000
		By Capital Profits	9,650
		By Revenue Profit	3,750
	43,400		43,400

CONSOLIDATED BALANCE SHEET
As on 31st March, 2005

Liabilities		Rs.	Assets		Rs.
Share Capital (Shares of Rs. 10 each)		5,00,000	Fixed assets:		
Reserves & Surplus :			Goodwill		
General Reserve			H Ltd.	70,000	
H Ltd.	1,70,000		S Ltd.	25,000	
S Ltd..	4,000	1,74,000		95,000	
Profit & Loss A/c			*Less* Capital Reserve	13,600	81,400
H Ltd.	55,500		Land & Building		3,30,000
S Ltd.(15,000 – 4,000)	11,000	66,500	Plant & Machinery		1,40,000
Current liabilities			Current Assets:		
Bills Payable			Stock		
H Ltd.	45,000		H Ltd.	2,55,000	
Less Mutual owings	30,000	15,000	S Ltd.	45,000	3,00,000
S Creditors			S. Debtors		
H Ltd.:	2,29,500		H Ltd.	1,75,000	
S Ltd.:	76,500	3,06,000	S Ltd.	80,000	
Loan		63,000		2,55,000	
Minority Interest		43,400	*Less* Loan paid	13,000	2,42,000
			Bills Receivable		
			H Ltd.	30,000	
			Less Mutual Owings	30,000	—
			Cash Bank		
			H Ltd.	25,000	
			S Ltd.	36,500	
				61,500	
			Cheque in Transit	13,000	74,500
		11,67,900			11,67,900

Illustration (20) (Preference Shares, Debentures and proposed dividend)

The following are the Balance Sheets of H Ltd. and S Ltd. as 31st March, 2005.

Liabilities	H Ltd. Rs.	S Ltd. Rs.
6% Preference Shares of Rs. 100 each	—	1,60,000
Equity Shares of Rs. 10 each	6,00,000	2,00,000
General Reserve	1,00,000	80,000
Profit & Loss Account	2,00,000	90,000
6% Debentures of Rs. 100 each	—	40,000
Proposed Dividend:		
On Equity Shares	60,000	20,000
On Preference Shares	—	9,600
Debenture Interest Accrued	—	2,400
S. Creditors	2,94,000	1,25,000
	12,54,000	7,27,000
Assets		
Fixed Assets	5,00,000	4,40,000
Investment:		
15,000 Equity Shares in S Ltd.	3,30,000	—
1,200 Preference Shares in S Ltd.	1,20,000	—
100 Debentures in S Ltd.	10,000	—
Current Assets	2,94,000	2,87,000
	12,54,000	7,27,000

Additional Information:

(i) General Reserve of S Ltd. as on 31.3.04 was Rs. 80,000

(ii) H Ltd. acquired shares in S Ltd. as on 31.3.04.

(iii) The balance of Profit & Loss A/c of S Ltd. is made up as follows :

		Rs.
	Balance as on 31.3.04	56,000
	Net Profit for year 2004-05	63,600
		1,19,600
Less	Provision for Proposed Dividend	29,600
		90,000

(iv) The balance of Profit & Loss A/c of S Ltd. as on 31.3.2004 is after providing for preference dividend of Rs. 9,600 and equity dividend of Rs. Rs. 10,000 both of which were subsequently paid and credited to Profit & Loss A/c of H Ltd.

(v) No entries have been made in the books of H Ltd. for Debenture interest due from or proposed dividend of S Ltd. for the year ended 31st March, 2005.

S Ltd. had issued fully paid bonus shares of Rs. 40,000 on 31st March, 2005 to the existing share holders out of general reserve. The transaction has not been given effect in the books of S Ltd.

You are required to prepare consolidated Balance Sheet of H Ltd. and it's subsidiary S Ltd. as on 31st March, 2005.

[CS (i) Dec. 91 Modified]

Solution:

			Rs.
	Capital Profits (Pre-acquisition)		
	General Reserve (31.3.04)	80,000	
Less	Bonus Issue	40,000	40,000
	Profit & Loss A/c (31.3.04)		56,000
			96,000
	H Ltd.'s share (75%)		72,000
	Minority Interest (25%)		24,000
	Bonus Issue:		40,000
	H Ltd.'s Share		30,000
	Minority Interest		10,000
	REVENUE (Post - acquisition) PROFITS		
	Profit & Loss A/c (31.3.05)		90,000
Less	Opening balance (31.3.04)		56,000
			34,000
Add	Provision for Proposed dividends		29,600
	(6% Preference dividend 9,600 + 10% Equity dividend 20,000)		63,600
	H Ltd.'s Share		47,700
	Minority Interest		15,900

COST OF CONTROL A/C

	Rs.		Rs.
To Investments	4,35,300	By Equity Share Capital	1,50,000
(*Less* dividend		By Preference Share Capital	1,20,000
(Out of pre-acquisition profit)		By Bonus Issue	30,000
(4,50,000–14,700)		By Capital Profits	72,000
		By Goodwill (B.F.)	63,300
	4,35,300		4,35,300

MINORITY INTEREST A/C

	Rs.		Rs.
To Proposed Dividend	7,400	By Equity Share Capital	50,000
(5000 + 2400)		By Preference Share Capital	40,000
To Balance c/d	1,32,500	By Bonus Issue	10,000
		By Capital Profits	24,000
		By Revenue Profits	15,900
	1,39,900		1,39,900

CONSOLIDATED BALANCE SHEET
As on 31st March, 2005

Liabilities		Rs.	Assets		Rs.
Share Capital			Fixed Assets		
Equity Shares of Rs. 10 each		6,00,000	Goodwill		63,300
Reserve & Surplus :			Other Fixed Assets		
General Reserve		1,00,000	H Ltd.	5,00,000	
Profit & Loss A/c [(1)]		2,33,600	S Ltd.	4,40,000	9,40,000
Secured Loans :			Investments		
6% Debentures	40,000		6% Debentures	10,000	
Less Mutual owings	10,000	30,000	*Less* Mutual Owings	10,000	—
O/s Debenture Interest	2,400		Current Assets		
Less Mutual owings	600	1,800	H Ltd.	2,94,000	
Current liabilities			S Ltd.	2,87,000	5,81,000
S Creditors : H Ltd.	2,94,000		Debenture Interest A/c	600	
S Ltd.	1,25,000	4,19,000	Less Mutual owings	600	—
Minority Interest		1,32,500			
Proposed Dividend					
H Ltd.	60,000				
S Ltd.	7,400	67,400			
		15,84,300			15,84,300

		Rs.
(1)	Profit & Loss A/c	
	H Ltd.	2,00,000
	Share in S Ltd.'s profit	47,700
	Debenture Interest	600
		2,48,300
Less	Dividend wrongly Credited	14,700
		2,33,600

Illustration (21) (Revaluation, Mutual owings and Goods-in-transit)

The following are the Balance Sheets of H Ltd. and S Ltd. as on 31st March, 2005

Liabilities	Rs.	Rs.
Equity Shares of Rs. 10 each	16,00,000	5,00,000
General Reserve	2,00,000	—
Profit & Loss Account	1,15,000	1,00,000
9% Debentures	1,00,000	—
Sundry Creditors:		
H Ltd.		48,000
Trade Creditors	1,12,000	1,12,000
	21,27,000	7,60,000

Assets		
Factory	11,00,000	80,000
Machinery	2,95,000	1,25,000
Investments in 37,500 shares of Rs. 10 each in S Ltd.	4,31,250	—
Stock	1,55,000	2,25,000
Bills Reservable	—	17,000
Sundry Debtors:		
S Ltd.	51,000	—
Trade Debtors	90,000	3,00,000
Cash & Bank balance	4,750	13,000
	21,27,000	7,60,000

Additional Information:

(i) On the date of acquiring shares in S Ltd. by H Ltd. there was a balance of Rs. 50,000 to the Credit of Profit & Loss Account of S Ltd.

(ii) For the purpose of fixing the price of shares of S Ltd. at Rs. 4,31,250 the factory was taken at Rs. 1,90,000 instead of its book figure of Rs. 1,70,000 on that day. (Depreciation to be ignored)

(iii) Goods were sold to S Ltd. by H Ltd. at cost plus 25% Stock of Rs. 2,25,000 of S Ltd. on 31.3.2005 included goods purchased from H Ltd. for Rs. 75,000. Goods sold to S Ltd. for Rs. 3,000 by H Ltd. were returned by S Ltd. on 28.3.2005 which however, reached H Ltd. on 5.4.2005.

Prepare consolidated Balance Sheet.

[C.S. (i) Dec. 82 Modified]

Solution : Percentage holding = $\frac{37,500}{50,000} \times 100 = 75\%$

Capital Profits	Rs.
Profit & Loss A/c (1.4.2004)	50,000
Profit on Revaluation of Factory (Rs. 1,90,000–1,70,000)	20,000
	70,000
H Ltd.'s Share (3/4)	52,500
Minority Interest (1/4)	17,500
Revenue Profits	
Profit & Loss A/c (31.3.2005)	1,00,000
Less Balance as on 1.4.2004	50,000
	50,000
H Ltd.'s share	37,500
Minority Interest	12,500

COST OF CONTROL A/C

	Rs.		Rs.
To Investment	4,31,250	By Share Capital	3,75,000
		By Capital Profits	52,500
		By Goodwill (B.F.)	3,750
	4,31,250		4,31,250

MINORITY INTEREST A/C

	Rs.		Rs.
To Balance c/d	1,55,000	By Share Capital	1,25,000
		By Capital Profits	17,500
		By Revenue Profits	12,500
	1,55,000		1,55,000

CONSOLIDATED BALANCE SHEET
As on 31st March, 2005

Liabilities		Rs.	Assets		Rs.
Equity Share Capital			Fixed Assets :		
Shares of Rs. 10 each		16,00,000	Goodwill		3,750
Reserve & Surplus :			Factory		
General Reserve		2,00,000	H Ltd.	11,00,000	
Profit & Loss A/c		1,36,900	S Ltd.	1,00,000	12,00,000
Secured Loan			(80,000 + 20,000)		
9% Debentures		1,00,000	Machinery		
Current liabilities:			H Ltd.	2,95,000	
Sundry Creditors			S Ltd.	1,25,000	4,20,000
S Ltd.	48,000		Stock:		
Less Mutual obligations			H Ltd.	1,55,000	
as per contra	48,000	—	S Ltd.	2,25,000	
Trade Creditors				3,80,000	
H Ltd.	1,12,000		In-Transit	2,400	
S Ltd.	1,12,000	2,24,000		3,82,400	
Minority Interest		1,55,000	*Less* Unrealised Profit	15,000	3,67,400
			Sundry Debtors		
			H Ltd.	51,000	
			Less Goods Returned	3,000	
				48,000	
			Less Mutual obligations	48,000	—
			as per Contra		
			Trade Debtors		
			H Ltd.	90,000	
			S Ltd.	3,00,000	3,90,000
			Bills Receivable (S. Ltd.)		17,000
			Cash & Bank balance		
			H Ltd.	4,750	
			S Ltd.	13,000	17,750
		24,15,900			24,15,900

		Rs.
(1)	Profit & Loss A/c (H Ltd.)	
	Balance as given	1,15,000
Less	Unrealised Profit on stock (75,000 × 25/125)	15,000
		1,00,000
Less	Unrealised Profit on goods-in-transit (3,000 × 25/125)	600
		99,400
Add	Share of Profit in S Ltd	37,500
		1,36,900

Illustration (22) (Interim dividend, Mutual owings and Unrealised Profit)

Following are the Balance Sheets of H Ltd. and S Ltd. as on 31st March, 2005.

Liabilities	H Ltd.	S Ltd.
	Rs.	Rs.
Equity Share Capital	10,00,000	2,50,000
Shares of Rs. 10 each		
General Reserve (1.4.2004)	3,50,000	10,000
Profit & Loss A/c	2,50,000	1,80,000
Sundry Creditors	2,50,000	1,10,000
	18,50,000	5,50,000
Assets:		
Fixed Assets	10,50,000	3,50,000
Investment in Shares in S Ltd.	3,50,000	—
Stock	2,20,000	1,10,000
Debtors	1,80,000	70,000
Cash & Bank Balance	50,000	20,000
	18,50,000	5,50,000

Additional Information :

(i) H Ltd. had acquired 20,000 shares in S Ltd. as on 1st July, 2004 at a cost of Rs. 3,50,000.

(ii) Balance in Profit and Loss Account as on 1.4.2004 of S Ltd. was Rs. 1,40,000. An interim dividend having been paid during the year out of the said undistributed profits

(iii) Profit & Loss Account of H Ltd. includes interim dividend received from S Ltd. in August 2004 @ 10%.

(iv) Sundry Creditors of H Ltd. includes Rs. 25,000 on account of purchase from S Ltd. who follow the practice of charging 25% extra on cost for determining the sales price.

(v) Stock in Trade of H Ltd. includes goods worth Rs. 15,000 purchased from S Ltd. who sells goods at cost plus 25%.

Presuming that profits have been earned on uniform basis through out the year 2004-05, prepare Consolidated Balance Sheet as on 31st March, 2005.

[CS (i) Dec. 1986 - Modified]

Solution:

$$\text{Percentage holding} = \frac{20,000}{25,000} \times 100 = 80\%$$

Capital Profits	Rs.
General Reserve (1.4.04)	10,000
Profit & Loss A/c (after dividend) (Rs. 1,40,000 – 25,000)	1,15,000
Current year's Profit (1.4.04 – 30.6.04) $(1,80,000 - 1,15,000) = \left(\frac{65,000 \times 3}{12}\right)$	16,250
	1,41,250
H Ltd.'s share (80%)	1,13,000
Minority Interest (20%)	28,250
Revenue Profits (Post-acquisition)	
Profit & Loss A/c (31.3.05)	1,80,000
Less Opening balance after dividend	1,15,000
	65,000
Less Profit for the pre-acquisition period	16,250
	48,750
H Ltd.'s share (80)%)	39,000
Minority Interest (20%)	9,750

COST OF CONTROL A/C

	Rs.		Rs.
To Investments (Rs. 3,50,000 – 20,000) Cost – dividend	3,30,000	By Share Capital	2,00,000
		By Capital Profits	1,13,000
		By Goodwill (B.F.)	17,000
	3,30,000		3,30,000

MINORITY INTEREST A/C

	Rs.		Rs.
To Balance c/d	88,000	By Share Capital	50,000
		By Capital Profits	28,250
		By Revenue Profit	9,750
	88,000		88,000

CONSOLIDATED BALANCE SHEET
As on 31st March, 2005

Liabilities		Rs.	Assets		Rs.
Equity Share Capital		10,00,000	Fixed Assets:		
Shares of Rs. 10 each			Goodwill		17,000
Reserve & Surplus :			Other Fixed Assets		
General Reserve		3,50,000	H Ltd.:	10,50,000	
Profit & Loss A/c (1)		2,66,000	S Ltd.:	3,50,000	14,00,000
Current liabilities:			Stock		
S. Creditors			H Ltd.:	2,20,000	
H Ltd.:	2,50,000		S Ltd.:	1,10,000	
S Ltd.:	1,10,000			3,30,000	
	3,60,000		*Less* Unrealised Profit	3,000	3,27,000
Less Mutual owings	25,000	3,35,000	Debtors		
Minority Interest		88,000	H Ltd.:	1,80,000	
			S Ltd.:	70,000	
				2,50,000	
			Less Mutual owings	25,000	2,25,000
			Cash Bank		
			H Ltd.	50,000	
			S Ltd.	20,000	70,000
		20,39,000			20,39,000

			Rs.
(1)	Profit & Loss A/c (H Ltd.)		
	Balance as on 1.4.2004		2,50,000
Less	dividend Wrongly credited	20,000	
Less	Unrealised Profits	3,000	23,000
			2,27,000
Add	Share of Profit in S Ltd.		39,000
			2,6,6000

Illustration (23) (Dividend declared but not paid, Dividend Receivable, cheque in transit and unrealised profit)

The following are the Balance Sheets of H Ltd. and it's subsidiary S Ltd. as on 31.3.2005.

	H Ltd.	S Ltd.
Sources :	Rs.	Rs.
Share Capital	25,00,000	7,50,000
Free Reserves	6,00,000	1,25,000
Profit & Loss Account	3,22,500	1,10,000
Bills payable	37,500	—
Sundry Creditors	8,37,500	2,00,000
	42,97,500	11,85,000

Application of Funds

Goodwill	5,00,000	1,10,000
Land & Building	6,00,000	2,50,000
Plant & Machinery	13,00,000	4,75,000
Investments in Shares in S Ltd. (at par)	7,20,000	—
Stock	3,50,000	1,25,000
Debtors	5,85,000	1,40,000
Other Current Assets	15,000	—
Bills Receivable	—	25,000
Cash & Bank balance	2,27,500	60,000
	42,97,500	11,85,000

Additional Information:

(i) Share Capital of H Ltd. is made of 5,000 12% Redeemable Preference Shares of Rs. 100 each and 2,00,000 equity Shares of Rs. 10 each, Share Capital of S Ltd. is made of fully paid up shares of Rs. 10 each.

(ii) The opening balance in Free Reserves of S Ltd. was Rs. 1,00,000

(iii) The particulars of Profit & Loss Account of Two companies are as under :

	H Ltd.	S Ltd.
	Rs.	Rs.
Opening Balance	40,000	30,000
Profit for the year	2,37,500	80,000
	2,77,500	1,10,000
Dividend declared		
(By S Ltd. in September 2004 out of the profits of 2004-05)	60,000	—
	3,37,500	1,10,000
Less Interim dividend on Preference Shares	(15,000)	—
	3,22,500	1,10,000

(4) Sundry Creditors of H Ltd. include Rs. 80,000 due to S Ltd. for supplies.

(5) Land & Building and Plant & Machinery of S Ltd. were revalued at the beginning of year at Rs. 2,90,000 and Rs. 5,10,000 respectively. These values are to be considered for the Consolidated Balance Sheet and have not been recorded in the books.

(6) Stock includes goods worth Rs. 1,10,400 to S Ltd. supplied by them to H Ltd. for Rs. 1,20,000

(7) Sundry Debtors of H Ltd. include Rs. 60,000 dividend receivable from S Ltd.

(8) Other current assets represent an advance made to S Ltd.

(9) H Ltd. had accepted the bills worth Rs. 37,500 in favour of S Ltd. Of these S Ltd. discounted the bills worth Rs. 12,500 which have not yet matured.

(10) Cash and Bank balances of S Ltd. is net of cheque for repayment of advance from H Ltd. However, H Ltd. did not receive it till 31.3.2004.

(11) H Ltd. acquired shares in S Ltd. at the close of business on 30.6.2004.

Prepare Consolidated Balance Sheet.

[ICWA (F) Dec. 94-Modified]

Solution :

Percentage holding = $\frac{7,200}{7,500} \times 100 = 96\%$

Capital Profits :

Free Reserve (1.4.04)	1,00,000
Profit & Loss A/c (1.4.04)	30,000
Profit for pre-acquisition period (1.05,000 × 3/12)	26,250
Revaluation Profit on :	
Land & Building (2,90,000 – 2,50,000)	40,000
Plant & Machinery (5,10,000 – 4,75,000)	35,000
	2,31,250
H Ltd.'s Share (96%)	2,22,000
Minority Interest (4%)	9,250
Revenue Profit = (Rs. 80,000 + 25,000) (Profit + Free Reserve) 1,05,000 × 9/12)	78,750
H Ltd.'s Share	75,600
Minority Interest	3,150

COST OF CONTROL A/C

	Rs.		Rs.
To Investment *	7,05,000	By Share Capital	7,20,000
Less dividend receivable for pre- acquisition period (1.4.04 to 30.6.04)		By Capital Profits	2,22,000
To Capital Reserve (B.F.)	2,37,000		
	9,42,000		9,42,000

*7,20,000 – 15,000 = 7,05,000

(60,000 × 3/12) = 15,000

MINORITY INTEREST A/C

	Rs.		Rs.
To Balance c/d	42,400	By Share Capital	30,000
		By Capital Profits	9,250
		By Revenue Profits	3,150
	42,400		42,400

CONSOLIDATED BALANCE SHEET
As on 31st March, 2005

Liabilities		Rs.	Assets		Rs.
Share Capital			Fixed Assets :		
12% Perference Share Capital		5,00,000	Goodwill : H Ltd.	5,00,000	
Equity Shares of Rs. 10 each		20,00,000	S Ltd.	1,10,000	
Reserves & Surplus :				6,10,000	
Free Reserves			*Less* Capital Reserve	2,37,000	3,73,000
H Ltd.	6,00,000		Land & Building		
S Ltd.	18,000	6,18,000	H Ltd.	6,00,000	
Profit & Loss A/c			S Ltd.	2,90,000	8,90,000
H Ltd.	3,22,500		Plant & Machinery		
Less Dividend Receivable	60,000		H Ltd.	13,00,000	
	2,62,500		S Ltd.	5,10,000	18,10,000
Add Share in S Ltd.	57,600		Current Assets :		
Less Unrealised Profit	3,20,100		Stock		
	9,600	3,10,500	H Ltd.	3,50,000	
Current liabilities :			S Ltd.	1,25,000	
Bills Payable				4,75,000	
H Ltd.	37,500		*Less* Unrealised Profit	9,600	4,65,400
Less Mutual debt	25,000	12,500	Sundry Debtors		
Sundry Creditors			H Ltd.	5,85,000	
H Ltd.	8,37,500		S Ltd.	1,40,000	
S Ltd.	2,00,000			7,25,000	
	10,37,500		*Less* Mutual debt	80,000	
Less Mutual debt	80,000			6,45,000	
	9,57,500		*Less* Dividend Receivable	60,000	5,85,000
Less Mutual Owings for [(4)] (Dividend receivable)	15,000	9,42,500	Bills Receivable		
			S Ltd.	25,000	
Minority Interest		42,400	*Less* Mutual debt	25,000	—
			Cash & Bank		
			H Ltd.	2,27,500	
			S Ltd.	60,000	2,87,500
			Cheque-in-Transit[(2)]		15,000
			Other Current Assets	15,000	
			Less Mutual owings as per Contra[(4)]	15,000	—
		44,25,900			44,25,900

Working notes :

(1) Profit of S Ltd. of Rs. 80,000 for the year 2004-05 is after transfer of Rs. 25,000 to free reserve. Hence actual profits for the current year are Rs. 1,05,000.

(2) Other current assets representing advance to S Ltd. has been adjusted against mutual debts, the cheque sent by S Ltd. against such advance but not received is shown as cheque in transit.

(3) Dividend declared by S Ltd. in September 04 out of current year's profits not yet paid, and which has been included in the Profit & Loss A/c and Debtors by H Ltd. has been adjusted by means of following entry.

Profit & Loss A/c	60,000	
To S. Debtors		60,000

Since S Ltd. has not recorded any entry for the dividend- the same has not been adjusted to P & L A/c of S Ltd.

(4) The dividend receivable for the pre-acquisition period (1.4.04 to 30.6.04) Rs. 15,000 represents capital receipt hence has been credited to Investment Account. Since this represents a liability of S Ltd. the same has been treated a mutual debt (owings) and hence eliminated from asset side and shown by way of deduction out of creditors of S Ltd.

(5) Dividend Receivable for the post acquisition period has not been given any separate treatment as the same has not been appropriated out of Profit & Loss A/c of S Ltd. as is clear from the statement sowing Profit & Loss Account balance.

Illustration (24) (Dividend paid, dividend proposed, contingent liability and Successive purchase of shares)

Following are the Balance Sheets of H Ltd. and S Ltd. as on 31st March, 2005

Liabilities	H Ltd. Rs.	S Ltd. Rs.
Share Capital		
Equity Shares of Rs. 10 each	7,00,000	1,00,000
General Reserve	50,000	30,000
Profit & Loss Account	1,00,000	30,000
Sundry Creditors	90,000	50,000
Bills Payable	10,000	15,000
Liability for Expenses	5,000	15,000
	9,55,000	2,40,000
Assets		
Land and Building	3,00,000	1,00,000
Plant & Machinery	2,80,000	50,000
7,000 Shares of S Ltd.	1,00,000	—
Stock	70,000	50,000
Sundry Debtors	1,50,000	20,000
Bills Receivable	10,000	—
Cash & Bank balance	45,000	20,000
	9,55,000	2,40,000
Contingent liability for Bills discounted	5,000	—

Additional Information :

(i) All Bills Receivable of H Ltd. including those discounted were accepted by S Ltd.

(ii) When 6,000 shares were purchased by H Ltd., S Ltd. had Rs. 5,000 credit balance in Profit & Loss Account and Rs. 20,000 in General Reserve.

(iii) At the time of acquisition of further 1,000 shares by H Ltd., S Ltd. had Rs. 25,000 in General Reserve and Rs. 28,000 credit balance in Profit & Loss Account from which 20% dividend was paid by S Ltd. and dividend received by H Ltd. on these shares was credited to Profit & Loss Account.

(iv) Stock of S Ltd. include Rs. 20,000 purchased from H Ltd. which has made 25% profit on cost.

(v) Both the companies have proposed dividend- H Ltd. -10% and S Ltd.:- 20% but no effect has been given in the Balance Sheets.

Prepare consolidated Balance Sheet as on 31st March, 2005.

[C.A. (F) Nov. 1990, Modified)

Solution :

First acquisition $= \frac{6,000}{10,000} \times 100 =$ 60%

Second acquisition $= \frac{1,000}{10,000} \times 100 =$ 10%

Total = 70%

Capital Profits (First Acquisition)

General Reserve	20,000
Profit & Loss A/c	5,000
	25,000
H Ltd.'s share (60%)	15,000

Second Acquisition

General Reserve	25,000
Profit & Loss A/c (Rs. 28,000 – 20,000 dividend paid)	8,000
	33,000
H Ltd.'s share (10%)	3300
Total share of H Ltd. in Capital Profits = (15,000 + 3,300)	18,300

COST OF CONTROL A/C

	Rs.		Rs.
To Investment (1,00,000 – 2,000)	98,000	By Share Capital	70,000
		By Capital Profits	18,300
		By Goodwill (B.F.)	9,700
	98,000		98,000

* Dividend wrongly credited to P & L A/c now corrected.

P & L A/C (S LTD.)

	Rs.		Rs.
To Cost of Control A/c (3)	3,800	By Balance c/d	30,000
To Minority Interest	9,000		
To Balance c/d	17,200		
	30,000		30,000

MINORITY INTEREST (30%)

	Rs.		Rs.
To Proposed dividend	6,000	By Share Capital	30,000
To Balance c/d	42,000	By General Reserve	9,000
		By Profit & Loss A/c	9,000
	48,000		48,000

CONSOLIDATED BALANCE SHEET
As on 31st March, 2005

Liabilities		Rs.	Assets		Rs.
Share Capital (Shares of Rs. 10 each)		7,00,000	Fixed Assets:		
Reserve & Surplus			Goodwill		9,700
General Reserve		56,500	Land & Building		
Profit & Loss A/c		41,200	H Ltd.:	3,00,000	
Current Liabilities			S Ltd.:	1,00,000	4,00,000
Sundry Creditors			Plant & Machinery		
H Ltd.	90,000		H Ltd.	2,80,000	
S Ltd.	50,000	1,40,000	S Ltd.	50,000	3,30,000
Expenses O/S			Current Assets		
H Ltd.	5,000		Stock		
S Ltd.	15,000	20,000	H Ltd.	70,000	
Bills Payable			S Ltd.	50,000	
H Ltd.	10,000		*Less* Unrealised Profit	4,000	1,16,000
S Ltd.	15,000		Debtors		
	25,000		H Ltd.	1,50,000	
Less Mutual owings	10,000	15,000	S Ltd.	20,000	1,70,000
Minority Interest		42,000	Bills Receivable		
Proposed Dividend			H Ltd.	10,000	
H Ltd.	70,000		*Less* Mutual owings	10,000	Nil
S Ltd.	6,000	76,000	Cash & Bank		
			H Ltd.	45,000	
			S Ltd.	20,000	65,000
		10,90,700			10,90,700

Working Profit & Loss A/c (H Ltd.)

(1)	Profit & Loss A/c (S Ltd.)		17,200
	Balance of P & L A/c	1,00,000	
Less	Dividend wrongly credited	(2000)	
Less	Unrealised Profit	(4000)	
Less	Proposed dividend	(70,000)	24,000
			41,200

(2) Of the dividend paid by S Ltd. @ 20% on Capital, dividend received on 1000 shares only (Second acquisition) has been credited to Profit & Loss A/c, hence the same has been corrected.

(3) The net amount taken out of Profit & Loss A/c to cost of control A/c arrived as follows:

60% of Rs. 5,000	= (Increase in General Reserve)	3,000
10% Rs. 8,000	= (Increase in General Reserve)	800
(28,000 – 20,000)		3,800

Illustration (25) (Revaluation, Bonus shares, Interest Receivable and contingent liability)

H Ltd. acquired 8,000 shares in S Ltd. on 31st March, 2005. The summarised Balance Sheets of the two companies as on that date were as follows :

Liabilities	H Ltd. Rs.	S Ltd. Rs.
Share Capital (Shares of Rs. 10 each)	3,00,000	1,00,000
Capital Reserve	—	52,000
General Reserve	25,000	5,000
Profit & Loss Account	38,200	18,000
Loans from S Ltd.	2,100	—
Bills Payable (including Rs. 500 to H Ltd.)	—	1,700
Creditors	17,900	5,000
	3,83,200	1,81,700
Assets		
Fixed Assets	1,50,000	1,44,700
Investment in shares of S Ltd. at cost	1,70,000	—
Stock	40,000	20,000
Loan to H Ltd	—	2,000
Bills Receivable (including Rs. 200 from S Ltd.)	1,200	—
Debtors	20,000	10,000
Bank	2,000	5,000
	3,83,200	1,81,700
Contingent liability for Bills discounted	1000	—

Additional Information :

(i) S Ltd. made a bonus issue on 31st March, 2005 of one share for every two shares held, reducing the Capital Reserve equivalently, but the transaction is not shown in the Balance Sheets.

(ii) Interest receivable Rs. 100 in respect of loan due by H Ltd. to S Ltd. has not been credited in the accounts of S Ltd.

(iii) The directors decided that the fixed assets of S Ltd. were over-valued and should be written down by Rs. 5,000

Prepare consolidated Balance Sheet as on 31st March, 2005.

[C.A. (F) May 1995 Modified]

Solution :

$$\text{Percentage holding} = \frac{8,000}{10,000} \times 100 = 80\%$$

Capital Profits

	Rs.
Capital Reserve after Bonus Issue (52,000 – 50,000)	2,000
General Reserve	5,000
Profit & Loss A/c (Rs. 18,000 + Rs. 100 Interest receivable from H Ltd.)	18,100
	25,100
Less Loss on Revaluation	5,000
	20,100
H Ltd. Share (80%)	16,080
Minority Interest (20%)	4,020

COST OF CONTROL A/C

	Rs.		Rs.
To Investment in Shares in S Ltd.	1,70,000	By Share Capital	80,000
		By Bonus Shares	40,000
		By Capital Profit	16,080
		By Goodwill (B.F.)	33,920
	1,70,000		1,70,000

MINORITY INTEREST A/C

	Rs.		Rs.
To Balance c/d	34,020	By Share Capital	20,000
		By Bonus Shares	10,000
		By Capital Profits	4,020
	34,020		34,020

CONSOLIDATED BALANCE SHEET
As On 31st March, 2005

Liabilities		Rs.	Assets		Rs.
Share Capital :		3,00,000	Fixed Assets:		
Shares of Rs. 10 each			Goodwill		33,920
Reserve & Surplus :			Other Fixed Assets		
General Reserve		25,000	H Ltd.	1,50,000	
Profit & Loss A/c		38,200	S Ltd.	1,39,700	2,89,700
Secured Loans			Current Assets		
Loan from S Ltd.	2,100		Stock		
Less Loan to H Ltd.	2,100	Nil	H Ltd.	40,000	
(Incl. Intt. Receivable)			S Ltd.	20,000	60,000
Current liabilities :			Debtors:		
Bill Payable	1,700		H Ltd.	20,000	
Less Mutual debt	200	1,500	S Ltd.	10,000	30,000
Creditors			Bills Receivable	1,200	
H Ltd.	17,900		*Less* Mutual debt	200	1,000
S Ltd.	5,000	22,900	Bank		
Minority Interest		34,020	H Ltd.	2,000	
			S Ltd.	5,000	7,000
		4,21,620			4,21,620

Note : Liability for bill discounted is Rs. 700*

* Of the bills of Rs. 500 accepted by S Ltd. bills for 300 have been discounted because Bill Receivable from S Ltd. for Rs. 200 are still in the hands of H Ltd. Hence of the total contingent liability of Rs. 1,000 Rs. 300 become the sure liability. Thus remaining contingent liability to be shown as a foot note amount to Rs. 700 only.

Illustration (26) (Revaluation and adjustment of depreciation retrospectively)

On 1.4.2002 H Ltd. acquired 8,000 shares of Rs. 100 each in S Ltd. at Rs. 9,00,000. The respective Balance Sheets as on 31st March, 2005 were as under :

	H Ltd.	S Ltd.
Liabilities		
Share Capital Shares of Rs. 100 each	10,00,000	10,00,000
General Reserve	4,00,000	2,60,000
Profit & Loss Account	3,60,000	3,50,000
Creditors	7,10,000	4,80,000
	24,70,000	20,90,000
Assets :		
Fixed Assets	6,00,000	11,00,000
Investments	10,00,000	1,50,000
Debtors	2,50,000	2,00,000
Stock	3,00,000	4,00,000
Bank	3,20,000	2,40,000
	24,70,000	20,90,000

Additional Information :

(i) At the time of acquiring shares S Ltd. had Rs. 2,40,000 in General Reserve and Rs. 1,50,000 in Profit & Loss Account.

(ii) S Ltd. paid 10% dividend in 2002-03,12% in 2003-04, and 15% in 2004-05 for 2001-02, 2002-03 and 2003-04 respectively. All dividends received have been Credited to Profit & Loss A/c of H Ltd.

(iii) Proposed dividend of S Ltd. for the year 2004-05 is 10%.

(iv) One bonus share for every five held has been declared by S Ltd. out of pre-acquisition reserve on 31st March 2005. No effect has been given in the above accounts.

(v) On 1st April 2000, Building of S Ltd. which stood in the books at Rs. 5,00,000 was revalued at Rs. 6,00,000 but no adjustment has been made in the books. Depreciation has been charged @ 10% p.a. on reducing balance method.

(vi) In 2004-05 H Ltd. purchased goods from S Ltd. for Rs. 1,00,000 on which S Ltd. made a profit of 20% on sale price, 25% of such goods were lying unsold on 31st March, 2005.

Prepare Consolidated Balance Sheet. *[CA (F) Modified]*

Solution : Percentage holding = $\frac{8,000 \times 100}{10,000} = 80\%$

Capital Profit :

	General Reserve (1.4.2002)	2,40,000	
Less	Bonus Issue (10,00,000 ×1/5)	2,00,000	40,000
	Profit & Loss A/c (1.4.2002)	1,50,000	
Less	Dividend (For 2001- 02) @ 10%	1,00,000	50,000
	Profit on Revaluation (Rs. 6,00,000 – 5,00,000)		1,00,000
			1,90,000
	H Ltd.'s Share (80%)		1,52,000
	Minority Interest (20%)		38,000

Revenue Profits :

	Profit & Loss A/c (31.3.2005)	3,50,000	
Less	Opening balance (1.4.2002) after dividend (as shown above)	50,000	3,00,000
Less	Depreciation on appreciated Value of Building for 3 years		
	Additional Depreciation on Rs. 1,00,000 @ 10% on W.D.V. basis		
	For the year 2002-03	10,000	
	For the year 2003-04	9,000	
	For the year 2003-04	8,100	27,100
			2,72,900
	H Ltd.'s share :		2,18,320
	Minority Interest:		54,580
	Bonus Shares		2,00,000
	H Ltd.'s Share		1,60,000
	Minority Interest		40,000
	Post- acquisition Reserve (2,60,000 – 2,40,000)		20,000
	H Ltd.'s Share		16,000
	Minority Interest		4,000

COST OF CONTROL A/C

	Rs.		Rs.
To Investments after dividend from pre-acquisition profit (9,00,000–80,000)	8,20,000	By Share Capital	8,00,000
		By Capital Profits	1,52,000
		By Bonus Shares	1,60,000
To Capital Reserve (B.F.)	2,92,000		
	11,12,000		11,12,000

MINORITY INTEREST A/C

To Proposed Dividend	20,000	By Share Capital	2,00,000
To Balance c/d	3,16,580	By Capital Profits	38,000
		By Bonus Shares	40,000
		By Revenue Profits	54,580
		By General Reserve (Post-acquisition)	4,000
	3,36,580		3,36,580

*Unrealised Profit on unsold stock Rs. 20% of (1,00,000 × 25/100) = Rs. 5,000

CONSOLIDATED BALANCE SHEET
As on 31st March 2005

Liabilities		Rs.	Assets		Rs.
Share Capital (Shares of Rs. 100 each)		10,00,000	Fixed Assets		
Reserve & Surplus			H Ltd.		6,00,000
Capital Reserve		2,92,000	S Ltd.	11,00,000	
General Reserve			*Add* Appreciation	1,00,000	
H Ltd.	4,00,000			12,00,000	
S Ltd.	16,000	4,16,000	*Less* Depreciation	27,100	11,72,900
Profit & Loss A/c			Investments		
H Ltd.	3,60,000		H Ltd.	1,00,000	
Less Dividend out of			S Ltd.	1,50,000	2,50,000
Pre-acquisition Profit	80,000		Current Assets		
	2,80,000		H Ltd.	2,50,000	
Add Share in S Ltd.	2,18,320		S Ltd.	2,00,000	4,50,000
	4,98,320		Stock		
Less Unrealised Profit	5,000	4,93,320	H Ltd.	3,00,000	
Current liabilities			S Ltd.	4,00,000	
Creditors				7,00,000	
H Ltd.	7,10,000		Less Unrealised Profit	5,000	6,95,000
S Ltd.	4,80,000	11,90,000	Bank		
Proposed Dividend (S Ltd.)		20,000	H Ltd.	3,20,000	
Minority Interest		3,16,580	S Ltd.	2,40,000	5,60,000
		37,27,900			37,27,900

Illustration (27) (Changing proportion of holding)

On 1.4.03 H Ltd. purchased 80,000 equity shares of Rs. 10 each in S Ltd. When S Ltd. had Rs. 10,00,000 share capital.

On 1.4.2004 it sold 5,000 such shares and purchased 10,000 shares on 1.4.2005.

S Ltd. paid dividend @ 15% each year in September and there was no change in the Share Capital up to 31.3.2006.

Profit and Loss Account balances in S Ltd. and Investments of H Ltd. in S Ltd. on different dates were as under :-

Year ending 31st March	Profit & Loss A/c of S Ltd.	Investments of H Ltd.
	Rs.	Rs.
2003	5,00,000	12,80,000
2004	6,20,000	12,80,000
2005	7,00,000	11,90,000
2006	8,00,000	14,00,000

The amount shown as Investments represent cost price as reduced by sales and increased by further purchase without making any adjustments for profit or loss on sale or purchase or for dividend.

Prepare statements to show the relevant figures as on 31st March, 2004, 2005, and 2006 for preparation of consolidated accounts in respect of :

(i) Goodwill or Cost of Control

(ii) Revenue Profits.

[C. S (F) May 1988 Modified]

Solution :

INVESTMENTS IN SHARES OF S LTD. A/C

		Rs.	31.3.04		Rs.
1.4.03	To Bank (80,000 Shares Purchased)	12,80,000		By P & L A/c (Dividend)	1,20,000
				By Balance c/d	11,60,000
		12,80,000			12,80,000
1.4.04	To Balance b/d	11,60,000	1.4.04	By Bank[(1)] (Sales of 5,000 Shares)	90,000
	To P & L A/c[(1)] (Profit on Sale of Shares)	17,500	31.3.05	By Balance c/d	10,87,500
		11,77,500			11,77,500
1.4.05	To Balance b/d	10,87,500	31.3.06	By P & L A/c[(2)] (Dividend)	15,000
	To Bank[(3)] (Purchase of Shares)	2,10,000		By Balance c/d	12,82,500
		12,97,500			12,97,500

(1) Sale proceeds of 5000 shares Rs. 12,80,00 – 11,90,000 = 90,000

Cost of 5000 shares (after dividend) $\left(\dfrac{11,60,000 \times 5000}{80,000}\right) =$ 72,500

Profit on sale of shares 17,500

(2) Dividend on 10,000 shares @ 15% Rs. 15,000.

(3) Purchase price of 10,000 shares – Rs. 14,00,000 – 11,90,000 = 2,10,000

STATEMENT SHOWING CAPITAL AND REVENUE PROFIT

Capital Profits as on 31.3.2004	Rs.
Profit & Loss A/c	5,00,000
(1.4.2003) *Less* Dividend @ 15% on Rs. 10,00,000	1,50,000
	3,50,000
H Ltd.'s share (80%)	2,80,000
Capital Profits As on 31.3.2005 (After H Ltd. Sold 5000 shares)	
Capital profits will be = 3,50,000 × 75% = (75,000/1,00,000 ×100 =75%)=	2,62,500
Capital Profits as on 31.3.2006 (After H Ltd. Purchased 10000 Shares)	
Profit & Loss A/c	7,00,000
Less 15% Dividend	1,50,000
	5,50,000
H Ltd.'s share (On 1000 shares) (10%) (10,000/1,00,000 ×100)	55,000
Add H Ltd.'s share on 75,000 shares calculated as above	2,62,500
Total Capital Profits	3,17,500

COST CONTROL A/C

31.3.04	Rs.		Rs.
To Investment in Shares in S Ltd. A/c (after dividend)	11,60,000	By Share Capital (80,000 Shares)	8,00,000
		By Capital Profits	2,80,000
		By Goodwill (B.F.)	80,000
	11,60,000		11,60,000
31.3.05			
To Investment in Shares in S Ltd. A/c	10,87,500	By Share Capital (75,000 Shares)	7,50,000
		By Capital Profits	2,62,500
		By Goodwill	75,000
	10,87,500		10,87,500
31.3.06			
To Investment in Shares in S Ltd. A/c	12,82,500	By Share Capital (85,000 Shares)	8,50,000
		By Capital Profits	3,17,500
		By Goodwill	1,15,000
	12,82,500		12,82,500

Revenue Profit	31.3.04 Rs.	31.3.05 Rs.	31.3.06 Rs.
Balance of P & L A/c	6,20,000	7,00,000	8,00,000
Less Capital Profits (31.3.04)	3,50,000	3,50,000	3,50,000
	2,70,000	3,50,000	4,50,000
Less Minority Interest (20%)	(54,000)	—	—
Less Minority Interest (25%)	—	(87,500)	—
Less Minority Interest (15%)	—	—	(67,500)
Less additional Capital Profits*	—	—	(20,000)
H Ltd.'s Share	2,16,000	2,62,500	3,62,500

*** Calculation of Additional Capital Profit**

		Rs.
	Balance of P & L A/c as on 31.3.2005	7,00,000
Less	dividend @ 15% on Rs. 10,00,000	1,50,000
		5,50,000
	Capital Profit already accounted for	3,50,000
		2,00,000
	Additional Capital Profit	
	H Ltd.'s share on additional acquisition 10%	20,000

Illustration (28) (Revaluation, dividend & Unrealised profit)

The following balances have been extracted from the books of H Ltd. and S Ltd. as on 31st March, 2005.

Liabilities	H Ltd.	S Ltd.
	Rs.	Rs.
Share Capital (Shares of Rs. 100 each)	6,00,000	1,00,000
General Reserve	60,000	20,000
Capital Reserve	1,00,000	30,000
Profit & Loss A/c	80,000	10,000

On 31st December, 2004, H Ltd. acquired 600 shares in S Ltd. by the issue to S Ltd. 1,200 shares in H Ltd. at a premium of Rs. 25 per share.

At the date of acquisition the fixed assets of S Ltd. were revalued and written-up by Rs. 1,00,000, the increase being added to Capital Reserve.

The profit of S Ltd. for the year ended 31st March, 2005 amounted to Rs. 1,20,000 and that of H Ltd. Rs. 1,60,000. The profits accrue evenly throughout the year.

At 31st March, 2005 dividends were recommended for the year 2004-05 @ 10% for H Ltd. and 15% for S Ltd. in respect of shares in issue at the close of the year.

The stock of S Ltd. included goods invoiced by H Ltd. in February 05 at a profit of Rs. 1000.

You are required to show how the relevant items would appear in the Consolidated Balance Sheet.

[ICWA (F) December, 1989 Modified]

Solution :

Percentage holding $\frac{600}{1,000} \times 100 = 60\%$

Capital Profits :

General Reserve	20,000
Capital Reserve	30,000
Profit & Loss A/c	10,000
Profit of the current year for pre-acquisition period (1.4.04 to 31.12.04) $\left(\text{Rs.}1,20,000 \times \frac{9}{12}\right)$	90,000
Profit on Revaluation of Fixed Assets	1,00,000
	2,50,000
H Ltd.'s Share (60%)	1,50,000
Minority Interest (40%)	1,00,000

Revenue Profits

Profit of the current year (1.1.2005 to 31.3.05) $\left(\text{Rs.}1,20,000 \times \frac{3}{12}\right)$	30,000
H Ltd.'s Share	18,000
Minority Interest	12,000
Cost of Investment 1,200 Shares @ 125	1,50,000

COST OF CONTROL A/C

	Rs.		Rs.
To Investment at cost	1,50,000	By Share Capital	60,000
To Capital Reserve (B.F.)	60,000	By Capital Profit	1,50,000
	2,10,000		2,10,000

MINORITY INTEREST A/C

	Rs.		Rs.
To Proposed Dividend	6,000	By Share Capital	40,000
To Balance c/c	1,46,000	By Capital Profits	1,00,000
		By Revenue Profit	12,000
	1,52,000		1,52,000

CONSOLIDATED BALANCE SHEET (RELEVANT ITEMS)
As on 31st March, 2005

Liabilities		Rs.
Share Capital (1) Shares of Rs. 100 each		7,20,000
Reserve & Surplus:		
Securities Premium (2)		30,000
Capital Reserve		1,60,000
Profit & Loss A/c (3)		1,97,000
General Reserve		60,000
Minority Interest		1,46,000
Proposed Dividend		
H Ltd.	60,000	
S Ltd.	6,000	66,000
		13,79,000

(1)	Share Capital (6,000 + 1200 Shares issued to S Ltd.)	7,20,000
(2)	Securities Premium 1200 Shares @ Rs. 25 per Share	30,000

PROFIT & LOSS A/C (H LTD.)

	Rs.		Rs.
To Proposed dividend	60,000	By Balance b/d	80,000
To Balance c/d	1,80,000	By Net Profit	1,60,000
	2,40,000		2,40,000

	Profit balance	1,80,000
Add	Share of Profit in S Ltd.	18,000
		1,98,000
Less	Unrealised Profit	1,000
		1,97,000

Illustration (29) (Dividend and treatment of hire purchase transaction)

Following are the Balance Sheets of H Ltd. and S Ltd. as on 31st March, 2005.

Liabilities	H Ltd. Rs.	S Ltd. Rs.
Equity Share Capital (Shares of Rs. 10 each)	5,00,000	2,00,000
General Reserve	2,40,000	1,00,000
Profit & Loss A/c	57,200	82,000
Bank Overdraft	80,000	—
Bills Payable	—	8,400
Creditors	47,100	9,000
	9,24,300	3,99,400
Assets		
Land & Building	1,50,000	1,80,000
Plant & Machinery	2,40,000	1,35,000
Investments in S Ltd.	3,40,000	—
Stock	1,20,000	36,400
Debtors	44,000	40,000
Bills Receivable	15,800	—
Cash	14,500	8,000
	9,24,300	3,99,400

H Ltd. had acquired 16,000 shares of S Ltd. On 1st October, 2004. The Profit and Loss Account of S Ltd. stood at Rs. 30,000 (Cr.) On 31st March, 2004 out of which a dividend of 10% was paid on 1st November, 2004.

H Ltd. had credited its share of dividend to its profit & Loss A/c. H Ltd. had sold an item of Machinery to S Ltd. on hire purchase basis whose details are as under :

	Rs.
Investments due	5,000
Investments not due	2,000
Hire Purchase stock Reserve	500

Prepare consolidated Balance Sheet as on 31st March, 2005.

[*CA (F) OS Modified*]

Solution :

Percentage holding $\frac{16,000}{20,000} \times 100 = 80\%$

Capital Profits:		Rs.
	Profit & Loss A/c	30,000
Less	Dividend	20,000
		10,000

General Reserve	1,00,000
Current year profit for pre-acquisition period (1.4.04 to 30.9.04)	
(82,000 – Op. Balance Rs. 10,000) $\frac{72,000 \times 6}{12}$	36,000
	1,46,000
H Ltd.'s Share (80%)	1,16,800
Minority Interest (20%)	29,200

Revenue Profit

(1.10.04 to 31.3.05)	36,000
H Ltd.'s Share	28,800
Minority Interest	7,200

COST OF CONTROL A/C

	Rs.		Rs.
To Investment (3,40,000 – 16,000)	3,24,000	By Share Capital	1,60,000
		By Capital Profits	1,16,800
		By Goodwill	47,200
	3,24,000		3,24,000

MINORITY INTEREST A/C

	Rs.		Rs.
To Balance c/d	76,400	By Share Capital	40,000
		By Capital Profit	29,200
		By Revenue Profit	7,200
	76,400		76,400

CONSOLIDATED BALANCE SHEET
As on 31st March, 2005

Liabilities	Rs.	Assets		Rs.
Share Capital	5,00,000	Fixed Assets :		
Equity Shares of Rs. 10 each		Goodwill		47,200
Reserve & Surplus :		Land & Building		
General Reserve	2,40,000	H Ltd.	1,50,000	
Profit & Loss A/c[(1)]	68,600	S Ltd..	1,80,000	3,30,000
Current Liabilities :		Plant & Machinery[(2)]		3,73,600
Bank Overdraft	80,000	Current Assets :		
Bill Payable	8,400	Stock[(3)]		1,54,400
Creditors[(5)]	49,100	Debtors[(4)]		79,000
Minority Interest	76,400	Bill Receivable		15,800
		Cash		
		H Ltd.	14,500	
		S Ltd.	8,000	22,500
	10,22,500			10,22,500

Working Notes

(1) Profit & Loss A/c (H Ltd.)

			Rs.
	Balance		57,200
Less	Dividend wrongly credited		16,000
			41,200
Add	Share in revenue profit of S Ltd.		28,800
			70,000
Less	Unrealised Profit included in Instalments due $\left(\frac{400*}{2,000} \times 5,000\right)$	1000	
Less	Unrealised Profit on H P. Stock (Instalments not due)	400	1,400*
			68,600

(2) Plant & Machinery

	H Ltd.		2,40,000
	S Ltd.		1,35,000
			3,75,000
Less	Unrealised Profit*		1,400
			3,73,600

(3) Stock

	H Ltd.		1,20,000
	S Ltd.		36,400
			1,56,400
Less	Investment not due		2,000
			1,54,400

(4) Debtors

	H Ltd.	44,000	
	S Ltd.	40,000	84,000
Less	Investments due		5,000
			79,000

(5) S Creditors

	H Ltd.		47,100
	S Ltd.		9,000
			56,100
Less	Investment due	5,000	
	Investment not due	2,000	7,000
			49,100

***Unrealised profit included in "Instalments due" and "Instalments not due" has been workedout to the extent of 80% being percentage holding.**

Illustration (30) (Dividend Corporate dividend tax, Bonus Issue and Unrealised Profit)

On 31st March, 2005, the Balance Sheets of H Ltd. and S. Ltd. stood as follows :

Liabilities	H Ltd.	S Ltd.
	Rs.	Rs.
Equity Share Capital (Authorised)	50,00,000	30,00,000
Issued & Subscribed Capital (Shares of Rs. 10 each fully paid)	40,00,000	24,00,000
General Reserve	9,28,000	690,000
Profit & Loss A/c	13,05,000	8,10,000
Bills Payable	1,24,000	80,000
S Creditors	4,87,000	4,27,000
Provision for Taxation	2,20,000	1,80,000
Other Provisions	65,000	17,000
	71,29,000	46,04,000
Assets		
Plant & Machinery	25,41,000	24,50,000
Furniture & Fittings	6,15,000	2,98,000
Investment in Equity Shares of S Ltd.	15,00,000	—
Stock	9,83,000	7,86,000
Debtors	7,00,000	6,83,000
Bills Receivable	1,20,000	95,000
Cash & Bank balance	4,10,000	1,02,000
Sundry Advances	2,60,000	1,90,000
	71,29,000	46,04,000

Additional Information :

(i) H Ltd. purchased 90,000 Equity Shares of S Ltd. on 1st April, 2004 when the following balances stood in the books of S Ltd.:

General Reserve	Rs.	15,00,000
Profit & Loss A/c	Rs.	6,33,000

(ii) On 24th July, 2004 S Ltd. declared a dividend of 20% out of pre-acquisition profits and paid corporate dividend tax *(Including surcharge) at 11% H Ltd. credited the dividend received to its Profit & Loss A/c.

(iii) On 19th November, 2004 S Ltd. issued 3 fully paid Equity Shares of Rs. 10 each for every 5 shares held as bonus shares out of pre-acquisition General Reserve.

(iv) On 31st March, 2005, the Stock of S Ltd. included goods purchased for Rs. 50,000 from H Ltd. which made a profit of 25% on cost. Prepare consolidated Balance Sheet as on 31st March 2005.

[CA (F) Nov., 2002 Modified

Note : The current rate of corporate dividend tax is 14.025% i.e.,[12.5% + 10% Surcharge + 2% Education cess). But for the sake of convenience the then rate prevailing in 2002 have not been changed

Solution :

	Equity Shares after bonus issue =		2,40,000
	Equity Shares before bonus Issue = 2,40,000 × 5/8 =		1,50,000
	Percentage holding = $\frac{90,000}{1,50,000} \times 100 = 60\%$		
	Bonus issue $\frac{1,50,000 \times 3}{5}$ = 90,000 Shares		9,00,000
	H Ltd.'s Share (60%)		5,40,000
	Minority Interest (40%)		3,60,000
Capital Profits:			
	General Reserve (1.4.04)		15,00,000
Less	Bonus Issue		9,00,000
			6,00,000
	Profit & Loss A/c (1.4.04)	6,33,000	
Less	Dividend @ 20% on Rs. 15,00,000	(3,00,000)	
	Corporate Dividend Tax @ 11%	(33,000)	3,00,000
			9,00,000
	H Ltd.'s Share (60%)		5,40,000
	Minority Interest (40%)		3,60,000

COST OF CONTROL A/C

	Rs.		Rs.
To Investments in Shares of S Ltd. (Rs. 15,00,000 – dividend* (Rs. 1,80,000)	13,20,000	By Equity Share Capital	9,00,000
		By Bonus Issue	5,40,000
		By Capital Profits	5,40,000
To Capital Reserve (B.F.)	6,60,000		
	19,80,000		19,80,000

* 60% of Rs. 3,00,000 = 1,80,000

MINORITY INTEREST A/C

To Balance c/d	15,60,000	By Equity Share Capital	6,00,000
		By Bonus Issue	3,60,000
		By Capital Profit	3,60,000
		By Revenue Profits	2,40,000
	15,60,000		15,60,000

PROFIT & LOSS A/C (ADJ.)

To Proposed Dividend	3,00,000	By Balance b/d	6,33,000
To Corporate Dividend Tax	33,000	By Net Profit	6,00,000
To Transfer to General Reserve	90,000		
To Balance c/d	8,10,000		
	12,33,000		12,33,000

Revenue Profit	6,00,000
H Ltd. Share (60%)	3,60,000
Minority Interest	2,40,000

CONSOLIDATED BALANCE SHEET
As on 31st March, 2005

Liabilities		Rs.	Assets		Rs.
Equity Share Capital (Authorised)		50,00,000	Fixed Assets:		
Issued & Subscribed Capital		40,00,000	Plants & Machinery		
(Shares of Rs. 10 each)			H Ltd.	25,41,000	
Reserve & Surplus			S Ltd.	24,50,000	49,91,000
General Reserve [1]		9,82,000	Furniture & Fittings		
Capital Reserve		6,60,000	H Ltd.	6,15,000	
Profit & Loss A/c[2]		14,21,000	S Ltd.	2,98,000	9,13,000
Current Liabilities and Provisions:			Current Assets :		
Bills Payable			Stock		
H Ltd.	1,24,000		H Ltd.	9,83,000	
S Ltd.	80,000	2,04,000	S Ltd.	7,86,000	
Sundry Creditors				17,69,000	
H. Ltd.	4,87,000		*Less* Unrealised Profit	10,000	17,59,000
S Ltd.	4,27,000	9,14,000	Debtors		
Provision for Taxation			H Ltd.	7,00,000	
H Ltd.	2,20,000		S Ltd.	6,83,000	13,83,000
S Ltd.	1,80,000	4,00,000	Bills Receivable		
Other Provisions			H Ltd.	1,20,000	
H Ltd.	65,000		S Ltd.	95,000	2,15,000
S Ltd.	17,000	82,000	S Advances		
Minority Interest		15,60,000	H Ltd.	2,60,000	
			S Ltd.	1,90,000	4,50,000
			Cash & Bank		5,12,000
		102,23,000			102,23,000

(1)	General Reserve (H Ltd.)	9,28,000
	60% of Rs. 90,000 transferred by S Ltd.	54,000
		9,82,000
(2)	**Profit & Loss A/c (H Ltd.)**	
	Balance as on 31.3.05 as per Balance Sheet	13,05,000
Less	Dividend Wrongly credited	1,80,000
		11,25,000
Add	Share in Revenue Profits (Rs. 3,60,000 – 54,000 transferred to General Reserve)	3,06,000
		14,31,000
Less	Unrealised Profit	10,000
	(Rs. 50,000 × 25/125)	14,21,000

Illustration (31) (Bonus Issue out of post acquisition profit)

On 31st March, 2000 H Ltd. acquired 1,05,000 shares of S Ltd. for Rs. 12,00,000 when the Balance Sheet of S Ltd. was as under :

Liabilities	Rs.	Assets	Rs.
1,50,000 Equity Shares of Rs. 10 each	15,00,000	Fixed Assets	10,50,000
Pre-incorporation Profit	30,000	Current Assets	6,45,000
Profit & Loss A/c	60,000		
Creditors	1,05,000		
	16,95,000		16,95,000

On 31st March, 2005 the Balance Sheet of two companies were as follows :

	H Ltd.	S Ltd.
Liabilities	Rs.	Rs.
Equity Shares of Rs. 10 each (before bonus issue)	45,00,000	15,00,000
Securities Premium	9,00,000	—
Pre incorporation Reserve		30,000
General Reserve	60,00,000	19,05,000
Profit & Loss A/c	15,75,000	4,20,000
Creditors	5,55,000	2,10,000
	135,30,000	40,65,000
Assets		
Fixed Assets	79,20,000	23,10,000
Investment in Shares of S Ltd. at cost	12,00,000	—
Current Assets	44,10,000	17,55,000
	135,30,000	40,65,000

Additional Information :

Directors of S Ltd. made bonus issue on 31st March, 2005 in the ratio of one equity shares of Rs. 10 each fully paid for every two equity shares held on that date.

Calculate (i) Cost of control/capital Reserve (ii) Minority Interest and prepare a consolidated Balance Sheet presuming that bonus issue was made out of post acquisition profits by using General Reserve.

[CA (F) May 2003]

Solution :

Percentage holding $= \frac{1,05,000 \times 100}{1,50,000} = 70\%$

Capital Profits :

	Rs.
Pre-incorporation Profits	30,000
Profit & Loss A/c (31.3.2000)	60,000
	90,000
H Ltd.'s Shares (70%)	63,000
Minority Interest (30%)	27,000

Bonus Issue

$1,50,000 \times \frac{1}{2} \times 10$	7,50,000
H Ltd.'s Share (70%)	5,25,000
Minority Interest	2,25,000

Revenue Profit

	General Reserve Balance as on 31.3.2005	19,05,000
Less	Opening balance (31.3.2000)	—
Less	Bonus Issue	7,50,000
		11,55,000
Add	Profit for the period (1.4.2000 to 31.3.2005) (4,20,000 – 60,000)	3,60,000
		15,15,000
	H Ltd.'s Share	10,60,500
	Minority Interest	4,54,500

COST OF CONTROL A/C

	Rs.		Rs.
To Investment in Shares of S Ltd.	12,00,000	By Share Capital	10,50,000
To Capital Reserve	4,38,000	By Capital Profits	63,000
		By Bonus Issue	5,25,000
	16,38,000		16,38,000

MINORITY INTEREST A/C

	Rs.		Rs.
To Balance c/d	11,56,500	By Share Capital	4,50,000
		By Bonus Issue	2,25,000
		By Capital Profit	27,000
		By Revenue Profits	4,54,500
	11,56,500		11,56,500

Profit & Loss A/c (H Ltd.)

	Balance as on 31.3.2005	15,75,000
Add	Share of Profit in S Ltd.	10,60,500
		26,35,500

CONSOLIDATED BALANCE SHEET
As on 31st March, 2005

Liabilities		Rs.	Assets		Rs.
Share Capital (Shares of Rs. 10 each)		45,00,000	Fixed Assets:		
Reserve & Surplus :			H Ltd.	79,20,000	
Securities Premium		9,00,000	S Ltd.	23,10,000	102,30,000
Capital Reserve		4,38,000	Current Assets		
General Reserve		60,00,000	H Ltd.	44,10,000	
Profit & Loss A/c		26,35,500	S Ltd.	17,55,000	61,65,000
Current Liabilities :					
Creditors					
H Ltd.	5,55,000				
S Ltd.	2,10,000	7,65,000			
Minority Interest		11,56,500			
		1,63,95,000			1,63,95,000

Illustration (32) Dividend correctly recorded, Revaluation and hire purchase instalments)

The following are the summarised Balance Sheets of H Ltd. and S Ltd. as on 31st March 2005.

Liabilities	H Ltd.	S Ltd.
	Rs.	Rs.
Authorised Capital (Shares of Rs. 10 each)	70,00,000	30,00,000
Issued & Subscribed Capital	50,00,000	20,00,000
Equity Shares of Rs. 10 each		
Capital Reserve	5,00,000	3,10,000
Revenue Reserve	8,50,000	75,000
Profit & Loss A/c	4,00,000	2,80,000
Sundry Creditors	2,50,000	2,25,000
Bills payable	1,00,000	10,000
	71,00,000	29,00,000
Assets		
Land & Building	20,00,000	15,20,000
Plant & Machinery	20,00,000	8,00,000
Furniture	5,00,000	1,60,000
Investments	16,10,000	—
Stock	3,40,000	1,00,000
Debtors	3,60,000	2,00,000
Bills Receivable	50,000	40,000
Cash & Bank	2,40,000	80000
	71,00,000	29,00,000

Additional Information :

(i) H Ltd. acquired 80% shares of S Ltd. on 30.9.2004 at a cost of Rs. 18,10,000. On 1.10. 2004 S Ltd. declared and paid dividend on equity shares. H Ltd. appropriately adjusted its shares of dividend in Investment Account.

(ii) On 1.4.2004 the Capital Reserve and Profit and Loss A/c stood in the books of S Ltd. at Rs. 50,000 and Rs. 2,75,000 respectively.

(iii) Land and Building standing in the books of S Ltd. at Rs. 16,00,000 on 1.4.2004 revalued at Rs. 20,00,000 on 1.10.2004 Furniture which stood in the books at Rs. 2,00,000 on 1.4.2004 revalued at Rs. 1,50,000 on 1.10.2004. In both the cases effects have not yet been given in the books.

(iv) S Ltd. bought an items of machinery from H Ltd. on hire-purchase basis. The following are the balances in respect of this machinery in the books on 31.3.2005.

Instalments due	20,000
Instalments not due	8,000
Hire purchase Stock Reserve	1,600

The above items stood included under appropriate heads in Balance Sheet of H Ltd. and it's subsidiary S Ltd. at 31st March, 2005 complying with the requirements of AS-21.

[CA (F) Nov. 2004]

Solution:

Capital Profits

		Rs.
	Capital Reserve (1.4.2004)	50,000
	Profit & Loss A/c (1.4.2004) Less Dividend	*25,000
	*Current year's Profit (Pre- Acq.) (1.4.2004 to 30.9.2004)	2,95,000
	Profit on Revaluation on Land & Building (1)	4,40,000
Less	Loss on Revaluation of Furniture (2)	(30,000)
		7,80,000
	H Ltd.'s Share	6,24,000
	Minority Interest	1,56,000

***PROFIT & LOSS APPROPREATION A/C**

	Rs.		Rs.
To Dividend	2,50,000	By Balance b/d	2,75,000
To Revenue Reserve	75,000	By Net Profit earned during the year	5,90,000
To Capital Reserve (3,10,000 – 50,000)	2,60,000		
To Balance c/d	2,80,000		
	8,65,000		8,65,000

COST OF CONTROL A/C

	Rs.		Rs.
To Investment in Shares of S Ltd. (Actual Cost Less dividend)	16,10,000	By Share Capital	16,00,000
		By Capital Profit	6,24,000
To Capital Reserve (B.F.)	6,14,000		
	22,24,000		22,24,000

CONSOLIDATED BALANCE SHEET
As on 31st March, 2005

Liabilities		Rs.	Assets		Rs.
Share Capital :			Fixed Assets :		
Authorised Share Capital		70,00,000	Land & Building		
Issued & Subscribed :			H Ltd.	20,00,000	
Equity Shares of Rs. 10 each		50,00,000	S Ltd.	19,50,000[1]	39,50,000
Reserves & Serplus[3]		12,18,000	Plant & Machinery		
Revenue Reserve[4]		8,80,000	H Ltd.	20,00,000	
Profit & Loss A/c[5]		4,92,400	S Ltd.	8,00,000	
Current Liabilities & Provisions :			*Less* Unrealised Profit	28,00,000	
S Creditors			on hire purchase	5,600	27,94,400
H Ltd.	2,50,000		Furniture		
S Ltd.	2,25,000		H Ltd.	5,00,000	
	4,75,000		S Ltd.	1,35,000[2]	6,35,000
Less H.P. Mutual owings	28,000	4,47,000	Current Assets :		
Bills Payable			Stock		
H Ltd.	1,00,000		H Ltd.	3,40,000	
S Ltd.	10,000	1,10,000	S Ltd.	1,00,000	
Minority Interest[6]		6,14,000		4,40,000	
			Less Instalments not due	8,000	4,32,000
			S Debtors		
			H Ltd.	3,60,000	
			S Ltd.	2,00,000	
			Less Instalments due	(20,000)	5,40,000
			Bills Receivable		90,000
			Cash at Bank		3,20,000
		87,61,400			87,61,400

Working notes :

		Rs.
(1)	Profit on Revaluation of Land & Building :	
	Revised Value as on 1.10.2004	20,00,000
Less	Written down as on 1.10.2004	15,60,000
	(Rs. 16,00,000 as on 1.4.2004	4,40,000
Less	Rs. 40,000 Depreciation for 6 months @ 5% p.a.)	
(2)	*Loss* on Revaluation of Furniture Revised Value as on 1.10.2004	1,50,000
Less	Written down Value on 1.10.2004	1,80,000
	(Rs. 2,00,000 W.D.V. as on 1.4.2004	30,000
Less	Rs. 20,000 Depreciation for 6 months @ 20% p.a.)	

(3) Capital Reserve

		Rs.
	Capital Reserve of H Ltd. as per Balance Sheet	5,00,000
Add.	Capital Reserve as per Cost of Control A/c	6,14,000
Add	Share in S Ltd. (80% (1/2 of Rs. 2,60,000) (Transfer out of post acquisition profit)	1,04,000
		12,18,000

(4) Revenue Reserve

	H Ltd.	8,50,000
	Share in S Ltd. (80% of (1/2 of Rs. 75,000)	30,000
		8,80,000

(5) Profit & Loss A/c

	H Ltd.	4,00,000
Add	Share of profit in S Ltd. (++)	98,000
		4,98,000
Less	Unrealised Profit on hire purchase transaction*	(5,600)
		4,92,400
	*Stock Reserve on H.P. stock	1,600
	Stock Reserve on Instalments due $\left(\frac{1,600}{8,000}\times 20,000\right)$	4,000
		5,600

(6) MINORITY INTEREST

	Rs.		Rs.
To Balance c/d	6,14,000	By Share Capital	4,00,000
		By Capital Profit	1,56,000
		By Revenue Profit	58,000*
	6,14,000		6,14,000

* **Post Acquisition Profit.** (1.10.2004 to 31.3.2005)

	Half of Rs. 5,90,000	2,95,000
Less	Additional Deprecation on Land & Building	(10,000)
		2,85,000
Add	Excess depreciation on Furniture	5,000
		2,90,000
	H Ltd.'s Share	2,32,000
	Minority Interest	58,000

(++)	H Ltd.'s share in Revenue Profit	2,32,000
Less	Transfer to **Capital** Reserve	(1,04,000)
Less	Transfer to **General** Reserve	(30,000)
		98,000

(7) Land & Building (S Ltd.)

		Rs.
	Book Value as per Balance Sheet (31.3.2005)	15,20,000
Add	Appreciation	4,40,000
		19,60000
Less	Additional Depreciation	10,000
		19,50,000

(8) Furniture (S Ltd.)

		Rs.
	Book value as per Balance Sheet (31.3.2005)	1,60,000
Less	Loss on Revaluation	30,000
		1,30,000
Add	Excess depreciation	5,000
		1,35,000

Illustration : (33) (Dividend, Bonus Issue, Preference Shares and successive acquisition of Equity shares)

The Balance Sheets of H Ltd. and it's subsidiary S Ltd. as on 31st March, 2005 were as follows.

Liabilities		
Equity shares of Rs. 10 each	48,00,000	20,00,000
10% Preference Shares of Rs. 10 each	7,00,000	3,80,000
General Reserve	5,50,000	4,20,000
Profit & Loss A/c	10,00,000	6,00,000
Bank Overdraft	1,20,000	70,000
S Creditors	4,30,000	4,80,000
Bills Payable	—	1,60,000
	76,00,000	41,10,000
Assets		
Goodwill	4,50,000	3,00,000
Plant & Machinery	12,00,000	5,00,000
Motor Vehicles	9,50,000	7,50,000
Furniture & Fittings	6,50,000	4,00,000
Investments	26,00,000	4,50,000
Stock	4,50,000	7,20,000
Debtors	9,30,000	7,80,000
Bills Receivable	1,45,000	—
Cash at Bank	2,25,000	2,10,000
	76,00,000	41,10,000

Details of acquisition of shares by H Ltd. are as under :

Nature of Shares	No. of Shares	Date of Acquisition	Cost of Acquisition
Preference Shares	14,250	1-4-2002	3,10,000
Equity Shares	80,000	1-4-2003	9,50,000
Equity Shares	70,000	1-4-2004	8,00,000

Other Information :

(i) On 1.4.2004 Profit & Loss A/c and General Reserve of S Ltd. had credit balances of Rs. 3,00,000 and Rs. 2,00,000 respectively.

(ii) Dividend @ 10% was paid by S Ltd. for the year 2003-04 out of its Profit & Loss A/c balance as on 1.4.2004. H Ltd. credited it's share of dividend to Profit & Loss A/c.

(iii) S Ltd. allotted bonus shares out of General Reserve at the rate of 1 share for every 10 shares held. Accounting thereof has not yet been made.

(iv) Bills Receivable of H Ltd. were drawn upon S Ltd.

(v) During the year 2004-05 H Ltd. purchased goods from S Ltd. Rs. 1,00,000 at a sale price of Rs. 1,20,000 40% of these goods remained unsold at the close of the year.

(vi) On 1.4.2004 Motor vehicles of S Ltd. were over valued by Rs. 1,00,000. Applicable depreciation rate is 20%.

(vii) Dividends recommended for the year 2004-05 in the holding and the subsidiary companies are 15% and 10% respectively.

Prepare Consolidated Balance Sheet as on 31st March, 2005.

[C.A. (F) May 2005. Modified]

Solution :

$$\text{Percentage holding} = \frac{1,50,000}{2,00,000} \times 100 = 75\%$$

Capital Profits		Rs.	Rs.
	General Reserve (1.4.04)	2,00,000	
Less	Bonus Issue	2,00,000	—
	Profit & Loss A/c (1.4.04)	3,00,000	
Less	Dividend for 2003-04 (10% of Rs. 20,00,000)	2,00,000	1,00,000
Less	Loss on Revaluation of Motor Vehicle		(1,00,000)
			Nil
Revenue Profits			
	Profit & Loss A/c as per Balance Sheet		6,00,000
Less	Balance as on 1.4.2004		1,00,000
	(after dividend)		5,00,000
Add	Transfer to General Reserve (Rs. 4,20,000 – 2,00,000)		2,20,000
			7,20,000
Add	Excess Depreciation charged on Motor		20,000
			7,40,000
Less	Preference dividend for 2004-05		38,000
			7,02,000
	Total Revenue Profit		7,02,000
	H Ltd.'s share (75%)		5,26,500
	Minority Interest (25%)		1,75,500

COST OF CONTROL A/C

		Rs.		Rs.
To Investments	20,00,000		By Shares Capital	15,00,000
(*Less* Dividend out of			By Equity Bonus Issue	1,50,000
Pre-acquisition Profit)	70,000	19,90,000	By Preference Share Capital	1,42,500
			By Goodwill (B.F.)	1,97,500
		19,90,000		19,90,000

MINORITY INTEREST

	Rs.		Rs.
To Balance	9,86,750	By Equity Share Capital	5,00,000
		By Bonus Issue	50,000
		By Preference Share Capital	2,37,500
		By Revenue Profit	1,75,500
		By Proposed Preference dividend	23,750
	9,86,750		9,86,750.

CONSOLIDATED BALANCE SHEET
As on 31st March, 2005

Liabilities		Rs.	Assets		Rs.
Share Capital			Fixed Assets		
Authorised Issued & Paid up Capital			Goodwill		9,47,500
Equity Shares of Rs 10 each		48,00,000	Plant & Machinery		
10% Preference Shares of Rs. 10 each		7,00,000	H Ltd.	12,00,000	
General Reserve[1]		7,15,000	S Ltd.	5,00,000	17,00,000
Profit & Loss A/c[2]		5,07,750	Motor Vehicle		
Current Liabilities & Provisions :			H Ltd.	9,50,000	
Bank Overdraft			S Ltd.	6,70,000[3]	16,20,000
H Ltd.	1,20,000		Furniture & Fittings		
S Ltd.	70,000	1,90,000	H Ltd.	6,50,000	
Sundry Creditors			S Ltd.	4,00,000	10,50,000
H Ltd.	4,30,000		Investments		
S Ltd.	4,80,000	9,10,000	H Ltd.	5,40,000[4]	
Bills Payable			S Ltd.	4,50,000	9,90,000
H Ltd.	1,60,000		Current Assets		
Less Mutual Owings	1,45,000	15,000	Stock		
Proposed Dividend			H Ltd.	4,50,000	
Equity (H Ltd.)		7,20,000	S Ltd.	7,20,000	
Preference (H Ltd.)		70,000		11,70,000	
Minority Interest		9,86,750	*Less* Unrealised Profit	8,000	11,62,000

CONSOLIDATED BALANCE SHEET

Liabilities	Rs.	Assets		Rs.
		Debtors		
		H Ltd.	9,30,000	
		S Ltd.	7,80,000	17,10,000
		Bills Receivable		
		H Ltd.	1,45,000	
		Less Mutual owings	1,45,000	—
		Cash at Bank		
		H Ltd.	2,25,000	
		S Ltd.	2,10,000	4,35,000
	96,14,500			96,14,500

Working Notes:

			Rs.
(1)	General Reserve (H Ltd.)		
	Balance as per Balance Sheet		5,50,000
Add	Share in S Ltd. (75% of Rs. 2,20,000 Transferred by S Ltd.)		1,65,000*
			7,15,000
(2)	Profit & Loss A/c (H Ltd.)		
	Balance as per Balance Sheet		10,00,000
Add	Share in S Ltd. (Rs. 5,26,500 – 1,65,000*) transferred to General Reserve)		3,61,500
Add	Share in Proposed Preference dividend of S Ltd.		14,250
			13,75,750
Less	Dividend out of pre-acquisition Profit	70,000	
	Unrealised Profit (40% of Rs. 20,000)	8,000	
	Proposed Dividend (Equity)	7,20,000	
	Preference Dividend	70,000	8,68,000
			5,07,750
(3)	**Motor Vehicle of S Ltd.**		
	Balance as per Balance Sheet		7,50,000
Less	Loss on Revaluation		1,00,000
			6,50,000
Add	Excess depreciation		20,000
			6,70,000
(4)	**Investments of H Ltd.**		26,00,000
Less	Cost of Investments in S Ltd. (Rs. 3,10,000 + 9,50,000 + 8,00,000)		20,60,000
			5,40,000

(5) For the purpose of calculating cost of investment, the dividend on 70,000 equity shares acquired on 1.4.2004 has been treated as dividend out of pre-acquisition profit because preference shares and 80,000 equity shares have already been purchased on 1.4.2002 and 1.4.2003 respectively.

QUESTIONS

1. Define holding company and subsidiary company as per Companies Act 1956.
2. Write a note on Consolidation Procedure as per AS-21.
3. Describe the merits and demerits of holding companies.
4. Write short notes on :
   - Cost of control
   - Minority Interest
   - Mutual owings
   - Unrealised profit
   - Revaluation of Assets
   - Capital Profits (Pre-acquisition Profit)
   - Revenue Profit (Post-acquisition Profit)
5. Explain the accounting treatment in the following cases when a holding company receives :
   - Bonus shares out of pre-acquisition profit.
   - Bonus shares out of post-acquisition profit.
   - Dividend out of pre-acquisition profit.
   - Dividend out of post-acquisition profit.

6 Write short notes on the following :
   - Interim dividend
   - Proposed dividend
   - Unclaimed dividend

PROBLEMS

1. (Pre-acquisition Loss)

The Balance Sheets of H Ltd. and S Ltd. as on 31st March, 2005 were as follows :

Liabilities	H Ltd.	S Ltd.
	Rs.	Rs.
Share Capital (Shares of Rs. 10 each)	1,00,000	60,000
General Reserve	40,000	—
Profit & Loss A/c	40,000	18,000
S Creditors	20,000	22,000
	2,00,000	1,00,000
Assets		
Sundry Assets	1,60,000	1,00,000
Investment in 4,000 shares in S Ltd.	40,000	—
	2,00,000	1,00,000

The shares were acquired by H Ltd. on 30th September, 2004. On 1.4.2004 the Profit & Loss Account of S Ltd. showed loss of Rs. 30,000 which was written off out of the profits earned during the year. Profits were earned uniformly over the year 2004-05.

Prepare a consolidated Balance Sheet of H Ltd. and S Ltd. as on 31st March, 2005.

[B. Com. (H) DU 1987 Modified]

Ans. : Cost of Control—Rs. 4,000
Minority Interest—Rs. 26,000
Balance Sheet Total—Rs. 2,64,000

2. (Common debts and Revaluation of stock)

The following are the Balance Sheets of H Ltd. and S Ltd. as on 31st March, 2005.

Liabilities	H Ltd..	S Ltd.
	Rs.	Rs.
Share Capital (shares of Rs. 10 each)	1,00,000	80,000
General Reserve	40,000	30,000
Profit & Loss A/c	40,000	20,000
Bills Payable	20,000	10,000
Creditors	50,000	40,000
	2,50,000	1,80,000
Assets		
Building	40,000	—
Plant & Machinery	10,000	60,000
Investment in Shares of S Ltd.	60,000	—
Stock	40,000	60,000
Debtors	50,000	30,000
Bills Receivable	30,000	20,000
Cash & Bank balance	20,000	10,000
	2,50,000	1,80,000

Additional Information :

(i) H Ltd. acquired 6000 shares in S Ltd. on 30th September 2004.

(ii) Debtors of H Ltd. include Rs. 20,000 receivable from S Ltd.

(iii) A loan of Rs. 10,000 given by H Ltd. to S Ltd. is also included in Debtors and creditors respectively.

(iv) S Ltd. has transferred Rs. 5,000 to General Reserve out of current year's profit.

(v) On 30th September, 2004 S Ltd. sold stock of Rs. 50,000 which was revalued at Rs. 40,000 by H Ltd. However, H Ltd. continued to show stock at cost.

Prepare Consolidated Balance Sheet as on 31st March 2005.

[B. Com (H) DU Modified]

Ans: Minority Interest — Rs. 30,000
Capital Reserve — Rs. 20,625
Total Balance Sheet— Rs. 3,30,000

Note: Treat loss on Revaluation of Stock as capital loss.

(Revaluation, Bonus Issue Proposed dividend)

3. The summarised Balance Sheets of H Ltd. and S Ltd. were as follows.

Liabilities	H Ltd.	S Ltd.
Preference Share (Capital Shares of Rs. 100 each)	1,00,000	40,000
Equity Share Capital (Shares of Rs. 10 each)	11,00,000	2,00,000
General Reserve	4,00,000	1,50,000
Profit & Loss A/c	2,00,000	50,000
Creditors	3,00,000	1,00,000
Proposed Dividend	—	40,000
	21,00,000	5,80,000
Assets		
Goodwill	20,000	10,000
Plant & Machinery	6,00,000	1,80,000
Furniture	1,00,000	34,000
Investments in 16,000 Shares of S Ltd.	3,20,000	—
Other Assets	10,60,000	3,46,000
Discount on Issue of Shares	—	10,000
	21,00,000	5,80,000

Additional Information :

(i) On the date of acquisition the books of S Ltd. had the following balances :

Profit & Loss A/c	Rs. 30,000
General Reserve	Rs. 50,000

(ii) Machinery (Book value — Rs. 2,00,000) of S Ltd. was valued at Rs. 3,00,000.

(iii) Furniture (Book value — Rs. 40,000) of S Ltd. was valued at Rs. 30,000.

(iv) During the year S Ltd. made a Bonus Issue out of pre-acquisition profit for Rs. 40,000 which has not been recorded in the books of accounts.

(v) Included in the creditors of S Ltd. is Rs. 20,000 for goods supplied by H Ltd. Also included in the Stock of S Ltd. are goods of the value of Rs. 8,000 which were supplied by H Ltd. at a profit of 25% on sales.

Prepare Consolidated Balance Sheet.

[B Com. (H) DU 1996 Modified

Ans: Minority Interest— Rs. 1,42,300
Cost of Control — Rs. 32,000
Total Goodwill — Rs. 62,000 in B/S
Total of B/S — Rs. 24,41,500

4. (Mutual Owings)

The following are the Balance Sheets of H Ltd. and it's subsidiary S Ltd. as on 31st March, 2005.

Liabilities	H Ltd.	S Ltd.
	Rs.	Rs.
Share Capital Shares of Rs. 10 each	6,00,000	2,00,000
General Reserve	3,40,000	80,000
Profit & Loss A/c	1,00,000	60,000
Creditors	70,000	35,000
	11,10,000	3,75,000
Assets		
Machinery	3,90,000	1,35,000
Furniture	80,000	40,000
Investment in 16,000 shares of S Ltd..	3,40,000	—
Debtors	50,000	30,000
Stock	1,80,000	1,20,000
Cash at Bank	70,000	50,000
	11,10,000	3,75,000

Additional Information :

(i) Profit & Loss A/c of S Ltd. stood at Rs. 30,000 on 1st April 2004 whereas general reserve remained unchanged since that date.

(ii) H Ltd. acquired 80% shares in S Ltd. on 1st October, 2004 for Rs. 3,40,000.

(iii) Included in debtors of S Ltd. is sum of Rs. 10,000 due from H Ltd. for goods sold at a profit of 25% on cost price. Till 31st March 2005 only half of the goods have been sold while remaining goods were lying in the godown of H Ltd. as on that date.

Prepare Consolidated Balance Sheet as on 31st March, 2005

[B Com. (H) DU 1994 Modified.

Ans: Cost of Control — Rs. 80,000
Minority Interest — Rs. 68,000
Total of Balance Sheet— Rs. 12,14,000

5. (Dividend, Unclaimed dividend, contingent liability and Mutual Owings.)

Following are the Balance Sheet of H Ltd. and S Ltd. as on 31st March, 2005.

Liabilities	H Ltd.	S Ltd.
	Rs.	Rs.
Equity Share Capital (Shares of Rs. 10 each)	5,00,000	2,00,000
General Reserve	2,40,000	1,00,000
Profit & Loss A/c	60,000	90,000
Unclaimed Dividend	—	1,000
Bills Payable	—	15,000
Sundry Creditors	2,00,000	44,000
	10,00,000	4,50,000

Assets		
Land & Building	2,00,000	2,20,000
Plant & Machinery	3,00,000	1,50,000
Investments	4,00,000	—
Stock	25,000	15,000
Debtors	20,000	25,000
Bills Receivable	5,000	10,000
Bank Balance	50,000	20,000
Preliminary Expenses	—	10,000
	10,00,000	4,50,000

Note: Contingent liability for Bills discounted Rs. 10,000

(i) H Ltd. acquired 16,000 equity shares of Rs. 10 each in S Ltd. on 1-10-2004 for Rs. 3,00,000.

(ii) The Profit & Loss A/c of S Ltd. showed a credit balance of Rs. 35,000, out of which a dividend of 10% was paid on 1.11.2004. The dividend was credited by H Ltd. to it's Profit & Loss A/c

(iii) Creditors of H Ltd. include an amount of Rs. 15,000 for purchases from S Ltd. The goods are still lying unsold. S Ltd. sells goods at cost plus 20%

(iv) Bills Payable of S Ltd. are all issued in favour of H Ltd. of which the latter company got discounted Rs. 10,000 bills receivable with its banker.

Prepare a Consolidated Balance Sheet as on 31st March,2005

[B Com. (H) DU 2003 Modified]

Ans : Minority Interest — Rs. 77,000 (including Unclaimed dividend)
Cost of Control (Goodwill)— Rs. 10,000
Total of Balance of Sheet — Rs. 11,27,500

6. (Interim Dividend, Revaluation, Mutual debts and Bonus Issue.)

Following Balance Sheets of H Ltd. and S Ltd. as on 31-3-2005.

Liabilities	H Ltd.	S Ltd.
Preference Share Capital (Shares of Rs. 100 each)	1,00,000	—
Equity Share Capital (Shares of 100 each)	5,00,000	1,50,000
General Reserve	3,40,000	6,000
Profit & Loss A/c	3,60,000	1,08,000
Creditors	1,00,000	44,150
Bills Payable	—	24,150
	14,00,000	3,32,300
Assets		
Land	3,56,000	70,000
Properties	3,76,000	40,000
Plant & Machinery	1,40,000	91,300
Investments in 1200 shares of S Ltd. on 1.4.2004	1,80,000	—
Stock	1,36,000	50,600
Debtors and Cash	2,12,000	80,400
	14,00,000	3,32,300

Additional Information :

(i) Profit and Loss A/c of H Ltd. includes an interim dividend of 10 % received from S Ltd.

(ii) On 1.4.2004 Profit & Loss A/c of S Ltd. stood at Rs. 77,500 and General Reserve at Rs. 3,000. Also H Ltd. revalued Plant and Machinery of S Ltd. at the time of purchase of shares by Rs. 20,000 more than its book value.

(iii) Stock of H Ltd. includes Rs. 8,000 of stock purchased from S Ltd. Further, debtors of S Ltd. includes Rs. 24,000 for sales to H Ltd. on which S Ltd. made a profit of Rs. 6,000.

(iv) S Ltd. made a bonus issue during the year out of pre-acquisition profits for Rs. 60,000 not recorded in the books.

Prepare consolidated Balance Sheet as on 31.3.2005

Ans. : Minority Interest — Rs. 56,800
Capital Reserve — Rs. 20,400
B/S Total — Rs. 15,46,300

[B Com. (H) DU, 1993 - Modified]

7. (Dividend, Revaluation, Mutual owings and contingent liability)

From the following Balance Sheets of H Ltd. and S Ltd. and additional information prepare 'Consolidated Balance Sheet as on 31 March, 2005.

Liabilities	H Ltd. Rs.	S Ltd. Rs.
Preference Share Capital (Shares of Rs. 100 each)	2,00,000	40,000
Equity Share Capital (Shares of Rs. 100 each)	8,00,000	4,00,000
General Reserve (1.4.04)	2,00,000	1,20,000
Profit & Loss A/c	2,80,000	1,80,000
Creditors	1,60,000	1,00,000
Bills Payable	—	40,000
	16,40,000	8,80,000
Assets		
Goodwill	80,000	60,000
Land & Building	4,00,000	2,60,000
Plant & Machinery	3,20,000	1,80,000
Debtors	40,000	1,50,000
Stock	2,00,000	1,80,000
3,000 Shares in S Ltd. (30.9.2004)	4,80,000	—
Cash & Bank	1,20,000	40,000
Preliminary Expenses		10,000
	16,40,000	8,80,000

Additional Information:

(i) Profit & Loss Account of S Ltd. showed a credit balance of Rs. 1,00,000 on 1.4.2004.

(ii) A Dividend of 15% was paid by S Ltd. in October 2004 for the year ended 31st March, 2004 which was credited to Profit & Loss A/c of H Ltd.

(iii) Included in Creditors of S Ltd. Rs. 40,000 for goods supplied by H Ltd. Also included in the stock of S Ltd. are goods to the value of Rs. 16,000 which were supplied by H Ltd. at a profit of 25% on sales.

(iii) Plant & Machinery were revalued at Rs. 3,00,000 which stood in the books at Rs. 2,00,000 in the beginning.

(v) There is a contingent liability of Rs. 2,000 for a pending suit in the court in the books of H Ltd.

[B Com. (H) DU -1995 Modified]

Ans.: Minority Interest — Rs. 2,38,625
Capital Reserve on acquisition — Rs. 1,12,500
Goodwill in the CBS — Rs. 27,500 (after adjustment of Capital Reserve)
Total of Balance Sheet — Rs. 19,78,000

8. (Dividend, Mutual debts and Unrealised profit)

Following are the Balance sheets of H Ltd. and its subsidiary S Ltd. as on 31st March, 2005.

Liabilities	H Ltd.	S Ltd..
	Rs.	Rs.
Equity Share Capital (Shares of Rs. 10 each)	4,00,000	1,00,000
General Reserve (1.4.04)	2,80,000	34,000
Profit & Loss A/c	1,70,000	42,000
S Creditors	70,000	35,000
	9,20,000	2,11,000
Assets:		
Plant & Machinery	4,80,000	90,000
Furniture	15,000	27,000
Investments	2,00,000	—
Stock	95,000	42,000
Debtors	60,000	32,000
Cash & Bank	70,000	20,000
	9,20,000	2,11,000

Additional Informational:

(i) H Ltd. acquired 8,000 equity shares of S Ltd. on 1st July, 2004 at a cost of Rs. 2,00,000.

(ii) Stock of H Ltd. includes Rs. 6,000 relating to stock purchased from S Ltd. which follows the practice of charging 25% extra on cost for determining the selling price.

(ii) Creditors of H Ltd. include Rs. 10,000 on account of purchase from S Ltd.

(iii) Profit & Loss A/c of H Ltd. includes dividend @ 10% for the year 2003-04 received from S Ltd. which was declared and paid in August 2004.

(v) Balance in S Ltd.'s Profit & Loss Account on 1st April, 2004 was Rs. 27,000. Dividend @ 10% for the year 2003-04 was declared out of this balance in August 2004. S Ltd. paid dividend tax @ 10%.

Prepare consolidated Balance Sheet as on 31st March 2005.

[B Com. (H) DU 1992 Adapted]

Ans: Minority Interest — Rs. 35,200
Cost Control — Rs. 66,800, Total of Balance Sheet — Rs. 9,86,000.

9. (Revaluation of Assets)

Following are the Balance Sheets of H Ltd. and S Ltd. as on 31st March 2005.

Liabilities	H Ltd. Rs.	S Ltd.. Rs.
Equity Share Capital (Shares of Rs. 10 each)	4,00,000	1,00,000
Profit & Loss A/c	50,000	20,000
Current Liabilities	7,50,000	4,80,000
	12,00,000	6,00,000
Assets		
Fixed Assets	2,50,000	95,000
Investment in 9,000 Equity shares of S Ltd.	1,40,000	—
Other Assets	8,10,000	5,05,000
	12,00,000	6,00,000

H Ltd. acquired shares in S Ltd. on 1.4.2004 when profit & Loss Account of S Ltd. showed a credit balance of Rs. 8,000. H Ltd. valued fixed assets at 20% above its book value of Rs. 1,00,000 but no such adjustment effected in the books of S Ltd.

Prepare consolidated Balance Sheet as on 31st March, 2005.

B Com. (H) DU 1985 Modified]

Ans.: Cost of Control — Rs. 24,800
Minority Interest — Rs. 13,900
Total Balance Sheet — Rs. 17,03,800

10. (Debentures mutually held & Pre-acquisition loss)

The following are the Balance Sheets of H Ltd. & S Ltd. as at 31st March, 2005.

Liabilities	H Ltd. Rs.	S Ltd. Rs.
Equity Share Capital Shares of Rs. 10 each	3,00,000	2,00,000
Capital Redemption Reserve	1,20,000	—
Capital Reserve	1,00,000	30,000
Profit & Loss A/c (before any appropriation)	60,000	40,000
Debentures	2,00,000	1,00,000
O/S Debenture Interest for one year	30,000	15,000
Other Liabilities	1,90,000	1,15,000
	10,00,000	5,00,000
Assets		
Fixed Assets	6,00,000	3,40,000
Investments in 15,000 shares in S Ltd. (30.9.2004)	2,00,000	—
Debentures of S Ltd. at par	50,000	—
Debentures of H Ltd. at par	—	60,000
Current Assets	1,50,000	1,00,000
	10,00,000	5,00,000

S Ltd. had a debit balance of Rs. 20,000 on 1.4.2004.

Prepare consolidated Balance Sheet.

B Com. (H) DU 1984 Modified

Ans. : Minority Interest — Rs. 67,500
Cost of control — Rs. 20,000
Balance Sheet — Rs. 11,93,500

11. (Bonus shares out of post acquisition Profits)

H Ltd. acquired 20,000 equity shares of Rs. 10 each in S Ltd. on 31st March, 2004. The summarised balance sheets of H Ltd. and its subsidiary S Ltd. were as follows :

Liabilities	H Ltd.	S Ltd.
	Rs.	Rs.
Equity Share Capital (Shares of Rs. 10 each)	8,00,000	2,50,000
General Reserve	3,00,000	50,000
Profit & Loss A/c	1,00,000	1,00,000
Creditors	2,00,000	50,000
	14,00,000	4,50,000
Assets		
Fixed Assets	7,00,000	2,50,000
Current Assets	4,00,000	2,00,000
Investment in Shares of S Ltd.	3,00,000	—
	14,00,000	4,50,000

Additional Information :

S Ltd. had a credit balance of Rs. 50,000 in the reserve and Rs. 20,000 in the profit & Loss Account when H Ltd. acquired shares S Ltd. issued bonus shares, in the ratio of one for every five shares held out of profits earned during the year 2004-05. This is not shown in the above balance sheet of S Ltd.

Prepare consolidated Balance Sheet of H Ltd.. and its subsidiary as on 31 March, 2005.

[B Com. (H) DU 1986 Modified]

Ans. : Minority Interest - Rs. 80,000
Cost of Control - Rs. 4,000
Total of Balance Sheet Rs. 15,54,000

12. (Interim dividend & Mutual owings)

Following are the Balance Sheets of H Ltd. and its subsidiary S Ltd. as on 31st March, 2005.

Liabilities	H Ltd.	S Ltd.
	Rs.	Rs.
Equity Share Capital (Rs. 10)	6,00,000	2,00,000
General Reserve	3,80,000	8,000
Profit & Loss A/c	3,20,000	1,44,000
S Creditors	60,000	64,400
	13,60,000	4,16,400

Assets

Building	4,12,000	1,20,000
Machinery	1,00,000	96,000
Furniture	20,000	12,400
Stock	1,36,000	80,800
Investments	4,48,000	—
Debtors	1,12,000	63,200
Cash & Bank balance	1,32,000	44,000
	13,60,000	4,16,400

Additional Information:

(i) H Ltd. acquired 80% Equity Shares in S Ltd. on 1st July at a cost price of Rs. 4,48,000

(ii) In the profit and Loss of H Ltd. interim dividend declared by S Ltd. on 1st July, 2004 at the rate of 10% per annum is included.

(iii) Creditors of H Ltd. include an amount of Rs. 24,000 in respect of purchase from S Ltd. and stock of H Ltd. also includes stock at cost price of Rs. 12,000 purchased from S Ltd. which sells the goods by adding 25% profit oncost price.

(iv) On 1.4.2004 S Ltd. had a credit balance of Profit & Loss A/c of Rs. 1,12,000 from which company declared 10% interim dividend. Prepare a Consolidated Balance Sheet as on 31st March, 2005.

[C.S. (1) Dec., 97 Modified]

Ans: Minority Interest — Rs. 70,400
Cost of Control — Rs. 1,81,600 Total of B/S — Rs. 14,83,600

13. (Dividend, proposed dividend & Unrealised Profit)

From the following prepare a Consolidated Balance Sheet as on 31st March, 2005.

Liabilities	H Ltd.	S Ltd..
Equity Share Capital Shares of Rs. 10 each	6,00,000	1,00,000
General Reserve	50,000	30,000
Profit & Loss A/c	80,000	40,000
Sundry Creditors	1,00,000	40,000
Bills Payable	10,000	15,000
	8,40,000	2,25,000
Assets		
Land & Building	2,00,000	1,00,000
Plant & Machinery	2,80,000	50,000
Investments in 7,000 shares of S Ltd.	1,00,000	
Stock	70,000	40,000
Bills Receivable	10,000	—
Debtors	1,50,000	20,000
Cash & Bank	30,000	15,000
	8,40,000	2,25,000

Additional Informations :

(i) When 6000 shares were acquired by H Ltd., S Ltd. had Rs 20,000 General Reserve and. Rs. 5000 credit balance of profit & Loss A/c

(ii) At the time of acquisition of further 1000 shares by H Ltd., S Ltd. had Rs. 25,000 General Reserve and Rs. 28,000 credit balance in Profit & Loss Account from which 20% dividend was paid by S Ltd. and dividend received by H Ltd. on these shares was credited to Profit & Loss A/c.

(iii) Stock of S Ltd. includes Rs. 20,000 purchased from H Ltd. which has made 25% profit on cost.

(iv) All the bills receivable of H Ltd.. including those discounted were accepted by S Ltd.

(v) Both the companies have proposed dividend - H Ltd. 10% and S Ltd. 15% but no effect has yet been given in the above balance sheets.

Prepare consolidated Balance Sheet as on 31st March, 2005.

[C.A. (F) Nov. 1990 Modified]

Ans. : Minority Interest — Rs. 45,000 excluding proposed dividend
Cost of Control — Rs. 9,700
Total of Balance Sheet — Rs. 9,60,700

Note: Show the proposed dividend for both the companies separately.

(Revaluation, Unrealised profit & Mutual Current Accounts)

14. The summarised Balance Sheets of H Ltd. & S Ltd. as on 31st March, 2005 was as follows :

Liabilities	H Ltd..	S Ltd..
Equity Shares of Rs. 100 each	24,00,000	12,00,000
Securities Premium	3,60,000	—
Capital Reserve (1.4.2004)	—	80,000
General Reserve	1,50,000	1,00,000
Profit & Loss A/c	6,00,000	1,00,000
Profit for the year 2004-05	1,80,000	60,000
Creditors	2,96,000	2,19,000
S Ltd. A/c Current A/c	34,000	
	40,20,000	17,59,000
Assets		
Goodwill	5,00,000	1,50,000
Plant & Machinery	9,60,000	8,10,000
Furniture & Fixtures	2,60,000	95,000
Stock	2,00,000	1,50,000
Debtors	8,20,000	4,10,000
Bank Balance	2,00,000	75,000
Trade Investments	—	30,000
Investment in 9600 shares of S Ltd.	10,80,000	—
H Ltd. Current A/c		39,000
	40,20,000	17,59,000

Additional Information :

(i) On 1.4.2004 H Ltd. acquired 9600 shares from the shareholders of S Ltd.. and allotted in consideration thereof 7,200 its own shares at a premium of Rs. 150 per share.

(ii) The consolidation for the shares of S Ltd. was arrived at inter alia by valuing the Plant & Machinery at Rs. 10,00,000 Furniture & Fixtures at Rs. 99,000 and placing no value for trade investments and goodwill.

(iii) The depreciation was charged @ 10% p.a. on Furniture & Fixtures during the year 2004-05.

(iv) The stock of S Ltd. includes Rs. 50,000 in respect of goods received from H Ltd. invoiced at cost plus 25%.

Prepare consolidated Balance Sheet as on 31st March, 2005.

[C.A. (F) Modified]

Ans: Minority Interest — Rs. 2,89,810
Goodwill — Rs. 5,00,000
Capital Reserve on Consolidation — Rs. 39,200
Total of CBS — Rs. 45,64,050

15. (Proposed dividend, Mutual owings, Cheque in-transit and unrealised profit)

Following are the Balance Sheets of H Ltd. and it's subsidiary S Ltd. as on 31st March 2005.

Liabilities	H Ltd. Rs.	S Ltd.. Rs.
9% Preference Share Capital (Shares of Rs. 10 each)	—	1,00,000
Equity Share Capital (Shares of Rs. 10 each)	6,00,000	4,00,000
General Reserve	1,60,000	80,000
Profit & Loss A/c	1,30,000	1,20,000
Bills Payable	20,000	25,000
S Creditors	2,30,000	2,85,000
Proposed Dividend	60,000	40,000
	12,00,000	10,50,000
Assets		
Goodwill	—	20,000
Fixed Assets	3,50,000	2,50,000
Investments	3,60,000	90,000
Stock	2,20,000	3,60,000
Debtors	2,10,000	2,50,000
Bills Receivable	40,000	35,000
Cash	20,000	45,000
	12,00,000	10,50,000

H Ltd. purchased interest in S Ltd. by acquiring 3/4th Equity Share Capital at a premium of 20% on 1.4.2004. Prepare a Consolidated Balance Sheet in the books of H Ltd. as on 31st March, 2005 after taking in to account the following information :

(i) Profit and Loss A/c of S Ltd. includes an amount of Rs. 20,000 brought forward from last year

(ii) Creditors of H Ltd. include an amount of Rs. 12,000 for purchase from S Ltd. which are still unsold. S Ltd. sells goods at cost plus 20%.

(iii) S Ltd. remitted a cheque of Rs. 10,000 on 31st March 2005 which was received by H Ltd. on 5th April 2005.

(iv) Bills Receivable worth Rs. 20,000 out of the bills of Rs. 25,000 received from S Ltd. were discounted by H Ltd. and S Ltd. had endorsed to its creditors all the bills received from H Ltd. amounting to Rs. 15,000

(v) The directors of H Ltd. and S Ltd. have proposed a dividend of 10% on equity share capital for the year 2004-05.

[CS (1) Adapted]

Ans: Minority Interest — Rs. 2,64,500
Cost of Control — Rs. 5,000
Total Balance Sheet— Rs. 18,56,000

16. (Revaluation, Unrealised profit & Cheque in transit)

The summarised Balance Sheets of H Ltd. and S Ltd. as on 31st March, 2005 were as follows :

Liabilities	H Ltd.	S Ltd.
Equity Share Capital (Shares of Rs. 100 each)	18,00,000	9,00,000
Securities Premium	2,70,000	—
Capital Reserve (1.4.04)	1,20,000	90,000
General Reserve (1.4.04)	2,25,000	1,50,000
Profit & Loss A/c (1.4.04)	6,00,000	1,20,000
Profit for the year 2004-05	2,40,000	75,000
S Ltd.	40,500	—
Creditors	5,25,000	1,65,000
	38,20,500	15,00,000
Assets		
Goodwill	3,75,000	1,12,500
Plant & Machinery	10,80,000	6,75,000
Computers	1,95,000	85,500
Investments at Cost:		
Trade Investments	—	37,500
Shares in S Ltd.	8,10,000	—
H Ltd.		48,000
Stock	2,70,000	1,80,000
Debtors	9,40,500	3,16,500
Bank Balance	1,50,000	45,000
	38,20,500	15,00,000

Additional Information:

(i) Plant and Machinery of S Ltd. was to be valued on 1st April, 2004 at Rs. 8,10,000, Computers at Rs. 75,000 and Trade Investments were deemed to be valueless. There was no sale or purchase of these assets during the year 2004-05.

(ii) Depreciation has been provided an Plant & Machinery at 10% and on Computers at 5%

(iii) The stock of S Ltd. included Rs. 60,000 goods purchased from H Ltd. who invoiced these goods at cost plus 25%.

(iv) A cheque of Rs. 7500 from H Ltd. to S Ltd. was in transit on 31st March 2005.

(v) H Ltd. acquired 7,200 equity shares of S Ltd. on 1.04.2004.

CA (F) 05 Modified

Ans: Minority Interest — Rs. 2,67,450, Capital Reserve — Rs. 2,04,000
Cost of Control (after adjusting Capital Reserve) — Rs. 2,83,500
Total of C B/S — Rs. 42,56,250

17. (Dividend, Mutual owings & Unrealised profit)

H Ltd. acquired 75% of Equity Shares and Preference Shares in S Ltd. on 1st April, 2004. The Balance Sheets of both the companies as on 31st March, 2005 were as under :

Liabilities	H Ltd. Rs.	S Ltd. Rs.
Share Capital		
Equity Shares of Rs. 10 each	5,45,000	1,00,000
6% Preference Shares of Rs. 100 each	—	50,000
Creditors	95,000	45,600
General Reserve	1,75,000	60,000
Profit & Loss A/c	90,000	46,000
	9,05,000	3,01,600
Assets		
Land & Building	2,60,000	95,000
Plant & Machinery	1,40,000	76,000
Investment in Shares of S Ltd.	2,00,000	—
Stock	1,15,000	77,000
Debtors	1,18,000	26,000
Cash at Bank	72,000	27,600
	9,05,000	3,01,600

Additional Information :

(i) On the date of acquisition of shares, Land & Building and Plant & Machinery of S Ltd. were valued at Rs. 1,15,000 and 70,000 respectively for which no effect has been given in the books.

(ii) The balance of Profit & Loss A/c of S Ltd. as on 1st April, 2004 was Rs. 20,000 out of which a dividend of 3% was paid on Equity Shares. The dividend in respect of preference shares is still payable for the year 2004-05.

(iii) The Profit & Loss Account of H Ltd. includes dividend @ 3% from S Ltd. Dividend was paid for the year ending 31st March, 2004.

(iv) Stock of H Ltd. includes Rs. 6,000 stock at cost purchased from S Ltd.

(v) Creditors of H Ltd. includes Rs. 12,000 for purchases from S Ltd. on which latter company made a profit of Rs. 2000.

Prepare a Consolidated Balance Sheet As on 31st March, 2005.

[CA (F) OS Modified

Ans. : Minority Interest — Rs. 67,500
Cost of Control — Rs. 17,000
Total of C B/S — Rs. 10,24,600

18. (Interim dividend, Mutual owings & Unrealised Profit)

On 1.7.2004 H Ltd. acquired 72,000 equity shares of Rs. 10 each for Rs. 8,00,000. On 31st March, 2005 following were the Balance Sheets of H Ltd. and it's subsidiary S Ltd.

Liabilities	H Ltd.	S Ltd.
Equity Share Capital (Shares of Rs. 10 each)	22,00,000	800,000
Securities Premium	1,20,000	—
General Reserve	1,75,000	90,000
Profit & Loss A/c	3,05,000*	2,50,000
*(including interim dividend received from S Ltd. Rs. 36,000)		
Bills Payable	—	80,000
S Creditors	1,95,000	1,10,000
H Ltd.	—	70,000
	29,95,000	14,00,000
Assets		
Goodwill	3,50,000	—
Plant & Machinery	7,00,000	6,30,000
Furniture	1,20,000	1,60,000
Investment in Shares of S Ltd.	8,00,000	—
Stock	4,50,000	3,10,000
Debtors	3,40,000	2,05,000
S Ltd.	75,000	—
Bills Receivable	50,000	—
Bank Balance	1,10,000	95,000
	29,95,000	14,00,000

The following additional information is provided to you :

(i) S Ltd. remitted a cheque for Rs. 5,000 to H Ltd. on 28th March, 2005 which was received by H Ltd. on 2nd April, 2005.

(ii) Bills accepted by S Ltd. were all drawn by H Ltd. and H Ltd. got bills for Rs. 30,000 discounted with the Bank.

(iii) S Ltd. had purchased goods from H Ltd. of which goods invoiced at Rs. 50,000 were in stock on 31st March, 2005. H Ltd. sells goods at cost plus 25%.

(iv) The balance of Profit & Loss A/c is arrived as under :

			Rs.
	Balance as on 1.4.2004		10,000
Add	Profit for the year 2004-05		3,20,000
			3,30,000
Less	Transfer to General Reserve	40,000	
	Interim dividend paid	40,000	80,000
			2,50,000

Prepare consolidated Balance Sheet

[CS (1) Dec. 2000 Modified]

Ans: Minority Interest — Rs. 1,14,000

Capital Reserve —Rs. 46,000

Total of CB/S— Rs. 34,19,000

19. (Dividend, Common transactions and Unrealised Profits)

The following are the Balance Sheets of H Ltd. and S Ltd. as on 31st March 2005.

Liabilities	H Ltd.	S Ltd.
	Rs.	Rs.
Equity Shares Capital (Shares of Rs. 10 each)	5,00,000	2,00,000
General Reserve (1.4.04)	1,00,000	60,000
Profit & Loss A/c	1,40,000	90,000
Bills Payable	—	40,000
S Creditors	80,000	50,000
	8,20,000	4,40,000
Assets		
Fixed Assets	3,60,000	2,20,000
Goodwill	40,000	30,000
Investments in 15,000 shares of S Ltd. at cost	2,40,000	—
Stock	1,00,000	90,000
Debtors	20,000	75,000
Cash & Bank balance	60,000	25,000
	8,20,000	4,40,000

Additional Information :

(i) The Profit & Loss A/c of S Ltd. showed a balance of Rs. 50,000 on 1st April, 2004. A dividend of 15% was paid on 15th October, 2004 for the year 2003-04. The dividend was credited by H Ltd. to its Profit & Loss A/c

(ii) H Ltd. acquired shares on 30th September, 2004.

(iii) The Bills Payable of S Ltd. were all issued in favour of H Ltd. which were discounted by the company.

(iv) Included in the creditors of S Ltd. are Rs. 20,000 for goods supplied by H Ltd. The stock of S Ltd. includes goods to the value of Rs. 8,000 which were supplied by H Ltd. at a profit of 33 $^{1}/_{3}$% profit on cost.

Prepare a consolidated Balance Sheet as on 31st March, 2005.

[C.S. (i) June 1997 Modified]

Ans: Minority Interest — Rs. 87,500

Capital Reserve — Rs. 18,750

Total of CB/S — Rs. 9,79,250

20. (Proposed, dividend, Mutual debts and Unrealised profit)

The following are the Balance Sheets of H Ltd. and S Ltd. as 31st March 2005.

Liabilities	H Ltd.	S Ltd.
	Rs.	Rs.
Equity Share Capital (shares of Rs. 10 each)	15,00,000	5,00,000
General Reserve	2,90,000	1,20,000
Profit & Loss A/c	2,40,000	1,05,000
S Creditors	2,50,000	70,000
Bills Payable	20,000	5,000
	23,00,000	8,00,000
Assets		
Goodwill	1,00,000	2,00,000
Freehold Property	9,00,000	3,00,000
Plant & Machinery	4,00,000	1,50,000
Investment in 40,000 shares of S Ltd.. at cost	4,70,000	—
Stock-in-Trade	1,50,000	50,000
Debtors	1,80,000	80,000
Bills Receivable	30,000	10,000
Cash & Bank balance	70,000	10,000
	23,00,000	8,00,000

Additional Information :

(i) On the date of acquisition of shares in S Ltd. by H Ltd. the undistributed profits and reserve of S Ltd. were Rs. 40,000 and Rs. 50,000 respectively

(ii) The Debtors of H Ltd. include Rs. 18,000 due from S Ltd.

(iii) Bills Receivable of S Ltd. include Rs. 5,000 due from H Ltd.

(iv) The Stock of S Ltd. includes goods purchased from H Ltd. at Rs. 15,000 which includes profit charged by H Ltd. at cost plus $33\,^1/_3$ %.

(V) H Ltd. and S Ltd. both have proposed dividend of 12% for 2004-05, but no effect has been given to the same in the books of accounts.

(v) In respect of H Ltd. there was a contingent liability of Rs. 20,000 in respect of bills discounted.

Prepare consolidated Balance Sheet as on 31st March 2005.

[ICWA (F) June 1994 Modified]

Ans. : Minority Interest — Rs. 1,33,000

Capital Reserve — Rs. 2000

Total of CBS — Rs. 26,01,250

21. (Revaluation of assets, & Unrealised profit)

On 1st October, 2004 H Ltd. acquired 13,500 shares of S Ltd. at a cost of Rs. 2,02,500. Following are the Balance Sheets of H Ltd. and S Ltd. as on 31st March, 2005

Liabilities	H Ltd.	S Ltd.
	Rs.	Rs.
Equity Shares of Rs. 10 each	3,60,000	1,80,000
General Reserve	36,000	30,000
Profit & Loss A/c	60,000	60,000
Creditors	60,000	42,000
Bills Payable (to H Ltd.)	—	6,000
	5,16,000	3,18,000
Contingent liability for Bills discounted	9,000	—
Assets		
Goodwill	6,000	24,000
Land & Building	60,000	60,000
Plant & Machinery	1,20,000	1,08,000
Stock-in-Trade	70,500	60,000
Debtors	30,000	54,000
Investment in Shares of S Ltd.	2,02,500	—
Cash at Bank	27,000	12,000
	5,16,000	3,18,000

Additional Information :

(i) S Ltd. had on 1.4.2004 Rs. 30,000 in General Reserve and Rs. 36,000 (Cr.) in Profit and Loss A/c.

(ii) Dividend @ 10% was received by H Ltd. in October 2004 from S Ltd. for the year 2003-04 and this was credited to Profit & Loss A/c of H Ltd.

(iii) Plant & Machinery was standing in the books of S Ltd. at Rs. 1,20,000 on the date of purchase was revalued at Rs. 1,44,000.

(iv) Stock of S Ltd. includes goods valuing Rs. 9,600 received from H Ltd. which made a profit of 25% on cost.

Prepare consolidated Balance Sheet as on 31.3.05.

[ICWA (F) Dec. 1995, Modified]

Ans.: Minority Interest — Rs. 73,200

Capital Reserve — Rs. 7,500

Total of C B/S — Rs. 6,29,880

22. (Revaluation, Mutual owings and Unrealised Profit)

The following were the Balance Sheets of H Ltd. and S Ltd. as on 31 March, 2005.

Liabilities	H Ltd.	S Ltd.
	Rs.	Rs.
Equity Share Capital (Shares of Rs. 100 each)	20,00,000	1,50,000
General Reserve	1,00,000	50,000
Profit & Loss A/c (1.4.04)	1,50,000	80,000
Profit for the year 2004-05	1,60,000	1,00,000
Bank overdraft	1,00,000	—
Bills Payable	40,000	—
S Creditors	1,20,000	90,000
	26,70,00	4,70,000
Assets		
Land & Building	5,00,000	—
Plant & Machinery	14,95,000	1,75,000
Investment in 1200 shares of S Ltd.	3,60,000	—
Stock	1,50,000	1,40,000
Debtors	1,40,000	1,30,000
Bills Reservable	—	15,000
Cash & Bank balance	25,000	10,000
	26,70,000	4,70,000

Additional Information:

(i) The Shares of S Ltd. were acquired by H Ltd. on 1.10.2004.

(ii) The Plant & Machinery of S Ltd. is to be valued at Rs. 2,25,000 on 1.4.2004. Depreciation at 12 $^1/_2$% has been charged in 2004-05.

(iii) Bills Receivable held by S Ltd. are all accepted by H Ltd.

(iv) The creditors of H Ltd. include Rs. 20,000 out of Rs. 40,000 purchased from S Ltd. on 1.12.2004 on which the latter company made a profit of Rs. 10,000.

(v) Stock of H Ltd. includes Rs. 16,000 at cost purchased from S Ltd. that is part of purchases of Rs. 40,000.

[ICWA (F) June 1993]

Ans. : Minority Interest — Rs. 83,950

Cost of Control — Rs. 58,500

Consolidated B/S — Rs. 28,43,250

23. (Revaluation, Depreciation, Dividend, Mutual owings & Unrealised profit)

The Balance Sheets of H Ltd. and S Ltd. as on 31st March 2005 were as under :

Liabilities	H Ltd.	S Ltd.
	Rs.	Rs.
Share Capital Shares of Rs. 10 each	1,20,000	1,00,000
General Reserve	20,000	36,000
Profit & Loss A./c	12,000	20,000
Sundry Creditors	4,000	7,000
Bills Payable	2,000	5,000
	1,58,000	1,68,000
Contingent liability for Bills Discounted (Not yet matured)	2,500	—
Assets		
Fixed Assets	44,000	84,000
Investments in S Ltd. (8,000 shares @ Rs. 11 each)	88,000	—
Stock	10,000	40,000
Sundry Debtors	6,000	15,000
Bills Receivable	4,000	16,000
Cash & Bank Balances	6,000	13,000
	1,58,000	1,68,000

Additional Information:

(i) Shares were purchased on 1.4.2002. On that date the General Reserve and Profit & Loss A/c stood at Rs. 30,000 and Rs. 16,000 respectively in the books of S Ltd.

(ii) Dividend has been paid @ 10% every year after the acquisition of shares. The first dividend being out of pre-acquisition profits. No, dividend has been proposed for the year 2004-05 as yet and no provisions need be made in consolidated Balance Sheet. H Ltd. has credited all the dividends received to Profit & Loss A/c.

(iii) On 31st March, 2005 Bonus Shares have been declared by S Ltd. @ 1 fully paid share for 5 held, but no effect has been made in the above accounts The bonus was declared out of profits earned prior to 1.4.2002 from General Reserve.

(iv) When the shares were purchased, agreed valuation of Fixed Assets was Rs. 1,08,000 although no effect has been given thereto in the books.

(v) Depreciation has been charged @ 10% p.a. on the book value of Fixed Assets as on 1.4.2002 on Straight Line Method, there being no addition or disposal since then. Out of current profits Rs. 2,000 has been transferred to General Reserve every year.

(vi) Bills Receivable of H Ltd. include Rs. 2000 accepted by S Ltd. and bills discounted by H Ltd. but not yet matured include Rs. 1500 accepted by S Ltd.

(vii) Sundry creditors of H Ltd. include Rs. 2000 due to S Ltd. whereas sundry debtors of S Ltd. include Rs. 4000 due from H Ltd. It is found that a cheque of Rs. 2000 has not yet been received by S Ltd.

Prepare consolidated Balance Sheet as on 31.3.2005

[CA (F) May 2000 Modified]

Ans: Minority Interest — Rs. 29,520
Capital Reserve — Rs. 19,200
Total of C B/S — Rs. 2,25,000

24. (Bonus, Issue, revaluation & Mutual debits)

H Ltd. acquired 80% of both classes of shares of S Ltd. on 1st April, 2004. The summarised Balance Sheets of H Ltd. and S Ltd. were as under :

Liabilities	H Ltd. Rs.	S Ltd. Rs.
Share Capital :		
10,000 Equity Shares of Rs. 50 each	5,00,000	—
6,000 Equity Shares of Rs. 50 each	—	3,00,000
6% 1000 Preference Shares of Rs. 100 each	—	1,00,000
Capital Reserve	—	1,50,000
Revenue Reserve	90,000	70,000
Profit & Loss A/c	1,60,000	60,000
Loan from H. Ltd. (including interest due Rs. 5,000)	—	25,000
Bills Payable (including Rs. 2,000 in favour of H Ltd.)	—	5,000
Sundry Creditors	80,000	30,000
	8,30,000	7,40,000
Assets		
Fixed Assets	2,25,000	4,00,000
Investment in Shares of S Ltd.	4,00,000	—
Loan to S Ltd.	20,000	—
Stock	65,000	80,000
Trade Debtors	50,000	1,30,000
Bills Receivable (including Rs. 2000 from S Ltd.)	4000	
Bank Balance	66,000	1,30,000
	8,30,000	7,40,000

Additional Information :

(i) S Ltd. made a bonus issue on 31st March, 2005 of one equity share for every two shares held, eliminating the capital reserve,. The Balance Sheet does not reflect this transaction.

(ii) The fixed assets of S Ltd. were overvalued at the time of acquisition and should be written down by Rs. 30,000.

(iv) Creditors of H Ltd. include an amount of Rs. 40,000 in respect of purchases from S Ltd. on which the latter company made a profit of Rs. 5,000.

(v) Stock of H Ltd. includes an amount of Rs. 20,000 out of the above purchases.

Prepare a Consolidated Balance Sheet assuming that S Ltd. Reserves on 1st April, 2004 were the same as on 31st March, 2005.

[CA (F) Modified]

Ans.: Minority Interest — Rs. 1,30,000
Capital Reserve — Rs. 1,20,000
Total of C B/S — Rs. 10,75,500

25. (Revaluation, Bonus Issue & Contingent liability)

H Ltd. acquired 12,000 equity shares of Rs. 10 each in S Ltd. on 31st March, 2005 cum-bonus. The summarised Balance Sheets of H Ltd. and S Ltd. on that were as follows :

Liabilities	H Ltd.	S Ltd.
Equity Share Capital Shares of Rs. 10 each	4,50,000	1,50,000
Capital Reserve	—	82,500
Revenue Reserve	45,000	7,500
Profit & Loss A/c	57,300	27,000
Loan from S Ltd. (including interest due)	3,150	—
Bills Payable (including Rs. 750 to H Ltd.)	—	2,550
Creditors	26,850	10,500
	5,82,300	2,80,050
Assets		
Fixed Assets	2,25,000	2,17,050
Investment in Shares of S Ltd.	2,55,000	—
Stock	60,000	30,000
Loan to H Ltd.	—	3,000
Bills Receivable (including Rs. 450 from S Ltd.)	1,800	—
Trade Debtors and Bank Balances	40,500	30,000
	5,82,300	2,80,050

Note : On Balance Sheet of H Ltd.

There is a Contingent Liability for Bills Receivable discounted for Rs. 1500.

Additional Information :

(a) S Ltd. made a bonus issue on 31st March, 2005 of one ordinary share for every two held, reducing the Capital Reserve equivalently. The transaction is not shown in the above Balance Sheet.

(b) The Directors decided to write-down the fixed assets of S Ltd. by Rs. 7,500.

Prepare consolidated Balance Sheet as on 31st March, 2005.

CA (F) O.S. Modified

Ans. : Minority Interest — Rs. 51,930
Cost of Control — Rs. 47,280
Total of C B/S — Rs. 6,43,680

26. (Investment in Equity, Preference Shares & Debentures, Dividend paid, Proposed dividend and Bonus Shares)

The following are the summarised Balance Sheets of H Ltd. and S Ltd. as on 31st March, 2005.

Liabilities	H Ltd. Rs.	S Ltd. Rs.
12% Preference Share Capital (Shares of Rs. 100 each)	—	2,00,000
Equity Share Capital (Shares of Rs. 10 each)	8,00,000	4,00,000
General Reserve	3,60,000	2,00,000
Profit & Loss A/c	2,40,000	1,40,000

	Rs.	Rs.
10% Debentures (Rs. 100)	—	50,000
Proposed Dividends on :		
Equity Shares	1,20,000	60,000
Preference Shares	—	24,000
Debenture Interest O/s	—	5,000
Trade Creditors	4,10,000	2,10,000
	19,30,000	12,89,000
Assets		
Fixed Assets	10,15,000	8,09,000
Investments in S Ltd.:		
15,000 Preference Shares	1,80,000	
30,000 Equity Shares	4,50,000	
250 Debentures	25,000	
Current Assets	2,60,000	4,80,000
	19,30,000	12,89,000

Additional Information:

(i)	The Balance of Profit & Loss A/c (1.4.2004)		40,000
Add	Current year's Profit		2,04,000
			2,44,000
Less	Transfer to General Reserve	20,000	
	Transfer to Proposed dividend	84,000	1,04,000
			1,40,000

(ii) The Profit & Loss A/c on 1.4.2004 was after providing for dividends on Preference Shares and 10% dividends on Equity Shares for the year ended 31st March, 2004. These dividends were paid in July 2004 and were credited to the Profit & Loss A/c by H Ltd.

(iii) No entries have been made in the books of H Ltd. for debentures interest due or proposed dividend of S Ltd. for the current year 2004-05.

(iv) H Ltd. owed Rs. 4,000 to S Ltd. and S Ltd. owed Rs. 20,000 to H Ltd. which is reflected in their respective Balance Sheets.

(v) S Ltd. issued fully paid bonus shares in the ratio of one for every four shares held in January 2005, utilising the general reserve which was not recorded in the books of both the companies.

Prepare Consolidated Balance Sheet as on 31.3.05.

M.U. (2003) Modified

Ans. : Minority Interest — Rs. 2,35,000
Capital Reserve — Rs. 33,000
Total C B/S — RS. 25,40,000

27. (Investment in Equity, Preference Shares and Other Securities, Unrealised Profit, Mutual debts and cheque-in- transit)

The Balance Sheets of H Ltd. and S Ltd. as on 31st March, 2005 were as follows :

Liabilities	H Ltd.	S Ltd.
10% Preference Shares of Rs. 100 each	8,00,000	—
8% Preference Shares of Rs. 100 each	—	9,60,000
Equity Shares of Rs. 10 each	20,00,000	15,00,000
Revenue Reserves	18,00,000	10,50,000
12% Debentures	20,00,000	—
Provision for Depreciation	8,00,000	1,46,000
Proposed Dividend	6,80,000	2,26,800
Sundry creditors	6,25,000	1,50,000
	87,05,000	40,32,800
Assets		
Freehold Property	10,00,000	19,60,000
Pant & Machinery	20,00,000	6,30,000
Investments	30,00,000	—
Stock	15,00,000	8,00,000
Debtors	11,00,000	6,00,000
Cash & Bank	1,05,000	42,800
	87,05,000	40,32,800

Additional Information :

(i) The Investment of H Ltd. consists of the following-

	Rs.
1,20,000 Equity Shares in S Ltd. at cost (Acquired on 1.10.2003)	20,26,000
3,200 Preference Shares in S Ltd. at cost (Acquired on 1.4.2004)	3,24,000
9% Tax free Govt. Securities at cost (Acquired on 31.3.2005)	6,50,000
	30,00,000

(iii) The Revenue Reserve of S Ltd. stood at Rs. 5,22,000 when H Ltd. made its equity investments in it. On 1.4.2004 S Ltd. revenue reserve balance stood at Rs. 6,00,000.

(iii) The closing stock of H Ltd. stood at Rs. 5,22,000 in respect of goods invoiced by S Ltd. at cost plus 25%)

(iv) Proposed dividends consist of :

	H Ltd.	S Ltd.
Equity	6,00,000	1,50,000
Preference	80,000	76,800
	6,80,000	2,26,800

(v) Intra-group balances including in debtors and creditors are as follows:

H Ltd.: Creditors S Ltd. - Rs. 80,000

S Ltd. Debtors H Ltd. - Rs. 1,15,000

(vi) A cheque of Rs. 35,000 drawn by H Ltd. on 29th March 2005 was received by S Ltd. on 3rd April 2005.

Prepare a consolidated Balance sheet of H Ltd. and it's subsidiary S Ltd. as on 31st March, 2005.

[ICWA (F) Dec. 1999 Modified

Ans: Minority Interest — Rs. 11,50,000
Cost Control — Rs. 4,12,400
Total C B/S — Rs. 96,39,160

(Sale of Shares)

28. From the following Balance Sheets of H Ltd. and S Ltd. as on 31st March, 2005 prepare a Consolidated Balance Sheet.

Liabilities	H Ltd. Rs.	S Ltd. Rs.
Share Capital (Shares of Rs. 10 each)	10,00,000	2,00,000
Investment Reserve	30,000	
Profit & Loss A/c 1.4.2004	60,000	72,000
Profit for the year	20,000	48,000
	11,10,000	3,20,000
Assets		
Sundry Assets	9,30,000	3,20,000
Investment in S Ltd. (12,000 shares at cost)	1,80,000	—
	11,10,000	3,20,000

H Ltd. bought 16,000 shares in S Ltd. at Rs. 15 per share when the Profit & Loss A/c of the latter company stood at Rs. 44,000 and sold 4,000 shares on 30th September, 2004 at Rs. 22.50 per shares crediting the profit on sale to Investment Reserve.

[CA (F) Modified]

Ans. : Minority Interest — Rs. 1,28,000
Cost control — Rs. 33,600
Total of C B/S — Rs. 12,83,600

(Sale of shares)

29. The summarised Balance Sheets of H Ltd. and S Ltd. were as follows :

Balance Sheets as on 31st March, 2005

	Sources of Funds	H Ltd. Rs.	S Ltd. Rs.
	Share Capital (Rs. 10)	20,00,000	5,00,000
	General Reserve	2,00,000	50,000
	Profit & Loss A/c (1.4.2004)	3,00,000	1,00,000
	Profit for the year	80,000	80,000
Add	Dividend from S Ltd.	40,000	
Less	Dividend paid		(50,000)
	Creditors	3,00,000	2,00,000
		29,20,000	8,80,000

Application of Funds

Fixed Assets	20,00,000	8,00,000
Investment in 30,000 Shares in S Ltd. at cost	6,00,000	—
Current Assets	3,20,000	80,000
	29,20,000	8,80,000

H Ltd. acquired 40,000 shares in S Ltd. at Rs. 20 each on 1st April, 2004 and sold 10,000 shares at the same price on 1st January 2005. The sale is cum-dividend. An interim dividend of 10% was paid on 1st October 2004 by S Ltd.

Draft Consolidated Balance Sheet.

CA (F) Nov. 2001 Modified

Ans : Minority Interest — Rs. 2,72,000
Cost of Control — Rs. 2,10,000
Total of C B/S — Rs. 34,10,000

30. (Successive Purchases, Dividend, Revaluation, Bonus shares, Mutual owings and unrealised profit)

The Balance Sheets of H Ltd. and S Ltd. as on 31st March, 2005.

Liabilities	H Ltd. Rs.	S Ltd.. Rs.
Share Capital :		
Preference Shares of Rs. 100 each	80,000	40,000
Equity Shares of Rs. 10 each	4,00,000	2,00,000
General Reserve	80,000	50,000
Profit & Loss A/c	1,30,000	1,00,000
Bank Overdraft	30,000	20,000
S Creditors	58,000	46,000
Bills Payable	—	3000
	7,78,000	4,59,000
Assets		
Goodwill	50,000	30,000
Plant & Machinery	80,000	50,000
Vehicles	1,60,000	75,000
Furniture	60,000	40,000
Investment	2,50,000	45,000
Stock	50,000	50,000
Debtors	70,000	80,000
Bills Receivable	1000	—
Cash & Bank balance	57,000	89,000
	7,78,000	4,59,000

Additional Information :

(i) H Ltd. acquired 8000 Equity shares of S Ltd. on 1st April, 2003 and further acquired 7000 Equity shares on 1st April, 2004 at cost of Rs. 95,000 and Rs. 80,000 respectively.

(iii) The Preference Share Capital of S Ltd. includes nominal value of Rs. 15,000 held by H Ltd. acquired on 1st April, 2002 at a cost of Rs. 35,000.

(iii) The Profit & Loss A/c of S Ltd. had a credit balance of Rs. 30,000 on 1st April, 2004 and that of General Reserve Rs. 20,000

(iv) S Ltd. had paid dividend @ 10% on its paid up capital out of its Profit & Loss A/c balance on 1st April, 2004 for the 2003-04. The entire dividend received by H Ltd. has been credited to its Profit & Loss A/c.

(v) S Ltd. allotted bonus shares @ 1:10 out of its General Reserve during January 2005.

(vi) Bills Receivable of H Ltd. were all accepted by S Ltd. out of which bills amounting to Rs. 2000 have been discounted with the bank.

(vii) During the year 2004-05 H Ltd. purchased goods from S Ltd. for Rs. 10,000 at a sale price of Rs. 12,000 40% of these goods remained unsold on 31st March, 2005.

(viii) On 1.4.2004 Machinery of S Ltd. was overvalued by Rs. 10,000 for which necessary adjustments are to be made. The company charges depreciation @ 10%.

(ix) The management of H Ltd. and S Ltd. wish to recommend 15% and 10% dividend respectively for the year 2004-05.

Prepare Consolidated Balance Sheet as on 31st March, 2005.

[CA (F) OS, Modified]

Ans.: Minority Interest — Rs. 1,11,750
Cost of Control — Rs. 26,000
Total Goodwill — Rs. 1,06,000
Total of C B/S — Rs. 10,42,000

31. (Dividend, Bonus Shares, Mutual Owings and Unrelised Profit)

On 31st March, 2005 the Balance Sheets of H Ltd. and it's subsidiary stood as follow :

Liabilities	H Ltd. (Rs. in Lacs)	S Ltd. (Rs. in Lacs)
Share Capital :		
Authorised	15,000	6,000
Issued & Subscribed (shares of Rs. 10 each)	12,000	4,800
General Reserve	2,784	1,380
Profit & Loss A/c	2,715	1,620
Bills Payable	372	160
S Creditors	1,461	854
Provision for Taxation	855	394
Proposed Dividend	1,200	—
	21,387	9,208
Assets		
Land & Building	2,718	—
Plant & Machinery	4,905	4,900
Furniture & Fittings	1,845	586

Investments in Shares in S Ltd.	3,000	—
Stock	3,949	1,956
Debtors	2,600	1,363
Cash & Bank balances	1,490	204
Bills Receivable	360	199
Sundry Advances	520	—
	21,387	9,208

Additional Information :

(a) H Ltd. purchased 180 lacs shares in S Ltd. on 1.4.2004 when the balances to General Reserve and profit & Loss stood at Rs. 3000 lac and Rs. 1,200 lac respectively.

(b) On 4th July, 2004 S Ltd. declared a dividend @ 20% for the year ended 31st March 2004. H Ltd. credited the dividend received to it's Profit & Loss A/c.

(c) On 1st January, 2005 S Ltd. issued 3 fully bonus shares for every 5 shares held aş bonus shares out of General Reserve balance as on 31st March, 2004.

(d) On 31st March, 2005 all the bills payable in S Ltd.'s Balance Sheet were accepted in favour of H Ltd. But on that date, H Ltd. held Rs. 45 lac of these acceptances in hand, the rest having been endorsed in favour of it's creditors.

(e) On 31st March, 2005 S Ltd. stock included goods which it had purchased for Rs. 100 lac from H Ltd. who made a profit @ 25% on cost.

Prepare a Consolidated Balance Sheet as on 31st March, 2005 keeping in mind the requirements of AS-21.

[CA (F) May 2004]

Ans. : Minority Interest — Rs. 3,120 lac

Capital Reserve — Rs. 1,320 lac

Total of C B/S — Rs. 27,520 lac.

9

Accounting for Banking Companies

A sound Banking system is an important pillar of an economy. The development and growth of banking system depends upon the trust that the society and customers have in it's reliability. Preparation of necessary ledger accounts and their disclosures are effective means of informing the society or market about the functioning, product and services, achievements, results & risks etc. For reasons of safety, soundness and transparency legal provisions require Banks to disclose information and make them publicly available. However, interpretation of accounting standards and disclosures differs from bank to bank or person to person Non-compliance of Accounting Standards could affect the confidence of the users of financial statements presented by the bank. It may well question the integrity of published financial statements. The Base Committee on Banking Supervision (BCBS) has underlined that disclosure should not be in conflict with the spirit of accounting standards and other statutory requirements. Where the disclosures are made under accounting requirements or are made to satisfy the listing requirements of regulators, the banks may rely on the guidelines to fulfill the expectations. In such situations banks should explain material difference between the accounting and other disclosures. A number of additional quantitative and qualitative disclosures are recommended by BCBS in the revised capital adequacy norms. Reserve Bank of India has been continuously making efforts to ensure convergence of it's supervisory norms and practices with a view to align the standards adopted by Indian banking system with global standards. It is observed that out of 29 Indian Accounting Standards, the banks in India are generally are complying with all the Accounting Standards except AS - 11 (Forex Transactions). Convergence should be possible in this AS-11 also with in short span.

According to the Preface to the Statements of Accounting Standards issued by the Council of the Institute of Chartered Accountants of India, the financial statements should be prepared in accordance with Accounting standards applicable on the following basis.

(i) Accounting Standards are intended to apply only to items, which are material.

(ii) These should enable to achieve uniformity in preparation and presentation of financial statements.

(iii) The emphasis is on laying down accounting principles and not the detailed rules for application and interpretation there of.

(iv) They should be in conformity with the provisions of applicable law, customs, usages and business environment in India.

(v) They cannot override the local regulations which govern the preparation and presentation of financial statements in the country.

The main objective of this chapter is to make students familiar with the various provisions relating to preparation of final accounts of banking companies, to enable them to understand the mode of disclosure of accounting policies adopted by the banking companies and to develop understanding of the accounting treatment of certain specific adjustments in the final accounts of banking companies. But first let us understand the nature of activities undertaken by the banking business in India which is governed by the Banking Regulation Act, 1949. The primary business of the bank is to accept the deposits from the public for lending and investment, repaying on demand or withdrawable by cheque, draft etc. Of late the Act has been amended by the Banking Regulation (Amendment) Act 1994 (w.e.f. 31st January 1994) followed by the Narsimham Committee II 1998. However, the Banking Act is not applicable to a primary agricultural society, a co-operative society, except in the manner and extent specified in the Act. Section 6(1) of the Banking Regulation Act 1949 lays down the primary functions as follows :

(i) Accepting deposits from the public

(ii) Lending or investing these deposits

(iii) Borrowing, raising or taking up money.

(iv) Accepting, drawing, discounting, buying, selling, collecting and dealing in bills of exchange, promissory notes and other instruments.

(v) Granting, issuing letter of credit (LC) and traveller's cheques.

(vi) Buying, selling on commission, dealing and underwriting shares, debentures and bonds etc.

(vii) Collecting and transmitting of money and securities

(viii) Buying, selling and dealing in bullion & specie

(ix) Receiving of all kinds of scrips or valuables on deposit or for safe custody.

(x) Acting as agents for any Government or local authority or any other person or persons: the carrying on the agency business of any description including the clearing and forwarding of goods.

(xi) Effecting, insuring, guaranteeing, underwriting, participating, in managing and carrying out of any issue of shares, debentures or bonds.

(xii) Carrying on and transacting every kind of guarantee and indemnity business.

(xiii) Managing, selling and realising any property which may come into the possession in satisfaction or part satisfaction of claims.

(xiv) Acquiring, holding and generally dealing with any property or any right, title or interest in any property which may form the security or part of security for any loan or advances.

(xv) Undertaking and executing trusts.

(xvi) Acquiring, constructing, managing and altering any building or works necessary for the purpose of banking company.

(xvii) Selling, improving, managing, developing, exchanging leasing, mortgaging, disposing of all or any part of property or rights of the banking company.

(xviii) Undertaking and administration of estates as executors, trustees or otherwise.

(xix) Acquiring and undertaking the whole or any part of business of any person or company when such business is of a nature described U/s 6 (1)

(xx) Doing all such things as are incidental or conducive to the promotion or advancement of the business of the company.

(xxi) Any other form of business which the central Government may notify in the official Gazette

Certain types of Business Prohibited for a Banking Company

As per the Banking Regulation Act 1949 the following types of business cannot be carried on by a banking company :

(i) Trading activities : (a) No banking company can directly or indirectly deal in buying, selling or bartering of goods except in connection with the realisation of security given or held by it, or (b) engage in any trade or buy or sell or barter goods for others except in connection with bills of exchange.

(ii) No banking company can deal in immovable property except that is required for it's own use. If acquired, must be disposed of within seven years from the date of acquisition. However, the Reserve Bank may in any particular case may extend the aforesaid period by a period not exceeding five years.

Certain Restrictions for a Banking Company

(a) Holding Shares: A banking company cannot hold shares of any other company (except of it's own subsidiary) exceeding 30% of it's own capital and reserves which over is less.

[Section 8]

(b) Payment of brokerage commission or discount beyond the limit : [Sec. 13]

No banking company can pay directly or indirectly an amount exceeding $2^1/_2\%$ of paid up value of shares.

(c) Charge on the unpaid capital: [Sec. 14]

No banking company can create any charge on the unpaid capital and if created it shall be void.

(d) Floating charge on assets: [Sec. 14A]

No banking company can create a floating charge on it's assets or part thereof except with the prior sanction from the Reserve Bank who will certify in writing that the charge is not detrimental to the interest of depositors.

(e) Payment of dividend [Sec. 15]

No banking company can pay dividend on it's shares until all it's capitalised expenses (including preliminary expenses, organisation expenses, share-selling expenses, brokerage, amount of losses incurred and any other item of expenditure not represented by tangible assets) have been completely written off.

However, a banking company is permitted to pay dividend without writing off the following :

(i) Depreciation in the value of it's investments in approved securities where such depreciation has not actually been capitalised or otherwise accounted for as a loss.

(ii) Depreciation in the value of it's investments in shares, debentures or bonds (other than approved securities) in any case where adequate provision for such depreciation has been made to the satisfaction of the auditors.

(iii) Bad debts, if any, where adequate provision has been made to the satisfaction of the auditors of the banking company.

(f) Granting of loans advances [Sec. 25]

(i) A banking company cannot grant any loans or advances on the security of it's own shares.

(ii) It cannot enter into any commitment for granting any loan or advance to or on behalf of:

(a) Any of it's directors

(b) Any firm in which any of it's directors is interested as a partner, manager, employee or guarantor.

(c) Any company in which any of it's directors is a director, manager, employee or guarantor or in which he holds substantial interest or

(d) Any individual in respect of whom any of it's directors is a partner or guarantor.

However, it does not apply to subsidiaries of the banking companies registered U/s 25 of the Companies Act or a Government Company.

OTHER LEGAL REQUIREMENTS

Capital and Reserves

Minimum Paid up Capital [Sec. 12] No banking company can commence banking business in India unless its subscribed capital is at least half of it's authorised capital and it's paid up capital is at least half of it's subscribed capital.

Minimum amount of Paid up Capital & Reserves

A Banking Company	Incorporated in India Rs.	Incorporated outside India Rs.
a. If it has a place of business in Mumbai or Kolkata or both	10,00,000	20,00,000
b. If it has no place of business in Mumbai or Kolkata	5,00,000	15,00,000
c. If all places of business in one state and if any place of business is Mumbai or Kolkata	Rs. 5,00,000 plus Rs. 25,000 for each place of business outside Mumbai or Kolkata subject to a maximum of Rs. 10,00,000.	
d. If all places of business are in one state and none of the places being in Mumbai or Kolkata	Rs. 1,00,000 plus Rs. 10,000 for each other place of business in the same district and Rs. 25,000 for each place of business outside district subject to a maximum of Rs. 5,00,000. If there is only one place of business the limit not to exceed Rs. 50,000.	

Statutory Reserve [Sec. 17] A banking company must create a reserve fund and transfer at least 25%* of it's annual profits to it. Such transfer will continue to be made even if the total of reserve fund and securities premium if any, exceeds it's paid up capital. However, the Central Government may grant exemption on the recommendation of Reserve Bank of India in this regard. The reserve fund so created has to be shown separately from the other reserves. It is to be noted that such transfer should be made out of the current year's profits before any appropriation.

(*raised from 20% to 25%)

CRR/Cash Reserves : [Sec. 18] According to this section of Banking Regulation Act every non scheduled bank is required to maintain by way of cash reserve with itself or in any current account with the State Bank of India or Reserve Bank of India or partly in cash with itself and partly in such account or accounts, a sum equivalent to 3%* of the total time and demand liabilities in India. Where as according to Sec. 42 of R.B.I all scheduled banks are required to maintain cash reserve equal to 3%* of total time and demand liabilities with the Reserve Bank of India who has the power to increase cash reserve percentage upto 20% through the notification in official gazette. It is 5% w.e.f. Oct. 2, 2004. The banks are entitled to get monthly interest on the deposits made out of cash reserve with Reserve Bank of India @ 3.5% w.e.f. September 18, 2004 from the earlier rate of 6%.

(*5% w.e.f. October 2, 2004); 5.75% w.e.f. Feb. 17, 2007; 6% w.e.f. March 3, 2007 at present 6.5%

SLR/Liquidity Reserve : [Sec. 24] Section 24 of Banking Regulation Act also requires that every banking company should maintain in India an amount equal to 25% of the time and demand liabilities in cash, gold and unencumbered approved securities over and above the cash reserve. The Reserve Bank of India is empowered to increase the ratio upto 40%. However, at present it stands at **25% w.e.f. October 26, 1997.**

Subsidiary Companies

A banking company is allowed to form a subsidiary company only for the purpose of undertaking of any business laid down U/s 6(1) of the Banking Regulation Act 1949 or with the written permission of the Reserve Bank of India to carry on the banking business exclusively outside India or to undertake such other business which the Reserve Bank may, with the prior approval of the Central Government consider conducive to the spread of banking in India or is in the public interest.

Licensing of Banking Companies

A banking company in India can function only if it acquires a licence from Reserve Bank of India in this behalf. Before granting licence the Reserve Bank of India must be satisfied after the inspection of books of accounts. Otherwise the following conditions must be satisfied.

1. That the company is or will be in a position to pay its future depositors in full as and when their claims accrue.
2. That the affairs of the company are not being conducted or are not likely to be conducted in a manner detrimental to the interest of its present or future depositors.
3. That the general character of the proposed management of the bank will not be prejudicial to the public interest of it's present and future depositors.
4. That the bank had adequate capital structure and earnings prospects.
5. That the public interest will be served by the grant of a licence to the company to carry on baking activities in India.
6. That having regard to the banking facilities available in the proposed principal area of bank already in existence and other relevant factors, the grant of the licence will not be prejudicial to the operation & consolidation system consistent with the monetary stability and economic growth.

Main Characteristics of a Bank's Book Keeping system

(i) Posting : Entries in the personal ledgers are made directly from vouchers (slips) instead of being posted from books of original entry.

(ii) Daily Summary Sheets : The vouchers entered into different personal ledgers are summarised each day on summary sheets, the totals of which are posted to the control accounts in the general ledger.

(iii) Daily Trial Balance : The general ledger trial balance is extracted and agreed every day.

(iv) Continuous Check : All entries in the personal ledgers and summary sheets are checked by persons other than those who have recorded entries. It helps in detecting the clerical mistakes immediately.

(v) Control Accounts : A trial balance of the detailed personal ledgers is prepared periodically also (weekly or fortnightly) which is agreed with general ledger control accounts.

(vi) Double Voucher System : Two vouchers are prepared for every transaction not involving cash - one debit voucher and other credit voucher.

I Principal Books of Accounts

Cash Book : Every transaction involving receipts and payments are recorded in the Receiving cashier Cash book and Paying Cashier Cash book respectively and there from posted to the concerned customer's/Depositor's/party's account on the basis of "pay-in-slip" or withdrawal form/cheque respectively. There after such transactions are recorded in the Master Cash Book for verification of all accounts.

General Ledger : It contains all personal accounts ledgers, nominal accounts ledgers, and real accounts ledgers whose closing balances are transferred to Trial Balance which helps in preparing the final accounts.

Other Ledgers : Some banks maintain separate books for debit revenue items and credit revenue items. The totals of debit and credit accounts are taken to Profit & Loss Account in the General Ledgers, while some banks record revenue items in the General Ledger itself. Even some banks maintain summary of revenue accounts in the General Ledger. In some cases, banks keep one account for Profit and Loss in the General Ledger and maintain separate books for detailed accounts.

II Subsidiary Ledgers

(a) Current Accounts Ledger : It contains the accounts of those persons who open current accounts in the bank. The bank does not allow any interest on the credit balance of account holder who, if required, sanctioned overdraft facility.

(b) Savings Bank Accounts Ledger : It contains the accounts of those customers who open saving bank accounts with the bank who allows interest on the monthly balance of customers.

(c) Fixed Deposit Accounts Ledger : This ledger contains the accounts of customers who have deposited money for a fixed period at a fixed rate of interest.

(d) Recurring Deposit Accounts Ledger : This ledger maintains the accounts of those customers who make deposit every weak, fortnight or month.

(e) Fixed Deposit Interest Ledger : It records the interest of every fixed deposit which is credited to each depositor's account by the end of each accounting year.

(f) Loan Accounts Ledger : It contains the account of each customer to whom loan is sanctioned. It also records amount of loan, rate of interest, the terms of payment, nature and amount of security pledged, mortgaged or hypothecated.

(g) Investments Accounts Ledger : This ledger contains the accounts of each investment the bank holds along with the details regarding face value, cost and rate of interest of each investment.

(h) Cash credit and overdrafts Ledgers : This ledger contains the accounts of customers who have been granted cash credit and overdraft facility.

(i) **Bills discounted and Purchased Ledgers** : These ledgers contain accounts of persons who got their bills discounted and those from whom bills have been purchased.

(j) **Customers' acceptances, endorsements and guarantee Ledger :** This ledger contains the accounts of bills accepted, endorsed or guaranteed by the other parties.

III Other Books and Registers

These include :

(1) **Statistical Books:** These are books contain information relating to :

(i) Number and amount of cheques paid

(ii) Number and amount of cheques collected including bills

(iii) Deposits received

(iv) Amount paid

(v) Balances of loans & advances on weekly or monthly basis.

(2) ***(a) Bills for Collection Register***

It contains the information about the bills deposited by customers for collection which includes names of the drawer and drawee, the nature of bill, whether payable on demand or at sight. These may further be classified as Inward or outward or Government bill for collection/bills lodged.

(b) Securities Register :

It contains the details of all securities held by the bank against loans sanctioned/advances given.

(c) Document Register :

This register contains the details of documents submitted by the customers against loans/advances.

(d) Jewellery Register :

This register shows the details of jewellery pledged by the parties against loans/advances.

(e) Cheques Dishonoured Register :

It records the details of dishonoured Cheques returned by bank and the reason of dishonour.

(f) Drafts Payable Register :

It records the details of drafts issued by other branches for payment at this branch.

(g) Drafts Issue Register :

It contains the details of drafts issued by the branch payable to other branches.

(h) Letters of Credit (LC) Register :

It contains the details of letters of credit issued by bank to it's clients.

(i) Letters of Guarantee Register :

It records the details of guarantee given by other parties (sureties) in case of loans/Advances granted by bank to other parties.

(j) Telegraphic Transfer/Mail Transfer (T.T/ M.T) Register :

It contains the details of Telegraphic transfer and Mail transfers made by order.

(k) Standing order Register

This register records the 'standing' instructions received from various account holders for the periodical payments or collection made on behalf of clients.

"Slip System" (Loose leaves Vouchers)

Slip refers to ay voucher such as pay-in-slip, cheques, dockets or withdrawal forms which are received from clients. These slips are passed on to the ledger keeper concerned for immediate posting on the same day. This way the bank keeps its ledgers upto date which helps in ascertaining the credit balance standing to the credit of any customer. A 'Day book' also records all such entries direct from such slips. Subsequently, entries in the customers accounts are tallied with entries in the 'Day Book'. Thus this system of double entry serves as an automatic check and ensures accuracy, saves time and efforts of recording in other subsidiary books, provides sound basis of accounting and auditing as the slips serve as perfect basis of evidence.

However, there is a risk of loss of slips and manipulation by dishonest employees. The illiterate customers face a lot of inconvenience while writing these slips.

A clarification of various types of slips will develop a thorough understanding of the slip system.

1. Pay-in-slip

A pay-in-slip is simply an acknowledgement of deposit made by the customer to his account in the bank. It is divided in two parts. The left side of the pay-in-slip is called "counterfoil" which is returned by the bank cashier (Receiving) after putting his signature and bank stamp. Thus 'counter foil' of the slip becomes the authentic receipt which serves as an evidence (proof) that amount as shown therein has been deposited in the bank account as per the details shown. The right side of pay-in-slip is kept by the receiving cashier for the purpose of recording entry in the personal account of the customer concerned.

2. Cheque or Withdrawal form

A cheque is an instrument which contains unconditional order to a specified bank to pay a certain sum of money to the bearer of instrument (cheque) or to a specified person. It simply means that when a customer (Account holder) wants to withdraw money from bank or wants to make payment to any other person, writes a cheque either in his own favour (i.e. self) or in favour of any third party. The paying cashier after making proper scrutiny of the cheque, relating to signature & amount standing to the credit of account holder makes the payment as directed. In the absence of cheque, the withdrawal form/slip serves the purpose and these become basis of recording entries in the personal accounts of the account holders.

3. Dockets

When there are no original vouchers then bank makes slips which are called dockets for such transactions. These dockets (slips) unlike other slips, are used for posting purposes. For example, when interest on loans or advances becomes due, the bank prepares a slip called docket on the basis of which posting is done in the ledger account concerned. Similarly if any amount is to be transferred from Current Account of a customer to his Saving Bank Account, a voucher will be prepared by the Current Account Department for posting.

Quick (Prompt) Payment System : (Teller) To facilitate customers banks continue to introduce various system of banking to make it easier and attractive. Under teller system tellers keep cash as well as ledger cards and the specimen signature cards of each customer in respect of Current and Saving Bank Accounts. A teller is authorised to make payment upto a particular amount say Rs. 2,000 or Rs. 5,000. On receipt of cheque, he checks, clears it, enters in the ledger card and makes the payment to the customer. The teller also receives the deposits which are credited to concerned customer's accounts.

Returns to be Filed by Banking Companies

Apart from the weekly return to be filed by scheduled banks, all banking companies have to file following returns with the Reserve Bank.

(a) Monthly return of unsecured loans and advances sanctioned or granted to companies in which any of the Bank's directors is interested as a director, managing agent or guarantor.

(b) Monthly return of assets maintained in accordance with Section 24 and time and demand liabilities at the close of business on every Friday.

(c) Quarterly return of assets and liabilities at the close of business on the last Friday of every quarter.

(d) Annual return of unclaimed accounts which have not been operated upon for 10 years or more.

(e) Monthly return of assets and liabilities at the close of business on the last Friday of every month.

(f) Annual return of remuneration paid to directors and the first ten (10) highest paid officers.

(g) Quarterly return of officers in India.

(h) Any other statement or information as may be required by the Reserve Bank of India.

Preparation of Financial Statements

With the onset of liberalisation and globalisation the economic and financial policies of the Government have changed the environment in which the banks operate. A committee, under the chairmanship of Shri A. Ghosh, Deputy Governor Reserve Bank of India was constituted to examine the desirability of greater disclosure in the published accounts of banks having regard to public accountability, maintenance of confidentiality, and maintaining the reputation and credit worthiness of the banks. The Committee after due deliberations suggested that there is need for better disclosure and need for improving the presentation of accounts.

On 18.1.1991 the Government of India under the Banking. Regulation Act 1949, notified it's intention to incorporate amendments to the third schedule of the above Act After examining the suggestions of Ghosh committee, the Government issued a fresh notification on 19.12.1990 accepting the revised formats after the expiry of three months. On 6.2.1992 the Reserve Bank of India issued a circular to the commercial banks advising them to ensure that their final accounts are compiled in the revised format for the accounting year 1991-92 and there after.

The revised formats of the Balance Sheet as per Form 'A' and Profit & Loss Account as per Form B and Eighteen other schedules including "Notes" and "Accounting Policies" are as under :

NEW REVISED FORMATS

The Third Schedule

(See Section 29)

Form 'A'

Form of Balance Sheet

Balance Sheet of (here enter name of the Banking company)

Balance Sheet as on 31st March (Year)

(000's omitted)

Capital & Liabilities	Schedule	As on 31. 3... (Current year)	As on 31. 3..... (Previous year)
Capital	1		
Reserve & Surplus	2		
Deposits	3		
Borrowings	4		
Other liabilities and provisions	5		
Total :			
Assets			
Cash and balances with Reserve Bank of India	6		
Balance with banks Money at call and short notice	7		
Investments	8		
Advances	9		
Fixed Assets	10		
Other Assets	11		
Total :			
Contingent liabilities	12		
Bills for collection			

Schedule 1 - Capital

I. For Nationalised Banks

Capital (Fully owned by Central Government)

II. For Banks Incorporated outside India : Capital

(i) (The amount brought in by banks by way of start-up capital as prescribed by RBI should be shown under this head)

(ii) Amount of deposit kept with the RBI under Section 11 (2) of the Banking Regulation Act, 1949.

Total :

III. For other Banks

Authorised Capital
(Shares of Rs. each)

Issued Capital
(Shares of Rs. each)

Subscribed Capital
(Shares of Rs. each)

Called-up Capital
(Shares of Rs. each)

Less : Calls unpaid

Add : Forfeited Shares

Schedule 2 - Reserves and Surplus

	As on 31. 3... (Current year)	As on 31. 3... (Previous year)
I. Statutory Reserves		
Opening Balance		
Additions during the year		
Deductions during the year		
II. Capital Reserves		
Opening Balance		
Additions during the year		
Deductions during the year		
III. Securities Premium		
Opening Balance		
Additions during the year		
Deductions during the year		
IV. Revenue and other Reserves		
Opening Balance		
Additions during the year		
Deductions during the year		
V. Balance in Profit & Loss Account		
Total : (I,II, III, IV and V)		

Schedule 3 - Deposits

A. I. Demand Deposits
- (i) From banks
- (ii) From others

II. Savings Bank Deposits

III. Term Deposits
- (i) From Banks
- (ii) From others

Total : (I, II and III)

B. (i) Deposits of branches in India
(ii) Deposits of branches outside India
Total I:

Schedule 4 - Borrowings

	As on 31. 3... (Current year)	As on 31. 3... (Previous year)
I Borrowings in India		
(i) Reserve Bank of India		
(ii) Other banks		
(iii) Other institutions and agencies		
II. Borrowings outside India		
Total : (I and II)		
Secured borrowings in I & II above - Rs.		

Schedule 5 - Other Liabilities & Provisions

I. Bills payable
II. Inter-office adjustments (net)
III. Interest accrued
V. Others (including provisions)
Total :

Schedule 6 - Cash and Balances With Reserve Bank Of India

I. Cash in hand (including foreign currency notes)
II. Balances with Reserve Bank of India
(i) In Current Account
(ii) In Other Account
Total : (I & II)

Schedule 7 - Balances With Banks & Money At Call & Short Notice

In India
(i) Balances with banks
(a) in Current Accounts
(b) in Other Deposit Accounts
(ii) Money at call and short notice
(a) with banks
(b) with other institutions
Total : (I & II)

Outside India
(i) In Current Accounts
(ii) In other Deposits Accounts
(iii) Money at call and short notice
Total : (I , II & III)
Grand Total (I & II):

Schedule 8 - Investments

	As on 31. 3... (Current year)	As on 31. 3... (Previous year)
I. Investments in India in		
(i) Government securities		
(ii) Other approved securities		
(iii) Shares		
(iv) Debentures and Bonds		
(v) Subsidiaries and/or joint ventures		
(vi) Others (to be specified)		
Total :		
II. Investments outside India in		
(i) Government securities (Including local authorities)		
(ii) Subsidiaries and/or joint ventures abroad		
(iii) Other investments (to be specified)		
Total :		
Grand Total : (I & II)		

Schedule 9 - Advances

A. (i) Bills purchased and discounted
(ii) Cash credits, overdrafts and loans payable on demand
(iii) Term loans
Total :

B. (i) Secured by tangible assets
(ii) Covered by Bank/ Government Guarantees
(iii) Unsecured
Total :

C. I. Advances in India
(i) Priority Sectors
(ii) Public Sector
(iii) Banks
(iv) Others
Total :

II. Advances outside India
(i) Due from banks
(ii) Due from others
(a) Bills purchased and discounted
(b) Syndicated loans
(c) Others
Total:

Grand Total: (C. I & II)

Schedule 10 - Fixed Assets

	As on 31. 3... (Current year)	As on 31. 3... (Previous year)
I. Premises		
At cost as on 31st March of the preceding year		
Additions during the year		
Deductions during the year		
Depreciation to date		
II. Other Fixed articles (including Furniture and Fixtures)		
At cost as on 31st March of the preceding year		
Additions during the year		
Deductions during the year		
Depreciation to date		
Total : (I & II)		
Grand Total:		

Schedule 11 - Other Assets

I. Inter-office adjustments (net)
II. Interest accrued
III. Tax paid in advance/tax deducted at source
IV. Stationery and stamps
V. Non-banking assets acquired in satisfaction of claims
VI. Other @
Total :

@ In case there is any unadjusted balance of loss the same may be shown under this item with appropriate foot-note.

Schedule 12 - Contingent Liabilities

I. Claims against the bank not acknowledged as debts
II. Liability for partially paid investments
III. Liability on account of outstanding forward exchange contracts
IV. Guarantees given on behalf of constituents
(a) In India
(b) Outside India
V. Acceptances, endorsements and other obligations
VI. Other items for which the bank is contingently liable
Total

Form 'B'

('000 omitted)

Form of Profit & Loss Account for the year ended 31st March

	Schedule No.	As on 31. 3... (Current year)	As on 31. 3... (Previous year)
I. Income			
Interest earned	13		
Other income	14		
Total			
II. Expenditure			
Interest expended	15		
Operating expenses	16		
Provisions and contingencies			
Total			
III. Profit/Loss			
Net profit/loss (–) for the year			
Profit/Loss (–) brought forward			
Total			
IV. Appropriations			
Transfer to statutory reserves			
Transfer to other reserves			
Transfer to Government/Proposed dividends			
Balance carried over to balance sheet			
Total			

Schedule 13 - Interest Earned

I. Interest/discount on advances/bills
II. Income on investments
III. Interest on balances with Reserve Bank of India and other inter-bank funds
IV. Others
Total

Schedule 14 - Other Income

I. Commission, exchange and brokerage
II. Profit on sale of investments
Less: Loss on sale of investments
III. Profit on revaluation of investments
Less: Loss on revaluation of investments
IV. Profit on sale of land, building and other assets
Less: Loss on sale of land, building and other assets
V. Profit on exchange transactions
Less: Loss on exchanges transactions

VI. Income earned by way of dividends etc. from subsidiaries/companies and/ or joint ventures abroad/in India

VII. Miscellaneous Income

Total :

Note : Under items II to V loss figures may be shown in brackets.

Schedule 15 - Interest Expended

I. Interest on deposits

II. Interest on Reserve Bank of India/inter-bank borrowings

III. Others

Total :

Schedule 16 - Operating Expenses

I. Payments to and provisions for employees

II. Rent, taxes and lighting

III. Printing and stationery

IV. Advertisement and publicity

V. Depreciation on Bank's property

VI. Director's fees, allowances and expenses

VII. Auditor's fees and expenses (including branch auditors)

VIII. Law Charges

IX. Postages, Telegrams, Telephones, etc.

X. Repair and maintenance

XI. Insurance

XII. Other expenditure

Total

Schedule 17 - Notes on Accounts

1. Reconciliation and consequential adjustments of pending items in inter-branch transactions including drafts payable and drafts paid without advice, accounts with other banks including foreign banks, clearing accounts and items in Sundries Receivable. Sundry Deposit Accounts are in progress. In some of the branches, balance in some of the accounts have not been tallied with those of subsidiary Ledger and Registers. Steps have already been taken to reconcile the differences. The effect of reconciliation of these pending items on the Profit & Loss Account and the Balance Sheet is not ascertainable at this stage.

2. In respect of un-audited branches, wherever information in regard to classification of advances were inadequate, the same has been classified to the extent possible on the basis of information available at the Administrative Offices/Head Office.

3. Advances due from sick units under nursing programmes, nationalised units, and in respect of various sticky, suit filed and decreed accounts have been considered good on the basis of-

(a) Available estimated value of existing and prospective primary and collateral securities including personal worth of the borrowers and the guarantors.

(b) The proposed/on-going revival/rehabilitation programmes.

(c) Pending settlement of claims by Government.

(d) The claims lodged/to be lodged under various credit guarantee schemes and the Agriculture and Rural Debt Relief Scheme, 1990.

4. The excess of the book value over market value of investments in Indian Government securities as on 31st March, 1992 amounts to Rs. 8,102.51 lakhs.

5. Premises include properties, book value of which is Rs. 245.93 lakhs, for which registration formalities are in progress.

6. The excess of liabilities over the readily realisable assets taken over from the erstwhile Bank of Thanjavur Limited is included under "Other Assets" pending settlement of claims lodged with Deposit Insurance and Credit Guarantee Corporation of India, realisation of assets taken over on collection basis and final settlement under the Scheme of Amalgamation.

7. The previous year's figures have been regrouped wherever practicable in accordance with the current year's classification as per the amended forms set out in Third Schedule to the Banking Regulation Act expect of classification of advances on securities/sectoral basis for which the information furnished by the Administrative Offices have been adopted.

Schedule 18 - Principal Accounting Policies

1. General - The accompanying financial statements have been prepared on the historical cost basis and conform to the statutory provisions and practices prevailing in the country.

2. Foreign Exchange Transactions

(a) Monetary and non-monetary assets and liabilities have been translated at the exchange rates prevailing at the close of year.

(b) Income and expenditure items in respect of Indian branches have been translated at the exchange rates ruling on the date of transactions and in respect of foreign branches at the exchange rates prevailing at the close of the respective half years.

(c) Profit or loss on foreign currency position including pending forward exchange contracts has been accounted for at the exchange rates prevailing at the close of the year, as per the guidelines of the foreign Exchange Dealer's Association of India.

3. Investments - Investments are shown at their book value.

4. Advances - Advances due from sick units under nursing programmes, nationalised units and in respect of various sticky, suit filed and decreed accounts have been considered good on the basis of :

(a) Available estimated value of existing and prospective primary and collateral securities including personal worth of the borrowers and guarantors.

(b) The proposed/on going revival/rehabilitation programmes.

(c) Pending settlement of claims by Government.

(d) The claim lodged/to be lodged under various credit guarantee schemes, and the Agriculture and Rural Debt Relief Scheme, 1990.

(e) Provisions to the satisfaction of auditors in respect of doubtful advances have been made and deducted from advances. Such provisions have been made on gross basis. Tax relief available when the advance is written off will be accounted for in the year of write off.

5. Fixed Assets - The premises and other fixed assets except for foreign branches are accounted for at their historical cost. Depreciation has been provided on written down value method at the rates prescribed in the Income Tax Rules, 1962 for Indian Assets. Depreciation in respect of Assets of Foreign branches has been provided as per the local laws.

6. Staff Benefits - Gratuity determined on actuarial basis has been paid to the approved gratuity fund constituted by the Bank.

NOTES AND INSTRUCTIONS FOR COMPILATION

General Instructions

1. Formats of Balance Sheet and Profit and Loss Account cover all items likely to appear in the statements. In case a bank does not have any particular item to report, it may be omitted from the formats.

2. Corresponding comparative figures for the previous year are to be disclosed as indicated in the format. The words "current year" and "previous year" used in the format are only to indicate the order of presentation and may appear in the accounts.

3. Figures should be rounded off to the nearest thousand rupees.

4. Unless otherwise indicated, the banks in these statements will include banking companies, nationalised banks, State Bank of India. Associate Banks and all other institutions including co-operatives carrying on the business of banking whether or not incorporated or operating in India. Hindi version of the balance sheet will be part of the annual report.

2.10 Note containing guidelines of Reserve Bank of India for compilation of Financial Statements :

Given below are the compilation notes of the Reserve Bank of India for balance sheet and profit and loss account as per the revised formats.

D. NOTE CONTAINING GUIDELINES OF RBI FOR COMPILATION OF FINANCIAL STATEMENTS

Balance Sheet

Item	Schedule	Coverage	Notes and instructions for compilation
Capital	1	**Nationalised Banks** Capital (Fully Owned by Central Government)	The Capital owned by Central Government as on the date of the Balance Sheet including contribution from Government, if any, for participating in World Bank Projects should be shown.
		Banking companies incorporated outside India	(i) The amount brought in by banks by way of start-up capital as prescribed by RBI should be shown under this head. (ii) The amount of deposit kept with RBI, under sub-section 2 of section 11 of the Banking Regulation Act, 1949 should also be shown. Authorised, Issued, Subscribed Called-up Capital should be given separately Calls-in-arrears will be deducted from Called up capital while the paid-up value of the forfeited shares should be added thus arriving at the paid-up capital.
		Other Banks (Indian) Authorised Capital (...Shares or Rs. each) Issued Capital (..Shares of Rs....each) subscribed Capital (...Shares of Rs...each) Called up Capital (....Shares of Rs....each. *Less :* Calls unpaid....... *Add:* Forfeited shares..... Paid up to capital......	

		Where necessary, items which can be combined should be shown under one head for instance 'Issued and Subscribed Capital'.
		Notes– General
		The changes in the above items, if any, during the years, say, fresh contribution made by Government, fresh issue of capital, capitalisation of reserves, etc. may be explained in the notes.
Reserves and Surplus	2 **(I) Statutory Reserves**	Reserves created in terms of Section 17 or any other section of Banking Regulation Act must be separately disclosed.
	(II) Capital Reserve	The expression 'capital reserves' shall not include any amount regarded as free for contribution through the profit and loss account. Surplus on revaluation should be treated as Capital Reserve Surplus on translation of the final instalment of foreign branches (which includes fixed assets also) is not a revaluation reserve.
	(III) Securities Premium	Premium on issue of share capital may be shown separately under this head.
	(IV) Revenue and other Reserves	The expression 'Revenue Reserve', called any reserve other than capital reserve created will include all reserves other than those separately classified. The expression Reserve shall not include any amount retained by way of providing renewals or diminution in value of assets or retained by way of providing fund for known liability.
	(V) Balance of Profit	Includes balance of profit after appropriations. In case of loss the balance may be shown as a deduction.
		Notes– General
		Movement in various categories of Reserves should be shown as indicated in the schedule.
Deposits	3 A. (I) Demand Deposits (i) from banks (ii) from others	Includes all bank deposit repayable on demand. Includes all demand deposits of the non-bank sectors. Credit balances in

		overdrafts, cash credit accounts, deposits payable at call, overdue deposits, inoperative current accounts, matured time deposits and cash certificates, certificates of deposits, etc. are to be included under this category.
	(II) Saving Bank Deposits	Includes all savings bank deposits (including inoperative savings bank A/c)
	(III) Term Deposits (i) from banks	Includes all types of bank deposits repayable after a specified term.
	(ii) from others	Includes all types of deposits of the non-bank sector repayable after a specified term. Fixed deposits, cumulative and recurring deposits, cash certificates, certificates of deposits, annuity deposits, deposits mobilised under various schemes, ordinary staff deposits, foreign currency non-resident deposits accounts, etc. are to be included under this category.
	B. (i) Deposits of branches in India	The total of these two items will agree with the total deposits.
	(ii) Deposits of branches outside India	**Notes - General** (a) Interest payable on deposits which is accrued but not due should not be included but shown under other liabilities. (b) Matured time deposits and cash certificates etc. should be treated as demand deposits. (c) Deposits under special schemes should be included under term deposits if they are not payable on demand. When each deposits have matured for payments they should be shown under demand deposits. (d) Deposits from banks will include deposits from the banking system in India co-operative banks, foreign banks which may or may not have a presence in India.
Borrowings	4 **(I) Borrowings in India** (i) Reserve Bank of India	Includes borrowings/refinance obtained from Reserve Bank of India.
	(ii) Other banks	Includes borrowings/refinance obtained from commercial banks (including co-operative banks).
	(iii) Other institutions	Includes borrowings/refinance obtained

	and agencies	from Industrial Development Bank of India, Export-Import Bank of India, National Bank for Agriculture and Rural Development and other institutions, agencies (including liability against participation certificates, if any).
	(II) Borrowings outside India	Includes borrowings of India branches abroad as well as borrowings of foreign branches.
	Secured borrowings included above.	This item, will be shown separately. Includes secured borrowings/refinance in India and outside India.

Notes - General

(i) The total of I & II will agree with the total borrowing shown in the balance sheet.

(ii) Inter-office transactions should not be shown as borrowings.

(iii) Funds raised by foreign branches by way of certificates of deposits, notes, bonds, etc. should be classified depending upon documentation, as 'deposits' 'borrowings', etc.

(iv) Refinance obtained by banks from Reserve Bank of India and various institutions are being brought under the head 'Borrowings'. Hence, advances will be shown at the gross amount on the assets side.

Other liabilities and provisions	5 **I.** Bills payable	Includes drafts, telegraphic transfers, travellers' cheques, mail transfers payable, pay slips, bankers cheques and other miscellaneous items.
	II. Inter-office adjustment	The inter-office adjustments balance, if in (net) credit, should be shown under this head. Only net position of inter-office accounts, inland as well as foreign should be shown here.
	III. Interest accrued	Includes interest accrued but not due on deposits and borrowings.
	IV. Others (including provisions)	Includes the net provision for income tax and other taxes like interest tax (less

advance payment tax deducted at source etc.), surplus in aggregate in provisions for bad debts provision account, surplus in aggregate in provisions for depreciation in securities, contingency funds which are not disclosed as a reserve but are actually in the nature of reserves, proposed dividend/transfer to Government, other liabilities which are not disclosed under any of the major heads such as unclaimed dividend, provisions and fund kept for specific purpose, unexpired discount, outstanding charges like rent, conveyance etc. Certain types of deposits like staff security deposits, margin deposits, etc. where the repayment is not free, should also be included under this head.

Notes-General

(i) For arriving at the net balance of inter-office adjustments all connected inter-office accounts should be aggregated and the net balance only will be shown, representing mostly items in transit and unadjusted items.

(ii) The interest accruing on all deposits, whether the payment is due or not, should be treated as a liability.

(iii) It is proposed to show only pure deposits under this head 'deposits' and hence all surplus provisions for bad and doubtful debts, contingency funds, secret reserves, etc. Which are not netted off against the relative assets, should be brought under the head 'Others (including provisions).

Cash and Balances with the Reserve Bank of India	6	I. Cash in hand (including foreign currency notes)	Includes cash in hand including foreign currency notes and also of foreign branches in case of banks having such branches.
		II. Balances with Reserve Bank of India (i) in Current Account	

	(ii) in other Accounts	
Balances with banks and money at call and short notice	7 **I. In India** (i) Balance with banks (a) in current accounts (b) in other Deposit accounts	Includes all balances with banks in India (including co-operative banks). Balances in current accounts and deposits accounts should be shown separately.
	(ii) Money at call and short notice (a) with banks (b) with other institutions	Includes deposits repayable within 15 days or less than 15 days notice lent in the inter bank call money market.
	II. Outside India (i) Current accounts (ii) Deposits accounts	Includes balances held by foreign branches and balances held by Indian branches of the banks outside India. Balance held with foreign branches by other branches of the bank should not be shown under this head but should be included in inter-branch accounts. The amount held in 'current accounts' and 'deposit accounts' should be shown separately.
	(iii) Money at call and short notice at call and short notice.	Includes deposits usually classified in foreign countries as money
Investments	8 **I. Investments in India** (i) Government securities	Includes Central and State Government securities and Government treasury bills. These securities should be shown at the book value. However, the difference between the book value and market value should be given in the notes to the balance sheet.
	(ii) Other approved securities	Securities other than Government securities, which according to the Banking Regulation Act, 1949 are treated as approved securities, should be included here.
	(iii) Shares	Investments in shares of companies and corporations not included in item (ii) should be included here.
	(iv) Debentures and Bonds	Investments in debentures and bonds of companies and corporations not included in item (ii) should be included here.
	(v) Investment in subsidiaries/ joint ventures	Investment in subsidiaries/joint ventures (including RRBs) should be included here
	(vi) Others	Includes residual investments, if any, like

		gold, commercial paper and other instruments in the nature of shares/ debentures/bonds.
	II. Investments outside India (i) Government securities (including local authorities)	All foreign Government securities including securities issued by local authorities may be classified under this head.
	(ii) Subsidiaries and/or joint ventures abroad	All investments made in the share capital of subsidiaries floated outside India and/ or joint ventures abroad should be classified under this head.
	(iii) Others	All other investments outside India may be shown under this head.
Advances	9 **A.** (i) Bills purchased and discounted (ii) Cash credits, overdrafts and loans repayable on demand	In classification under section 'A'. All outstandings in India as well as outside- less bad debt, will be classified under three heads as indicated and both secured and unsecured advances will be included under these heads.
	(iii) Term loans	Including overdue instalments.
	B. (i) Secured by tangible assets	All advances or part of advances which are secured by tangible assets may be shown here. The item will include advances in India and outside India.
	(ii) Covered by Bank/ Government	Advances in India and outside India to the extent they are covered by guarantees of Indian and foreign governments and Indian and foreign banks and DICGC & ECGC are to be included.
	(iii) Unsecured	All advances not classified under (i) and (ii) will be included here.
		Total of 'A' should tally with the total of 'B'
	C. I. Advances in India (i) Priority sectors (ii) Public sector (iii) Banks (iv) Others **C. II. Advances outside India** (i) Due from banks (ii) Due from others	'Advances in India' and 'Advances outside India'. Advances should be broadly classified into Advances in India will be further classified on the sectoral basis as indicated. Advances on sectors which for the time being are classified as priority sectors according to the instructions of the Reserve Bank are to be classified under the head 'Priority sector'. Such advances should be excluded from item (ii) *i.e.* advances to public sector. Advances to

Head	Items	Notes
	(a) Bills purchased and discounted (b) Syndicate loans (c) Others	Central and State. Governments and other Government undertaking including Government companies and corporations which are are, according to the status, to be treated as public sector companies are to be included in the category "Public Sector". All advances to the banking sector including co-operative banks will come under the head 'Banks'. All the remaining advances will be included under the head 'Others' and typically this category will include non-priority advances to the private, joint and co-operative sectors. **Notes - General** (i) The gross amount of advances including refinance and rediscounts but excluding provisions made to the satisfaction of auditors should be shown as advances. (ii) Term loans will be loans not repayable on demand. (iii) Consortium advances would be shown net of share from other participating banks/institutions.
Fixed Assets 10	**I. Premises** (i) At cost as on 31st March of the preceding year (ii) Additions during the year (iii) Deductions during the year therefrom (iv) Depreciation to date	Premises wholly or partly owned by the banking company for the purpose of business including residential premises should be shown against 'Premises'. In the case of premises and other fixed assets, the the previous balance, additions thereto and deductions during the year as also the total depreciation written off should be shown. Where sums have been written off on reduction of capital or revaluation of assets, every balance sheet after the first balance sheet subsequent to the reduction or revaluation should show the revised figures for a period of five years with the date and amount of the revision made.
	II. Other Fixed Assets (including furniture and fixtures) (i) At cost on 31st March	Motor vehicles and other fixed assets other than premises but including furniture should be shown under this head.

		of the preceding year	
		(ii) Additions during the year	
		(iii) Deductions during the year	
		III. Depreciation to date	
Other Assets	11	**I.** Inter/office adjustments (net)	The inter-office adjustments balance, if in debit, should be shown under this head. Only net position of inter-office accounts, inland as well as foreign, should be shown here. For arriving at the net balance of inter-office adjustment accounts, all connected inter-office accounts should be aggregated and the net balance, if in debit, only should be shown representing mostly items in transit and unadjusted items.
		II. Interest accrued	Interest accrued but not due on investments and advances and interest due but not collected on investments will be the main components of this item. As banks normally debit the borrowings' accounts with interest due on the balance sheet date, usually there may not be any amount of interest due on advances. Only such interest as can be realised in the ordinary course should be shown under this head.
		III. Tax paid in advance/tax deducted at source	The amount of tax deducted at source on securities, advance tax paid etc. to the extent that these items are not set off against relative tax provisions should be shown against this item.
		IV. Stationery and stamps	Only exceptional items of expenditure on stationary like bulk purchase of securities paper, loose leaf or other ledgers, etc. which are shown as quasi-asset to be written off over a period of time should be shown here. The value should be on a realistic basis and cost escalation should not be taken into account, as these items are for internal use.
		V. Non-banking assets acquired in satisfaction of claims	Immovable properties/tangible assets acquired in satisfaction of claims are to be shown under this head.
		VI. Others	This will include items like claims which have not been met, for instance, clearing

			items, debit items representing addition to asset or reduction in liabilities which have not been adjusted for technical reasons, want of particulars, etc. advances given to staff by a bank as employer and not as a banker, etc. Items which are in the nature of expenses which are pending adjustments should be provided for and the provision netted against this item so that only realisable value is shown under this head. Accrued income other than interest may also be included here.
Contingent Liabilities	12	**I.** Claims against the bank not acknowledged or debts	
		II. Liability for partly paid investments	Liabilities on partly paid shares, debentures, etc. will be included under this head.
		III. Liability on account of outstanding forward exchange contracts	Outstanding forward exchange contract may be included here.
		IV. Guarantees given on behalf of constituents (i) In India (ii) Outside India	Guarantees given for constituents in India and outside India may be shown separately.
		V. Acceptances, endorsements and other obligations customers.	This item will include letters of credit and bills accepted by the bank on behalf of
		VI. Other items for which the Bank is contingently liable	Arrears of cumulative dividends, bills rediscounted under underwriting contract, estimated amounts of contracts remaining to be executed on capital account and not provided for, etc. are to be included here.
Bills for collection			Bills and other items in the course of and not adjusted will be Collection shown against this item in the summary version only. No separate schedule is proposed.
		Profit & Loss Account	
Interest earned	13	**I.** Interest/discount on advances/bills	Includes interest and discount on all types of loans and advances like cash credit, demand loans, overdraft, export loans, term loans, domestic and foreign bills purchased and discounted (including those rediscounted), overdue, interest and also interest subsidy, if any, relating to such

			advances/bills.
		II. Income on Investments	Includes all income derived from the investment portfolio by way of interest and dividend.
		III. Interest on balances with Reserve Bank of India and other Interbank funds	Includes interest on balances with Reserve Bank and other banks, call loans, money market placements, etc.
		IV. Others	Includes any other interest/discount income not included in above heads. not included in above heads.
Other Income	14	**I.** Commission, exchange and brokerage	Includes all remuneration on services such as commission on collections, commission/exchange on remittances and transfers, commission on letter of credit, letting out of lockers and guarantees, commission on Government business, commission on other permitted agency business including consultancy and other services, brokerage, etc. on securities. It does not include foreign exchange income.
		II. Profit on sale of investments *Less*: Loss on sale of investments etc. **III.** Profit on revaluation of investments *Less*: Loss on revaluation of investments	Includes profit/loss on sale of securities, furniture, land and buildings, motor vehicle, gold, silver. Only the net position should be shown. If the net position is a loss, the amount should be shown as a deduction. The net profit/loss on revaluation of assets may also be shown under this item.
		IV. Profit on sale of land, building and other assets *Less*: Loss on sale of land, buildings and other assets	
		V. Profit on exchange transactions *Less*: Loss on exchange transactions **VI.** Income earned by way of dividends etc. from subsidiaries, companies, joint ventures abroad/in India	Includes profit/loss on dealing in foreign exchange, all income earned by way of foreign exchange, commission and charges on foreign exchange transactions excluding interest which will be shown under interest. Only the net position should be shown. If the net position is a loss, it is to be shown as a deduction.
		VII. Miscellaneous income	Includes recoveries from constituents for the godown rents, income from bank's

			properties, security charges, insurance etc. and any other miscellaneous income. In case any item under this head exceeds one percentage of the total income, particulars may be given in the notes.
Interest	15	**I.** Interest on deposits	Includes interest paid on all types of deposits including deposits from banks and others institutions.
		II. Interest on Reserve Bank of India/inter-bank borrowings	Includes discount/interest on all borrowings and refinance from Reserve Bank of India and other banks.
		III. Others	Includes discount/interest on all borrowings/refinance from financial institutions. All other payments like interest on participation certificates, penal interest paid, etc. may also be included here.
Operating expenses	16	**I.** Payments to and Provisions for employees	Includes staff salaries/wages, allowances, bonus, other staff benefits like provident fund, pension, gratuity liveries to staff, leave fare concessions, staff welfare, medical allowance to staff etc.
		II. Rent, taxes and lighting	Includes rent paid by the banks on building and other municipal and other taxes paid (excluding income tax and interest tax) electricity and other similar charges and levies. House rent allowance and other similar payments to staff should appear under the head 'Payments to and provisions for employees'.
		III. Printing and Stationery	Includes books and forms and stationery used by the bank and other printing charges which are not incurred by way of publicity expenditure.
		IV. Advertisement and publicity	Includes expenditure incurred by the bank for advertisement and publicity purposes including printing charges of publicity matter.
		V. Depreciation on Bank's property	Includes depreciation on bank's own property : motor cars and other vehicles, furniture, electric fittings, vaults, lifts, leasehold properties, non-banking assets, etc.

VI. Director's fees, allowances and expenses	Includes sitting fees and all other items of expenditure incurred on behalf of directors. The daily allowances, hotel charges, conveyance charges, etc. which though in the nature of reimbursement of expenses incurred may be included under this head. Similar expenses of local Committee members may also be included under this head.
VII. Auditor's fees and expenses (including branch auditors' fees and expenses)	Includes fees paid to the statutory auditors and branch auditors for professional services rendered and all expenses for performing their duties, even though they may be in the nature of reimbursement of expenses. If external auditors have been appointed by banks themselves for internal inspections and audits and other services the expenses incurred in that context including fees may not be included under this head but shown under 'other expenditure'.
VIII. Law charges	All legal expenses and reimbursement of expenses incurred in connection with legal services are to be included here.
IX. Postage, telegrams, telephones, etc.	Includes all postal charges like stamps, telegram, telephones, teleprinter, etc.
X. Repairs and maintenance	Includes repairs to bank's property, their maintenance charges, etc.
XI. Insurance	Includes insurance charges on bank's property, insurance premia paid to Deposit Insurance and Credit Guarantee Corporation, etc. to the extent they are not recovered from the concerned parties.
XII. Other expenditure	All expenses other than those not included in any of the other heads like, licence fees, donations, subscriptions to papers, periodicals, entertainment expenses, travel expenses, etc. may be included under this head. In case any particular item under this head exceeds one percentage of the total income particulars may be given in the notes.

Provisions and contingencies	Includes all provisions made for bad and doubtful debts, provisions for taxation, provisions for diminution in the value of investments, transfers to contingencies and other similar items.

2. 11 Disclosure of Accounting Policies

In order to bring the true financial position of banks to pointed focus and enable the users of financial statements to study and have a meaningful comparison of their positions, the banks should disclose the accounting policies regarding key areas of operation at one place along with notes on accounting in their financial statements - this is the content of a Circular No. DBOD.BP. 91/C. 686/ 91 dated 28-2-1991 of the Reserve Bank of India issued to the Chief Executives of all Scheduled Commercial Banks Excluding Regional Rural Banks. RBI also issued a specimen form in which the accounting policies may be disclosed. The specimen indicates broadly the areas where the accounting policies followed by each bank should be disclosed and the banks can make necessary modifications to suit their individual needs. The specimen form is given below:

SPECIMEN FORM OF ACCOUNTING POLICIES

I. Principal Accounting Policies

(1) General: The accompanying financial statements have been prepared on the historical cost basis and conform to the statutory provisions and practices prevailing in the country.

(2) Transactions involving foreign exchange: (a) Monetary assets and liabilities have been translated at the exchange rate prevailing at the close of the year. Non-monetary assets have been carried in the books at the historical cost.

(b) Income and expenditure items in respect of the Indian branches have been translated at the exchange rates ruling on the date of the transaction and in respect of overseas branches at the exchange rates prevailing at the close of the year.

(c) Profit or loss on pending forward contracts has been accounted for.

(3) Investments : (a) Investments in Government and other approved securities in India are valued at the lower of cost or market value.

(b) Investment in subsidiary companies and in some companies (*i.e.* companies in which at least 25% of the share capital) have been accounted for on the historical cost basis.

(c) All other investments are valued at the lower of cost or market value.

(4) Advances : (a) Provisions for doubtful advances have been made to the satisfaction of the auditors :

(i) in respect of the identified advances, based on a periodical review of advances and after taking into account the portion of advance guaranteed by the Deposit Insurance Credit Guarantee Corporation, the Export Credit and Guarantee Corporation and similar statutory bodies.

(ii) in respect of general advances as a percentage of total advances taking into account guidelines issued by the Government of India and the Reserve Bank of India.

(b) Provisions in respect of doubtful advances have been deducted from advances to the extent necessary and the excess has been included under "Other liabilities and provisions".

(c) Provisions have been made on a gross basis. Tax relief which will be available when the advance is written off will be accounted for in the year of write off.

(5) Fixed Assets

(a) Premises and other fixed assets have been accounted for at their historical cost. Premises which have been revalued are accounted for at the values determined on the basis of such revaluation made by professional valuers. Profit arising on revaluations has been credited to Capital Reserve.

(b) Depreciation has been provided for on the straight line/diminishing balance method.

(c) In respect of revalued assets, depreciation is provided for on the revalued figure and an amount equal to the additional depreciation consequent on revaluation is transferred annually from the Capital Reserve to the General Reserve/Profit and Loss Account.

(6) Staff Benefits: Provisions for gratuity/pension benefits to staff has been made on as accrual/ cash basis. Separate funds for gratuity/pension have been created.

(7) Net Profit : (a) The net profit disclosed in the profit and loss account is after :

(i) provisions for taxes on income in accordance with statutory requirements.

(ii) provision for doubtful advances.

(iii) adjustments to the value of "current investments in Government and other approved securities in India valued at lower of cost or market value".

(iv) transfers to contingency funds.

(v) other usual or necessary provisions.

(b) Contingency funds have been grouped by the Balance Sheet under the head "Other Liabilities and Provisions".

PRUDENTIAL NORMS AND INCOME RECOGNITION

Assets of the banks are classified as "performing assets" and "non-performing assets" for the purpose of income recognition. In line with the international practice and as per the recommendations made by the Narasimham Committee the Reserve Bank of India has introduced, in a phased manner, prudential norms for income recognition, asset classification and provisioning for the advances portfolio of the banks so as to move towards greater consistency & transparency in the published accounts.

The policy of income recognition should be objective and based on record of recovery rather than on any subjective considerations Like wise classification of assets of the banks has to be done on the basis of objective criteria which would ensure uniform and consistent application of the norm. Similarly provisioning should be made on the basis of classification of assets based on the period for which the asset has remained non-performing and the availability of security and the realisable value thereof.

"Non-performing assets"

An asset, including a leased asset, becomes non-performing when it ceases to generate income for the bank. The non-performing asset (NPA) is defined as any credit facility in respect of which interest or/and instalment of principal has remained unpaid for a specified period of time. The specified period has been reduced in a phased manner as under :

Year ending 31st March	Specified period
1993	4 Quarters
1994	3 Quarters
1995 onwards	2 Quarters
2004 onwards	1 Quarter

An amount due under any credit facility is treated as "past due" when it has not been paid within 30 days from the due date. However, the concept of "past due" has been dispensed with effect from March 31, 2001.

With a view to moving towards international best practices and to ensure greater transparency it has been decided to adopt the 90 days overdue for identification NPAs from the year ending 31st March 2004 as given below :

(i) Term Loans : Interest and/or instalment of principal remain over due for a period of more than 90 days (one quarter)

(ii) Cash credit and Overdrafts : A cash credit or overdraft account will be treated as Non-performing Asset (NPA) if the account remains out of order for a period of more than 90 days (one quarter)

An account is treated as "out of order" if outstanding balance remains continuously in excess of the sanctioned limit/drawing power. In cases where outstanding balance in the principal operating account is less than the sanctioned limit/drawing power, but there are no credits continuously for six months as on the date of Balance Sheet or credits are not enough to cover the interest debited during the same period, these accounts should be treated as "out of order".

(iii) Bills purchased and discounted

The bills purchased and discounted account should be treated as Non-performing Asset (NPA) if the bills remain "overdue" for a period of more than 90 days.

Any amount due to the Bank under any credit facility is "overdue" if it is not paid on the due date fixed by the Bank.

(iv) Agricultural Advance :

With effect from September 30, 2004, a loan granted for short duration crops will be treated as NPA, if the instalment of principal or interest there on remains over due for two crop seasons. A loan granted for long duration crops will be treated as NPA if instalment of principal or interest there on remains overdue for one crop season.

A long duration crop means a crop having a crop-season longer than one year and crops which are not long duration crops would be treated as short duration crops. These NPA norms would also be made applicable to agricultural term loans availed by the agriculturists.

(v) Any Other Credit Facility :

In case of any other credit facility if the amount to be received remains overdue for a period of more than 90 days norm, then such a facility will be classified as NPA. To facilitate the smooth transition to 90 days norm the banks have shifted to charging of interest at monthly rests with effect from 1st April 2002. However, the date of classification of an advance as NPA cannot be changed on account of charging of interest at monthly rests. Therefore, a credit facility will continue to be classified as NPA only if the interest charged during any quarter is not serviced within 90 days from the end of the quarter w.e.f. 31st March, 2004.

Income Recognition

In case of Non-performing Assets (NPA) the interest is recognised when it is actually received and not on accrual basis. This is also in accordance with the AS-9 on Revenue Recognition which also states that recognition of interest should be deferred where there is uncertainty regarding it's collection. However this rule does not apply in case of advances against term deposits, NSCs, IVPs, KVPs, and Life Policies provided adequate margin is available.

Fees and Commission earned by the banks as a result of re-negotiations or rescheduling of outstanding debts should be recognised on an accrual basis over the period of time covered by the renegotiated or rescheduled extension of credit.

If the **Government guaranteed advances** become NPA, the interest on such advances should not be taken to income unless interest has been realised.

An advance which become NPA the interest accrued and credited to income has to be revised or provided for if the same is not realised. This applies to Government guaranteed advances also.

In respect of NPAs, fees, commission and similar income that have accrued ceases to accrue in the current period, should be reversed or provided for with respect to past periods, if uncollected.

The finance charges as per AS-19 : Leases, which have accrued and credited to Income Statement before the asset become non-performing, and remaining unrealised, should be reversed or provided for in the current accounting period.

As far as the adjustment for partial recoveries is concerned, the RBI has in recent past advised the banks to adopt an accounting principle and exercise the right of appropriation of recoveries in an uniform and consistent manner. Classification of Bank Advances on the basis of Asset Performance

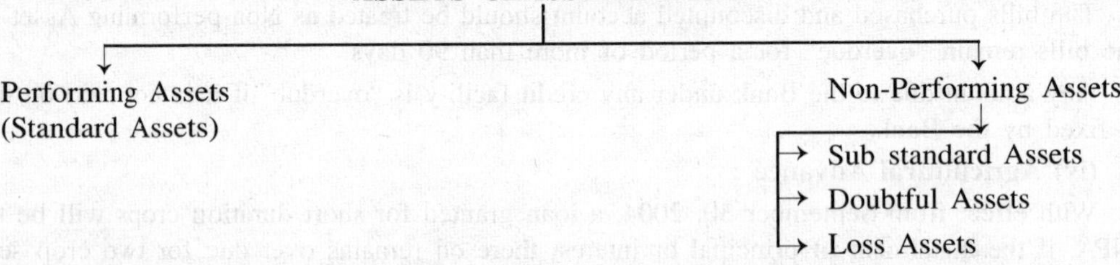

The Banks have to classify their advances into four broad categories:

(i) **Standard Assets :** Assets which do not carry any risk which is in addition to normal risk attached to the banking business. In other words these are the assets (advances) which continue to generate income (interest) on regular basis without any default or risk. These are known as performing assets or standared assets.

(ii) **Substandard Assets :** With effect from 31st March 2005 Sub-standard assets are those assets which have been classified as NPA for a period less than or equal to twelve (12) months. In such cases the current net worth of the borrower/guarantor or the current market value of the security charged is not enough to ensure recovery of the dues (principal & interest) in full. Thus the earlier period of 18 months has been reduced to 12 months.

(iii) **Doubtful Assets :** With effect from 31st March, 2005 an asset would be classified as doubtful if it remained in the sub-standard category for twelve (12) months. Thus the earlier period of exceeding 18 months has been reduced to 12 months.

A loan classified as doubtful has all the characteristics/weaknesses inherent in that classified as "sub-standard" assets which makes recovery in full uncertain on the basis of currently known facts, conditions and values highly questionable and improbable.

In case there is a fall in the value of security by more than 50% of the value assessed by the Bank or accepted by RBI at the time of last inspection, such NPAs may directly be classified in the Doubtful category.

(iv) **Loss Assets :** A loss asset is one where loss has been identified by the bank or internal or external auditors or the RBI inspection but the amount has not been written off wholly. In other words, such an asset is considered wholly bad or uncollectible and of such little value that its continuance as a bankable asset is not warranted although there may be some salvage or recovery value. The accounts where DICGC/ECGC cover is available or where claim is already received cannot fall under this category. However, where DICGC claim has already been adjusted and for the balance there is no security to fall back upon, then such accounts will become loss assets.

PROVISIONING NORMS

In conformity with the prudential norms, provisions are required to be made on the non-performing assets on the basis of classification of assets into prescribed categories. Taking into consideration the time leg between an account becoming doubtful of recovery, its recognition as such the realisation of the security and erosion overtime in the value of security charged to the bank, the banks have to make provisions against sub-standard, doubtful and loss assets.

1. Loss Assets

The entire asset should be written off, if the assets are permitted to remain in the books for any reason, 100 percent of the outstanding need be provided for

2. Doubtful Assets

(a) 100 percent to the extent to which the advance is not covered by the realisable value of the security to which bank has a valid recourse and the realisable value is estimated on a realistic basis

(b) With regard to the secured portion, provision may be made, depending upon the period for which asset has remained doubtful as shown below :

Period for which the Advances have remained in doubtful category	Provision Required (%)
Upto one year	20%
One to three years	30%
More than three years :	
(i) Outstanding balance of NPAs as on 31st March, 2004	50%
(w.e.f. 31. 3. 2005)	60%
(w.e.f. 31. 3. 2006)	75%
(w.e.f. 31. 3. 2007)	100%
(ii) Advances classified as doubtful as on or after 1st April, 2004	100% (w.e.f. 31.3.2005)

(c) Banks are permitted to phase the additional provisioning consequent upon the reduction in the transition period from sub-standard to doubtful asset from 18 to 12 months over a four year period commencing from the year ending 31st March 2005, with a minimum of 20% each year

(d) With a view to bringing down the divergence arising out of difference in assessment of the value of security, in cases of NPAs with balance of Rs. 5 crore, stock audit at annual intervals by external agencies appointed as per the guidelines approved by the Board is mandatory in order to enhance reliability on stock valuation. Collaterals such as immovable properties charged in favour of bank have to be valued once in three years.

3. Sub-Standard Assets : A general provision of 10 percent on total outstanding is required to be made without making any allowance for DICGC/ECGC guarantee cover and securities available. The unsecured exposures which are identified as "sub-standard" would attract additional provision of 10 percent *i.e.* a total of 20 percent on the outstanding balance. Unsecured exposure means an exposure where the realisable value of the security, as assessed by the bank/approved valuer/RBI's inspecting officials is not more than 10 percent *ab initio* of the outstanding exposure.

4. Standard Assets : From the year ending 31st March, 2000, the banks have to make a general provision of a minimum of 0.25* percent on standard assets on global loan portfolio basis.

The provisions on standard assets is not reckoned for arriving at net NPAs. The provisions towards Standard Assets need not be netted from gross advances but shown separately as "Contingent Provisions" against Standard Assets under "Other Liabilities and Provisions in schedule 5 of the Balance Sheet.

* Revised to 0.4 percent

Provisions on Leased Assets

(i) *Sub-Standard Assets*

(a) 10 percent of the sum of the "net investment" in the lease and the unrealised portion of "finance income" net of "finance charge component as per AS - 19 Leases.

(b) Unsecured lease exposures which are identified as 'standard' would attract additional 10 percent provision *i.e.* total 20%.

(ii) *Doubtful Assets*

100 percent of the extent to which the finance is not secured by the realisable value of the leased asset. Realisable value to be estimated on a realistic basis. The quantum of provision in the three categories of doubtful leased assets is the same as in case of other doubtful advances.

(iii) *Loss Assets*

The entire assets should be written off. If for any reason, an asset is allowed to remain in books, 100 percent of the sum of the net investment in the lease and the unrealised portion of finance income net of finance charge component should be provided.

* **Government Guaranteed Advances.** If the guarantee in respect of Government Guaranteed advances sanctioned on or after 31st March, 2000, is invoked and remains in default for more than 90 days the banks are required to make normal provisions as explained above.

* Advances Granted under Rehabilitation Packages Approved by BIFR/Term Lending Institutions.

(i) In this case provision is to be made in respect of dues to the bank on the existing credit facilities as per their classification as substandard or doubtful asset.

(ii) As regards the additional facilities sanctioned as per packages finalised by BFIR and/ or Term Lending Institutions, provision on additional facilities sanctioned need not be made for a period of one year from the date of disbursement.

* Advances Against term deposits, NSCs eligible for surrender, IVPs, KVPs and life policies would attract provisions as applicable to their asset classification status.

* Advances Against gold ornaments, government securities & all other kinds of securities are not exempted from provisioning requirements.

* Treatment of interest suspense account :

Amounts held in Interest Suspense Account is not be reckoned as part of provisions. Amounts is to be deducted from the relative advances and thereafter, provisioning as per the norms, should be made on the balance after such deduction.

* Advances Covered by DICGC/ECGC

In the case of advances guaranteed by DICGC/ECGC the provision should be made only in excess of the amount guaranteed by these corporations. Further, while arriving at the provision required to be made for doubtful assets, realisable value of securities should first be deducted from the outstanding balance in respect of the amount guaranteed by these corporations and then provision should be made.

* Advance Covered by CGTSI guarantee :

In case advance covered by CGTSI guarantee becomes non-performing no provision need be made towards the guaranteed portion. The amount outstanding in excess of guaranteed portion should be provided for as per the extant guidelines on provisioning for non-performing advances.

ADVANCES CLASSIFICATION (SECURITY-WISE)
As per Third schedule of Banking Regulation Act, 1949

1.	Staff Provident Fund Loan against their own contribution where Bank holds letters of lien on their P.F. Contribution	Unsecured
2.	Advances against book debts/receivable	Unsecured
3.	Advances balances in Deposit Accounts treated as advanced	Unsecured
4.	Advances against demand promissory notes but not supported by marketable securities	Unsecured
5.	Advances to staff co-operative housing societies where equitable mortgage has been created and a memorandum of agreement has been executed by society	Secured
6.	Advances against pledge of machinery (When outstanding less than the market value)	Secured
7.	Where the outstandings are secured but the security is relating to which is not charged to Bank	Unsecured

8. Where excess drawings are permitted in clean cash credit account guaranteed by the Central/State Government. Indian/Foreign Banks and DICGC/ECGC outstanding upto the limit of guarantee, which is unexpired — Guaranteed
9. Where excess drawings are permitted in clean cash credit account guaranteed by one or more parties excepting Central/State Government, Indian/Foreign Banks and DICGC/ECGC — Unsecured
10. The balance in excess of limit of the guarantee given by Central/State Government, Indian/Foreign Banks and DICGC/ECGC and where guarantee has been repudiated. — Unsecured
11. Advances against supply bills (including Government Supply bills) not secured by tangible security either as primary security or collateral. — Unsecured
12. Where the advance is irregular the position of the outstandings covered by the market value of the stock (without deduction of margin) — Secured

Classification of Bills Discounted & Purchased.

Indian Bills

13. Demand Purchases (Documentary) — Secured
14. Unsance Bill (Documentary)
    (a) Where documents have been delivered to draw against acceptance — Unsecured
    (b) Before acceptance — Secured
15. Inland Bills/Bills of Exchange (Usance bills discounted inland as well as exports) — Unsecured
16. Clean bills — Unsecured
17. Clean usance bills and/or other bills guaranteed by third party other than Central/state Government, Indian/Foreign Banks and DICGC/ECGC — Unsecured

Protested Bills

18. Where the aggregate value of security (Primary/collateral) exceed the outstandings — Secured

Otherwise :

(i) The realisable value from Central/State Government, Indian/Foreign Bank guarantees and DICGC/ECGC etc. — Guaranteed

(ii) Balance outstanding — Unsecured

Example : A loan Rs. 12,00,000 was advanced on 1.10.2005 @ 10% p.a. interest payable half yearly, but loan was outstanding as on 31st March, 2006 without paying any amount either interest or principal. The security for loan was 20,000 fully paid equity shares of Rs. 10 each (market value Rs. 98 as on 1.10.2005) But due to volatility in the market the price plunged to Rs. 48 per share. However, the market recovered and price, as per Stock Exchange quotation was Rs. 80 per share. How will you classify loan as secured/unsecured?

Ans. : The value of security as on 31.3.2006 is Rs. 16,00,000 as against the loan of Rs. 12,00,000. Since it covers amount of loan as well interest there on, it will be treated as fully secured.

Illustration : 1

Given below are details of interest on advances of a Commercial Bank as on 31st March, 2006.

	Interest on			Rs. '000'
	Performing Assets		Non-Performing Assets	
	Earned	Received	Earned	Received
Term Loans	6,000	4,000	3,750	250
Cash Credit & Overdrafts	37,500	31,000	7,500	600
Bills Purchased & Discounted	7,500	7,500	5,000	1,000

Find out the income to be recognised for the year ended 31st March, 2006.

[ICWA (F) Adapted]

Solution :

Interest on **performing assets** are recognised on accrual basis and Interest on non-performing assets are recognised on cash basis (receipt basis)

		Rs. '000'
Interest on Term Loans :	Performing Assets	6,000
	Non-performing Assets	250
Cash credits & Overdrafts :	P.A.	37,500
	NPA	600
Bills Purchased & Discounted :	PA	7,500
	NPA	1,000
		52,850

Illustration : 2

From the following particulars, Compute the amount of provision for doubtful debts relating to a Commercial Bank

		Rs. "000"
(i)	Loans & Advances (Total)	10,000
(ii)	Fully secured loans & Advances	6,000
(iii)	Advances Overdue for 11 months	2,000
(iv)	Advances Overdue for 15 months (Secured by mortgage of Machinery worth Rs. 2,00,000)	1,000
(v)	Non-recoverable unsecured Advances	6,000
(vi)	Small advance not exceeding Rs. 20,000 to each borrower	400

Solution :

(a) Classification of Assets

		Rs.
(1)	Standard Assets (only fully secured)	6,000
(2)	Sub-Standard Assets (Advances over due for less than or equal to 12 months)	2,000
(3)	Doubtful (Overdue for more than 12 months)	1,000
(4)	Loss Assets (Non-recoverable)	600
(5)	Small advances	400

(b) Computation of Provision

	Types of Assets	Amount Rs.	Provision %	Required Rs.
1.	Standard Assets	60,00,000	0.25%*	15,000
2.	Sub-standard Assets	20,00,000	10%	20,000
3.	Doubtful Assets	10,00,000		
	Unsecured	8,00,000	100%	8,00,000
	Secured	2,00,000	30%	60,000
4.	Loss Assets	6,00,000	100%	6,00,000
5.	Small Advances	4,00,000	15%	60,000
				15,55,000

Illustration : 3

From the following details, compute the amount of provision required to be made in the Profit and Loss Account of a Commercial Bank for the year 2005-06

Assets	Rs. in "000"
Standard	80,000
Sub-Standard	60,000
Doubtful :	
For one year (secured)	24,000
For Two to three years (Secured)	18,000
For more than three years (Secured by mortgage of Plant worth Rs. 50,00,000)	9,000
Non-recoverable Assets	15,000

[C.S. (I) June 2003- Modified]

Solution :

Computation of Provision

Types of Assets	Rs. '000'	Percentage	Provision Rs. '000'
Standard	80,000	0.25%*	200
Sub-Standard	60,000	10%	6,000

* Revised to 0.4 percent

Doubtful for :

One year	24,000	20%	4,800
Two to three years	18,000	30%	5,400
More than three years :			
Unsecured	4,000	100%	4,000
Secured	5,000	50%	2,500
Non-recoverable	15,000	100%	15,000
Total			37,900

Illustration : 4

A Commercial Bank provides you the following information for the year ended 31st March, 2005

(i)	Export Credit given	Rs. 200 lacs
	ECGC cover	40%
	Securities held	Rs. 40 lacs
		(Relisable value Rs. 48 lacs)
	Period for which the advance has remained doubtful	More than 3 years
(ii)	Term Loans	Rs. 3,00 lacs
	DICGC Cover	50% (Max. limit Rs. 80 lacs)
	Securities held	Rs. 80 lacs (Realisable Value Rs. 72 lacs)
	The period for which the loan remained doubtful	More than 3 Years

You are required to calculate provision required on the above advances.

Solution :

Computation of Provision

			Rs. "00,000"
(i)	Total Amount of Export Credit		200.00
Less	Realisable Value of securities		48.00
			152.00
Less	ECGC Cover 40%		60.80
	Unsecured Balance		91.20
Provision Required :			
	Unsecured balance 100%		91.20
	Provision for Secured Portion :		
	50% of for secured portion	24.00	
Less	ECGC Cover @ 40%	9.60	
			14.40
	Total Provision required		105.60

(ii)	Amount of Term Loans	300.00
Less	Realisable Value of Securities	(72.00)
		228.00
Less	DICGC Cover 50% (Limited to Rs. 80 Lacs)	(80.00)
	Unsecured Portion	148.00
Provision Required :		
	Provision for Unsecured Portion 100%	148.00
	Provision for Secured Portion 50% of 72 lacs (Realisable Value of securities)	36.00
		184.00

SPECIAL TRANSACTIONS OF BANKS

1. Discounting and Collection of Bills

A bank may purchase a bill or collect it on behalf of the customers. When a bill is drawn by one party and accepted by other (whether a Trade bill or accommodation bill) the drawer has the following options after the acceptance.

(i) The bill may be retained till maturity or

(ii) It may be discounted from the bank or

(iii) It may be sent for collection or

(iv) It may be endorsed to thirty party.

If the bill is discounted the Bank records the following entry.

Bills Discounted A/c	Dr.	(Amount of Bill)
To Customer's A/c		(Net amount)
To Discount A/c		(Discount Amount)

When the bill is either purchased by the bank or is realised on the date of maturity the following entry is recorded :

Cash A/c	Dr.	(Full Amount)
To Bills Discounted A/c		(Full Amount)

If however, some bills remain unrealised on the date of closing of books of accounts the same shall be shown in Balance Sheet under the heading "Advances" and details to be shown in the Schedule 9.

Bills for Collection : A Bank receives bills from it's customers for collection on the due dates. The bills are kept by the Bank to be collected on behalf of customers. The Bank records particulars of the bills in "Bills for collection Register" only. There is no any other entry till the date of maturity. On the date of maturity when the bills are realised, following entry is recorded.

Cash A/c	Dr.	(Full Amount)
To Customer's A/c		(Net)
To Commission A/c		(Commission)

If however, some bills remain outstanding, the same are shown by means of footnote under to Balance Sheet.

2. Rebate on Bills Discounted

When a bill is discounted from the bank the whole amount of the discount earned is credited to "Discount Account". However, some bills discounted may not mature for payment by the end of the accounting year. Thus the total discount will represent discount earned for the expired period and "unearned discount" for the unexpired period. The discount earned is credited to Profit and Loss Account where as unearned discount for the unexpired period is carried forward by debiting the Discount Account and crediting the Rebate on Bills Discounted Account which is shown on the liabilities side of the Balance Sheet as "Discount Received but not Earned" or "Discount Received in Advance", under the heading "Other liabilities & Provisions".

Example : A customer discounts a bill of Rs. 30,000 for 3 months at 6% on 1st March while bank closes its books on 31st March each year. Record journal entry.

Solution :

Discount on Rs. 30,000 @ 6% for 3 months

$$= 30{,}000 \times \frac{6}{100} \times \frac{3}{12} \qquad = \text{Rs. } 450$$

Discount earned for one month (1st March to 31st March)	= Rs. 150
Discount unearned for two months (April & May)	= Rs. 300

Bills Discounted A/c	Dr.	30,000	
To Customer's A/c			29,550
To Discount A/c			150
To Rebate on Bills Discounted A/c			300

Illustration (5)

On 31st March 2006, a Bank had the following Bills Discounted Outstanding.

Date of Bill	Amount Rs.	Duration in (Months)	Discount %
1.12.2005	42,000	5	7%
1.2.2006	60,000	4	6.5%
1.3.2006	48,000	3	6%

Calculate Rebate on Bills Discounted and record the journal as on 31st March 2006.

Solution :

Amount of the bill	Duration in (Months)	Discount Rate	No. of months after 31st March	Total Discount	Unearned Discount
42,000	5	7%	1	1225	245
60,000	4	6.5%	2	1300	650
48,000	3	6%	2	720	480
1,50,000				3,245	1,375

Bills Discounted A/c	Dr.	1,50,000	
To Customers A/c			1,46,755
To Discount A/c			1,870
To Rebate on Bills Discounted			1,375

Alternatively :

Journal entry at the time for discounting

Bills Discounted A/c	Dr.	1,50,000	
To Customer's A/c			1,46,755
To Discount A/c			3,245
(Being bills discounted)			

Journal Entry as on 31st March, 2006

Discount A/c	Dr.	1,375	
To Rebate on Bills Discounted A/c			1,375
(Being unearned discount adjusted)			

Illustration (6)

The following particulars are extracted from the books of a Commercial Bank for the year ended 31st March, 2006.

	Rs.
1. Interest and discount	8,75,750
2. Rebate on Bills Discounted (1. 4. 2005)	32,500
3. Bills Discounted and Purchased	

It is ascertained that proportionate discount not yet earned on the bills discounted which will mature during the year 2005-06 amounted to Rs. 46,000.

Record journal entries and prepare relevant ledger accounts.

[C.A. (F) Adapted]

Solution :

Journal Entries

				Rs.	Rs.
1.4.2005	Rebate on Bills Discounted A/c	Dr.		32,500	
	To Interest and Discount A/c				32,500
	(Being opening balance of Rebate on Bills Discounted credited to Interest and Discount A/c				
31.3.2006	Interest and Discount A/c	Dr.		46,000	
	To Rebate on Bills Discount A/c				46,000
	(Discount not yet earned transferred to Rebate on Bills Discounted A/c)				

INTEREST & DISCOUNT A/C

		Rs.			Rs.
2006 March 31	To Rebate on Bills Discounted	46,000	2005 April 1	By Rebate on Bills Discounted	32,500
March 31	To Profit & Loss A/c (Transfer)	8,62,250	March 31	By Bills Purchased & Discounted A/c	8,75,750
		9,08,250			9,08,250

REBATE ON BILLS DISCOUNTED A/C

2005		Rs.	2005		Rs.
April 1	To Interest & Discount A/c	32,500	April 1	By Balance b/d	32,500
2006			2006		
April 1	To Balance c/d	46,000	March 31	By Interest & Discount A/c	46,000

3. Acceptances, Endorsements & Other Obligations

This represents banks liability on account of bills accepted or endorsed on behalf of its customers. As against this liability, the bank has a corresponding claim against the customer on whose behalf it has undertaken to be a party to the bill, either as an acceptor or as an endorser. Such liabilities which are outstanding at the close of the year and the corresponding assets are disclosed as contingent liability as per the new format. As a safeguard against the default on the part of customer, usually the bank requires the customer to deposit the security equivalent to the amount of bill accepted on his behalf. If the bill is not met on maturity and the amount is not collected from the customer on demand, the bank disposes of the security deposited by the customer.

Illustration (7)

On 1.4.2005, Acceptances, Endorsements and other obligations stood at Rs. 43,50,000. During the year Acceptances, Endorsements and Guarantees amounted to Rs. 1,33,00,000. Bank honoured acceptances to the extent of Rs. 75,00,000 and the customers paid Rs. 25,00,000 against the guaranteed liability. The customers failed to pay Rs. 5,00,000 which the bank had to pay.

Prepare Acceptances, Endorsements & Other obligations A/c.

ACCEPTANCES, ENDORSEMENTS & OTHER OBLIGATIONS ACCOUNT

March		Rs.	April 1		Rs.
2005-06	To Constituents liabilities for Acceptances and Endorsements etc.	75,00,000	2005	By Balance b/d	43,50,000
	To Constituents liabilities for Acceptances and Endorsements etc.	25,00,000		By constituents liabilities for Acceptances & Endorsements etc.	1,33,00,000
	To Constituents liabilities for Acceptances & Endorsements etc. (Paid on default)	5,00,000			
March 31 2006	To Balance c/d	71,50,000			
		1,76,50,000			1,76,50,000

4. Letters of Credit (LC) and Traveller's Cheques (TC)

These are issued to facilitate customers travelling within the country or abroad. In either case the desiring customers are required to deposit the full value of letter of credit or traveller's cheques issued in their favour: This amount is credited to Letter of Credits Account or Traveller's Cheques Account as the case may be. When a bill is drawn against the Letter of Credit, the amount is debited to Letters of Credits Account. Similarly when Traveller's Cheques are presented these are debited to Travellers Cheques Account. If the Cheques are in foreign currency, the equivalent value there of in home currency is collected at the rate of exchange prevailing on the date of issue of traveller's cheques and the bank either purchases immediately the amount of foreign exchange equal to the value of travellers cheques issued or transfers out of foreign currency balances. The same procedure is followed in case of Letters of Credits in foreign currency.

5. Money at Call and Short notice

These represent inter-bank loans. Under this arrangement, money is borrowed by one bank from another bank usually for 1 to 15 days. This is done to use surplus money as advance for a very short duration. Banks having shortage of cash funds contact brokers to cope with their requirements who in turn arrange money from the banks having surplus money. These brokers charge brokerage usually at 5%. The rate of interest charged by the bank is usually very high.

6. Interest on Doubtful Debts

Interest on doubtful debts can be treated in any of the following manners :

a. Cash Basis : The interest is recognised only when it is received. Such interest is credited to Profit & Loss Account under the heading "Interest & Discount".

b. Accrual basis : Under this method the interest due is credited to Interest & discount Account with the corresponding entry of adequate provisions against doubtful debts.

It is to be noted that if the "Doubtful debts" falling within the category of NPAs then the interest income there on will not be recognised.

c. Interest Suspense Method : Under this method the interest on doubtful debts is credited to Interest Suspense Account and there from it is adjusted, depending upon the realisation of debts/or doubtful turning into bad.

Illustration (8)

On 31st March, 2005 a bank shows an unsecured Loan balance of Rs. 5,00,000 in the account of Mr. X whose position is being considered as bad and doubtful. Interest on the same for the year 2004-05 which amounted to Rs. 50,000 has not been recorded.

During the year 2005-06 the back realised 70 paise in a rupee on account of the total payment of debt from Mr. X as on 31st March, 2005.

Record journal entries and prepare necessary ledger accounts under:

(a) Cash Method

(b) Accrual Method

(c) Interest Suspense Method

[C.A. (i) Adapted]

(a) Cash Method

JOURNAL ENTRIES

2006			Rs.	Rs.
March 31	Profit and Loss A/c	Dr.	5,00,000	
	To Provision for Bad & Doubtful Debts A/c			5,00,000
	(Being provision for bad debts created)			
	Cash A/c	Dr.	3,85,000	
	To Interest A/c			35,000
	To X's A/c			3,50,000
	(Being 70% of the total dues recovered)			
	Bad debts A/c	Dr.	1,50,000	
	To X's A/c			1,50,000
	(Being irrecoverable amount charged to Bad debts)			
	Provision for bad debts A/c	Dr.	1,50,000	
	To Bad debts A/c			1,50,000
	(Being bad debts written off against provision)			

X'S A/C

		Rs.			Rs.
2004 April 1	To Balance b/d	5,00,000	2005 Mar. 31	By Balance c/d	5,00,000
2005 April 1	To Balance b/d	5,00,000	2006 Mar. 31	By Cash A/c	3,50,000
				By Bad debts A/c	1,50,000
		5,00,000			5,00,000

INTEREST A/C

		Rs.			Rs.
2006 Mar. 31	To Profit & Loss A/c	35,000	2006 Mar. 31	By Cash A/c	35,000

BAD DEBTS A/C

2006 Mar. 31	To X A/c	1,50,000	2006 Mar. 31	By Provision for Bad debts	1,50,000

(b) Accrual Method

JOURNAL ENTRIES

2005			Rs.	Rs.
Mar. 31	X's A/c	Dr.	50,000	
	To Interest for bad debts A/c			50,000
	(Being interest due on loan)			
	Cash A/c	Dr.	3,85,000	
	Bad debts A/c	Dr.	1,65,000	
	To X's A/c			5,50,000
	(Being 70% of the dues realised from X and the balance transferred to Bad Debts A/c)			

Contd.

Provision for Bad debts A/c Dr.		1,65,000	
To Bad debts A/c			1,65,000
(Being bad debts written off against provision)			

X'S A/C

		Rs.			Rs.
2004 April 1	To Balance b/d	5,00,000	2005 Mar. 31	By Balance c/d	5,50,000
2005 Mar. 31	To Interest A/c	50,000			
		5,50,000			5,50,000
2005 April 1	To Balance b/d	5,50,000	2006 Mar. 31	By Cash A/c	3,85,000
				By Bad debts A/c	1,65,000
		5,50,000			5,50,000

INTEREST A/C

		Rs.			Rs.
2005 Mar. 31	To Profit & Loss A/c	50,000	2005 Mar. 31	By X's A/c	50,000

PROVISION FOR BAD DEBTS A/C

		Rs.			Rs.
2005 Mar. 31	To Balance c/d	5,50,000	2005 Mar. 31	By Profit & Loss A/c	5,50,000
2006 Mar. 31	To Bad debts	1,65,000	2005 April 1	By Balance b/d	5,50,000
	To Balance c/d	3,85,000			
		5,50,000			5,50,000

BAD-DEBTS A/C

		Rs.			Rs.
2006 Mar. 31	To X's A/c	1,65,000	2006 Mar. 31	By Provision for Bad debts A/c	1,65,000

III Interest Suspense Method

JOURNAL ENTRIES

2005			Rs.	Rs.
Mar. 31	X's A/c Dr.		50,000	
	To Interest Suspense A/c			50,000
	(Being interest due doubtful debts transferred to Interest Suspense A/c)			
	Profit & Loss A/c Dr.		5,00,000	
	To Provision for bad debts A/c			5,00,000
	(Being provision for bad debts created)			
2006	Cash A/c Dr.		3,85,000	
Mar. 31	To X's A/c			3,85,000
	(Being 70% of dues recovered)			

Particulars		Dr. (Rs.)	Cr. (Rs.)
Interest Suspense A/c	Dr.	15,000	
Bad debts A/c	Dr.	1,50,000	
To X's A/c			1,65,000
(Being amount of interest not received reversed and the balance transferred to bad debts)			
Interest Suspense A/c	Dr.	35,000	
To Profit & Loss A/c			35,000
(Being Interest received credited to Profit & Loss A/c)			
Provision for bad debts A/c	Dr.	1,50,000	
To Bad debts A/c			1,50,000
(Being bad debts written off)			

X'S A/C

Date	Particulars	Rs.	Date	Particulars	Rs.
2004 April 1	To Balance b/d	5,00,000	2005 Mar. 31	By Balance c/d	5,50,000
2005 Mar. 31	To Interest Suspense A/c	50,000			
		5,50,000			5,50,000
2005 April 1	To Balance b/d	5,50,000	2006 Mar. 31	By Cash A/c	3,85,000
				By Interest Suspense A/c	15,000
				By Bad debts A/c	1,50,000
		5,50,000			5,50,000

INTEREST SUSPENSE A/C

Date	Particulars	Rs.	Date	Particulars	Rs.
2005 Mar. 31	To Balance c/d	50,000	2005 Mar. 31	By X's A/c	50,000
2006 Mar. 31	To X's A/c	15,000	2005 April 1	By Balance b/d	50,000
	To Profit & Loss A/c	35,000			
		50,000			50,000

CAPITAL ADEQUACY NORMS

In step with Bank for International Settlements (BIS) norms and in consonance with international practice, the Reserve Bank of India prescribed new capital adequacy norms for banking institutions in April 1992. BIS standards specify capital into two tiers, viz, Tier I Capital and Tier II capital known as core capital, consists of the most permanent and readily available support to bank in the event of unexpected losses.

According to the norms established by RBI Tier I Capital for **Indian Bank** consists of:

(i) Paid up Capital

(ii) Statutory Reserves and

(iii) Other free reserves if any,

From Tier I Capital are **deducted**

(i) Investments in subsidiaries

(ii) Intangible assets

(iii) Losses for the current year and losses brought forward from the previous years.

Tier II Capital consists of

(i) Undisclosed reserves and cumulative perpetual cumulative preference shares.

(ii) Revaluation reserves

(iii) General provisions and loss reserves

(iv) Hybrid debt capital instruments

(v) Subordinated debts

(vi) Investment fluctuation reserve, including realised gains from sale of investments.

For foreign banks, Tier I capital consists of

(i) Interest free funds from head office kept in a separate account in Indian books.

(ii) Remittable surplus written in Indian books which is not repatriable so long as bank functions in India.

(iii) Statutory reserves kept in Indian books

(iv) Capital reserves representing surplus arising out of sale of assets in India held in a separate account and which is not eligible for repatriation so long as the bank functions in India and

(v) Interest free funds remitted from abroad for the purpose of acquisition of property and held in a separate account in Indian books.

The net credit balance, if any, in the inter-office account with head office or overseas branches will not be recommended as capital funds. At the same time, ay debit balance in the head office account will have to be set-off against the capital.

Tier II capital for foreign banks consists of:

(i) Undisclosed reserves and cumulative perpetual preference shares.

(ii) Revaluation reserves

(iii) General provisions and loss reserves and

(iv) Hybrid debt instruments and subordinated reserves.

It may be noted that the capital to risk weighted assets ratio (CRAR) was originally fixed at 8 percent in 1992 which was revised subsequently. It has been stipulated that banks should achieve CRAR of 9 percent by March 31, 2000.

RISK WEIGHTED ASSETS AND OFF BALANCE SHEET ITEMS

Risk weighted assets signify weighted aggregate of funded and non-funded items. Off Balance Sheet items signify items which are not shown in the Balance Sheet. Each asset is assigned percentage weight and off Balance Sheet factors. The value of each asset of item is multiplied by the relevant weight or of assets and off Balance Sheet items. On arriving at the risk weighted asset ratio, the aggregate is taken into consideration. The following tables show the percentage weight and credit conversion factors.

I Domestic Operations

A. Funded Risk Asset

TABLE 1

Sl. No.	Item of asset or liability	Risk weight %
I.	**Balances**	
1.	Cash, balances with RBI	0
2.	i. Balances in current account with order banks	20
	ii. Claims on Bank/Financial Institutions (Fis)	20
II.	**Investments**	
1.	Investments in Government Securities	2.5
2.	Investments in other approved securities guaranteed by Central/State Government.	2.5
3.	Investments in other securities where payment of interest and repayment of principal are guaranteed by Central Govt. (This will include investments in Indira/Kisan Vikas Patra (IVP/KVP) and investments in Bonds and Debentures where payment of interest and principal is guaranteed by Central Govt.)	2.5
4.	Investments in other securities where payment of interest and repayment of principal are guaranteed by State Governments.	2.5
Note:	Where guarantee has been invoked and the State Government concerned has remained in default, banks should assign 102.5% risk weight. However, the banks need to assign 102.5% risk weight only on those State Government guaranteed securities issued by the defaulting entities and not on all the securities issued or guaranteed by that State Government.	
5.	Investments in other approved securities where payment of interest and repayment of principal are not guaranteed by Central/State Govt.	22.50
6.	Investments in Government guaranteed securities of Government Undertakings which do not form part of the approved market borrowing programme.	
Note :	In order to provide sufficient time to comply with this provision, banks are permitted to account for the risk weight on the outstanding stock of such securities in the portfolio of the banks as on 31.03.2000 in two phases of 10 percent each in 2001-2002 and 2002-2003. This implies that on purchases after 31.03.2000, full 20 percent risk weight will have to be assigned during the year of purchase. Further, above securities will also attract uniform risk weight of 2.5 percent towards market risk.	
7.	Claims on commercial banks and public financial institutions	22.50
8.	Investments in bonds issued by other banks/PFIs	22.50
9.	Investments in securities which are guaranteed by banks or PFIs as to payment of interest and repayment of principal	22.50
10.	Investments in subordinated debt instruments and bonds issued by other banks or Public Financial Institutions for their Tier II capital	102.50
11.	Deposits placed with SIDBI/NABARD in lieu of shortfall in lending to priority sector	102.50
12.	Investment in Mortgage Backed Securities (MBS) or residential assets of Housing Finance Companies (HFCs) Which are recognised and supervised by National Housing Bank (subject to statisfying terms & conditions)	52.50
13.	All other investments	102.50

Note:	Equity Investments in subsidiaries, Intangible assets and losses deducted from Tier I capital should be assigned zero weight.	
III	**Loans & advances including bills purchased and discounted and other credit facilities**	
1.	Loans guaranteed by Govt. of India	0
2.	Loans guaranteed by State Govts.	0
Note:	Loans guaranteed by State Govts. where guarantee has been invoked and the State Govt. concerned has remained in default as on March 31, 2000, a risk weight of 20 percent should be assigned on such advances. Where State Govts. continue to be in default, even after March 31, 2001, a risk weight of 100 percent should be assigned.	
3.	Loans granted to public sector undertakings of Govt. of India	100
4.	Loans granted to public sector undertakings of State Govts.	100
5.	Others	100
6.	Leased assets	100
7.	Advances covered by DICGC/ECGC	50
Note:	The risk weight of 50% should be limited to the amount guaranteed and not the entire outstanding balance in the accounts. In other words, the outstandings in excess of the amount guaranteed, will carry 100% risk weight.	
8.	SSI Advances Guaranteed by Credit Guarantee Fund Trust for Small Industries (CGTSI) up to the guaranteed portion	0
Note:	Banks may assign zero risk weight for the guaranteed portion. The balance outstanding in excess of the guaranteed portion would attract a risk-weight as appropriate to the counter-party	
9.	Advances against term deposits, life policies, NSCs, IVPs and KVPs where adequate margin is available	0
10.	Loans and advances granted to staff of banks which are fully covered by superannuation benefits and mortgage of flat/house	20
11.	Housing loans to individuals against the mortgage of residential housing properties	50
12.	Takeout finance	20
	(i) Unconditional takeover (in the books of lending institution)	
	a. Where full credit risk is assumed by the taking over institution	
	b. Where only partial credit risk is assumed by taking over institution	
	i. the amount to be taken over	20
	ii. the amount to be taken over	100
	(ii) Conditional take-over (in the books of lending and Taking over institution)	100
IV	**Other Assets**	
	1. Premises, furniture and fixtures	100
	2. (i) Income tax deducted at source (net provision)	0
	(ii) Advance tax paid (net of provision)	0
	(iii) Interest due on Government securities	0

(vi)	Accrued interest on CRR balances and claims on RBI on account of Government transactions (net of claims of Government/RBI on banks on account of such transaction)	0
(v)	All other assets	100

B. *Off-Balance Sheet Items*

The credit risk exposure attached to off-Balance Sheet items has to be first calculated by multiplying the face value of each of the off-Balance Sheet items by 'credit conversion factor' as indicated in the table below as in Table 9.2. This will have to be again multiplied by the weights attributable to the relevant counter-party as specified above.

TABLE 2

Sl. No.	Instruments	Credit Conversion Factor (%)
1.	Direct credit substitutes such as general guarantees of indebtedness (including stand-by L/Cs serving as financial guarantees for loans and securities) and acceptances (including endorsements with the character of acceptance)	100
2.	Certain transaction-related contingent items (*e.g.* performance bonds, bid bonds, warranties and stand-by L/Cs related to particular transactions).	50
3.	Short-term self-liquidating trade-related contingencies (e.g. documentary credits collateralised by the underlying shipments)	20
4.	Sale and repurchase agreement and asset sales with recourse, where the credit risk remains with bank	100
5.	Forward asset purchases, forward deposits and partly paid shares and securities, which represent commitments with certain draw down	100
6.	Note issuance facilities and revolving underwriting facilities	50
7.	Other commitments (*e.g.* formal stand-by facilities and credit lines) with an original maturity of over one year	50
8.	Similar commitments with an original maturity upto one year, or which can be unconditionally cancelled at any time	0
9.	Aggregate outstanding foreign exchange contracts of original maturity—	
	*less than one year	2
	*for each additional year or part there of	3
10.	Take-out Finance in the books of taking-over institution	
	(i) Unconditional take-out finance	100
	(ii) Conditional take-out finance	50

Note: As the counter-party exposure will determine the risk weight, it will be 100 percent in respect of all borrowers or zero percent of covered by Government guarantee.

II Overseas Operations (only applicable to Indian banks having branches abroad)

A. Funded Risk Assets

TABLE 3

Sl. No.	Item of asset or liability	Risk weight %
(i)	Cash	0
(ii)	Balances with Monetary Authority	0
(iii)	Investments in Government securities	0
(iv)	Balances in current account with other banks	20
(v)	All other claims on banks including but not limited to funds loaned in money markets, deposit placements, investments in CDs/FRNs, etc.	
(vi)	Investment in non-bank sectors	100
(vii)	Loans and advances, bills purchased and discounted and other credit facilities	
	(a) Claims guaranteed by Government of India	0
	(b) Claims guaranteed by State Governments	0
	(c) Claims on public sector undertakings of Government of India	100
	(d) Claims on public sector undertakings of Sate Governments	100
	(e) Others	100
(viii)	All other banking and infrastructural assets	100

B. Non-funded Risk Assets

TABLE 4

Sl. No.	Instruments	Credit conversion factor (%)
(i)	Direct credit substitutes, such as general guarantees of indebtedness (including stand-by letters of credit serving as financial guarantees for loans and securities) and acceptances (including endorsements with the character of acceptances)	100
(ii)	Certain transaction-related contingent items (e.g. performance bonds, bid bonds, warranties and stand-by letters of credit related to particular transactions)	50
(iii)	Short-term self-liquidating trade related contingencies such as documentary credits collateralised by the underlying shipments	20
(iv)	Sale and repurchase agreement and asset sales with recourse, where the credit risk remains with the credit risk remains with the bank	100
(v)	Forward asset purchases, forward deposits and partly paid shares and securities, which represent commitments with certain draw down	100
(vi)	Note issuance facilities and revolving underwriting facilities	50
(vii)	Other commitments (*e.g.* formal stand-by facilities and credit lines) with an original maturity of over one year	50
(viii)	Similar commitments with an original maturity up to one year, or which can be unconditionally cancelled at any time	0

The New Basel Capital Accord

Internationally, capital adequacy has gained credence with the move towards the adoption of the new Basel Capital Accord. The proposed new Capital Accord is both far reaching and path breaking. It redefines the regulatory approach to bank supervision and provides new incentives for banks supervision and provides new incentives for banks to improve their risk measurement procedures. It also takes cognizance of the fact that technology and market practices have substantially altered since the days of the old accord and consequently, envisages a change in the oversight function of the regulatory authorities. The accord is at an advanced stage of implementation and is likely to be operationalised sometime around 2007.

Three features of the new accord are significant. The first relates to credit risk sensitivity. Inadequate differentiation in credit quality, as prevalent in the old accord, had become increasingly apparent It was, therefore, proposed in the new accord to increase the scale of risk weights and employ external credit ratings to categorise credit. Illustratively, the measurement of credit risk requires to be disaggregated into individual components, viz., probabilities of default, loss given default, exposure at default and correlation of defaults across exposures. The second is the wide applicability of the new accord. The applicability of the old accord was uniform across institutions with varying degrees of sophistication and countries with wide ranging legal traditions and business cultures, thereby resulting in 'one-size-fits-all' approach. The answer has been to introduce a menu approach, with options capable of catering to a heterogeneous banking populace. Third is the responsibility for measuring risk away from regulators towards banks. Such a shift inevitably necessitates strengthening oversight on banks' risk measurement and management. Consequently, supervisory review and market discipline through heightened disclosure have been explicitly incorporated in the new accord.

The implementation of the new accord envisages the development of a comprehensive and efficient internal system for assessment and management of risks, setting up and adhering to adequate internal exposure limits and improving internal control systems in banks. This is important not only from the viewpoint of deciding the quantum of capital allocation, but also from the systemic stability angle to ensure that there are no disruptions in the capital structure.

Classification and Regulation of Investments

The investment portfolio of a bank normally consist of both "approved securities" and "Other securities". Approved securities include predominantly Government securities where as other securities include shares, debentures and bonds. However, the approved securities are bifurcated into permanent and current investments Permanent investments are those which the bank intends to hold till maturity and current investments are those which a bank intends to deal in *i.e.* buying and selling of securities. The ratio of current and permanent investments has been changing over the years in view of measures to adopt prudent accounting standards. With effect from 1998-99 the banks classified a minimum of 70 percent of investments in approved securities as current. And all subsequent purchases to be classified suitably. There is no objection to banks interchanging investments from one category to other with the prior permission of Board of Directors.

Since a significant proportion of banks investments in securities are through private placement. In order to allay concerns arising from the non-transparent practices prevalent in the market, guidelines have been issued in June 2000 regarding undertaking of due diligence obtaining disclosures and credit risk with regard to privately placed investments. Accordingly the banks are required to classify their entire investments portfolio (*w.e.f.* 30.9.2000) under three categories:

I Held to Maturity

II Available for sale

III Held for trading

I The Banks are required to decide the category of investment at the time of acquisition and the decision should be recorded on the investment proposals.

The securities acquired by Banks with intention to hold them till maturity will be classified under 'held to maturity". The ratio of permanent investments (held to maturity) to current investments not to exceed 25 : 75 (1 : 3) or 25% of the total investments. Now, the following investments will be classified under "held to maturity" (permanent) investments.

a. Re-capitalisation bonds received from the Government of India towards their recapitalisation requirements and held in their investment portfolio.

b. Investments in subsidiaries and joint ventures.

c. Investments in debentures/bonds, which are deemed to be in the nature of an advance. Profit on sale of investments on these investments should be first taken to the Profit & Loss Account and there after transferred to "Capital Reserve". Loss on the investments, however, should be charged to Profit & Loss Account only. These investments should be carried at acquisition cost. The premium (excess of purchase price over face value) should be amortised over the period of maturity. A permanent fall in the value of securities should be recognised by the Banks and determined separately for each investment.

II The second category 'Available for sale' should be marked to market at quarterly intervals at least. While the net depreciation under each classification should be ignored. The book value of the individual securities would not change after the revaluation.

A provision for depreciation is required to be made and charged to Profit and Loss Account. However, an equivalent amount net of tax benefit, and net of consequent reduction in the transfer to Statutory Reserve or balance available in Investment Fluctuation Reserve Account, which ever is less, shall be credited to Investment Fluctuation Reserve Account to be shown under the heading 'Revenue and other Reserves'.

III These investments are to be marked to market at monthly or more frequent intervals. The book value of the individual security will not change.

Of course in the Balance Sheet, the investments will continue to be disclosed as per the existing six categories under Investments in India and three categories under Investments Outside India (as shown under schedule 8)

Investment Fluctuation Reserve

Banks are advised to follow a more prudent policy for utilising gains realised on sale of investments in securities arising from the decline in Interest rate and also for building up adequate reserves to guard against any possible reversal of interest rate environment due to unexpected developments. Alternatively banks are required to transfer maximum amount of gains realised on sale of investments in securities to the Investment Fluctuation Reserve. Banks are required to achieve an IFR at a minimum of 5 percent of all investments "held for trading" and "Available for sale" with in a period of five years. However, the unrealised gains on valuation of investment portfolio are not to be taken to Profit & Loss Account or Investment Fluctuation Reserve. The Banks are free to build up a higher percentage of IFR upto 10 percent of the portfolio depending on the size and composition of their portfolio with the permission of Board. The transfer to IFR is treated as an appropriation of net profit "below the line" after statutory reserve.

Transparency and Disclosure in Final Accounts

Transparency and disclosure of Bank accounts play an important role in encouraging healthy competition. Transparency not only helps the Depositors (creditors) whose funds are at risk to make optimal decisions regarding their investment portfolio, but also imposes market discipline on banks to perform well in competitive manner. Accordingly, the banking sector's allocative efficiency and the enhanced private sector participation would be best facilitated if there is increased transparency in banking operations. In case of highly diversified banks, it becomes difficult to make a prior judgment regarding their ability to control the risk component. Therefore, public disclosure acts as a speed breaker in funding risky activities. Adequate and timely disclosures can help to reduce bank failures.

The second Narasimham Committee has already suggested larger disclosure of accounts by Banks in a phased manner keeping in line with the emerging regulatory and supervisory standards at international level, the RBI initiated some micro-level monitoring techniques to assess the true health of the banks. Besides RBI's formats for financial statements, the international accounting standards are broadly followed along with the specific valuation standards prescribed for the investments and foreign exchange positions.

GRADED ILLUSTRATIONS

Illustration (1) (Provision for Taxation & Contingencies)

From the following information calculate the amount of Provisions and contingencies and prepare Profit and Loss Account of a Commercial Bank for the year ended 31st March, 2005.

	(Rs. in '000')
Interest and Discount (including interest accrued on investments)	44,300
Other income	1,100
Interest Expended	13,600
Operating Expenses	14,150
Interest accrued on investments	50

Additional Information :

(a) Rebate on bills discounted to be provided for	150
(b) Classification of advances :	
(i) Standard Assets	20,000
(ii) Sub-standard Assets	11,200
(iii) Doubtful Assets (Fully unsecured)	1,950
(iv) Doubtful Assets- Cover fully by security	
Less than one year	500
More than one year but less than 3 years	3,000
More than three years	3,000
(v) Loss Assets	1,880

(c) Provide 35% of the profit towards provision for taxation

(d) Transfer 25% of the profit to Statutory Reserve

[C.A. (I) May 2005 Modified]

Solution :

COMMERCIAL BANK LTD.
PROFIT & LOSS ACCOUNT
for the year ended 31st March, 2005

	Particulars	Schedule	Rs. (in '000)
I	Income		
	Interest Earned	13	44,150
	Other Income	14	1,100
			45,250
II	Expenditure		
	Interest Expended	15	13,600
	Operating Expenses	16	14,150
	Provisions and Contingencies [4]		11,000
			38,750
III	Profit/Loss		
	Net Profit for the year		6,500
	Profit (Loss) brought forward		Nil
		Total	6,500
IV	Appropriations :		
	Transfer to Statutory Reserve @ 25%		1,625
	Balance carried to Balance Sheet		4,875
		Total	6,500

Working Notes :

(1) Schedule 13 - Interest Earned

(i) Interest & Discount	44,300
Less Rebate on Bills Discounted	(150)
Less Interest Accrued on Investments	(50)
(ii) *Add* Interest Accrued on Investments	50
	44,150

2. Calculation of Provision and Contingencies

Assets	Rs. '000'	%	Provision (Rs. '000')
Standard Assets	20,000	0.25*	50
Substandard Asset	11,200	10	1,120
Doubtful (Unsecured)	1,950	100	1,950
Doubtful (Secured)			
Less than 1 year	500	20	100
More than 1 but less than 3 years	3,000	30	900
More than 3 years	3,000	50	1,500
Loss Assets	1,880	100	1,880
Total Provision			7,500

* Revised to 0.4 percent

3. Provision for Taxation

35% of Net profit before Tax

(45,250 – (13,600 – 14,150 – 7,500)

Rs. 10,000 35% = 3,500

4. Total Provisions and Contingencies = 11,000

(7,500 + 3,500)

Illustration (2) (Provisions and Contingencies)

From the following information relating to a Commercial Bank Ltd. Prepare Profit and Loss Account for the year ended 31st March 2005.

Previous year (Rs. '000')	Items	Current year (Rs. '000')
7,135	Interest and Discount	10,225
570	Income from Investments	560
775	Interest on Balances with RBI	885
3,610	Commission and Brokerage	3,560
60	Profit on sale of Investments	610
3,060	Interest on Deposits	4,110
635	Interest paid to RBI	735
3,635	Payment to and Provision for Employees	4,275
790	Rent and Taxes	895
735	Printing & Stationery	1,060
560	Advertisement	490
490	Depreciation	490
740	Director's Fees	1,060
550	Auditor's Fees	550
250	Legal Charges	760
240	Postage & Telephone	310
210	Insurance	260
285	Repairs & Maintenance	330

Additional Information :

(i) The following items are already adjusted with Interest and Discount (cr.)

	Rs. '000'
Provision for Taxation	740
Provision for Doubtful debts	460
Loss on sale of Investments	60
Rebate on Bills Discounted	275

(ii) 25% of the profit to be transferred to Statutory Reserve and 5% of profit to Revenue Reserve.

Solution : 2

COMMERCIAL BANK LTD.
PROFIT AND LOSS ACCOUNT
for the year ended 31st March 2005

(Rs. '000')

		Schedule	Current year	Previous year
I	Income			
	Interest Earned	13	13,205	8,480
	Other Income	14	4,110	3,670
	Total		17,315	12,150
II	Expenditure			
	Interest Expended	15	4,845	3,695
	Operating Expenses	16	10,480	8,485
	Provisions and contingencies(1)		1,475	—
	Total		16,800	12,180
III	Profit/Loss for the year		515	(30)
	Balance brought forward		(30)	
	Total		485	(30)
IV	Appropriations			
	Transfer to Satutory Reserve		128.75	
	Transfer to Revenue Reserve		25.75	
	Balance carried to Balance Sheet		330.50	
	Total		485.00	

Schedule 13 : Interest Earned (Rs. '000')

(i)	Interest & Discount		11,760
(ii)	Income from Investments		560
(iii)	Interest from RBI		885
	Total		13,205

Schedule 14: Other Income

(i)	Commission and Brokerage		3,560
(ii)	Profit on Sale of Investments	610	
	Less loss on sale of Investments	(60)	550
	Total		4,110

Schedule 15: Interest Expended

(i)	Interest on Deposits	4,110
(ii)	Interest on RBI/Other Bank borrowings	735
	Total	4,845

Schedule 16: Operating Expenses

(i)	Payment to and provision for employees	4,375
(ii)	Rent & Taxes	895

(iii)	Printing & Stationery	1,060
(iv)	Advertisement	490
(v)	Depreciation	490
(vi)	Director's Fees	1,160
(vii)	Auditors Fees	550
(viii)	Legal Charges	760
(ix)	Postage & Telephone	310
(x)	Repairs & Maintenance	330
(xi)	Insurance	260
	Total	10,480

Working note (1)

Provision & Contingencies	Rs. '000'
Provision for Taxation	740
Provision for Doubtful debts	460
Rebate on Bills Discounted	275
	1,475

Illustration (3) (Interest earned and Provision for contingencies)

From the following particulars prepare Profit & Loss Account of Zed Bank Ltd. for the year ended 31st March, 2005.

	Rs. '000'
Interest on Term Loans	9,240
Interest on Over draft	4,500
Interest on Cash Credit	10,920
Income on Investments	5,040
Interest on balances with RBI	900
Commission on remittances & transfer	450
Commission on Letter of Credit	708
Commission on Government business	492
Profit on sale of Land & Building	162
Loss on exchange transactions	312
Interest paid on deposit	16,320
Auditor's Fees & Allowances	720
Directors Fees and Allowances	1,500
Advertisements	1,080
Salaries, Allowances & Bonus to employees	7,440
Payment to Provident Fund	1,680
Printing and Stationery	840
Repairs and Maintenance	300
Postage & Telephones	480

Other Information:

(i) Interest on NPA is as follows :

	Earned (Rs. '000')	Collected (Rs. '000')
Cash Credit	4,920	2,400
Overdraft	2,700	600
Term Loans	4,500	1,500

(ii) Classification of Advances

Sub-standard Assets	6,720
Doubtful Assets not covered by security	1,200
Doubtful Assets covered by security for 1 year	300
Loss Assets	1,200

(iii) Investments 16,500

Bank should not keep more than the required limit as permanent investments. The market value of it's 75% investment is Rs. 10,50,000 as on 31st March 2005.

Solution :

ZED BANK LTD.
PROFIT AND LOSS ACCOUNT
For the year ended 31st March, 2005

		Schedule	(Rs. '000')
I	Income		
	Income Earned	13	22,980
	Other Income	14	1,500
			24,480
II	Expenditure		
	Interest Expended	15	16,320
	Operating Expenses	16	14,040
	Provision and Contingencies		5,007
			35,367
III	Profit (Loss)		(10,887)
IV	Appropriations		Nil

Schedule 13: Interest Earned

		(Rs. '000')
(i)	Interest on Cash Credit (10,920 – 250)	8,400
(ii)	Interest on Overdraft (4,500 – 2,100)	2,400
(iii)	Interest on Term Loans (9,240 – 3,000)	6,240
(iv)	Income from Investments	5,040
(v)	Interest on Balances with RBI	900
		22,980

Schedule 14: Other Income

		(Rs. '000')
I	Commission, Exchange & Brokerage	
	Commission on remittances & transfer	450
	Commission on Letter of Credit	708
	Commission on Government business	492
		1,650
II	Profit on sale of Land & Building	162
III	Loss on Exchange Transactions	(312)
		1,500

Schedule 15: Interest Expended

Interest on Deposits	16,320

Schedule 16: Operating Expenses

(i)	Salaries, Allowances & Bonus to Employees	7,440
(ii)	Provident Fund Contribution	1,680
(iii)	Printing & Stationery	840
(iv)	Advertisement	1,080
(v)	Director's Fee & Allowances	1,500
(vi)	Auditor's Fees and Allowances	720
(vii)	Postage and Telephones	480
(viii)	Repairs and Maintenance	300
		14,040

Working Notes:

			(Rs. '000')
(i)	Provisions and Contingencies		
	Provision for Non-Performing Assets		
	Sub standard Assets	@ 10%	672
	Doubtful Assets not Covered by Security	100%	1,200
	Doubtful Assets Covered by Security:		
	Doubtful for 1 year	20%	60
	Loss Assets	100%	1,200
			3,132
Depreciation on Current Investments			
	Cost of 75% Rs. 16,500	12,375	
Less	Market Value of Current Investments	10,500	1,875
			5,007

(1) As per the RBI guidelines effective from 30.9.2000 a bank should not hold investments till maturity (Permanent) more than 25% of total investments.

(2) Depreciation is calculated on the current investments.

Illustration (4) (Interest and Rebate on Bills discounted)

From the following particulars of a Commercial Bank prepare Profit and Loss Account for the year ended 31st March, 2005.

	Rs. '000'
Interest paid on Deposits :	
— On Fixed Deposits Accounts	20,480
— On Saving Bank Deposits Accounts	4,000
— On Recurring Deposits Accounts	6,000
Interest Received	35,225
Discount Received	20,200
Commission	2,150
Exchange and Brokerage	850
Rent Received	827
Profit on sale of Investment	3,000
Salaries & Allowance of Staff	2,950
Director's Fees & Allowances	600
Rent & Rates etc.	1,500
Printing and Stationery	750
Postage and Telephones	700
Auditor's Fees	125
Preliminary Expenses	225
Depreciation on Bank property	450

Additional Information :

(i) Rebate on bills discounted as on 31st March, 2004 and as on 31st March, 2005 were Rs. 1,80,000 and Rs. 2,40,000 respectively.

(ii) An advance of Rs. 1,50,00,000 was extended to X Ltd. who went into liquidation due to heavy losses. The Official Receiver assured that a recovery of 50% is certain.

(iii) There were other debts also for which a provision of Rs. 22,50,000 is required as per the report of Auditors.

(iv) Write off preliminary expenses

(v) Provide Rs. 32,50,000 for income tax.

Solution:

COMMERCIAL BANK LTD.
PROFIT & LOSS ACCOUNT
for the year ended 31st March, 2005

	Schedule	(Rs. '000')
I Income		
Interest Earned	13	55,365
Other Income	14	6,827
		62,192

			(Rs. '000')
II	**Expenditure**		
	Interest Expended	15	30,480
	Operating Expenses	16	7,300
	Provisions & Contingencies		13,000
			50,780
III	**Profit/Loss**		11,412
	Balance brought forward		Nil
			11,412
IV	**Appropriations**		
	Transfer to Statutory Reserve* (25% of Rs. 11,412)		2,853
	Balance carried forward		8,559
			11,412

* As per the provisions of Banking Regulation Act 1949.

Schedule 13: Interest Earned

Interest	35,225
Discount	20,140
	55,365

Schedule 14: Other Income

Commission	2,150
Exchange & Brokerage	850
Profit on sale of Investments	3,000
Rent Received	827
	6,827

Schedule 15: Interest Expended

Interest on Deposits:	
Fixed Deposits Accounts	20,480
Saving Bank Accounts	4,000
Recurring Deposits Accounts	6,000
	30,480

Schedule 16: Operating Expenses

Staff Salaries & Allowances	2,950
Rent & Rates	1,500
Printing & Stationary	750
Postage & Telephones	700
Director's Fees & Allowances	600
Auditor's Fees	125
Depreciation	450
Preliminary Expenses	225
	7,300

Working Notes :

			(Rs. in '000'
(1)	Provisions & Contingencies		
	Provision for Bad & Doubtful Debts (75,00,000 + 22,50,000)		9,750
	Provision for Taxation		3,250
			13,000
(2)	Interest Earned		
	Interest Received		35,225
	Discount Received	20,200	
Add	Rebate on Bills discounted (as on 31.3.2004)	180	
		20,380	
Less	Rebate on Bills discounted (as on 31. 3. 2005)	240	20,140
			55,365

Illustration (5) (Reserve for unexpired discounts)

Following information has been extracted from the books of Modern Bank Ltd. for the year ended on 31st March, 2005.

(Rs. '000')

		Dr.	Cr.
Share Capital			25,000
Reserves			40,000
Dividend Fluctuation Fund			15,000
Bills Payable			50,000
Borrowings from Banks in India			6,250
Non Banking Assets		1,750	
Interest Accrued on Investments		6,500	
Advance Payment of Tax		2,750	
Silver	5,000		
Branch Adjustment		1,44,850	
Loans, Advances, Cash Credit & Overdraft in India		1,25,000	
Unclaimed Dividend			600
Unexpired Discount			1,250
Cash with RBI		85,000	
Cash with SBI		30,000	
Depreciation Fund on Premises			2,00,000
Premises at Cost		2,50,000	
Additions to Premises		50,000	
Reserve for Buildings			25,000
Profit & Loss A/c including 5,200 thousand for the year			10,250
Investments at Cost : Government Securities		1,25,000	
Debentures		10,000	
Bullion		60,000	
Bills Discounted & Purchased in India		22,500	
Money at Call and Short notice in India		5,000	

	Dr.	Cr.
		(Rs. '000')
Fixed Deposits		1,00,000
Savings Bank Deposits		1,50,000
Current Accounts		3,00,000
	9,23,350	9,23,350

Additional Information :

The bank had bills for collection for Rs. 25,00,000 and for Acceptances Rs. 40,00,000. There was a claim of Rs. 50,00,000 against the Bank not acknowledged as debt. The Liabilities for bills discounted was Rs. 7,50,000 and liability for forward exchange contract was Rs. 10,00,000. The Directors decided to reserve Rs. 50,000 for unexpired discounts and transfer reserve for Building to Depreciation Fund. Draw up the Balance Sheet as per the latest provisions of Banking Regulation Act, 1949.

{C.S. (I) Adapted]

Solution:

MODERN BANK LTD.
BALANCE SHEET
As on 31st March, 2005

Capital and Liabilities	Schedule	(Rs. '000')
Share Capital	1	25,000
Reserve and Surplus	2	65,200
Deposits	3	5,50,000
Borrowings	4	6,250
Other liabilities & Provisions	5	2,76,900
		9,23,350
Assets		
Cash and Balance with RBI	6	85,000
Balance with SBI and Money at Call and Short notice	7	35,000
Investments	8	1,95,000
Advances	9	1,47,500
Fixed Assets	10	3,00,000
Other Assets	11	1,60,850
		9,23,350
Contingent liabilities:	12	10,750
Bills for collection		2,500

Schedule: 1 Share Capital

Issued, Subscribed & Paid up	25,000

Schedule: 2 Reserve & Surplus (Rs. '000')

(i) Statutory Reserve	40,000	
Add Current year's transfer	1,300	41,300
(ii) Revenue and Other Reserve		
Dividend Equalisation Fund		15,000
Profit & Loss Account		8,900
(10,250 – 1,300 – 50)		65,200

(Balance as per Balance Sheet Less statutory transfer @ 25% of current year's profit less reserve for unexpired discount)

Schedule 3: Deposits

Demand Deposits (Current Accounts)	3,00,000
Savings Bank Deposits	1,50,000
Term Deposits (Fixed Deposits)	1,00,000
	5,50,000

Schedule 4: Borrowings

Borrowings in India	6,250

Schedule 5: Other Liabilities & Provisions

Bills payable	50,000
Unclaimed dividends	600
Unexpired discount (1,250 + 50)	1,300
Depreciation Fund	2,00,000
Reserve for Building	25,000
	2,76,900

Schedule 6 : Cash and Bank Balances with RBI

Balances with RBI	85,000

Schedule 7: Balance with Banks and Money at Call and Short notice

Balance with SBI	30,000
Money at call and at short notice	5,000
	35,000

Schedule 8: Investments

Government Securities	1,25,000
Debentures	10,000
Bullion	60,000
	1,95,000

Schedule 9 : Advances

Bills purchased and discounted	22,500
Loans Cash Credits, advances and overdrafts	1,25,000
	1,47,500

Schedule 10: Fixed Assets

Premises at cost	2,50,000
Addition made during the year	50,000
	3,00,000

Schedule 11: Other Assets

Branch Adjustment	1,44,850
Silver	5,000
Advance payment of tax	2,750
Interest Accrued on investments	6,500
Non-banking Assets	1,750
	1,60,850

Schedule 12: Contingent Liabilities

Claims against not acknowledged as debt	5,000
Liability for bill discounted	750
Liability for forward exchange contract	1,000
Acceptances, Endorsements and other obligations	4,000
	10,750

Illustration (6) (General)

Following balances have been extracted from the books of Hill Top Bank Ltd. for the year ended 31st March, 2005.

Particulars	Dr. (Rs. '000')	Cr. (Rs. '000')
Share Capital		30,000
Creditors		1,800
Salaries	4,800	
Rent	1,800	
Bills discounted	30,000	
Bills payable		48,000
Profit & Loss Account (1.4.2004)		9,600
Interest and discount		27,000
Unclaimed Dividends		1,800
Interest Accrued and paid	12,000	
Money at call and Short notice	18,000	
Cash with RBI	90,000	
Cash with SBI	78,000	
Cash in hand	3,600	
Buildings	72,000	
Investments in India in :		
Government Securities	60,000	
Shares & Debenture	50,000	
Bullion	70,000	

Borrowed from Bank		12,000
Current Accounts		4,20,000
Saving Bank Deposits		1,80,000
Fixed Deposits		1,20,000
Statutory Reserve		60,000
Loans, Advances, Overdrafts and Cash Credits	4,20,000	
	9,10,200	9,10,200

Additional Information :

(i) The Bank has the bills for Rs. 50,00,000 as collection for it's constituents and acceptances and endorsement for Rs. 15,00,000.

Solution :

HILL TOP BANK LTD.
BALANCE SHEET AS ON 31ST MARCH 2005

Capital & Liabilities	Schedule	(Rs. '000')
Share Capital	1	30,000
Reserve & Surplus	2	78,000
Deposits	3	7,20,000
Borrowings	4	12,000
Other Liabilities & Provisions	5	51,600
		8,91,600
Assets		
Cash and Balance with RBI	6	93,600
Balance with other bank and Money at call at short notice	7	96,000
Investments	8	1,80,000
Advances	9	4,50,000
Fixed Assets	10	72,000
Other Assets	11	—
		8,91,600
Contingent Liabilities	12	1,500
Bills for Collection		5,000

PROFIT AND LOSS ACCOUNT
FOR THE YEAR ENDED 31ST MARCH 2005

		Schedule	(Rs. '000')
I	Income		
	Income	13	27,000
	Other Income	14	—
			27,000
II	Expenditure		
	Interest Expended	15	12,000
	Operating Expenses	16	6,600
	Provision & Contingencies	—	—
			18,600

III	Profit/Loss	
	Net Profit for the year	8,400
	Balance brought forward	9,600
		18,000
IV	Appropriations	
	Transfer to Statutory Reserve (25%)	2,100
	Balance Carried forward	15,900
		18,000

Schedule 1 : Share Capital

Share Capital	30,000
Shares of Rs...... each	

Schedule 2 : Reserve and Surplus

Statutory Reserve (op. Balance)	60,000
Addition made during the year	2,100
	62,100
Capital Reserve	—
Securities Premium	—
Revenue and Other Reserves	—
Balance in Profit and Loss A/c	15,900
	78,000

Schedule 3: Deposits

Demand Deposits	4,20,000
Savings Bank Deposits	1,80,000
Term Deposits	1,20,000
	7,20,000

Schedule 4: Borrowings

Borrowings from other Banks	12,000

Schedule 5: Other Liabilities and Provision

Bills payable	48,000
S. Creditors	1,800
Unclaimed Dividends	1,800
	51,600

Schedule 6 : Cash and Balance with RBI

Cash and balance with RBI	93,600

Schedule 7: Balance with Other Bank and Money at Call and at Short notice

Balance with SBI	78,000
Money at Call and Short notice	18,000
	96,000

Schedule 8: Investments

	Rs. '000'
Investments in India :	
Government Securities	60,000
Shares and Debentures	50,000
Bullion	70,000
	1,80,000

Schedule 9: Advances

Bills discounted & purchased	30,000
Loans, advances, Cash credits, and overdrafts	4,20,000
	4,50,000

Schedule 10: Fixed Assets

Buildings	72,000
Other Fixed Assets	—
	72,000

Schedule 12: Contingent liabilities

Acceptances, Endorsements and other obligations	1,500

Schedule 13: Interest Earned

Interest and discount received	27,000

Schedule 15: Interest Expended

Interest accrued and paid	12,000

Schedule 16: Operating Expenses

Payment to employees (Salaries)	4,800
Rent & Rates etc.	1,800
	6,600

Illustration (7) (CRR and LSR)

From the following ledger balances, prepare Balance Sheet of Maha-Luxmi Bank Ltd. as on 31st March, 2005.

	(Rs. '000') Dr.	Cr.
Share Capital		99,000
Statutory Reserve		1,15,500
Term Loans	3,96,440	
Furniture	35,060	
Government Securities	55,085	
Gold	27,615	
Premises	77,850	
Money at Call & short notice	1,05,060	
Net Profit before appropriation		75,000
Profit and Loss Account		2,06,000
Fixed Deposits		2,58,500
Savings Deposits		2,25,000
Current Accounts	14,000	2,60,060

Borrowings from other Banks		55,000
Bills payable		50
Cash credits	4,06,050	
Cash in hand	80,075	
Cash with RBI	18,940	
Cash with Other Banks	77,935	
	12,94,110	12,94,110

(i) 50% of term loans are secured by Government guarantee. 10% of cash credits are unsecured. Other portion is secured by tangible assets.

(ii) Necessary transfer is to be made from cash with other Banks to maintain 5% cash reserve on fixed, savings and current deposits with RBI.

(iii) Check if 25% of demand and time liabilities is maintained in cash, gold or unencumbered securities if not, identify the deficit/excess.

		(Rs. '000')
(iv)	Bills for collection	9,050
(v)	Acceptances and Endorsements	7,060
(vi)	Claims against bank not acknowledged as debt	2,750
(vii)	Depreciation on:	
	Premises	550
	Furniture	390

Prepare final Balances Sheet.

MAHA LUXMI BANK LTD.
BALANCE SHEET AS ON 31ST MARCH 2005

Capital and Liabilities	**Schedule**	**(Rs. '000')**
Share Capital	1	99,000
Reserve and Surplus	2	3,96,500
Deposits	3	7,43,560
Borrowings	4	55,000
Other Liabilities & Provision	5	50
		12,94,110
Assets		
Cash and balance with RBI	6	1,17,253
Balances with other Banks and Money at call and short notice	7	1,64,757
Investments	8	82,700
Advances	9	8,16,490
Fixed Assets	10	1,12,910
Other Assets	11	Nil
		12,94,110
		(Rs. '000')
Contingent liabilities	12	
Bills for collection		

Schedule 1: Share Capital	(Rs. '000')
Subscribed and Paid up Capital (99,00,000 shares of Rs. 10 each	99,000
	99,000

Schedule 2: Reserve and Surplus	
Statutory Reserve (Op. Balance)	1,15,500
Addition made during the year (25% of current year's profits)	18,750
	1,34,250
Balance in Profit & Loss A/c (3)	2,62,250
	3,96,500

Schedule 3: Deposits	
Demand Deposits	2,60,060
Savings Bank Deposits	2,25,000
Fixed Deposits	2,58,500
	7,43,560

Schedule 4 : Borrowings	
Borrowings from Banks in India	55,000

Schedule 5: Other liabilities & Provisions	
Other liabilities & Provisions	50

Schedule 6: Cash and Balance with RBI	
Cash in hand	80,075
Balances with RBI in Current Accounts	37,178
	1,17,253

Schedule 7: Balance with Banks & Money at call and short notice	
Balances with Banks in India	59,697
Money at call and short notice	1,05,060
	1,64,757

Schedule 8: Investments	
Government Securities	55,085
Gold	27,615
	82,700

Schedule 9: Advances	
Cash credits & Overdraft	4,20,050
Term Loans	3,96,440
	8,16,490
Secured by tangible assets (B. Figure)	5,76,265
Secured by Government Guarantee (50% of Term Loan)	1,98,220
Unsecured (10% of Cash Credits)	42,005
	8,16,490

(Rs. '000')

Schedule 10: Fixed Assets

	Premises at cost	78,400	
Less :	Depreciation	550	77,850
	Furniture at cost	35,450	
Less :	Depreciation	390	35,060
			1,12,910

Schedule 11: Other Assets Nil

Schedule 12: Contingent liabilities

Claims against banks not acknowledged as debt	2,750
Acceptances and Endorsements	7,060
	9,810

Working Note :

(1) The Banks are required to maintain 5% of total demand and time liabilities as cash reserve with RBI. 5% of (Fixed Deposits + Savings deposit and current accounts deposits)

= 7,43,560 × 5%	= 37,178
Balance with RBI	18,940
Amount to be transferred	18,238

(2) Liquidity Reserve: Banks are required to maintain 25% of total demand and time liabilities as liquidity Reserve i.e. 25% of 7,43,560 = 1,85,890

Liquid Assets	
Cash in hand	80,075
Cash with Other Banks	77,935
Money at call & at short notice	1,05,060
Gold	27,615
Government Securities	55,085
	3,45,770

Excess Liquidity = 3,45,770 – 1,85,890 = 1,59,880

(3) Appropriation

	Net Profit	75,000
	Balance of Profit & Loss A/c b/d	2,06,000
		2,81,000
Less:	Transfer to Statutory Reserve (25% of 75,000)	18,750
		2,62,250

Illustration (8) (Contingent liabilities in the Trial Balance)

From the following information relating SRK Bank Ltd. Prepare Profit and Loss Account for the year ended 31st march 2006 and a Balance Sheet as on that date.

(Rs. '000')

Particulars		Dr.	Cr.
Share Capital (Rs. 10 each)			95,000
Branch Adjustments		10,000	
Loss on Sale of Invesments		10,000	
Postage		625	
Directors Fees		500	
Depreciation Reserve (Building)			400
Miscellaneous Income			1,950
Cash in hand and with RBI		37,500	
Rent Rates & Taxes		6,000	
Salaries		10,600	
Depreciation Reserve (Furniture)			100
Audit Fees		2,500	
Rent Received			300
Discount Received			21,000
Interest paid		3,975	
Bills discounted		6,250	
Loans		90,500	
Interest Received			31,000
Bills for Collection		21,750	21,750
Profit & Loss Account			3,250
Reserve Fund			70,000
Current Accounts Control			48,500
Employees Security Deposits			3,710
Government Bonds		47,185	
Gold Bullion		7,565	
Silver	1,000		
Constituents liabilities for acceptances and endorsements		28,250	28,250
Borrowings from Banks			38,615
Buildings		32,500	
Furniture		2,500	
Money at call and short notice		13,000	
Commission and Brokerage			12,650
Savings Deposits			7,500
Fixed Deposits			11,525
Balances with Other Banks		23,175	
Other Investments		27,815	
Interest Accrued on Investments		12,310	
		3,95,500	3,95,500

Other Information

You are required to prepare the Profit and Loss Account for the year ended and a Balance Sheet of the Bank as per the provisions of Banking Regulation Act 1949 as amended upto date after taking into account the following information:

		(Rs. '000')
(a)	Rebate on bills discounted to be provided :	20,000
(b)	Depreciation for the year on :	
	Building	2,500
	Furniture	2,50
(c)	Included in the current accounts	
	Ledger are accounts over drawn by	1,250

[C.A. (I) Adapted]

Solution :

SRK BANK LTD.

BALANCE SHEET AS ON 31ST MARCH, 2006

Capital and Liabilities	**Schedule**	**(Rs. '000')**
Share Capital	1	95,000
Reserves & Surplus	2	1,01,200
Deposits	3	68,775
Borrowings	4	38,615
Other liabilities & Provisions	5	5,710
		3,09,300
Assets		
Cash and balance with RBI	6	37,500
Balance with Other Banks and Money at Call and short notice	7	36,175
Investments	8	83,565
Advances	9	98,000
Fixed Assets	10	31,750
Other Assets	11	22,310
		3,09,300
Contingent liabilities	12	28,250
Bills for Collection		21,750

SRK BANK LTD.
Profit & Loss Account
For the year ended 31st March, 2006

		Schedule	(Rs. '000')
I	Income		
	Interest and Discount	13	52,000
	Other Income	14	4,900
			56,900
II	Expenditure		
	Interest Expended	15	3,975
	Operating Expenses	16	22,975
	Provisions and Contingencies		2,000
			28,950
III	Profit/Loss		
	Net profit for the year		27,950
	Balance b/d		3,250
			31,200
IV	Appropriations		
	Transfer to Statutory Reserve		6,987.50
	(@ 25% of Current year's profit)		
	Balance c/d		24,212.50
			31,200.00

Schedule 1: Share Capital

	Issued, Subscribed & Paid up Capital	
	Shares of Rs. 10 each	95,000

Schedule 2: Reserves & Surplus

1.	Statutory Reserves	70,000.00
Add	transferred during the year	6,987.50
		76,987.50
II	Balance in Profit & Loss A/c	24,212.50
		1,01,200.00

Schedule 3: Deposits

I	Demand Deposits	49,750
	(Current Accounts + Overdrawn)(48,500 + 1,250)	
II	Saving Bank Deposits	7,500
III	Term Deposits	11,525
		68,775

Schedule 4 : Borrowings

	Borrowings from other Banks in India		38,615

Schedule 5 : Other Liabilities & Provisions

	Rebate on Bills discounted		2,000
	Employees Security Deposits		3,710
			5,710

Schedule 6: Cash Balance with RBI

	Cash and balance with RBI		37,500

Schedule 7: Balance with Other Banks and Money at Call and Short notice

(i)	Balances with other banks		23,175
(ii)	Money at Call and short notice		13,000
			36,175

Schedule 8: Investments

(i)	Government Securities		47,185
(ii)	Other Investments		27,815
(iii)	Gold		7,565
(iv)	Silver		1,000
			83,565

Schedule 9: Advances

(i)	Bills purchased & Discounted		6,250
(ii)	Cash Credits & Overdrafts and loans (90,500 + 1,250)		91,750
			98,000

Schedule 10: Fixed Assets

(i)	Buildings at Cost	32,500	
Less	Acc. Depreciation	(2,900)	29,600
(ii)	Furniture at cost	2,500	
Less	Acc. Depreciation	(350)	2,150
			31,750

Schedule 11: Other Assets

(I)	Inter-Branch Adjustments		10,000
(II)	Interest Accrued		12,310
			22,310

Schedule 12: Contingent liabilities

	Acceptances, Endorsements and Other obligations		28,250

Schedule 13: Interest Earned

	Interest & Discount		39,690
	Income on Investments		12,310
			52,000

Schedule 14: Other Income (Rs. '000')

(i)	Commission, Exchange & Brokerage	12,650
(ii)	(Loss) on sale of Investments	(10,000)
(iii)	Miscellaneous Incomes Rent & other receipts	2,250
		4,900

Schedule 15: Interest Expended

(i)	Interest on Deposits	3,975

Schedule 16: Operating Expenses

(i)	Salaries	10,600
(ii)	Rent & Rates etc.	6,000
(iii)	Director's Fees	500
(iv)	Auditor's Fees	2,500
(v)	Postage	625
(vi)	Depreciation	2,750
		22,975

Working Notes:

(1) The amount of Rs. 1,250 thousand overdrawn as shown by Current Accounts Ledger has been treated under "Demand Deposits" (as per Schedule 3) and "Advances" (as per Schedule 9). It is to be noted that every item of adjustment requires double treatment.

(2) Constituents liabilities for acceptances, endorsements generally do not form part of trial balance. If shown (as given in this question) will not affect the preparation of Balance Sheet. These contingent liabilities have to be shown under schedule 12.

Illustration (9) Classification of Advances: Security wise, priority wise)

From the following particulars prepare Profit and Loss Account and the Balance Sheet of Bright Bank Ltd. for the year ending 31st March 2006.

(Rs. '000')

Particulars	Dr.	Cr.
Share Capital		5,487
Money at Call and short notice	1,200	
Cash Balance: In India	1,656	
Outside India	984	
Balance with other Banks	600	
Deposits:		
Current		7,800
Savings Bank		10,500
Fixed		21,000
Borrowings:		
In India		12,000
Outside India		750

Particulars			
Advances:			
Bills purchased & discounted		4,800	
Cash Credits & Overdrafts		10,800	
Term Loans		6,900	
Fixed Assets:			
Premises	16,200		
Additions made during the year	75		
	16,275		
Less Accumulated Depreciation	(3,000)	13,275	
Furniture	5,700		
Additions made during the year	450		
	6,150		
Less Accumulated Depreciation	(300)	5,850	
Other liabilities:			
Bills payable			1,050
Branch Adjustments			30
Interest Accrued			300
Operating Expenses:			
Salaries	900		
Rent, Rates & Taxes	72		
Printing & Stationery	18		
Legal Charges	42		
Directors Fees	12		
Insurance	15		—
Depreciation on:			
Premises	600		
Furniture	120		
Interest and Discount			4,500
Interest on Investment			1,500
Commission, Exchange and Brokerage			300
Profit on sale of Investments			60
Interest paid on deposits		1,980	
Reserves and Surplus		3,000	
Investments: Govt. Securities		12,300	
Shares & Debentures		153	
Other Investments		6,000	
		68,277	68,277

Additional Information

		(Rs. '000')
(i)	Bills for collection amounted to	2,100
(ii)	Acceptances, endorsements and other obligations	1,500
(iii)	Provision for taxation is to be Credited to the extent of	451
(iv)	Statutory Reserve as on 1. 4. 2005 and the balance Capital Reserve	1,800
(v)	Advances :	
	(a) Security-wise	
	Secured by tangible assets	18,600
	Covered by Bank guarantees	1,800
	Unsecured	2,100
	(b) Sectors-wise	
	Priority Sector	9,900
	Public Sector	3,000
	Others	9,600
	(c) Bad & Doubtful debts	
	An unsecured advance considered doubtful	150
(vi)	A dividend of 10% has been proposed	

BRIGHT BANK LTD.
BALANCE SHEET
As on 31st March, 2006

Capital and Liabilities	**Schedule**	**(Rs. '000')**
Share Capital	1	5,487.00
Reserves & Surplus	2	4,451.30
Deposits	3	39,300.00
Borrowings	4	12,750.00
Other liabilities & provisions	5	2,379.70
		64,368
Assets		
Cash and Balance with RBI	6	2,640
Balances with other Banks and Money at call and short notice	7	1,800
Investments	8	18,453
Advances	9	22,350
Fixed Assets	10	19,125
Other Assets	11	—
		64,368
Contingent liabilities	12	1,500
Bills for collection		2,100

BRIGHT BANK LTD.
PROFIT AND LOSS ACCOUNT
for the year ended 31st March, 2006

		Schedule	(Rs. '000')
I	Income:		
	Interest Earned	13	6,000
	Other Income	14	360
			6,360
II	Expenditure:		
	Interest Expenditure	15	1,980
	Operating Expenses	16	1,779
	Provisions & Contingencies		601
			4,360
III	Profit/Loss		
	Net profit for the year		2,000.00
IV	Appropriation:		
	Transfer to Statutory Reserve(25%)		500.00
	Proposed Dividend (10%)		548.70
	Balance c/d		951.30
			2,000.00

Schedule 1: Share Capital

Issued, subscribed and Paid up Capital	
Shares of Rs. 10 each	5,487

Schedule 2: Reserves and Surplus

I	Statutory Reserve	
	Opening Balance	1,800.00
	Addition made during the year (25% of Current year's profit)	500.00
II	Capital Reserve	1,200.00
III	Balance in Profit & Loss A/c	951.30
		4,451.30

Schedule 3 : Deposits

(i)	Demand Deposits	7,800
(ii)	Savings Bank Deposits	10,500
(iii)	Term Deposits	21,000
		39,300

Schedule 4: Borrowings

(i)	Borrowings From other Banks in India	12,000
(ii)	Borrowings From other Banks outside India	750
		12,750

Schedule 5: Other liabilities & provisions

(i)	Bills payable	1,050.00
(ii)	Inter-office adjustments	30.00
(iii)	Interest accrued	300.00
(iv)	Others including provisions	999.70
	(1.Tax + Proposed dividend)	2,379.70

Schedule 6: Cash and Balance with RBI

Cash in hand & Balance with RBI	2,640
(In India 1,656 + outside India 984)	

Schedule 7: Balance with Banks and Money at call and at short notice

(i)	Balance with other Banks	600
(ii)	Money at call and at short notice	1,200
		1,800

Schedule 8: Investments

Investments in India:

Government Securities	12,300
Shares and Debentures	153
Other Investments	6,000
	18,453

Schedule 9: Advances

(A)	(i)	Bills purchased and discounted	4,800
	(ii)	Cash Credit, overdrafts & loans (Less bad debts)	10,650
	(iii)	Term loans	6,900
			22,350
(B)	(i)	Secured by Tangible assets	18,600
	(ii)	Covered by Bank Guarantee	1,800
	(iii)	Unsecured (less Bad Debts)	1,950
			22,350
(C)		Advances in India	
	(i)	Priority Sectors	9,900
	(ii)	Public Sectors	3,000
	(iii)	Banks	—
	(iv)	Others	9,450
			22,350

Schedule 10: Fixed Assets

(i)	Premises at Cost	16,200	
	Addition made during the year	75	
		16,275	
Less	Depreciation to date	(3,000)	13275
			13,275

	Balance b/d		13,275
(ii)	Other Fixed Assets		
	Furniture at cost	5,700	
	Addition made during the year	450	
		6,150	
Less	Depreciation to date	(300)	
			5,850
	Total (i) + (ii)		19,125

Schedule 11: Other Assets

Nil

Schedule 12: Contingent liabilities

	Acceptances, endorsements and other obligations1,500	
		1,500

Schedule 13: Interest Earned

(i)	Interest and Discount	4,500
(ii)	Income on Investments	1,500
		6,000

Schedule 14: Other Income

(i)	Commission, exchange & brokerage	300
(ii)	Profit on sale of investment	60
		360

Schedule 15: Interest Expended

(i)	Interest on deposits	1,980

Schedule 16: Operating Expenses

(i)	Payments to and provisions for employees (Salaries)	900
(ii)	Rent, taxes & lighting	72
(iii)	Printing and Stationery	18
(iv)	Depreciation on Banks property	720
(v)	Director's fees	12
(vi)	Legal Charged	42
(vii)	Other Expenditure	15
		1,779

Working Notes :

(i) Calculation of Provisions and contingencies.

Provision for Bad debt debts	150
Provision for Income Tax	451
	601

Illustration (10) (Provision against Advances and Taxation)

From the following Trial Balance as on 31st March, 2005, prepare Profit & Loss Account of Atlantic Bank Ltd. for the year ended 31st March, 2006 and a Balance Sheet as on that date.

(Rs. '000')

	Dr.	Cr.
Cash Credits, Overdrafts & Loans	5,700	
Term Loans	5,100	
Interest on Advances		3,200
Interest from Investments		500
Premises (net)	5,500	
Furniture	1,000	
Interest paid	480	
Salaries	300	
Commission, Brokerage etc.		800
Profit on sale of Investments		80
Other revenue receipts		320
Printing & stationery	140	
Postage & Telegrams	80	
Repairs	100	
Interest Accrued	200	
Share Capital		8,000
Statutory Reserve		3,600
Fixed Deposits		1,100
Savings Deposits		1,300
Current Accounts		500
Borrowings from other Banks		1,200
Cash Balance	800	
Balance with Other Banks	1,600	
Cash with RBI	400	
Investment in Govt. Securities	1,200	
Other approved Securities	400	
Profit & Loss Account		2,600
Bills purchased & Discounted	1,000	
Borrowings from RBI		400
Bills payable		100
Interest Accrued		300
	24,000	24,000

Additional Information :

(i) Bills for collection as on 31st March 2006 amounted to Rs. 940 thousand

(ii) Income tax @ 40% is to be provided.

(iii) Advances have been classified as under :

(Rs. '000')

	Cash Credits Overdrafts etc.	Term Loans	Bills Discounts and purchased
(i) Standard Assets	4,000	3,900	900
(ii) Sub-standard Assets	500	400	100
Doubtful Assets:			
— Up to one year	400	80	—
— One to three years	480	200	—
— More than three years	200	320	—
Loss Assets	120	200	—

No provision has been made against these assets. Doubtful Assets are secured to the extent of 50% of the amount due.

[C.A. (I) Adapted]

Solution:

ATLANTIC BANK LTD.
BALANCE SHEET
As on 31st March, 2006

Capital and Liabilities	**Schedule**	**(Rs. '000')**
Share Capital	1	8,000
Reserves and Surplus	2	7,534
Deposits	3	2,900
Borrowings	4	1,600
Other liabilities & Provisions	5	1,326
Total		21,360
Assets		
Cash and Balance with RBI	6	1,200
Balances with Banks and Money at call and short notice	7	1,600
Investments	8	1,600
Advances		10,260
Fixed Assets		6,500
Other Assets	11	200
		21,360
Bills for collection		940

PROFIT AND LOSS ACCOUNT
For the year ended 31st March 2006

		Schedule	(Rs. '000')
I	Income:		
	Interest Earned	13	3,700
	Other Income	14	1,200
			4,900

II	Expenditure		
	Interest Expended	15	480
	Operating Expenses	16	620
	Provision and contingencies*		2,466
			3,566
III	Profit/Loss		
	Net profit for the year		1,334
	Profit brought forward		2,600
			3,934
IV	Appropriations		
	Transfer to Statutory Reserve (25% of current year's profit)		333.50
	Balance carried to Balance Sheet		3,600.50
			3,934.00

*(Provision against advances and provision for taxation)

Schedule 1: Capital (Rs. '000')

Issued Subscribed and paid up capital	8,000

Schedule 2: Reserves and Surplus

(i)	Statutory Reserves	
	Opening balance	3,600.00
	Addition made during the year	333.50
		3,933.50
(ii)	Balance in Profit & Loss Account	3,600.50
		7,534.00

Schedule 3: Deposits

(i)	Demand deposits	500
(ii)	Savings Bank Deposits	1,300
(iii)	Terms Deposits	1,100
		2,900

Schedule 4: Borrowings

I	Borrowings in India :	
	(i) Reserve Bank of India	400
	(ii) Other Banks	1,200
		1,600

Schedule 5: Other Liabilities & Provisions

(i)	Bills payable	100
(ii)	Interest Accrued	300
(iii)	Provision for Income Tax	926
		1,326

Schedule 6: Cash and Balance with RBI

(i)	Cash in hand	800
(ii)	Balance with RBI	400
		1,200

Schedule 7: Balance with Bank and Money at call and short notice

	Balance with other Banks in India	1,600

Schedule 8: Investments

I	Investments in India	
	(i) Government Securities	1,200
	(ii) Other approved securities	400
		1,600

Schedule 9: Advances

(A)	(i) Bills purchased & Discounted	990
	(ii) Cash credits, overdrafts and loans repayable on demand	4,828
	(iii) Terms loans	4,442
		10,260

Schedule 10: Fixed Assets

(i)	Premises	5,500
(ii)	Other Fixed Assets	1,000
		6,500

Schedule 11: Other Assets

(i)	Interest Accrued	200

Schedule 13: Interest Earned

(i)	Interest and Discount	3,200
(ii)	Income on Investments	500
		3,700

Schedule 14: Other Income

(i)	Commission, Exchange & Brokerage	800
(ii)	Profit on sale of Investments	80
(iii)	Miscellaneous Income	320
		1,200

Schedule 15: Interest Expended

(i)	Interest paid on Deposits	480

Schedule 16: Operating Expenses

(i)	Payments to and Provision for employees	300
(ii)	Printing & Stationery	140
(iii)	Postage and Telegrams	80
(iv)	Repairs and Maintenance	100
		620

CALCULATION OF PROVISION AGAINST ADVANCES

	Amount	%	Provision
Standard Assets	8,800	0.25*	22
Sub-standard Assets	1,000	10	100
Doubtful Assets (secured) 50%			
upto one year	240	20	48
One to three years	340	30	102
More than three years	260	50	130
Doubtful Assets (Unsecured) 50%			
Upto one year	240	100	240
One to three year	340	100	340
more than three years	260	100	320
			1,562

* raised to 0.4%

Illustration (11) (Rebate on Bills discounted)

Excel Bank Ltd. has an authorised capital 60,000 shares of Rs. 100 each. It's trial balance as on 31st March 2006 was as follows :

(Rs. '000')

	Dr.	Cr.
Cash in hand	1,200	
Bills payable		300
Reserve Fund		1,500
Interest and Discount		2,400
Investment in Govt. Securities	7,500	
Current Accounts		3,600
Savings Bank Deposits		3,000
Fixed Deposits		7,500
Furniture less Depreciation	195	
Bills discounted	600	
Money at call and short notice	1,800	
Premises less Depreciation	1,500	
Issued & subscribed Capital		3,000
Loans and Overdrafts	6,900	
(Term Loans Rs. 3,000)		
Cash Credits	2,700	
Director's Fees	24	
Sundry Expenses	18	
Non-Banking assets	120	
Depreciation on Bank's property	60	
Postage	30	
Advertisement	15	
Printing and stationery	51	

Salaries	450	
Interest paid on Deposits	900	
Audit Fees	54	
Cash with RBI	345	
Commission	30	540
Unclaimed dividends		30
Rent Received		60
Borrowing from other Banks		2,400
Pension Fund		150
Cash with Other Banks	438	
Profit & Loss Account (1.4.2004)		450
	24,930	24,930

Additional Information: (Rs. '000')

(i)	Interest occurred on investments	69
(ii)	The bills discounted mature at an average date of June 13 (including grace days). All bills were discounted at 10% p.a	
(iii)	Bills for collection amounted to	600
(iv)	Provide for doubtful debts	60
(v)	Acceptances on behalf of customers	120
(vi)	Create a provision for taxation	@ 40%
(vii)	Liability on Bills of Exchange rediscounted	75
(viii)	Directors propose dividend	@ 10%

Prepare Profit and Loss Account for the year ending 31st March 2006 and a Balance Sheet as on that date.

Solution:

EXCEL BANK LTD.
BALANCE SHEET
As on 31st March 2006

Capital & Liabilities	**Schedule**	(Rs. '000')
Capital	1	3,000
Reserves & Surplus	2	2,469
Deposits	3	14,100
Borrowings	4	2,400
Other liabilities & Provisions	5	1,338
		23,307
Assets		
Cash in hand balance with RBI	6	1,545
Balances with Other Banks and Money at call and short notice	7	2,238
Investments	8	7,500

	Schedule	
Advances	9	10,140
Fixed Assets	10	1,695
Other Assets	11	189
		23,307
Contingent liabilities	12	195
Bills for collection		600

PROFIT AND LOSS ACCOUNT
for the year ended 31st March, 2006

		Schedule	(Rs. '000')
I	Income		
	Interest Earned	13	2,457
	Other Income	14	600
			3057
II	Expenditure		
	Interest Expended	15	930
	Operating Expenses	16	702
	Provisions and Contingencies		606
			2,238
III	Profit/Loss		
	Net profit for the year		819
	Profit brought forward		450
			12,69
IV	Appropriations		
	Transfer to Statutory Reserve		204.75
	Proposed dividend		300.00
	Balance Carried over to Balance sheet		764.25
			1,269.00

Schedule 1: Capital

Authorised Capital	
60,000 Shares of Rs. 100 each	6,000
Issued, subscribed & paid up capital	
30,000 shares of Rs. 100 each	3,000

Schedule 2: Reserves & Surplus

(i)	Statutory Reserve (Op. Balance)	Nil
	Addition during the year	204.75
(ii)	Revenue Reserve	
	Reserve Fund	1,500.00
(iii)	Balance in the Profit & Loss A/c	764.25
		2,469.00

Schedule 3: Deposits

(i)	Demand Deposits	3,600
(ii)	Savings Bank Deposits	3,000

(iii)	Term Deposits	7,500
		14,100

Schedule 4: Borrowings

I	Borrowing in India	
	(i) Reserve Bank of India	Nil
	(ii) Borrowings from other Banks	2,400
		2,400

Schedule 5: Other liabilities & Provisions

(i)	Bills payable	300
(ii)	Rebate on Bills discounted (1)	12
(iii)	Pension Fund	150
(iv)	Others:	
	Provision for taxation (2)	546
	Proposed dividend	300
	Unclaimed dividend	30
		1,338

Schedule 6: Cash in hand and balance with RBI

(i)	Cash in hand	1,200
(ii)	Cash with RBI	345
		1,545

Schedule 7: Balance with Other Banks and Money at call and short notice

(i)	Balances with other Banks	438
(ii)	Money at call and short notice	1,800
		2,238

Schedule 8: Investments

I	Investments in India	
	Investment in Govt. Securities	7,500

Schedule 9: Advances

A	(i) Bills discounted & purchased	600
	(ii) Cash credits, overdrafts and loans repayable on demand	6,600
	(iii) Term loans	2,940*
		10,140

*Less Bad debt provision

Schedule 10: Fixed Assets

(i)	Premises Less Depreciation	1,500
(ii)	Furniture	195
		1,695

Schedule 11: Other Assets

(i)	Interest Accrued	69
(ii)	Non-Banking Assets	120
		189

Schedule 12: Contingent liabilities

(i)	Acceptances on behalf of customers	120
(ii)	Liability on bills rediscounted	75
		195

Schedule 13 : Interest Earned

(i)	Interest and Discount	2,388
(ii)	Interest Accrued on Investment	69
		2,457

Schedule 14: Other Income

(i)	Commission, Exchange & Brokerage	540
(ii)	Rent Received	60
		600

Schedule 15: Interest Expended

(i)	Interest paid on Deposits	900
(ii)	Commission	30
		930

Schedule 16: Operating Expenses

(i)	Payments and provision for employees	450
(ii)	Printing and Stationery	51
(iii)	Advertisement & Publicity	15
(iv)	Depreciation on Bank's property	60
(v)	Director's fees allowances & expenses	24
(vi)	Auditors fees and expenses	54
(vii)	Postage, telegrams & telephones	30
(viii)	Other Expenditure	18
		702

Working note:

(1) Calculation of Rebate on bills discounted.

Since the average due date is 13th June including 3 days for the grace period, the rebate has been calculated from the period starting from 1st April to 12th June *i.e.* excluding the due date

April; 30 days + May; 31 days + June: 12 day

Total 73 days $6,00,000 \times \frac{10}{100} \times \frac{73}{365} = \text{Rs.}\, 12,000$

(2) Provision for Taxation has been computed as under:

	Total Income		3,057
Less	Interest Expended	930	
	Operating Expenses	702	
	Provision for Bad debts	60	1,692
			1,365
	Tax @ 40%		546
	Current year's profit		819

REFERENCES

(1) Master Circular issued by RBI (30.6.2002)
(2) Narasimham Committee 1991, and 1998
(3) RBI Guide lines Nov. 2001
(4) Reports on Currency and Finance.
(5) RBI Bulletins.
(6) Annual Reports of RBI
(7) Reports on Trends and Progress of Banking in India.
(8) The Chartered Accountant - April 2005

QUESTIONS

1. Describe the main functions of a commercial bank.
2. Is there any restriction imposed by The Banking Regulation Act 1949 on banks? If yes, what are these restrictions?
3. Explain the legal provisions relating to final accounts of a banking company.
4. Explain the salient features of prudential norms relating to income recognition and provisioning norms.
5. Differentiate and explain the following terms:
   (a) Standard Assets
   (b) Sub-standard Assets
   (c) Doubtful Assets
   (d) Loss Assets
6. What are non-performing assets? What criteria will you adopt to declare an asset as "non-performing one".
7. Once an asset becomes non-performing it remains non-performing asset forever,"
   Comment CS (I) Dec. 2002
8. Write notes on :
   (i) Advance
   (ii) Deposits
   (iii) Money at Call and Short notice.
9. Differentiate and explain the terms with regard to investments.
   (a) Held to Maturity
   (b) Available for Sale
   (c) Held for Trading
10. Write short notes on :
    (i) Acceptances, Endorsements & Other obligations
    (ii) Bills for collection
    (iii) Rebate on Bills discounted
11. Explain the latest RBI guidelines with regard to Statutory Reserve and Liquidity Reserve.
12. How will you judge the Capital adequacy of a commercial bank?

PROBLEMS

(1) From the following information find out the amount of provisions to be shown in the Profit and Loss Account of a Commercial Bank Ltd.

Assets	(Rs. in '000')
Standard	4,00,000
Sub-standard	2,00,000
Doubtful upto one year	90,000
Doubtful upto three years	40,000
Doubtful more than three years	30,000
Loss Assets	50,000

P.E.E. (II) Nov. 2004

Note : Treat doubtful assets as fully secured.

Ans : Rs. 1,16,000 thousand. Calculated @ 0.25% on Standared Assets but now raised to 0.4%

(2) The following particulars are extracted from the (Trial Balance) books of a commercial Bank Ltd. for the year ending 31st March 2006. (Rs. in '000')

(i)	Interest and Discounts	98,312
(ii)	Rebate on Bills Discounted (Balance on 1.4.2005)	325.2
(iii)	Bills Discounted & Purchased	33,727

It is ascertained that proportionate discount not yet earned on the Bills Discounted which will mature during 2006-07 amounted to Rs. 463.8 thousand.

Pass necessary journal entries adjusting the above and show.

(a) Rebate on Bills Discounted Account &

(b) Interest and Discount Account.

[PEE (II) Nov. 2003 Adapted]

Ans: Closing balance (Rs. in '000')

(a) Rebate on Bills Discounted A/c	463.8
(b) Interest and Discount transferred to Profit & Loss Account	98,173.4

(3) From the following information, calculate the amount of Provisions and contingencies and prepare Profit and Loss Account of Zed Bank Ltd. for the year ended 31st March, 2006.

	(Rs. in '000')
Interest and Discount (includes Interest accrued on investments)	8,860
Other income	220
Interest Expended	2,720
Operating Expenses	2,830
Interest accrued on investments	10

Additional Information

(a) Rebate on bills discounted to be provided for 30

(b) Provide 35% of the profits towards taxation.

(c) Transfer 25% of the profits to statutory reserve

(d) Advances have been classified as under :

(i)	Standard Assets	4,000
	Sub Standared Assets	2,240
(ii)	Doubtful Assets (fully Unsecured)	390
(iii)	Doubtful Assets (fully secured)	
	*Less than one year	100
	*More than one year but less than three years	600
	*More than three years	600
(v)	Loss Assets	376

[PEE (II) May 2005]

Ans: Net Profit Rs. 1,300 thousand

(4) R. Bank Ltd. had extended the following credit lines to a small scale Industry which had not paid any interest since March, 2000.

(Rs. in '000')

Term Loan	Export Credits	
Balance Outstanding (31.3.2006)	3,500	3,000
DICGC/ ECGC Cover	40%	50%
Securities held	1,500	1,000
Realisable Value of Securities	1,000	800

Compute necessary provisions to be made for the year ended 31st March, 2006.

[PEE (II) May 2004]

Ans: Total provisions required: (Rs. in '000')

Term Loan - Rs. 1,800 & Export Credit Rs. 1,300

(5) The following balance have been extracted from the Trial Balance of ABC Bank Ltd. as on 31st March, 2006.

	(Rs. in '000')
Rebate on bills discounted (1.4.2005)	640
Discount received	9,200
Bills discounted & purchased	63,094
Bills for collection	2,400

The Bank's rate of discounting has been 18% and rate of commission on Bills for collection 4% whereas the average due date for the Bills discounted and purchased and Bills for collection is calculated as 15th May and 15th April 2006 respectively.

Show the calculation of the amount to be credited to Bank's Profit & Loss Account as Discount earned for the year 2005-06. Pass journal entries.

C.A. (I) O.S. Adapted

Ans: Rs. 84,39,833

(6) From the following calculate Rebate on Bills discounted as on 31st March, 2006.

Date of Bill	Amount of Bill	Period	Rate of discount
15.1.2006	75,000	5 months	8%
10.2.2006	45,000	4 months	7%
25.2.2006	60,000	4 months	7%
20.3.2006	90,000	3 months	9%

[ICWA (F) Adapted]

Ans: Rs. 4,531

(7) **The Books of a Bank include a loan of Rs. 25,00,000 advanced on 31. 12. 05, interest chargeable @ 16% per annum compounded quarterly . The security for the loan being 35,000 shares of Rs. 100 each of a public limited company valued at Rs. 90 each. There is no repayment till 31st March 2006. On 31st March 2006 the value of shares declined to Rs. 80 per share. How would you classify the loan as secured or unsecured in the Balance Sheet?**

[ICWA (F) Adapted]

Ans: Secured Loan - Rs. 28,00,000
Unsecured Loan - Rs. 2,41,630

(8) On 31st March, 2006 the Loan account in the books of a bank showed a debit balance of Rs. 5,00,000 including Rs. 1,00,000 due from a merchant which is doubtful. The interest accrued on this loan upto 31.3.06 was Rs. 25,000 including Rs. 5,000 on doubtful debt. The merchant became insolvent and the official receiver paid a dividend of Re. 0.25 in the rupee on 30th April, 2006.

Pass journal entries in the books of the Bank on 31st March, 2006 and 30th April, 2006. Also prepare Loan Account

[C.S. (I) Adapted]

Ans: Bad debts to w/o Rs. 75,000

(9) From the following information prepare profit and Loss Account of a Commercial Bank Ltd. for the year ended 31st March, 2006.

	(Rs. in '000')
Interest earned	1,295
Discount on bills discounted (net)	975
Interest on cash credit	1,115
Interest on Fixed Deposits	1,375
Rebate on bills discounted required	245
Commission	41
Establishment	270
Interest on Current A/c	210
Rent & Taxes	90
Interest on Overdraft	770
Director's Fees	15
Auditors Fees	6
Interest on Saving Bank Deposits	340

Postage and telephones	7
Printing and Stationery	15
Sundry charges	8

Bad debts to be written off amounted to Rs. 2,00,000. Provision for Taxation may be made at 40%. Balance of Profit and Loss Account from last year was Rs. 6,00,000. The Directors have recommended a dividend of Rs. 1,00,000 for the shareholders.

[ICWA (F) & CA (I) Adapted]

Ans: Profit - Rs. 8,49,000

(10) From the following particulars, prepare Profit and Loss Account of Star Bank Ltd. for the year ended 31st March 2006.

	(Rs. in '000')
Interest on Loans	3,600
Interest on Fixed Deposits	3,300
Commission	120
Exchange and Brokerage	240
Salaries and Allowances	1,800
Discount on bills (Gross)	1,824
Interest on Cash credits	2,880
Interest on overdrafts in Current Accounts	360
Interest on Saving Bank Deposits	1,044
Postage, telegram and stamps	120
Printing & Stationary	240
Sundry Expenses	120
Rent	180
Taxes and licences	120
Audit Fees	120

Additional Information :

(i) Rebate on bills discounted	360
(ii) Salary of Manager	360
(iii) Bad debts	480
(iv) Provision for Taxation 40%	
(v) Interest on doubtful debts wrongly credited to interest on loan account	480

[CA (I) Adapted]

Ans: Net Profit - Rs. 4,32,000

(11) From the following information, prepare Profit and Loss A/c of India Bank Ltd. as on 31st March, 2006.

	(Rs. in '000')
Interest and discount	3,045
Income from Investment	115
Interest on balance with R.B.I.	180
Commission, exchange and brokerage	820

Profit on sale of Investments	110
Interest on deposits	1,225
Interest to R.B.I.	161
Payments to and provision for employees	1,044
Rent, taxes and lighting	210
Printing and stationery	180
Advertisement and publicity	95
Depreciation	92
Directors' fees	220
Auditors' fees	120
Law charges	230
Postage, telegrams and telephone	70
Insurance	56
Repairs and maintenance	48

Other Information:

(i) Interest and discount mentioned above is after adjustment for the following.

Tax provision for the year	220
Provision during the year for doubtful debts	102
Loss on sale of investments	12
Rebate on bills discounted	58

(ii) 25% of profit is transferred to statutory reserve.

5% of profit is transferred to revenue reserve.

Profit brought forward from the previous year	16

(CA Inter, Nov. 1992)

Ans: Net Profit for the year Rs. 5,19,000

(12) From the following information relating to Zed Bank Ltd. prepare Profit & Loss Account for the year ended 31st March, 2006 along with the necessary schedules :

Items	Amount for the year ended 31.3.1996 Rs. '000'
Interest/discount on advances/bills	31,628
Income on investments	11,810
Interest on balances with Reserve Bank of India	4,243
Commission, exchange and brokerage	2,907
Profit on sale of investments	114
Interest on deposits	31,404
Interest on Reserve Bank of India borrowings	3,362
Payments to and provisions for employees	9,717
Rent, taxes and lighting	955

Printing and stationery	213
Advertisement and publicity	87
Depreciation on bank's property	292
Director's fees, allowances and expenses	7
Auditor's fees and expenses	41
Law charges	22
Postage, telegrams, telephones, etc.	312
Repairs and maintenance	91
Insurance	915
Other expenditure	884
Balance of Profit and loss A/c b/f	1,524

The following adjustments are to be made:

(i) Make provision for income-tax (including surcharge) @ 51.75%.

(ii) Every year, the bank transfers 25% of profit to statutory reserves and 5% of profit to revenue reserve.

(iii) Dividend amount to Rs. 2,00,000 for the year ended 31st March, 2004 is proposed by the Board

(CS Inter June, 1995)

Ans: Net Profit for/the year Rs. 11,58,000

(13) The following figures are extracted from the books of Exe Bank Ltd. as on 31st March, 2006.

(Rs. in '000')

Interest and discount received	4,060
Interest paid on deposits	2,404
Issued and subscribed capital	1,000
Reserve under section 17	700
Commission, exchange and brokerage	180
Rent received	60
Profit and sale of investments	190
Salaries and allowances	210
Directors fees and allowances	24
Rent and taxes paid	108
Stationery and printing	48
Postage and telegraph	40
Preliminary expenses	10
Audit fees	8
Depreciation on banks properties	25

The following further information is given :

(a) A customer to whom a sum of Rs. 5,00,000 has been advanced has become insolvent and it is expected only 40% can be recovered from his estate. Interest due at 15 per cent on his debt has not been provided in the books.

(b) Provision for bad and doubtful debts on other debts necessary Rs. 1,00,000.

(c) Rebate on Bills Discounted as on 31st March, 2005 Rs. 10,000. Rebate on Bills Discounted as on 31st March, 2006 Rs. 15,000.

(d) Provide Rs. 3,00,000 for income tax.

(e) The Director desire to declare 10% dividend.

Prepare the Profit & Loss A/c in accordance with law. Make necessary assumptions.

(CA Inter New Scheme, November, 1976)

[Ans. : Net Profit Rs. 8,08,000]

(14) From the following trial balance as on 31st March, 2006 prepare final accounts of Cyma Bank Limited.

Rs. in '000

Particulars	Dr.	Cr.
Interest on advances		800
Interest from investments		125
Commission, exchange and brokerage		200
Profit on sale of investments		20
Other revenue receipts		80
Share Capital		2,000
Statutory reserves		900
Profit & Loss A/c		650
Fixed deposits		275
Savings deposits		325
Current account		125
Borrowing from other banks		300
Borrowing from RBI		100
Bills payable (Net)		25
Interest accrued		75
Cash balance	200	
Balance with other banks	400	
Cash with RBI	100	
Investments In Govt. securities	300	
Other approved securities	100	
Bills purchased and discounted	250	
Cash credits, overdrafts and demand loans	1,425	
Term loans	1,275	
Premises (net)	1,375	
Furniture	250	
Interest paid	120	

Salary	75	
Printing and stationery	35	
Postage and telegram	20	
Repairs	25	
Interest accrued	50	
	6,000	6,000
Bills for collection	235	

Additional Information :

Advances made have been classified as under :

Particulars	Cash Credits Overdrafts, etc.	Term Loans	Bills Purchased
Standard assets	1,000	975	225
Sub-standard assets	125	100	25
Doubtful upto one year	100	20	—
One to three years	120	—	50
More than three years	50	80	—
Loss assets	30	50	—
	1,425	1,275	250

No provision has been made so far against these assets. Doubtful assets are secured to the extent of 50% of the dues.

(CA Inter, May 1994)

[Ans : Net Profit for the year Rs. 5,65,000 Total of Balance Sheet Rs. 57,25,000]

(15) The following particulars are available from the books of the P Bank Ltd. as on 31st March, 2006. You are required to prepare Balance Sheet as on 31st March 2006

	(Rs. in '000')
Cash with Reserve Bank of India	500
Cash in hand	370
Current and contingency A/c (after setting off overdrawn balance of a customer of Rs. 1,00,000)	2,500
Saving bank A/c	4,000
Fixed deposit A/c	1,500
Bills discounted and purchased	2,000
Loans, cash credits, etc. (Dr.)	9,000
Acceptance, endorsement and other obligations	300
Rebate on bills discounted	150
Bills payable	250
Investments	1,600
Reserve fund	1,200

Non-banking assets	100
Gold	200
Furniture	125
Premises	375
Profit and Loss A/c (Cr.)	140
Interest accrued on investments	40
Bills for collection outstanding on 31st March, 1997	225
Outstanding liabilities	60
Contingent liability for public issue of shares underwritten on behalf of a client	400
Margin money held against letter of credit issued	70
Borrowing from other banks	200
Compulsory deposit received under (ITP) schemes	100

The difference in Balance Sheet represents issued and fully-paid up Equity Share Capital of Rs. 10 each, being 50% of the amount of authorised capital.

Classification of Total Advances is as Follows:

(a) Secured by tangible assets	60% of advances
(b) Covered by bank or Govt. guarantees	20% of advances
(c) Unsecured	15% of advances
(d) Bad or doubtful to be provided for	5% of advances

Advances in India :

Priority Sector	40%
Public sector	20%
Banks	10%
Others	30%

The advances considered to be doubtful are out of unsecured advances in the form of Cash Credits granted to Priority Sectors.

C.A. (F) Adapted OS

Ans. : B/s Total : Rs. 1,38,55,000

(16) Following are the balances from the books of National Bank Ltd. as on 31st March, 2006

	Rs.
Current deposits	2,27,50,000
Savings A/c	82,60,000
Fixed and time deposits	1,75,90,000
Compulsory deposits of Income tax payers	10,00,000
Sundry creditors	2,27,500
Debts due to banks (secured)	61,00,000
Bills receivables	90,50,000
Rebate on bills discounted	7,500
Branch adjustments (credit)	22,77,500
Reserve fund	62,50,000

Capital (authorised, issued, subscribed and paid up)	
1,00,000 shares of Rs. 50 each	50,00,000
Interest and discount received	29,00,000
Exchange and commission received	8,77,500
Profit & Loss A/c balance as on 1.4.96	4,26,000
Cash in Hand	6,53,500
Cash at Bank	30,00,000
Bills for collection	90,50,000
Liabilities for customer's acceptances	75,84,000
Investments	
Governments securities	1,70,00,000
Shares	79,50,000
Interest accrued on investments	4,37,500
Loans	2,08,50,000
Bills purchased and Discounted	1,77,50,000
Furniture & Fixtures	2,50,000
Depreciation on assets	2,50,000
Interest paid	6,00,000
Exchange and Commission paid	50,000
Salaries	12,00,000
Director's Fees	50,000
Stationery and Postage	2,00,000
Miscellaneous Expenses	1,50,000
Land and Building	15,00,000
Money at Call and at short notice	7,50,000
Non-Banking Assets	25,000

You are required to prepare Profit and Loss Account for the year ending 31st March, 2006 and a Balance Sheet as on that date after taking into account the following :

Provision for Taxation 40%

Current Accounts includes Rs. 42,50,000 debit balances being overdraft. One of the accounts of Rs. 50,000 (including interest Rs. 5,000) is doubtful. During the year a property was acquired in the satisfaction of a claim amounting to Rs. 25,000 and was sold for Rs. 18,000. The loss resulting there from remained unadjusted in the books.

[C.A. (I) Nov. 1980]

Ans: Net Profit: Rs. 7,32,300; Balance Sheet Total- Rs. 9,19,98,000.

10

Statement of Changes in Financial Position (SCFP) Working Capital Basis and Cash Basis

Financial Statements (Profit and Loss Account and Balance Sheet) are the only statements to judge the results of business operation and financial position of an enterprise. The Profit and Loss Account (Income Statement) shows the revenues, expenses, gains, losses and discloses the resources generated and used in business operations. The Balance Sheet discloses the over all financial position of an enterprise on a specific date when books of accounts are closed. These statements have a limited role to perform. The Profit and Loss Account does not show the effects of each transaction and event which affect the liquidity of an enterprise there by having a bearing on ability to meet future obligations and commitments. Infact these statements leave many a questions unanswered such as :

(i) The magnitude of funds generated from operations.

(ii) Whether or not the liquidity position is improved?

(iii) What is the extent of inflow and outflow of resources?

(iv) What is the direction of movement of funds?

(v) What are the key factors responsible for changes in assets, liabilities and capital?

(vi) How the fixed assets have been financed?

(vii) Whether the working capital is adequate?

(viii) What is the extent of flow of funds from investing and financing activities.

(ix) What is the prudence of dividend policy in retaining or releasing resources for dividend purpose?

(x) Can the enterprise pay long-term debts as per schedule.

To answer these pertinent questions statement called "Statement of Changes in Financial Position" (Fund Flow Statement/Cash Flow Statement) is prepared which also meets the requirements of AS-3 (Revised)

Concept of Statement of Changes in Financial Position (SCFP)

Statement of Changes in Financial Position helps to understand how and why a change in financial position of an enterprise is brought about and discloses the extent and source of inflow and out flow both during an accounting period. In other words it measures the changes that have taken place in the financial position of an enterprise. The changes in financial position are attributed to 'sources of funds' and 'application or uses of funds', which tells the efficiency and effectiveness of the finance management because SCFP shows the financial health of the enterprise in an unambiguous term. The basic and relevant quarry as to "where the money (funds) come from and where it is gone" can be answered after analysing the Statement of Changes in Financial Position (SCFP). It helps to judge management's effectiveness in utilising the resources of an enterprise. According to Accounting Principles Board, USA," Information concerning the financing and investing activities of a business enterprise and the changes in the financial position for a period is essential for financial statement users, particularly owners and creditors, in making economic decisions. When financial statements purporting to present both financial positions (Balance Sheet) and results of operations (Statement of Income and retained earnings) are issued, a statement summarising changes in financial position should also be presented as a basic financial statement for which an income statement is presented".

Accounting Standard 3 (Revised) issued by Institute of Chartered Accounts of India has made it mandatory for listed companies and other enterprises whose turnover exceeds Rs. 50 crore to prepare and present the Statement of Changes in Financial Position along with the Financial Statement Realising the importance of such a statement, a number of companies in India have started providing an analysis of their funds and cash flow position in their annual reports. Companies who are required to comply with Accounting Standard (Revised), the presentation of cash flow statement has become a part of the financial statements. The Statement of changes in Financial Position presents condensed and summarised information (prepared from data collected from Income Statement and Balance Sheet) which is not readily available in these statements. In fact the statement of changes in Financial Position is a refined form or an extension of the funds flow or cash flow statement. It is more informative and comprehensive in indicating the financial position of an enterprise.

Approaches

In order to get better insight and get a comprehensive information the Statement of Changes in Financial Position can be prepared on the following basis.

1. Working Capital basis (Funds Flow Statement)
2. Cash basis (Cash Flow Statement)

1. SCFP – WORKING CAPITAL BASIS
(Funds Flow Statement)

The Statement of Changes in Financial Position prepared to determine the sources and uses of working capital during an accounting period is known as Funds Flow Statement.

The term 'Funds', in common or 'general use' refers to cash. However, in a broader sense, it means working capital which represents excess of current assets over current liabilities. In other words the terms "Funds" stands for net working capital or net current assets. And, net current asset or net working capital is that portion of current assets which is financed by long term liabilities/funds.

The statement of changes in working capital reveals to management the way in which the working capital is generated and used. During each accounting period, the current assets are continuously converted into Cash a portion of which is used to pay current liabilities or finance a fixed assets. Likewise a loan may be raised to finance current assets. Normally, a company may have transactions which may affect the working capital while some transactions may not affect working capital at all. Transactions which affect (increase or decrease) working capital are those transactions which affect simultaneously both current and non-current items such as :

- Issue of shares for cash
- Purchase of fixed assets for cash

- Redemption of shares and debentures
- Sale of fixed assets
- Raising of loan from a bank
- Repayment of a loan.

In the above examples cash or bank account involved is a current asset item while issue or redemption of shares, purchase or sale of a fixed asset or raising or repayment of loan involved are non-current (items). To be more specific, if a company acquires a computer for cash; the cash account which is a current (asset) account and the computer, which is a non-current (asset) account are affected. Thus company acquires a fixed asset by paying cash. This transaction decreases the working capital. Likewise sale of any fixed asset will increase the working capital (Net Current assets).

Hence it can be concluded that **working capital is affected when current and non-current items are affected simultaneously.**

On the other hand there are some transactions which do not affect working capital, such as :

- Cash received from debtors
- Purchase of goods (stock) for cash
- Purchase of goods (stock) on credit
- Payment to creditors

In the above examples both the accounts involved in any transaction are current hence there will be no change in the working capital.

- Cash A/c and Debtors A/c both current,
- Cash A/c and Stock A/c both current,
- Stock A/c and Creditors A/c both current,
- Cash A/c and Creditors A/c both current,

As we know —

Working Capital = Current Assets – Current Liabilities
(WC = CA – CL)

Thus, if both items are of current nature there may be change in the composition of current assets or current liabilities but not a change in working capital. For example receipt from debtors increases cash but will decrease debtors hence total current assets remaining unchanged leading to no change in working capital.

Similarly, working capital will also not be affected if both the accounts involved are non-current, such as—

- Purchase of a fixed asset against issue of shares or debentures.
- Transfer to General Reserve or any other fund.
- Writing off intangible assets
- Conversion of debentures in to shares.
- Transfer to Provision for Taxation.

In the above example both the accounts involved are non-current in nature and do not affect current assets or current liabilities. Therefore, there will be no change in the amount of working capital.

Thus, it may be concluded that a transaction will affect the working capital only when one of the accounts affected is a current account (current asset or current liability) and other account is of non-current nature (long term asset (Fixed Asset) or Long term liability). In case both the accounts are of current nature or non-current nature, the working capital (Funds) will remain unaffected.

SOURCES OF WORKING CAPITAL (FUNDS)

(1) Funds from Operations

It is the major source of working capital in the form of net-profit. However, the net profit as disclosed by the Income Statement does not reveal the actual inflow of working capital (funds). The Profit and Loss Account contains number of items which do not result either in inflow or outflow of funds. These include non-cash charges, write-offs, adjustments, amortisation and transfers in respect of which no payment has been made to outside agencies. Therefore, necessary adjustments have to be made to the net-profit as disclosed by Profit and Loss Account to arrive at actual figure of "Funds from operation". Therefore if these items of **non-cash charges** (such as depreciation) **write-offs** (such as discount on issue of shares and debentures, Preliminary Expenses) **Adjustments** (such as Loss on Sale of fixed assets) **Amortisation** (such as goodwill, patents, copyrights or trade marks written off) **Appropriations and Transfers** (to general reserve or other funds) are added back to net profit and non-operating incomes (such as dividend, Rent and interest etc.) if credited to Profit and Loss Account are deducted, then the actual "funds from operations can be ascertained.

In other words—

(i) All such expenses which have been charged to Profit and Loss Account but do not result in out flow (do not reduce working capital) should be added back and

(ii) All such items which have been credited to Profit and Loss Account but do not result in inflow (do not increase working capital) should be deducted and

(iii) All items of revenue which are non-operating in nature (non-operating incomes) should also be adjusted (deducted) and shown separately in the Statement of Changes in Financial Position (SCFP).

The following methods may be used to as certain funds from operation :

(a) *When profit figures relating to only current year's are given* :

	Net Profit as per Profit and Loss A/c	***
Add	Depreciation written off	**
	Preliminary Expenses w/o	**
	Discount on Issue of shares and debentures w/o	**
	Goodwill, Patents, Copyright, w/o	
	Loss on sale of fixed assets w/o	
	Proposed dividend/Provision for Taxation	
Less	Gain on sale of fixed assets	**
	Provision written back	
	Non-business (Non-operating) incomes (such as dividend, rent and interest etc.)	**
	FUNDS FROM OPERATIONS	***

(b) *When figures of profits for two years are given.*

PROFIT AND LOSS A/C (ADJUSTED)

	Rs.		Rs.
To Depreciation w/o	* *	By Balance b/d	* *
To Preliminary Expenses w/o	* *	By Gain on sale of any fixed asset	* *
To Discount on Issue of Shares and debentures w/o	* *	By Dividend	* *
		By Interest	* *
To Goodwill w/o	* *	By Rent etc.	* *
To Copyrights, Trademarks W/o	* *	By Excess Provisions written back	* *
To Loss on sale of Machinery	* *	By Funds from Operations (Balancing figure)	* *
To Provision for Taxation	* *		
To Proposed Divided	* *		
To Interim Dividend	* *		
To Transfer to Reserves etc.	* *		
To Premium on Redemption of Preference Shares/Debentures	* *		
To Balance c/d	* *		
	* * *		* * *

Illustration (1) (Calculation of Funds from operation from current years figures)

From the following Profit and Loss A/c of A Ltd. for the year ending 31st March, 2005 Calculate Funds From Operations.

		Rs.		Rs.
To Opening stock		2,80,000	By Sales	25,00,000
To Purchases		8,20,000	By Closing Stock	3,50,000
To Wages	2,00,000			
Add O/s	50,000	2,50,000		
To Gross Profit c/d		15,00,000		
		28,50,000		28,50,000
To Salaries		2,75,000	By Gross Profit b/d	15,00,000
To Rent	90,000		By Gain on sale of Land	50,000
Less Prepaid	15,000	75,000		
To Discount on issue of debentures w/o		25,000		
To Depreciation		1,25,000		
To Preliminary Exp. w/o		15,000		
To Goodwill w/o		35,000		
To Patents w/o		23,000		
To Loss on sale of Plant		17,000		
To Net Profit		9,60,000		
		15,50,000		15,50,000

Solution :

Calculation of "Funds from Operation"

		Rs.	Rs.
	Net Profit as per Profit and Loss A/c		9,60,000
Add	**Items not resulting in outflow :**		
—	Depreciation	1,25,000	
—	Discount on Issue of Debentures w/o	25,000	
—	Preliminary Expenses w/o	15,000	
—	Goodwill w/o	35,000	
—	Patents w/o	23,000	
—	Loss on Sale of Plant	17,000	2,40,000
			12,00,000
Less	**Items not resulting in inflow :**		
	Gain or sale of Land		50,000
	Funds From Operations		11,50,000

** **Alternatively**, 'FFO' can also be calculated as under : ***(Direct Method)***

			Rs.	Rs.
	Sales			25,00,000
Less	Cost of Goods Sold:			
	Op. Stock	2,80,000		
Add	Purchases	8,20,000		
		11,00,000		
Less	Cl. Stock	3,50,000	7,50,000	
	Wages		2,50,000	
	Salaries		2,75,000	
	Rent		75,000	13,50,000
	Funds From Operations			11,50,000

Working notes :

(1) Outstanding and prepaid are to be adjusted as usual but will not have any impact on flow of funds otherwise.

(2) Opening stock and closing stock are to be adjusted with purchases to ascertain actual flow of funds.

(3) Items which do not involve any inflow or out flow are ignored under 'Direct Method'.

Illustration (2) (Funds From operations)

X Ltd. earned a net profit of Rs. 75,500 after making following adjustments.

	Rs.
Salaries	1,20,000
Rent	60,000
General Expenses	15,000
Provision for Bad debt.	5,000
Depreciation on fixed assets	2,10,000

Profit on Sale of Building	75,000
Loss on Sale of Investments	25,000
Discount on Issue of Shares w/o	10,000
Preliminary Expenses w/o	18,000
Goodwill w/o	32,000
Transfer to General Reserve	50,000
Transfer to Sinking Fund	45,000
Proposed Dividend	1,25,000
Rent Received	25,000
Dividend from UTI	50,000

Calculate Funds from Operations.

Solution :

		Rs.	Rs.
	Net Profit as per Profit and Loss		7,75,500
Add :	Non-Cash Charges/write-offs and Appropriations:		
	Depreciation	2,10,000	
	Discount on Debentures w/o	10,000	
	Preliminary Expenses w/o	18,000	
	Goodwill w/o	32,000	
	Loss on sale of Investments	25,000	
	General Reserve	50,000	
	Sinking Fund	45,000	
	Proposed Dividend	1,25,000	5,15,000
			12,90,500
Less :	Non-operating items		
	Profit on Sale of Building	75,000	
	Dividend from UTI	50,000	
	Rent Received	25,000	1,50,000
	Funds From Operations		11,40,500

(2) Sale of non-current (Fixed) Assets.

Sale or disposal of fixed assets for cash results in generation of funds, because sale proceeds of such assets increases the current assets (cash, bank or cash equivalents) without any corresponding increase in current liability. Hence such transactions are a source of working capital. It should be noted that profit or loss on sale of fixed assets is immaterial, the working capital is bound to increase by the amount of "sale proceeds".

(3) Long Terms loans or borrowings.

Long term borrowings such as issue of debentures, loans from banks or financial institutions or public deposits result in increase in current assets and thereby increasing working capital (funds). However, short-term loans or borrowings do not provide any additional working capital as they result in corresponding increase in current liability.

(4) Issue of Shares

Issue of equity or preference shares for cash or in exchange for current assets or in discharge of a current liability increases the flow of funds which increases the working capital. However, issue of shares in exchange for **fixed assets** will not affect working capital at all. Such transaction does not result in inflow of funds either by increasing current assets or by reducing current liabilities.

The initial or additional capital introduced by a proprietor or a partner in the form of current assets represent source of funds.

(5) Non-operating Incomes

Rent, interest or dividend received on investments constitute a source of funds. However, these are shown separately in the Statement of Changes in the Financial Position. (SCFP)

USES OR APPLICATION OF WORKING CAPITAL

(1) Release from Operations

The loss from operations after due adjustments of non-cash charges and write offs, if any, involves application of working capital. In other words if a loss disclosed by a firm cannot be set-off against non-cash charges (such as depreciation) the balance of loss will result in loss of funds or working capital in operations.

(2) Purchase or Acquisition of fixed (non-current) Assets for Cash

Purchase of tangible fixed assets like land, building, plant, machinery and equipments, purchase of intangible assets such as goodwill, patents and copyrights, and purchase of long-term investments like shares, debentures, bonds etc. for cash or on short term credit reduces the working capital and hence such transactions result in usage of working capital.

(3) Repayment of long term debts/borrowings

Any repayment of non-current liabilities (debentures/bonds/Loans) results in reduction of current assets and there by reduces the working capital to the extent of such repayment. Hence it is treated as application of funds.

(4) Redemption or buy back of Shares

Redemption (repayment of share capital) and buy back of shares whether equity or preference, also result in outflow or usage of funds hence these transactions reduce working capital and result in application of funds.

(5) Payment of dividend*

Any payment of cash dividend to equity or preference shareholders reduces the working capital. It is an application of funds. Proposed dividend as already stated, is treated under "source from operation" and added back to current year's profits.

(6) Payment of Tax*

Payment of tax is an application of funds because it results in reduction of working capital.

> ***Note :** Students are advised to treat Proposed dividend and "Provision for taxation" as non-current items. Any transfer to proposed dividend/Provision for taxation should be treated under funds from operation" and added back to current year's profits whereas cash payment of dividend whether interim or final and Tax payment should be treated as application of funds separately in the Funds Flow Statement. (AS-3)

USES OF FUNDS FLOW STATEMENT

(1) A tool of management for financial planning

Funds flow statement is an useful tool in the hands of management. It provides necessary inputs for taking financial, operating and investment decisions. Since it shows the flow of funds management can choose the appropriate time to make best use of the available funds. It can plan payment of cash dividend, payment to creditors, purchase or acquisition of fixed assets for expansion, temporary investment of idle funds, if any, raising of loan, redemption of debentures/preference shares etc. This way management makes optimum use of every available funds with the help of Funds Flow Statement.

(2) Basis of Budgeting

Since Funds Flow Statement provides the details of internally generated funds, the company can prepare an estimate for the available funds for the next year. Since funds are the basis of carrying on every business operation, the management can workout how much funds the company requires, how much can be generated internally and how much funds from outside sources are required. This way Funds Flow Statement helps management in preparing the Cash Budget and Capital Budget of the enterprise.

(3) Basis of decision-making for the users

Funds Flow Statement also provides necessary information required by users of accounting information. For example, Banks and financial institutions want to satisfy themselves about the ability of an enterprise to repay the loan. Similarly suppliers and creditors can form their credit policy after ascertaining company's short term solvency and liquidity position on the basis of Funds Flow Statement. Hence users can ascertain as to whether or not the enterprise will be able to meet financial commitments or obligation in time. This way Bankers, creditors and financial institutions can assess the degree of risks involved in granting the loan/credit to the company.

(4) Funds Flow Statement also serves as a control device while comparing the actuals with budgeted figures. In the event of major deviations, the financial manager can take remedial measures. Thus Funds Flow Statement points out sound or weak financial policies of the company. The management can rearrange the firms' financing on the basis of requirements to ensure effective utilisation of company's resources.

(5) Funds Flow Statement points out the causes of changes in working capital and also discloses whether the sources of funds are increasing, decreasing or constant. The National Association of Accountants states the following uses of funds flow statement.

(i) FFS helps in estimating the amount of funds needed for growth, expansion or diversification.

(ii) It plans the investment of idle funds for a very short period during which funds are required by the enterprise.

(iii) It helps in securing the additional working capital as and when required.

(iv) It avoids the liquidity crunch by easing the effect of an insufficient cash balance.

(v) An effective utilisation of funds improves the rate of income on assets.

(vi) FFS helps in planning the timely payment of dividends and interest.

(vii) It helps in securing economies in the centralised management of cash.

LIMITATIONS OF FUND FLOW STATEMENT (FFS)

(i) Historical in nature

Funds Flow Statement is like any other financial statement which is purely historical in nature and hence it serves no purpose unless another projected FFS is prepared for future.

(ii) FFS ignores non-fund transactions

FFS does not take into consideration those transactions which do not affect working capital. Issue of shares or debentures for a consideration other than cash (and current assets), conversion of debentures in to shares and vice versa etc. are some of the transactions which are ignored altogether. Hence, FFS fails to give a complete and clear picture of company's operating, investing and financing activities. Thus it fails to disclose structural changes in the financial relationship.

(iii) Based on secondary data

FFS is prepared from the data contained in the Income Statement and Balance Sheet. If the figures given in these statements are not authentic or those are tampered or adjusted to suit managerial motives, the FFS become useless statement and will not help users in arriving at appropriate decisions. Further, FFS does not include any new or additional item to enhance it's usefulness. It lacks originality.

(iv) Fails to disclose vital changes

FFS statement does not disclose or reveal continuous changes in the policy regarding investment in current assets and short term financing. It is treated as a static statement. Even the changes in the cash position are not analysed. Hence, it is not considered an ideal tool for financial analysis.

(v) Not a precise tool of fund measurement

The measurement of working capital flow is less precise than for cash because working capital includes inventory and prepaid items which creates a problem of proper valuation of funds. Further postponement of purchase of goods/inventory on open account does not influence working capital flow. Similarly, addition to inventories financed by short term loans would not be shown because two items are offset in the computation of net working capital.

Despite the limitations, FFS provides a meaningful link between the Balance Sheets (opening and closing) and Profit and Loss Account for the period and presents information which may not be readily available in either of the two (Balance Sheet and Profit and Loss A/c) statements.

Preparation of SCFP on working Capital basis

Funds Flow analysis requires preparation of two statements

(a) Statement of Changes in Working Capital

(b) Statement of Changes in Financial Position (FFS)

(a) Statement of changes in Working Capital

The Statement of Changes in working capital shows the change in the amount of working capital over an accounting period. Working Capital represents the excess of current assets over current liabilities. Since all current assets and current liabilities are the essential components of working capital, it is necessary to measure the increase or decrease there in. For this purpose a Statement or Schedule of changes in Working Capital is prepared. This Statement or Schedule of changes in Working Capital provides information concerning the changes in each individual items of current assets and current liabilities and their effect on working capital. To ascertain the net effect on working capital total increase is compared with total decrease. The resultant is either the net increase or net decrease in working capital. Changes (+/–) are ascertained by comparing current years figures with last years.

Points to remember : Working Capital = Current Assets – Current Liabilities

While comparing items of Current assets/liabilities :

(i) An **increase** in Current Assets means **increase** in Working Capital.

(ii) A **decrease** in Current Assets means **decrease** in Working Capital.

(iii) An **increase** in Current liabilities means **decrease** in Working Capital.

(iv) A **decrease** in Current liabilities means **increase** in Working Capital.

Thus Current Assets have direct positive relationship with Working Capital while Current liabilities have inverse relationship with **WC**

SCHEDULE OF CHANGES IN WORKING CAPITAL (A FORMAT)

	Figures of Previous Year Rs.	Figures of Current Year Rs.	Changes in Working Capital	
			(Dr.) Increase Rs.	(Cr.) Decrease Rs.
(A) Current Assets:				
Cash balance				
Bank balance				
Marketable Securities				
Bills Receivable				
Debtors				
Stock				
Prepaid Expenses				
(B) Current Liabilities:				
Creditors				
Bills Payable				
Bank Overdraft				
Outstanding Expenses				
Income received in Advance				
Provision for bad & doubtful debts*				
(C) Working Capital (A – B)				
(D) Increase or Decrease in Working Capital				

* If all debtors are good, the provision is treated as a non-current item and any transfer, if made out of current year's profit, is added to Net profit to calculate "Funds from operation".

Point to remember : Schedule of changes in Working Capital is prepared with the items of current assets and current liabilities appearing in the Balance Sheets only. Additional information has nothing to do with the amount of changes in Working Capital.

Steps for the preparation of schedule of changes in Working Capital

(1) Compare the amount of each current asset of current year with it's amount of previous year if it has increased, put the excess in the "(Dr.) Increase" column and if it has decreased put the shortfall in the "(Cr.) Decrease" Column.

(2) Compare the amount of each current liability of the current year with it's corresponding amount of item of previous year, put the excess to the (credit) decrease column and in case there is a short fall (decrease) put the same to the (Dr.) Increase column.

(3) Make sure that all items of current assets and current liabilities appearing in the two Balance Sheets are considered and difference is properly recorded.

(4) Findout the total (Dr.) Increase column and (Cr.) Decrease column.

(5) If the total of (Dr.) Increase column is more, it means there has been an increase in Working Capital and if (Cr.) Decrease column exceeds, such excess represents decrease in Working Capital.

Net "Increase" in Working Capital shows **application of funds** and "net decrease" refers to **source of funds**. This difference (Increase/Decrease) should be equal to the amount disclosed by Funds Flow Statement.

Preparation of Statement of Changes in Financial Position (SCFP) (Funds Flow Statement)

Once the "Funds From Operation" is ascertained and "Schedule of Changes in Working Capital" is prepared, then finally the Statement of Changes in Financial Position is prepared which shows overall position of movement (Total inflow and outflow) of funds, the amount of funds generated from various sources and their usages. This statement takes into consideration those items of non-current assets and non-current liabilities which have not been accounted for or analysed so far. Besides, all additional information or adjustments given, have to be analysed and their impact is ascertained on inflow or outflow of funds during the accounting period.

There are two ways of preparation of Funds Flow Statements :

(a) Statement Form

(b) 'T' form or Account form.

(A) SCFP—WORKING CAPITAL BASIS (A FORMAT/STATEMENT FORM)

	Rs.
A : *Sources of Working Capital*	
(i) Working Capital from operation*	--- -
(ii) Issue of shares for cash	-----
(iii) Issue of Debentures for cash	-----
(iv) Raising of Loan (Long term) borrowings	-----
(v) Sale of fixed Assets	-----
(vi) Sale of long term Investments	-----
(vii) Financing and Investing Activities not affecting Working Capital	-----
B : *Uses of Working Capital*	Rs.
(i) Release of Working Capital from operation*	-----
(ii) Redemption of Preference shares/Debentures	------
(iii) Buy back of shares	------

(iv)	Repayment of long term loans.	-----
(v)	Acquisition of Fixed Assets	-----
(vi)	Purchase of long term Investments	-----
(vii)	Payment of dividends (Interim/Final)	-----
(viii)	Payment of Tax	-----
(ix)	Financing and Investing activities not affecting working capital as per contra	-----
	Increase or Decrease in Working Capital	-------

(B) ACCOUNT FORM/ 'T' FORM

Statement of changes in Financial Position (Working Capital Basis) for the year ending on 31st

Sources	Rs.	Uses	Rs.
To Funds From Operations*		By Release of Working Capital from operations	
To Issue of shares for cash		By Redemption of Preference Shares/ Debentures	
To Issue of Debentures for cash		By Buy back of Shares	
To Long term borrowings		By Repayment of loans	
To Sale of Fixed Assets		By Acquisition of Fixed Assets	
To Sale of long term Investments		By Purchase of long term Investments	
To Other receipts (Non-business)		By Payment of dividend	
To Financing and Investing Activities not affecting Working Capital as per contra		By Payment of Tax	
To Decrease in Working Capital		By Financing and Investing activities not affecting Working Capital as per contra	
		By Increase in Working Capital	
	---		---

HIDDEN TRANSACTIONS

Quite often the information required for the preparation of Funds Flow Statement is not given in the problem, and it becomes quite difficult to ascertain the nature of transactions that took place during the accounting period. Balance Sheet items and additional information do give some indications but do not spell out exact nature of transactions which may help to ascertain it's impact on inflow or outflow of funds. In such circumstances, it is advisable to prepare all such relevant accounts to findout exact in-flow (source) and out-flow (application) of funds. The following steps may be taken.

1. Open all relevant non-current accounts (assets/liabilities) with their opening and closing balance as shown in the Balance Sheets.
2. Account for the adjustments given one by one.
3. Findout the "balancing figure" which indicates the missing (hidden) source or application of funds. Each such account may be closed by transferring the balancing figure either to Profit & Loss (Adjusted) Account or to Cash or Bank Account.

Following examples will make it more clear and understandable :

Example (1)

Figure extracted from the Balance Sheets of X Ltd. as on :

	31.3.2002	31.3.2003
	Rs.	Rs.
Plant and Machinery	6,50,000	7,80,000

A depreciation of Rs. 65,000 was charged during the year on Plant and Machinery.

Working : Apparently it appears that there has been an application of funds to the extent of Rs. 1,30,000 (Rs. 7,80,000 – 6,50,000) but the analysis of information speaks other wise.

PLANT AND MACHINERY A/C

	Rs.		Rs.
To Balance b/d	6,50,000	By Depreciation	65,000
To Bank* -Purchased (Balancing figure)	1,95,000	By Balance c/d	7,80,000
	8,45,000		8,45,000

* Balancing figure indicates usage of working capital (funds) to the extent of Rs. 1,95,000.

Example (2)

Extract of Balance Sheets of Y Ltd. as on 31st March, ...

Liabilities	2003 Rs.	2004 Rs.	Assets	2003 Rs.	2004 Rs.
Provision for Depreciation	1,50,000	1,75,000	Plant and Machinery	4,50,000	6,00,000

During the year a part of plant costing Rs. 50,000 (Accumulated depreciation thereon being Rs. 35,000) was sold for Rs. 12,000.

Working :

PROVISION FOR DEPRECIATION A/C

	Rs.		Rs.
To Plant & Machinery Disposal A/c	35,000	By Balance b/d	1,50,000
To Balance c/d	1,75,000	By Profit and Loss A/c (Balance figure)	60,000
	2,10,000		2,10,000

PLANT AND MACHINERY A/C

	Rs.		Rs.
To Balance b/d	4,50,000	By Plant & Machinery Disposal A/c	50,000
To Bank-Purchased (Balance figure)	2,00,000	By Balance c/d	6,00,000
	6,50,000		6,50,000

PLANT & MACHINERY DISPOSAL A/C

	Rs.		Rs.
To Plant and Machinery A/c	50,000	By Provision for Depreciation A/c	35,000
		By Bank-sale	12,000
		By Profit and Loss A/c (Balancing figure)	3,000
	50,000		50,000

Preparation of relevant accounts reveals :

(i) Depreciation provided during the year Rs. 60,000 to be transferred to Profit & Loss (Adjusted) A/c to ascertain Funds From Operation.

(ii) Addition made to Plant & Machinery to the extent of Rs. 2,00,000.

(iii) Loss on sale of disposal of Plant & Machinery Rs. 3,000 to be adjusted against profit for the year to ascertain Funds from operation.

Example (3)

Extracts from Balance Sheets of Roaming Ltd. as on 31st March......

Liabilities	2003	2004	Assets	2003	2004
	Rs.	Rs.		Rs.	Rs.
Share Capital			Goodwill	—	30,000
(Shares of Rs. 10 each)	6,00,000	8,00,000	Machinery (at cost)	2,50,000	3,75,000

During the year Roaming Ltd. acquired the assets of Boaring Ltd. for Rs. 1,50,000 payable in fully paid shares. Assets included Machinery Rs. 75,000 and stock Rs. 45,000.

Working :

SHARE CAPITAL A/C

	Rs.		Rs.
To Balance c/d	8,00,000	By Balance b/d	6,00,000
		By Machinery	75,000
		By Stock (source)*	45,000
		By Goodwill	30,000
		By Bank (Bal. figure)	50,000
	8,00,000		8,00,000

MACHINERY A/C

	Rs.		Rs.
To Balance b/d	2,50,000	By Balance c/d	3,75,000
To Share Capital	75,000		
To Bank-purchased for cash Bal. figure)	50,000		
	3,75,000		3,75,000

* Any change in any current asset item due to change in non-current liability will result in inflow (source) of funds.

** Issue of shares for a consideration other than cash and current assets will not result in inflow (source) of funds.

Example (4)

Extracts from the Balance Sheet of Ajanta Ltd. as on 31st March......

Liabilities	2003 Rs.	2004 Rs.
Provision for Taxation	1,25,000	1,65,000
Proposed Dividend	85,000	95,000

During the year income tax paid amounted to Rs. 1,50,000.

An interim dividend of Rs. 40,000 was paid in October, 2003.

Working :

PROVISION FOR TAXATION A/C

	Rs.		Rs.
To Bank (Tax paid)	1,50,000	By Balance b/d	1,25,000
To Balance c/d	1,65,000	By Profit & Loss A/c (Bal. figure)	1,90,000
	3,15,000		3,15,000

PROPOSED DIVIDEND A/C

	Rs.		Rs.
To Bank*	1,25,000	By Balance b/d	85,000
To Balance c/d	95,000	By Profit & Loss A/c (Bal. figure)	1,35,000
	2,20,000		2,20,000

* Rs. 85,000 + Rs. 40,000

Actual payment of tax is to be treated as application and shown in the Funds Flow statement while balancing figure of Rs. 1,90,000 will be adjusted in Profit and Loss Account to ascertain Funds from operation.

In case of dividend, proposed dividend of last year plus interim dividend of current year is treated as application while balancing figure which is equal to interim dividend and current year's proposed dividend is to be adjusted in Profit and Loss Account to ascertain Funds from operation.

Example (5)

From the following information ascertain the amount to be shown in the Funds Flow Statement.

	31.12.2003 Rs.	31.12.2004 Rs.
Provision for Taxation	75,000	85,000

Income tax provided during the year amounted to Rs. 90,000.

PROVISION FOR TAXATION A/C

	Rs.		Rs.
To Bank (Tax paid-Bal. figure)	80,000	By Balance b/d	75,000
To Balance c/d	85,000	By Profit and Loss A/c	90,000
	1,65,000		1,65,000

Since in the adjustments income tax provided during the year is given, the balancing figure Rs. 80,000 shall be treated as application during the year 2004.

Example (6)

From the following information show the accounting treatment of the undermentioned items in respect of SCFP. As on ....

	31.3.2004	31.3.2005
Discount on Issue of Debentures	25,000	10,000
Preliminary Expenses	20,000	15,000

DISCOUNT ON ISSUE OF DEBENTURES A/C

	Rs.		Rs.
To Balance b/d	25,000	By Profit and Loss A/c (B.F.)	15,000
		By Balance c/d	10,000
	25,000		25,000

PRELIMINARY EXPENSES A/C

	Rs.		Rs.
To Balance b/d	20,000	By Profit & Loss A/c (Bal. figure)	5,000
		By Balance c/d	15,000
	20,000		20,000

Similar treatment shall be given to other fictitious assets (such as underwriting commission etc.) if the same are shown on the date of Balance Sheets Any amount written off shall be adjusted against Profit & Loss A/c while computing funds from operation.

Example (7)

Extract of liabilities side of Balance Sheets of Resham Ltd.

	As on	
	31.3.2004	31.3.2005
General Reserve	1,20,000	1,75,000

GENERAL RESERVE A/C

	Rs.		Rs.
To Balance b/d	1,75,000	By Balance b/d	1,20,000
		By Profit and Loss A/c (Balancing figure)	55,000
	1,75,000		1,75,000

Similarly, if there are undistributed profits in any other form, the difference will be shown on the debit or credit side of Adjusted Profit & Loss A/c. If a balance of such accumulated profit increases, it will be shown on the debit side of the Profit & Loss A/c (Adjusted) where as if decreases, then such decrease will be put on the credit side of Profit & Loss A/c (Adjusted).

GRADED ILLUSTRATIONS
(Interim dividend)

Illustration (1) From the following information you are required to prepare :

(i) Schedule of Changes in Working Capital (ii) Funds Flow Statement.

BALANCE SHEETS OF X LTD. AS ON 31ST MARCH.....

Liabilities	2003 Rs.	2004 Rs.
Equity Share Capital (Shares of Rs. 10 each)	5,00,000	5,50,000
General Reserve	70,000	90,000
Profit & Loss A/c	80,000	65,000
Creditors	46,000	31,000
Provision for Taxation	80,000	90,000
Provision for Doubtful Debts	2,000	3,000
	7,78,000	8,29,000
Assets		
Building	2,00,000	1,90,000
Plant & Machinery	1,85,000	1,80,000
Investments (Long term)	80,000	1,35,000
Stock	1,60,000	1,33,000
Debtors	90,000	95,000
Cash and Bank	33,000	76,000
Preliminary Expenses	30,000	20,000
	7,78,000	8,29,000

Additional Information :

(i) Depreciation on Plant charged during the year amounted to Rs. 20,000

(ii) A part of plant was sold for Rs. 40,000 during the year. The cost of the part of the plant was Rs. 60,000 on which depreciation of Rs. 35,000 was charged before it's disposal.

(iii) Provision for Taxation provided during the year Rs. 95,000

(iv) Interim dividend of Rs. 40,000 was paid during the year.

Solution : **Schedule of changes in Working Capital**

	31.3.03 Rs.	31.3.04 Rs.	Changes in Working Capital Increase	 Decrease
Current Assets :				
Stock	1,60,000	1,33,000	—	27,000
Debtors	90,000	95,000	5,000	
Cash and Bank	33,000	76,000	43,000	
Current liabilities :				
Creditors	46,000	31,000	15,000	
Provision for Doubtful Debts	2,000	3,000	—	1,000
			63,000	28,000
Net Increase in Working Capital				35,000
			63,000	63,000

COMPUTATION OF WORKING CAPITAL FROM OPERATION

Profit and Loss A/c (Adjusted)

	Rs.		Rs.
To Depreciation:		By Balance b/d	80,000
Plant	20,000	By Profit on Sale of Machinery	15,000
Building	10,000	By Working Capital from operations	1,65,000
To Preliminary Expenses	10,000		
To Provision for Taxation	95,000		
To Interim Dividend	40,000		
To General Reserve	20,000		
To Balance c/d	65,000		
	2,60,000		2,60,000

SCFP - Working Capital Basis

	Rs.
Sources :	
Working Capital from Operations	1,65,000
Issue of Share Capital (1)	50,000
Sale of Plant	40,000
	2,55,000
Application :	
Purchase of Plant (2)	40,000
Purchase of Investments (3)	55,000
Payment of Tax (4)	85,000
Payment of Interim Dividend	40,000
	2,20,000
Increase in Working Capital	35,000
	2,55,000

Working notes

(1) EQUITY SHARE CAPITAL A/C

	Rs.		Rs.
To Balance c/d	5,50,000	By Balance b/d	5,00,000
		By Bank (B.F.)	50,000
	5,50,000		5,50,000

(2) PLANT AND MACHINERY A/C

	Rs.		Rs.
To Balance b/d	1,85,000	By Bank (Sale)	40,000
To Profit on Sale of Plant	15,000	By Depreciation	20,000
To Bank (Purchased) (Bal. Figure)	40,000	By Balance c/d	1,80,000
	2,40,000		2,40,000

(4) PROVISION FOR TAXATION A/C

	Rs.		Rs.
To Bank A/c (Tax paid-Bal. figure)	85,000	By Balance b/d	80,000
To Balance c/d	90,000	By Profit and Loss A/c	95,000
	1,75,000		1,75,000

(3) INVESTMENTS A/C

	Rs.		Rs.
To Balance b/d	80,000	By Balance c/d	1,35,000
To Bank- (Purchased Bal. figure)	55,000		
	1,35,000		1,35,000

Illustration (3)

(Financing and Investing activities not affecting Working Capital)

From the following Balance Sheets of Rama Ltd. prepare statement of changes in Working Capital and Statement of Changes in Financial Position for the year ended 31st March 2005.

BALANCE SHEETS AS ON 31ST MARCH

	2004	2005
Liabilities	Rs.	Rs.
Equity Share Capital (Shares of Rs. 10 each)	6,00,000	7,00,000
General Reserve	2,00,000	3,00,000
Profit & Loss A/c	1,20,000	1,40,000
6% Debentures	3,00,000	5,00,000
Provision for Depreciation on Machinery	1,80,000	2,60,000
Sundry Creditors	1,50,000	2,20,000
Bills Payable	20,000	30,000
	15,70,000	21,50,000
Assets		
Goodwill	2,00,000	1,60,000
Machinery	8,20,000	10,80,000
Investments	60,000	1,60,000
Stock	80,000	1,10,000
S. Debtors	1,60,000	3,80,000
Cash and Bank	2,40,000	2,60,000
Discount on Issue of Debentures	10,000	—
	15,70,000	21,50,000

During the year investments costing Rs. 60,000 were sold for Rs. 56,000. A new machine was purchased for Rs. 90,000 and the payment was made in fully paid shares.

Solution :

I STATEMENT OF CHANGES IN WORKING CAPITAL

	31.3.03	31.3.04	Changes in Working Capital	
	Rs.	Rs.	Increase	Decrease
Current Assets :			Rs.	Rs.
Stock	80,000	1,10,000	30,000	—
Sundry Debtors	1,60,000	3,80,000	2,20,000	—
Cash and Bank	2,40,000	2,60,000	20,000	—
Current Liabilities :				
S. Creditors	1,50,000	2,20,000		70,000
Bills Payable	20,000	30,000		10,000
			2,70,000	80,000
Net Increase in Working Capital				1,90,000
			2,70,000	2,70,000

II COMPUTATION OF WORKING CAPITAL FROM OPERATIONS PROFIT AND LOSS A/C (ADJUSTED)

	Rs.		Rs.
To Depreciation	80,000	By Balance b/d	1,20,000
To Goodwill w/o	40,000	By Working Capital from operations	2,54,000
To Discount on Issue of debentures	10,000		
To Loss on sale of Investment	4,000		
To General Reserve	1,00,000		
To Balance c/d	1,40,000		
	3,74,000		3,74,000

II SCFP — WORKING CAPITAL BASIS

	Rs.
Sources :	
Working Capital from operations	2,54,000
Issue of shares (for cash)(1)	10,000
Issue of Debentures (Rs. 3,00,000 to Rs. 5,00,000)	2,00,000
Sales of Investments (2)	56,000
	5,20,000
Application :	
Purchase of Machinery (3)	1,70,000
Purchase of Investments (2)	1,60,000
	3,30,000
Net Increase in Working Capital	1,90,000
	5,20,000

Note : Financing and Investing Activities not affecting Working Capital 90,000

Working notes

(1) SHARE CAPITAL A/C

	Rs.		Rs.
To Balance b/d	7,00,000	By Balance b/d	6,00,000
		By Machinery	90,000
		By Bank (Balance Fig.)	10,000
	7,00,000		7,00,000

(2) INVESTMENTS A/C

	Rs.		Rs.
To Balance b/d	60,000	By Bank (Sale)	56,000
To Bank-(Purchased) (Bal. figure)	1,60,000	By Profit & Loss A/c (Loss)	4,000
		By Balance c/d	1,60,000
	2,20,000		2,20,000

(3) MACHINERY A/C

	Rs.		Rs.
To Balance b/d	8,20,000	By Balance c/d	10,80,000
To Share Capital	90,000		
To Bank (Bal. figure) (Addition made)	1,70,000		
	10,80,000		10,80,000

Illustration (4)

(Redemption of Debentures at Par)

Following are the Balance Sheets of Good luck Co. Ltd. as on 31st March.

Liabilities	2004 Rs.	2005 Rs.
Share Capital	25,00,000	27,50,000
General Reserve	5,00,000	5,00,000
Profit and Loss A/c	2,75,000	4,75,000
6% Debentures	12,50,000	7,50,000
S. Creditors	1,25,000	1,00,000
Bills Payable	50,000	75,000
Provision for Doubtful debt.	75,000	60,000
Provision for Taxation	1,00,000	2,75,000
	48,75,000	49,85,000

Assets	Rs.	Rs.
Goodwill	1,25,000	1,00,000
Land & Building	10,50,000	16,50,000
Plant & Machinery	15,00,000	20,00,000
Stock	6,25,000	5,25,000
Debtors	7,50,000	600,000
Cash and Bank	7,50,000	60,000
Preliminary Expenses	75,000	50,000
	48,75,000	49,85,000

Additional Information :

(i) A part of machine costing Rs. 18,750 (Accumulated depreciation there on being Rs. 6,250) was sold for Rs. 7,500 during the year ending 31st March 2005.

(iv) Depreciation provided during the year amounted to Rs. 25,000 and Rs. 1,25,000 on Land and Building and Plant and Machinery respectively.

(iii) During the year company paid Rs. 1,25,000 for income tax and Rs. 2,50,000 as dividend.

You are required to prepare :

(a) A Schedule of Changes in Working Capital

(b) A statement showing the Sources and Application of Funds.

Solution:

I SCHEDULE OF CHANGES IN WORKING CAPITAL

	31st March		Changes is Working Capital	
	2004 Rs.	2005 Rs.	Increase Rs.	Decrease Rs.
Current Assets :				
Stock	6,25,000	5,25,000		1,00,000
Debtors	7,50,000	6,00,000		1,50,000
Cash and Bank	7,50,000	60,000		6,90,000
Current Liabilities :				
S. Creditors	1,25,000	1,00,000	25,000	
Bills Payable	50,000	75,000		25,000
Provision for D. Debts	75,000	60,000	15,000	
			40,000	9,65,000
Net Decrease in Working Capital			9,25,000	—
			9,65,000	9,65,000

II CALCULATION OF WORKING CAPITAL FROM OPERATIONS

Profit and Loss A/c (Adjusted)

	Rs.		Rs.
To Depreciation		By Balance b/d	2,75,000
On Machinery	1,25,000	By Working Capital from Operations	9,55,000
On Land & Building	25,000		
To Goodwill w/o	25,000		
Preliminary Exp. w/o	25,000		
To Loss on Sale of Machinery	5,000		
To Provision for Taxation (3)	3,00,000		
To Dividends	2,50,000		
To Balance c/d	4,75,000		
	12,30,000		12,30,000

III STATEMENT OF CHANGES IN FINANCIAL POSITION (SCPP)

(Working Capital Basis)

	Rs.
Sources	
Working Capital from Operations	9,55,000
Issue of Share Capital	2,50,000
Sale of Machinery	7,500
	12,12,500
Application	
Purchase of Land and Building (1)	6,25,000
Purchase of Plant and Machinery (2)	6,37,500
Redemption of Debentures	5,00,000
Income Tax paid	1,25,000
Dividend paid	2,50,000
	21,37,500
Decrease in Working Capital	(9,25,000)
	12,12,500

Working notes

(1) LAND AND BUILDING A/C

	Rs.		Rs
To Balance b/d	10,50,000	By Depreciation	25,000
To Bank- (Addition) (Balancing figure)	6,25,000	By Balance c/d	16,50,000
	16,75,000		16,75,000

(2) PLANT AND MACHINERY A/C

	Rs.		Rs.
To Balance b/d	15,00,000	By Bank (Sale)	7,500
To Bank (Addition)	6,37,500	By Profit and Loss A/c (Loss)	5,000
(Bal. figure)		By Depreciation	1,25,000
		By Balance c/d	20,00,000
	21,37,500		21,37,500

(3) PROVISION FOR TAXATION A/C

	Rs.		Rs.
To Bank (Tax paid)	1,25,000	By Balance b/d	1,00,000
To Balance c/d	2,75,000	By Profit and Loss A/c	3,00,000
		(Bal. figure)	
	4,00,000		4,00,000

Illustration (5) (Excess Depreciation)

From the following Balance Sheets of ABC Ltd. prepare a Schedule of Changes in Working Capital and Statement of Changes in Financial Position a for the year ended 31st March, 2005.

Liabilities	2004	2005
	Rs.	Rs.
Equity Share Capital	2,75,000	3,25,000
Profit & Loss Appropriation A/c	1,86,250	1,97,500
Provision for Depreciation	1,01,250	60,000
Current Liabilities	2,75,000	2,60,000
	8,37,500	8,42,500
Assets		
Goodwill	25,000	—
Fixed Assets	3,50,000	4,25,000
Marketable Securities	87,500	37,500
Other Current Assets :		
Stock	1,75,000	1,60,000
Debtors	1,50,000	1,65,000
Cash and Bank	50,000	55,000
	8,37,500	8,42,500

Additional Information:

During the year depreciation of Rs. 33,750 was charged on fixed assets and a machinery costing Rs. 25,000 (accumulated depreciation Rs. 7,500) was sold for Rs. 15,000. Due to change in policy of charging depreciation the excess depreciation of past years has been charged to Profit & Loss A/c of the current year.

Solution :

I SCHEDULE OF CHANGES IN WORKING CAPITAL

	As on 31st March		Changes in Working Capital	
	2004 Rs.	2005 Rs.	Increase Rs.	Decrease Rs.
Current Assets :				
Stock	1,75,000	1,60,000	—	15,000
Debtors	1,50,000	1,65,000	15,000	—
Cash and Bank	50,000	55,000	5,000	—
Marketable Securities	87,500	37,500	—	50,000
Current liabilities :	2,75,000	2,60,000	15,000	—
			35,000	65,000
Net Decrease in Working Capital			30,000	—
			65,000	65,000

II COMPUTATION OF WORKING CAPITAL FROM OPERATIONS

Profit and Loss Appropriation A/c (Adjusted)

	Rs.		Rs.
To Depreciation	33,750	By Balance b/d	1,86,250
To Goodwill w/o	25,000	By Provision for Depreciation	67,500
To Loss on Sale of Machinery	2,500	(Excess Dep.)	
To Balance c/d	1,97,500	By Working Capital from operations	5,000
	2,58,750		2,58,750

III STATEMENT OF CHANGES IN FINANCIAL POSITION (SCFP)
(Working Capital basis)

	Rs.
Sources	
Working Capital from Operations	5,000
Issue of Share Capital	50,000
Sale of Machinery	15,000
	70,000
Application	
Purchase of Machinery (Fixed Assets)	1,00,000
Decrease in Working Capital	(30,000)
	70,000

Working note :

(1) FIXED ASSETS A/C

	Rs.		Rs.
To Balance b/d	3,50,000	By Machinery Disposal A/c	25,000
To Bank (Addition) (Bal. figure)	1,00,000	By Balance c/d	4,25,000
	4,50,000		4,50,000

(2) PROVISION FOR DEPRECIATION A/C

	Rs.		Rs.
To Machinery Disposal A/c	7,500	By Balance b/d	1,01,250
To Profit and Loss A/c (Bal. figure) (Excess Depreciation)	67,500	By Depreciation	33,750
To Balance c/d	60,000		
	1,35,000		1,35,000

MACHINERY DISPOSAL A/C

	Rs.		Rs.
To Fixed Assets A/c	25,000	By Provision for Depreciation A/c	7,500
		By Bank (Sale)	15,000
		By Profit and Loss A/c (Loss on sale)	2,500
	25,000		25,000

Illustration (6) (Financing and Investing activities not affecting Working Capital)

The following are Balance Sheets of Arnold Ltd. as on 31st March, 2004 and 2005.

Liabilities	2004 Rs.	2005 Rs.
Share Capital	2,00,000	2,60,000
Reserves	50,000	50,000
Profit and Loss A/c	39,690	41,220
S. Creditors	39,500	41,135
Bills Payable	33,780	11,525
Bank Overdraft	59,510	—
Provision for Taxation	40,000	50,000
	4,62,480	4,53,880
Assets:		
Goodwill	—	20,000
Land & Building	1,48,500	1,44,250
Plant & Machinery	1,12,950	1,16,200

	Rs.	Rs.
Stock	1,00,000	90,000
S. Debtors	85,175	72,625
Bills Receivable	11,040	7,370
Prepaid Expenses	2,315	735
Cash at Bank	2,500	2,700
	4,62,480	4,53,880

Additional Information:

(i) During the year ended March 2005 an interim dividend of Rs. 26,000 was paid.

(ii) The assets of another company were purchased for Rs. 60,000 payable in fully paid shares. These assets consisted of :

Stock	Rs. 22,000
Machinery	Rs. 18,000
Goodwill	Rs. 20,000

In addition a part of planı

(iii) Income Tax paid during the year amounted to Rs. 25,000.

(iv) The net profit for the year amounted to Rs. 62,530.

Prepare :

(a) Statement of Changes in Working Capital

(b) Statement of Changes in Financial Position.

C.A. (I) and B.Com. D.U.- Modified

Solution :

I SCHEDULE OF CHANGES IN WORKING CAPITAL

	As on 31.3.04	As on 31.3.05	Changes in Working Capital	
	Rs.	Rs.	Increase	Decrease
Current Assets:				
Stock	1,00,000	90,000		10,000
S. Debtors	85,175	72,625		12,550
Bills Receivable	11,040	7,370		3,670
Prepaid Expenses	2,315	735		1,580
Cash at Bank	2,500	2,700	200	—
Current Liabilities :				
Sundry Creditors	39,500	41,135		1,635
Bills Payable	33,780	11,525	22,255	
Bank Overdraft	59,510	—	59,510	—
			81,965	29,435
Net Increase in Working Capital				52,530
			81,965	81,965

II COMPUTATION OF WORKING CAPITAL FROM OPERATIONS

Profit and Loss A/c (Adjusted)

	Rs.		Rs.
To Depreciation (Rs. 4,250 + 20,350)(2)	24,600	By Balance b/d	39,690
To Provision for Taxation(3)	35,000	By Working Capital from operations	87,130
To Interim Dividend	26,000	(Bal. figure)	
To Balance c/d	41,220		
	1,26,820		1,26,820

III STATEMENT OF CHANGES IN FINANCIAL POSITION

(Working Capital Basis)

	Rs.
Sources	
Working Capital from Operations:	87,130
Issue of Share Capital (for stock) (1)	22,000
Issue of Share Capital for Machinery and Goodwill as per contra(1)	38,000
	1,47,130
Application	
Purchase of Plant and Machinery for cash (2)	5,600
Payment of Tax	25,000
Payment of Interim Dividend	26,000
Purchase of Machinery & Goodwill by issue of Share Capital as per contra (2)	38,000
	94,600
Increase in Working Capital	52,530
	1,47,130

Working notes:

(1) SHARE CAPITAL A/C

	Rs.		Rs.
To Balance c/d	2,60,000	By Balance b/d	2,00,000
		By Plant and Machinery	18,000
		By Goodwill	20,000
		By Stock (Source)	22,000
	2,60,000		2,60,000

(2) PLANT AND MACHINERY A/C

	Rs.		Rs.
To Balance b/d	1,12,950	By Depreciation (Bal. figure)	20,350
To Share Capital	18,000	By Balance c/d	1,16,200
To Bank	5,600		
	1,36,550		1,36,550

(3) PROVISION FOR TAXATION A/C

	Rs.		Rs.
To Cash	25,000	By Balance b/d	40,000
To Balance c/d	50,000	By Profit & Loss A/c (Bal. figure)	35,000
	75,000		75,000

Illustration (6) (Statement of Income and it's reconciliation)

The following are the summarised Balance Sheets of Pratibha Ltd. as on 31st March, 2004 and 2005.

Liabilities	31.3.2004 Rs.	31.3.2005 Rs.
Share Capital	5,00,000	9,20,000
Retained Earnings	4,62,000	4,22,000
9% Debentures	4,40,000	1,20,000
Social Security Tax Accrued	6,000	10,000
Estimated Income Tax	1,72,000	24,000
Notes Payable	56,000	16,000
Accounts Payable	1,16,000	1,88,000
	17,52,000	17,00,000
Assets		
Building & Equipments	8,40,000	9,60,000
Less Accumulated Depreciation	(2,10,000)	(2,40,000)
	6,30,000	7,20,000
Land	1,20,000	1,20,000
Patents	1,10,000	1,30,000
Inventories	6,24,000	5,54,000
Accounts Receivable	1,08,000	94,000
Prepaid Expense	12,000	8,000
Cash and Bank	1,48,000	74,000
	17,52,000	17,00,000

STATEMENT OF INCOME AND RECONCILIATION OF EARNINGS
for the year ending 31. 3. 2005

	Rs.
Turn over (Net)	39,40,000
Less Cost of Goods sold	(29,60,000)
	9,80,000
Less Operating Expenses (including depreciation on Building and Equipments - Rs. 46,000 Amortisation of Patents Rs. 12,000	(10,00,000)
Net Loss from Operation	(20,000)

Net Loss from Operation	(20,000)
Other Incomes	14,000
Net Loss	(6,000)
Loss on sale of assets	(2,000)
Retained Earnings of last year	4,62,000
	4,54,000
Dividend Paid	(32,000)
Retained Earnings 31st March, 2005	4,22,000

An item in the Building and Equipments Account sold during the year was a specialised machine that originally cost Rs. 30,000. The accumulated depreciation on this machine at the time of sale was Rs. 16,000. The machine was sold for Rs. 12,000 and full payment was received in cash :

(a) A Statement of Changes in Working Capital

(b) A statement of Changes in Financial Position.

Solution:

I STATEMENT OF CHANGES IN WORKING CAPITAL

	As on 31.3.04	As on 31.3.05	Changes in Working Capital	
	Rs.	Rs.	Increase	Decrease
Current Assets:				
Inventories	6,24,000	5,54,000	—	70,000
Accounts Receivable	1,08,000	94,000	—	14,000
Prepaid Expenses	12,000	8,000	—	4,000
Cash and Bank	1,48,000	74,000	—	74,000
Current Liabilities:				
Accounts Payable	1,16,000	1,88,000	—	36,000
Notes Payable	56,000	16,000	40,000	
Social Security Tax Accrued	6,000	10,000	—	4,000
			40,000	2,38,000
Net Decrease in Working Capital			1,98,000	—
			2,38,000	2,38,000

II COMPUTATION OF WORKING CAPITAL FROM OPERATIONS

Profit and Loss A/c (Adjusted)

	Rs.		Rs.
To Provision for Depreciation (4)	46,000	By Balance b/d	4,62,000
To Patents w/o	12,000	By Working Capital from operations	52,000
To Loss on sale of machine	2,000	(Bal. figure)	
To Dividend	32,000		
To Balance c/d	4,22,000		
	5,14,000		5,14,000

III STATEMENT OF CHANGES IN FINANCIAL POSITION (SCFP)

(Working Capital basis)

	Rs.
Sources:	
Working Capital from Operations	52,000
Issue of shares for cash (1)	4,20,000
Sale of machine	12,000
	4,84,000
Application	
Purchase of Building and Equipment(2)	1,50,000
Purchase of Patents (4)	32,000
Dividend Paid	32,000
Tax Paid	1,48,000
Redemption of Debentures	3,20,000
	6,82,000
Decrease in Working Capital	(1,98,000)
	4,84,000

Working Notes :

(1) SHARE CAPITAL A/C

	Rs.		Rs.
To Balance c/d	9,20,000	By Balance b/d	5,00,000
		By Bank (Bal. figure)	4,20,000
	9,20,000		9,20,000

(2) BUILDING AND EQUIPMENTS A/C

	Rs.		Rs.
To Balance b/d	8,40,000	By Bank (Sale)	12,000
To Bank-Purchased (Bal. figure)	1,50,000	By Acc. Depreciation	16,000
		By Profit and Loss A/c (Loss on sale)	2,000
		By Balance c/d	9,60,000
	9,90,000		9,90,000

(3) PROVISION FOR DEPRECIATION A/C

	Rs.		Rs.
To Building and Equipments A/c	16,000	By Balance b/d	2,10,000
To Balance c/d	2,40,000	By Depreciation	46,000
	2,56,000		2,56,000

(4) PATENTS A/C

	Rs.		Rs.
To Balance b/d	1,10,000	By Profit and Loss A/c	12,000
To Bank-Acquired (Bal. figure)	32,000	By Balance	1,30,000
	1,42,000		1,42,000

Illustration (7) (Conversion of Debentures)

Following are the Balance Sheets of X Co. Ltd. as on 31st March 2004 and 2005.

Liabilities	31.3.04 Rs.	31.3.05 Rs.
9% Preference Share Capital	—	2,00,000
Equity Share Capital	4,20,000	5,20,000
General Reserve	1,00,000	1,10,000
Profit and Loss A/c	61,000	71,200
12% Debentures	2,00,000	—
Creditors	4,40,000	2,68,000
Unclaimed Dividend	—	2,000
Provision for Taxation	60,000	70,000
	12,81,000	12,41,200
Assets :		
Goodwill	20,000	30,000
Building	6,00,000	5,80,000
Machinery	3,00,000	3,38,000
Stock	2,00,000	1,48,000
Debtors	1,40,400	1,08,000
Cash and Bank	20,600	37,200
	12,81,000	12,41,200

Additional Information :

During the year ending 31st March, 2005

(i) Dividend was paid in cash Rs. 50,000

(ii) Assets worth Rs. 1,00,000 were acquired :

Stock Rs. 50,000, Machine Rs. 40,000 and goodwill.

(iii) Machine was purchased for cash Rs. 12,000

(iv) Provision for tax was made for Rs. 66,000

(v) Debentureholders accepted preference shares in settlement of their claims.

(vi) Depreciation on Building was provided Rs. 20,000.

Prepare : Funds Flow Statement and Schedule of Changes in Working Capital.

B. Com (H) D.U. (1996) Modified

Solution :

I SCHEDULE OF CHANGES IN WORKING CAPITAL

	As on 31st March		Changes Working Capital	
	2004	2005	Increase	Decrease
Current Assets:	Rs.	Rs.	Rs.	Rs.
Stock	2,00,000	1,48,000	—	52,000
Debtors	1,40,400	1,08,000	—	32,400
Cash and Bank	20,600	37,200	16,600	—
Current Liabilities:				
Creditors	4,40,000	2,68,000	1,72,000	—
Net Increase in Working Capital				1,04,200
			1,88,600	1,88,600

II COMPUTATION OF WORKING CAPITAL FROM OPERATIONS PROFIT AND LOSS A/C (ADJUSTED)

	Rs.		Rs.
To Depreciation on :		By Balance b/d	61,000
Building	20,000	By Working Capital from operations	1,72,200
Machinery	14,000		
To General Reserve	10,000		
To Provision for Taxation	66,000		
To Dividend	52,000		
To Balance c/d	71,200		
	2,33,200		2,33,200

III STATEMENT OF CHANGES IN FINANCIAL POSITION (WORKING CAPITAL BASIS)

	Rs.
Sources :	
Working Capital from operations	1,72,200
Issue of share Capital (Stock)	50,000
Financing and Investing Activities not affecting Working Capital as per contra:	
Issue of Share Capital for Goodwill	10,000
Issue of Share Capital for Machinery	40,000
Issue of Preference Shares in lieu of debentures' redemption	2,00,000
	4,72,200
Application :	
Purchase of Machinery for Cash	12,000
Payment of Tax	56,000
Payment of Dividend	50,000
Financing and Investing Activities not affecting Working Capital as per contra	
Purchase of Goodwill	10,000
Purchase of Machinery	40,000

Redemption of Debentures	2,00,000
	3,68,000
Net Increase in Working Capital	1,04,200
	4,72,200

Important Note: Students should note that any item of liability which requires adjustment cannot be treated as current liability. In the absence of adjustments "Unclaimed dividend" could have been treated as current liability.

Working Notes

(1) Unclaimed dividend has been treated as non-current. Out of Rs. 52,000 proposed dividend only Rs. 50,000 has been paid Rs. 2,000 is still the o/s remaining balance. Hence actual application (outflow) is Rs. 50,000 and not Rs. 52,000.

(2) PROVISION FOR TAXATION

	Rs.		Rs.
To Bank (Bal. figure)	56,000	By Balance b/d	60,000
To Balance c/d	70,000	By P and L A/c	66,000
	1,26,000		1,26,000

(3) MACHINERY A/C

	Rs.		Rs.
To Balance b/d	3,00,000	By Depreciation (Bal. figure)	14,000
To Share Capital	40,000	By Balance c/d	3,38,000
To Bank	12,000		
	3,52,000		3,52,000

Illustration (8) (Missing figures)

From the following information prepare

(i) a Statement of Changes in Working Capital and

(ii) a Statement of Changes in Financial Position

Liabilities	31.3.05	31.3.04
Equity Share Capital	11,00,000	8,00,000
Securities Premium	1,20,000	—
Retained Earnings	6,72,000	6,50,000
9% Debentures	10,00,000	5,00,000
Provision for Depreciation	5,50,000	3,00,000
S. Creditors	2,00,000	1,50,000
Bills Payable	1,00,000	50,000
	37,42,000	24,50,000

Assets		
Land and Building	12,70,000	4,70,000
Plant and Machinery	10,00,000	7,00,000
Inventories	1,90,000	1,40,000
Investments (Long Term)	1,40,000	2,20,000
Debtors (Net)	3,00,000	2,50,000
Marketable Securities	2,12,000	1,00,000
Cash and Bank balance	6,30,000	5,70,000
	37,42,000	24,50,000

INCOME STATEMENT
for the year ended 31st March, 2005

	Rs.	Rs.
Turnover		12,00,000
Less Cost of Goods sold		6,74,000
		5,26,000
Operating Expenses :		
Depreciation — Machinery	1,00,000	
— Building	1,60,000	
Other Expenses	2,00,000	4,60,000
		66,000
Gain on Sale of Investments		24,000
		90,000
Less Loss on Sale of Machinery (Sale proceeds - Rs. 30,000)		10,000
Net Profit		80,000

SOLUTION : I STATEMENT OF CHANGES IN WORKING CAPITAL

	As on 31st March		Changes Working Capital	
	2004	2005	Increase	Decrease
Current Assets:	Rs.	Rs.	Rs.	Rs.
Inventories	1,40,000	1,90,000	50,000	—
Debtors	2,50,000	3,00,000	50,000	—
Marketable Securities	1,00,000	2,12,000	1,12,000	—
Cash and Bank Balance	5,70,000	6,30,000	60,000	—
Current liabilities				
S. Creditors	1,50,000	2,00,000	—	50,000
Bills Payable	50,000	1,00,000	—	50,000
			2,72,000	1,00,000
Net Increase in Working Capital			—	1,72,000
			2,72,000	2,72,000

II STATEMENT OF CHANGES IN FINANCIAL POSITION
(Working Capital Basis)

Sources :	Rs.
Working Capital from operations (1)	3,26,000
Issue of share Capital	3,00,000
Receipt of Securities Premium	1,20,000
Issue of Debentures	5,00,000
Sale of Investments	1,04,000
Sale of Machine	30,000
	13,80,000
Application :	
Purchase of Land and Building (2)	8,00,000
Purchase of Plant (3)	3,50,000
Payment of Tax (4)	58,000
	12,08,000
Net Increase in Working Capital	1,72,000
	13,80,000

Working notes:

(1) Working Capital from operations

		Rs.
	Net Profit as per Income Statement	80,000
Add.	Non Cash Charges:	
	Depreciation (Rs. 1,00,000 + 1,60,000)	2,60,000
	Loss on sale of machinery	10,000
		3,50,000
Less	Gain on sale of Investments	24,000
		3,26,000

(2) LAND AND BUILDING A/C

	Rs.		Rs.
To Balance b/d	4,70,000	By Balance c/d	12,70,000
To Bank (Bal. fig) (Purchase)	8,00,000		
	12,70,000		12,70,000

(3) PLANT AND MACHINERY A/C

	Rs.		Rs.
To Balance b/d	7,00,000	By Machinery Disposal A/c	50,000*
To Bank (B.F.) (Purchased)	3,50,000	By Balance c/d	10,00,000
	10,50,000		10,50,000

MACHINERY DISPOSAL A/C*

	Rs.		Rs.
To Plant and Machinery A/c (Bal. figure)	50,000	By Provision for Depreciation A/c	10,000
		By Profit and Loss A/c (Loss)	10,000
		By Bank	30,000
	50,000		50,000

PROVISION FOR DEPRECIATION A/C

	Rs.		Rs.
To Machinery Disposal A/c (B.F.)	10,000	By Balance b/d	3,00,000
To Balance c/d	5,50,000	By Profit and Loss A/c	2,60,000
	5,60,000		5,60,000

(4) RETAINED EARNINGS A/C

	Rs.		Rs.
To Provision for Tax* (Bal. figure)	58,000	By Balance b/d	6,50,000
To Balance c/d	6,72,000	By Profit and Loss A/c (Net Profit)	80,000
	7,30,000		7,30,000

* The balancing figure may be assumed to be a provision for tax or a proposed dividend.

Illustration (9) (Stock Valuation and Redemption of Preference shares)

From the following information, prepare:

(i) A Schedule of Changes in Working Capital

(ii) A Statement of Changes in Financial Position.

BALANCE SHEETS OF ROAMER INDIA LTD.
as on 31st March, 2004 and 2005

	31.3.04	31.3.05
Liabilities	Rs.	Rs.
9% Preference Share Capital	3,00,000	1,50,000
Equity Share Capital	4,50,000	5,25,000
Profit and Loss A/c	1,65,000	4,05,000
6% Debentures	1,50,000	3,00,000
Provision for Doubtful debts	15,000	22,500
Current Liabilities	1,05,000	2,17,500
	11,85,000	16,20,000
Assets		
Net Block	7,65,000	9,30,000
Investments	45,000	1,20,000
Current Assets	3,60,000	5,62,500

Discount on Debentures	15,000	7,500
	11,85,000	16,20,000

Additional Information :

(i) On 1. 4. 2005 Preference Shares were redeemed at a premium of 5%

(ii) Dividend @ 15% was paid on equity shares for the year ending 31. 3. 04.

(iii) A machine costing Rs. 1,05,000 book value Rs. 60,000 was disposed off for Rs. 37,500

(iv) The Provision for depreciation stood at Rs. 2,25,000 on 31. 3. 2004 and at Rs. 2,85,000 on 31. 3. 2005.

(v) Stock which was valued at Rs. 1,35,000 as on 31. 3. 2004 was written up to it's cost Rs. 1,50,000 for preparing the Profit and Loss A/c for the year ending 31. 3. 2005

(vi) All debtors are good.

Solution :

(I) SCHEDULE OF CHANGES IN WORKING CAPITAL

	As on 31st March		Changes in Working Capital	
	2004 Rs.	2005 Rs.	Increase Rs.	Decrease Rs.
Current Assets:				
Current Assets (Adjusted for stock)*	3,75,000*	5,62,500	1,87,500	—
Current liabilities				
Current liabilities	1,05,000	2,17,500	—	1,12,500
			1,87,500	1,12,500
Net Increase in Working Capital			—	75,000
			1,87,500	1,87,500

(II) WORKING CAPITAL FROM OPERATIONS
PROFIT AND LOSS A/C (ADJUSTED)

	Rs.		Rs.
To Depreciation (2)	1,05,000	By Balance b/d (1)	1,65,000
To Discount on Debentures	7,500	By Stock (Adj.)	15,000
To Provision For D. Debts (3)	7,500	By Working Capital from	4,69,500
To Loss on Sale of Machinery	22,500	Operations	
To Premium on Redem. of Pref. Shares	7,500		
To Dividend (4)			
Preference @ 9%	27,000		
Equity @ 15%	67,500		
To Balance c/d	4,05,000		
	6,49,500		6,49,500

III STATEMENT OF CHANGES IN FINANCIAL POSITION
(Working Capital Basis)

	Rs.
Sources :	
Working Capital from operations	4,69,500
Issue of E. Share Capital	75,000
Issue of Debentures	1,50,000
Sale of Machinery	37,500
	7,32,000
Uses :	
Redemption of Preference Shares	1,57,500
Purchase of Fixed Assets (5)	3,30,000
Purchase of Investments	75,000
Payment of Dividend (27,000 + 67,500)	94,500
	6,57,000
Net Increase in Working Capital	75,000
	7,32,000

Working notes:

(1) An upward valuation of closing stock of last year will increase the profit for the last year hence the same has been transferred to Profit and Loss (Adjusted) A/c so as to increase the opening balance of Profit and Loss A/c.

(2) PROVISION FOR DEPRECIATION A/C

	Rs.		Rs.
To Machinery Disposal A/c (Cost– Book value)	45,000	By Balance b/d	2,25,000
To Balance c/d	2,85,000	By Profit and Loss A/c (Bal. figures)	1,05,000
	3,30,000		3,30,000

(3) When debtors are good, any transfer to provision for doubtful debts is treated as an appropriation and not a charge.

(4) Equity dividend can not be paid prior to Preference dividend hence while paying equity dividend the preference dividend has also been paid.

(5) NET BLOCK (FIXED ASSETS) A/C

	Rs.		Rs.
To Balance b/d	7,65,000	By Bank (Sale)	37,500
To Bank (Purchase Bal. figure)	3,30,000	By P & L A/c (Loss)	22,500
		By Depreciation	1,05,000
		By Balance c/d	9,30,000
	10,95,000		10,95,000

Alternatively Fixed Assets can be prepared at cost. (WDV + Provision)

Fixed Assets A/c (at cost)

	Rs.		Rs.
To Balance b/d	9,90,000	By Machinery Disposal A/c	1,05,000
To Bank (Bal. Figure)	3,30,000	By Balance c/d	12,15,000
	13,20,000		13,20,000

and

MACHINERY DISPOSAL A/C

	Rs.		Rs.
To Fixed Assets A/c	1,05,000	By Provision for Depreciation A/c	45,000
		By Bank	37,500
		By P and L A/c (Loss)	22,500
	1,05,000		1,05,000

Illustration (10) (Hidden information)

From the following information you are required to prepare a Statement of Changes in Financial Position on working capital basis.

	31.3.2004	31.3.2005
	Rs.	Rs.
Fixed Assets (net of depreciation)	9,05,000	9,30,000
Long Term Loans	—	2,25,0000
Share Capital	7,50,000	6,25,000
Profit and Loss A/c	10,80,000	8,40,000

During the year depreciation of Rs. 95,000 was charged to Profit and Loss A/c. Dividend amounting to Rs. 75,000 was paid during the year 2004-05. Also a Machinery having net book value of Rs. 2,40,000 was sold and the gain of Rs. 15,000 was credited to Profit and Loss A/c.

M.Com. D.U. - Adapted

STATEMENT OF CHANGES IN FINANCIAL POSITION
(Working Capital basis)

	Rs.
Sources	
Working Capital from Operation (1)	3,95,000
Issue of Share Capital	1,25,000
Sale of Machinery	2,55,000
	7,75,000
Uses	
Repayment of loan	2,25,000
Payment of Dividend	75,000
Purchase of Fixed Assets (2)	3,10,000
	6,10,000
Increase in Working Capital (Bal. fig)	1,65,000
	7,75,000

Working notes

(1) PROFIT AND LOSS A/C (ADJUSTED)

	Rs.		Rs.
To Depreciation	95,000	By Balance b/d	8,40,000
To Dividend	75,000	By Profit on Sale of Machinery	15,000
To Balance c/d	10,80,000	By Working Capital from operations (Bal. figure)	3,95,000
	12,50,000		12,50,000

FIXED ASSETS A/C

	Rs.		Rs.
To Balance b/d	9,30,000	By Depreciation	95,000
To Profit & Loss A/c (Profit on sale)	15,000	By Bank (2,40,000 + 15,000)	2,55,000
To Bank (Purchase) (Bal. figure)	3,10,000	By Balance c/d	9,05,000
	12,55,000		12,55,000

Illustration (11) (Revaluation and pre-acquisition dividend)

From the following Balance Sheets of a company as on 31st March 2004 and 2005 prepare :

(i) A Statement of Changes in Working Capital

(ii) and A Statement of Changes in Financial Position.

	31. 3. 04	31. 3. 05
Liabilities	Rs.	Rs.
8% Preference Share Capital	1,50,000	1,00,000
Equity Share Capital	1,50,000	2,50,000
General Reserve	20,000	30,000
Capital Reserve	—	25,000
Profit and Loss A/c	18,000	27,000
Proposed Dividend	27,000	33,000
Provision for Taxation	28,000	32,000
S. Creditors	26,000	53,000
Bills Payable	18,000	12,000
	4,37,000	5,62,000
Assets		
Goodwill	60,000	47,000
Land and Building	1,00,000	75,000
Plant and Machinery	90,000	1,91,000
Long Term Investments	10,000	35,000
Stock	85,000	78,000
S. Debtors	60,000	90,000
Bills Receivable	15,000	18,000

Cash at Bank	10,000	22,000
Cash in hand	7,000	6,000
	4,37,000	5,62,000

Additional Information

(i) During the year ending 31. 3. 2005 a depreciation of Rs. 18,000 has been written off Plant and Machinery where as no depreciation has been charged on Land and Building.

(ii) A piece of land has been sold and balance has been revalued. Profit on such sale and revaluation has been transferred to Capital Reserve. There is no other entry in Capital Reserve Account.

(iii) A part of plant was sold for Rs. 12,000 (W.D.V. Rs. 15,000)

(iv) Rs. 2,100 dividend has been received but it includes Rs. 600 pre-acquisition dividend.

(v) An interim dividend of Rs. 10,000 has been paid during the current year.

(vi) Proposed dividend and Provision for Taxation are to be treated as non-current liabilities.

(B.Com (D.U.) - 2001 - Modified)

Solution:

I STATEMENT OF CHANGES IN WORKING CAPITAL

	As on 31st March		Changes in Working Capital	
	2004 Rs.	2005 Rs.	Increase Rs.	Decrease Rs.
Current Assets				
Stock	85,000	78,000	—	7,000
S. Debtors	60,000	90,000	30,000	
Bills Receivable	15,000	18,000	3,000	
Cash at Bank	10,000	22,000	12,000	
Cash in hand	7,000	6,000	—	1,000
Current liabilities				
S. Creditors	26,000	53,000	—	27,000
Bills Payable	18,000	12,000	6,000	
			51,000	35,000
Net Increase in Working Capital				16,000
			51,000	51,000

II STATEMENT OF CHANGES IN FINANCIAL POSITION
(Working Capital Basis)

Sources:	Rs.
Working Capital from operations (1)	1,26,500
Issue of Equity Share Capital	1,00,000
Sale of Fixed Assets :	
Land (2)	50,000
Plant	12,000
Other receipts - Dividend	2,100
	2,90,600

Uses:

	Rs.
Redemption of Preference Shares	50,000
Purchase of Plant (3)	1,34,000
Purchase of Investments (5)	25,600
Payment of Tax	28,000
Payment of Dividend* (Rs. 27,000 + 10,000)	37,000
	2,74,600
Net Increase in Working Capital	16,000
	2,90,600

* Last year's proposed dividend plus current year's interim dividend.

Working notes

(1) WORKING CAPITAL FROM OPERATIONS
Profit and Loss A/c (Adjusted)

	Rs.		Rs.
To Depreciation on :		By Balance b/d	18,000
Plant and Machinery	18,000	By Dividend Received excluding	1,500
To Goodwill	13,000	pre-acquisition dividend Rs. 600	
To Loss on Sale of Plant	3,000	By Working Capital from operation	1,26,500
To Provision for Taxation	32,000	(Bal. figure)	
To General Reserve	10,000		
To Proposed Dividend (4)	43,000		
To Balance C/d	27,000		
	1,46,000		1,46,000

(2) LAND AND BUILDING A/C

	Rs.		Rs.
To Balance b/d	1,00,000	By Bank (Bal. figure)	50,000
To Capital Reserve	25,000	By Balance c/d	75,000
(Profit on sale and on revaluation)			
	1,25,000		1,25,000

(3) PLANT AND MACHINERY A/C

	Rs.		Rs.
To Balance b/d	90,000	By Depreciation	18,000
To Bank-Purchased	1,34,000	By Bank	12,000
(Bal. figure)		By Loss on Sale	3,000
		By Balance c/d	1,91,000
	2,24,000		2,24,000

(4) PROPOSED DIVIDEND A/C

	Rs.		Rs.
To Bank (27,000 + 10,000)	37,000	By Balance b/d	27,000
To Balance c/d	33,000	By Profit and Loss A/c (Bal. figure)	43,000
	70,000		70,000

(5) INVESTMENTS A/C

	Rs.		Rs.
To Balance b/d	10,000	By Bank (Dividend)	600
To Bank A/c (Bal. figure)	25,600	(Pre. Acquisition	
		By Balance c/d	35,000
	35,600		35,600

Illustration (11) (Rectification, Bonus Shares and Revaluation)

From the following summarised Balance Sheets of a company as an 31st March, 2004 and 2005 prepare :

(i) A Schedule of Changes in Working Capital and

(ii) Statement of Sources and Uses of Funds.

Liabilities	31.3.04	31.3.03
	Rs.	Rs.
10% Redeemable Preference Share Capital	1,50,000	1,20,000
Equity Share Capital	1,00,000	1,50,000
Reserve for Replacement of Machinery	22,500	15,000
Bank Loan	—	60,000
Trade Creditors	80,000	75,000
Bank Overdraft	33,000	—
Proposed Dividend on :		
Equity Shares	18,000	36,000
Profit and Loss A/c	1,00,000	1,03,500
	5,03,500	5,59,500
Assets		
Fixed Assets at Cost	3,60,000	3,75,000
Less Depreciation	1,35,000	1,45,000
	2,25,000	2,30,000
Investments	60,000	75,000
Stock	95,000	1,05,000
Trade Debtors	90,000	85,000
Bank	33,500	64,500
	5,03,500	5,59,500

Additional Information

(i) During the year, additional equity capital was issued to the extent of Rs. 20,000 by way of bonus shares fully paid up.

(ii) Change in Reserve for Replacement of Machinery represents transfer to Profit and Loss A/c.

(iii) Final dividend on Preference Shares and interim dividend on of Rs. 5,000 on equity shares were paid on 31. 3. 2005.

(iv) Proposed dividends for the year ended 31st March 2004 were paid in October 2004.

(v) During the year one item of plant was overvalued by Rs. 5,000 and credit for this was taken to Profit and Loss Account.

(vi) Rs. 2,500 being expenditure on fixed assets for the year ended 31st March 2004 wrongly debited to Trade Debtors then, was corrected in the next year.

(vii) Fixed Assets costing Rs. 10,000 (accumulated depreciation Rs. 5,500) were sold for Rs. 2,000 Loss arising there from was written off.

(viii) Preference shares redeemed in the year (June 2004) were out of a fresh issue of equity shares Premium paid on redemption was 10%.

[C.A. (I) Adapted]

Solution :

I SCHEDULE OF CHANGES IN WORKING CAPITAL

	31st March		Changes in Working Capital	
	2004 Rs.	2005 Rs.	Increase Rs.	Decrease Rs.
Current Assets				
Stock	95,000	1,05,000	10,000	—
Trade Debtors (90,000 – 2,500)*	87,500*	85,000	—	2,500
Bank	33,500	64,500	31,000	—
Current liabilities				
Bank Overdraft	33,000	—	33,000	—
Trade Creditors	80,000	75,000	5,000	—
			79,000	2,500
Net Increase in Working Capital				76,500
			79,000	79,000

II COMPUTATION OF WORKING CAPITAL FROM OPERATIONS

Profit and Loss A/c (Adjusted)

	Rs.		Rs.
To Depreciation (4)	15,500	By Balance b/d	1,00,000
To Loss on sale of Plant (5)	2,500	By Reserve for Replacement of Machinery	7,500
To Bonus Issue	20,000		
To Proposed dividend on Equity Shares (2)	41,000	By Revaluation Profit (Fixed Assets)	5,000
To Preference dividend	12,000	By Working Capital from operations	85,000
To Premium on Redem.. of Pref. shares	3,000		
To Balance c/d	1,03,500		
	1,97,500		1,97,500

III STATEMENT OF CHANGES IN FINANCIAL POSITION
(Working Capital Basis)

Sources	Rs.
Working Capital from operations	85,000
Issue of Equity Capital (1)	30,000
Bank Loan	60,000
Sale of Fixed Assets	2,000
	177,000
Uses	
Purchase of Fixed Assets (3)	17,500
Purchase of Investments	15,000
Redemption of Preference Share	33,000
Payment of Dividend	
Equity (18,000 + 5,000)	23,000
Preference @ 10% on Rs. 1,20,000	12,000
	1,00,500
Net Increase in Working Capital	76,500
	1,77,000

Working notes:

(1) EQUITY SHARE CAPITAL A/C

	Rs.		Rs.
To Balance c/d	1,50,000	By Balance b/d	1,00,000
		By Bonus Issue	20,000
		By Bank (Bal. figure)	30,000
	1,50,000		1,50,000

(2) PROPOSED DIVIDEND (EQUITY)

	Rs.		Rs.
To Bank A/c (18,000 + 5,000)	23,000	By Balance	18,000
To Balance c/d	36,000	By Profit & Loss A/c (Bal. figure)	41,000
	59,000		59,000

(3) FIXED ASSETS A/C

	Rs.		Rs.
To Balance b/d	3,60,000	By Plant Disposal A/c	10,000
To Trade Debtors	2,500	By Balance c/d	3,75,000
To Profit and Loss A/c (Revaluation)	5,000		
To Bank-(Addition) (Bal. figure)	17,500		
	3,85,000		3,85,000

(4) ACCUMULATED DEPRECIATION A/C

	Rs.		Rs.
To Plant disposal A/c	5,500	By Balance b/d	1,35,000
To Balance c/d	1,45,000	By Profit and Loss A/c (Bal. figure)	15,500
	1,50,500		1,50,500

(5) PLANT DISPOSAL A/C

	Rs.		Rs.
To Fixed Assets A/c	10,000	By Acc. Depreciation A/c	5,500
		By Bank	2,000
		By Profit & Loss A/c (Loss)	2,500
	10,000		10,000

Illustration (12) (Inter-Company Account and Winding up)

From the following Balance Sheet of a wholly owned subsidiary Company, prepare :

(i) A Statement of Changes in Working Capital

(ii) Statement of changes in Financial Position

Liabilities	31.3.04 Rs.	31.3.05 Rs.
Equity Share Capital	10,00,000	—
Retained Earnings	8,40,000	—
Capital Reserve	3,60,000	—
Current liabilities	2,10,000	3,00,000
Inter Company Account	1,20,000	16,50,000
	25,30,000	19,50,000
Assets		
Fixed Assets (Net)	12,50,000	12,70,000
Goodwill	7,50,000	85,000
Current Assets	4,80,000	5,65,000
Deferred Charges	50,000	30,000
	25,30,000	19,50,000

Adjustments

(1) On 31st March 2004, Rs. 7,00,000 of goodwill was charged off Rs. 3,60,000 to Capital Reserve and Rs. 3,40,000 to Retained Earnings.

(2) In the first half of the year the subsidiary company bought the assets of a business consisting of some fixed assets and goodwill and Rs. 60,000 for stock. The amount paid was Rs. 2,00,000.

(3) An old machinery was sold for Rs. 1,500 (Book value Rs. 15,000) on which 10,000 has been charged as depreciation.

(4) On 31st October 2004 the subsidiary company was wound up and made a division of the parent company. It's account continued in separate divisional ledger.

(5) A net profit of Rs. 4,50,000 after providing Rs. 95,000 for depreciation and Rs. 10,000 for amortisation of goodwill, has been credited to Intercompany Account.

(6) Deferred charges consists of un-expired insurance and prepaid current expenses.

C.A. (I) Adapted

Solution:

I SCHEDULE OF CHANGES IN WORKING CAPITAL

	As on 31st March		Changes in Working Capital	
	2004 Rs.	2005 Rs.	Increase Rs.	Decrease Rs.
Current Assets	4,80,000	5,65,000	85,000	
Current liabilities	2,10,000	3,00,000		90,000
Net Decrease in Working Capital			5,000	
			90,000	90,000

II WORKING CAPITAL FROM OPERATIONS

		Rs.
	Net Profit earned during the year	4,50,000
Add:	Depreciation	95,000
	Goodwill w/o	10,000
	Loss on Sale of machinery	3,500
	Deferred charges w/o	20,000
		5,78,500

STATEMENT OF CHANGES IN FINANCIAL POSITION (Working Capital Basis)

	Rs.
Sources	
Working Capital from operations	5,78,500
Sale of Machinery	1,500
Loan from Parent Company (1)	10,80,000
	16,60,000
Uses	
Purchase of Fixed Assets (2)	1,20,000
Purchase of Goodwill (3)	45,000
Payment of dividend (4)	5,00,000
Payment of Share Capital (5)	10,00,000
	16,65,000
Net Decrease in Working Capital	(5,000)
	16,60,000

(1) INTER COMPANY A/C

	Rs.		Rs.
To Balance c/d	16,50,000	By Balance b/d	1,20,000
		By Profit and Loss A/c	4,50,000
		By Loans from Parent Co. (Bal. figure)	10,80,000*
	16,50,000		16,50,000

(2) FIXED ASSETS A/C

	Rs.		Rs.
To Balance b/d	12,50,000	By Depreciation	95,000
To Bank (Addition) (Bal. figure)	1,20,000	By Bank (Sale)	1,500
		By Loss on Sale	3,500
		By Balance c/d	12,70,000
	13,70,000		13,70,000

(3) GOODWILL A/C

	Rs.		Rs.
To Balance b/d	7,50,000	By Retained Earnings	3,40,000
To Bank (Bal. figure)	45,000	By Capital Reserve	3,60,000
		By P and L A/c	10,000
		By Balance c/d	85,000
	7,95,000		7,95,000

(4) RETAINED EARNINGS A/C

	Rs.		Rs.
To Goodwill	3,40,000	By Balance b/d	8,40,000
To Dividend** (Bal. figure)	5,00,000		
	8,40,000		8,40,000

(5) SHARE CAPITAL A/C

	Rs.		Rs.
To Bank A/c	10,00,000	By Balance b/d	1,00,000
	10,00,000		1,00,000

* Any increase in Inter Company's A/c, after adjusting for profit or loss of the current year, represents loan from the parent company.

** The balancing figure of Retained Earnings is presumed to be utilised for paying dividend.

Illustration (13) (Defalcation by Cashier and Records destroyed)

The following is the audited Balance Sheet of a Trader as or 31st March 2004

Liabilities	Rs.	Assets	Rs.
Capital	3,24,000	Computer	80,000
Creditors for goods	60,000	Furniture	20,000
		Stock	70,000
		Debtors	1,80,000
		Bank	22,000
		Cash	12,000
	3,84,000		3,84,000

On 31st March, 2005, all the books of account were destroyed due to outbreak of fire. The cashier absconded with the available cash. However, the following information was made available by the trader:

(i) Sales are effected as to 20% cash and the balance on credit. His total sales for the current year was 20% higher than the previous year.

(ii) Terms of credit were as under

Debtors — 2 months

Creditors — 1 month

(iii) Stock level was maintained at Rs. 70,000 throughout the year.

(iv) Rate of Gross Profit of 331/3% was maintained throughout. Payments to creditors are made by cheques only. There was no cash purchase.

(v) His private records and the Bank Pass Book Kept with him disclosed the following transactions for the year:

(a) Repairs Rs. 5,000 (paid in cash)

(b) Addition to computer Rs. 1,00,000 (cheque)

(c) Travelling Expenses Rs. 24,000 (Cash)

(d) Drawings @Rs. 6,000 p.m. Rs. 72,000 (Cash)

(e) Miscellaneous business Expenses:- Rs. 3,60,000 (including o/s on 31. 3. 2005 - Rs. 10,000) out of which Rs. 70,000 paid by cheque.

(vi) Collections from debtors (including Rs. 60,000 in cash) and payment to creditors were prompt all along.

(vii) Depreciation is to be provided @10% of the closing book value.

(viii) Defalcation by cashier is to be charged to Profit and Loss A/c

Prepare : (i) Relevant Accounts

(ii) A Statement of Changes in Working Capital

(iii) and Statement of Changes in Financial Position

C.A. (F) Adapted.

Solution :

I TRADING, PROFIT & LOSS A/C
for the year ended 31st March 2005

		Rs.		Rs.
To Opening Stock		70,000	By Sales:	
To Purchases (2)		10,80,000	Cash	3,24,000
To Gross Profit b/d		5,40,000	Credit	12,96,000
			By Closing Stock	70,000
		16,90,000		16,90,000
To Repairs		5,000	By Gross Profit b/d	5,40,000
To Travelling Exp.		24,000		
To Miscellaneous Exp.	3,50,000			
Add O/s	10,000	3,60,000		
To Depreciation		18,000		
To Defalcation by Cashier		15,000		
To Net Profit		1,18,000		
		5,40,000		5,40,000

CASH BOOK (TWO COLUMN)

	Cash Rs.	Bank Rs.		Cash Rs.	Bank Rs.
To Balance b/d	12,000	22,000	By Creditors	—	10,50,000
To S. Debtors	6 0,000	12,00,000	By Repairs	5,000	—
To Sales	3,24,000	—	By Travelling Exp.	24,000	—
			By Drawings	72,000	—
			By Miscellaneous Exp.	2,80,000	70,000
			By Computer	—	1,00,000
			By Balance c/d (Bal. figure)	15,000*	2,000
	3,96,000	12,22,000		3,96,000	12,22,000

*Defalcation by cashier

II STATEMENT OF CHANGES IN FINANCIAL POSITION
(Working Capital Basis)

	As on 31st March		Changes in Working Capital	
	2004	2005	Increase	Decrease
Current Assets :	Rs.	Rs.	Rs.	Rs.
Stock	70,000	70,000	—	—
Debtors (3)	1,80,000	2,16,000	36,000	—
Bank	22,000	2,000	—	20,000
Cash	12,000	—	—	12,000
Current Liabilities:				
Creditors for goods (4)	60,000	90,000	—	30,000
Creditors for Expenses	—	10,000	—	10,000
			36,000	—
Net Decrease in Working Capital			36,000	—
			72,000	72,000

I STATEMENT OF CHANGES IN FINANCIAL POSITION
(Working Capital -Basis)

Sources		Rs.
	Working Capital from Operations (Net Profit + Depreciation)	1,36,000
Uses:		
	Purchase of Computer	1,00,000
	Drawings	72,000
		1,72,000
	Decrease in Working Capital	(36,000)
		1,36,000

Working notes :

(1) Calculation of Sales for the year ending 31st March, 2004 collection period 2 months

Debtors Turnover being 12 $\div$ 2 = 6 Times

Credit sales being Average Debtors $\times$ 6

= 1,80,000 $\times$ 6 =	10,80,000
Cash Sales being 20% of Total Sales or 25% of Credit sales =	2,70,000
Total Sales (for 2003 – 04)	13,50,000

Sales for 2004-05

Sales for the current year is 20% more as compared to last year.

= 13,50,000 $\quad 13{,}50{,}000 \times \frac{120}{100}$ 16,20,000

Cash sales = 20% of Rs. 16,20,000 = Rs. 3,24,000

Credit Sales = 80% of Rs. 16,20,000 = Rs. 12,96,000

(2) Calculation of Purchases

	Sales for the year 2004-05	1 6,20,000
Less	Gross Profit @ $33^1/_3$%	5,40,000
	Cost of Goods Sold	10,80,000

Purchases = Cost of goods Sold + Closing Stock – Opening Stock.

Since there is no change is stock level Purchases will be Rs. 10,80,000

(2) DEBTORS A/C

	Rs.		Rs.
To Balance b/d	1,80,000	By Cash (Bal. figure)	12,60,000
To Credit Sales	12,96,000	By Balance c/d	2,16,000*
	14,76,000		14,76,000

*Equal to 2 months credit sales or = $\frac{12,96,000}{6}$ 2,16,000

(4) CREDITORS' A/C

	Rs.		Rs.
To Cash (Bal. fig.)	10,50,000	By Balance b/d	60,000
To Balance c/d	90,000*	By Credit Purchases	10,80,000
	11,40,000		11,40,000

*Equal to month's credit purchase $\frac{10,80,000 \times 1}{12}$ = Rs. 90,000

Illustration (14) (Sale and Purchase of Investments)

The Balance Sheets of H Ltd. are given below for the years 2004 and 2005.

Liabilities	2004 Rs.	2005 Rs.
Share Capital	12,00,000	14,00,000
General Reserve	4,00,000	5,00,000
Profit on Sale of Investments		20,000
Profit and Loss Account	2,00,000	4,00,000
7% Debentures	6,00,000	4,00,000
Creditors for Expenses	20,000	24,000
Trade Creditors	3,20,000	5,00,000
Proposed Dividend	60,000	70,000
Provision for Taxation	1,40,000	1,50,000
	29,40,000	34,64,000

Assets

	Fixed Assets at Cost	20,00,000	24,00,000
Less	Accumulated Depreciation	4,00,000	5,00,000
		16,00,000	19,00,000
	Investments at Cost	3,60,000	3,60,000
	Stock at Cost	4,00,000	5,40,000
	Sundry Debtors (*Less* provisions Rs. 40,000 and Rs. 50,000)	4,50,000	4,90,000
	Bills Receivable	80,000	1,30,000
	Prepaid Expenses	20,000	24,000
	Miscellaneous Expenditure	30,000	20,000
		29,40,000	34,64,000

Additional Information:

(i) During the year 2005 fixed assets valued at Rs. 20,000 (accumulated depreciation Rs. 60,000) was sold for Rs. 16,000.

(ii) The proposed dividend of last year was paid during 2005.

(iii) During the year 2005, investments costing Rs. 1,60,000 were sold and later in the year investments of the same cost were purchased.

(iv) Debentures were redeemed at a premium of 10%.

(v) Liability for taxation for 2004 came to Rs. 1,10,000.

(vi) During the year 2005, bad debts written off were Rs. 30,000 against the provision amount.

Prepare

(i) A Statement of Changes in Working Capital

(ii) and Statement of Changes in Financial Position.

ICWA (F) Modified.

Solution:

I STATEMENT OF CHANGES IN WORKING CAPITAL

	As on 31st March		Changes in Working Capital	
	2004	2005	Increase	Decrease
Current Assets:	Rs.	Rs.	Rs.	Rs.
Stock	4,00,000	5,40,000	1,40,000	—
Debtors less provision	4,50,000	4,90,000	40,000	—
Bills Receivable	80,000	1,30,000	50,000	—
Prepaid Expenses	20,000	24,000	4,000	—
Current liabilities:				
Creditors for Expenses	20,000	24,000	—	4,000
Trade Creditors	3,20,000	5,00,000	—	1,80,000
			2,34,000	1,84,000
Net Increase in Working Capital	—			50,000
			2,34,000	2,34,000

II WORKING CAPITAL FROM OPERATIONS

Profit and Loss A/c (Adjusted)

	Rs.		Rs.
To Depreciation (4)	1,60,000	By Balance b/d	2,00,000
To Loss on Sale of Fixed Assets	4,000	By Working Capital from operations	6,84,000
To Premium on Redem. of debentures	20,000		
To Miscellaneous Exp. w/o	10,000		
To General Reserve	1,00,000		
To Proposed Dividend	70,000		
To Provision for Tax (6)	1,20,000		
To Balance c/d	4,00,000		
	8,84,000		8,84,000

III STATEMENT OF CHANGES IN FINANCIAL POSITION

(Working Capital basis)

	Rs.
Sources:	
Working Capital from Operations	6,84,000
Issue of Share Capital (1)	2,00,000
Sale of Investments (2)	1,80,000
Sale of Fixed Assets	16,000
	10,80,000
Uses:	
Purchase of Fixed Assets (3)	4,80,000
Purchase of Investments	1,60,000
Redemption of Debentures	2,20,000
Payment of Tax	1,10,000
Payment of Dividends	60,000
	10,30,000
Net Increase in Working Capital	50,000
	10,80,000

Working notes

(1) SHARE CAPITAL A/C

	Rs.		Rs.
To Balance c/d	14,00,000	By Balance b/d	12,00,000
		By Bank A/c (Bal. figure)	2,00,000
	14,00,000		14,00,000

(2) INVESTMENTS A/C

	Rs.		Rs.
To Balance b/d	3,60,000	By Bank	1,80,000
To Bank (Purchased)	1,60,000	By Balance c/d	3,60,000
To Profit on Sale of Investments (Capital Reserve)	20,000		
	5,40,000		5,40,000

(3) FIXED ASSETS A/C

	Rs.		Rs.
To Balance b/d	20,00,000	By Fixed Assets Disposal A/c	80,000
To Bank-Addition (Bal. figure)	4,80,000	By Balance c/d	24,00,000
	24,80,000		24,80,000

(4) ACCUMULATED DEPRECIATION A/C

	Rs.		Rs.
To F.A. Disposal A/c	60,000	By Balance b/d	4,00,000
To Balance c/d	5,00,000	By Profit & Loss A/c (Bal. figures)	1,60,000
	5,00,000		5,60,000

(5) FIXED ASSETS DISPOSAL A/C

	Rs.		Rs.
To Fixed Assets A/c	80,000	By Bank	16,000
		By Acc. Depreciation A/c	60,000
		By Profit and Loss A/c (Loss)	4,000
	80,000		80,000

(6) PROVISION FOR TAX A/C

	Rs.		Rs.
To Bank (Tax Liabilities Paid)	1,10,000	By Balance b/d	1,40,000
To Balance c/d	1,50,000	By Profit & Loss A/c (Bal. figure)	1,20,000
	2,60,000		2,60,000

Illustration (15) (Bonus shares, conversion and Reserves)

Fairdeals Ltd. presents the Balance Sheets as an 31st December 2004 and 2005

Liabilities	31.12.04	31.12.05
	Rs.	Rs.
Share Capital	20,00,000	25,00,000
Reserves and Surplus	8,00,000	8,70,000
9% Convertible Debentures	10,00,000	8,00,000
Public Deposits	3,00,000	2,50,000

	Current liabilities and Provisions	6,20,000	7,10,000
	Proposed Dividend	2,00,000	2,50,000
		49,20,000	53,80,000
Assets			
	Fixed Assets at Cost	25,00,000	30,00,000
Less	Depreciation till date	6,80,000	8,20,000
		18,20,000	21,80,000
	Trade Investments	12,50,000	13,50,000
Current Assets			
	Marketable Securities	60,000	30,000
	Inventories	4,10,000	5,20,000
	Book-Debts	5,30,000	5,05,000
	Cash and Bank Balance	1,20,000	1,40,000
	Preliminary Expenses	1,00,000	50,000
	Capital Work-in-Progress	6,30,000	6,05,000
		49,20,000	53,80,000

You are informed that during 2005:

(i) Rs. 2,00,000 of Debentures were converted in equity shares at par.

(ii) A bonus issue was made in the ratio of 1:10 out of reserves before conversion.

(iii) Rs. 1,00,000 shares were issued to the vendor of fixed assets who had supplied a machine costing Rs. 1,20,000.

(iv) A Computer costing Rs. 50,000 (book value Rs. 30,000) was disposed of for Rs. 20,000.

(v) Change in Marketable Securities represents sale of securities for Rs. 3 6,000.

You are required to prepare :

(i) A Schedule of Changes in Working Capital

(ii) A Statement of Changes in Financial Position.

ACS (F) Modified

Solution:

I SCHEDULE OF CHANGES IN WORKING CAPITAL

	As on 31st March		Changes in Working Capital	
Current Assets:	2004 Rs.	2005 Rs.	Increase Rs.	Decrease Rs.
Marketable Securities	60,000	30,000		30,000
Inventories	4,10,000	5,20,000	1,10,000	
Book-Debts	5,30,000	5,05,000		25,000
Cash and Bank balance	1,20,000	1,40,000	20,000	—
Current liabilities	6,20,000	7,10,000	—	90,000
			1,30,000	1,45,000
Net Decrease in Working Capital			15,000	—
			1,45,000	1,45,000

II WORKING CAPITAL FROM OPERATIONS

RESERVES AND SURPLUS A/C

	Rs.		Rs.
To Depreciation (3)	1,60,000	By Balance b/d	8,00,000
To Loss Sale of Machine	10,000	By Securities Premium	20,000
To Preliminary Exp.	50,000	By Working Capital from operations	7,20,000
To Bonus Issue	2,00,000		
To Proposed Dividend	2,50,000		
To Balance c/d	8,70,000		
	15,40,000		15,40,000

III STATEMENT OF CHANGES IN FINANCIAL POSITION (WORKING CAPITAL BASIS)

	Rs.
Sources	
Working Capital from Operations	7,20,000
Sale of Machinery	20,000
Financing and Investing Activities not affecting working Capital as per contra	
Issue of Shares for conversion of debentures	2,00,000
Issue of Shares for fixed Assets (at 20% Premium)	1,20,000
	10,60,000
Uses	
Purchase of Fixed Assets for Cash (4)	4,05,000
Dividends paid	2,00,000
Purchase of Trade Investment	1,00,000
Repayment of Public Deposits	50,000
Financing and Investing Activities not affecting working Capital as per contra.	
Purchase of fixed assets against shares	1,20,000
Redemption of Debentures for shares	2,00,000
	10,75,000
Net Decrease in Working Capital	(15,000)
	10,60,000

Working notes :

(1) Since Premium on issue of Shares issued against purchase of machinery has not been transferred separately to "Securities Premium" A/c it should have been transferred to Reserves and Surplus A/c, hence adjusted.

(2) SHARE CAPITAL A/C

	Rs.		Rs.
To Balance c/d	25,00,000	By Balance b/d	20,00,000
		By 9% Debentures	2,00,000
		By Fixed Assets	1,00,000
		By Bonus Issue	2,00,000
	25,00,000		25,00,000

(3) ACCUMULATED DEPRECIATION A/C

	Rs.		Rs.
To Machinery Disposal A/c	20,000	By Balance b/d	6,80,000
To Balance c/d	8,20,000	By Profit & Loss A/c (Bal. figure)	1,60,000
	8,40,000		8,40,000

(4) FIXED ASSETS A/C (AT COST INCLUDING CAPITAL WIP)

	Rs.		Rs.
To Balance b/d	31,30,000	By Machinery Disposal A/c	50,000
To Share Capital	1,00,000	By Balance c/d	
To Reserve and Surplus (Premium)	20,000	(30,00,000 + 6,05,000)	36,05,000
To Bank A/c - Purchase (Bal. Figure)	4,05,000		
	36,55,000		36,55,000

(5) MACHINERY DISPOSAL A/C

	Rs.		Rs.
To Fixed Assets A/c	50,000	By Accumulated Depreciation A/c	20,000
		By Bank	20,000
		By Reserve and Sup. (Loss)	10,000
	50,000		50,000

Illustration (16) (Redemption of Preference shares and Miscellaneous Expenditure)

Following are the Balance Sheets of V. Lal Ltd. as on 31st March, 2004 and 2005.

Liabilities	31.3.2004	31.3.2005
	Rs.	Rs.
10% Redeemable Preference Shares	5,00,000	2,50,000
Equity Share Capital	5,00,000	10,00,000
Securities Premium	50,000	25,000
Capital Redemption Reserve	—	2,50,000
General Reserve	4,00,000	2,25,000
Provision for Taxation	2,50,000	3,00,000
Current liabilities	3,00,000	1,12,500
	20,00,000	21,62,500
Assets		
Fixed Assets	6,50,000	7,87,500
Stock	4,00,000	4,75,000
Debtors	7,50,000	7,25,000
Bank Balance	1,50,000	1,25,000
Miscellaneous Expenditure	50,000	50,000
	20,00,000	21,62,500

Additional Information:

(1) The Company declared a dividend of 20% for the year ended 31st March 2004 to equity shareholders on 30. 6. 2004. Dividend on Preference Share Capital for the year ended 31. 3. 2005 was paid on 31st March, 2005.

(2) The Company issued notice to preference shareholders holding preference shares of Rs. 2,50,000 for redemption at a premium of 10% on 1. 10. 2004 and the entire proceedings were completed before 31.10.2005 in accordance with law.

(3) The Company provided depreciation at 10% on closing balance of Fixed Assets. During the year a machinery costing Rs. 1,50,000 (Book Value - Rs. 1,00,000) was sold at loss of Rs. 15,000.

(4) Miscellaneous expenditure incurred during the year ended 31.3.2005 Rs. 12,500 for share issue and other expenses.

(5) A sum of Rs. 2,00,000 has been provided for taxation for the year.

Prepare : (i) A Statement of Changes in Working Capital and (ii) Statement of changes in Financial Position.

C.A. (F) Adapted.

Solution:

I SCHEDULE OF CHANGES IN WORKING CAPITAL

	As on 31st March		Changes in Working Capital	
	2004	2005	Increase	Decrease
Current Assets:	Rs.	Rs.	Rs.	Rs.
Stock	4,00,000	4,75,000	75,000	
Debtors	7,50,000	7,25,000	—	25,000
Bank Balance	1,50,000	1,25,000	—	25,000
Current liabilities	3,00,000	1,12,500	1,87,500	
			2,62,500	50,000
Net Increase in Working Capital				2,12,500
			2,62,500	2,62,500

II CALCULATION OF WORKING CAPITAL FROM OPERATION

General Reserve A/c (Adjusted)

	Rs.		Rs.
To Depreciation	87,500	By Balance b/d	4,00,000
To Loss on Sale of fixed assets	15,000	Working Capital from operations	5,27,500
To Capital Redemptions Reserve	2,50,000		
To Dividend on: Equity Shares	1,00,000		
Preference Shares	37,500		
To Provision for Tax	2,00,000		
To Share Issue Expenses	12,500		
To Balance c/d	2,25,000		
	9,27,500		9,27,500

III STATEMENT OF CHANGES IN FINANCIAL POSITION

	Rs.
Sources:	
Working Capital from operations	5,27,500
Issue of Equity Shares	5,00,000
Sale of Fixed Assets	85,000
	11,12,500
Uses:	
Redemption of Preference Shares	2,75,000
Payment of Dividend	1,37,500
Payment of Tax	1,50,000
Purchase of Fixed Assets	3,25,000
Share Issue Expenses	12,500
	9,00,000
Net Increase in Working Capital	2,12,500
	11,12,500

(1) FIXED ASSETS A/C

	Rs.		Rs.
To Balance b/d	6,50,000	By Bank	85,000
To Bank (Purchased)	3,25,000	By Loss on Sale	15,000
		By Depreciation	87,500
		By Balance c/d	7,87,500
	9,75,000		9,75,000

(2) PROVISION FOR TAXATION A/C

	Rs.		Rs.
To Bank (B.F)	1,50,000	By Balance b/d	2,50,000
To Balance c/d	3,00,000	By Profit and Loss A/c	2,00,000
	4,50,000		4,50,000

	Rs.
(3) Preference Dividend (for the year ending 31st March, 2005)	
On Rs. 5,00,000 @ 10% for 6 months =	25,000
On Rs. 2,50,000 @ 10% for 6 months =	12,500
	37,500
(4) Equity Dividend (for the year ending 31. 3. 2004)	
On 5,00,000 @ 20%	1,00,000

Illustration (17) (Current Assets and Current liabilities not given)

From the following information of X Ltd. at the beginning and end of the year 2004 prepare.

(i) A Statement of changes in Working Capital

(ii) A Statement of Changes in Financial Position.

	1st Jan, 04	31st Dec.04
	Rs.	Rs.
Fixed Assets (Net)	2,54,000	5,70,000
Investments	5,28,000	11,60,000
6% Debentures	10,00,000	2,80,000
Equity Share Capital	16,00,000	16,00,000
Retained Earnings	9,52,000	16,42,000

Additional Information:

(i) Dividend paid during the year Rs. 1,50,000 (ii) A gain on sale of plant of Rs. 52,000 has been included in the net income. The fixed assets (gross) increased by Rs. 3,72,000 even though plant costing Rs. 1,16,000 with a net book value of Rs. 76,000 was sold.

Solution:

In order to calculate Working Capital the information may be put in a Balance Sheet form.

Assets	1st Jan 04	31st Dec.,04
Fixed Assets	2,54,000	5,70,000
Investments	5,28,000	11,60,000
	7,82,000	17,30,000
Liabilities		
Share Capital	16,00,000	16,00,000
Retained Earnings	9,52,000	16,42,000
6% Debentures	10,00,000	2,80,000
	35,52,000	35,22,000

In the absence of Current assets and current liabilities, the excess of Capital and long term liabilities over fixed assets and investments will represent Working Capital. Hence Working Capital as on 1st January, 2004 = (Rs. 35,52,000 – 7,82,000 = 27,70,000

and as on 31st December, 2004 (35,22,000 – 17,30,000) = 17,92,000

Thus Decrease in Working Capital = 9,78,000

III WORKING CAPITAL FROM OPERATION
RETAINED EARNINGS A/C (ADJUSTED)

	Rs.		Rs.
To Dividends	1,50,000	By Balance b/d	9,52,000
To Balance c/d	16,42,000	By Profit on sale of plant	52,000
		By Appreciation in Fixed Assets	20,000
		By Working Capital from operations	7,68,000
	17,92,000		17,92,000

III STATEMENT OF CHANGES IN FINANCIAL POSITION (SCFP)

Sources:	Rs.
Working Capital from Operations	7,68,000
Sale of Plant	1,28,000
	8,96,000

Uses:		Rs.
	Purchase of Fixed Assets	3,72,000
	Purchase of Investments	6,32,000
	Redemption of Debentures	7,20,000
	Payment of Dividend	1,50,000
		18,74,000
Less	Decrease in Working Capital	(9,78,000)
		8,96,000

Working notes:

(1) FIXED ASSETS A/C

	Rs.		Rs.
To Balance b/d	2,54,000	By Bank (Sale of Plant)	1,28,000
To Profit Sale of Plant	52,000	By Balance c/d	5,70,000
To Bank (Addition)	3,72,000		
To Appreciation (Bal. figure)	20,000		
	6,98,000		6,98,000

(2) INVESTMENTS A/C

	Rs.		Rs.
To Balance b/d	5,28,000	By Balance c/d	11,60,000
To Bank (Addition)	6,32,000		
	11,60,000		11,60,000

Illustration (18) (Interim and Final dividend)

The Balance Sheets of Shalinee Ltd. as on 31st March 2004 and 2005 were as under :

Liabilities		31.03.05	31.03.04
		Rs.	Rs.
	Equity Share Capital (Shares of Rs. 10 each)	8,00,000	7,20,000
	General Reserve	1,20,000	2,20,000
	Profit and Loss A/c	1,06,900	40,900
	S. Creditors	3,50,700	3,67,300
	Proposed Dividend	30,000	57,600
	Provision for Taxation	64,000	—
		14,71,600	14,05,800
Assets:			
	Fixed Assets	10,40,000	9,60,000
Less	Provision for Depreciation	2,80,000	2,16,000
		7,60,000	7,44,000
	Investments at Cost	1,00,000	2,00,000
	Stock	1,81,000	1,11,200

S. Debtors	3,35,600	2,36,600
Cash and Balance at Bank	95,000	99,600
Preliminary Expenses	—	14,400
	14,71,600	14,05,800

The net profit for the year 2004-05 (after providing depreciation Rs. 80,000 and writing off preliminary expenses Rs. 14,400 and making a provision for taxation Rs. 64,000) amounted to Rs. 1,16,000. During the year the company sold machinery costing Rs. 18,000 for Rs. 6,000. The accumulated depreciation on that machinery was Rs. 16,000.

A portion of investments found worthless was written off against General Reserve during the year. No other transaction has been effected in the Investments Account.

Company paid Rs. 20,000 as interim dividend and recommended a final dividend of Rs. 30,000 for the year 2004-05.

Prepare (i) A Statement of Changes in Working Capital and (ii) Statement of Changes in Financial Position.

[C.A. (F) Adapted]

Solution:

I SCHEDULE OF CHANGES IN WORKING CAPITAL

	As on 31st March		Changes in Working Capital	
	2004	2005	Increase	Decrease
Current Assets:	Rs.	Rs.	Rs.	Rs.
Stock	1,11,200	1,81,000	69,800	
S. Debtors	2,36,600	3,35,600	99,000	
Cash Bank Balance	99,600	95,000		4,600
Current liabilities				
S. Creditors	3,67,300	3,50,700	16,600	—
Net Increase in Working Capital			—	1,80,800
			1,85,400	1,85,400

II STATEMENT OF CHANGES IN FINANCIAL POSITION

	Rs.
Sources:	
Working Capital from operations (1)	2,70,400
Sale of Fixed Assets	6,000
Issue of Shares	80,000
	3,56,400
Uses:	
Acquisition of Fixed Assets (2)	98,000
Payment of dividend (3) (Rs. 57,600 + 20,000)	77,600
	1,75,600
Net Increase in Working Capital	1,80,800
	3,56,400

Working notes :

(1) Working Capital from operation

PROFIT & LOSS A/C (ADJUSTED)

	Rs.		Rs.
To Depreciation	80,000	By Balance b/d	40,900
To Dividend:		By Profit on sale of Machinery	4,000
Interim	20,000	By Working Capital from operations	2,70,400
Final (Proposed)	30,000		
To Preliminary Expenses	14,400		
To Provision for Taxation	64,000		
To Balance c/d	1,06,900		
	3,15,300		3,15,300

(2) FIXED ASSETS A/C (AT COST)

	Rs.		Rs.
To Balance b/d	9,60,000	By Machinery Disposal A/c	18,000
To Bank (B.F.) (Acquired)	98,000	By Balance c/d	10,40,000
	10,58,000		10,58,000

PROVISION FOR DEPRECIATION A/C

	Rs.		Rs.
To Machinery Disposal A/c	16,000	By Balance b/d	2,16,000
To Balance c/d	2,80,000	By Profit and Loss A/c	80,000
	2,96,000		2,96,000

MACHINERY DISPOSAL A/C

	Rs.		Rs.
To Fixed Assets A/c	18,000	By Provision for Depreciation A/c	16,000
To Profit on Sale (B.F.)	4,000	By Bank	6,000
	22,000		22,000

(3) PROPOSED DIVIDEND A/C

	Rs.		Rs.
To Bank* (57,600 + 20,000)	77,600	By Balance b/d	57,600
To Balance c/d	30,000	By Profit and Loss A/c	50,000
	1,07,600		1,07,600

* Company has to pay last year's final dividend besides current year's interim dividend.

2. STATEMENT OF CHANGES IN FINANCIAL POSITION

(Cash Basis) as per AS-3 (Revised)

Funds Flow Statement (Statement of Changes in Financial Position—on Working Capital basis) makes analysis of inflow and outflow of funds. As explained earlier the term "funds" is used to refer Working Capital. However, the term "Funds" may also be used to refer **"Cash and cash equivalents".** In view of certain limitations and lack of Standard format of preparation and presentation of Funds Flow Statement, the Institute of Chartered Accountants of India issued AS-3 (Revised) in March 1997.

AS-3 (Revised) aims to provide a "standard format of information" about the cash flow of an enterprise for the users of financial statements who assess the ability of an enterprise to generate cash and cash equivalents and the application there of.

As per AS-3 (Revised) the objective of cash flow statement is to provide information about the cash flows of an enterprise which is useful in providing the users of financial statements with a basis to assess the ability of an enterprise to generate cash and cash equivalents to utilise those cash flows. The economic decisions which are taken by users require an evaluation of ability of an enterprise to generate cash and cash equivalents and the timing and certainty of their generation. The Statement deals with the provisions of information about the historical changes in cash and cash- equivalents. It classifies flow of cash into operating, investing and financing activities".

Uses of Cash Flow Statement

1. A managerial tool : For an efficient cash management, cash flow statement helps to prepare and formulate sound financial policies. It also provides necessary input to evaluate current cash position and estimate future flow of cash. It is an effective tool in the hands of management to be used for future planning of cash requirement and cash generation. It helps in taking short term and long-term investment decisions.

2. Basis of decisions for the Bank and Financial Institutions : Cash flow Statement helps to raise loan from Banks and other Financial Institutions who easily determine the repaying capacity of the enterprise through its cash flow statement. It suggests the upper limit for making advance after judging company's credit worthiness. Company's expansion and diversification programme can easily be financed and materialised with certainty as the lenders can satisfy themselves after careful study of cash flow statement.

3. Investors' guide : The investment decisions of the various types of investors (institutional or individual) are guided by the economic performance of the enterprise. The rationality of the investment decisions can be judged by operating, investing and financing activities as disclosed in the cash flow statement. Thus the information contained in the cash flow statement may substantiate viability of present project in which investments are to be made. The cash flow statement helps to understand liquidity and solvency of the enterprise concerned.

4. Other uses : Cash Flow Statement is a test of total financial position. It arranges the information in it's historical retrospect. The enterprise can have a rational dividend policy based on the cash flow from various activities. The weakness of a policy or it's strong aspects an be gauged by the analysis of cash flow statement. An enterprise may decide—

(i) Timing and amount of issue of shares, debentures or raising of loan and it's repayment/ redemption.

(ii) Implementing an expansion or diversification programme in view of availability of cash resources and.

(iii) Review it's wage policy, credit policy, sales promotion schemes, production policy and purchase policy etc. which involve flow of cash.

LIMITATIONS OF CASH FLOW STATEMENT

(1) It shows the past record only :

Cash flow statement is purely historical in nature. It rearranges the information as shown in the Income Statement and Balance Sheet. However, a projected cash flow can be more useful which can be prepared with the help of existing cash flow.

(2) Non-cash transactions are ignored : The cash flow statement recognises cash basis of accounting and ignores prepaid and accured items. Hence it sounds unreasonable in the light of accrual concept of income.

(3) Gap between inflow and net income : When fixed assets are acquired for cash it results outflow of cash in the year of purchase, but depreciation, which is a charge against the operating income is recorded gradually in future. This results in big gap between inflow of cash and net income.

(4) Neither a substitute of Income Statement nor a substitute of Balance Sheet : Cash Flow statement can not be a substitute of Profit and Loss Account or a substitute of Balance Sheet because it shows only flow of cash as against the net income and financial position of the enterprise.

In spite of these limitations cash flow statement is an important tool of financial planning and control which an be used to evaluate an enterprise's performance for the purpose of taking operating financing and investing decisions.

AS-3 (Revised) requires that an enterprise should prepare a cash flow statement for each accounting period along with the financial statements.

DISTINCTION BETWEEN 'FUNDS FLOW STATEMENT' AND 'CASH FLOW' STATEMENT

	FFS	CFS
(1) Basis of Accounting	FFS recognises the accrual basis of accounting and shows the causes of changes in Working Capital.	CFS recognises the cash basis of accounting and shows the causes of changes in cash.
(2) Meaning	It is based on wider concept of Working Capital	It is based on narrow concept of cash and cash equivalents.
(3) Format	It does not have any specific or standard format of preparation and presentation of inflow or outflow of funds.	AS-3 provides an standard format and studies the flow of cash under operating, financing and investing activities.
(4) Usefulness	It is useful for long term financial analysis.	It is useful for short term financial planning.
(5) Scope	Funds from operations are calculated without considering current assets and current liabilities.	Cash from operation is computed after accounting for current assets and current liabilities.

DEFINITIONS OF CERTAIN TERMS AS PER AS-3 (REVISED) AND SCFP

(i) **Cash** comprises cash in hand and demand deposits with banks.

(ii) **Cash Equivalents:** These are short term, highly liquid investments that are readily convertible into known amount of cash and which are not subject to any significant risks of changes in value. An investment qualifies as "Cash equivalent" only when it has a very short period of maturity - say - three months or less from the date of acquisition (issue) such as:

- Treasury bills
- Commercial paper
- Money market funds
- Preference shares redeemable within three months.

(iii) **Cash flows :** It refers to inflow and outflow of cash and cash equivalents. An inflow increases the total cash and cash equivalents where as an out flow decreases cash and cash equivalents. An **inflow** is treated as "source" while a outflow is termed as "application" of cash. The excess of sources over uses represents "net cash inflow" while excess of application (uses) over sources refers to net cash outflow.

> **Please remember—**
>
> **Cash flow does not include :**
>
> Movement between items which constitute cash or cash equivalents because such movements are part of cash management which includes the investment of excess cash in cash equivalents.

Classification of activities resulting in cash flows as per AS-3 (Revised) According to AS-3 (Revised), the activities which result in inflow or outflow of cash are classified into:

(i) Operating Activities
(ii) Investing Activities
(iii) Financing Activities

Operating Activities

These are the principal revenue producing activities of the enterprise Cash flows from operating activities generally result from transactions and events which enter into the determination of net profit or loss, such as :

(i) Cash received from sale of goods and rendering of services.
(ii) Cash received from royalties, fees, commission and other revenue.
(iii) Cash paid to supplier for goods and services.
(iv) Payment of operating expenses such as wages, salaries, rent, electricity, printing and stationary etc.
(v) Receipts and payment of an insurance premium/claims by an Insurance company.
(vi) Payments or refunds of income taxes.

> **Note :** In fact operating cash flows arise from activities relating to business in which the enterprise deals in *e.g.* Interest and dividend received by financial institutions will be treated as operating cash flow. Similarly, if a financial institution deals in securities, cash flow from sale and purchase of securities will be treated as cash flow from operating activities.

Investing Activities

Investing activities refer to acquisition and disposal of long-term assets and other investments not included in cash equivalents. These include transactions involving sale and purchase of long term assets like land and building, plant and Machinery, furniture and fictures etc. which are not held for resale. Cash flows from investing activities are :

(i) Cash payments to acquire fixed assets

(ii) Cash receipts from disposal of fixed assets including intangibles

(iii) Sale and purchase of shares, debentures or bonds held as investments.

(iv) Cash advances and loans made to third parties by a trading or manufacturing enterprise (other than the Financial Enterprise)

(v) Cash receipts from the repayment of loans and advances by an enterprise other than the financial enterprise.

(vi) Cash receipts relating to future contracts forward contracts, option contracts and swap contracts (excluding contracts held for trading purposes)

(vii) Cash payments relating to future contracts, forward contracts, option contracts and swap contracts (excluding contracts held for trading purposes).

Financing Activities

These activities include those activities which affect the long term funds. In other words financing activities result in changes in the size and composition of Capital (including preference) and borrowings of an enterprise. Cash flow from such activities include :

(i) Cash proceeds from issue of shares and other securities.

(ii) Cash proceeds from issuing debentures, loans bonds, notes or other borrowings

(iii) Cash repayments of amount borrowed.

(iv) Cash payment for redemption of bonds, debentures or preference shares.

(v) Cash payment against buy back of shares.

(vi) Interest paid by a company other than a financial institutions.

(vii) Dividend paid to shareholders.

(viii) Tax on dividend

It is to be noted that "Dividend Paid" will always be classified as "Financing Activity" whether it is paid by a Financial institution or by a non-financial enterprise.

Note : It is to noted that interest and dividend received by a financial institution will be treated as cash flow from "operating activities" and similarly interest paid by such financial institution will be covered under operating activities."

Consider the following items—

1. Cash sales and other selling expenses
2. Cash purchases and other factory/office expenses.
3. Cash received from debtors/cash paid to creditors
4. Cash paid to employee as :
   - Salaries, bonus, commission etc.
   - Provident Fund

- Gratuity

5. Cash receipts and payments for:
   - Future Trading contract
   - Forward trading contract
   - Option and swap trading contract
   - Currency forward contract (for import of goods)
6. Interest and dividends received by financial institutions
7. Interest paid by financial institutions
8. Income Tax on operating income
9. Acquisition of fixed tangible and intangible assets
10. Loans and advances made and collected and Investment in equity or debt securities by an enterprise other than the financial institutions.
11. Interest and dividend received by companies other than the financial institutions.
12. Acquisition/redemption of shares or debentures in joint ventures, associates or subsidiaries
13. Inter Corporate Loans and repayment there of
14. Issue of shares or other securities for cash
15. Buy-back of shares for cash
16. Redemption of preference shares and debentures.
17. Interest paid by companies by other than the financial institutions.
18. Dividend paid to shareholders including Tax there on.
19. Purchase of fixed assets on hire-purchase or on instalment.

Ans. : Operating Activities: 1 to 8
Investing Activities: 9 to 13
Financing Activities: 14 to 18

Item 19 includes part of cash price and part of interest in instalments. Hence cash price element is treated as cash flow from investing activities while interest element" as financing activities.

PREPARATION OF CASH FLOW STATEMENT

The following steps are required :

(I) Computation of cash flow from operating activities.
(II) Calculation of cash flow from investing activities
(III) Determination of cash flow from financing activities.
(IV) Reporting of investing and financing activities not affecting cash flow.
(V) Adjusting for the net increase or decrease made in cash and cash equivalents.

I CALCULATION OF CASH FLOW FROM "OPERATING ACTIVITIES"

As per AS-3 (Revised) there are two methods of calculating the cash-flow from operating activities.

(A) Direct Method
(B) Indirect Method

Under Direct Method the cash flow from operating activities is calculated by accounting for gross **cash** (operating) **receipts** and gross **cash** (operating) **expenses** only.

It is to be noted that :

(i) Non-cash, charges are not accounted for.

(ii) Outstanding for the last year's are added and outstanding for the current year's are substracted to find out actual inflow or out flow from each individual item of receipt and payment.

(iii) No adjustment is made for :

- Loss or gain on sale of fixed assets and investments
- Non-operating items as rent received, dividend interest received or paid.

(iv) Prepaid for the current year's are added while that of last year's are substracted.

(v) All appropriations like transfer to General Reserve, Sinking Fund, Capital Redemption Reserve, dividends etc. are totally ignored.

(vi) While calculating the cash received from debtors and cash paid to creditors, it is advisable to prepare Debtors A/c and S. Creditors A/c.

(vii) In case some of the items are represented by outstandings and prepaids simultaneously at the beginning and at the end of an accounting year then actual cash flow should be worked out by preparing relevant items account.

Illustration (1)

From the following Profit and Loss Account of ABC Ltd. for the year ended 31st March 2004, calculate cash generated from "operating activities" by "Direct Method".

PROFIT AND LOSS ACCOUNT
For the year ended 31st March, 2004

		Rs.		Rs.
To Opening Stock		1,60,000	By Sale (cash)	42,50,000
To Purchases (Cash)		31,00,000	By Commission Accrued	40,000
To Wages	4,40,000		By Dividend Received	60,000
Add Outstanding	60,000	5,00,000	By Profit on sale of plant	2,40,000
To Salaries	2,20,000		(Sale Proceeds-Book value)	
Add o/s	20,000		(22,40,000 – 20,00,000)	
	2,40,000		By Closing Stock	2,20,000
Less prepaid	10,000	2,30,000		
To Office Expenses		80,000		
To Selling Expenses		1,20,000		
To Depreciations		1,10,000		
To Income Tax Paid		20,000		
To Goodwill w/o		44,000		
To Preliminary Exp. w/o		20,000		
To Net Profit		4,26,000		
		48,10,000		48,10,000

Solution:

CASH FLOW FROM OPERATIONS

			Rs.
(A)	Operating cash Receipts:		
	Cash Sales		42,50,000
Less			
(B)	Operating Cash Payments:		
	Purchases	31,00,000	
	wages	4,40,000	
	Salaries	2,20,000	
	Office Expenses	80,000	
	Selling Expenses	1,20,000	39,60,000
	Cash flow from operations before tax		2,90,000
Less	Income Tax paid		20,000
	Net cash inflow from operations		2,70,000

Notes. (1) Non cash charges such as depreciation, Goodwill w/o and Preliminary Expenses w/o have been ignored as these do not involve any cash flow.

(2) Dividend received and profit on sale of plant are to be treated under cash flow from 'Investing Activities'.

(3) Commission Accured does not involve any cash inflow, hence ignored.

(4) Changes in the current assets and current liabilities are ignored.

Illustration (2) (Cash flow from operations - Missing figures)

From the following Profit and Loss A/c and additional information of M/s. Shalini Enterprises, compute cash flow from operations.

PROFIT AND LOSS ACCOUNT
for the year ended 31st March, 2004

		Rs.		Rs.
To Opening Stock		80,000	By Sales:	
To Purchases			Cash	3,00,000
Cash	1,00,000		Credit	5,00,000
Credit	3,00,000	4,00,000	By Closing Stock	1,04,000
To Wages		24,000	By Commission	56,000
To Office Expenses		88,000	By Royalties	40,000
To Selling Expenses		48,000	By Discount Received	20,000
To Bad debts		8,000		
To Discount Allowed		16,000		
To Depreciation		60,000		
To Provision for Tax		1,20,000		
To Net Profit		1,76,000		
		10,20,000		10,20,000

Additional Information

	March 31 2003	March 31 2004
Debtors	60,000	72,000
Creditors	56,000	40,000
O/s Selling Expenses	12,000	16,000
Prepaid office Expenses	8,000	12,000
Accured Royalties	48,000	44,000
Advance Commission	36,000	32,000
Provision for Tax	1,60,000	2,40,000

Solution :

CASH FLOW FROM OPERATIONS:

			Rs.
(A)	Receipts from Operations :		
	Cash Sales		3,00,000
	Cash received from Debtors		4,64,000
	Cash from Royalties		44,000
	Cash from Commission		52,000
			8,60,000
Less (B)	Operating Cash Payments:		
	Cash Purchase	1,00,000	
	Cash paid to creditors	2,96,000	
	Cash Selling Expenses	44,000	
	Cash Office Expenses	1,16,000	5,56,000
	Cash inflow from operations before tax		3,04,000
Less	Income Tax paid (on operating Incomes)		40,000
	Net Cash flow from operations		2,64,000

Note : It is to be noted that under Direct Method the current assets/current liabilities are automatically adjusted while calculating actual cash paid or actual cash received hence such items do not require any adjustment.

II CALCULATION OF CASH FLOW FROM INVESTING ACTIVITIES

Cash flow from Investing Activities is worked out as under "Direct and Indirect Method".

		Rs.
(+)	Sale of Fixed Assets for cash	- --
(+)	Sale of Investments for Cash	- - -
(+)	Cash Dividend/Interest received in cash	- - -
(+)	Loans and Advances (in case of financial enterprise)	- - -
(–)	Purchase of Fixed Assets/Goodwill for cash	(--)
(–)	Purchase of Investments for cash	(--)
Net Cash flow from Investing Activities		***

III CALCULATION OF CASH FLOW FROM FINANCING ACTIVITIES

(+)	Issue of Shares and Debentures for cash	---
(+)	Long Term borrowings	---
(–)	Interest/Dividend paid	(- -)
(–)	Redemption of Shares/Debentures	(- -)
(–)	Buy back of shares	(- -)
(–)	Repayment of Loans/Borrowings	(- -)
Net cash flow from Financing Activities		***

(A) DIRECT METHOD

Statement of Changes in Financial Position (SCFP)
(Cash Flow Statement - A Format as per AS - 3)

		Rs.	Rs.
1.	Cash Flow from Operating Activities		
(a)	Operating Cash Receipts:		
	Cash Sales	***	
	Cash Received from Debtors	***	
	Commission Received	***	
	Royalties Received	***	
		***	
(b)	Operating Cash Payments:		
	Cash purchases	***	
	Cash paid to creditors	***	
	Cash Expenses (Manufacturing)	***	
	Office, Selling and distribution Exp.)	***	
	Cash flow from operating Activities (a – b)	***	
(–)	Income Tax Paid (Net of Tax Refund)	***	
	Cash flow before Extraordinary items	***	
(+/–)	Extraordinary Item	***	
	Net Cash Flow from Operation		***
2.	Cash Flow from Investing Activities*		***
3.	Cash Flow from Financing Activities*		***
4.	Net Increase/Decrease in Cash and Cash Equivalents		***
Add	Cash and Cash Equivalent at the beginning		***
	Cash and Cash Equivalents at the end		***

*As explained earlier

(B) INDIRECT METHOD

Statement of changes in Financial Position (SCEP)

(Cash Flow Statement - A Format as per AS - 3)(Revised)

	Rs.	Rs.
1. Cash Flow From Operating Activities		
Net Profit before Tax and Extra-Ordinary items		***
Adjustments for Non-cash and Non-operating items		
Add: Depreciation	+	
Intangibles w/o (Goodwill, Patents etc.)	+	
Fictitious Assets w/o (Preliminary Exp etc.)	+	
Loss on sale of fixed assets	+	
Interest on Loans/Debentures*	+	***
(To be shown under Financing Activities)		***
Less Profit on sale of Fixed Assets	(–)	
Non-operating Incomes**	(–)	
(**Dividend, Rent, Interest etc. to be shown under Investing activities)	(–)	***
Operating Profit before Working Capital changes		
Add decrease in Current Assets and	+	
Increase in Current liabilities	+	
Less Increase in Current Assets and	(–)	***
Decrease in Current liabilities	(–)	***
Cash flow from operations		***
Less Income Tax paid (Net of tax refund)		(–)
Cash Flow before Extraordinary Items		***
Extra Ordinary Items		(+/–)
(Claims for loss of stock/damages paid)		
Net Cash Flow from operating Activities		***
2. Cash Flow from Investing Activities:		
(a) Sale of Fixed Asset for cash	+	
Sale of Investments for cash	+	
Sale of Intangible assets for cash	+	
Dividend, Interest and Rent Received	+	
	***	
(b) Acquisition of Fixed Assets	(–)	
Purchase of Investments	(–)	
Purchase of Intangibles (Goodwill etc.)	(–)	
Cash flow from Investing Activities before		
Extraordinary items (a – b)	***	
(–/+) Adjustment for Extraordinary items	(+/–)	
(Claims for loss of Property etc.)		
Net Cash Flow from Investing Activities		***

Contd.

	Rs.	Rs.
3. Cash Flow from Financing Activities		
(a) Issue of shares debentures for cash	+	
Long Term borrowings	+	
(b) Interest/Dividend Paid	(–)	
Redemption of Shares/Debentures	(–)	
Repayment of Loan/Overdraft	(–)	
Cash flow from Financing Activities before Extraordinary item (a – b)	***	
(+/–) Extra -ordinary items	(+/–)	
Net Cash flow from Financing Activities		***
Net Increase/Decrease in cash and Cash Equivalents (1 + 2 + 3)		(+/–)
Cash & Cash Equivalent in the beginning		***
Cash and Cash Equivalent at the end		***

SPECIAL TREATMENT FOR CERTAIN ITEMS
"A Clarification"

1. Extra-Ordinary Items:

The Cash flow associated with extraordinary items should be classified as arising from operating, investing or financing activities. These are :

Claim for

1. Loss of Stock	—	Under operating activity
2. Claims for loss of Assets	—	Under Investing Activity
3. Bad debts Recovered	—	Under Operating Activity
4. Damages paid/Received for breach for contract	—	Under Operating Activity
5. Winning from lotteries	—	Under Investing Activity
6. Cost of Legal action to protect property title	—	Under Investing Activity

2. Provision for Taxation and Income Tax Paid

Provision for Taxation for the current year should be treated as non- cash charges under operating activity while tax paid should be shown as operating cash out flow after adjusting for tax refund. However, **Capital gain tax** should be classified as investing activity, and the **corporate dividend tax** should be recorded as part of **financing activity.**

3. Interest and Dividends

Cash flows from interest and dividends received and paid should be disclosed separately and classified on the basis of nature of the enterprise as shown below.

Items	In case of	
	Financial Enterprise	**Non-financial Enterprise**
Interest Paid	Operating	Financing
Dividend Paid	Financing	Financing
Interest Received	Operating	Investing
Dividend Received	Operating	Investing
Overdraft	Operating	Financing

4. Foreign Currency Cash Flows

Transactions in a foreign currency should be in reporting currency after converting these flows by applying the exchange rate between foreign currency and reporting currency on the date of cash flow.

However, unrealised gains/losses arising from change in exchange rate do not involve any cash flow and thus not reported in Cash flow statement.

5. Non-Cash Transactions

Investing and financing transactions which do not require use of cash or cash equivalents are not shown in the cash flow statement. Such transactions are-

(i) Issue of shares or debentures for a consideration other than cash *i.e.* against building, machinery

(ii) Conversion of Debentures into shares

(iii) Purchase of business by issue of shares/debentures.

However, AS-3 (Revised) recommends that such transactions may be disclosed under foot note to cash flow statement.

6. Enterprises dealing in Securities

The cash flows arising from sale and purchase of securities including interest and dividend received on such securities are classified as cash flow from operating activities.

> **Note:** Cash flow from operating activities may be calculated either by "Direct Method" or "Indirect Method" However, SEBI has provided that listed companies should follow the "Indirect Method." only.

7. Investments in Subsidiaries, Associates and joint ventures

Acquiring interest in any subsidiary, associates or in any joint venture is treated as "Investing Activity". Similarly sale or disposal of such interest and receipt of interest or dividends on such investments is treated as "Investing activity".

> It should be noted that only such transactions shall be reported which result Cash flow.

"GRADED ILLUSTRATIONS"

Illustration (1) (Cash flow from operation-Indirect Method

From the following, calculate cash from operation by Indirect Method.

PROFIT AND LOSS ACCOUNT
For the year ended 31st March, 2004

		Rs.		Rs.
To Opening Stock		2,00,000	By Sales	45,00,000
To Purchases		36,40,000	By Closing Stock	2,40,000
To Wages	2,25,000			
+ Outstanding	25,000	2,50,000		
To Manufacturing Expenses		75,000		
To Gross Profit c/d		5,75,000		
		47,40,000		47,40,000
To Salaries	1,37,500		By Gross Profit b/c	5,75,000
Add Outstanding	62,500	2,00,000	By Rent Received	37,500
To Insurance	30,000		By Commission Accured	17,500
Less Prepaid	7,500	22,500	By Net Loss	55,000
To Office Expenses		1,17,500		
To Selling Expenses		1,45,000		
To Depreciation		1,25,000		
To Share Issue Expenses w/o		75,000		
		6,85,000		6,85,000

Solution:

CALCULATION OF CASH FROM OPERATING ACTIVITIES
"Indirect Method"

			Rs.
	Net Loss as per Profit and Loss A/c (before tax and Extraordinary item)		(55,000)
	Adjustments for Non cash charges and Non-operating items.		
Add	Depreciation	1,25,000	
Add	Share Issue Expenses w/o	75,000	2,00,000
			1,45,000
Less	Rent Received (Non-operating)		(37,500)
	Operating profit before Working Capital Changes		1,07,500
Adjustment for current assets/liabilities:			
Add	Increase in Current liabilities		
	Wages O/s	25,000	
	Salaries	62,500	87,500
			1,95,000

	Balanced b/d		1,95,000
Less	Increase in Current Assets		
	Stock	40,000	
	Prepaid Insurance	7,500	
	Accrued Commission	17,500	(65,000)
Net Cash from operating Activities			1,30,000

Illustration (2) (Cash from operation and Extra ordinary Activities)

From the following information calculate cash from operations.

PROFIT AND LOSS ACCOUNT
for the year ended 31st March 2005

	Rs.		Rs.
To Opening Stock	1,50,000	By Sales	32,75,000
To Purchases	14,50,000	By Closing Stock	3,25,000
To Wages	70,000		
To Gross Profit c/d	19,30,000		
	36,00,000		36,00,000
To Operating Expenses	11,10,000	By Gross Profit b/d	19,30,000
To Interest on debentures	18,000	By Interest on Investments	15,000
To Depreciation	1,20,000	By Dividend Received	18,000
To Loss on Sale of Plant	40,000	By Profit on Sale of Land	20,000
To Discount on Issue of shares	10,000	By Rent Received	12,000
To Goodwill w/o	15,000	By Refunds of Tax	8,000
To Provision for Tax	30,000	By Insurance claims for Loss of Stock	1,25,000
To General Reserve	25,000		
To Proposed Dividend	1,80,000		
To Interim Dividend	70,000		
To Net Profit	5,10,000		
	21,28,000		21,28,000

Additional Information:

	31.03.04 Rs.	31. 03. 05 Rs.
Stock	1,40,000	1,00,000
Debtors	25,000	1,00,000
Creditors	15,000	50,000
Provision for Tax	50,000	60,000
Prepaid Expenses	18,000	20,000
Outstanding Salaries	20,000	25,000
Accrued Commission	15,000	30,000

Solution :

CASH FLOW FROM OPERATING ACTIVITIES

		Rs.	Rs.
	Net Profit before Tax and Extraordinary items (1)		6,82,000
	Adjustment for: Non Cash Charges and Non-operating items		
Add:	Depreciation	1,20,000	
	Goodwill	15,000	
	Discount on issue of shares	10,000	
	Loss on sale of plant	40,000	
	Interest on Debentures (2)	18,000	2,03,000
			8,85,000
Less	Profit on Sale of Land (3)	20,000	
	Interest Received (3)	15,000	
	Dividend Received (3)	18,000	(53,000)
	Operating profit before working Capital Changes		8,32,000
Adjustment for Working Capital :			
Add	Decrease in Current Assets and Increase in current liabilities:		
	Stock	40,000	
	Debtors	35,000	
	O/s Salaries	5,000	80,000
			9,12,000
Less	Increase in current assets and decrease in current liabilities:		
	Debtors	75,000	
	Accrued Commission	15,000	
	Prepaid Expenses	2,000	(92,000)
			8,20,000
Less	Tax Paid		(12,000)
	Cash flow before Extraordinary items		8,08,000
Add	Cash from Extra ordinary items (Insurance claims for loss of Stock (4))		1,25,000
Net	Cash Flow from Operations		9,33,000

Working notes

			Rs.
(1)	Net Profit as per P and L A/c		5,10,000
Add	Tax and Appropriations:		
	Provision for Tax	30,000	
	Proposed Dividend	1,80,000	
	Interim Dividend	70,000	
	General Reserve	25,000	3,05,000
			8,15,000
Less	Tax Refund and Extra Ordinary Receipts (8,000 + 1,25,000)		1,33,000
			6,82,000

(2) Interest on Debentures to be adjusted against Financing Activities.

(3) Interest Received, Dividend Received, Profit on sale of Fixed Assets are covered by Investing Activities.

(4) Insurance claims for loss of Stock is treated under Operating Activities while loss of assets under "Investing Activities".

Illustration (3) (Direct and Indirect Methods)

From the following particulars, prepare Cash Flow Statement for the year ended 31st March, 2005 using.

(a) Direct Method

(b) Indirect Method

(a) Income Statement of M/s Ali Pvt. Ltd.
For the year ended 31st March 2005

			Rs.
	Turnover		12,80,000
Less	Cost of Goods Sold		8,00,000
Add	Other Receipts		4,80,000
	Insurance Claims for loss of Stock due to fire		20,000
			5,00,000
Less	Operating Expenses	3,16,000	
	Interest on Debentures	6,000	
	Depreciation	84,000	
	Discount on Debentures w/o	400	4,06,400
	Profit before Tax		93,600
Less	Provision for Tax		36,800
	Profit after Tax		56,800

(b) The Assets and liabilities as on 31. 3. 2004 and 31st March 2005 were as under.

	31.03.2004	31.03.2005
	Rs.	Rs.
Stock	72,000	88,000
Debtors	16,000	15,200
Bills Receivable	12,000	22,000
Cash and Bank balance	44,800	99,200
Creditors	31,200	38,000
Bills Payable	8,000	6,000
O/s Expenses	12,400	17,600

(C) Additional Information:

(i) Fully paid Equity shares of the face value of Rs. 80,000 were allotted at a premium of @20%

(ii) Fixed assets were acquired for Rs. 60,000 and the payment was made in 6% convertible debentures at par.

(iii) Income Tax paid during the year amounted to Rs. 38,000.

(iv) Company paid a dividend and corporate dividend tax there on for the year ended 31st March 2004 amounting to Rs. 44,000.

(v) 9% Debentures for Rs. 1,20,000 were redeemed at a premium of 2%

Solution (a) Cash Flow Statement (Direct Method)

	Rs.	Rs.
Cash Flow from Operating Activities:		
(a) Operating Cash Receipts:		
Cash from customers (1)	12,70,800	
(b) Operating cash Payments (2)	11,22,000	
Cash Flow from Operations (a – b)	1,48,800	
Income Tax Paid	(38,000)	
	1,10,800	
Cash Flow from Extra Ordinary items:		
Add Claims Received	20,000	
Net cash Flow from operating activities :		1,30,800
Cash Flow from Financing Activities:		
Issue of shares at premium (3)	96,000	
● Redemption of Debentures	(1,22,400)	
● Interest on Debentures	(6,000)	
● Dividend and Corporate dividend Tax	(44,000)	
Net cash used in financing Activities		(76,400)
Net Increase in cash and Cash Equivalents		54,400
Cash and Cash equivalents in the beginning		44,800
Cash and Cash equivalents at the end		99,200

Financing and Investing Activities not affecting	
Cash flow— Issue of debentures against acquisition of land -	Rs. 60,000

Working Notes:

(1) RECEIVABLES A/C (DEBTORS + BILLS RECEIVABLES)

	Rs.		Rs.
To Balance b/d	28,000	By Cash Received (B.F.)	12,70,800
To Sales (credit)	12,80,000	By Balance c/d	37,200
	13,08,000		13,08,000

(2) PAYABLES A/C (CREDITORS + BILLS PAYABLE)

	Rs.		Rs.
To Cash Paid	8,11,200	By Balance b/d	39,200
To Balance c/d	44,000	By Purchases*	8,16,000
	8,55,200		8,55,200

OPERATING EXPENSES A/C

	Rs.		Rs.
To Cash Paid (Bal. Figure)	3,10,800	By Balance b/d	12,400
To Balance c/d	17,600	By Profit and Loss A/c (Income statement)	3,16,000
	3,28,400		3,28,400

*Purchases = Closing Stock + Cost of Goods sold – Opening stock
Purchases = 88,000 + 8,00,000 – 72,000 = 8,16,000

Thus operating cash payment =	8,11,200 (To creditors)
and operating Expenses paid	3,10,800
	11,22,000

		Rs.
(3)	Face Value of Shares issued	80,000
	Add Premium @ 20%	16,000
		96,000

(3) CASH FLOW STATEMENT AS PER AS-3 (REVISED)
(Indirect Method)

		Rs.	Rs.
I Cash Flow from Operating Activities:			
	Net Profit before Tax and Extraordinary Item	73,600	
	Adjustment for Non Cash and Non operating items Depreciation	84,000	
	Discount on Issue of Debentures	400	
	Interest on Debentures	6,000	
	Operating profit before Working Capital Changes	1,64,000	
Adjustment for current items.			
–	Increase in Stock	(16,000)	
–	Increase in Bills Receivable	(10,000)	
–	Decrease in Bills Payable	(2,000)	
+	Decrease in Debtors	800	
+	Increase in creditors	6,800	
+	Increase in o/s Expenses	5,200	
	Cash generated from operation	1,48,800	
Less	Income Tax paid	38,000	
	Cash flow from operation before Extraordinary. item	1,10,800	
Add	Insurance Claim for loss of stock	20,000	
	Net Cash generated from operation		1,30,800
II	**Cash Flow from Investing Activities**	—	—
III	**Cash Flow from Financing Activities**		
	Issue of shares at premium	96,000	
	Redemption of Debentures	(1,22,400)	
	Interest on Debentures	(6,000)	

Contd.

	Rs.	Rs.
Dividend and corporate dividend Tax	(44,000)	
Net cash used in Financing Activities		(76,400)
Net Increase in Cash and Cash Equivalents		54,400
Cash and Cash Equivalents in the beginning		44,800
Cash and Cash Equivalents at the end		99,200

Illustration (4) (Cash Flow Statement – General)

From the following particulars prepare a Cash Flow Statement as per AS-3 (Revised)

Liabilities	31.03.04	31.03.05
	Rs.	Rs.
Share Capital – Shares of Rs. 10 each	4,00,000	4,00,000
Profit and Loss A/c	1,92,000	1,96,000
Loan from Bank	1,20,000	1,00,000
Loan from Association	—	80,000
S. Creditors	1,44,000	1,64,000
	8,56,000	9,40,000
Assets		
Fixed Assets (Depreciating)	4,28,000	4,88,000
Less Provision for Depreciation	(1,08,000)	(1,44,000)
	3,20,000	3,44,000
Fixed Assets (Non-Depreciating)	2,80,000	3,40,000
Stock in Trade	1,00,000	88,000
Debtors	1,40,000	1,53,600
Cash and Bank	16,000	14,400
	8,56,000	9,40,000

*During the year the company paid a dividend of Rs. 1,04,000.

Solution :

CASH FLOW STATEMENT AS PER AS-3 (REVISED)
for the year ended 31st March, 2005.

	Rs.	Rs.
I Cash Flow from Operation :		
Net profit before tax and extraordinary items (1)	1,08,000	
Adjustment for non-cash and Non-operating items :		
Depreciation	36,000	
Cash flow before working Capital changes	1,44,000	
Adjustment for working Capital:		
Decrease in stock	12,000	
Increase in creditors	20,000	
Increase in Debtors	(13,600)	
Net cash flow from operations		1,62,400

II Cash flow from Investing Activities		
Acquisition of Fixed Assets (Non-Depreciating)	(60,000)	
Purchase of Fixed Assets (Depreciating)	(60,000)	
Net Cash used in Investing Activities		(1,20,000)
III Cash Flow from Financing Activities		
Loan from Associates	80,000	
Repayment of Bank Loan	(20,000)	
Payment of Dividend	(1,04,000)	
Net Cash used in Financing Activities		(44,000)
Net decrease in cash and cash Equivalents		(1,600)
Cash and Cash equivalents in the beginning		16,000
Cash and Cash equivalents at the end		14,400

Working notes :

(1) PROFIT AND LOSS A/C

	Rs.		Rs.
To Dividend	1,04,000	By Balance b/d	1,92,000
To Balance c/d	1,96,000	By Net Profit before tax & Extraordinary item (B.F)	1,08,000
	3,00,000		3,00,000

(2) FIXED ASSETS (DEPRECIATING) A/C

	Rs.		Rs.
To Balance b/d	3,20,000	By Depreciation	36,000
To Cash (Purchased) (B.F.)	60,000	By Balance c/d	3,44,000
	3,80,000		3,80,000

Illustration (5) (Loss on Machinery discarded)

Following are the Balance Sheets of Suhani Ltd. as on 31st March, 2004 and 2005.

Liabilities	31. 03. 05	31. 03. 04
	Rs.	Rs.
Share Capital	4,00,000	3,00,000
General Reserve	1,00,000	80,000
Profit & Loss A/c	50,000	30,000
Debentures	1,00,000	1,50,000
Provision for Taxation	40,000	50,000
Proposed Dividend	40,000	30,000
Trade Creditors	70,000	90,000
	8,00,000	7,30,000
Assets		
Goodwill	90,000	1,00,000
Plant and Machinery	4,29,250	2,98,000

Investments	60,000	1,00,000
S. Debtors	1,10,000	1,60,000
Stock	80,000	50,000
Prepaid Expenses	5,750	4,000
Cash and Bank balance	20,000	10,000
Discount on Debentures	5,000	8,000
	8,00,000	7,30,000

Additional Information :

(i) Depreciation on Plant and Machinery has been charged @ 15%.

(ii) A machine costing Rs. 10,000 (W.D.V. Rs. 3,000) has been discarded. An old machine costing Rs. 50,000 (W.D.V. Rs. 20,000) has been sold for Rs. 35,000.

(iii) A profit of Rs. 10,000 has been earned by sale of investments.

(iv) Debentures have been redeemed at 5% premium.

(v) Rs. 45,000 income tax has been paid and adjusted against provision for taxation. Prepare Statement of Changes in Financial Position -cash basis.

C.A. (Adapted)

Solution:

STATEMENT OF CHANGES IN FINANCIAL POSITION (CASH BASIS) for the year ended 31st March 2005

		Rs.	Rs.
Cash Flow from operating Activities			
	Net Profit before tax and extraordinary items	1,75,000	
Adjustment for Non cash and Non-operating items:			
	Depreciation	75,750	
	Goodwill w/o	10,000	
	Loss on machine discarded	3,000	
	Profit on sale of Investment	(10,000)	
	Profit on sale of Machine	(15,000)	
	Loss (premium) on Redemption of Debentures	2,500	
	Discount on Issue of Debentures	3,000	
	Cash generated from operation before Tax	1,84,250	
Less	Tax paid	45,000	
	Cash generated from Operating activities before Working Capital	1,39,250	
Adjustments for Working Capital			
	Decrease in Debtors	50,000	
	Increase in Stock	(30,000)	
	Increase in Prepaid Expenses	(1,750)	
	Decrease in Trade creditors	(20,000)	
	Net cash flow from Operating Activities		1,37,500

II Cash Flow from Investing Activities :		
Sale of Investments	50,000	
Sale of Machinery	35,000	
Purchase of Machinery	(2,30,000)	
Net cash used in Investing Activities		(1,45,000)
III Cash Flow from Financing Activities:		
Issue of Shares	1,00,000	
Redemption of Debentures	(52,500)	
Payment of Dividend	(30,000)	
Net Cash generated from Financing Activities		17,500
Net Increase in Cash and Cash Equivalents		10,000
Cash and Cash equivalents at the beginning		10,000
Cash and Cash equivalents at the end		20,000

Working notes:

(1) PROFIT AND LOSS A/C (ADJUSTED)

	Rs.		Rs.
To Provision for Tax	35,000	By Balance b/d	30,000
To General Reserve	20,000	By Net Profit before Tax and Extraordinary items	1,15,000
To Proposed dividend	40,000		
To Balance c/d	50,000		
	1,45,000		1,45,000

(2) PLANT AND MACHINERY A/C

	Rs.		Rs.
To Balance b/d	2,98,000	By Depreciation*	75,750
To Profit on sale (Tr. to P and L A/c)	15,000	By Bank (sale)	35,000
To Bank (Purchased) (Bal. figure)	2,30,000	By Loss on sale (Tr. to P and L A/c)	3,000
		By Balance c/d	4,29,250
	5,43,000		5,43,000

		Rs.
	* W.D.V. as on 1. 4. 2004	2,98,000
Less	W.D.V. of machine sold (20,000 + 3,000)	23,000
		2,75,000
	* Depreciation @ 15%	41,250
	W.D.V. after Depreciation	2,33,750
	Cost of Machinery acquired	2,30,000**
	*Depreciation on Machinery Purchased	34,500
	W.D.V.	1,95,500
	*Thus total Depreciation charged Rs. (41,250 + 34,500) =	75,750

** Rs. $(4,29,250 - 2,33,750) = \left(1,95,500 \times \frac{100}{85}\right) =$ Rs. 2,30,000

(3) PROVISION FOR TAX A/C

	Rs.		Rs.
To Bank	45,000	By Balance b/d	50,000
To Balance c/d	40,000	By P and L A/c (B.F.)	35,000
	85,000		85,000

Illustration (6) (Investing and Financing activities not affecting Cash)

The Following are the Balance Sheets of Huda Ltd. as on 31st March, 2004 and 31st March, 2005.

Liabilities	31.03.04	31.03.05
	Rs.	Rs.
Share Capital	4,00,000	5,20,000
General Reserve	1,00,000	1,00,000
Profit & Loss Account	79,380	82,440
S. Creditors	79,000	82,270
Bills Payable	67,560	23,050
Bank Overdraft	1,19,020	—
Provision for Tax	80,000	1,00,000
	9,24,960	9,07,760
Assets		
Goodwill	—	40,000
Land & Building	2,97,000	2,88,500
Plant and Machinery	2,25,900	2,32,400
Stock	2,22,080	1,94,740
Advances	4,630	1,470
Debtors	1,70,350	1,45,250
Cash at Bank	5,000	5,400
	9,24,960	9,07,760

Additional Information

(i) During the year ended 31st March, 2005, an additional dividend of Rs. 52,000 was paid.

(ii) The assets of another company were purchased for Rs. 1,20,000 payable in fully paid shares of the company. The assets consisted of Stock Rs. 43,280, Machinery Rs. 36,720 and Goodwill Rs. 40,000. In addition plant was purchased amounting to Rs. 11,300.

(iii) Income tax paid during the year was Rs. 50,000.

(iv) The net-profit for the year before tax amounted to Rs. 1,25,060.

Prepare Cash Flow Statement as per AS-3 (Revised)

C.S. (F) Adapted

Solution :

CASH FLOW STATEMENT
for the year ended 31st March, 2005

		Rs.	Rs.
I	**Cash from operating Activities :**		
	Net Profit before tax and Extraordinary items	1,25,060	
	Adjustment for Non cash and Non-operating items :		
+	Depreciation (*)	50,020	
		1,75,080	
	Adjustment for Working Capital		
+	Decrease in Debtors	25,100	
+	Decrease in Advances	3,160	
+	Decrease in Stock (2)	70,620	
+	Increase in Creditors	3,270	
–	Decrease in Bills Payable	(44,510)	
	Cash flow operating activities	2,32,720	
Less	Income Tax paid	50,000	
	Net cash flow from operating activities		1,82,720
II	**Cash Flow from Investing Activities:**		
–	Purchase of Plant	(11,300)	
	Net Cash used in Investing Activities		(11,300)
III	**Cash Flow from Financing Activities:**		
	Payment of Overdraft	(1,19,020)	
	Payment of Dividend	(52,000)	
	Net Cash used in Financing Activities		(1,71,020)
	Net Increase in Cash and Cash Equivalents		400
	Cash and Cash Equivalents in the beginning		5,000
	Cash and Cash Equivalents at the end		5,400

Working notes

(*) PLANT AND MACHINERY A/C

	Rs.		Rs.
To Balance b/d	2,25,900	By Depreciation (Bal. figure)	41,520
To Cash (Addition)	11,300		
To Share Capital (Addition)	36,720	By Balance c/d	2,32,400
	2,73,920		2,73,920

LAND AND BUILDING A/C

	Rs.		Rs.
To Balance b/d	2,97,000	By Depreciation (Bal. figure)	8,500
		By Balance c/d	2,88,500
	2,97,000		2,97,000

Total Depreciation - Rs. 41,520 + 8,500 = Rs. 50,020

Decrease in Stock = Opening + Acquired – Closing

(2) Rs. 2,22,080 + 43,280 – 1,94,740 = Rs. 70,620

(3) SHARE CAPITAL A/C

	Rs.		Rs.
To Balance c/d	9,20,000	By Balance b/d	8,00,000
		By Stock	43,280
		By Plant and Machinery	36,720
		By Goodwill	40,000
	9,20,000		9,20,000

(4) As per AS-3 (Revised) Financing and Investing Activities which do not affect cash flow are not required to be shown in the Cash flow statement. However the same may be reported as a footnote.

Illustration (7) (Interest and Premium on Redemption of Debentures)

From the following Balance Sheets of Twenty First Century Ltd. and additional information prepare a Cash Flow Statement as per AS - 3 (Revised)

Liabilities	31.3.2004 Rs.	31.3.2005 Rs.
Equity Share Capital	12,00,000	15,00,000
General Reserve	3,00,000	3,50,000
Profit and Loss A/c	1,00,000	1,50,000
9% Debentures	6,00,000	4,00,000
Creditors	4,90,000	5,60,000
Proposed Dividends	1,20,000	1,80,000
Provision for Taxation	1,00,000	1,30,000
	29,10,000	32,70,000
Assets		
Building	8,00,000	7,60,000
Machinery	5,00,000	7,20,000
Short-Term Investments	3,00,000	4,50,000
Inventories	4,00,000	4,70,000
Debtors	6,70,000	5,30,000
Cash at Bank	2,20,000	3,30,000
Prepaid Expenses	20,000	10,000
	29,10,000	32,70,000

Additional Information:

(i) Debentures were redeemed at a premium of 10% on 1st April, 2004.

(ii) Income tax paid during the year amounted to Rs. 1,40,000.

(iii) A machine which appeared at a W.D.V. of Rs. 80,000 was sold for Rs. 1,30,000 and a new machine costing Rs. 3,60,000 was acquired during the year.

B.Com (H) D.U. 1999 (Adapted)

Solution :

CASH FLOW STATEMENT AS PER AS-3 (REVISED)
for the year ended 31st March, 2005

		Rs.	Rs.
I	**Cash Flows from operating Activities:**		
	Net Profit before Tax and Extraordinary items (1)	4,50,000	
	Adjustment for Non-cash and Non-operating items:		
+	Depreciation (60,000 + 40,000) (2)	1,00,000	
–	Profit on sale of machinery	(50,000)	
+	Premium on Redemption of Debentures	20,000	
+	Interest on Debentures	36,000	
	Cash flow before Working Capital Changes	5,56,000	
	Adjustment for Working Capital changes:		
–	Increase in Inventories	(70,000)	
+	Decrease in Debtors	1,40,000	
+	Decrease in Prepaid Expenses	10,000	
+	Increase in Creditors	70,000	
	Cash Flow before Tax	7,06,000	
Less	Income Tax	1,40,000	
	Net Cash Flow from Operating Activities		5,66,000
II	**Cash Flow from Investing Activities**		
+	Sale of Machinery	1,30,000	
–	Purchase of Machinery	(3,60,000)	
–	Purchase of S.T. Investments	(1,50,000)	
	Net Cash used in Investing Activities		(3,80,000)
III	**Cash Flow from Financing Activities**		
+	Issue of share Capital	3,00,000	
–	Redemption of Debentures	(2,20,000)	
–	Payment of Interest	(36,000)	
–	Payment of Dividend	(1,20,000)	
Net Cash used in Financing Activities			(76,000)
	Net Increase in Cash and Cash Equivalents		1,10,000
	Cash and Cash Equivalents in the beginning		2,20,000
	Cash and Cash Equivalents at the end		3,30,000

Working notes:

(1) MACHINERY A/C

	Rs.		Rs.
To Balance b/d	5,00,000	By Bank (Sale)	1,30,000
To Bank (Addition)	3,60,000	By Depreciation (B.F.)	60,000
To Profit on Sale (Tr. to P & L A/c)	50,000	By Balance c/d	7,20,000
	9,10,000		9,10,000

BUILDING A/C

	Rs.		Rs.
To Balance b/d	8,00,000	By Depreciation (B.F.)	40,000
		By Balance c/d	7,60,000
	8,00,000		8,00,000

(2) PROFIT AND LOSS A/C (ADJUSTED)

	Rs.		Rs.
To General Reserve	50,000	By Balance b/d	1,00,000
To Proposed Dividend	1,80,000	By Net Profit before tax and	
To Provision for Tax	1,70,000	Extra-Ordinary items	4,50,000
To Balance c/d	1,50,000		
	5,50,000		5,50,000

(3) PROVISION FOR TAXATION A/C

	Rs.		Rs.
To Bank	1,40,000	By Balance b/d	1,00,000
To Balance c/d	1,30,000	By P and L A/c	1,70,000
	2,70,000		2,70,000

(4) PROPOSED DIVIDEND A/C

	Rs.		Rs.
To Bank*	1,20,000	By Balance b/d	1,20,000
To Balance c/d	1,80,000	By P and L A/c	1,80,000
	3,00,000		3,00,000

*Last year's proposed dividend to be paid this year.

(5) Debentures are presumed to redeemed on 1.4.2004.

Illustration (8)

The Balance Sheets of Harrison Ltd. as on 31st March, 2004 and 2005 were as follows :

	31.3.04	31.3.05
	Rs.	Rs.
Share Capital	6,00,000	8,00,000
Capital Reserve	—	20,000
General Reserve	3,40,000	4,00,000
Profit and Loss A/c	1,20,000	1,50,000
10% Debentures	4,00,000	2,80,000
Current liabilities	2,40,000	2,60,000
Provision for Taxation	1,80,000	1,70,000

Proposed Dividend	60,000	72,000
Unclaimed Dividend		8,000
	19,40,000	21,60,000
Assets		
Fixed Assets at cost	16,00,000	19,00,000
Less Depreciation	(4,60,000)	(5,80,000)
	11,40,000	13,20,000
Trade Investments	2,00,000	1,60,000
Current Assets	5,60,000	6,60,000
Preliminary Expenses	40,000	20,000
	19,40,000	21,60,000

Additional Information

During the year 2004-05 the company :

(i) Sold one machine for Rs. 50,000, the cost of which was Rs. 1,00,000 and the depreciation provided on it was Rs. 40,000.

(ii) Provided Rs. 1,80,000 as depreciation.

(iii) Redeemed 30% of the Debenture @ Rs. 105.

(iv) Sold some Trade Investments at a profit of Rs. 20,000 which was credited to capital Reserve.

(v) Decided to value Stock at cost, where as previously practice was to value stock at cost less 10%. The Stock according to books on 31st March 2004 was Rs. 1,08,000. The Stock on 31st March 2005 was correctly valued at Rs. 1,50,000 and

(vi) Decided to write off Fixed Assets costing Rs. 28,000 on which depreciation amounting to Rs. 20,000 has been provided.

You are required to prepare the Statement of Change in Financial Position (Cash basis) as per AS-3 (Revised)

C.A. (F) Adapted

Solution :

STATEMENT OF CHANGES IN FINANCIAL POSITION
(Cash-basis As per AS-3 (Revised)

		Rs.	Rs.
I Cash Flow from Operating Activities :			
	Net Profit before tax and extraordinary item:	3,20,000	
+	Depreciation	1,80,000	
+	Preliminary Expenses w/o	20,000	
+	Loss on Sale of Machinery	10,000	
+	Fixed Assets w/o (28,000 – 20,000)	8,000	
+	Premium on Redemption of Debentures	6,000	
+	Interest on Debenture	28,000	
		5,72,000	
Less	Income Tax Paid	1,80,000	
		3,92,000	

		Rs.	Rs.
Adjustment for Working Capital Changes			
–	Increase in current Assets	(88,000)	
+	Increase in current liabilities	20,000	
	Net cash flow from Operating Activities		3,24,000
II Cash Flow from Investing Activities			
	Sale of Machinery	50,000	
	Sale of Trade Investments	60,000	
	Purchase of Fixed Assets	(4,28,000)	
	Net cash used in Investing Activities		(3,18,000)
III Cash Flow from Financing Activities			
	Redemption of Debentures	(1,26,000)	
	Payment of Interest	(28,000)	
	Payment of Dividend	(52,000)	
	Issue of Shares	2,00,000	
	Net Cash used in Financing Activities		(6,000)
	Net Increase in Cash and Cash Equivalents		Nil
	Cash and Cash Equivalents in the beginning		Nil
	Cash and Cash Equivalents at the end		Nil

Working notes:

(1) PROFIT AND LOSS A/C (ADJUSTED)

			Rs.
To General Reserve	60,000	By Balance b/d	1,20,000
To Dividend	72,000	By Adjustment in the value of Stock	12,000
To Provision for Tax	1,70,000	By Net Profit before tax and	
To Balance c/d	1,50,000	Extraordinary items	3,20,000
	4,52,000		4,52,000

(2) ADJUSTMENT IN THE VALUE OF STOCK

Rs. $1,08,000 \times \frac{100}{70} = 1,20,000$ Adjusted value

Difference Rs. 12,000 = (1,20,000 – 1,08,000) credited to last year's profit because an increase in the value of closing stock of last year will increase the profit of that year.

(3) Debentures are presumed to be redeemed on 1st April, 2004.

Illustration (9) (Miscellaneous)

From the following information of Rising Waves Ltd. prepare a Statement of Changes in Financial Position – (Cash basis) as per AS-3 (Revised)

	Rs. in '000'
Net profit after tax	1,00,000
Dividend (including dividend tax) paid	34,140
Provision for Income Tax	20,000
Income Tax paid during the year	16,992
Loss on sale of fixed Asset	160
Book value of fixed asset sold	740
Depreciation charged	80,000
Amortisation of Capital grant	24
Profit on sale of Investments	400
Carrying amount of Investments sold	1,11,060
Interest Income on investments	10,024
Interest Expenses	40,000
Interest paid during the year	42,080
Increase in Working Capital (excluding cash and Bank Balance)	2,24,300
Purchase of Fixed Assets	58,240
Investments in joint venture	15,400
Expenditure on construction Work-in-progress	1,38,960
Proceeds from calls in Arrears	8
Receipt of grant for Capital projects	48
Proceeds from long term borrowings	1,03,920
Proceeds from short term borrowings	82,300
Cash and bank balance in the beginning	20,012
Cash and bank balance the end	27,952

{C.A. (F) Adapted)

Solution:

STATEMENT OF CHANGES IN FINANCIAL POSITION
(Cash basis as per AS - 3 (Revised)

		Rs.'000'	Rs.'000'
I Cash Flow from Operating Activities:			
	Net Profit before tax and extra ordinary items (Net Profit + Provision for Tax)	1,20,000	
	Adjustments for Non Cash and Non-operating items:		
+	Depreciation	80,000	
+	Loss on sale of fixed asset	160	
–	Amortisation of Capital grant	(24)	
–	Profit on sale of Investments	(400)	
+	Interest Expenses	40,000	
–	Interest Income on Investments	(10,024)	
	Operating profit before Working Capital changes	2,29,712	
	Increase in Working Capital (excluding cash and bank balance)	(2,24,300)	
	Cash generated form Operation	5,412	
Less	Income Tax paid	(16,992)	
	Net Cash used in Operating Activities		(11,580)

	Rs.	Rs.
II Cash Flow from Investing Activities:		
* Sale of Fixed Asset (740 - 160)	580	
* Sale of Investments (1,11,060 + 400)	1,11,460	
Interest Income on Investments	10,024	
Purchase of Fixed Assets	(58,240)	
Investments made in joint venture	(15,400)	
Expenditure on Construction Work-in-progress	(1,38,960)	
Net Cash used in Investing Activities		(90,536)
III Cash Flow from Financing Activities:		
Proceeds from long term borrowings	1,03,920	
Proceeds from short term borrowings	82,300	
Capital grant receipts	48	
Proceeds from Calls-in-Arrears	8	
Payment of Interest	(42,080)	
Net Cash generated from Financing Activities		1,10,056
Net Increase in Cash and Cash equivalents		7,940
Cash and Cash equivalents in the beginning		20,012
Cash and Cash equivalents at the end		27,952

Working notes

(*) While calculating proceeds of asset sold loss on sale has to be deducted while profit there on has to be added

(2) It should be noted that an item of income, while amortising, has to be credited to profit and Loss Account in the same manner when an item of expense (goodwill, patents) has to be debited to Profit and Loss Account.

(3) Increase in Working Capital represents either an increase in current assets or decrease in current liabilities which results in outflow of cash.

(4) Expenditure on construction work-in-progress is a Capital expenditure covered by Investing activities.

(5) Capital grant receipt is a Financing Activity.

Illustration (10) (Direct and Indirect Method)

From the following summarised Cash Book of a limited company, prepare Cash Flow Statement for the year ended 31st March, 2005 as per AS-3 (Revised) using "Direct and Indirect" Methods.

1.4.2004	Rs.'000'		Rs.'000'
To Balance b/d	1,250	By Payment to Creditors	50,000
To Equity Share Capital	7,500	By Purchase of Fixed Assets	5,000
To Receipts from Customers	70,000	By Overhead Expenses	5,000
To Sale of Plant	2,500	By Wages and Salaries	2,500
		By Taxation	6,250
		By Dividend	1,250
		By Repayment of Bank Loan	7,500
		By Balance c/d (31.03.05)	3,750
	81,250		81,250

[C.A. (F) Adapted]

Solution: (a) Direct Method Approach

CASH FLOW STATEMENT
For the year ended 31st March 2005

	Rs.'000'	Rs.'000'
I Cash Flow from Operating Activities:		
Receipts from Customers	70,000	
Less Payment to Creditors	(50,000)	
Wages and Salaries paid	(2,500)	
Over head expenses paid	(5,000)	
Cash generated from operations	12,500	
Less Income Tax paid	(6,250)	
Net Cash generated from Operating Activities		6,250
II Cash Flow from Investing Activities		
Sale of Plant	2,500	
Purchase of Fixed Assets	(5000)	
Net Cash used in Investing Activities		(2,500)
III Cash Flow from Financing Activities:		
Issue of Share Capital	7,500	
Repayment of Bank Loan	(7,500)	
Dividend Paid	(1,250)	
Net Cash used in Financing Activities		(1,250)
Net Increase in Cash and Cash equivalents		2,500
Cash and Cash equivalents in the beginning		1,250
Cash and Cash equivalents at the end		3,750

(b) Indirect Method Approach

CASH FLOW STATEMENT
For the year end 31st March, 2005

Rs. in '000'

I Cash Flow from Operating Activities		
Net Profit before tax and extraordinary items:	12,500	
Add Non cash and Non-operating items	--	
Less Income Tax paid	(6,250)	
Net Cash generated from operating activities		6,250
II Cash flow from Investing Activities		
Sale of Plant	2,500	
Purchase of Fixed Assets	(5,000)	
Net cash used in Investing Activities		(2,500)
III Cash flow from Financing Activities		
Issue of equity shares	7,500	
Repayment of Bank Loan	(7,500)	
Dividend Paid	(1,250)	
Net Cash used in Financing Activities		(1,250)

Net Increase in Cash and Cash Equivalents	2,500
Cash and Cash equivalents in the beginning	1,250
Cash and Cash equivalents at the end	3,750

Illustration (11) (Valuation of Stock and Redemption at Premium)

The Balance Sheets of New Light Ltd. for the years ended 31st March, 2004 and 2005 are as under :

Liabilities	31.03.2004	31.03.2005
	Rs.	Rs.
10% Preference Share Capital	4,00,000	2,80,000
Equity Share Capital	12,00,000	16,00,000
Capital Reserve		40,000
General Reserve	6,80,000	8,00,000
Profit and Loss Account	2,40,000	3,00,000
9% Debentures	4,00,000	2,80,000
Current liabilities	4,80,000	5,20,000
Proposed Dividend	1,20,000	1,44,000
Provision for Tax	3,60,000	3,40,000
Unpaid dividend	—	16,000
	38,80,000	43,20,000
Assets		
Fixed Assets	32,00,000	38,00,000
Less Depreciation (Accumulated)	(9,20,000)	(11,60,000)
	22,80,000	26,40,000
Investments	4,00,000	3,20,000
Cash and Bank balance	10,000	10,000
Other Current Assets	11,10,000	13,10,000
Preliminary Expenses	80,000	40,000
	38,80,000	43,20,000

Additional Information :

(i) The Company sold one fixed asset for Rs. 1,00,000 the cost of which was Rs. 2,00,000 and the depreciation provided on it was Rs. 80,000.

(ii) The Company also decided to write off another fixed assets costing Rs. 56,000 on which depreciation amounting to Rs. 40,000 has been provided.

(iv) Depriciation on fixed assets provided Rs. 3,60,000.

(iii) Company sold some investments at a profit of Rs. 40,000 which was credited to capital reserve.

(v) Debentures and Preference shares are redeemed at 5% premium on 31. 3. 2005.

(vi) Company decided to value stock at cost where as previously the practice was to value stock at cost less 10%. The stock according to books on 31. 3. 2004 was Rs. 2,16,000. The Stock on 31. 3. 2005 was correctly valued at Rs. 3,00,000.

Prepare Cash Flow Statement as per revised Accounting Standard 3 by Indirect Method.

C.A. (I) Nov. 2003

Solution :

CASH FLOW STATEMENT [AS PER AS-3 (REVISED)]
for the year ended 31st March, 2005

	Rs.	Rs.
I Cash Flow from Operating activities :		
Net Profit before tax and extraordinary items (1)	6,40,000	
Adjustment for Non Cash and Non-operating items :		
+ Depreciation (5)	3,60,000	
+ Preliminary Expenses w/o	40,000	
+ Loss on sale of fixed assets	20,000	
+ Fixed assets w/o	16,000	
+ Premium on Redemption of Preference Shares	6,000	
+ Premium o Redemption of Debentures	6,000	
+ Interest on Debentures	36,000	
Operating Profit before Working Capital Changes	11,24,000	
Adjustment for Working Capital		
Increase in Current Assets (2)	(1,76,000)	
Increase in Current liabilities	40,000	
Cash generated from operations	9,88,000	
Less Income Tax paid	(3,60,000)	
Net Cash generated from Operating Activities		6,28,000
II Cash Flow from Investing Activities :		
Sale of fixed assets	1,00,000	
Sale of Investments (3)	1,20,000	
Purchase of fixed assets (4)	(8,56,000)	
Net Cash used in Investing Activities		(6,36,000)
III Cash Flow from Financing Activities :		
Issue of Share Capital	4,00,000	
Redemption of Preference Shares*	(1,26,000)	
Redemption of Debentures*	(1,26,000)	
Interest paid	(36,000)	
Dividend paid (6)	(1,04,000)	
Net Cash from Financing Activities		8,000
Net increase/decrease in Cash and Cash equivalents		Nil
Cash and Cash equivalents in the beginning		10,000
Cash and Cash equivalents at the end		10,000

*Including premium on redemption

Working notes

(1) PROFIT AND LOSS A/C (ADJUSTED)

	Rs.		Rs.
To General Reserve	1,20,000	By Balance b/d	2,40,000
To Provision for Tax	3,40,000	By Stock Adjustment	24,000*
To Proposed dividend	1,44,000	By Net Profit before tax and	
To Balance c/d	3,00,000	extraordinary items	6,40,000
	9,04,000		9,04,000

$$\text{*Stock Adjustment} = 2{,}16{,}000 \times \frac{100}{90} = \text{Rs. } 2{,}40{,}000$$

Adjusted Value = Rs. 2,40,000 – 2,16,000 = 24,000

(2) Increase in Current Assets

Current Assets as on 31.3.2005	13,10,000
Less Current assets as on 31.3.2004	11,34,000
(11,10,000 + 24,000*)	1,76,000

(3) INVESTMENT A/C

	Rs.		Rs.
To Balance b/d	4,00,000	By Bank A/c	1,20,000
To Capital Reserve	40,000	(Bal. figure)	
(Profit or Sale)		By Balance c/d	3,20,000
	4,40,000		4,40,000

(4) FIXED ASSETS A/C (AT COST)

	Rs.		Rs.
To Balance b/d	32,00,000	By Bank (Sold)	1,00,000
To Bank (Bal. figure)	8,56,000	By Acc. Depreciation (on asset sold)	80,000
		By Loss on sale	20,000
		By Acc. Dep. (on asset discarded)	40,000
		By Loss on asset discarded	16,000
		By Balance c/d	38,00,000
	40,56,000		40,56,000

(5) ACCUMULATED DEPRECIATION A/C

	Rs.		Rs.
To Fixed Assets A/c	80,000	By Balance b/d	9,20,000
To Fixed Assets A/c	40,000	By P and L A/c	3,60,000
To Balance c/d	11,60,000	(dep. provided)	
	12,80,000		12,80,000

(6) In the absence of any specific information relating to preference or equity dividend it is always presesumed that proposed dividend includes preference and equity dividend both.

PROPOSED DIVIDEND A/C

	Rs.		Rs.
To Bank (Bal. figure)	1,04,000*	By Balance b/d	1,20,000
To Balance c/d (C.Y.)	1,44,000	By P and L A/c	1,44,000
(L.Y.)	16,000		
	2,64,000		2,64,000

Out of last year proposed dividend Rs. 16,000 is still unpaid, hence actual cash flow is Rs. 1,04,000. (Rs. 1,20,000 – 16,000)

Illustration 12 (Pre-acquisition dividend)

From the following Balance Sheets and information prepare Cash flow Statement of Ryan Ltd. for the year ended 31st March, 2005.

Liabilities	31.3.05	31.3.04
	Rs.	Rs.
Equity Share Capital	6,00,000	5,00,000
10% Preference Share Capital	—	2,00,000
Capital Redemption Reserve	1,00,000	—
Capital Reserve	1,00,000	—
General Reserve	1,00,000	2,50,000
Profit & Loss A/c	70,000	50,000
9% Debentures	2,00,000	—
Sundry Creditors	95,000	80,000
Bills Payable	20,000	30,000
Liabilities for Expenses	30,000	20,000
Provision for Taxation	95,000	60,000
Proposed Dividend	90,000	60,000
	15,00,000	12,50,000
Assets		
Land and Building	1,50,000	2,00,000
Plant and Machinery	7,65,000	5,00,000
Investments	50,000	80,000
Inventories	95,000	90,000
Bills Receivable	65,000	70,000
Sundry Debtors	1,75,000	1,30,000
Cash at Bank	65,000	90,000
Preliminary Expenses	10,000	25,000
Voluntary Separation Payment	1,25,000	65,000
	15,00,000	12,50,000

Additional Information

(i) A piece of land has been sold for Rs. 1,50,000 (Cost Rs. 1,20,000) and the balance land was revalued. Capital reserve consisted of profit on sale of land and profit on revaluation.

(ii) On 1. 4. 2004 a plant was sold for Rs. 90,000 (original cost – Rs. 70,000 and W.D.V. Rs. 50,000) and Debentures worth Rs. 1,00,000 were issued at par as part of consideration for plant of Rs. 4,50,000 acquired.

(iii) Part of the investments (Cost Rs. 50,000) was sold for Rs. 70,000.

(iv) Pre-acquisition dividend received Rs. 5,000 was adjusted against cost of investments.

(v) Directors have proposed 15% dividend for the current year.

(vi) Voluntary separation cost of Rs. 50,000 was adjusted against general reserve.

(vii) Income Tax liability for the current year was estimated at Rs. 1,35,000.

(viii) Depreciation @ 15% has been written off from Plant Account but no depreciation has been charged on Land and Building.

Apply "Indirect Method" as per AS-3 (Revised)

C.A.(I) May 2003-Modified

Solution :

CASH FLOW STATEMENT
for the year ended 31st March, 2005

		Rs.	Rs.
I Cash Flow from Operating Activities:			
	Net Profit before tax and Extraordinary items (1)	2,45,000	
Adjustments for Non Cash and Non operating items			
Add	Depreciation (2)	1,35,000	
Add	Preliminary Expenses	15,000	
Add	Interest on Debentures	18,000	
Less	Profit on sale of Plant	(40,000)	
Less	Profit on sale of Investments	(20,000)	
Operating Profit before Working Capital Changes		3,53,000	
Adjustment for Working Capital Changes			
Less	Increase in inventory	(5,000)	
Less	Increase in debtors	(45,000)	
Less	Decrease in Bills payable	(10,000)	
Add	Decrease in Bills receivable	5,000	
Add	Increase in Creditors	15,000	
Add	Increase in o/s Expenses	10,000	
	Cash generated from operating activities	3,23,000	
Less	Income Tax paid (8)	1,00,000	
		2,23,000	
Less	Voluntary Separation Payment (6) (Extraordinary item)	(1,10,000)	
Net Cash generated from operating activities			1,13,000

	Rs.	Rs.
II Cash Flow from Investing Activities		
Sale of Land	1,50,000	
Sale of Plant	90,000	
Sale of Investments	70,000	
Purchase of Plant	(3,50,000)	
Purchase of Investments	(25,000)	
Pre-acquisition dividend	5,000	
Net Cash used in Investing activities		(60,000)
III Cash Flow from Financing Activities		
Issue of equity shares	1,00,000	
Issue of Debentures for cash	1,00,000	
Redemption of Preference Shares	(2,00,000)	
Payment of Interest on Debentures	(18,000)	
Payment of Dividend (7)	(60,000)	
Net Cash used in Financing Activities		(78,000)
Net decrease in Cash and Cash equivalents		(25,000)
Cash and Cash equivalents in the beginning		90,000
Cash and Cash equivalents at the end		65,000

Working notes:

(1) PROFIT AND LOSS A/C (ADJUSTED)

	Rs.		Rs.
To Provision for Tax	1,35,000	By Balance b/d	50,000
To Proposed Dividend	90,000	By Net Profit before tax and extraordinary items	2,45,000
To Balance A/c	70,000		
	2,95,000		2,95,000

(2) PLANT AND MACHINERY A/C

	Rs.		Rs.
To Balance b/d	5,00,000	By Bank (Sale)	90,000
To Profit on sale	40,000	By Depreciation (B.F.)	1,35,000
To Debentures	1,00,000	By Balance c/d	7,65,000
To Bank (Addition)	3,50,000		
	9,90,000		9,90,000

(3) LAND AND BUILDING A/C

	Rs.		Rs.
To Balance b/d	2,00,000	By Bank (Sale)	1,50,000
To Capital Reserve (Profit on Sale)	30,000	By Balance c/d	1,50,000
To Capital Reserve (Profit on Revaluation)	70,000		
	3,00,000		3,00,000

(4) INVESTMENTS A/C

	Rs.		Rs.
To Balance b/d	80,000	By Bank (Sale)	70,000
To Profit & Loss A/c (Profit on Sale)	20,000	By Dividend	5,000
To Bank (Purchased) (B.F.)	25,000	By Balance c/d	50,000
	1,25,000		1,25,000

(5) CAPITAL RESERVE A/C

	Rs.		Rs.
To Balance c/d	1,00,000	By Profit on Sale of Land	30,000
		By Profit on Revaluation (B.F.)	70,000
	1,00,000		1,00,000

(6) VOLUNTARY SEPARATION PAYMENTS A/C

	Rs.		Rs.
To Balance c/d	65,000	By General Reserve	50,000
To Bank (Bal. figure)	1,10,000	By Balance c/d	1,25,000
	1,75,000		1,75,000

(7) PROPOSED DIVIDEND A/C

	Rs.		Rs.
To Bank (Bal. figure)	60,000	By Balance b/d	60,000
To Balance c/d	90,000	By Profit and Loss A/c	90,000
	1,50,000		1,50,000

(8) PROVISION FOR TAX A/C

	Rs.		Rs.
To Bank (Bal. figure)	1,00,000	By Balance b/d	60,000
To Balance c/d	95,000	By P & L A/c	1,35,000
	1,95,000		1,95,000

(9) GENERAL RESERVE A/C

	Rs.		Rs.
To Capital Red. Reserve	1,00,000	By Balance b/d	2,50,000
To Voluntary Separation Payment	50,000		
To Balance c/d	1,00,000		
	2,50,000		2,50,000

Illustration (13) (Changes in Assets and liabilities and Cash Flow Statement)

The following changes are noted in the various items of assets and liabilities of Exe Ltd. during the year ending 31st March, 2005 over the last year ending 31st March, 2004.

Particulars of Assets/liabilities	Changes Debits/(credits) Rs.
Equity Share Capital 1,50,000 Shares of Rs. 10 each fully paid	Nil
Capital Reserve	(2,46,000)
8% Debentures	(2,50,000)
Debentures discount	5,000
Free hold Property at Cost/revaluation	2,15,000
Plant and Machinery at Cost	3,00,000
Depreciation on Plant and Machinery	(72,000)
Debtors	2,50,000
Stock and Work-in-progress	1,92,500
Creditors	(59,000)
Net Profit for the year	(3,82,500)
Dividend paid for the year 2004	1,50,000
Provision for Doubtful debts	(16,500)
Trade Investments at Cost	2,35,000
Bank	(3,21,500)
	0

You are informed that :

(i) Capital reserve as at the end of the year 31st March 2005 represented realised profits on sale of one freehold property together with surplus arising on revaluation of remaining freehold properties.

(ii) During the year plant costing Rs. 90,000 against which depreciation provision of Rs. 67,500 was charged sold for Rs. 35,000.

(iii) During the middle of the year Rs. 2,50,000 debentures were issued for cash at a discount of Rs. 5,000.

(iv) The net profit for the year was after crediting the profit on sale of plant and charging debenture interest.

You are required to prepare a statement which will explain, why bank borrowing has increased by Rs. 3,21,500 during the year ending 31st March 2005. Ignore taxation.

C.A. (Final) Nov. 1998 (Adapted)

Solution :

CASH FLOW STATEMENT
For the year ended 31st March, 2005

		Rs.	Rs.
I	**Cash Flow from Operating Activities**		
	Net profit before tax and Extraordinary items	3,82,500	
Adjustments for Non Cash and Non-operating items			
Add	Depreciation (1)	1,39,500	
Add	Interest on Debentures	10,000	
Less	Profit on sale of Plant (2)	(12,500)	
	Operating profit before Working Capital changes	5,19,500	

		Rs.	Rs.
	Balance b/d	5,19,500	
Adjustment for Working Capital Changes :			
	Increase in Creditors	59,000	
	Increase in debtors (*Less* provision) (Rs. 2,50,000 – 16,500)	(2,33,500)	
	Increase in Stock and Work in progress	(1,92,500)	
Net Cash generated from Operating Activities			1,52,500
II Cash Flow from Investing Activities			
	Sale of Plant	35,000	
	Sale of Freehold property (3)	31,000	
	Purchase of Plant and Machinery (4)	(3,90,000)	
	Purchase of Trade Investments	(2,35,000)	
Net cash used in Investing Activities			(5,59,000)
III Cash Flow from Financing Activities			
	Issue of Debentures at a discount (5)	2,45,000	
	Debentures Interest Paid	(10,000)	
	Dividend Paid	(1,50,000)	
	Net Cash from Financing Activities		85,000
Net decrease in cash (as reported)			(3,21,500)

Working notes:

	(1) Depreciation on Plant Machinery provided	**Rs.**
	Increase in Provision for Depreciation (as given in the question)	72,000
Add	Depreciation on Plant sold	67,500
	Depreciation provided during the year	1,39,500

	(2) Profit on Sale of Plant	Rs.
	Sale Proceeds	35,000
Less	Written down value (Cost less Depreciation) (Rs. 90,000 – 67,500)	22,500
		12,500

	(3) Sale of Freehold Property	Rs.
	Capital Reserve (Profit on Sale + Revaluation Profit)	2,46,000
Less	Increase in Freehold Property (as given)	2,15,000
	Sale Proceeds	31,000

	(4) Purchase of Plant and Machinery	Rs.
	Increase in Value (at cost) (as given)	3,00,000
Add	Cost of Plant sold	90,000
	Net Addition made	3,90,000

(5) Proceeds from Issue of Debentures:	Rs.
Face value of Debentures	2,50,000
Less Discount on Debentures	5,000
	2,45,000

Illustration (14) Direct and Indirect Method & Conversion)

From the following particulars prepare a Cash Flow Statement as per AS-3 (Revised) under :

(i) Direct Method

(ii) Indirect Method

BALANCE SHEETS OF EXE LTD. AS ON

Liabilities	31.3.05 Rs.	31.3.04 Rs.
Equity Share Capital (Rs. 100)	7,50,000	5,50,000
10% Redeemable Preference Shares (Rs. 100)	50,000	2,00,000
Capital Redemption Reserve	50,000	—
General Reserve	75,000	50,000
Profit and Loss A/c balance	1,50,000	1,00,000
8% Convertible Debentures	1,00,000	2,00,000
Terms Loans	75,000	1,50,000
	12,50,000	12,50,000
Assets		
Fixed Assets Less Depreciation	6,50,000	5,00,000
Long Term Investments	2,00,000	2,50,000
Working Capital	4,00,000	5,00,000
	12,50,000	12,50,000

STATEMENT OF PROFIT AND LOSS
for the year ended 31st March, 2005

		Rs.	Rs.
	Sales		30,00,000
Less	Cost of goods Sold		(20,00,000)
	Gross Profit		10,00,000
Less	Establishment charges	1,50,000	
	Selling and Distribution Expenses	3,00,000	
	Interest Expenses	25,000	
	Loss on Sale of Machine	75,000	
	(Book Value = Rs. 2,00,000)		(5,50,000)
			4,50,000
	Interest Received	20,000	
	Dividend Received	10,000	
	Foreign Exchange Gain	50,000	
	Damages received for Loss of reputation	70,000	1,50,000
			6,00,000

	Rs.
Balance c/d	6,00,000
Less Depreciation	(2,50,000)
	3,50,000
Taxes	(1,50,000)
	2,00,000
Dividend	(75,000)
Net Profit carried to Balance Sheet	1,25,000

Additional Information:

	31.3.05	31.3.04
	Rs.	Rs.
Dividend Receivable	10,000	20,000
Interest Receivable	15,000	10,000
Cash in hand and at Bank	35,000	50,000
Investments (maturing within 2 months)	15,000	10,000
Interest Payable	20,000	25,000
Taxes Payable	30,000	15,000
Current Ratio	1.5	1.4
Acid Test	1.1	0.8

Debentureholders holding 50% of the Debentures outstanding as on 31st March, 2004 exercised the option for conversion into equity shares, and same was put through during the year 2004-2005.

[C.A. (F) Adapted]

Solution:

(a) Direct Method

CASH FLOW STATEMENT
for the year ended 31st March, 2005

	Rs.	Rs.
I Cash From Operating Activities		
Cash Received from Debtors (5)	31,05,000	
Less Cash Paid to Creditors (6) and	(20,30,000)	
Employees (2) Establishment + Selling and Distribution Expenses)	(4,50,000)	
Cash generated from operations	6,25,000	
Less Taxes Paid (7)	(1,35,000)	
Net Cash flow from Operating Activities		4,90,000
II Cash Flow from Investing Activities:		
Sale of Machinery (9)	1,25,000	
Sale of Long Term Investments	50,000	
Interest Received (10)	15,000	
Dividend Received (11)	20,000	
Purchase of Fixed Assets (9)	(6,00,000)	
Cash used in Investing Activities before extraordinary items	(3,90,000)	
Damages received for loss of Reputation (goodwill)	70,000	
Net Cash used in Investing Activities		(3,20,000)

III Cash Flow from Financing Activities		
Issue of Shares for Cash	1,00,000	
Redemption of Preference Shares	(1,50,000)	
Repayment of Term Loans	(75,000)	
Interest Paid (8)	(30,000)	
Dividend Paid	(75,000)	
Net Cash used in Financing Activities		(2,30,000)
Net Decrease in Cash and Cash equivalents		(60,000)
Cash and Cash equivalents in the beginning		60,000
Cash and Cash equivalents at the end		Nil

RECONCILIATION STATEMENT*

	RS.
Cash and Cash equivalents at the end (35,000 + 15,000) Cash + Investments (2 months)	50,000
Effect of Foreign Exchange Rate Fluctuation (as reported in Income Statement)	(50,000)
Cash and Cash equivalents	Nil

* This statement is drawn in accordance with the requirements of AS-3 (Revised). Otherwise if the gain is realised in Cash on account of foreign exchange received from customers the same could have ben considered under operating activities. If it could have been the payment in foreign exchange against purchase of an asset, the same would have been accounted for under "Investing Activities".

Working notes:

(1) Calculation of Debtors, Creditors and Stock as on 31st March

	2005	2004
Current Ratio	1.5:1	1.4:1
Hence Working Capital	0.5	0.4
Therefore Current Assets	$\frac{4,00,000\times1.5}{0.5}$	$\frac{5,00,000 \times 1.4}{0.4}$
	Rs. 12,00,000	Rs. 17,50,000
Current liabilities	Rs. 12,00,000 – 4,00,000	Rs. 17,50,000 – 5,00,000
(CL = CA – WC)	= 8,00,000	= 12,50,000
(2) Stock = Current Ratio – Acid Test		
	1.5 – 1.1	1.4 – 0.8
	= 0.4	= 0.6
Stock to Current liabilities	0.4 : 1	0.6 : 1
Stock	= 0.4 × 8,00,000	0.6 × 12,50,000
	= Rs. 3,20,000	Rs. 7,50,000
(3) Total Current Assets:		
Stock	3,20,000	7,50,000
Debtors (Bal. figure)	8,05,000	9,10,000
Other Current Assets*	75,000	90,000
	12,00,000	17,50,000

***Other Current assets include**

- Dividend Receivable
- Interest Receivable
- Cash in hand and at Bank
- Investment maturing within 2 months

(4) Current liabilities

Creditors (B.F.)	7,50,000	12,10,000
Others	50,000	40,000
	8,00,000	12,50,000

(5) DEBTORS' A/C

	Rs.		Rs.
To Balance b/d	9,10,000	By Cash (B.F.)	31,05,000
To Sales	30,00,000	By Balance c/d	8,05,000
	39,10,000		39,10,000

(6) CREDITOR'S A/C

	Rs.		Rs.
To Cash (B.F.)	20,30,000	By Balance b/d	12,10,000
To Balance c/d	7,50,000	By Purchase	15,70,000
	27,80,000		27,80,000

Cost of goods sold = Op. Stock + Purchase – Cl. Stock

Purchases = Cost of goods sold + Cl. Stock – Op. Stock

20,00,000 = 3,20,000 – 7,50,000 = Rs. 15,70,000

(7) TAXES PAYABLE A/C

	Rs.		Rs.
To Cash Paid	1,35,000	By Balance b/d	15,000
To Balance c/d	30,000	By P & L A/c	1,50,000
	1,65,000		1,65,000

(8) INTEREST PAYABLE A/C

	Rs.		Rs.
To Cash Paid (B.F.)	30,000	By Balance b/d	25,000
To Balance c/d	20,000	By P & L A/c	25,000
	50,000		50,000

(9) FIXED ASSETS A/C

	Rs.		Rs.
To Balance b/d	5,00,000	By Depreciation	2,50,000
To Cash (B.F.)	6,00,000	By Cash (Sale)	1,25,000
(Purchased)		By Loss on Sale	75,000
		By Balance c/d	6,50,000
	11,00,000		11,00,000

(10) INTEREST RECEIVABLE A/C

	Rs.		Rs.
To Balance b/d	10,000	By Cash Received (B.F.)	15,000
To P and L A/c	20,000	By Balance c/d	15,000
	30,000		30,000

(11) DIVIDEND RECEIVABLE A/C

	Rs.		Rs.
To Balance b/d	20,000	By Cash (B.F.)	20,000
To P and L A/c	10,000	(Received)	
		By Balance c/d	10,000
	30,000		30,000

Note: Damages received for loss of reputation has been considered under Investing Activities because reputation being goodwill falls under intangible assets which are covered under Investing activities as per AS-3 (Revised)

(b) Indirect Method

CASH FLOW STATEMENT
for the year ended 31st March, 2005

		Rs.	Rs.
I Cash Flow from Operating Activities:			
	Net Profit before Tax and Extraordinary items	2,80,000	
	Adjustment for Non Cash and Non-operating items:		
	Depreciation	2,50,000	
	Interest Expenses	25,000	
	Dividend Received	(10,000)	
	Interest Received	(20,000)	
	Cash flow before Working Capital changes	5,25,000	
Add	Decrease in Working Capital	1,00,000	
Adj.	for Extraordinary item:	6,25,000	
	Damages (under Investing Activities)		
Less	Income Tax Paid	(1,35,000)	
	Net Cash Flow from Operating Activities		4,90,000

II Cash Flow from Investing Activities		
Sale of Machinery	1,25,000	
Sale of long term Investments	50,000	
Interest Received	15,000	
Dividend Received	20,000	
Purchase of Fixed Assets	(6,00,000)	
Cash used in Investing Activities before Extraordinary item	(3,90,000)	
Damages for loss of Reputation	70,000	
Net Cash used in Investing Activities		(3,20,000)
III Cash Flow from Financing Activities:		
Issue of Shares for Cash	1,00,000	
Redemption of Preference Shares	(1,50,000)	
Repayment of Term Loan	(75,000)	
Interest Paid	(30,000)	
Dividend Paid	(75,000)	
Cash used in Financing Activities		(2,30,000)
Net Decrease in Cash and Cash Equivalents		(60,000)
Cash and Cash Equivalents at the beginning		60,000
Cash and Cash Equivalents at the end*		Nil

*** Please refer to Reconciliation Statement which shows the adjustment of foreign exchange rate fluctuations. (Already shown under Direct Method).**

QUESTIONS

1. What do you mean by term "Funds"? How the funds from operations are computed?
2. What are the advantages of Funds Flow Statement? Also describe it's limitations.
(B. Com (H) D.U. - 1992)
3. Enumerate and explain the major sources of Working Capital.
4. List any seven examples of uses of Working Capital. Explain, how the funds from operations are different from net operating profit.
5. Distinguish between Funds Flow Statement and "Cash Flow Statement"
6. Write a note on uses and limitations of Cash Flow Statement.
7. What do you understand by "Cash from operations"? How is it computed?
8. Distinguish between Operating, Investing and Financing activities as per AS - 3 (Revised) Give 3 examples in each case.
9. How the "Direct Method" is different from "Indirect Method" of computing cash from operation.

PROBLEMS

Funds Flow Statement

(1) From the following compute Funds from Operations.

PROFIT AND LOSS A/C OF X LTD.

for the year ended 31st March, 2005

	Rs.		Rs.
To Office Expenses	1,20,000	By Gross Profit b/d	7,50,000
To Selling Expenses	45,000	By Profit on sale of Building	75,000
To Depreciation	75,000	By Dividend Received	20,000
To Goodwill w/o	45,000	by Interest Received	15,000
To Preliminary Expenses	30,000	By Rent Received	25,000
To Provision for Tax	60,000	By Insurance Claim for loss of stock	5,000
To Proposed dividend	60,000		
To General Reserve	30,000		
To Net Profit c/e	4,25,000		
	8,90,000		8,90,000

Ans. : Funds from operations – Rs. 5,90,000

Hint : Insurance claim for loss of stock is treated operating receipt.

(b) Will it made any difference if the above mentioned Profit and Loss A/c relates to Financial Institution.

Ans. : Funds From operations – Rs. 6,25,000

(b) Dividend and interest received will be treated as operating incomes.

(2) From the following information relating to "Investment Corporation, Calculate sources and uses of funds

	2004	2003
Investment in other Companies	1,40,000	1,70,000
Profit and Loss Appropriation A/c	3,37,500	2,85,000

The corporation sold it's 40% investments for Rs. 1,17,500. There was a gain for Rs. 67,500 on such sale which has been transferred to P and L Appropriation A/c.

Ans : Source of funds – Rs. 1,17,500
Uses of Funds – Rs. 20,000
Loss from operation – Rs. 15,000

(3) The following balances appeared in the books of a Limited Company.

	31.3.2004 Rs.	31.3.2005 Rs.
Plant and Machinery	7,50,000	15,00,000
Provision for Depreciation	1,87,500	2,62,500

A piece of plant costing Rs. 1,50,000 (accumulated depreciation Rs. 75,000) sold at a gain of Rs. 18,750. Calculate :

(i) Funds provided by sale of piece of plant

(ii) Funds used to acquire plant and Machinery

(iii) Depreciation provided during the year.

Ans: **(i)** Rs. 93,750 **(ii)** 9,00,000 **(iii)** Rs. 1,50,000

(4) From the balances given below, calculate the Funds from operations.

	31.3.2004	31.3.2005
	Rs.	Rs.
Profit and Loss A/c	2,50,000	2,25,000
General Reserve	5,00,000	6,25,000
Provision for Tax	1,00,000	1,25,000
Provision for Depreciation	50,000	62,500
Goodwill	50,000	37,500
Discount on issue of debentures	20,000	7,500
Proposed dividend	25,000	30,000
Prepaid Rent	5,000	6,000
O/s Expenses	7,000	4,500
Cash and Bank Balance	21,000	18,500
Dividend Receivable	6,000	4,000
Interest Payable	7,000	7,000

Ans. : Rs. 2,92,500

(5) From the following information prepare a Statement of Sources and Application of Funds for the year ended 31st March, 2005

(i) Net profit Rs. 1,29,000 before writing off goodwill and Preliminary expenses.

(ii) Depreciation on Fixed Assets Rs. 21,000

(iii) Goodwill Rs. 15,000

(iv) Dividend Paid Rs. 42,000

(v) Shares issued for Cash Rs. 60,000.

(vi) Increase in Working Capital Rs. 48,000.

(vii) Machinery purchased for Cash Rs. 1,20,000

(viii) Preliminary expenses - Rs. 12,000

(ix) Company issued 9% Debentures having a face value of Rs. 5,00,000 at 10% premium as a part of purchase consideration of Building acquired during the year.

Ans. : Funds from Operations - Rs. 1,50,000

Total Sources of Funds - Rs. 2,10,000

Total Application of Funds - Rs. 1,62,000

(6) The net profit after making a provision of Rs. 3,30,000 for income tax for the year ended 31st March, 2005 amounted to Rs. 3,00,000 after taking into account the following :

		Rs.
(i)	Depreciation on fixed assets	65,000
(ii)	Preliminary Expenses w/o	7,000
(iii)	Bad debts	1,000
(iv)	Loss on Sale of furniture	1,500
(v)	Profit on Sale of long term investments	5,000

Calculate funds from operations

[B. Com (H) D.U. 1992 Modified]

Ans. : Rs. 3,68,500

(7) The following are the Balance Sheets of Asian Electronics Ltd. as on 31st March, 2004 and 2005.

Liabilities	31.3.2004	31.3.2005
	Rs.	Rs.
7% Redeemable Preference Shares	—	1,00,000
Equity Shares	4,00,000	4,00,000
General Reserve	20,000	20,000
Profit and Loss Account	10,000	12,000
Debentures	60,000	70,000
Provision for Taxation	30,000	42,000
Creditors	1,20,000	1,10,000
Proposed Dividend	50,000	58,000
Bank Overdraft	1,25,000	68,000
	8,15,000	8,80,000
Fixed Asset	4,10,000	4,00,000
Less Depreciation	1,10,000	1,50,000
	3,00,000	2,50,000
Current Assets:		
Debtors	2,00,000	2,40,000
Stock	3,00,000	3,50,000
Prepaid Expenses	3,000	5,000
Cash	12,000	35,000
	8,15,000	8,80,000

You are required to prepare—

(i) A Statement showing changes in the working capital and

(ii) A Statement of sources and applications of funds.

B.Com (H) D.U. Adapted

Ans. : Increase in Working Capital — Rs. 1,82,000

Funds from Operations — Rs. 1,42,000

Total Sources — Rs. 2,62,000

Total Applications — Rs. 80,000

(8) From the following Balance Sheets of Aruna Ltd. prepare

(i) Statement of changes in Working Capital and

(ii) Funds Flow Statement.

Liabilities	31. 3. 04	31. 3. 05
	Rs.	Rs.
8% Redeemable Preference Share Capital	1,50,000	1,00,000
Equity Share Capital	3,00,000	4,00,000
General Reserve	40,000	70,000
Profit & Loss A/c	30,000	48,000
Proposed Dividend	42,000	50,000
Creditors	55,000	83,000
Bills Payable	20,000	16,000
Provision for Taxation	40,000	50,000
	6,77,000	8,17,000
Assets		
Goodwill	1,15,000	90,000
Land and Building	2,00,000	1,70,000
Plant	80,000	2,00,000
Stock	77,000	1,09,000
Debtors	1,60,000	2,00,000
Bills Receivable	20,000	30,000
Cash at Bank	10,000	8,000
Cash in hand	15,000	10,000
	6,77,000	8,17,000

Additional Information :

(i) Depreciation of Rs. 10,000 and Rs. 20,000 has been charged on Plant and Land and Building respectively during the year ending 31st March, 2005

(ii) During the year an interim dividend of Rs. 20,000 and Income tax of Rs. 35,000 has been paid.

[B.Com (H) D.U. - Modified]

Ans. : Increase in Working Capital — Rs. 51,000

Funds from Operations — Rs. 2,18,000

Sources of Funds — Rs. 3, 28,000

Applications of Funds — Rs. 2,77,000

(9) From the following particulars prepare

(i) A Schedule of changes in Working Capital and

(ii) A Statement of Sources and uses of funds.

(A) BALANCE SHEET

	As on 31st March 2004	2005
Liabilities	Rs.	Rs.
Share Capital	6,00,000	6,00,000
Surplus	2,00,000	2,40,000
Long Term Loans	6,00,000	4,00,000
Accounts Payable	3,00,000	5,00,000
Cash Credit	2,60,000	2,00,000
O/s Expenses	40,000	60,000
	20,00,000	20,00,000
Assets		
Fixed Assets (Net)	12,00,000	13,00,000
Loans and Advances	1,00,000	—
Inventories	4,00,000	5,00,000
Accounts Receivable	2,00,000	1,60,000
Cash and Bank balance	1,00,000	40,000
	20,00,000	20,00,000

INCOME STATEMENT

		Rs.
	Turnover	40,50,000
Less	Cost of goods sold	34,50,000
	Gross Profit	60,00,000
Less	Operating Expenses (including depreciation of Rs. 2,00,000)	4,00,000
		2,00,000
Less	Tax paid @ 50%	1,00,000
		1,00,000
Less	Dividend Paid	60,000
	Retained in Business	40,000

Ans: Decrease in Working Capital — Rs. 2,60,000
Funds from Operations — Rs. 4,00,000
Total Sources — Rs. 4,00,000
Total Applications — Rs. 6,60,000

(10) Following are the Balance Sheets of Sunami Ltd. as on 31st March, 2004 and 2005.

Liabilities	2004 Rs.	2005 Rs.
Equity Share Capital	3,00,000	3,50,000
Securities Premium	—	40,000
Revenue Reserves	15,000	21,000
9% Debentures	80,000	40,000
Current liabilities	96,000	87,000
Proposed Dividend	30,000	49,000

Provision for Tax	15,000	20,000
	5,36,000	6,70,000
Assets	Rs.	Rs.
Goodwill	15,000	12,000
Building	1,90,000	1,80,000
Machinery	1,30,000	2,15,000
Current Assets	2,01,000	2,00,000
	5,36,000	6,07,000

Additional Information

(i) A machine which appeared at a written down value of Rs. 22,000 was sold for Rs. 18,000.

(ii) New machine costing Rs. 1,20,000 was installed during the year, and

(iii) Taxes paid during the year amounted to Rs. 22,000

Prepare Funds Flow Statement

[B.Com (H) D.U. 1998 - Modified]

Ans. : Funds From Operations - Rs. 1,12,000
Increase in Working Capital - Rs. 8,000
Total Sources - Rs. 2,20,000
Total Applications - Rs. 2,12,000

(11) The summarised Balance Sheets of SRK Ltd. as on 31st March 2004 and 2005 were as under:

Liabilities	31.3.2004	31.3.2005
	Rs.	Rs.
Equity Share Capital	12,00,000	15,00,000
14% Debentures	6,00,000	4,00,000
General Reserve	3,00,000	3,50,000
Profit and Loss A/c	1,00,000	1,50,000
Creditors	4,90,000	5,60,000
Proposed dividend	1,20,000	1,80,000
Provision for taxation	1,00,000	1,30,000
	29,10,000	32,70,000
Assets		
Building	8,00,000	7,60,000
Machinery	5,00,000	7,20,000
Short/Term Investments	3,00,000	4,50,000
Inventories	4,00,000	4,70,000
Debtors	6,70,000	5,30,000
Cash at Bank	2,20,000	3,30,000
Prepaid Expenses	20,000	10,000
	29,10,000	32,70,000

Additional Information :

(i) Debentures were redeemed at a premium of 10%

(ii) Taxes paid during the year amounted to Rs. 1,40,000.

(iii) A machine which appeared at a written down value of Rs. 80,000 was sold for Rs. 1,30,000 and a new machine costing Rs. 3,60,000 was acquired during the year.

Prepare a statement of sources and uses of funds showing changes in the working capital.

B.Com (H) D.U. 1999

Ans.: Funds from operations — Rs. 5,20,000
Total Sources — Rs. 9,50,000
Total Applications — Rs. 8,40,000
Increase in Working Capital — Rs. 1,10,000

(12) Following are the Balance Sheets of Fair and Lovely Ltd. as on 31st March, 2004 and 2005.

Liabilities	31.3.04	31.3.05
	Rs.	Rs.
Equity Share Capital	3,10,000	3,60,000
General Reserve	50,000	55,000
Profit and Loss A/c	30,500	35,600
Bills Payable	70,000	—
Creditors	1,50,000	1,35,200
Provision for tax	30,000	35,000
	6,40,500	6,20,800
Assets		
Goodwill	10,000	15,000
Building	3,00,000	2,90,000
Machinery	1,50,000	1,69,000
Stock	1,00,000	74,000
Debtors	80,000	64,200
Cash and Bank balance	500	8,600
	6,40,500	6,20,800

Additional Information :

(i) Dividend of Rs. 25,000 was paid during the year.

(ii) Assets of another company were purchased for Rs. 50,000 payable in shares. Assets purchased were stock Rs. 20,000, Machinery Rs. 25,000.

(iii) Machine was further purchased for cash Rs. 6,000.

(iv) Taxes paid during the year Rs. 28,000.

Prepare Funds Flow Statement and schedule of changes in working Capital.

[B.Com. (H) D.U. 1993 Modified]

Ans. : Funds from operations — Rs. 90,100

Total Source — Rs. 1,10,100

Total Applications — Rs. 59,000

Increase in Working Capital — Rs. 51,100

Investing and Financing Activities not affecting Working Capital Rs. 30,000

(13) From the following Balance Sheets of Hi-Fi-Ltd., prepare a statement of changes in financial position-Working Capital basis

	31.3.04	31.3.05
Liabilities	Rs.	Rs.
Share Capital	4,50,000	5,40,000
Reserve and Surplus	2,10,000	2,85,000
9% Debentures	75,000	—
Creditors	1,65,000	1,35,000
Unclaimed dividend	—	15,000
	9,00,000	9,75,000
Assets		
Goodwill	90,000	75,000
Machinery	3,75,000	3,00,000
Stock	1,80,000	2,70,000
Debtors	2,25,000	2,85,000
Cash and Bank	30,000	45,000
	9,00,000	9,75,000

Additional Information :

(i) On 1.4.2004 a Machinery for Rs. 45,000 Stock worth Rs. 15,000 and Goodwill were acquired by issue of shares and a machinery of the book value of Rs. 90,000 was sold for Rs. 97,500.

(ii) On 31. 3. 2005 the Debentures were redeemed for Rs. 73,500 and Shareholders were paid Rs. 37,500 cash for dividend.

[B.Com (H) D.U. Adapted]

Ans: Funds from Operation — Rs. 1,93,500

Total Sources — Rs. 3,06,000

Total Uses — Rs. 1,26,000

Increase in Working Capital — Rs. 1,80,000

Investing and Financing Activities not affecting Working Capital— Rs. 75,000

(14) The Balance Sheets Zohra Ltd. as on 31st March 2004 and 2005 were as under.

	31.3.04	31.3.05
Liabilities	Rs.	Rs.
Equity Share Capital	3,00,000	4,00,000
Capital Reserve	—	10,000
General Reserve	1,70,000	2,00,000
Profit and Loss A/c	60,000	75,000
Debentures	2,00,000	1,40,000
Current liabilities	1,20,000	1,30,000

	Provision for Taxation	90,000	85,000
	Proposed dividend	30,000	36,000
	Unpaid dividend	—	4,000
		9,70,000	10,80,000
Assets			
	Fixed Assets at Cost	8,00,000	9,50,000
Less	Depreciation	(2,30,000)	(2,90,000)
		5,70,000	6,60,000
	Trade Investments	1,00,000	80,000
	Current Assets	2,80,000	3,30,000
	Preliminary Expenses	20,000	10,000
		9,70,000	10,80,000

During the year 2004-2005 the company—

(i) Sold one machine for Rs. 25,000 the cost of which was Rs. 50,000 and the depreciation provided on it was Rs. 21,000.

(ii) Provided depreciation Rs. 95,000.

(iii) Redeemed 30% of Debentures @ 103

(iv) Sold some investments at a profit which was credited to Capital Reserve.

(v) Decided to value the Stock at cost where as previously the practice was to value Stock at cost less 10%. The Stock according to books on 31st March 2004 was Rs. 54,000. The Stock on 31st March 2005 was correctly valued at cost Rs. 75,000.

(vi) Decided to write off Fixed Assets costing Rs. 14,000 (fully depreciated).

You are required to prepare the Statement of Sources and Applications of Funds and a Schedule of changes in Working Capital.

[C.A. (F) O.S. Modified]

Ans. : Funds from Operations — Rs. 2,70,800
Sources — Rs. 4,25,800
Applications — Rs. 3,91,800
Increase in Working Capital — Rs. 34,000

(15) You have been given the following statement of a company as on 31st March, 2004 and 31st March, 2005.

	31.3.04	31.3.05
Assets	Rs. '000'	Rs.'000'
Fixed Assets less Depreciation	1,440	2,400
Investments	45	40
Stock in Trade	570	784
S. Debtors	362.8	560
Cash at Bank	520	180
Prepaid Expenses	56	84
	2,993.8	4,048

Liabilities		
Share Capital	788	920
Reserves and Surplus	592	1,248
Bank Loan (Secured)	348	—
Provision for Taxation	260	688
S. Creditors	1,005.8	1,192
	2,993.8	4,048

The following additional information is available—

(1)	Reserve and Surplus balance as on 1st April, 2004	5,92,000
	Net Profit for the year	7,94,000
		13,86,000
Less	Dividend	1,38,000
		12,48,000

(2) On 31st March, 2005 the accumulated depreciation on fixed assets was Rs. 8,00,000 and on 31st March, 2004 Rs. 7,20,000. Machinery costing Rs. 80,000 which was one-half depreciated was discarded and written off in the year ending 31.3.2005. Depreciation for the year just ended amounted to Rs. 1,20,000.

(3) Investments costing Rs. 20,000 were sold for Rs. 19,200 and Government Securities of the face value of Rs. 16,000 were purchased for Rs. 15,000 during the year.

Required :

(i) Statement Showing the detail the item-wise increase or decrease in Working Capital.

(ii) Statement sources and application of funds.

[ICWA (F) O/s Modified]

Ans: Funds from Operation Rs. 16,42,800
Sources Rs. 17,94,000
Applications Rs. 18,81,000
Decrease in Working Capital Rs. 87,000

(16) The Balance Sheets of Zed Ltd. as on 31st March, 2004 and 2005 are given below :

	31.3.04	31.3.05
Liabilities	Rs.	Rs.
Share Capital	3,00,000	4,50,000
Securities Premium	—	15,000
General Reserve	1,50,000	1,80,000
Profit and Loss A/c	30,000	51,000
6% Debentures	2,10,000	1,50,000
Provision for Depreciation on Plant	1,50,000	1,68,000
Provision for Depreciation on Furniture	15,000	18,000
Provision for Taxation	60,000	90,000
S. Creditors	2,58,000	2,85,000
	11,73,000	14,07,000

Assets		
Freehold Land	3,00,000	3,00,000
Plant at Cost	3,12,000	3,00,000
Furnitures at Cost	21,000	27,000
Investment at Cost	1,80,000	2,40,000
Debtors	90,000	2,10,000
Stock	1,80,000	1,95,000
Cash and Bank	90,000	1,35,000
	11,73,000	14,07,000

Additional Information :

(i) A plant purchased for Rs. 12,000 (Depreciation Rs. 6,000) was sold for cash Rs. 2,400 on 31st December, 2004. On 30th September, 2004, an item of furniture was purchased for Rs. 6,000. These were the only transactions concerning the fixed assets during 2004-2005. Depreciation on plant provided at 8% on cost (the sold out item is not taken into consideration) and on furniture at 12.5% on average cost. A dividend of 22.5% on original shares was paid.

You are required to prepare a statement showing sources and uses of funds.

C.A. (F) O.S. Adapted

Ans:

Funds from Operation	Rs. 2,39,100
Increase in Working Capital	Rs. 1,53,000
Total Sources	Rs. 4,06,500
Total Uses	Rs. 2,53,500

(17) From the following particulars you are required to prepare a Statement of Sources and Uses of Funds for the year ending 31st March, 2005.

	31.3.04.	31.3.05
Liabilities	Rs.	Rs.
Equity Share Capital	2,00,000	3,00,000
Securities Premium	30,000	70,000
Profit and Loss A/c	56,000	1,40,000
9% Debentures	1,40,000	60,000
Bank Overdraft	28,000	—
Creditors	68,000	96,000
Proposed dividends	30,000	40,000
Depreciation - Plant	90,000	1,08,000
- Fixtures	26,000	30,000
	6,68,000	8,44,000
Assets		
Freehold Property at Cost	2,20,000	2,60,000
Plant and Machinery at Cost	2,40,000	3,02,000
Fixtures and Fittings at Cost	48,000	58,000
Stock	74,000	1,02,000

Debtors	86,000	88,000
Bank Balance	—	32,000
Premium on Redemption of debentures		2,000
	6,68,000	8,44,000

Additional Information :

(i) A machine which had cost Rs. 16,000 and in respect of which Rs. 12,000 depreciation had been provided was sold for Rs. 6,000, and fixtures (Cost Rs. 10,000 and Depreciation Rs. 4,000) was sold for Rs. 2,000. The profits and losses of these transactions had been dealt through the Profit and Loss A/c.

(ii) Actual premium paid on redemption of the debentures was Rs. 4,000 of which Rs. 2,000 had been written off to the Profit and Loss A/c.

(iii) No interim dividend has been paid.

ICWA (F) O.S. Adapted

Ans. : Funds from Operations — Rs. 1,66,000
Increase in Working Capital — Rs. 62,000
Total Sources — Rs. 3,14,000
Total Uses — Rs. 2,52,000

(18) Following are the Balance Sheets of Rayon Ltd. as on 31st March, 2004 and 2005.

	31.3.04	31.3.05
Liabilities	Rs.	Rs.
Equity Share Capital (Rs. 100)	4,00,000	6,00,000
Securities Premium	1,00,000	1,10,000
General Reserve	2,00,000	2,20,000
Debenture Redemption Reserve	1,00,000	1,10,000
Debentures	3,00,000	2,90,000
Secured Loans	2,00,000	1,00,000
Provision for Taxation	40,000	35,000
Current Liabilities	24,000	30,000
	13,64,000	14,95,000
Freehold Property	5,70,000	5,00,000
Plant and Machinery	3,60,000	3,51,000
Furniture	90,000	81,000
Investments	—	2,10,000
Stock	1,55,000	1,45,000
Debtors	1,80,000	1,60,000
Bills Receivable	4,000	40,000
Cash in hand	5,000	8,000
	13,64,000	14,95,000

Additional Information :

(i) During the year the company paid 12% dividend on it's equity share capital of Rs. 4,00,000.

(ii) Taxation provision of last year was utilised to the extent of Rs. 30,000 for income tax paid in the current year.

(iii) Depreciation was charged as follows—

Building	5%
Plant and Machinery	10%
Furniture	10%

(iv) A building worth Rs. 70,000 was sold on 1.4.2004 at Rs. 60,000 and a new Building was constructed at a value of Rs. 25,000 on 31.3.2005.

(v) A machine was purchased at a cost of Rs. 40,000 on 1.4.2004 while a machine having a book value of Rs. 10,000 was sold on 1.10.2004 for Rs. 20,000.

Prepare :

(i) A Schedule of Changes in Working Capital

(ii) A Funds Flow Statement

C.S. (F) O.S. Modified

Ans. : Funds form Operations — Rs. 1,76,000
Total Sources — Rs. 4,66,000
Total Applications— Rs. 4,63,000
Increase in Working Capital— Rs. 3,000

(19) The following are the Balance Sheet of Amisha Ltd. as on 31st March, 2005. Anisha Ltd. is a wholly owned subsidiary of SRK Ltd.

Liabilities	Rs.	Rs.
Equity Share Capital	8,00,000	—
Capital Surplus	3,00,000	—
Reserve Surplus	7,00,000	—
Inter Company Account	1,00,000	13,67,000
Current liabilities	2,00,000	2,50,000
	21,00,000	16,17,000
Assets		
Goodwill	6,50,000	60,000
Fixed Assets less Depreciation	10,00,000	10,16,000
Current Assets	4,00,000	5,01,000
Deferred Charges	50,000	40,000
	21,00,000	16,17,000

On June 30 2004 Rs. 6,00,000 of goodwill was charged off Rs. 3,00,000 to Capital Surplus and Rs. 3,00,000 to Revenue Surplus.

In the first half of the year, the subsidiary bought the assets and goodwill and Rs. 50,000 for inventory and accounts receivable. The amount paid Rs. 1,70,000.

An old machinery (book value Rs. 12,000) on which Rs. 8,000 was charged as depreciation sold for Rs. 1,000.

On 30th September, 2004 the Subsidiary company was dissolved and made a division of a parent company It's accounts continued in a separate divisional ledger.

A net profit of Rs. 3,17,000 after providing Rs. 80,000 for depreciation and Rs. 10,000 for amortisation of goodwill, had been made and was credited to inter-company account. The deferred charges consist of unexpired insurance and prepaid current expenses.

[C.A.(F) O.S. Modified]

Ans: Funds from Operations Rs. 4,20,000
Total Sources Rs. 13,71,000
Total Applications Rs. 13,20,000
Increase in Working Capital Rs. 51,000

Hint : Please refer to illustration 12.

(20) From the following particulars you are required to prepare :

(i) A Schedule of Changes in Working Capital

(ii) A Statement of Changes in Financial Position

Liabilities	31.3.2004	31.3.2005
	Rs.	Rs.
Equity Share Capital (Rs. 100)	10,00,000	15,00,000
9% Preference Share Capital (Rs. 100) (Rs. 50 paid)	5,00,000	
Securities Premium	25,000	—
Capital Redemption Reserve	—	5,00,000
General Reserve	10,00,000	7,00,000
Profit and Loss A/c	2,75,000	3,00,000
Other liabilities	10,00,000	6,00,000
	38,00,000	36,00,000
Assets		
Fixed Assets	15,00,000	18,00,000
Current Assets	22,00,000	14,00,000
Miscellaneous Expenditure	1,00,000	4,00,000
	38,00,000	36,00,000

Additional Information :

(i) The Company declared a dividend of 20% to Equity Shareholders on 30.6.2004.

(ii) The Company issued notice to Preference Shareholders for redemption at a premium of 5% on 1.7.2004 and the entire proceedings were completed before 15th September, 2004 in accordance with the legal provisions of redemption.

(iii) The Company provided depreciation at 10% on the closing balance of fixed assets. During the year one plant whose book value was Rs. 1,00,000 was sold at a loss of Rs. 25,000.

(iv) There was no change in the schedule of debtors as on 31st March, 2004. However as the company felt that certain debtors were doubtful of recovery a provision was made in the accounts.

(v) Miscellaneous expenses included Rs. 50,000 share issue and other expenses paid during the year.

C.A. (F) O.S. Modified

Ans: Funds From operations— Rs. 5,75,000
Total Sources—Rs. 15,50,000
Total Applications— Rs. 19,50,000
Decrease in Working Capital— Rs. 4,00,000

Hint : CRR Created Rs. 3,00,000 from General Reserve and Rs. 2,00,000 from P & L A/c and Miscelleneous Expenses of Rs. 1,00,000 only are to be treated as non-cash charges written off

(21) From the following particulars and additional information prepare (i) Statement of Changes in Working Capital and (ii) Statement of changes Financial Position.

	31.03.04 Rs.	31.03.05 Rs.
Credit balances		
Equity Share Capital	8,00,000	8,00,000
Capital Reserve	—	2,00,000
8% Debentures	—	2,50,000
Profit and Loss A/c	3,00,000	4,50,000
Net Profit for the year	2,30,000	3,00,000
Provision for Depreciation	4,00,000	5,00,000
Provision for Doubtful debts	20,000	35,000
Current liabilities	3,50,000	2,50,000
Bank Overdraft	2,80,000	1,00,000
	23,80,000	28,85,000
Debit Balances		
Land and Building	5,00,000	4,00,000
Plant and Machinery	10,00,000	12,50,000
Trade Investments at Cost	1,00,000	3,00,000
Current Assets	7,00,000	8,50,000
Dividend for the previous year	80,000	80,000
Discount on Issue of Debentures	—	5,000
	23,80,000	28,85,000

Additional Information :

(i) During the year, land and building having an original cost of Rs. 1,00,000 and a written down value of Rs. 75,000 have been sold for Rs. 3,00,000. The Capital Profit has been transferred to Capital reserve and profit equivalent to the depreciation written off in the past has been included in the profit for the year.

(ii) On 1st April, 2004, the company issued debentures of the face value of Rs. 2,50,000 at a discount of 5%. Part of the discount has been written off out of the profits.

C.A. (F) O.S. Modified

Ans: Total Sources Rs. 9,45,000
Total Application Rs. 5,30,000
Increase in Working Capital Rs. 4,15,000
Funds from Operation Rs. 4,07,500

Hint: Of the Capital profit and Rs. 2,25,000 Rs. 2,00,000 has been transferred to Capital Reserve and balance Rs. 25,000 to Profit and Loss A/c.

CASH FLOW STATEMENT

(22) From the following particulars Calculate Cash from operating activities by applying :

(a) Direct Method

(b) Indirect Method.

PROFIT AND LOSS A/C
for the year ended 31st March, 2005

To Opening Stock	60,000	By Sales	6,00,000
To Purchases	3,00,000	By Stock	85,000
To Wages	75,000	(Closing)	
To Gross Profit c/d	2,50,000		
	6,85,000		6,85,000
To Salaries	50,000	By Gross Profit b/d	2,50,000
To General Expenses	15,000		
To Insurance	10,000		
To Depreciation	75,000		
To Provision for Tax	30,000		
To Net Profit	70,000		
	2,50,000		2,50,000

Additional Information

	31.3.04.	31.03.05
	Rs.	Rs.
Salaries o/s	5,000	7,500
Prepaid Insurance	5,000	5,000
Debtors	50,000	70,000
Bills Receivable	25,000	15,000
Creditors	35,000	25,000

Income Tax paid during the year amounted to Rs. 25,000.

Ans. : Rs. 97,500.

(23) From the following Profit and Loss A/c Calculate Cash from operating activities.

To Salaries	1,80,000	By Gross Profit b/d	5,40,000
To Rent	90,000	By Profit on Sale of Land	28,000
To Office Expenses	30,000	By Dividend Received	20,000
To Depreciation	24,000	By Income Tax Refund	8,000
To Loss on Sale of Plant	12,000	By Rent Received	40,000
To Goodwill w/o	30,000		
To Discount on Issue of Debentures w/o	10,000		
To Preliminary Expenses w/o	8,000		
To Proposed Dividend	60,000		
To Provision for Tax	60,000		
To Net Profit c/d	1,32,000		
	6,36,000		6,36,000

Income Tax paid during the year amounted to Rs. 50,000.

Ans. : Cash generated from operating activities Rs. 1,98,000

(24) From the following information compute :

(1) Cash flow from Operating activities

(2) Cash flow from Investing activities

(3) Cash flow from Financing activities.

		Rs.
(i)	Sales made during the year	
	Cash —	2,00,000
	Credit —	3,50,000
	Purchases Cash —	Nil
	Credit —	3,00,000
(ii)	Salaries incurred during the year	62,500
(iii)	Depreciation	1,50,000
(iv)	Goodwill w/o	12,500

(v) Issue of 1,00,000 equity shares of Rs. 10 each at premium of 20%.

(vi) Issue of equity shares of Rs. 25,00,000 as purchase consideration of Building of Rs. 30,00,000

(vii) Purchase of Machinery for cash - 4,20,000

(viii) Dividend of last year amounting to Rs. 1,00,000 was paid. Dividend of Rs. 2,50,000 was declared but not yet paid.

(ix) An equipment (Book value Rs. 50,000) sold for Rs. 60,000

(x) Closing Balances- Debtors- Rs. 85,000

Creditors - Rs. 1,00,000, Salaries o/s Rs. 12,500

Ans. : Cash from Operating activities — Rs. 2,15,000

Cash used in Investing activities — Rs. (3,60,000)

Cash Flow from financing activities — Rs. 11,00,000

(25) Following are the Balance Sheets of Virnda Ltd. as on 31st March, 2004 and 2005

Liabilities	31.3.04 Rs.	31.3.05 Rs.
Equity Share Capital	12,00,000	12,75,000
Profit and Loss Appropriation A/c	2,17,500	3,67,500
Mortgaged Loans	—	75,000
S. Creditors	1,35,000	75,000
	15,52,500	17,92,500
Fixed Assets	11,10,000	12,60,000
Stock	1,35,000	1,05,000
Debtors	2,47,500	2,92,500
Cash and Bank Balance	60,000	1,35,000
	15,52,500	17,92,500

Prepare Cash Flow Statement as per AS- (Rev.)

Ans. : Cash From Operating Activities — Rs. 75,000
Cash used in Investing Activities — Rs. (1,50,000)
Cash flow from Financing Activities — Rs. 1,50,000
Increase in Cash and Cash Equivalents — Rs. 75,000

(26) From the following Balance Sheets of Ahmed Ltd. prepare a Cash Flow Statement.

Liabilities	31.3.04 Rs.	31.3.05 Rs.
12% Preference Share Capital	—	90,000
Equity Share Capital	7,20,000	8,10,000
General Reserve	36,000	45,000
Profit and Loss Account	18,000	21,600
15% Debentures	1,08,000	1,17,000
S. Creditors	2,16,000	1,98,000
Bank overdraft	2,25,000	1,22,400
Provision for Taxation	54,000	75,600
Proposed Dividend	90,000	1,04,400
	14,67,000	15,84,000
Assets		
Fixed Assets	7,38,000	7,20,000
Less Provision for Depreciation	(1,98,000)	(2,70,000)
	5,40,000	4,50,000
Stock	5,40,000	6,30,000
Debtors	3,60,000	4,32,000
Prepaid Expenses	5,400	9,000
Cash and Bank	21,600	63,000
	14,67,000	15,84,000

Interest paid on debentures - Rs. 16,200
Prepare Cash Flow Statement

Ans. : Cash from Operating activities — Rs. 43,200
Cash from Investing Activities — Rs. 18,000
Cash used in Financing Activities — Rs. 82,800
Net Increase in Cash and Cash equivalent — Rs.1,44,000

(27) From the following Balance Sheets of Mr. Exe as on 31st March, 2004 and 2005, prepare a Cash Flow Statement as per AS-3 (Revised)

Liabilities	31.3.04 Rs.	31.3.05 Rs.
Share Capital	5,00,000	6,12,000
Loan from Bank	1,60,000	2,00,000
Loan from a Friend	1,00,000	—
Creditors	1,60,000	1,76,000
	9,20,000	9,88,000

Assets		
Land	1,60,000	2,00,000
Building	1,40,000	2,40,000
Machinery	3,20,000	2,20,000
Stock	1,40,000	1,00,000
Debtors	1,20,000	2,00,000
Cash and Bank	40,000	28,000
	9,20,000	9,88,000

During the year a machine costing Rs. 40,000 (accumulated depreciation Rs. 12,000) was sold for Rs. 20,000. Provision for depreciation against Machinery as on 31st March, 2004 and 31st March, 2005 was Rs. 1,00,000 and Rs. 1,60,000 respectively. Net Profit for the year amounted to Rs. 1,80,000.

Ans. : Cash flow from Operating Activities — Rs. 2,36,000
Cash used in Investing Activities — Rs. (1,20,000)
Cash used in Financing Activities — Rs. (1,28,000)
Decrease in Cash and Cash equivalents — Rs. (12,000)

(28) S. S. Ltd. wants you to prepare a Cash Flow Statement as per AS-3 (Rev.). The Balance Sheets for the ending on 31st March, 2004 and 2005 are as under :

Liabilities	31.3.04 Rs.	31.3.05 Rs.
Equity Share Capital	4,50,000	5,25,000
General Reserve	1,50,000	2,25,000
Profit and Loss A/c	90,000	1,05,000
10% Debentures	2,25,000	3,75,000
S. Creditors	1,12,500	1,65,000
Bills Payable	15,000	22,500
Provision for Depreciation	1,35,000	1,95,000
	11,77,500	16,12,500
Goodwill	1,50,000	1,20,000
Machinery	6,15,000	8,10,000
10% Investments	45,000	1,20,000
Stock	60,000	82,500
Debtors	1,20,000	2,85,000
Cash and Bank balance	1,80,000	1,95,000
Discount on Issue of Debentures	7,500	—
	11,77,500	16,12,500

Additional Information :

(i) Investments costing Rs. 45,000 were sold for Rs. 42,000 during the year 2004-2005.

(ii) A new machine costing Rs. 1,95,000 was purchased for cash.

(iii) The Company paid dividend @ 10% for the last year.

(iv) Company received a sum of Rs. 10,000 as claim for loss of stock due to fire from the Insurance company. This claim was credited to Profit and Loss Account.

Ans. : Cash from Operating Activities — Rs. 81,000
Cash used in Investing Activities — Rs. (2,68,500)
Cash from Financing Activities — Rs. 2,02,500
Net Increase in Cash and Cash Equivalents — Rs. 15,000

(29) From the following Balance Sheets of Diana and Daisy Ltd. prepare a Cash Flow Statement for the year end 31st March, 2005.

Liabilities	31. 3. 04	31. 3. 05
	Rs.	Rs.
8% Preference Share Capital	1,50,000	1,00,000
Equity Share Capital	3,00,000	4,00,000
General Reserve	40,000	70,000
Profit and Loss A/c	30,000	48,000
Proposed Dividend	42,000	50,000
Creditors	55,000	83,000
Bills Payable	20,000	16,000
Provision for Taxation	40,000	50,000
	6,77,000	8,17,000
Assets		
Goodwill	1,15,000	90,000
Land and Building	2,00,000	1,70,000
Plant and Machinery	80,000	2,00,000
Stock	77,000	1,09,000
Debtors	1,60,000	2,00,000
Bills Receivable	20,000	30,000
Cash at Bank	15,000	10,000
Cash in hand	16,000	8,000
	6,77,000	8,17,000

Additional Information:

(i) Depreciation of Rs. 20,000 and Rs. 10,000 have been charged on Plant and Machinery and on Building respectively.

(ii) An interim dividend of Rs. 20,000 has been paid during the year.

(iii) Income Tax Rs. 35,000 was paid during the year.

B.Com (H) D.U. Adapted.

Ans. : Cash from Operating activities — Rs. 1,25,000
Cash used in Investing activities — Rs. (1,20,000)
Cash used in Financing activities — Rs. (12,000)
Net decrease in Cash and Cash equivalents— Rs. (7,000)

(30) The following are the summarised Balance Sheets of Tony Tyres Ltd. as on 31st March, 2004 and 31st March, 2005.

Liabilities	31.3.04	31.3.05
	Rs.	Rs.
Share Capital	2,00,000	2,50,000
General Reserve	50,000	60,000
Profit and Loss A/c	30,500	30,600
Bank Loan	70,000	—
S. Creditors	1,50,000	1,35,200
Provision for Taxation	30,000	35,000
	5,30,500	5,10,800
Assets		
Land and Building	2,00,000	1,90,000
Machinery	1,50,000	1,69,000
Stock	1,00,000	74,000
S. Debtors	80,000	64,200
Bank	—	8,000
Cash in hand	500	600
Goodwill	—	5,000
	5,30,500	5,10,800

Additional Information :

During the year ended 31st March, 2005

(i) Dividend of Rs. 23,000 was paid.

(ii) Assets of another Company were purchased for a consideration of Rs. 50,000 payable in shares. The following assets were purchased: Stock - Rs. 20,000, Machinery - Rs. 25,000

(iii) Machinery was further purchased for Rs. 8,000.

(iv) Depreciation written off machinery Rs. 12,000.

(v) Income Tax provided during the year Rs. 33,000.

(vi) Loss on sale of machinery Rs. 200 was written off to General Reserve.

You are required to prepare Cash Flow Statement as per AS-3 (Revised)

Ans. : Cash from Operating Activities — Rs. 1,07,300

Cash used in Investing Activities — Rs. (6,200)

Cash used in Financing Activities — Rs. (93,000)

Net Increase in Cash and Cash Equivalents— Rs. 8,100

(31) Following are the Balance Sheets of Abdullah Ltd. as on 31st March, 2004 and 2005.

		31.3.04.	31.3.05
Liabilities		Rs.	Rs.
	Share Capital	12,00,000	14,00,000
	General Reserve	4,00,000	5,00,000
	Profit and Loss A/c	2,00,000	4,00,000
	Capital Reserve	—	20,000
	7% Debentures	6,00,000	4,00,000
	Creditors for Expenses	20,000	24,000
	Creditors for Supply of goods	3,20,000	5,00,000
	Proposed Dividend	60,000	70,000
	Provision for Taxation	1,40,000	1,50,000
		29,40,000	34,64,000
Assets			
	Fixed Assets	20,00,000	24,00,000
Less	Accumulated Depreciation	(4,00,000)	(5,00,000)
		16,00,000	19,00,000
	Investments at cost	3,60,000	3,60,000
	Stock at cost	4,00,000	5,40,000
	S. Debtors	4,50,000	4,90,000
	Bills Receivable	80,000	1,30,000
	Prepaid Expenses	20,000	24,000
	Miscellaneous Expenses	30,000	20,000
		29,40,000	34,64,000

Additional Information :

(i) During the year 2004-2005 fixed assets (valued at Rs. 20,000, depreciation written off Rs. 60,000) was sold for Rs. 16,000.

(ii) Proposed dividend of last year was paid during the year.

(iii) During the year investment costing Rs. 1,60,000 were sold and later in the year investments of the same cost were purchased. Profit on sale of investments was credited to Capital Reserve.

(iv) Debentures were redeemed at a premium of 10%.

(v) Liability for taxation came to Rs. 1,10,000.

You are required to prepare cash flow statement.

ICWA (I) Modified

Ans. : Cash from Operating Activities — Rs. 5,24,000

Cash used in Investing Activities — Rs. (4,44,000)

Cash used in Financing Activities (Rs. 80,000)

(32) From the following data compute cash flow from operating activities, cash flow from investing activities and cash from financing activities.

INCOME STATEMENT OF A LTD. FOR THE YEAR ENDED 31ST MARCH, 2005

		Rs.
	Sales	12,60,000
Less	Cost of goods	(7,20,000)
	Depreciation	(60,000)
	Interest Expenses	(90,000)
	Other Expenses	(3,45,000)
	Discount on issue of debentures	(6,000)
	Net Income	39,000

BALANCE SHEET OF A LTD.
As on 31st March, 2004 and 2005

Liabilities	2005 Rs.	2004 Rs.
Equity Share Capital (Shares of Rs. 10 each)	3,60,000	2,10,000
Retained Earnings	1,44,000	1,05,000
Debentures	3,00,000	3,00,000
Creditors	1,80,000	2,10,000
	9,84,000	8,25,000
Assets		
Fixed Assets :		
Gross Block	3,60,000	3,00,000
Less Depreciation	(1,20,000)	(60,000)
	2,40,000	2,40,000
Current Assets		
Cash	3,00,000	2,40,000
Stock	2,40,000	2,10,000
Debtors	1,80,000	1,05,000
Miscellaneous Expenditure		
Discount on issue of Debentures	24,000	30,000
	9,84,000	8,25,000

Ans. : Cash from Operations — Rs. 1,20,000
Cash used in Investing Activities — (Rs. 60,000)
Cash from Financing Activities — Rs. 60,000
Increase in Cash and Cash Equivalents — Rs. 60,000

Hint: Presume dividend paid — Rs. 60,000

11

Ratio Analysis

Published accounts presented by a company in an annual general meeting do not serve the inherent purpose of every user of accounting information. The information contained in these financial statements does not give any instant suggestion or direction with regard to solvency, liquidity, operating efficiency, debt capacity, or future prospects of the company. It is believed that figures do not speak themselves, we have to make them speak. For this purpose the information contained in these financial statements is used (analysed) by the management, creditors, investors, bankers, employees, shareholders and others to form judgements and to get better insight about the financial strength and weakness of the company concerned. This analysis is done by means of various tools such as :

- Comparative Statements
- Common size Statements
- Trend Analysis, and
- Ratio Analysis.

These tools of analysis help in estimating earning capacity of the enterprises, assessing the financial position of the company, ascertaining the future prospects of the firm, measuring the efficiency of operation, judging the solvency of an enterprise, determining the debt capacity of the company, assessing the financial performance of the business and to know the progress and take future course of action. The present chapter focuses only on last and the most reliable tool of analysis *i.e.* "Ratio Analysis".

Meaning and Nature

"Ratio" refers to a relationship between the two numerical variables in quantitative term. It simply means expressing one item in relation to another in numerical term. It is a yardstick which measures and compares the relationship between two or more items (accounting figures). Infact accounting ratio shows and describes the significant relationships between accounting data so as to arrive at certain conclusion or form judgement. An isolated or a single figure does not convey any significant improvement, change or deterioration in a company's financial health, profitability, solvency or liquidity position unless expressed in relation to other figure. For example a profit of Rs. 5,00,000 earned by a company during the current year does not convey any significant information unless the other constituent (variable) such as sales or capital employed is not given. Then, we can measure profit margin in relation to sales or earning capacity on capital employed. This information when compared with last year's figures or with the figures of other firm in the same industry will convey a significant information about company's profitability and earning capacity in terms of good, better, bad or worse. Thus the rationale of ratio analysis lies in the fact that it makes related information comparable. The ratios reveal or disclose the relationship in a more meaningful way so as to draw certain conclusions. Ratios help to summarise the large number of financial data into a smaller fraction, percent or ratio to form quick opinion or make judgements on some of the aspects of company's affairs. In nutshell it indicates quantitative relationship to make quantitative judgement.

Bench marks (Standards)

It is to be noted that ratio analysis involves comparison for the purpose of proper interpretation of accounting data. These ratios relating to current year are compared with the 'standards'. (Benchmarks) These "standards" may be :

- Past ratios of the same company
- Projected ratios (predetermined norms, taking future into account)
- Competitors ratios or
- Industry's ratios

When **"past ratios"** of a company are taken as standard for comparison for evaluating the performance over a period of time, it is known as "**Trend** or **Time-series** Analysis. This analysis shows the direction of change which may be favourable or unfavourable as compared to previous year.

The use of 'pre-determined projected ratios' as standards to compare the current and past performance is covered under **"proforma analysis"**. If projected (future) ratios indicate unfavourable position, then the corrective measures must be taken.

When ratios of one enterprise are compared with ratios of other enterprise of the same industry at the same point of time, it is known as cross sectional analysis. Inter-firm comparisons reflect the performance of a firm in relation to its competitors.

Under Industry analysis the ratios are compared with the average ratios of the industry under which it operates. This analysis helps in ascertaining the variation in profitability, liquidity, solvency and financial position of the enterprise as against the overall industry's position.

Forms of Ratios

Ratios may be expressed in any of the following forms

(1) **Pure ratios :** When a variable is divided by other variable the quotient shows the relation of numerator with denominator, which may be expressed as 4 : 1, 3 : 1, 2 : 1 or 1 : 1 or 0.5 : 1 and so on.

(2) **Rate :** Ratios may be expressed in terms of rate such as two times, three times or four times and so on.

(3) **Percentage :** Ratios may be expressed in relation to hundred *i.e.* in the form of percentage also, such as 20%, 25%, 30% 50% or 80% and so on.

(4) **Fraction :** The ratios may also be expressed in the form of fractions, such as 1/4th 1/3rd, 2/5th or 3/4th and so on.

Objectives of Ratio Analysis

(i) To judge the earning capacity, operating efficiency, financial soundness, and liquidity position of an enterprise in an unambiguous manner.

(ii) To assess the comparative changes and the degree of improvement or deterioration in the financial health of the enterprise, profitability or liquidity position.

(iii) To provide a proper base for decision making purposes for the users of financial statements.

(iv) To pin point areas of shortcomings which facilitates to take corrective measures by the management.

(v) To provide base for future planning and preparing various budgets.

(vi) To highlight the company's performance by giving at a glance information to the management and others.

USES/IMPORTANCE

As already explained the figures as shown in the financial statements do not convey or explain themselves unless grilled and converted into ratios. Ratio analysis summarises and simplifies the huge figures systematically into a small understandable figures which helps in the following ways.

(1) Simplifies accounting figures and makes them understandable

Ratio analysis simplifies the financial statements. It tells the whole or essence of story of changes in the financial position, liquidity position, solvency, profitability or operating efficiency etc. Its main contribution lies in communicating the relationship between two or more accounting variables. These ratios are highly useful because absolute figures do not communicate anything. Ratio analysis shows the result of detailed and complicated computation in a very short and brief form. One may draw certain conclusions by inference just after studying ratios.

(2) It provides data for inter-firm and intra-firm comparison

Ratio analysis provides the data for inter-firm comparison. *i.e.* comparing the various results and ratios with other firms of same industry and intra-firm comparison *i.e.* comparing the performance of one unit with other units of the same firm. This analysis will enable the management to measure the progress of an enterprise year after year in relation to other firms of the same industry and different units of the same firm. At the same time necessary corrective measures can be taken by management by reviewing the various policies to improve the overall performance.

(3) It helps in understanding the financial statements

Ratios are useful for understanding the financial statements. Even a layman develops interest in analysing the results of operations of an enterprise. Various ratios relating to profitability, liquidity, solvency and activity provide a proper direction to users of accounting information. It helps them to take appropriate decisions.

(4) It helps in forecasting and Planning

Ratios form the basis of future planning and forecasting. Trend analysis (ratios calculated for a number of years relating to an enterprise) is used as guide to future planning which assists management in its basic functions of forecasting, planning, organising, co-ordinating and controlling.

(5) Useful in Credit and other analysis

Liquidity and current ratios judge the firms' credit worthiness and debt paying capacity, debt-equity ratios determine the degree of risk attached to their stakes and the extent to which the firm can use borrowed funds, which in turn determine the long term solvency of an enterprise. A favourable or unfavourable liquidity and solvency ratios will determine suppliers and lenders (Banks/financial institutions) policy to extend credit/loans or not.

(6) Useful in security analysis

Investments in securities are guided by long term profitability which depends on number of factors such as stock-turnover, debtors turnover, creditors turnover, return on capital employed etc. Investment decisions are based on safety of principal, consistency and adequacy of return. These ratios provide greater insights into the fundamentals of a company to draw certain conclusions.

(7) It helps in strategic analysis

A strategic analysis shall reveal the goals and strategies of company and how far the same have been achieved. If not, how far the changes in investments pattern, financing needs and its pressure, usage of resources and generation of funds for financing activities will help to meet the desired level of expectations.

Thus the importance of ratio analysis lies in the fact that it presents figures and facts on a comparative basis and enables the users to draw inferences regarding the liquidity profitability solvency, operating efficiency of an enterprise. Ratios are exceptionally useful tools of financial statement analysis which provide a sound base for decision-making purposes.

LIMITATIONS OF RATIO ANALYSIS

(1) Inferences may be misleading

Ratios are computed from figures taken from the financial statements. Hence inferences from such accounting ratios are as reliable as the data on which these ratios are based. If the figures are not true and fair, the ratios may mislead the users. For example, valuation of inventories at market price (inflated price) over-valuation of fixed assets, charging less depreciation, treating revenue expenditures as capital expenditure and vice-versa, will distort the entire profitability and financial position of the enterprise which will render the whole exercise of ratios futile.

(2) Problem of standard terms

The absence of use of standard accounting terms also creates a problem of proper interpretation. For example while calculating profitability ratio some companies take PBIT (Profit before interest and Tax) while some take PAT Profit after Interest and Tax, where as others may take Profit after Interest but before Tax (PAIBT). Thus ratios based on different notions may not be compared appropriately.

(3) Difficulty in comparison

Intra-firm and inter-firm (including trend analysis) comparisons suffer from many drawbacks which renders the comparison very difficult.

This is due to following reasons—

(i) Different policies of valuation of stock/inventories such as FIFO, LIFO, Average etc. adopted by various firms.

(ii) Different methods of charging depreciation such as Straight Line Method, Written Down Value Method etc. applied by them.

(iii) Different policies followed by the firms in respect of amortisation of intangible assets, writing off discount on issue of shares/debentures, and preliminary expenses etc.

Such differences in policies and methods render the ratios uncomparable in true sense. If compared the results are bound to be misleading.

(4) Impact of Price-level changes

Financial statements are based on historical cost which ignores the changes in the price level taken place over a period of time. Assets acquired by the two firms at different point of time will be shown at different costs as the same will not be adjusted for changes in price level. For example an asset acquired in 1998 will show a lower asset turnover ratio as compared to the asset acquired in 2005 due to rising price level. Thus price level changes often make comparison of figures very difficult.

(5) Ignores qualitative (Non-monetary) factors

Accounting figures do not provide any non-monetary information howsoever important it may be. Accounting ratios as a matter of fact are tools of quantitative analysis only which totally ignore qualitative aspects. For example, though credit may be granted to a customer on the basis of information regarding his financial position yet the grant of credit depends on customer's past record, honesty and integrity. Hence decisions based on ratios would be misleading. The qualitative factors are needed to draw definite conclusions.

(6) Ratios without absolute figures are meaning less

Ratios should be studied and analysed in the light of absolute figures also. Otherwise, the conclusions drawn may not be dependable and reliable. For example if a company's turnover is Rs. 5,00,000 in the first year and Rs. 10,00,000 in the next year. This shows an increase of 100% in turnover where as other company's turnover is Rs. 50,00,000 in the first year and Rs. 75,00,000 in the next year. This indicates an increase of 50% only. If one looks at the absolute figures, one may notice an increase of Rs. 5,00,000 in turnover in the first case while that of Rs. 25,00,000 in the second case. That is five times more than the first company's growth sales.

(7) Past does not reflect future

Past (historical cost) is not an exact indicator of future. Accounting ratios are computed on the basis of past facts and figures which do not reflect the present or future conditions of the business. Hence any forecast based on past records (data) is not desirable for forecasting current and future events. These ratios may be effective only when they take into account the probable happenings in future.

(8) No common benchmarks (standards)

It is difficult to evolve common standard ratios in terms of liquidity, profitability, debt equity, solvency and so on because the conditions prevailing differ from firm to firm and industry to industry. For example a firm with 2 : 1 current ratio may not be able to discharge its current obligations due to uneven distribution of current assets in relation of liquidity. Where as, other firm with a current ratio of 1.5 : 1 may not have any liquidity crunch due to favourable (even) distribution of current assets in relation to liquidity.

(9) Window-dressing and personal judgements

Manipulation of facts and figures to present an improved financial position than the actual one is known as window dressing. It is a technique which is applied by management (Directors) to achieve certain inherent objectives: Thus the ratios based on over-stated assets and understated liabilities are bound to be deceptive and unreliable. Similarly, personal judgements with regard to certain estimates may be biased. For example, estimating the life of an asset for depreciation purposes or providing provision for bad and doubtful debts may be affected by personal judgements of the accountant and management.

(10) Irrelevant ratios

Ratios may be worked out for any two variables even if these are not related to each other. For example ratio of gross profit to investments in government securities is totally unrelated and insignificant. Such ratios have no relevance in any decision making process. Since ratios are easy to compute and simple to understand, there is a tendency to over-employ them. Hence, it should be noted that ratios are simply tools of analysis, the usefulness lies in it's proper application and on the analytical ability of users.

Thus, it may be concluded that ratios are only tools of making observations and not sure indicators of good or bad financial position, liquidity or solvency position. These ratios should be studied in it's totality. They are simply means of diagnoses, proper treatment depends upon the wisdom of the analysts (users).

Classification of Ratios

Ratios can be classified in number of ways to suit any particular purpose depending upon the circumstances and requirements of the users. Different types of ratios are selected for different types of situations. Now-a-days ratios are used as basis of prediction of events such as resource crunch, technical insolvency or total or partial bankruptcy or possible failure to honour loan agreement etc. The following table shows functional classification of ratios objectives and users theirof.

Ratios	Objectives	Users
(A) Profitability Ratios: • Gross Profit Ratio • Net Profit Ratio • Operating Profit Ratio • Return on Capital Employed or (Return on Investments) • Return on Net worth • Return on Proprietors Fund • Return on Equity (ROE) • Return on Assets (ROA) • Earning Per Share (EPS) • Price Earning Ratio (PER) • Dividend Payout Ratio • Dividend Yield Ratio • Dividend Cover Ratio	To test profitability of a concern in relation to **turnover** and Capital employed, and to ascertain how successfully is the business growing.	Sharesholders, Owners, Investors, Management, Govt. Agancies. Lenders, Employees and Competitors
(B) Expenses Ratios • Prime Cost Turnover Ratio • Factory Overhead T.O. Ratio • Administrative O.H. Ratio • Selling and Distribution O.H. Ratio • Financial O/H Ratio • Operating (Expenses) Ratio	To judge the operating (Cost) efficiency of the firm.	Management

Ratios	Objectives	Users
(C) Liquidity Ratios : • Current Ratio • Quick (liquid) Ratio (Acid Test) • Super Quick Ratio	To test the short term solvency and the ability of the firm to meet current (day today) obligations.	Creditors, Lenders, Bankers, Suppliers
(D) Solvency Ratios : • Debt-Equity Ratio • Debt to total Funds Ratio • Debt-service Coverage Ratio • Proprietory Ratio • Fixed Assets Ratio or Shareholders Equity to Fixed Assets Ratio	To test long term solvency of a concern. It judges the long term financial position and soundness of financial policies of the firm.	Long term Creditors Debentureholders and Financeirs
(E) Activity Ratios: • Stock Turnover Ratio • Debtors Turnover Ratio • Creditors Turnover Ratio • Working Capital Turnover Ratio • Assets Turnover Ratio Capital Turnover Ratio	To Judge the overall efficiency of an enterprise by measuring the effectiveness with which a firm uses resources at it's disposal.	Management
(F) Financial Ratio : • Capital gearing Ratio	To ascertain the cost of capital and return to shareholders.	Shareholders, leders, Management and Creditors.

(A) Profitability Ratios

For survival and growth it is essential that an enterprise must earn sufficient profits The profits are the indicators of firm's operating efficiency and continued success. Management is always interested in maximising the profits year after year. Profitability is the end product of the policies and decisions taken by a firm and is his single most important measure of success.

Profitability should be distinguished from profits which can be expressed in terms of absolute figures such as Rs. 50,000 Rs. 5,00,000 or Rs. 7,50,000 and so on. Whereas profitability is the ability to earn profits. It is a measure of efficiency, growth and success.

Profitability ratios are computed to assess as to how efficiently the business is being run by the management. Profitability provides a solid base for liquidity and solvency. Profitability ratios can be computed either on the basis of turnover (Sales) or on the basis of investments (Capital employed).

PROFITABILITY RATIOS BASED ON SALES/TURNOVER

1. Gross Profit Ratio

Gross profit Ratio establishes the relationship between profits and sales. It shows the result of trading operations. This ratio is of great importance especially where there is fixed profit margin. Any shortfall in fixed mark-up (standard) may result into losses. A low ratio reflects the poor sales and marketing policy, ineffective inventory control, inefficient utilisation of current as well fixed assets, low or falling sales price due to intense competition, low volume of sales either due to inferior quality of the product or lack of demand, increase in over all cost of goods sold or a faulty purchase policy or a hike in wage and direct expenses.

A high Gross Profit Ratio is an indicator of efficient and effective management. It may be due to low cost of goods sold through optimum use of available resources or an increasing selling price, undervaluation of opening stock and over-valuation of closing stock or an hike in sales volume of products having high profit margin.

The term "Sales" (Turnover) should be used when the main source of revenue of the business is "Sale of goods", where as "Revenue" may be used in case of service sector enterprises.

The Gross Profit Ratio is calculated by dividing the gross profit by sales.

$$\text{Gross Profit Ratio} = \frac{\text{Gross Profit}}{\text{Sales}} \times 100$$

where :

Gross Profit = Sales – Cost of goods sold

Cost of goods sold = Opening Stock
Add Purchases
Less Closing Stock
Add Direct expenses

Gross Profit margin is usually different for different types of industry and also for different units within the same industry and even for different products for the same unit. However a standard Gross profit Ratio helps to judge efficiency and competence of management.

2. Net Profit Ratio

Net profit represent excess of gross profit and other incomes (such as rent, interest, dividend etc.) over total indirect expenses. This ratio takes into account income from operations and also from non-operating activities (such as investments). It measures the overall performance of an enterprise. A high net profit ratio indicates the concern's capacity to withstand adverse economic conditions such as falling sales price, rising cost of production or declining demand because falling gross profit margin may be made good by additional non-business incomes. In order to understand firm's overall profitability prospect, both gross and net profit ratios should thoroughly be investigated to ascertain the actual causes of deviations from the standards.

A high net profit ratio ensures good return to shareholders whereas a low net profit margin has adverse implications.

$$\text{Net Profit Ratio} = \frac{\text{Net Profit}}{\text{Sales}} \times 100$$

Where "Net Profit" refers to Profit after tax (PAT)

3. Operating Profit Ratio

Operating profit refers to the profit (after operating expenses). Operating ratio does not consider non-operating incomes (such as rent, interest and dividend etc.) and non-operating expenses such as interest on loans or borrowings.

Illustration (1)

From the following information calculate.

(i) Gross Profit Ratio

(ii) Net Profit Ratio, and

(iii) Operating Profit Ratio

TRADING AND PROFIT & LOSS ACCOUNT

	Rs. '000'		Rs. '000'
To Opening Stock	380	By Sales	2,500
To Purchases	1,575	By Closing Stock	490
To Carriage & Freight	10		
To Wages	25		
To Gross Profit c/d	1,000		
	2,990		2,990
To Office Overheads	530	By Gross Profit b/d	1,000
To Selling & Distribution O/H	95	By Interest on Securities	5
To Loss on Sale of Investments	5	By Dividend	24
To Net Profit c/d	400	By Profit from sale of securities	1
	1,030		1,030

Solution:

(i) Gross Profit Ratio

$$= \frac{\text{Gross Profit}}{\text{Sales}} \times 100 = \frac{1,000}{2,500} \times 100 = 40\%$$

(ii) Net Profit Ratio $= \frac{\text{Net Profit}}{\text{Sales}} \times 100 = \frac{400}{2,500} \times 100 = 16\%$

(iii) Net Operating Profit Ratio =

NOP = Net Profit + Non-operating Expenses – Non-Operating Incomes

Net Operating Profit = Rs. 4,00,000 + 5,000 – 30,000 = 3,75,000

$$\text{NOP Ratio} = \frac{3,75,000}{25,00,000} \times 100 = 15\%$$

Illustration (2)

Following is the Trading and Profit & Loss Account of A Ltd. for the year ended 31st March, 2005.

	Rs. '000'		Rs. '000'
To Opening Stock	375	By Sales	3,000
To Purchases	1,550	By Closing Stock	200
To Freight	75		
To Gross Profit c/d	1,200		
	3,200		3,200
To Administrative O/H	4,00	By Gross Profit b/d	1,200
To Selling & Distribution O/H	290	By Dividend	25
To Financial Expenses	5	By Interest	15
To Other non-operating Exp.	5		
To Net Profit	540		
	1,240		1,240

Calculate :

(i) Gross Profit Ratio
(ii) Net Profit Ratio &
(iii) Operating Profit Ratio

Solution :

(i) Gross Profit Ratio $= \frac{\text{Gross Profit}}{\text{Sales}} \times 100$

$= \frac{1,200}{3,000} \times 100 = 40\%$

(ii) Net Profit Ratio $= \frac{\text{Net Profit}}{\text{Sales}} \times 100$

$= \frac{540}{3,000} \times 100 = 18\%$

(iii) Net Operating Profit Ratio $= \frac{\text{NOP}}{\text{Sales}} \times 100$

NOP = Net Profit + Financial Expenses + Other Non-operating expenses – Non-operating incomes

NOP = 540 + (5 + 5) – (25 + 15) = 510

NOP Ratio $= \frac{510}{3,000} \times 100 = 17\%$

PROFITABILITY RATIOS BASED ON CAPITAL EMPLOYED

(i) Return on Capital Employed or Return on Investments

This is one of the key profitability ratios. It measures the overall efficiency/performance of an enterprise and discloses as to how efficiently the borrowed funds are being used by the management. It also indicates a firm's ability to exercise "trading on equity" which can be determined by comparing the "rate of return" on capital employed and prevailing rate of interest. This ratio is very useful in intra-firm and inter-firm comparison and suggests the maximum limit of equity dividend.

$$\text{ROI or ROCE} = \; = \frac{\text{PBIT}}{\text{Capital Employed}} \times 100$$

where :

PBIT = Profit before Interest and Tax

(And before any adjustment for any abnormal loss or gain). The effect of abnormal items if any, should be neutaralised

Capital Employed = Total Assets (excluding fictitious assets) less current liabilities or

Alternatively = Share Capital (both Preference and Equity) + Reserves & Surplus + long term borrowings – Fictitious assets and Non-business assets.

Great care must be exercised in measuring this ratio. For a proper evaluation the capital employed needs to be an average figure for the accounting period in which the profit was calculated. Since the year end is by no means likely to be representative of the average for a period, any calculated figure must be taken with caution.

Hence, in order to calculate Capital employed exclude :

(i) Self generated intangible assets — such as goodwill, Trade mark, copyrights etc. However, if same has been acquired, then these should not be excluded.

(ii) Non-business assets such as investments.

(iii) Fictitious assets such as preliminary expenses, discount on issue of shares/debentures and advertisement suspense account etc.

(iv) Half of the current year's profit to get the average capital employed.

(v) Idle assets *i.e.* assets which are not used in business due to some abnormal factors.

Similarly while calculating PBIT :

(i) Income from Non-business assets should be excluded.

(ii) Exclude abnormal and non-recurring profits and gains/losses such as loss or profit on sale of fixed assets, loss due to fire, any penalty or fine paid for breach of law or profit or gains on foreign currency transactions or from speculative transactions. Infact operating profits represent PBIT.

Illustration (3)

Consider the Income Statement of illustration 2 along with the following information :

		31.3.2004	31.3.2005
		Rs. in '000'	
		Rs.	Rs.
	Equity Share Capital	500	500
	9% Preference Share Capital	100	100
	General Reserve	100	150
	Profit & Loss A/c	185	250
	10% Debentures	150	200
	12% Term Loan	250	300
	Unsecured Loan	150	125
		1,435	1,625
	Gross Block	1,400	1,600
Less	Accumulated Depreciation	400	500
	Net Block	1,000	1,100
	Investments	200	250
	Working Capital (Current assets less Current liabilities)	235	275
		1,435	1,625

Calculate Return on Capital Employed (ROCE).

Solution :

$$\text{ROCE} = \frac{\text{PBIT (operating Profit)}}{\text{Capital Employed}} \times 100$$

PBIT or Operating profit as per illustration '2' is Rs.. 5,10,000

Capital employed = Share Capital + Reserves & Surplus + long term borrowings – fictitious Assets & Non business assets

$$\text{Average Capital Employed} = \frac{\text{Opening} + \text{Closing}}{2}$$

$$\text{ACE} = \frac{14{,}35{,}000 + 16{,}25{,}000}{2}$$

$$= \frac{30{,}60{,}000}{2}$$

$$= 15{,}30{,}000$$

$$\text{ROCE} = \frac{5{,}10{,}000}{15{,}30{,}000} \times 100 \qquad = 33.33\%$$

(2) Return on Net Worth or Return on proprietors Funds or Return on Shareholders' Funds

Return on Capital Employed (ROCE) shows the relationship of return to total funds (owned and borrowed) where as Return on Net Worth (RONW) measures the return on shareholders' (owners') funds only.

$$\text{RONW} = \frac{\text{Net Profit (after interest \& Tax)}}{\text{Shareholders' Funds}} \times 100$$

Net profit represents net income which includes net non-operating incomes. *i.e.* (Non operating income less non operating expenses)

Shareholders' Funds include both preference and equity share capital and all reserves and surplus.

(3) Return on Equity: (ROE)

This ratio determines the earning power of equity share capital which helps equity shareholders to judge the effectiveness of management in running, the enterprise. The potential investors decisions are based on this ratio because they can forecast their probable future earnings in the form of dividend. It is the single most important ratio to judge whether the enterprise has earned a satisfactory return or not

$$\text{Return on Equity} = \frac{\text{Net Profit (after Interest \& Tax and Preference dividend)}}{\text{Equity Shareholders' Funds}}$$

Equity Shareholders funds = Equity Share Capital + Reserves & Surplus – Fictitious assets and Non-business assets.

(4) Return on Assets (ROA)

This ratio measures the profit after tax against total amount invested in all the assets. (*i.e.* in current & fixed both). In other words it also takes into account the short term loans and creditors dues.

$$\text{ROA} = \frac{\text{Net Profit (after Tax)}}{\text{Total assets}}$$

Illustration (4)

From the following balance sheet and other information, calculate :

(i) Return on Capital Employed (ROCE)

(ii) Return on Net Worth (RONW)

(iii) Return on Equity (ROE)

(iv) Return on Assets (ROA)

BALANCE SHEET OF N A LTD. AS ON 31st MARCH, 2005

Liabilities	**Rs.**
10% Preference Share Capital (Rs. 100 each)	3,00,000
Equity Share Capital (Rs. 10 each)	5,00,000
General Reserve	2,00,000
Capital Reserve	1,20,000
8% Debentures	2,50,000
S. Creditors	1,50,000
	15,20,000

Assets

	Gross Block	12,50,000
Less	Accumulated Depreciation	2,50,000
	Net Block	10,00,000
	10% Investments	2,00,000
	Current assets	3,00,000
	Preliminary Expenses	20,000
		15,20,000

Net Profit before tax is Rs. 3,30,000. Assume rate of tax at 40%.

Solution :

(i) $\text{ROCE} = \dfrac{\text{PBIT (operating Profit)}}{\text{Capital Employed}} \times 100$

PBIT = Net Profit + Interest on Debentures – Income from Investment
= Rs. 3,30,000 + 20,000 – 20,000
= Rs. 3,30,000

Capital Employed = 15,20,000 – 20,000 – 1,50,000
(Total assets – Fictitious assets – S. Creditors) = 13,50,000

$$= \frac{3{,}30{,}000}{13{,}50{,}000} \times 100 = 24.44\%$$

(ii) $\text{RONW} = \dfrac{\text{Net Profit After Tax}}{\text{Shareholders' Funds}} \times 100$

PAT = 3,30,000 – 40% Tax (Rs. 1,32,000)
= 1,98,000.

Shareholders' Funds = Rs. 5,00,000 + 3,00,000 + 2,00,000 + 1,20,000 – 20,000
= (Equity Capital + Pref. Capital + Reserves & Surplus – Preliminary Expenses)
= Rs. 11,00,000

$$\text{RONW} = \frac{1{,}98{,}000}{11{,}00{,}000} \times 100 = 18\%$$

(iii) Return on Equity (ROE)

$$= \frac{\text{Net Profit after Tax and Preference dividend}}{\text{Equity Shareholders' Funds}} \times 100$$

Return = Rs. 1,98,000 – 30,000 = 1,68,000

Equity= Shareholders funds – Preference Share Capital

$$\text{ROE} = \frac{1{,}68{,}000}{11{,}00{,}000 - 3{,}00{,}000} \times 100 = 21\%$$

(iv) $\text{Return on Assets} = \dfrac{\text{Net Profit after Tax}}{\text{Total Assets}} \times 100$

$$= \frac{1,98,000}{15,00,000} \times 100$$
$$= 13.2\%$$

Important Note : Students should note that when the basis or yardstick of measurement includes loans/debentures (as in case of capital employed) interest on loans/debentures will be included in the profits. Similarly when shareholders funds includes preference share capital then preference dividend will not be deducted from net profit.

(v) Earning Per Share (EPS)

EPS measures the amount of profits available for shareholders on per share basis. The profits available to the shareholders (Equity) are calculated by deducting the tax and preference dividend out of net profit. EPS is worked out by dividing the profits (after tax and preference dividend) by the number of equity shares.

$$\text{EPS} = \frac{\text{Net Profit after tax and Preference dividend}}{\text{No. of equity shares}}$$

This ratio is used to draw certain conclusions by establishing the trend over a period of time of the same firm and by making inter-firm comparison with regard to EPS. However, this ratio should be used very cautiously because it does not reveal the actual amount paid to shareholders in the form of dividend. In spite of this EPS plays an important role and is considered an important factor while judging the fundamentals of a company. However, if a company's capital structure consists of convertible preference shares or convertible debentures (Partly or wholly) such options may be treated as potential equity shares equivalents while computing the earnings per share. Such a computation, based on potential equity shares, is termed as Diluted Earnings per share (DEPS)

Illustration (5)

A Ltd. Shows the following balances as on 31. 3. 2005

	Rs.
8% 5,000 Preference Shares of Rs. 100 each	5,00,000
50,000 Equity shares of Rs. 10 each	5,00,000
7%, 2000 Debentures of Rs. 100 each	2,00,000
Net Profit for the year (after interest)	2,50,000

Preference shareholders and Debentureholders have the option to convert their 50% and 25% holdings in to equity shares respectively @ 10 : 1.

Calculate EPS and DEPS.

Solution :

		Rs.
	Net Profit for the year	2,50,000
Less	Preference Dividend	40,000
	(on Rs. 5,00,000 @ 8%)	2,10,000

$$\text{EPS} = \frac{\text{Rs. } 2,10,000}{50,000 \text{ Equity Shares}} = \text{Rs. } 4.2$$

DEPS :

		Rs.
	Net Profit	2,50,000
Add	interest on debentures on	
	(Converted portion not payable) Rs. 50,000 @ 7%	3,500
		2,53,500
Less	Preference dividend (on Rs. 2,50,000 @ 8%) after conversion)	20,000
		2,33,500

$$\text{DEPS} = \frac{2,33,500}{50,000+25,000+5,000} = \frac{2,33,500}{80,000}$$

Rs. 2.918

(vi) Price-Earning-Ratio

This ratio shows the relation between Earnings and market price of the share. A high ratio indicates that share is overvalued while a low price-earning ratio shows that the share is undervalued. P/E ratio measures investors expectations and helps in deciding whether to make investment in equity shares or not. A high ratio is the outcome of investors confidence in the stability and growth of company P/E ratio is workedout as follows :

$$\text{P/E Ratio} = \frac{\text{Market Price per share}}{\text{Earning per share}}$$

If P/E ratio is given, the market price can be ascertained by multiplying the EPS with P/E ratio.

Market price = EPS × P/E ratio

(vii) Payout Ratio or Dividend Payout Ratio

This ratio reveals as to what extent of amount of earnings have been paid to the shareholders in the form of dividend. It indicates the proportion of earnings retained and the proportion of earnings utilised in paying dividend. It can be calculated by dividing the total dividend paid to equity shareholders by the total profits available for equity shareholders.

$$\text{Dividend Payout Ratio} = \frac{\text{Total dividend to Equity shareholders}}{\text{Total profits (earnings) available for equity shareholders}} \times 100$$

It can also be worked out by dividing the 'Dividend Per Share' by the 'Earning Per Share' *i.e.*

$$\text{D/P Ratio} = \frac{\text{Dividend per Equity Share (DPS)}}{\text{Earning per share (EPS)}} \times 100$$

The ratio so computed and expressed in percentage, if deducted out of 100 will show the percentage of earnings retained in the business.

(viii) Dividend Yield Ratio

It establishes the relationship between dividend and market price of share. This ratio is calculated by dividing the dividend per share by the market price per share. Infact this ratio shows the real return based on the current market price of share which forms the basis of investment decisions for the investors.

$$\text{Dividend Yield Ratio} = \frac{\text{Dividend per share}}{\text{Market price per share}} \times 100$$

Potential investors would invest in companies having high dividend yield ratio and dispose off the shares of those companies indicating low dividend yield ratio.

(ix) Dividend Coverage Ratio

This ratio measures the ability of the firm to pay dividend to Preference shareholders and Equity Shareholders. It can be calculated by dividing the Profits after tax by the dividend payable to Preference shareholders and profit after tax and preference dividend by the dividend payable to equity shareholders as shown below.

(i) $\text{Preference dividend coverage} = \frac{\text{Profit after Tax}}{\text{Preference dividend Payable}}$

(ii) $\text{Equity dividend coverage} = \frac{\text{Profit after Tax \& Preference dividend}}{\text{Equity dividend Payable}}$

Illustration (6)

	Rs.
8% Preference Share Capital : Shares of Rs. 100 each fully paid	2,50,000
Equity Share Capital : Shares of Rs. 10 each fully paid	5,00,000

The following information is made available to you :

(i)	Profits before Tax	4,00,000
(ii)	Rate of Tax	40%
(iii)	Interest Charged to P & L A/c	20,000
(iv)	Depreciation Charged during the year	50,000
(v)	Equity dividend payable	20%
(vi)	Market price of Equity Share	25

You are required to calculate

(a) Dividend Yield Ratio

(b) Dividend Coverage Ratio for preference and equity shares

(c) Dividend Payout Ratio

(d) Price-Earning Ratio

Solution :

(a) $\text{Dividend Yield Ratio} = \frac{\text{Dividend per Equity Share}}{\text{Market Price of Equity Share}} \times 100$

$$= \frac{2}{25} \times 100 = 8\%$$

[Dividend per Equity Share = 20% of Rs. 10 = Rs. 2]

(b) Dividend Coverage Ratio

$$\text{Preference Dividend Coverage Ratio} = \frac{\text{Profit after Tax}}{\text{Preference dividend}}$$

Profit after Tax = Rs. 4,00,000 – 40% Tax $= \dfrac{2,40,000}{20,000} =$ 12 Times.

(Preference dividend 8% Of Rs. 2,50,000)

$$\text{Equity Dividend Coverage Ratio} = \frac{\text{Profit after Tax \& Pref. dividend}}{\text{Equity dividend Payable}}$$

Profit after Tax & Preference dividend = 2,40,000 – 20,000

= 2,20,000

(Equity dividend Payable 20% of Rs. 5,00,000) $= \dfrac{2,20,000}{1,00,000}$

= 2.2 Times.

(c) Dividend Payout Ratio $= \dfrac{\text{Dividend Per Equity Share}}{\text{Earnings Per Share}} \times 100$

Dividend per Equity share = 20% of 10 = Rs. 2

$$\text{EPS} = \frac{\text{Profit after Tax \& Pref. dividend}}{\text{No. of Equity shares}}$$

$$= \frac{2,20,000}{50,000 \text{ shares}} = \text{Rs. 4.40 per share}$$

$$\text{D/P Ratio} = \frac{2}{4.4} \times 100 = 45.45\%$$

$$\text{or alternatively} = \frac{\text{Total Equity dividend}}{\text{Profit after Tax \& Pref. dividend}} \times 100$$

$$\text{D/P Ratio} = \frac{1,00,000}{2,20,000} \times 100 = 45.45\%$$

(d) Price Earnings Ratio $= \dfrac{\text{Market Price per share}}{\text{Earnings per share}}$

$$= \frac{25}{4.40} = 5.68\% \text{ Times}$$

(B) Expenses Ratios

These ratios are also termed as "supporting ratios" to operating and profitability ratios. In order to understand and analyse the profitability in a wider prospective it is imperative to ascertain factors contributing to profitability of a concern. The main objective of calculating expenses ratio is to explain the increase or decrease in profitability ratio. Ratios so calculated are compared either with the same ratios of the previous year or with the predetermined standard ratios so as to ascertain the efficiency of the management and its ability to control cost. The lower the ratio higher is the efficiency and greater the profitability. These ratios reveal the relation of different expenses to net sales. There are many expenses ratios which can be computed as under :

(i) Prime Cost Turnover Ratio = $\frac{\text{Prime Cost}}{\text{Sales}} \times 100$

Prime Cost = Raw material consumed +Productive Wages + Direct (Production) Expenses.

Separate ratio of each component of prime cost can also be worked out to ascertain the individual expense effectiveness or ineffectiveness such as :

(a) $\frac{\text{Raw Material Consumed}}{\text{Sales}} \times 100$

(b) $\frac{\text{Direct Wages}}{\text{Sales}} \times 100$

(c) $\frac{\text{Direct (Production) Expenses}}{\text{Sales}} \times 100$

Similarly various Overheads (Indirect expenses) ratios can be calculated which can be classified in to four heads.

(ii) Factory Overheads Ratio = $\frac{\text{Factory O/H}}{\text{Sales}} \times 100$

(iii) Administrative O/H Ratio = $\frac{\text{Administration O/H}}{\text{Sales}} \times 100$

(iv) Selling & Distribution O/H Ratio = $\frac{\text{Selling \& Distribution O/H}}{\text{Sales}} \times 100$

(v) Financial overheads Ratios = $\frac{\text{Financial O/H}}{\text{Sales}} \times 100$

(vi) Operating Ratio

This ratio establishes the relationship between "Cost of Sales" and "Sales". It indicates the proportion that cost of sales bears to total sales.

Cost of sales (Operating Cost) = Cost of goods sold + Factory O/H + Administrative O/H + Selling & Distribution O/H + Financial O/H.

It does not take into account non-operating expenses and losses i.e. those expenses which have no bearing on production or sales such as loss on sale of fixed asset/investments Interest on long term debt, penalties and fines etc.

Operating Ratio = $\frac{\text{Operating Cost}}{\text{Sales}} \times 100$

Illustration (7)

The following is the Trading and Profit & Loss Account of a Limited Company for the year ended 31st March, 2005.

	Rs.		Rs.
To Opening Stock	1,21,600	By Sales	
To Purchases	5,04,000	Cash	3,00,000
To Carriage Inward	3,200	Credit	5,00,000
To Wages	8,000	By Closing Stock	1,56,800
To Gross Profit c/d	3,20,000		
	9,56,800		9,56,800
To Office Overheads	1,28,000	By Gross Profit b/d	3,20,000
To Selling & Distribution O/H	32,000	By Dividend	15,000
To Finance Expenses :		By Interest	12,000
Interest	2,000	By Rent	25,000
Discount	1,500		
Bad debts	4,500		
To Loss on Sale of Investment	3,000		
To Provision for legal suit	1,000		
To Net Profit c/d	2,00,000		
	3,72,000		3,72,000

Calculate :

(1) Expenses Ratios

(2) Operating Ratio and

(3) Operating Profit Ratio

Solution :

(1) *Expenses Ratios*

(i) Administrative O/H Ratio $= \dfrac{\text{Office O/H}}{\text{Sales}} \times 100$

$= \dfrac{1,28,000}{8,00,000} \times 100 = 16\%$

(ii) Selling & Distribution O/H Ratio

$= \dfrac{\text{Selling \& Distribution O/H}}{\text{Sales}} \times 100 = \dfrac{32,000}{8,00,000} \times 100 = 4\%$

(iii) Financial O/H Ratio

$= \dfrac{\text{Finance Expenses}}{\text{Sales}} \times 100 = \dfrac{8,000}{8,00,000} \times 100 = 1\%$

(iv) Non-operating Expense Ratio

$= \dfrac{\text{Non-operating Expenses}}{\text{Sales}} \times 100 = \dfrac{4,000}{8,00,000} \times 100 = 0.5\%$

(2) Operating Ratio $= \dfrac{\text{Cost of Goods Sold + Operating Expenses}}{\text{Sales}} \times 100$

Cost of Goods Sold = Opening Stock + Purchases + Direct Expenses – Closing Stock

$= \text{Rs. } 1{,}21{,}600 + 5{,}04{,}000 + 3{,}200 + 8{,}000 - 1{,}56{,}800 = 4{,}80{,}000$

Operating Expenses = Office O/H + Selling & Distribution O/H + Financial Expenses

$= \text{Rs. } 1{,}28{,}000 + 32{,}000 + 8{,}000 = 1{,}68{,}000$

$$\text{Operating Ratio} = \frac{4{,}80{,}000 + 1{,}68{,}000}{8{,}00{,}000} \times 100 = 81\%$$

(3) Operating Profit Ratio : $\dfrac{\text{Operating Profit}}{\text{Sales}} \times 100$

Operating Profit = Net Profit + Non-Operating Expenses – Non-operating incomes

$= \text{Rs. } 2{,}00{,}000 + 4{,}000 - 52{,}000$

$= \text{Rs. } 1{,}52{,}000$

$$= \frac{1{,}52{,}000}{8{,}00{,}000} \times 100 = 19\%$$

Please note that operating ratio and operating profit ratio should be equal to 100. In the above illustration it is 81% and 19% respectively.

(C) LIQUIDITY RATIOS

Liquidity refers to ability of the business enterprise to meet its short term liabilities and to finance day to day operations. These ratios are calculated to measure short term solvency of a concern and its ability to meet short term obligations. If a firm fails to pay its short term liabilities it is deemed to be technically insolvent. Its credit rating is affected adversely. The lack of sufficient liquidity will result in a poor credit worthiness and loss of creditors' confidence. However, a high ratio (excess liquidity) results in idle funds which contribute nothing to firms earnings. Therefore, it is necessary to maintain required degree of liquidity by striking a balance between high liquidity and low liquidity. It is used by creditors, bankers, lenders and employees.

The most common ratios which show the extent of liquidity are as follows :

(i) Current Ratio (ii) Quick Ratio (iii) Super Quick and (iv) Net Working Capital Ratio

(1) Current Ratio

The current ratio measures the short term or current financial liquidity of the firm by showing the relation between Current Assets and Current Liabilities which indicates firm's short term solvency. It is calculated by dividing the current assets by current liabilities.

$$\text{Current Ratio} = \frac{\text{Current Assets}}{\text{Current Liabilities}}$$

Current assets are those assets which can be converted into cash within an accounting year in the ordinary course of business. These include Cash and Bank balance, Marketable securities, Bills Receivable, Book-debts (good), Inventories, Advance Tax, Prepaid Expenses and those assets which can be realised within one year.

Current liabilities are those liabilities which are to be paid within an accounting year in the normal course of business. Current liabilities include Creditors, Bills Payable, Bank Overdraft, Provision for Taxation, Proposed Dividend, Outstanding Expenses and any other liability maturing in current year.

Significance

The comparison between Current Assets and Current Liabilities reveals the ability of the business to meet short term obligations. However, while determining the benchmark (standard) current ratio, the nature of business (speculative or non-speculative), Character of business (seasonal or non-seasonal), requirements of business, credit period allowed and availed etc. should be taken into consideration. Any-how, in the absence of any such peculiar condition the ideal ratio of 2 : 1 is treated as satisfactory. The idea of keeping current assets double of current liabilities is to tide over certain contingencies, overcome delays in assets realisation and to provide required cushion in view of shrinkage in the value of current assets.

An ideal current ratio shows short-term financial strength, short-term solvency, credit worthiness, capacity to carry on effective operations and discloses over-trading or under capitalisation.

The Tandon Committee and Chore Committee, appointed by Reserve Bank of India recommended that business enterprises should progressively improve their liquidity position. Initially they should set 1.33 : 1 and gradually achieve the target of 2 : 1.

Current Ratio represents margin of safety for creditors and other short term obligations. The higher the ratio, the greater is the margin of safety, the more is the ability of the firm to meet current obligations.

However, while analysing current ratio, the quality and composition of assets should also be taken into account. The Current assets may have bad, doubtful or slow paying debtors, slow moving and obsolete stock which disturb or impair the firm's ability to meet its current obligations in time. Hence too much reliance should not be placed on current ratio without making comprehensive analysis.

(2) Quick Ratio (Liquid Ratio)

$$\text{Quick Ratio} = \frac{\text{Quick Assets}}{\text{Quick Liabilities}}$$

It is also known as acid test. All the constituents of current assets are not equally liquid. An asset is liquid if it can be converted into cash immediately without loss of time and value. Cash and bank balance is considered the most liquid asset. Other liquid assets include Debtors (only good). Bills Receivable, and Marketable Securities, Stock and Prepaid Expenses are excluded from the list of quick (liquid) assets, because slow moving inventories or stock take some time before these are converted into cash and Prepaid Expenses which can not be converted into cash.

Similarly quick (liquid) liabilities do not include Bank overdraft, Cash credit and other short-term borrowings which are used to finance current assets. These feature generally on a permanent basis because they are renewable and go year after year even with an increasing level of cash credit and overdraft limits. Thus

Quick (liquid) Assets = Current assets − Inventories − Prepaid Expenses

Quick (liquid) liabilities = Current liabilities − Cash Credit − Bank over-draft or short term bank borrowings.

Acid Test (Quick Ratio) is treated as the best measure of a firm's ability to meet short term liabilities. A bench mark of 1 : 1 is considered satisfactory. The quick ratio is more rigorous and penetrating test of liquidity position of a concern than the current ratio. Even then this ratio should be used with caution because slow paying debtors may cause cash crunch especially in the wake of mounting operating expenses.

(3) Super Quick Ratio (Cash Ratio)

This ratio is calculated by dividing super quick assets by the current liabilities. While calculating super quick ratio, the Inventories, prepaid expenses, Debtors and Bills Receivables are excluded from the list of current assets. An acceptable norm of 1 : 3 is considered sufficient. It is worked out as under

$$\text{SQ Ratio} = \frac{\text{Cash \& Bank balance} + \text{Marketable Securities (Cash \& Cash equivalents)}}{\text{Current Liabilities}}$$

This ratio is significant only when it is used with current ratio and quick ratio. It is to be noted that if a firm enjoys reserve (extra) borrowing power, it will always be placed in a better position even with a lower standard ratio.

(4) Net-Working Capital Ratio

The excess of current assets over current liabilities represents net working capital which is also used to measure the liquidity of a concern. It can be derived by dividing Net-Working Capital by Net Assets. It is considered that a high ratio represents a greater liquidity because it reflects larger proportion of investment in current assets. Thus a company with a larger proportion of working capital in relation to total capital employed or net assets, has the greater ability to meet it's current obligations.

$$\text{Net Working Capital Ratio} = \frac{\text{Net Working Capital}}{\text{Net Assets}}$$

However, it should be noted that although liquidity is desirable as well as essential but too much liquidity results in unwise or irrational use of funds which could be better employed elsewhere. It should also be kept in mind that during peak demand period a larger portion of funds are required for working operations due to a increased activity whereas during recessionary period the amount or proportion of desired or required working capital will be less.

(5) Interval Measure

Interval Measure shows the ability of the firm to meet cash expenses out of cash reservoir (cash funds). It determines the number of days the cash funds will last, if there is no inflow of cash. A higher reservoir provides a better protection against the unforeseen events as the business depends mainly on it's cash reservoir. Interval measure is calculated by dividing the cash reservoir by the average daily cash expenses.

$$\text{Interval Measure} = \frac{\text{Cash Reservoir}}{\text{Average daily Cash Expenses}}$$

Cash Reservoir is the sum total of "Cash and Cash Equivalents" *i.e.* cash in hand, cash at Bank and Marketable securities (at market value).

Average daily cash expenditure is the sum total of expenses charged to Profit & Loss A/c excluding non-cash charges such as depreciation, preliminary expenses written off, discount on issue of shares written off etc. which is divided by the number of days in a year.

Illustration (8)

Following is the Balance Sheet of Asia Pacific Ltd. as on 31st March, 2005.

Liabilities	Rs. in '000'
Equity Share Capital	2,000
Reserve & Surplus	575
9% Debentures	425
Cash Credit	300
S. Creditors	300
Provision for Taxation	250
Proposed dividend	250
	4,100

Assets	
Gross Block less Depreciation	2,025
Investment	350
Marketable Securities	250
Inventories	750
Book Debts	450
Advances	100
Cash & Bank balance	175
	4,100

The marketable securities are worth Rs. 2,85,000. The annual cash expenditure is Rs. 2,09,87,500

Calculate :

(i) Current Ratio (ii) Quick Ratio (iii) Super Quick Ratio (iv) Net Working Capital Ratio and (v) Interval Measure

Solution :

(i) Current Ratio = $\dfrac{\text{Current Assets}}{\text{Current Liabilities}}$

Current Assets	Rs.
Inventories	7,50,000
Book-Debts	4,50,000
Advances	1,00,000
Cash & bank balance	1,75,000
Marketable Securities	2,85,000
	17,60,000

Current liabilities	
Cash Credit	3,00,000
S. Creditors	3,00,000
Provision for Taxation	2,50,000
Proposed dividend	2,50,000
	11,00,000

$$\text{Current Ratio} = \frac{17,60,000}{11,00,000} = 1.6$$

(ii) $$\text{Quick Ratio} = \frac{\text{Quick Assets}}{\text{Quick Liabilities}}$$

Quick Assets = Current Assets – Inventories

= 17,60,000 – 7,50,000 10,10,000

Quick liabilities = Current liabilities – Cash credit

= 11,00,000 – 3,00,000 = 8,00,000

$$\text{Quick Ratio} = \frac{10,10,000}{8,00,000} = 1.2625$$

(iii) $$\text{Super Quick Ratio} = \frac{\text{Cash \& Bank balance + Marketable Securities}}{\text{Current Liabilities}} = \frac{1,75,000 + 2,85,000}{11,00,000}$$

= 0.418 : 1

(iv) $$\text{Net Working Capital Ratio} = \frac{\text{Net Working Capital}}{\text{Net Assets}}$$

Net Working Capital = Current Assets – Current liabilities

= 17,60,000 – 11,00,000

= 6,60,000

Net Assets = 41,00,000 + Appreciation in Marketable securities

= 41,00,000 + 35,000 = 41,35,000

$$= \frac{6,60,000}{41,35,000} = 0.16 \text{ App.}$$

(v) $$\text{Internal Measure} = \frac{\text{Cash + Marketable Securities}}{\text{Average daily Cash Expenditure}} = \frac{1,75,000 + 2,85,000}{57,500} = 8 \text{ days}$$

$$\text{Average daily Cash Expenditure} = \frac{\text{Annual Cash Expenditure}}{\text{365 days}} = \frac{209,87,500}{365} = 57500$$

(D) Solvency Ratios

To judge the long term financial position of a concern, the ability of the firm to pay long-term debts and servicing thereof is to be examined by solvency ratios. These ratios throw light on the long term solvency of an enterprise as reflected in its ability to pay contractual obligations such as:

(i) periodic payment of interest as and when due

(ii) repayment of principal on maturity.

These ratios are also called stability, leverage or capital structure ratios. Long term creditors such as debentureholders, financial institutions and banks are interested in judging the long term financial position of the concern. They want to know how the assets of the company are financed

Whether these ratios indicate appropriate mix of funds (debt and equity) or not. The company has a legal obligation to pay interest to debentureholders and other lenders/financiers irrespective of profit or loss. Failure to pay interest may result in unnecessary litigation or even liquidation. These ratios can be studied under following heads :

(i) Debt Equity Ratio

As already stated, assets of a concern are financed by partly by owners (shareholders) funds and partly by borrowed funds *i.e.* It shows the extent of owners equity (internal equity) as well as outside debts (external equity). The ratio studies the relationship between borrowed funds and owners funds to determine the long term solvency of the company. This ratio discloses the relative proportion of debts and equity in financing the assets of an enterprise. This ratio is worked out in many ways as shown below :

$$\text{Debt-Equity Ratio} = \frac{\text{Debts*}}{\text{Equity**}} = \frac{\text{External Equity*}}{\text{Internal Equity**}}$$

$$\text{or } \frac{\text{Debts*}}{\text{Debts + Equity***}} = \frac{\text{External Equity*}}{\text{Total long term funds***}}$$

Significance

A high ratio shows the claims of creditors are greater than shareholders' claims. A company with high ratio is known as highly geared or leveraged and has limited ability to borrow funds from outside. In case of low profitability, the company finds it difficult to meet working capital requirements and as a consequence company may borrow on highly unfavourable terms which may lead to debt-trap.

A low debt-equity ratio indicates a satisfactory situation since high proportion of equity provides greater cushion (safety margin) to creditors. However, during boom and high return period, a low leveraged or geared company will not be able to take advantage of trading on equity. Thus there is a need to strike a balance between debt & equity in the light of risk and return.

> It is to be noted that while calculating debt-equity ratio, the liability arising out of possible payment of pension, gratuity funds and other contingent liabilities becoming real liabilities should not be ignored.

2. Debt to Total Funds Ratio

When long term funds includes both debts and equity it is known as "Debt to total funds ratio" It discloses the share of outsiders' funds in relation to total funds employed by a concern.

---

*Debts or External Equity refers to **"Total Outside liabilities"** which includes short-term as well long term debts. However, when Long term financial ratio is calculated it takes into account the **"long term debts"** only.

**Equity or Internal Equity refers to shareholders funds which includes:

Equity Share Capital

Preference Share Capital and all Reserves & Surpluses

Less Fictitious assets

***Debt + Equity refers to total long term funds both as defined above. Hence such ratio is known as "Debt to Total Funds Ratio".

Illustration (9)

From the following particulars calculate debt-equity ratio & debt to total funds ratio.

Liabilities	Rs.'000'	Assets	Rs.'000'
Share Capital	5,000	Net Block	10,000
Reserve & Surplus	3,750	Current Assets	9,100
Secured Loans*	7,500	Preliminary Expenses	50
Unsecured Loans	2,500		
Current liabilities & provision:			
S. Creditors	250		
Bank overdraft	150		
	19,150		19,150

*Secured loans include cash credit from bank Rs. 4,30,000

Solution :

(1) $$\text{Debt-Equity ratio} = \frac{\text{Debts}}{\text{Equity}} = \frac{10{,}000 - 430}{8750 - 50}$$

$$= \frac{9{,}570}{8{,}700} = 1.1$$

Debts = Secured Loans – Cash credit + Unsecured Loans

Equity = Capital + Reserve & Surplus – Preliminary Expenses

Debt – Equity Ratio = 1.1:1

(2) $$\text{Debt to total funds ratio} = \frac{\text{Debts}}{\text{Debts + Equity}}$$

$$= \frac{9{,}570}{8{,}700 + 9{,}570} = \frac{9{,}570}{18{,}270} = 0.52 \text{ App.}$$

$$= 0.52 : 1$$

(3) Debt service coverage Ratio

This ratio measures the debt-servicing capacity of an enterprise with regard to long term debts. This ratio is also known as interest coverage ratio. Whenever any enterprise, raises funds either by issuing debentures or taking loans from banks or by way of public deposits, these lenders are interested in knowing the debt-servicing capacity. The lenders want timely payment of loan instalments and interest. This ratio is worked out by dividing the "Earning Before Interest and Tax (EBIT) by the fixed interest charges as shown below.

$$\text{Debt-service} = \frac{\text{EBIT*(*before deducting non cash charges)}}{\text{Interest + Loan Instalments}}.$$

Significance

This ratio shows how many times the interest charges are covered by earnings (before interest & tax) out of which interest charges will be met. Higher the coverage better is the repaying capacity of the business to service its debts. This ratio establishes the relationship between the profits available from operations and the claims of lenders. However, a very high ratio may imply unused debt capacity and very low ratio runs the risk of a sunk debt and indicates towards possible bankruptcy. It is to be noted that a higher ratio is an indicator of better credit rating.

Illustration (10)

From the following particulars, calculate debt-service coverage ratio.

Net profit after charging depreciation Rs. 45,000 Preliminary expenses Rs. 3,500 and the interest on the following loan funds amounted to Rs. 2,00,000.

(i) 9% Debentures Rs. 3,00,000 – 20% repayable at the end of current year

(ii) 10% Term loans Rs. 2,00,000 – 20% repayable at the end of current year.

(iii) 12% Cash Credit Rs. 1,50,000

(iv) 15% Loan from a friend Rs. 80,000 – 50% repayable at the end of the current year.

Solution :

$$\text{Debt-service coverage Ratio} = \frac{\text{EBIT (and non-cash Charges)}}{\text{Interest + Loan instalments}}$$

(i) EBIT = Net Profit + Depreciation + Interest + Prel. Expenses

(ii) Interest on:	Rs.
9% Debentures	27,000
10% Term Loans	20,000
12% Cash Credit	18,000
15% Loan from friend	12,000
	77,000

(ii) Loan Instalments falling due during the year:	Rs.
20% of 9% Debentures	60,000
20% of 10% Term loans	40,000
50% of 15% loans from friend	40,000
	1,40,000

$$\text{Debt. service coverage Ratio} = \frac{2,00,000 + 45,000 + 3,500 + 77,000}{77,000 + 1,40,000} = \frac{3,25,500}{2,17,000}$$

$$= 1.5 \text{ times}$$

This shows the company's ability to service the debt for $1^1/_2$ times.

(4) Proprietory Ratio

Proprietory ratio shows the owners' contribution to total assets or capital employed. Proprietory Fund refers to Equity and Preference share Capital, Reserves & Surplus minus losses and fictitious assets. It indicates share of proprietory fund against each rupee of investment in the assets. This ratio is also known as 'Net worth to Total Assets' or 'Shareholders' Equity to Total Equity ratio. It is calculated by dividing the shareholders' Funds by the 'Total Assets'.

$$\text{Proprietory Ratio} = \frac{\text{Shareholders' Funds}}{\text{Total assets (Fixed \& Current)}}$$

Significance

Propietory Ratio indicates the long-term solvency of the firm and shows the proportion of assets financed by the proprietors (owners). Thus it measures the extent of cushion available to creditors. A high ratio shows lesser dependence on external sources and a low ratio indicates greater dependence on external sources. It also determines the extent of trading on equity and is an indicator of firm's financial position.

Illustration (11)

Following is the Balance Sheet of Anderson Ltd. as on 31st March, 2005.

Liabilities	Rs.'000'	Assets	Rs. '000'
9% Preference Share Capital		Net Block	1,790
Shares of Rs. 100 each	250	Current Assets Loans & Advances:	
Equity Share Capital		Stock	750
Shares of Rs. 10 each	750	Debtors	450
Reserves & Surplus :		Cash & bank	200
General Reserve	550	Loans to Employees	150
Capital Reserve	150	Miscellaneous Expenses :	
Securities Premium	150		
Profit & Loss A/c	250	Preliminary Expenses	50
Secured loans :			
9% Debentures	300		
11% Bank Loan	200		
Unsecured loans :			
Loan from X Ltd.	190		
Current Liabilities & Provisions :			
S. Creditors	250		
Proposed Dividend	150		
Provision for Taxation	200		
	3,390		3,390

Additional information : Stock is overvalued by Rs. 50,000, Provision for bad debts is estimated at Rs. 20,000. A claim for damages for breach of contract is estimated at Rs. 30,000. Fixed Assets are undervalued by Rs. 2,50,000. Calculate proprietory ratio.

Solution :

$$\text{Proprietory Ratio} = \frac{\text{Shareholders' Funds}}{\text{Total Assets}}$$

Shareholders' Funds :	Rs.
9% Preference Share Capital	2,50,000
Equity Share Capital	7,50,000
General Reserve	5,50,000
Capital Reserve	1,50,000

	Securities Premium		1,50,000
	Profit & Loss A/c		2,50,000
			21,00,000
Less	Fictitious assets & liabilities not provided for:		
	Preliminary Expenses	50,000	
	Over-valuation of Stock	50,000	
	Provision for Bad debts	20,000	
	Claims for damages	30,000	1,50,000
			19,50,000
Add	Appreciation in Fixed Assets		2,50,000
			22,00,000
Total Assets :			
	Net Block		17,90,000
Add	Appreciation in Fixed Assets		2,50,000
			20,40,000
	Stock	7,50,000	
Less	Over-valuation	50,000	7,00,000
	Debtors	4,50,000	
Less	Provision	20,000	4,30,000
	Cash & Bank		2,00,000
	Loans to Employees		1,50,000
			35,20,000

$$\text{Proprietory Ratio} = \frac{22,00,000}{35,20,000} = 0.6.25 \text{ or } 62.5\%$$

(5) Fixed Assets Ratio (Fixed assets to Shareholders' Funds)

This ratio expresses the relationship of fixed assets with proprietors' or shareholders' funds. This ratio discloses the extent to which fixed assets are financed out of proprietors' (Shareholders') funds.

Taking illustration (11) Calculate fixed assets ratio

$$\text{Fixed assets ratio} = \frac{\text{Fixed Assets}}{\text{Proprietors' Funds}}$$

$$= \frac{20,40,000}{22,00,000} = 0.9272 \text{ or } 92.72\%$$

(E) Performance or Activity Ratios

Activity ratios are computed to evaluate the efficiency with which assets are used by the management. These ratios are also called "Turnover Ratios" because these ratios indicate the speed with which assets are converted into sales. Activity ratios are calculated on the basis of sales or cost of sales and are expressed in number of times an asset (especially current assets) is converted into sales during a year. A higher ratio reflects greater efficiency with regard to usage of current assets. A lower ratio expresses under utilisation of resources. These ratios are explained as under.

(i) ***Stock-Turn over Ratio***

Stock or Inventory turnover ratio measures the speed with which stock/inventory is converted into sales. It is infact a test of efficient or inefficient inventory management. In order to judge the efficiency of inventory management the ratio so calculated is compared with the past ratios and with the ratios of other firms of the same industry.

A high ratio implies a good inventory management but a very high ratio may be the result of under-investment in inventories which in turn affects ability to meet demand requirements of the product/raw materials.

A low ratio reflects the excessive investment in inventory which shows under utilisation of funds contributing to higher cost of storage and possible deterioration due to obsolescence or losses through pilferage and low liquidity.

Stock Turnover-ratio establishes relationship between cost of goods sold and average inventory held during a period of time. It is calculated as follows :

$$\text{Stock-Turnover Ratio} = \frac{\text{Cost of goods sold}}{\text{Average Stock (inventory)}}$$

where :

$$\text{Average Stock} = \frac{\text{Opening Stock} + \text{Closing Stock}}{2}$$

and Cost of Goods Sold = Sales − Gross Profit

or Opening Stock + Purchases + Direct Expenses − Closing Stock

This ratio shows the **"Velocity of Stock"** which turns stock into sales (Turnover). The components of ratios are shown at cost. However, some authorities favour computation at sales price as shown below :

$$\text{Stock Turnover Ratio} = \frac{\text{Net Sales}}{\text{Average Stock at selling price}}$$

Of the two methods, the former (at cost) is the best because inventories are normally maintained at cost price. However, where cost of goods sold cannot be ascertained for lack of information, the same may be calculated at selling price. Anyhow, while analysing or interpreting stock turnover ratio, the following factors should carefully be considered.

(i) Price volatility or trend (in future)

(ii) Volume of business in near future (increasing/decreasing)

(iii) Availability and proximity to supply or replenish stock (Terms of supply)

(iv) Nature of business (whole sale vs. retail) and

(v) Seasonal factors, if any.

Illustration (12)

From the following information calculate "Stock Turnover Ratio".

TRADING ACCOUNT OF NELSON LTD.
for the year ended 31st March, 2005

	Rs.		Rs.
To Opening Stock	2,00,000	By Sales :	
To Purchases:		Cash	3,00,000
Cash	3,25,000	Credit	12,00,000
Credit	6,00,000	By Closing Stock	3,00,000
To wages	2,75,000		
To Manufacturing Exp.	1,50,000		
To Gross Profit	2,50,000		
	18,00,000		18,00,000

Solution :

$$\text{Stock Turnover Ratio} = \frac{\text{Cost of goods sold}}{\text{Average Stock (inventory)}}$$

Cost of Goods sold = Opening Stock + Purchases + Direct Expenses – Closing Stock
= Rs. 2,00,000 + 9,25,000 + 4,25,000 – 3,00,000
= Rs. 12,50,000

Average Stock = Opening. Stock + Closing Stock/2
= Rs. 2,00,000 + 3,00,000/2
= Rs. 2,50,000

$$\text{Stock Turnover Ratio} = \frac{12,50,000}{2,50,000} = 5 \text{ Times}$$

$$\text{Average number of days to Turnover} = \frac{\text{No. of days in a year}}{\text{Stock Turnover Ratio}}$$

$$= \frac{365}{5} = 73 \text{ days.}$$

(ii) ***Debtors Turnover Ratio***

It expresses the relationship between credit sales and debtors (accounts receivable). It helps in judging the adequacy of working capital as it discloses the average credit period enjoyed by the debtors (credit customers)

A high ratio indicates the efficiency and economy with which receivables (Debtors & Bills Receivable) are being collected. Higher the ratio, shorter is the time lag (duration) of debt collection period and lesser are chances of bad debts.

On the other hand, a low ratio is an indication of long collection period and consequent greater risk or loss due to possible bad debts. This will require a comparatively higher amount of working capital.

Thus it reflects the company's credit granting policy. Any departure from the set policy may quickly be reviewed to minimise loss and resultant blockage of working capital. If debtors are collected as scheduled, the company is able to meet its day-to-day obligations promptly which reflects a sound liquidity and short term solvency position. A comprehensive analysis of Debtors Turnover Ratio helps in preparing the ageing schedule of debtors that pinpoints possible bad debts.

Debtors Turnover Ratio is worked out as follows :

$$\text{Debtors Turnover Ratio} = \frac{\text{Net Credit Sales}}{\text{Average Receivable}}$$

Where:

Net Credit Sales means sales of goods on credit basis in which the firm deals in. It excludes all other sale-such as cash sale and sale of fixed assets, if any, and sales returns.

Average Receivable = Debtors and Bills Receivable in the beginning and at the end divided by two.

$$\text{Collection Period} = \frac{\text{No. of Days in a year } (i.e.\ 365/360)}{\text{Debtors Turnover Ratio}}$$

$$\text{Average daily Credit Sales} = \frac{\text{Net Credit Sales}}{\text{No. of Days in a year } (i.e.\ 365/360)}$$

$$\text{Collection Period may also be calculated as under} = \frac{\text{Average Receivable}}{\text{Net sales (Credit)}} \times 365/360$$

Illustration (13)

From the following particulars calculate

(i) Debtors Turnover Ratio

(ii) Collection period (Taking 360 days in a year)

(iii) Average daily credit sales.

	Rs.
Trade Debtors in the beginning	54,000
Bills Receivable in the beginning	6,000
Debtors at the end	70,000
Bills Receivable at the end	10,000
Cash Sales during the year	8,50,000
Credit Sales during the year	12,65,000
Sales Returns	5,000
Provision for Bad debts to be provided	10,000

Solution :

$$\text{Debtors Turnover Ratio} = \frac{\text{Net Credit Sales}}{\text{Average Receivable}}$$

Net Credit Sales = Rs. 12,65,000 – 5,000 = 12,60,000

$$\text{Average Receivable} = \frac{(54{,}000 + 6{,}000) + (70{,}000 + 10{,}000)}{2}$$

$$= \frac{1{,}40{,}000}{2} = 70{,}000$$

$$\text{Debtors Turnover Ratio} = \frac{12{,}60{,}000}{70{,}000} = 18 \text{ Times}$$

Debt Collection Period = 360/18 = 20 days.

> It is to be noted that average receivable (Debtors + B/R) will be equal to "Sale for the debt collection period. In the above example = $\frac{12{,}60{,}000 \times 20}{360}$ = Rs. 70,000

(iii) *Working Capital Turnover Ratio*

This ratio expresses relationship between working capital and sales (Turnover). It indicates the number of times an unit invested in Working Capital produces sale. It reflects the overall working capital management, i.e. the effectiveness with which current assets are put to use by the management. It is calculated as under.

$$\text{Working Capital Turnover Ratio} = \frac{\text{Net Sales}}{\text{Working Capital}}$$

Where : **Net sales** includes both cash & credit sales but excludes sales returns and sale of fixed assets.

Working Capital represents excess of current assets over current liabilities.

(iv) *Fixed Assets Turnover Ratio*

It shows the extent to which the fixed assets contribute to sales (Turnover) A high ratio reflects better utilisation of fixed assets whereas a low ratio is the indication of poor or inefficient use of fixed assets. It should be noted that volume of sales not only depends on efficient utilisation of current assets but on the usage factor of fixed assets as well, especially that of Land & Building and Plant & Machinery in case of a manufacturing concern. It is worked out as under

$$\text{Fixed Assets Turnover Ratio} = \frac{\text{Net Sales}}{\text{Net Fixed assets}}$$

(v) *Capital Turnover Ratio*

This ratio discloses the relationship between capital employed and sales. It highlights how effectively the firm's total resources are being put to use to generate sales. The amount of capital employed and volume of turnover reveal the margin of each unit of capital invested.

A high ratio is an indication of efficient utilisation whereas a very high ratio may be the out come of paucity of capital funds. It is computed as under:

$$\text{Capital Turnover Ratio} = \frac{\text{Net Sales}}{\text{Capital Employed*}}$$

Capital Employed = Net total assets

*(Please see Proprietory Ratio)

(vi) *Creditors Turnover Ratio*

This ratio shows the relationship between credit purchases and accounts (average) payables. It calculates the velocity (speed) with which payment is made by the company to the suppliers of goods.

A higher ratio is an indication of shorter credit period while a low ratio is an expression of larger credit period enjoyed by the company. A comparative study of creditors turnover ratios over the years helps in evolving a trend to determine the soundness of policy of prompt payment to creditors.

Creditors Turnover Ratio is calculated as under:

$$\text{Creditors T.O. Ratio} = \frac{\text{Net Credit Purchases}}{\text{Average Accounts payable}}$$

Average Accounts Payable = Creditors & Bill Payable in the beginning and at the end divided by 2.

> It is to be noted that creditors are those who supply goods on credit basis in which a company deals in. Bills payable refer to trade bills and not accomodation bills.

$$\text{(APP) Average Payment Period} = \frac{\text{No. of days in a year}}{\text{Creditors T.O. Ratio}}$$

Average payment period shows the average number of days taken by a company to pay the creditors as against the credit period allowed by suppliers. This will reveal whether or not the company is making payment to creditors in time.

> In case creditors (Payable) are not given, then the same may be taken equal to purchases (credit) and for the creditors payment period *i.e.* $\frac{\text{Credit Purchases}}{\text{No. of Days in a year}} \times \text{APP}$

(F) Capital Gearing Ratio

Capital gearing refers to the proportion of various types of securities used to raise long term funds. These securities may be grouped in two categories viz:

(i) Those carrying fixed commitments such as Debentures, term loans and cumulative preference shares. On these securities interest/preference dividend has to be paid for each year irrespective of profits or losses made by a business.

(ii) Those carrying no commitment-such as equity shares including ploughing back *i.e.* Equity S/H funds.

Capital gearing ratio shows the relationship between fixed commitment bearing securities and the securities without any such commitment. This ratio is calculated as under :

$$\text{Capital Gearing Ratio} = \frac{\text{Funds bearing Fixed Commitment}}{\text{Equity Shareholders' Funds}}$$

If the ratio is more than one the company is said to be highly geared. It shows that funds carrying fixed rate of interest/dividend are in larger proportion. This situation will be better if rate of interest/fixed dividend remains low as compared to overall earnings rate. This state of affairs is known as "Trading on Equity" and is considered beneficial to the equity shareholders. However, a low rate of earnings indicates a higher risk of insolvency as company's debt repaying capacity is hampered to a greater extent. Capital gearing ratio should be analysed in the light of rate of actual earnings, otherwise mere high or low ratio will not convey anything.

Illustration (14)

From the following particulars calculate capital gearing ratio.

	Rs.
9% Preference Share Capital	5,00,000
Equity Share Capital	7,00,000
10% Debentures	12,00,000
Reserve & Surplus	8,00,000
11% Term Loans	3,00,000
Profit before interest & Tax @ 40%	9,78,000

Solution :

	Profit before interest and Tax		9,78,000
Less	Interest on Debentures	1,20,000	
	Interest on 11% Term Loans	33,000	1,53,000
			8,25,000
Less	Tax @ 40%		3,30,000
			4,95,000
Less	Preference dividend		45,000
			4,50,000

$$\text{Return on Equity Shareholders' Funds} = \frac{4{,}50{,}000 \times 100}{15{,}00{,}000} = 30\%$$

$$\text{General Rate of Return} = \frac{9{,}78{,}000 - 3{,}30{,}000}{35{,}00{,}000} = \frac{6{,}48{,}000 \times 100}{35{,}00{,}000} = 18.5\%$$

$$\text{Capital Gearing Ratio} = \frac{20{,}00{,}000}{15{,}00{,}000} = 1.333\,\text{Time}$$

This shows the company is highly geared. While taking returns into account the company is thriving on Trading on Equity. As against the general rate of return of 18.5% Equity Shareholders are enjoying a higher return of 30%.

GRADED ILLUSTRATIONS

(1) From the following particulars calculate :

(i) Gross Profit Ratio

(ii) Net Profit Ratio

(iii) Operating Profit Ratio

(iv) Stock Turnover Ratio

PROFIT & LOSS A/C OF A LTD.
for the year ended 31st March, 2005

	Rs.		Rs.
To Opening Stock	3,60,000	By Sales	48,00,000
To Purchases	26,20,000	By Closing Stock	2,40,000
To Productive Expenses	1,40,000		
To Gross Profit c/d	19,20,000		
	50,40,000		50,40,000
To Administrative Expenses	5,30,000	By Gross Profit b/d	19,20,000
To Selling & Distribution Expenses	4,30,000	By Dividend	70,000
To Loss on Sale of Investments	50,000	By Rent	60,000
To Loss on Sale of Machinery	20,000		
To Interest on Debentures	60,000		
To Provision for Tax	1,92,000		
To Net Profit	7,68,000		
	20,50,000		20,50,000

Solution:

(i) Gross Profit Ratio: $\frac{\text{Gross Profit}}{\text{Sales}} \times 100$

$$= \frac{19,20,000}{48,00,000} \times 100 = 40\%$$

(ii) Net Profit Ratio = $\frac{\text{Net Profit}}{\text{Sales}} \times 100$

$$= \frac{7,68,000}{48,00,000} \times 100 = 16\%$$

(iii) Operating Profit Ratio $\frac{\text{Operating Profit}}{\text{Sales}} \times 100$

$$= \frac{9,60,000^*}{48,00,000} \times 100 = 20\%$$

(*Gross Profit – Adm. Exp – Selling & Dist. Exp)

(v) Stock Turnover Ratio $= \dfrac{\text{Cost of Goods Sold}}{\text{Average Stock}}$

Cost of goods sold $= \text{Sales} - \text{Gross Profit}$

$= 48{,}00{,}000 - 19{,}20{,}000 = 28{,}80{,}000$

Average Stock $= \dfrac{\text{Opening Stock} + \text{Closing Stock}}{2}$

Stock Turnover Ratio $= \dfrac{28{,}80{,}000}{\dfrac{3{,}60{,}000 + 2{,}40{,}000}{2}}$ 4.8 Times

(2) From the following particulars, you are required to calculate :

(i) Current Ratio

(ii) Liquid Ratio

(iii) Debt Collection period & Debtors Turnover Ratio

(iv) Debt Equity Ratio

(v) Stock Turnover Ratio

BALANCE SHEET OF A LTD.
as on 31st March, 2005

Liabilities	Rs.	Assets	Rs.
Equity Share Capital Shares of Rs. 10 each	15,00,000	Fixed Assets	15,00,000
		Stock	6,50,000
Reserves	5,00,000	Debtors	6,00,000
9% Debentures	5,00,000	Cash & Bank	1,50,000
Loan from Directors	3,00,000	Profit & Loss A/c	2,50,000
S. Creditors	2,50,000		
Bills Payable	1,00,000		
	31,50,000		31,50,000

Sales during the year amounted to Rs. 30,00,000. The company maintains an uniform rate of 20% profit on cost price.

Solution:

(1) Current Ratio $= \dfrac{\text{Current Assets}}{\text{Current Liabilities}}$

$= \dfrac{14{,}00{,}000}{3{,}50{,}000} = 4 : 1$

(ii) Liquid Ratio $= \dfrac{\text{Liquid Assets}}{\text{Current Liabilities}}$

$= \dfrac{7{,}00{,}000}{3{,}50{,}000} = 2 : 1$

(iii) Debtors Turnover Ratio $= \dfrac{\text{Sales}}{\text{Average Debtors}}$

$= \dfrac{30,00,000}{6,00,000} = 5 \text{ Times}$

Average Collection Period $= \dfrac{365}{\text{Debtors Turnover}}$

$= \dfrac{365}{5} = 73 \text{ days}$

(iv) Debt-Equity Ratio $= \dfrac{\text{Long Term Debts}}{\text{Equity capital} + \text{Reserves} - \text{Dr. Balance of P \& L A/c}}$

$= \dfrac{8,00,000}{20,00,000 - 2,50,000}$

$= \dfrac{8,00,000}{17,50,000} = 0.457$

(v) Stock Turnover Ratio $= \dfrac{\text{Cost of Goods Sold}}{\text{Average Stock}}$

Cost of Goods Sold = Sales – Gross Profit

= Rs. 30,00,000 – 5,00,000

= Rs.25,00,000

Stock Turnover Ratio $= \dfrac{25,00,000}{6,50,000} = 3.846 \text{ Times}$

Illustration (3)

From the following particulars compute necessary ratios to comment on the solvency position of the firm.

	Year ending 31st March		
	2003	2004	2005
	Rs.	Rs.	Rs.
Inventories	2,40,000	1,60,000	3,00,000
Debtors	3,20,000	4,80,000	4,50,000
Prepaid Expenses	5,000	10,000	-
Cash & Bank Balance	—	2,50,000	1,50,000
Sundry Creditors	—	3,75,000	3,25,000
Bills Payable	—	75,000	1,75,000
Bank Overdraft	—	—	1,00,000
Sales	—	10,00,000	17,25,000
Rate of Gross Profit to Sales	—	20%	20%

Solution :

Since Capitals, long-term loans and fixed assets are not given, long-term solvency ratios can not be calculated. However, in order to assess short term solvency position various ratios indicating the liquidity positions and some activity ratios showing inflow of cash can be workedout.

(i) Current Ratio $= \frac{\text{Current Assets}}{\text{Current Liabilities}}$

31st March, 2004 $= \frac{1,60,000 + 4,80,000 + 10,000 + 2,50,000}{3,75,000 + 75,000}$

$= \frac{9,00,000}{4,50,000} = 2:1$

31st March, 2005 $= \frac{3,00,000 + 4,50,000 + 1,50,000}{3,25,000 + 1,75,000 + 1,00,000}$

$= \frac{9,00,000}{6,00,000} = 1.5 : 1$

(ii) Liquid Ratio $= \frac{\text{Quick Assets*}}{\text{Quick Liabilities}}$

31st March, 2004 = *Current Assets – Prepaid Exp. – Stock

$= \frac{7,30,000}{4,50,000} = 1.622 : 1$

31st March, 2005 $= \frac{6,00,000}{5,00,000^*} = 1.2 : 1$

*Current Liabilities – Bank overdraft

(iii) Inventory Turnover Ratio $= \frac{\text{Cost of Goods Sold}}{\text{Average Inventory}}$

Cost of Goods Sold = Sales – Gross Profit

= 10,00,000 – 2,00,000

= 8,00,000

31st March, 2004 $= \frac{8,00,000}{(2,40,000 + 1,60,000) \div 2}$

$= \frac{8,00,000}{2,00,000} = 4 \text{ Times}$

31st March, 2005 Cost of goods sold = 17,25,000 – 3,45,000 = 13,80,000

Stock T.O. Ratio $= \frac{13,80,000}{(1,60,000 + 3,00,000) \div 2}$

$= \frac{13,80,000}{2,30,000} = 6$ Times

(iv) Debtors T.O. Ratio $= \frac{\text{Net Sales}}{\text{Average Debtors}}$

2004 $= \frac{10,00,000}{(3,20,000 + 4,80,000) \div 2}$

$= \frac{10,00,000}{4,00,000} = 2.5$ Times

2005 $= \frac{17,25,000}{(4,80,000 + 4,50,000) \div 2}$

$= \frac{17,25,000}{4,65,000} = 3.71$ Times

Average Collection Period (2004) = 365/2.5 = 146 days

Average Collection Period (2005) = 365/3.71 = 98 days

These ratios indicate that over all short term solvency position is improving. Despite the decrease in current and liquid ratio, the overall repaying capacity has improved due to higher Inventory Turnover Ratio, Debtors T.O. Ratio and falling collection period.

Illustration (4)

A firm has a liquidity ratio of 2 : 1 if the Stock is Rs. 75,000 and total current liabilities are 1,50,000 ascertain the current ratio.

Solution :

Liquid ratio = 2 : 1

i.e. liquid Assets : Current Liabilities

		Rs.
	Liquid assets = 1,50,000 × 2	3,00,000
Add	Stock	75,000
	Current Assets	3,75,000

Current Ratio $= \frac{\text{Current Assets}}{\text{Current Liabilities}} = \frac{3,75,000}{1,50,000} = 2.5 : 1$

Illustration (5)

X Ltd. has a current ratio of 3.5 : 1 and liquid ratio of 2 : 1. If the value of stock is Rs. 60,000, find out the total current liabilities and total current assets.

Solution :

Current ratio	3.5 : 1
Liquid ratio	2.0 : 1
Stock to current liabilities.	1.5 : 1

$$\text{Current liabilities} = \frac{60,000}{1.5} \times 1 = 40,000$$

$$\text{Current assets} = 40,000 \times 3.5 = \text{Rs. } 1,40,000$$

Illustration (6)

Y Ltd. shows the following position for the year ending 31st March, 2004 and 31st March, 2005

	Year ending 31st March	
Liabilities	2004	2005
	Rs.	Rs.
Equity Share Capital	5,00,000	5,00,000
Reserve & Surplus	5,00,000	15,00,000
Borrowed Funds (Long Term)	35,00,000	30,00,000
Current liabilities	10,00,000	15,00,000
	55,00,000	65,00,000
Assets		
Net Block	15,00,000	15,00,000
Current Assets:		
Stock	10,00,000	15,00,000
Debtors	15,00,000	15,00,000
Cash & Bank balances	10,00,000	5,00,000
Other Current Assets	5,00,000	15,00,000
	55,00,000	65,00,000
Sales	150,00,000	135,00,000

Calculate :

(i) Debt-Equity Ratio, Quick Ratio and Working Capital Turnover ratio for the year 2004 and 2005.

(ii) Compute the amount of sales for the year 2004-2005 if the company is to maintain its Working Capital Ratio.

[C.A. (I) Adapted)

Solution :

	Year ending 31st March	
	Rs. 2004	Rs. 2005

(i) Debt-Equity Ratio = $\frac{\text{Debt}}{\text{Equity}}$

$$\frac{\text{Long Term Borrowed Funds}}{\text{Equity Capital + Reserve and Surplus}} = \frac{35,00,000}{10,00,000} \qquad \frac{30,00,000}{20,00,000}$$

3.5 : 1   1.5 : 1

(ii) Quick Ratio

$$\frac{\text{Quick Assets}}{\text{Quick Liabilities}} = \frac{\text{Debtors + Cash \& Bank}}{\text{Quick Liabilities}} = \frac{15,00,000 + 10,00,000}{10,00,000} \qquad \frac{15,00,000 + 5,00,000}{15,00,000}$$

= 2.5 : 1   1.33 : 1

(iii) Working Capital T.O. Ratio

(a) $$\frac{\text{Sales}}{\text{Working Capital*}} = \frac{150,00,000}{30,00,000} \qquad \frac{135,00,000}{35,00,000}$$

5 Times   3.86 Times

(b) Required Sales to maintain W.C.T.O Ratio

$$\text{WCTO Ratio} = \frac{\text{Sales}}{\text{Working Capital}}$$

$$5 = \frac{\text{Sales}}{35,00,000}$$

Sales = 35,00,000 × 5 = Rs. 175,00,000

*Working Capital = Current Assets – Current liabilities

Illustration (7)

From the following particulars calculate for the year 2004-2005.

(i) Current Ratio
(ii) Stock Turnover Ratio
(iii) Return on Capital Employed
(iv) Return on Net worth
(v) Proprietory Ratio

Liabilities	31.3.04 Rs.	31.3.05 Rs.
Equity Share Capital	12,50,000	12,50,000
Reserves & Surplus	5,00,000	5,75,000
Term Loans	6,00,000	5,00,000
Current Liabilities	1,25,000	6,50,000
	24,75,000	29,75,000

Assets

Fixed Assets (Net)	10,00,000	13,00,000
Investments	1,50,000	2,05,000
Stock	5,00,000	6,00,000
Debtors	2,50,000	3,50,000
Cash & Bank balance	1,00,000	1,00,000
Other Current Assets	1,25,000	1,20,000
Miscellaneous Expenses	3,50,000	3,00,000
	24,75,000	29,75,000
Sales	-	30,25,000
PBIT	-	8,05,000
Interest	-	1,24,325
Provision for Tax	-	3,15,000
Proposed Dividend	-	2,50,000

[C.A. (I) Adapted]

Solution:

(i) Current Ratio $= \dfrac{\text{Current Assets}}{\text{Current Liabilities}} = \dfrac{11,70,000}{6,50,000}$

$= 1.8 : 1$

(ii) Stock Turnover Ratio $= \dfrac{\text{Cost of Goods Sold}}{\text{Average Stock}}$ or $\dfrac{\text{Sales*}}{\text{Average Stock}}$

*When COGS cannot be worked out

$= \dfrac{30,25,000}{5,00,000 + 6,00,000 \div 2} = \dfrac{30,25,000}{5,50,000}$

$=$ 5.5 Times

(iii) Return on Capital Employed

$= \dfrac{\text{PBIT}}{\text{Average Capital Employed}} \times 100$

$= \dfrac{8,05,000}{20,12,500} \times 100 = 40\%$

(iv) Return on Net-Worth

$= \dfrac{\text{PAT}}{\text{Average net worth}} \times 100$

PAT $=$ PBIT – Interest – Tax

$=$ 8,05,000 – 1,24,325 – 3,15,000 = Rs. 3,65,625

Net worth = Equity Share Capital + Reserves & Surplus – Miscellaneous Expenses.

		2004	2005
	Equity Share Capital	12,50,000	12,50,000
	Reserves & Surplus	5,00,000	5,75,000
		17,50,000	18,25,000
Less	Miscellaneous Exp.	3,50,000	3,00,000
		14,00,000	15,25,000

$$\text{Average Net worth} = \frac{14,00,000 + 15,25,000}{2} = 14,62,500$$

$$\text{Return on Net worth} = \frac{3,65,625}{14,62,500} \times 100 = 25\%$$

(v) $$\text{Proprietory Ratio} = \frac{\text{Proprietory Funds}}{\text{Net Assets}}$$

$$= \frac{15,25,000}{29,75,000 - 3,00,000}$$

$$= \frac{15,25,000}{26,75,000} = 0.57 \text{ Times or } 57\%$$

Working note: Computation of Average Capital Employed

		31.3.04 Rs.	31.3.05 Rs.
	Total Assets (Excluding fictitious)	21,25,000	26,75,000
Less	Current liabilities	1,25,000	6,50,000
		20,00,000	20,25,000

$$\text{Average Capital Employed} = \frac{\text{Opening Balance + Closing balance}}{2}$$

$$= \frac{20,00,000 + 20,25,000}{2} = \text{Rs. } 20,12,500$$

Illustration (8)

The Balance Sheets of P Ltd. for the last 3 years read as below : (Rs. in lacs)

Sources:	2003 Rs.	2004 Rs.	2005 Rs.
Share Capital (Rs. 10 each)	2,000	2,000	3,000
Securities Premium	1,500	1,500	500
Reserves (after 10% dividend)	1,500	1,700	1,800
Long Term Loans	1,000	800	800
	6,000	6,000	6,100
Represented by:			
Fixed Assets	2,000	2,500	3,000
Less Depreciation	700	950	1,250
	1,300	1,550	1,750
Capital Work-in-progress	800	900	700
Investments	200	200	200
	2,300	2,650	2,650

Net Current Assets:			
Debtors	1,700	1,800	1,850
Stock	1,800	1,900	2,400
Cash & Bank	500	500	500
Others	400	600	1,400
	4,400	4,800	6,150
Less Current liabilities	(700)	(1,450)	(2,700)
	3,700	3,350	3,450
Total Assets	6,000	6,000	6,100
Sales	3,900	4,000	5,000

Sales excludes excise duty & sales tax @ 20% Calculate for the 2004 and 2005 :

(i) Fixed Assets Turnover Ratio

(ii) Stock Turnover Ratio

(iii) Debtors Turnover Ratio in terms of number of days

(iv) Earnings per share.

[C.A. (I) May 1996-Modified]

Solution :

(Rs. in lacs)

	2004	2005
(i) Fixed Assets Turnover Ratio :		
$= \dfrac{\text{Sales}}{\text{Average Fixed Assets}}$	$= \dfrac{4,000}{1,425}$	$\dfrac{5,000}{1,650}$
	= 2.8 Times	= 3.03 Times
(ii) Stock Turnover Ratio :		
$= \dfrac{\text{Sales}}{\text{Average Stock}}$	$= \dfrac{4,000}{1,850}$	$\dfrac{5,000}{2,150}$
	= 2.16 Times	= 2.33 Times
(iii) Debtors Turnover Ratio :		
$= \dfrac{\text{Average Receivables}}{\text{Credit Sales}} \times 365$	$= \dfrac{1,750}{4,800} \times 365$	$= \dfrac{1,825}{6,000} \times 365$
	= 133 days	= 111 days
(iv) Earnings Per Share:		
$= \dfrac{\text{Profit after Tax}}{\text{No. of equity shares}}$	$\dfrac{400}{200}$	$\dfrac{400}{300}$
	Rs. 2 per share	Rs. 1.33 per share

Working notes

(1) Average Fixed Assets have been workedout by adding the fixed assets for the previous year and current year and dividing by two.

(2) Similarly average stock and average receivables have been calculated.

(3) Profit after Tax (PAT) have been calculated as follows :

(Rs. in lacs)

		Year 2004	Year 2005
	Opening balance (Reserve)	1,500	1,700
	Closing balance	1,700	1,800
	Addition made (Profit after dividend)	200	100
Add	Dividend (10% on Capital)	200	300
	Profit After Tax	400	400

Illustration (9)

From the following calculate 'Average Collection Period' by taking 360 days in an year.

Average Inventory	Rs. 3,60,000
Debtors	Rs. 2,30,000
Stock Turnover Ratio	6 Times
Gross Profit Ratio	10%
Credit Sales to Total Sales	20%

[C.A. (I) May 1993]

Solution :

(i) Calculation of Cost of Sales:

$$\text{Inventory T.O. Ratio} = \frac{\text{Cost of Goods Sold}}{\text{Average Inventory}}$$

or Cost of goods Sold = Average Inventory × Inventory T.O. Ratio

$= 3,60,000 \times 6 =$ Rs. 21,60,000

(ii) Calculation of Sales

Gross Profit Ratio is 10%

$$\text{Hence Total Sales} = \text{Cost of goods sold} \times \frac{100}{90} = \frac{21,60,000 \times 100}{90}$$

= Rs. 24,00,000

(iii) Credit Sales

Since Credit sales is 20% of Total Sales the credit sales will be :

20% of Rs. 24,00,000

= Rs. 4,80,000

(iv) $$\text{Average Collection Period} = \frac{\text{Debtors}}{\text{Daily Credit Sales*}}$$

$$= \frac{2,30,000}{4,80,000/360} = 172.5 \text{ days or } 173 \text{ days}$$

*Daily credit sales = Credit sales divided by number of days in a year.

Illustration (10)

(a) From the following particulars, Calculate :

(i) Sales

(ii) Debtors

(iii) Closing Stock, and

(iv) Creditors

Gross Profit Ratio	25%
Stock Velocity	8 months
Creditors' Velocity	2 months
Debtors' Velocity	3 months

Gross Profit for the year ended 31st March, 2005 amounted to Rs. 6,00,000.

(b) Will it make any difference if closing stock of the year is Rs. 30,000 more than the opening stock. Bills Receivable amount to Rs. 50,000 and Bills Payable Rs. 25,000.

Solution :

(i) Calculation of Sales

$$\text{Sales} = \frac{\text{Gross Profit} \times 100}{\text{G.P. Ratio}}$$

$$= \text{Rs. } 6{,}00{,}000 \times \frac{100}{25} = \text{Rs. } 24{,}00{,}000$$

(ii) "Debtors" = Sales × Debtors Velocity or Sales/Debtors T.O. Ratio

$$= 24{,}00{,}000 \times \frac{3}{12} = \text{Rs. } 6{,}00{,}000$$

(iii) Closing Stock

$$\text{Stock T.O. Ratio} = \frac{\text{Cost of Goods Sold}}{\text{Average Stock}} \text{ or } \frac{\text{No. of months}}{\text{Stock velocity}}$$

$$\text{Stock T.O. Ratio} = \frac{12}{\text{Stock Velocity}} = \frac{12}{8} = 1.5$$

Cost of goods sold = Sales – Gross Profit

or 24,00,000 – 6,00,000 = 18,00,000

$$\text{Average Stock} = \text{Cost of Goods Sold} \times \frac{\text{Stock Velocity}}{12}$$

$$= 18{,}00{,}000 \times \frac{8}{12} = \text{Rs. } 12{,}00{,}000$$

Alternatively:

$$\text{Average Stock} = \frac{18{,}00{,}000}{1.5} = \text{Rs. } 12{,}00{,}000$$

Hence average stock = Closing Stock

Rs. = 12,00,000

(iv) Creditors

Cost of goods sold = Purchases + Opening stock – Closing Stock

or Purchases = Cost of goods sold – Opening Stock + Closing Stock

Since Opening & closing stock are equal = Cost of goods sold is equal to purchases. *i.e.* Rs. 18,00,000.

Creditors = Purchases × creditors velocity/12 = $\frac{18,00,000 \times 2}{12}$ = Rs. 3,00,000

(b) Calculation of Closing Stock if it is Rs. 30,000 more than the opening stock.

Let the opening stock be x then.

Closing Stock will be Rs. 30,000 + x

$$\text{Average Stock} = \frac{x + (x + 30,000)}{2}$$

$$12,00,000 = 2x + 30,000/2$$

$$12,00,000 = x + 15,000$$

$$12,00,000 - 15,000 = x$$

$$x = 11,85,000$$

Closing Stock = 11,85,000 + 30,000

= Rs. 12,15,000

*Since Total Debtors (Receivables) include Rs. 50,000 Worth of Bills Receivable, then Sundry Debtors will be

= Rs. 6,00,000 – 50,000 = 5,50,000

Similarly

*Total Creditors (Payables) include an amount of Rs. 25,000 on account of Bills Payable. then sundry creditors will be calculated after adjusting for the stocks and thereafter deducting Bills payable therefrom as shown under :

Purchases = Cost of goods sold – Opening Stock + Closing Stock

= Rs. 18,00,000 – 11,85,000 + 12,15,000

= Rs. 18,30,000

Total Creditors = $\frac{18,30,000 \times 2}{12}$ = 3,05,000

Sundry Creditors = Rs. 3,05,000 – 25,000 (Bills Payable) = Rs. 2,80,000

Illustration (11)

From the following information compute:

(i) Sales
(ii) Cost of Sales
(iii) Credit Sales
(iv) Total Assets
(v) Inventory
(vi) Long Term Debt
(vii) Current liabilities
(viii) Current Assets
(ix) Debtors

Gross Profit (20% of Sales)	Rs. 3,00,000
Credit Sales to total sales	80%
Total assets to Turnover	3 Times
Inventory Turnover Ratio	8 Times
Average Collection period (Taking 360 days in a year)	9 days
Current Ratio	2 : 1
Long Term Debt to Equity	40%
Shareholders' Equity	Rs. 2,50,000

Solution :

(i) Sales

$$\text{Gross Profit} \times \frac{100}{\text{G.P.Ratio}}$$

$$= 3{,}00{,}000 \times \frac{100}{20} = \text{Rs. } 15{,}00{,}000$$

(ii) Cost of Sales = Sales – Gross Profit
Rs. 15,00,000 – 3,00,000 = 12,00,000

(iii) Credit Sales = 80% of Total Sales
= 80% of Rs. 15,00,000
= Rs. 12,00,000

(iv) Total Assets
Total Assets T.O. Ratio = 3 Times

$$\text{Total Assets} = \frac{\text{Sales}}{\text{Total Assets T.O Ratio}} = \frac{15{,}00{,}000}{3}$$

= Rs. 5,00,000

(v) Inventory
Inventory T.O. Ratio = 8 Times

$$\text{Inventory} = \frac{\text{Cost of Sales}}{\text{Inventory T.O Ratio}} = \frac{12{,}00{,}000}{8} = \text{Rs. } 1{,}50{,}000$$

(vi) Long Term Debt:

Long Term Debt-Equity Ratio = 40%

Shareholders Equity is Rs. = 2,50,000

Hence Long Term Debt = 40% of Rs. 2,50,000

= Rs. 1,00,000

(vii) Current liabilities :

Current liabilities = Total Assets – (Shareholders Equity + Long Term Debt)

= 5,00,000 – (2,50,000 – 1,00,000)

= Rs. 1,50,000

(viii) Current Assets :

Current Ratio is 2 : 1

Current liabilities are Rs. 1,50,000

Current Assets = 1,50,000 × 2 = Rs. 3,00,000

(ix) Debtors

$$\text{Debtors} = \frac{\text{Credit Sales} \times \text{Average Collection Period}}{\text{No. of days in a year}}$$

$$= \frac{12,00,000 \times 9}{360} = \text{Rs. } 30,000$$

Illustration : 12 (Turnover Vs. Velocity)

From the following particulars you are required to calculate :

(i) Sales and Cost of goods sold.

(ii) Capital

(iii) Creditors

(iv) Fixed Assets

(v) Closing Stock

(vi) Debtors

Gross Profit	2,40,000
Gross Profit Margin	20%
Stock Velocity	6
Capital Turnover Ratio	2
Fixed Assets Turnover Ratio	4
Debt Collection Period	2 months
Creditors Payment Period	73 days
Excess of Closing stock over opening Stock	Rs. 40,000

Solution :

(i) Calculation of Sales

$$\text{Sales} = \frac{\text{Gross Profit} \times 100}{\text{Gross Profit Ratio}}$$

$$= \frac{2,40,000 \times 100}{20} = \text{Rs. } 12,00,000$$

Cost of Goods sold

COGS = Sales – Gross Profit

= 12,00,000 – 2,40,000 = Rs. 9,60,000

(ii) Capital:

Capital Turnover Ratio = 2

$$\text{Capital T. O. Ratio} = \frac{\text{Sales}}{\text{Capital}}$$

$$2 = \frac{12,00,000}{\text{Capital}}$$

$$\text{Capital} = \frac{12,00,000}{2} = \text{Rs. } 6,00,000$$

(iii) Creditors

Creditors Payment period = 73 days

$$\text{or Creditors Turnover Ratio} = \frac{365}{73} = 5$$

$$\text{Creditors} = \frac{\text{Purchases*}}{\text{Creditors T.O. Ratio}} = \frac{10,00,000}{5} = \text{Rs. } 2,00,000$$

$$\text{or } \frac{\text{Purchases} \times 73}{365} = \frac{10,00,000 \times 73}{365}$$

$$= \text{Rs. } 2,00,000$$

*Purchases = Cost of Goods sold + Excess of closing Stock over opening stock
or COGS – Excess of opening Stock over closing stock

(iv) Fixed Assets

Fixed Assets Turnover Ratio = 4

$$\text{Fixed Assets T.O. Ratio} = \frac{\text{Sales}}{\text{Fixed Assets}}$$

$$4 = \frac{12,00,000}{\text{Fixed Assets}}$$

$$\text{Fixed Assets} = \frac{12,00,000}{4} = \text{Rs. } 3,00,000$$

(v) Closing Stock:

$$\text{Stock Turnover Ratio} = \frac{\text{Cost of Goods Sold}}{\text{Average Stock}}$$

$$6 = \frac{9,60,000}{\text{Average Stock}}$$

Average Stock $= \dfrac{9,60,000}{6} = Rs.\,1,60,000$

Let the Opening Stock be x

Closing Stock $= (x + 40,000)$

Average Stock $= \dfrac{x + (x + 40,000)}{2}$

$1,60,000 = \dfrac{2x + (40,000)}{2}$

$1,60,000 = x + 20,000$

$1,60,000 - 20,000 = x$

$1,40,000 = x$

Hence Closing Stock = 1,40,000 + 40,000 = 1,80,000

(vi) Debtors Collection Period = 2 months

Debtors T.O. Ratio $= \dfrac{12}{2} = 6$

Debtors $= \dfrac{\text{Sales}}{\text{Debtors T.O. Ratio}} = \dfrac{12,00,000}{6}$

= Rs. 2,00,000

Velocity *vs.* Turnover Ratio

Students Should note that :

(i) If Stock Velocity, Debtors Velocity or Creditors Velocity is given interms of period (month/days) then the respective Turnover ratio will be calculated by dividing the yearly period (months/days) by the respective velocity period.

Say stock Velocity 4 months.

then Stock T.O. Ratio = $\dfrac{12}{4}$ = 3 Times

If however stock Velocity is given only as 4 then Stock T.O. Ratio and Stock Velocity will be the same. Because 4 refers to 4 times and not 4 months.

Illustration (13) (Return on Capital Employed and on Net worth)

The following information has been abstracted from the annual accounts of a company.

	Rs.
Share Capital	10,00,000
General Reserve	7,50,000
Investment Allowance Reserve	2,50,000
15% Long Term Loans	15,00,000
Profit before tax	6,50,000

Provision for tax	3,50,000
Proposed Dividends	50,000

Calculate Return on Capital Employed and on Net worth.

Solution

(i) Return on Capital Employed

$$= \frac{\text{EBIT (PBIT)}}{\text{Capital Employed}} \times 100$$

$$\text{EBIT} = \text{Net Profit} + \text{Interest} + \text{Tax}$$
$$= 6{,}50{,}000 + 2{,}25{,}000 \text{ (Interest)}$$
$$= \text{Rs. } 8{,}75{,}000$$

Capital Employed = Share Capital + General Reserve + Investment Allowance Reserve + Long Term Loans

$$= 10{,}00{,}000 + 7{,}50{,}000 + 2{,}50{,}000 + 15{,}00{,}000$$
$$= \text{Rs. } 35{,}00{,}000$$
$$= \frac{8{,}75{,}000 \times 100}{35{,}00{,}000} = 25\%$$

(ii) Return on Net Worth

$$= \frac{\text{Profit after Tax}}{\text{Net Worth (Shareholders' Equity)}} \times 100$$

$$= \frac{6{,}50{,}000 - 3{,}50{,}000}{10{,}00{,}000 + 7{,}50{,}000 + 2{,}50{,}000} = \frac{3{,}00{,}000}{20{,}00{,}000} \times 100 = 15\%$$

Illustration (14) Calculation of Proprietors Funds (Preference and Equity Share Capital)

Working Capital of a company is Rs. 5,40,000 and current ratio is 2.5. Liquid Ratio is 1.5 and the proprietory ratio 0.75. Bank Overdraft is Rs. 1,20,000. There are no long term loans and fictitious assets. Reserves and surplus amount Rs. 3,60,000 and Capital gearing ratio (Equity-preference Capital) is 2.

Your are required to calculate :

(i) Current Liabilities
(ii) Current Assets
(iii) Quick liabilities
(iv) Quick Assets
(v) Stock
(vi) Net Block
(vii) Proprietory Fund
(viii) Preference Share Capital and
(ix) Equity Share Capital

[C.A. (I) May 1991 Adapted]

Solution :

Calculation of Current Liabilities

(i) Working Capital is Rs. 5,40,000 and Current Ratio = 2.5 : 1

Working Capital = Current Asset – Current liabilities

Let Current liabilities be x

Working Capital = $2.5\,x - x$

$5{,}40{,}000 = 1.5x$

$3{,}60{,}000 = x$

Hence Current liabilities = Rs. 3,60,000

(ii) Current Assets

Working Capital = Current Assets – Current liabilities

Rs. 5,40,000 = Current Assets – 3,60,000

Current Assets = Rs. 9,00,000

* Alternatively current assets are 2.5 times of Current Liabilities. Thus Current Assets = 3,60,000 × 2.5 = Rs. 9,00,000

(iii) Quick liabilities

= Current liabilities – Bank Overdraft

= 3,60,000 – 1,20,000 = 2,40,000

(iv) Quick Assets

Quick (liquid) Ratio = Quick Assets : Quick liabilities

= 1.5 : 1

Quick liabilities are Rs. 2,40,000

Hence Quick (liquid) assets = 2,40,000 × 1.5

= Rs. 3,60,000

(v) Stock = Current Assets – Quick Assets

= Rs. 9,00,000 – 3,60,000

= Rs. 5,40,000

(vi) Net Block = Fixed Assets

Total Assets = Net Block + Current Assets

Let the Net Block be x

Total Assets = x + 9,00,000

Proprietory Fund is 75% of (x + 9,00,000)

Hence (x + 9,00,000) – 3,60,000 = 75% (x + 9,00,000)

(Fixed Assets) x = 5,40,000

(vii) Proprietor's Funds : Equity Share Capital + Preference Share Capital + Reserves and surplus.

Where as Proprietory Fund given is 75% of Fixed Assets and Current Assets.

i.e. 75% (5,40,000 + 9,00,000)

= Rs. 10,80,000

(viii) Equity & Preference Share Capital = Proprietory Funds – Reserves & Surplus

= Rs. 10,80,000 – 3,60,000 = Rs. 7,20,000

Equity Capital = 7,20,000 × 2/3 = Rs. 4,80,000
Preference Share Capital = 7,20,000 × 1/3 = 2,40,000

Illustration (15) (Missing figures & Balance Sheet)

From the following calculate :

(i) Cost of goods sold
(ii) Sales
(iii) Closing Stock
(iv) Accounts Receivable and Debtors
(v) Accounts Payable and Creditors
(vi) Fixed Assets

Also prepare a Balance Sheet.

Gross Profit	Rs. 4,00,000
Gross Profit to Cost of good sold ratio	1/3
Stock Velocity	6 Times
Opening Stock	Rs. 1,80,000
Accounts Receivable Velocity (360 days in a year)	72 days
Accounts Payable Velocity (360 days in a year)	90 days
Current Assets	7,50,000
Bills Receivable	1,00,000
Bills Payable	25,000
Fixed Assets Turnover Ratio	8 Times

Solution :

(i) Cost of Goods Sold = Gross Profit × G.P. Ratio
= Rs. 4,00,000 × 3 = 12,00,000

(ii) Sales = Cost of Goods sold + Gross Profit
= Rs. 12,00,000 + 4,00,000 = Rs. 16,00,000

(iii) Closing Stock

$$\text{Stock Velocity} = \frac{\text{Cost of goods sold}}{\text{Average stock}}$$

$$6 = \frac{12{,}00{,}000}{\text{Average Stock}}$$

$$\text{Average Stock} = \frac{12{,}00{,}000}{6} = \text{Rs. } 2{,}00{,}000$$

$$\text{Average Stock} = \frac{\text{Opening Stock} + \text{Closing Stock}}{2}$$

$$\text{Rs. } 2,00,000 = \frac{1,80,000 + \text{Closing Stock}}{2}$$

Closing Stock = 2,00,000 × 2 – 1,80,000

= 4,00,000 – 1,80,000 = Rs. 2,20,000

(iv) Accounts Receivable

$$\text{Accounts Receivable Turnover Ratio*} = \frac{\text{Credit Sales}}{\text{Average Receivable}}$$

$$\text{ARTO. Ratio *} = \boxed{\frac{360}{72} = 5 \text{ Times}} \qquad 5 = \frac{16,00,000}{\text{Average Receivable}}$$

Average Receivable = 16,00,000/5 = Rs. 3,20,000

Debtors = Accounts Receivable – Bills Receivable

= Rs. 3,20,000 – 1,00,000 = Rs. 2,20,000

(v) Accounts Payable

$$\text{Account Payable Turnover Ratio*} = \frac{\text{Credit Purchases}}{\text{Average Payable}}$$

$$\boxed{\text{Accounts Payable T. O*} \quad \frac{360}{90} = 4 \text{ Times}} \qquad 4 = \frac{12,20,000\text{**}}{\text{Average Payable}}$$

Credit Purchases** = Cost of goods sold – Opening Stock + Closing Stock

= Rs. 12,00,000 – 1,80,000 + 2,20,000

= 12,40,000

$$\text{Average Payable} = \frac{12,40,000}{4} = 3,10,000$$

Creditors = Average Payable – Bills Payable

= Rs. 3,10,000 – 25,000 Rs. 2,85,000

(vi) Fixed Assets

$$\text{Fixed Assets Turnover Ratio} = \frac{\text{Sales}}{\text{Fixed Assets}}$$

$$\text{Fixed Assets} = \frac{\text{Sales}}{\text{F.A.T.O. Ratio}}$$

$$\text{Fixed Assets} = \frac{16,00,000}{8}$$

= Rs. 2,00,000

All sales and Purchases are treated on credit basis

BALANCE SHEET
as on ———

Liabilities	Rs.	Assets	Rs.
Capital (Bal. figure)	6,40,000	Fixed Assets	2,00,000
		Current Assets:	
Creditors	2,85,000	Stock	2,20,000
Bills Payable	25,000	Debtors	2,20,000
		Bills Receivable	1,00,000
		Cash & Bank*	2,10,000
	9,50,000		9,50,000

* Cash & Bank = Total Current Assets – (Stock + Debtors + B/R)

Illustration (16) (Ascertaining Working Capital)

From the following particulars ascertain the amount of working capital:

Sales	Rs. 30,00,000
Gross Profit margin	25%
Credit Purchases	2/3rd of cost of goods sold
Average payment period	72 days
Average collection period	60 days
Inventory holding period	90 days
Cash and Bank balance	2.5% of Sales
Assume 1 year = 360 days	

[C.A. (I) Nov, 1992 Modified]

Solution:

Working Capital = Current Assets – Current liabilities

I Calculation of various item of Current Assets

(i) Inventory (Stock)

$$\text{Inventory} = \frac{\text{Cost of goods Sold*}}{\text{Inventory T. O. Ratio**}}$$

*Cost of goods sold = Sales – Gross Profit

= 30,00,000 – 7,50,000 = Rs. 22,50,000

$$\text{**Inventory T.O. Ratio} = \frac{360}{90} = 4 \text{ Times}$$

$$\text{Inventory} = \frac{22,50,000}{4} = \text{Rs. } 5,62,500$$

$$\text{(ii) Debtors} = \frac{\text{Total Credit Sales}}{\text{Debtors T. O. Ratio}}$$

$$\text{Debtors T.O. Ratio} = \frac{360}{60} = 6 \text{ Times}$$

$$\text{Debtors} = \frac{30,00,000}{6} = \text{Rs. } 5,00,000$$

(iii) Cash & Bank Balance = Sales × 2.5%

$$30,00,000 \times \frac{2.5}{100} = \text{Rs. } 75,000$$

II Calculation of Current liabilities

$$\text{Creditors} = \frac{\text{Credit Purchase}}{\text{Creditors T.O. Ratio}}$$, whereas credited purchses are equal to 2/3rd of Cost of Goods sold

∴ Credit Purchases = 2/3rd of Rs. 22,50,000 = Rs. 15,00,000

$$\text{Creditors T.O. Ratio} = \frac{360}{72} = 5 \text{ Times}$$

$$\text{Creditors} = \frac{15,00,000}{5} = 3,00,000$$

Total Current Assets		Rs.
	Inventory	5,62,500
	Debtors	5,00,000
	Cash & Bank balance	75,000
		11,37,500
Less	Current liabilities :	
	Creditors	3,00,000
	Working Capital	8,37,500

Illustration (17) (Preparation of Final Accounts)

Following information has been extracted from the books of SRK Ltd. for the year ended 31st March 2005. You are required to prepare a Trading and Profit & Loss Account and a Balance Sheet.

Current Ratio	2.5 : 1
Quick Ratio	1.3 : 1
Proprietory Ratio (Fixed Assets/Prop. Fund)	0.6 : 1
Gross Profit Ratio	10%
Debtors Velocity	40 days
Sales	Rs. 7,30,000
Working Capital	Rs. 1,20,000
Bank-Overdraft	15,000
Share Capital	2,50,000

Closing Stock is 10% more than Opening Stock Net profit is 10% of Proprietory Funds.

[C.A. (I) Nov. 1993]

Solution :

Calculation of missing figures

(i) Calculation of Current assets and Current liabilities

Current Ratio as given 2.5 : 1

Let Current liabilities be x

Current Assets = 2.5 x

Working Capital = 2.5 $x - x$

1,20,000 = 1.5x

80,000 = x

Thus, current liabilities = Rs. 80,000 & Current Assets Rs. 80,000 × 2.5 = Rs. 2,00,000

(ii) Closing Stock

Quick liabilities = Current liabilities – Bank Overdraft

Quick Ratio = Quick assets/Quick liabilities

(1.3)

Quick liab. = 80,000 – 15,000 = 65,000

Quick Assets = 65,000 × 1.3 = 84,500

Closing Stock = Current Assets – Quick Assets

2,00,000 – 84,500 = Rs. 1,15,500

(iii) Opening Stock = Rs. 1,15,500 × $\frac{100}{110}$ = Rs. 1,05,000

(iv) Debtors: Debtors T.O. Ratio = $\frac{\text{Credit Sales}}{\text{Average Debtors}}$

or Debtors = $\frac{\text{Credit Sales}}{\text{Debtors T. O. Ratio*}}$

*Debtors T.O. Ratio = $\frac{365}{40}$ = 9.125 Times

Debtors = $\frac{7,30,000}{9.125}$ = Rs. 80,000

or $\frac{7,30,000 \times 40}{365}$ = Rs. 80,000

(v) Gross Profit: 10% of Rs. 7,30,000 = Rs. 73,000

(vi) Proprietory Funds

Proprietory Ratio = 0.6 : 1

Proprietary Ratio = $\frac{\text{Fixed Assets}}{\text{Proprietory Fund}}$ = 0.6

or in relation to Working Capital it is 0.4

Since Working Capital is Rs. 1,20,000

Proprietory Fund = $\frac{1,20,000}{0.4}$ = Rs. 3,00,000

(vii) Fixed Assets = Rs. 3,00,000 × 0.6 = Rs. 1,80,000

(viii) Net Profit is 10% of Rs. 3,00,000 = Rs. 30,000

(ix) Opening balance of Profit & Loss A/c (or reserve)

Proprietory Fund = Share Capital + Current Year Profit + Opening Balance

Rs. 3,00,000 = 2,50,000 + 30,000 + 20,000 (Bal. figure)

(x) Other Current Assets (Bank and Cash Balance)

Total Current Assets – Debtors – Stock

Rs. 2,00,000 – 1,15, 500 – 80,000 = Rs. 4,500

TRADING & PROFIT & LOSS ACCOUNT
for the year ended 31st March, 2005

	Rs.		Rs.
To Opening Stock	1,05,000	By Sales	7,30,000
To Purchases (Bal. figure)	6,67,500	By Closing Stock	1,15,500
To Gross Profit c/d	73,000		
	8,45,500		8,45,500
To Opening Expenses (Bal. figure)	43,000	By Gross Profit b/d	73,000
To Net Profit c/d	30,000		
	73,000		73,000

BALANCE SHEET
As on 31st March 2005

Liabilities		Rs.	Assets	Rs.
Share Capital		2,50,000	Fixed Assets	1,80,000
Reserves & Surplus			**Current Assets:**	
Profit & Loss A/c			Stock	1,15,500
Opening balance	20,000		Debtors	80,000
Current years	30,000	50,000	Cash & Bank balance	4,500
Current liabilities				
Bank Overdraft		15,000		
S. Creditors		65,000		
		3,80,000		3,80,000

Illustration (18) (Calculation of Cash & Bank balance by Balance Sheet/Trial Balance)

From the following Calculate —

(i) Sales

(ii) Cost of Goods sold

(iii) Purchases

(iv) Proprietor's Funds

(v) Fixed Assets
(vi) Debtors
(vii) Creditors
(viii) Stock
(ix) Share Capital
(x) Cash & bank balance

Inventory Turnover Ratio	6 Times
Debtors outstanding at the end for	2 months
Creditors outstanding at the end for	73 days
Ratio of Cost of goods sold to:	
(a) Proprietory Fund	2 : 1
(b) Fixed Assets	4 : 1
Ratio of Gross Profit to Sales	20%
Closing Stock is greater than opening Stock by	Rs. 25,000
Gross Profit for the year	Rs. 3,00,000
Reserves & Surplus at the end	Rs. 1,00,000

[C.A. (I) May, 1998 Modified]

Solution:

Calculation of :

(i) $\text{Sales} = \dfrac{\text{Gross Profit} \times 100}{\text{Gross Profit Ratio}}$

$3{,}00{,}000 \times \dfrac{100}{20} = \text{Rs. } 15{,}00{,}000$

(ii) Cost of Goods Sold = Sales – Gross Profit

Rs. 15,00,000 – 3,00,000 = Rs. 12,00,000

(iii) Purchases

Purchases = Cost of Goods Sold + Excess of Closing Stock over Opening Stock

= 12,00,000 + 25,000 = Rs. 12,25,000

(iv) Proprietor's Funds

Ratio of Cost of goods sold to proprietory funds is 2 : 1

$\text{Proprietors Funds} = \dfrac{\text{Cost of Goods Sold}}{2}$

$= \dfrac{12{,}00{,}000}{2} = \text{Rs. } 6{,}00{,}000$

(v) Fixed Assets

Ratio of Cost of Goods Sold to Fixed assets is 4 : 1

$\text{Fixed Assets} = \dfrac{\text{Cost of Goods Sold}}{4}$

$= \dfrac{1{,}20{,}000}{4} = \text{Rs. } 3{,}00{,}000$

(vi) Debtors at the end are outstanding for 2 months which is equal to 2 months of annual sales.

$$\text{Debtors} = \frac{\text{Sales} \times 2}{12} = \frac{15{,}00{,}000 \times 2}{12} = \text{Rs. } 2{,}50{,}000$$

(vii) Creditors at the end are outstanding equal to 73 days of the annual purchases

$$\text{Creditors} = \frac{12{,}25{,}000 \times 73}{365} = \text{Rs. } 2{,}45{,}000$$

(viii) Inventory

Inventory Turnover Ratio is 6 times

$$\text{Average Inventory} = \frac{\text{Cost of Goods Sold}}{6}$$

$$= \frac{12{,}00{,}000}{6} = \text{Rs. } 2{,}00{,}000$$

Opening & Closing Stock

Let the opening Inventory be x

Closing inventory = $x + 25{,}000$

$$\text{Average Inventory} = \frac{x + (x + 25{,}000)}{2}$$

$$\text{Rs. } 2{,}00{,}000 = \frac{2x + 25{,}000}{2}$$

Rs. 2,00,000 = x + 12,500

Rs. 2,00,000 – 12,500 = x

x = 1,87,500 opening Inventory

Closing inventory = 1,87,500 + 25,000 = Rs. 2,12,500

(ix) Share Capital

Share Capital = Proprietory Funds – Reserve & surplus

= Rs. 6,00,000 – 1,00,000 = Rs. 5,00,000

(x) Cash & Bank Balance

BALANCE SHEET

As on ——

Liabilities	Rs.	Assets	Rs.
Share Capital	5,00,000	Fixed Assets	3,00,000
Reserve & Surplus	1,00,000	**Current Assets**	
S. Creditors	2,45,000	Stock	2,12,500
		Debtors	2,50,000
		Cash & Bank (Bal. figure)	82,500
	8,45,000		8,45,000

Cash & Bank Balance can also be ascertained by preparing Trial Balance as shown below:

	Dr.		Cr.
Fixed Assets	3,00,000	Share Capital	5,00,000
Stock	2,12,500	Reserve & Surplus	1,00,000
Debtors	2,50,000	S. Creditors	2,45,000
Cash & Bank balance (Balancing figure)	82,500		
	8,45,000		8,45,000

Illustration (19)

Current Ratio	1.70
Quick Ratio	0.80
Sales to total assets	1.25
Sales to Working Capital	5 times
Credit Sales	80%
Cash to Total Assets	0.05
Opening Debtors	Rs. 1,38,000
Working Capital	Rs. 2,10,000

Calculate

(i) Current assets and Current Liabilities
(ii) Quick Assets and Stock
(iii) Total Sales and Credit Sales
(iv) Total Assets
(v) Closing, Average Debtors & Debtors Turnover Ratio
(vi) Cash

Solution:

Calculation of

(i) Current Assets and Current Liabilities:

Let Current liabilities be x

Current Assets = $1.7x$

Current Assets – Current liabilities = Working Capital

$1.7x - x = 2{,}10{,}000$

$.7x = 2{,}10{,}000$

$x = 3{,}00{,}000$

When Current liabilities are Rs. 3,00,000

Current Assets will be = 3,00,000 × 1.7

= Rs. 5,10,000

(ii) Quick Assets : Quick Ratio is 0.8 : 1

When Quick (Current) liabilities are Rs. 3,00,000

The Quick assets = 0.8 × 3,00,000 = Rs. 2,40,000

(Assuming that there is no bank overdraft)

Stock = Current Assets – Quick Assets

= Rs. 5,10,000 – 2,40,000 = Rs. 2,70,000

(iii) Total Sales

Sales to Working Capital Ratio is 5

= Working Capital × 5

= Rs. 2,10,000 × 5 = Rs. 10,50,000

Credit Sales = 80%

80% of Rs. 10,50,000 = 8,40,000

(iv) Total Assets: Sales to total Assets is 1.25

$$= \frac{\text{Sales}}{\text{Total Assets}} \quad \frac{10,59,000}{1.25} = \text{Rs. } 8,40,000$$

(v) Closing & Average Debtors

Closing Debtors = Current Assets – Stock – Cash

= Rs. 5,10,000 – 2,70,000 – 42,000*

= Rs. 1,98,000

$$\text{Average Debtors} = \text{Rs. } \frac{1,38,000 + 1,98,000}{2} = \text{Rs. } 1,68,000$$

(vi) Debtors T.O. Ratio = Credit Sales/Average Debtors

= 8,40,000/1,68,000 = 5 Times

(vii) Cash = 0.05 of Total Assets

$$= \text{Rs. } 8,40,000 \times \frac{8,40,000 \times 5}{100} = \text{Rs. } 42,000^*$$

Illustration (20) (Calculation of Projected Ratio)

The Balance Sheet of Magha Ltd. as on 31st March 2005 was as under.

Liabilities	Rs.	Assets	Rs.
Equity Share Capital	2,00,000	Fixed Assets	3,40,000
9% Preference Share Capital	1,00,000	(Cost Rs. 5,00,000 – Dep. 1,60,000)	
General Reserve	60,000	Stock	60,000
12% Debentures	60,000	Bank	20,000
S. Creditors	80,000	Debtors	80,000
	5,00,000		5,00,000

Additional Information

(i) Fixed Assets costing Rs. 1,00,000 have been installed on 1. 4. 2005 but the payment will be made on 31. 7. 2005.

(ii) Fixed Assets - Turnover Ratio on the basis of Gross Value of Fixed Assets would be 1.5

(iii) Stock - Turnover Ratio would be 14.4 Calculated on the basis of average stock

(iv) The break-up of Cost and profit would be as follows :

Materials Consumed	40%
Labour	25%
Manufacturing Expenses	10%
Office and selling Expenses	10%
Depreciation	5%
Profit	10%
	100%

(v) Debtors would be 1/9th of sales

(vi) Creditors would be 1/5th of material consumed.

(vii) 12% Debentures of Rs. 25,000 have been issued on 1. 4. 2006.

(viii) The Bank balance after these adjustment would be Rs. 32,800

You are required to find out relevant figures to compute (after adjustment)

(i) Current Ratio

(ii) Fixed Assets/Net worth Ratio

(iii) Debt-Equity Ratio.

Ignore profit & Tax

Solution:

Calculation of figures after adjustment

(i) Sales

Projected Fixed Assets (Gross Value) Turnover Ratio = 1.5

Gross Fixed Assets = Rs. 5,00,000 + 1,00,000 = Rs. 6,00,000

Sales = Rs. 6,00,000 × 1.5 = Rs. 9,00,000

(ii) Cost of Goods Sold = Material + Labour + Manufacturing Expenses + Depreciation

= 40% + 25% + 10% + 5% = 80%

COGS = 80% of Rs. 9,00,000 = Rs. 7,20,000

(iv) $\text{Average Stock} = \dfrac{\text{Cost of goods Sold}}{\text{Stock Turnover Ratio}}$

$= \dfrac{7,20,000}{14.4} = 50,000$

Closing Stock = Rs. 50,000 × 2 – Rs. 60,000 = Rs. 40,000

(v) Debtors = 1/9th of Rs. 9,00,000 = Rs. 1,00,000

(vi) Creditors = 1/5th of Material Consumed

= 1/5 of (40% of Rs. 9,00,000) = Rs. 72,000

(1) $\text{Current Ratio} = \dfrac{\text{Current Assets}}{\text{Current Liabilities}}$

Current Assets (as calculated above)

Closing Stock	40,000
Debtors	1,00,000
Bank	32,800
	1,72,800

Current liabilities (creditors) Rs. 72,000

Current Ratio = 1,72,800/72,000 = 2.4 : 1

(2) Fixed Assets to Net worth

Fixed Assets = Rs. 3,40,000 + 1,00,000 = Rs. 4,40,000

Net Worth = Equity Capital	2,00,000
Preference Capital	1,00,000
Reserves	60,000
	3,60,000

$$\text{Fixed Assets to Net worth} = \frac{4,40,000}{3,60,000} = 1.22 : 1$$

(3) Debt-Equity Ratio :

$$= \frac{\text{Debt}}{\text{Equity}} \textit{ or } \frac{\text{Debt}}{\text{Debt + Equity}}$$

Debt = 12% Debentures Rs. 60,000 + 25,000 = Rs. 85,000

Equity = Net worth as calculated Rs. 3,60,000

$$\text{Debt-Equity Ratio} = \frac{85,000}{3,60,000} = 0.236 : 1$$

$$\text{or} = \frac{85,000}{85,000 + 3,60,000} = 0.191 : 1$$

Illustration (21) (Estimation of Working Capital & Increase in sales)

Important ratios of a firm for the year 2005 are given below :

1.	Stock velocity	4
2.	Debt Collection period	2 months
3.	Creditors payment period	73 days
4.	Gross Profit	Rs. 2,00,000
5.	Gross Profit margin	20%
6.	Cash & bank balance	5% of sales
7.	Credit purchases	25%

The firm expects an increase of 50% in sales in the ensuing year. Estimate the working capital requirements for the ensuing year.

[C.A. (I) May 2000]

Solution:

(1) Sales for the year 2005

$$\text{Sales} = \frac{\text{Gross Profit} \times 100}{\text{Gross Profit Ratio}}$$

$$= \frac{2,00,000 \times 100}{20} = \text{Rs. } 10,00,000$$

(2) Estimated Sales for the year 2006:

Current year's sales + 50% thereof Rs. 10,00,000 + 5,00,000

= Rs. 15,00,000

(3) Gross Profit = 20% of Sales

$$= \text{Rs. } 15,00,000 \times \frac{20}{100} = \text{Rs. } 3,00,000$$

(4) Cost of Goods Sold (Sales – G.P.)

(Rs. 15,00,000 – 3,00,000) = Rs. 12,00,000

(5) Debtors:

$$\text{Average Debtors} = \frac{\text{Credit Sales}}{\text{Debtors Turnover Ratio*}}$$

$$\boxed{\text{DTOR} = \frac{12}{2} = 6 \text{ Times}} = \frac{15,00,000}{6} = \text{Rs } 2,50,000$$

(6) Purchases :

Purchases = Cost of Goods Sold – Opening Stock + Closing Stock

Since the difference in opening and closing stock is not given, purchases will be equal to cost of goods sold = Rs. 12,00,000

(7) Credit Purchases = 25% of Total purchases

= Rs. 12,00,000 × 25% = Rs. 3,00,000

(8) Creditors

Creditors payment period = 73 days

$$\text{Creditors T.O. Ratio} = \frac{365}{73} = 5 \text{ Times}$$

$$\text{Average Creditors} = \frac{\text{Credit Purchases}}{\text{Creditors T.O. Ratio}}$$

$$= \frac{3,00,000}{5} = \text{Rs. } 60,000$$

(9) Cash & Bank balance = 5% of sales

= Rs. 15,00,000 × 5% = Rs. 75,000

Estimated Working Capital for the year 2006

		Rs.
Current Assets		
	Stock	3,00,000
	Debtors	2,50,000
	Cash & Bank	75,000
		6,25,000
Less	Current liabilities (Creditors)	60,000
	Working Capital	5,65,000

Illustration (22) (Calculation of Operating Cycle)

A Company furnishes you with the following details :

			Rs.
(i)	Opening Stock		50,000
(ii)	Closing Stock		70,000
(iii)	Sales :		
	Cash		1,50,000
	Credit		2,10,000
(iv)	Gross Profit		60,000
(v)	Year end Debtors	20,000	
	Less Provision	2,000	18,000
(vi)	Year end Bills Receivable		15,000

A year may be taken for 360 days. You are required to workout

(i) Stock-Turnover and Debtors Turnover ratios;

(ii) Operating Cycle.

[C.A. (I) Nov. 1999 - Modified]

Solution:

(1) Stock Turnover Ratio $= \dfrac{\text{Cost of Goods sold}}{\text{Average Stock}}$

Cost of Goods Sold = Sales – Gross Profit

= Rs. 3,60,000 – 60,000 = Rs. 3,00,000

Average Stock $= \dfrac{50,000 + 70,000}{2} =$ Rs. 60,000

STOR $= \dfrac{3,00,000}{60,000} = 5$ Times

(2) Operating Cycle

Operating Cycle Period = Inventory Conversion period + Debt Collection period

Inventory Conversion period $= \dfrac{360}{\text{Stock Turnover Ratio}} = \dfrac{360}{5} = 72$ days

Debt Collection period $= \dfrac{360}{\text{Debtors Turnover Ratio}}$

Debtors' Turnover Ratio $= \dfrac{\text{Credit Sales}}{\text{Average Receivable}}$

$= \dfrac{2,10,000}{20,000 + 15,000} = 6$ Times

Debt Collection period $= \dfrac{360}{6} = 60$ days

Operating Cycle Period = 72 days + 60 days = 132 days

Illustration (23)

The following is the Balance Sheet of a company as on 31st March 2005

Liabilities	Rs.	Assets	Rs.
Share Capital	10,00,000	Fixed Assets	4,00,000
Trade Creditors	1,40,000	Stock	3,00,000
Profit & L A/c	60,000	Debtors	1,50,000
		Cash & Bank	3,50,000
	12,00,000		12,00,000

The management estimates the purchases and sales for the year ended 31st March, 2006 as under :

	upto 28.2.2006	March 2006
	Rs.	Rs.
Purchases	14,10,000	1,10,000
Sales	19,20,000	2,00,000

It was decided to invest Rs. 1,00,000 in purchases of fixed assets which are depreciated @ 10% on cost. The time lag for payment to creditors for purchases and receipt from sales is one month. The company earns a gross profit of 30% on turnover. The expenses against gross profit amount to 10% of turnover. The amount of depreciation is not included in these expenses. Prepare Trading & P & L A/c and Balance Sheet as on 31st March, 2006, assuming that creditors are all trade creditors for purchases and debtors for sales. There is no other item of current assets and liabilities apart from stock and Cash & bank balances.

[CA(I) Modified]

Solution :

PROJECTED TRADING & PROFIT & LOSS A/C
for the year ended 31st March 2006

	Rs.		Rs.
To Opening Stock	3,00,000	By Sales**	21,20,000*
To Purchases*	15,20,000*	By Closing Stock (Bal. figure)	3,36,000
To Gross Profit c/d (30% of Sales)	6,36,000		
	24,56,000		24,56,000
To Sundry Expenses (10% of sales)	2,12,000	By Gross Profit b/d	6,36,000
To Depreciation	50,000		
To Net Profit	3,74,000		
	6,36,000		6,36,000

* Rs. 14,10,000 + 1,10,000 = 15,20,000

** Rs. 19,20,000 + 2,00,000 = 21,20,000

PROJECTED BALANCE SHEET
As on 31st March, 2006

Liabilities		Rs.	Assets	Rs.
Share Capital		10,00,000	Fixed Assets	4,00,000
Profit & Loss A/c			Addition made	1,00,000
Opening balance	60,000			5,00,000
Current year	3,74,000	4,34,000	*Less* Deprecation @ 10%	50,000
Trade Creditors (1)		1,10,00		4,50,000
			Stock	3,36,000
			S. Debtors (1)	2,00,000
			Cash & bank balance (2)	5,58,000
		15,44,000		15,44,000

Working notes:

(1) Trade Creditors and Debtors are equivalent to purchases & sales of last months of the accounting year (March) because there is one month's time lag for creditors payment and debt collection.

(2) Cash & Bank balance has been calculated as under :

	Rs		Rs.
To Balance b/d	3,50,000	By S. Creditors**	15,50,000
To Sundry Debtors*		(1,40,000 + 14,10,000)	
(1,50,000 + 19,20,000)	20,70,000	By Expenses	2,12,000
		By Fixed Assets	1,00,000
		By Balance c/d	5,58,000
	24,20,000		24,20,000

* Collection of last year's debtors + equal to 11 months sale.

** Payment of last year's Creditors + equal to 11 months purchases

Illustration (24) (Projected financial Statements)

You have been asked by the Management of Global Suppliers Ltd. to prepare a projected Trading and Profit & Loss Account and the Balance Sheet on the basis of following estimated figures and ratios, for the next financial year ending March 31, 2007

Ratio of Gross Profit	25%
Stock Turnover Ratio	5 Times
Average Debt Collection Period	3 months
Creditors' Velocity	3 months
Current Ratio	2
Proprietory Ratio (Fixed Assets to Capital employed)	80%
Capital Gearing ratio (Preference Shares & Debentures to Capital Employed)	30%
Net Profit to Issued (Equity) Capital	10%
General Reserve and Profit & Loss A/c to issued (Equity) Capital	25%

Preference Shares to Debentures	2
Cost of goods sold consists of 50% of Materials	
Gross Profit	Rs. 12,50,000

[C.A. (F) Modified]

Solution :

Calculation of missing figures

(i) Sales :

$$\text{Sales} = \frac{\text{Gross profit} \times 100}{\text{Gross profit Ratio}}$$

$$= \frac{12,50,000 \times 100}{25} = \text{Rs. } 50,00,000$$

(ii) Cost of Goods Sold: Sales – Gross Profit

= Rs. 50,00,000 – 12,50,000 = Rs. 37,50,000

(iii) Materials Consumed = 50% of Cost of Goods Sold.

$$= \frac{\text{Rs. } 37,50,000 \times 50}{100} = \text{Rs. } 18,75,000$$

(iv) Stock $\dfrac{\text{Cost of Goods Sold}}{\text{Stock Turnover Ratio}} = \dfrac{\text{Rs. } 37,50,000}{5} = \text{Rs. } 7,50,000$

(v) Debtors $= \dfrac{\text{Credit Sales}}{\text{Debtors Turnover Ratio*}}$ $\boxed{\dfrac{12^*}{3} = 4}$

$$= \frac{50,00,000}{4} = \text{Rs. } 12,50,000$$

Alternatively say equal to 3 month's sale $\left(\text{Rs. } 50,00,000 \times \dfrac{3}{12}\right) = \text{Rs. } 12,50,000$

(vi) Current Assets = Stock + Debtors

= Rs. 7,50,000 + 12,50,000 = Rs. 20,00,000

(vii) Creditors: Creditors velocity is 3 months. It means Creditors are equal to three months credit purchases. Since the difference in opening and closing stock is not given, the (credit) purchases will be equal to cost of goods sold. Creditors = 18,75,000 × 3/12 = Rs. 4,68,750

(viii) Current liabilities

Current Ratio = 2 : 1

Total Current Assets = Rs. 20,00,000

Total Current liabilities = Rs. 10,00,000

Other current liabilities = Rs. 10,00,000 – Creditors (4,68,750)

= Rs. 5,31,250

(ix) Fixed Assets = Fixed Assets are 80% of Capital employed. It means Working* Capital is 100 – 80 = 20% (*Net Current Assets) Thus fixed assets are 4 Times of Working Capital. Fixed Assets = 10,00,000 × 4 = 40,00,000

(x) Capital Employed = Rs. 40,00,000 × $\frac{100}{80}$ = Rs. 50,00,000

(or Fixed Assets + Working Capital)

(xi) Capital Gearing Ratio = $\frac{\text{Preference Shares + Debentures}}{\text{Capital Employed}}$ = 30%

Preference Shares & Debentures = 30% of Rs. 50,00,000 = 15,00,000

(xii) Equity Shareholders' Funds = Rs. 35,00,000
(Rs. 50,00,000 – 15,00,000)

(xiii) Preference Share Capital = 2/3 × 15,00,000 = Rs. 10,00,000
& Debentures 1/3 of Rs. 15,00,000 = Rs. 5,00,000

(xiv) General Reserves & Profit = 25% of Equity Capital It means ratio of Reserve & Profit to Total Equity is 25/125 or 1/5

Hence General Reserve & Profit = 35,00,000 × $\frac{1}{5}$ = 7,00,000 and

Issued Equity Capital = Rs. 28,00,000 (i.e. Rs. 35,00,000 – 7,00,000)

(xv) Net Profit = 10% of Rs. 28,00,000 = 2,80,000
General Reserve = Rs. 7,00,000 – 2,80,000 = Rs. 4,20,000

PROJECTED TRADING & PROFIT & LOSS A/C

	Rs.		Rs.
To Opening Stock	7,50,000	By Sales	50,00,000
To Material Purchases	18,75,000	By Closing Stock	7,50,000
To Labour & Direct Expenses	18,75,000		
To Gross Profit c/d	12,50,000		
	57,50,000		57,50,000
To Indirect Expenses (Bal. figure)	9,70,000	By Gross Profit b/d	12,50,000
To Net Profit	2,80,000		
	12,50,000		12,50,000

PROJECTED BALANCE SHEET
As on 31st March, 2006

Liabilities	Rs.
Preference Share Capital (Shares of Rs... each)	10,00,000
Equity Share Capital (Shares of Rs... each)	28,00,000
Reserve & Surplus:	
General Reserve	4,20,000
Profit & Loss A/c	2,80,000
Secured Loans :	
Debentures	5,00,000

Current liabilities	
S. Creditors	4,6 8,750
Other liabilities	5,31,250
	60,00,000
Assets	
Fixed Assets	40,00,000
Current Assets	
Stock	7,50,000
Debtors	12,50,000
	60,00,000

QUESTIONS & PROBLEMS

1. **What do you understand by term "Ratio Analysis"? Describe it's uses and limitations**

   (B.Com (H) D.U. 1989)

2. **Give a brief description of limitations of the "Analysis of Financial Statements"**

   [B.Com (H) D.U. 1994]

3. **Explain the significance of accounting ratios in financial Statetment analysis.**

   [B Com. (H) DU 1977]

4. **Explain any two of the following :**
   (i) Gross Profit Ratio
   (ii) Stock Turnover Ratio
   (iii) Proprietory Ratio

   [B.Com (H) D.U. 1993]

5. **Explain the following ratios :**
   (i) Current Ratio
   (ii) Debtors Turnover Ratio

   [B.Com (H) D.U. 1995]

6. **Distinguish between Current Ratio and Quick Ratio.**

   [B.Com (H) D.U. 1997]

7. **Write formula to calculate the following :**
   (i) Quick or liquidity ratio
   (ii) Selling Expenses Ratio
   (iii) Debt-Equity Ratio.
   (iv) Debtors Turnover Ratio & Debt Collection Period.
   (v) Creditors Turnover Ratio & Creditors Payment period

   [B.Com (H) D.U. 1991]

8. **State the significance and mode of determining following ratios :**
   (i) Inventory Turnover Ratio
   (ii) Debtors Turnover Ratio
   (iii) Operating Ratio *C.A. (I)*

9. Describe the following ratios and briefly explain their application:
   (i) Gross Profit Ratio
   (ii) Net Profit Ratio
   (iii) Operating Profit Ratio

C.A. (I)

10. Explain briefly the meaning and usefulness of the following ratios:
   (i) Liquidity ratios
   (ii) Current Ratio
   (iii) Liquid Ratio
   (iv) Return on Net Worth

C.A. (F)

11. State in each case the effect of the following transactions on Debt-Equity Ratio of company.
   (i) Issue of new equity for cash
   (ii) Issue of Bonus Shares
   (iii) Conversion of Debentures in to shares
   (iv) Raising of Loan from IFCI
   (v) Issue of Debentures to vendor for supply of machinery.

B.Com (H) D.U. 1990

Ans.: Decrease: (i), (iii), No Change (ii); Increase (iv), (v)

12. The Current Ratio of a Company is 2 : 1. Which are the following suggestions would improve the ratio, reduce the ratio or not change at all.
   (i) To sell a motor car for cash at a slight loss
   (ii) To borrow money on interest bearing promissory note.
   (iii) To Purchase stock for cash and
   (iv) To give an interest bearing promissory note to a creditor of goods:

C.A. (F)

Ans: Improve: (i), (ii); Reduce (iii); No Change: (iv), (v)

13. Assume the Current Ratio is 2.5 : 1 State in each case whether the Current ratio will improve, decline or not change.
   (i) Payment of a current liability
   (ii) Purchase of Fixed Assets for cash
   (iii) Cash Collected from customers
   (iv) Bills Receivable dishonoured
   (v) Issue of new shares for cash *[C.A. (F) May 1990]*

Ans: Improve: (i), (v); Decline (ii); No Change (iii) (iv)

(14) A Ltd. made a sale of Rs. 8,00,000 during the year ending 31st March, 2005. If Debtors Turnover is 8 times, Calculate debtors as on 31st March, 2005. It is ascertained that debtors as on 31st March, 2005 are Rs. 20,000 more than the Debtors on 1st April, 2004.

Ans: Debtors at the end - Rs. 1,10,000

(15) A Company's Current Ratio is 2 : 1 and Quick ratio is 1.5 : 1 as on 1st March, 2005. If the company sells goods for Rs. 2,00,000 at a profit of 20% on cost during the month of March, what difference will it make on both the ratios:

Ans: Increase both ratios

(16) A Ltd. maintains an average stock of Rs. 1,60,000 and turns this over five times in a year. If company marks up selling price at 25% on cost, what shall be the amount of sales and gross profit.

Ans: Sales; Rs. 10,00,000; Gross Profit : Rs. 2,00,000

(17) During the year ending 31st March 2005 the gross profit ratio of a company workedout to be 20% on a Turnover of Rs. 8,40,000. The net profit was 12.5% on turnover and rate of stock turnover was 6.

During the year 2005-06, it was estimated that the rate of turnover can increase to 10 while carrying the same average stock if the company reduces it's price by 10% and expenses by 2.5% on turnover.

Calculate (i) Gross Profit, Net Profit and Expenses for the year 2004-05 and

(ii) Estimated sales, Estimated gross profit, Estimated expenses and Estimated net profit for the year 2005-06.

Ans: 2004-05 - Gross Profit: Rs. 1,68,000 = 20% of T.O.

Net Profit : Rs. 1,05,000 = 12.5% of T.O.

Expenses : Rs. 63,000 = 7.5% of T.O.

2005-06 - Estimated Sales: Rs. 12,60,000

Estimated Gross Profit: Rs. 1,40,000

Estimated Expenses: Rs. 63,000

Estimated Net Profit: Rs. 77,000

Hint: $\text{Average Stock} = \dfrac{\text{Cost of Goods Sold}}{\text{Stock T.O. Ratio}} = \dfrac{6,72,000}{6}$

COGS = Sales – G.P. (Rs. 8,40,000 – 1,68,000)

Average Stock Rs. 1,12,000 which will remain unchanged. However, after calculating the sales for the year 2005-06, reduce it by 10% due to reduction in selling price.

(18) From the following particulars, Calculate debt Collection period.

	Rs.
Total Gross Sales	23,50,000
Cash Sales	5,08,000
Sales Returns	17,000
Debtors as on 31. 3. 2005	2,25,000
Bills Receivable as on 31. 3. 2005	50,000
Provision for Doubtful debts	25,000

Ans: 55 days

Hint: Take the year of 365 days.

(19) **From the following particulars of X Ltd. Calculate, Debtors Turnover Ratio and Average Collection period.**

	Year ending 31st March 2004 Rs	2005 Rs.
Gross Sales	22,60,000	18,90,000
Sales Returns	10,000	18,000
Debtors in the beginning	2,15,000	2,00,000
Debtors at the end	2,85,000	2,16,000
Year may be taken for		360 days
Ans: Debtors T.O. Ratio	9 Times	9 Times
Average Collection period	40 days	40 days

(20) **A Ltd. has a Capital of Rs. 50,00,000. It's turnover is three times of Capital and the margin on sales is 10%. What is the return on investment?**

Ans: 30%

(21) **The Balance Sheet of ABC Ltd. as on 31st March, 2005 was as follows:**

Liabilities	Rs.	Assets	Rs.
Share Capital	35,00,000	Goodwill	1,20,000
Securities Premium	4,00,000	Building	18,00,000
Revenue Reserves	2,10,000	Machinery	21,50,000
14% Debentures	4,00,000	Current Assets	20,00,000
Current liabilities	8,70,000		
Proposed Dividend	4,90,000		
Provision for Taxation	2,00,000		
	60,70,000		60,70,000

Calculate: (i) Current Ratio (ii) Debt-Equity Ratio

[B.Com (H) D.U. 1998]

Ans: Current Ratio = 1.282 : 1

Debt-Equity Ratio = 1 : 10. 28

(22) **Following is the Balance Sheet of YR Ltd. as on 31st March, 2005**

Liabilities	Rs.	Assets	Rs.
Share Capital	15,00,000	Building	7,60,000
General Reserve	3,50,000	Machinery	7,20,000
Profit & Loss A/c	1,50,000	Short-Term Investments	4,50,000
14% Debentures	4,00,000	Inventories	4,70,000
S. Creditors	5,60,000	Debtors	5,30,000
Proposed Dividend	1,80,000	Cash at Bank	3,30,000
Provision for Taxation	1,30,000	Prepaid Expenses	10,000
	32,70,000		32,70,000

Calculate :

(i) Long Term Funds to Fixed Assets Ratio

(ii) Debt Equity Ratio

(iii) Liquidity Ratio

[B.Com (H) D.U. 1999]

Ans: (i) 1.62 : 1 ; (ii) 1 : 5 (iii) 1. 5 : 1

(23) Following is the Balance Sheet of XL Ltd. as on 31st March 2005

Liabilities	Rs.	Assets	Rs.
Preference Share Capital	4,00,000	Land & Building	3,50,000
Equity Share Capital	3,00,000	Plant & Machinery	3,00,000
General Reserve	50,000	Furniture	40,000
Profit & Loss A/c	50,000	Debtors	2,00,000
12% Debentures	2,00,000	Stock	1,50,000
Trade Creditors	60,000	Cash	40,000
Outstanding Expenses	15,000	Prepaid Expenses	10,000
Provision for Taxation	20,000	Preliminary Expenses	35,000
Proposed Dividend	30,000		
	11,25,000		11,25,000

Calculate :

(i) Current Ratio (ii) Liquid Ratio (iii) Debt-Equity Ratio (iv) Capital Gearing Ratio

[ICWA (I) Adapted], B.Com (H) D.U. 2000

Ans: (i) 3.2 : 1 (ii) 1.92 : 1 (iii) 0.62 : 1 (iv) 1.5 : 1

(24) Following information relates to the trading activities of A Ltd. for year ended 31st March, 2005

Debtors' Velocity	3 months
Stock Velocity	6 months
Creditors' Velocity	2 months
Gross Profit Ratio	20%
Gross Profit for the year ended	Rs. 5,00,000

Stock at end was Rs. 40,000 more than the stock in the beginning of the year. Bills Payable and Receivable were Rs. 40,000 and Rs. 60,000 respectively calculate :

(i) Sales, (ii) Debtors, (iii) S. Creditors, (iv) Stock

Ans. : (i) Rs. 25,00,000, (ii) Rs. 5,65,000 (iii) Rs. 3,00,000 (iv) Rs. 10,20,000

(25) Following information has been extracted from the financial statement of SN Ltd.

Gross Profit Margin on Sales	36%
Inventory Turnover Ratio	20 Times
Average Inventory	Rs. 48,000
Average Debtors	Rs. 5,00,000
Income Tax	40%
Net Income after tax as percentage to sales	12%

Calculate :

(i) Gross Profit (ii) Sales (iii) Profit before Tax (iv) Profit after Tax

Ans: (i) Rs. 5,40,000 (ii) Rs. 15,00,000 (iii) Rs. 3,00,000 (iv) Rs. 1,80,000

(26) Following figures relate to Z Ltd.

	Rs.
Share Capital	5,00,000
Reserves & Surplus	4,00,000
Total Debts of the net worth	2/3rd
Turnover to total assets	2 Times

Calculate : (i) Total Debts (ii) Total Assets (iii) Sales

Note : There are no fictitious assets.

Ans. : (i) Rs. 6,00,000 (ii) Rs. 15,00,000 (iii) Rs. 30,00,000

(27) From the following ascertain

(i) Net-worth

(ii) Current Liabilities

(iii) Long-Term Liabilities

Sales for the year	Rs. 35,00,000
Sales to Net Worth	5 Times
Current liabilities to Net worth	40%
Total Debts to Net Worth	70%

Ans: Net worth Rs. 7,00,000, Current liabilities Rs. 2,80,000, Total-Debts Rs. 4,90,000.

(28) The following is the Balance Sheet of S J Ltd. as on 31st March, 2005

Liabilities	Rs.	Assets	Rs.
Share Capital	6,00,000	Fixed Assets	14,70,000
General Reserve	1,20,000	Stock-in Trade	6,50,000
Profit & Loss A/c	90,000	S. Debtors	3,00,000
Development Rebate Reserve	1,10,000	Bills Receivable	80,000
Bank-Overdraft	12,00,000	Cash & Bank	50,000
S. Creditors	3,00,000		
Bills Payable	1,30,000		
	25,50,000		25,50,000

Calculate : (i) Current ratio (i) Acid Test, (iii) Debt-Equity and (iv) Proprietory ratio.

C.A. (I) Adapted

Ans: (i) 1 : 1.51 (ii) 1 : 1 (iii) 1.77 : 1 (iv) 0.36 : 1

(29)

Sales	Rs. 20,00,000
Net Profit Ratio	15%
Non-Operating Loss	Rs. 60,000
Indirect Expenses Ratio	14%
Opening Inventory	Rs. 80,000
Closing Inventory	Rs. 56,000

Calculate : Inventory Turnover ratio

Ans: 20 Times

Hint : GP ratio (32%) = Net Profit Ratio + N.O. Exp. Ratio + Indirect Expenses ratio

(30) Following are the ratios relating to the trading activities of National Traders Ltd.

Debtors' Velocity	3 months
Stock Velocity	8 months
Creditors' Velocity	2 months
Gross Profit Ratio	25%

Gross Profit for the year ended 31st December 2005 amounts to Rs. 4,00,000. Closing Stock of the year is Rs. 10,000 above the opening stock. Bills Receivable amount to Rs. 25,000 and Bills Payable amount to Rs. 10,000.

Find out:

(i) Sales (ii) Sundry Debtors (iii) Closing Stock and (iv) Sundry Creditors

[C.A. (I) May 2002]

Ans: (i) Rs. 16,00,000 (ii) Rs. 3,75,000* (iii) Rs. 8,05,000 (iv) Rs. 1,91,667*

(*after deducting B/R & B/P)

(31) Prepare a Balance Sheet from the particulars furnished hereunder:

Stock Velocity	6
Gross Profit Margin	20%
Capital Turnover Ratio	2
Fixed Assets Turnover Ratio	4
Debt Collection Period	2 months
Creditors Payment Period	73 days
Gross Profit	Rs. 60,000

Excess of Closing stock over opening Stock Rs. 5,000 Difference in Balance Sheet represents Bank balance. The entire sales and purchases are made on credit basis.

[B.Com (H) D.U. 2001]

Ans: Total of Balance Sheet : Rs. 1,69,000

(32) Using the following data, Complete the Balance Sheet of X Ltd. as on 31.3.2005

(a) Gross Profit 25% of Sales

(b) Gross Profit Rs. 1,20,000

(c) Shareholders Equity Rs. 20,000

(d) Credit Sales to total sales 80%

(e) Total turnover to total assets = 4 times

(f) Cost of goods sold to inventory = 10 times

(g) Average Collection period = 5 days

(h) Long term debt = ?

(i) Current Ratio = 1.5

(j) Sundry Creditors = Rs. 60,000

BALANCE SHEET OF X LTD. AS ON 31. 3. 2005

Liabilities	Rs.	Assets	Rs.
S. Creditors	—	Cash	—
Long Term Debt.	—	S. Debtors	—
Share Capital	—	Inventory	—
		Fixed Assets	—
	—		—

[C.A. (I) Nov. 2000]

Ans.: Total of Balance Sheet- Rs. 1,20,000
Long Term Debt (Bal. figure) Rs. 40,000

(33) The Balance Sheet of Y Ltd. Stood as follows as on :

	31. 03. 04	31. 03. 05
	(Rs. in lacs)	
	Rs.	Rs.
Liabilities		
Share Capital	250	250
Reserves	100	116
Long Term Loans	120	100
Creditors and other Current liabilities	25	129
	495	595
Assets		
Fixed Assets	300	400
Less Depreciation	100	140
	200	260
Investments	30	40
Stock	100	120
Debtors	50	70
Cash/Bank	20	20
Other Current Assets	25	25
Miscellaneous Expenditure	70	60
	495	595

You are given following information for the year 2004-05.

	(Rs. in lacs)
Sales	600
PBIB	150
Interest	24
Provision for Tax	60
Proposed Dividend	50

You are required to calculate :

(a) Return on Capital Employed Ratio

(b) Stock Turnover Ratio

(c) Return on Net worth Ratio

(d) Current Ratio

(e) Proprietory Ratio

[C.A. (I) Nov. 1995 Modified[

Ans: (a) 32.05% (b) 5.45 Times
(c) 22.53% (d) 1.82 : 1 (e) 57%

(34) From the following information and ratios prepare Profit & Loss Account for the year ended 31st March 2005

Current Assets to Stock	3.2
Current Ratio	3
Acid Test Ratio	1
Financial Leverage	2.2
Earnings Per Share (each of Rs. 10)	Rs. 10
Book Value per share	Rs. 40
Average Collection Period (assume 360 days in a year)	30 days
Stock-Turnover Ratio (based on Sales)	5
Fixed Assets Turnover Ratio	1.2
Total liabilities to Networth	2.75
Net Working Capital	Rs. 10,00,000
Net Profit to Sales	10%
Variable Cost	60%
Long term Loan interest	12%
Taxation	to be ignored

[C.A. (I) Nov. 94-Modified]

Ans: Sales : Rs. 50,00,000
Long Term Loans Rs. 50,00,000
Shareholder's Funds (Net worth) Rs. 20,00,000
Fixed Assets Rs. 41,66,667
Stock Rs. 10,00,000
EBIT Rs. 11,00,000 (Net Profit × 2.2)
Interest Rs. 6,00,000 (EBIT – NP)
Fixed Cost 40% of sales – EBIT = 9,00.000
Net Profit Rs. 5,00,000
Total of Balance Sheet - Rs. 70,00,000

(35) The following figures are extracted from the books of A Ltd. and B Ltd.

	A Ltd.	B Ltd.
	Rs.	Rs.
Sales	8,00,000	10,00,000
Net Profit	60,000	50,000
Capital employed	4,00,000	2,50,000

Judge the performance of both the companies by calculating primary ratio and secondary ratio.

C.S. (F) Modified

Hint: Primary ratio = Return on Capital employed; Secondary ratio = Profitability ratio.

Ans: From primary ratio point of view B Ltd. is more profitable From Secondary ratio point of view A Ltd. is more profitable.

(36) Prepare Trading & Profit & Loss A/c and a Balance Sheet from the following particulars.

Stock Velocity	6
Gross Profit margin	20%
Capital Turnover Ratio	4
Debt Collection Period	3 months
Creditors payment period	2 months
Gross Profit	Rs. 6,00,000
Excess of closing stock over opening Stock	Rs. 50,000

Assume that no cash purchases and cash sales are made. Bank balance is the balancing figure in the Balance Sheet.

[B.Com (H) D.U. 2002]

Ans: Capital - Rs. 7,50,000, Closing Stock - Rs. 4,25,000

Creditors - Rs. 4,08,333, Debtors - Rs. 7,50,000

Cash & bank balance - Rs. 5,83,333

Note: Since expenses are not given, the gross profit will be treated as net profit

(37) The assets of ABC Ltd. consists of fixed assets and current assets while it's current liabilities comprise bank credit and trade credit in the ratio of 2 : 1. From the following figures relating to the company for the year 2005, prepare it's Balance Sheet. Show your working as part of your answer.

Share Capital	Rs. 19,95,000
Working Capital (CA – CL)	Rs. 4,50,000
Gross Margin	20%
Inventory Turnover	6
Average Collection Period	2 months
Current Ratio	1.5
Quick Ratio	0.9
Reserves and Surplus to Cash	3

[C. A. (F) Modified]

Ans:		
	Current Assets	Rs. 13,50,000
	Current liabilities	Rs. 9,00,000
	Stock	Rs. 5,40,000
	Debtors	Rs. 6,75,000
	Cash	Rs. 1,35,000
	Reserve & Surplus	Rs. 4,05,000
	Total of Balance Sheet	Rs. 33,00,000
	Fixed Assets (Bal. figure)	Rs. 19,50,000